BK 923.173 J45S
THOMAS JEFFERSON
/SCHACHNER,
1957 .00 FV
D1030505

Thomas Jefferson

A BIOGRAPHY

BY NATHAN SCHACHNER

THOMAS JEFFERSON: A BIOGRAPHY

ALEXANDER HAMILTON

THE WANDERER

THE SUN SHINES WEST

THE KING'S PASSENGER

BY THE DIM LAMPS

THE MEDIAEVAL UNIVERSITIES

AARON BURR: A BIOGRAPHY

ALEXANDER HAMILTON: NATION BUILDER

THE FOUNDING FATHERS

THE PRICE OF LIBERTY

Courtesy of Percy S. Straus, Jr.

THOMAS JEFFERSON

Painting by Gilbert Stuart

NATHAN SCHACHNER

Thomas Jefferson

A BIOGRAPHY

THOMAS YOSELOFF

NEW YORK · LONDON

Thomas Yoseloff, *Publisher*
8 East 36th Street
New York 16, N. Y.

Thomas Yoseloff Ltd
18 Charing Cross Road
London W.C.2, England

First printing (two volumes), 1951
Second printing (one volume), 1957
Third printing, 1960
Fourth printing, 1964

To Helen, my wife, and Barbara, my daughter, who necessarily suffered during the hermitlike existence of an author in the throes of research and composition, but who never once complained, and stimulated and encouraged when he faltered or despaired.

PRINTED IN THE UNITED STATES OF AMERICA

Foreword

Of all the great figures in American history, Thomas Jefferson is perhaps the most difficult to write about adequately. Yet at the same time he is the most fascinating. To him may truly be applied the famous Shakespearian line: "Age cannot wither, nor custom stale (his) infinite variety."

His long life spanned the birth and establishment of a new nation, and no man contributed more to both than he did. Yet he was much more than a political leader. In an era of complex and many-sided men, he was without doubt the most complex and many-sided of them all. He literally took all knowledge to be his province, and his insatiable curiosity and probing intellect took him along amazing highways and byways. In all he did supremely well.

Had not fate and the times destined him to preside at the birth pangs of a nation and to help guide it along the broad vistas of democracy as he envisioned them, he could have been famous in any one of innumerable other fields. He wrote with clarity and precision, and phrases tipped with immortality rolled happily from his pen. The *mot juste*, the pregnant apothegm and the ringing affirmation may be culled from every page. His contributions to political philosophy were many and various, and have formed a significant underpinning to any understanding of America. He was an educator par excellence, and no one has done more to set this country upon the path of the free and universal diffusion of knowledge. His powerful advocacy of religious liberty and the eternal freedom of the human mind are too well known to require any comment.

He was an extraordinary architect as well, and an artist in landscaping and gardening. He dabbled in many sciences, and helped illuminate them all—ethnology, archaeology, practical astronomy, geology and geography. He conducted researches in scientific farming and the breeding of animals. He sought to transplant new strains of olives, vines, rice and cotton from the Old World to the New. He invented an improved plough, and numerous ingenious mechanical gadgets that still delight and astound the visitor to Monticello today. He explored history and the former institutions of men, and sought to apply their lessons to the problems of his own day. He profoundly believed in the perfectability of mankind, and foresaw an endless vista of upward and onward progress. He forged for himself a religion and an ethic peculiarly his own, though he firmly refused to impose them on others; and he compiled a Bible for himself, stripped bare, as he said, of the excrescences of later obscurantists.

At the same time, Jefferson was no mere intellectual machine. No matter how many-sided and various his genius, he would then have been but poor material for a personal biography. He was a warm-blooded, passionate, sensitive, breathing human being. He had faults as well as virtues. He could be rigorously logical, and simultaneously wildly inconsistent. In short, he was neither god nor devil, as only too many commentators have sought in the past to depict and fit into the iron mold of a thesis. His complexity and humanity defy such easy simplifications.

For example, he was the proud aristocrat and spokesman for the common man; an awkward lover and an ideal husband; the creator of a brave new world and an eminently practical politician; the rigid economist in government and a private spendthrift; a dyed-in-the-wool local Virginian and a national expansionist on a grandiose scale; an advocate of the inalienable right to revolution and the relentless suppressor of revolutionary attempts during his terms of office; capable of both bold and decisive strokes and of endless trimmings and hesitations.

It is no wonder then that Jefferson is at once the delight and despair of biographers. And when, to the innumerable ramifications of the man himself, are added the truly staggering amount of material and the endless array of manuscripts that exist all over the world, the difficulties involved become almost insuperable.

Yet the biography of Jefferson has been in the past and must continue in the future to be attempted. Without a close study of the man, his philosophy and works no proper understanding of America as it was and as it is today can be arrived at. He is an integral part of the warp and woof of this country, and the problems with which he wrestled and the solutions he arrived at are still with us, and vital to our continued existence. Whether it be states' rights versus national centralization, isolationism versus internationalism, war versus peace, government controls versus laissez faire, debit spending versus balanced budget, strict versus liberal construction of the Constitution–these are just as controversial and just as important issues to the nation of the nineteen-fifties as they were to the earlier decades when Jefferson pondered and acted on them.

I can only plead in defense for this addition to the huge body of Jefferson literature that I have worked diligently at the task for past twenty years; and have been able perhaps to gain some new insights and some fresh viewpoints through my studies in connection with previous biographies of Alexander Hamilton and Aaron Burr, whose lives and fortunes were inextricably interwoven with those of Thomas Jefferson. I have gone to the contemporary documents themselves–both printed and manuscript–and sought to appraise them afresh and without any preconceptions and theses ready-made in advance. I have tried to portray men and events objectively–though this, of course, is an ideal that can never be fully achieved–and without, what has been too often the case, either uncritical panegyric or biased prejudice.

I have gone to every known source and some which have hitherto been unknown, and I have had my share of rewards in unearthing new material from which new light can be thrown on moot points and intrenched errors corrected. I have tried to make this biography as complete and as accurate as possible. Anyone who has ever written must know, however, that inaccuracies and proof-reading mistakes inevitably creep in, and the indulgence of the reader is craved for any such. I have also sought to make this book as readable as possible, and as interesting to the general reader as to the scholar and student. Certainly Jefferson himself would not have wished the story of his life and career to be wrapped up in the unintelligible jargon of the schools and limited to the esoteric few.

Whether I have succeeded is another matter, and must now be left to the judgment of others.

NATHAN SCHACHNER

Contents

Contents (continued)

List of Illustrations

List of Illustrations (continued)

Thomas Jefferson

A BIOGRAPHY

CHAPTER I

In the Beginning

JUST when the first Jefferson came over to Virginia from his ancestral home in the British Isles it is difficult to say. Thomas Jefferson himself never knew nor, it seems, did he very much care. It is true that when he contemplated marriage and a family of his own, interest stirred somewhat in him. He went so far as to commission his agent, Thomas Adams, who was about to sail to England, to "search the Herald's office for the arms of my family. I have what I have been told were the family arms, but on what authority I know not. It is possible there may be none. If so, I would with your assistance become a purchaser, having Sterne's word for it that a coat of arms may be purchased as cheap as any other coat." [1]

Adams, no doubt, fully appreciated the mixture of earnestness and jest, for he brought back neither the true Jeffersonian arms nor a purchased substitute; and Jefferson continued at infrequent intervals to use the putative seal in his possession until, in later years, he shifted to another of his own contriving, bearing the eminently satisfactory motto: REBELLION TO TYRANTS IS OBEDIENCE TO GOD.

The only other time Jefferson saw fit to ponder on genealogy was in old age when he wrote his memoirs. Then he set down the family tradition that their paternal ancestor had come to the New World from Wales, near Snowdon mountain, though in what year or even decade no one knew. Jefferson had also come across the family name in a Welsh case cited in the law reports, and had noted it in the records as belonging to the secretary to the Virginia Company; but he frankly admitted that his own particular knowledge went back no further than to his grandfather.[2]

Today we know something more of Jefferson's ancestry than he did, and can push definite knowledge back at least to his great-grandfather. Beyond that, however, all is conjecture. The Welsh habitation of his forebears has never been documented, and the records of the Virginia Company disclose no Jefferson as its secretary.

Nevertheless, three Jeffersons do appear in the earliest accounts of the Colony, two of them bearing the same given name, John, and the third anonymously described as "Mr."

"Mr." Jefferson was evidently a man of some consequence, for he represented "Flouer dieu Hundred" in the first legislative assembly in the New World when it met at Jamestown in 1619.[3] Inasmuch as Flower de Hundred was on that same stretch of the James River where the first known Jefferson later appeared on the scene, there is a possibility that the two were related;

but the hiatus between 1619 and 1678 is too great for anything but unsubstantiated surmise.

One of the John Jeffersons was also a man of considerable standing; for he was chosen by the Privy Council of Great Britain on October 24, 1623, as a commissioner to investigate the admittedly disordered state of affairs in the newly erected Colony. The commission of appointment set him down as a "Gentleman"; [4] but here the possibility of a connection with the later Jeffersons is much more remote than in the case of "Mr." Jefferson.

The other John Jefferson of whom the records speak was of a different sort. He was no "gentleman" in the sense that his namesake had been so described. Rather, he was a blacksmith and apparently an indentured servant to boot, whose sole doubtful claim to immortality resides in a warrant issued for his arrest on May 2, 1625, by the Council and General Court of Virginia: "Yt is ordered yt there be A warrant granted to Capt' Hamer for the Attachinge of John Jefferson the Smith and Capt' Hamers Maide in any Plantation where they shall be found." [5] Whether the runaways were ever apprehended is not disclosed; nor has any link been discovered between the errant blacksmith and the Jeffersons with whom we are concerned.

That line authentically enters history with Jefferson's great-grandfather, named, like himself, Thomas Jefferson. Of the date or place of his birth nothing is known; he comes before us full-blown in 1678 as a married man and the owner of a plantation in the "Curles" of the James River.[6] The Curles are those snakelike convolutions through which the James meanders for some distance below the fall line at Richmond and which constituted, in the early part of the seventeenth century, the frontier of Virginia. However, by 1678 enterprising settlers had pushed beyond them and the falls into the true Piedmont section and were engaged in staking out huge territorial claims and fighting off hostile Indians. By that time, indeed, the Curles were well settled according to the standards of the day, and the surrounding area was dotted with plantations, large and small, of such well-known families in Virginian history as the Cockes, the Blands, the Farrars, the Eppes' and the Randolphs.

Nathaniel Bacon had been one with them, too, but he had died two years before, an outlaw and a rebel against the royal governor and the king. It would be interesting to know what position the young plantation-owner, Thomas Jefferson, took on that first revolt against British overlordship in America; a revolt whose principles pregnantly foreshadowed by a full century the Declaration of Independence of his great-grandson. Certainly he expressed no active sympathy; had he done so, his holdings would have vanished in the general confiscation, he himself would have been banished or executed, and the famous Declaration would perforce have been penned by another hand. Of such are the ironies of history.

So that, when the tumult and the shouting died, Thomas Jefferson, as a loyal subject of his king, remained firmly ensconced in his possessions and able to continue with his proper business of rearing a family. That family consisted of his wife Mary, the daughter of William and Jane Branch, and their two children, Thomas, Jr., and Martha. His alliance with the Branches indicates that Thomas Jefferson, Sr., was considered a solid, substantial young man and the record bears it out. His name appears with some frequency in the archives of Henrico County. He was a surveyor (in which profession his descendants dutifully followed him); he appeared on the roll of jurors and appraised estates; he paid taxes for the maintenance of soldiers; and he was evidently an excellent shot, for he collected a good many bounties which the colony offered for the extermination of wolves.[7] He showed enterprise, too, for he entered as a squatter on some virgin forest land further up the river, only to discover that it had already been granted to that prince of speculators, William Byrd. The defect in title was cured in 1682, however, by the purchase of the 167 acres in question.[8]

When Thomas Jefferson, Sr., died in 1697 he left a fairly adequate estate for the benefit of his wife and two children. Exclusive of Negro slaves and crops, it came to a valuation of some £97, a respectable total for the period.[9] Mary Jefferson, the widow, took herself a second husband about three years later, a man named Joseph Mattocks, and passes out of our story. But by that time her children by her first husband were grown and able to fend for themselves.

Thomas Jefferson, Jr., had been born about 1677 and was therefore twenty years old when his father died.[10] By the terms of the will he received a one-third share of the estate; a small enough amount with which to start out in life. But he was evidently vigorous and alert, and not only managed to advance the family fortunes during his lifetime but achieved a recognized position among the gentry as well. This, of course, was a much simpler achievement than it would have been in England, where caste lines were rigid and inflexible, or in a later Virginia when the molds had hardened and genealogical inquiries became a study of much import. Any personable young man with a talent for acquisition and an eye to the main chance could break into the still ill-defined circle; even indentured servants, after their terms had expired, were able eventually to carve out a career of respectability and esteem.

Barely had his father's body been lowered into its grave when Thomas Jefferson, Jr., took the first step toward the advancement of his position. On October 20, 1697, he took out a license to marry Mary Field, the daughter of Peter and Judith Field of New Kent County, and consummated the marriage in the following year.[11] Again a Jefferson had done well for himself in taking a wife; for the Fields were solid in lands and connections. Peter Field was a major of militia, and his wife Judith was not only the daughter of a former speaker of the House of Burgesses but, as the erstwhile widow of Henry Randolph, was connected with one of the most powerful and far-flung clans of Virginia. The fortunes of the Randolphs were to continue to be closely entwined with those of the Jeffersons.

The newly wedded couple established themselves at Osborne's, a small, straggling community on the James about a dozen miles from Bermuda Hundred. The property on which they settled, according to their grandson, was later acquired by the parish for its glebe.[12] It was here that six children were born to them—three sons, Thomas, Field and Peter; and three daughters, Judith, Mary and Martha. Thomas had become a traditional appellation in each generation for the eldest son; while Martha and Mary were regularly to recur among the daughters.

Thomas, Jr., or Captain Jefferson as he later became known by virtue of a militia command,[13] proceeded to enlarge his estate. Some lands were added by judicious purchase; others were received as headrights for the importation of colonists from England; but his most ambitious acquisition took the form of a patent to 1,500 acres on Fine Creek, on the south side of the James and above the falls, granted to him and three partners in 1718 by Governor Spotswood.[14]

Within a reasonable time Captain Jefferson became a man of substance and standing; due partly, no doubt, to his own efforts and partly to the influence of his wife's connections. In 1714 he was appointed justice of the peace and continued in that honorable station for about twenty years.[15] From 1718 to 1719 he filled the equally honorable position of sheriff of Henrico County.[16] In 1723 his financial condition was such that he was able to build a church for the benefit of Bristol parish, and in return the church became known as "Jefferson's church." [17] Yet not all his progress was forward; he suffered setbacks as well. On December 8, 1720, he presented a petition to the Virginia Assembly "setting forth his great loss sustained by fire and praying relief thereon." [18] Where the fire occurred or what damage was done was not stated, nor does the record disclose what disposition was made of his petition.

Captain Jefferson must have been quite a sporting character, at least as a young man. Just before his marriage he owned a racing mare which he pitted against the coursers of his neighbors. On April 1, 1698, one such race ended up in the law courts. Jefferson's mare, Bony, had run against a horse named Watt for a wager of five pounds, quite a substantial sum in those days. Bony won, but the owner of Watt refused to pay up. Whereupon young Jefferson entered suit at the Varina Courthouse and won his case.[19]

Mary Jefferson, the wife of the Captain, died on August 13, 1715, after having borne six children. There is some evidence that her bereaved husband remarried and was again, within a short period, widowed.[20] In any event, when Captain Jefferson himself died on February 18, 1731, at the age of fifty-three, he mentioned no wife in his will but divided his estate among his five remaining children. Thomas, the eldest, had not survived young manhood; he had perished in 1723 while on a voyage of the ship *Williamsburg*, commanded by Captain Isham Randolph.[21] It was this same Isham Randolph whose daughter was to become the mother of the Thomas Jefferson in whom we are particularly interested.

Captain Jefferson's will left only a "mourning ring of the value of twenty shillings" to his eldest surviving son, Field. No doubt the property at Osborne's also went to him as a result of the legal system of entails which Virginia had taken over from the mother country, England, and which remained in effect until a later Jefferson caused it to be abolished.

But it is evident that Peter, the youngest son, was the Captain's favorite. To him was left the major portion of the estate—the acquired lands at Fine and Manakin Creeks, the "two Negro's Farding and Pompey," feather beds, couch, tables and other household equipment, half the stock of cattle, sheep and hogs. "I also give unto my son Peter my chest and wearing cloaths with the cloth and trimming that is in the chest, my cane, my six silver spoons which I bought of Turpin, Two Horses named Norman and Squirrell, my Trooping Arms and Gunn I had of Joseph Wilkinson." The remainder of the estate was divided among the three daughters.[22]

Field Jefferson, the elder brother, lived on to the age of sixty-two and eventually sired a considerable family.[23] For a short period after their father's death both he and Peter remained at Osborne's. Together they operated a ferry across the James for which the parish duly paid them in pounds of tobacco, the legal tender of the time. Field also received payment for "Siting up horse blocks at the Church." [24] But neither stayed on in the place in which he was born. Field moved to Lunenberg and became a justice of the peace, while Peter decided to settle at Fine Creek on the lands which he had inherited.

Peter Jefferson, born on February 29, 1708, was now in the prime of manhood. He was obviously a young man of sound qualities and sense, or Captain Jefferson would not have left him the larger portion of the unentailed estate and named him executor to the exclusion of Field. He was also, both in youth and later age, a man of extraordinary physical strength. Tradition ascribed to him various feats which are the common coin of frontier legend, such as the simultaneous lifting to an upright position of two hogsheads of tobacco, each weighing approximately a thousand pounds, and the hauling down of an old shed unaided after three slaves had failed in the attempt.[25]

According to his son, Peter Jefferson's formal education had been neglected, "but being of a strong mind, sound judgment and eager after information, he read much and improved himself."[26] Obviously Thomas Jefferson did not mean that his father had not received the usual elementary training in the three R's; he was referring to the classical education which he himself had been given and which included Latin, Greek and the higher mathematics. But very few of the lesser gentry of Virginia were educated in that sense; only the wealthy could afford to send their sons to England or even to the struggling little institution of William and Mary down at Williamsburg, and private tutors of any competence were with difficulty induced to venture into the interior.

By the end of his career, however, Peter Jefferson had managed to overcome some of the deficiencies of his youth. True, he never learnt the ancient tongues; but the library of forty-two volumes which he left at the time of his death discloses a reasonably wide range of interests. Aside from the omnipresent Bible and prayer books, as well as such practical compendiums as Nelson's *Office of a Justice*, the *Scrivener's Guide* and *The London and Country Brewer*, it contained maps of various sections of the world, volumes of history, one on astronomy, a dictionary and, for literature, Addison, the *Spectator*, the *Tattler* and the *Guardian*.[27] Not an impressive list, to be sure, but probably as good as could be found in most plantations along the middle and upper James. Even more important for his purposes, perhaps, was his acquisition of sufficient mathematics to attain a definite niche in the history of early American surveying. Of that, more will be said shortly.

Young Peter entered upon his promised inheritance at Fine Creek prior to the death of his father and evinced his intention of settling there permanently. Three years before, in fact, he had cleared some of the land and erected a small, cabinlike dwelling at a cost of three pounds, ten shillings, and two tobacco houses for nine pounds, both of which items were charged to his father as legal owner.[28] Seemingly he continued to live there, returning only to Osborne's in 1731 to take charge of his father's estate. His accounts as executor, running from October 19, 1731, to November 5, 1732, show total entries of forty-three pounds, ten shillings, six pence.[29] It was this very modest sum, evidently, which represented the residuary estate to be divided up among his three sisters.

With his legal duties completed, Peter returned to his cabin on Fine Creek and set about the business of life. Fine Creek flowed northeasterly into the James and lay in the newly erected County of Goochland. The surrounding territory was fertile, well watered and timbered; well adapted after clearing to the cultivation of the money crop of tobacco. It was sparsely settled at the time; the north bank of the James was relatively more thickly populated and included such establishments as Dungeness, the court house of the county, and Tuckahoe. But the river made a broad highway on which intercommunication between the abutting plantations was easy, and Peter did not lack for neighbors.

Among these were the omnipresent Randolphs; one of whom, William, lived at Tuckahoe, and another, Isham, his uncle, was the master of Dungeness. It has until recently been a matter of astonishment to biographers that Peter Jefferson was able to gain the equal friendship of such an aristocratic clan and eventually to marry one of its daughters.

But newly ascertained data on the Jeffersons have lessened the gap between the two families to one of more manageable proportions. In a society in which the ownership of land was the chief determinant of status, the Randolphs were at this time middle gentry and the Jeffersons lesser gentry, but gentry nevertheless. From the moment that both appear on the American scene they were neighbors, friends, and in a sense related. Peter's maternal grandmother had been the prior widow of a Randolph; and Isham Randolph, his current neighbor, had been on cordial terms with his father. It was on Isham's ship, in fact, that Peter's eldest brother had come to a tragic end.

The Randolphs, indeed, thought very well of themselves. As Thomas Jefferson was rather dryly to remark: "They trace their pedigree far back in England & Scotland, to which let every one ascribe the faith & merit he chooses."[30] But by the time he wrote this, Jefferson had had several unfortunate experiences with descendants of the stock.

In any event, the first Randolph to come to Virginia was William, who proudly set himself down in his will as a "Gentleman" of Warwickshire.[31] Arriving at the age of twenty-three, he settled in 1674 at Turkey Island on the Curles of the James and thereby became a neighbor to Thomas Jefferson, Sr. In 1680 he married Mary Isham, the daughter of Colonel Henry Isham of Bermuda Hundred.

William Randolph's rise to fortune was spectacular. Whatever he touched turned literally to gold. His crops grew strong and plentiful; his ships bore profitable cargoes to England and back; and his land speculations were lucky. The domed mansion which he erected on Turkey Island dazzled his neighbors and made a beacon for the river mariners on the James. Nor was he less successful in his family; nine of whom survived the fevers and the accidents of childhood to produce in turn the most bewilderingly abundant progeny that even Virginia, notable in such matters, has ever seen. Indeed, so luxuriant had they become by 1787 and their ramifications so intricate that a French traveler, the Marquis de Chastellux, declared: "One must be fatigued with hearing the name of Randolph in travelling in Virginia (for it is one of the most ancient families in the country); a Randolph being among the first settlers, and is likewise one of the most numerous and rich. It is divided into seven or eight branches, and I am not afraid of exaggerating when I say that they possess an income of upwards of a million livres."[32]

Isham Randolph, the third son of William, was born in 1685. He received an excellent education and was almost as much at home in England as in his native Virginia. He took to the sea at an early age and, when twenty-five, was recommended for the captaincy of a ship by William Byrd of Westover.[33] Thirteen years later he was still sailing the Atlantic, this time with the unfortunate young scion of the Jeffersons on board.

Yet Isham did not neglect the more solid earth in the furtherance of his fortunes. On his father's death in 1711 he shared with five brothers in a tract of over 3,000 acres on the upper reaches of the James, and later added to it 8,800 acres more.[34] It was on this land at Dungeness, and only ten miles from Fine Creek where Peter Jefferson later installed himself, that Isham made his permanent home. From all accounts it was one of the better establishments on the upper James, and his numerous acres were tended by a hundred slaves.

To this wilderness grandeur he finally brought as mistress a young English girl, Jane Rodgers, whom he had met and married in 1717 while representing Virginia as its Colonial Agent in England. He remained in London for several years in that capacity, and his first child, Jane, was born there and baptized at St. Paul's in the parish of Shadwell, on February 20, 1720. He also found time to father ten more children in the intervals of sea voyages and public activities. Those public activities were many; aside from his official representation of Virginia in the mother country, he sat in the House of Burgesses at home, became a colonel of militia and was appointed Adjutant General of the colony.[35] He was also an enthusiastic amateur naturalist, and it was to him that Peter Collinson, the English man of science, recommended John Bartram of Philadelphia when the latter wished in 1737 to study the flora of Virginia.[36]

While Jane Randolph was growing to maturity at Dungeness, Peter Jefferson, down at Fine Creek, was establishing himself as an eminently respectable citizen. He had already, in 1731, been appointed one of the first magistrates of Goochland County. No doubt he visited the Isham Randolphs regularly and noted their eldest daughter as she ripened into womanhood. He also established cordial relations with William Randolph of Tuckahoe, a nephew of Isham and cousin to Jane. So that in 1737, when Peter was awarded the important post of sheriff of the county, it was Isham Randolph and William Randolph who bound themselves in the sum of £1,000 sterling for the faithful performance of his duties.[37]

The same year, Peter Jefferson embarked on an ambitious campaign to increase his land holdings that was to continue almost to the time of his death. Together with his friend William Randolph and four other interested parties, he petitioned the Council of Virginia for and received a grant of "fifty thousand Acres beginning at a place called the Crabb Orchard near the Ridge of Mountains on the head Springs of Sherrando & running South Westerly between the blue Ridge & third Ridge provided the same do not interfer[e] with any former Entry." [38] There is considerable doubt, however, whether the partners ever perfected their title to this enormous grant.

The next year Peter Jefferson sought on his own and received a grant of 2,000 acres on Davis's Creek, near the Great Pass;[39] and in 1741 the obliging Council disposed of 15,000 more acres in Brunswick County to the ambitious young speculator and two other partners. But here the Council called a halt. Faced with still another petition by the same trio for 40,000 acres on Blackwater Creek, it administered a sharp rebuke, declaring the petition "rejected as being judged too great a Grant to what is already granted the Pet'rs." [40]

The rebuff put an end for some years to Peter Jefferson's attempts to carve out a princely domain for himself in the still-unpeopled western areas of Virginia. Proceeding at too rapid a pace, and perhaps counting too confidently on the influence of the Randolphs, he had come in conflict with other empire-builders, whose claims merited more respectful consideration from the august members of the Council. It was not until 1748 that he resumed operations on a large scale in the public domain and, by now a man of some standing, was once more rewarded with sizable grants.

More modestly, he picked up choice parcels by purchase whenever the occasion arose. Of particular interest in this category was the acquisition of a mountaintop in 1735 on the south side of the Rivanna,[41] which his son was later to make world-famous under the name of Monticello. Another acquisition was a plat of 11,770 acres on the branches of Black Water Creek which the Council granted in 1751 to Jefferson and an influential group of associates; including the Honorable William Dawson, Colonel Joshua Fry and three others.[42] Peter's share in this, consisting of 2,000 acres, was similarly to become dear to his son, if not of equal renown to the world at large, under the name of Poplar Forest.

One more parcel, small in size, merits mention. It totaled 400 acres on the Northanna in St. James Parish, Goochland County. Two hundred acres of this was acquired by Peter on May 18, 1736 from his friend William Randolph. The terms of the transfer were unusual, to say the least. The only consideration cited in the deed was the due delivery to young Randolph of tavern-keeper "Henry Wetherburn's biggest bowl of Arrack punch." [43] No doubt equal parts of generosity and conviviality were compounded in the transaction. Later on, in 1741, when Peter had a much more legitimate claim on Randolph's generosity, though perhaps not on his conviviality, a more sober financial note entered into their dealings. This time Peter *purchased* from Randolph an adjoining 200 acres, the whole becoming known as Shadwell, in honor of the birthplace of his bride.[44]

In estimating the total of Peter Jefferson's holdings, it must be remembered that not all of the Council's grants ripened into legal title; certain technical requirements had first to be complied with which the hopeful recipients did not always find feasible. And Jefferson, in common with land speculators generally, sold as well as purchased. But sufficient remained on his death to make a goodly inheritance for his son, though perhaps not as much as some recent biographers have estimated. According to Thomas Jefferson's own account of his holdings in 1794 and the sources from which they were derived, about 5,000 acres seems to be the most likely figure.[45]

In October, 1739, Peter Jefferson married Jane, the eldest daughter of Isham Randolph.[46] Peter was then thirty-one, and Jane was nineteen. By the standards of the colony Peter was late in getting himself a wife; perhaps he had been waiting for Jane to grow up, perhaps eligible young girls were scarce in the neighborhood of Fine Creek. In any event he had, from a material point of view, done very well for himself.

Thomas Jefferson was to keep an almost impenetrable silence about his mother. His few references are dry, curt and uncommunicative; even though she survived her husband by a good many years. Nothing is known of her except some stray items of doubtful tradition; the mother of no other great man is as singularly devoid of embodiment for posterity.

Isham Randolph was obviously satisfied with his daughter's marriage. He settled on her the sum of £200 sterling; but doubtless because hard money was scarce, the marriage portion was not paid over to Peter until after Randolph's death in November, 1742.[47]

Now that Peter was a married man, newer territory beckoned as the place where fortune could better be wooed than at Fine Creek; and he determined to settle in St. James Parish on the Northanna, on the land which he had previously traded in part and purchased in part from William Randolph.

For several years, while still residing at Fine Creek, Peter intermittently prepared Shadwell for future dwelling. He first built, in accordance with the usual custom, a small, cabinlike dwelling which could later be made into an outbuilding of a more formal and elaborate home. Then, early in 1743, he quit Fine Creek permanently for Shadwell. With him went his wife, Jane, and their two baby daughters: Jane, born June 17, 1740, and Mary, born October 1, 1741. Also traveling with them, as invisible baggage, was still another child. Barely, in fact, had they settled themselves in their rude new quarters when a son was born—Thomas Jefferson, fourth of the eldest males so to be named in the known line of the Jeffersons. The date of his birth was April 2, 1743, Old Style; but it is celebrated, because of the subsequent shift to the Gregorian calendar, on April 13th.

CHAPTER 2

Father and Son

SHADWELL, though not on the real frontier of Virginia, lay in the midst of a sufficiently unpopulated territory. To the west loomed like a cloud the faint outlines of the Blue Ridge Mountains; to the south sloped the waters of the Northanna, or, as it became more popularly known, the Rivanna. Other settlers in the vicinity were few and scattered—Thomas Jefferson later thought that his father was among the first three or four to enter the district [1]—but the Three Notch'd Road, main artery of east-west travel, passed close to Peter's land and brought welcome relief from the monotony of wilderness existence.

A year after Peter arrived with his family the Virginia Assembly created a new county, Albemarle, out of this western part of Goochland.[2] In so doing it displayed a spirit of optimism in the rapid growth of the colony's western domain which the future was amply to justify, though currently the total population of Albemarle County consisted only of about one hundred whites and a proportionate number of Negro slaves.[3]

Since Peter Jefferson had already officiated as magistrate and sheriff of Goochland County it was natural for him to be appointed one of Albemarle's six new justices of the peace and, in February, 1745, a judge of the Court of Chancery.[4] The following month he was named Lieutenant Colonel of militia—comprising all the able-bodied men in the county entitled to bear arms—and ten years later achieved the high station of county lieutenant, or general commander.[5]

But the Jeffersons and their four small children (a further daughter, Elizabeth, had been born in November, 1744) had barely acclimated themselves to their new surroundings when a most unusual demand was transmitted to them. William Randolph, cousin to Jane Jefferson, bosom friend to Peter and imbiber of the famous punch bowl, died suddenly at Tuckahoe in 1745. Only thirty-three years of age, he was already a widower with three daughters, Judith, Mary and Priscilla, and one son, Thomas Mann, aged four. When his will came to be read, it was found to contain a remarkable provision. After specifying that he had nominated Peter Jefferson as his executor, it declared: "Whereas I have appointed by my will that my Dear only Son Thomas Mann Randolph should have a private education given him at Tuckahoe, my will is that my Dear and loving friend Mr. Peter Jefferson do move down with his family to my Tuckahoe house and remain there till my son comes of age with whom my dear son and his sisters shall live." [6]

If Peter evinced any hesitation in complying with this singular request the record does not disclose it. Actually it was no mere request; though all commentators have treated it as such and attributed Peter's compliance to a natural deference to the wishes of a dead friend. But it is hard to believe that a man with four small children and a laboriously prepared future of his own would readily pull up stakes and return to the neighborhood he had quitted in order to supervise the private education of the son of a friend, no matter how close. Furthermore, Randolph's statement was not couched in the form of a request; it was in effect a command. It is "my will"; and Peter obeyed that will. Was Randolph's calm certitude based on a definite prearrangement between them or on claims which he knew that Jefferson must acknowledge as irresistible? Unfortunately we do not know the answers; nor is it likely that we ever shall.

Whatever the motivation may have been, the Jeffersons packed up their few possessions and with their four children, one an infant in arms, rode the fifty mud-tracked miles to Tuckahoe. That journey constituted the earliest recollection of Thomas Jefferson, barely two years old. In later years he was to recall being seated on a jogging horse, with a slave to hold him steady, and a pillow underneath to cushion him from the jolts and jars of the rutted road.[7]

They came to Tuckahoe early in August, 1745, and remained there for seven years, until 1752. Certainly their adopted home was a far cry from the rude little wilderness cabin they had just quitted. In 1791 an English traveler visited Tuckahoe and described it in the following terms: "It is in the form of an H and has the appearance of two houses, joined by a large saloon; each wing has two stories, and four large rooms on a floor; in one the family reside, and the other is reserved solely for visitors; the saloon that unites them is of considerable magnitude and on each side are doors; the ceiling is lofty, and to these they principally retire in summer... The outhouses are detached at some distance, that the house may be open to air on all sides."[8]

Such an arrangement no doubt made it convenient for the Jeffersons. They were assured of privacy in one wing, and the orphaned Randolphs and their personal servants could occupy the other.

Peter Jefferson set about the management of his deceased friend's estate and the cultivation of his lands with his customary vigor and prudence. The lands were divided into seven noncontiguous farms and necessitated a good deal of overseeing. Tobacco and corn had to be planted and harvested, the slaves superintended, and provision made for the sale and shipment of the tobacco. Peter began his accounts with the "Estate of Coll. William Randolph" on August 19, 1745, and continued them until 1756. They are written in a precise hand and evidence both his careful management and the varied nature of the operations.[9] In spite of his efforts, however, the period of his stewardship ended with a deficit. His entries disclose a total of some £617 in receipts for these years, against which he drew

£644. But such a deficit in net return would excite no comment from the average Virginia planter. From year to year, and generation to generation, the Virginia gentleman ran behind in hard cash, and thought little of it. British merchants were patient and added the current year's debit—with accrued interest, of course—to the total already on their books, passing it on to their sons, just as the Virginian blithely bequeathed the debt to *his* son. By the time of the Revolution, the accrued sums were so enormous that they helped color the attitude of the Virginia planters toward the question of severance from England.

In Peter Jefferson's case, too, it must be remembered that the running expenses were heavy. They included the upkeep of two families and the rearing and education of two groups of children. There is nothing in his accounts, however, to show that he received any compensation besides living expenses for his services as executor, manager and guardian; [10] and he was compelled, in order to provide for the future, to seek additional employment. He sought it as a surveyor, as his father and grandfather had done before him.

Surveyors were greatly in demand at the time. It was an age of easy and almost careless grants by the Council of Virginia to the unestablished wilderness, and in most cases the boundaries were ill-defined. Sometimes, indeed, the Council itself did not know whether its present munificence did not conflict with prior largesse.[11] Therefore it was essential, before perfecting titles, to make exact surveys and file the resultant maps in the county courts. The requirements for a surveyor were simple—a knack with figures, a certain dexterity with instruments, and the physical stamina to break through untraveled wilderness and live, so to speak, off the land. Peter Jefferson taught himself the first two; the third was the gift of nature.

He had already begun the practice of his new profession prior to his removal to Tuckahoe. From the end of 1744 to the end of 1745 he had received around £20 as compensation for his services; [12] but his first big job came the following year. Joshua Fry, a university-trained Englishman, had emigrated to Virginia early in the century and established himself, first as master of a grammar school in Williamsburg, and then as professor of mathematics at William and Mary College. The rewards of teaching being insufficient, he moved on to the newly erected County of Albemarle, where his talents received instant recognition. Together with his new neighbor, Peter Jefferson, he was appointed a justice of the peace; he became County Lieutenant and Colonel of the militia, with Jefferson as his lieutenant colonel; and he also received the post of County Surveyor, again with Jefferson as his assistant.[13]

In 1746, Joshua Fry was called in as one of the surveyors to settle definitively the limits of what was probably the largest patent ever issued in Virginia—the grant to Lord Fairfax, embodying the whole of Northern Neck. From the very beginning there had been sharp dispute between Fairfax and the colony of Virginia as to the exact limits of that regal gift.

An attempt at a survey had been initiated in 1736, but the British Council for Plantation Affairs later determined to run a new dividing line from the south branch of the Rappahannock to the source of the Potomac. A group of "Gentlemen Commissioners," representing both sides to the controversy, was selected to supervise the operation. Among them were such dignitaries as the Hon. William Fairfax, Col. William Beverley, Col. Lomax and others. The surveyors were chosen and Fry, as one of the first to be selected, obtained an appointment for his assistant, Peter Jefferson.

Thomas Lewis, surveyor for the Fairfax interests, kept a journal of this epic survey.[14] He met Fry and Jefferson on September 12, 1746, and the entire expedition, surveyors, instruments, pack men and animals, together with the "Gentlemen Commissioners," set off from Capt. Downs' place on September 19th to plunge directly into the difficult mountain area of the Blue Ridge. The very next day witnessed their first defection. "The mountains made Such a Dismal appearance that John Thomas one of our men took Sick on the Same & So Returned home." [15] Weak-livered John Thomas was not the only one to quit before the survey was finished.

By noon of the 20th the expedition had pushed its way to the head of the river where the earlier survey of 1736 had taken its start, only to discover that the blazed tree markers were lost or obliterated. While other members of the party beat the bush for the vital markers, Peter Jefferson and Captain Winslow surveyed the south branch of the river and Brooke and Lewis plotted the north branch. Still at a loss for the exact point from which to start line surveys the perspiring men moved over the tops of the "Blew Ridge." The Gentlemen Commissioners looked thoughtfully at the tangled steeps and decided that the scramble was not for them. As the working surveyors toiled up the mountainside the commissioners took the easier valley roundabout. Through the trackless mountains went Peter Jefferson and his company, hauling their unwieldy instruments, setting them up on precarious ledges, chopping down trees that masked their sight, scribbling down lengths and angles, until finally they descended on the other slope to the river where they found the commissioners comfortably ensconced in camp. There, narrated Lewis, we "Regald ourselves with Several Black Jacks of Punch." [16]

Thus refreshed, the surveyors clambered up Peaked Mountain, suffering intensely from thirst until, at the very top, they came upon a gush of water which in gratitude they named "the fountain of life." On September 30th, Jefferson and Brooke struggled on ahead with their instruments, while the rest of the party followed at a more leisurely pace. By October 3rd, they reached the top of "Divels Back Bone," a knifelike ridge on which the pack horses went "tumbling over Rocks and precipices & ourselves often in the outmost Danger. This tirable place was Called Purgatory." [17]

Sunday, October 5th, found them deep in the savage mountains, their provisions gone, their horses exhausted and starving; yet they continued indomitably through tangled brush, rotting logs, precipices and sliding rocks, suffering repeated falls and stumbling in the encroaching dark until, at ten that night, they wearily made camp. The next day Jefferson and Lewis struggled down to the river to seek provisions, but they found only "one familey of poor Duch people" in the wild valley, themselves on the verge of starvation, and the two men were compelled to return to their fellows empty-handed.[18]

Yet the surveyors did not give up. While a messenger made his way to the camp of the commissioners for supplies they tightened their belts on empty stomachs and plunged deeper into the mountains, surveying as they went. On October 8th they finally made contact with the commissioners and, once more supplied with food, hacked a path to the top of Allegheny Mountain, matted with laurel and rhododendron and marshy underfoot. This was the highest point of their trek. From there they descended to a river "called the Styx from the Dismal apperance of the place Being," as Lewis described it in his own wonderful spelling, "Sufficen to Strick terror in any human Creature ye Lorals Ivey & Spruce pine so Extremly thick in ye Swamp through which this River Runs that one Cannot have the Least prospect Except they look upwards." The horses slipped in the muddy bottoms and tumbled their loads down the high, encroaching banks into the Stygian waters. Finally the straining men were forced to portage the heavy instruments and supplies themselves through the most dangerous spots. The next day, however, when fortitude and strength seemed wholly at an end, they broke through to pleasant timbered land and a spring of pure, abundant water. "Neve[r] was the Elysian feilds more Wellcome to a Departed Soul than this place," Lewis recorded thankfully.[19]

On October 20th, fortune finally smiled on them. One of the party stumbled on some blazed trees, the first tangible evidence of the earlier survey of 1736. With these as anchor, they could now proceed with the survey of the division line of the Fairfax Grant. After a short rest they commenced their proper task.

Five days later Lewis laconically reported that Peter Jefferson was "very much Indisposed"; but seemingly the ailment was not sufficient to keep him from wading with the rest of the party through the interminable swamps. More of the hardy surveyors went down with fevers and dysentery, among them Brooke and Winslow, but there was no place for stopping. They had to go on.

Finally, on November 13th, they emerged from the wilderness hell, so accurately oriented in their surveys that the camp of the commissioners, their circuitous destination after 76½ miles of measurement, beckoned gratefully a bare hundred yards away. They received a well-earned welcome, and they "Dined Drank his majesties & L. Fairfax hea[l]ths which was accompanyd with a Discharge of nine Guns to Each health."[20] An epic survey had been completed.

Two days later Peter Jefferson set out for Tuckahoe and his family. The next step was to embody in definitive map form the results of their arduous expedition. While all of the members of the party joined in the task, it was Peter Jefferson, representing Virginia, and Robert Brooke, for the Fairfax interests, who affixed their names to the final document.

In 1749, Fry and Jefferson, now well known in their profession, were commissioned to continue the dividing line between Virginia and North Carolina from the place where William Byrd had carried it in 1728. The perils and toils of this new survey, equally as arduous as those of the Fairfax line, have come down to us only as oral tradition, but the satisfaction of the Virginia Council with their reports and maps was sufficiently made tangible in the shape of a grant of £300 sterling to each of them, over and above all expenses.[21]

These travels and explorations whetted Peter's land hunger. That same year he joined with Fry, Dr. Thomas Walker and others, thirty-nine in all, in a tremendous speculation. Under the name of the Loyal Company they received from the Council a vast grant of 800,000 acres on the southern rim of the Virginia frontier,[22] a grant which was to be attended with innumerable later vicissitudes and from which the promoters gained little current profit. But these accomplishments and associates, in addition to Col. Fry's prestige, were sufficient to gain them a respectful hearing in their next venture.

As far back as 1738 Fry and two other surveyors had proposed to the Assembly that they make a comprehensive survey of the entire colony and publish a map. The advantages of the plan were obvious, but the Assembly hemmed and hawed for six years before finally rejecting it. In 1749, Fry returned to the attack, this time in association with Jefferson. The success that had attended their efforts in the Fairfax and the Carolina line surveys and the growing need for accurate and detailed information no doubt swayed the Assembly, and it was graciously indicated to them that they might proceed. They commenced work at once, using old surveys of specific districts and adding to them from all available sources of information. In 1751 they completed their map of "the most inhabited part of Virginia containing the whole province of Maryland with parts of Pensilvania, New Jersey & North Carolina," and signed their names thereto. This map, duly engraved and published in London, still represents the fundamental map of Virginia and its environs, and remained for many years the sole geographical arbiter for the territory it presumed to cover. Virginia awarded Fry and Jefferson each the sum of £150 sterling in appreciation of their efforts;[23] to which must be added the trifling amount cryptically recorded by Peter in his account book: "By drawing 1 map of Virginia, 1½ pistoles."[24]

Fry and Jefferson continued to be close friends and associates in surveying and as officers of the county militia until Fry's sudden death in 1754.

That was the year of Braddock's ill-fated expedition against the French. Fry had been placed in command of the Virginia forces under Braddock, and George Washington had been named his Lieutenant Colonel. While actually on his way to Fort Cumberland, Fry took ill and died; and Washington assumed command. From that sudden death and Washington's promotion were to flow events of incalculable consequence to America. In his will Fry left "to his good friend Col. Jefferson, all his surveying instruments," and nominated him as executor of his estate.[25]

Peter Jefferson remained at Tuckahoe for seven years, obedient to the behest of his deceased friend, William Randolph. For some unknown reason Randolph had a deep-rooted prejudice against the educational practices of both William and Mary College and the institutions of learning in England and specified in his will that Jefferson was not to send his son, Thomas Mann, to either of these places but to provide private tutors at Tuckahoe. His daughters, too, were to receive training according to their "quality and circumstances."

Jefferson followed the main lines of the will and obtained the services of a tutor. To Randolph's children as pupils were added the young Jeffersons of sufficient age, notably little Thomas, two years younger than Thomas Mann Randolph, the pupil in chief. Of this tutor or of the education they received nothing is known. Doubtless it followed the general pattern of elementary instruction in those days: reading, writing and a little arithmetic, together with a degree of moral and religious training. Thomas Jefferson refers to it in his Autobiography as the "English school" and dates his attendance in it from the age of five.

In 1752, when young Thomas was nine years old, the Jeffersons moved back to Shadwell. Peter had not fully complied with the behest of his deceased friend, for Thomas Mann Randolph had certainly not come of age—he was eleven at the time—but doubtless he felt that he had sacrificed enough for friendship. The boy was old enough to proceed under other auspices; Shadwell could not properly thrive under absentee management; Peter's own family was steadily enlarging—Martha had been born in 1746; a son, christened Peter Field in 1748, survived barely a month; another son was stillborn in 1750; but a daughter Lucy, born in 1752, managed to pass the danger point. Twins, Anna Scott and Randolph, who came upon the scene in 1755, completed the sum of Peter's offspring.

Returned to Shadwell, the Jeffersons found that their initial cabin was neither sufficient for their numerous family nor adequate for their enhanced dignity and station in life. Peter proceeded to remedy the defect. He called in a master carpenter, John Bissell, who, together with Jefferson's artisan slaves, built additional tobacco houses, a mill and some ovens, moved and finished the stable, mended the hen house, added several small houses and, in 1753, set down the sills for a "Dwelling House" which was roofed over in 1754.[26] Thus Peter laid the foundation for an establishment at Shadwell which, modest though it always remained in comparison with the noble plantation homes of some of his compatriots, nevertheless represented the comfortable average of the inhabitants of Albemarle county. Excavations, commenced in 1941 and still continuing, disclose the general ground plan of Peter Jefferson's final home as it existed during his lifetime and the youth of his son Thomas, until fire wiped it out in 1770.[27]

It was here that Peter passed the remainder of his life, watching the semiwilderness burgeon into settled territory, achieving the respect and friendship of his neighbors, and participating in the communal activities of the district. In 1747, he had been appointed to the vestry of St. James—the hallmark of substantial citizenry;[28] now in 1755 he was already a churchwarden of St. Anne Parish.[29] But the crowning point of his career was the accolade awarded him by the citizens of Albemarle when they sent him to the House of Burgesses as their representative for the years 1754-55.[30] These public duties, together with his surveying, land speculations, farming and the care of a numerous family, rounded out a busy and honorable life.

The education of young Thomas, as his eldest son and chief heir, called for careful planning. In a sense it had been a stroke of good luck that Peter had been called to Tuckahoe to take charge of the Randolph children; for those years of guardianship concentrated his attention sharply on the processes of learning, so that he was able to employ them to good effect in bringing up his son. It is quite likely that otherwise Peter would have been content to provide Thomas with the normal schooling of their class, but no more. Now, however, he developed more ambitious plans, involving a thorough classical education for his son and heir. Thomas Jefferson more than once was to remember with deepest gratitude this decision of his father. "I have often heard him say," declared Thomas's grandson, "that if he had to decide between pleasure derived from the classical education which his father had given him, and the estate left him, he would decide in favor of the former."[31]

At Tuckahoe, Thomas had received the fundamentals of English. Now, aged nine, he was to obtain Latin. But there were no teachers then competent to teach in the vicinity of Shadwell nor, for that matter, anywhere in the comparatively raw county of Albemarle. Some five miles away from Tuckahoe, however, at Dover Church, preached the Rev. William Douglas, a Scot who had come to Virginia in 1748 or 1749, tutored for a while in Westmoreland County, then returned to England for ordination, and come back to assume clerical duties in St. James Parish. As was customary with the low-paid clergy of the interior, Douglas eked out his salary with teaching.[32] Peter Jefferson was vestryman of the parish at the time and, in 1752, when he made his move back to Shadwell, determined to leave young Thomas behind in Douglas's care.

The Rev. William Douglas was not a brilliant scholar nor a particularly good teacher. Jefferson was to remember him as a superficial Latinist, a worse Grecian and somewhat acquainted with the French tongue. Nevertheless, the boy managed to gain some knowledge of the rudiments of these three languages from the clergyman, for which Peter paid at the rate of £16 a year for tuition and board.[33]

Young Thomas remained at Dover under Douglas's tutelage for five years, until his father's death. That took place on August 17, 1757, after an illness of several months. Peter Jefferson was only forty-nine at the time, and in the full vigor of manhood. Behind him he left a widow and eight children, the oldest of whom was seventeen and the youngest not quite two.

The boy naturally hastened to Shadwell on receipt of the tragic news. He was fourteen now and male head of the family. Most of his formative years had been spent away from the scene of his birth, first at Tuckahoe and then at Dover. Only during vacation periods had he been for any length of time at Shadwell. What stuck chiefly in his memory of those infrequent stays were the Indians who on occasion traveled the great road that swept past Shadwell to distant Williamsburg. In particular he remembered "the great Outassetè, the warrior and orator of the Cherokees," who always stopped at Shadwell as Peter's guest when he journeyed down the highway. The boy would haunt the camp which the Indian chief and his entourage pitched on the Jefferson lands and drink in vivid impressions of stately red men that remained to color his future dealings with the race. One scene he then witnessed stirred the young lad profoundly and remained fixed in his imagination to extreme old age. "I was in his camp," he reminisced in 1812, "when he made his great farewell oration to his people the evening before his departure for England. The moon was in full splendor, and to her he seemed to address himself in his prayers for his own safety on the voyage, and that of his people during his absence; his sounding voice, distinct articulation, animated action, and the solemn silence of his people at their several fires, filled me with awe and veneration, although I did not understand a word he uttered." [34]

CHAPTER 3

Education of a Virginian

PETER JEFFERSON left a comfortable estate to his family and in sound, manageable condition. Nor was it laden with the burden of debt that only too often frittered away the ostensible substance of the average Virginia holding. A life of unremitting activity and prudent investment had borne fruit. His lands at Shadwell, Monticello and its environs, Poplar Forest and elsewhere totaled somewhere around 7,500 acres, and were largely good, cultivable property. The group of buildings he had erected at Shadwell were sufficient for the current needs of his family. They were surprisingly well furnished; the inventory of his personal possessions discloses a cherry-tree desk, a walnut desk, two bookcases which housed his little library, black walnut tables and chairs to match, arm chairs, mirrors, dressing tables, the inevitable beds and bedding, and fine silver services that were doubtless imported from England. Nor was his farm less well stocked: twenty-one horses, a goodly number of cows, hogs and sheep, and fifty-three slaves to tend the fields and take care of personal wants. The Jeffersons would not be poor.[1]

To his wife, Jane, Peter left the house and lands at Shadwell for life, one-sixth of the household goods and slaves, two work horses and one-third of the other farm animals. To the six daughters went body servants and the sum of £200 each, payable to them either on marriage or the attainment of twenty-two years of age. The slaves otherwise undisposed of went to his sons, Thomas and the infant Randolph; and the balance of his livestock was to be sold and the avails used "for the support and maintenance of my Family and for the benefit of my two sons equally." To Thomas, as the elder son, went the largest portion of the estate: "my mulatto fellow Tawny, my books, mathematical instruments, and my cherry tree desk and bookcase"; the choice of either his lands on the Rivanna or on the Fluvanna, election to be made within one year after he reached twenty-one; and the residuary estate. To Randolph went the lands which Thomas did not choose. However, all lands, no matter to whom granted, were made subject to "the maintenance of my family, the education of my younger children, and the payment of my daughters' Portions." [2]

As executors and guardians Peter chose an impressive assemblage: Colonel Peter Randolph, who was Jane's cousin; Thomas Turpin, who had married Peter's sister Mary; Dr. Thomas Walker of Castle Hill, who had attended Peter in his last illness; and John Harvie of Belmont, lawyer and associate of Peter in some of his more grandiose speculations. Of these only Walker and Harvie did any real work, and it was Harvie who did the most. Both men played a considerable role in young Thomas Jefferson's life, and the son of Dr. Walker was to continue the part in a manner at once amazing and sinister.[3]

Thomas Jefferson eventually elected to take the lands on the Rivanna which, together with those received as part of the residuary estate, came to almost 5,000 acres. The Rivanna tract alone, comprising about 2,500 acres, was appraised at £2,129, 10 s., 1½ d.[4] In addition, he became the owner of some thirty slaves, considerable personal belongings, and the rights to the Shadwell property on his mother's death. So he received an excellent start in life, both in worldly goods and in sound guardianship, even though in later years he was to throw a veil of pathos over his predicament. "When I recollect that at fourteen years of age," he then wrote, "the whole care and direction of myself was thrown on myself entirely, without a relation or friend qualified to advise or guide me, and recollect the various sorts of bad company with which I associated from time to time, I am astonished I did not turn off with some of them and become as worthless to society as they were."[5] This was untrue both in substance and detail. He was extremely fortunate in having such able, conscientious and understanding guardians as Harvie and Dr. Walker, and none of his youthful associates turned out to be as worthless as he pretended. But then he was writing a hortatory letter to his young grandson, and there is a tendency to exaggerate the hardships of one's own childhood in such circumstances.

Nevertheless the death of his father did mark a distinct turning point in Jefferson's life. He could look forward to an assured place in society and he was back at Shadwell from which he had been absent, except for intermittent periods, almost all his life. In one particular, however, the wishes of his father as well as his own held his course unchanged. He was to obtain the best classical education that Virginia could afford.

It was unfeasible for young Thomas to return to the tutelage of the inept Mr. Douglas, and fortunately there was no necessity for it. A school had recently been instituted in the parish of Fredericksville at Hanover, in the shadow of the Southwest Mountains, by the pastor of the parish, the Reverend James Maury. Born in Dublin in 1718, he was the son of Matthew Maury, whose French Huguenot ancestors had fled the revocation of the Edict of Nantes to the safety of the English domain. Attracted by the lure of the New World, Matthew voyaged to Virginia before his wife gave birth to his son James and, in 1719, sent funds for them to join him. James grew up destined for the church. After attending William and Mary College he went to England to be ordained, as was essential under the rules of the Anglican Church, and returned to Virginia to officiate first as rector of King William Parish and then of Fredericksville in 1752.

In view of the later clamor against the allegedly munificent perquisites of the clergymen of the established church, it is significant that so many of Virginia's men of the cloth had to eke out their incomes by teaching and boarding scholars. Maury set up a little school in a log cabin on his land and invited the neighboring planters to send him their sons. His reputation was good, his classical learning adequate and, more important perhaps, his wife's uncle was Dr. Thomas Walker, one of the guardians of young Jefferson, now in search of just such an establishment. Accordingly Thomas, nearing fifteen, was sent off to become a boarder at Fredericksville, whose nearness to Shadwell enabled him to spend the week ends at home.

The Reverend James Maury was a sorely harassed and despondent man, albeit a man of learning, a good clergyman and the author of a treatise on education. For one thing, he disliked his sprawling parish which necessitated laborious journeys on horseback; for another, he had eight growing children to support, and the income he received, fixed by law, was inadequate to their demands. Further to exasperate him and to reduce his income came the Act of the Virginia Assembly in 1755 which in its effect cut the salaries of the clergy to a bare pittance. In 1748 the Assembly, with royal approval, had fixed the amount at 16,000 pounds of tobacco a year. But by 1755 the price of tobacco had gone up considerably, and it was felt that such a variable scale imposed too much of a hardship on the tithe-paying parishioners. Accordingly, the Assembly shifted from a tobacco base to cash, and set the equivalent at two pence per pound of tobacco. At the current price for tobacco, this was a distinct loss of income to the clergy. They protested vigorously, appealing to the bishop in London for relief. None was forthcoming. The triumphant Assembly re-enacted the law in 1758.[6] This time the clergy sent an advocate to England to plead their cause, and the king in council now disallowed both acts—those of 1755 and 1758.

James Maury, who perhaps had felt the pinch most and had been among the loudest protestants, brought suit against his parishioners to recover the difference in salaries paid him under the annulled Acts and the then current price of tobacco. The case, which was finally tried at Hanover Courthouse in 1763, became a *cause célèbre*, brought unwelcome notoriety to Maury and the beginning of immortality to a youthful and almost briefless lawyer named Patrick Henry, and did much to sharpen the dispute between Church and State in Virginia which led to eventual disestablishment. Maury won his case, as the law was plain; but Henry's oratorical assault on tyranny, together with the Presbyterian leanings of the jury, made the victory a hollow one. The verdict was exactly one penny in damages.[7] Of the implications of this famous trial more will be said hereafter.

Young Jefferson found Maury's school much more to his liking than those of his previous instructors. For one thing, the pastor grounded him thoroughly in Latin and Greek, those languages which were fundamental to the education of a gentleman; for another, Maury, whose range of interests was wide even for that encyclopedic age, initiated the lad into the mysteries of natural philosophy and the elements of geology. It was Maury who first discovered the prints of fossil sea shells on the crests of the Blue Ridge Mountains, a discovery which was later to color the thinking of his greatest pupil and bring him to much speculative assertions on the nature of the world and of Deity itself.[8]

Maury had vigorous and strongly held opinions on the subject of education, and expressed them at some length in a letter to a friend several years after Jefferson had moved on to other fields; but there is no doubt that he had held them as well in 1758.[9] Maury was obviously no liberal, nor an equalitarian; yet there was a sound vein of common sense in his views, some of which reappeared in Jefferson's own ideas on education at a later time. Greek and Latin, thought Maury, were "absolutely necessary" for the student of divinity, medicine or law, and were useful and ornamental for those who could be classed as "gentlemen." For the lower classes, he doubted their value. And even for gentlemen, especially of the Virginia persuasion, he placed more emphasis on a general knowledge of their own country, of history, literature, geography and "Chronology." In fact, he questioned the whole theory of the current educational practices with their almost exclusive preoccupation with the ancient tongues and their antiquarian bypaths. Unless considerably supplemented by more practical studies, he inquired, of what earthly value were they to the average Virginia planter, immersed in daily affairs, the rearing of his family and the management of his estate?

How much of this iconoclastic doctrine he passed on to his pupils is conjectural. Certainly it did not interfere with a rigorous training in those classics which he had called merely "useful and ornamental"; yet it is possible that enough of his attitude seeped through to influence Jefferson's thought, at least in retrospect.

Jefferson's two years at Maury's school were pleasant and fruitful. We have no description of him at the time, but there is no doubt that he was already tall and gangling, with reddish-sandy hair and a light, freckled skin that illy took the sun. His classmates were few—only four in number—but select. All of them were to exercise a considerable influence on his career, and their ties were to be of the closest.

First among them was James Maury, Jr., the pastor's own son. Maury was younger than Jefferson, and the latter felt paternally toward the lad, for he would bring him along to Shadwell "of a Saturday." Though their paths diverged in later life, Maury going to England and becoming a merchant, they kept up an intermittent correspondence, and on Jefferson's death, Maury lamented "much on hearing my antient class mate had left me the sole survivor of the *five* who were together somewhat more than *three score and ten years ago*."[10]

James Madison was the second of the pupils; *not* the James Madison who later became Jefferson's closest personal and political associate as well as President of the United States, but his cousin. This James Madison was an important figure in his own right, becoming a bishop of the Anglican Church, president of William and Mary College, and a man of broad intellectual and scientific interests. They could not have had too much in common at the time, for Madison was six years younger than Jefferson, but in later years the tie grew stronger and they maintained a steady correspondence, chiefly concerned with their mutual intellectual pursuits.

The third was Dabney Carr. Young Carr, six months younger than Jefferson, fast became his dearest friend. Their relationship assumed the classic mantle of Damon and Pythias. They roamed the neighboring hills together; they confided their innermost thoughts and most secret dreams; they went on together to William and Mary and to the practice of law. Dabney Carr achieved a quick reputation at the bar, rivaling the redoubtable Patrick Henry in forensic eloquence, and entered the House of Burgesses under the best auspices. When, on July 20, 1765, he married Martha Jefferson, Thomas's younger sister, Thomas's happiness was complete. The two young men continued the close conjuncture of their lives in politics and in the early stages of the struggle with England. In 1773, Carr became a member of the colonial Committee of Correspondence and was chosen to move the resolutions of protest against the British Parliament. He did so with force and eloquence, and it was generally agreed that a remarkable career lay ahead for the young advocate. Just thirty-five days later, however, on May 16, 1773, he was dead. The tragedy of his passing left a deep and ineradicable mark on Jefferson's mind and heart; he never forgot the close companion of his youth and early manhood, of whom his widowed sister remained a constant reminder. It is doubtful whether Jefferson was ever again to lavish such unrestrained affection on any friend.[11]

The last of Jefferson's classmates was John Walker, familiarly known as "Jack." Young Jack was the son of Dr. Walker, Jefferson's guardian, and related to the Rev. James Maury. On all counts, therefore, it was natural that he and Jefferson should become good friends; and that friendship continued for many years until politics and an ugly scandal destroyed it beyond all possible repair.

Thomas Jefferson was the oldest of Maury's little group of pupils, and it may plausibly be assumed that he was their leader, both in studies and in their extracurricular activities. They found time from their construing of Latin and Greek authors to roam the woods and hunt small game in the neighboring mountains, and to play boyish tricks on one another. One of these, attributed to the boy Jefferson by Maury, Jr. in reminiscent old age, discloses a sense of humor and a turn for obfuscation that it is a pity did not survive in Jefferson the man. Dabney Carr owned a horse of whose fleetness of foot he was inordinately proud; young Jefferson possessed a pony whose snail-like pace excited the risibilities of his comrades. Whereupon Thomas challenged Dabney to a race, a challenge which was speedily accepted. The site for the epic match was marked out; a flat stretch of ground near Belvoir, part of Dr. Walker's estate. Thomas set the time. The race, he gravely announced, would be run on February the thirtieth. The unsuspecting lads eagerly awaited the fated day, no doubt speculating what possessed Jefferson to pit his slow-paced mount against Carr's agile steed. Not until February came to a close did they realize the hoax that had been played on them.[12]

Jefferson remained with Maury until the beginning of 1760 and, for all his escapades, received a thorough grounding in the classics and an awareness of earth's processes on which the later superstructure of his life was based. At the end of each year the schoolmaster sent a bill for board, lodging and tuition to the executors of the estate, and both bills were duly paid. For the year 1758 he charged £22; for 1759 only £20, perhaps because Jefferson did not quite complete the term.[13]

Nor did the guardians feel that their duties were ended with the processes of formal education. They provided young Thomas with sufficient pocket money and they hired a dancing master, a Mr. Alexander Ingles, to teach five of the Jefferson brood, of whom it is likely that Thomas was one, the intricacies of the dance.[14] Perhaps it was from him also that the boy learned to play the violin. Such knowledge was indispensable to the Virginia gentry; dancing ranged alongside of riding, hunting and racing as one of the essential accomplishments of the day. Jefferson became a good, though possibly not a too graceful, dancer. He sat his horse with the best of them and felt himself, like a true Virginian, happiest when on the back of a fine, blooded steed. As a boy he shouldered his gun and scoured the woods for game; but he lost his taste for hunting in maturity, preferring rather to observe the habits of wild life than to shoot them for sport. Aside from the abortive match with Dabney Carr, however, he never developed a passion for racing; that was a species of gambling which had ruined many an old Virginia house, and Jefferson steadfastly steered clear of any excess. But the violin did become a passion. For years he fiddled assiduously, and when compelled by circumstances to give up its daily practice, he harked back with nostalgic longing to the days when melody poured forth from the administration of his bow.

It has been too often assumed that during these boyhood years at Shadwell Jefferson was immersed in a semiwilderness, from which he did not emerge and enter into the social air and clime until he went to Williamsburg to become a student at William and Mary. But an attentive reading of the documents discloses that, if anything, Shadwell and its neighborhood possessed too many distracting gaieties and streams of company for sober, continuous study. The Jeffersons were a large family and their connections were good. Only too often, young Thomas was to complain, were his week ends at home from Maury's school devoted to the entertainment of visitors instead of to his books. Besides, his two elder sisters were grown young women and the second of them, Mary, was already engaged to John Bolling of Goochland, whom she was to marry on January 24, 1760. Jane, the elder, remained unmated until her untimely death at the age of twenty-five, some five years later.

Whether it was these distractions and their consequent expense that led the boy to consider quitting Shadwell and Maury's tutelage for more distant fields, as he alleged, is a matter of doubt. The great world, as embodied in the small colonial capital, beckoned enticingly; and without question a more varied curriculum was available in the colonial college.

The Christmas holiday of 1759 brought to a decision what the youth of sixteen had probably been meditating for some time. He had been invited to the home of Nathan Dandridge in Hanover to spend the season of cheer. He remained a fortnight and found himself in a large, gay company which, according to custom, made the rounds of the hospitable houses in the neighborhood, eating, drinking, dancing, flirting and playing games. Perhaps some young collegians from William and Mary were present, whose *savoir-faire* and stories fired young Jefferson to the final determination.

But only one recognizable name of the festive company has come down to us—Patrick Henry. That rawboned, loose-jointed young man, seven years older than Jefferson, was reading law at the time after unsuccessful attempts to become either a storekeeper or a farmer, and he was the life of the party. Jefferson, remembering the occasion in old age when he cordially detested the man, thought then that Henry's manners "had something of the coarseness of the society he had frequented; his passion was fiddling, dancing and pleasantry. He excelled in the last, and it attached every one to him." [15]

Filled with his new determination, Thomas quit the party to pay a courtesy call on Col. Peter Randolph, one of his guardians. To him he spoke of his eagerness to attend college. Randolph approved. But the final decision rested with John Harvie. When the boy returned to Shadwell, therefore, he wrote a carefully composed, if somewhat ingenuous, letter pleading his cause to the arbiter of his fortunes.

SIR,—I was at Colo. Peter Randolph's about a Fortnight ago, & my Schooling falling into Discourse, he said he thought it would be to my Advantage to go to the College, & was desirous I should go, as indeed I am myself for several Reasons. In the first place as long as I stay at the Mountains the Loss of one fourth of my Time is inevitable, by Company's coming here & detaining me from School. And likewise my Absence will in a great Measure put a Stop to so much Company, & by that means lessen the Expences of the Estate in House-Keeping. And on the other Hand by going to the College I shall get a more universal Acquaintance, which may hereafter be serviceable to me; & I suppose I can pursue my Studies in the Greek & Latin as well there as here, & likewise learn something of the Mathematics. I shall be glad of your opinion.[16]

Harvie saw the advantages to be derived from attendance in Williamsburg, even though he may not have quite followed his young ward's argument that financially the estate would benefit from such an arrangement, and added his approval.

Joyfully the young lad set his affairs in order, packed his clothes and books, said good-by to his erstwhile mentor, the Reverend James Maury, and to his small band of fellow pupils, some of whom were to follow him at a later date to the common goal, and bade farewell to his mother, his sister Jane and the younger children. Mary had already departed in the guise of Mrs. Bolling to set up an establishment of her own. Mounting his horse and accompanied by a body servant with his baggage, young Jefferson took the Three Notch'd Road toward Williamsburg.

It was the middle of March, 1760, and spring was in the air. The first green was covering the bare red earth and the mountains fell away behind as they jogged down the muddy, thawing highway toward the flat Tidewater and the capital of Virginia. Within several days they arrived in town. But an unforeseen hitch arose. Most of the students who attended William and Mary came up from the grammar school attached to the college, and Jefferson had to convince the faculty that his preparatory schooling was adequate. After a two weeks' delay, during which his qualifications were examined, the applicant was duly admitted and commenced residence on March 25, 1760.[17]

William and Mary was the oldest institution of higher learning in the South, and the second oldest in the American Colonies, having been preceded only by Harvard. Already sixty-seven years in existence, the college was still a comparatively small affair, limited both in faculty and in instruction. Situated at the western terminus of the Duke of Gloucester Street and fronting on the Jamestown Road, it consisted of a main building modeled on plans of Christopher Wren, the great English architect, a smaller building called the Brafferton House, and the living quarters of the president of the college. The Wren building in particular was stately and gracefully planned, and Jefferson must have thought so at the time, though in later years he was to sneer at the college architecture, together with that of the hospital for the insane, as "rude misshapen piles, which, but that they have roofs, would be taken for brick-kilns." [18]

But by that time he was deeply infatuated with the neoclassic forms of architecture and considered that there was scarcely a building, public or private, worthy of note in all Virginia. In fact, only two public buildings—both in Williamsburg—were deemed worthy of even grudging praise.

They were the capitol, which he thought "a light and airy structure," though it could be critized in detail as sinning against severe canons of art, and the Governor's Palace which, while "not handsome without," was "spacious and commodious within," and "prettily situated." As for the rest of it, "the genius of architecture seems to have shed its maledictions over this land... the first principles of the art are unknown, and there exists scarcely a model among us sufficiently chaste to give an idea of them." [19] This, it must be repeated, was hindsight and certainly not Jefferson's first impressions of either the college or the town.

The same held good for the government of the college and the courses of instruction. In his *Notes on Virginia*, Jefferson's strictures on his alma mater were severe. "The admission of the learners of Latin and Greek [from the grammar school]," he declared, "filled the college with children. This rendering it disagreeable and degrading to young gentlemen already prepared for entering on the sciences, they were discouraged from resorting to it, and thus the schools for mathematics and moral philosophy, which might have been of some service, became of very little." [20] Here again, the harsh judgment did not represent either his earlier or his later more considered views. For, within a few years after, he was advising young men to go to William and Mary rather than an English or European university, and to the end of his life he remained enthusiastic over the caliber of the instruction he had received.

The college was governed by a Board of Visitors with inquisitorial powers. The faculty consisted of a president, who at the moment was the Reverend Thomas Dawson, to be succeeded within a year by the Reverend William Yates, and six professors. Neither of the incumbent presidents seems to have made any impression on Jefferson; the case was far different with at least one of the professors. The chairs of instruction followed chiefly the usual lines of the times: Greek and Latin, mathematics, moral philosophy and divinity; but one was of a different sort—the chair for teaching Indians on the campus and seeking their conversion to Christianity.

At the time of Jefferson's arrival, however, not all of these chairs were filled. The struggle over the Two Penny Act, previously mentioned, had led to the dismissal of three of the professors; and another one, Jacob Rowe, who incongruously attempted to teach Jefferson moral philosophy, was righteously dismissed within a few months for overconviviality and for participating too enthusiastically in town and gown affrays. Dawson himself, the president, was accused and convicted of drunkenness; so that, despite the theologic background of the college, the atmosphere at the time of Jefferson's entrance could not be said to have been too uplifting.[21]

In a sense, however, these defections and dismissals proved fortunate for the career of the youthful student. It brought him into enforced and intimate contact with a truly great scholar and an even greater teacher, one of the two happy influences that molded Jefferson's early life and colored all his days with grateful memories. This was Dr. William Small; the other, who came on the scene a little later, was George Wythe.

William Small was a Scot who had come to Virginia in 1758 to accept the chair of mathematics at William and Mary. When the time of troubles came, Small found himself teaching, in addition, natural history and metaphysics; and when Rowe, who occupied the chair of moral philosophy, disappeared from view, he took that over as well. In effect he was the entire faculty, with the exception of Latin and Greek, so far as Jefferson's first year was concerned. It was in truth a happy concatenation of circumstances, as Jefferson later testified. "It was my great good fortune," he wrote, "and what probably fixed the destinies of my life that Dr. Wm. Small of Scotland was then professor of Mathematics, a man profound in most of the useful branches of science, with a happy talent of communication, correct and gentlemanly manners, & an enlarged & liberal mind. He, most happily for me, became soon attached to me & made me his daily companion when not engaged in the school; and from his conversation I got my first views of the expansion of science & of the system of things in which we are placed." When, as Jefferson delicately put it, the chair of philosophy became vacant, Small was "appointed to fill it per interim" and became the first to give regular lectures at the college in "Ethics, Rhetoric & Belles lettres."[22]

It is a pity that so little is known of this commanding personality, for other students similarly testified to the quality of his teaching, his eloquence and logic, and the liberality of his views. He was responsible, without doubt, for the turn which Jefferson's thoughts took toward scientific investigation, though Maury perhaps had here paved the way; and it is quite likely that his undogmatic and naturalistic approach toward the problems of philosophy and the nature and governance of the universe were similarly responsible for his greatest pupil's deistic tendencies. It was he also who brought Jefferson to the attention of George Wythe and the new governor of Virginia, Francis Fauquier. But of these memorable acquaintances, and the "*partie quarrée*" they formed, more shortly.

Small quit the college in 1764 under disagreeable circumstances. He had come over under temporary appointment to the chair of mathematics, and when the former professor, dismissed over the Two Penny Act controversy, won his appeal in England for reinstatement, Small continued in moral philosophy alone. But the Board of Visitors insisted on the right to remove any professor at will, no doubt because of the recent unpleasantness. Small refused to remain under these circumstances and departed for England in 1764. An acrimonious exchange of letters ensued, and he never returned. Instead, he entered on the practice of medicine and became the friend of some of the greatest and most enlightened spirits then resident in England. Together with Erasmus Darwin, James Watt, Joseph Priestley, Josiah Wedgwood and others of a similar inquiring turn of mind, he formed the Lunar Society of Birmingham, where scientific and philosophical matters were discussed at the various members' houses with great acumen and much enthusiasm. William Blake was to satirize the Lunar Society in his poetical *An Island in the Moon* because of the endless scientific advances they envisaged and their sceptical attitude toward any mystical or spiritual foundation for the world. Small died in 1775, on the very verge of the American Revolution.[23]

It is incredible that Jefferson did not correspond with his beloved master after his departure for England, but only one letter has survived, written May 7, 1775, which evidently did not arrive in England until after Small's death. In spite of the fact, as Jefferson put it, that Lexington and Concord had "cut off our last hope of reconciliation" with Great Britain, he was sending Small three dozen bottles of Madeira now and three dozen later, "genuine from the island, & has been kept in my own cellar eight years." [24] It is a pity that Small was never able to enjoy the wine sent him by his most beloved pupil.

If Jefferson was fortunate in his association with Dr. Small on an intellectual level during his college days, he was almost equally happy in his associations with his classmates. They were the sons of the middle gentry of Virginia and in many respects represented its sturdiest stock. They came rather from central and western Virginia than the Tidewater, whose aristocratic families preferred to send their heirs for education to England. Among Jefferson's bosom companions were Dabney Carr and John Walker, who had followed him from Maury's school to William and Mary, John Page of Rosewell, who next to Carr became his closest friend, John Tyler and Francis Willis of Gloucester County.

All of his fellows agreed on Jefferson's remarkable application to his studies which, they cheerfully admitted, far surpassed their own. Page recalled that he himself had never "made any great proficiency in any study, for I was too sociable, and fond of the conversation of my friends, to study as Mr. Jefferson did, who could tear himself away from his dearest friends, to fly to his studies." [25] Page was of an age with Jefferson, and had come to the college from the attached grammar school. He lived in style in the house of the president of the college who, as Page made no bones in acknowledging, "my Father had feed handsomely to be my private tutor." [26] His lack of book knowledge did not prevent him from later becoming governor of his native state.

Jefferson, on the other hand, requiring no such special attention, roomed with John Tyler and Francis Willis. Tyler was four years younger than Jefferson, and took his elder roommate as a model for applying himself to his studies. He too was to become a governor of Virginia. But Willis was of a different sort. He preferred the recreations and dissipations of the town to poring over dull repositories of knowledge. Coming home at midnight from some escapade and perhaps a trifle overburdened with wine, he would consider it the height of comedy to surprise his roommates still at the midnight lamp, tip over the table and run off with their books. He also stabled his horse in the cellar of their domicile.[27] What Jefferson thought of his comrade's sense of humor has not been revealed.

Not that Jefferson was a mere devotee of books, and nothing else. He was young, a Virginia gentleman of spirit, and sociable. The students of William and Mary seem to have been pretty much as college students have always been through the ages, ready for a fight or a frolic The fight, still in accordance with tradition, was usually with the town. Jacob Rowe had been dismissed for leading his students in the affrays, but his enforced absence had not put a stop to continued struggles. In later years Jefferson was to recall with obvious enjoyment "the regular annual riots and battles between the students of William and Mary with the town boys, before the Revolution, *quorum pars fui* [of which I was a part]."[28]

All his life Jefferson remained grateful for the education he had received, and particularly for his training in the classics. To the Latin and Greek models he attributed "the chaste and rational style of modern composition, instead of the inflated & vague manner of the Eastern & Northern nations." Even as a luxury, he declared long after, "I should feel myself more indebted to my father for having procured it to me, than for any other luxury I derive from his bounty."[29]

CHAPTER 4

Law, Life and Love

TWO years of assiduous application to his studies exhausted the potentialities of William and Mary for Jefferson. He was now nineteen, and it was necessary for him to come to a decision as to the future. For most of his fellow students the path was simple and direct. They returned to their estates and became gentlemen managers of broad plantations, tilling the soil with the aid of slaves and overseers, establishing families, riding and hunting, and partaking in the local affairs of their counties. For those who wished to do otherwise, only three courses were open—to practice law, to enter the ministry, or to study medicine. Politics as a career was as yet subsidiary in colonial Virginia, and was chiefly engaged in as an adjunct to the law. Trade was out of the question.

It does not seem likely that at the moment young Jefferson had any hankering to return to Shadwell and develop his holdings. His mother was resident there and in possession for life of its perquisites. The acres on the Rivanna and elsewhere, of which he held the fee, were still on the rim of what might be called civilization and would have required arduous and exacting toil to bring them to the level of Tidewater estates. Besides, his appetite for the life of learning and for the gracious variety of Williamsburg had grown on that with which it had been fed. The ministry held no charms for him; his emerging deism and the sceptical influence of Dr. Small closed that avenue quite effectively. Medicine, though fitted for a gentleman, held no high estate, and Jefferson never thought much of the ministrations of doctors. That left the law which, as a learned profession, highly esteemed and centered in Williamsburg, fitted all requirements.

The young man discussed the matter with his preceptor, Dr. Small, in their innumerable walks and talks. There were no schools of law anywhere in America and, unless one went to England to attend the Inns of Court, the procedure to follow was to study with some practicing attorney and under his guidance. Dr. Small's most intimate friend in Williamsburg was George Wythe, perhaps the most learned and scholarly lawyer in all Virginia, if not in the colonies generally. On Small's advice, Jefferson entered Wythe's law office and thereby came under the second great influence of his early career.[1]

George Wythe, then thirty-five years of age, had never received any formal schooling and, according to Jefferson, had unassisted become the best Latin and Greek scholar in the state, teaching himself as well mathematics, natural and moral philosophy.[2] But a British traveler made a more romantic tale of it, insisting that Wythe obtained "a perfect knowledge of the Greek language" on his mother's knee in the "back woods" in which he was born.[3] Whatever the merits of the story it is obvious from his handwriting that he had never properly learned the art of penmanship; for he formed large, quavering, sprawling letters that might easily be attributed to the painful efforts of a child of six. Trumbull's portrait of him as he ostensibly appeared at the signing of the Declaration of Independence, discloses a plain-featured man, with a recessive, baldish forehead and an overlong Roman nose. But his dark brown eyes are deep-set and contemplative as befits a philosophic turn of mind, and there is an air of kindliness and general benevolence that fits well with all pen portraits that have come down to us.

If Jefferson had been deeply impressed with Dr. Small, he became equally so with his new teacher. Perhaps even more, since his friendship with Small terminated unavoidably on the latter's departure for England; while Wythe continued, first as mentor and then as valiant co-worker in the cause of revolution and on behalf of their mutually beloved Virginia until his tragic death by poisoning in 1806 at the hands of a grand-nephew.

But before he died, Wythe managed to secure a solid niche in American history. As a lawyer and jurist he was pre-eminent. His manner of reasoning was logical and precise; according to Jefferson, he never employed a "useless or declamatory thought or word." As a member of the House of Burgesses he exercised a salutary restraining influence on his more hot-headed associates during the turbulent years that preceded the Revolution, yet he was bold enough when the occasion demanded. His signature to the Declaration of Independence may have seemed shaky, but there was no inward quavering over the act itself. Appointed one of the first judges of the Court of Chancery in 1778, and the first incumbent of the chair of law at William and Mary in 1780, he helped chart the future course of American jurisprudence; while his work in revising the laws of Virginia, in conjunction with Jefferson and others, was epochal.

Of Wythe's character the testimony is unanimous and approaches the panegyric. He was likened in virtue, integrity and purity of manners to the ancient Roman senators of whom Plutarch wrote; while Jefferson never could find sufficient laudatory phrases to express his gratitude and affection for the man who had first taught him law. Wythe, he declared, was "the Cato of his country, without the avarice of the Roman"; he was "my second father," "my antient master, my earliest & best friend; and to him I am indebted for first impressions which have had the most salutary influence on the course of my life."[4]

Even after the pupil had achieved overwhelming fame and station, he always deferred with respect to the opinions of the master, and sought his advice whenever possible. The news of Wythe's death in 1806, and the manner of its making, shocked Jefferson to the cry that "such an instance of depravity has been hitherto known to us only in the fables of the poets."

And the information that Wythe had bequeathed to him his books and philosophical apparatus, his silver cups and gold-headed cane, touched the sensibilities of the then President of the United States to the quick.[5]

Jefferson settled down to his study of law in the office of George Wythe with the same pertinacity and thoroughness that he had displayed from his earliest days. The student who placed himself under the tutelage of a practicing attorney usually helped around the office, acted as messenger boy and clerk, looked up points of law and carried his master's books for him to court in return for the training he received. In addition, as in all apprenticeships, he paid a fee for the privilege. In Jefferson's case, however, there is no record of any sums being turned over to Wythe or of any articles of apprenticeship between the two. This may explain what has troubled previous biographers: why, in view of Jefferson's known gratitude to Wythe, did he shortly thereafter advise his cousin, young Philip Turpin, against any such apprenticeship if he wished to study law. "I always was of opinion," he then declared, "that the placing a youth to study with an attorney was rather a prejudice than a help. We are all too apt by shifting on them our business, to incroach on that time which should be devoted to their studies. The only help a youth wants is to be directed what books to read, and in what order to read them." [6]

It is highly probable, therefore, that no relationship of apprentice and master existed between Jefferson and Wythe; that their footing was similar to that which he suggested to young Turpin—guidance in the reading of the law books themselves and assistance in clearing up obscure points.

Jefferson was eminently well qualified to profit from such a system of independent study. From his earliest childhood he had learnt how to apply himself with single-minded absorption and eliminate all distracting influences. The story is told of his days at Maury's school that in the intervals between lessons, while his comrades joyously raced to games and play, young Thomas betook himself instead to a Greek grammar. The same informant, who doubtless got it from Jefferson himself, asserts that "when young he adopted a system, perhaps an entire plan of life from which neither the exigencies of business nor the allurements of pleasure could drive or seduce him. Much of his success is to be ascribed to methodical industry." [7] And, of course, to a measure of genius.

The incredible regimen of studies which Jefferson was in later years to expound sagely to young neophytes and which has been believed to represent his own experience at Williamsburg must be taken with a grain of salt. For example, a timetable for students which he drew up shortly after he commenced the practice of law and which he passed on to others some fifty years after, begins at dawn and terminates at bed time without a gap for either meals or recreation. Not merely law, he exhorts, but a foundation of Latin, French, mathematics and natural philosophy is essential, as well as ethics, natural religion, politics, history, belles-lettres, rhetoric and oratory.[8] Obviously, such a routine is impossible for any human being and represents merely that ideal which those too enthusiastically immersed in educational theories are prone to offer as the pattern for others. Nor can it be taken as an accurate report of Jefferson's own day-to-day work in Williamsburg; the "distractions," as we shall soon see, were too numerous and extensive.

Nevertheless, the evidence is positive that Jefferson applied himself diligently and methodically to his studies. If nothing else, his commonplace books would indicate that. Written in a neat, immensely fine hand, these bound volumes of abstracts of cases and comments trace the course of his readings in the law from the days of his studentship to his final abstention from practice. Some fifty years later he explained his method of work. "When I was a student of the law, now half a century ago," he wrote to his friend, Thomas Cooper, "after getting through Coke Littleton, whose matter cannot be abridged, I was in the habit of abridging and common-placing what I read meriting it, and of sometimes mixing my own reflections on the subject." Surveying that far-off youth from the vantage point of his current eminence, Jefferson permitted himself a little wistful pride. "They were written at a time of life when I was bold in the pursuit of knowledge, never fearing to follow truth and reason to whatever results they led, and bearding every authority which stood in their way." [9]

The reading of law in those days followed a well-established pattern. Sir Edward Coke's commentaries on Littleton, who had written the fundamental text on the laws of property and tenures, was the first volume placed in the hands of the student. Blackstone's Commentaries, which were largely to supersede Coke, did not appear in print until some years after.

Coke's volume, as Jefferson indicated, was itself an abridgment and commentary, and therefore could not be further digested. It was all bone and sinew, dry and unclothed in fleshly graces, and the young student, packing it in his trunk to take back to Shadwell for a winter's study that first year, was tempted to cry out: "I do wish the Devil had old Coke, for I am sure I never was so tired of an old dull scoundrel in my life." [10]

But Jefferson was to change his mind about the "old dull scoundrel," so much so that it was Coke to whom he turned in drafting his bill on crimes and punishments for the new state of Virginia. And he was later to hail Coke as the greatest lawyer England ever had, even greater than Lord Holt, whom he esteemed highly.[11]

For Blackstone, when he later swam into his view, Jefferson had nothing but contempt. That contempt, however, was based not so much on the legal doctrines adduced in that famous Bible for lawyers as on the political consequences which Blackstone drew therefrom, and which became one of the sturdiest pillars of Toryism and the English monarchy. Together with Hume and Montesquieu, Blackstone became Jefferson's special *bête noire*. But these deep dislikes were the result of Jefferson's later violent reaction against all English institutions and their theoretical upholders, and cannot be retraced to these earlier years when England was still the "mother country." In 1814, he was to ascribe the new and disturbing toryism of American lawyers to "the substitution of Blackstone for my Lord Coke, as an elementary work," and coupled him with Hume as the responsible poisonous influence. "In truth," he asserted, "Blackstone and Hume have made tories of all England, and are making tories of those young Americans whose native feelings of independence do not place them above the wily sophistries of a Hume or a Blackstone." [12]

From Coke's first volume, based on Littleton, Jefferson went on to the other three volumes of his *Institutes*, to the various existing compilations of English Reports, and came to the legal, historical and politico-philosophical volumes of Lord Henry Home Kames. With the apparition of this Scottish lord, jurist, philosopher and inquirer into the principles of morality and natural religion a new and fascinating world opened to the youthful student. In Kames he found another master whose mode of reasoning touched congenial springs in his own nature and brought to flowering hitherto vague and inchoate concepts in wide-ranging fields. For Kames was just such a universalist as Jefferson was coming to be, and wrote of the history of law, of property, of natural right, of religion, of aesthetics and the principles of criticism with ease and an eighteenth-century sceptical, yet at the same time dogmatic, approach that appealed immensely to Jefferson's own trends of thought. The fact that he had been vehemently attacked by some of the Scottish clergy for his *Essays on the Principles of Morality and Natural Religion*, if anything, enhanced him in Jefferson's eyes.[13]

The first volumes of Kames that Jefferson read (he persistently spelt the name "Kaims") were his *Historical Law Tracts* and his *Tract on Property*. The care and fullness with which Jefferson abstracted his treatment of the various phases of the law in these and other legal dissertations disclose his enthusiastic reception of the new authority, even though later he acknowledged that Kames was perhaps too metaphysical and theoretical; that "though he has given us what should be the system of equity, yet it is not the one actually established, at least not in all parts." [14]

But by and large Jefferson yielded enthusiastic assent to the major portion of Kames's propositions and it is doubtless through him that the young man first became practically acquainted with the doctrines of natural rights and natural morality as they were expounded in the eighteenth century. It is true that Kames's ideas were derivative from Locke, and that Jefferson read Locke himself. But it seems evident from the progression of the items in the commonplace books that the reading of Locke came after, and not before Kames.

Kames wrote that "man, by his nature is fitted for society, and society by its conveniences, is fitted for man. The perfection of human society, consists in that just degree of union among individuals, which to each reserves freedom and independency, as far as is consistent with peace and good order. The bonds of society may be too lax, but they may also be overstrained." It is obvious that Jefferson copied this passage because it agreed fully with, and helped mature, his own ideas.[15]

When Kames denounced the prevailing system of entails as a pernicious locking up of land and a conversion of its natural blessings into a curse, declaring that it subverted "that liberty and independency, to which all men aspire, with respect to their possessions as well as their persons," he was helping lay the foundation for Jefferson's vehement aversion to all such species of restrictions which ended, at least in Virginia, in their early abolition.[16]

If young Jefferson was a diligent student of the law, and thought much on what he read in this and in kindred fields, he did not therefore eschew society and the company of friends. On his graduation from William and Mary he joined an alumni group in what was jocularly, if obscurely, known as the Flat Hat Club. Founded in 1750, it constituted what was perhaps the first secret society in American colleges, antedating the more seriously organized Phi Beta Kappa, with which it was nevertheless confused, by about a quarter of a century. Little is known of the club except what Jefferson himself has written. Its purposes were evidently purely social and skylarking, and it was confined to six members at any given period. Among them were St. George Tucker, John Walker, the Reverend Thomas Gwatkin, James Innes and others. Jefferson in grave old age disparaged it as having "no useful object"; but at the time, no doubt, he did not worry particularly about such pragmatic sanctions.[17]

As late as 1769, in fact, when Jefferson had reached alleged years of discretion and the dignified practice of law, he was penning a weird, schoolboyish, pig-Latin letter to his friend and fellow member, Jack Walker, in what was obviously the best tradition of the Flat Hats. The puns are really atrocious: "*Galfridi-filius Ambulatori S.* [Jeffrey-son to Walker greeting]. *Ero apud* Society spring on Tuesday *per quator. fortasse et I. Lepus-aemula veniet. apis ibi et tu quoque.* [I shall be at the Society spring on Tuesday at four. Perhaps J. Harestone will also come. *Bee* there and you also]." Bring a chessboard (*tabulam*); Jefferson will bring the pieces.[18]

But the Flat Hats were mere adolescent high jinks. On a much higher and more serious level was Jefferson's association with Francis Fauquier and the circle in which he moved. Fauquier was perhaps the most attractive and generally intelligent of all the royal governors that England sent to preside over a colony. Indeed, had even a majority of them possessed his charm, tact, wit and sympathetic approach, and had the ministry at home been heedful of his suggestions, the Revolution might never have come to pass.

Born in 1704, he was the son of another one of those Huguenots whose expulsion from France did so much to impoverish that country and enrich England which gave them shelter. Young Francis flourished exceedingly in the adopted land of his father. After a short military career he was appointed deputy master of the Mint and a director of the notorious South Sea Company. Addicted to intellectual pursuits, he became a fellow of the Royal Society and published in 1756, during the current war with France and its allies, "An Essay on Ways and Means of Raising Money for the Support of the Present War without Increasing the Public Debts." In effect, he advocated the pay-as-you-go policy of a graduated income tax which would have spread the load over all, instead of descending, as taxes then did, with crushing weight upon the ultimate consumer. Sufficient to say that his advice was not followed.

In January, 1758, he was appointed Lieutenant Governor of Virginia and, arriving in his new office on June 7th, promptly ingratiated himself with the proud and independent colonials. The fact that he followed Dinwiddie, whose handling of the French and Indian War and general fumbling had made him exceedingly unpopular, was also in his favor.

At the time that young Jefferson met him Fauquier was already well established. He was a handsome man, with short, cropped hair slightly curled at the nape, a bold nose over delicate lips, with wide-arched, penetrating eyes, and eyebrows that seemed almost penciled. His manner was gallant and charming, his conversation witty, and his interest in scientific pursuits endeared him to the intellectuals of William and Mary. He was a passionate devotee of music and himself partook in the string concerts which he inaugurated in the Governor's Palace.

If he had one fault, it was an equally passionate devotion to gaming; the story being that in one night's session at cards in England he had lost his fortune and that it was this untoward circumstance which brought him to seek the governorship of the colony. True or not, the additional story that it was he who introduced the mania into Virginia is definite fable. The Virginia gentlemen required no such adventitious aid to their native propensities.

It is unquestionable that Fauquier introduced a new and liberal tone in manners and conversation into the colony, and when he died in 1768, it was to universal mourning and the knowledge that they would not soon see his like again.[19]

Dr. Small and George Wythe formed part of the Governor's circle and both of them brought Jefferson to his attention. Fauquier welcomed the young man to his house and table and immediately charmed him with his learning, wit and social graces. The four of them—Small, Wythe, Fauquier and Jefferson—habitually dined together and, Jefferson was to declare, "at these dinners I have heard more good sense, more rational and philosophical conversations, than in all my life besides. They were truly Attic societies."[20]

It speaks volumes for the essential qualities of the youth and for their transparence to the outer world that these three established and middle-aged men welcomed him so readily to their intimacy and conversation. It is doubtless true that he was more the worshipful listener than an equal participator; but from the wide-ranging talk, the easy flow of wit and knowledge, Jefferson gained more perhaps than from his formal readings. It was a liberal education of the finest sort.

When Fauquier discovered that his young friend played the violin he invited him to join him in his weekly concerts.[21] The names of the other members of the amateur group are not known, but they probably included John Randolph, later attorney general of the colony, and from whom Jefferson was to purchase his violin under curious circumstances, and Robert Carter, member of the Executive Council, who lived next door to the Palace and installed an organ which Jefferson tried in vain to obtain. In these soirees Jefferson deepened and enriched his love of music, a love which remained with him through life.

Thus, as a member of the "*partie quarrée*" which provided feasts for the intellect and of the musical group which stirred the emotions and the soul, Jefferson received during these formative years an education far beyond the average. It was memories such as these that roused Jefferson to remark retrospectively to his grandson that Williamsburg had been "the finest school of manners and morals that ever existed in America." [22]

Williamsburg may have been all of that, particularly to Jefferson, but it was also a town where amusements, the theater, dancing, gaming, horse racing, convivial eating and drinking, and flirtations could be had in full measure.

The youthful student was no Puritan, nor did he disdain this lighter and gayer side of the little capital. That he participated fully in the various activities, with the sole exception of serious gambling, is undeniable. The theater, the famous Apollo Room in the Raleigh Tavern, some card playing on a minor scale, the balls and rounds of entertainment in the houses of the gentry, all divided his attention with his books and his older friends. They cost money, too; more, as Jefferson readily admitted, than his guardians had anticipated or provided for.

In 1790, when Jefferson was attempting to settle his father's estate, he wrote to the executor, Dr. Walker: "During a part of the time that I was a student in Williamsburg my expences were greater than they ought to have been. It was therefore agreed that they should be paid by the estate, but that I should repay so much as they exceeded." John Harvie, now dead, had left a statement of the amounts actually disbursed, and Jefferson wanted Walker to estimate what his "reasonable expences" during the years 1760-1763 should have been, and charge the balance against his share of Peter Jefferson's estate.[23]

In the process of being a young-man-about-town, Jefferson fell in love. It was normal and in the natural course of events, and left no abiding marks on either of the parties concerned. Jefferson was nineteen at the time and just beginning the study of law; the beloved object, Rebecca Burwell, was a bare sixteen.

Lewis Burwell, the young lady's father, had been an important figure in Virginia. He first sat in the House of Burgesses and then became a member of the Executive Council, its president in 1750, and acting governor during the interregnum before Dinwiddie arrived. He was alleged to be "a scholar and a gentleman," but he had fallen off a horse while in England and the ensuing trepanning operation had left him, in the words of Virginia's historian, "occasionally subject to derangements." [24] These fits of insanity evidently were deemed no bar to his legislative and executive duties. He died in 1752, leaving four orphaned children; his wife, the former Mary Willis of Gloucester, having departed at an earlier date.

Rebecca, the youngest of the daughters, was brought up by her aunt, Elizabeth, who had married William Nelson of Yorktown. Since Nelson was also a member of the Council, the family came often to Williamsburg and it was there that young Jefferson first met the young lady.[25] Nothing is known of her looks or appearance. Of her character, then or later, all that has come down is a pious description attributed to her daughter by a clerical author, that in the opinion of her more worldly companions, it was stamped with religious enthusiasm.[26] But a certain common sense and an air of having her feet solidly on the ground, even as a girl, appears by indirection in the sole source we have of this youthful affair—Jefferson's own letters.

Jefferson was probably introduced to young Rebecca by her brother and his fellow classmate, Lewis Burwell, sometime in the spring of 1762. She was then one of a bevy of girls with whom he partied, danced and flirted in the approved manner of Virginia society and young folks anywhere. They included Sukey Potter, Alice Corbin, Nancy Wilton, Jenny Taliaferro and a host of others; on the male side of the intermingling group were John Page, Jack Walker, William Fleming, Willis and other youthful blades.

In the nature of things the initial random attraction of male and female tended to a more specific focus, and Tom Jefferson's eye tended more and more to linger on the fair Rebecca. By the time he had packed his law books, including that "old dull scoundrel" Coke, for winter transfer to Shadwell and uninterrupted study, he had advanced so far in Rebecca's regard that he carried in his watch case a miniature silhouette of her lineaments.

On his way to Shadwell, however, he first paused at Fairfield, the ancestral home of the Burwells, to partake of Christmas cheer with his friend and the brother of his beloved, young Lewis Burwell. There "tragedy" befell him; or so he wrote to his boon companion, Page, who had remained behind in Williamsburg. The young men had fashioned a code between them; one of those mock-serious and mock-heroic affairs that no doubt befuddled the begetters as much as the outer world. Williamsburg became "Devilsburg"; the dear object of Jefferson's affections was transformed into "Belinda," and then twice transformed into "Adnileb" (Belinda in reverse), "Campana in die (Bell in day); and sometimes, to make confusion worse confused, the palindrone was spelled out in Greek characters. It was all pretty heavy-handed stuff, liberally besprinkled with Latin tags and youthful rodomontade that passed for humor between the young men.

From Fairfield, Jefferson informed Page of the misfortunes that had overwhelmed him. They were, he gravely announced, greater than "have befallen a descendant of Adam," with the exception of Job, "since the creation of the world." What were they? For one thing, "the cursed rats" had eaten his pocket book while he slept, and had carried away his "jemmy-worked silk garters, and half a dozen new minuets I had just got, to serve, I suppose, as provision for the winter." For another, it had rained during the night, the roof had leaked, and he had awakened to find his watch "all afloat in water," the case penetrated and "the particles of paper, of which my dear picture and watch-paper were composed," completely disintegrated. This was indeed disaster, for the obliterated picture was the portrait of Belinda, or Rebecca Burwell. But the disconsolate youth soon brightened with the thought that although her picture was defaced, "there is so lively an image of her imprinted in my mind, that I shall think of her often." But another thought disturbed this new-found equanimity. Page had attended a wedding in Williamsburg. "Was she there?" he anxiously inquired, "because, if she was, I ought to have been at the Devil for not being there too." [27]

Having thus had the Christmas season spoiled for him, Jefferson went on to Shadwell, where "all things here appear to me to trudge on in one and the same round." But in the midst of his legal studies and sojourn with his family, the young man's thoughts recurred to Williamsburg and the problems he had left behind. Rebecca Burwell was the chief of these. In the monotonous round of Shadwell his love for the absent damsel grew, and a longing to know his fate once and for all. "How does R. B. do?" he asked his confidant, Page. "Had I better stay here and do nothing, or go down and do less? . . . Inclination tells me to go, receive my sentence, and be no longer in suspense: but reason says, if you go, and your attempt proves unsuccessful, you will be ten times more wretched than ever." His eyes were sore, and he could not read. So his mind wandered restlessly. "I have some thoughts of going to Petersburg, if the actors go there in May." He was building "a full-rigged flat" boat to be christened *Rebecca.* Suppose Page and he hoisted sail and away to "England, Holland, France, Spain, Italy (where I would buy me a good fiddle) and Egypt." To be sure, the journey "would take us two or three years, and if we should not both be cured of love in that time, I think the devil would be in it." [28] Page, it seems, was supposed at this time to be in love with Nancy Wilton.

Jefferson wrote this letter in one of those fits of discouragement that come upon the victims of youthful love, especially when the fair one is absent and has perhaps not given sufficient indications of reciprocity. The usual cure in cases such as these is a contemplated sea voyage; the farther off the better. Yet, after having penned the letter, Jefferson held it for two months, as though awaiting some indication from Williamsburg that the beloved was showing signs of interest in him before committing himself to this half-serious proposal. None came. In fact, there is no evidence that Rebecca ever wrote to him, or that he in turn addressed directly the object of his affections.

Instead, a letter came from his friend Jack Walker, announcing the prevalence of smallpox in Williamsburg. The news banished from Jefferson's mind any idea of coming down to pin Rebecca to a definite answer. "You may scratch out that sentence of my letter," he exhorted Page in a postscript dated February 12th. A very prudent and cautious young man, indeed! He had more news which caused him to indulge in some self-pitying sighs. "Miss Willis is to be married next week to Dangerfield. Why can't you and I be married too, Page, when and to whom we would choose? Do you think it would cause any such mighty disorders among the planets? Or do you imagine it would be attended with such very bad consequences in this bit of a world, this clod of dirt, which I insist, is the vilest of the whole system? . . . I verily believe I shall die soon and yet I can see no other reason for it but that I am tired of living. At this moment when I am writing I am scarcely sensible that I exist." This was the stuff of sentimental *Weltschmerz* which Goethe was later to immortalize in his *Sorrows of Werther*.

But still Jefferson held on to the letter. It was not until March 11th that he finally sent it on, with an additional inconsequential postscript.[29]

All that winter and through the spring and summer of 1763 Jefferson remained at his home in Shadwell, steadily at work on his law books, interspersed with broodings on Rebecca Burwell in Williamsburg. His passion could not have been too unmanageable, for he made no move to journey down to see her, even after the smallpox that had first held him back subsided. Then John Page sent him news that should have been alarming—and was not. On May 30th that stanch "attorney" advised him that a rival had appeared on the scene and was making progress with the young lady while Jefferson tarried. Come down immediately, Page exhorted, and lay siege "*in form*," if you do not wish to be definitely ousted.

Even this admonition failed to shake Jefferson from his lethargy. He waited until July 15th to reply and then only to announce his resolution to go to England. "And to begin an affair of that kind now, and carry it on so long a time in form, is by no means a proper plan. No, no, Page; whatever assurances I may give her in private of my esteem for her, or whatever assurances I may ask in return from her, depend on it—they must be kept in private. Necessity will oblige me to proceed in a method which is not generally thought fair; that of treating with a ward before obtaining the approbation of her guardian." In other words, the proposed trip abroad bulked larger in his dreams than the hand of Rebecca Burwell. He was sensible enough to realize that her guardian would disapprove of committing his ward to an engagement from which the swain would depart for some years of travel; therefore, the most he could do would be to speak *informally* to her direct and obtain her private consent to await his return.

"If Belinda [Rebecca] will not accept of my service, it shall never be offered to another. That she may, I pray most sincerely; but that she will, she never gave me reason to hope." He admitted that he was "scared to death at making her so unreasonable a proposal as that of waiting until I return from Britain, unless she could first be prepared for it." The implication was obvious; Page was to pave the way for the timid suitor. Jefferson intended to be in Williamsburg by October 1st, and would like to build a house there; "no castle though, I assure you; only a small house, which shall contain a room for myself and another for you, and no more, unless Belinda should think proper to favour us with her company, in which case, I will enlarge the plan as much as she pleases." [30]

Jefferson actually started for Williamsburg in September to learn his fate, but tarried en route at Richmond and elsewhere to enjoy some good company and survey the lively young beauties of the section, particularly a certain Miss Jenny Taliaferro; though he professed, to his friends at least, a "most philosophical indifference" to all the beauties of the world.[31]

At length, this most dilatory lover reached Williamsburg. On October 16th, he met the idol of his heart. He danced with her in the Apollo Room of the Raleigh Tavern, scene of many a famous dance and convivial entertainment. The assembled company was most agreeable and the maiden in his arms divine. "I was prepared to say a great deal," he mournfully informed Page after the event. "I had dressed up in my mind, such thoughts as occurred to me, in as moving language as I knew how, and expected to have performed in a tolerably creditable manner. But, good God! When I had an opportunity of venting them, a few broken sentences, uttered in great disorder, and interrupted with pauses of uncommon length, were the too visible marks of my strange confusion! The whole confab I will tell you, word for word, if I can, when I see you." And the first sincere cry now burst from Jefferson; an imploring "For God's sake come," to his loyal friend.[32]

We do not know whether Page, then at his home at Rosedale, rushed to Williamsburg in response to this despairing call for aid and consolation. Nor could the dejected suitor depart, for life must go on. He had actually returned to the capital after almost a year's absence to gain some practical knowledge of the law under Wythe's tutelage, and was in constant attendance with his mentor in the courts to observe and assist in the trial of cases.

Some time later, in October, he plucked up sufficient courage for another "confab" with Rebecca. This time, as he reported it to Page, "I . . . opened my mind more freely, and more fully. I mentioned the necessity of my going to England, and the delays which would consequently be occasioned by that." He made no formal proposal that would have required a "categorical answer," but assured her that some day he would. Rebecca evidently asked for time to consider the proposal that was not a proposal, and just as evidently she had already received more forthright and unconditional offers from others. Jefferson ended his account of the proceedings with Spartan fortitude: "My fate depends on [Belinda's] present resolutions, by them I must stand or fall." [33]

What was the necessity which Jefferson conceived as compelling him to England, even at the cost of love and marriage? It was no longer the vague longing toward distant lands, even to Egypt, of some months before, but a specific, limited and therefore obviously more practical purpose. The question has never been resolved; but it seems highly probable that the mother country beckoned on several counts: first, the urbane discourse and scientific attainments of Dr. Small and Governor Fauquier had created an appetite to seek the original fount from which their qualities flowed; second, a term of residence at the Inns of Court might add, if not to his knowledge of the law, at least to the prestige of the youthful lawyer who intended to practice in Williamsburg. Aside from all this, however, one gets the impression that, consciously or subconsciously, the reluctant lover used the proposed journey as a means for staving off such a formal engagement as would inevitably end in binding ties and responsibilities.

Whatever the reason, simple or complex, Jefferson never did get to England. Instead, he remained, as he himself put it, "indolently" in Williamsburg, not bothering to seek out or persuade Rebecca again, and awaiting her final decision with suspicious fortitude.

That decision came to him secondhand the following March. Rebecca Burwell had considered the situation. Either from a romantic or a sensible point of view what profit was there in binding oneself to a proposal which in effect was not a proposal or to await a youth whose passion was not sufficiently urgent to seek her out during months of uncertainty?

On March 18, 1764, kind souls informed Jefferson that Rebecca was going to marry Jacquelin Ambler. That young man had placed no strings on his proposal, he was eminently eligible, and very sensibly Rebecca accepted him. Young Ambler was not quite a year older than the unsuccessful suitor and came from a good family. He became a Councillor of Virginia during the Revolution and later on, the State Treasurer. There is no reason to believe that Rebecca ever regretted her choice or looked back longingly on the opportunity missed. Ironically, one of her daughters was to marry John Marshall, Jefferson's great antagonist of later years; while another laughed her mother's early suitor to scorn for his alleged cowardice in fleeing from the enemy during the British invasion of Virginia.

The news gave Jefferson a violent headache for at least two days. The shock was more to his vanity than to the roots of his being. Late at night he passed on the information to William Fleming, another of his cronies. All their schemes for marrying and living close together, he mournfully informed him, have been "totally frustrated by Miss R. B.'s marriage with Jacquelin Ambler, which the people here tell me they daily expect: I say the people here tell me so, for (can you believe it?) I have been so abominably indolent as not to have seen her since last October." [34]

Within a few weeks, however, he was cynically ridiculing to Page the love passion of a mutual friend, Warner Lewis, and affecting the misogynist.[35] That usual pose of the rejected lover remained with him for some years and filled his commonplace books with the accepted tags and echoes from the writings of others. From the *Medea* of Euripedes he copied out with considerable unction: "Mortals should beget children from some other source and there should be no womankind; thus there would be no ill for men." In Milton he contemplated with melancholy satisfaction those blasts against women that so liberally adorn the pages of *Paradise Lost*.[36]

No doubt he was certain that he was destined to remain a bachelor; that no more would he "offer to another." He watched his friends sheepishly depart and take unto themselves wives with an amusement mingled with disdain. John Page yielded to the blandishments of Fanny Burwell, a cousin of the faithless Rebecca. Jack Walker married Betsey Moore, in whom Jefferson was later to display an undue interest. Warner Lewis, Benjamin Harrison, William Bland, one by one the gay blades vanished into domesticity, leaving young Jefferson to his solitary pride and the remembrance of his wounds. One desertion, and one only, did he welcome with enthusiasm—the marriage of his dearest friend, Dabney Carr, to his sister Martha.

CHAPTER 5

The Shape of Things to Come

NOW that his abortive love affair with Rebecca Burwell had collapsed, young Jefferson once more devoted himself to the serious business of life. The projected journey to England, on which his love had foundered, never did materialize. Instead, he alternated between Shadwell and Williamsburg, continuing a leisurely reading of the law and commencing, on a more grandiose scale, that omnivorous and insatiable inquiry into all the kingdoms of knowledge that was to mark him through life.

The surprising thing about his legal preparation, indeed, was that it took so inordinately long. He commenced his studies under Wythe in 1762; it was not until 1767 that his mentor led him for induction to the bar of the General Court. Five years is a lengthy period for preparation even today, when the corpus of law has immensely expanded; in the eighteenth century it was practically unheard of. Two years was more than ample then, and the record is full of cases in which a year or less was deemed sufficient. The names of Alexander Hamilton, Aaron Burr, John Marshall and Patrick Henry come immediately to mind.

It is obvious, therefore, that Jefferson was in no hurry to commence practice. His conception of preparation, not merely for the law, but for the business of life itself, included a broader field of knowledge than that envisaged by almost anyone else of his time.[1] His several commonplace books mark the progression of his wide readings for many years to come.

Languages he considered the fundamental tool. Already possessed of an excellent foundation in Latin and Greek—for which he never ceased expressing his gratitude to his father—he read deeply in the classics and excerpted those passages which touched responsive chords in his own being. In the Greek, Homer, Euripides and Anacreon seem to have been his favorites in those early years, and chiefly he copied down their comments on life, destiny and woman. He read Herodotus among the historians, but not yet Thucydides. The philosophers he did not touch at all, though later he sampled Plato and conceived a violent aversion to him. He liked his philosophy rational, as became a child of the Enlightenment, and professed a vast scorn for metaphysics of all kinds. Later on he discovered Epicurus and became his disciple, and admired the Stoics, at least in their ethical pronouncements. Why he found no pabulum in Aristotle is a mystery; for the great Stagyrite was certainly a rationalist. The answer may lie in the ill repute into which that philosopher had fallen because of his identification with and incorporation into the structure of medieval metaphysical thought.[2]

As was natural, Jefferson's readings in Latin were far more extensive than in Greek. Cicero, especially in his *Tusculan Disputations*, proved the most congenial author. His aphorisms, reflections and moral sayings, his eclectic discourses on life and death, were distinctly agreeable to Jefferson's gradually unfolding deistic and materialistic tenets. Especially did he approve of Cicero's conception of death as either a change to a better state or a "deep sleep," and in either case not to be feared by the wise man. Carefully he copied out a statement which became one of the foundations of his own career: "Death which threatens us daily from a thousand accidents, and which by reason of the shortness of life, can never be far off, does not deter a wise man from making such provision for his country and his family as he hopes may last forever; and from regarding posterity, of which he can never have any real perception, as belonging to himself." [3]

Vergil, Horace, Terence and Ovid completed the tale of Jefferson's early Latin readings. In French he read Racine, and later on Montesquieu, Voltaire, Helvetius, d'Holbach and the Encyclopedists. But not Rousseau, whose romantic and egalitarian tenets had practically no influence on the course of Jefferson's, or indeed any American, thought.

At an early date Jefferson commenced the study of Italian and applied himself to it with such effect that he was able to read, write and speak it with a considerable degree of fluency.[4] He read Machiavelli in the original, rather for his *Discourses* on Roman themes than for his statecraft as exemplified in the *Prince;* and particularly the great Italian penologist, Beccaria, whose humane principles for the treatment of criminals materially affected Jefferson's later revisions of the penal code of Virginia. Indeed, Jefferson would have gone further along Beccaria's lines if he had been permitted. In his Autobiography he comments that "Beccaria and other writers on crimes and punishment had satisfied the reasonable world of the unrightfulness and inefficacy of the punishment of crimes by death... The Revisors had adopted their opinions; but the general idea of our country had not yet advanced to that point." [5]

A working knowledge of Spanish was to come later; but German he never attempted, even though there is in existence a crude interlinear translation in his handwriting of a German song.[6] Anglo-Saxon, however, became his favorite study. His abiding interest in it extended all through life; in 1798 he wrote a learned and ingenious essay in which he attempted to simplify its grammar, "by reducing the infinite diversities of its unfixed orthography to single and settled forms." [7] It was one of the subjects he insisted on incorporating into the curriculum of his beloved University of Virginia and, at an age when others are content to hug the fireside, he revised his essay to the form of a text for classroom purposes.

The young law student was first led to Anglo-Saxon by the numerous legal terms stemming from that language. In his efforts to run down precise meanings he soon found himself involved in a study of institutions. That interest grew with the increasing quarrel with England, when American publicists sought eagerly for theoretical bases in the early history of England to justify their stand. Jefferson found his justifying arguments and the cradle of liberty in the ancient systems of government of the Celts and the Germanic tribes, which in turn became the base for the Anglo-Saxon system.[8]

To his Anglo-Saxon forebears, indeed, he came to attribute all the virtues and believed that the current corruption of England was due solely to the Norman invasion and the consequent introduction of the feudal system.[9] Jefferson might be considered one of the first to support in America the Teutonic hypothesis which became so fashionable in the second half of the nineteenth century. In extreme old age he still clung to the thesis, remarking that "it has ever appeared to me that the difference between the Whig and the Tory of England is, that the Whig deduces his rights from the Anglo-Saxon source, and the Tory from the Norman."[10]

English literature also engaged his attention during these formative years. He read the novelists, and especially Sterne, with delight; though when he grew older he thrust them aside as vain toys and considered their influence pernicious.[11] Shakespeare he thought highly of, especially the historical plays, but he also digested *Troilus and Cressida*, the misogynist's bible; and when he read Milton it was with a similar eye, copying down those passages from *Paradise Lost* and *Samson Agonistes* which took a jaundiced view of the female sex. Pope, Young's *Night Thoughts*, Thomson's *Seasons*, Butler's burlesque *Hudibras*, Akenside and the Restoration dramatists all found a place on his shelves. But particularly he fell under the spell of Ossian.

When that most famous of all literary forgeries came into his hands he sighed and swooned over it as did countless others. Nothing like the enthusiasm exhibited over its high-flown, romantic strains had been seen before or since. There were few who had Dr. Johnson's sturdy common sense to disbelieve its ancient Gaelic origin. Jefferson was not among the critical. So deeply impressed was he that he naïvely wrote to an Edinburgh merchant named Charles McPherson, a relative of the mighty James McPherson, imploring him to ask his cousin to send him copies of the poems in their original Gaelic dress, together with a grammar, dictionary and catalogue of books in that language. "These pieces have been and will, I think, during my life," avowed Jefferson, "continue to be to me the sources of daily pleasures. The tender and the sublime emotions of the mind were never before so wrought up by the human hand. I am not ashamed to own that I think this rude bard of the north the greatest poet that has ever existed." If the originals had appeared in print, he would want a copy; "but if there is none such, be so good as to use your interest with Mr. McPherson to obtain leave to take a manuscript copy of them, and procure it to be done. I would choose it in a fair, round hand, on fine paper, with a

MAIN STREET, FROM THE COLLEGE WINDOWS

THE RALEIGH TAVERN

WILLIAM AND MARY COLLEGE

WILLIAMSBURG SCENES

Scribner's Monthly, November 1875

A Declaration by the Representatives of the UNITED STATES OF AMERICA, in General Congress assembled.

When in the course of human events it becomes necessary for one people to dissolve the political bands which have connected them with another, and to assume among the powers of the earth the separate and equal station to which the laws of nature & of nature's god entitle them, a decent respect to the opinions of mankind requires that they should declare the causes which impel them to the separation.

We hold these truths to be self-evident; that all men are created equal; that they are endowed by their creator with [inherent &] inalienable rights; that among these are life, liberty, & the pursuit of happiness; that to secure these rights, governments are instituted among men, deriving their just powers from the consent of the governed; that whenever any form of government becomes destructive of these ends, it is the right of the people to alter or to abolish it, & to institute new government, laying it's foundation on such principles & organising it's powers in such form, as to them shall seem most likely to effect their safety & happiness. prudence indeed will dictate that governments long established should not be changed for light & transient causes: and accordingly all experience hath shewn that mankind are more disposed to suffer while evils are sufferable, than to right themselves by abolishing the forms to which they are accustomed. but when a long train of abuses & usurpations [begun at a distinguished period &] pursuing invariably the same object, evinces a design to reduce them under absolute Despotism, it is their right, it is their duty, to throw off such government, & to provide new guards for their future security. such has been the patient sufferance of these colonies; & such is now the necessity which constrains them to [expunge] their former systems of government. the history of the present king of Great Britain is a history of [unremitting] injuries and usurpations, [among which appears no solitary fact to contradict the uniform tenor of the rest, but all have] in direct object the establishment of an absolute tyranny over these states. to prove this, let facts be submitted to a candid world, [for the truth of which we pledge a faith yet unsullied by falsehood.]

Courtesy the Library of Congress

FACSIMILE OF FIRST PAGE OF JEFFERSON'S DRAFT OF THE DECLARATION OF INDEPENDENCE

Nor have we been wanting in attentions to our British brethren. we have warned them from time to time of attempts by their legislature to extend a jurisdiction over [these our states]. we have reminded them of the circumstances of our emigration & settlement here, [no one of which could warrant so strange a pretension: that these were effected at the expence of our own blood & treasure, unassisted by the wealth or the strength of Great Britain: that in constituting indeed our several forms of government, we had adopted one common king, thereby laying a foundation for perpetual league & amity with them: but that submission to their [illegible] credited: and] we have appealed to their native justice & magnanimity, [as well as to] the ties of our common kindred to disavow these usurpations which [were likely to] interrupt our connection & correspondence. they too have been deaf to the voice of justice & of consanguinity, [& when occasions have been given them, by the regular course of their laws, of removing from their councils the disturbers of our harmony, they have by their free election re-established them in power. at this very time too they are permitting their chief magistrate to send over not only soldiers of our common blood, but Scotch & foreign mercenaries to invade & destroy us. these facts [illegible] unfeeling brethren. we must endeavor to forget our former love for them, and to hold them as we hold the rest of mankind, enemies in war, in peace friends. we might have been a free & a great people together; but a communication of grandeur & of freedom it seems is below their dignity. be it so, since they will have it: the road to happiness & to glory is open to us too; we will tread it apart from them, and] acquiesce in the necessity which denounces our [eternal] separation!

We therefore the representatives of the United States of America in General Congress assembled, do, in the name & by authority of the good people of these [states] reject & renounce all allegiance & subjection to the kings of Great Britain & all others who may hereafter claim by, through, or under them; we utterly dissolve all political connection which may heretofore have subsisted between us & the people or parliament of Great Britain; and finally we do assert and declare these colonies to be free and independant states, and that as free & independant states they have full power to levy war, conclude peace, contract alliances, establish commerce, & to do all other acts and things which independant states may of right do. And for the support of this declaration] we mutually pledge to each other our lives, our fortunes, & our sacred honour.

Courtesy the Library of Congress

FACSIMILE OF LAST PAGE OF JEFFERSON'S DRAFT OF THE DECLARATION OF INDEPENDENCE

Courtesy the New York Public Library

GEORGE WASHINGTON

Painting by Rembrandt Peale

good margin, bound in parchments as elegantly as possible, lettered on the back, and marbled or gilt on the edges of the leaves. I would not regard expense in doing this." [12]

One can well understand James McPherson's embarrassment when this request was forwarded to him by his cousin. He took refuge in evasion. "I should be glad to accommodate any friend of yours," he told Charles; "especially one of Mr. Jefferson's taste and character. But I cannot, having [refused] them to so many, give a copy of the Gaëlic poems, with any decency, out of my hands. The labour, besides, would be great. I know of none, that could copy them. My manner and my spelling differ from others; and I have the vanity [to] think, that I am in the right. Make my humble respects to your American friend." [13]

The rebuff did not inhibit Jefferson's continued enthusiasm for Ossian. When the Marquis de Chastellux visited Jefferson at Monticello in 1782 they discovered over a bowl of punch their mutual delight in the poems. "It was a spark of electricity which passed rapidly from one to the other," he narrates; "we recollected the passages in those sublime poems which particularly struck us.... In our enthusiasm the book was sent for, and placed near the bowl, where, by their mutual aid, the night far advanced imperceptibly upon us." [14]

But the master to whom Jefferson most yielded himself in these early days was far removed from the cloud-cuckoo romanticism of Ossian. He was the brilliant, licentious, high-monarchical, irreligious Viscount Henry St. John Bolingbroke. The Tory aristocrat was everything that Jefferson ordinarily despised, but his philosophical writings and attacks on revealed religion chimed in with Jefferson's own deistic sentiments. Those writings, which had been published only a few years before and which were denounced by Dr. Samuel Johnson as "the blunderbuss charged against religion and morality," were given the most extensive space of any author in Jefferson's literary commonplace book.

He copied out those passages in particular which argued against the uncritical acceptance of revelation in Christianity and which declared it nonsensical to accept as proof of the "word of God" such evidence as would not stand up for an instant in a court of law if the sum of ten pounds were at stake. Bolingbroke considered Christ's ethics not entire and not deduced from reason. "A system," he wrote, and Jefferson faithfully copied, "thus collected from the writings of antient heathen moralists of Tully, of Seneca, of Epictetus, and others, would be more full, more entire, more coherent, and more clearly deduced from unquestionable principles of knowledge." He also thought it "absurd" and "impious" to ascribe "mosaical laws to god," and ridiculed the belief that "God sent his only begotten son, who had not offended him, to be sacrificed by men, who had offended him, that he might expiate their sins, and satisfy his own anger." [15]

Violent sentiments such as these, and others of a similar cast, were excerpted by Jefferson. It must not be assumed that he agreed to the full with the free-thinking Bolingbroke, but there is no question that he had reservations then, and later, concerning the authority of revelation and the divinity of Christ. His opinion of the *ethical* teachings of Christ, however, was to clash in later years with that here expressed by Bolingbroke. He then saw within what he termed "the rubbish" under which it was buried "the outlines of a system of the most sublime morality which has ever fallen from the lips of man"; and he set himself the task of clearing away that "rubbish" and setting forth the ethical teachings in their pristine purity.[16]

Jefferson's favorable opinion of Bolingbroke never changed. In old age he hailed both Bolingbroke and Thomas Paine as "alike in making bitter enemies of the priests and pharisees of their day. Both were honest men; both advocates for human liberty." And he considered Bolingbroke's writings "certainly the finest samples in the English language, of the eloquence proper for the Senate. His political tracts are safe reading for the most timid religionist, his philosophical, for those who are not afraid to trust their reason with discussions of right and wrong." [17]

Thus, while preparing himself for the bar, young Jefferson was reading widely in many fields. Without scanting his legal books he ranged through the green pastures of literature, both ancient and modern, sharpened his language tools, and pondered much on religion and the applications of reason to the problems of the universe. He studied history, too, particularly that of England as portrayed in the persuasive pages of Hume, and dipped somewhat into the origins of institutions, feudal and Anglo-Saxon chiefly, thereby laying the groundwork for some of his leading ideas when he himself stepped upon the stage of history. But by and large his intensive application to the lessons of history and political theory came later, as the special need arose and their practical significance for the work at hand was urgent.

Already the first faint adumbrations of that special need were beginning to show along the horizon, though no one at the moment, and certainly not the youthful law student, realized the full import of what was taking place.

When the so-called "French and Indian War" ended in 1763 with total victory for the British and the eradication of French influence on the North American continent, neither the exultant mother country nor her equally exultant colonies could have foreseen that this victory would prove the catalyst that hastened the eventual breach between them. For one thing, the colonies no longer required the might of England to protect them against Indian depredations and French encroachments; for another, the heavy costs of the war compelled England to explore new sources of revenue to fill her depleted treasury. What more natural than to seek such revenue from the colonies partly in whose behalf the war had been fought and who had gained so much from its successful conclusion?

The whole philosophy of mercantilism under which England operated, in common with most of the great powers of the day, treated colonies as essentially constituted for the benefit of the mother country; with both forming a closed system whereby the raw materials of the former flowed to the latter and the manufactured articles of the latter were marketed in the former. England had long had on the statute books a series of navigation and other acts embodying that philosophy and sharply channeling the trade of the colonies in the directions indicated. But they had never been too stringently enforced, and as long as the colonies could evade or disregard them they were deemed nothing more than an irritating nuisance.

The first notification from England that such evasions would no longer be tolerated came in 1760 when William Pitt determined to enforce the dormant Sugar Act of 1733 and thereby put a stop to the flourishing trade in molasses, fish and other essential products between New England and the enemy West Indies islands. The writs of assistance by which he proposed to put an end to smuggling and the evasion of duties raised a storm in Boston, the chief offender. It was then that James Otis first raised the query as to the relations between England and America, between a king and his people.

In Virginia, however, and the South generally, the enforcement of the Sugar Act roused less of a furore. What touched them was not the fate of molasses, fish and lumber, but that of tobacco, their chief money crop. In this connection there had been grumblings for some time. Through the working of the various navigation acts that trade was almost exclusively with England, and just as exclusively it lay in the hands of English and Scottish merchants and factors. For a variety of reasons, but chiefly due to the Virginia planters' reckless disregard of the elementary principles of bookkeeping and the balance of expenditures and income, the planters were invariably in the debt of the merchants and sank in deeper from year to year.

When, therefore, Virginia sought to relieve itself of an onerous burden by directing that the clergy be hereafter paid in cash and not in high-priced pounds of tobacco, and England annulled the several acts, the fat was in the fire. Richard Bland declared that they were being stripped of the rights and privileges of British subjects; that is, to determine their own domestic good without let or hindrance: while Patrick Henry leaped into fame in the Parson's Cause with his bold pronouncement that all government was a conditional compact, and that the king, by vetoing the Assembly's reasonable and beneficial measures, had forfeited his right to their obedience. Thereby Bland and Henry took the same stand for Virginia that Otis had taken for Massachusetts.

The fat simmered for a while; then burst forth into flames. The inciting spark was the passage of the Stamp Act by Parliament in 1764. On this issue both northern and southern colonies could unite, for the interests of both were equally involved. Through this act and its companion American

Revenue Act the British Parliament openly avowed its intention of seeking a direct revenue from the colonies sufficient to pay for their defense and administration.

The issue was joined. Heretofore Parliament had contented itself with laying requisitions upon the colonies for such purposes, and permitting the colonial assemblies themselves to raise the necessary funds by whatever means they deemed fit. Now, for the first time, Parliament was taxing directly, and in a fashion that no longer could be evaded by the resourceful colonists.

Violent outcries came from practically every colony. They had submitted, albeit not without grumbling, to the management of their external trade by Parliament; but they would never consent, so they declared, to the imposition of taxes by a Parliament in which they were not represented.

On March 22, 1765, the Stamp Act, in spite of petitions and protests from the colonies, was finally signed and copies shipped across the Atlantic. The answering explosion came from Virginia, rather than Massachusetts, where it might properly have been expected. At first glance, indeed, Virginia ought to have been one of the last colonies to take revolutionary steps in opposition. The King's representative in the colony, Governor Fauquier, was the mildest and most deservedly popular of all the royal governors; and the Tidewater planters were notoriously conservative and proud of their connection with England.

But for some time there had been a slow but steady shift in the complexion of the Virginia Assembly. By 1765, the middle and western counties—where dissenters, Pennsylvania Germans and Scotch-Irish were numerous and bound by no ties of affection to England—were leavening the original mass of aristocrats from the Tidewater with a new group of representatives in the Assembly. The leader of these was Patrick Henry, the young lawyer whose flaming declamation in the Parson's Cause had catapulted him into fame.

Since the Stamp Act, by its terms, was not to become effective until November, Governor Fauquier prudently withheld its contents from the Assembly then in session. The time was the end of May, and on the last day of the month the current session would expire and the members disperse. As a matter of fact, most of the members had already departed and a bare 39 out of a total membership of 116 lingered to wind up their desultory affairs. Governor Fauquier breathed easier; by the time they reconvened in the fall much might have happened to take the edge off an act of which he himself disapproved.[18]

Unfortunately, as Fauquier was rather plaintively to explain, a copy of the obnoxious law had somehow "crept into the House," and on May 29th the members still in town resolved themselves into a Committee of the Whole "immediately, to consider of the Steps necessary to be taken in Consequence of the Resolutions of the House of Commons of Great Britain relative to the charging certain Stamp Duties in the Colonies and Plantations of America." [19]

Patrick Henry, the new member, was ready prepared. In his pocket lay seven resolutions for offer. The first asserted that the settlers of Virginia had brought with them "all the privileges, franchises, and immunities, that have at any time been held, enjoyed, and possessed, by the people of Great Britain." The second declared that the royal charters of James I had officially so stated. The third avowed that taxation by the people themselves, or their chosen representatives, "is the distinguishing characteristic of British freedom." The fourth recounted that Virginia had uninterruptedly enjoyed the right of being governed by its own Assembly in matters of taxation and internal police.

So far the resolutions were preamble, statements of general principles. But the fifth resolution got down to cases and breathed revolutionary defiance. "Resolved, therefore," it read, "That the General Assembly of this colony have the only and sole exclusive right and power to lay taxes and impositions upon the inhabitants of this colony, and that every attempt to vest such power in any person or persons whatsoever, other than the General Assembly aforesaid, has a manifest tendency to destroy British as well as American freedom."

The delegate from Hanover County had two other resolutions in his pocket, but he waited to determine the fate of the first five before he brought them into the open. He displayed a proper caution, for if the fifth resolution was bold and revolutionary in tenor, the withheld pair were immediate incitements to revolt. The sixth was really the logical extension of the fifth, declaring that the people of Virginia were not bound to yield obedience to any tax not duly levied on them by their own Assembly. The seventh burst all bounds of legal procedure. Any person, it fulminated, who maintained that any other than the Assembly had the right to impose taxes on Virginians, "shall be deemed an enemy to his Majesty's colony." [20] The phrase strikes an ominous note; it is uncomfortably reminiscent of the dread accusation of "enemy of the people" which caused the guillotine to work overtime during the French Revolution and of the even more sanguinary cries in modern totalitarian states.

The five resolutions proffered by Patrick Henry were considered by the rump session behind closed doors and reported out for open debate on the following day. Young Jefferson and his fellow law student, John Tyler, hurried over to the House of Burgesses on May 30th to hear what promised to be a spate of oratory. Among the membership present were George Wythe, Jefferson's legal mentor, Speaker John Robinson, Richard Bland, Edmund Pendleton, Robert Carter Nicholas, Peyton Randolph and John Randolph, Attorney General of Virginia. These were names to conjure with, representing the learning, solidity and aristocracy of the colony; but it was not to them that all eyes turned when the session opened. That was reserved for the new and fiery member from the hinterland, the plainly dressed, awkward-seeming Patrick Henry.

The two law students stationed themselves at the open door of the lobby and peered eagerly into the solemn, well-proportioned chamber as Henry rose. Jefferson had not thought much of him when he first met him at the home of Col. Dandridge, nor had more recent acquaintance in Williamsburg caused him to change his opinion. He considered him coarse and uncouth, a good fiddler and jokester, perhaps, but ignorant of the classics and not much of a lawyer. While he, Jefferson, was spending years of arduous preparation for the law, Patrick Henry had dashed through Coke *et al.* in a miraculous six weeks and been admitted to practice under confused and cloudy circumstances.[21] But his gift for oratory—the kind that sweeps even coldly cautious men from their feet and leaves them breathless—Jefferson was ever ready to admit, especially after the signal demonstration with which he was now confronted.

Patrick Henry rose to present his resolutions. Behind him sat a solid phalanx of young, hotheaded supporters from Virginia's interior. The Tidewater members, who had hitherto swayed the Burgesses with their influence and prestige, were perturbed and uneasy. They had already heard the explosive resolutions the day before, and were resolved to prevent their passage. It was not that they were in favor of the obnoxious Stamp Act; far from it. But they thought that the resolutions were radical, revolutionary, and bound to start a convulsion whose end they could not see. Petitions, dignified remonstrances, were more to their liking. They had been caught off base; their fellows, the great majority of whom would have followed their leadership, had already departed and were unavailable on this crucial vote. They had been defeated in the Committee of the Whole by narrow margins; they marshaled their strength against this final vote.

Henry launched into his speech. In this open session he was addressing not merely the delegates, not alone the students who harkened from the lobby, but Virginia and all the colonies. It was a tremendous effort; impassioned, eloquent, soaring to flights that left one spectator at least limp with excitement. To Jefferson, listening to the coruscating flow of words, it seemed that never again would he hear such a remarkable display. Here, he thought, was speech as mighty as anything in Homer's pages.[22]

Jefferson was to hear the orator again in later days, and each time the effect was somewhat similar. But his analytical powers came into play after the first overwhelming impression. As he described it in old age to Daniel Webster, himself no mean orator: "Although it was difficult when he had spoken to tell what he had said, yet, while he was speaking, it always seemed directly to the point. When he had spoken in opposition to my opinion, had produced a great effect, and I myself been highly delighted and moved, I have asked myself when he ceased: 'What the d[evi]l has he said?' "[23]

It is a pity that the text of Henry's speech has not come down to us, and there has been endless dispute over the peroration. It is agreed that first he alluded to "those examples of successful resistance to oppression which rendered glorious the annals of Greece and Rome." There is reasonable agreement that he electrified his auditors with the declaration that "in former times Tarquin and Caesar had their Brutus, Charles his Cromwell, and George III–" Here he paused dramatically, and with his pause, confusion enters the scene. The most famous and widely known account credits the shocked burgesses with loud interruptions of "Treason! Treason!" and Henry's almost immediate continuation, as though he had not heard the outcries: "And George III may profit by their examples." Then, defiantly: "Sir, if this be treason, make the most of it." [24]

Edmund Randolph, however, later averred that after the alleged cries of treason, Henry deftly switched to "–and George the Third, may he never have either." But a French traveler, eye-witness to the exciting scene, gave still another and much less dramatic version: that Henry, interrupted by Speaker Robinson alone, was not permitted to continue until he had apologized and declared his loyalty to the King.[25]

The leaders of the House vigorously opposed each resolution as Henry introduced it, not, as Jefferson remembered it, because they differed in principle but because, in the preceding session, they had already put themselves on record somewhat to the same effect, if in much milder tone, and an answer from England was still to be expected.[26] Word had not yet come that their respectful remonstrances had been wholly disregarded.

After furious debate the five resolutions were put to a vote, and passed by the barest majorities. The largest was 22 to 17; while the fifth, the most controversial of all, squeezed through by a single vote–20 to 19.[27]

Jefferson had remained transfixed through the entire "most bloody" debate and saw Peyton Randolph, his kinsman, stalk violently out of the door, exclaiming: "By God, I would have given one hundred guineas for a single vote." [28]

Whether the hundred guineas were duly delivered, or whether it was because Patrick Henry showed himself still a tyro in practical politics by triumphantly leaving for his home, the next day brought about what Fauquier called "a small alteration in the House."

The Old Guard had remained firmly seated in Williamsburg, determined to get rid of at least that combustible fifth resolution. Jefferson narrates how he, fascinated, watched Peter Randolph of the Council leaf through the old Assembly Journals seeking in vain for a precedent whereby the offending resolution could be expunged. Overnight, also, they worked on some of the less determined members who had voted for it. On May 31st, the House reconvened; with the redoubtable, if unwary, Henry missing from his seat. Now the Old Guard was in the saddle. They tried to undo all the hot work of the previous day; but the wavering members refused to follow on the first four resolutions. On the fifth, however, they were victorious, and it was stricken from the Journals.[29]

The victory was a Pyrrhic one; for copies of all *seven* resolutions, including even the two that Henry had decided finally not to submit, had been secretly sent to the newspapers of the Colonies, and appeared in the full panoply of print in *The Newport Mercury* of June 24th and in the *Boston Gazette* of July 1st. In fact, for a long while it was thought that all seven had been passed by the embattled burgesses of Virginia.

In Virginia there was no doubt that Henry and his resolutions had the support of the central and upper counties, as Jefferson carefully noted, no matter what the Tidewater sections felt. Even the Rev. James Maury, Jefferson's old teacher, who had cause enough to be bitter against Patrick Henry, nevertheless approved of the opposition to the Stamp Act, even though thereby "some may brand us with the odious name of rebels." [30]

Governor Fauquier promptly dissolved the Assembly, and enclosed copies of the four offending resolutions to England as justification for his conduct. Yet he was sufficiently conversant with the temper of the Virginians to doubt that elections to a new Assembly would bring in "cool reasonable men." [31]

The Governor's doubts and prescience of trouble were fully realized. When the hated stamps actually arrived in Virginia the ensuing October, he was compelled to intervene to save Colonel Mercer, their distributor, from physical harm. Only Fauquier's popularity and, as he informed his superiors in England, "the respect they bore to my character and ... the love they bore my person" protected the embarrassed Mercer from being roughly handled.[32] In Massachusetts and elsewhere, where the governors were not equally beloved, there were riots and bloody turmoils.

The widespread publication of the Virginia Resolves, including those which had never been offered, proved "an alarum bell to the disaffected," according to the gloomy report of the Massachusetts governor.[33] On June 8th, Massachusetts called for the convocation of a congress of all the colonies to meet at New York to discuss the situation. This so-called Stamp Act Congress, the harbinger of more to come, passed a series of resolutions of protest, much more moderate than the resolves of Virginia; but a precedent for concerted, independent action was established that was to bear fruit in the not too distant future.

It is probable that Jefferson was not in Williamsburg at the time of the Mercer incident, for his sister Jane had died on October 1st, and no doubt he hastened to Shadwell to join his sorrowing family. All that we know of Jane, who was twenty-five at the time of her death, is that she had a sweet singing voice, and loved especially the stately psalms of the Church of England.[34]

During all this turmoil, indeed, young Jefferson seems to have been an interested spectator rather than a participant. We have little knowledge of his movements or activities from the end of May in 1765, when he harkened breathlessly to the matchless eloquence of Patrick Henry, until the following May of 1766. But it is highly probable that the period was devoted to his law books and his readings in other fields, alternating, as was his wont, between Williamsburg and Shadwell.

In May, 1766, however, he determined to see the world; if not as far as England and Egypt, at least to Pennsylvania and New York. The exact motivation for the journey is obscure. Certainly he wished to be inoculated against the smallpox, and the nearest medical practitioners equipped to handle the dangerous transfer of infected material were in Philadelphia. All his life Jefferson was intensely interested in the theory and practice of inoculation, and pioneered in introducing it into his beloved state of Virginia.

At all events, armed with a letter of introduction to a leading medical luminary in Philadelphia, he started out on his travels on May 11th or 12th, 1766.[35] He traveled in style, with horse and carriage and driven by a Negro slave. His first stop was Annapolis, the capital of Maryland, and the journey was not without its excitement. "Surely never," he reported ruefully to his friend Page, "did small hero experience greater misadventures than I did on the first two or three days of my travelling."[36] Twice his horse ran away with him; then he drove through a terrific rain for two hours without a single shelter in sight. Crossing the Pamunkey River, he missed the ford and his carriage submerged over the cushions of the seat and almost capsized on a jutting rock.

But all was well that ended well and he came safely to Annapolis. To his fresh but appraising eyes the town seemed about the size of Williamsburg; its houses were finer, but its gardens were not as good. What particularly interested him, however, was the colonial Assembly then in session. It was not an inspiring sight to a young man who was accustomed to the dignity and decorum of the Burgesses of Virginia. The Maryland members looked like a "mob" and made "as great a noise and hubbub as you will usually observe at a publick meeting of the planters of Virginia." The clerk of the Assembly would read a proposed bill in "a schoolboy tone," while the members lounged in little groups and addressed the Speaker without taking the trouble to rise from their chairs. Votes were always *viva voce*, and no one bothered to demand a poll even when the votes seemed evenly divided. "In short," the youthful spectator disgustedly declared, "every thing seems to be carried without the house in general's knowing what was proposed."

But there was no gainsaying the enthusiasm and the rejoicings when, during Jefferson's stay, the news came that the British Parliament had finally repealed the hated Stamp Act.[37]

On May 26th, Jefferson continued his journey to Philadelphia. He traveled alone, though he had hoped that his friend Francis Willis would accompany him. But Willis had left Williamsburg several weeks earlier, and so Jefferson jogged into Philadelphia without a companion to share his wonder at the size and bustle of the largest town in America.[38]

How much time the young Virginian spent in Philadelphia there is no way of knowing. He submitted to inoculation, probably at the hands of Dr. John Morgan, to whom he had a letter of introduction; though his first biographer claims that the administering doctor was William Shippen.[39] Fortunately, there were no ill effects, such as happened only too often in the crude state of the process.

After duly seeing the sights and tasting something of the intellectual ferment of the metropolis, Jefferson proceeded to New York, the terminus of his trip. New York was somewhat smaller than Philadelphia; nor was it at the time an equal center of men of science and the arts. While viewing the town on the Hudson and assimilating its life, Jefferson took lodgings at a house in which Elbridge Gerry of Massachusetts was similarly lodged. The two young men became friendly, and parted on their several paths with mutual polite expressions of regard. They did not meet again until 1775, when both were members of the Continental Congress. From then on, however, their lives were to be conjoined on numerous occasions.[40]

Early in July, Jefferson returned to Virginia by boat, agreeably satisfied with his journey through the middle colonies. He had seen other towns and other manners, and had learned something of the way in which men who were not Virginia planters thought. He was no longer a provincial.

The rest of the year passed without further incident. Jefferson buckled down to his law and, early in 1767, came to the end of five years of apprentice study. His teacher and guide, George Wythe, led him before the General Court of Virginia where, after due examination into his qualifications, Thomas Jefferson was admitted to the bar.

CHAPTER 6

Public Forum and Private Mansion

THE practice of law was not excessively lucrative in the Virginia of the time. It could not hope to attain the generous rewards to be found in the trading and commercial colonies of Pennsylvania, New York and Massachusetts. Hard money was scarce, and the litigation that inevitably arose from mercantile establishments, shipping, financial transactions and trade by land and sea was still scarcer. Aside from the usual petty material of personal disputes—assaults and batteries, slander, trespasses, sales of chattels, etc.—the chief source of a lawyer's business was transactions in land and the clearing of titles. And, since Virginia gentry were notoriously short of cash and accustomed to paying their bills, if at all, from their estates, the pickings were slender enough. If the newly fledged lawyer had had to rely upon his legal earnings as the sole source of livelihood his situation would have been parlous indeed. Fortunately for Jefferson, and for most of his compeers, law was in effect an avocation. Their true vocation, and their mainstay, were their lands and the crops they raised thereon with their slaves and overseers.

In fact, even during his active practice, Jefferson spent much of his time at Shadwell personally superintending his own crops and those of his mother. His love for the land was deep and strong, and nothing—law, politics, or even the Presidency of the United States—could prove an adequate substitute for direct contact with the earth and the life of a working country gentleman. In 1766 he began a Garden Book, in which he jotted down the daily minutiae of plants and flowers, fruit-bearing trees and bushes. Later he was to add to this a series of account books in which, with daily accuracy, he noted expenses, journeys, the state of the weather, practical rules, formulae, and whatever came into his mind that seemed worth recording.

The first entry in his Garden Book is dated March 30, 1766, at Shadwell and characteristically notes that the "purple hyacinth begins to bloom." Within a week "narcissus and puckoon open" and, as he was preparing for his journey north, he entered the fact that the purple flag, violets and wild honeysuckle were still in full flower.[1]

The following year, when final preparation for the bar and the beginning of a legal career should properly have held him busy in Williamsburg, saw him devoting most of his time to Shadwell and the practical processes of farming. On February 20, 1767, he sowed peas and took time out to ascertain some quantitative scientific data. Five hundred peas, he noted, weighed 3 oz., 18 pennyweight; and about 2500 of them filled a pint. On March 15th, he planted asparagus, and a week later celery and Spanish onions. On April 2nd, he started his garden with carnations, Indian pink, marigold, globe amaranth and a score of other common and rare varieties; to which he added shrubs and trees like the lilac, Spanish broom, umbrella, laurel, "muscle plumbs" and the gooseberry. By May 28th he was able to write that "strawberries come to table" and the "forwardest" of the peas. Late that autumn he observed, with the true fervor of a scientific agriculturalist, that a horse will generally eat eight or ten bundles of fodder during a night and that therefore 1,170 bundles will keep him through the winter.[2]

Nevertheless, he found time in February to go down to Williamsburg to make a start at law. His first case was given him by Gabriel Jones on February 12, 1767, and involved a transaction in land.

From then on he obtained business in reasonable volume. The usual cases that are grist to a country lawyer's mill flowed in—land contracts, slanders, trespasses and suits on securities. More important matters also came his way, and requests from older attornies to join them in the preparation and trial of cases. Some of these required travel to the various county seats; on August 22nd, we find him at Staunton getting his soiled linen washed; on the 26th, having his horse shoed afresh; on the 31st, he was dining at Culpepper Court House; each item of expense being meticulously entered in his accounts.[3]

Aside from humdrum cases of land and contracts, the young lawyer also handled matters that brought him in contact with interesting aspects of Virginia life and manners. One such was scandalous in the extreme. Jefferson entered the facts frankly in his case book: "David Frame (Augusta) directs me to issue writ in Scandal agt James Burnside (Augusta). Burnside said he caught Frame (who is a married man) in bed with Eliza Burkin put his [hand] on Frame's as he lay in bed with the girl and felt it wet, and then put his hand on his [*erased and inked through*] and felt it wet also." [4] Evidently Burnside was able to prove his scandalous story, for later on Jefferson was notified by his client to drop the proceedings.

More, perhaps, to Jefferson's liking, even though he refused a fee for it, was his defense, "*totis viribus*," of his law teacher and revered friend, George Wythe, against the suit of a "seafaring man." Both the nature of the action and its outcome are unknown.

Interspersed, however, with the endless lists of cases and notes for drafting complaints are other memoranda of a more social and intimate nature. In April, 1768, for example, appears the sudden notation in reminder: "send Mrs. Charwell 7 oz. yellow silk from Charlottesville, not doubled and twisted. The deepest yellow half, and the other half lighter." And a month earlier, a list of items for himself to purchase: "Coarse

Dowlas for Jupiter . . . broadcloth for myself . . .cotton stockings . . . silk dittos . . . buckskin gloves . . . buck handle knives and forks." [5]

By the end of his first year in practice, Jefferson added up his accounts and found that he had been retained in 67 cases and had sent out bills for £293 in fees. This would have been a respectable sum for a beginning attorney, if collected; unfortunately, only £43 in actual cash came in. The volume of business continued steadily to mount: 115 cases in 1768 for a total of £304; 198 cases in 1769, billed at £370; and in 1770 came the high water mark, at least in theoretical earnings—the sum of £521.

But, alas, the actual returns bore little relation to the figures which Jefferson so carefully entered in his books. The monies that came into his pocket ranged from one-quarter to one-half of the amounts which he billed to his clients with monotonous regularity and were ignored by them with blithe insouciance. During the first six years that Jefferson practiced law he earned £2,177, a fair enough sum for a Virginia lawyer; but his actual collections amounted only to £792; certainly not enough to keep him in gentlemanly style without other sources of income.[6]

This state of affairs was not unique with Jefferson; it was the sad experience of all Virginia lawyers. In 1770, one Thomson Mason exploded into a series of public advertisements. "As I am determined for the future," he announced, "to receive more money, or have less business in the way of my profession, I take this method . . . of declaring that I will not for the future undertake the management of any cause unless my fee is first paid down, or a bond given for it." He was tired, he continued with pardonable exasperation, of those "who, at the time they pretended to be my friends, could coolly sit still and see me reduced to the necessity of selling my slaves to a very great disadvantage, and yet withhold the small sums due to me." [7]

Thus being pilloried in the public prints evidently did not stir the conscience of delinquent clients for, in 1773, six of the most respected lawyers of Virginia—Edmund Pendleton, John Randolph, Patrick Henry, James Mercer, Gustavus Scott and Thomas Jefferson—published a formal notice to all and sundry: "On serious Consideration of the present state of our practice in the General Court we find it can no longer be continued on the same terms. The Fees allowed by Law, if regularly paid, would barely compensate our incessant Labours, reimburse our expences and the losses incurred by Neglect of our private Affairs; yet even these Rewards, confessedly moderate, are withheld from us, in a great Proportion, by the unworthy Part of our Clients. Some regulation, therefore, is become absolutely requisite to establish Terms more equal between the Client and his Council. To effect this, we have come to the following Resolution, for the invariable Observance of which we mutually plight our Honour to each other: 'That after the 10th day of *October* next we will not give an Opinion on any Case stated to us but on Payment of the whole Fee, nor prosecute or defend any Suit or Motion unless the Tax, and one half of the Fee, be previously advanced, excepting those Cases only where we choose to act *gratis*;' and we hope no person whatever may think of applying to us in any other way." [8]

It is to be feared that the effect of this pronunciamento was null, and that litigious Virginians continued to ask counsel and to make no payment. But by this time Jefferson was seeking other fields for the just display of his talents and had withdrawn from the profitless practice of law.

As a lawyer, he was a good desk and brief man. He prepared his cases with painstaking care and delved into ancient precedents, history and legal philosophy to bolster them. He achieved the respect of his fellow lawyers and clients. In one case in particular, Howell v. Netherland, submitted on an agreed state of facts in April, 1770, he sought to give a higher philosophic tone to the argument than either the court or the *mores* of Virginia would permit. Curiously enough, his victorious adversary was George Wythe, his old teacher and friend.

Jefferson appeared for the plaintiff, a mulatto, who sought freedom from servitude under an original term imposed by the churchwardens of the parish against his grandmother, the daughter of a Negro father and a free white mother. In his plea before the General Court, Jefferson argued that "the purpose of the act was to punish and deter women from that confusion of species, which the legislature seems to have considered as an evil, and not to oppress their innocent offspring." It was unjust, he insisted, to visit the sins upon the third generation. With the courage of his convictions Jefferson boldly told the court that "under the law of nature, all men are born free, every one comes into the world with a right to his own person, which includes the liberty of moving and using it at his own will." It was a sufficient violation of the laws of nature, he declared, for the plaintiff's *mother*, herself innocent, to have been continued in servitude; certainly the continuance of that violation to her issue "and that too without end," was legally and morally unjustifiable.[9]

This was dangerous doctrine to propound in Virginia at the time, even though it is understood that a lawyer has a wide latitude in the advocacy of his client's case. That the court brooked it ill is evidenced by the fact that when Wythe rose to reply to Jefferson's argument, the judges brusquely interrupted and gave immediate judgment to Wythe's client.

It is doubtful that Jefferson was a good trial lawyer, in the sense that he could sway a jury to his side, regardless of the merits of the case. Certainly he could not be compared with Patrick Henry in this respect. Jefferson was no orator; he possessed neither the physical qualities of voice nor the extrovert personality required. He shrank from appearances before large audiences, and hated to bare his emotions, sincere or assumed for the occasion, for the delectation of the groundlings. His voice, if raised much above the loudness of ordinary conversation, began, with a few moments' effort, to "sink in his throat"; in other words, to become husky and inarticulate.[10] He was happiest in the calm appraisal of points of law before a bench of judges; the oratorical appeal to a jury was not for him. Edmund Randolph later compared him with Patrick Henry. "Mr. Jefferson," he said, "drew copiously from the depths of the law, Mr. Henry from the recesses of the human heart."[11]

Jefferson spent a part of each year at Shadwell and in the management of his private affairs. During the periods that the General Court was in session, however, he was down in Williamsburg. He was no mere dry-as-dust scholar; life itself, the gracious amenities and varied activities of the capital, found him an active participant. He was young, unattached and a Virginia gentleman.

His liquor cellar was well stocked; in 1769, he found himself with 279 bottles on hand, 26 empties and 89 "being carried off or broke." He was an ardent admirer of the theater and attended performances whenever he could; nor did he disdain the more vulgar shows of traveling magicians, exhibition of tigers, enormous hogs, elks and puppet entertainments. He drank his arrack punch with the best of them, and spent convivial evenings at the various clubs and taverns: Raleigh's, Ayscough's, Singleton's and Charlton's. He visited the homes of his friends, male and female, and tipped the servants generously when he left. He went to the races, but never bet; his gambling was restricted to small stakes at backgammon and similar games. A lover of horseflesh, he purchased a mare that struck his fancy; he saw to it that his Negro body servant, Jupiter, was well supplied with powder for his wig. In short, he lived the normal life of a fashionable young man. Yet, generous as he was, he entered every penny he spent in his little account books and, when overcharged, had no hesitation in demanding a return of the excess.[12]

But other items give us a different side of Jefferson. In 1768, he bought a violin for £5, and its constant use is testified to by the number of replacement strings he required. Nor is the repair item for a "microscope & perspect[ive] glass" one that ordinarily appears in the expenditures of a Virginia gentleman of the period. On a more serious plane also is the constant purchase of books either at the local stationers or on order from England. And there is one item, set down on April 17, 1769, that intrigues the attention: "pd. towards printing poem I never saw nor even wish to see—2/6."[13] What mendicant poet had waylaid Jefferson and cadged an unwilling contribution from him?

Music was one of his passions. He played the violin all his life. The Italian musician Alberti came to Williamsburg with a troop of players and gave concerts as well as lessons. Certainly Jefferson attended the concerts, and perhaps took lessons then on his beloved instrument. In any event, after he was established at Monticello, Alberti went there at Jefferson's invitation and taught him the finer points of the art. Jefferson was to reminisce that he played no less than three hours a day for many years; but that when the Revolution broke out, he laid aside the violin and never took it up again.[14] Once more his memory played him tricks, for his account books show purchases of violin strings long after the Revolution.

His chief passion, however, was building, landscaping and architecture. To these noble pursuits he remained faithful through life; studying the classical models, modifying and improving on them until he emerged as one of the greatest and most original of the early American architects. He became the inspirer of a neoclassical form of architecture whose impetus is not yet entirely spent.

The first evidence of his abiding interest in these subjects appears during his law student days. In 1765, he was purchasing volumes on gardening and landscaping, particularly William Shenstone's *Works;* and later on he got, immediately after its publication in England, Thomas Whately's *Observations on Modern Gardening*. The latter volume, with its detailed description of the great landscaped parks of England, became in effect a handbook and guide for his own more modest ventures in that direction.

By 1768, he had acquired the notable volume of Andrea Palladio, entitled *Four Books of Architecture*. The more he studied Palladio the more enthusiastic he became. That great Italian architect of the sixteenth century, the designer of numerous palaces and country villas, had revolted against the prevalent baroque incrustations of his day and gone back to the stately and simple designs of ancient Rome for his models.

Jefferson's instinctive distaste for the architectural construction of his time has already been noted. The Tudor, Georgian, and even the authentically indigenous Colonial American schools, repelled him. He was essentially a classicist in his artistic and literary tastes, and Palladio furnished him with designs that evoked an immediate response. Yet Jefferson was no slavish imitator; even as Palladio had modified the ancient Roman to conform to sixteenth-century Italian conditions, so his disciple changed and added to his designs to meet the needs of eighteenth and nineteenth century Virginia.[15]

Just when Jefferson decided to build a home for himself is not known, but by the time he had purchased Palladio his plans were well advanced. The first known reference to the place of his proposed new habitation occurs in 1767, when he mentions grafting cherry trees at Monticello.[16] This was the mountaintop he had inherited from his father and which he now named, from his Italian studies, "the little mountain." The name did not become final until 1770. For a while he thought of changing it to the Hermitage; then he shifted back again.[17] Similarly, he gave a name derived from the Greek to the hilly stretch of farmland to the east of the mountain: Pantops, meaning "place with a view everywhere."

What prompted Jefferson, a young beginning lawyer with no present interest in marriage, to a permanent habitation and a rooted home, situated so far away from Williamsburg where his practice would lie, and especially so contrary to the fixed Virginia tradition of a manor on a river bank or on a level, traveled road?

He had been alternating between Shadwell and Williamsburg and there is reason to believe that he was satisfied with neither. At Shadwell, his mother had the life tenancy; and there does not seem to have been any close ties of affection between mother and son. His sister Jane, for whom he had felt a greater warmth, was newly dead. Mary was long married; and Elizabeth, younger than himself by a year and a half, was displaying those deficiencies of intellect which within a few years was to lead to tragic death. Martha, three years younger, had married in 1765; Lucy was fifteen; while the twins, Anna Scott and Randolph, were nearly twelve. Randolph, who had joined in the inheritance with Thomas, and whom Jefferson was soon to send to William and Mary for his education, was, if not as deficient as Elizabeth, at least simple-minded. It was obviously not an atmosphere in which Thomas Jefferson could feel completely at home.

Williamsburg, on the other hand, though possessing marked advantages, was hardly considered as the permanent residence of a Virginia landowner. He might have a town house there, and descend for some months to enjoy the pleasant social life and the round of entertainments; but home was where his broad acres yielded their crops of tobacco and corn, and his slaves toiled under his personal supervision.

Jefferson was a true Virginian in his love of the land, his observation of the processes of nature and his practical concern with the tillage of the soil. Similarly, he yearned for a spacious place of abode, built to his own desires and furnished with fine mahogany and silver plate. In one particular, however, he sharply differed. Whereas his fellows sought broad valleys or tidewater levels, he alone lifted his eyes to the mountaintops. Bold scenery, magnificent horizons, remarkable convulsions of nature uplifted his spirit and filled him with rapturous awe. His recorded ecstasies over the cleft of the Potomac through the Blue Ridge, his emotions at the sight of the arching Natural Bridge, are justly famous. In this he was at one with the romantics; in most other respects he was essentially a rationalist and a child of the Enlightenment.

And, as has been pointed out, he found in Palladio sketches and praise of the ancient Roman villas or country houses where the cultivated Roman gentlemen retired in elegance from the seething life of the city. These villas were chiefly on the slopes of the Alban Hills or in the foothills of the Apennines, and classical literature teems with eloquent descriptions of noble vistas and genial retreats. Palladio himself advised that the country house be built "in elevated and agreeable places... upon an eminence."[18]

Under the spell of these new-found enthusiasms Jefferson found the exact location in his own possession. The crest of the hill which he named Monticello was surrounded on all sides by light and air, with noble vistas of distant mountains and closer valleys whichever way a contemplative eye was cast. Here, too, the heat of the Virginia summer was tempered with cooling winds, and newly established Charlottesville, the county seat of Albemarle, nestled in the valley below.

As the young lawyer toiled at the preparation of his cases in distant Williamsburg and sought musty precedents with which to bolster his arguments, his thoughts would wander. Salked's *Reports of Cases in the King's Bench* would close and Palladio, ever at hand, would open. In his memorandum books, interspersed with law, Jefferson would make quick sketches of floor plans and scribble supporting data. He envisaged a house with pedestals, entablatures and pediments, with "wings 48 f. sq. to water table." In Palladio (Book 4, Plate 36) he found the proper disposition of the paneling. He set down particulars of two-story "outhouses" to flank the central structure. He went into minute details, specifying cartridge paper of Prussian blue and Spanish white for the dining room. The furnishings, too, engaged his absorbed attention. An Aeolian harp, a refracting telescope, Venetian blinds, a backgammon table, a chessboard and men, a reading desk—all these he noted down as they sprang into his mind. And later, as his ambition grew, a small clavichord "to be made at Hamburgh in Germany" according to his own specifications. A most unusual instrument, for he called for a "compass from Double tr. to F in alt. to be made for holding in the lap, or laying on a table as light and portable as possible. The wood deal veneered over with the finest mahogany. The keys ivory flats and sharps tortoise shell." [19]

The young man of twenty-five dreamed of a country home to outshine anything in the colonies, a villa that Pliny or Horace might have been proud to occupy. It would be equipped with music and with instruments to measure the earth and contemplate the stars. A grandiose vision that might indeed come to a young man, and end in a sigh of aspiration. The amazing thing with this particular young man is that he went through with it; and still more amazing is the practical particularity with which he drafted his plans, measured dimensions and calculated quantities with all the accuracy of an architect, a bricklayer and a working carpenter. If any thoughts of eventual cost entered his mind, there is no mention anywhere.

Toward the end of 1767, he actually commenced work on Monticello. Lumber was sawn into planks and rails; glass was ordered for windows, and contracts made to level the top of the mountain. During 1768, he brought in a crop of tobacco on the lower fields totaling 9,787 lbs. In March, 1769, he commenced on the upper reaches what would eventually become a flourishing orchard. Slips and young trees were hauled toilsomely up the mountain—pear, cherry, apple, peach, apricot, nectarine and the more exotic almond, pomegranate and fig. He levied on his friends for choice botanical specimens, including a nectarine from George Wythe. He noted that he must set out raspberry, gooseberry and currant bushes, imbed asparagus, strawberries and artichokes, and build a henhouse. A road to the top was a prime essential and that called for wagonloads of wood and sand. Even a canal to deepen the water in the Rivanna at the foot of the mountain, so that produce and supplies could be floated to market, called for exact specifications. By July, he started work on the south outbuilding, to be used as a dwelling while he superintended the larger construction of the whole.[20]

And, in the midst of these manifold activities of law and estate-building, politics suddenly beckoned.

CHAPTER 7

The Study of Man—and of Woman

WHEN the abhorred Stamp Act was repealed in 1766 the colonies had responded with loud rejoicings and new affirmations of their loyalty to England and the King. Very strangely they paid little attention to the accompanying Declaratory Act which completely nullified the effect of the repealer and notified the recalcitrant colonists in plain language that Parliament had full power to legislate for the British possessions in America "in all cases whatsoever," including taxation.

The purport of this proclamation of powers did not strike home until Charles Townshend, Chancellor of the Exchequer, sought new revenues for England in the following year. He had already publicly declared that he knew no "distinction between internal and external taxes; it is a distinction without a difference, it is perfect nonsense."[1] Whether it was or not—and the point is arguable—the colonists were decidedly and vehemently to the contrary. They had fought the Stamp Act with seeming success because it *was* an internal tax, and they were in no mood to take on another.

Therefore, when Townshend pushed through Parliament a series of duties on such essential articles as paper, painters' colors, glass and tea, payable at the ports of entry in the colonies, and reorganized the customs service in the chief port, Boston, with full powers to seek out smuggled goods and untaxed commodities, once more Massachusetts rose figuratively, and to some degree literally, in arms. So threatening was their mien that the frightened Customs Commissioners called for troops and ships of war. In turn, the Massachusetts legislature circularized the sister colonies for concerted measures to oppose both the duties and the alleged illegalities of the Commissioners. When it refused to rescind the call on the demand of the British authorities, the House was dissolved. But the storm was thereby increased rather than allayed. Confronted with riots and disorders both in Boston and elsewhere, Parliament threatened to adopt repressive measures of the sternest kind. The most alarming of these was the decision to hale political offenders to England for trial.

Virginia observed the struggles of her sister colonies to the north with indignant sympathy. The one man who might have placated or modified her sentiments—Francis Fauquier—had died on March 3, 1768. All Virginia mourned his passing. "He was," declared the *Virginia Gazette*, "a Gentleman of a most amiable disposition,—generous, just, and mild; and possessed, in an eminent degree, of all the social virtues." For once an obituary was not sufficiently laudatory. Fauquier's death was a blow to the cause of good relations between England and her colony; and a personal loss to Thomas Jefferson, who had dined with him, fiddled with him, and indulged in much profound and stimulating talk.

The new governor, Norborne Berkeley, Baron de Botetourt, arrived in Williamsburg to assume his duties in October, 1768. He was no Fauquier, though a kindly and well-meaning enough man; even his popular predecessor would have found it difficult to settle the storm that was brewing.

With his coming, writs were issued for the election of a new Assembly. In December, 1768, the electors of Albemarle County assembled at the tiny town of Charlottesville to select two burgesses for the forthcoming Assembly. They voted publicly, each man announcing his vote to the tally clerk; and when they were through—Dr. Thomas Walker was one burgess, and Thomas Jefferson the other.

What had induced Jefferson to become a candidate at this particular juncture is unknown; but the circumstances may plausibly be reconstructed. He was a rising young lawyer, with friends and kinsmen already seated in the House. John Page, of the same age as himself, had achieved a status in the Council the year before. George Wythe had just been chosen as Mayor of Williamsburg. Through Fauquier and others Jefferson was well acquainted with the workings of government, and ever since he had heard Patrick Henry's first famous speech, the Assembly had exercised an undoubted fascination on him. Then, too, he was a substantial landholder, intelligent and accomplished, and his father had represented Albemarle in his day and exercised authority in the county. His connections were influential in Albemarle, and the other successful candidate, Dr. Walker, was a friend of the family and his old guardian.

Besides, the times were ripe. He had watched with a keen and discerning eye the steady progression of events, and the Assembly now called into being would be confronted with issues at least as important as those it had faced during the turmoil over the Stamp Act. He had definite ideas on the relations of England and America, and on the theory of government itself, which required the forum of the Assembly for their unfolding and maturing.

On April 3, 1769, Jefferson journeyed down to Williamsburg from Shadwell. The new Assembly did not convene until May 8th, but he had legal matters to attend to and the puppet show was in town. He saw the latter three times and viewed, in company with a crowd of gaping onlookers, an exhibited hog that weighed over 1,050 lbs.[2]

More serious business was soon on tap, however, and it is probable that the members of the forthcoming Assembly were already in private conference, mapping out a plan of action and allotting roles to the various individuals. The new member from Albemarle was no doubt included in the meetings; the celerity with which he was given a part in the proceedings indicates that.

On May 8, 1769, the House convened. Its membership included some of the most prominent citizens of Virginia; men whose names were to become firmly established in the annals of their native state and of the nation which they helped build. Peyton Randolph, Speaker of the House, Edmund Pendleton, George Wythe, the haughty and austere Robert Carter Nicholas, Richard Bland, whose trenchant pamphlet *An Enquiry into the Rights of the British Colonies* had drawn first blood in the controversy with England, Patrick Henry, George Washington, Richard Henry Lee, Benjamin Harrison, John Blair, Jr., Thomas Nelson, Carter Braxton, Archibald Cary, and Thomas Jefferson—few legislative bodies then or after could boast such a roster of talents.

The session opened mildly enough. Peyton Randolph, who had been the King's attorney in the colony and was a man of probity and moderation, was quickly elected Speaker of the House. Lord Botetourt made a short speech of welcome to His Majesty's loyal subjects and spoke graciously of their "zeal and wisdom." To these remarks the Assembly interposed the conventional thanks and appointed a committee to incorporate them in proper flowery language. The new member from Albemarle was placed on that committee.[3]

Too much, perhaps, has been made of this assignment. It was innocuous enough and a decent introduction for a fledgling legislator to the work of the House. Even the fact that he was asked by the other and older committee men to draft the responsive address to the Governor meant little. It gave him a chance to try his powers under the supervision of more experienced heads.

It turned out exactly that way. Jefferson, confronted with this first public paper, followed the text of the resolutions too stiffly and too literally. When he presented his draft to his fellow committee members, Robert Carter Nicholas objected to it as not sufficiently ample and redrafted it. Even after many years Jefferson remembered that blow to his youthful pride. Writing of the incident in 1815, it still quivered a trifle. "Being a younger man as well as a young member," he recalled, "it made on me an impression proportioned to the sensibility of that time of life." [4] Whether as a young man or an old man, Jefferson was always sensitive to any criticism, expressed or implied.

This abortive address seems to have been his sole contribution to that first short session, though in his Autobiography he speaks of an attempt, which similarly failed, to ameliorate the strict rules prohibiting the private emancipation of slaves.[5] But no record of it exists in the House Journals.

There was much more important business on hand, however, than a pleasant exchange of compliments between Governor and Assembly. The circular appeal of the Massachusetts House of Representatives against the Townshend Acts was at hand, together with news of rioting to the north and the contemplated restrictive measures of the British Parliament. All groups in the Virginia Assembly agreed that they called for action on their part. There is no question that the more radical members headed by Patrick

Henry—with whom Jefferson seems to have been in sympathy—would have wished for some clarion blast equal in vigor to the famous expunged resolution of 1765, but memories of what had then happened led them to agree to the milder and more dignified protest submitted by the moderates.

It was the beginning of a strategy that was to prove eminently successful. Though the radicals champed at the bit, they realized that they had to make haste slowly, and do nothing to alarm the moderate and influential members. Jefferson later described their tactics: "Subsequent events favored the bolder spirits of Henry, the Lees, Pages, Mason &c., with whom I went in all points. Sensible, however, of the importance of unanimity among our constituents, although we often wished to have gone faster, we slackened our pace, that our less ardent colleagues might keep up with us; and they, on their part, differing nothing from us in principle, quickened their gait somewhat beyond that which their prudence might of itself have advised, and thus consolidated the phalanx which breasted the power of Britain. By this harmony of the bold with the cautious, we advanced with our constituents in undivided mass, and with fewer examples of separation than, perhaps, existed in any other part of the Union." [6]

On May 16th, accordingly, the House unanimously passed what seemed to them moderate and respectful resolutions: (1) a reiteration of the earlier doctrine that only *they* had the right to impose taxes on the people of Virginia; (2) that they had the right to petition the King for redress of grievances; (3) that any trial of a Virginian for alleged crimes could only be held in Virginia, and they viewed transportation of the accused to England as "highly derogatory of the Rights of British Subjects." [7]

Much to the surprise of the moderates, the Governor summoned the House to his Council Chamber the following day and informed them sternly: "I have heard of your Resolves, and augur ill of their Effect. You have made it my Duty to dissolve you; and you are dissolved accordingly." [8] The honeymoon was over.

Nothing that Botetourt could have done could have pushed the moderates more violently into the arm of the radicals. They had thought they were stating mere basic principles and employed the most respectful language; yet they had been rudely dismissed and Virginia left without a representative body. Now wholly at one, the legislators went in a body to the Raleigh Tavern and reconvened in the Apollo Room. That famous scene of dances and entertainments was the only nongovernmental place in Williamsburg sufficiently large to house the wrathful delegates. There they promptly elected Peyton Randolph, their late Speaker, as moderator and proceeded to consider their course.

With the dissent of only a few of their number they resolved upon a boycott to bring England to her senses. Already, in anticipation of just such a contingency, George Mason had drafted an "Association." He was not present at the Assembly, but he had thoughtfully given his draft to George Washington, the member from Fairfax County; and Washington now pulled it out of his pocket.[9] It was passed almost by acclamation and on the following day, May 18, 1769, one by one the members came up to the table and signed it. The signature of Thomas Jefferson, though not of course the first, was written with a precise and unfaltering hand.

The "Association" was completely revolutionary. While the Resolves that followed the Stamp Act were more violent in tone, they were nevertheless mere words. Here was action; and action of the kind that, it was thought, would hit England in her most tender spot, her purse.

While vowing "our inviolable and unshaken fidelity and loyalty to our most gracious sovereign," but "at the same time being deeply affected with the grievances and distresses with which his majesty's American subjects are oppressed," particularly the late taxes on tea and other items, the signatories bound themselves into an Association and recommended that others do the same. They would not, they declared, import any goods now or hereafter taxed by Parliament for the purpose of raising a revenue in America; they would not import from Great Britain or the continent of Europe liquors, beef, pork, fish, cheese, sugar, furniture, jewelry, woolens, shoes and a host of other enumerated articles until the Parliamentary taxes were revoked; they would cancel all previous orders to British merchants for goods; and they would import no slaves.[10]

Thomas Jefferson was receiving his first lesson in the theory and practice of boycott, nonimportation and embargo that he was to impose as President of the United States with legal compulsions and on a much more drastic scale. But the ill success of this first tentative venture might have taught him another lesson as well. For, in spite of the hullaballoo and the social pressures of resolved patriots on the lukewarm, in spite of similar "Associations" in other colonies, it cannot be said that this one, or its later revivals, did anything to bring the English merchants clamoring to Parliament.

In the late summer of 1770, Arthur Lee, then in England, appraised the situation. "From the best intelligence that can be gained from the merchants here," he wrote disgustedly, the Virginians "did not keep one article of it before, and why shou'd I hope that the honour they have already violated, will bind them now! The Association of last year, was as solemnly entered as this, yet it is constantly, and confidently declared here, that the exports to Virginia, of the prohibited articles, was never more considerable." [11]

After signing the document, the members dispersed to their home counties to arouse the people and await the inevitable call for new elections. Jefferson was more leisurely about it, remaining in Williamsburg for about a month. Probably he had some legal business to wind up; but by the middle of July he was back in Charlottesville superintending the building of his heart's desire on the mountaintop.[12]

Botetourt duly called for a new election; and just as duly, in September, 1769, Jefferson, as well as practically every other member who had signed the Association, was returned triumphantly to the House. The electorate may not have been willing to inflict on themselves the hard abstentions from English goods, but they righteously approved the principle and the delegates who had enunciated it.

The new session opened on November 7, 1769. This time Botetourt was most conciliatory. He had just received a letter from England, he informed the recalcitrant Assembly, to the effect that "his Majesty's present Administration have at no Time entertained a Design to propose to Parliament to lay any further Taxes upon America for the Purpose of raising a Revenue, and that it is their intention to propose in the next Session of Parliament, to take off the Duties upon Glass, Paper, and Colours, upon Consideration of such Duties having been laid contrary to the true Principles of Commerce." [13] Significantly, tea was not mentioned.

England seemingly had backed down. The omission of any reference to tea in the proposed repealer might have been an oversight. Since the letter was dated May 13th, it could not have been inspired by fear of the Association. Nevertheless, it was a great victory, and the Assembly ought to have been thankful. It was, and duly proffered its most humble thanks, but watered them down with a sceptical aside that "we will not suffer our present Hopes . . . to be dashed by the bitter Reflection that any future Administration will entertain a Wish to depart from that Plan." [14]

What had happened in England to bring about the seeming *volte-face* was the death of Townshend, the resignation of William Pitt and the appearance of Lord North as Prime Minister. North thought that the idea of adding to the cost of British manufactures in the colonies limited their sale and therefore affected his own constituents adversely. It was therefore on a strictly self-interested basis that he moved for repeal of the offending duties. The tax on tea, however, since this was not an article of English manufacture, was retained. By keeping merely this inconsiderable tax, he believed, he managed at one and the same time to placate the colonists and reaffirm the vital principle of the powers of Parliament. He was mistaken on the first count, at least.

Temporarily, however, the commotion subsided. The ensuing session of the Assembly was a dull one. Both the legislators and the people marked time. As Jefferson put it, "our countrymen seemed to fall into a state of insensibility to our situation. The duty on tea not yet repealed & the Declaratory act of a right in the British parl[iament] to bind us by their laws in all cases whatsoever, still suspended over us." [15]

Obviously Jefferson was not one of the insensible ones. He did nothing in this particular session, it is true, except to offer a private bill to "dock the Intail of certain lands" belonging to a neighbor.[16] But he was busy preparing himself against future eventualities in the only way that at the time seemed effective.

Hitherto Jefferson's studies, rigorous as they were, had been along linguistic, legal, ethical and scientific lines. He had delved somewhat into the history of institutions, insofar as they were a natural appendage to his readings in general history, but he had studied them only to satisfy an insatiable intellectual curiosity that might well have been diverted to other and equally fascinating subjects. Now that he was a political figure, however, and involved in the inner mechanism of the ever-widening and deepening struggle with England, his studies took a definite and specific turn.

The climate of the eighteenth century was conducive to the search for a theoretical and rational base for every course of action. It was the Age of Reason, of Enlightenment, when human beings rediscovered themselves as rational, sentient creatures, and prided themselves on their ability to find a sufficient reason for everything they did, founded solidly on immutable laws of nature that were as majestic and eternal in their course as the wheelings of the stars above. Was not the universe a grandiose mechanism, set in motion by a beneficent if somewhat vague Deity, and its workings, when rightly understood, wholly for the benefit of mankind? Man, it is true, had perverted nature through a series of institutions formulated by the power-greedy few for their own aggrandizement over the unorganized many. Such had been the kingships, the oligarchies, the religious hierarchies which had, by force and cunning, stripped the mass of mankind of their inherent, natural rights; those rights with which Nature, Deity, call it what you will, had originally invested them.

It was the duty, therefore, of rational man to remove these accreted layers of usurpation and restore that original status which must necessarily bring justice and a golden age to the world. Man, by his nature, declared these children of the Enlightenment, was good. His unspoiled nature, still unperverted by artificial institutions imposed on him for the benefit of the few, could best be studied in his early history. Therefore we must go back in time, not so much to the later classical world, when powerful perversions of the original state had already taken place, but to the primitive Greeks and the more individualistic and loosely grouped tribes of northern Europe.

Today we might use the term "rationalization" in its modern sense to describe the processes of mind through which the eighteenth-century theoreticians on government worked. The conclusion to which they wished to come was pushed back into the premise. The natural law from which they argued was merely the logical construct of their own desires, and they carefully chose from the limited and distorted history available to them those facts and factors which fitted the thesis they had already evolved. Just as Locke had deduced from man in a state of nature the triumphant principles of the "glorious revolution" of 1688, so, with equal facility, Hobbes had been able to find in that same natural man a fatal necessity for total submission to government and absolutism.

The American colonists—or at least their leaders—found it necessary to appeal to these same rational processes and precedents to justify their struggle with England. They were not revolutionaries—as yet; they sought to convince England and themselves that their claims were founded first, on the immutable rights of all men, and second, on the history and primary institutions of England itself. That required a good deal of reading in the right places, and the American theoreticians did an amazing amount of it. Characteristically, Jefferson was one of them.

In the summer of 1769, after his first legislative session, he ordered a large number of books from England. They were all of a piece—inquiries into the nature of government and the factual material from which that nature could be deduced. The prime movers of eighteenth-century thought were there—Locke on *Government*, Burlamaqui on *Natural Law*, and the *Works* of Montesquieu. Buttressing these were volumes on political economy, civil society, parliamentary history and the history of specific countries and peoples.[17]

The precious volumes arrived in December, 1769, while Jefferson was in the midst of the Assembly's second session. He fell on them with the eagerness of a neophyte and wrote down in his commonplace book those passages which particularly struck his attention or bolstered his own private beliefs. Especially did he seek for material which could be used for ammunition in the battle of pamphlets that was already under way.

Before going to the great theorists, however, he read the volumes which purported to deal with historical facts. A long series of entries discloses his systematic study of the history of the early populations of Europe, their modes of inheritance, forms of government, customs and manners. They all relate to a definite purpose—to prove that the ancient, primitive forms all rested on popular will and popular sovereignty, freely expressed and unfettered by coercions.

For example, from Simon Pelloutier's *Histoire des Celtes* he culled such assertions as that, among the Celts, it was the people who elevated kings or deposed them at their own pleasure, and that the freemen, capable of bearing arms, decided by a majority vote "all matters which affected the well-being of the state."[18]

Even among the Greeks, at least in the beginning, he discovered corroborative material. His authority was Abraham Stanyan's *Grecian History*. It was with much evident satisfaction that Jefferson wrote down in his book: "Stanyan sais that the first kings of Greece were elected by the free consent of the people. They were considered chiefly as the leaders of their armies." Later they enlarged their powers to become absolute; but, abusing their trust, "the people, as opportunity offered, resum'd the power in their own hands."[19]

This preoccupation on the part of Jefferson, at so early a period, with historical instances of the power of the people to depose their kings, is extremely enlightening. Perhaps its full implications have been overlooked. For at this time there were few, if any, in the colonies who concerned themselves with the nature of their relations to the king of England. It was against alleged Parliamentary usurpations that their heaviest batteries were directed; indeed, the kingly tie was used as a sort of stick with which to beat Parliament over the head. But Jefferson, this early, was obviously cutting through to the heart of the issue. In their eagerness to affirm the king as against Parliament, were not the colonies laying themselves open—granted that Parliament claims were withdrawn—to an equally odious assumption of similar powers by the king?

Jefferson noted the dilemma and fortified himself against any such admissions. But, as he was later to declare in his Autobiography, haste could be made only slowly. The timid must not be alarmed; nor the conservatives made to recoil. In his *Summary View*, several years later, he attacked the pretensions of both king and Parliament with equal avidity. In the Declaration of Independence he went all out against the king alone.

The nature of the relations between England as mother country and Virginia as colony similarly interested Jefferson. In the history of the Greek colonies he found ready-made to his hand a wealth of fascinating examples. Again using Stanyan as his source book, he carefully abstracted every example of a Greek colony that threw off its dependence on its mother country. Syracuse, Corcyra, Mycenae and others, "as they increased their power, they renounced their obedience." [20] What better precedents could there be for similar action some day on the part of the American colonies?

Among Jefferson's manuscripts is a copy which he had made of the articles of surrender of Virginia to the Parliamentary emissaries after the overthrow of Charles I. On this copy Jefferson wrote the comment that the pact was "a voluntary act not forced . . . by a conquest of the country." [21] Evidently what was uppermost in his mind when he took the trouble to copy the articles was the point that any pact that was voluntary in nature could justly be dissolved by a similar voluntary act.

Thus fortified from history, Jefferson next proceeded to an examination of the great theoretical authors. Strangely, the one from whom he should have derived most sustenance, John Locke, appears but once in his commonplace book.[22] Certainly, if we remember the famous similarities between the phrases of Locke and the phrases of the Declaration of Independence, the debt was large. But Locke was a common part of the American scene; his treatises on Civil Government were the stock in trade of every publicist and well-read man. Perhaps Jefferson felt that it was not necessary to copy down the pertinent sections in order to fix them in his memory. He already had them at his finger tips. The same observations apply to Burlamaqui and Puffendorf, whose discourses on the laws of nature and of nations had similarly passed into the current coin of the realm. But Montesquieu's *Esprit des Lois* was of a different order.

That epoch-making work was still a novelty in Virginia and Jefferson, in his first contact with the Frenchman's vast and systematic treatment, displayed an immediate enthusiasm. His transcriptions from Montesquieu are voluminous and second only in extent to those from Bolingbroke.

What interested him was not so much Montesquieu's predilection for a constitutional monarchy, as his definitions of popular sovereignty, his theory of federative republics, his examples of the relativity of laws and constitutions and the necessity for their constant modification to conform to new circumstances, and particularly his comments on civil liberties and the processes by which democracies prosper or become corrupted.[23]

It is obvious, therefore, that Jefferson absorbed those sections which agreed with or factually confirmed his own natural predilections and omitted, or contradicted, those which did not. How much, or how far, Montesquieu "influenced" Jefferson's thinking has been hotly debated. But such influences, and the degree thereof, so dear to the hearts of Ph. D. candidates, are usually subject to an important psychologic law: that men ordinarily take over from their readings and studies that which is consonant with their own ideas, and mostly ignore that which is contradictory.

Similarly, this explains what has puzzled many commentators: why, if Jefferson at this stage was so engrossed with Montesquieu, did he later turn and rend him limb from limb? The answer is comparatively simple. At first reading the areas of agreement bulked large in the particular problems with which Jefferson—and the colonies—were confronted; they were water over the dam after the Revolution. *Then,* faced with other problems, and especially with what Jefferson called the "monarchical principles" of his enemies, the areas of disagreement assumed a portentous aspect that had not been visible before. Two phases of Montesquieu's thinking then excited Jefferson's wrath and alarm—his advocacy of an English-type monarchy, and his doctrine that a republic could exist only in a small area and must inevitably be destroyed once the territorial extent expanded beyond town-meeting proportions. Both these dogmas had been employed with telling effect by Jefferson's opponents, and it is no wonder he reacted violently against their author.

By 1790, he was weighing Montesquieu's merits and demerits with an even hand; by 1810, he was exclaiming vehemently that "I am glad to hear of everything which reduces that author to his just level, as his predilection for monarchy, and the English monarchy in particular, has done mischief everywhere, and here also, to a certain degree."[24]

On February 1, 1770, Jefferson was in Shadwell. He ate at the family table, then mounted horse and rode on business to Charlottesville, the county seat. A few hours later a slave spurred into the little town, mud-spattered and distraught. "Master," he gasped, "the old place is burnt down. Everything's gone." Jefferson was thunderstruck. "Everything?" he echoed. "Didn't you save my books?" The slave shook his head. "No, Master, all lost." Then he grinned hopefully. "Not all. We saved your *fiddle.*"[25]

This was disaster. Shadwell, his birthplace, the home of his mother, remaining sisters and younger brother, was completely destroyed. Yet

Jefferson's first thought and later bewailment was for his books and papers. His law books, his records and memoranda of law cases, his own and his father's memorabilia, letters, notes, perhaps some early essays—and the solid beginnings of a library. For a bookish man like Jefferson—and for his biographers—this was irretrievable loss. The books might eventually be replaced, but the precious scraps of paper from which his early life could have been more fully reconstructed had vanished forever into char and dismal smoke. Fortunately, his small pocket account books and commonplace books were not involved in the holocaust; doubtless the current one accompanied him to Charlottesville and the earlier volumes reposed in safety in his Williamsburg quarters.

That Jefferson was quick to realize the relative importance of his several losses is evidenced by the letters he wrote to his friends. To John Page he wrote in his first despair: "My late loss may perhaps have reached you by this time; I mean the loss of my mother's house by fire, and in it of every paper I had in the world, and almost every book. On a reasonable estimate I calculate the *cost* of the books burned to have been £200 sterling. Would to god it had been the money. *Then* had it never cost me a sigh." Of his law books, only one was left. "Of papers too of every kind I am utterly destitute. All of these, whether public or private, of business or of amusement, have perished in the flames." His records of cases, his prepared notes for trials, all were gone. What, he asked plaintively, was he going to do at the April term of the General Court? He would not be ready for trial, and the Court had specifically forbidden any adjournments.[26]

He also wrote to his friend Thomas Nelson, Jr., of York, to the same effect and sent him a list of volumes to forward to his bookseller in England for replacement. Young Nelson, whose father was Secretary of the Council and a man of weight, wrote back not to worry. The cases would be adjourned to permit adequate preparation, the books would be ordered and, in the meantime, Nelson, Sr., would lend him whatever law books he needed.[27]

It is strange that Jefferson's whole concern—at least as far as his letters go—was for his books and papers. No word of regret is spoken of the complete loss to his mother of home and belongings, of the cramped quarters to which she and the rest of the family were driven by the destruction of the main buildings at Shadwell. His total silence goes far to establish the belief that his relationship with his mother was not of the best.

As for himself, he was already engaged in building a new home on the mountaintop at Monticello, and the fire at Shadwell merely hastened his efforts to make it habitable as soon as possible.

He rushed the work and, in accordance with Virginia custom, prepared a single room in which he could dwell while supervising building operations on the rest. Into this single room "which, like the cobblers, serves me for parlour for kitchen and hall. I may add, for bedchamber and study too," he moved on November 26, 1770. There, as he somewhat shamefacedly avowed, "my friends sometimes take a temperate dinner with me and then retire to look for beds elsewhere. I have hope however of getting more elbow room this summer." [28]

By the time of Jefferson's removal to Monticello he had already become one of the leading figures in his native county. On June 9, 1770, Baron de Botetourt, Governor of Virginia, appointed him Lieutenant of Albemarle County and "Chief Commander of all his Majesty's Militia, Horse and Foot" in that county. The actual commission was issued on December 15th.[29] This was the same station that Peter Jefferson had achieved at a much later period in life and gave its possessor considerable prestige. Though it carried with it certain responsibilities it was, at least in times of peace, somewhat honorific. Certainly Thomas Jefferson was no military man, either now or at any other period of his life, and his current command of the county militia did little or nothing to initiate him into the mysteries of the military profession.

As a person of considerable importance, an established lawyer, a member of the legislature, the owner of considerable landed property and a future home in progress, it was high time for a young man nearing the ripe age of twenty-eight to marry. Such, at least, was the custom of the country. Jefferson's friends had practically all achieved that "blessed" state; only Thomas seemed to be the perennial bachelor.

There is hardly any doubt that the eligible maidens of Albemarle and of Williamsburg, with the advice and concurrence of their mothers, had already set their caps at him. Yet he had managed to escape the lure of their undeniable attractions thus far. How much of his unwillingness to submit to the proffered yoke stemmed from his early experience with Rebecca Burwell, how much flowed from the same hesitations which finally decided that young lady against him, and how much came from his unwillingness to include a bride in the family circle around his mother at Shadwell, cannot be measured with rule and compass. Probably all three had their due share in his wariness.

But now, with Monticello already assuming the outlines of concrete accomplishment, faint adumbrations began to stir in its master. The first evidence, curiously paradoxical, appears in the interleaved copy of the *Virginia Almanack* for 1770 which he used for his account book. On the inside front cover, in his usual precise handwriting, is a string of Latin quotations. All of them, in hearty classical language, berate the fairer sex and decry its capacity for fidelity, goodness and general mental capacity. *Foemina nulla bona est* is the general theme.[30]

Such a sudden outbust of misogynist fervor in a grown man of twenty-seven may be attributed to one of two things: either he had just suffered a reverse in an encounter with a lady, or he feared the consequences of an involvement already in being and consciously sought to fortify himself against them by apt citations from those who had similarly been once bitten and twice shy. The second alternative seemed Jefferson's case and his literary attempts at self-defense proved singularly futile.

On October 6, 1770, appeared this portentous entry in his account book: Gave a "Smith at Wayles's 1/3," evidently for shoeing his horse. Twice in December he was again at "Wayles's," each time tipping the servants when he left.

What was the magnet that drew Jefferson to the place called "The Forest" on the banks of the James River in Charles City County, where John Wayles, attorney and wealthy man of affairs, resided? It soon became evident that the stellar attraction was his daughter, Martha Wayles Skelton, recently widowed and with a child by her deceased husband.

John Wayles had come from England to practice law in Williamsburg. His practice was large, Jefferson later declared, not so much because of his legal knowledge as his "great industry, punctuality and practical readiness." He was also, to quote the same informant, "a most agreeable companion, full of pleasantry and good humor, and welcomed in every society," and, what made him doubly welcome, the possessor of "a handsome fortune." [31]

What Jefferson forgot to mention, however, and what seems to have been hitherto overlooked, was another and perhaps even more potent contributor to Wayles's fortune than the practice of law. On October 22, 1772, appeared this significant advertisement in *The Virginia Gazette:*

> Just arrived from *Africa*, the Ship *Prince of Wales*, *James Bivins* Commander, with about four Hundred fine healthy SLAVES; the Sale of which will begin at *Bermuda Hundred*, on *Thursday*, the 8th of *October*, and continue until all are sold. [Signed] JOHN WAYLES. RICHARD RANDOLPH.

Two days before this advertisement appeared, evidently the last of several, Wayles complained to his then son-in-law, Thomas Jefferson, that the current slave sale "goes on slowly." [32] The slave trade was an exceedingly profitable business, though already subject to uneasy consciences on the part of a good many Virginians. Jefferson was to become one of its most vigorous opponents in the future.

Wayles married three times. His daughter Martha was the fruit of his first marriage with Martha Eppes, the daughter of Col. Francis Eppes of Bermuda Hundred. The child's birth on October 30, 1748, was no doubt responsible for the mother's death a few days later.

Young Martha grew up under the care of two successive stepmothers, the second of whom had been, prior to her marriage with John Wayles, the widow of one Reuben Skelton. Reuben had a younger brother, Bathurst, who doubtless came to visit his erstwhile sister-in-law at her new ménage at The Forest, and thereby became acquainted with the growing girl in her charge.

Bathurst Skelton had attended William and Mary in 1763 and 1764 and had been friendly with the group of young men which included Jefferson and Page.[33] Later he became a sheriff, justice of peace and the amasser of a small library which betrayed a certain literary taste. He was twenty-two when, on November 20, 1776, he married Martha Wayles, then barely eighteen. They moved to Elk Hill on the James, and on November 7th of the following year a son named John was born to the newly wedded pair. The marriage was short-lived; on September 30, 1768, Bathurst Skelton died, and the bereaved widow, with her infant son, returned to her father's domicile.

Widows did not usually remain long in that condition in eighteenth-century Virginia, especially when they were young, the possessor of an estate in their own right and expectant of a larger one in the not too distant future. Since no portrait of Martha Skelton has come down to us, either painted or contemporaneously verbal, we have no means of determining what degree of beauty she possessed in addition to her other merits. The traditional account, based on the memories of her family and therefore not impartial, describes her as a little above medium height, slight in frame, and with a brilliant complexion, hazel eyes, and auburn-tinged hair. That she played the spinet and harpsichord with taste and feeling may be taken as authentic; that she was a good housewife is otherwise attested to by the few household accounts which have come down to us.[34]

Jefferson must have first met Martha Skelton in Williamsburg sometime in 1770 and been attracted to the young widow. In due time he visited her at The Forest, and the attraction deepened. That he was wrestling violently with himself is evident both from the Latin tags previously quoted and from his mournful complaint to his friend James Ogilvie, a London minister in search of a Virginia parish. Adverting to the dilemma of a mutual friend who was estopped from marrying the girl he loved because of her mother's disapproval, he continued: "I too am in that way; and have still greater difficulties to encounter, not," he hastened to add, "from the frowardness of parents, nor perhaps want of feeling in the fair one, but from other causes as unpliable to my wishes as these."[35]

What those causes were he did not mention. Perhaps they were the lingering remains of his former aversion to matrimony; perhaps they had to do with the current cramped state of his quarters at Monticello. That they were not insuperable, even to himself at the moment, is indicated by his order to his agent on the same day for a clavichord to be purchased in Hamburg and for a search to be instituted in London for the putative Jeffersonian arms.[36]

During the winter and spring of 1771, Jefferson became a regular visitor at The Forest. Obviously his doubts and the alleged impediments were gradually being dissolved. He was an extremely busy young man, what with his legal career, his legislative duties, his courtship and the immense building project at Monticello.

All that was finished on the mountaintop was the single-roomed brick building in which he lived and which later became the "southeast pavilion" of the finished structure. Now the tempo was stepped up and he hired a builder to assist him and help him supervise his workmen. The actual planning and architectural details were peculiarly his own; that he would not depute to another. His ideas were definite and his capabilities amazing. With Palladio constantly at hand, together with several other architectural volumes, he filled his notebooks with quick, rough sketches of elevations, front and side views and drew on his table large-scale plans with supporting data of which any professional architect could justly be proud.[37]

Jefferson's first idea was not too remote from the normal Virginia mansion. He proposed a large two-story building, flat-roofed, and differing from the norm chiefly in two sets of frontal columns superimposed one on the other, the lower one Doric and the upper Ionic. A little later he added—on paper—supporting single-story wings, and devised a series of service rooms—cookrooms, servants' quarters, stables and storerooms to run submerged at either flanking wing and at right angles to the main house.[38]

But these were merely his first thoughts on the magnificent abode he envisioned. The eventual structure we now know was the product of many years of incessant planning and constant modifications. Jefferson never hesitated, when a new idea struck him, to change his plans and even to rip and tear down what had already been built in order to rear something new to conform with his latest heart's desire. The item of expense was dismissed with a lordly indifference. It became an abiding passion with him, this mountaintop—one that overshadowed for him the more famous sections of his career. Even the overmastering absorption of his final years—the University of Virginia—was as much the result of his itch to put architectural plans on paper and see them transformed into glowing reality as of his admitted interest in educational schemes.

Mingled with the classical influence, however, were elements of the romantic and Gothic which, aside from his infatuation with Ossian, evidenced themselves in the landscaping which he proposed for the grounds around Monticello.

He would train the spring on the northern end of his park, he mused, into a waterfall which would then cascade into a cistern under a temple. He was not quite sure in which style he would build the temple—Chinese or Grecian—but he was quite certain that underneath it he would install an Aeolian harp to vibrate mournfully in the wind. Nearby he would place a sleeping marble figure recumbent on a slab bearing a Latin inscription; while all around jasmine, honeysuckle, sweetbrier and other fragrant flowers would waft perpetual fragrance on the air.

But soon his romantic mood took new flights and his imagination a new track. "This would be better," he wrote. Form a grotto above the spring, cover it with moss, spangle with translucent pebbles and beautiful shells, and channel the spring in at one corner of the grotto, to fall through a spout into a basin and then emerge at the other end. In this grotto, he decreed, the recumbent figure would most appropriately repose, and on the supporting slab the Latin inscription would be Englished into verse:

> Nymph of the grot, these sacred springs I keep,
> And to the murmurs of these waters sleep:
> Ah! spare my slumbers! gently tread the cave!
> And drink in silence or in silence lave!

As if this were not enough to sate his Gothic yearnings, he moved on to a melancholy contemplation of the graveyard. "Chuse out for a Burying place some unfrequented vale in the park where is 'no sound to break the silence.' . . . Let it be among antient and venerable oaks; intersperse some gloomy evergreens. . . . In the center of it erect a small Gothic temple of antique appearance, appropriate one half to the use of my own family; the other of strangers, servants, &c. . . . In the middle of the temple an altar, the sides of turf, the top a plain stone. Very little light, perhaps none at all, save only the feeble ray of an half extinguished lamp."[39]

Decidedly, Jefferson was solitary on his mountaintop and in love!

Yet even while he was jotting down such moonstruck visionings in one small pocket book he prosaically entered in another: "Cart. H. Harrison tells me it is generally allowed that 250 lb green pork makes 220. lb pickled"; and "Old Sharpe sais a bushel of Lime-stone will weigh 114 lb and if well burnt will make 2. bushels of slacked lime."[40] The first was a passing mood; *this* was the permanent man.

When down in Williamsburg, however, Jefferson became again the young man of the world. He attended the theater regularly and entered into a very curious agreement with John Randolph, Attorney General of Virginia, concerning a violin which Jefferson coveted. Drawn in full legal dress, properly attested for recording and witnessed by a host of eminent witnesses, it set forth the following: if Randolph survived Jefferson, he would be entitled to books of the latter to the value of one hundred pounds sterling or, if there were a deficiency, to sufficient cash to make up the sum. But if Jefferson survived Randolph, then he was to get "the violin which the said John brought with him into Virginia, together with all his music composed for the violin, or in lieu thereof, if destroyed by any accident, 60 pounds sterling worth of books of the said John, to be chosen by the said Thomas."[41] The discrepancy in the mutual sums to be paid out, or their equivalents, was obviously based on the different life expectancies of the parties to the agreement.

This might be taken as a ponderous jest were it not for the surprising sequel. In 1775, when the colonies were aflame and John Randolph, English-born and loyal to his king, determined to quit rebellious Virginia for the country of his birth, he bethought himself of his earlier legal commitment. As an honorable man, and not knowing what the future might have in store for either of them, he proposed an immediate transfer of the precious violin to Jefferson for thirteen pounds and a cancellation of the old agreement.

Jefferson eagerly seized the opportunity. "I received your message by Mr. Braxton," he replied, "& immediately gave him an order on the Treasurer for the money which the Treasurer assured me should be answered on his religion. I now send the bearer for the violin & such music appertaining to her as may be of no use to the young ladies. I believe you had no case to her. If so, be so good as to direct Watt Lenox to get from Prentis's some bags or other coarse woollen to wrap her in & then to pack her securely in a wooden box." [42] At the same time he prudently entered in his account book a memorandum of the new agreement and a notation that "this dissolves our bargain recorded in the General Court, and revokes a legacy of £100 sterling to him now standing in my will, which was made in consequence of that bargain." [43]

The distractions of the theater and of music did not interfere with the progress of Jefferson's love affair. Through the summer and autumn of 1771 he journeyed frequently to The Forest, where the young widow doubtless gave him comforting welcome. Each time he went he tipped another servant, but on November 11th, moderation vanished and he scattered largesse with a generous hand.[44] Was this the day, perhaps, on which the final plans were made for the wedding?

On November 23rd, the marriage bond was signed. On December 29th, there appears for the first time any mention of his beloved in his account books, and then most discreetly as "Mrs. Sk." On the following day he dispatched forty shillings for a marriage license.[45]

On New Year's Day, January 1, 1772, the wedding was solemnized at The Forest, with two ministers in attendance. Thomas Jefferson was twenty-eight, and Martha Wayles Skelton, now Martha Jefferson, was twenty-three. In true Virginia fashion the ensuing festivities lasted for several weeks. The relatives, guests and friends on either side had assembled from considerable distances and were in no hurry to return home. After a short intervening journey to Shirley, where Jefferson's phaeton required considerable mending, the bride and groom finally departed on January 18th from The Forest for Monticello.[46]

The snow was falling as they drove off in Jefferson's phaeton, and it increased in depth and violence as the horses plodded over submerging roads, first to Richmond and then upcountry toward Charlottesville and

Monticello. Finally the snow became so deep that they had to abandon the carriage at Blenheim and continue on horseback.

It was late at night on January 25th that the half-frozen and buffeted bridal pair took the final winding road up the mountain to their still unfinished home. The servants had gone to bed, not expecting them, and the fires were out. Under such untoward circumstances was Martha introduced to Monticello.[47]

CHAPTER 8

Revolutionary Remonstrance

LIFE was not easy for the young married couple those first months at Monticello. Living quarters were confined; the single bachelor room which was adequate for Jefferson had now to hold a young wife as well, accustomed to the spaciousness of her father's home. The mountaintop was littered with unfinished structures, piles of lumber, stone and earth, and the constant hammering and disorder of building operations. But Virginia women, plantation-reared, showed a surprising adaptability to pioneer conditions, and Martha, or Patty as she came to be affectionately called, no doubt adjusted herself readily to housekeeping under difficulties. Jefferson remained with her at Monticello for several months until she became acclimated, leaving both his law business and the affairs of the colony to take care of themselves.

Martha's young son by her former marriage, John Skelton, had probably been left behind at The Forest in the custody of her father, though she doubtless intended to bring him to Monticello in the spring. There is no evidence, however, that the transfer was ever made, and young John died in his grandfather's home sometime in 1772.[1]

His mother was not long left childless. On September 27, 1772, not quite nine months after the wedding ceremony, a daughter was born to the Jeffersons. Named Martha after her mother—and nicknamed Patsy by her father—the infant ailed at first, but soon grew robust and became a staff of comfort to Jefferson in his later widowed existence.

In the due rotation of the moons five more children came in regular sequence, but of them only one other besides Martha survived. This was Mary or Maria—nicknamed Polly—born on August 1, 1778. The others, all daughters, except for one impermanent son, did not survive the ailments of childhood. The last, and doubtless the one that finally contributed—with several intervening miscarriages—to Martha Jefferson's death, was Lucy Elizabeth, born May 8, 1782.

Martha Jefferson brought to her husband what seemed to be a substantial fortune. Her first husband had left her some property, and her father, John Wayles, was reputed rich and was certainly possessed of considerable lands and a luxurious way of life. On May 28, 1773, Wayles died at the age of fifty-eight, leaving three daughters to divide his estate. Their three husbands, Thomas Jefferson, Francis Eppes and Henry Skipwith, were named as executors in his will. Much of Martha's inheritance was already provided for by her mother's will and a substantial settlement made by her father and mother jointly on her first marriage.[2] At first blush the total was considerable, and Jefferson, even in later years when he should have known better, wrote with obvious satisfaction that the portion which came to his wife "was about equal to my own patrimony, and consequently doubled the ease of our circumstances." [3]

This was true, insofar as accretions of land were concerned. Elk Island had come to Jefferson through Bathurst Skelton. John Wayles's holdings, scattered over half a dozen counties, totaled some 19,770 acres which Jefferson valued at over £20,000.[4] This was certainly substantial, even after being divided three ways. Martha's share, from all quarters, came to the highly respectable figure of about 11,000 acres and 35 slaves. But—and it was a big *but*—John Wayles had died heavily in debt. It was again the case of land-rich and money-poor which plagued so many Virginia gentlemen during the pre-Revolutionary years. With the estate went an enormous mortgage of debt to English and Scottish merchants. Martha Jefferson's share alone, encumbering the land and slaves, was about £3,750.[5]

His wife's indebtedness was to become an incubus around Jefferson's neck that eventually almost strangled him. In the long run it would have been far better had Martha come to him penniless, without assets and without obligations. Hard cash, and certainly in the amount with which he was now confronted, was difficult to come by at all times in Virginia; special circumstances within the next few years made it impossible; and the original sum, large enough in all conscience, snowballed with accrued interest and depreciated land and tobacco values until the unfortunate husband grew almost frantic in his attempts to stave off creditors. But this was in the distant future.

Even at the moment, however, he realized that some provision must be made for payment. With what he considered prudent foresight—though it was always painful for him to divest himself of a single acre—from 1774 to 1778 he sold almost half of Martha's inherited lands, amounting in all to some 5,000 acres, for a combined purchase price of over £5,800. This would have been ample enough to clear off the entire debt, had the transactions been for cash. But land sales in Virginia never were for cash; a token down payment was indicated, and the balance was met with long-term promissory notes which required frequent renewals before they were, if ever, finally paid.

He offered to turn these promissory notes or bonds, as they were then known, over to the English firm of William Jones, the largest creditor; but the American agent flatly refused to accept them as a substitute for Jefferson's obligation. This was during the war years, and no doubt the agent was quite right in rejecting the doubtful paper of obscure Americans for the primary obligation of such a well-known figure as Jefferson. But the latter was to comment bitterly after the war that had the agent done so, his principal in England would have been protected under the terms of the treaty of peace and eventually been paid, dollar for dollar, in hard coin; while Jefferson, as a fellow-American, was not so protected and had to accept payment in depreciated paper which, in effect, wiped out most of the receipts, yet left him still compelled to meet his English obligations at face value.[6]

At the same time, however, that he was selling land to satisfy the encumbered estate, Jefferson could not resist making new purchases. These included 266 acres in Goochland called Elk Hill, 819 acres in Albemarle known as Hickman's and 483 acres from Col. Edward Carter situated on "the high mountain Albemarle."[7]

There was something of the agility of a juggler in the way Jefferson was handling a whole series of complicated accounts and estates. Besides the new headaches created by the Wayles and Skelton accessions, he still had problems to solve in connection with the estate of his own father, with its manifold ramifications involving his mother, his sisters, and his brother, Randolph Jefferson.

He sent the brother to William and Mary for an education.[8] Randolph remained a year or so, but gained little profit from his sojourn. While he later managed to marry, have offspring and cultivate his land, all the evidence points to the fact that his grade of intelligence was barely sufficient, with his brother's aid, to grapple with the ordinary difficulties of life.[9]

With his mother, as always, Jefferson's relations continued on a purely formal basis. At stated intervals he sent her corn, beef and hogs and charged it against her estate. He duly entered in his accounts the eleven slaves which she conveyed to him as a set-off for his payment of her debts. And when she finally died on March 31, 1776, the sole notice he took was the dry statement in his account book: "My mother died about 8. oclock this morning. In the 57th. year of her age."[10]

Other and earlier losses had touched him closer. On May 16, 1773, Dabney Carr, his closest friend and the husband of his sister Martha, died suddenly. As schoolboys they had bound themselves with solemn vows that the survivor would bury the other under a certain favorite oak on Monticello. Jefferson remembered the oath and undertook its fulfillment. On May 22nd he sent two slaves to "grub" a graveyard eighty feet square in which the body of his friend would be the first to rest. But even in the performance of this sad duty Jefferson could not resist taking note of certain practical farming data. The two hands, he observed, took three and a half hours to turn over the soil. That meant that a single hand would have taken seven hours for the task; therefore one man could do an entire acre in forty-nine hours of four working days. This bit of information he put down for future reference.[11]

On February 24, 1774, came the second tragedy. Three days before, an earthquake had shaken the houses at Monticello so sensibly that everyone had run out of doors in great fright. On the following day, another shock sent them scurrying again. In the hurry and confusion Jefferson's sister Elizabeth disappeared. Search was immediately instituted and two days later she was found. Where she was discovered, whether alive or dead, is not indicated. But seemingly she was still alive, though in a desperate condition; for, on March 7th, her body was interred as the second occupant of the family burial plot.[12] Elizabeth was nearing thirty at the time of her death and had never married. Something had been wrong with her from the time of her birth; if not wholly imbecilic, she was perilously close to that unfortunate state.

Jefferson owed the preacher forty shillings for the funeral ceremony, and another forty for performing a similar service for Dabney Carr the year before. Instead of paying in cash, however, Jefferson gave the reverend gentleman two old bookcases of his at a valuation of five pounds, and generously waived the remaining twenty shillings as a gratuity. But at the same time he was careful to note that the cost of Dabney's sermon should be charged to his estate.[13]

Jefferson's life with Martha was very happy. The evidence of his prostration with grief over her untimely death and his long period of mourning leave no doubt of that. Yet of the wife of no other great man is there so little knowledge. She left few visible evidences of her existence and Jefferson's reticence concerning her verged on the morbid. There certainly were letters that passed between them during his frequent absences from Monticello, yet not a single one of them remains. Jefferson, who meticulously saved every scrap of paper, no matter how unimportant, during his long life, permitted no sign of her to remain behind after his own death. For years after her passing he bemoaned his grief and the loneliness of his state, but not once did he refer to her by name or except by indirection.

Of her physical appearance we have only the traditional account of her family previously referred to, and the reminiscences of an old family slave long after the event. She was "small" of body, he remembered, and pretty; for he described the second surviving daughter, Maria—nicknamed Polly—as "low like her mother & long ways the handsomest: pretty lady just like her mother." Martha—nicknamed Patsy—the older daughter, on the other hand was described as tall like her father and evidently not handsome.[14]

Martha Jefferson could play the spinet and the harpsichord, and probably Thomas fiddled away to her accompaniment in their hours of leisure. But constant pregnancies, miscarriages and child-bearings wore her down, and her health was not good for years before her eventual demise. That she had charm, kindliness and an equable temper is attested to by visitors to Monticello.[15]

Lord Botetourt had died in October, 1770, and John Murray, Earl of Dunmore, appeared leisurely on the scene in September of the following year to assume the duties of Governor of Virginia. He had neither the intelligence of Fauquier nor the sympathetic kindliness of Botetourt; and in New York, from which he had been transferred, he had become accustomed to the supine complaisance of the dominant merchant class. For the first time in a generation Virginia was to know what it meant to be ruled by a narrow-minded and arrogant governor who knew nothing of their problems and cared less. Perhaps, as Jefferson later remarked, this was fortunate for the Revolution. Had Botetourt lived, "he could have embarrassed the measures of the patriots exceedingly." [16]

However, there was an interval of comparative quiet in the hitherto exacerbated relations between England and her colonies. Yet the old Association whereby the colonies agreed to boycott English goods until Parliament repealed the obnoxious taxes was still in effect, and Jefferson tried conscientiously to live up to it. In February, 1771, he had given his agent a list of items to purchase in England, but with an appended caution. "You will observe," he wrote, "that part of these articles (such as are licensed by the association) are to be sent at any event. Another part (being prohibited) are only to be sent if the tea act should be repealed before you get home.... I am not without expectation that the repeal may take place. I believe the parliament want nothing but a colorable motive to adopt this measure. The conduct of our brethren of New York affords them this." [17]

By June, he was certain that the Association would abandon the boycott on all but the specific goods on which the duties had been levied. He therefore ordered his agent to purchase the contingent items previously listed. But, he significantly added, "I must alter one item in the invoice. I wrote therein for a Clavichord. I have since seen a Forte-piano and am charmed with it. Send me this instrument then instead of the Clavichord: let the case be of fine mahogany, solid, not veneered, the compass from Double G. to F. in alt, a plenty of spare strings; and the workmanship of the whole very handsome and worthy the acceptance of a lady for whom I intend it. I must add also ½ doz pr India cotton stockings for myself @ 10/ sterling pr pair, ½ doz pr best white silk do.; and a large umbrella with brass ribs, covered with green silk, and neatly finished." [18] The lady, of course, was Martha Wayles Skelton.

With the Association rapidly slipping into oblivion and with Lord North's seemingly more tolerant policy toward the recalcitrant colonies there ensued an era of good feeling that required little in the way of legislative activities from the Virginia Assembly. It is true that on June 27, 1770, the House of Burgesses had sent another expostulatory petition to the King of England,[19] but no notice had been taken of it and, except for a short interlude, all further sessions were prorogued until the beginning of 1772.

This long vacation gave Jefferson a chance to catch up with his private affairs; notably marriage, the building of Monticello and the practice of law. He must also have made the acquaintance of Lord Dunmore—though he mentions nothing of him during this period—for among his papers is a "Plan for an addition to the College of William and Mary, drawn at the request of Ld. Dunmore." It was in the form of an Italian palace, enclosed and arcaded, such as he had seen in Palladio.[20] The plan was never acted on, but it is interesting to note that Jefferson's abilities as an architect were already attracting favorable attention.

He also found time to continue his readings and researches in widely scattered fields. He was building afresh, slowly and expensively, that library of books whose loss at Shadwell had been a matter of such anguish to him. By 1773, he was able to note proudly in his account book that in all his bookcases and shelves 1,256 new volumes stood erect and solid, exclusive of bound music and the books he had at Williamsburg.[21]

What particularly fascinated Jefferson were the old records and public documents of Virginia. From the moment that he first started studying law until the Revolution sent him abroad to other fields he spent diligent hours in the office of the Secretary of the Colony examining the already ancient and yellowing records of the early days of his beloved Virginia.[22] Nor was this mere idle antiquarian curiosity. It can never be too often reiterated that Jefferson did everything with an eye to practical results. At the beginning of these studies he was equipping himself for the better practice of law; later on, he was exploring old charters for the purpose of better withstanding the alleged pretensions of King and Parliament to subvert the original liberties of Virginia. He realized the true value of original documents and the necessity of their preservation, and he later carefully collected files of the newspapers of Virginia with the same object in mind.

So meticulous was he and so complete were the files of original documents which he salvaged from the ravages of time and the wreckage of the Revolution that later Virginia historians found them essential to any accurate reporting of past events. Robert Burk, Virginia's first great historian, could not have done the job he did, had he not had access to Jefferson's collection of documents.

Jefferson's fame as a collector of books was already beginning to spread and others applied to him for aid in erecting their own libraries. Young Robert Skipwith, newly married to Tabitha Wayles, Martha's half-sister, had fifty pounds to expend for books. Which would his prospective brother-in-law recommend? But Jefferson refused to be bound by such narrow limits. He would, he declared, frame a general collection adequate to a gentleman of parts, and let Skipwith purchase its components gradually over a period of years. The list was impressive and included solid volumes in criticism, politics, trade, law, religion, history, natural philosophy and—fiction.[23]

He hesitated before recommending books in that last category. They would, he confessed, "extort a smile from the face of gravity." He felt impelled to defend their inclusion on the ground that "the entertainments of fiction are useful as well as pleasant." They were useful because they implanted in the reader the principles and practices of virtue. "When any original act of charity or of gratitude, for instance, is presented either to our sight or imagination, we are deeply impressed with its beauty and feel a strong desire in ourselves of doing charitable and grateful acts also. On the contrary when we see or read of any atrocious deed, we are disgusted with its deformity, and conceive an abhorrence of vice.... I appeal to every reader of feeling and sentiment whether the fictitious murther of Duncan by Macbeth in Shakespeare does not excite in him as great a horror of villany, as the real one of Henry IV. by Ravaillac as related by Davila?" History, considered as a moral exercise, offers lessons too infrequent when confined to real life. In fiction—in which he included the drama—there are an infinitude of better examples, more livelily portrayed and more illustrative of every moral rule of life. "Thus a lively and lasting sense of filial duty is more effectually impressed on the mind of a son or daughter by reading King Lear, than by all the dry volumes of ethics, and divinity that ever were written."

The didactic and essentially moral strain in Jefferson is present here in its full flower. Pleasure, entertainment and unsupported intellectual curiosity are not enough. To justify any effort or activity of mind there must be some practical, useful or improving moral end involved. Art for art's sake, aestheticism in any form, or the sheer delight in speculation as an intellectual good in itself had no place in Jefferson's ordered scheme of things.

It is interesting to note that in later years he dismissed the novel, with some few exceptions, as a means of self-improvement. Especially for women were they anathema and an obstacle to their true education. "When this poison infects the mind," he then asserted, "it destroys its tone and revolts it against wholesome reading. Reason and fact, plain and unadorned, are rejected. Nothing can engage attention unless dressed in all the figments of fancy, and nothing so bedecked comes amiss. The result is a bloated imagination, sickly judgment, and disgust towards all the real business of life." [24] But this reversal of judgment, coupled with a similar prohibition against most poetry, was based on the same criteria he enunciated in younger days. Maturity had brought him to the conviction that fiction and poetry were *not* conducive to higher ethical standards, especially in the female sex, towards whom he always expressed the most gallant sentiments but of whose intellectual capacities he thought little.

Jefferson had been regularly and almost automatically re-elected to the House of Burgesses for each succeeding session, but it was not until the meeting which opened on March 4, 1773, that the pot of imperial relations began to simmer again. In the preceding year the hotheads of Rhode Island, enraged at the way in which the British patrol boats off shore were cramping their "legitimate" smuggling activities, had attacked and burnt the *Gaspee*, one of the most irritatingly vigilant of the ships. The infuriated British officials promptly instituted a court of inquiry and threatened to send the culprits to England for trial, where they would not have the benefit of sympathetic juries.

The younger members of the Virginia Assembly, and particularly those from the "back" districts, secretly applauded the terroristic act and indignantly inveighed against the proposed invasion of the legal rights of the putative defendants. The older members from the Tidewater regions, however—and they had hitherto been the leaders of the Assembly—were considerably more cautious. While they deplored the threatened infringement of colonial liberties, they disavowed the act on which it was predicated.

Confronted with this inexplicable lack in the leaders of that "forwardness & zeal which the times required"—to use Jefferson's own phrase—a number of the more ardent spirits gathered one evening in a private room of the Raleigh Tavern. Among those present, besides Jefferson, were the inevitable Patrick Henry, Richard Henry Lee, Francis Lightfoot Lee, Dabney Carr and one or two others. The tiny but determined caucus agreed that the only way of effectively countering British usurpation was for all the colonies to make common cause and unite in action as in complaint. This could best be accomplished by instituting committees of correspondence in each colony for swift and constant intercommunication and by providing for a meeting of delegates from each colony whose function it would be to direct and unify such measures as the colonies would decide upon. In other words, a Continental Congress.[25]

The plan was enthusiastically adopted by the conspirators and a series of conforming resolutions drawn. It was proposed that the honor of moving them in the Assembly go to Jefferson, but he insisted that the privilege be given to his brother-in-law, Dabney Carr. Carr was a new member, Jefferson argued, and he wanted him to be given a chance to bring himself to the attention of the House. And so it was decided.[26]

The secret meeting ended with a plan of operations carefully drawn. The next day Dabney Carr rose in the House and proposed the famous resolutions.

WHEREAS, The minds of his Majesty's faithful Subjects in this Colony have been much disturbed, by various Rumours and Reports of proceedings tending to deprive them of their ancient, legal and constitutional rights,

AND WHEREAS, The affairs of this Colony are frequently connected with those of Great Britain, as well as of the neighboring Colonies, which renders a Communication of Sentiments necessary; in Order therefore to remove the Uneasiness, and to quiet the minds of the People . . .

Be it resolved, That a standing Committee of Correspondence and inquiry be appointed to consist of eleven Persons, to wit, the Honourable Peyton Randolph, Esquire, Robert Carter Nicholas, Richard Bland, Richard Henry Lee, Benjamin Harrison, Edmund Pendleton, Patrick Henry, Dudley Digges, Dabney Carr, Archibald Cary, and Thomas Jefferson, Esquires, any six of whom to be a Committee, whose business it shall be to obtain the most early and Authentic intelligence of all such Acts and Resolutions of the British Parliament, or proceedings of Administration, as may relate to or affect the

British Colonies in America, and to keep up and maintain a Correspondence and Communication with our Sister Colonies, respecting these important Considerations; and the result of such their proceedings, from Time to Time, to lay before this House.[27]

It is to be noted that the public resolutions sounded innocuous on the surface; nor did they proclaim the full intentions of their proponents. Nothing was said of the Continental Congress; nothing of the *Gaspee* incident which had been one of the prime causes. It was essential to placate and lull the moderate members into a sense of security; and, by giving them a majority of the proposed committee, what harm could they fear from a mere exchange of information?

Dabney Carr made his maiden speech with brilliance and persuasive power, much to the pride and satisfaction of his brother-in-law. Alas, two months later he was dead, and Jefferson, as well as the infant nation, had lost a devoted and able advocate.

On March 12th, the resolutions were passed without a dissenting voice; on the next day the committee, with Jefferson actively present, held an organizing meeting.

But now Lord Dunmore stepped into the picture. In a rage at what he deemed arrant impudence in the Assembly he prorogued that body indefinitely and sent them packing.

Jefferson and his friends had no doubt envisaged that they could obtain control of the Committee of Correspondence; but they were doomed to disappointment. The moderate majority took over the reins and appointed a select committee of three to whom they delegated the actual work. The three men named were safe and sound—Peyton Randolph, Robert Carter Nicholas and Dudley Digges.

Thus frustrated, the radical members lost all interest and went home. But the select committee was conscientious. On April 6th, it held a second meeting and wrote letters to the other colonies and to friends in England. Replies were not long in forthcoming. Rhode Island, primarily interested, eagerly agreed to co-ordinate action. So did New Hampshire, Massachusetts, Georgia, Connecticut, South Carolina, North Carolina, Delaware and Maryland. Pennsylvania wrote that the matter would be laid over to the next session with a recommendation for adoption. New Jersey was the last to approve; leaving New York solitary and alone in the failure to take positive action. But its legislature was not in session.[28] It was the first general meeting of minds in the colonies, aside from the abortive Stamp Act Congress, and laid the foundation for that Continental Congress towards which Jefferson and his fellows had pointed.

For the balance of 1773 and the spring of 1774 Jefferson had no opportunity to dabble officially in politics. Once more his private affairs claimed his attention. His law practice had suffered for a variety of reasons; chiefly, his preoccupation with other matters. His income from that source fell off from the earlier years and what he did manage to earn, was largely uncollectible. In 1774, he decided that law was not for him, even though his fees took a jump upward in that year. He was spending too much time at Monticello enjoying the felicities of marriage and the management of his estate; when he came down to Williamsburg, politics absorbed more and more of his time.

Accordingly, on August 11, 1774, Jefferson turned over his law practice to Edmund Randolph, listing 132 clients whose active cases required Randolph's attention and in whose behalf advance payment of fees had to be credited. The total amount involved, of which Jefferson estimated that two-thirds would eventually come to Randolph, amounted to about £519.[29]

Thus Jefferson washed his hands of the law, seemingly with considerable relief, and never returned to it. He was undoubtedly a good "brief" lawyer, and would have enjoyed that phase of practice; but unfortunately neither Virginia nor any of the other colonies required much specialization. Trial practice was the mainstay of a legal career and demanded a certain rough-and-tumble and jury-convincing brand of oratory from which Jefferson shrank and for which he was singularly unfitted.

There were compensations for his new leisure. When in Williamsburg, Jefferson was a regular frequenter of the playhouse and even, when nothing else afforded, attended a concert of musical glasses. At home he added to his books and laid down a stock of hard liquors for his slaves and the more robust of his company; for himself and his more discriminating friends he served fine French wines, with an occasional sip of port, Madeira and beer. He knew there was no fear of the slaves raiding his less intoxicating wines, but he kept a tally on his Jamaica rum to make certain that Martin, the slave who held the keys to the cellar, did not surreptitiously make off with some.[30]

On October 14, 1773, his old college, William and Mary, which had the disposal in its hands, appointed him Surveyor of Albemarle County; a position which Peter, his father, had held before him.[31]

But chiefly he was engrossed in being a farmer and a builder. The constant construction going on at Monticello absorbed him, and he delighted in exercising his ingenuity in architecture. He paid a great deal of attention to his crops and eagerly sought information of more scientific and profitable methods of cultivation. As a business man, however, he was not very successful. On May 5, 1773, for example, he took a little speculative flier in tobacco. Purchasing 5,758 pounds at 18 shillings the hogshead, he had to sell it the same day for 17 shillings. That evening he attended a lecture "on ye eye." Evidently he thought he needed it.[32]

The management of his farms was really a full-time job. They were scattered over three counties, plus the famous Natural Bridge in a fourth, and totaled some 10,000 acres. To till these widely separated acres and to keep his private establishment going necessitated numerous slaves. Life in Virginia was self-contained; practically everything, with the exception of luxury imports, was grown or manufactured directly on the plantation. Slave labor was employed both for the crops and the manufactures. They were the nailers, the field hands, the blacksmiths, the carpenters, the spinners, the weavers, the millers, the house servants, the distillers, the nurses, the bakers and the grooms. No wonder Jefferson—or any Virginian, for that matter—was unable to understand the manufacturing needs of the Northern colonies.[33]

What with the slaves he inherited and those which came to him on marriage, he had a sufficiency for his purposes. By the end of 1774, they numbered 187; in 1783, they totaled 204. They answered to classical, mythological and biblical names: Jupiter, favorite body servant and coachman, Hercules, Scilla, Caesar, Goliath, Juno, Luna and the like; but there was a sprinkling of prosaic appellations as well: Gill, Fanny, Suckey, Quash and Hannah. Very rarely did Jefferson deal in these articles of human flesh, and then only for reasons of weight. In 1773, he sold only one slave, and him to a neighbor; probably to keep a family together. Between 1774 and 1778 he parted with two more and purchased four.[34] He was a kindly master and had inner qualms about the nature and ethics of the institution. He would have liked to see it eventually abolished; but since the hard fact was there, he sensibly made use of it with an equal eye to the slave's welfare and his own.

It was tea—the fragrant brew associated with fragile cups, crooked fingers and cozy gossip—that finally sent the ball rolling on the road to revolution. Or rather, it was the stern necessities of the East India Company, its chief purveyor. Bankrupt and distraught, its directors felt that all would be well if the tax were removed and the recalcitrant Americans brought to buy *their* tea again instead of wallowing in the smuggled Dutch variety. Lord North refused to yield the principle of taxation, yet he wished to help the straitened Company. He evolved what he thought, and every sensible man thought, a clever scheme. While retaining the tax, he absolved the Company's tea of all the usual restrictions which had increased the cost to the consumer, thereby making it possible for the Company actually to undersell the smuggled variety in America. Patriotism, he thought gleefully, could never withstand the lure of cheapness.

He was mistaken, or perhaps he underestimated the ramifications and profits of the smuggling trade. The cargoes of tea which entered American ports were turned back by threats or left to rot in warehouses; in Boston, where British military power was invoked to prevent either course, a strange band of hideously painted "Indians" dumped the offending chests into the harbor.

When the news of the Boston "Tea Party" reached England all ranks closed—even among the Whigs—and North had no difficulty in pushing through Parliament in March, 1774, the first of the so-called Coercive

Acts to close the port of Boston until adequate satisfaction was made to the East India Company.

In Virginia Lord Dunmore had kept the Assembly out of the way for a full year. Unknowing what had happened in England he thought it now safe to reconvene the troublesome lawmakers.

On May 5, 1774, the Assembly opened. Jefferson came down to Williamsburg to attend. The first few days were devoted to routine matters. On May 9th, Jefferson was placed on the Committee on Religion; but more important to him personally at the moment was the fate of a petition which he filed the same day for the removal of the entail on a tract of land in Cumberland County belonging to his wife, which he wished to sell. The House graciously granted the petition of its member, and the entail was eventually lifted.[35]

While the Assembly droned along, the news of the retaliatory closing of Boston Port reached that threatened city on May 11th. Faced with the prospect of complete economic prostration, the beleaguered patriots sent postriders racing to all the colonies with appeals for aid.

Virginia got the news on May 22nd or 23rd. Immediately the young radicals met in private caucus to determine on a course of action. They considered themselves now as the spearhead of the struggle with England and were resolved to take the initiative away from the older members.

The meeting included Jefferson, who had become one of the mainstays of the group, Patrick Henry, the two Lees and a few others. How best, they wondered, could they arouse the Virginians from the lethargy into which they had fallen during the past two years and make them dramatically aware of the danger impending to their liberties?

Jefferson modestly makes no mention in his recollections of who it was that finally proposed a day of fasting to startle and electrify the people into an awareness of the seriousnes of the occasion. But Edmund Randolph gives the honor to Jefferson and to one of the Lees.[36]

The others agreed and the night was spent in looking up old forms of proclamations which the Puritans had used during *their* Revolution. With these in hand they "cooked up a resolution" in which the thunderous Puritanic phrases were somewhat modernized and appointing June 1st, the day when the Boston Port Bill became effective, as "a day of fasting, humiliation & prayer." [37]

It was a curious business for the deistic, sceptical Jefferson to be associated with. But Randolph later gave a cynical explanation of the transaction. "Such is the constitution of things," he wrote, "that an act of public devotion, will receive no opposition from those, who believe in its effect to appease offended heaven, and is registered in the cabinet of the politician, as an allowable trick of political warfare." [38]

Much later, when Jefferson was President, and *he* was asked to proclaim a day of fasting and prayer in a public emergency, he flatly refused, using ostensible constitutional grounds to conceal his aversion to the act itself.

The youthful members, however, knew that such a resolution, if proposed by them, would carry little weight. It was decided therefore to ask Robert Carter Nicholas, chairman of the Committee on Religion, "whose grave & religious character was more in unison with the tone of our resolution," to father it.[39] That haughty and austere individual agreed, and on the morning of May 24th, the bill was presented to a full House and passed without a dissenting vote. Conservatives and radicals alike joined to show a solid front against the repressive tactics of the British Parliament.[40]

Lord Dunmore did the expected; on May 26th he promptly dissolved the defiant Assembly. And similarly, the Assembly just as promptly repaired to the Raleigh Tavern. Action and counteraction were beginning to take on all the aspects of a formal game of chess.

Once more Peyton Randolph took the chair. Once more the embattled legislators adopted a series of resolutions declaring that an attack on one colony was an attack on all, and must be unitedly opposed. It was agreed therefore to write to the legislatures of all the colonies, calling for the appointment of deputies to meet annually in a General Congress and to deliberate on measures to be taken in common. Eighty-nine of the members, including Jefferson, affixed their names to the resolutions.[41]

Their work seemingly accomplished, most of the members scattered to their homes. This was on May 27th. But some two days later the frantic dispatches for help came posthaste from Boston. Faced with appeals that could not wait for the deliberate assemblage of a general Congress, Peyton Randolph reconvened on May 30th those of the legislators who were still in Williamsburg. Only twenty-five appeared, among whom was Jefferson.

It was not deemed wise, therefore, to attempt any binding action on the specific measures proposed by Massachusetts, but to inform her of their belief that Virginia would back her to the full, even to an association to boycott importations and perhaps even exportations. But, they added hastily, this must not be considered as a definite engagement. That must wait on a convention which they were calling for the first of August.[42]

This time Jefferson went home. But before he went, in spite of the strained political relations with the Governor of Virginia, he contributed twenty shillings towards a ball to be given in honor of Lady Dunmore, his wife.[43] Political differences were not as yet carried over into personal enmities. That was to come later for most of the patriots; for Jefferson, never.

Back in Monticello again, Jefferson saw to it that the men of the cloth in all Albemarle obeyed the instructions of the Assembly to make June 1st a day of "fasting, humiliation and prayer." Similar measures were taken in the other counties by their representatives.

The appointed day came, and from practically every pulpit in Virginia the assembled people were exhorted to mourn appropriately for the stricken city of Boston and call on God to redress their common wrongs. "The effect of the day through the whole colony," Jefferson was to write with much retrospective satisfaction, "was like a shock of electricity, arousing every man & placing him erect & solidly on his centre."[44]

Obedient to the call of the dissolved Assembly for an election of delegates to a convention to consider the state of the colonies, and aroused by the fastings and the prayers, the various counties gathered during July, 1774, to select their deputies. Jefferson and Walker were triumphantly chosen on July 26th; in fact, Virginia re-elected every member of the former Assembly as "proof of their approbation of what had been done."[45]

Not content with mere re-election, Jefferson drafted a series of resolutions for the assembled freeholders of Albemarle to sign. They were accepted by acclamation.

The Albemarle resolutions were in Jefferson's happiest vein; forthright, uncompromising and setting up a model on which the forthcoming Congress could act. They minced no words in denouncing any attempt by Parliament to legislate for them, excoriated the Boston Port Bill, and declared their readiness to join with the other colonies "in executing all those rightful powers which God has given us, for the re-establishment and guaranteeing such their constitutional rights, when, where, and by whomsoever invaded."

These were generalities, but Jefferson wrote in immediate, specific steps. Stop at once all imports from Great Britain, with certain exceptions essential to the welfare of the colonies; and stop all exports to her after October 1, 1775. Stop exports from any other part of the world which were subject to the payment of duties in America.[46]

Jefferson was finished with his political apprenticeship. The sore memory of what had been done with his earlier attempt at a political document was temporarily forgotten. Heartened by the acclaim of his neighbors he sat down to draft proposed instructions from the forthcoming Convention to the men they would send to the General Congress.

Jefferson was later to apologize for the haste with which they were written, the number of blanks he was compelled to leave, and "some uncertainties & inaccuracies of historical facts, which I neglected at the moment, knowing they could be readily corrected at the meeting."[47]

He need not have apologized. With this *A Summary View of the Rights of British America*, as it came to be known, Jefferson moved in one swift step to the forefront of the great pamphleteers of the Revolution; and even more so, to a radical philosophic and political position that made it inevitable for him to be chosen to pen the Declaration of Independence when that revolutionary document came to be written.

The long years of hard reading and hard thinking were now bearing fruit. The meticulous care with which he searched old precedents and old authors gave a solid substratum to his work. More than that, however, he had gained a style, inimitable, just, expressing thought in happiest phrases, and fitting matter to words in a fashion that was to gain him the title of "the penman of the Revolution." He had finally found his métier, this man to whom it was agony to rise in public and deliver a set speech.

The *Summary View* was much more than a series of instructions for delegates. It was a reasoned historical and philosophical setting for the proposed meeting of a Congress, and it was a bold look forward toward that Revolution which Jefferson now realized was definitely on its way. It was a marked advance on all the disquisitions which the other colonial pamphleteers had hitherto written. It put in plain words what they had shrunk from envisaging; the logical end toward which their arguments tended. James Wilson, James Otis and Richard Bland, "that antiquary in learning" who had "attacked with boldness every assumption of power," [48] had stopped short of the ultimate assault. They were right; neither they nor the colonies were prepared for the final step. Nor were they prepared when Jefferson took it. It had to wait on additional events and additional provocations; but when they came, the *Summary View* was there to point the way.

It started off conservatively enough in the usual form of a "humble and dutiful address" to be made by Congress to His Majesty as Chief Magistrate of the British Empire, petitioning against the "many unwarrantable encroachments and usurpations, attempted to be made by the Legislature of one part of the empire, upon those rights which God and the laws have given equally and independently to all."

Thus far Jefferson was following the conventional form—the appeal to a common king against a usurping parliament. But now a new and revolutionary note appeared. Hitherto the King had been presumed by a convenient fiction to be above the battle. No more. Jefferson reminded him sharply of the many petitions by individual colonies he had not deigned to answer; perhaps he would answer a *united* petition. The threat was unmistakable; but to make certain that it was not missed, Jefferson called on him to reflect "that he is no more than the chief officer of the people, appointed by the laws, and circumscribed with definite powers, to assist in working the great machine of government, erected for their use, and consequently subject to their superintendence." Jefferson's researches into ancient history had not been in vain.

With this significant introduction, Jefferson turned to the history of the colonies themselves. Just as their common Saxon ancestors had migrated to England and established new laws, without any claim on the part of *their* mother country to sovereignty over them, so it was, he declared, with Americans "going in quest of new habitations, and of there establishing new societies, under such laws and regulations as to them shall seem most likely to promote public happiness."

It was *individuals* who had conquered this land, spilled their own blood and used their own fortunes. Only when they were already firmly established and "valuable to Great Britain for her commercial purposes" did Parliament deign "to lend them assistance against the enemy." Such assistance gave Parliament no title of authority, however. The union was merely one through a common sovereign, "who was thereby made the central link connecting the several parts of the empire thus newly multiplied."

Lest the King take heart from this statement Jefferson, with astonishing boldness, called attention to the Stuarts, "whose treasonable crimes against their people brought on them afterwards the exertion of those sacred and sovereign rights of punishment reserved in the hands of the people for cases of extreme necessity."

Turning from King to Parliament again, Jefferson attacked as a series of void acts each and every prohibition and abridgement of the "natural right" of America to "the exercise of a free trade with all parts of the world." All too plainly they now pointed to " a deliberate and systematical plan of reducing us to slavery."

"Not only the principles of common sense," Jefferson continued vehemently, "but the common feelings of human nature, must be surrendered up before his majesty's subjects here can be persuaded to believe that they hold their political existence at the will of a British parliament. Shall these governments be dissolved, their property annihilated, and their people reduced to a state of nature, at the imperious breath of a body of men, whom they never saw, in whom they never confided, and over whom they have no powers of punishment or removal, let their crimes against the American public be ever so great? Can any reason be assigned why 160,000 electors in the island of Great Britain should give law to four millions in the states of America, every individual of whom is equal to every individual of them, in virtue, in understanding, and in bodily strength?"

Parliament and the rotten borough system had been castigated before, but never in such savage terms. In his enthusiasm Jefferson permitted himself some rodomontade and an inaccuracy as to the total American population.

Having polished off Parliament, Jefferson turned once more to the king. Divesting himself of all the fictions which had hitherto held the monarch sacred against attack, he launched into a direct and bitter assault. In language that adumbrates the future impeachments of the Declaration of Independence, he accused the King of deviating from his duty, of rejecting the most salutary laws passed by the colonial assemblies, of negativing all attempts to rid themselves of the institution of slavery, of causing his governors to dissolve American legislatures for daring to declare their rights, of instituting feudal tenures in America, of sending armed forces into the colonies, though he had "no right to land a single armed man on our shores."

These are our grievances, he concluded. We lay them before you "with that freedom of language and sentiment which becomes a free people claiming their rights, as derived from the laws of nature, and not as the gift of their chief magistrate. Let those flatter who fear, it is not an American art."[49]

It is an amazing document, blistering and revolutionary in content, and though Jefferson ends it on a discreet note of not wishing to separate from Great Britain, the implication is unmistakable. Treat us generously and justly, or else we may come to revise that wish.

CHAPTER 9

Coming of the Revolution

THE extralegal Convention was scheduled to meet in Williamsburg on August 1, 1774. Jefferson set out from Monticello a few days before. In his traveling bags were several copies of the proposed instructions he had drawn in such haste.

But somewhere on the road—the exact place is unknown—he took ill with dysentery and could proceed no further. Nothing could have been more unfortunate. Virginia was on the broad highway to decisive action, the ultimate consequences of which no one could foresee. Measures would be taken in which he would have no part. Delegates would be elected to a general Congress of all the colonies, and now there was no chance that he would be among them. The white-hot indictment he had drawn rested passive in his bags, their drafting futile, their mission at an end. At least *they* must reach the Convention, and stand for him *in loco parentis.*

Returned to Monticello, Jefferson expressed from his bed of weakness two copies to the assembled delegates; one under cover to Peyton Randolph, who doubtless would preside; the other to Patrick Henry, in whose energy and boldness he confided. Then, impatiently, he awaited the result.

Alas, Patrick Henry did not live up to the trust that Jefferson had in him. The draft Jefferson sent to him in such haste never emerged from his hands. Afterwards, Jefferson reflected bitterly that either he had deemed it too bold for presentation or he had been too lazy to read it; "for he was the laziest man in reading I ever knew." [1] It is possible that Jefferson's disillusionment and later break with Patrick Henry had its seeds in this episode.

Peyton Randolph, on the other hand, though fundamentally at odds with the whole tenor and violence of the *Summary View*, conscientiously presented it to the delegates for their consideration. But before he did so he tried it out on a large company in his own house, among whom were members of the forthcoming Convention. Edmund Randolph, who was present, distinctly remembered that most of the paragraphs were greeted with applause, though the more fiery ones were not equally approved. "The young," he remarked, "ascended with Mr. Jefferson to the source of these rights; the old required time for consideration, before they could tread this lofty ground." They marched, he believed, "far beyond the politicks of the day." [2]

The older heads prevailed when the document came up again formally in the Convention. "Tamer sentiments were preferred," and, Jefferson conceded at a much later date, wisely so; "the leap I proposed being too long, as yet, for the mass of our citizens." But he could not forbear adding that "the distance between these, and the instructions actually adopted is of some curiosity however, as it shews the inequality of pace with which we moved, and the prudence required to keep front and rear together." [3]

The Convention members, of course, were unexceptionably correct in adopting a "tamer" set of instructions. The vehemence and rashness of Jefferson's proposals would have definitely barred the way to any possible *rapprochement* between England and the colonies, a situation which very few as yet were prepared to view with equanimity. Furthermore, their submission to the general Congress would have affrighted the timid, and caused the moderate to reflect; and doubtless would have hamstrung any efforts at solid achievement. But as a private document, it served a valuable purpose as a goad and a signpost for the all too immediate future.

Yet the instructions which the Convention actually adopted were not as "tame" as Jefferson somewhat contemptuously indicates. Couched in the usual frame of diplomatic respect they nevertheless warned England in clear enough language that unless the British Parliament paused in its unconstitutional courses the colonists were ready and willing to redress their grievances by instituting a boycott of all English goods and prohibiting exports to her.

Some of Jefferson's friends, not content to see his discourse lost to view, undertook to print it privately in Williamsburg as a pamphlet under a lengthy title of their own choosing: *A Summary View of the Rights of British America. Set Forth in Some Resolutions Intended for the Inspection of the Present Delegates of the People of Virginia now in Convention. By a Native, and Member of the House of Burgesses.* Though printed without his knowledge and, as customary, anonymously, Jefferson did not betray that annoyance with which, in later years, he met unauthorized printings of his writings.

The pamphlet met with immediate and widespread diffusion. Everywhere throughout the colonies it was read with eager interest and a knowledge of the true author under the transparent "Native." It brought his name, hitherto unknown except within the confines of Virginia, to the attention of leaders to the north.

Within a few months it was reprinted in Philadelphia and, *mirabile dictu,* in the England whose King and Parliament it so bitterly attacked. There, it seems, the printing was instigated by Arthur Lee, colonial agent, who furnished it with a daring preface under the pseudonym of "Tribunus." According to Jefferson, the revolutionary pamphlet was taken up by the opposition party in England and used for their own purposes, even to the extent of interpolating some sentiments of Edmund Burke.[4] But Jefferson was wrong as to Burke; the English text of the

Summary View was identical in all respects with the American. Nor was his name proposed for a bill of attainder by an infuriated Parliament, as he thought.

Jefferson was not chosen as one of the delegates from Virginia to the Continental Congress. It is doubtful that he would have been picked even if he had been present at the deliberations of the Convention. He was still not considered as one of the leaders in Virginia and his *Summary View* might have disqualified him as a firebrand in any event. The men chosen were representative and well known—Peyton Randolph, Richard Henry Lee, George Washington, Patrick Henry, Richard Bland, Benjamin Harrison and Edmund Pendleton.

The Continental Congress—first of its kind and precursor to others—met in Philadelphia on September 5, 1774. In this concert of the colonies there was no talk of independence or of armed resistance; the assembled delegates agreed with the Virginia instructions that a firm stand, a vigorous declaration of their rights and an Association forbidding imports immediately, and exports at a later date, would bring sufficient pressure on England to cause the repeal of obnoxious taxes and restrictive acts.

To enforce the proposed boycotts, committees of safety were set up in every colony and its subdivisions. These committees, without legal standing, were nevertheless remarkably effective. They took upon themselves the right to inquire into the accounts of the merchants and to examine suspected persons for deviations against the rules. They enforced their decrees by social and commercial excommunication and, in some instances, by grimmer methods. No appeal was possible from their findings and the violator had no recourse but to pay fines and promise abjectly to comply in the future before he could be restored to the bosom of the community.[5]

Jefferson had no qualms about the Association or the vigilante tactics employed in enforcing it. If anything, he thought the Association did not go far enough, and that it contained too many defects and loopholes. "We have left undone those things which we ought to have done," he noted with some asperity. "And we have done those things which we ought not to have done."[6]

Jefferson shortly discovered, however, that the restrictions were perhaps more rigorous than he would have liked, and he was forced into lengthy explanations of what might have proved an embarrassing situation. He had himself violated the earlier Association of May, 1774, by ordering from England fourteen pair of sash windows for his Monticello establishment. On the plea that the original terms were vague and that the later embargoes were all subject to further action, he failed to countermand the order. When Congress passed its final comprehensive Association, however, he hastily wrote to England in cancellation. It was too late, for the offending sashes were already on the way.

Realizing that the local Committee would inspect and confiscate the shipment on arrival, and that the name of the consignee would be bruited abroad, Jefferson in considerable perturbation explained the history of the unfortunate transaction to the Committee members at Norfolk, the port of entry. He was willing, he ended, to submit to their disposal and condemnation.[7]

Evidently the Committee, composed of friends and fellow delegates, accepted the explanation and laid the mantle of charity over the proceedings. For the errant window frames were not confiscated, and later duly made their appearance at Monticello.[8]

The contretemps did not prevent Jefferson from heading the list of candidates to the Albemarle Committee in the voting of his fellow citizens.[9] And similarly they elected him a delegate to another Convention for the Colony of Virginia to be held at Richmond. That inland town at the falls of the James was chosen in order to be far removed from the royal seat of power in Williamsburg and possible interference from the Governor.

Lord Dunmore watched with helpless fury the succession of illegal assemblages and the increasing vanishment of authority from the regular tribunals. "There in not a Justice of the Peace in Virginia that acts, except as a committee-man," he complained bitterly to his superiors at home.[10] The extralegal Association Committees, not the courts, were ruling the colony, and exercising controls over the lives and property of the people that the British suzerainty would never have dared inaugurate.

The Richmond Convention convened at St. John's Church on March 20, 1775; but Jefferson was in Richmond at least by March 18th, tipping the doorkeeper with a lordly gesture and hiring a coach to convey him about the town.[11]

Inevitably Peyton Randolph was elected president and the Convention got down to business. On March 22nd, it unanimously approved of the proceedings and resolves of the Continental Congress. On March 23rd, it resolved to put Virginia "into a posture of defence," and appointed a committee, of which Jefferson was made a member, to prepare a plan for raising and arming a militia.[12]

The die of revolution was cast. Petitions, remonstrances and protests had been tried and found wanting. Armed resistance was in the offing. Thereafter events moved at an accelerated pace.

It must not be considered that this final step was taken by the assembled delegates without opposition or vigorous protest. Patrick Henry, as might have been expected, offered the resolution and Richard Henry Lee seconded him. Bland, Harrison, Pendleton and Nicholas vehemently objected that this was war and where were the stores, the arms and the soldiers with which to fight it? In reply Patrick Henry rose to white-heat oratory and the great cry that has resounded ever since: "Gentlemen may cry peace, peace—but there is no peace. . . . Is life so dear, or peace so sweet, as to be purchased at the price of chains and slavery? Forbid it, Almighty God! I know not what course others may take; but as for me... give me liberty, or give me death!" [13]

For the first and almost the only time Jefferson rose in a public assembly and made a speech. He supported Henry in an address that "argued closely, profoundly and warmly." [14] It is a pity that no copy of his remarks have survived, nor other reference to its contents than this adverbial vagueness.

The resolution was passed, but by an uncomfortably small majority. On March 24th, Jefferson introduced a resolution declaring that the alleged defection of New York from the Association "would be a perfidy too atrocious to be charged on a sister colony but on the most authentic information," and instructing the Virginia Committee of Correspondence to take the necessary steps to discover the truth.[15] The resolution was passed in a somewhat altered form.

The next day the Convention suspended all courts and legal proceedings in Virginia, with certain exceptions, and voted a list of delegates to Congress. Jefferson was not on the original list; but since Peyton Randolph, head of the delegation, might be detained from attending in Philadelphia through illness or the pressure of duties at home, Jefferson was selected as an alternate. He might now be considered as having reached at least the outer edges of the inner circle of men who were leading Virginia in peace or to war.

Jefferson quit Richmond and returned to Elk Hill, where his family had been sojourning for some time. He totaled the number of hogsheads he might expect this year from his various plantations, and found that they came to a mere forty-six; certainly not enough to provide him with much of an income. He estimated his stock of wines and discovered that he was using it up at the rate of ten bottles a month. His affairs were obviously not in good order, though the winter had been the most favorable "ever known in the memory of man." [16]

Yet the preceding year he had been diligently engaged at Monticello in extended plantings and improvements. He laid off an area on the southeast slope of the mountain as a future garden, though the actual work of leveling was not completed until after he had retired from the Presidency. And he put in large amounts of vegetables and grape vines, noting them down in a strange mixture of English and Italian nomenclature.[17]

The reason for the sudden burst of Italian was the advent of one Philip Mazzei in the neighborhood of Monticello. This Italian by birth, whose career was to become so intimately connected with Jefferson's and whose indiscreetness was to lead to one of the most embarrassing episodes in Jefferson's life, had been forced to quit Italy because he persisted in importing such prohibited books as Giordano Bruno, Voltaire and Rousseau.

Fleeing to England, he met Benjamin Franklin and Thomas Adams, Jefferson's agent, who suggested America to him as a haven for all liberal spirits. Adams specified Virginia as the particular paradise and advised him to seek out Jefferson as a man whose talents, beliefs and philosophical leanings were similar to his own.

Hearing that the wine grape was still unknown in America, Mazzei brought along with him some Tuscan wine makers and special cuttings of the delectable vine. Arriving in Virginia at the end of 1773 he visited the Jeffersons at Monticello. They took to each other at once and, through Jefferson's efforts, Mazzei purchased 400 acres and a cabin at Colle, adjoining Jefferson's own property.

Jefferson's Italian was self-taught, but Mazzei found that he could understand the Tuscan tongue quite well, even though he had never heard it spoken. "Nevertheless, he could converse with my men in Italian, and they were so pleased by the fact that he could understand them that I was touched. Among his slaves, there were many skilled workmen of all trades, but no tailors. As soon as he saw our spades and bill hooks, he ordered some made for use on all his estates. He liked our hunting coat, and adopted it too. The neighbors imitated him, with the result that it became very popular." [18]

Mazzei was a true European liberal, his head filled with the gospel of the Enlightenment and the more radical teachings of the *philosophes*. He threw himself heart and soul into the turbulent career of his adopted country, and even joined a volunteer company on the outbreak of hostilities, though he saw no service. He was to influence Jefferson considerably, though the reverse influence was even more profound.

It was through him that Jefferson tried the culture of the vine on his own and later became interested in the possibilities of the olive and the silkworm in America. But his first attempt was unfortunate. An unseasonable frost destroyed all the shoots he had so carefully planted, half his fruit and practically all his wheat, corn, rye and tobacco. The year 1774 was a bad one for him financially.[19]

Back in Williamsburg, Lord Dunmore hurried from blunder to blunder. Though he had been in Virginia for several years he still had no conception of the character of the people he was supposed to govern. On March 28, 1775, he issued a proclamation ordering all civil officers of the colony to prevent any appointment of delegates to the Continental Congress. The officers he addressed prudently ignored it. On April 20th, he sent a company of armed men to seize twenty barrels of gunpowder from the colonial magazine in Williamsburg and remove them to the armed schooner *Magdalen*. He might have known that the sudden seizure would cause a different sort of explosion. An aroused Williamsburg demanded the immediate return of its powder. He evaded. Whereupon men took down their muskets in all the surrounding counties and prepared to march. Dunmore, now thoroughly frightened, backed down and paid in full for the confiscated powder.[20]

But before he did so, Virginia rocked to the startling news from Lexington and Concord. The first blood had been shed on American soil between British troops and American colonists in battle array. The Revolution had commenced, and there was little that either side could now do to prevent it from rolling on its predestined course.[21]

At his wits' end, Dunmore determined to reconvoke the legal Assembly. Certain allegedly conciliatory proposals had been received from Lord North and he thought that they might do much to allay the threatening mien of his unruly subjects.

The session was called for June 1st and Jefferson went down to the capital for the opening. He might have gone instead to Philadelphia, for Peyton Randolph, whose alternate to the Continental Congress he was, had hastened down to Williamsburg to preside. But Jefferson preferred to see first what was going on in Virginia before he departed for the north.

Dunmore presented to the assembled delegates Lord North's assurances that no specific taxes would henceforth be levied and that they might, as in the halcyon past, contribute free-will offerings of their own. But matters had gone too far to be averted by soothing promises from a source which had only too often broken its plighted word. The Assembly listened in ominous silence and appointed a committee which included Jefferson to draft a reply.

Peyton Randolph privately asked Jefferson to prepare the document, fearing, as Jefferson was to recollect, that "Mr. Nicholas, whose mind was not yet up to the mark of the times, would undertake the answer."[22]

But before the reply could be delivered, events had moved at a breakneck pace. The Assembly had sent a committee to investigate the magazine from which the gunpowder had been removed, and three men were wounded by a booby trap that someone had recklessly installed. Indignation flamed again. Lord Dunmore was accused of setting the trap, and once again armed men prepared to march. Dunmore, who had fortified his palace against possible attack, now gathered his family and effects and fled in haste on June 8th to the security of the British warship *Fowey* lying off Yorktown. From there he threatened and fulminated dark threats, but he never returned to the land he had governed with such ineptitude.

Unperturbed by the flight of its Governor, the Assembly proceeded grimly with its work. On June 12th, Archibald Cary, chairman of the committee, rose to report the reply to Lord Dunmore's speech just as though the latter were present. Jefferson had drafted it and was therefore entitled to read it, but perhaps he preferred to let Cary, a known moderate, introduce it and help disarm the expected opposition.

For the "reply" was forthright, direct, and minced no words. Jefferson was fast gaining a polemic style that might have later enabled him to meet the redoubtable Hamilton on somewhat even terms, had he not then yielded the pen to Madison.

He declared flatly that "the British Parliament has no right to intermeddle with the support of civil Government in the Colonies. For us, not for them, has Government been instituted here. Agreeable to our ideas, provision has been made for such officers as we think necessary for the administration of publick affairs; and we cannot conceive that any other legislature has a right to prescribe either the number or pecuniary appointments of our offices."

The Colonies had the right to give their money without coercion and in their own discretion, so that any offer on the part of Parliament to forbear levying taxes, provided the Colonies undertake to make future grants, contradicted fundamental principles and must be rejected. Furthermore, Parliament still had left unrepealed all of the acts against the Colonies on which protests had been made in the past and must continue to be made.

"We are now represented in General Congress," Jefferson wrote, and "we consider ourselves as bound in honour, as well as interest, to share one general fate with our sister Colonies; and should hold ourselves base deserters of that union to which we have acceded, were we to agree on any measures distinct and apart from them....

"What, then, remains to be done?" he concluded. "That we commit our injuries to the even-handed justice of the Being who doth no wrong, earnestly beseeching him to illuminate the counsels, and prosper the endeavours of those to whom America hath confided her hopes, that through their wise direction we may again see reunited the blessings of liberty, property, and harmony with Great Britain." [23]

In effect, Jefferson was burning bridges, even though he gave lip service at the end to a possible reunion with England. Nothing in the body of his reply justified such a possibility, unless she was willing to back down completely under a show of force and grant her American Colonies what was tantamount to Dominion status.

There was considerable debate in the House over the tone of the proffered response. Robert Carter Nicholas and James Mercer were in the forefront with what Jefferson disgustedly called "long and doubtful scruples." In spite of their objections it was carried, though with "a dash of cold water on it here & there, enfeebling it somewhat." [24]

But Jefferson was not present either at the reading, the ensuing debate or the final passage. For, on June 11th, he started for Philadelphia to take Peyton Randolph's place as a Virginia delegate to the Continental Congress.[25]

It was quite likely that Jefferson knew, as he jolted in his phaeton toward the north, that he was on his way to momentous decisions and the birth of a continental idea. Yet there was no urgency in his travel;

his was the leisured journey of a gentleman tourist with an inquiring turn of mind and time in which to satisfy it. Accompanied by a postilion and a body servant, he drove to Fredericksburg where he purchased a horse that struck his fancy and which later became his favorite mount. The steed was called The General and cost him fifty pounds. Other items, including harness and a postilion's whip, ended a small shopping spree. Three days of restful sojourn and he was on the road again. As he crossed the Maryland border it struck him forcibly once more that currency was a local colonial affair and that the differential in exchange from colony to colony varied as the occasion warranted it. Virginia was in a particularly favorable position; 100 of its shillings rated 125 in the currency of Maryland, Pennsylvania and Delaware. Nevertheless, the varying rates were serious obstacles to the free flow of trade, and Jefferson filed away the possibility of uniform currency for future consideration.

By June 17th he was in Annapolis, the capital of Maryland, where he had once noted with disgust the disorderly proceedings of an ill-mannered Assembly. None was now in session; but he found some books he wanted at the stationer's to the tune of 31 shillings. On to Wilmington in Delaware, where he had to hire a guide for fear of losing his way on the road to Philadelphia. The guide charged him 28 shillings. The equipage clattered into the cobblestone streets of Philadelphia on June 20, 1775. It had taken ten days to make the journey.[26]

The first thing he did was to find lodgings for himself, his servants and his horses. He put up at the establishment of a cabinetmaker named Benjamin Randolph; his horses were cared for by one Jacob Hiltzheimer; and he took his meals in company with a group of other delegates at the City Tavern. They were chiefly Virginians, as was to be expected; but there was also a scattering of men from the other colonies.[27]

Thus comfortably established, Jefferson presented his credentials to the Continental Congress on the following day, June 21st, and was duly installed as delegate from Virginia.[28]

The Congress had been in session for some time now and was faced with the herculean task of binding the colonies together in a common struggle against the British. The news from Boston was increasingly ominous; Lexington and Concord had touched off bloody war, and George Washington set off several days after Jefferson's arrival to take command as generalissimo of the rapidly mobilizing colonial troops around Boston.

Whether Congress was doing a proper job depended on the viewpoint of the particular delegate. John Adams of Massachusetts thought the proceedings "tedious beyond expression," and the members unacquainted "with each other's language, ideas, views, designs." Intensely jealous of one another, each delegate considered himself at once "a great man, an orator, a critic, a statesman," and felt called upon to prove his greatness on every question.[29]

But John Adams was notoriously intolerant of those who did not meet with his high intellectual standards. Richard Henry Lee, on the other hand, declared that "there never appeared more perfect unanimity among any sett of Men than among the Delegates, and indeed all the old Provinces not one excepted are directed by the same firmness of union and determination to resist by all ways and to every extremity." [30]

Jefferson was cordially welcomed by the Virginian delegation, and doubly so because he brought with him a *douceur* of back pay for distribution.[31] They knew him and respected his talents; and the impression which he made upon the delegations from the other colonies was equally favorable. The *Summary View* had spread his name and fame, and the news he brought of Virginia's vigorous response to Lord Dunmore (which he had drafted) added to the impression.

Even John Adams warmed to this youthful delegate from Virginia; the youngest in point of years in all the Congress. The crusty New Englander later remembered Jefferson's "reputation for literature, science, and a happy talent of composition. Writings of his were handed about, remarkable for the peculiar felicity of expression. Though a silent member of Congress, he was so prompt, frank, explicit and decisive upon committees and in conversation . . . that he soon seized upon my heart." [32] That "seizure" was to be reciprocated and survived years of misunderstanding and political enmities.

Jefferson's "silence" in public debate became almost proverbial; but, as Adams noted, he was a valiant committee man and could draft a document with precision and literary grace. Congress came to recognize the positive traits and to take advantage of them. On June 23rd, two days after Jefferson was accredited, the question of drafting a Declaration stating the grounds for America's taking up arms came up for consideration. It was felt that Washington, about to proceed to the encampment near Boston, should publish it on his arrival to the assembled troops and to the world. The news of Bunker Hill had just arrived in Philadelphia; but it was not yet known whether it was in truth a victory or a defeat.

The committee appointed to draft the Declaration turned the task over to John Rutledge of South Carolina. He did the job overnight, but when it was presented to Congress on the following day, objections were raised to the phraseology and the contents. On June 26th it was recommitted and John Dickinson of Pennsylvania, one of its most vehement critics, and Thomas Jefferson of Virginia were added to the committee. The task of revamping the unsatisfactory Declaration was given to Jefferson; according to him, on the proposal of William Livingston of New Jersey.[33] If so, then Livingston soon had cause to repent of his recommendation. Had he read carefully his protégé's former tracts, he would have realized his error. For Jefferson was even more of a firebrand than Rutledge, whom both Livingston and Dickinson had thought too "harsh."

Yet the young Virginian believed he was weighing his words carefully and with due restraint when he drafted, and then redrafted, the Declaration on Taking up Arms. To a large extent it followed the historical and argumentative thesis of his *Summary View;* bringing it up to date, however, with appropriate allusions to Concord and the "avowed course of murder & devastation" followed by General Gage around Boston. "To oppose his arms we also have taken up arms," Jefferson asserted. "We should be wanting to ourselves, we should be perfidious to posterity, we should be unworthy that free ancestry from which we derive our descent, should we submit with folded arms to military butchery & depredation, to gratify the lordly ambition, or sate the avarice of a British ministry."

At the end, however, Jefferson sought to soothe any alarm which "our good fellow subjects in any parts of the empire" might feel over his bold pronouncements and violent language by assuring them that "we mean not in any wise to affect that union with them in which we have so long & so happily lived and which we wish so much to see again restored." [34]

It is to be doubted whether the "good fellow subjects" could be so easily placated with this halfhearted sop; certainly Dickinson and Livingston, who were strongly opposed to any steps being taken by the colonies which might forever preclude an amicable agreement with Great Britain, were justifiably sceptical that Jefferson's Declaration would promote that laudable end.

The committee met to consider the draft. Besides Dickinson and Livingston, it consisted of Rutledge, Benjamin Franklin, John Jay and Johnson. Dickinson, perhaps the foremost advocate of reconciliation in Congress and author of the famous *Letters of a Pennsylvania Farmer*, thought it harsh and full of offensive statements. And Livingston privately considered that both Rutledge's and Jefferson's drafts "had the faults common to our Southern gentlemen. Much fault-finding and declamation, with little sense or dignity. They seem to think a reiteration of tyranny, despotism, bloody, &c. all that is needed to unite us at home and convince the bribed voters of [Lord] North of the justice of our cause." [35] It all depended, of course, on what was wanted. As propaganda for home consumption, it *was* effective. As propaganda abroad, it was not.

By and large Congress was not prepared for an irremediable break at this time, and Dickinson spoke for the majority. Reluctantly, and because of his honesty and ability, even those "who could not feel his scruples," as Jefferson later put it, decided to turn the objectionable draft over to him for rewriting.

Curiously enough, Dickinson's revision incorporated much of Jefferson's thoughts and language and, particularly at the end, where Jefferson had attempted to soothe, had gone far beyond him in boldness and plain-speaking.[36] In this modified form, the Declaration was finally passed on July 6th.

Jefferson, sensitive as always to criticism, could not but be taken aback by this revision of his handiwork. Though he tried to gloss over his hurt in his Autobiography, it found vent in the manifest delight with which he recounted Benjamin Harrison's remark on a petition to the King which Dickinson immediately thereafter drew. Dickinson had observed of his own writing that there was but one word in the paper of which he disapproved, and that was the word *Congress*. Whereupon Harrison declared: "There is but one word in the paper, Mr. President, of which I approve, and that is the word *Congress*."[37]

But Jefferson's feelings were soon salved. On July 22nd, he was joined with Franklin, John Adams and Richard Henry Lee in a committee to report on Lord North's conciliatory motion of February 20, 1775, in the House of Commons. Since Jefferson had already drafted the reply of the Virginia Assembly to the same proposals, it was only logical that he repeat the performance for the Continental Congress. His answer, much along the same lines, was similarly approved by Congress on July 31st.[38]

While Jefferson was thus engaged in the employment of his pen for the benefit of Congress—and sitting silently through the interminable debates—he did not lose sight of more humane pursuits or private relaxation. He sought new books and new music eagerly for his library at home; kept up with his violin playing and snapped strings in the process that required replacement; bought a sword chain, though he was the last one in the world to swash it with a weapon at his side; went to see the current waxworks exhibition; mended his phaeton; and purchased a tomahawk that struck his fancy.[39]

On August 1st, Congress recessed and Jefferson started home with Benjamin Harrison, who accompanied him part of the way. The Virginia Convention was in session at Richmond, and Jefferson stopped off to report on the proceedings of the Congress and to be re-elected—this time in his own right—as a delegate to the next meeting of Congress. Jefferson was third in the voting, being topped only by Peyton Randolph and Richard Henry Lee. He received 85 ballots to their 89 and 88 respectively.[40] This rise in reputation and popularity should have contented him, for he led such men as Benjamin Harrison, Thomas Nelson, Jr., Richard Bland and George Wythe. Bland begged off because of age, and Francis Lightfoot Lee took his place. Patrick Henry remained at home to take command of the Virginia forces in the field.

Within a week Jefferson left the Convention to proceed to Monticello and his family, only to find tragedy in the offing. His infant daughter, Jane Randolph, died shortly after his arrival.

A short month's interval with his wife and private affairs, and public duty called again. On September 25th, he started out for Philadelphia to resume his place in Congress. That body had already been in session since September 13th, and Jefferson occupied his old lodgings, with Peyton Randolph and Thomas Nelson as co-tenants. Randolph, however, died suddenly of an apoplexy on October 22nd. He was only fifty-four at the time and, though a moderate, had been one of the mainstays of Virginia strength.

Congress was immersed in the accelerating pace of military affairs, and much of its business concerned the raising and equipping of armies. In this type of legislation Jefferson could be of little help, even though the Virginia Committee of Safety had seen fit, a day after his departure, to commission him County Lieutenant for Albemarle.[41] What Jefferson was much more deeply concerned with were leading principles and the future of the controversy with England.

More and more he was seeing that future plain and clear, as a definite break and eventual independence. His famous letter to the Loyalist John Randolph—he of the precious violin and now a fugitive from Virginian shores to the mother country—has been quoted as evidence that at this period Jefferson was *not* thinking of independence. Particularly are quoted those sections which declare himself "sincerely one of those [who still wish for re-union with their parent country,] and would rather be in dependence on Great Britain, properly limited, than on any other nation on earth, or than on no nation." It must be remembered that Jefferson possessed singular delicacy, almost feminine in its aspects, and he would never have been brutally frank with an old friend who was sacrificing so much for political principles. He *had* to soften the blow, and permit him the hope of some day returning. Nevertheless he owed it to his own integrity to add that "I am one of those, too, who, rather than submit to the rights of legislating for us, assumed by the British Parliament, and which late experience has shown they will so cruelly exercise, would lend my hand to sink the whole Island in the ocean."[42]

John Randolph knew better the turn of Jefferson's mind, and passed over Jefferson's proposal that he enlighten the British Ministry on the true state of affairs and thereby help bring about a reconciliation. He replied only that "tho we may *politically* differ in Sentiments, yet I see no Reason, why *privately* we may not cherish the same Esteem for each other which formerly I believe subsisted between us."[43] He had set sail minus his violin, but with his books, which Jefferson eagerly offered to buy. "My collection of classics," Jefferson had written, "& of books of parliamentary learning particularly, is not so complete as I could wish. As you are going to the land of literature & of books you may be willing to dispose of some of yours here & replace them there in better editions." Randolph ignored the offer.

This second session of Congress, vital though it was for the success of the commencing Revolution, proved unbearably tedious for Jefferson. There were two reasons for his state of mind; first, he had little or nothing to do with the technical bills to raise and furnish armies that currently absorbed the legislators, and his few appointments to committees were on minor matters;[44] second, he was getting extremely worried over the lack of news from home. Martha (or Patty) had evidently not been in the best of health when he quit Monticello, and she did not answer his letters. Nor did anyone else.

On October 31st, he wrote ironically to his friend Page: "I have set apart nearly one day in every week since I came here to write letters. Notwithstanding this I have never received the scrip of a pen from any mortal breathing. I should have excepted two lines from Mr. Pendleton to desire me to buy him 24. lb of wire from which I concluded he was alive."[45]

A week later, the irony had given way to frantic urgency. "I have never received the scrip of a pen from any mortal in Virginia since I left it; nor been able by any enquiries I could make to hear of my family," he told his brother-in-law, Francis Eppes. "The suspense under which I am is too terrible to be endured. If any thing has happened, for god's sake let me know it."[46]

Some of his alarm was due to news which came to Philadelphia of the ravagings by British forces in Virginia. The port of Norfolk was being threatened and shortly thereafter in fact destroyed; and Lord Dunmore's troops were moving inland, aiming, as Jefferson feared, toward Charlottesville and Monticello. He sent off a letter to Patty urging her to remove the family to a place of refuge until the danger was over,[47] and to this also he seemingly received no reply.

On December 28th, though Congress was still in session, the anxious paterfamilias could stand the ominous silence no longer, and set off for Virginia. He found his family safe and in no immediate danger; though Patty was not in the best of health and his mother was shortly to die. He was at Monticello when the event took place and he noted it with Spartan brevity in his account book.[48]

Jefferson remained at home for four months. What prompted him to stay away from the center of things during that period is obscure. War evidently was not as total in those days, nor politics as unremitting. Virginia's vote in Congress could be cast without him, and the members came and went with considerable nonchalance.

In any event, Jefferson busied himself with his private concerns, duly broached a pipe of Madeira, "vintage of 1770," and no doubt found it flavorful; watched the foaling of a colt whom he named Caractacus and made up a careful list of all his horses (he was a passionate lover of horseflesh); and in general conducted himself as a retired gentleman at peace with himself and the world.[49] He did, it is true, draw up a list of militia volunteers from Albemarle, but this seems to have been about all he did in connection with his duties as County Lieutenant.[50]

On May 7, 1776, he finally started out from Monticello to resume his post in Philadelphia, first leaving with his wife ten pounds in cash to take care of household expenses.[51] Seemingly he had intended to leave earlier, around the middle of March, but an illness for which he was treated by his friend, Dr. George Gilmer, incapacitated him.[52] Probably it was the beginning of those severe headaches which came on him at periodic intervals in later life.

CHAPTER 10

Immortal Declaration

JEFFERSON reached Philadelphia on May 14, 1776. It was high time he made his appearance; the delay of an additional month or so in his return and he would have missed his chance of entering the company of the immortals and perhaps have shifted his entire career to one of modest obscurity.

Events were moving at a furious pace. The once limited revolt had flamed to a full-fledged revolution. Benedict Arnold had invaded Canada in the hope of capturing that base of operations from the British and lost most of his army; the tide of war engulfed North and South together; Tom Paine's wing-tipped words in *Common Sense* were being eagerly absorbed in every village and hamlet; and France, the traditional enemy of England, was pondering possible intervention in the heaven-sent struggle.

The movement for outright independence was growing apace. More and more the once-dreaded phrase was coloring the thoughts and speech of the colonists. Tom Paine clad it in roseate hues and thundered it aloud. John Adams and his cousin Sam harkened to the thunder and exulted. "Every Post and every Day rolls in upon us Independence like a Torrent," cried John. South Carolina instructed its delegates to Congress to proclaim independence. John Page, Jefferson's boyhood friend, wrote vehemently to him: "For God's sake declare the Colonies independant at once, & save us from ruin." [1] The "Torrent" was indeed beginning to roll.

But the radicals—and these included Jefferson—realized that they had to make haste slowly. As late as February 13, 1776, a Congressional committee had actually reported out an address to the Colonies written by James Wilson of Pennsylvania which emphatically disavowed any intention of seeking independence and declared "that what we aim at, and what we are entrusted by you to pursue, *is the Defence and the Re-establishment of the constitutional Rights of the Colonies*." [2]

Richard Henry Lee, one of the more radical members of Congress, was champing at the bit. Vehemently he exhorted the equally fiery Patrick Henry: "Ages yet unborn, and millions existing at present, must rue or bless that Assembley [of Virginia], on which their happiness or misery will so eminintly depend. Virginia has hitherto taken the lead in great affairs, and many now look to her with anxious expectation, hoping that the spirit, wisdom, and energy of her councils, will rouse America from the fatal lethargy into which the feebleness, folly, and interested views of the Proprietary governments, with the aid of Tory machinations, have thrown her most unhappily."[3]

That meeting of the Virginia Convention to which Lee so anxiously referred was in truth poised on the edge of momentous decisions. As Virginia went, so, it might be considered, would the other colonies go. Independence, or supine dependence, waited on the result. Jefferson, newly come to Philadelphia, felt himself away from the center of the struggle. As a delegate, he was bound by the instructions that emanated from Williamsburg. In Philadelphia, he was a rubber stamp; in Williamsburg, the true decisions were being made. Aside from the question of independence or no, Virginia was engaged in drafting a new form of government for herself to take the place of the old. And again Jefferson, who had precise ideas as to what that form should be, was not there to help mold it.

He poured out his troubled thoughts to Thomas Nelson and hinted slyly at the remedy. "Should our Convention propose to establish now a form of government," he wrote, "perhaps it might be agreeable to recall for a short time their delegates. It is a work of the most interesting nature and such as every individual would wish to have his voice in. In truth it is the whole object of the present controversy; for should a bad government be instituted for us in future it had been as well to have accepted at first the bad one offered to us from beyond the water without the risk and expence of contest."

As for independence, he was waiting to hear what Virginia's instructions would be; though, as far as the upper counties were concerned, he had found nine out of ten in favor of it.[4]

Yet, while thus fuming at his absence from Virginia almost as soon as he had quit it, Jefferson managed to beguile his time in hot Philadelphia. He first took quarters in his old lodgings, but the impending heat determined him to seek new ones on the outskirts, where the air was fresher. On May 23rd, he found what he wanted in a three-story brick house at 230 High Street, on its southwest corner. Later on, the building was renumbered as 700 Market Street. It was owned by a young bricklayer of German parentage named Jacob Graff (Jefferson wrote it *Graaf*) and Jefferson rented the second floor—parlor and bedroom—for 35 shillings a week.[5] The house has since become enshrined in American memory as the birthplace of the Declaration of Independence.

Probably the parlor resounded to the strains of his fiddle, for he had to purchase new strings. A luxurious silver cover to an ivory book caught his fancy and it cost him 45 shillings; more than the price of a week's lodging. A monkey was on exhibition, and Jefferson gaped with the rest.[6]

In a sense Congress was marking time until Virginia determined on its course, though it sensibly accelerated the train of events by approving, on May 15th, the resolution which John Adams of Massachusetts and Richard Henry Lee of Virginia had introduced on May 10th: advice to the colonies that they adopt "such government as shall in the opinion of the representatives of the people, best conduce to the happiness and safety of their constituents in particular and America in general."

By the time the text of this resolution reached Virginia, however, that powerful colony had already acted. On the very day that Congress moved thus tentatively toward eventual independence, Virginia instructed its delegates in Congress to declare for independence at once. Thus, at one stroke, Virginia was prepared to cut the umbilical cord which had bound the American possessions to the mother country, England.

The electrifying news was presented to Congress on May 27th by the Virginia delegation, and the machinery began ponderously to move. But back in Williamsburg the Convention, with instructions for independence out of the way, was moving with great speed to effectuate that ultimate separation, so far as it was concerned, by forming a new Constitution suitable to a newly sovereign State.

On May 24th, Edmund Pendleton wrote privately to Jefferson to advise him of the train of events: "You'l have seen yr. Instructions to propose Independance, your resolutions to form a Government. The Political Cooks are busy in preparing the dish, and as Colo. Mason seemed to have the ascendancy in the great work, I have sanguine hopes it will be framed so as to Answer its end, Prosperity to the Community & Security to Individuals."[7]

The receipt of this private communication galvanized Jefferson into activity. He had evinced a strange apathy—at least outwardly—toward the furiously boiling topic of independence. His letters had mentioned it almost in passing; he had taken no overt steps in Congress. Richard Henry Lee had borne the brunt for the Virginia delegation; perhaps by agreement of the delegates themselves. This was indeed curious, for Jefferson had been among the first to foresee that inevitable conclusion to the long controversy. It is possible, of course, that he felt his activity was not currently required; that others were carrying the work adequately toward the desired end.

But the proposed constitution for Virginia was another matter. Though his views were continentally enlarged, Virginia was his beloved "country," and what was happening at home touched him to the quick. He would have preferred that Virginia had waited; a constitution that would permanently bind Virginia for the future should not, he thought, be drafted in haste nor by a temporary Convention that had not been elected for that purpose. There were many things wrong in Virginia—feudal tenures, echoes of aristocratic forms, voting privileges, clerical establishments—which required fundamental changes; and the current Convention did not represent, to his mind, the true sentiments of the people on these great matters.[8]

According to Edmund Randolph, Jefferson conveyed his views to a "youthful friend" in the Convention (probably Randolph himself) and asked him to oppose the drafting of a permanent constitution until the people could elect delegates for that particular purpose. There is no doubt that Jefferson expected to be one of the delegates. The "youthful friend" dutifully submitted his mentor's objections to the Convention leaders—Pendleton, Patrick Henry and George Mason—but "these gentlemen saw no distinction between the conceded power to declare independence, and its necessary consequence, the fencing of society by the institution of government." [9]

Whether Jefferson knew of this denouement in time, or was spurred by Pendleton's letter, he deemed it wise to make the best of a bad situation by conveying forthwith to the Convention his own ideas for a constitution. George Mason, whom Pendleton had declared the probable draftsman, was, to Jefferson's mind, not as tender as himself on the relations of government and the *people*.

In hot haste, therefore, and within a few days, Jefferson composed his own draft constitution for Virginia to consider. He put it, however, in the form of an act rather than a definitive constitution, so that it might readily be amended at some future date and not made into a strait jacket for the fundamental liberties of the people of Virginia. Two copies exist; one, the original draft, and the second, what he called a fair copy, though it was itself considerably interlineated and erased.[10]

It opened with what certainly would have no place in a permanent constitution—an extended account of the crimes committed by King George of England against the colonies which is reminiscent of the similar list in the *Summary View* and heralds the more compact denunciations of the Declaration of Independence.

Using these crimes as the justification for a deposition of the kingly prerogative—tantamount to a declaration of independence from England, since Jefferson and other American publicists had consistently contended that the only tie between the two was based on a common king—he proceeded to the constitution proper.

There would be three branches of government—the Legislative, Executive and Judiciary—all to be forever separate. The legislature was to be divided into a House of Representatives and a Senate; the former to be elected by all males of full age possessing a quarter acre of land in a town or twenty-five acres in the country, or who had paid "scot and lot" during the preceding two years. Representatives were to be apportioned to the number of qualified electors in each town or borough.

Since, in Jefferson's scheme of things, the House of Representatives was to be the most powerful body of the new government, these electoral provisions disclosed his preoccupation not merely with broadening the base for voting but ensuring that the Tidewater aristocrats could no longer, as in the past, by weighted representation, dominate the back counties of

Virginia. It is true that he still held to landholding as the chief qualification for an elector, but the number of acres he set as the minimum qualification was so small that the overwhelming majority of freemen could easily qualify. Since he also provided that every adult who did *not* possess fifty acres of land was entitled to a grant of that much from the unappropriated or forfeited lands of Virginia, he was in effect providing for universal male suffrage.[11]

The Senate was neither to be appointed by the Executive nor elected by the people. Appointed by the House of Representatives, and incapable of reappointment after the expiration of their terms, its members would ordinarily conform to the general trend of the appointing House.

The Executive, or Administrator, was similarly a creature of the House. Annually appointed by that all-powerful body, he was a pale simulacrum of the usual Executive—he could not veto a bill, dissolve or adjourn the legislature, declare war or peace, raise armed forces, coin money, erect courts and offices, or create dignities. With these and other negatives to his powers, it is difficult to determine exactly what functions were left to him. Thus early, Jefferson was betraying that suspicion of executive authority which pervaded his thinking through life and which, hamstringing his actions while Governor of Virginia, had to be ingeniously evaded by various subterfuges when President of the United States.

The powers and structure of the Judiciary were sharply defined and jury trials safeguarded in all cases, civil, criminal and ecclesiastical. Further to limit the power of the judges, provision was made for jury determinations even of contempts of court.

With a bold insight into the future of America, Jefferson proposed that the great inchoate territories west of the Alleghenies to which Virginia laid claim should eventually be established into new colonies, "on the same fundamental laws contained in this instrument, and shall be free and independent of this colony and of all the world."

Just as important as the political clauses—perhaps even more important in Jefferson's thought—were those which added up to a fundamental bill of rights: "No person hereafter coming into this country shall be held within the same in slavery under any pretext whatever.... All persons shall have full and free liberty of religious opinion, nor shall any be compelled to frequent or maintain any religious institution.... No freeman shall be debarred the use of arms.... There shall be no standing army but in time of actual war.... Printing presses shall be free, except so far as by commission of private injury cause may be given of private action."

Jefferson thought he was being conservative in these proposals: they did not interfere with the system of land tenures and other matters close to his heart; but they were sufficiently radical to ensure their defeat by the present, or indeed, for some time to come, by future Virginia conventions and assemblies.

He sent them off with George Wythe, who was returning from Philadelphia to Williamsburg, for submission to Edmund Pendleton as president of the Convention. They reached the Convention on the very day that its own plan of government was being reported out from the Committee of the Whole to the House itself. Wythe promptly showed Jefferson's draft to Pendleton and other leaders. But all agreed that it was too late to consider any fundamental changes in the document at hand.

The Virginia plan had been debated so vigorously and contentiously, the several proposals had been disputed in such minute detail, and everyone was so tired of the long-drawn-out struggle, that they deemed it wise not to reopen the subject. Then, too, which the leaders did not stress, there were radical elements in Jefferson's version to which neither they, nor the members at large, could possibly agree. They would, however, and did, insert some minor phrases from Jefferson's copy and, more importantly, tack on to the beginning of the instrument Jefferson's entire preamble which arraigned King George in such violent terms.[12]

The Constitution, as George Mason had drafted it, with Jefferson's Preamble, was unanimously adopted on June 29, 1776. There were striking differences between the two. The right of suffrage for both Houses of the legislature was left as before; and Jefferson's dream of an extended electorate and a more equitable scheme of apportionment had to wait for future developments. The Governor, elected by *both* Houses, instead of the lower one, had a Council of State to assist him, and was given far more vigorous powers and personality than inhabited Jefferson's pale wraith.[13]

In one point, however, Mason's form was superior to Jefferson's—it provided for a Senate elected by the people. Jefferson very curiously called for its *appointment* by the lower House. With the appointment of the Administrator similarly in its hands, there would have been hardly that complete and absolute separation of powers among the several branches of government which Jefferson had envisaged. He did not realize, in his determination to make the popular branch primary, that he might thereby set up a new tyrant.

Pendleton objected strongly to the method which Jefferson had proposed for choosing the Senate and, ironically enough, the radical was compelled to defend his proposal to the moderate by impugning the wisdom of the electorate. Biographers and historians have generally shied away from this strange document.

"You seem to have misapprehended my proposition for the choice of a Senate," wrote Jefferson. "I had two things in view: to get the wisest men chosen, & to make them perfectly independent when chosen. *I have ever observed that a choice by the people themselves is not generally distinguished for its wisdom. This first secretion from them is usually crude & heterogeneous. But give to those so chosen by the people a second choice themselves, & they generally will chuse wise men.* For this reason it was that I proposed the representatives (& not the people) should chuse the Senate, & thought I had notwithstanding that made the Senators (when chosen) perfectly independent of their electors." Though he would prefer a nonrecurring term of years for the Senators, "yet I could submit tho' not so willingly to an appointment for life, *or to anything rather than a mere creation by & dependance on the people*." [14]

This is indeed a far cry from Jefferson's later public utterances, and might have been proposed with complete good grace by Alexander Hamilton, his future great antagonist.

Of much more importance to the future of Virginia—and of America—was the prior passage on June 12th of the Declaration of Rights. This famous document—the first of its kind, and a remarkable preview of both the Declaration of Independence and the Bill of Rights amendments to the federal Constitution—was similarly prepared by George Mason.

The very first paragraph proclaimed the fundamental thesis, one which Jefferson was later to lift almost bodily: "That all men are by nature equally free and independent [Mason's own draft used the word "created"], and have certain inherent rights, of which, when they enter into a state of society, they cannot, by any compact, deprive or divest their posterity; namely, the enjoyment of life and liberty, with the means of acquiring and possessing property, and pursuing and obtaining happiness and safety." [15]

Nor is the second paragraph any less fundamental: "That all power is vested in, and consequently derived from, the people; that magistrates are their trustees and servants, and at all times amenable to them."

And the third, as a necessary corollary, upheld the right of revolution: "... whenever any government shall be found inadequate or contrary to these purposes, a majority of the community hath an indubitable, unalienable, and indefeasible right, to reform, alter, or abolish it, in such manner as shall be judged most conducive to the public weal."

Practically every one of the safeguards of the later federal Bill of Rights and of those which Jefferson sent down in his own plan of government are here incorporated: freedom of religion and press, right to bear arms and to jury trials, etc. In one respect only would Jefferson's proposals have added significantly to Mason's draft: a prohibition against compulsory maintenance of any church. But Mason, while omitting this prohibition—in effect, the disestablishment of the Anglican Church—was eloquent enough on the general topic of religious freedom: "That Religion, or the Duty which we owe to our Creator, and the Manner of discharging it, can be directed only by Reason & Conviction, not by Force or Violence, and therefore that all Men should enjoy the fullest Toleration in the Exercise of Religion, according to the Dictates of Conscience, unpunished, & unrestrained by the Magistrate ..." [16]

A youthful delegate to the Convention, named James Madison, tried indeed to amend this section to include a way station to disestablishment, but the opposition was too great. He did manage, however, to change

Mason's phraseology of "toleration" to the more powerful statement that "all men are equally entitled to the free exercise of religion."[17]

While Virginia was thus proclaiming her own independence, Congress was moving rapidly toward a similar proclamation for *all* the colonies.

On June 7, 1776, with the instructions of the Virginia Convention before him, Richard Henry Lee rose in the Continental Congress to move three memorable resolutions:

> *Resolved*, That these United Colonies are, and of right ought to be, free and independent States, that they are absolved from all allegiance to the British Crown, and that all political connection between them and the State of Great Britain is, and ought to be, totally dissolved.
>
> That it is expedient forthwith to take the most effectual measures for forming foreign Alliances.
>
> That a plan of confederation be prepared and transmitted to the respective Colonies for their consideration and approbation.[18]

Though long expected, the shock of final recognition sobered both sides to the tremendous argument—to be, or not to be, independent. The leaders of the opposing factions girded their loins for what they thought must prove a Homeric battle.

Consideration was adjourned until the following day, Saturday, June 8th. At 10 A.M. the delegates assembled. Lee, Wythe and John Adams, who had seconded the resolutions, led the debate for the proponents. James Wilson and John Dickinson of Pennsylvania, Robert R. Livingston of New York, and Edward Rutledge of South Carolina, led the opposition.

The latter group, who considered themselves "the sensible part of the House," fought a delaying action. They realized that in the present temper of some of the colonies outright opposition would be fatal. Therefore they proclaimed that they too believed in eventual independence, but that the time was not yet ripe for action. What was the point of giving England definite notice of their intentions, they inquired, before they had the means to execute them? It would be wiser, they insisted, first to pass the second and third resolutions, calling for foreign alliances and confederation at home, before making the futile gesture of independence. Furthermore, they argued, the colonies which they represented and others were not yet ready for the final plunge. They would come to it in time, and *then* Congress could act with a good grace, since it would rightly be said that the voice of the people had driven them into it.[19]

It was a plausible argument, and Adams, Lee and Wythe found it difficult to surmount it. If the only objection was one of timing, they countered, Congress might as well declare a fact that already existed. The people were waiting for them to lead the way. In fact, the people were in favor of the measure, even though some of their representatives had instructions to the contrary. Only a Declaration of Independence would make it possible for the European powers to enter into alliances with the embattled colonies; and not the reverse, as the opposition claimed.[20]

The debate spilled over into Monday, June 10th. The delegates of New Jersey, Maryland and Delaware joined the arguers for delay; while all New England and Georgia backed Virginia and Massachusetts in pressing for immediate action. In the end, rather than face a divided and resentful House, the proponents deemed it prudent to postpone final decision on independence until the 1st of July. By that time the assemblies of the middle colonies, whose instructions to their delegates had not been consonant with independence, would have a chance to meet and remove the restrictions.[21]

At the same time, however, the proponents of independence were determined that such delay be not stretched to unconscionable lengths. They therefore proposed and carried a proposition that a committee be appointed immediately to get to work on an appropriate declaration and have it ready by the adjourned date. On June 11th, the committee was duly selected. On it were Thomas Jefferson, John Adams, Benjamin Franklin, Roger Sherman and Robert R. Livingston. Jefferson, who had received the greatest number of votes, became its chairman.

Jefferson's appointment to the committee and its chairmanship was a decided surprise. All through the great debate he had sat in silence, not once opening his mouth; busy, rather, in taking notes on the arguments of others which late in life he incorporated into his Autobiography. Certainly, Richard Henry Lee, the author of the resolution and conspicuous all through the debate, deserved the place rather than he. Even Benjamin Harrison, who had reported it out of committee, had a prior claim. But both of these Virginians were excluded in favor of Jefferson. Why?

Political and personal feuds among the Virginia delegation were the answer, according to Adams. Political expediency had dictated that the place of honor be given to a Virginian. Even before Congress met, the Massachusetts delegation had been advised by delegates from other colonies, notably Pennsylvania, to yield the palm in everything to Virginia. With the middle and some of the southern colonies hostile to the idea of independence, with Virginia populous and proud, the latter's vanity would be served by giving her the leadership and the former would be more apt to follow her than Massachusetts.[22]

Therefore, a Virginian was indicated for the chairmanship of the committee to frame the Declaration. But Lee and Harrison, the two most likely candidates, were engaged in a bitter feud of their own. The choice of either would have split an already mutually jealous and quarrelsome delegation wide open. George Wythe explained the background to Adams. "Mr. Lee had," Wythe said, "when he was very young, and when he first came into the House of Burgesses, moved and urged on an inquiry into the state of the treasury, which was found deficient in large sums, which had been lent by the treasurer [John Robinson] to many of the most influential families of the country, who found themselves exposed, and had never forgiven Mr. Lee." [23]

Lee was placated with the chairmanship of the committee to prepare articles of confederation. In any event, within two days he departed for Virginia to be with his sick wife and to attend the proceedings of the Convention. As for Harrison, the argument against Lee held equally in reverse for him, and in addition, he was not too well liked by the delegates from the other colonies.

Under these circumstances Adams, on whom Jefferson, in spite of his silence, had made a profound impression, worked unceasingly in behalf of his young friend. Jefferson received the most votes, he noted in his diary, "because we united in him to the exclusion of R. H. Lee, and to keep out Harrison." The further tale that the Virginia group, hating Lee, set up Jefferson to rival and supplant him, may have some truth in it, even though Jefferson was probably an unwitting beneficiary. Of this supplanting, Adams was to remark that "this could be done only by the pen, for Mr. Jefferson could stand no competition with [Lee] or any one else in elocution and public debate." [24]

The mechanism whereby Jefferson was chosen to draft the Declaration, and the various forms it took before it was finally submitted to Congress for approval, have been overlaid with interminable clouds of controversy and evoked a staggering literature of historical dispute. The chief cause for the controversy lies in the several versions written many years later by the main participants—Adams and Jefferson—as the result of an attempt by Timothy Pickering, embittered Federalist, publicly to play down Jefferson's authorship in the immortal document. The attempt did not succeed; Jefferson's name, and none other, is eternally wedded to the Declaration he fashioned; but historians have had a field day ever since attempting to provide a provenance for every word and every comma that went into the final paper.

In reality, the two versions before us are not essentially different, except for minutiae of no great importance. Adams sought honestly to recount, as far as memory could serve, the several steps; and doubtless Jefferson would not have contested his version so vehemently had he not been made unduly sensitive by Pickering's political decrial.

Adams's account is largely contained in his autobiographical reminiscences, written about 1805, and secondarily in a letter to Pickering, written in 1822. Jefferson's version is contained in a letter to Madison, written in 1823, intended to confute a Fourth of July speech made that year by Pickering, who claimed it was based on the information sent him by Adams.[25]

Adams averred that the Committee of Five met in session, decided on "the articles of which the declaration was to consist," and then appointed

Jefferson and himself as a subcommittee to "draw them up in form." Thereafter he and Jefferson met, Adams continued, and Jefferson "proposed to me to make the draught, I said I will not; You shall do it. Oh no! Why will you not? You ought to do it. I will not. Why? Reasons enough. What can be your reasons? Reason 1st. You are a Virginian and a Virginian ought to appear at the head of this business. Reason 2nd. I am obnoxious, suspected and unpopular; you are very much otherwise. Reason 3rd. You can write ten times better than I can. 'Well,' said Jefferson, 'if you are decided I will do as well as I can.' Very well, when you have drawn it up we will have a meeting." [26]

Jefferson, for his part, denied that any subcommittee had been appointed on which Adams was a member as well as himself. He insisted that the Committee "unanimously pressed on myself alone to undertake the draught. I consented; I drew it. . . . " As the basis for his recollection, Jefferson claimed support from notes in his possession which he had taken "at the moment and on the spot." But these notes, alas, no longer exist, and the final version he set down in his Autobiography is severely bald and noncommittal.

The palm for accurate recollection must, however, go to Jefferson, in spite of Adams's colorful precision of detail. Everyone—Adams himself as well as later historians—seems to have overlooked the entry in Adams's own Diary, dated June 23, 1779, only three years after the event, of a short colloquy with Marbois, the French minister. Marbois had asked him: "Who made the Declaration of Independence?" "Mr. Jefferson, of Virginia," said I, "was the draughtsman. The committee consisted of Mr. Jefferson, Mr. Franklin, Mr. Harrison [sic], Mr. R. and myself; and we appointed Jefferson a subcommittee to draw it up." [27] No mention here of Adams as a member of the subcommittee.

What happens then to Adams's later recollection of that wonderful discussion with Jefferson? It ought not to be assumed that he deliberately made it up out of whole cloth. Perhaps the answer is that it took place during the session of the *entire* committee; that it had first been suggested that Adams and Jefferson collaborate; that Jefferson pressed it on Adams, as was only proper for the younger man; that Adams refused in language somewhat as indicated; and *then* the Committee of Five turned over the job to Jefferson alone.

What is certain is that Jefferson *did* draw up the Declaration on his own. According to Adams, the first draft was completed within a day or two, and was based on written minutes of the Committee's proposals as to form and contents. Those minutes, if they ever existed, have also vanished into the limbo of forgotten things.

On subsequent events Adams's memory faded, while Jefferson's continued precise. Both agreed that Jefferson showed the draft first to Adams, though the latter was unable to recollect if he suggested any changes. Actually, he did; and his interlineations show clearly on the original draft. So, too, do those of Franklin, to whom Jefferson later brought the draft, no doubt, at the house of Edward Duffield, several miles north of Philadelphia on the Bristol Pike, where that aged philosopher lay ill with the gout.[28]

Jefferson claimed that the corrections made by Adams and Franklin to his draft were two or three only; and that they were purely verbal. From this so-called "Rough Draft," he declared, he made a "fair copy" which he submitted to the entire Committee. They approved it unaltered, and it was reported to the Congress.[29]

But here confusion becomes worse confounded. The task of disentangling the various drafts has been diligently and minutely performed by several historians, and the reader must be referred to them for the details. It is as fascinating a bit of detective work and learned ingenuity as we possess, though the historians themselves do not altogether agree in assignment of phrases and chronology. Suffice it to say that most agree that Adams made two corrections, Franklin five, and Jefferson some sixteen or so. Whether some of these last were written in by Jefferson at the behest of the Committee as a whole must forever remain in obscurity, though he asserts, as we have seen, that they made no alteration whatever.

John Adams made a copy, evidently from the document as first submitted to him by Jefferson. Franklin made no copy at all. The "rough draft" or a reasonable facsimile thereof which has since been lost, went to the Committee. The final text, with excisions in Congress, went to the printer for use in setting up what is now known as the "engrossed copy." After its approval, Jefferson made copies for his friends—R. H. Lee, George Wythe, John Page, Edmund Pendleton and Philip Mazzei, showing the variations between his own handiwork and the one approved by Congress. Only one of these is now extant—that of R. H. Lee—in snug harbor with the American Philosophical Society. The Adams copy resides with the Adams Papers on deposit in Boston; while the "rough draft" draws crowds whenever it is exhibited in the Library of Congress. Madison later had a copy; and there were one or two others.

But all this is mere scaffolding or, from another point of view, skeletonizing. In the painstaking analysis of the several drafts and copies, in the attempted attribution and chronology of each word and mark on the famous "rough draft" which, as someone remarked, is "scored and scratched like a schoolboy's exercise," we must not lose sight of the document as a whole, as a finished product.

When Jefferson sat down with his writing materials in the front parlor of his quarters at young Jacob Graff's, he knew that he was confronted with a difficult and important assignment. On the assumption that Lee's resolution for independence would pass in Congress, it was the job of the Declaration to justify that explosive pronouncement to the people of America and the world at large. It was therefore as propaganda, as special pleading, as impassioned argumentation that the document had to be considered; not as a calm and objective statement of philosophic principles intended for the closet and the lamp. Too often this guiding rule is forgotten in the innumerable discussions of the Declaration.

What has made the Declaration perhaps the most influential document the world has ever seen, and its author immortal, however, is the patent fact that Jefferson did manage to place philosophic principles into intimate conjunction with propaganda, and wedded them in such wise that conviction irresistibly follows even at this late date when the original passions have subsided and some of the leading principles have become outmoded, if not indeed suspect. As literary art, as articulated structure and concatenated cadence, as a repository of magical and immortal phrases that burn in the mind and sing in the heart, the Declaration of Independence has no political peer.

The colonies were in revolt; armies were trampling the land. What had caused the revolt? What moral and legal justifications were there for severing all connections with the mother country and setting up a new nation? Large and important sections of the American people were not yet convinced that irremediable independence was either necessary or desirable; numerous individuals throughout all the colonies clung stubbornly to the belief that the revolt itself was sacrilege and treason. At least the first group must be convinced; the second, if not open to conviction, must be overborne.

Jefferson's role, as he himself later declared, was not to be strikingly original or to unearth new and ingenious philosophic formulae for the course they were taking. It was rather, "not to find out new principles, or new arguments, never before thought of, not merely to say things which had never been said before; but to place before mankind the common sense of the subject, in terms so plain and firm as to command their assent, and to justify ourselves in the independent stand we are compelled to take. Neither aiming at originality of principle or sentiment, nor yet copied from any particular and previous writing, it was intended to be an expression of the American mind, and to give to that expression the proper tone and spirit called for by the occasion." [30]

It is exactly because everything which Jefferson put down had already existed in the American mind and, as Adams was to remark without any attempt at denigration, "there is not an idea in it but what had been hackneyed in Congress for two years before," [31] that made the Declaration so powerful in its effects and its truths so "self-evident."

It commenced fairly and moderately, and with a decent respect for the opinions of mankind.

> When in the Course of human events, it becomes necessary for one people to dissolve the political bands which have connected them with another, and to assume among the powers of the earth, the separate and equal station to which the Laws of Nature and of Nature's God entitle them, a decent respect

to the opinions of mankind requires that they should declare the causes which impel them to the separation.

The "Laws of Nature and of Nature's God," as well as their correlative, "natural rights," were the current coin of the eighteenth century and known to every literate American through the writings of Locke, Hobbes, Harrington, Montesquieu, Vattel, Burlamaqui, Grotius and a host of others. As for those not so literate they had acquired that soothing patina of rightness and truth which demands no further emendation.

Logically, Jefferson should have passed on immediately to a consideration of the causes, but instead, with a felicitous instinct, he penned those magnificent affirmations of human rights which gave depth, solidity and philosophic tone to the entire discussion and have reverberated ever since in the consciousness of mankind.

We hold these truths to be self-evident, that all men are created equal, that they are endowed by their Creator with certain inalienable rights, that among these are Life, Liberty, and the Pursuit of Happiness.—That to secure these rights, Governments are instituted among Men, deriving their just powers from the consent of the governed.—That whenever any Form of Government becomes destructive of these ends, it is the right of the People to alter or abolish it, and to institute new Government, laying its foundation on such principles, and organizing its powers in such form, as to them shall seem most likely to effect their Safety and Happiness.

The most obvious and immediate source of these splendid phrases was the Virginia Declaration of Rights, penned by George Mason, a copy of which had unquestionably come to Jefferson's hand even before its final passage in the Assembly. A point-to-point correspondence can be shown between the two documents, even to the famous lines on life, liberty and the pursuit of happiness. What Jefferson did was to take the somewhat pedestrian phraseology of Mason, heighten and condense, sharpen and make swift, and then tip with immortal flame. They became as much his own as Shakespeare's new-modeling of lines lifted bodily from the pages of others.

Nor can it be said that Mason was original, either. John Locke might perhaps be considered the godfather of them all. Mason took the items of life, liberty and property from him, and added the pursuit of happiness. Jefferson dropped the property, and kept the pursuit of happiness. But Mason might just as well have copied his exordium from James Wilson, the Pennsylvania pamphleteer, as from Locke. Wilson's *Considerations on the Nature and Extent of the Legislative Authority of the British Parliament*, written around 1770 and published in 1774, could similarly be subjected to a point-to-point correspondence with both Mason and Jefferson.[32] The "truths" were in the air and part of the common heritage.

Having established the nature of government and the rights of man, the next step was to show how that government had been subverted and the rights denied through the tyrannical acts of the English king. Parliament, the original *bête noire*, no longer merited attack now that independence was the goal. It was the king, and the king alone, who held the colonies to England; and if he could be indicted for high crimes and misdemeanors against his faithful subjects, then all ties fell to the ground. Therefore Jefferson proceeded with a long catalogue of those crimes.

Since he had already enumerated them in detail in his draft constitution for Virginia, it was a comparatively simple matter to lift them bodily from their original context and set them down again in the Declaration. Several new ones were added for good measure. But what a vast difference stylistically between the sprawling catalogue which Jefferson had drawn for the constitution only two weeks or so before, and the serried ranks in which the same indictments march in the Declaration. Their reiterated and cumulative beat storm the senses and pound the veins until, perhaps, their truth or falsity are no longer matters of calm discourse. For this was polemics and intended to arouse, rather than a study in historical causation. King George became the villain of the piece; it was easier to personify injustice in and to direct hatred against an individual than a large and heterogeneous Parliament or abstract institutions.

Having thus detailed in full the tyrannous acts of the king and voiced the appeals which the colonists had made in vain both to him and to the British people, Jefferson had prepared the way for the ultimate step—separation and independence.

> We, therefore, the Representatives of the United States of America, in General Congress Assembled . . . solemnly publish and declare, that these United Colonies are, and of Right ought to be Free and Independent States. . . . And for the support of this Declaration . . . we mutually pledge to each other our Lives, our Fortunes, and our Sacred Honor.[33]

On June 28, 1776, the Committee of Five reported Jefferson's draft Declaration to Congress. Since its consideration would have been premature until Lee's resolution for independence was first disposed of, it was ordered to lie on the table.[34]

On July 1st, as had been previously agreed, Lee's resolution came up for debate.

In the period of delay, the doubtful and recalcitrant colonies had had an opportunity to reconsider their position. As Congress entered on its momentous task, heartening news came from Maryland that its convention had unanimously repealed its former instructions and now required its delegates to vote for independence.[35]

Resolved into a Committee of the Whole, Congress debated the fundamental issue. All day long the debate raged. The New York delegation sorrowfully assured their fellows that while they personally were for the resolution and they were certain their constituents were for it, nevertheless their hands were tied by their twelve-months-old instructions.

John Dickinson of Pennsylvania tried eloquently and at length to stem the tide for independence, and Adams answered him at equal length. "It was," Adams assured a correspondent that evening, "an idle mispense of time, for nothing was said but what had been repeated and hackneyed in that room before a hundred times for six months past." [36]

Perhaps it was not as idle as Adams thought, for it helped swing doubtful delegations and brought pause even to those opposed. When the vote was finally taken at the end of the day nine colonies voted *yes;* two, South Carolina and Pennsylvania, voted *no;* Delaware, with only two delegates present, was evenly divided; and New York, bound by ancient instructions, refrained.

Technically, Congress could have immediately resolved itself back into open session and, by the same vote, have forced through the resolution of independence. Then the opposing colonies could either have ultimately reversed themselves and joined their brethren, or remained aloof as British subjects.

But Edward Rutledge of South Carolina, one of those who had said *nay*, now rose to request an overnight delay. Though he and his colleagues disapproved, he thought that they might, for the sake of unanimity, change their position by the morrow. To this bright prospect Congress assented.[37]

The next morning, July 2nd, Congress reconvened. The previous evening had obviously been well spent by the missionaries for independence; South Carolina announced her adherence; the missing third member of the Delaware delegation made his appearance and cast his deciding ballot in favor; and even the Pennsylvania delegation, swollen by last-minute arrivals, overrode the redoubtable Dickinson and his valiant compeer, James Wilson. Only New York mournfully abstained, as before; within a few days, however, tidings came that the New York convention had met and voted new instructions which permitted its representatives to assent.

Independence became official as of July 2nd; that is, insofar as a resolution could make it so. The British, naturally, had something to say about it; and did say it for many weary years to come, amid the thunder of cannon, the crackle of small arms, and broadsides from stately ships at sea.

John Adams had no present qualms, however, The following morning he awoke to exult: "Yesterday, the greatest question was decided, which ever was debated in America, and a greater, perhaps, never was nor will be decided among men. You will see, in a few days, a Declaration setting forth the causes which have impelled us to this mighty revolution, and the reasons which will justify it in the sight of God and man." [38]

What Jefferson's emotions were at the sight of independence are not recorded; but it is easy to surmise that they too were eloquent. For he, as well as Adams, had been steadily pointing toward this day for many more months than most of his fellows. The exultation in Jefferson's case, however, was tempered by two considerations. The first was that his beloved brain child was being subjected to the ruthless excisions of men who had not known the agonies of authorship. The second was the most unwelcome news which had just arrived from Virginia; of which more in the next chapter.

With the fact of independence established, Congress now took up the Declaration which was to explain and justify it to the world. For three full days—July 2nd, 3rd and 4th—it was debated, paragraph by paragraph, clause by clause, word by word; while its sole progenitor sat and writhed in helpless silence.

Since Congress was sitting as a Committee of the Whole no official record of the discussions exists, but their thoroughness may be deduced from the time consumed, Jefferson's discomfort and the important changes which appeared in the document when it finally emerged into the light of day.

Some anecdotes and later comments disclose the tenor of the objections raised from the floor. What Jefferson contemptuously called "the pusillanimous idea that we had friends in England worth keeping terms with, still haunted the minds of many"; and therefore they struck out those passages in the indictment which censured the English people rather than the English king.[39]

If this aroused Jefferson's contempt, the next slash ought to have aroused his laughter. He had animadverted on the employment of "Scotch and other foreign auxiliaries" by the king to overawe the colonies, and several gentlemen in Congress who hailed from Scotland raised their voices in protest at the slur. The offending phrase obediently vanished.

As if this had been the signal, Congress now went to work with a will. Whole paragraphs, on which Jefferson had lavished such care, were removed *in toto*. Too vehement accusations against King George, which cooler heads realized might provide their own reaction, were expunged. Words were changed, phrases modified, and the whole text cut for economy and concision. In several places, particularly in the peroration, Congress inserted references to God and Divine Providence which Jefferson had not contemplated.

As change after change was made, or "mutilations," as Jefferson termed them, the unhappy author showed his anguish plain in every lineament. Old Ben Franklin, recovered from his gout, noted the younger man's vexation and sought kindly to turn aside his thoughts. "I have made it a rule," he said, "whenever in my power, to avoid becoming the draughtsman of papers to be reviewed by a public body. I took my lesson from an incident which I will relate to you." The incident was the tale of a hatter who, after proposing a handsome and extended sign for his establishment, unfortunately sought the advice of his friends. Successively they cut out all the fine phrases he had savored, until finally all that remained on the flapping board were his bare name and the picture of a hat.[40] Whether Jefferson then saw the humor of the situation may be doubted, whatever his relish of the tale in retrospect.

One change there was, or rather complete excision, which boded ill for the future of the country, even though it was perhaps wisdom's part to eliminate it at the moment.

Jefferson, like most thoughtful men, was no proponent of the institution of slavery. Morally, philosophically and politically he deemed it an evil that must eventually be extirpated. As far back as the *Summary View* he had listed as a major abuse of power by the British king the vetoing of a Virginia act forbidding further importation of slaves.

In the Declaration, therefore, where every possible complaint against the king was resurrected and expanded, where the rights of man constituted the fundamental premise, was it not proper to list once again this most shameful of abuses?

> He has waged cruel war against human nature itself, violating its most sacred rights of life and liberty in the persons of distant people, who never offended him, captivating and carrying them into slavery in another hemisphere, or to incur miserable death in their transportation thither.... Determined to keep open a market where Men should be bought and sold, he has prostituted his negative for suppressing every legislative attempt to prohibit or to restrain this execrable commerce: and that this assemblage of horrors might want no fact of distinguished dye, he is now exciting those very people to rise in arms among us, and to purchase that liberty of which he has deprived them by murdering the people upon whom he also obtruded them; thus paying off former crime committed against the liberties of one people, with crimes which he urges them to commit against the lives of another.

It was one thing, however, to inveigh against slavery in a polemical pamphlet; it was another to incorporate an open assault on the institution in an official paper. True, there were polemics enough in the Declaration; but they were directed against England and therefore impermanent in nature, once the tie was broken. Slavery, on the other hand, would remain as an *American* problem and one in which the Southern States were vitally involved.

It is no wonder then that certain "Southern gentlemen," notably from South Carolina and Georgia, disapproved of the lengthy paragraph or that it was struck out "in complaisance" to them. Jefferson believed that the disapproval was based on the desire of those colonies to continue importation, and that Northern members voted with them because their consciences sat uneasy under the imputation of their former complicity in the slave trade.[41] Perhaps; but Jefferson's abhorrence went plainly beyond the trade to the institution itself; and the issue, thus baldly stated in the Declaration, would probably have split the colonies wide open and aborted all possibility of a confederate union.

On the evening of July 4th the rapid fire of changes, alterations and excisions ceased, and the Declaration of Independence became a fact—one of the most notable in the history of the world. So overwhelming has been its impression, indeed, that the day of its passage has become the legal holiday for the celebration of Independence, instead of July 2nd, the proper date.

Congress ordered the Declaration to be engrossed on parchment for future signature. On August 2nd the suitably engrossed document lay on the desk and the members came up one by one to affix their names. Some fifteen, however, were not in Philadelphia at the time, and they straggled in to sign until November.

But publication to the people did not wait on engrossment. Copies were immediately printed for distribution; on July 8th, it was brought in procession to the State House yard and there read to a large and excited concourse of people, even though one spectator at least thought that very few "respectable" persons were present.[42]

In other towns the news was received to the accompaniment of parades, the beating of drums and shrilling of fifes; in New York all debtors were released from jail; while Williamsburg, which had the most cause for joyous celebration, waited until the 25th; but then it made up for the delay by a fervor of applause, the discharge of cannon and firing of small arms, and fireworks and illuminations in the evening.[43]

CHAPTER II

The Great Revisions

DURING the great debate on independence and the Declaration which was to proclaim it to the world, Jefferson did not relinquish his other pursuits. On July 1st, for example, he began a detailed and meticulous series of weather observations which were continued, with but few interruptions, through most of his life.[1] Each morning and evening he noted the exact temperature and, dissatisfied with the accuracy of his instrument, he took time on July 4th—the great day itself—to buy a new and expensive thermometer for £3, 15 s. To this he added on the 8th a barometer, costing £4, 10 s.

As time went on, more information was jotted down in his notebooks—wind direction and velocity; the first appearance and final departure of leaves, flowers, fruits, insects and birds; observations on solar eclipses and the aurora borealis. No press of private or public business was permitted to interfere; and eventually he entered into correspondence with like-minded amateur meteorologists in other sections of the country for an interchange of information and observational data. In effect he was instituting, without quite realizing it, the first general weather bureau in the world.

Nor did he forget his family at home during this trying period. On that same notable 4th of July he visited the Philadelphia purveyors of fine articles for ladies and chose seven pairs of gloves to send to Monticello and, at a later date, six pairs of shoes.[2]

While all the colonies celebrated the Declaration of Independence with parades, speeches, fireworks and the noise of guns, Jefferson viewed his handiwork, as it emerged in final form from the deliberations of Congress, with mixed feelings. They had mutilated his precious phrases, he thought, and his auctorial vanity suffered intensely.

While under the spell of his fancied grievance he sent copies of the public Declaration to all his friends, taking care at the same time to forward copies of his original draft, so that they might be able to compare the two and note the differences.

The friends rose to the occasion and responded in terms calculated to soothe his wounded pride. Edmund Pendleton obliged with the remark that Congress had treated Jefferson's draft "as they did yr Manifestto last summer, altered it much for the worse. Their hopes of a reconciliation might restrain them from plain truths then, but what could cramp them now." [3]

Richard Henry Lee was even more obliging. "I wish sincerely," he declared, "as well for the honor of Congress, as for that of the States, that the Manuscript had not been mangled as it is. It is wonderful, and passing pitiful, that the rage of change should be so unhappily applied—However the *Thing* is in its nature so good, that no Cookery can spoil the Dish for the palates of Freemen." [4]

John Page, his boyhood friend, was not as tactful. He permitted himself unrestrained praise. "I am highly pleased with your Declaration—God preserve the united States—We know the Race is not to the swift nor the Battle to the strong—Do you not think an Angel rides in the Whirlwind & directs this Storm?" [5]

In reality the Declaration of Independence had been memorably improved by its ordeal in Congress. Offensive passages had been eliminated; the texture of the prose had been tightened and rambling passages made swift; certain historical inaccuracies, if not all, had been corrected; and, in general, it was a good editorial job well done.

Yet the fundamental text was Jefferson's, and the glory must immortally remain his. In later years, when vanity had cooled and more just appraisals were possible, Jefferson wrote down the Declaration of Independence as one of the three great achievements of his life by which he wished to be remembered to posterity.

He had other cause, however, during this period, for a sense of injury and an exacerbation of feelings. Virginia, his beloved country, seemed to have turned abruptly on her devoted son.

From the moment Jefferson heard that Virginia was framing a new form of government, his thoughts had turned toward Williamsburg and he increasingly resented his enforced presence in Philadelphia. As has already been pointed out, he conceived Congress as merely the obedient instrument of the colonies and the delegates in attendance as the transmitters of their will. Primary decisions were made in the local legislatures, and it was there that ample room existed for initiative, original planning and the remaking of the future. Even the assignment of the Declaration of Independence did not assuage his fundamental unease at being absent from the seat of power.

As early as the middle of May he had hinted to Nelson that he wished to be recalled in order to participate in the work at hand. The hint fell on stony ground. Because of his absence, he had not been able to influence to any marked degree the new constitution of his state; a document he considered far removed from his wishes in many respects. The foundations were being laid for a permanent Virginia, and he had no hand in their proper building. He might become, so he conceived, the forgotten man.

Accordingly, he determined to return to Virginia when his term of office expired, and wrote letters to his friends asking that he not be renominated for another term in Congress. One of these letters was addressed to his co-delegate to the Convention, Dr. George Gilmer.

But the affair was mismanaged. The first news that Jefferson received of what had taken place came in the form of a cryptic note from his friend and fellow delegate, William Fleming. "As some of your friends have, no doubt, given you a history of our late Election of delegates to serve in Congress, and of the spirit (evil spirit I had almost said) and general proceedings of our convention, I shall, for the present, forbear any animadversions thereon." [6]

This alarmingly obscure missive reached Jefferson on July 1st. He had *not* received any account of the proceedings from others, as Fleming had so easily assumed. What *had* come through was the bald report of the election vote for delegates to Congress and that, in conjunction with Fleming's dark intimations, was enough to harry Jefferson's soul. For the vote disclosed several disturbing things: the size of the delegation to Congress had been reduced from seven to five; Jefferson had been re-elected in spite of his expressed desire to the contrary; and, having been re-elected, he stood fourth in a list of five—indication of dissatisfaction or insult.

Disturbed, alarmed, and conjuring up dark visions of disaster to his political fortunes at home while he was helplessly away, Jefferson wrote immediately in return: "I wish you had depended on yourself rather than others for giving me an account of the late nomination of delegates. I have no other state of it but the number of votes for each person. The omission of Harrison and Braxton and my being next to the lag give me some alarm. It is a painful situation to be 300 miles from one's country, and thereby opened to secret assassination without a possibility of self-defence. I am willing to hope nothing of this kind has been done in my case, but yet I cannot be easy. If any doubts has arisen as to me, my country will have my political creed in the form of a 'Declaration' &c. which I was lately directed to draw. This will give decisive proof that my own sentiments concurred with the vote they instructed me to give." [7]

In a day or so, however, the delayed explanation came in a letter from Edmund Randolph, and Fleming hastened to amplify his cryptic remarks after receipt of Jefferson's agitated complaint.

Gilmer, it seemed, had been absent from the Convention on the day when the new delegates to Congress were being elected. Jefferson's formal request to Pendleton, its president, that he be not chosen, had not arrived until the day after the voting. Gilmer, unable to be present, had sent a memorandum to Randolph, asking him to place Jefferson's refusal before the members. "I urged it in decent Terms," Randolph explained, "but stirred up a Swarm of Wasps about my Ears, who seemed suspicious, that I designed to prejudice you. However, fortunately for my Credit, your

Letter to the President was yesterday read to the House, confirming, what I had asserted. Your Excuse was rejected, as made by me. Whether they will admit it, as now made by yourself, I know not. If they do, for God's sake, be with us quickly. Our Counsels want every Thing, to stamp Value on them." [8]

Fleming confirmed Randolph's account, adding details. Randolph's announcement had given rise to an extended debate, in which was maintained by some that Jefferson was merely "jesting" in his refusal, and by others that he was in earnest. When it came to the vote, "many of your warmest friends (myself among the rest) erased your name out of their ballots, taking it for granted that your services in congress were to be dispensed with. . . . Had it not been for these circumstances, I much doubt whether there would have been three votes against you." [9]

Jefferson's alarm at his status in Virginia was thus allayed, but the news only hardened his determination to return. In addition, he was, as always, anxious about the state of his wife's health.[10] She seems to have been frequently ailing, and a notably poor correspondent. Jefferson's letters to friends and relations in Virginia are full of complaints about her failure to write, in spite of appeals and solicitations.

Some time in July he sent a formal note of resignation to Pendleton, basing his desire on the situation of his domestic affairs, and asking that a substitute be sent to Congress at least by the end of the year.[11]

As the days rolled by, his impatience increased, especially as the reports he received of Martha's condition were not too favorable. To all and sundry, he announced his intention of quitting Philadelphia some time in August. To Richard Henry Lee, he wrote that he hoped his successor would come before that; "in that case, I shall hope to see you & Mr. Wythe in Convention, that the business of government, which is of everlasting concern, may receive your aid." [12]

By July 20th, as the news from Martha grew more ominous, it was with difficulty that he restrained himself from quitting incontinently. But only he and Carter Braxton remained of the entire Virginia delegation, and Braxton had already made plans to go home within two days. If Jefferson left also, Virginia would be wholly unrepresented and her vote lost.[13]

Indeed, the Convention itself was demanding his presence. Pendleton called for him to come. "I wish you could be here, if you could be Spared from Congress, indeed you must be Spared, to sustain one of the Important Posts in the Judiciary, where I most fear our deficiency, and conceive it to be of the greatest importance in the rearing our Commonwealth." In addition, "you are also wanting much in the Revision of our Laws & forming a new body, a necessary work for which few of us have adequate abilities & attention." [14]

Jefferson declined the judiciary appointment.[15] He was not interested in returning to the law, whether as practitioner or judge. And it would have meant his retirement from political affairs. He was, however, intensely concerned with the revision of Virginia's laws, and he was shortly to become one of the prime architects of that revision.

Meanwhile, he was compelled to possess his soul in patience in Philadelphia during the summer months. After the blaze of glory that had surrounded his production of the Declaration, there was a distinct letdown in the remainder of his sojourn in Congress. He was placed on several minor committees and dutifully drafted reports on such matters as terms of office for delegates to Congress (Jefferson proposed short terms and rotation); the preparation of a seal for the new United States (as far back as 1774 he thought of "the Father presenting the bundle of rods to his sons"; but now he suggested for one side, the children of Israel in the wilderness, led by a cloud by day and a pillar of fire by night; and on the other, Hengist and Horsa, his favorite Saxon heroes); gold and silver coins; Indian affairs and the post office.[16]

On only one matter was his ardor so intense that he was moved to rise from his seat in Congress and participate in the debate. This, as might be expected, related to Virginia's interests. It had been proposed, in the Articles of Confederation submitted to Congress, that the boundaries of the several colonies be fixed, and that their large inchoate claims to the western lands be turned over to the new Confederation for present disposition and eventual erection into independent states.

Jefferson had been prepared, when he drafted a constitution for Virginia, to lay out new colonies in her western domain and grant them independence of the mother colony; but he was not ready to turn that domain over to the unrestricted disposal of the Confederation. He feared that Congress, at the behest of some of the land-poor states, might curtail the westward expansion of settlers out of Virginia and their present settlements across the Alleghenies; and he raised his voice in protest against the power of Congress to sit in judgment on the rights of Virginia. Virginia, he argued, could be relied on to do the proper thing without outside intervention.[17]

It was due to the determined opposition of the Southern States that the proposition was dropped, and Jefferson took credit to himself for having a part in that opposition. His stand would on the surface seem contradictory to his later yeoman service in turning over the vast Northwest Territory to the United States. But he bottomed it on several leading ideas which were applicable at the time. It was intended, he thought, that Congress sell these lands to individual settlers and use the income to help pay the Continental debt. But he was unalterably opposed to selling the lands at all. They were free, and should remain free to all settlers. The newcomers would, in any event, have to assume their share of the debt load; why should they, by payment, take on an additional burden? He feared speculations and land grabs, if Congress became the disburser; he wanted the lands to be allotted to legitimate settlers in small parcels; and he believed that the several states would better protect their interests than the federal government.[18]

Meanwhile, Jefferson was getting desperate at his continued enforced stay in Philadelphia. By July 29th, he was truly frantic. He appealed to Lee, who was supposed to have relieved him: "For god's sake, for your country's sake, and for my sake, come. I receive by every post such accounts of the state of Mrs. Jefferson's health that it will be impossible for me to disappoint her expectation of seeing me at the time I have promised, which supposed my leaving this place on the 11th. of next month." As if this were not urgent enough, he added a postscript: "I pray you to come. I am under a sacred obligation to go home." [19]

But Lee was unable to come until at least the 20th.[20]

During this trying period Jefferson was watching the course of war with keen and anxious interest. The Canadian expedition had been a disaster, and the news from New York and the Jerseys was ominous. To meet the impending threat of Lord Howe's powerful armament against New York, Congress had called two battalions of Virginia troops to the north. The Virginia Council protested the transfer, and Jefferson rapped them sharply across the knuckles. "Other colonies of not more than half their military strength have 20 battalions in the field," he pointed out. "Think of these things & endeavor to reconcile them not only to this, but to yield greater assistance to the common cause if wanted. I wish every battalion we have was now in New York." [21]

All through the war the reluctance of the various states to permit their troops to be employed in theaters of war distant from their own borders gravely hampered operations. Time and again Washington, Greene, von Steuben and other generals found their best-laid plans gone awry because state contingents on which they had counted were refused or, when granted, never showed up at the appointed time and place. Jefferson fought mightily against this local particularism when Governor; but only too often his own state failed to back up his attempts to get desperately needed troops to outside theaters of war.

In this particular instance, Virginia's excuse was that the Indians on her own borders had commenced war upon the outlying settlements. But Jefferson insisted that the local militia was ample to take care of these incursions and even to pursue the marauders into their own country. There were times when he could be vindictive and this was one of them. "Nothing will reduce those wretches so soon," he exclaimed to Page, "as pushing the war into the heart of their country. But I would not stop there. I would never cease pursuing them while one of them remained on this side the Mississippi. So unprovoked an attack & so treacherous a one should never be forgiven while one of them remains near enough to do us injury." [22]

At length the long-awaited day arrived. His new term of office as member to Congress had commenced on August 11th, but he quit before he served a bare three weeks of it. Back home, his own Albemarle constituents had re-elected him to the Virginia Convention and he wanted to be present at its opening in October. "I knew that our legislation under the regal government had many very vicious points which urgently required reformation," he wrote much later, "and I thought I could be of more use in forwarding that work." [23]

Toward the end of August, he busied himself in settling his affairs and accounts in Philadelphia. He purchased some hats, new guitar strings, turned over to John Hancock $98 which Virginia had collected for the poor of Boston and, on September 1, 1776, took horse for Monticello.[24]

On September 9th he was home. Home! All through his life that word held passionate meaning for Jefferson. Whether war engulfed the nation, or political battles equally convulsed, his thoughts ever turned eagerly to his haven on the mount, where he could withdraw "from the noise and bustle of the world," and follow those domestic, intellectual and scientific pursuits for which he panted.

Now, for a brief halcyon spell, he could relax, Just what his wife's continued illness was, is not known. It could not have been too serious, for, after paying twenty shillings on October 1st to Dr. Brydon for a professional visit, he was able to take her with him on October 6th to Williamsburg to attend the opening session of the Virginia Assembly.

In the meantime, just as though war and politics were far removed, he busied himself with barometric observations of the surrounding terrain. On September 15th, he calculated the height of Monticello above the Tobacco Landing at the river as 512.17 feet, and similarly measured the height of Montalto, the neighboring mountain.[25]

He had barely reached Williamsburg when an express from Congress announced his appointment on September 26th as a Commissioner to France, in conjunction with Benjamin Franklin and Silas Deane.[26]

The commission was one of the greatest importance; no less, indeed, than to negotiate a treaty of alliance against England. Richard Henry Lee, who had returned to Congress so that Jefferson might leave, wrote privately urging him to accept. "In my judgement, the most eminent services that the greatest of her sons can do America, will not more essentially serve her and honor themselves, than a successful negotiation with France." [27]

Jefferson was faced with a dilemma. There was no question of the importance of the mission or of the honor that would accrue to him from its fulfillment. But it meant a stay of at least a year or more abroad; and again he would be parted from family and Monticello, and from the basic construction of a new Virginia.

For three days, while the messenger cooled his heels and waited, Jefferson wrestled with his conscience. Then, apologetically, he dispatched his refusal to Philadelphia, and Arthur Lee was appointed in his stead. He excused himself on the ground "that the state of his family will not permit him to accept." [28]

Richard Henry Lee did not think the excuse sufficient, and read him a sharp lesson on the ethics of his stand. "No Man feels more deeply than I do," he exclaimed, "the love of, and the loss of, private enjoyments; but let attention to these be universal, and we are gone, beyond redemption lost in the deep perdition of slavery." [29]

But Jefferson remained immovable. He had other axes to grind which, perhaps, he was not willing to avow to Lee.

Jefferson first took up quarters, at Wythe's invitation, in the latter's residence facing the Palace Green. On December 2nd, he moved his family to Pinkney's establishment, where he occupied two rooms. No rent had been agreed on in advance, but Jefferson thought that since Pinkney was paying £25 for the whole house, if he gave him half of that, "it will be a plenty." [30]

The Assembly opened its doors on October 7, 1776, and Jefferson was promptly in his seat. After the usual organizational problems were out of the way, which included the election of the perennial Pendleton as Speaker and the choice of Benjamin Harrison to fill Jefferson's vacant position in Congress, the Assembly got down to work.

Jefferson had prepared himself with a comprehensive and revolutionary plan for the remodeling of the goverment and for the revision of its social, religious, political and legal institutions. For years he had pondered the inequities and abuses which existed in his beloved "country," and he was determined to refashion it nearer to his heart's desire. Now, if ever, was the time to do so, while Virginia was still in flux, and the revolutionary ardor which animated its leaders and population in throwing off the political yoke of England might be harnessed to the even more fundamental job of overthrowing the outworn and outmoded institutions which, like incubi, had weighted down and oppressed the people.

As a true child of the Enlightenment he was deeply concerned with human rights and their vigorous operation and growth, unhampered by governmental interference. The people—and by that term it must be remembered that he had in mind chiefly a sturdy yeomanry of small, landowning farmers—could flourish best without outside restrictions on thought or deed. That government governed best, he always held, which governed least.

In Virginia, however, the restrictions were numerous and, to his mind, barbarous and symptomatic of an ancient tyranny. The nature of landholding, in particular, excited his wrath. The system of entails, which restricted the free dispositions of land, and the laws of primogeniture, which tended to create an aristocracy and a host of dispossessed younger sons, were feudal in concept and practice and stemmed, according to him, from that fountainhead of all abuses, the Norman conquest of England.[31]

His second great passion related to freedom of religion and the complete independence from each other of Church and State. Religion was the sole concern of the individual and his conscience, and no concern of the State. He himself was no believer in the supernatural aspects of Christianity, and he sought for others that right of dissent from the formal tenets of any revealed religion which he claimed for himself. He held compulsory attendance on an Established Church and enforced support of its institutions by law to be an outrageous spiritual tyranny and an economic disaster. They were the products of the ingenious machinations of kings and priests who thereby sought to cement their tyrannical overlordship and the pretended divinity of their rule.[32]

The third great head of his program involved a complete and thoroughgoing revision of the laws of Virginia. As a student of law he had observed numerous cruelties and inequities, as well as the confused jargon of the current legal system. This he considered in urgent need of reformation, both because it stemmed from a monarchical system and was therefore not adapted to a republican form of government, and because it represented a barbarous and savage code that was sadly out of line with modern, progressive criminology.

Included in his scheme of revision were proposals for revamping the educational system of the state. Only through proper education, he was profoundly convinced, could the people be qualified to understand their rights, to maintain them, and to exercise with intelligence their parts in self-government.[33] If any passion became his overmastering one, it was this, and the last years of his life were devoted to making his dream of an informed and rational electorate a reality.

The fourth section of his program occupied at the moment a comparatively minor place in his thinking. Since the institution of slavery in all its phases was repugnant to him, he hoped some day that Virginia might point the way to a gradual emancipation; though he acknowledged that for the present there were almost insuperable difficulties in the way. But, at least, some modifications might be introduced that would eventually lead to the abolition of the evil.

These four prongs of a comprehensive program—though the item of slavery might not, perhaps, be considered as such for the time being—would, in his estimation, form a system "by which every fibre would be eradicated of ancient or future aristocracy; and a foundation laid for a government truly republican."[34]

Jefferson was taking the eloquent words of his Declaration of Independence as a practical guide to action. Theoretical considerations had no value to him except insofar as they furnished such a guide.

Collection of Mrs. Page Kirk. Courtesy the Frick Art Reference Library

EDMUND RANDOLPH

Painting by J. A. Elder

Collection of the Old South Meeting House Association.
Courtesy the Frick Art Reference Library

GOUVERNEUR MORRIS

American School

Jefferson found the new House divided into bitter and opposing factions. The first families of Virginia had bitterly resented Richard Henry Lee's exposure of their complicity in the tangled accounts of the former treasurer, John Robinson, and they were determined to break his influence. Benjamin Harrison was their instrument, and because of their mutual feud Jefferson had been given the opportunity of drafting the Declaration of Independence.

But Lee, returning to Virginia, had rallied his cohorts and succeeded in retiring Harrison and Braxton, another of the planter party, from the halls of Congress. In the process, Jefferson almost went by the board as well.

It must not be considered, however, that the sole reason for the dangerous feud was the Robinson affair. Now that Patrick Henry had, as it were, retired from the fray to the governorship, Lee was the head and front of the radical party in Virginia. Opposed to him and all he stood for was the aristocracy of the Tidewater, who considered him a leveler and a would-be disrupter of the social and political scheme of things that had given them security and power. Their leaders were Edmund Pendleton, Robert Carter Nicholas, Benjamin Harrison, Landon Carter, Mann Page, Carter Braxton and others.

Strangely enough, Jefferson, at least as radical as Lee and far more dangerous to the entrenched Tidewater aristocracy, was personally on as good terms with the members of the right as with the members of the left. He had cordial friends in both camps, Certainly, his relations with Pendleton and Wythe were closer and more enduring than those with Lee and Patrick Henry, the firebrands of his own group.

The reasons for his ability to move at will among all parties were several. In the first place, he had not been involved in the personal feuds and financial machinations of the times. In the second place, the lines of party were still not clear-cut: men voted as individuals and not by caucus; and some of Jefferson's most thoroughgoing measures received valiant support from those who vehemently opposed the rest. And, thirdly, Jefferson seems at this time to have been possessed of a degree of tact and moderation in epithet which would have stood him in good stead had he still possessed them during the great debate with Hamilton and the later struggles with the Federalists.

On October 11, 1776, four days after the session opened, Jefferson moved for leave to bring in the first of his bills—the establishment of courts of justice. The leave was granted and he was appointed chairman of a committee to draft the bill.[35]

On the surface this appeared noncontroversial. The system of courts had been disrupted by the Revolution and it was vital to get the wheels of justice moving again. But it was not as simple as it seemed. The House divided the bill into five parts, corresponding to five kinds of courts. On

November 25th, Jefferson brought in three, setting up Courts of Appeals, Chancery and Assize; on December 4th, he brought in two more—Admiralty and County.

The bill for the Admiralty Court was passed without difficulty—its advantages were immediate and obvious. Thereby, captured enemy ships could be brought into Virginia ports and sold as prizes. But the establishment of the other courts, essential though they were to the regular processes of law and order, commerce and the daily transactions of life, were bitterly opposed. The motives which underlay this surprising opposition were the same that haunted the internal and external relations of the several states and the United States for many years to come—the unwillingness or inability of the debtor class to meet its obligations under disadvantageous circumstances. Once the regular courts were established, the instrumentalities of the law could be invoked by creditors; and the planters, the chief debtors, were without funds. Their money crop, tobacco, had practically no market.

As a result, the four bills were laid over. Regular courts were not finally established until the end of the following year and, in the case of the Court of Appeals, not for two years.[36]

On the day after he brought in his court bill, Jefferson launched the first of his major assaults on the ancient regime—a request for leave to bring in a bill "to enable tenants in taille to convey their lands in fee simple." And, as if this revolutionary attack on the fundamental base for an aristocracy were not sufficient for a day, he followed it immediately with a demand for a complete and drastic revision of the laws of Virginia.[37]

Just as though they were routine measures, the House granted leave and the usual committees were appointed to draft the bills. But this time Jefferson, though made a member of both committees, was not given the chairmanships. They went to Richard Bland as perhaps a moderating influence.

If that was the intention, the stratagem did not succeed, for Bland permitted Jefferson to draft and present the bill on entails to the House on October 14th.[38]

The system of entailing lands was the true cornerstone of any aristocracy. By proper legal provision, the foresighted founder of a family could limit in perpetuity the distribution of the lands to which the entail was attached. They could neither be sold nor seized for debt; they must descend from generation to generation to the heir or heirs specified in the original entailment—usually, the eldest son. There could be no dissipation among a number of children, nor loss by reckless or wasteful possessors. The real title was in the biological family, and not in the temporary individual. As a result, wealth, power and influence accreted through the years. In Virginia, slaves too might be entailed and they and their increase passed on from heir to heir.

To Jefferson, this feudal method of holding land represented everything that he hated. Whatever might have been the reason for its existence in England, it had no place in America. He conceived of the New World as a land of fluidity and boundless opportunities, where energy and merit could find their just rewards and not be hampered by the rigid mold of mortmain, the dead hand of earlier individuals who had procured large grants of land for little or nothing. It meant an ultimate aristocracy with its corollary, a monarch, and the death of the egalitarian principles that were so deeply imbedded in his thought. By abolishing entails, by permitting the unrestricted sale, disposition and division of land in fee simple, he considered that he was laying the ax to the roots from which an aristocracy of wealth and power inevitably sprang, and was truly ensuring the birth of a new aristocracy based on virtue and talents—qualities that could not be hoarded in any one family or transmitted by legal fiat.[39] The wonder is that Jefferson effectuated this radical revision of the social and economic base for Virginian life as quickly as he did.

The chief of the opposition was Edmund Pendleton, to whom Jefferson later gave the accolade of being "the ablest man in debate I have ever met with." His speech was lofty, yet persuasive; he was quick, acute and resourceful; and he never admitted defeat. When overwhelmed on the main issue, he maneuvered to such advantage and nibbled away in such persevering detail that sometimes he regained important sectors of the ground he had seemingly lost. Yet, even in the heat of bitter debate, he managed to keep it on an intellectual level and to hold the firm friendship of his opponents. Such was Jefferson's admiring estimate of Pendleton in later years.[40]

In spite of Pendleton's maneuvering and crippling amendments—one came within a bare few votes of passage—the bill passed the House on October 23rd, was approved in the Senate on November 1st, and became the law of the land. Virginia became the first of the states to abolish entails; in some, indeed, the system lingered on into the nineteenth century.

There were several reasons for the speed and comparative ease with which this fundamental change in the methods of land ownership went through the Assembly. Not all lands, even among the so-called aristocracy, were entailed. Jefferson's, for example, were not. It was possible to get rid of an entail by obtaining a special act of the Assembly. This had become an increasingly prevalent practice—Jefferson had obtained such a release on behalf of certain lands belonging to his wife—though it was expensive and time-consuming. At this particular period, too, when money was scarce and credit difficult to get, many of the aristocracy welcomed the chance to dispose of their estates as they wished and without archaic hindrances.

One recalcitrant aristocrat, however, invoked the curses of posterity on those responsible for the abolition of entails and, rather incoherently, likened "the famous T. J——n!" to a "mid-day" drunkard who dared take from his neighbor "his will and pleasure in giving his own property away." [41] But this was a solitary ebullition in an otherwise rippleless stream.

CHAPTER 12

Shackles from the Mind

THE second bill proposed on that notable day of October 12, 1776, was for a thorough revision and codification of the laws of Virginia. Inasmuch as the bill merely called for the appointment of revisors to consider the vast subject and bring in a report on which further action might be based, it had no difficulty in passing both the House and Senate.[1]

On November 5th, a committee of revisors was accordingly selected. It consisted of Thomas Jefferson, chairman, Edmund Pendleton, George Wythe, George Mason and Thomas Ludwell Lee. It was a strong group, comprising some of the best and most acute minds to be found in all Virginia.

The act calling for revision alleged that the change in government required corresponding changes in the laws "heretofore in force, many of which are inapplicable to the powers of government as now organized, others are founded on principles heterogeneous to the republican spirit, others which, long before such change, had been oppressive to the people, could yet never be repealed while the regal power continued," and that new laws, "friendly to liberty and the rights of mankind," ought to be adopted in their stead.[2]

It was a large order, and perhaps not all the legislators who voted for it knew exactly what it entailed. But Jefferson knew.

While sitting through the long sessions of Congress in Philadelphia, Jefferson had been giving this problem much earnest thought. He was persuaded then, he related in his Autobiography, that "our whole code must be reviewed, adapted to our republican form of government; and, now that we had no negatives of Councils, Governors, and Kings to restrain us from doing right, that it should be corrected, in all its parts, with a single eye to reason, and the good of those for whose government it was framed."[3]

Two leading principles governed Jefferson in rearing a new legal structure. The first was that there should be a minimum of laws, and he quoted approvingly, in support, the dictum of Tacitus that the more corrupt the commonwealth, the greater the number of its laws. The second called for terseness, simplicity and such plainness that the ordinary layman could understand and plead his own case in court without the help of any counsel.[4]

It was January 13, 1777, before the committee met at Fredericksburg to consider the procedures they were to follow in the gigantic task before them.

The first question to be decided was whether they should scrap the entire legal system as it then existed and start *de novo*, or merely modify and adapt that system to current needs. On this fundamental question there was a surprising division of opinion. Pendleton, the conservative, argued for a total fresh start; and Thomas Ludwell Lee joined with him. Wythe, Mason and Jefferson, on the other hand, objected that this was too bold a project and went far beyond what the legislature had intended. Furthermore, the rearing of such a code, similar in structure and extent to Justinian, Bracton or Blackstone, was too vast and arduous and would, by virtue of its lack of precedent and expounded interpretation, become the subject of ages of litigation and uncertainty before a new body of adjudications was built up. Therefore they plumped for mere modification and revision.[5]

The arguments of the majority were sensible and prevailed. The next step was to apportion the work. George Mason declined to take a share on the ground that he was no lawyer, and later resigned from the committee. Lee offered the same excuse, and his participation ended shortly thereafter with his death. That left the whole burden on Pendleton, Wythe and Jefferson.

Jefferson took for his particular province the common law and appropriate statutes of Great Britain up to the time that the Virginia legislature was separately established; Wythe undertook the British statutes from the Virginia establishment to the date of separation; and Pendleton was assigned the laws of Virginia itself. All of these, naturally, had made up the corpus of Virginia law until the Revolution.

Since the common law thus became Jefferson's peculiar domain—and therefore the laws governing real property, inheritance, and criminal procedures—he proposed certain principles concerning them to his coadjutors.

For one thing, he proposed the abolition of the law of primogeniture—whereby real property not specifically devised by will went to the eldest son—and instead, to permit its distribution on the same terms as personalty among the next of kin. This was a logical addendum to the removal of entails.

Pendleton, as was to be expected, objected. On being overruled by Wythe and Jefferson, he suggested that at least a double portion go to the eldest son. To which Jefferson sardonically observed that such a double share depended on no natural fact, unless it could be proved that the eldest was able to eat twice as much or work twice as hard as his younger brothers and sisters.[6]

As for the criminal law, all were agreed that the death penalty should be abolished, except in cases of treason and murder. For all other felonies, hard labor on public works was to be substituted. In some cases, however, the *lex talionis*—the eye for an eye, tooth for a tooth principle—was to apply. In his Autobiography, Jefferson expressed wonder and forgetfulness at how "this last revolting principle came to obtain our approbation." And though he obediently placed in the code such punishments for rape and sodomy as castration for male offenders and nose-boring for female, for maiming of another a similar maiming to the guilty party, he nevertheless wrote to Wythe: "I have strictly observed the scale of punishments settled by the Committee, without being entirely satisfied with it. The *Lex Talionis,* although a restitution of the Common law, to the simplicity of which we have generally found it so advantageous to return, will be revolting to the humanized feelings of modern times.... This needs reconsideration."[7]

It was not reconsidered, and the whole question of responsibility for the inclusion of the *lex talionis* is a puzzling one. Probably the suggestion came originally from Pendleton. While Jefferson was still in Congress there had been some correspondence between them on the subject of crimes and punishments. Replying to a letter from Jefferson which, unfortunately, seems to have disappeared, Pendleton had retorted: "I don't know how far you may extend your reformation as to our Criminal System of Laws. That it has been too sanguinary, punishing too many crimes with death, I confess, & could wish to see that changed for some other mode of Punishment in most cases; but if you mean to relax all punishments, and rely on Virtue & the Public Good as sufficient to prompt Obedience to the Laws, you must find a new race of men to be the Subjects of it, but this I dare say was not your meaning. However I have heard it insisted on by others."[8]

Doubtless Jefferson had been advocating the advanced penal system of the Italian penologist Beccaria, whose works had long been his Bible in the field and from which he had copied such copious extracts in his commonplace book.[9]

But, strangely enough, on receiving Pendleton's realistic response, Jefferson assented to the infliction of that very *lex talionis* at which, in retrospect, he wondered so audibly. Rape and buggery, he agreed then, should be punished by castration. Murder and treason deserved death; all other crimes terms at hard labor. Slaves found guilty of any offense were to be sold into slavery in foreign lands.[10]

After the allocation of their respective parts and agreement on moot points, the three men departed from Fredericksburg for their homes and commenced their laborious task.

With his law books and volumes of British statutes spread out around him, Jefferson settled down to work. The entire job, with normal interruptions, occupied him almost two years. He was much taken with the simplicity of the ancient statutes, and was careful not to modernize their language or attempt new turns of expression, for fear that the changes would create new doubts in cases where adjudications had long been settled. But the later British statutes and the acts of the Virginia Assembly were another matter. They had achieved a verboseness, a complication of parenthesis within parenthesis, tautologies and endless *whereases* and *aforesaids* as to make them the despair, not merely of the layman, but of the lawyer himself. Here he pruned and simplified ruthlessly.[11]

When Jefferson came to draft his new bill for "proportioning crimes and punishments in cases heretofore capital," the principles which guided him are best expressed in his own language. "In its style, I have aimed at accuracy, brevity, and simplicity, preserving, however, the very words of the established law, wherever their meaning had been sanctioned by judicial decisions, or rendered technical by usage. The same matter, if couched in the modern statutory language, with all its tautologies, redundancies, and circumlocutions, would have spread itself over many pages, and been unintelligible to those whom it most concerns. Indeed, I wished to exhibit a sample of reformation in the barbarous style into which modern statutes have degenerated from their ancient simplicity."[12]

Jefferson, unfortunately, was unable to initiate the reformation he hoped for, as a moment's glance at current statutes and administrative rulings will make immediately plain.

The bill for proportioning crimes and punishments was Jefferson's most extensive contribution to the revisions and, indeed, constituted his *opus magnum* in the field. The number of capital crimes in Virginia, based on rigorous British law, was appalling. Already humane voices had been raised against the infliction of the death penalty in so many instances, and enlightened penologists like Beccaria had justified mitigation by arguments against its effectiveness as a deterrent to crime.

Jefferson substituted hard labor for hanging in all cases except murder and treason. Nevertheless, he listed a fatal duel as murder, and provided for gibbeting of the challenger. The cruel punishments for rape and buggery have already been mentioned, and Jefferson included deliberate polygamy in this category of crimes. Reluctantly, as we have seen, he decreed the retaliation of the eye for an eye, nose for a nose, etc., in maimings. The "pretended arts of witchcraft, conjuration, enchantment, or sorcery, or by pretended prophecies, shall be punished by ducking and whipping, at the discretion of a jury, not exceeding fifteen stripes." All other crimes, hitherto punishable by death or otherwise, were to be penalized by varying terms of labor on public works.[13]

This bill was considered by the Virginia lawmakers, when they finally got around to it, as too advanced and too lenient to lawbreakers; and it was lost by a single vote. But Jefferson, by that time, had changed his own views as to the efficacy of hard labor on public works. Pennsylvania had tried the scheme, and the spectacle of shaven criminals at work, subject to the jeers and taunts of the spectators, convinced the reformers that, instead of reformation, the exhibited criminals hardened into depravity and corruption.[14]

The labor of revision took over two years for completion and resulted in one hundred and twenty-six bills. Meeting again in Williamsburg in February, 1779, the three revisors ironed out their several difficulties and divergences of opinion. On June 18, 1779, they submitted their report to the Assembly.[15]

The Assembly never considered the Report of the Revisors as a whole. Instead, special bills were taken out of it at intervals and debated. Indeed, at the time of its submission, important sections were already under advisement. But the unified code that Jefferson and his co-workers had contemplated was never put into effect. It became, rather, what Madison late in life called "a mine of Legislative wealth," into which the Assembly dipped from time to time to extract nuggets for enactment or refusal.[16]

By 1786, fifty-six of the original one hundred and twenty-six bills, with varying amendments, were finally made into law. One of these was the bill for the abolition of primogeniture, drafted by Jefferson after Pendleton's reluctant acquiescence. This bill, together with the repeal of entails and the acts for religious freedom and the diffusion of knowledge, were considered by Jefferson as four great weapons in the fight against the old aristocracy and the prevention of any further revival.

The problem of slavery and its material and moral defects had exercised Jefferson's conscience for a long time. While acknowledging that complete abolition was impossible for the present, he sought at least to prevent the increase of the evil. One of his bitterest arraignments of the English king had been provoked by the latter's veto of local attempts to prohibit the further importation of slaves. Now that Virginia was free, Jefferson hastened to promulgate a code that would not only prevent importation from abroad, but from sister states as well. Nevertheless, in conformity with his settled conviction that the white and black races could not live together in a state of freedom, he insisted that those Negroes who gained their liberty by operation of the laws, emancipation or otherwise must, within a specified period, depart the state or lose their new-found liberty. Similarly, a white woman with child by a Negro or mulatto must depart the commonwealth or be bound out to service.[17]

But this was merely a digest of laws already in existence or previously annulled by royal veto. The revisors agreed after considerable discussion that nothing more drastic could be attempted at the moment. While they were convinced that gradual emancipation was the ideal and its principles were agreed on—freedom to all Negro children born after a definite date, and deportation from the state on reaching maturity—it was deemed better to defer that violently controversial issue until the bill reached the House and then propose it in the form of amendments from the floor.

Nothing came of the scheme, either then or later, because, as Jefferson put it, "the public mind would not yet bear the proposition, nor will it bear it even at this day." Confronted, when he wrote these lines as an old man, with the echoing repercussions of intersectional strife, he penned an eloquent warning to his countrymen: "Yet the day is not distant when it must bear and adopt [emancipation], or worse will follow. Nothing is more certainly written in the book of fate, than that these people are to be free; nor is it less certain that the two races, equally free, cannot live in the same government. Nature, habit, opinion have drawn indelible lines of distinction between them. It is still in our power to direct the process of emancipation and deportation, peaceably, and in such slow degree, as that the evil will wear off insensibly, and their place be, *pari passu*, filled up by free white laborers. If, on the contrary, it is left to force itself on, human nature must shudder at the prospect held up." [18] He never deviated from this solution—emancipation and deportation.

The great bills, however, which Jefferson drafted for incorporation into the fundamental law of Virginia were two in number—the bill "for establishing religious freedom" and the bill "for the more general diffusion of knowledge." The first became law after an epic struggle and many vicissitudes; the second never achieved success.

It is in the architecture of these two bills that Jefferson is at his happiest and appears most congenial to modern eyes. It is here that he takes his rightful position with the great liberating influences of all time. His activities toward the abolition of entails and primogeniture, which he erected into equal pillars with the statute for religious freedom and the Declaration of Independence, while meritorious, fall far below them in primary importance. These were relics of an ancient feudal system that were alien to the boundless American scene and already were tottering. Sooner or later they would have collapsed of their own weight—even in Virginia they were already riddled with loopholes and easy of evasion. Jefferson merely hastened their inevitable demise.

But the theory and practice of unchallenged religious freedom and of universal and unfettered education were neither inevitable nor, as of today, honored in the practice as completely as in the theory. Particularly in the field of religion it requires no great stretch of the imagination to surmise that, without the herculean efforts of Jefferson and his valiant co-workers, the course of American history in this respect might well have been different. The passions of sects are easily aroused, and tend to be illiberal toward differing beliefs. Those who occupy the seats of influence and are in possession of vested powers, do not voluntarily make the gesture of refusal or permit minorities to escape lightly from their control.

The idea that religion was a private affair had rarely penetrated into the consciousness of man. Just as men were organized into a civil polity for purposes of material government, so it was deemed necessary for them to be organized into a spiritual polity for the better government of their souls. The single problem to be decided was which should govern the other—State or Church?

That problem had been finally settled in England in favor of the State. The Church of England became the official arm of the State of England, and its tenets, dogmas and hierarchical organization officially prescribed. In return for such subordination, the Church received vast privileges. Disobedience to its doctrines became disobedience to the State. Dissenters could be prosecuted by the civil arm and compulsory attendance enforced. Its perquisites and fees, its salaries and cost of operation, were the responsibility of the State and provided for by tithes and taxes, payable by the entire population—communicants, dissenters and nonbelievers alike.

It was inevitable, therefore, that the first colonists in America brought with them these accustomed attitudes toward the relation of Church and State. The institutions and beliefs to which they had subscribed at home were transplanted with only minor modifications to the new world. The settlers in Virginia and the Carolinas were communicants of the Church of England and that Church therefore became the legal establishment. In New England they were chiefly Calvinist, and the frame of government reflected the theocratic dogmas of the founder. Only in Rhode Island, under the initial impulse of Roger Williams, was the peculiar doctrine promulgated that religion was a matter of man's individual conscience, and no concern of the State. The heresy did not last long; within a short period Rhode Island joined her sister colonies in imposing a religious frame of reference upon her inhabitants.[19]

Issue became joined in Virginia with the advent of dissenters from the Church of England. Fleeing the mother country because of persecution for their beliefs, the Quakers, Presbyterians, Methodists and Baptists found similar persecutions in their new home of Virginia. Later, when the Ulster Irish and Germans came in large numbers, chiefly to the Piedmont and the western borders, the situation became exacerbated.

Harshly persecuted at first for their beliefs, their growing numbers achieved in time a certain degree of tolerance. But tithes and taxes continued to be levied on them for the support of the Established Church, and onerous restrictions—civil, political and religious—still burdened their existence. At every session of the Assembly their clamors and complaints rose in steady crescendo.

Something of Jefferson's private religious convictions has already been indicated. Though formally a communicant of the Church of England, his readings in history and in the seventeenth and eighteenth century philosophers, together with his own meditations, had created in him a sceptical attitude toward revealed religion and a disbelief in all clerical establishments and their hierarchical pretensions. The relations of man to God and the universe were strictly the affair of the individual conscience, and neither State nor organized Church had a right to intervene.

"The error seems not sufficiently eradicated," he wrote eloquently in his *Notes on Virginia*, "that the operations of the mind, as well as the acts of the body, are subject to the coercion of the laws. But our rulers can have authority over such natural rights, only as we have submitted to them. The rights of conscience we never submitted, we could not submit. We are answerable for them to our God. The legitimate powers of government extend to such acts only as are injurious to others. But it does me no injury for my neighbor to say there are twenty gods, or no god. It neither picks my pocket nor breaks my leg.... Reason and free inquiry are the only effectual agents against error.... Had not the Roman government permitted free inquiry, christianity could never have been introduced. Had not free inquiry been indulged, at the aera of the reformation, the corruptions of christianity could not have been purged away. If it be restrained now, the present corruptions will be protected, and new ones encouraged. ... It is error alone which needs the support of government. Truth can stand by itself." [20]

These pronouncements, though some of them are historically arguable, represented his deepest and most steadfast convictions; and later became the basis for the most violent attacks against his person and his public position, even by those who now received the greatest benefits from their promulgation.

The Revolution presented a heaven-sent opportunity to the dissenting sects. Their members were overwhelmingly Whig in politics and ardent in rebellion. The Tories and the Loyalists stemmed just as overwhelmingly from the ranks of the Established Church. To the patriots, all of England's institutions had become suspect; and one of the many complaints against the king had been the disallowance of the Virginia law which sought to fix a different base for the salaries of the Anglican ministers. The clergy itself had lost in prestige and respect through the dilatoriness and inattention to their duties of many of its constituents. Now, if ever, was the time to change the entire system.

The Bill of Rights drafted by George Mason had been the opening gun in the struggle. Yet, though asserting the important general principle of freedom of religious thought and its exercise, it neither affected the regular establishment of the Anglican Church nor freed dissenters from the obligation to contribute to its support. That issue was now joined.

The new Assembly had barely commenced its proceedings when it was confronted with a flood of petitions from various dissenting groups clamoring for relief. On October 11, 1776, the Assembly appointed a Committee on Religion "to take under their consideration all matters and things relating to religion and morality." It was a large committee; on its roster were Thomas Jefferson, Carter Braxton, Richard Lee, Richard Bland, William Fleming, Mann Page, Robert Carter Nicholas and others.[21] It was a true mingling of liberals and conservatives; if anything, the conservatives were in the majority.

On the same day that the committee was appointed, the first of the petitions was submitted. Coming from Prince Edward County it was radical and thoroughgoing in its demands. Hailing the Bill of Rights as "the rising sun of Religious liberty, to relieve them from a long night of Ecclesiastical bondage," it requested the House "to complete what is so nobly begun," and insisted that, "without delay, all Church establishments might be pulled down, and every tax upon conscience and private judgment abolished." [22]

This was but the beginning of the flood. Similar petitions, in almost similar language, poured in from the dissenters of Albemarle, Amherst and Buckingham counties, from a German congregation of Culpepper, from the Presbytery of Hanover, and elsewhere. All were referred to the Committee on Religion.

In great alarm, the clergy of the Established Church countered with a mournful and somewhat agitated plea. To the petitions which sought to abolish establishment, they argued their own vested interest in its continuance. When they had accepted the charge of their parishes, they declared, "they depended on the publick faith for the receiving that recompense for their services, during life... which the laws of the land promised, a tenure which to them appears of the same sacred nature as that by which every man in the State holds, and has secured to him, his private property... that from the nature of their education they are precluded from gaining a tolerable subsistence in any other mode of life." [23] There is an element of the pathetic in the language of this memorial. Seemingly unaware of the larger issues involved, the clergy shrank affrighted from the loss of their perquisites. They realized only too well that no such burning faith infused their congregations as would yield them voluntarily the style of living to which they were accustomed,

Nor were the dissenters immune from economic preoccupations. While all joined joyfully in the demand that the Church of England be dethroned from its predominant position, not all agreed on the theory of disestablishment. Some of them, indeed, demanded *multiple* establishments—in which, naturally, their own church would be included—and the use of the power of the State to compel the communicants of each adequately to support, through tithes and taxes, the church of which they were members; or, better still, a general collection by the State and due allocation to the respective churches.

Though the committee which considered these petitions was large and representative—nineteen in number—the tidal wave of them and the passions which they aroused caused the Assembly on November 6th to agree that *any* interested member of the House might sit and vote on the committee and, on November 9th, to throw the whole matter into the House as a Committee of the Whole.[24]

After a bitter and desperate contest, which Jefferson afterward declared the most severe in which he had ever been engaged, the House resolved to repeal all acts of Parliament which had made criminal offenses of dissenting religious opinions, failure to attend the Established Church, and the exercise of different modes of worship. It was also decided to exempt dissenters from enforced contributions to the Established Church; and it was agreed, as a temporary war measure, to suspend the compulsory support of that Church by its own members.[25]

There was immediate agitation, in view of these developments, to create a *general* assessment, to be distributed to all designated churches; and a counteragitation to leave every religious society to the voluntary contributions of its own members. Pendleton and Nicholas, who had been the pillars of the opposition to any form of disestablishment, now argued for the former; Jefferson and Madison for the latter. In the end, it was agreed to reserve this most controversial of issues for future determination.[26]

Jefferson was placed on the committee to bring in the requisite bills, but it was Starke, the chairman, who actually brought them in. The debate went on for days, centering chiefly around the bill providing exemption for dissenters from the necessity of supporting the Anglican Church, and finally, on December 5th, it was passed. On December 9th, the Senate agreed to it with immaterial amendments and, the House concurring, it became law.[27]

Nothing in the record discloses what part Jefferson took in these vital proceedings, except for his membership on the various committees which handled the problem. But there is no doubt that it was considerable. There is in existence a series of notes and heads of arguments on the general subject which probably served him as ammunition in the debates. "Each church is to itself orthodox," he jotted down; "to *others* erroneous or heretical. . . . Truth will do well enough if left to shift for herself. She seldom has received much aid from the power of great men to whom she is rarely known & seldom welcome. She has no need of force to procure entrance into the minds of men. . . . Why have [Christians] been distinguished above all people who have ever lived, for persecutions? Is it because it is the genius of their religion? No, its genius is the reverse."[28]

The battle had been hard, but the gains achieved were enormous, even though Jefferson at the time and later expressed his disappointment at the compromises which the radicals were forced to accept. Certainly, the problem of *total* disestablishment and the concomitant separation of Church and State had been relegated to the future. But freedom of worship had been established, nonmembers of the Church of England were relieved of the burden of supporting a church in whose doctrines they disbelieved, and even support by its own members had been temporarily shifted from a compulsory to a voluntary basis. And that temporariness, as was inevitable, eventually became permanent. Suspended regularly each year, the taxes were permanently repealed in 1779.[29]

The wonder, rather, is that so much was immediately achieved. As Jefferson pointed out, the majority of the Assembly were sound Church of England men and partial to its established position. But the forces of revolution were too great for them to oppose *in extremis*, and the best they could do was to fight a delaying battle. When they ultimately came to grips with the fundamental question of the separation of Church and State they were to find powerful allies in those same dissenting churches which had opposed them so vehemently in the initial skirmishes.

The struggle now proceeded in several steps and phases, and it is in these that Jefferson took over the chief role for several years, yielding it only to Madison to bring to a memorable conclusion when perforce he quit Virginia for the Court of France in 1784.

All through this period, Jefferson was diligently at work on what was perhaps his greatest document, with the possible exception of the Declaration of Independence—A Bill for Establishing Religious Freedom. He envisaged it as part of the general revision of the laws, and incorporated within three short sections some of the noblest utterances ever pronounced on this delicate and controversial question.

Well aware [it began] that the opinions and belief of men depend not on their own will, but follow involuntarily the evidence proposed to their minds; that Almighty God hath created the mind free, and manifested his supreme will that free it shall remain by making it altogether insusceptible of restraint; that all attempts to influence it by temporal punishments, or burthens, or by civil incapacitations, tend only to beget habits of hypocrisy and meanness, and are a departure from the plan of the holy author of our religion... That to compel a man to furnish contributions of money for the propagation of opinions which he disbelieves and abhors, is sinful and tyrannical; that even the forcing him to support this or that teacher of his own religious persuasion, is depriving him of the comfortable liberty of giving his contributions to the particular pastor whose morals he would make his pattern... that our civil rights have no dependence on our religious opinions, any more than our opinions of physics or geometry; and therefore the proscribing any citizen as unworthy the public confidence by laying upon him an incapacity of being called to offices of trust or emolument, unless he profess or renounce this or that religious opinion, is depriving him injudiciously of those privileges and advantages to which, in common with his fellow-citizens, he has a natural right ... that the opinions of men are not the object of civil government, nor under its jurisdiction... that truth is great and will prevail if left to herself; that she is the proper and sufficient antagonist to error, and has nothing to fear from the conflict unless by human interposition disarmed of her natural weapons, free argument and debate....[30]

In this tremendous preamble Jefferson laid down for all time the fundamental nature of the relations between man and his fellow men, between man and State, between State and Church, in the field of ideas, of religious beliefs and practices. The argument is as good now as it was then, and as timely.

With the philosophical and logical ground thus carefully prepared, Jefferson moved on to the positive law:

> We the General Assembly of Virginia do enact that no man shall be compelled to frequent or support any religious worship, place or ministry whatsoever, nor shall be enforced, restrained, molested, or burthened in his body or goods, or shall otherwise suffer, on account of his religious opinions or belief; but that all men shall be free to profess, and by argument to maintain, their opinions in matters of religion, and that the same shall in no wise diminish, enlarge, or affect their civil capacities.

In such sweeping language Jefferson sought to create an unbreachable wall of separation between Church and State and make religious opinions forever private and sacrosanct from intrusion. So fundamental and unalterable was this concept that he sought, by legislative fiat, to bind the consciences of future lawmakers against any retrogression.

"That the rights hereby asserted are of the natural rights of mankind," he solemnly pronounced, "and that if any act shall be hereafter passed to repeal the present or to narrow its operations, such act will be an infringement of natural rights."

The path to the ultimate triumph of these principles proved long and hard. The actual submission of the act to the consideration of the Assembly did not take place until after Jefferson became Governor. On June 12, 1779, John Harvie, his old friend, formally brought in the bill. Immediately the forces in opposition interposed objections and sought delay. These now included, besides the staunch proponents of the Anglican Church, many of the dissenting churches. The latter, as has already been indicated, felt that Jefferson was going too far. They were willing enough to haul down the Anglican Church, but they were not prepared to cut themselves off irrevocably from all possibility of future State support. They now insisted, with but few honorable exceptions like the Baptists,[31] that *all* Christian churches be considered as established and entitled to support; that toleration be extended only to those believing in "one God, and a future State of rewards and punishments"; and that every freeholder and possessor of tithables be compelled to enroll and declare to which of the established churches he chose to contribute. Not even the Roman Catholic Church would have come within the definition.

The combined opposition succeeded, after two readings of Jefferson's bill, in postponing the third until August 1st. In the meantime, they prepared a counterbill for multiple establishments based on the above principles. James Henry of Accomac introduced it on October 25th into the Assembly.[32] The issue was now clearly joined.

Jefferson had early sought to ward off any such proposal for multiple establishments by attempting to prove that the ministers of the respective sects could be adequately provided for on a voluntary basis. As far back as February, 1777, on the first temporary stoppage of compulsory tithes, he had personally drawn and headed a subscription list for the Reverend Charles Clay, minister of the Calvinistical Reformed Church. "We, the subscribers, professing the most Catholic affection for other religious sectaries who happen to differ from us in points of conscience . . . and moreover, approving highly the political conduct of the revd. Charles Clay who, early rejecting the tyrant and tyranny of Britain, proved his religion genuine by its harmony with the liberties of mankind," thereupon made up a substantial sum for his support. Jefferson contributed the largest amount—six pounds.[33]

Since such voluntary gestures did not serve to appease the dissenters, Jefferson privately circulated his bill among friends and influential Virginians, without naming its author. But they found no difficulty in reading him aright. "I guess at the Author of the bill," John Todd wrote back, "& I love and esteem the man." He was pessimistic, however, of the triumph of its principles, because of "the gross ignorance of some on the subject, & the little narrow soul'd bigotry & blind ungenerous attachment of others to the peculiarities of parties." One further passage from Todd's reply is worth quoting—it is fully as eloquent as anything Jefferson himself said on the subject. "I am not affrighted with tolerating papists in the State," he asserted, "but think they will be our true friends, & that people of different sentiments in religion will be all one in their love & fidelity to the State: which secures them every thing dear and valuable."[34]

But the conduct of the fight necessarily passed, with Jefferson's elevation to the governorship, into other hands. Young James Madison, hitherto almost unknown to Jefferson, took over the largest share of the responsibility for the legislative maneuvers. If Jefferson's bill was unable at the time to muster sufficient votes for passage, Madison and others were similarly able to postpone consideration of Henry's bill.

Steadily the friends of religious freedom pressed toward the goal, through the distractions of war and the violent problems of peace. Jefferson could no longer aid, except from a distance. From the gubernatorial chair he returned to Congress, and then removed completely from the scene to France. It was there, in 1786, that young Madison reported triumphantly to him the tidings that, in spite of the determined opposition of such former stalwarts as Richard Henry Lee and Patrick Henry, and despite the deletion of certain too sweeping affirmations from the preamble, Jefferson's bill for religious freedom had finally passed both Houses and become the law of the land.[35] More basic and fundamental in its terms than even the First Amendment to the Constitution, and more philosophic in its implications, the Virginia statute is a noble landmark in the historic panorama of human rights and of human freedom.

Jefferson's second great cornerstone for the liberties of Virginia was his Bill for the More General Diffusion of Knowledge. Indeed, he considered this the most important of all his proposals for his native state; even though, at the time he was so informing his friend Wythe, the bill for religious freedom had only recently been enacted.[36]

Jefferson was a profound believer in the liberating influence of knowledge. With the optimistic ardor that characterized all disciples of the Enlightenment he held that, once mankind was given the truth, error and superstition must inevitably slink back into their holes, defeated. A properly educated people meant a free people, against whom tyranny will beat in vain. Laws, too, could only be "wisely formed, and honestly administered, in proportion as those who form and administer them are wise and honest." But wisdom and honesty were inherent virtues, independent of wealth, birth or other accidental circumstances; and their efflorescence could best be achieved by proper education. The problem then was twofold: to provide for *all* a sufficient modicum of education so as to enable them to differentiate the true from the false; and to educate for leadership those whom nature had endowed with genius and virtue. Since these latter were not confined to any one class of society and since, among the poor, it was impossible for the parents to provide the necessary education, they should, declared Jefferson boldly, "be sought for and educated at the common expence of all."[37]

With these concepts Jefferson was laying the preliminary foundation for a system of free and universal public education. But only the preliminary, as is too often forgotten in hailing him as the father of the public school system in America. In a sense, indeed, he was; but only in a sharply defined and limited area. Everyone, he held, was entitled to education on the primary level—the practical arts of reading, writing and computation. After that, those who could pay for it, might go as far as they liked and their finances permitted. But for the vast majority of the poor, education would end with the primary school. Only for the rigorously sifted few among them, those who gave solid evidences of fitness and talent—genius even—and whose better education would serve the purposes of the state, should the higher reaches be available at the public expense. The present theory and practice in the large that *all* are entitled to a complete education—primary, intermediate, college and even university—regardless of special talents other than the mere ability to pass courses, would have been repudiated by Jefferson with considerable vehemence. Education, to him, constituted a form of selective hierarchy, pyramidal in form, broad and universal at the base, and tapering at the top to a small and select few.

The scheme he proposed for free education—and it must be remembered that it applied only to the children of those too poor to pay for it privately—was in form that pyramid.

Each county would be divided into "hundreds," in each of which a primary school was to be established. For a period of three years, all the children resident in the "hundred" would be entitled to free tuition in reading, writing and arithmetic, "and the books which shall be used therein for instructing the children to read shall be such as will at the same time make them acquainted with Graecian, Roman, English, and American history."

For each ten schools of the "hundreds," a more advanced "grammer" school would be provided. These would accept private pupils whose parents could afford to pay. But they would also accept what we might call "scholarship" pupils from among those too poor to pay the regular board and tuition. An appointed overseer would choose from the ten primary schools in his jurisdiction *one* pupil "of the best and most promising genius and disposition" to be educated and boarded at public expense in the grammar school. Here they would receive instruction in "the Latin and Greek languages, English Grammer, geography, and the higher part of numerical arithmetick, to wit, vulgar and decimal fractions, and the extrication of the square and cube roots."

At the end of the first year, one-third of these "foundationers" would be dropped; at the end of the second, *all* would end their studies with the exception of one only, "the best in genius and disposition," who would continue for four years longer.

The final tip of the apex was reached at the end of this four-year period. From each county, from all the grammar schools therein, and at intervals of two years, *one* was to be chosen "among the said seniors, of the best learning and most hopeful genius and disposition, who shall be authorized by [the visitors] to proceed to William and Mary College; there to be educated, boarded, and clothed, three years," at the public expense.

This was indeed a rigorous, almost ruthless series of eliminations. The overwhelming majority of the children of the poor could hope to go no further than the primary school; a tiny proportion might envisage the grammar schools; and only a blessed few, one from each county, could attain the heights of a college education. And these, by the very process of their selection, would be destined to public service and the devotion of their encouraged talents to the common good.

The bill never passed. It was considered too expensive an undertaking for the limited finances of Virginia. Perhaps there were other reasons, decently concealed. Consideration, begun in 1786 under the auspices of the indefatigable Madison, was postponed from year to year, and it was only in 1796 that a highly limited provision was made for a certain number of scholarships. But the fundamental base of the universal primary schools was left for future generations to accomplish.

Jefferson never gave up hope. Almost to the day of his death he worked unweariedly for the effectuation of his program and drew up plans and schemata in profusion for the realization of his noble dream.

While thus concerned with foundations, Jefferson did not ignore the apex of the educational system of the state, the College of William and Mary. He had had ample opportunity while in attendance as a student to measure its merits and defects. The latter outweighed the former in his estimation, and he was determined to remedy them if he could.

Though amply endowed with public lands, quitrents and public donations, the College, he asserted, had not during its hundred years of existence answered the public expectations. It was therefore the "peculiar" duty of the legislature "to aid and improve that seminary, in which those who are to be the future guardians of the rights and liberties of their country may be endowed with science and virtue, to watch and preserve the sacred deposit." [38]

Jefferson drafted a bill providing for five visitors or governors, to be appointed by the joint ballots of both branches of the Assembly, who in turn would appoint the Rector. Eight professors would compose the Faculty: one in moral philosophy, laws of nature and nations; one in fine arts; one in law and "police" (politics); one in civil and ecclesiastical history; one in mathematics; one in anatomy and medicine; one in ancient, oriental and northern languages; and one in natural philosophy and natural history.

Two things are noteworthy in this curriculum: the emphasis laid on scientific and practical studies; and the elimination of the time-honored Biblical and divinity instruction which had occupied so important a place in the old scheme of things. True, the professors were to appoint a missionary "of approved veracity" to the Indian tribes; but not, as heretofore, to seek their conversion to Christianity. Instead, the missionary was "to investigate their laws, customs, religions, traditions, and more particularly their languages," construct grammars and vocabularies thereof, and deposit them in the college library for the benefit of such enthusiasts in Indian lore as Jefferson himself.

In addition—and this displayed another enthusiasm of the father of the bill—the famous astronomer, David Rittenhouse, was to be authorized to construct a model of the solar system for installation in the college precincts. Doubtless Jefferson had seen during his term in Congress the orrery which Rittenhouse had on exhibition in Philadelphia, and been fired with emulation to place a similar one in his native state where he could examine it at his leisure.

The ambitious bill did not pass in its original form; both the entrenched interests of the current board of governors and the suspicions of the dissenting churches anent this stronghold of Anglicanism were sufficient to keep it from enactment. But Jefferson was able during his governorship to introduce certain improvements and much later, when his University of Virginia was taking slow shape and form, he had the satisfaction of seeing a then moribund William and Mary petition in vain for a share in the program it had so cavalierly turned down at the earlier date.

The final bill which Jefferson introduced in his rounded scheme for raising the educational tone of Virginia had to do with the establishment of a public library in Richmond, endowed with £2,000 a year to purchase books and maps "for indulging the researches of the learned and curious." [39] This too failed of passage.

Yet it must not be considered from the general failure of his educational ideas to achieve statutory embodiment that they were wholly lost. The seeds were sown, the ideas germinated, and eventually most of them came to fruition, reaching final glory in the University of Virginia. Truly, Jefferson may be considered as the progenitor of many of the leading ideas of modern educational theory, and the precursor of the public education and university systems of the United States of today.

CHAPTER 13

Domesticity in Time of War

WHILE diligently engaged in the preparation of an entire corpus of laws for the permanent use of Virginia, Jefferson did not neglect his immediate duties in the Assembly. The exigencies of war permitted no cloistered calm and the threat of British invasion was ever imminent.

The capital of Williamsburg was peculiarly exposed to sudden raids from the hovering fleet and the defenses were weak and inadequate. Accordingly, on October 14, 1776, Jefferson brought in a bill proposing the removal of government to the safe interior.[1] But he had more in mind than a mere temporary displacement. He called for a permanent capital at Richmond as approximating the geographic and population center of the state, arguing that thereby business could be facilitated and the convenience of the inhabitants consulted. What he failed to say was that thereby the influence of the Tidewater conservatives might also be diminished and that of the more radical upcountry stock enhanced.

The Tidewater delegates mustered sufficient strength to defeat the bill at the moment, and it was not until May, 1779, when the British were actually converging on the exposed capital, that the reluctant lawgivers yielded and Richmond was designated as Virginia's seat of government.[2]

Jefferson was responsible for other abortive bills, such as an attempt to suspend executions for debt until the restoration of normal conditions, provided the defendant gave proper security for eventual payment.[3] The reasoning was plain; in the desperate condition of the planters any attempt at collection of their long-outstanding debts might be disastrous, and the planters had accordingly opposed any organization of the courts to prevent it. Jefferson hoped to allay their alarm with this compromise and at the same time permit legal processes to be reinstated. The planters refused to take the bait, and both went down to defeat.

The momentous session ended rather darkly for the ambitious architect of a brave new world. He had gained some resounding successes, notably in the abolition of entails and in the beginning at least of a far-reaching revision and codification of the laws. But the conservatives had rallied toward the end and consistently defeated, or delayed, other sections of his vast schemes of improvement. But he was willing to wait, realizing that time was on his side and that the forces behind him were steadily growing in confidence and strength.

With a sigh of relief he returned to his beloved Monticello, to minister to his ailing and once-more pregnant wife, to prepare for spring plantings, and to work steadily at the codification of the laws.

It was the severest winter he so far remembered; and, to add to his troubles, his wells ran dry and remained so all through the year. Nevertheless, when warm weather came, he planted strawberry shoots, Italian types of cabbage—no doubt at Mazzei's instigation—and the more usual crops.[4]

Actual war may have been remote from the mountaintop, but the rumors came with increasing regularity; and the visible signs of drilling militia and of sullen British prisoners sent to Albemarle for safe-keeping were all about. As County Lieutenant and newly appointed Justice of the Peace, it was Jefferson's responsibility to train the militia, feed and clothe the prisoners, and to keep order.[5]

Rumblings, somewhat exaggerated, perhaps, came also from the outer world. His militant compatriot, Thomas Nelson, wrote wrathfully from Baltimore: "Could we but get a good Reglar Army we should soon clear the Continent of these damned Invaders. They play the very Devil with the Girls and even old Women to satisfy their libidinous appetites. There is scarcely a Virgin to be found in the part of the country that they have pass'd thro and yet the levies will not turn out. Rapes, Rapine, and Murder are not sufficient to rouse the resentment of these people."[6]

Nelson was echoing, at least so far as the militia was concerned, a complaint that rose like fuming incense all through the Revolution. Recruitments for the regular army, enlisted for long terms and amenable to service anywhere, were painfully slow; while the militia levies, bound to limited terms and local service, either failed to appear when called or dropped arms the moment their terms expired. Jefferson was to find them his heaviest headache during his turbulent incumbency as Virginia's governor.

The next session of the Assembly was scheduled to commence on May 5, 1777. Jefferson left twenty pounds with Martha to pay Dr. Gilmer for medical care and the impending confinement and, on May 4th, rode toward Williamsburg.[7]

He arrived probably on the 7th, and that same evening purchased a ticket to attend a concert. The next morning there were sufficient delegates present to constitute a quorum and the session was formally opened.[8]

Jefferson put George Wythe in nomination for Speaker, and his old friend was elected over Robert Carter Nicholas and Benjamin Harrison. The wheels began to turn. Jefferson was placed on the Committee for Religion, the Committee for Courts and on some general committees. On May 9th, he prepared a bill "providing against invasions and insurrections" which, with modifications, was enacted into law on May 21st.[9] On May 12th he was ordered to prepare a bill "for regulating the appointment of delegates to General Congress," and this was passed on May 16th.[10]

This last bill was the climax of the bitter feuds which had disorganized

Virginia's representation in Congress from the earliest days. The Lee faction had temporarily gained control of the delegation and the Harrison group sought to oust Lee himself by limiting any one term of office to two years and providing for an interim period of a year before re-election was possible. Jefferson believed in the principle, though personally allied with the Lee group rather than the Harrison contingent. He drafted the bill which had the effect of removing Lee from Congress, yet managed by some incredible legerdemain not to incur the enmity of the man he ousted. All Lee's bitterness was directed at Harrison as the chief manipulator of the strings.

Jefferson was not present to witness all the denouements of his respective measures. Martha's confinement was approaching fast and, on May 20th, he asked for and received leave to absent himself for the remainder of the session.[11]

He hastened back to Monticello in ample time to witness the birth of a son on May 28th. But the child proved sickly and, on June 14th, without seemingly ever having received a name, it died.[12] Jefferson never did have a son to survive him.

Life went on, nevertheless, and there was much to be done on his mountain eyrie to dull the edge of grief. Martha had to be nursed back to health and strength; crops had to be tended and water hauled painfully up the hill from the valley streams because his wells were dry; there was his growing library of books to absorb him evenings when outdoor activities ceased. All in all, it might have been an idyllic existence had there not been a war and the sweaty struggle of forming a stable continental union out of disparate parts.

Richard Henry Lee, involved in some of the sweaty details, wrote somewhat sarcastically to Jefferson: "It will not perhaps be disagreeable to you in your retirement, sometimes to hear the events of war, and how in other respects we proceed in the arduous business we are engaged in."[13]

Indeed, this was neither the first nor the last time that Jefferson's friends viewed with a jaundiced eye his attempts to retire from the dust and heat of the market place to the clear, clean air of Monticello. Each time, it is true, he attributed his defection to the health of his wife and domestic concerns, but the others properly replied with varying degrees of asperity that they too had wives who sometimes ailed and lands that had to be tended.

Biographers have generally avoided an impartial examination of this trait, and have usually taken Jefferson's protestations at face value. But, surprising as it may sound in the light of his truly amazing industry, Jefferson was never capable of prolonged and sustained political effort. Particularly was this true when the wheel of fortune turned against him and defeat, either personal or in connection with measures which he advocated, stared him in the face. He had a tendency then to view with overwhelming longing the secure delights of Monticello and discover domestic difficulties which required instant attention. Once thus snugly ensconced, however, he seemed to draw Antaeus-like sustenance from the soil; and the problems he had incontinently quit welled once more in his mind and ripened to reflective solution. When that occurred, he returned to the hustings, yielding amiably to the protestations of his friends and followers, for another bout and wrestling with the things of the world.

During this current retreat he did pay some attention to his duties as County Lieutenant, but they were cursory and absorbed little of his time. Meanwhile, in Philadelphia, the job of finding a means of consolidating the independent States was dragging wearily on. Until some proper confederation could be evolved, the outlook for a successful termination of the struggle with England was dark indeed. Yet just as dark was the prospect of the mutually suspicious local governments yielding up that measure of sovereignty which the situation required.

Jefferson was well aware both of the need and the obstacles. Before he quit Williamsburg he had proposed to John Adams that he attempt to reconcile the dispute over the ratio of representation between the large and the small states by granting a veto on any proposition to the representatives of either a majority of the *people* or of the States. The first type of veto would secure the large states from the tyranny of the smaller; while the second would similarly keep the smaller from being overborne by the larger.[14] In effect, if not in method, this was exactly what the Constitution eventually did, with the respective representations in the Senate and the House of Representatives. But it took years of conflict and rancorous discussion before this solution could be worked out.

Adams expressed his willingness to offer Jefferson's proposition to Congress if his own plan for proportional voting failed of adoption. At the same time he thought Jefferson's place was in Congress, though he was a trifle more tactful in the telling than Lee had been. "Your Country is not yet, quite secure enough," he wrote, "to assure your Retreat to the Delights of domestic Life. Yet, for the soul of me, when I attend to my own Feelings, I cannot blame you."[15]

If Jefferson felt the implied reproof he gave no sign. But from Monticello he began to give increasing attention to the problems that beset the struggling colonies. Hearing that Franklin was proposing to sail shortly for France, he seized the occasion to unburden himself of some reflections. Virginia, he considered, had made the transition from a monarchical to a republican state "with as much ease as would have attended their throwing off an old, and putting on a new suit of clothes. Not a single throe has attended this important transformation. A half-dozen aristocratical gentlemen, agonizing under the loss of pre-eminence, have sometimes ventured their sarcasms on our political metamorphosis. They have been thought fitter objects of pity, than of punishment."

From his vantage point in Monticello, Jefferson took a benign and optimistic view of ultimate American success. The only possibility of failure, he instructed Franklin, lay in the event of the collapse of the paper currency. But that contingency could be avoided either by an alliance with a naval power like France who could protect their trade or, if that was impossible, by shutting American ports to the entire world and converting at home to manufactures. Thus early was Jefferson adumbrating the embargo policy of his Presidential years.

Rather wistfully he concluded: "I wish my domestic situation had rendered it possible for me to join you in the very honorable charge confided to you. Residence in a polite Court, society of literati of the first order, a just cause and an approving God, will add length to a life for which all men pray . . ." [16] The leaven was beginning to work.

What had put Jefferson on the subject of credit was a letter from John Adams expressing concern over the situation. Money had to be raised; but the usual sources, such as France and Holland, were coy. Why not, Jefferson inquired, make application to a smaller power like the Grand Duke of Tuscany? Obviously, the suggestion had come from Philip Mazzei, Jefferson's new neighbor. Indeed, Mazzei would be willing to revisit his native land and take care of the negotiations.[17] Nothing came of it at the moment; but so impressed was Jefferson with Mazzei's ability and zeal that, later on, he procured for him a somewhat similar mission on behalf of Virginia alone.

Jefferson's leave of absence had been for the unexpired duration of the spring session of the Assembly. The fall session ostensibly began on October 20, 1777, but so dilatory were the delegates that it took the services of the sergeant-at-arms and ten days before a quorum could be assembled.

Jefferson was in his seat on the 30th, and was placed on his usual committees. It was now that he brought in his bills for the establishment of courts, discussed in an earlier chapter. He also participated in Virginia's ratification of the Articles of Confederation which Congress had laboriously hammered out and which, in spite of Adams's efforts and Jefferson's proposals, permitted an absolute veto to a small minority of dissenting states.[18]

He was also responsible for the drafting of a bill, of which the best that can be said is that it was a war measure. This was the Bill for Withholding British Property. It provided for the sequestration of all property in Virginia belonging to British subjects and the payment of all avails into the Virginia loan office for eventual disposition. It also permitted patriotic Virginia debtors of English merchants to pay their debts into the loan office in the depreciated currency of the state at face value and receive a discharge in full from the Governor of the state.[19]

Jefferson was among those who took advantage of its final passage to hypothecate their debts. In Jefferson's case, however, it led to untold difficulties in the future. By 1779, the Assembly acknowledged the error of this sort of bookkeeping and after the peace, the courts were obliged to consider such payments as invalid. Much of Jefferson's later financial entanglements stemmed from this unfortunate act which he had sponsored, and for years he struggled to repay a second time, and in solid currency, too, the debts he now thought he was rid of forever.

On January 24th, two days after its passage, the Assembly adjourned and Jefferson returned to Monticello. But not before he had purchased a new theodolite from the Rev. Mr. Andrews for forty-five pounds and had sold to John Cocke some superfluous books of his own for over twenty-two pounds.[20]

Home again, he hastened to try out the theodolite in fixing the latitude and true meridian of his mountain home, and took observations on an almost total eclipse of the sun which providentially occurred on June 24.[21] These were the things he reveled in, rather than the hurly-burly of politics.

He also recommenced building operations. The rearing of the noble structure he envisaged on the mountaintop, temporarily halted because of his extended absences and the exigencies of war, was now resumed full speed ahead. He contracted for three stone columns to support the portico of the house, and ordered 100,000 more red bricks in addition to the 90,000 already made. Spring planting was upon him again, and this year he was particularly assiduous in setting out an orchard of assorted fruits and nuts. The preceding severe winter had killed off most of his young trees, and these were replacements as well as additions. Later in the fall he took from Mazzei's establishment at Colle olive and orange shoots and set them out, too.[22] He was truly building for permanence.

All too soon for his numerous activities the Assembly reconvened. On May 4, 1778, Jefferson was promptly in his seat again; but, as usual, it was May 12th before a quorum could be gathered. On May 12th, the election for Speaker of the House was held. For the first time Jefferson was placed in nomination; but Benjamin Harrison, leader of the conservative faction, defeated him overwhelmingly by a vote of 51 to 23.[23]

The lines of party were now increasingly evident, chiefly because of the violent fight over the religious issue. Harrison showed his hand immediately in the first failure to place Jefferson on the all-important Committee for Religion. Instead, he was given less controversial committee assignments. For the remainder of the session Jefferson was perforce comparatively impotent.

The Assembly rose at the beginning of June, but Jefferson lingered a week or so in Williamsburg attending to his private affairs. It also gave him a chance to catch up on his correspondence. One of his most interesting letters was addressed to Giovanni Fabbroni, a compatriot of Mazzei, who had hoped to come to America with his friend, but was never to quit Europe. Through the good offices of Mazzei the two men, Jefferson in America and Fabbroni in Paris and elsewhere, conducted a scientific and learned correspondence for many years.

Picking up an exchange that had lain fallow since 1776, Jefferson now complained to his unseen friend of the little leisure he had, because of political duties, to indulge his fondness for philosophical studies. By philosophy, of course, he meant *natural* philosophy or science, as we would call it today. Philosophy in the sense of metaphysics was completely foreign to Jefferson's temperament, and was always treated with contempt as not merely fruitless but obscurantist in effect.

He would like, he wrote, to compare observations with Fabbroni on the respective climates of Virginia and France. Each morning he took the temperature reading on awakening, and again at four in the afternoon. These, he considered, gave the maxima of cold and heat for the day. In botany, he confessed, he knew only the first principles; but he was willing to exchange specimens. He was really being modest, for his curious and roving eye had combed the countryside for rare specimens, and what he could not himself find, he begged his friends all over Virginia to send him.

What excited an almost lyrical quality in Jefferson, however, was music. "If there is a gratification which I envy any people in this world," he told Fabbroni, "it is to your country its music. This is the favorite passion of my soul, & fortune has cast my lot in a country where it is in a state of deplorable barbarism." Would Fabbroni be good enough to send over someone "who may be a proficient in singing, & on the Harpsichord. I should be contented to receive such an one two or three years hence"; that is, when the war would probably be over. "The bounds of an American fortune will not admit the indulgence of a domestic band of musicians," he observed mournfully, "yet I have thought that a passion for music might be reconciled with that economy which we are obliged to observe." Already among his servants were a gardener, a weaver, a cabinet-maker, a stonecutter and a "vigneron." In Italy, he supposed, such skilled craftsmen were sufficiently versed in musical instruments so that "one might have a band of two French horns, two clarinets, & hautboys and a bassoon, without enlarging their domestic expenses. A certainty of employment for a half dozen years, and at the end of that time to find them if they choose a conveyance to their own country might induce them to come here on reasonable wages." Would Fabbroni be able to find out such men and send them along?

Alas, Jefferson's passion was destined to go unslaked; for the letter, on its way abroad, was intercepted and captured by an unfeeling British warship.[24] It never reached Fabbroni.

At about the same time he wrote to Fabbroni, he was inquiring of the Rev. Dr. Samuel Henley, a Loyalist refugee who had fled to England, whether he would sell his books. These had been left in the care of James Madison, professor at William and Mary. They were damaged by damp, but, said Jefferson hopefully, he would be glad to buy them.[25] It does not seem that Henley ever replied.

A little later, after his return to Monticello, he wrote to David Rittenhouse. The eclipse, he informed the Philadelphia astronomer, for whose observation he had purchased a new theodolite, had proved most disappointing. The day had been cloudy and the obscured sun appeared only at intervals. In addition, he had found himself without an accurate timepiece. Rittenhouse had promised, when he was in Philadelphia, to construct one for him for astronomical use. Would he now oblige?

Rittenhouse and Franklin, he pursued in laudatory vein, were too great in genius to occupy themselves with governmental affairs. "There is an order of geniusses above that obligation," he declared, "& therefore exempted from it. Nobody can conceive that nature ever intended to throw away a Newton upon the occupations of a crown.... Cooperating with nature in her ordinary economy we should dispose of and employ the geniusses of men according to their several orders and degrees. I doubt not there are in your country [Pennsylvania] many persons equal to the task of conducting government; but you should consider that the world has but one Ryttenhouse, & that it never had one before." [26]

If this was fulsome praise for a man certainly not in the first rank of genius, the principle involved was nevertheless important. It was only in World War II that we came reluctantly, and almost too late, to the realization that genius might be better employed than on the battlefield; though, of course, the realization was strictly confined to that type of genius which could help win the war.

On August 1, 1778, Martha gave birth to a daughter, the third in number, but only the second to survive.[27] Though there were two children born after her, neither lived sufficiently long to make any impact; and Jefferson was perforce content with two daughters to grow to maturity. Martha (Patsy) was now almost six; and the newborn child was named Mary (Maria, Polly).

Little Polly gave him an additional reason for remaining at Monticello. Besides, was there not a rumored treating of peace which would render unnecessary any further great efforts? His nimble mind looked to the future. In the event of peace, he wrote Lee, would it not be wise to exclude the British and everyone else except our "tres grands & chers amies & alliees" from that nursery for seamen, the Newfoundland fisheries?

There was also the problem of filling up this country with immigrants as fast as possible. Where should they come from? From the Latin Mediterranean countries, he thought, rather than from the Teutonic northern ones. The influence of the enthusiastic Italian, Mazzei, is plainly visible; in fact, Jefferson admitted to long conversations with him on the subject. Italian immigrants, he pursued, "would bring with them a skill in agriculture & other arts better adapted to our climate. I beleive [*sic*] that had our country been peopled thence we should now have been farther advanced in rearing the several things which our country is capable of producing," such as wine, oil and silk. Perhaps it would be wise to send

Mazzei with William Lee to Italy to procure such skilled agricultural laborers for Virginia.[28]

One wonders how far Jefferson would have been willing to push this thesis, in the light of his firm belief that free institutions and the love of independence had something of a Teutonic and Anglo-Saxon tinge to them. In his enthusiasm he had overstated his thought. The rapid expansion of the agricultural resources of Virginia, and particularly the development of new money crops, were uppermost in his mind; and for this Italian workers were more immediately valuable. The prospect of an Italianate state, in which Anglo-Saxon planters and small farmers were supplanted by Mediterranean immigrants, would doubtless have dismayed him.

He continued for a considerable period under the spell of Mazzei's glib tongue and facile enthusiasms. In October, he was suggesting to John Hancock, president of the Continental Congress, that Mazzei was just the man to send to Italy to borrow large sums of money from the wealthy Grand Duke of Tuscany and from the Genoese, the richest people in Europe.[29]

By this time, however, he was back in Williamsburg to attend the fall session of the Assembly. He was not a very faithful attendant, it seems; on several occasions he was ordered taken into custody by the sergeant-at-arms and brought forcibly to meetings, and on at least two occasions he had to pay a fine before he was released.[30]

It was a comparatively short session, commencing on October 5, 1778, and ending on December 19th. Jefferson's name is absent from the proceedings except in connection with the sergeant-at-arms; but his former guardian, Dr. Thomas Walker, petitioned the Assembly on behalf of himself and the estate of Peter Jefferson for leave to survey 1,456 acres on the New River which had been assigned to them out of a former 10,000 acre grant. The petition was granted.[31]

The beginning of the new year of 1779 found Jefferson once more back in Monticello, with the comfortable feeling that the war was progressing satisfactorily and that his intermittent attendances in Williamsburg represented the sum total of his duties to his country.

It is true that a similar tendency to regard the war as almost ended and to feel that it was time to relax existed all through the colonies. Had not Burgoyne's army been captured en masse at Saratoga and the flower of British infantry been removed from battle? Had not the French joined in the combat, and was it not possible for that noble ally to handle the British alone?

But George Washington was under no such optimistic illusions. He saw the British comfortably ensconced in the chief ports, well-equipped, well-fed; while his own Continentals shivered with cold, starved on occasion and were ill-supplied with arms. His constant complaints to Congress for the sinews of war were either ignored or insufficiently attended to; while the states behind Congress became increasingly immersed in their own affairs. Virginia, his native state, was equally an offender with the rest. With great tact he called Benjamin Harrison's attention to the situation, and delicately named some of Virginia's chief delinquents.

"I am alarmed and wish to see my Countrymen roused," he wrote to the Speaker of the House. "I have no resentments, nor do I mean to point at any particular characters... but in the present situation of things I cannot help asking: Where is Mason, Wythe, Jefferson, Nicholas, Pendleton, Nelson, and another I could name [Harrison]; and why, if you are sufficiently impressed with your danger, do you not... send an extra Member or two [to Congress] for at least a certain limited time till the great business of the Nation is put upon a more respectable and happy establishment." [32]

Washington's complaint against the immersion of the leading Virginians in their own affairs and their inability to see that their presence in Congress was essential, aroused no particular flurry of activity among them. They continued to remain in their native state, unmoved by this or other pleas. They felt that their primary responsibility lay in building up Virginia; and they could not, and perhaps did not wish to, envisage in Congress a national body whose strengthening was desirable. It is no wonder then that the war dragged wearily along and dark times came.

If the war did enter into the consciousness of Albemarle at this particular time, it was in a fashion that helped reinforce their belief that it was soon to end. Burgoyne's army had surrendered under a convention that it was to be returned to England on the pledge that the troops involved would remain out of the war for the duration. But once transferred to Boston, Congress broke the pledge and held them in this country. Four thousand of them, mixed British and Hessians, were marched cross-country to Virginia and installed in hastily constructed barracks not far from Charlottesville.

Jefferson was at Monticello when they arrived in January, 1779, and, as was proper to his position as County Lieutenant, rode over to familiarize himself with the situation. He found it bad enough. The weather was cold and rainy, the proposed barracks for the shivering prisoners were as yet unfinished, the food decayed and uneatable. What he saw enlisted his humanitarian impulses, and closer acquaintance with some of the officers, particularly among the Hessians, stirred him to considerable activity in their behalf.

With the British he remained on generally formal terms. They were the enemy, and their arrogance, even as prisoners, repelled him. But the Hessians—or rather, the Brunswickers, for most of them hailed from that small German state—were a different lot. The private soldiers had come unwillingly, and the officers, unlike their British counterparts, were polite, well-mannered and, best of all, from Jefferson's viewpoint, cultured and worldly men, acquainted with books, and lovers of music. General William

Phillips, the chief British officer, represented the former element, and with him and his fellows Jefferson's relations were always somewhat cold, if entirely correct. But he took the Germans to his heart. Among them were Major General Baron Frederick Adolphus Riedesel, Captain Baron de Geismar and Jean Louis de Unger.

Riedesel's wife and three children followed him into captivity, but came about a month after the troops arrived. To provide for their coming, and with Jefferson's aid, he rented Mazzei's home at Colle. Mazzei was finally on his way to Europe, not as the agent of Congress, as Jefferson had suggested to Hancock, but as an agent for Virginia. On the voyage across, however, he was captured by a British privateer and it was only after many difficulties that he was able, late in 1779, to reach France and enter upon his duties.

Riedesel found Mazzei's home too small for his flourishing family and built an additional log house on the grounds. He also installed cows, pigs and chickens and planted vegetables. His soldiers did the same around their barracks and soon the prison camp took on the appearance of a permanent, orderly establishment complete with womenfolk and the shouts of playing children.[33]

Baroness Friderike von Riedesel, when she finally appeared on the scene, proved to be a buxom, handsome dame, with a penetrating eye and a habit of riding booted and spurred that evoked the astonishment of the Virginia ladies. And they and their climate in turn evoked both her wonderment and terror. She dreaded the rattlesnakes, the flitting bats, the sultry heat, the forest fires and the terrific thunderstorms. She didn't like the institution of slavery and thought that many of the planters, though not all, treated their slaves badly.

But of the Virginians themselves she stood in no fear; rather, they excited her risibility. "The Virginians are generally inert," she wrote, "a fate which they attribute to their hot climate; but on the slightest inducement, in a twinkling, they leap up and dance about; and if a reel . . . is played for them, immediately the men catch hold of the women who then jump up as if they were possessed; but as soon as they are led back to their chairs they sit on them like blocks of wood."[34]

Jefferson formally exchanged calls with the British officers, but he delighted in the Germans. The Riedesel and Jefferson ménages were soon on reciprocally cordial terms, and the Baroness sang Italian airs to the violin accompaniment of young Captain Geismar. According to Mazzei, Geismar and Jefferson played duets together, Geismar performing very well on the violin and Jefferson "passably" on the violoncello.[35] With young Unger, Jefferson discussed philosophy, and the wives and children visited back and forth. It was all very civilized, and neither the brute fact of continuing war nor controversial politics passed the lips of the courteous host.

When Riedesel suffered a stroke from the hot Virginia sun, Jefferson

Museum of the Arts, Boston

ABIGAIL ADAMS

Painting by Gilbert Stuart

Courtesy the Frick Art Reference Library

JOHN ADAMS

Portrait by Saint-Memin

was able to get him permission to take the waters at the Berkley Springs, together with General Phillips' family.[36] When Geismar found his prospects impaired by further imprisonment, Jefferson obligingly obtained an exchange for him and sent him back to Germany.[37]

The Germans remembered his efforts in their behalf with deep gratitude and continued a correspondence with their former host for a considerable period after the end of war and their safe re-establishment in their native land. One, indeed, who evidently painted, anonymously sent a letter home while still a prisoner. A Hamburg newspaper published it.

"My only Occupation at present is to learn the English language," he said. "It is the easier for me, as I have free Access to a copious & well chosen Library of Colo. Jefferson's, Governor of Virginia. . . . The Governor possesses a Noble Spirit of Building. He is now finishing an elegant building, projected according to his own fancy. In his parlour he is creating on the Cieling a Compass of his own invention by wich he can know the Strength as well as Direction of the Winds. I have promised to paint the Compass for it. . . . As all Virginians are fond of Music, he is particularly so. You will find in his House an elegant Harpsichord, Pianoforte & some Violins. The latter he performs well upon himself, the former his Lady touches very skilfully & who, is in all respects a very agreeable, sensible & accomplished Lady."[38] Of particular interest is this description of Martha Jefferson, one of the very few in existence.

In a sense, even before he became Governor, Jefferson considered the Convention troops as under his protective wing. When, in March, the report circulated that the prisoners might be removed, in whole or in part, from Charlottesville and sent elsewhere, he sent a strong protest to the then Governor, Patrick Henry. Any partial separation of officers and men would be a direct breach of the terms of the Convention, he insisted. Let them go in a body or not at all. But what was the necessity for their removal? It had cost over £25,000 to build the barracks, and the prisoners were spending at the rate of $30,000 a week, to the "great and local advantage" of Virginia. Here they were safe from rescue by the enemy, healthy, and had established themselves with gardens, cattle and homes. They were happy and content. "Does not every sentiment of humanity revolt against the proposition of stripping them of all this, and removing them into new situations," where they would have to start afresh?[39] The rumored removal did not take place; but not before Jefferson had appeared before the Council of State with a tale of their possible insurrection and a demand for arms to be furnished to the militia of the surrounding counties to counteract any such attempt.[40]

The spring session of the Assembly commenced on May 3, 1779; and this time Jefferson was prompt in attendance. That he seriously contemplated dropping all political activities at this time is evidenced by Pendleton's remonstrance: "You are too young to Ask that happy quietus from the public, and should not [*sic*] at least postpone it til you have taught the rising Generation the forms as well as the substantial principles of legislation."[41]

Whether it was his senior's kindly expostulation or the rapid course of events, Jefferson was shortly immersed to the hilt. A new Governor was to be elected in place of Patrick Henry who, after three terms in office, was no longer eligible according to law. On June 1st, the two branches of the Virginia legislature met in joint ballot to choose the Governor. Probably Jefferson had been advised in advance that he would be nominated, and had indicated to Pendleton his distaste for the assignment. In any event there were three candidates—Jefferson, General Thomas Nelson, who had made a fine military record, and John Page.

Page was Jefferson's oldest living friend, an amiable but not too able gentleman who had managed to elevate himself to the presidency of the Council of State and to the lieutenant-governorship under Patrick Henry. That he was a logical candidate is clear; that Jefferson at first had not wanted the job is equally clear; but the sudden juxtaposition of their two names in opposition created an immediate constraint.

On the first ballot, Jefferson led his competitors, but had not the majority required under the constitution. The vote stood: Jefferson—55; Nelson—32; Page—38. On a second vote, the followers of Nelson shifted their support overwhelmingly to Page; but there were sufficient defections to permit Jefferson barely to squeeze through. The final vote stood: Jefferson—67; Page—61.[42]

The next day, Page shamefacedly sent a little note of disavowal to his friend, protesting that the competition had not been of his making, but had been due to the zeal of his friends. Jefferson passed it off with a warm note of his own, reiterating their ancient friendship—and the shadow was gone.[43]

Thus suddenly, and seemingly without much prior thought or excessive electioneering, Jefferson became the second Governor of Virginia.

CHAPTER 14

War Governor

JEFFERSON always looked back upon the period of his governorship as a painful episode in an otherwise long and fruitful life, and sought as much as possible to bury it in oblivion. His Autobiography, meticulously detailed before and after, dismisses these two years in a single paragraph and hastens on to more congenial topics.

For this highly self-conscious attitude there is much justification. With all his talents, zeal and undoubted patriotism, Jefferson was not the man for the job in the peculiar chaos of Virginia at the time. The war, which had nibbled on its borders and coast line for several years, was now to march full-panoplied into its very vitals; finances, the life blood of a beleaguered commonwealth, were disintegrating under the impact of an uncontrolled inflation; a jealous individualism and a suspicion of all authority, local or continental, hamstrung systematic endeavor; while a constitution that would have proved inefficient in time of peace literally fell to pieces in time of war.

To surmount these obstacles required a strong and even ruthless executive; one who was willing, when necessary, to overlook the letter of the constitution and the limitations on his powers; to act first in an emergency and seek the legal justification for the act later. In short, to be something of a dictator. Jefferson was not that man.

The chief trouble was the Virginia constitution. In the reaction against the "tyrant of Britain," Virginia had placed practically all power in the legislative as against the executive. The Governor was in effect the arm of the Assembly, its faithful follower of instructions. And, to make certain that those instructions were properly adhered to, a Council of State had been created, appointed by the Assembly, ostensibly to assist and advise the Governor but actually, as it turned out, to make decisions for him to follow. Further to complicate matters, a Board of War and a Board of Trade had been instituted (and this had been a recommendation of the Revisors, of which Jefferson was a member), appointed by the Assembly and subject to the control of the Council of State and the Governor.

The machinery, in short, was cumbersome and unwieldy, and wholly unfit for the rapid decisions required in a state of war and invasion.

The tendency has been to blame the constitution of Virginia, as prepared by other hands, for these shackles on Jefferson's regime. But his own draft constitution had insisted on practically similar restraints. Indeed, his definition of an executive was remarkable for its negativism; the powers were only vaguely specified, but the restrictions were detailed, numerous and sweeping.[1]

That they could be overcome by a bold executive was shown by the experience of Thomas Nelson, Jefferson's unsuccessful competitor in the present election and his successor when Jefferson finally retired from the scene. But the qualities required were those which Jefferson held in abhorrence. While not a total advocate of an uncontrolled, all-powerful legislature, he feared even more a constitutionally strong executive. All his experience, all his readings in history, had convinced him that the liberties of a people could not survive under an executive clad in fundamental power. Where the Assembly ordered, and the Council of State ruled, he obeyed; where they failed to order, or were not in attendance, he waited their assemblage, no matter what the emergency. Religiously he stayed within his legal powers.

When Jefferson took office on June 2, 1779, it is extremely doubtful that he was fully aware of the difficulties ahead. As a member of the Assembly he had, of course, been immersed in the general situation; but he had devoted his attention primarily to those broad reforms which were intended to revolutionize the base of Virginia society and bring true freedom to its people. They had little or nothing to do with the hard facts of a current war, with the welter of day-to-day decisions immediately required. Now he was catapulted into a situation where such decisions became his chief province.

One of the hard facts with which he was confronted was inflation. It cost money to run a government and a war, and there was little solid money on hand. The people, remembering their resistance to taxes imposed by England, similarly objected to, and then evaded, taxes imposed by their own Assembly. To solve the situation, the Assembly resorted to the printing press and ran into the same consequences that have always attended the emission of *fiat* paper money. Prices rose; more money was printed to pay the increased prices; and prices jumped again. The gap ever widened.

In October, 1776, the Assembly had voted £500,000 more paper money; in May, 1779, an additional £1,000,000. By October of the same year, that enormous emission (if face value alone were considered) was already exhausted. This time the Assembly realized that it was losing the race and, as the only alternative to "the ruinous expedient of future emissions of paper money," decreed new taxes—a poll tax, a tax on slaves, carriages, liquors, imports and retail stocks.[2] But the machinery of collection was primitive and evasion rampant. Little was collected, and that little was swallowed up in the maw of war. Later on, other desperate remedies were resorted to, but always it was a losing race.

Jefferson's own accounts give a graphic picture of the steady perpendicular rise of inflation. His salary as Governor—geared, supposedly, to inflated prices—was £375 a month. But four days after he received this seemingly munificent sum he was paying over £5 for some pins, and five months before had given £13 for twelve bottles of anchovies. By September, a bonnet for Martha stood him £36. This was nothing, however, compared to what happened in 1780. His salary, it is true, tried to keep pace, reaching the astronomical figure of several thousand pounds a month; but prices soared even more astronomically. Six handkerchiefs for Martha set him back £159, and a pair of shoes, £84/6. Two quarts of oysters went for £15, and 112 lbs. of sugar cost £436/16.[3]

How then could Virginia hope to supply its militia with arms, munitions, tents, clothing, shoes and all the requisites of war? How could they send to Congress the assessments demanded for the running of the central government and the maintenance of the Continental armies in the field? This was the problem which confronted not Virginia alone, but most of the other state governments; and it remained hopelessly insoluble throughout the war.

Nor was the military picture as bright as most Virginians, including Jefferson liked to think. The surrender of Burgoyne, with its visible evidence in their midst—the Convention prisoners—and the open entry of France into the war, had generated an easy optimism. There was a tendency to let the French take over, and attend to one's private affairs. Surely the war, now that France was in, could not last much longer.

Richard Henry Lee, from his vantage point in Congress, had written bitterly to Jefferson of the "speculating harpies" with hard money who were taking advantage of the general depreciation in currency to buy up such solid, tangible goods as land and Negroes. "Our misfortune is," he complained, "that the bulk of the people, throut [*sic*] the States seem to have lost sight of the great object for which we had recourse to arms, and to have turned their thoughts soley [*sic*] to accumulating *ideal* wealth and preying upon the necessities of their fellow Citizens."[4]

In fact, there was a general feeling that it was Congress who was unconscionably delaying an immediate peace. Reports were abroad that the French minister had urged on Congress that, in exchange for a Spanish alliance, it cede all claims to Florida and the control of the Mississippi; that Congress had balked and, as a result, the disgusted French minister intended to leave for home. The reports, based partly on fact, stirred up a hornet's nest. Jefferson was as outraged as the rest. He talked of reestablishing the old committees of correspondence and bypassing a reluctant Congress with direct negotiations between the States and the French minister. Jefferson was willing enough to yield the American claims in return for a Spanish alliance; though he cannily looked to the future to abrogate the arrangement, by force if necessary. The thing that mattered most to him at the moment was an immediate cessation of the current war. "It would surely be better," he declared, "to carry on a ten years' war some time hence than to continue the present an unnecessary moment."[5]

Jefferson was thus insistent on an immediate peace, even at the cost of expansionist claims, because the picture of the war, as far as the South was concerned, had definitely darkened. Georgia had been invaded and Savannah was fallen; just a month before Jefferson took office, the British landed at Portsmouth and were ravaging the countryside, contemptuous of the hastily levied Virginia militia. The whole system of defense on a militia basis was laid bare in all its inadequacy for those who had eyes to see.

While these vital problems of inflation, militia and the proper conduct of the war were pending, almost the first question that engaged Jefferson's attention and absorbed much of his energies for months to come was an individual case.

George Rogers Clark and a band of Virginians had marched into Kentucky and across the Ohio to whip Indians and British alike in a series of brilliant exploits. In the course of these actions he had the good fortune —or misfortune, as it turned out for Jefferson—to capture the British commander in the area, Governor Henry Hamilton.

The news of the final victory reached Williamsburg just after Jefferson was inaugurated. Hamilton, and several of his aides, came some time later —in chains. This was not the usual practice in so-called civilized warfare, but in Clark's view—and in Jefferson's—there was good justification in this case. Hamilton had gained an unenviable reputation on the frontier for cruelties and barbaric practices, notable among which was the public purchase of American scalps from his Indian allies.

Jefferson welcomed the victory, and viewed his manacled prisoners with a grim satisfaction. He had cause to rejoice in the success of Clark's expedition. His eye had ever been fixed on the western lands as a natural area of expansion, and he had been an interested party in laying the groundwork for the original expedition and bringing it to the attention of the then Governor, Patrick Henry. Clark was a realist—and so were the adventurers who followed his banner. Before they started out, they first sought and obtained assurances from those in power—Patrick Henry as Executive, and Jefferson, Wythe and George Mason as influential members of the Assembly—that liberal grants of land would be theirs in any territories they might conquer.[6]

All through the war, indeed, the minds of a good many Virginians were obsessed with visions of the vast, untrodden lands to the west, and they were eager to stake out claims in that expanse before the rush of settlers inevitable at war's end. Jefferson had fought turning over sovereignty to the Northwest to Congress because he feared Congress, as then constituted, would favor large-scale speculators over small yeoman farmers. With the same end in view he now pushed through a Virginia land office and established safeguards for granting these "waste and unappropriated lands."[7]

One of the first things that the land office did, however, was to register the outstanding claim of the Loyal Company to 200,000 acres of land, pending a formal court adjudication. Jefferson had an interest in the Loyal Company, through inheritance from his father; and his former guardian, Dr. Thomas Walker, was one of its active promoters. The grant dragged through interminable proceedings and finally petered out; and Jefferson's share never amounted to anything. But the end result of Jefferson's efforts was indeed ironic—the land measure he helped draft in effect turned over huge tracts to speculators instead of the small settlers he had envisaged.[8]

The three prisoners who came to Williamsburg and thereby dumped a problem in Jefferson's lap were Governor Henry Hamilton, Captain William Lamothe and Philip Dejean. By the usual courtesies of war, particularly when high officers were involved, they should have been paroled within the limits of Williamsburg and eventually exchanged. But neither Jefferson nor his Council of State was in any mood for observing the amenities. Not even the interposition of General William Phillips, Jefferson's former Convention prisoner, availed. The reports of Hamilton's indiscriminate murder of men, women and children on the frontier, his direct instigation of the most fiendish Indian cruelties, shocked Jefferson into a passion and a stubborn, almost vindictive relentlessness that consort ill with the usual picture of the mild, humane, easy-going man. And unfortunately, as it turned out, the matter was further complicated by the fact that Clark had entered into a capitulation agreement with Hamilton whereby he was entitled to special privileges.

Jefferson brushed all such considerations aside. Murderers such as these were entitled to nothing but the harshest treatment. By order of the Council, the three men were thrust into the public jail, clapped into irons and forbidden writing materials and visitors. It was, declared Jefferson, "impossible for any generous man to disapprove his [Hamilton's] sentence."[9]

Certainly the Virginians did not disapprove nor, in the beginning, did General Washington.[10] But the harassed commander was shortly compelled to change his mind. The British were raising quite a fuss about the treatment of their officers and vowed retaliations on American prisoners in their hands. They also charged a violation of the capitulation, and this goaded Jefferson into a spirited defense which convinced him, at least, that his course was justified.[11]

Washington now tactfully told Jefferson that "this subject, on mature consideration, appears to be involved in greater difficulty than I apprehended." After all, there *was* that little matter of the capitulation; perhaps a publication to the world of Hamilton's cruelties might help; perhaps it might be wise to mitigate his treatment; though, Washington added, don't give him *too* many privileges.[12]

Jefferson was away when Washington's letter reached Williamsburg.

The Council hurriedly complied and removed the prisoners' irons. Jefferson bowed to the inevitable on his return; and a formal parole was drafted. But the prisoners refused to sign because a special clause had been inserted which, so they said, restricted their "freedom of speech" by forbidding them, during their parole, from making remarks prejudicial to the United States. Whereupon Jefferson, with what was probably considerable satisfaction, remanded them again to jail.[13]

The controversy grew in intensity and acerbity; one gets the impression, indeed, that so much energy was involved in this, after all, somewhat less than vital dispute, that far more important matters were for the moment sidetracked. Seemingly, Jefferson was determined to stand on his honor in the matter and yield, if at all, only by small grudging retreats. The day after he had clapped Hamilton back in jail, a paroled American officer appeared from New York with a letter from the British Commissary of Prisoners threatening retaliation against Virginia officers in his hands if Hamilton was not properly treated. The American–Col. George Matthews, himself a Virginian–made a personal plea to Jefferson and produced a letter along the same lines from Washington.[14]

The effect on Jefferson was just the reverse of what had been intended. "Were I to speak from present impressions," he told Washington vehemently, "I should say it was happy for Governor Hamilton that a final determination of his fate was formed before this new information. As the enemy have released Capt. Willing [an imprisoned Virginian] from his irons the Executive of this State will be induced perhaps not to alter their former opinion. But it is impossible they can be serious in attempting to bully us in this manner. We have too many of their subjects in our power & too much iron to clothe them with & I will add too much resolution to avail ourselves of both to fear their pretended retaliation."[15]

Washington wisely ignored this astonishing violence. The flood of correspondence continued unabated, and it was not until October, 1780, a year later, that the embattled Governor finally gave way and permitted Hamilton to be paroled to New York. Even then, Jefferson refused to let him go until he had signed the disputed wording of the parole.[16] Perhaps, as has been remarked, Jefferson showed a vein of iron on this occasion; but one wonders whether that vein would not have been more appropriate in connection with other matters relating to his governorship.

On Jefferson's Council of State were two of his boyhood friends–John Page and John Walker. There was also a third young man–younger by seven years than Jefferson–who eventually became his closest friend and most valiant collaborator–James Madison. Young Madison had traveled north to the newly established college at Princeton to get his education and had returned to Virginia to enter eventually into the Revolutionary House of Delegates. There, at first, he had been quiet in debate, though effective in committee; and Jefferson, while noting him as a supporter of liberal measures, had had no chance to make his closer acquaintance. Toward the end of 1777, however, the House recognized his abilities sufficiently to appoint him to the Council of State, where Jefferson now found him.

The older man and the younger discovered under the pressure of this close relationship those qualities in each other which admirably complemented and mutually strengthened them both. Madison's mind was as keen as Jefferson's, though not as large in contemplation nor as all-embracing in vision. But he was much more logical and analytical, and he tended to limit soaring projects to the immediately practicable. Time and again, his sense of timing and practical consideration held Jefferson from bumping his head against immovable obstacles. Short, spare of frame, dry, precise, almost timid in manner though fearless of intellect, he was just the foil that Jefferson required. Jefferson furnished the larger frame of speculation; Madison seized upon the workable essentials and gave them solidity and logical form. The nation was mightily to benefit from the constant friction of these two minds.

Aside from the Hamilton episode, with its aspects of the *opéra bouffe*, the problem that most absorbed Jefferson's attention was the state of the finances. He was hopeful in the beginning. With the opening of the land office, the proposed sale of confiscated British property and the new tax bill, he expected that the financial situation would improve and enable Virginia, in co-operation with the other States, to bring within workable limits the enormous sums of paper money then in circulation. "Every other remedy," he rightly insisted, "is nonsensical quackery." [17] He saw clearly the dangers of an uncontrolled inflation; and this became one of the numerous points on which he finally broke with his predecessor in office and former political associate, Patrick Henry.

But his optimism soon faded in the cold light of the realities. The demon of inflation was not thus simply exorcised and, within ten days, he was writing despairingly to Richard Henry Lee: "It is a cruel thought, that, when we feel ourselves standing on the firmest ground, in every respect, the cursed arts of our secret enemies, combining with other causes, should effect by depreciating our money, what the open arms of a powerful enemy could not. What is to be done? Taxation is become of no account, for it is foreseen, that, notwithstanding its increased amount, there will still be a greater deficiency than ever. I own I see no assured hope, but in peace, or a plentiful loan of hard money." [18]

Who those "secret enemies" were he did not specify. He may have meant obstructionists in the Assembly, or those outside who refused service, evaded taxation and were ready, either from personal toryism or hope of private gain, to interpose false claims of ownership to forfeited British estates and throw their sale "into a course of legal contestation which under the load of business now on the docquet of the general Court, may not be terminated in the present age." [19]

Meanwhile, the frantic requisitions from Congress to carry on the war continued to flow in unabated; and Jefferson became equally frantic in his attempts to comply. The ever-increasing printing of paper money was certainly not the answer, though the Assembly manfully tried it; the sale of British property was doomed to failure; the land office brought in very little. Only a rigorous collection of taxes would have helped; and Virginians hated taxes. Was not this one of the main reasons why they were throwing over the British yoke? Besides, with the best will in the world, there was little enough real money in Virginia. Their chief money crop, tobacco, was effectualy blockaded from export by, as Jefferson put it, "a parcel of trifling privateers under the countenance of two or three larger vessels who keep our little naval force from doing anything." He complained bitterly to John Jay, the President of Congress, of the supposition that the American fleet should concentrate its efforts on the protection of the northern ports and let the southern ones go hang. Similarly, why did the navy, when it took a British prize off the southern coast, promptly carry it for condemnation into a northern port, and cause the South to lose its just rewards? "A British prize would be a more rare phenomenon here than a comet," he remarked sarcastically, "because the one has been seen, but the other never was." [20]

Whichever way he turned, Jefferson found almost insurmountable difficulties. The food situation was getting more and more serious; the militia, when they deigned to answer the repeated calls to arms, had to be fed, clothed and armed; and it seemed that certain Virginians were more eager to sell provisions to the British, who paid in hard money, than to their own countrymen, who could offer only depreciated paper.

It was therefore determined to place an embargo on the export of all provisions from the state, such as beef, pork, corn, wheat, grain and flour, until the following May 1st, and Jefferson issued a proclamation to that effect.[21] The embargo was continued in force by appropriate acts from time to time, but it was not very effective. The "engrossers and monopolizers" still managed to ship provisions, at enormous profits, everywhere but where they were needed most—in the camps of the American troops.

The problem of troops, arms and munitions was another that engaged Jefferson's closest attention. There was an understandable lack of these important items, and the question was how to allocate what little there was. Congress and the respective States engaged in a constant tug of war over their allocation; the former, under Washington's proddings, insisted that *national* strategy was necessarily uppermost; the latter as vehemently called attention to the requirements for their own defense.

The problem was never really solved. It is easy today to blame the States for their shortsightedness; but it is readily comprehensible that a people, threatened with the horrors of imminent invasion, would turn deaf ears to demands which shifted their sole protection to distant fields and left them naked to the enemy. Such heroic self-sacrifice requires a degree of statesmanship and long-range vision which few possess.

Jefferson tried honestly to co-operate with the demands of Washington and Congress for arms, troops, and more troops. He acknowledged the continental requirements and though he realized the implications to his own beloved state, was willing, wherever possible, to shift troops and munitions to meet those requirements.

With the best will in the world, however, it was easier acknowledged than done. At times he even rebelled. During the summer of 1779, Virginia expected an invasion of her borders and commandeered certain Continental arms within the state. The indignation of Congress brought a vigorous defense from Jefferson. These arms, he stated, were justly due Virginia; seven battalions had been raised in the face of the threat and the troops had to be armed. "In this situation of things a vessel, loaded with arms, seemed to be guided by the hand of providence, into one of our harbours. They were it's true the property of our friends, but of friends indebted to us for those very articles. They were for the common defence too, and we were a part of the Body to be defended." [22]

Though the rumor of invasion proved groundless at the moment, the alarms continued and eventually precipitated into fact. Virginia had furnished large contingents of her able-bodied men to the Continental army and had to rely on rapidly mobilized militia for the protection of the home territory. The militia was always an unpredictable quantity. The Assembly might pass the necessary laws, the Governor and the Council of State might order and threaten dire penalties, but the men assembled reluctantly, if at all; and on numerous occasions refused to march to distant points within the state if there was a possibility their own homes might be threatened, or it was planting or harvest time.

Such, for example, was the state of affairs at the end of 1779. Jefferson and the Council had received intelligence that an invasion was imminent. "It is our duty to provide against every event," Jefferson wrote in the name of the Council to the Speaker of the Assembly, "and the Executive are accordingly engaged in concerting proper measures of defence." They wished to call out the militia to defend York and the south side of the James River, the danger points; but the expense, the exhausted condition of the treasury, the difficulties of the call, the rigor of the season, and the disgust of the militia should no enemy appear, "induce us to refer to the decision of the general assembly" whether the call should be made.[23]

This, of course, was a deliberate avoidance of responsibility that plainly points up Jefferson's failure as a war governor. The difficulties, it is true, were immense; and the obstacles he lists in such detail were there; but it was the duty of a strong executive to surmount difficulties and overcome obstacles, and not drop them into the lap of a legislative body for long debate and enactments that could prove no more effective than his own executive orders. And, if invasion had actually come at this time as was expected, the results of delay would have been disastrous.

By May, 1780, the Assembly realized that the Executive must be given full powers, at least in times of public emergency, and granted extraordinary powers for limited periods to the Governor and the Council. It gave them the right to call out as many as 20,000 men and send them out of the state, if necessary; it authorized them to imprison or remove disaffected persons in the event of invasion or insurrection; and it granted them power to commandeer provisions, cattle, tent linens, horses, wagons and boats for military use and to pay for them at appraised prices.[24] These were indeed large grants of authority and sufficient for strong executive action. But, in spite of occasional flurries of decisiveness, the granted powers were frittered away or left unemployed.

Jefferson was well aware of his own limitations and acknowledged them with candor. Only four months after the Assembly had given him what was practically *carte blanche* in the conduct of the war, he was announcing his determination to quit. He wrote to R. H. Lee: "The application requisite to the duties of the office I hold is so excessive, and the execution of them after all so imperfect, that I have determined to retire from it at the close of the present campaign. I wish a successor to be thought of in time who to sound whiggism can join perseverance in business and an extensive knowledge of the various subjects he must superintend. Such a one may keep us above water even in our present moneyless situation." [25] And, he might have added, furnish a boldness and promptitude in execution which he never possessed. Even when he was President, there were occasions when action was too much sicklied over with the pale hue of thought.

Another example ought to prove sufficient. From April 7, 1780, until May 13th, in the midst of war, Jefferson had been unable to get his Council together. As a result, he confessed, no business was transacted during this period of five weeks! [26]

Yet, for all the turmoil and confusion at home, Jefferson was taking bold steps to rivet the vast western territory irrevocably to Virginia and the infant United States. He may not have been the right man to cope with the endless day-to-day decisions of local administration; he may have observed too strictly the legal limitations of his office when it came to seeming infringements on the sacred rights and privileges of his fellow citizens; yet all indecision and all constitutional inhibitions dropped like a cloak when he faced the problems of the western lands and the eventual expansion of his country. Here he was prompt, far-seeing, bold in conception and decisive in deed. He moved freely and unhampered, and without a single qualm. The same change occurred in him during his Presidency in dealing with Louisiana.

The touchstone he applied to any assumption of power seemed to be:

will this, as a precedent, tend eventually to subvert the liberties of the American people? In domestic matters, he answered himself, it probably would. In foreign affairs, however—particularly when new lands were gained thereby—it would not. Late in 1779, Clark expressed a desire to build a fort at the juncture of the Ohio River with the Mississippi, and the plan fired Jefferson's imagination. Thereby two ends would be served. One, the safeguarding of the western frontier; two, the protection of American trade with New Orleans as it moved along these vital waterways.[27] He sent prompt approval to Clark, together with detailed, almost minute instructions for building the fort, recruiting and storing of provisions. Anything that related to construction operations evoked his enthusiasm; his fingers itched for the drafting board and the precise arithmetical calculations of cubic yards of earth, linear feet of lumber, number of bricks, sizes, shapes, dimensions. Yet he did not forget in these details the more philosophic aspects.

"We approve very much," he wrote, "of a mild conduct towards the inhabitants of the French villages. It would be well to be introducing our Laws to their knowledge and to impress them strongly with the advantages of a Free Government." In like vein, Clark was to cultivate peace and friendship with the various Indian tribes, and to encourage their forays against those Indians who were at war with the United States. But not against the English. "Notwithstanding their base example we wish not to expose them to the inhumanities of a savage enemy. Let this reproach remain on them, but for ourselves we would not have our national character tarnished with such a practice." Of course, he added almost as an afterthought, should the English attack the Indians, "these will have a natural right to punish the aggressors and we none to hinder them. It will then be no act of ours. But to invite them to a participation of the [war] is what we would avoid by all possible means."[28]

What also motivated Jefferson in this close preoccupation with the West, and his eagerness to send expeditions into the wilderness, even at the risk of weakening defenses at home and hampering the Continental effort, was his fear that Virginia might lose her claimed rights to that noble area. He had fought the first attempts to place the territory without adequate safeguards under the sole control of Congress; and he was now deeply concerned over the conflicting claims of Pennsylvania. In particular, Pittsburg, at the head of navigation on the Ohio, was in dispute.

Mason and Dixon had surveyed the line between Pennsylvania and Maryland in 1767, but had failed to run it farther west, where Pennsylvania and Virginia faced each other across a disputed territory. Pennsylvania men had rushed into the troubled area in large numbers and spilled across the Ohio into what Virginia claimed was her private domain. Virginia men followed suit. As a result, there ensued a bewildering complexity of irregular titles, opposing claims and threats to maintain possession by force.

Virginia ordered all new settlements to cease; but her ukase was disregarded by the land-hungry pioneers on both sides. She therefore established a land office, laid out districts of her own in the disputed areas, and sent commissioners to clean up the titles. When Pennsylvania protested to Congress, Jefferson assured that body that no attempts would be made at actual dispossession until the Virginia legislature had first made an attempt to settle matters with Pennsylvania; even though, on the statute books as of October, 1779, provision had been made to use military force, if necessary, to remove recalcitrant squatters from the northern banks of the Ohio.[29] True to his word, on July 1, 1780, the legislature passed a resolution to appoint joint commissioners with Pennsylvania to settle the line between them.[30]

Nevertheless, while this was pending, Jefferson continued to urge Clark on to further efforts, even to an ambitious expedition against Detroit, the outpost of British power in the northwest territory. When informed of the proposed expedition, Washington gave cautious approval, though acknowledging that he had neither the force nor the means to effect it. He was willing to leave the project to Jefferson and Clark jointly.[31]

This eminently suited Jefferson, as a *Virginia* success against Detroit would have firmly fixed her claims to the entire area; and he drove ahead as fast and hard as he could. But Clark soon discovered the difficulties to be insuperable: money and supplies were woefully limited; essential Indian auxiliaries could not be raised in the numbers required nor, if raised, kept satisfied with sufficient gifts; and Washington, in spite of his earlier disclaimer, had ordered Colonel Daniel Brodhead at Pittsburg to join in the proposed expedition. Conflicts of authority and personal clashes between the two commanders followed, and Clark reluctantly abandoned the plan. With it went glimmering all hopes of a Virginia empire in the West, and Jefferson thereupon pitched his sights on a more national scale.[32] But the West, and the illimitable prospects of American expansion across wilderness and prairie, never left his mind and bore startling fruit during the period of his Presidency.

While his attention was thus engaged in vast plans to the west, more immediate problems rose to plague him at home. The British had shifted the main theater of their operations to the south; North Carolina had been raided and South Carolina was under concerted attack. General Horatio Gates, the hero of Saratoga, and General Nathanael Greene commanded the defending American forces. For the first time, Virginia stood in danger of invasion by land as well as from sea. From his new capital at Richmond, to which the government had removed in obedience to legislative decision, Jefferson was compelled during his second term in office to face an increasingly grave situation.

Frantic requests for troops poured in from Greene and Gates almost daily. Jefferson agreed that the need was urgent, and offered Greene the militia of four counties already in camp on the southern border. But he added an astonishing proviso to the offer. As he told General von Steuben, he would send them, "provided they can be induced to go willingly. The length of their march heretofore and having been some time in service seems to give them a right to be consulted." [33]

The imagination falters over the nature of Steuben and Greene's thoughts at such a reservation. The Carolinas were in grave danger of being wholly overrun, with nothing but poorly equipped and insufficient forces in their path; Charleston was being bombarded and eventually surrendered on May 12; and the whole future of the United States wavered in the balance. Yet the wishes of each individual Virginia militiaman had first to be consulted before he could be sent to the rescue. This, Steuben must have thought, accustomed as he was to the iron discipline of European armies, was indeed a strange war.

But it must be said in partial defense that Jefferson knew his fellow Virginians—at least those who had not patriotically volunteered for Continental service and remained behind to act as militia. Many of them were imbued with the most narrowly parochial views; many of them, particularly from the western counties, were either wholly weary of the war or Tory in sympathies.

In July, 1780, the frightening information came to Richmond that an insurrection had raised formidable head on the New River. Colonel Preston, the commander in the area, feared that the insurgents intended to march on the lead mines—Virginia's chief source for the raw materials of bullets—and destroy them. Jefferson promptly called on Colonel William Campbell to drop his other duties and "take in hand those Parricides, and if they have proceeded as we have heard to actual murder, to recommend that you take such effectual measures of punishment as may secure the future safety of that quarter." To that end Campbell was to apply "the means & powers put into your hands for the Indian expedition." [34]

Within a month the insurrection had been suppressed, but Jefferson was determined to make an example of the leaders. He was willing to countenance philosophical Tories, especially when they fled to England and did nothing to impede the Revolution; but he was ruthless against those who remained at home and in active opposition. He wrote Colonel Charles Lynch, the judge in charge of proceedings—and whose name has since been offered in evidence, because of what followed, as the origin of the current word *lynch*—that "the most vigorous, decisive measures shou'd be continued for seizing every one on whom probable proof of guilt shall appear;" to try the leaders and officers for high treason and let the smaller fry go, provided they repented and turned State's evidence.[35]

At the same time he congratulated Campbell for having so effectually put down the rebellion. Campbell raised a nice question, however. His militia had not only suppressed the insurrectionists, but had enthusiastically and indiscriminately looted. Campbell asked for power to restore the loot. Jefferson shrugged away the main issue and engaged in some rather curious quibbling. "You are too well acquainted with our government," he replied, "not to know that no power of doing that is lodged with the executive. You can also judge whether if the appropriation is made by the people themselves and nothing said about it, there will be any danger of the former proprietors troubling them with actions. It would seem probable they will hardly ever hazard their lives by stirring such a question, unless they were really innocent, in which case it ought to be restored to them. This is all I think myself at liberty to say on this question." [36]

The May, 1780, meeting of the Assembly, under the prodding of events and the insistence of Washington and Congress, had passed a series of bills designed to cope with the emergency. They recalled the paper money in circulation for redemption, in accordance with a Congressional resolution, at twenty to one of new bills of credit, bearing interest, and redeemable in 1786 on the pledge of the United States. They voted to complete their unfilled quota to the Continental army by raising 3,000 men for service until the end of 1781. They abolished the boards of War and Trade, which had proved inefficient, and substituted a Commercial Agent, a Commissioner of Navy and one for War, to be appointed by the Governor with the advice of his Council. They gave to Jefferson those extraordinary powers in time of danger to which reference has already been made. They voted to raise militia for service in invaded South Carolina. And they voted a new emission of £2,000,000 in treasury notes and imposed new taxes.[37]

But it took more than mere legislative sanctions to put these laudable steps into action. Washington, it is true, was happy to hear that his native state finally contemplated new additions to his forces. But he was not so happy over the limit of service to eighteen months; he would have preferred enlistment for the duration. "Short inlistments," he complained, "have subjected Us to such distresses, to such enormous expences, have so intimately hazarded our liberties that I never reflect on them, but with a degree of horror." [38]

He continued to reflect on Virginia's unwillingness to extend the period and found it most unpalatable. A month later he returned to the attack. "To our army's being levied on a short and temporary footing, the War has been protracted already to a period, to which I am doubtful whether it would ever have otherwise extended; to this we may ascribe near all our other misfortunes and present embarrassments, and to this the loss of our liberties and Independence, if the fatal event should take place. This system of politics has brought us very low indeed, and had we not been held up by providence and a powerful Ally, we must have submitted before this to the Yoke of bondage." [39]

Even this strong plea did not shake Virginia's—nor, for that matter, most of the other states'—determination to keep their levies on a carefully rationed basis. Nor did Jefferson do anything to bring pressure on the Assembly. He hated standing armies with an abiding hatred, considering them sure weapons for the overthrow of liberty. Even in time of war he put all his faith, in spite of present experiences to the contrary, in a militia of the people, springing to arms democratically in defense of their hearths and their institutions.

From the South, too, came urgent calls for help. General Gates had made a special trip to Richmond to plead his cause and had been warned by Jefferson "to look forward to much Difficulty and a perplexed Department." Yet now, ensconced in headquarters at Hillsborough, he renewed his pleas. Never, he declared, had he seen such terrible want as his command exhibited. Of the militia voted by Virginia to go to his assistance, only 1,438 were on the ground, and these were practically without arms. They had few guns, and many of those they had were useless; they had few cartridge boxes, and no bayonets at all. In short, they needed arms, ammunition, provisions, tents—everything! [40]

As though this was not bad enough, he forwarded a report the very next day, "so extraordinary in itself, that your Excellency [Jefferson] will be necessarily led into an Enquiry of the State in which they (the Cartridge Boxes &c) left Virginia, and to whom intrusted as it carries exceedingly the Appearance of Neglect or Fraud." [41]

Almost every day Gates wrote imploring letters to Jefferson, all chanting the same monotonous litany: what good are your soldiers if they lack every supply, have neither guns nor bullets, nor tents under which to sleep? By August 3rd, he was writing with prophetic despair: unless the unpardonable backwardness of Virginia and North Carolina in sending supplies is remedied immediately, there will be no army soon to defend the South.[42]

Jefferson tried hard to respond to all the calls that came in from every quarter. Yet he did not know quite which way to turn. Everyone was asking *him* for help when it seemed to him that Virginia stood most in need of it herself. The flower of her troops had been trapped in the Charleston surrender; military intelligence reached him at a snail's pace; military stores, which only the North could supply, never reached him and therefore could not be transmitted to the clamoring troops in the South; and the cry of Congress for money—and more money—was eternal. Which way indeed ought he to face? he asked Washington almost pathetically. He was situated between two fires—to the north and to the south; and both Congress and Virginia were divided as to where Virginia's battered resources should go.[43]

Yet, at a time when he was thus harried with matters of war and possible collapse, he was astonishingly able to exult over a victory in a totally different field. George Wythe had opened a law school! "Our new institution at the College," he wrote Madison, "has had a success which has gained it universal applause. Wythe's school is numerous, they hold weekly Courts & Assemblies in the Capitol. The professors join in it, and the young men dispute with elegance, method & learning. This single school by throwing from time to time new hands well principled, & well informed into the legislature, will be of infinite value." [44]

Certainly the man who could write like this had an abiding faith in the eventual triumph of the Revolutionary cause.

Within three weeks, however, that faith was to suffer a shattering blow. On August 16, 1780, the main Continental army in the South was routed and cut to pieces at Camden in South Carolina. Gate's gloomy prognostications had only too literally been fulfilled, and Gates himself was compelled to spur hard and furiously to avoid capture by the triumphant British. It was one of the great disasters of the war, and Virginia's ill-equipped contingents seem to have contributed to it by scattering hastily at the first impact of the enemy.

The news came as a tremendous blow to Jefferson, both for its far-reaching consequences and the shock to State pride. He expressed his deep mortification to Gates, now at Hillsborough again, and apologized for the faint hearts of the Virginia militia. He was calling out new levies, and would send down more regulars "as fast as they come out of the Hospital." Virginia was in truth scraping the bottom of the barrel. But alas, they had no arms to put in their hands, aside from the few Congress had supplied. And, once more, the old refrain: "Our treasury is utterly exhausted and cannot again be replenished till the Assembly meets in October. We might however furnish considerable Quantities of Provision were it possible to convey it to you." To which Gates retorted with considerable asperity that he wanted no more Virginia troops either in the field or in camp unless they were furnished with shoes, blankets and other necessities.[45]

It was a sad commentary on the situation that while Rome metaphorically burned, the members of the Assembly could go unconcernedly about their private affairs and reconvene only when legally compelled; leaving both the state and the Executive helpless to cope in the interim with disaster. At least Jefferson tried his best, within the legal limits of his circumscription. He scribbled down some headings for possible emergency measures: call up a troop of horse and 10,000 men; call vessels and stores from the shipyard, and provide bateaux for quick removal of material from the foundry in case of invasion; order the Convention prisoners to the interior; get beeves for the barracks and impress wagons and provisions.[46] None of these came to anything, except the eventual removal of the prisoners. He had to seek aid elsewhere.

He convened the Council, and sent his tale of woe along to those patient ears, Washington and Samuel Huntington, the president of Congress. To the latter he told also of the insurrection in the four upland counties, which involved many hundreds who had "actually enlisted to serve his

Britannic Majesty" and taken an oath of allegiance to him; and of his fears that in the hour of trial other counties would similarly fail.[47]

At the same time, however, he was still able to rise above the immediate disaster to a broad, continental viewpoint. In statesmanlike fashion he wrote to the Chevalier de la Luzerne, the French commander: "The interest of this State is intimately blended, so perfectly the same with that of the others of the confederacy that the most effectual aid it can at any time receive, is where the general cause most needs it. Of this yourself, Congress, and General Washington, are so perfect judges that it is not for me to point it out.... If their action in the north will have more powerful influence towards establishing our Independence, they ought not to be wished for in the south, be the temporary misfortunes there what they will."

Wise and brave words, indeed. Yet he could not help but insinuate that the aid of the French fleet to clear out Chesapeake Bay, "the unavoidable channel of all our commerce," might well contribute to the total cause. Virginia's own fleet, pitifully comprised of a single fourteen-gun brig and two armed boats, was certainly insufficient for the job, even when combined with Maryland's similarly small naval force.[48]

And, as if to fill the cup of present and impending disaster to the brim, came simultaneous warnings from the north and the south that Virginia was about to be invaded. Cornwallis, flushed with recent triumphs, was moving up from Carolina; while Sir Henry Clinton was embarking from New York to join in a gigantic pincer operation.[49]

CHAPTER 15

Time of Troubles

THERE had been alarms before of invasion, but aside from a brief raid on Portsmouth in May, 1779, none of them had actually materialized.[1] This time, however, the cry of *wolf* proved only too true. On the morning of October 20, 1780, a formidable British fleet appeared in Hampton Roads, packed with soldiery, part of whom were promptly debarked near Portsmouth.

An express arrived in Richmond with the news on October 22nd, and Jefferson put into motion the pitiful means he had to oppose them. Whatever scattered militia were on hand in the threatened area turned out; but they had, as usual, few arms and practically no cartridge paper, without which no bullets could be fired. And, even if properly equipped, the militia on foot was helpless against the enemy's horse. Fears were expressed that the British intended to press on to Richmond itself, and once again measures were taken to move the Convention prisoners further into the interior.

But by the middle of November, the seemingly overwhelming storm had blown over. Clinton had performed his share of the maneuver by sending an army down from New York; Cornwallis, however, poised in the South, had not moved. Even so, had the British force on hand acted energetically, it could have swept over a practically undefended Virginia. After seizing Portsmouth and raiding sporadically into the surrounding country, the enemy lost heart and re-embarked their troops on the night of November 15th; leaving behind them a large number of Negro slaves who had joined them in the hope of gaining freedom.[2]

Jefferson breathed a little more freely; but he realized that what had once happened could happen again, and with more determination. The dilatory Assembly had reconvened, and he demanded of them increased preparations for defense rather than congratulation on the enemy's retirement. They could well be expected to return, this time with a force "to which the southern states have yet seen nothing equal." The other southern states could do nothing to help; on Virginia alone would rest the total burden.

He was now ready to advocate a permanent army. The disastrous ventures with the militia convinced him that Washington had been right. Let the Assembly do something about it, and vote the necessary supplies as well. "The proposals herewith transmitted for raising a standing body of forces for the defence of this state," he added, "requiring conditions beyond the powers of the executive, I beg leave to submit them to the wisdom of the General Assembly."[3]

The Assembly did not respond to these appeals. They felt they had done enough at the beginning of their session when they had voted 3,000 men to the Continental army to serve for three years or the duration, with attractive bounties which included "a healthy, sound negro, between the ages of ten and thirty years, or sixty pounds in gold or silver, at the option of the soldier," if he volunteered for the duration. They had also voted suitable supplies of clothes, provisions and wagons, and had ordered seizure in the event they were not otherwise forthcoming. They had, in addition, voted the emission of up to £6,000,000 in paper money and authorized the Governor to issue £4,000,000 more at his discretion.[4] What more, they thought, could mortals do? Nothing, perhaps, except to see to it that the orders were translated into action.

In the midst of turmoil and invasion, threatened and actual, several things happened. General Nathanael Greene superseded Gates as commander of the paper army of the South, and Gates retired northward, his laurels sadly tarnished, to sulk in his tents.[5] Mazzei, from Paris, en route to Italy, was writing enthusiastically of the possible fruition of Jefferson's dream of peopling Virginia with Mediterranean laborers. He had met a Neapolitan prince, of "an old branch of the Medicean family, who assured me that with a moderate fortune & families of labourers & mechanicks, he will bring to Virginia true Republican Sentiments. The notions of Equality among mankind have made of late a most rapid & surprising progress."[6] This news doubtless encouraged Jefferson mightily in his hour of need!

Yet perhaps it did; for Jefferson had the amazing faculty of withdrawing himself completely from the immediacies of the occasion into an almost unrestrained absorption in intellectual pursuits. How else can one explain his taking this particular moment in the war, amid his excessive duties as Governor, to commence research for what was to develop as his famous *Notes on Virginia*, in response to a formal general request from the French Minister?

"I am at present busily employed for Monsr. Marbois," he wrote the Chevalier d'Anmours, "without his knowing it, and have to acknolege to him the mysterious obligation for making me much better acquainted with my own country than I ever was before. His queries as to this country just [came] into my hands by Mr. Jones. I take every occasion which presents itself of procuring answers. Some of them however can never be answered till I shall go to Monticello where alone the materials exist which can enable any one to answer them."[7]

So absorbed did he become, in fact, in this fascinating new venture that he was ready to resign his governorship and devote his entire time to the project. He had been keeping his own meteorological journal right through the war, but he wanted similar data from other parts of the state. He wrote

John Page who, in spite of his position on the Council of State, was currently enjoying his leisure amid domestic scenes at Rosewell, for his meteorological observations as well as his copy of the list of tithes for Virginia. Page sent what he could; at the same time begging Jefferson not to resign, as he had intimated he would.[8]

Perhaps it would have been better had Jefferson carried out his present intention of resigning. His reputation might then have been spared the worst blot of all.

For the balance of the year, however, the skies seemed to have brightened somewhat. The enemy had retired; George Rogers Clark's western adventure seemed fraught with happy omens and met with the approval of Washington; and a daughter, weighing 10½ pounds, had been born to Martha Jefferson on November 3rd.[9] Lucy Elizabeth, as she was christened, unfortunately survived only a few months, but this was naturally not foreseen at the time of her birth.

True, the Assembly did not view full co-operation with General Greene with the same urgency that Jefferson did. Greene had come to Richmond with the expectation of making Virginia an effective base for his proposed campaign against Cornwallis; but he found Virginia absorbed solely in her own defense. He proceeded in disgust to the Carolinas to take command, first leaving, however, an estimate with Jefferson of his requirements in men, money and supplies. He pointed out that Virginia's best defense lay in the defeat of Cornwallis, and that the success of the entire war depended on his success in the Carolinas.[10] Jefferson duly passed on the information to the Assembly, but that body failed to react.

Greene had left Steuben in charge of operations at Richmond, and it was with him that Jefferson dealt from now on. Jefferson tried to get the Assembly to send General Lawson's corps to the South, but they refused, on the ground that the terms of enlistment of the men had nearly expired. Somewhat taken aback, Jefferson inquired of Steuben whether he should not attempt to get the corps to agree to serve on a voluntary basis. Steuben, annoyed at this most unmilitary procedure, indicated that he would prefer to see the men dismissed; and Jefferson with his Council acquiesced in the following language: "The Diversion of their services to an object different from that to which they had attached their original views seems to have had a considerable influence on their minds; as also on the Militia who were under marching orders for Carolina & stopped in like manner." [11]

This was the state of affairs when the thunderbolt finally struck. On October 10, 1780, Washington had sent a second warning that another expedition out of New York directed toward the South was impending, though he did not know whether Virginia or the Carolinas was the objective. Included in the warning was advice to remove all public stores from the vicinity of navigable waters and to take all precautions for defense.

On January 2, 1781, he sent actual news: a large British fleet had sailed out of New York, destination south, under the command of Benedict Arnold, the American traitor.[12] But the information was too late; before the letter arrived in Richmond, Jefferson knew only too well that Arnold's destination was Virginia.

Richmond, the new capital, was situated at that point on the James River where the waters tumbled down from the mid-central plateau to the plain which stretched flat and straight to the sea. It was a small, provincial town; its houses all of simple, unadorned wood except for two aristocratic brick dwellings. The "governor's house," on the brow of what is now Capitol Hill, was wooden and plain; and in it Jefferson was installed with his family, who had descended from Monticello with their personal slaves to keep him company. The Assembly met in a larger house, similarly of wood, and "shedded round like a barn on the hill." A saddler shop shared quarters with the Assembly; and Billy Wiley, the saddler, doubled as doorkeeper when the legislature was in session. It was all a far cry from Williamsburg.[13]

On Sunday, December 31, 1780, the final day of the year, at 8 a.m., a messenger rode up to the door of the Governor's "palace" and handed Jefferson a letter. It came from General Nelson, to whom it had been addressed by Jacob Wray, a Hampton merchant. Wray reported that he had sighted on the morning of Friday, December 29th, twenty-seven sail proceeding down Chesapeake Bay, just below Willoughby's Point, the southern cape of the James River. They were manifestly warships, but whether friend or foe, or what their destination was, Wray did not know.[14]

Why Nelson merely sent along the information to Jefferson without taking immediate measures is not known—for it was obvious that this was the long-heralded British fleet out of New York, of which the warnings had come thick and fast. Nor is it known why a leisurely two days elapsed before the message reached Richmond.

Questions were hurled at Jefferson later on: Why, for example, had there been no lookouts posted along those strategic shores, and why did such vital information depend on a casual encounter by a militia officer? Where were the series of postriders which Congress had established at its own expense the preceding summer? Why was there such a delay in taking measures even after the information was received?

Some of these questions Jefferson was able later to answer with a fair degree of satisfaction; others he was hard put to it to answer at all.

William Tatham, attached to Nelson's staff, happened to be in Richmond at the time. Hearing of the news, he rode over to Jefferson's house. He found him calmly walking out, seemingly unperturbed. Jefferson acknowledged that an express had just arrived; but he believed that the enemy fleet meditated nothing more than a foraging party ashore and, unless he received further information, he had no intention of disturbing the country by calling out the militia.[15]

For two days, in fact, Jefferson did nothing, except to write some letters asking for information that was most dilatory in coming, and sending Nelson down to investigate.[16] Since it was Sunday, Jefferson did not even trouble to convene his Council.

On the next day, Monday, January 1, 1781, the Council met in regular session. It consisted, besides Jefferson in the chair, of David Jameson, William Fleming, Andrew Lewis, George Webb and Jacquelin Ambler—Jefferson's successful rival for the hand of Rebecca Burwell.

No further news had arrived in the interim, and Jefferson laid before the Council Wray's letter to Nelson and explained that he had written to the latter and various militia officers along the coast "requiring several necessary measures to be taken, & had given orders for stationing expresses for obtaining proper intelligence." [17] The Council approved of what had been done and adjourned.

On the following morning, January 2nd, fifty hours after the first information, the damning news at length arrived. Col. Nathaniel Burwell reported that this was no mere foraging party; a powerful British fleet had initiated a full-scale invasion of Virginia. The ships had entered the James River and were already at Warrasqueak Bay.

At once the hitherto calm atmosphere of Richmond was transformed into feverish activity. No one knew just how far up the river the British intended to penetrate. The Council came up with a flurry of orders: that half of the militia of the three surrounding counties and a fourth of three more further up be called out for mobilization at Petersburg; that Nelson be commissioned a Brigadier during the invasion and ordered to call out the militia of the lower counties; that the arms and stores at Petersburg, the logical goal of the British, be removed to Richmond; that the gunpowder at the powder mills be transferred to Westham, and canoes commandeered to remove the stores, if necessary, farther up the river; and that the Convention troops be shifted out of rescue reach into Maryland.[18]

The members of the Assembly promptly arose and hastened to their respective counties to supervise the raising of the militia. General Steuben, with a total Continental force of 200 new recruits, hastened to the defense of Petersburg which, as the depot for the Southern army, he thought might well be the enemy's aim.

Jefferson sat down to send broadcast to the various County Lieutenants the necessary orders. Up to this moment he had not believed that more than the coast would be invaded; but now it seemed clear that either Petersburg or Richmond would be the focal point of invasion. Two vital days had been lost in mobilizing the neighborhood militia. He was then, and later, to complain that he was not at fault; that the first report had not been sufficient to put him on his guard.[19]

On the night of the 3rd more news came. The enemy ships had cast anchor at Jamestown. Jefferson relaxed. Perhaps *that* was their destination. But when he was aroused at 5 a.m. on the 4th to be told that the ships had lifted anchor and were sailing past Kennon's and Hood's, the realization finally broke on him that this was a serious, full-scale invasion and that the capital itself was threatened. The time for piecemeal measures was over. Still another day had been partially wasted.

He immediately convened the Council and now *all* the militia of the surrounding counties were ordered out, instead of by halves and quarters, this time to rendezvous at Westham, some seven miles above Richmond and across the river. And Col. Taylor was urged to start moving the Convention prisoners to Maryland without even waiting for their baggage to be packed.[20] A sense of urgency was beginning to pervade the scene.

By the evening of the 4th, they heard that the enemy had landed at Westover and that Richmond was therefore definitely their destination. Benedict Arnold was moving fast, aiming to strike at the heart of Virginia, and capture the entire government if he could. He almost succeeded.

With this startling information before him, Jefferson reversed some of his previous orders. Instead of loading the precious stores by wagon along the Richmond side of the river, where they could easily be pursued by light cavalry, he shipped them directly across the river; then crossed personally that evening and rode to the arms foundry six miles up, where he ordered all-night wagoning of arms and stores to Westham and across the river. Then on to Westham, and finally to Tuckahoe where he had already sent his family for safekeeping. He arrived there at one in the morning, and spent what remained of the night.[21]

He knew by now that the time had been too short for a straggling militia to reach Richmond in time for any real defense. But the myth of an armed militia springing to battle, full-panoplied and aroused, was to die hard with him, if at all.

Benedict Arnold was marching with all speed. With only 900 lightly accoutered troops he quit Westover and the safety of his ships at 2 P.M. on January 4th and covered the twenty-five miles to Richmond by 1 P.M. on the 5th. It was a daring, well-timed exploit; a dash through the heart of an enemy country which ought to have been swarming with militia. Yet he was wholly unopposed. In fact, aside from a few shots fired at the ships further down the river, the whole expedition had met with no resistance.

Richmond itself was deserted except for cowering civilians. The Governor was gone; so were his Council and the members of the Assembly.

The British entered in triumph; though they were disappointed to find that their quarry had fled. According to Isaac, one of Jefferson's slaves who had been left behind, they wanted particularly to catch Jefferson, and had brought along a pair of silver handcuffs to clap on him. But Isaac's story was pretty considerably embroidered in the later telling.[22]

They plundered his wine cellar, however, though they left the furniture intact. George, another of Jefferson's slaves, saved the silver by hiding it in the bed tick; for which quick-wittedness he was later granted his freedom, but elected to continue in Jefferson's employ.

Arnold blew up the powder magazine and destroyed or carried off the public records, some of which in the hurry of the occasion had not been removed. He wasted no time, however, in mere destruction. He was after bigger game. A regiment of infantry and 30 horse, under Lt. Col. John G. Simcoe, pursued the lumbering wagons toward the foundry and Westham, burned the foundry, the boring mill and other buildings which had been the center of Virginia arms manufacture, destroyed whatever stores they found still on this side of the river and returned to Richmond.

On January 6th, Arnold decided it was time to retire. The entire countryside had been alarmed, and even the lackadaisical militia was beginning to form. Steuben and Nelson, whom he had outguessed, were hastily approaching from Petersburg. He burnt both public and private buildings, gathered up all the slaves he could find or persuade to go along with him, and retreated at noon to Westover, where the guns of the ships protected him.

Among the slaves thus captured were ten belonging to Jefferson. Isaac, then a young boy, was one of them. The British, he admitted afterward, treated them quite well, giving them plenty of fresh meat and wheat bread. But the fever raged at Yorktown, where they were eventually carried, and many of the Negroes died, though none of Jefferson's. These hid in a cave after the battle of Yorktown, and Washington brought them back to Richmond, where Jefferson picked them up. Their brief taste of freedom was over.[23]

Steuben and Nelson, by now reinforced with a considerable body of militia which even his enemies later admitted had been raised by Jefferson's unwearied exertions,[24] followed Arnold cautiously down to Westover. Unable to attack his intrenchments under the guns of his ships, Steuben contented himself with throwing screens of troops around the neighborhood to guard against further raids; and eventually Arnold boarded ship with his booty and dropped down the river to Yorktown. He had ruthlessly exposed Virginia's undefended condition and destroyed its seat of government.

During these eventful proceedings, Jefferson was engaged in a literal frenzy of activity, sparing neither himself nor his mount. On the morning of January 5th he rose early, took his family across the river and sent them to Fine Creek, his father's first establishment. Even Tuckahoe might not be immune from enemy raids. Then he spurred to Westham and supervised the removal of the stores. On to Chetwood's, which Steuben had appointed as his headquarters, riding so hard that his horse foundered and he was compelled to borrow another. Steuben was not there, and after a fruitless search, Jefferson returned to Westham to work far into the night. He slept briefly at Daniel Hylton's house and awoke on the 6th to renew operations.

About fifteen tons of munitions were rescued by the time Simcoe's party came up. Three hundred stand of arms had hastily to be dumped in the river and afterward recovered. But those public records which had been shifted from Richmond were ferreted out and destroyed.[25]

That evening he rode indefatigably to Fine Creek to be with Martha and his three children; and on the following morning returned to Westham to inspect the damage—all in a downpour of rain—and down to Manchester. By now it was Sunday, January 8th, and Arnold had quit Richmond. The next morning Jefferson crossed to the partially burnt capital and ruefully surveyed his losses.

These, according to his calculations, amounted to the 300 muskets thrown into the river, uniforms, leather, tools and wagons, five brass cannon which the enemy dragged from the river into which Jefferson had dropped them, five to six tons of powder, public records, buildings and manufactories destroyed. All in all, a serious loss to a state at best ill-equipped with the sinews of war.

Jefferson claimed that "the parracide Arnold" had 1,500 infantry with him and 50 to 120 horse. Opposed to them at the initial start of the raid were 200 militiamen, who fled from Richmond at the first shot.[26]

He promptly convened the Council on the 8th; but only three others beside himself had returned; and it adjourned from day to day until January 19th before an additional member ventured out of hiding to constitute a quorum and the business of government could be resumed. The Assembly could not collect itself until March. The Council listened gravely to an account by Jefferson of what he had done during the recess and of events in general. These had been considerable. With over 2,000 militia embodied in four groups, Steuben had seen Arnold quit Westover on the 10th in his ships. He had raced across country in an attempt to cut him off at Hood's, but failed to get there in time and the British continued down the river unscathed.

They also heard and approved of Jefferson's proposed proclamation declaring paroles forced by the British on "peaceable Citizens" as null and void; and continued the embargo on provisions before they adjourned.[27]

Laboriously Jefferson began to pick up the pieces. He was sufficiently stout of heart to provide for Clark's ever-recurrent Detroit expedition and to express to Congress the assent of Virginia to the resolution of the preceding year which ceded the lands claimed on the north side of the Ohio to the general government, provided the States ratified the Articles of Confederation. "This single event," he declared, "could it take place shortly would overweigh every success which the Enemy have hitherto obtained and render desperate the hopes to which those successes have given birth."[28]

Similarly, he issued a call for a special session of the Assembly for March 1st. Since the public funds were exhausted and men like Washington,

Greene and Steuben had stated that "our Defence could not be rested on militia . . . men and money will be the Subject of your Deliberations."[29]

But the humiliation he had suffered during that one disastrous week turned to bitter wrath against the author of his ills. Benedict Arnold, the man who had been responsible, the traitor to his country and his cause, must be made to suffer for it. Jefferson conjured up visions of what he would do with him if only he had him in his power. With vengeful pen he wrote to an unnamed officer, probably General John P. G. Muhlenburg: "[I want you] to drag [Arnold] from those under whose wing he is now sheltered. On his march to and from this place I am certain it might have been done with facility by men of enterprise & firmness. I think it may still be done though perhaps not quite so easily. Having peculiar confidence in the men from the Western side of the Mountains, I meant as soon as they should come down, to get an enterprize proposed to a chosen number of them, such whose courage and fidelity would be above all doubt." Let Muhlenburg pick "from among them proper characters, in such number as you think best, to reveal to them our desire, & engage them to undertake to seize and bring off this greatest of all traitors." Jefferson engaged to get them a reward of 5,000 guineas if they captured Arnold alive, besides the satisfaction of knowing that their names would be gloriously recorded in history.[30]

Thus far, though melodramatic enough, the plan might be considered as permissible. But Jefferson went further, in an unpublished section which, on calmer consideration, he crossed out from his original draft and never sent. Here his white-hot rage truly reveals itself. "I shall be sorry to suppose that any circumstances may put it out of their power to bring him off alive and after they shall have taken him, & of course oblige them to put him to death. Should this happen however [illegible word] and America be deprived of the satisfaction of seeing him exhibited as a public spectacle of infamy & of vengeance, I must give my approbation to their putting him to death. I do this considering him as a deserter from the American army." But, in that case, "I must reduce the reward proposed to 2000 guineas, in proportion as our satisfaction would be reduced."[31]

Jefferson could not, however, afford to waste his energies in wild plots such as this. A letter from Washington helped put him back on the proper track. Though mortified at Arnold's unopposed depredations, he warned Jefferson that "the evils you have to apprehend from these predatory incursions are not to be compared with the injury to the common cause and with the danger to your state in particular, from the conquest of those states southward of you," and "I am persuaded the attention to your immediate safety will not divert you from the measures intended to reinforce the Southern army and put it in a condition to stop the progress of the enemy in that Quarter." It was Cornwallis that had to be watched; Arnold's operations were merely a covering feint.[32]

Even before this admonition arrived, however, Jefferson had received a most remarkably vehement, almost incoherent communication from Gates, who was still smarting from the defeat he had suffered at Camden. It was high time, Gates declaimed, that there was an army in the field to oppose Cornwallis, well armed and equipped, superior in numbers, and prepared to take the offensive. Once Cornwallis conquered most of North Carolina, he warned, "you must expect the Weight of War, will penetrate into your Bowels, and cause such an Inflammation there, as may, (if timely Remedies are not applied) consume the Life Blood of the State.—Have you cried aloud to Congress, and to the Commander in Chief of the Army, for Succour?—have they listened to your Cry?—if they have not, are you doing the best Thing for Yourselves.—Military Wisdom has heretofore been imputed to Virginia. Is there a Rotteness [*sic*] in the State of Denmark?—find it out.—and cut it off.—This is the Letter of One Chess Player, to Another —not the Letter of General Gates, to Governor Jefferson." [33]

From all sides, then, fell these hammer blows of urgency on Jefferson's head. Virginia was pivotal. On what that state could do immediately, depended the fate of the war.

It was easy enough for outsiders to demand action. It was infinitely more difficult to comply. For the first time, the whole unsupported weight rested on Jefferson himself. The Assembly was not in session and would not reconvene until March. The Council, which had hitherto in many respects taken the lead, was now content to act as a rubber stamp for the Governor. Still stunned by the hurry of events, and only slowly regathering its membership, it initiated nothing and obediently approved whatever Jefferson proposed. Yet in one vital instance it took the bit in its mouth and stubbornly reversed his decision. Thereby it started a feud between Jefferson and Steuben that bore festering consequences.

Steuben had already grown impatient with what he conceived to be the lax, dilatory and inept measures of the Virginia administration. And he was smarting at the disgrace of Arnold's raid, of which inevitably, though to his mind innocently, he must share the blame. Now came the incident which caused him to explode.

Even before the advent of Arnold, he had proposed that Hood's, located in the bend of the James River a little below Richmond, be fortified to prevent just such an attempt on the capital. His proposals had met with the usual failure to obtain materials and men. Now he urged his plan even more strongly on Jefferson and, according to him, Jefferson agreed to press into service by February 7th some forty Negroes and ten mechanics to labor on the works.

When the appointed day arrived, not a man showed up. Steuben sharply demanded to know the reason. Whereupon Jefferson blandly denied that any such agreement had been made, at least insofar as impressment was concerned. "The Executive," he explained, "have not by the laws of this state any power to call a freeman to labor even for the public without his consent, nor a slave without that of his master." He would, however, try to hire labor on a voluntary basis; but that might take a long time.[34]

To Steuben this was the last straw. How in Heaven's name could a war be fought under conditions like this? Sarcastically he wrote to Washington: "The executive power is so confined that the Governor has it not in his power to procure me 40 negroes to work at Hood's."

On February 15th, Jefferson called a meeting of the Council to see what could be done, and also to provide some measure of co-operation with the French fleet expected shortly off the Capes. Steuben attended to explain the situation.

The Council agreed to erect the defensive work at Hood's, but gave Jefferson only that power which he himself had asked for: to hire slaves with the consent of their masters. When it came to Steuben's demand, however, that all armed vessels in the James be immediately impressed to aid the French, something went wrong. Steuben departed in the assurance that the Council had granted his request. And Jefferson, red-faced, was compelled the next day to inform him that such was not the case.

"I make no doubt," he wrote, "from what passed in council in your presence you were led to beleive [*sic*] as I was that I should be advised to impress immediately all armed vessels in James river to cooperate with the French force. The board however decide against an impress, so that I am only to endeavor to engage the willing." [35] What Steuben's thoughts were on this final example of futility, evasion or worse is not on record.

Yet, when Jefferson really wanted action from the Council, he got it. Witness its appropriation of funds to buy for public use the great, many-volumed French Encyclopedia, which Jefferson had been eyeing covetously for some time, but had been unable to buy for himself because of the expense.[36]

Meanwhile, if possible, the situation was daily getting worse. The one bright spot was the advice from Washington that a powerful French fleet was on the way to attack Arnold's ships, and that General Lafayette had been placed in command of an army similarly on the way to confront Cornwallis.[37] This was wonderful news; but, in the meantime, how could they hold out?

Greene had sent Jefferson the alarming information that Cornwallis had burnt his wagons and was marching without impedimenta for an invasion of Virginia, and that he, Greene, was retiring before him. Jefferson thereupon called on the County Lieutenants to raise the militia and proceed to Greene's assistance. To encourage their efforts, he added somewhat optimistically: "By this movement of our Enemy he has ventured his all on one stake. Our stroke is sure if the force turns out which I have ordered & without delay. In such a crisis expedition decides the event of the contest." [38] The reasoning was correct; its implementation improbable. It was to be left finally to Washington, Lafayette and the French to destroy Cornwallis and bring the war practically to an end.

Cornwallis was really moving fast, seeking to catch up with Greene's retreating troops and smash them. Barely had Greene crossed the Dan at Boyd's Ferry when Cornwallis appeared on the opposite bank. This time, however, the militia actually turned out and, hovering on his flanks and rear, compelled him to retreat, with Greene now the pursuer. This novel situation did not last too long, and Cornwallis moved up again.

The Assembly convened on March 2, 1781, and to them Jefferson gave an account of the state of affairs, which included the doleful news that considerable numbers of militia had failed to take the field when ordered, and others, once provided with precious guns, had promptly decamped, taking the guns with them. More stringent laws were the answer, he said. Furthermore, not a shilling remained in the public coffers.[39]

But all such misfortunes were forgotten in the glorious news that the French fleet had finally arrived and that Lafayette's army was on the scene. Jefferson welcomed them both with almost pathetic joy. Yet he could not forbear, in view of his clashes with Steuben, to warn this other foreign soldier that while he intended to co-operate to the hilt, "mild Laws, a People not used to prompt obedience, a want of provisions of War & means of procuring them render our orders often ineffectual, oblige us to temporize & when we cannot accomplish an object in one way to attempt it in another." [40] And again, two days later, in sending down what boats he could for Lafayette's use, he resumed this very sore topic. Apologetically he wrote: "I know that you will be satisfied to make the most of an unprepared people, who have the war now for the first Time seriously fixed in their Country and have therefore all those habits to acquire which their Northern Brethren had in the year 1776...." [41]

Luckily, Lafayette had already received a thorough training in the invincible disinclination of the Americans to submit to discipline and military orders; and he was able to get along much better with Jefferson and his Virginians than Steuben had. As a result, the two men formed a friendship that extended over two continents and many decades. It must be confessed, however, that Lafayette's patience and understanding were sorely tried in the months to come.

Nor were Jefferson's troubles over. He tried faithfully to comply with the numerous demands on him that came from every side. Generals Phillips and Arnold lay at Portsmouth, besieged by Lafayette, and it was important to supply the investing army with food, means of transport and supporting militia. Steuben as liaison begged, implored and threatened for these essential articles; but, in spite of a stream of orders from Jefferson, nothing much materialized. Nor did the Council co-operate. They had the bit in their teeth again, and turned down with what must have seemed to Steuben sadistic glee practically every attempt to get the militia into action.

As far back as February 24th, Jefferson had informed Steuben that the nakedness of the militia around Williamsburg was such that mutiny impended "and that there is no hope of being able longer to keep them in service. The precedent of an actual mutiny would be so michevious [*sic*] as to induce us to believe an accommodation to their present temper most prudent." [42] In other words, let them go home.

Col. James Jones, in command of the disaffected militia, thought differently. Steuben had sent him marching orders; when Jefferson's order came to disband his troops, he deemed it "expedient" to conceal Jefferson's order and follow Steuben's. But a *second* order from Jefferson and one from General Nelson made it plain to him that he had better obey. All he could do now, he explained to Steuben, was to *hope* that he would soon be able to collect another force and follow him.[43]

These forces had been intended to march to Muhlenburg's support in a trap they were setting for Cornwallis and Arnold. Steuben's mortification and anger were complete when he heard that the Virginia militia could no longer be counted on. He wrote an excoriating letter to Jefferson.

Muhlenburg had been unable to act, he blazed, because the expected troops had failed to appear. And, as the last straw, *twelve* men had shown up from New Kent of the hundred and four ordered, and *they* had no arms. "I am extremely sorry to declare," he proceeded furiously, "I shall give neither Arms nor Orders—On the Assurances I recd from Government by Colo. Walker I had the Weakness to write Genl Washington & Marquis De la fayette that every thing was ready for the Expedition; my Credulity however is punished at the expence of my honor and the only excuse I have is my Confidence in Government [Jefferson].

"The Quarter Master writes me that he has in vain implored the Assistance of Government in procuring Horses for the Expedition—In fact if the powers of Government are inadequate to the furnishing what is indispensably necessary the Expedition must fail.

"In this Situation I am determined to suspend giving any orders till I receive your Excellencys answer to this—which answer I will lay before the Marquis & the Commander of the french fleet that they may not engage too far in an Enterprize which there is no prospect of carrying through." [44] Plain speaking could proceed not much further.

Yet Steuben's misfortunes were not yet complete. He asked that 2,000 militia on the south side of the James be sent over into North Carolina to help Greene. The Council refused, agreeing to send only one-fourth of the available militia from the bordering counties, and *hoping* that these "may be able to furnish, in great measure their own arms." [45]

When Steuben further urged the necessity of strengthening the army below and asked the immediate raising of 200 cavalry, the Council being, as they put it, "very unwilling to harrass the Militia more than shall be absolutely unavoidable," piously rejoined that perhaps an application from Jefferson to the County Lieutenants to call up for service those who had already been delinquent in answering former calls would be sufficient.[46]

Finally goaded by Steuben's bitter complaints to sharp language in his own turn, Jefferson informed him that "we can only be answerable for the orders we give, and not for the execution. If they are disobeyed from obstinacy of spirit or want of coercion in the laws it is not our fault; we have done what alone remained for us to do in such case, we have ordered other militia from other counties." [47] This is what the lawyers call confession and avoidance. Unfortunately, it is also clear indication that Jefferson's government had reached the nadir of impotence.

What might have happened had the Virginia militia marched to aid Greene can only remain in the realm of historical conjecture. The idea was that Greene, who had suffered a defeat at Guilford Court House on March 15th at the hands of Cornwallis, might, thus reinforced, be able to turn and crush Cornwallis decisively. So, at the time, thought Steuben, Lafayette, Washington and even a good many Virginia leaders.

As for Lafayette, who was hoping similarly to seize Phillips and Arnold at Portsmouth, the lack of everything compelled him to sit tight until the French fleet arrived. But that fleet had been encountered on the high seas by a British squadron and compelled to turn back to Newport. Instead, therefore, of the French flag, it was the *British* colors that sailed into Chesapeake Bay; and Lafayette had to raise his siege and return to headquarters on the Head of Elk. The two-pronged campaign, which had started off so hopefully, had ended in futility.

In the midst of these dark events, Jefferson bestirred himself to activity in quite another direction. The line between Virginia and Pennsylvania had not yet been drawn, and he had thought of a good method of doing it which involved the activities of two sets of astronomers; one taking the longitude at Philadelphia and the other at Fort Pitt. But this required proper astronomical instruments at Fort Pitt, and Jefferson accordingly solicited the loan of these from the Reverend James Madison and Robert Andrews of William and Mary. He also asked for the use of the college timepiece which had been provided for the college by public subscription, and therefore "the loan of it is now asked for a purpose important to the public Interest & in no small degree to Geographical science." Horses would be furnished Madison and a covered wagon so that the precious clock might be "well packed laid on a feather bed which you may find it necessary to carry for yourself or otherwise on straw or perhaps swung it cannot receive Injury." [48] The relief with which he turned to scientific considerations such as these is obvious.

He was not long permitted, however, such withdrawals of the spirit. The tide of war rolled back on him again, and with it the angry expostulations of the Continental officers who were trying to fight it. Lafayette had been tactful and delicate in his approach. When he signed a warrant to impress local horses for his artillery he did it with Gallic apologies for the necessity he was under to distress the inhabitants of Virginia.[49] Steuben, however, exploded with truly Prussian anger at the ineptitude and selfishness of the civilians with whom he had to deal; and Jefferson would sometimes flash back in the anger of a man harassed beyond his powers. He did not intend to allow any regular army quartermaster to impress horses at will, he said sharply. The people of Virginia had volunteered their mounts for service only too readily. Nor did he intend to harass the militia in cases "where we had reason to suspect they were not wished by the Quarter-master as *Militia*, but as servants." [50]

This matter of the impressment of horses touched the horse-minded Virginians in their most tender sensibilities. And particularly when they saw their finest mounts commandeered for wagon and artillery service. Revolutions have been started for less. Clamors, more anguished than even during invasion, rose to the Assembly and the Assembly spoke sharply to the Continental offenders.

Jefferson, himself a lover of horseflesh, was embarrassed by the Assembly action. He wrote privately to General Greene in apologetic vein. The Assembly, he said, had unfortunately passed a resolution "that all horses impressed & valued to more than £5000 [in depreciated paper] should be returned to their owners. This was in fact requiring them all to be returned. Should this be complied with fully I apprehend that it must have the most fatel [*sic*] effect on your operations which depend so much on your superiority in cavalry." Therefore, would Greene see to it that abuses in impressments were rectified, especially when it came to taking stud horses, and then write publicly to Jefferson pointing out the danger to the war effort of the Assembly action, so that Jefferson could lay Greene's letter before them.[51]

Under such circumstances it is no wonder that Greene was ready to agree with Steuben's outspoken disgust with these parochially minded Virginians. "One point is absolutely necessary to be settled by Congress," he declared, "which is, whether the militia or State Troops shall be under the orders of the continental officers or not. If the views of a State, are opposed to the general plan of operations, and the force in the field can only be employed at such points as they shall think proper, no Officer can be safe in his measures, nor can the War be prosecuted upon a general Scale." [52] The truth of these observations was incontestable, but nothing was ever done to remedy the situation.

To add to Jefferson's troubles came personal tragedy. His baby daughter, Lucy Elizabeth, died on April 15th. He had but little time to grieve. On April 19th he laid before his Council the alarming intelligence that the British were on the move again. Reinforced by sea, with Lafayette gone to the north and Steuben futile in the face of local inertia, Phillips and the hated Arnold were sailing once more up the broad highway of the James. On the 20th they had landed and were marching on Williamsburg.

This time both Jefferson and the Council remembered the lesson of the previous invasion, and called out immediately all the militia of the neighboring counties and half of those from the remoter ones. Couriers spurred with appropriate orders to the County Lieutenants, to Steuben and elsewhere. Preparations were made for removing records and stores.[53]

Yet, in spite of promptitude in orders and commands, it seemed that again all would be lost because of the failure of the militia to assemble. Jefferson's order went out on April 19th; two full days later not a single man had yet showed up. "This fatal Tardiness will I fear," Jefferson fumed, "be as unfortunate for Williamsburg on this Occasion as formerly it was for Richmond."[54]

His prognostication was correct so far as Williamsburg was concerned. Col. James Innes, in command of the militia forces, was compelled to fall back and the British entered Williamsburg, raided the shipyard on the Chickahominy where a twenty-gun ship was being built and destroyed it; and the way seemed wide open into the interior. Again Virginia was helpless before a show of enemy force.

The same alarm gripped Richmond as in previous days, and the same confusion both as to the plans of the British and of requisite counter-measures. On April 23rd the enemy was up the river as far as Westover, within striking distance of the capital; yet only 200 armed men and 300 without arms had gathered to defend it. Steuben called for a bold stroke—to gather all public and private vessels and send them down the river to attack the enemy's shipping at City Point where they lay at anchor. Had this been done, and the British ships destroyed or seriously damaged, the landing force would have been cut off and perhaps annihilated.

But neither the Board of War nor the Council favored such drastic measures. Let an observer go down to the scene of operations, they said, examine our strength and that of the enemy, and return with a report to Jefferson and Baron Steuben.[55] No wonder Steuben was in a perpetual state of apoplectic wrath!

Having thus performed their duty, at least to their own satisfaction, a majority of the Council members disappeared from the scene. From April 26th until May 10th—during the days of greatest peril—no quorum could be had. Jefferson dutifully called daily sessions, at which one to three members showed up; and as dutifully adjourned. The business of the Commonwealth was at a standstill. Civil government had abdicated.

Jefferson valiantly remained on the spot and did his utmost to co-operate with Steuben's forces. But all he could do was write letters and orders that no one seemed even to pretend to obey. Yet still he justified the militia when, on receipt of news that their home counties were under threat of invasion, they deserted with their arms and returned to their families.[56] But he met downright disobedience with stern, if futile, reprimands. When seven out of eleven counties ordered to send reinforcements to Greene pleaded off, alleging the necessity of attending to their crops, he declared sarcastically that "the enemy will not suspend their operations till we sow or reap."[57] When actual mutiny arose among individuals called up for service at Pittsburg, he advised that they be taken "out of their Beds, singly, and without Noise, or if they be not found the first time to go again & again so that they may never be able to remain in quiet at home."[58]

The defeat of this latest invasion was due, not to local efforts, but to the exertions of Continental officers and Continental troops. The British, 2,300 strong, had eventually landed at City Point and marched on Petersburg where Steuben was encamped with less than 1,000 militia. A battle was fought and the militia retreated, though in good order. The enemy ravaged the country, burnt all the tobacco in the vicinity and moved up to Manchester, opposite Richmond. Here the same depredations were repeated, and Richmond seemed at their mercy.

But Lafayette, warned in time of the expected invasion, had been hurrying with his Continentals by forced marches to the rescue. On April 29th, he hurled his wearied regulars, 900 in all, into Richmond on one side of the river just as the British made their appearance on the other. Jefferson welcomed him joyously. This was the first time the thirty-eight-year-old Governor and the slim young French nobleman had met, though they had long corresponded.

By now a sizable group of militia had assembled, and Lafayette promptly incorporated them into his little army. The British, in the face of this determined force and a river to cross, with the knowledge that Steuben lay in back of them with a steadily increasing force, decided to take the part of discretion. After some days of indecision, they packed up and departed, dropping down the river to their base of operations. The immediate peril was over.

But not for long. By May 20th, the British were on the march again, this time in full force and in juncture with Lord Cornwallis, who had finally come up from the south and thrown his main army into Petersburg. Only Lafayette's much inferior force lay between them and a complete occupation of Virginia that would effectively cut the embattled Colonies in two.

The civilian government made some dying gestures at the pretense that it was still a government; but even the participants were oppressed with the futility of it all. The Council held one legal meeting on May 10th—and even then a bare quorum attended—approved some emergency measures a rump had previously taken, and vanished into limbo again. The Assembly prudently decided that Richmond was too exposed for comfort, and nominated Charlottesville as a safer place of meeting.

On May 24, 1781, the Assembly—or those members of it who were willing to venture out—met in the temporary capital and voted Jefferson and the Council practically unlimited powers.[59] But even as they voted, they must have realized that the powers were meaningless at this stage of the game and unenforceable.

The Council evidently so construed the grant for, from May 24th until

May 30th, Jefferson and a solitary member—George Webb—met each day solemnly, stared at one another, and adjourned. On May 30th, William Fleming bravely joined them; but Webb by this time had had enough, and he departed the following day. On the three days of May 31st through June 2nd, Jefferson and Fleming met, adjourned and met. On that final day, Jefferson quit, and Fleming sat in solitary splendor—a mournful reminder of the state into which Virginia had fallen—until June 12th, when Webb returned to join him. Not until Thomas Nelson was elected Governor on June 12th did the Council—and the Executive—begin to function again.[60]

CHAPTER 16

Aftermath

THUS abruptly, and most ingloriously, Jefferson ended his two years as Governor of Virginia. He handed in his resignation on June 1, 1781, which he conceived marked the legal date of termination of his office; on the next day he shook the dust of government from his shoes and departed for Monticello and home. Bitterness must have welled in him, and a sense of release. True, another Governor had yet to be elected, and an interregnum of eleven days elapsed, during which time—with the defection of both Governor and Council—no Executive existed in Virginia.

But what did it matter? If the truth were known, and Jefferson in his heart knew it, none had existed for some time. As far back as May 14th, Jefferson had practically thrown in the sponge. On that day he had candidly told Lafayette that it was vain to call out a militia that would not come. "I could perhaps do something," he added pathetically, "by Reprimands to the County Lieutenants by repeating and even increasing the Demands on them by way of penalty." And one of his last official letters to the Assembly repeated vaguely that something had to be done about the backward militia; though what, exactly, he failed to mention.[1]

He made one last desperate appeal to Washington to come down in person and save the state they both loved. By the time the reply came—for the moment, at least, in the negative—Jefferson had resigned. Nor could Washington's kindly accolade do much to relieve the burden of Jefferson's bitterness. "Give me leave . . ." wrote the commander, "to Express the obligations I am under for the readiness and Zeal with which you have always forwarded and supported every measure which I have had occasion to recommend thro' you." [2]

Jefferson was always to remain on the defensive with respect to his term as Governor; the very vehemence with which he defended himself discloses his uneasy feeling that he had not shone particularly in the office. He had been conscientious and had not spared himself. During the first invasion he had remained in the saddle until he had practically dropped from fatigue; he had maintained a stream of correspondence and orders that is amazing in its volume. Perhaps that was one of his failings—the belief that dispatching a letter could solve a given situation. Yet it must be confessed that as a civilian he could do little more. He had neither the military type of mind nor the flair for action that the times demanded; both of which his successor was finally to furnish. And the veneration which he paid to the legal limitations on his powers did not make the problem more easy. Not until much later, during his Presidency, did he understand the methods of achieving the substance while respecting the outward forms.

Jefferson thought he was finished with humiliations and any further active part in the war when he retired to the mountain fastness of Monticello. He was mistaken. Fate had one more humiliation in store for him.

Cornwallis was lying with his main body in Hanover County when he received word that the Assembly and Governor of Virginia had removed to Charlottesville. Also that Steuben had gone to the Point of Fork, at the extremity of the James River, to cover a Continental store of arms. Naïvely considering the constituted government of Virginia to be of more importance than the facts warranted, Cornwallis sent Lt. Col. Bonastre Tarleton, one of the most brilliant of his cavalry leaders, to seize if possible the persons of the Assembly and the Governor; and dispatched Lt. Col. John G. Simcoe to capture the stores.[3]

Tarleton's force, consisting of 180 dragoons and 70 mounted infantry, started out on June 3, 1781. Time and the element of surprise were of the essence in a venture such as this, and Tarleton's troops rode hard and fast, reaching Louisa Court House by eleven in the evening. There Tarleton permitted his wearied men and blown horses a short respite of three hours —from 11 P.M. until 2 A.M.—and thereby lost his chance for a complete bag.

John Jouett, a militia captain better known to fame as Jack, was regaling himself late in the Cuckoo Tavern at Louisa when Tarleton's men pulled rein. Jouett, rightly surmising the destination of the British, slipped quietly out, mounted horse and rode furiously to warn the unsuspecting government. A native of the country, knowing every back trail, Jouett cut across fields and woods with whipping brambles and overhanging trees, through the black of the night, and spurred up the mountain to Monticello before dawn—another Paul Revere—to shout his warning.

Jefferson, hurriedly aroused, took the news calmly. With him, spending the night, were the Speakers of the two branches of the Assembly, as well as some of the members. As Jefferson was to tell it later, he ordered a carriage to be made ready to transport his family to a place of safety; then he roused his guests and they all breakfasted leisurely. After breakfast, the men of the Assembly rode down to Charlottesville to warn their fellows.[4]

Meanwhile, Tarleton had not been idle. He was moving faster than even Jouett had thought, and almost on his heels. Before dawn he had captured and burnt twelve wagons filled with arms and clothing destined for South Carolina; immediately after daybreak he had routed "some of the principal gentlemen of Virginia" from their beds, paroled some and took the others with them; near Dr. Thomas Walker's place he captured Francis Kinlock of North Carolina, a member of the Continental Congress.

Tarleton paused for breath and breakfast at Walker's for half an hour, and lost another opportunity. When he finally clattered into Charlottesville, after routing a hasty guard at the ford of the Rivanna, he was so close on the heels of the warning of his approach that he was able to gather up seven members of a too leisurely Assembly and a brigadier general. The rest of the lawmakers, pausing only long enough to designate Staunton as their next temporary capital, had fled just in time.

Dispatching Captain McLeod to Monticello to capture Jefferson, Tarleton pursued the fleeing assemblymen and destroyed all stores in Charlottesville, including, according to his own estimate, 1,000 new firelocks, 400 barrels of gunpowder and several hogsheads of tobacco.[5]

Meanwhile Jefferson was unaccountably dilatory. He was still gathering up his papers, and his family were still on the grounds, when one Christopher Hudson, passing through Charlottesville on his way to join Lafayette, saw Tarleton, and galloped up the mountain to warn Jefferson.

This time Jefferson acted with speed. He sent his family at once in the carriage to Blenheim, Col. Carter's place. Making some last-minute arrangements, which were almost too late, he mounted horse. By now McLeod's dragoons were painfully visible coming up the mountain, and Jefferson spurred into the woods from the gap and scrambled up the neighboring Carter's Mountain.

Five or ten minutes later the dragoons stood on the level plateau of Monticello to find their prey escaped. Either one or two slaves had remained on the premises, and legend has embroidered some fanciful tales of secreted plate and involuntary imprisonment in an airless hole. But McLeod proved a gentleman. He remained on the grounds for eighteen hours before he descended to rejoin the main force; but during that time nothing was taken and nothing was harmed.[6]

Jefferson caught up with his family at Carter's, and eventually sent them on to his second residence at Poplar Forest. As far as he was concerned, the incident was over. But the public did not forget nor, in later years, did his political enemies allow him to forget. For some curious reason this tale of escape from Monticello excited their risibilities and, much embroidered, gave rise to repeated charges of cowardice that literally drove Jefferson frantic. Would it be believed, he demanded passionately, that this episode "has been the subject, with party writers, of volumes of reproach on me, serious or sarcastic? that it has been sung in verse, and said in humble prose" that he had cravenly declined combat?[7]

Certainly no fair-minded person could have expected Jefferson to remain alone and do battle with the British dragoons; if anything, all that he could be justly accused of was delaying too long before making off. The Assembly, with some militia on hand, had run for it without any undue sneers.

Had he only known of it, the most unkindest cut of all was the contemporary ridicule heaped on him by, of all persons, Eliza J. Ambler, the daughter of that Rebecca Burwell whom Jefferson had lackadaisically courted in youth. In a pert letter which poked fun at another individual who had somewhat similarly fled the British, she proceeded: "But this is not more laughable than the account we have of our illustrious Gov. who they say took neither rest or food, for man or horse, til he reached Carters Mountain."[8] The laughter of the daughter throws a revealing light on the attitude of the mother toward her former suitor.

If Tarleton's men had acted honorably toward Jefferson's possessions, the same could not be said for his chief, Cornwallis. That British lord had encamped his army on the James River in the vicinity of Elk Hill, one of Jefferson's estates. He remained there for ten days and used Jefferson's house for headquarters. With vindictive thoroughness he destroyed the growing crops of corn and tobacco, burned the barns and the fences, stole the cattle, sheep and hogs, and carried off the horses and about thirty slaves when he retired. Had the slaves been taken, said Jefferson in later years, "to give them freedom he would have done right, but it was to consign them to inevitable death from small pox & putrid fever then raging in his camp. This I knew afterwards to have been the fate of 27. of them. I never had news of the remaining three, but presume they shared the same fate." Jefferson was certain that Cornwallis had singled him out for the total extermination of his possessions.[9]

As if to keep before him a constant reminder of his wrongs, Jefferson meticulously listed all the losses he had sustained from the British during this disastrous year of 1781. They were spread over his various plantations–Cumberland, Elk Hill, Shadwell, and a few slaves from Monticello itself.

It is interesting to note, though, that so many slaves voluntarily took the road to freedom with the British, in spite of their master's well-attested kindliness and even-handed treatment. Most of them died in the enemy's camp from the prevalent fevers; some returned to die and infected their fellows who had faithfully remained behind. In all, Jefferson estimated that the British had cost him a total of twenty-nine slaves.

In property that was not human his losses were even greater. Nine blooded mares, 59 head of cattle, 60 hogs; corn, wheat, barley, cotton and tobacco, both in the field and in storage; houses and fences burnt; plantation utensils; medical bills for infected slaves; expenses for pursuing runaway slaves–a staggering total that may go far to explain Jefferson's consistent hatred for all things British that marked the rest of his life.[10]

Even yet, the cup of Jefferson's humiliation was not complete. Safely ensconced with his family and what remained of faithful slaves in Poplar Forest, he may have thought that, once more a private citizen, he was rid of further bludgeonings. But he reckoned without the natural desire of other humiliated men to seek a scapegoat.

The Assembly–those who had managed to escape capture at Tarleton's hands–finally reconstituted themselves at Staunton, across the Blue Ridge. They met in bitterness and defeat, seeking to place the blame for the parlous state of Virginia everywhere but on themselves. Even at Chantilly, somewhat aloof from the blinding dust of passions and recriminations, Richard Henry Lee, once a staunch co-worker with Jefferson, displayed impatience with his former friend. Jefferson had resigned, he complained to Washington; the Assembly was in flight; and "we remain without government at a time when the most wise and most vigorous administration of public affairs can alone save us from the ruin determined for us by the enemy." [11]

At the very moment he was penning this jeremiad, however, the Assembly was in session under the aegis of Patrick Henry and taking decisive action. Thomas Nelson was elected Governor; there is a tradition that Jefferson, in spite of his "resignation," received a few votes in the upper House. They also resolved to present Captain John Jouett with an "elegant sword and pair of pistols" in gratitude for his timely warning of the approach of the enemy. Then bitterness overflowed. "Resolved, That at the next session of the Assembly an inquiry be made into the conduct of the Executive of this State for the last twelve months." [12]

The motion for the inquiry had been made by George Nicholas, a new member from Hanover County; but Patrick Henry, the radical, joined in the action with outspoken censure of Jefferson's conduct in office. It is not without reason, therefore, that Jefferson was later to date his break with the great orator from this time. According to Edmund Randolph, the friends of the late Governor as well as his enemies voted for the resolution, though for a different reason. Ugly rumors were circulating—of personal cowardice, of omissions in duty and even malfeasance. An official inquiry might set all rumors aright.[13]

Jefferson, however, was unable to view the proceedings with the same degree of calmness of his friends in the Assembly. The news struck him like a thunderbolt. His already lacerated pride suffered the ultimate agony. Nor did the soothing words of his friend Archibald Cary soften the blow. "Your Friends confident an Inquiry would do you Honor second the Motion. . . . I had heard something of this kind was to be brought on the Carpet; and if I know you, it will Give you no pain." [14] Fair speech; or else Cary did *not* know Jefferson.

At about the same time that this startling information reached him, the tired ex-Governor received a much more flattering communication—that Congress had appointed him, together with Adams, Franklin, Jay and John Laurens, Minister Plenipotentiary for negotiating peace through the good offices of the Empress of Russia. Jefferson declined the appointment and, quivering with indignation, moved to the defense of his conduct at home.

To climax the tale of his misfortunes, he had suffered a bad fall on June 30th from his favorite mount, Caractacus, and the resulting injuries, which included a broken arm, laid him up for almost six weeks. Even this was later distorted by his enemies to a sneer that the fall had occurred during his cowardly flight from the British at Monticello.[15]

Jefferson had returned to Monticello to recuperate, and from that base of operations found a member of the Assembly from Albemarle, one Isaac David, who was willing to resign so that Jefferson might be sent to Staunton to seek his vindication. The next step was to write a letter to George Nicholas demanding a formal bill of particulars of the charges on which the motion for an inquiry had been predicated. "It could not be intended," he declared with ill-concealed bitterness, "first to stab a reputation by a general suggestion under a bare expectation that facts might be afterwards hunted up to boulster it." [16]

Young Nicholas was a stout, ungainly youth and a novice in politics, though he had already earned a commission as colonel. His family had been on the closest terms of intimacy with the man he was now attacking; Archibald Cary was his uncle and Robert Carter Nicholas, though a conservative, had been on personal good terms with Jefferson. He himself was later to join Jefferson's party of Republicans.

The motives for his present assault are obscure; perhaps he had fallen under the influence of Patrick Henry, who used him as a stalking horse for his own devious plans to regain the governorship eventually and eliminate a formidable rival whose ideas had steadily drifted apart from his own.

Nicholas was obviously embarrassed by this formal demand. "You consider me in a wrong point of view when you speak of me as an accuser," he wrote back. "As a freeman and the representative of free men I considered it as both my right and duty to call upon the executive to account for our numberless miscarriages and losses so far as they were concerned in or might have prevented them. In doing this I had no private pique to gratify, and if (as I hope it may) it shall appear that they have done everything in their power to prevent our misfortunes I will most readily retract any opinion that I may have formed to their prejudice." After this preamble, he proceeded to enumerate certain charges which had chiefly to do with the failure to take adequate measures to repel Arnold's raid on Richmond.[17]

With specific accusations on hand, Jefferson proceeded to answer them *seriatim.*

Item, that Washington had sent advance warning of an expedition. *Answer*, that the warning had been a general one, without any intimation that the British aim was Virginia. Such intimations were always being forwarded, "but we (for some time past at least) never thought any thing but actual invasion should induce us to the expence of calling the militia into the field." *Item*, where were the postriders that had been established last summer? *Answer*, they had been instituted by Congress to get news of the arrival of the French fleet and had been discontinued by it. *Item*, why were only a few militia called out and and then too late? *Answer*, that as many were ordered up as Steuben required, and the orders went out immediately on news of the actual invasion. And so on and so on.[18]

Each charge was plausibly answered, and there were no chinks in the defensive armor. Yet the uneasy feeling persists that, while Jefferson had gone through the requisite motions, the results had been grossly insufficient. Both sides sheered gingerly away from the main issue—the reluctance of the people of Virginia to sacrifice their private concerns in time of war and invasion.

While thus preparing his defense, Jefferson announced his irrevocable determination, once he had cleared his name, to retire forever from public life. To the remonstrances of his friends he remained obdurate. "I have taken my final leave of everything of that nature. I have retired to my farm, my family & books from which I think nothing will evermore separate me." [19]

The new Assembly set December 12th as the day for taking up the resolution of inquiry, and Jefferson appeared as a delegate from Albemarle to answer the charges in person. Meanwhile, a committee had been appointed to gather evidence. It was headed by John Banister and included Nicholas, the prime mover. Significantly, Patrick Henry was not a member.[20]

In the extended interim, however, Jefferson's friends had rallied, and the bitterness had departed from the opposition. Cornwallis had surrendered at Yorktown and bygones could be bygones. Furthermore, as the committee of investigation discovered, there was nothing tangible on which definite hold could be laid. Nicholas himself failed to come forward; and the committee was left without anything but mere unsubstantiated rumors on which to act.

All parties, therefore, agreed to close the books. A resolution that left nothing to be desired was unanimously passed: "Resolved, That the sincere thanks of the General Assembly be given to our former Governor, Thomas Jefferson, Esq. for his impartial, upright, and attentive administration of the powers of the Executive, whilst in office; popular rumors gaining some degree of credence, by more pointed accusations, rendered it necessary to make an inquiry into his conduct, and delayed that retribution [*sic*] of public gratitude, so eminently merited; but that conduct having become the object of open scrutiny, tenfold value is added to an approbation, founded on a cool and deliberate discussion. The Assembly wish therefore, in the strongest manner, to declare the high opinion which they entertain of Mr. Jefferson's ability, rectitude and integrity, as Chief Magistrate of this Commonwealth; and mean by thus publicly avowing their opinion, to obviate all future, and to remove all former, unmerited censure." [21]

This was both handsome and flowery. The Senate, notoriously more conservative in thought and economical in language, cut out the extensive verbiage and the protestations, but left the essentials of approval and vindication. In this barer form, the resolution was jointly adopted on December 19th; and the incident was seemingly closed.[22]

But the scars were to remain, even though old friends like John Harvie assured Jefferson that no one believed the rumors and that "all men" were lauding his administration.[23] A letter written shortly after the event discloses how deep was the wound and its festering state. When Jefferson thought of young George Nicholas, the author of his attempted disgrace, his pen dipped in venom: "The trifling body [Nicholas] who moved this matter was below contempt; he was more an object of pity. His natural ill-temper was the tool worked with by another hand [Patrick Henry?]. He was like the minners [*sic*] which go in & out of the fundament of the whale. But the whale himself was discoverable enough by the turbulence of the water under which he moved." [24] The agitation of Jefferson's own spirits is sufficiently discernible in the mixture and confusion of metaphors and epithets.

CHAPTER 17

Notes on Virginia

VINDICATED, yet with bitter memories, Jefferson resigned his seat in the House the same day he had triumphed. His resolve was firm; he was shaking the dust of politics from his feet, and even the flattering amends offered by the Assembly in appointing him as a delegate to Congress was thrust aside.[1]

The Monticello to which he returned had been spared most of the crippling damage that his other plantations had sustained. True, it had been temporarily occupied by the enemy, but the particular enemy had scrupulously refrained from harm. Some slaves, however, had wandered off in the confusion; and Jefferson tried to get them back. George Wythe, in Williamsburg, reported that one such had been found and was being returned under guard; if Jefferson would send him descriptions of the missing servants, he would search for them. The recession of the British power had left these pathetic seekers after freedom stranded, and some were hiding in the neighborhood.[2]

What Monticello looked like at about this time, and what Jefferson himself looked like to an observing Frenchman, may be gleaned from the account of the Marquis de Chastellux, who during this period of war and turmoil, amused himself by traveling leisurely through the distracted States and jotting down notes of what he saw.

He came to Monticello in the spring of 1782 and described its master as "not yet forty, tall, and with a mild and pleasing countenance, but whose mind and understanding are ample substitutes for every exterior grace. An American, who without ever having quitted his own country, is at once a musician, skilled in drawing, a geometrician, an astronomer, a natural philosopher, legislator, and statesman." To complete the idyllic picture, this paragon had "a mild and amiable wife, charming children, of whose education he himself takes charge, a house to embellish, great provisions to improve, and the arts and sciences to cultivate." [3] To add to the noble marquis's delight, he and his host discovered a mutual enthusiasm, Ossian, and discoursed that fabled poet's merits over many a bowl of punch.

The buildings at Monticello evoked a similar, if perhaps more critical enthusiasm. "This house," he wrote, "of which Mr. Jefferson was the architect, and often one of the workmen, is rather elegant, and in the Italian taste, though not without fault; it consists of one large square pavilion, the entrance of which is by two porticos, ornamented with pillars. The ground floor consists chiefly of a very large, lofty salon which is to be decorated entirely in the antique style; above it is a library of the same form; two small wings with only a ground floor and attic story are joined to this pavilion, and communicate with the kitchen, offices, etc., which will form a kind of basement story, over which runs a terrace." Indeed, the marquis could "safely aver that Mr. Jefferson is the first American who has consulted the fine arts to know how he should shelter himself from the weather."

In truth, the building of Monticello remained one of the great passions of Jefferson's life. It was actually a lifetime job, and nothing was permitted to interfere with the course of construction—war, illness, absence or plethora of other duties. He was constantly changing his plans, as he read in the architectural books, traveled abroad, or devised newer and loftier structures in the recesses of his own mind. Always he saw room for improvement, and did not hesitate to tear down what had already been constructed, or go to fabulous expense to shift designs in mid-career. The grounds were always in a clutter of bricks, lumber and semicompleted buildings.

Fiske Kimball, in his monumental volume and special studies, has sufficiently traced the emergence of the final Monticello which, as restored, we know today. Originally inspired by the Englishman James Gibbs, Jefferson quickly shifted his allegiance to the great Italian classicist Andrea Palladio, who in turn based his *Four Books of Architecture* on the existing monuments of ancient Rome and on the descriptions by Pliny and Vitruvius of those which had yielded to time. But Jefferson was no mere slavish copier. He invented new forms, combined the best features of old ones, and created an architecture which was to bear solid fruit on the American scene. He employed the Ionic, the Corinthian, the Tusçan and the Roman rotunda styles with equal facility and in happy combinations.

As may be noted from the description of Chastellux, the first building was square in structure; but later on that too was changed to the present octagonal form, which was then unknown in Virginia, though Jefferson had doubtless seen examples in Philadelphia, Annapolis and New York. The dependencies were similarly embryonic and were later considerably extended and enlarged. The vast number of extant drawings, architectural plans and minute working calculations testify both to Jefferson's genius and his tremendous delight in the home he was building. It was never fully completed, in the sense that he was satiate and content.[4]

But even this fascinating preoccupation was not sufficient to keep such an active and eternally fertile mind as Jefferson's entirely busy. The particular spark that set him off in another direction was generated by a polite request transmitted to him as Governor of Virginia by the French Government. That power, entering the war on the side of America, thought it might be well to be provided with a fund of information concerning the geography, flora and fauna, climate, people, resources and customs of its new ally.

François, Marquis de Barbé-Marbois, Secretary of Legation in America, prepared a series of questions in accordance with the desires of his home Government and sent them to those men in the several states whom inquiry had developed as most likely to know the answers. On the recommendation of Joseph Jones, member of Congress from Virginia, one set came to Jefferson.

He received the questions at the end of 1780 and, as has already been pointed out, fell upon them with such avidity that he almost resigned his governorship to devote himself entirely to seeking out the answers.

On March 4, 1781, at a time when the entire administration of Virginia was a hopeless wreck, he was apologizing to Marbois that he had been unable to do more than the preliminary work on his project, and assuring him that very shortly he would be in "a condition" really to buckle down to it.[5]

He was as good as his word; indeed, better. The moment Jefferson washed his hands of the governorship, and perforce had to leave Monticello, he betook himself to the privacy of Poplar Forest, where he surrounded himself with books, documents and years of meteorological and botanical notes which he had unwittingly been gathering against just such a day. Even the unfortunate contretemps with his horse and the resultant broken arm did no more than temporarily impede his absorption in this new task.

The matter grew under his hands, and the appeals and inquiries he made to his friends for additional data broadened the scope of his answers to such a degree that a book-length, compendious history of Virginia resulted which, even to this day, is *sui generis*. Politics, laws, geography, climatology, natural history, anthropology, geology, economics, industries, agriculture, ethics, religion, manners, architecture and a host of other topics, together with reflective observations on each item, make up what ought to have been an indigestible mass, yet actually constitute a coherent, orderly whole—the modestly entitled *Notes on the State of Virginia.*

Jefferson worked diligently on these *Notes* all through his convalescence at Poplar Forest and continued them on his return to Monticello. Finally, on December 20, 1781, he finished the voluminous manuscript, with another apology for the long delay. "I retired from the public service in June only," he explained, "and after that the general confusion of our state put it out of my power to procure the information necessary till lately. Even now you will find them very imperfect and not worth offering but as a proof of my respect for your wishes."[6] Modesty could go no further.

Jacquelin Ambler, to whom he entrusted the bulky packet for transmission, was unable to send it for some months, and Jefferson utilized the intervening period to revise and enlarge his manuscript. The final product, with still more humble apologies, finally went on its journey the end of March, 1782.[7]

It is not known whether the French Government derived any benefit from this philosophical and penetrating study. Certainly it received nothing comparable from any other of the States. But to Americans ever since, it has proved a mine of information on matters that extended far beyond the borders of Virginia, with which it was intended to deal; and, of equal value, it presents a chart to the workings of a reflective and insatiably inquiring mind. The *Notes* have become something of a classic in American literature.

In his Autobiography, Jefferson explains the provenance of the *Notes:* "I had always made it a practice whenever an opportunity occurred of obtaining any information of our country, which might be of use to me in any station public or private, to commit it to writing. These memoranda were on loose papers, bundled up without order, and difficult of recurrence when I had occasion for a particular one. I thought this a good occasion to embody their substance, which I did in the order of Mr. Marbois' queries, so as to answer his wish and to arrange them for my own use."[8]

What added, perhaps, to his enthusiasm for the venture was his recent election to the American Philosophical Society, a small but ambitious group of inquirers into natural phenomena dedicated to the promotion of useful knowledge, which Benjamin Franklin, Charles Thomson and others had organized in Philadelphia in imitation of the Royal Society of Great Britain.[9] Jefferson took great pride in his membership in this learned society, and later became its president. The association stimulated him and enlarged his powers; while his constant correspondence with members such as David Rittenhouse, Charles Thomson, Benjamin Rush, Caspar Wistar, Francis Hopkinson, Thomas Cooper and other intellectual worthies clarified his concepts and crystallized them on paper.

The *Notes*, following the order of Marbois's queries, commenced with a description of the geography of Virginia, its boundaries, rivers, mountains, cascades and caverns. But Jefferson did not limit himself to the bare bones of answers; he amplified, illustrated, commented and produced a luxuriance of supporting material and curious information.

When he came to the rivers of Virginia, for example, he included data on depths, navigability, harbors, the exact tonnage of ships that could sail their lengths, and ranged out to other rivers and lakes like the Mississippi, Missouri, Ohio, Illinois, and even those as remote from Virginia as the Hudson and Lake Erie. Nor did he refrain from aesthetic and intellectual considerations. "The *Ohio*," he would break into rhapsody, "is the most beautiful river on earth. Its current gentle, waters clear, and bosom smooth and unbroken by rocks or rapids, a single instance only excepted."[10]

His knowledge of the Ohio was derivative, but of his native Potomac entirely firsthand; and his apostrophe to the passage of its waters through the great gap is justly famous. He himself had stood on the pinnacle he described, and the ecstasies were his own, though perhaps tinged with reminiscenses of Ossian and the cult of romantic poetry.

> The passage of the Patowmac through the Blue ridge is perhaps one of the most stupendous scenes in nature. You stand on a very high point of land. On your right comes up the Shenandoah.... On your left approaches the Patowmac.... In the moment of their junction they rush together against the mountain, rend it asunder, and pass off to the sea. The first glance of this scene hurries our senses into the opinion that this earth has been created in time, that the mountains were formed first, that the rivers began to flow afterwards, that in this place particularly they have been dammed up by the Blue ridge of mountains, and have formed an ocean which filled the whole valley, that continuing to rise they have at length broken over at this spot, and have torn the mountain down from its summit to its base.... But the distant finishing which nature has given to the picture, is of a very different character. It is a true contrast to the foreground. It is as placid and delightful as that is wild and tremendous. For the mountain being cloven asunder, she presents to your eye, through the cleft, a small catch of smooth blue horizon, at an infinite distance in the plain country, inviting you, as it were, from the riot and tumult roaring around, to pass through the breach, and participate of the calm below.[11]

In similar vein he described the Natural Bridge, in which, as its owner, he had a particular pride. "It is impossible," he exclaimed, "for the emotions arising from the sublime to be felt beyond what they are here; so beautiful an arch, so elevated, so light, and springing as it were up to heaven, the rapture of the spectator is really indescribable!"[12]

But such raptures soon yielded to those more precise and *useful* facts which were considerably more congenial to Jefferson's mind. Madison's Cave, for example, one of the numerous limestone recesses with which Virginia is honeycombed, is given dimensions, distances, temperatures, winds and topographical drawings with no more than a glancing aside at the fantastic formations and faery beauty of the place.

By far the largest section of the *Notes* is devoted to the mines, minerals, trees, plants, fruits, Indians and general natural history of Virginia. These were his true interests—scientific, practical, anthropological—yet with more than a cursory interest in the beginnings of this world, if not of the next.

The scientific world at the moment was distracted between two theories as to the surface origin of the earth—one, the cataclysmic theory; the other, a universal deluge. Darwin and Sir Charles Lyell were still in the future.

Jefferson injected himself into the controversy with a curious mixture of penetrating observations and fantastic theories. He had seen and remarked on fossil shells which were to be found on high mountains and rightly noted their dissimilarities from the living shells of the Tidewater. But, to the prevalent opinion that these were the remains of a universal deluge, he countered with calculations that if the whole atmosphere were water, its precipitation would not have been sufficient to rise to the level of the mountains. The hypothesis of alternate risings and lowerings of land masses and the theory of sedimentary deposits had not yet occurred to any one. Therefore, faced with insurmountable objections to any prevalent hypothesis, Jefferson could only conclude that these seeming fossil shells were not real animal shells at all, but mineral simulacra which nature ingeniously made "by passing the same materials through the pores of calcareous earths and stones." [13]

When he came to descriptions of the mammals of North America, however, he was on solid ground, and he took violent issue with the theoretical philosophizings of the Comte de Buffon as to their natures and types. Such public divergence required a notable degree of courage on Jefferson's part; for Buffon was the greatest naturalist alive, and his lightest pronouncement was received with almost superstitious veneration by other scientists. One small point, however, militated in Jefferson's favor in the ensuing dispute. *He* was in America, had studied the animals of which he spoke, had measured their various dimensions and examined their organs when dead, and watched them in the fields and woods when alive. Buffon, on the other hand, had never been to America, had examined no specimens, relied for his information on the tales of travelers and cogitated his theories from what he conceived to be the nature of things. The result, therefore, could not too long be in doubt.

Buffon had delivered himself of the pontifical opinion that the animals of the New World whose species corresponded to those of Europe were smaller in size and generally degenerate as contrasted with their more favored brethren. He attributed this pretended fact to the richer natural food, the friendlier heats and the dryer climate of the Old World.

Such superior theorizing—sight unseen—offended not only Jefferson's realistic observations, but his patriotism. He dryly remarked that "all the manna of heaven would never raise the Mouse to the bulk of the Mammoth," and denied first, that America was moister and colder than Europe, and second, that any evidence existed that climatic conditions regulated size. More conclusive and scientific, however, were the careful series of comparison tables he drew up between the comparable American and European quadrupeds, in which the evidence triumphantly pointed to the contrary of Buffon's thesis—the American animals were generally larger and heavier than the European.

He also took issue with Buffon's insistence that the mammoth, the fossil remains of which were to be found equally in Europe and America, was merely a species of elephant; and thought that perhaps living specimens might still be roaming the unexplored western and northern sections of America. So far Jefferson was on fairly solid ground; but he added a theory of his own which was just as fantastic as any which Buffon had offered. "Such is the economy of nature," he wrote in support of his belief that the mammoth still survived, "that no instance can be produced, of her having permitted any one race of her animals to become extinct; of her having formed any link in her great work so weak as to be broken." [14] It was probably this teleological hypothesis which forced Jefferson to deny that fossil shells, like none now in existence, were real accretions of animal life.

He was not through with Buffon yet. He tilted at still another preconception of the eminent Frenchman—that the American aborigines were as proportionately degenerate to European man as the American mammal to the European one. Buffon's account, remarked Jefferson, was "an afflicting picture, indeed, which for the honor of human nature, I am glad to believe has no original." He knew nothing, he continued, of the South American Indian, but he *did* know the red man of North America.

Sharply contradicting Buffon's assertions, *that* Indian "is neither more defective in ardor, nor more impotent with his female, than the white reduced to the same diet and exercise"; he is brave and enduring; he is a faithful friend; affectionate to his children; and possessed of a keen sensibility even though assuming an outward stoicism. It was true, Jefferson admitted, that the Indian women were drudges; but this, he insisted, was the case with every barbarous people. "It is civilization alone which replaces women in the enjoyment of their natural equality." And, with manifest approval, he cited the Indian practice of voluntary abortion and the use of contraceptives.

As for any comparisons in eloquence and oratory, Jefferson believed that the balance lay wholly in favor of the Indian. "I may challenge the whole orations of Demosthenes and Cicero," he declared, "and of any more eminent orator, if Europe has furnished any more eminent, to produce a single passage, superior to the speech of Logan, a Mingo chief, to Lord Dunmore, when governor of this state." [15] He proceeded to give the background and the text of this famous Indian speech.

Briefly, as Jefferson stated them, the facts were these. In 1774, two Shawnee Indians had robbed and murdered a Virginia settler. The whites, under Col. Michael Cresap, "a man infamous for the many murders he had committed on those much injured people," ambushed and slew an unarmed canoeload of Indian men, women and children. The slain Indians were of the family of Logan who, though he had previously been a friend of the whites, now took to the warpath. He and his allies were defeated; the others sued for peace, but Logan did not. Instead, he sent a speech by messenger to Lord Dunmore, Governor of Virginia. This was the speech which Jefferson held up for comparison with the best efforts of antiquity and modern times.[16]

Jefferson was always enamored of the Indians, their speech and customs, even though, at a later date, he urged that many of them be driven across the Mississippi; and an extended consideration of this passage concerning Logan and Col. Cresap would not have been necessary had not the eventual publication of the *Notes* stirred up a veritable hornet's nest of personal and political invective because of it. For Luther Martin, whom Jefferson was to call "the bulldog of Federalism," challenged the account in a Baltimore paper in 1797. Martin was not only politically opposed to Jefferson but, as the son-in-law of the defamed Cresap, reacted violently to what he considered unjust and untrue aspersions on his father-in-law's character.

Jefferson wrote to all and sundry who might have knowledge of the original facts for corroboration of his account. Unfortunately, some of the evidence he collected, including a letter from his old friend George Rogers Clark, held Cresap blameless for the particular massacre or for any other.

Involved by this time in a controversy that had assumed formidable political dimensions, Jefferson failed to publish this letter, though he did admit certain minor errors in his original account. The letter, and other evidence tending to exculpate Cresap, came to light long after Jefferson's death, with consequent unfavorable comments on Jefferson's suppression. The comments must stand, even though it now appears—what Jefferson then did not know—that contemporary first-hand evidence existed to the effect that Cresap *was* responsible for the massacre.[17]

Not content with thus raising up present and future antagonists, Jefferson proceeded to attack another famous French natural philosopher, Abbé Guillaume Raynal. The Abbé had remarked in his *History of Philosophy* that "one ought to be astonished that America has not yet produced a good poet, an able mathematician, a man of genius in a single art, or a single science." To which Jefferson countered that "when we shall have existed as a people as long as the Greeks did before they produced a Homer, the Romans a Virgil, the French a Racine and Voltaire, the English a Shakespeare and Milton," and *then* produced no one of similar caliber, that would be the time to express astonishment. But that applied only to poetry. In the other fields mentioned by Raynal, however, what was wrong with a Washington for the art of war, a Franklin for science, and a Rittenhouse for astronomy? Certainly they could take their place alongside anyone that Europe could show.[18] Patriotic fervor and facts were mingled in equal quantities.

Returning to the Virginia scene after having thus ranged the entire continent and spilled over into other parts of the world, Jefferson gave current population statistics and figured that, at the present rate of increase, Virginia would have six to seven million in ninety-five years. This estimate planted a more general doubt in Jefferson's mind: whether the desire to produce a large population in America as rapidly as possible by the importation of foreigners was founded in good policy. He foresaw that in the future it would be impossible to feed and clothe adequately such a multitude of people.

But what troubled him even more was the probable effect of such an influx of foreigners on the American form of government. We possessed a peculiar republican government; "a composition of the freest principles of the English constitution, with others derived from natural right and natural reason. To these nothing can be more opposed than the maxims of absolute monarchies. Yet from such we are to expect the greatest number of emigrants. They will bring with them the principles of the governments they leave, imbibed in their early youth; or, if able to throw them off, it will be in exchange for an unbounded licentiousness, passing, as is usual, from one extreme to another. It would be a miracle were they to stop precisely at the point of temperate liberty. These principles, with their language, they will transmit to their children. In proportion to their numbers, they will share with us the legislation. They will infuse into it their spirit, warp and bias its directions, and render it a heterogeneous, incoherent, distracted mass." [19]

Jefferson had forgotten his first enthusiasm for peopling Virginia with Mediterranean laborers and agriculturalists. The specter he now conjured before him was to haunt the sessions of the later "nativist politicians" and be repeated almost verbatim in the pages of future "nativist" historians. He wobbled several times during the course of a long career on this point, but his instincts always brought him back to the fear that American institutions would be inundated and subverted by any large-scale immigration from the absolutist countries of Europe.

The same fear motivated his almost pathological horror of the industrial artisans and mechanics, who, to his imagination, inevitably swarmed in the rabbit warrens of large cities. Fortifying this dread was his almost religious belief that agriculture was a divine institution; that only tillers of the soil were free enough and intelligent enough to value properly freedom and a heritage of liberty.

"We have an immensity of land courting the industry of the husbandman. Is it best then," he inquired, "that all our citizens should be employed in its improvement, or that one half should be called off from that to exercise manufactures and handicraft arts for the other? Those who labour in the earth are the chosen people of God, if he ever had a chosen people, whose breasts he has made his peculiar deposit for substantial and genuine virtue. . . . Corruption of morals in the mass of cultivators is a phaenomenon of which no age nor nation has furnished an example. It is the mark set on those, who not looking up to heaven, to their own soil and industry, as does the husbandman, for their subsistence, depend for it on casualties and caprice of customers. Dependance begets subservience and venality, suffocates the germ of virtue, and prepares fit tools for the designs of ambition. . . . While we have land to labour then, let us never wish to see our citizens occupied at a workbench, or twirling a distaff." Let us rather send our provisions and raw materials to Europe, and get in return their manufactures.

"The loss by the transportation of commodities across the Atlantic will be made up in happiness and permanence of government. The mobs of great cities add just so much to the support of pure government, as sores do to the strength of the human body. It is the manners and spirit of a people which preserve a republic in vigour. A degeneracy in these is a canker which soon eats to the heart of its laws and constitution." [20]

Jefferson was never to overcome his distrust of large cities, manufactures and the workers who made them possible. Even when he was compelled, in the formation of his Republican party, to accept their aid, it was always an uneasy alliance, and he distrusted profoundly their leaders. Even when, during the embargo of his Administration and in the later War of 1812, it was essential to encourage manufactures, he envisaged them as much as possible in the home, the farmhouse and the plantation.

This dithyrambic exaltation of agriculture over industry became one of his chief points of difference with Alexander Hamilton. Jefferson sought an Arcadian state, a nation of small cultivators; Hamilton foresaw a thriving industrial economy, the land filled with belching chimneys and the seas thronged with freighted argosies. The facts of history favored Hamilton.

In 1805, when Continental war and British blockades posed the problem afresh, Jefferson found some of the forthright statements of the *Notes* a source of embarrassment. They had been improperly construed, he complained, and perhaps he ought to qualify certain expressions. He had been thinking only of "the great cities in the old countries, at the present time, with whom the want of food and clothing necessary to sustain life, has begotten a depravity of morals, a dependence and corruption, which renders them an undesirable accession to a country whose morals are sound. My expressions look forward to the time when our own great cities would get into the same state. But they have been quoted as if meant for the present time here." [21] Meaning, of course, that considerable political ammunition had been furnished by the passage.

The problem of slavery and the status of the Negro was always to trouble Jefferson. Every humanitarian, philosophical and political instinct in him revolted against the subjection of one man to another; and the rapid increase of the slave population made him apprehensive that eventually they would far outnumber the whites. He hoped, however, that the prohibition of any further importation "will in some measure stop the increase of this great political and moral evil, while the minds of our citizens may be ripening for a complete emancipation of human nature."

Some of his ideas about emancipation and eventual colonization elsewhere have already been discussed in connection with the Report of the Revisors; yet it should be emphasized that Jefferson did not at any time consider the Negroes as the possible political and social equals of the whites in this country. They could not live side by side, once the Negroes were set free, he said, because of the "deep rooted prejudices entertained by the whites; ten thousand recollections, by the blacks, of the injuries they have sustained; new provocations; the real distinctions which nature has made; and many other circumstances will divide us into parties, and produce convulsions, which will probably never end but in the extermination of the one or the other race."

There were essential physical and mental differences, he believed, between the two races, and he resolved all comparisons in favor of the whites; so that, though he was careful to state that the matter required further objective study, he suspected that "the blacks, whether originally a distinct race, or made distinct by time and circumstances, are inferior to the whites in the endowments both of body and mind." Hence the two races ought to be kept separate, and "removed beyond the reach of [blood] mixture." [22] It was difficult, indeed, for even a philosopher to rise wholly superior to his environment.

Certainly, he was far more sympathetic to the Indians and "the melancholy sequel of their history" in Virginia; perhaps because they were not as inextricably involved in the social and economic structure of the state and could be viewed with a due concern for their present problems and the romantic glamour of their past. The memory of that moonlit convocation he had witnessed as a boy and the impressive bearing of the Indian orator colored his mature thoughts; while their mysterious origin, the unknown etymology of their language, stirred his scientific ardor.

He had, it seems, discovered an ancient Indian barrow on the banks of the Rivanna near his home, and he had opened it carefully by means of perpendicular test cuts. The procedures, in fact, which he employed in examining these prehistoric remains have excited the admiration of archeologists as far in advance of his time and consonant with the most approved modern methods. From the thousands of bones he discovered within the barrow, including those of children, and the lack of evidence of violence, he deduced that these were no sepulchers of warriors fallen in battle, as was then generally held, but the normal accretions of a settled community.[23]

Where did the Indians originally come from? Probably, he thought, across the narrow waters between Asia and North America. Again he was anticipating modern archeology. He was also a firm believer in the comparative study of languages as a method of disclosing the kinship of nations, and he particularly wished to compare the various Indian tongues with the languages of the Old World to seek out possible derivations and affinities. Lamenting that so many tribes had died out "without our having previously collected and deposited in the records of literature, the general rudiments at least of the languages they spoke," he was himself to attempt such collections in the future, through his own personal efforts and commissions to travelers and explorers in the farther West. These compilations, with studies of their grammars and inflections, should, he declared, be deposited in all the public libraries for the use of scholars.[24]

He discussed the political situation and institutions of Virginia with the same candor and frankness that he employed on less controversial topics. He openly declared his discontent with the Virginia constitution, which he explained as having been "formed when we were new and inexperienced in the science of government.... No wonder then that time and trial have discovered very capital defects in it." He listed the defects: the majority of the men who pay and fight for its support were unrepresented in the legislature; the weighting of representation from the Tidewater counties as against the others; the essential sameness of the Senate and the House; that "all the powers of government, legislative, executive, and judiciary, result to the legislative body."

Such a concentration of powers in the same hands was abhorrent to him. It was "precisely the definition of despotic government." Nor did it matter that it rested not in a single hand, but in a legislative group. "173 despots would surely be as oppressive as one," he declared. Nor did the fact that the people chose the legislature alter the matter. "An *elective despotism* was not the government we fought for," he insisted, "but one which should not only be founded on free principles, but in which the powers of government should be so divided and balanced among several bodies of magistracy, as that no one could transcend their legal limits, without being effectually checked by the others."[25]

This profound principle of checks and balances in government became the later cornerstone of the Constitution of the United States. Yet Jefferson did not himself always adhere to the principle he now so flatly maintained. He tended to subordinate the executive to the legislature, and the judiciary to both. And, as between legislatures, Federal and State, he was to uphold the supremacy of the State. But his later practice does not vitiate the wisdom he displayed in this discussion of what constitutes despotism—the irresponsible employment of power by a single body, whether that body consists of one or many.

Here, too, Jefferson recapitulated his work on the revision of the laws of Virginia, including his scheme of education and the story of his struggles for religious liberty. Much of this has already been discussed in connection with his legislative career; but some of his present comments further illuminate his ideas in these fields.

On Education: "By that part of our plan which prescribes the selection of the youths of genius from among the classes of the poor, we hope to avail the state of those talents which nature has shown as liberally among the poor as the rich, but which perish without use, if not sought for and cultivated.—But of all the views of this law none is more important, none more legitimate, than that of rendering the people the safe, as they are the ultimate, guardians of their own liberty." Hence their first, and necessarily for most, their *whole* education should be chiefly historical: "By apprising them of the past, will enable them to judge of the future.... Every government degenerates when trusted to the rulers of the people alone. The people themselves therefore are its only safe depositories. And to render even them safe, their minds must be improved to a certain degree." [26]

On Religion: "Subject opinion to coercion: whom will you make your inquisitors? Fallible men; men governed by bad passions, by private as well as public reasons. And why subject it to coercion? To produce uniformity. But is uniformity of opinion desirable? No more than of face and stature.... Difference of opinion is advantageous in religion. The several sects perform the office of a *censor morum* over each other. Is uniformity attainable? Millions of innocent men, women, and children, since the introduction of Christianity, have been burnt, tortured, fined, imprisoned; yet we have not advanced one inch towards uniformity. What has been the effect of coercion? To make one half the world fools, and the other half hypocrites. To support roguery and error all over the earth." [27]

On War and Peace: "Young as we are, and with such a country before us to fill with people and with happiness, we should point in that direction the whole generative force of nature, wasting none of it in efforts of mutual destruction. It should be our endeavor to cultivate the peace and friendship of every nation, even of that which has injured us most [Great Britain], when we shall have carried our point against her. Our interest will be to throw open the doors of commerce, and to knock off all its shackles, giving perfect freedom to all persons for the vent of whatever they may chuse to bring into our ports, and asking the same in theirs. Never was so much false arithmetic employed on any subject, as that which has been employed to persuade nations that it is their interest to go to war. Were the money which it has cost to gain, at the close of a long war, a little town, or a little territory, the right to cut wood here, or to catch fish there, expended in improving what they already possess, in making roads, opening rivers, building ports, improving the arts, and finding employment for their idle poor, it would render them much stronger, much wealthier and happier. This I hope will be our wisdom." [28]

Such were the *Notes on Virginia*—a wide-ranging, comprehensive survey not merely of his native state, but of America as a whole, and the philosophy which Jefferson conceived it should mirror for the edification of the rest of the world. Its variety is amazing; its philosophic grasp and general wisdom profound. It displays the many-faceted mind of a citizen of the world and a firm believer in the perfectibility of the human race and the uniqueness of the American experiment.

Yet Jefferson, when he was finished with it, realized that it was not for current publication. He had been too frank, too honest in his opinions; he had trodden on too many prejudices and touched too many tender spots. The storm which eventually ensued when it *did* reach the general public proved the justness of his fears.

He sent one copy to Marbois, and held another for circulation among his friends for suggestions and corrections. Charles Thomson, secretary of Congress and member of the American Philosophical Society, sent extended comments which Jefferson added in the form of notes to later copies. He added, revised and enlarged as new material came in or his thoughts elaborated, almost up to the time that he departed for Europe.

The response of his friends was so enthusiastic, and the demand for copies so great that he thought seriously of having the Philadelphia printer William Dunlap strike off a private edition for personal distribution before he sailed; but the time was too short, and it had to wait for his sojourn in Paris.[29]

CHAPTER 18

Domestic Tragedy

JEFFERSON'S retirement brought long expostulations from his friends. They refused to accept his reasons for taking the step and urged him to come forth again on the public stage and lend his talents to the state and nation which he claimed he loved. In particular, their anger was aroused by his declination of the office of delegate to the Assembly which his neighbors in Albemarle had tendered to him.[1]

What precipitated the great debate was a letter which Jefferson wrote to James Monroe, in reply to his exhortations to return to the arena. Monroe, barely twenty-four at this time, had made Jefferson's acquaintance two years before while Jefferson was Governor and Monroe had returned to his native state after a term as aide to Washington to seek more active field service than the secretarial position he held. Not content with the openings at hand, he thought to turn his attention to the study of law; but Jefferson, who took to the lad, sent him southward as a commissioner to report on the situation in that troubled theater of war, and later directed his studies. The kindly attention touched Monroe's heart, and he became Jefferson's man for practically the rest of his life—with certain later reservations and intermissions.[2] Next to Madison, he was Jefferson's closest friend and political co-worker; and the trio became fixed in the public mind as "the Virginia dynasty." But there never was that intellectual equality of partnership between Jefferson and Monroe which existed between Jefferson and Madison. It was more a case of teacher and disciple.

Jefferson now pleaded to Monroe's expostulations that he was thoroughly cured of all political ambition. He cited the ruined state of his private affairs and the needs of his family; but the true reason for his decision peeped out in the bitterness with which he spoke of the charges levied against him in the Assembly, even though they had been followed, as he said, by "an exculpatory declaration. But in the meantime I had been suspected & suspended in the eyes of the world without the least hint then or afterwards made public which might restrain them from supposing that I stood arraigned for treason of the heart and not merely weakness of the head." [3] This, of course, was unfair; the Assembly had made handsome public amends. But Jefferson's pride had received such a wound that only time could salve the hurt; and he preferred now, like another Achilles, to sulk in his tents.

Edmund Randolph, to whom Monroe showed the letter, put his finger understandingly on the true cause. "The pathos of the composition is really great," he told Madison in turn; "and the wound, which his spirit received by the late impeachment, is, as he says, to be cured only by the all-healing grave. His triumph might certainly be an illustrious one over his former enemies, were he to resume the legislative character; for in the constant division between the two leaders, Henry and Lee, he might incline the scale to whichsoever side he would."[4]

But Madison, the cold intellectual, refused to waste sympathy or sentimentalize over Jefferson's assumed wrongs. For once he displayed a touch of impatience toward his revered elder friend. "Great as my partiality is to Mr. Jefferson," he retorted, "the mode in which he seems determined to revenge the wrong he received from his country does not appear to me to be dictated either by philosophy or patriotism. It argues, indeed, a keen sensibility and strong consciousness of rectitude. But this sensibility ought to be as great towards the relentings as the misdoings of the Legislature, not to mention the injustice of visiting the faults of this body on their innocent constituents."[5]

As men who were in the thick of the conflict then convulsing Virginia, both Madison and Randolph realized how evenly that conflict was balanced. Patrick Henry was moving rapidly away from his former radicalism; only his demagoguery and unrivaled talents for rousing the populace remained. The great bills which Jefferson had drafted—especially those for religious liberty and disestablishment—were undergoing hard sledding, and Patrick Henry was joined in opposition with the conservatives. *They* were on the spot, suffering the bludgeons of that opposition; while Jefferson, their natural leader, sulked and preferred to meditate on his wrongs.

Nevertheless, Jefferson continued to remain at Monticello, occupied with transplanting fruit trees and strawberry plants to his second domicile at Poplar Forest, noting the birth of another daughter (named Lucy Elizabeth, after the baby recently deceased), watching a fine aurora borealis, and observing domestically that "a quart of Currant juice makes 2. blue teacups of Jelly, 1 quart of juice to 4. of puree."[6]

But this preoccupation with minutiae was soon to be jarred abruptly by the onset of tragedy. His family had grown in extent, not merely by the birth of his own child, but by the accession of his widowed sister Martha, and her six children by the late Dabney Carr. These had now come to Monticello to be cared for and sheltered; and the education of the children, notably of Peter Carr, the eldest, absorbed much of his attention.

Jefferson's wife, Martha, had never been a healthy woman. And now, under the strain of the recent events—the hurried flight from Monticello, her husband's broken arm immediately thereafter, her pregnancy and eventual delivery—her health began to fail alarmingly.

By the end of June, 1782, in fact, her condition was such that reports were already abroad that she was dead.[7] She lingered on, however, until September 6th, when she died. More, perhaps, than all other accounts of the shock to Jefferson, the simple entry in his account book discloses the depths of his feeling. "Sept. 6—my dear wife died this day at 11-45 AM."[8] It was the first and last time he permitted an endearing adjective to appear in these most impersonal jottings.

So little is known of Martha Jefferson that it is hard to envisage the state of his despair. But everything we know of Thomas Jefferson confirms certain salient facts: he had loved her devotedly; he was thrown by her loss into such a frame of mind that for years he viewed the world through distraught eyes; he spoke always of the event by indirection, and never used her name on paper again; he never remarried, though such prolonged widowerhood was most unusual among the Virginia gentry; and he carefully destroyed prior to his own death—at least, it must have been he—every vestige of the letters that had passed between them.

Of his emotions during her illness and final death we have the vivid account of his eldest daughter, named like her mother, Martha. "As a nurse," she recalled, "no female ever had more tenderness or anxiety. He nursed my poor mother in turn with Aunt Carr and her own sister—sitting up with her and administering her medicines and drink to the last. For four months that she lingered, he was never out of calling; when not at her bedside, he was writing in a small room which opened immediately at the head of her bed. A moment before the closing scene, he was led from the room almost in a state of insensibility by his sister Mrs. Carr, who, with great difficulty, got him into his library, where he fainted, and remained so long insensible that they feared he never would revive.... He kept his room three weeks, and I was never a moment from his side. He walked almost incessantly night and day, only lying down occasionally, when nature was completely exhausted.... When at last he left his room, he rode out, and from that time he was incessantly on horseback, rambling about the mountain, in the least frequented roads, and just as often through the woods...."[9]

Martha Jefferson was buried in the little family cemetery which Jefferson had planned on the side of the mountain. On her tomb he placed a single inscription—a quotation from the *Iliad* in the original Greek. It has been said that he employed the Greek characters to veil his loss from the common herd. Perhaps; but most of his friends and visitors as they passed up the mountainside could read the Greek with ease.

Even in translation, the words of Homer resound with ineffable pathos:

> If in the house of Hades men forget their dead,
> Yet will I even there remember my dear companion.

If Jefferson had had reason to withdraw himself from the world before, that reason was thrice-compounded now. He wrote few letters—and those merely formal—and the entries in his ordinarily meticulously kept account and garden books are sparse and end with abrupt finality. The single item in the Garden Book, however, made only five days after the tragedy, is quite enlightening. In it he noted down the details of stuffing and preserving birds, as given to him by a neighbor.[10] Even in his great grief his mind accepted practical scientific information and made it permanent.

His friends respected his retirement for two months; then they decided that his entry into public affairs was essential, not only for himself, but for the good of his country. If he refused to return to the Virginia Assembly because of his pride, he ought not to refuse to accept an appointment from Congress, that had never done him harm. As a delegate *to* Congress, he would have had to pass through the Assembly; as a representative abroad, Congress had the power of direct appointment. Furthermore, a mission to Europe, among novel scenes and new activities, would help remove the brooding which had overcome him.

Madison found the instrument of his translation immediately at hand. Once more—and this time more solidly based in fact—a mission was being sent to France to negotiate a general peace. The British were weary of the war; to all intents and purposes it had ended with the surrender of Cornwallis at Yorktown. Armies were still in the field; but they remained inactive, content to sit and wait out the final disposition of their respective governments.

On November 12, 1782, Congress unanimously reappointed Jefferson as a Minister Plenipotentiary for the purpose of negotiating a peace. Not a single adverse remark was made, Madison noted, and the decision was reached after someone (most likely Madison) had said that the death of Mrs. Jefferson would probably change his views on public life and a stay in Europe.[11]

As his friends had suspected, Jefferson welcomed the appointment. Already he had begun to chafe at his self-imposed confinement, and had half-contemplated a trip to Philadelphia or some other northern point. Europe would be even better to take his mind off his troubles. When the notification came, he was away from home, having his children inoculated against the smallpox; he promptly returned, arranged his affairs and sent off his acceptance.[12]

The Marquis de Chastellux was sailing for France in a convoy some time in December, and Jefferson hastened his own preparations so that he might have the company of that congenial Frenchman, with whom he could discuss scientific matters, his *Notes on Virginia*, and perhaps indulge in a game of chess or two to ease the long voyage.[13]

Leaving his affairs in the hands of two good friends, Francis Eppes and Nicholas Lewis, Jefferson set out from Monticello for "Philadelphia, France &c." on December 19, 1782. His oldest daughter, Patsy, went along with him.[14]

He was not to get to France this time, however. When he arrived in Philadelphia on the 27th he found, first, the usual delays. The French frigate *Romulus*, on which he was scheduled to sail, was locked in ice below Baltimore, and Jefferson cooled his heels in Philadelphia for almost a month waiting for news of its release. He regaled himself during the interim in the company of Madison and made the acquaintance of Mrs. Elizabeth Trist, daughter of the house in which he boarded. Patsy, aged ten, and Mrs. Trist took to one another immediately, and became fast friends. Jefferson seized the opportunity to purchase some books (he never went anywhere that he did not buy profusely), mended his gunlock, sword and watch, bought maps of Europe, and prepared himself generally for shipboard and the European scene. He also visited the Philosophical Society and donated thirty-five shillings to their fund.[15]

Around the middle of the month, he decided it might be wiser to be in Baltimore, ready to board the *Romulus* as soon as the ice broke up. By January 31st he was in that town, purchasing tickets for the playhouse, a set of chess, "raw silk" stockings for himself, knee buckles, and a generous assortment of sundries for little Patsy. His phaeton, too, which he intended to take across to Paris, needed repairs.[16]

But again he was disappointed. The weather got colder and the *Romulus* was compelled to drop some miles down the bay. Jefferson set out in a small boat to board the vessel, was caught in the floating ice, and finally, after transshipment to a stouter sloop, managed to reach the frigate.

Here, however, he heard for the first time that the British were cruising in strength outside the Capes to waylay the *Romulus* and her sister ship, the *Guadeloupe*. In some perplexity, he asked Congress for instructions.[17]

While waiting for a response, and back on shore again, Jefferson amused himself with speculations to Madison about his fellow commissioner, John Adams. Would he be a good man to work with? "His vanity is a lineament in his character which had entirely escaped me. His want of taste I had observed. Notwithstanding all this he has a sound head on substantial points, and I think he has integrity. I am glad therefore that he is of the commission & expect he will be useful in it." He had been observing his secretary, too. Major David S. Franks, who had been assigned to him in that capacity, seemed to have "a good eno' heart, and understanding somewhat better than common, but too little guard over his lips." Women were his besetting vice, though; and Jefferson feared that "his temperature would not be proof against their allurements, were such to be employed as engines against him." [18] Certainly this was no recommendation for a confidential secretary on a diplomatic mission.

He had plenty of time to write letters. Baltimore bored him. He sent a long, important communication to Edmund Randolph in Virginia. He had just read the British king's speech on the peace negotiations and thought that he "seems to part with us with a sigh" and that "there is much lying & some puffing" in it. The news that Randolph intended to enter the legislature again pleased him, "as I have seen with depression of spirit the very low state to which that body has been reduced." It had attempted to exclude the Loyalist refugees from return and insisted on the forfeiture of their property. It talked "of the dissolution of the social contract on a revolution of government, and much other little stuff by which I collect their meaning to have been that on changing the form of our government all our laws were dissolved, & ourselves reduced to a state of nature." But this was precisely the doctrine against which Virginia had been adamant in the past.

"For my part," Jefferson declared, "if the term *social contract* is to be forced from the theoretical into practical use, I shall apply it to all the laws obligatory on the state, & which may be considered as contracts to which all the individuals are parties." Any changes made in particular laws, whether involving administration of government or "the transmission or regulation of private property," applied only to the ones amended and to no other.

Jefferson may have been a revolutionist; but he was a cautious revolutionist. He believed that the "return to a state of nature" doctrine had been grossly overworked. He did *not* believe in making a clean sweep of existing institutions and starting from scratch. Let those laws be changed which require changing, he argued; but keep those laws and institutions which have stood the test of time. He was a gradualist; not a doctrinaire radical.

The local particularism of the states similarly disturbed him. He had seen only too many evidences of it in his own Virginia. "I find also the pride of independance taking deep & dangerous hold on the hearts of individual states," he wrote. "I know no danger so dreadful & so probable as that of internal contests. And I know no remedy so likely to prevent it as the strengthening the band which connects us. While subject to Gr. Britain she preserved peace among us. We have substituted a Congress of deputies from every state to perform this task; but we have done nothing which would enable them to enforce their decisions. What will be the case? They will not be enforced." He feared internecine wars, in which the aid of foreign powers would be invoked. "Can any man be so puffed up with his little portion of sovereignty," he exclaimed, "as to prefer this calamitous accompaniment to the parting with a little of his sovereign right and placing it in a council from all the states?"

Let Randolph, Madison and a young friend of his, William Short, go into the legislature, he urged; and ended with a noble peroration that betrayed both his concern and his deepest feelings: "My humble & earnest prayer to Almighty god will be that you . . . will first lay your shoulders to the strengthening the band of our confederacy & averting those cruel evils to which its present weakness will expose us, & that you will see the necessity of doing this instantly before we forget the advantages of union, or acquire a degree of ill-temper against each other which will daily increase the obstacles to that good work." [19] A vision of a nation had dawned on Jefferson.

When Congress finally replied to his letter, it contained disappointing information. Inasmuch as it now seemed likely that peace was about to be consummated, it would be best to suspend the mission pending further information.[20]

Jefferson was also left suspended, so to speak. It was not advisable to return to Monticello, when any day might bring definite word of new plans for him. So he remained rather unhappily in Baltimore until the end of the month, and then rode back to Philadelphia to be closer to the sources of information.

While still in Baltimore, he received a proposal from Abner Nash, Governor of North Carolina, who was in the city, inviting him to enter into a land speculation with him and a group of associates. The plan was to have a select party of friends and politicians purchase the escheated lands in North Carolina at a nominal figure—Nash would obviously see to that—and thereby eventually obtain a fortune. There would be twenty partners, and each one would be entitled to 100,000 acres of the 2,000,000 that would be thrown open to public sale when the land office opened in the spring. The cost would be ten shillings per 100 acres. The plan, Governor Nash enjoined, was to be held in the deepest secrecy.

It was a glittering bait that was thus dangled before Jefferson. At first he had some qualms, having, as he told Francis Eppes, "never adventured in this way in my own country because being concerned in public business I was ever determined to keep my hands clear of every concern which might at any time produce an interference between private interests and public duties." Nevertheless the bait was too tempting, and Jefferson took one share for himself and another share jointly for Eppes, Nicholas Lewis and Henry Skipwith.[21]

In March, however, after he had gone on to Philadelphia, his uneasiness over the ethics of the deal returned to him, especially as it was possible that the interests of the various land companies might be discussed in the European negotiations. He therefore decided to withdraw from the scheme, and wrote Nash tactfully that, were he merely a private citizen, he would unhesitatingly proceed with the venture; but, since he was not, he had better withdraw. He had made it a rule, he explained, "while concerned in the direction of public affairs ... to avoid engaging in any of those enterprises which ... might lay my judgment under bias or oblige me from fear of that to withdraw from that decision altogether."[22] What Nash thought of this nice point of honor, since he would be far more intimately involved in public decisions on his private interest, is not known.

It was fortunate that Jefferson changed his mind. Aside from the purely practical consideration that the scheme died a-borning, unscrupulous speculators in western land-jobbing later pretended to act as his agents and a scandal was in the making. He was in Paris when the whisperings reached him, and he promptly wrote to Madison giving him a true picture of what had taken place.[23]

Philadelphia held him until the middle of April, 1783. Congress finally notified him that peace was so far advanced in Europe that it would not be necessary for him to take the trip, and they therefore terminated his commission.[24]

Once again Jefferson packed his baggage, placed Patsy in the phaeton, and drove back to Monticello, reaching home on May 15th. He had been away almost five months. But the time was not wholly wasted. The stupor into which he had fallen on his wife's death had vanished; the indignity he had suffered at the hands of Virginia was pushed into a recess of his mind; and his political faculties and interests were fully reawakened. Once more he was ready to take his proper place in the councils of his country.

Several things happened before his arrival in Monticello. For one, the faculty of William and Mary honored their famous alumnus with a degree of Doctor of Law.[25] For another, he stopped at Richmond for two weeks, renewing his associations with the members of the legislature. Technically, he was still a member himself, though he had declined to serve.

What he particularly wanted was to get votes for two pet projects of his: a new constitution for Virginia through a convention; and the adoption of the Congressional plan for a closer union based on a federal system of import duties and an assumption of the state debts by a federal government.

The first had been close to Jefferson's heart ever since Virginia had failed to accept his draft for a tentative constitution and had adopted another which was unsatisfactory to him. It had been put over on the people, he thought, without a formal mandate and without adequate consideration. During his sojourn in Richmond, he found a movement looking to such a convention. Accordingly, on his return to Monticello, Jefferson drafted a proposed new constitution for Virginia. It embodied some of his ripest political thinking.

After a preamble which stressed the temporary status of the present constitution, Jefferson proceeded to his own specific proposals. The powers of government were to be divided into three equal and independent departments—executive, legislative and judicial. Both branches of the legislature were to be chosen by an electorate consisting of all free male citizens either resident in the county, enrolled in the militia, or possessing real property therein. In other words, universal male suffrage. The Governor was to be chosen by both Houses, to serve five years and thereafter be ineligible for re-election. Advising him was a Council of State, likewise chosen by both Houses, to serve for seven years and be similarly ineligible for reappointment. The Judiciary was to be chosen in like manner, to hold office during good behavior. A Council of Revision—a body for which there was precedent in New York and elsewhere—was granted a veto power over all Assembly bills which, if rejected by them, could become law only after repassage by a two-thirds vote.

Specific limitations were invoked against possible infractions by the several branches of government of civil liberties and rights. The General Assembly was forbidden to abridge civil rights because of religious beliefs, to interfere in their free exercise or compel contributions to any church, to ordain the death penalty except for certain heinous offenses, to pass ex post facto laws, to permit the further importation of slaves, or to continue slavery in Virginia except for those already slaves on December 31, 1800. All born after that date were to be free. Trial by jury was provided for except in impeachments, appeals and military offenses; habeas corpus and freedom of the press were to remain inviolate; and the military was always to be subordinate to the civil power.[26]

Had this constitution been adopted, Virginia would have become, by virtue of it, the most advanced state in the Union. Except for the principle of ineligibility and the concept of a Council of Revision, practically all of its clauses eventually became the law of the land, State and Federal; but many weary years were to pass before that happened.

At the moment, however, the idea of a convention to form a new constitution was dropped, and Jefferson's proposals had no other immediate effect than to obtain the commendations of his friends. He thought so much of it, however, that he printed it later in Paris in pamphlet form, and still later attached it as an appendix to his *Notes on Virginia.*

The second matter that motivated his stopping at Richmond—the Congressional impost—seemed more immediately likely of action. While the legislature was indisposed to grant Congress the right to levy import duties, it liked the idea of the assumption of its debts, an interesting fact in connection with Virginia's—and Madison and Jefferson's—later violent opposition to that very proposal when Hamilton offered it. But the situation, of course, had changed considerably by that time.

Since the two parts were bound together in a single package, sentiment at first was pretty evenly divided. "Henry as usual," remarked Jefferson, "is involved in mystery: should the popular tide run strongly in either direction, he will fall in with it."[27]

By June 1st, the tide seemed to take the right turn, and Patrick Henry came out in favor of the impost. "This will ensure it," Jefferson exulted.[28] The exultation was premature, however. When the question actually was put in debate, Henry sat in a dead silence. He had changed his mind; and with him Virginia.[29]

Though Jefferson had failed in both the projects which brought him to Richmond, the stay bore other fruit. His friends had been busy among themselves with schemes to get him back into legislative life. Randolph thought he ought to resume his seat in the Virginia Assembly; others, among whom was Madison, considered his presence in Congress even more essential. The latter view prevailed; and, on June 6, 1783, Virginia duly appointed him a delegate to Congress, to take office on November 1st. So eager, indeed, was everyone to get him back into circulation that a Massachusetts man nominated him in Congress for the post of Secretary of Foreign Affairs; and withdrew his name only after being assured that Jefferson would not accept.[30]

With ample time before his attendance in Congress, Jefferson spent the summer and early fall at Monticello, rearing his own children and those of his sister, Martha Carr, and amusing himself with drawing up a complete catalogue of the books in his library. He drafted it with the meticulous care that he employed in all his projects; and he noted on the fly leaf that his collection numbered 2,640 volumes. These had been laboriously and expensively collected since that day at Shadwell when all his possessions had vanished in flame.

Even at this early date, it represented one of the finest collections in America, both in number and quality. But what is intensely interesting in this catalogue is the system of classification which he set forth for its orderly arrangement, and which he was to follow, with minor variations, in all future catalogues. It had been Francis Bacon's scheme originally, and Jefferson added some ideas of his own.

He divided books according to their conformity to the faculties of the mind: I, Memory, exemplified in History; II, Reason, under which went books of philosophy; III, Imagination, to which adhered the Fine Arts. History he divided into Civil and Natural, with appropriate subbranches; Philosophy into Moral and Mathematical, appending a significant footnote that "the term and division of Metaphysics is rejected as meaning nothing or something beyond our reach or what should be called by another name." And the Fine Arts flowered into Gardening, Architecture, Sculpture, Painting, Poetry, Oratory and Criticism. It is tempting to believe that the careful ordering of the divisions of the Fine Arts represents his own critique on their relative importance.

In addition to his books, Jefferson had a large collection of volumes of music that showed impeccable taste. Among the composers were such giants as Bach, Haydn, Corelli, Vivaldi, Pergolesi, Purcell and others. For lighter occasions he had a group of drinking songs.[31]

Jefferson might well be proud of his library. It was first-rate in every respect, though perhaps it leaned more to the solid material of law, history and government than a more elegant man might fancy. But more and more, Jefferson was to read for instruction and moral elevation than for entertainment and delight. Poetry, except for the Greek and Latin, occupied less and less of his time; novels vanished altogether from the scene. Architecture, however, as he became engrossed in building schemes–Monticello, Washington, the University of Virginia–grew continually in importance. The single wholly non-utilitarian pursuit that remained with him all through life was music.

On October 12th, Jefferson purchased two horses for his phaeton and asked for a third matching mount as a relief horse for his servant, when on the road to Philadelphia and Congress.[32] Three days later he was actually on his way.

Once more his daughter Patsy accompanied him. It was a good method of broadening her education while at the same time it afforded him the pleasure of her company. He was a thoroughly domestic man and, as he frequently said, never happier than when surrounded by his family. Polly and the infant Lucy Elizabeth were unfortunately still too young to travel extensive distances, and were left in the care of Mrs. Eppes, his sister-in-law.

CHAPTER 19

Return to Life

JEFFERSON arrived in Philadelphia on October 29, 1783; but Congress was no longer there. A mutinous soldiery, unpaid for months and swollen with the discontent of manifold grievances, had assumed such a threatening aspect that Congress had decamped in fright to Princeton to resume its sessions. The trouble had largely abated by the time of Jefferson's arrival; but Congress deemed it wiser not to return to the turbulent city.

Before proceeding farther, Jefferson placed Patsy in the care of Elizabeth Trist and provided a dancing master to give her instruction in the pleasant art. Then he journeyed on to Princeton, only to discover that Congress was adjourning to Annapolis, in Maryland, as still further removed from the camps of a sullen army. He therefore turned his horses back again to Philadelphia and found that Patsy had again to be moved. Mrs. Trist was departing from the city, and he now domiciled her with Mrs. Hopkinson, the mother of Francis Hopkinson, who had signed the Declaration of Independence with him. The change-over took place on November 19th; the following day he mended his violin, which seemed always in need of repairs, and arranged to give his daughter music lessons. Then he set out for Annapolis with Madison to catch up with a peregrinating Congress.[1]

The education of Patsy, however, remained much in his mind. He had barely settled himself in new lodgings (with a Mrs. Gheeseland, at a guinea a week and two and sixpence a day for firewood) when he was formulating a rigid schedule of studies and activities for the eleven-year-old girl to follow.

"From 8 to 10," he instructed her, "practice music. From 10 to 1, dance one day and draw another. From 1 to 2, draw on the day you dance, and write a letter next day. From 3 to 4, read French. From 4 to 5, exercise yourself in music. From 5 till bed-time, read English, write, etc." And, rather pathetically, consider Mrs. Hopkinson "as your mother, as the only person to whom, since the loss with which Heaven has pleased to afflict you, you can now look up."[2]

He explained his system of education to Marbois who, as a Frenchman, had definite ideas of his own on what was fitting for the fair sex. "The plan of reading which I have formed for her," he wrote, "is considerably different from what I think would be most proper for her sex in any other country than America." He had, for example, placed in the little girl's hands *Don Quixote* and the picaresque *Gil Blas*. "I am obliged in it," he pursued, "to extend my views beyond herself, and consider her as possibly at the head of a little family of her own. The chance that in marriage she will draw a blockhead I calculate at about fourteen to one, and of course that the education of her family will probably rest on her own ideas & direction without assistance. With the best poets and prose writers I shall therefore combine a certain extent of reading in the graver sciences."[3]

Jefferson's estimate of the intellectual capacities of his Virginia neighbors, from whom naturally Patsy would eventually pick a mate, sounds surprisingly cynical. Certainly his fears, at least in that direction, were not to be realized; for Thomas Mann Randolph, who became the husband of a grown Martha, was no "blockhead," whatever other faults he may have possessed.

Perhaps at this moment Jefferson was generally cynical. Witness his ironic description of the new dress affected by the ladies of Philadelphia during his short stay in their midst. "The high head is made as flat as a flounder. Instead of the burthen of lawn, ribbon, false hair &c. the head is covered with a plain chip-hat with only a ribbon round the crown. The shoulders are where the chin used to be, and the hips have succeeded to the place of the shoulders. The circumference of the waste [*sic*] is the span of the lady's own hands in order to preserve due proportion. All the residue of the figure is resigned to the possession of a hoop which at each angle before projects like two bastions of a fort. I am impatient to see whether our married ladies will be able to reduce & keep themselves to this form."[4]

Congress was supposed to have reconstituted itself at Annapolis on November 26th, but Jefferson arrived to find that demoralized body still unable to gather a quorum. By December 11th, the representatives of only six States were on the spot (a majority of seven was necessary for ordinary business; nine for ratification of the peace treaty). Rhode Island was expected shortly; but *when* two more would appear, complained Jefferson, "seems as insusceptible of calculation as when the next earthquake will happen."[5] Actually, as soon as Rhode Island arrived on the 13th, Congress commenced sessions, even though there could be no final action on the treaty.

By now, Jefferson was pretty much disgusted with the entire situation; nor had his useless additional four hundred miles of traveling in pursuit of the Congress sweetened his spirits. There is in existence the mutilated draft of a letter, undated and addressee not given, which indicates the reasons for his disgust at this particular moment.

For one thing, the treatment meted out to the Tories, in flagrant violation of the terms of the peace treaty, excited his anger. "The unseasonable & unnecessary resolves of various towns on this subject," he wrote, "the actual expulsion of tories from some places, & the avowed implacability of almost all who have published their sentiments about the matter, are circumstances which are construed not only to the prejudice of our national magnanimity & good faith but also to the prejudice of our government."

For another, the "situation of the army, the reluctance of the people to pay taxes, & the circumstances under which Congress removed from Philadelphia, have diminished the admiration in which the people of America were held among the nations of Europe." His reason for being sensitive to European opinion was frankly stated. Unless we could establish good faith in Europe and unity at home, he argued, America could only be an unimportant consumer of European goods and a reservoir of laborers to furnish her with raw materials.[6] This last fear is somewhat surprising. Had not Jefferson, in his *Notes on Virginia* and elsewhere, proclaimed the desirability of just such a state of affairs—America to furnish raw materials to Europe and receive in turn manufactured goods?

It was with such gloomy forebodings that Jefferson took his seat in a sparsely populated Congress. In addition, he was not feeling too well physically.

The ratification of the peace treaty was the most important business before Congress. It had been signed by the plenipotentiaries abroad on September 3, 1783; but it contained a clause which made it effective only if ratifications were exchanged between the signatory powers within six months thereafter. By the beginning of 1784, four months had already elapsed of the six, and there still did not seem a sufficient interest among the States to send delegates to ensure its permanence.

The leaders of Congress were understandably anxious—and Jefferson, though perhaps not a leader at this moment, agreed with them. For the peace treaty, as it had finally been shaped in the deliberations in Europe, was an amazing document. It gave the former colonies across the seas far more than even the most optimistic had ever dared dream possible: territorial extensions, recognition, delivery of border forts and other plums that ordinarily are demanded from an enemy beaten to its knees. England definitely was not in this condition. In exchange, England asked for only two items: generous treatment for those who had been loyal to her during the Revolution, and the right of her merchants to collect private debts owing to them prior to the war.

But all these advantages were likely to be thrown away if the treaty was not ratified in time. Already England was having second thoughts; and France was miffed because the terms with America had been consummated behind her back and in violation of an agreement that she would be an equal party to any negotiations. Time was therefore of the essence.

Jefferson was appointed chairman of a committee to consider the treaty. It was hoped that by the time the committee completed its work and reported, the necessary nine States would be present. But the prospects were not bright. Even as General Washington, amid affecting scenes of solemnity, laid down his command, a delegate decided to depart for home, which would have left only six States present; thereby putting an end even to routine matters.[7]

Meanwhile Jefferson's committee was active in considering the treaty. Several members, including Jacob Read, Hugh Williamson and others, were so alarmed at the shortness of time available that they violently demanded unconstitutional ratification on the basis of seven States. They argued that these were sufficient for legality. Jefferson opposed them just as strenuously, on the ground that *nine* States were essential to constitute a legal ratification. Tempers rose; the proponents demanded a vote of the members for the record; and Jefferson informed them that he would place a resolution on the record spreading the whole controversy.

This he did by motion on January 2, 1784. It declared that since the terms of the treaty called for an exchange of ratifications by March 3rd (and this meant actual delivery of the signed document in Europe), and since there was a dispute whether or not *seven* States might not ratify the provisional treaty with instructions to enter into a definitive one later on, "the states now present in Congress do declare their approbation and so far as they have power, their ratification of the sd treaty," thereby offering this temporary expedient to Europe until a *full* ratification was received. If the latter did not arrive in time, then a three-month extension was to be requested.[8]

Fortunately, it was unnecessary to try such a ticklish procedure. Congress had sent out urgent expresses to round up the lagging States and, on January 14th, New Jersey and New Hampshire appeared on the scene, the delegate who had thought to go home was persuaded to stay, and the magic number of nine was achieved.

The ratification, prepared by Jefferson, was rushed to a vote; the nine States duly voted *aye*; and the crisis was over—at least as far as Congress was concerned.[9]

The next step was to hurry the ratification to Europe. Col. Harmer and Col. Franks (the young man had been promoted since Jefferson had proposed to take him on his mission as private secretary) hastened on board a waiting vessel, but sailing conditions being what they were, Jefferson never expected them to arrive before the deadline. As a matter of fact, they did not; but England raised no objections, and the final exchange took place without incident in May.

This supreme act of resolution over, Congress relapsed into its wonted state of inertia. Two days later, though nine States were still officially present, they were largely represented by such skeleton crews that a *single* delegate of any one of several States could, by his bare negative, halt any legislation. And there was a host of matters for consideration—treaties of alliance and commerce, domestic administration, arsenals and frontier posts, the western territory, Indian treaties and, most important of all, finances.[10]

Congress, Jefferson gloomily foreboded, would have to adjourn and tell the States in plain language why they did so. By February 20th, in fact, one State had departed in the person of its representative, and now there were eight. Congress had sat in session only three times in three weeks. Protest after protest had been sent to the delinquent States, but to no avail.[11]

Yet these forebodings were only for confidential ears. To the outer world, and especially the European, Jefferson maintained a bright optimism. To the Marquis de Chastellux he delivered himself with serene aplomb: "As yet every thing has gone smoothly since the war. We are diverted with the European accts. of the anarchy & opposition to gov [ern] ment in America. Nothing can be more untrue than these relations." True, he admitted, it was difficult to get money from the State governments, but the reason, he protested, "is not founded in their unwillingness, but in their real inability." [12]

Yet a little while later he was receiving a startling communication from no less a person than the secretary to Congress: "Unless a different spirit prevail from what has of late appeared there is reason to apprehend a dissolution of the Confederacy." [13]

And, in later years, Jefferson described the Congress of these days with acid pen. "Our body was little numerous, but very contentious. Day after day was wasted on the most unimportant questions." When a fellow delegate, John F. Mercer, who was himself "afflicted with a morbid rage of debate" and a "copious flow of words," expressed astonishment that Jefferson could sit in silence and listen to so much false reasoning which a word would refute, Jefferson retorted that "to refute indeed was easy, but to silence was impossible." He was duty bound to participate in debate when measures which he had brought forward were being considered; at other times he was content to listen. He did not believe in belaboring every matter to extremities, and adducing every conceivable argument in its behalf. He remembered that Washington in the Virginia legislature, and Franklin at prior sessions of Congress, had never taken more than ten minutes to discuss a question. If the present delegates would do the same, they could accomplish in a day what now took a week. But what could you expect, he wound up, with a hundred and fifty lawyers gathered together? It was their trade "to question everything, yield nothing, and talk by the hour." [14] How much of this Jefferson actually said at the time, and how much of it was brilliant afterthought, is another matter.

In spite of the interminable talk, however, the state of the nation—and, for Jefferson, the state of Virginia—required that business be somehow transacted. The most important item now on the agenda was the organization of the great Northwest Territory. Virginia had finally ceded all its rights in that vast area unconditionally to the United States and instructions were sent to her delegates in Congress to execute the necessary deeds.[15]

On March 1, 1784, the Virginia delegation offered the title deeds. New Jersey, Pennsylvania and Rhode Island, who feared that their own claims to the same territory might be jeopardized by Virginia's generous waiver, offered an amendment to the effect that, by acceptance, Congress did not attempt to validate Virginia's original all-embracing claim of title. All the other States joined to defeat the amendment. Whereupon New Jersey stubbornly voted *no* when the matter of acceptance finally came up, while South Carolina, for reasons of its own, was divided.[16]

With the title duly passed, Jefferson was appointed chairman of a committee to prepare a plan for the temporary government of the Northwest. The report, brought in on March 22nd, is one of Jefferson's greatest documents; indeed, it has been held by Paul Leicester Ford to be second only to the Declaration of Independence in importance and statesmanship. That, perhaps, is an overstatement, when we remember the Statute for Religious Liberty; but there is no question that, in its original form, adherence would have averted some of the major ills that afflicted the United States in the future.

The Report had two major theses: *first,* that the territory and all future cessions, whether from the States or by Indian tribes, be subdivided into new states; *second,* that the settlers be permitted to form temporary governments until their particular state had as many free inhabitants as the least numerous of the original States, after which they could organize a permanent government and a constitution, and be admitted to the Union on a vote of the existing States.[17]

Thus far, the Report was sufficiently epoch-making; for it set up the principle that new states could be carved out of the illimitable West, eventually even to the Pacific Ocean. Jefferson even drew the boundaries of his proposed states, and gave names to some of them. These names, largely of classical origin—though, in deference to Washington, one was given his name—excited considerable ridicule afterwards. Two, however, nonclassical in style, eventually took hold in shorter form: Michigania and Illinoia. But Cherronesus, Assenisipia, Metropotamia, Polypotamia and Pelisipia died natural deaths. So, for less natural reasons, did Sylvania and Saratoga. Washington was much later chosen for the extreme northwest corner of the United States.[18]

But the heart of the Report lay in the conditions which Jefferson attached to the formation of permanent governments in the carved-out states: 1. That they shall forever remain a part of this confederacy of the United States of America. 2. That they shall be subject to the Government of the United States in Congress assembled. 3. That they shall be subject to pay a part of the federal debts. 4. That their respective governments shall be in republican forms. 5. That after the year 1800 there shall be neither slavery nor involuntary servitude in any of the said states except as punishment for a crime.

It was chiefly the last condition that was extraordinary. Just as Jefferson had labored unsuccessfully to remove the blight of slavery from Virginia, where it was firmly entrenched, now he seized the opportunity to save from all future problems the great virgin territory where it did not as yet exist. As state after state of free territory came into the Union, the influence of the peculiar institution must progressively diminish in the older areas, and he hoped that the example might eventually dispose the South to yield it up gracefully and voluntarily. It was a noble dream, but doomed to defeat for the present, just as his similar attempt in writing it into the Declaration of Independence.

The South reacted promptly and violently. The Report was recommitted and, when it reappeared on the floor on April 19th with the offending clause still intact, a motion was offered to strike it out. Ten States were present at the time, and the vote was surprisingly close. The question was put in the affirmative: Should the slavery clause be allowed to *stand?* The Northern States—New Hampshire, Massachusetts, Rhode Island, Connecticut, New York, Pennsylvania—lined up solidly in back of the clause; New Jersey had only a single delegate present, so that, though he voted *yes,* it lost its vote; Maryland and South Carolina were unanimously opposed; North Carolina was divided and also lost its voice; while in the Virginia delegation, Jefferson voted *yes,* but his colleagues, Hardy and Mercer, voted *no.* Had another of the Virginia delegation, who was ill, been present, he would have voted *yes,* so Jefferson claimed, and thereby neutralized the State delegation instead of its vote being cast, as now, in the negative.[19]

Since only six States voted to retain the slavery prohibition, and seven were needed, it was stricken out. Had the missing New Jersey delegate been present, it would have passed. As it was, the prohibition had to wait on the final and definitive Ordinance of 1787 for inclusion. But by then it was sharply limited to the Northwest Territory itself, whereas Jefferson had attempted to include all future accessions from the States and from Indians.

One more clause—unimportant in character—was stricken out; a prohibition against hereditary honors in the territory. With these two excisions, the Western Territory Act was passed on April 23rd, with South Carolina solitary in dissent.[20]

Jefferson never saw the United States as merely a stretch of thirteen states along the Atlantic littoral; his vision flamed outward over an expanding nation of numerous sovereign subdivisions, bound indissolubly together in mutual amity and accord. If he later hesitated over the indissolubility of the compact, he never wavered on the imperial dream, and he was to do more than anyone else to make it a reality.

He felt, too, that by carving new states out of the wilderness, instead of maintaining it as an adjunct of already established states, an impetus would be afforded to quick settlement and growth.

The pioneers who had peopled Kentucky, for example, were clamoring to be separated from Virginia and be set up as a separate state. A petition had been sent to Congress; but Congress had no powers in the matter. Jefferson and his fellow delegates sent a copy of it to Virginia; and Jefferson urged upon his state that it be granted. Kentucky will eventually separate in any event, he argued; and if they do it in wrath, it will sweep into its orbit all the other Virginia lands beyond the Allegheny. It would therefore be the part of wisdom to grant the petition voluntarily, and thereby save the rest.

What he particularly had in mind was to save control of the shortest water route between the Atlantic and the western waters—via the Potomac and the branches of the Ohio—and thereby gain a practical monopoly of the western and Indian trade. Pennsylvania was already making surveys for a canal to absorb that trade, and unless Virginia acted swiftly, she would lose the opportunity. Not only Jefferson, but Washington, had much at heart this plan of an inland canal stretching from the Potomac to the Ohio.[21]

There were no specialists in the legislative bodies of the day. Every delegate was presumed to be able to handle any matter that came before an Assembly or Congress, no matter how technical. But it is doubtful if any single delegate possessed the wide-ranging mind or the versatility of talents displayed by Thomas Jefferson. With equal conversance and ease he ranged from treaties to disquisitions on commerce; from technical points of law to currency systems.

As far back as 1776, he had reported to Congress on the variety of coins employed in the several states. Each state set up its own values—and English, French, Dutch, Spanish and Portuguese coins, all legal tender, were convertible in bewildering array. Obviously, a uniform coinage and uniform values were a necessity if commerce was to flow unimpeded.

Robert Morris, the Financier, had proposed at the end of 1782 that a standard unit be adopted, and a Congressional Committee, of which Jefferson was a member, had studied his report. Jefferson thought his general views were sound, but objected that the proposed unit—a coin representing $1/1440$ of a dollar—was too minute, too fractional, and would involve arithmetical calculations "entirely unmanageable for the common purposes of society." To Jefferson, the important considerations in fixing a unit were (1) that it be of convenient size; (2) that its parts and multiples be in simple proportions; (3) that its value be close enough to that of already existing coins as to make its adoption easy.

With what was tantamount to a stroke of genius he fastened on the Spanish dollar as more nearly fulfilling these conditions than any other coin, and set up a decimal system of subdivisions and multiples. He suggested, therefore, the silver Spanish dollar as the base; together with a gold piece worth ten dollars, a silver dime and a copper cent. Each of these new coins, he pointed out, had practical equivalents among coins already in circulation. As for the conversion rate between silver and gold, he suggested fifteen to one.

Morris agreed in principle with Jefferson's proposals, with two exceptions. He thought the market ratio between silver and gold was higher than fifteen to one, and Jefferson agreed to accept a higher one. And, while admitting that perhaps his original penny had been too small, Morris merely wanted to multiply it by 1,000, which brought it up to $^{25}/_{36}$ of a dollar. This was sheer stubbornness, involving a complicated fractional arithmetic, and Jefferson refused to yield.[22]

As a result, nothing was done about it at the moment. Jefferson later issued a pamphlet embodying his plan, Morris's objections and his own supplementary notes in reply. Eventually, Congress finally got around to legislating on coinage, and adopted Jefferson's system of decimal coinage, with the dollar as the unit. The amateur had shown himself more flexible and far-seeing than the professional specialist.

Various other projects engaged Jefferson's activity, in spite of the fact that he was ill most of the session, suffering from what seemed to be a migraine headache which attacked him with incapacitating force at regular intervals all through life. One of the most important of these lesser matters was to arrange for a continuing executive arm of government during adjournments of Congress. That legislative body, according to the Articles of Confederation, was also the Executive. Suggestions had been made at various times for a separate Executive, either a single President or a Committee of Three; but they had failed of adoption. The fear of empowering one man or even three to take over the reins of government was still strong. The memory of King George the Third rose like Banquo's ghost.

Nevertheless, something had to be done, if government was not to lapse altogether in the frequent intermissions. As early as December, 1775, Jefferson had proposed a solution: that a committee of Congress sit with executive powers during adjournments. It had failed of passage then; but now the need was obviously overwhelming; and a committee, of which Jefferson was chairman, was ordered in December, 1783, to consider the matter *de novo*. He now proposed that a Committee of States be appointed to act during recesses, with power to transact all business that an ordinary quorum of seven states could have transacted in full Congress. It was a very lengthy report, and he had to redraft it in curtailed form, specifying certain exceptions to the Executive Committee's powers. In this final form it was passed on May 29, 1784.[23]

As might be expected, the Committee of States did not function very well; and the problem of a proper executive branch of government had to wait for solution for the eventual revamping of the entire system in the Constitution. The Committee, consisting of a member from each state, were more interested in their respective states than in the general welfare; quarrels arose; and the members dispersed, leaving the country once more without anyone to function. The experience made Jefferson a believer in a *single* Executive; and what he saw in France under the Directory only confirmed that belief.[24]

But his days in the United States were now numbered. For some time, Congress had realized the necessity of negotiating treaties of commerce with the nations of Europe. During the period of dependency on England, the colonies had been firmly held within a mercantile system whose whole basis was the advantage of the mother country and not that of her colonies. England would have liked to continue her monopoly, now that her colonies had broken loose; but again on her own terms. In order to break that stranglehold, it was essential therefore to enter into mutually beneficial trade relations with countries like France, Holland, Portugal, the Scandinavian countries and Prussia. That was not as simple as it sounded, for most of these nations were similarly involved in mercantile systems which sought their own advantage and were indifferent to the interests of others.

On May 7, 1784, Congress decided to send Jefferson abroad to join Franklin and Adams, already on the spot, as Ministers Plenipotentiary in the negotiation of proper treaties.[25] What motivated his choice, besides general agreement on his ability, was the fact that the others were northern men and a southerner, who would know southern problems and southern needs for markets, ought to be joined to them.

Jefferson accepted the post with a certain eagerness. Twice before he had been on the verge of going, and each time there had been a last-minute change of heart. Monticello still held bittersweet memories of his unforgotten wife, and Europe with its infinite variety of scenes and occupations, would help ease the hurt. He had always yearned toward Europe—in particular, France—as the ancient seat of civilization, of culture, of the arts and sciences. He had corresponded with some of her leading scientists and entered into controversies with others. Now was the chance to meet them face to face and help influence, by a species of cross-fertilization, both sides of the Atlantic.

But before he could go, there were preparations to be made and matters to be cleaned up.

Washington, for example, had asked him what he thought of a proposed society, to be composed of the ex-officers of the Revolutionary Army, and hereditary in principle. It sounded innocuous enough—this society of the Cincinnati—but Jefferson foresaw grave dangers in its initiation. Himself a civilian, and therefore ineligible for membership, perhaps he saw more danger than there really was. But some of the objections he listed for Washington's benefit were pertinent: the line of separation it would draw between the military and the civilian; the hereditary principle which might eventually lead to the establishment of a new type of aristocracy in America; and, perhaps, most potent of all, the likelihood that such an organization of officer veterans (the common soldier was not eligible) might be used for political purposes.[26]

That these were no idle warnings, especially the last one, may be gathered from the history of later veterans' groups that were much more democratic in inception and theory. Furthermore, the very airing of the proposal to set up such a society of the (as it were) elite, had already touched off violent reactions. Aedanus Burke, a furious democrat of South Carolina, had already inveighed against the purposes of such a society in a series of pamphlets; and within a little while, a candidate to the Virginia Assembly was defeated on the sole ground that he was a member of the Cincinnati.[27]

In spite of Jefferson's objections, however, Washington finally decided to join the organization; and it later became, if not itself a power in politics, at least the political ground for such a fear in its opponents.

The remissness of Virginia in contributing her proper share to the Continental expenses distressed Jefferson exceedingly. Could not Madison, he asked, get Virginia to appropriate for that purpose the receipts on the slave tax, so that it might be "bearable to any man of feeling to represent her in Congress?" South Carolina, notwithstanding her troubles, was far ahead of Virginia in answering the requisitions of Congress. "Whence does this proceed?" he inquired indignantly, and answered himself. "From a difference of spirit solely; from a pride of character; from a rejection of the unmanly supineness which permits personal inconvenience to absorb every other sentiment. There is no man who has not some vice or folly the starving of which would not pay his taxes."

Having thus indicted his native state, he returned to more personal affairs. He was going away, he told Madison, and he wanted to leave in his care young Peter Carr, the son of his sister and his deceased friend, Dabney Carr. Peter was then fourteen, and Jefferson had been both father and teacher to him. Would Madison see to it that the lad completed his studies in Latin, Greek, French, Italian and Anglo-Saxon, so that, at sixteen, he could go to college? His other nephew, aged ten, was to be placed in a good school.[28]

Madison expressed his readiness to comply with both the political and private requests. He was not too happy, however, over Jefferson's impending departure for Europe. He felt he was needed at home, particularly for the aid he might render in revising the Virginia constitution. But he intended to go on fighting on his own, and to use Jefferson's ideas in that connection.[29] How redoubtable were his efforts, and his valiant employment of Jefferson's ideas—as well as his own—was later evidenced by the triumphant passage of the famous Statute for Religious Liberty.

Meanwhile, Madison in turn had dumped a problem in Jefferson's lap. Mazzei, Jefferson's volatile Italian neighbor, had returned from his mission to Europe in 1783. His own activities there had been obscure and without obvious results; but he had brought back with him one fixed idea—a bitter enmity toward Benjamin Franklin, whom he had met in Paris. He told Madison, and Madison passed it on to Jefferson, that "the exquisite cunning of the old fox has so enveloped his iniquity, that its reality cannot be proved by those who are thoroughly satisfied of it." Of John Adams, he had a higher opinion. Now he wanted an appointment to a European consulate, and he was on his way to Annapolis for Jefferson to use his influence to get him one.[30]

But Jefferson had received a previous intimation of Mazzei's coming from Madison, and the thought had alarmed him. A renewed acquaintance with Mazzei had served to temper some of Jefferson's old enthusiasm. "I tremble at the idea," he had written Madison. "I know he will be worse to me than a return of my double quotidian head-ach." [Tell him that Congress has a resolution pending to give no foreign jobs to any but native Americans. No doubt, he thought, Mazzei had collected in Paris "facts true or false to *impeach* [Franklin]. You know there are people here who, on the first idea of this will take him to their bosom & turn all Congress topsy turvy. For God's sake then save us from this confusion if you can."[31] He was unable to stave off the persistent Mazzei for long, however; for, within a short period, the latter appeared on the European scene to complicate Jefferson's life.

Jefferson decided to take Patsy with him. He had become accustomed to her company in his travels, and Europe would provide a finishing school for her education. Nor had he forgotten her during their separation. He wrote regularly to her, inquiring after her studies, and giving her fatherly advice on deportment and conduct. He was a true pedagogue. He wanted to know what books she read, what tunes she could play, and to receive specimens of her drawings. She had met a French drawing teacher at the Rittenhouses', a M. Cimitiere, and Jefferson was pleased to have her take lessons from him. (Later, Cimitiere proved unreasonable about an additional guinea of payment and had to be dropped.) Jefferson hoped she would not trespass too often on the hospitality of the Rittenhouses, though she would witness there "the best examples of national life and learn to esteem and copy them."[32]

His two younger daughters again had to be left behind, in the care of relatives.

One more problem confronted Jefferson—whom to take along as his secretary. The last time he was scheduled to go he had intended to take David S. Franks, but Franks was already in Europe on a mission, and he had been afraid of his wagging tongue and weakness for women. He required someone he could wholly trust.

There was Monroe, with whom he had become very friendly and whom he had earlier considered for the post. But Monroe was fast making his way politically on the domestic scene; and his eyes therefore turned instead to a young man named William Short.

Since Short was to become an integral part of Jefferson's life from now on and, in a sense, that "son" to him which nature had unfortunately withheld, it is proper to devote some space to that interesting young gentleman.

William Short was born at Spring Garden, Virginia, in 1759, and was therefore now twenty-five. Educated at William and Mary, he had decided to enter politics in 1783. His brother, Peyton, gave him some excellent advice on the nature and business of politics. "Let me insist that you offer at the first Opportunity," wrote brother Peyton. "If you succeed you enter immediately the proper School for calling your Talents into Play—if you do not you lose no time to give the People warning that you will be at their Service—Believe me my dear Brother there is nothing in this Business equal to being known personally to the People." [33]

Acting on this sage advice, William Short offered, was duly elected and became almost immediately a member of the Executive Council. Just when Jefferson made his acquaintance is not known, but by February of the following year he was urging that Short be sent as a delegate from Virginia to Congress. "I see the best effects produced by sending our young statesmen here," he observed. "They see the affairs of the Confederacy from a high ground; they learn the importance of the Union & befriend federal measures when they return. Those who never come here, see our affairs insulated, pursue a system of jealousy & self interest, and distract the Union as much as they can."

Both Short and Monroe were buying land near Monticello on which to build. Jefferson hoped that Madison would do the same. "With such a society," and he meant it sincerely, "I could once more venture home & lay myself up for the residue of life, quitting all its contentions which grow daily more and more insupportable.... Life is of no value but as it brings us gratifications. Among the most valuable of these is rational society. It informs the mind, sweetens the temper, chears [*sic*] our spirits, and promotes health." [34] But this was before he was nominated for Europe, and the dream of an earthly Paradise had to wait many long years.

When Jefferson heard of his appointment as Minister Plenipotentiary, he promptly offered Short a personal secretaryship, even though the general secretaryship to the Commission was not available. "You have said you would condescend to be the index of a book," he wrote. "So dispose then of your matters as to be *in utrumque paratus*, & on short warning. If I am enabled to offer you no other advantage than a bed & board free, I am also enabled to assure you I shall give you very little trouble." [35]

Short gladly accepted the offer, no matter what the capacity, and in an accompanying letter told of a private conference he had attended, at which Patrick Henry, Madison and Joseph Jones were present. Henry had expressed his readiness to support on the floor of the Assembly any measures that Madison and Jones would draft to give greater powers to the Federal Government. He had declared that this was the only inducement for his attending the current Assembly; that he saw "Ruin inevitable unless something was done to give Congress a compulsory Process on delinquent States." [36]

If Short was reporting accurately, and was not merely being misled by youthful enthusiasm, then this was a most amazing conversation which contradicted Henry's whole past, present and future course and bore no visible fruits. No one was to be a more vociferous opponent of the Constitution on the very ground that the Federal Government was given too much power over the States than this same Patrick Henry—unless it was Governor George Clinton of New York. It was not until late in the 1790's, when Henry's political and private fortunes had changed, that he became a Federalist.

On May 10, 1784, Jefferson quit Annapolis and Congress in preparation for his journey to Europe. He was forty-one years of age and a new, if paradoxically older, world was beckoning.

He had spoken to Short of his indifference to his ultimate destination, whether at home or abroad, and had hinted to others of the frame of mind in which he still was as a result of Martha's death. That there was a real basis for what might otherwise be taken as pretense, is evident from the observations of a young Dutch nobleman, Count Gijsbert Karel van Hogendorp, who had come to Annapolis in March, just a month before, to observe the workings of an American Congress. What he saw did not prepossess him in its favor; but a single month was to make him an admirer of Jefferson for life. He found him a man of many affairs, leading a life retired from social distractions, occupying himself solely with public matters and indulging in no amusements but those of belles-lettres.

Hogendorp thought his conversation serious, though reserved, and "more usefull to me than that of any Gentleman in town." Jefferson attributed his retired life to his poor health at the time, but the Dutch traveler discerned a deeper reason—that, "accustomed to the agreeable society of an amiable wife, he is not attracted to ordinary society now that she is gone." After he left Annapolis, Hogendorp was emboldened to write and tell him so. "I pitied your situation," he wrote, "for I thought you unhappy. Why, I did not know; and though you appeared insensible to social enjoyments, yet I was perfectly convinced you could not have been ever so. One evening I talked of love, and then I perceived that you still could feel, and express your feelings." [37]

Perhaps the impetuousness of the assault, or a weakness for the young man, made Jefferson open his heart in return. "Your observation on the situation of my mind is not without foundation," he told his young admirer. "Yet I had hoped it was unperceived, as the agreeable conversations into which you led me, often induced a temporary inattention to those events which have produced that gloom you remembered. . . . I have known what it is to lose every species of connection which is dear to the human heart: friends, brethren, parents, children—retired, as I thought myself to dedicate the residue of life to contemplation and domestic happiness, I have been again thrown by events on the world without an object on which I can place value." [38]

It was high time, obviously, that he went to Europe.

Yet, while thus discoursing of gloom and the aridity of the world, Jefferson could at the same time throw himself with tremendous ardor into all sorts of scientific matters. How otherwise explain his enthusiastic account to a relative, only a few days before, of a book he had read on the newly discovered art "of traversing the air in ballons," complete with tables, charts and free hand drawings of balloons? [39]

How also account for Jefferson's passionate interest in obtaining "big bones" of every description—elk bones, mammoth bones? To George Rogers Clark, on whom he made the request repeatedly, he declared that "there is no expence of package or of safe transportation which I will not gladly reimburse to procure them safely." And, with reports abroad that money had been raised in England to explore the vast region from the Mississippi to California on the pretense of promoting knowledge but, as Jefferson believed, actually to colonize, he hoped that perhaps Virginia might send out its own party of exploration. "How would you like to lead such a party?" he concluded.[40] Thus early came the inception of the idea of that future exploration undertaken in Jefferson's Presidency.

But then, Jefferson was a highly complex individual, and it may well be that compartments in his mind opened and shut automatically without too great an intercommunication among them.

Jefferson's first stop was Philadelphia, to pick up Patsy, settle her affairs and outfit himself for an extended stay abroad. He did not know at the time just how long that stay was going to be.

Among the curious things that he purchased in the metropolis was a panther's skin, for which he paid forty-five shillings.[41] This was a large specimen of its kind, and he wanted to prove to M. Buffon by irrefutable tangible evidence that his strictures on the degenerate smallness of American animals were unfounded. He was later to put himself and others to infinite trouble and expense to obtain other specimens of American mammalia for the same purpose. Patriotic pride, as well as scientific truth, was involved.

At Philadelphia, too, he had hoped to get Dunlap, the printer, to print privately some copies of his *Notes on Virginia* for distribution among his friends at home and for the use of savants abroad. But Dunlap was unable to promise delivery before he sailed; so perforce he took the manuscript to Europe for printing there.[42]

He was sailing from Boston; and he welcomed the opportunity of journeying leisurely by land to that port of embarkation, as giving him a chance to visit for the first time some of the New England States and inform himself of the commercial practices and needs of those Northern communities. After all, he was going to Europe to negotiate trade treaties, and Jefferson was not one to proceed blithely without as careful a background of facts and figures as he could possibly amass.[43]

He carried with him also a set of official instructions which he himself had helped draft, and final copies of which came to him during his stay at Philadelphia. The magnitude and extent of the task which confronted the three Ministers were amazing, and ought to have daunted any man. But the representatives of the infant Republic possessed a supreme confidence in themselves and in the destiny of the nation whose credentials they held and, by the very virtue of a certain audacity, were able to perform magnificent feats in its behalf that, knowing all the circumstances, might otherwise sound incredible today.

The Ministers, for example, were empowered to treat with Russia, Austria, Prussia, Denmark, Saxony, Hamburg, Great Britain, Rome, Turkey—the full list is staggering. They were to negotiate agreements which in effect would have given to American shipping and trade the full freedom of the seas—rights which would have broken down the monopolistic restrictions of the various national mercantilist systems and permitted commerce to flow unimpeded in spite of war, of colonial barriers or the navies of the world.[44] It was a gargantuan task that confronted these new-fledged diplomats, and impossible of full execution as long as Great Britain ruled the seas. That they achieved even a measure of success was due to a concatenation of circumstances, which will be developed at the appropriate time.

With Patsy ensconced in the coach with him—and accompanied by Col. David Humphreys, who had been appointed as secretary of the Commission—Jefferson left Philadelphia on May 28th. His first stop was New York where he spent a week. He bought a Spanish dictionary to brush up on his knowledge of that language and to be able to read *Don Quixote* in the original; [45] then proceeded to New Haven, where he visited the learned Dr. Ezra Stiles, president of Yale College. That extraordinary divine, broad-minded in religion and curious about the phenomena of nature as well as the things of the spirit, promptly took to his eminent visitor.

They discoursed with mutual profit and delight of a wide range of subjects. Jefferson told Stiles that the ownership of land was so widely diffused in Virginia that there was no question in his mind that eventually "the plebeian Interest will prevail over the old aristocratical Interest in that State." He also described an electrostatic machine which a British officer had left behind in Philadelphia and discussed at length the ridiculous theories of the unwitting Buffon anent the nature of the mammoth. Could Stiles get him additional information on this rapidly enlarging scientific controversy and send it along to him? "The Gov. [Jefferson] is a most ingenous [*sic*] Naturalist & Philosopher," Stiles noted delightedly in his Diary, "a truly scientific & learned Man—every way excellent." He was so impressed that two years later he caused Yale to confer the degree of Doctor in Laws on his visitor.[46]

From New Haven Jefferson proceeded to Hartford, then into Massachusetts in easy stages. On the morning of June 18th, he was breakfasting with Fisher Ames in Dedham;[47] that same Ames who was later to become one of his most bitter political enemies and would no more have thought of eating at the same table with Jefferson than with the devil himself. But party animosities were still a thing of the future. In the afternoon, the coach with its accompanying entourage was jolting into Boston.

Sailing times in those days were highly irregular, and Jefferson was unable to find a proper ship until July 5th. But the delay was not wasted. There was Boston, the cradle of the Revolution, to explore; old friends from the various Congresses to meet; and its commerce to consider. He also had time to take a short jaunt up the coast into the ports of New Hampshire to find out the requirements of that state and embodied his discoveries in a series of memoranda listing the state of trade in the various communities, the laws governing it and immigration, and their imports and exports, all meticulously compiled either from his own observations or from information received from correspondents at his request.[48] He intended to be well armed with pertinent facts and figures when he spoke to the various chancelleries of Europe.

He almost had the company of the redoubtable Abigail Adams on the way to Europe. She had sailed to join her husband, John, some thirty-six hours after Jefferson's arrival in Boston, and Jefferson would have loved to have gone with her. But the time was too short for him, and he would have offended his numerous friends by a too hasty departure. He was overwhelmed "by the hospitality & civilities of this place which I have experienced in the highest degree."[49]

On July 5, 1784, at six in the morning, the great day finally arrived. The fine new merchantman *Ceres*, owned by Nathaniel Tracy of Newburyport and captained by St. Barbe, hoisted its sails and beat its way out of Boston harbor. On board, besides Jefferson and his company, were only six other passengers, with all of whom he was acquainted. At long last, after many false starts, Jefferson was on his way to the Old World, that swarming focus of humanity which exercised both an infinite attraction and an almost equally infinite repulsion upon one whose spirit clung parochially to Virginia yet, at the same time, ranged the entire world for sustenance and delight.

CHAPTER 20

Minister to France

THE voyage was calm, pleasant and surprisingly rapid. It took only nineteen days from landfall to landview, something of a record for that time, and the sun was out practically every day.

Jefferson busied himself with the usual minutiae of a landsman taking his first sea voyage, entering in his account book such information as the daily log, the ship's bearings, the temperature, wind direction; and duly noting the gannets and "pettrils" that circled the vessel, and the whales, sharks and Portuguese man-of-war that inhabited the depths. Since the sea was calm as a lake, the little party suffered no seasickness.[1]

On July 26, 1784, they landed at West Cowes on the Isle of Wight, and transshipped to Portsmouth. Patsy had been running a fever the last few days of the voyage, and Jefferson called in a doctor, nurses and an apothecary to care for her. The child recovered rapidly and Jefferson was able to proceed on the 31st.

He took passage to Havre de Grace, posted to Rouen and on August 6th was in Paris.[2] Patsy, now well again, had viewed the strange country through which they passed with delight, and kept her friend Mrs. Trist, in Philadelphia, informed of all the details. What impressed her most, perhaps, was the venerable habit of cheating strangers, from which, it seems, her father was not immune.[3]

The first thing Jefferson did on arrival in the French capital was to get himself set. He took lodgings at the Hôtel d'Orléans, on the Rue Richelieu, where six days' house rent cost him 72 francs. The next thing was to go on a buying spree. He had no intention of being out of fashion in Paris. He purchased a complete outfit for Patsy; a map, cambric, lace ruffles, hat, sword and sword belt, knee and shoe buckles for himself. And, of course, the inevitable books. He was literally to indulge in an orgy of book-buying all through his European stay. Here were in abundance the volumes whose titles he had surveyed with longing eyes in America, and whose physical possession had been possible, if at all, only through extended negotiations and survival of the lengthy ocean voyage between. Within a few days he was giving young William Franklin, his old friend's illegitimate son, who was departing for London, a commission and 16½ guineas to buy him more books and a copying press in England.[4] The latter was important. Jefferson liked to have copies on hand of every letter he wrote, of every scrap of paper on which he scribbled notations; and the copying press, though only taking wet impressions (the ink spreading and blurring, to the despair of all later researchers), was the most modern method available at the time, aside from the laborious hand-copying of the document.

The Hôtel d'Orléans in the Rue Richelieu was a temporary stopping place, and Jefferson transferred to the similarly named hotel in the Rue Petits Augustins on August 10th. Here he paid 20 louis a month for his quarters; took on a substantial entourage of servants, including one Gaspard and a *valet de chambre* named Marc. He bought dishes, silverware, glasses and began laying down an extensive wine cellar; subscribed to all the great newspapers of Europe, hired a coach, even though he had brought his famous phaeton along with him, and was ready to entertain in style.[5] He was determined that these sophisticated Frenchmen should understand that Americans were not barbarians. But Benjamin Franklin had already taken care of that in a wholly different way—by affecting a plainness of dress and simplicity of speech which delighted the French perhaps even more than Jefferson's ruffles, lace and abundant wines.

Jefferson had posted down to Passy, where that sage and philosopher was the cynosure of neighboring eyes, and paid his respects to his older confrere. They discussed old times, plans for the joint mission, and sent to John Adams, the third of the triumvirate, now at The Hague, to join them in Paris.

The next thing was to take care of Patsy. Jefferson had no intention of interrupting her education, or keeping her amid the constant comings and goings that were inevitable in his own lodgings. He made careful inquiries to find her a suitable place and, on the advice of Madame de Lafayette, the wife of his friend from those unfortunate war days in Virginia, settled her at the Abbaye de Panthemont where the nuns taught school to a cosmopolitan group of girls, Protestants as well as Catholics.[6] It was considered one of the best institutions of its kind in Europe, and Jefferson was assured that no attempt would be made to convert his daughter to Catholicism. Patsy liked it very much, and Jefferson found no reason for misgivings as to his choice; though later, Abigail Adams, with proper Puritan suspicion, was to denounce him for having thus exposed his daughter to possible contamination.

The school was not inexpensive, costing 500 francs a month, besides a small *douceur* for charity; but at this time he was spending money in the grand manner. Jefferson was never one to scrimp and save, even when his finances were at a low ebb and debts mountainous. The true Virginia blood coursed in his veins.

Now that Patsy was safely ensconced, he did all the things that could only be done in Paris, and continued his extravagant expenditures. He attended an Italian comedy, then a French comedy and a "*concert spirituel*"; saw the gardens at Versailles and a balloon ascension—he had already witnessed one during his stay in Philadelphia.

The quarters in the Rue Petits Augustins cramped him; and he moved once more on October 17th—this time with some permanence—to a house at No. 5, Rue Taitbout. For this new establishment he invested in more furniture, to the tune of 1,632 francs, picked up two "small laughing busts," two "pictures of heads," and two somewhat fuller portraits, of which one was an "*Ecce homo*." He also saw and coveted a plaster statue of Hercules, received the first volumes of the great French Encyclopedia, installed a fountain and cistern, and ran riot with lamps, china plate, silver and gifts "for my children" at home, pictures, books and more books, and wines. Nor did he forget his beloved music. He replaced his fiddle strings, purchased music and a music stand, and hired a pianoforte. No doubt he scraped away on his violin before the stand, but to whose accompaniment on the pianoforte is not known.

By this time he was tired of paying hire for his rented carriage, and the Virginia phaeton was not suitable. Therefore, on March 15th of the next year, he became the proud possessor of a lavish new chariot, costing 800 francs, which he forthwith lined with "green marocco." [7] With his staff of four servants, at 242 francs a month, with house rent, food, clothes, accoutrements, Patsy's education and keep, it is no wonder that he was later to complain that the sums which a grudging Congress devoted to the maintenance of its representatives abroad could not begin to pay the expenses; even when they were forwarded, which often they were not.

With Jefferson lived his private secretary, young William Short, and Col. David Humphreys, the Secretary of Legation. Their living expenses were also a part of his ménage. Col. David Franks, that lively young man, was also in and out; and usually out of pocket, as well.

Strangely enough, though Jefferson read French fluently and had met and discoursed with numerous Frenchmen in the States, on his landing in France he found that he understood the French in their native habitat "so imperfectly as to be incertain [*sic*] whether those to whom I speak and myself mean the same thing." [8] But the long years in France gave him both fluency and a proper accent.

In spite of the round of buying, house seeking and sightseeing, however, Jefferson did not forget the precious manuscript of his *Notes on Virginia*, which he was so anxious to put into print.

He found a printer who agreed to strike off two hundred copies at a price about a quarter of what he had been asked in Philadelphia. Now, for the first time, he gave it what has become its final title; but he was careful to append no name to it as author. For this caution he had sound and sufficient reasons, as he surmised then and the sequel proved only too true. He gave those reasons when he sent a copy to Chastellux, returned to Paris from his travels, and warned him against allowing the copy out of his hand or betraying the name of the author. He repeated the same warning in forwarding a copy to Madison.

As he told Chastellux, he did not fear the publication of extracts which dealt with purely physical matters. But "the strictures on slavery and on the constitution of Virginia are not of that kind, and they are the parts which I do not wish to have made public, at least till I know whether their publication would do most harm or good. It is possible that in my own country these strictures might produce an irritation which would indispose the people towards the two great objects I have in view, that is the emancipation of their slaves & the settlement of their constitution on a firmer & more permanent basis. If I learn from thence, that they will not produce that effect, I have printed & reserved just copies enough to be able to give one to every young man at the College. It is to them I look," he ended eloquently, "to the rising generation, and not to the one now in power, for these great reformations." But, as he told Madison, he was ready to burn those copies if the replies were unfavorable.[9]

In due time, Madison's eagerly awaited response came back from distant America. That careful and conscientious friend had read the *Notes* himself and discussed their contents with a select group of friends, among whom was the judicious George Wythe. They were all most enthusiastic but, at the same time, realized that the parts relating to slavery and Virginia politics would displease certain groups of people. Nevertheless, it was the consensus that this consideration be not allowed to weigh against Jefferson's plan. "We think," wrote Madison for himself and the others, "both the facts and remarks which you have assembled too valuable not to be made known, at least to those for whom you destine them." Wythe suggested that copies be placed in the College library, instead of an indiscriminate distribution to students. As he pointed out, the latter course might "offend some narrow-minded parents." [10]

Curiously enough, while the Virginians were ready to chance at least a limited circulation, Charles Thomson from Pennsylvania warned against it. He felt Jefferson's fears justified; though slavery, he exclaimed prophetically, "is a cancer which we must get rid of. It is a blot in our character that must be wiped out. If it cannot be done by religion, reason and philosophy, confident I am that it will one day be by blood." [11]

Thomson was a deeply religious man, well versed in Biblical literature and, in 1808, was to translate the Septuagint and the New Testament into English. At the same time, he was an enthusiastic dabbler in science and natural history, active in the Philosophical Society, and corresponded with Jefferson on such subjects as animal magnetism, balloons, rocks, the theory of the earth and kindred matters. He was also a radical in politics, having earned the soubriquet during the Revolution of the "Sam Adams of Philadelphia," and had been a faithful and conscientious secretary to the several Continental Congresses.[12]

But before Jefferson could make up his mind what to do, his hand was forced for him. One of the copies which he had given to a certain Mr. Williamos found its way into the hands of an unscrupulous French printer named Barrois. Barrois had caused the *Notes* to be translated into French, and had the impudence to ask Jefferson to correct the proofs. "I never had seen so wretched an attempt at translation," moaned the unhappy author. "Interverted, abridged, mutilated, and often reversing the sense of the original, I found it a blotch of errors from beginning to end."[13]

In self-defense, Jefferson was compelled to correct at least the most glaring errors, and it was published in 1786 with a preface by Abbé Morellet, the translator.

The fat was in the fire. Willy-nilly, his observations on Virginia were in the public domain. So bad was the Abbé's rendition—Jefferson drew up in parallel columns the original English and the wrong French of it—that he was determined not to allow it to stand as the sole evidence of his work.

He therefore wrote to John Stockdale, a well-known London printer who, on the publication of the French edition, had proposed to publish the English original, that he could go ahead. Jefferson had, moreover, made some revisions in the text and had engraved a new map for it, taking in the territory from Albemarle Sound to Lake Erie which, he modestly thought, would be worth more than the book itself.[14]

Having learnt his lesson about the ways of printers, Jefferson insisted that Stockdale publish exactly what he received, without any "additions, alterations, preface, or any thing else but what is there." Furthermore, the plate of the map, which had come back to him from a London engraver, was full of "a prodigious number of orthographical errors," and Jefferson had to hire another engraver to correct them.[15]

The English edition appeared in 1787, and has been the basis of all later ones. Jefferson shipped fifty-seven copies to his factor, Alexander Donald, in Richmond, with instructions to distribute seventeen among friends, relatives and leaders like Washington, Edmund Randolph, Joseph Jones, Francis Eppes, R. H. Lee and George Mason. The balance of forty was to be put on sale at ten shillings, Virginia money, and half that for the maps.[16]

The reception of the volume from most of those who received copies was enthusiastic. Benjamin Vaughan in London sent high critical praise, declaring that Jefferson had confuted the erroneous opinions of Buffon and others concerning America; while David Rittenhouse called it "an inestimable treasure." Rittenhouse, however, quarreled with Jefferson's notion that fossil shells were imitative stones, and more sharply pointed ridicule on that strange theory also appeared in the French press.[17]

But the real storm did not come until later, when American printers, who had sought in vain for Jefferson's permission to publish official American editions, defiantly brought out pirated ones. The American reading public did not bother too much about scientific inaccuracies; but vociferous groups fell upon the sections on slavery, Biblical history, religion and Christianity. These, with the story of Logan and Cresap, turned up regularly in every political campaign, and often in between, to plague their promulgator.

Jefferson always contemplated a new, enlarged and authorized edition, and made diligent notes and corrections in anticipation; but he never got around to it; and it was only in 1853 that his executor finally published the *Notes* with the additional material.

While thus engaged in a multitude of activities, news came from Virginia that struck another of those many blows that Jefferson seemed fated to undergo in his personal life. Elizabeth Eppes, his sister-in-law, wrote to convey the sad information that little Lucy Elizabeth, aged two, had died of the whooping cough. Polly, aged six, had almost died of the same disease, but was now recovered.[18]

Jefferson's health had not been too good after his arrival in Paris. The dampness of the climate, the unwholesomeness of the water, and the recurrence of his migraine headaches incapacitated him for some six weeks. Nor did the news from Virginia help to restore him quickly to health. It was only in the spring of 1785, when the sun finally appeared again, that he recovered.[19] To a Virginia sun-worshipper, the Parisian climate of rain, mist and overcast was a dire calamity. On October 16, 1785, over a year after his arrival in Europe, he entered this significant observation in his Weather Book: "The first day of uninterrupted sunshine from sunrise to sunset which I have seen in Paris." [20]

Illness, however, did not prevent him from casting a perceptive eye on the state of Europe—political, social, economic, scientific and artistic. He tried to keep his friends in America informed of the latest developments on all fronts, and they in turn sent him the news from his native land. Since the mails were often opened by solicitous agents of government or by merely curious postmasters, it was customary to send confidential communications in cipher. Jefferson had arranged several such ciphers—nine, in fact, for official use, and others by private prearrangement with his friends. Most of them were simple substitution codes of numerals for words and syllables. Of one of these, Jefferson wrote a comment: "Frequently throw in numbers higher than 1545 [the top number in that code], which meaning nothing will serve to perplex." It is to be doubted, however, that any of these would have long perplexed a modern expert. One code was based on a column arrangement of the Lord's Prayer, and another on a French-English pocket dictionary, which might have made more trouble for the inquisitive.[21]

It was in a number cipher that Jefferson reported to Madison his thoughts on Patrick Henry and his attitude toward a new constitution for Virginia. Even if a Convention were held for that purpose, Jefferson feared that at the present time it might do more harm than good. "While Mr. Henry lives," he wrote with great bitterness, "another bad constitution would be formed & forever on us. What we have to do I think is devotedly to [252.746] for his death."[22] Jefferson's editor discreetly left the verb in the original cipher; but the meaning is plain enough.

Yet he was compelled to enter into a formal correspondence with the man whose death was so devoutly to be wished; for Patrick Henry was again Governor of Virginia, and the Virginia Assembly, voting to erect a heroic statue of General Washington, had asked Jefferson to find an appropriate sculptor in Europe. Jefferson informed Henry that Houdon of Paris was unrivaled for that purpose; but he must make the statue from life. Houdon, in fact, was "so anxious to be the person who should hand down the figure of the General to future ages, that without hesitating a moment he offered to abandon his business here, to leave the statues of kings unfinished, & to go to America to take the true figure by actual inspection and mensuration." The fee, he had assured Jefferson, would be reasonable.[23]

Jean-Antoine Houdon was in truth, as Jefferson enthusiastically declared, the greatest living sculptor of the day and one of the great of all time. His portrait heads of Voltaire and Franklin are inimitable, and eminent men fought to sit for him.

Both Washington and the Virginia Assembly agreed to grant him the commission and Jefferson thereupon engaged him. The price was 25,000 livres in cash, the expenses of the journey and insurance on his life. He also hoped, and Jefferson urged it on his friends in Congress, for a commission to do an equestrian statue of Washington for the nation.[24]

The latter project never developed, and Houdon was at first reluctant to make the long journey simply on the basis of the standing statue for Virginia. Then illness intervened, and the trip was again delayed. He finally went in July, 1785—after Jefferson had devoted an undue part of his time to endless correspondence on the subject—made a life mask of Washington, took all measurements, and returned to France to complete the statue. But should it be in classical or in modern dress? There was more delay while Washington was consulted. Washington's decision for the modern met with Jefferson's approval.

"I am happy to find," he wrote, "that the modern dress for your statue would meet your approbation. . . . I think a modern in antique dress as just an object of ridicule, as a Hercules or Marius with a periwig and a *chapeau bras*."[25]

It was not until 1796 that, after many vicissitudes, the statue was finally finished and shipped to Virginia, where it now stands in the Capitol, solitary and impressive.

On France itself, as it unfolded in all its manifestations, Jefferson was of two minds. He envied the French their architecture, sculpture, painting and music; but nothing else. Fresh from the spaciousness of America, where institutions, no matter how far behind the ideal, at least were liberal and progressive, where the people walked with an independent air and poverty was practically unknown, the swarming alleys of Paris, the contrast between resplendent Court and the hopeless masses, the ironbound castes and the feudal regime, filled him with a sense of horror.

Back in Virginia was a Florentine savant, Carlo Bellini, whom the indefatigable Mazzei had brought with him in 1773 and whom Jefferson, during his term of governorship, had caused to be appointed to William and Mary as its first professor of modern languages. Bellini, who is the only person known to have addressed Jefferson in a letter familiarly as "dearest Thomas,"[26] had been anxious to obtain Jefferson's impressions of Europe. Jefferson obliged about a year after his arrival.

"Behold me," he wrote, "at length on the vaunted scene of Europe!" Perhaps Bellini was curious to know "how this new scene has struck a savage of the mountains of America. Not advantageously I assure you. I find the general fate of humanity here most deplorable. The truth of Voltaire's observation offers itself perpetually, that every man here must be either the hammer or the anvil." In science, the masses were far behind their counterparts in America; while even the literati were only a half dozen years ahead, the exact time it took for Europe's books to filter through to America. Socially, "intrigues of love occupy the younger, & those of ambition the more elderly part of the great. Conjugal love having no existence among them, domestic happiness, of which that is the basis, is utterly unknown."[27]

To Monroe he was even more direct. Come and see France, he exhorted. "It will make you adore your own country.... My God, how little do my country men know what precious blessings they are in possession of, and which no other people on earth enjoy."[28]

He had always been opposed to sending American youth to study in Europe, and his opposition to that practice of the wealthy increased with firsthand knowledge. Practically every branch of learning, he informed an inquirer with some vehemence, was as well taught at William and Mary as at any place in Europe. Only for medicine, he reluctantly conceded, was Europe essential. And look what happened to the morals of the young man who unwittingly came across. In excoriating language he described the corruption that awaited him.

"If he goes to England, he learns drinking, horse racing and boxing. These," he added, forgetting that the first two at least were not uncommon in Virginia, "are the peculiarities of English education." In Europe generally, the unhappy youth acquires "a fondness for European luxury and dissipation, and a contempt for the simplicity of his own country"; he contracts "a partiality for aristocracy or monarchy"; he is led "into a spirit for female intrigue, destructive of his own and others' happiness, or a passion for whores, destructive of his health, and, in both cases, learns to consider fidelity to the marriage bed as an ungentlemanly practice, and inconsistent with happiness"; he returns to his native land filled with a hankering for the foreign fleshpots and himself a foreigner, "unacquainted with the practices of domestic economy, necessary to preserve him from ruin, speaking and writing his native tongue as a foreigner, and therefore unqualified to obtain those distinctions, which eloquence of the pen and tongue ensures in a free country." [29]

It is indeed an amazing indictment, true perhaps in part, but grossly exaggerated. There existed in Jefferson two concurrent strains; one of fierce local patriotism, and the other of a distinct Puritanism that kept cropping up at frequent intervals.

It may be that at this particular time he had come across some examples of American youth in Paris who fitted his description; and he had himself as an example of the luxurious living of which he complained, and which was fast running him into debt. In fact, not long before he thus gave vent to his feelings, he was describing the tangled state of his own affairs to an applicant for a loan. "My outfit here, for the articles of furniture, clothes & carriage only has cost me fifteen hundred guineas. No allowance of this kind being made [by Congress] I have been obliged to run in debt for it. The uneasiness which this has given me for some time past has preyed on my spirits night and day." He was in mortal fear that some creditor might complain to the king, which would expose him "to censure and recall. These circumstances have not only reduced me to a rigid economy, but render it impossible for me either to advance money or further hazard my credit." [30]

Later, after a longer stay in France, Jefferson was to modify some of his ideas to such an extent that he was willing to remain indefinitely in this sink of iniquity; and when he *did* return to America, looked upon France as his second home.

The three Ministers Plenipotentiary—Franklin, Adams and Jefferson—met to consider their course of action as soon as Adams, who had gone to England to welcome his wife Abigail on her arrival, could reach the French capital.

The instructions which Jefferson had brought over with him called for treaties of commerce to be negotiated with practically every nation in Europe. This was a large order, as the ministers were soon to discover. The first thing to be done was to prepare a general form of treaty which they could exhibit to those nations who might be willing to negotiate. This was comparatively simple, for the instructions from Congress covered most of the points, and these were duly inserted: exemption of capture during war of peaceful merchantmen engaged in normal trade; freedom from molestation of unarmed citizens, fishermen and farmers by an occupying power; abolition of the concept of contraband of war and, most important of all, the principle that free bottoms made free goods.[31]

It was simple enough to incorporate such provisions, but none of the ministers could have been naïve enough to believe that maritime powers like Great Britain would submit tamely to agreement on these proposals.

Courtesy the New York Public Library

MARQUIS DE LAFAYETTE

Painting by Samuel F. B. Morse

Courtesy the New-York Historical Society, New York City

BENJAMIN FRANKLIN

Painting by Joseph S. Duplessis

England's source of strength in war lay in her ability to sweep the seas of all enemy ships and prevent neutral vessels from bringing to her enemies the food, supplies and raw materials that were essential for their continued fighting of the war. If the American principles were adopted, the English navy lost its excuse for being. True, it could make the hostile fleet run to cover; but of what avail was that when neutral vessels—American, Dutch, Danish, Swedish—could flaunt unmolested on the high seas, with laden cargoes for enemy ports and bearing enemy goods, while they stood helplessly by? Even the carrying trade of the world, on which England depended for its very existence, would find its way into neutral bottoms, instead of English ships.

England never yielded to American demands, at this or any other time; and she fought a war with the United States in 1812, based in large part on her refusal so to yield; and was on the verge of war on other occasions, ranging from 1793 to as late as World War I. It was only when the United States herself joined in that later conflict, that this principle of the freedom of the seas, which had for more than a century been a cardinal creed in American diplomacy, was quietly shelved; if not in theory, certainly in practice.

If the American ministers had any illusions, they were soon disabused. By January, 1785, Jefferson was writing home that "we do not find it easy to make commercial arrangements in Europe. There is a want of confidence in us."[32]

There was good reason for this lack of confidence. Even those powers to whose advantage it was to establish the principle of the freedom of the seas, as Denmark, Sweden, Prussia and the Netherlands, might well hesitate before entering into commitments with a nation still in its swaddling clothes, with a Congress whose powers were vague and limited, and which were certain to expose them to the ire and possible retribution of England. Even France, though now interested in the doctrine and bound by treaty to her former ally, realized that some day she might in turn find it necessary to invoke a contrary doctrine against her perennial enemy, Great Britain.

Nevertheless, the three ministers went to work. Their first, and prime, target was England. They officially notified the British ambassador in Paris, David Hartley, that they had full powers to negotiate a treaty with England. His response was evasive. Let Congress send a person direct to London, he told them; he would not take up the questions with them in Paris.

Jefferson took this as an indication that England wanted to delay any definite showdown until she could see how far she could throttle American trade and exalt her own without a treaty. But, he wrote with grim resolution to Monroe, "we shall bring them to an issue. I suppose it will probably end in our going to London."[33] Eventually he did go, but without any greater success than he now had in Paris.

The only way to beat England to her knees and force concessions from her, Jefferson thought, was to forbid all American trade with her as long as there was no treaty. "Deaf to every principle of common sense, insensible to the feelings of man, they firmly believe they shall be permitted by us to keep all the carrying trade and that we shall attempt no act of retaliation because they are pleased to think it our interest not to do so." [34] But Congress, in spite of resolutions, was not yet ready for any such drastic step.

With negotiations with England thus aborted, the three commissioners had to turn their attention elsewhere.

The first place, at least as far as Jefferson was concerned, had nothing to do with the powers with whom they had been authorized to treat. He had been in Europe only a short while when he received information that pirates from the Barbary States had seized three American vessels. One, which had been taken by the Moroccans, had been given up; but two, seized by the Algerians, were still in their hands and would remain there, unless the United States agreed to pay tribute.

Nothing was more calculated to make Jefferson's blood boil than this bit of news. Fresh from a victory over the mightiest power on earth, he could not understand the strange tactics employed by all the great European seafaring nations in paying annual tribute to a nest of pirates on the African coast for the privilege of letting their ships proceed unmolested.

To Jefferson this was incredible. His first impulse was to go to them with an equal treaty, uncontaminated by tribute, in one hand, and a declaration of war in the other. If they refused the one, let them have the other. Actually, he preferred the idea of war; and his reasoning is most interesting in the light of later developments. "We ought to begin a naval power," he told Monroe, now in Congress and therefore in a position to do something about it, "if we mean to carry on our own commerce. *Can we begin it on a more honorable occasion, or with a weaker foe?*" [35]

Two months later, after he had gained a deeper insight into the complexities and obliquities of European diplomacy, his faculties were "absolutely suspended between indignation & impotence." It was not as easy to clean out the piratical nest as he had thought—not because of lack of naval power to do the job, but because the kettle of Europe could be too easily upset thereby. Nevertheless, if the United States *had* to pay any tribute for the privilege of navigating European waters, then she ought to retaliate on the European powers by imposing a separate impost on their goods to make up the amount of the tribute.[36]

The more he thought of the situation the more his anger mounted, until he completely lost his head, and was proposing to Monroe—and therefore, through him to Congress—one of the most fantastic schemes ever propounded by a responsible diplomat. Let us declare war on the Barbary pirates, he exclaimed, and should the European powers refuse to join us in the venture, "such as should refuse would give us a just right to turn pyrates also on their West India trade, and to require an annual tribute which might reimburse what we may be obliged to pay to obtain a safe navigation in their seas. Were we possessed even of a small naval force what a bridle would it be in the mouths of the West Indian powers and how respectfully would they demean themselves towards us. Be assured," he continued, veering to another source of indignation, "that the present disrespect of the nations of Europe for us will inevitably bring on insults which must involve us in war. A coward is much more exposed to quarrels than a man of spirit." [37]

Fortunately, both Congress on the other side of the Atlantic, and Franklin and Adams in Europe, were keeping their heads at this particular juncture, or Jefferson's curious hotheadedness might have hurried their infant nation into courses that could only have ended in disaster.

Only a month later, indeed, Jefferson was joining with his colleagues in a normally worded and cautiously diplomatic note addressed to the Comte de Vergennes, the French Minister of Foreign Affairs. They had just received authority from Congress to treat with the Barbary Powers, they said. But, having heard that the Emperor of Morocco had commenced hostilities on the United States by capturing an American ship, they were asking Vergennes' advice whether they should invite the Moroccan representative in Paris to treat with them, or should they conduct the negotiation wholly by letter; in which case would Vergennes be good enough to transmit one for them?

Furthermore, since the French treaty with Algiers was soon expiring, "and we are desirous of knowing (if it is not improper that we should enquire) whether this treaty is, or is likely to be renewed, because if there is a probability of a war Congress would probably prefer joining in the war, rather than to treat with nations who so barbarously & inhumanly commence hostilities against others who have done them no injury." [38] The fiery Mr. Jefferson had been properly bridled.

Charles Gravier, Comte de Vergennes, around whose figure American diplomacy on the Continent perforce gravitated, was an extremely interesting man. Almost singlehanded he had brought France into the war against England on the side of America, and now, in spite of the rebuff he had received through the secret negotiations between America and England on the terms of a peace treaty, he still conceived himself to be America's friend. Naturally, his course was motivated as much by policy as by friendship, just as his entry into the war had given France the opportunity of avenging former defeats at the hands of England.

Later on, after a considerable acquaintance, Jefferson was able to estimate his character with some correctness. "He is a great minister in European affairs," he wrote Madison, "but has very imperfect ideas of our institutions, and no confidence in them. His devotion to the principles of pure despotism renders him unaffectionate to our governments. But his fear of England makes him value us as a makeweight. He is cool, reserved in political conversations but free and familiar on other subjects, and a very attentive, agreeable person to do business with. It is impossible to have a clearer, better organized head; but age had chilled his heart." [39] Vergennes was over seventy at this time; and shortly thereafter was dead.

It was with this minister that Jefferson was to deal almost exclusively. For Congress had decided it was unnecessary to continue three commissioners concentrated in Paris. Franklin, aged and sufficiently covered with laurels, had asked permission to return to the United States. John Adams was appointed Minister to England; and Jefferson, on March 10, 1785, was appointed sole Minister to France.[40] Adams left for England in June, and Franklin departed home in July.

But before the three commissioners parted company they had won at least one victory. They had successfully consummated the first commercial treaty with a European power—Prussia. It is true that Prussia's trade with the United States was inconsiderable and that she had no navy to speak of; nevertheless the treaty possessed some novel, if not revolutionary, ideas on international law which render it notable.

Negotiations had been commenced by Adams with "old Frederic of Prussia" through his minister at The Hague prior to Jefferson's arrival, and they continued satisfactorily after Jefferson took a hand. It was doubtless Jefferson who penned the finely moralizing phrases of the "Reasons in Support of the New Proposed Articles in Treaties of Commerce," which the commissioners forwarded to Frederick. They invoked the law of nations in the past, and inquired "why should not this law of nations go on improving?" Why should not a future law of nations permit, during war, such categories of men as cultivators of the earth, fishermen, merchants, artists and mechanics, unarmed and peaceful and laboring for the benefit of mankind, to go undisturbed in person and property about their regular business? [41]

Whatever the Prussian king thought of these fine phrases, he was ready to sign a pact with the country which had unaccountably given them birth. The treaty, which was concluded on September 10, 1785, and later ratified by Congress, contained a sufficiency of unusual provisions. Besides the usual commercial clauses, it abolished the concept of contraband in connection with privately owned property at sea and forbade the seizure of private property on land even though enemy-owned. Since the likelihood of war between the United States and Prussia by land was slim, and since Prussia had no navy that could pretend to conduct searches on the high seas, it is obvious that "old Frederic" was yielding very little in this treaty. Nevertheless, to the United States it was important as delivering to them a handle for achieving the same concessions from other nations.

On May 14, 1785, Jefferson presented his credentials as United States Minister to France to the Comte de Vergennes; and three days later paid his respects to King Louis the Sixteenth at a private audience and "went through the other ceremonies usual on such occasion."[42]

By this time he was sufficiently sobered from his earlier outbursts and was ready to conduct himself as a proper diplomat. Indeed, his skill and self-possession were to grow from this time on until, by the end of his mission, he was able to deal with European courts on their own terms and yet, at the same time, maintain the fresh viewpoint and high level of statesmanship essential to the representative of a country that had insufficient power to back up its demands abroad.

In his first faltering steps he had the aid of Philip Mazzei; at least, so that gentleman was later to claim. Mazzei was once more in Paris in 1785 and Jefferson welcomed him cordially, even though he had soured somewhat on him in the last days at home.

Mazzei had had dealings with Vergennes in his former mission abroad and had submitted to him a series of "*Réflexions . . . sur le commerce de la France avec les Etats Unis*" which attempted to convince Vergennes that a free trade between the United States and the French West Indies would be of mutual profit.[43] Vergennes had listened politely and, as Mazzei described it, "conceived the propriety of the arguments, though it is not to be expected that he will openly agree to it, unless the times were so altered as to admit a reform. I wish it may be the case, & that Mr. Jefferson may have the satisfaction & honor of bringing it about; but my hope is not sanguine."[44]

In addition, Mazzei, again according to his hitherto unpublished "Notes," had lauded Jefferson to Vergennes and the latter gentleman had expressed a great desire to see him in France. Now that Jefferson was here, Mazzei wanted to take him around and get him acquainted with the men who could be of service to him. The American Commissioners, Mazzei commented, "have too much neglected the proper Attention to Men in Office at Court." He jotted down memoranda of the people to see—and there is no question that they were important—Pierre-Michel Hennin and Joseph-Mathias Gérard de Reineval of the American office in the Foreign Ministry, de Marmontel and the Duc de la Rochefoucauld, as well as other prominent figures; together with tips on their characters, attitudes toward the United States and other pertinent data. Let all these people know, he advised Short, that Jefferson was engaged to the best of his abilities "to promote the intercourse between France & America, & to keep off *Anglomany*."[45]

Jefferson's official dealings with France were confined to specific commercial matters, since the two countries already had a treaty between them. They included, in Jefferson's own words, "the receipt of our whale-oils, salted fish, and salted meats on favorable terms, the admission of our rice on equal terms with that of Piedmont, Egypt & the Levant, a mitigation of the monopolies of our tobacco by the Farmers-general, and a free admission of our productions into their islands." [46]

In his efforts to achieve these vital objects Jefferson was to receive inestimable assistance from Lafayette, now returned to France and at the height of popularity. Jefferson not only gratefully acknowledged his aid, but added the comment that the French government was disposed to be friendly. As for the man with whom he had directly to deal: "The Count de Vergennes had the reputation with the diplomatic corps of being wary & slippery in his diplomatic intercourse; and so he might be with those whom he knew to be slippery and double-faced themselves. As he saw that I had no indirect views, practiced no subtleties, meddled in no intrigues, pursued no concealed object, I found him as frank, as honorable, as easy of access to reason as any man with whom I had ever done business." [47] Shirt-sleeve diplomacy such as this was evidently a refreshing experience to the French Court, and paid off in dividends now as it did on other occasions in United States history.

The matters of which Jefferson had to treat with Vergennes meant much to the States back home. Tobacco was Virginia's lifeblood; whale oil, salted fish and meats were a considerable item in the economy of Massachusetts, Rhode Island and Connecticut; rice interested South Carolina; and the West India trade involved practically all the country. France had imposed strict limitations on each of these items; and Jefferson had found during his tour of the northern states, and knew of his own knowledge concerning the southern, how desperately important it was to obtain concessions from France.

He placed the entire business before Vergennes in a long communication on August 15, 1785. "No two countries are better calculated for the exchanges of commerce," he argued. "France wants rice, tobacco, potash, furs and ship-timber. We want wines, brandies, oils, and manufactures." Remove the restrictions on American imports to France and mutual trade will rise and the King's revenues increase.

It was the King's revenues that happened to be the sticking point; for on such a considerable item as tobacco, the King had granted a monopoly of the trade to farmers-general who, in return for a sum paid into the King's treasury, admitted what tobacco they wished, and paid for it on a take-it-or-leave-it basis. Naturally, as a Virginian and a grower of tobacco himself, Jefferson devoted most of his attention to a consideration of this ticklish problem.[48]

This letter had resulted from a preliminary conference with Vergennes a few days before, in which the French Minister had complained that little of American commerce came to France while, at the same time, it "covered the Thames." Jefferson admitted the fact, remarking, however, that while Americans would much prefer to deal with France, "the Impossibility of making Paiments here prevented our making Purchases"; and that, on items like tobacco, the monopoly discouraged our trade.

Vergennes observed as to tobacco that "the King recieved such a Revenue on that as could not be renounced." Jefferson promptly countered with a solution—abolish the monopoly and have the importer pay a duty on the tobacco equal to what the King had heretofore received from the farmers-general for the same amount. The thought struck Vergennes forcibly. "*Ma foi,*" he exclaimed, "*c'est une bonne Idée: il faut y penser.*" Jefferson was not certain as he recorded the conversation later in the evening whether the Count had said *y penser* or *y travailler*.[49] The difference, of course, was most important: whether Vergennes was going to *think* about it, or get to *work* on Jefferson's plan.

Nothing further developed, however, in spite of Vergennes' admiring exclamation; and Jefferson was compelled to await another opportunity to bring the matter forcibly before him. The opportunity arose early in November. A Mr. Boylston of Massachusetts had brought a cargo of whale oil into Havre, together with letters addressed to Lafayette and Jefferson requesting their assistance in disposing of it. Lafayette had been able to secure a special exemption from duty on a similar cargo the preceding year, and Boylston asked that the process be repeated. But Jefferson now considered that the time was ripe to get a *general* exemption for United States citizens on whale oil, and asked Lafayette to see what he could do. Lafayette promptly applied to de Calonne, the Comptroller General, on that basis. Within a few days Calonne agreed to accept American whale oils on the same footing as those shipped from the Hanseatic towns, which meant that the duties charged Americans would be cut to less than one-third of the former rate. But, he added, the agreement was to be limited to one year, and the oil must be shipped in either American or French bottoms.[50]

Limited as it was, it nevertheless represented the first breach of the stalemate; and Jefferson followed up the advantage by a double-barreled attack: he wrote Vergennes that the interests and friendship of the two nations would best be conserved by treating each other's citizens as they treated their own, instead of using the *most favored nation* formula;[51] and he asked for another personal interview.

On December 9, 1785, he saw Vergennes at the Court of Versailles. Vergennes took the offensive, repeating his ancient complaint that American trade favored England over France. Jefferson patiently repeated that "Merchants would not & could not trade but where there was to be some Gain; that the Commerce between two Countries could not be kept up but by an Exchange of Commodities"; and that such a condition was the case with England, but *not* with France. In other words, said Jefferson plainly, if France chooses to restrict the purchase of American commodities, she cannot expect to sell her own.

Vergennes saw the point, Jefferson noted that evening—indeed, he had laid himself open to Jefferson's retort by his complaint—but the American pressed home his victory in detail.

Why, for example, did not France take American rice, when it was of a better quality than that procured from the Mediterranean littoral? This was not so, as Jefferson was to discover later; but Vergennes let it pass.

Peltry and furs. These commodities France was willing to accept; but we did not ship. On this point Jefferson had to take the defensive, explaining that as long as England was in possession of our frontier posts, that trade was almost completely in her hands.

Whale oil. Jefferson acknowledged that the late diminution in duty granted by de Calonne might bring more to France; but, since whaling voyages took years, he delicately hinted that the one-year grace period was not enough. Vergennes did not take the hint.

Tobacco. Jefferson recalled to Vergennes the letter of August 15th, in which he had discussed the all-important tobacco problem. Tobacco, he pointed out, was *the* big crop we could furnish France and, with the money received in payment, buy French products in return. Just as though Vergennes had never been struck with Jefferson's "good idea" before, he now repeated his old argument of the King's revenue and the long-standing arrangements. Just as patiently Jefferson repeated *his* solution. But this time Vergennes did not exclaim; he merely ended the interview with the remark that no promises could be made.[52]

It was most discouraging for a diplomatic novice, after the high hopes he had allowed himself following that first interview. What infuriated him particularly was the fact that Robert Morris, a Pennsylvanian, *not* a Virginian, had been able by appropriate means to obtain a monopolistic contract from the farmers-general, whereby he could ship 60,000 hogsheads of American tobacco to France, and no other Americans need apply.[53]

What the "double monopoly" meant to Virginia tobacco Jefferson was only too well aware. Morris could compel her merchants to sell to him at his own figure—since the excess that normally would have gone to France had now no other outlet, and the commerce of that article would be thrown "in agonies," while Morris made enormous profits.[54]

Such manifest injustice was not to be borne, and Jefferson called once more on the ever-obliging Lafayette to use his influence. That gallant young man, tender toward the nation he had helped set free, considered America practically as much his country as France.

He fell in readily with Jefferson's appeal. He had already conceived the happy idea of gathering together certain French gentlemen of influence in a committee to promote commerce with America. The plan succeeded, the committee was organized on an official basis, and Lafayette became a member of it.

Lafayette reported to Jefferson on March 18, 1786. He had made a speech before the Committee on American Tobacco and had been asked to put it in writing. "I am considered as one that Has got a very strange idea—and don't think I can get anything now But the Hatred of the financee[r]ing people—But as M. de Malesherbes was telling me in His Botanic style I am sowing seeds which will bear fruit in time."[55]

This sounded bad; and in a low ebb of spirits, Jefferson wrote home to John Jay, invested with Foreign Affairs, that "with this country nothing is done; and that nothing is intended to be done, on their part, admits not the smallest doubt." It was not that they did not think American commerce important to them. They did. But "they are sure of keeping it on their own terms." To prove the point, since those first meetings he had not received "one scrip of a pen, or one word from a minister, except a vague proposition at an accidental meeting. We availed ourselves even of that, to make another essay to extort some sort of declaration from the court. But their silence is invincible."[56]

Even as he wrote, the skies were clearing. Vergennes had attended some meetings of Lafayette's committee and had decided on a change of tactics. On May 30, 1786, Jefferson received official word that "notwithstanding the treaty which the Farmers General have made with Mr. Robert Morris, for the delivery of a certain quantity of tobacco they have just concluded to take in the way of trade [from other American merchants] as much as fifteen thousand hogsheads per annum. . . . I beg that you will make it known both in America, as also to the American owners of vessels who may be found in our ports, so that they may direct their commercial speculations accordingly."[57]

It was a small enough concession, but it helped break the Pennsylvania financier's monopoly and set prices soaring in America. This, in addition to a better attitude by France on the question of whale oils, and the expressed desire of a wealthy French group to go into partnership with an American company in the fur trade and thereby gain French government support,[58] proved to Jefferson that steady pressure—plus Lafayette—eventually obtained results.

CHAPTER 21

The Sights and Sounds of Europe

THE duties of an American minister in a foreign Court were not exacting. Negotiations usually proceeded at a very leisurely pace, and there were long intervals during which there was nothing officially to do except wait in patience for the next move. Diplomacy, as then practiced, resembled nothing so much as a long-drawn-out chess game, in which both parties had ample time on their hands; and it was not sporting to complain if one's opponent took time out for lunch before contemplation of the ensuing gambit.

The negotiations with France, as we have seen, were of such a nature. The treaty with Prussia had been arranged with remarkable speed, and with little effort. There were certain explorations with Denmark and Tuscany through their representatives in Paris, but they amounted to very little; and the American commissioners had been in no hurry to press these comparatively unimportant countries. Indifference, it seemed, was the keynote of most of the other powers. To them, the new nation that now appeared on the scene offering them gifts was only a vague report of remote rebels who had proved successful in their rebellion, but of whose commerce and possibilities they knew nothing.[1] It was agreed, therefore, that attention should be concentrated on major objectives—and these were England, France and the Barbary States. But matters were in train in all these areas—and Jefferson had plenty of time on his hands.

He employed his leisure well. Paris, France and the scene of Europe opened to him large possibilities. If the masses, as he had written, were far behind the average American in scientific knowledge, at least the elite were a half dozen years ahead; and he worked hard at catching up with them. He relayed his findings home to other eager spirits in the States as rapidly as he obtained them; particularly to the members of the Philosophical Society, whose acquaintance he had made while in Philadelphia.

They were a surprisingly notable group. At one time it was the fashion to decry the state of the arts and sciences in early America, but that time had long since past. No young nation which could point to such figures as Franklin, Charles Thomson, David Rittenhouse, Dr. Benjamin Rush, Charles Wilson Peale, Benjamin Smith Barton, Francis Hopkinson, Tom Paine, John Trumbull, Ezra Stiles—and, later, Joseph Priestley—needed to blush in the company of its elders.

It was with men such as these that Jefferson hobnobbed and corresponded, and made one of their company. With them, with the Reverend

James Madison at William and Mary, and with such distinguished amateurs as that other more famous James Madison, he was able to converse at length with a full mind and a full pen, in the satisfying realization that their interests ran in similar grooves and dug as deeply, if perhaps not as widely, as his own.

He had barely been settled in Paris when he was discoursing enthusiastically across the Atlantic with Thomson, Madison and others concerning a newly invented cylinder lamp he had seen. Using olive oil as a fuel and with a wick forced through a hollow cylinder large enough to permit the passage of air, it gave a brilliant light equal to that of six to eight candles. But even more enthusiastic was his description of the new phosphorus matches. "They are a beautiful discovery and very useful," he exclaimed, "especially to heads which like yours and mine cannot at all times be got to sleep. The convenience of lighting a candle without getting out of bed, sealing letters without calling a servant, of kindling a fire without flint, steel, punk, &c., are of value." But one had to be careful, he warned, not to let the phosphorus drip on one's hand, "because it is inextinguishable & will therefore burn to the bone if there be matter enough. It is said," he added, "that urine will extinguish it." [2]

All new inventions, in fact, were eagerly to be sought out, especially if they were "useful." That, above all, was the first criterion for Jefferson's immediate interest. Contrary to popular opinion, he was an eminently practical man, to whom beauty was well enough, but when utility was added, it then took on true value. He was delighted, for example, with the copying press he had acquired, and offered to buy additional ones for the use of his friends at home. Though it cost ten guineas, "I would give ten times that sum," he averred, "that I had had it from the date of the stamp act." [3] Historians can only echo that wish; for lack of a copying instrument, too few manuscripts have survived from that important period.

The newly invented balloon—new, at least, for human ascensions—fascinated him. He had eagerly read whatever material he could lay his hands on about it, and he had witnessed a balloon ascension in Philadelphia. His prophetic mind had even then grasped the possibilities of this triumph over gravity, and he had envisaged its use in future wars so as to make static fortifications obsolete and cities open to bombardment from above. Now, located in the very heart of the experiments, he reported on them with avid delight. At Javel, some four miles from Paris, two "artists" were successfully experimenting with a balloon that could be directed by its occupants. "They ascend & descend at will," he reported, "without expending their gaz [*sic*], and they can deflect 45 ° from the course of the wind when it is not very strong. We may certainly expect that this desideratum will be found. As the birds & fish prove that the means exist, we may count on human ingenuity for its discovery." [4] That human ingenuity on which Jefferson so confidently counted has since given us the jet-propelled plane and the huge bomber with its load of atom bombs.

Francis Hopkinson of Philadelphia, with whose mother Jefferson had placed Patsy during his Congressional duties at Annapolis, was almost as universal a man as Jefferson himself. Active in politics—he had been a member of Congress and had signed the Declaration of Independence on behalf of Pennsylvania; a poet, judge, composer, musician, satirist and writer of essays and political tracts; an inventor and scientist; there was little in which his mind did not partake. Among his numerous inventions was a proposed improvement of the harpsichord—the substitution of tongues of leather and cork for the usual quill picks.

Jefferson had seen it when in Philadelphia and had been impressed. Now in Paris, the heart of the musical world, Jefferson sought to advance his friend's invention. He placed an advertisement in a Paris paper in the summer of 1785 but, as he ruefully reported to Hopkinson, only one application for the invention had been received. This was due to the season, he explained, "as all the beau monde leave Paris in the summer, during which the musical entertainments of a private nature are suspended." As soon as winter came, however, he hoped to get acquainted with the principal musicians and call the invention to their attention. "I communicated to Doctr. Franklin," he continued enigmatically, "your idea of Mesmerising the harpsichord. He has not tried it, probably because his affairs have been long packed & packing. As I do not play on that instrument I cannot try it myself." Unfortunately, as it later turned out, Jefferson was to find in an English shop a duplicate of Hopkinson's invention. The English had forestalled the American.[5]

But more, perhaps, than anything else, Jefferson was eager to convince Buffon and other European scientists that their contemptuous strictures on American flora and fauna were founded in ignorance. There is a touch of comedy in the controversy and in Jefferson's patriotic counterendeavors to prove that in fact everything in America grew on a much larger scale than in the Old World. He had devoted much space in his *Notes on Virginia* to convince the scientific world of his position; but print was not nearly as convincing as tangible evidence. It was with this in mind that Jefferson had taken along with him a panther's skin with which to confute Buffon.

It was some time, however, before he was able to meet this scientific pontiff whose published volumes had at one and the same time aroused his veneration and repelled him. The opportunity finally came through the good offices of Chastellux, with whom Jefferson had renewed acquaintance after those pleasant hours in Monticello over a bowl of punch and a copy of Ossian.

Chastellux carried him down to Buffon's country house toward the end of 1785 and introduced him as that Mr. Jefferson who had combated the great man's opinions in his *Notes*. The great man did not deign to argue with this upstart from a savage land. Instead, he took down from his shelves a copy of his latest work and presented it to Jefferson with a gesture.

"When Mr. Jefferson shall have read this," he said, "he will be perfectly satisfied that I am right."

This was the moment Jefferson had been waiting for. He unpacked his panther skin and presented it for Buffon's inspection. Panther, *not* cougar, and certainly larger than any European specimen. The great man rose to the occasion. He had been wrong, he handsomely admitted, and would correct the error in the next edition. *Imprimis,* he never did.

Pressing his advantage, Jefferson moved to the next attack. Buffon had confused American deer with the smaller deer of Europe; and the gigantic American moose with the lesser reindeer of northern Europe. Jefferson declared that in America the deer had horns two feet in length. Buffon scoffed. Show him even *one-foot* horns, he said. Jefferson insisted that a reindeer could actually walk, head up, under the belly of an American moose. Buffon laughed out loud. The panther was one thing—the skin was before him—but such tall tales as these! And on that note the interview ended.[6]

But Jefferson was no man to be put down that easily. He promptly wrote to his friend Archibald Cary in Virginia, as well as to others. Get me the largest pair of buck's horns you can, he demanded; and send them along to me with the skin and interior bones so that it can be stuffed to full dimensions in Paris. In return, Jefferson was sending to America for colonization some of Europe's products—hares, rabbits, pheasants, partridges, wine grapes, cork and oak trees.[7]

In due time, horns arrived, not of two, but of *four* feet in length. Jefferson rushed them to Buffon in triumph, and once again the great man had to acknowledge his error.

But the business of a moose was not as easy to accomplish. Moose were notoriously hard to get, and they dwelt in almost inaccessible wilderness. Jefferson refused to be daunted, however. He had appealed to Governor John Sullivan of New Hampshire, in whose mountainous regions the moose lurked, to get him a specimen and charge the cost to him. He was later to rue the carte blanche thus blithely given.

For Sullivan had a one-track mind. His friend, Jefferson, wanted a moose and, by God, he would get him one, no matter what the difficulty! No specimen could be found within easy reach, so the conscientious Governor sent out a veritable army of trappers and hunters in the dead of winter to find one. It turned out to be a truly Homeric expedition; but Sullivan was able finally to send a moose to Jefferson, together with a long account of the terrific difficulties that had been encountered by his men in shooting, dressing and transporting the hapless animal, which included the cutting of a road for twenty miles. And he also sent a bill. The bill amounted to over forty-six pounds sterling! [8]

Jefferson stared at the moose. It was not in the best of condition—a good deal of the hair had fallen off in transit to France. Then he stared at the bill. When the draught for its payment had arrived, seemingly before the moose itself, he complained bitterly to the presenter of the bill. "I did indeed, when in America, ask him to send me the skin & some of the bones of a Moose, which I imagined would have been bought of some hunter for a guinea or two. But I have never heard that he has got these for me, & much less expected, or can yet suppose any body would have asked, or he have given such a sum for them." [9] The agitation of Jefferson's mind may readily be gleaned from the complexity of that last sentence.

To Sullivan, of course, nothing of this appeared except by indirection. Jefferson thanked him for the moose, and even asked that if any large horns of deer, moose or elk should happen to "fall into your way by accident," to ship them; but only, Jefferson was quick to add, "on condition they should occasion you no trouble, and me little expense." [10]

Some measure of satisfaction was derived, however, from sending this specimen of a gigantic American mammal, denuded of hair though it was, to the sceptical M. Buffon. That gentleman was finally compelled to admit that his thesis on American mammalia required considerable revision.[11]

Other scientific interest did not require as vast an expenditure of energy; though, in some instances, Jefferson's expense was almost equally great. All things mechanical aroused his instant attention. He went to see a new type of steam vessel propelled by a screw operating against air pressure. He justly observed that the screw would be "more effectual if placed below the surface of the water." [12] He paid three francs to examine a plough operated by a windlass.[13] He went nowhere, on business or pleasure, that he would not stop to look at a new mechanical contrivance, particularly if it could be employed in agriculture; and noting if a copy could be made for use back home.

The progress of science enraptured him. It was science, he was profoundly convinced, that would eventually bring a state of utopia to the world, enlarge men's minds and ease their toil.

He voiced thoughts such as these to his young nephew, Peter Carr, now fifteen, who had acknowledged that he had not made the headway he might have in his studies; sometimes, as he put it, "for the want of horses and sometimes for the want of money." [14]

Jefferson reproved the errant youngster sharply. "I can assure you," he wrote, "that the possession of [science] is, what (next to an honest heart) will above all things render you dear to your friends, and give you fame and promotion in your country." He was sending him books in mathematics, astronomy and physics. And he was sending him others in the liberal arts, in which he set down at length a proper course of studies. Begin with ancient history, he advised, "reading everything in the original and not in translations." Then on to modern history. Study the Greek and Latin poets; also Milton, Shakespeare, Ossian, Pope and Swift among the moderns. Read the great ancient moralists and ethical teachers; learn French and Spanish; and be sure to take exercise, of which walking was the best form.[15] It was an extended educational course that Jefferson outlined for his benefit; one of the many that he was always ready to offer to youth when the occasion arose. Among his other qualities, Jefferson was definitely a pedagogue.

Poetry, in fact, was also engaging his attention at this time; more so than it ever would again. Perhaps the necessity for directing his nephew's education had something to do with it; perhaps his association with the Marquis de Chastellux, who loved it devotedly and admired the English poets. It was around this time that Jefferson purchased the twenty-two volume set of Bell's English Poets.[16] It was a little later that he embarked on the ambitious project of setting down his thoughts on English prosody for the benefit of Chastellux and other non-English readers. In this long essay he explained the different measures and accents, quoting heavily in illustration from a minor English poet, William Shenstone; to whom he was drawn, very likely, more for his descriptions of gardens than for his poetry. But he did not neglect Pope, Milton, Addison, Gray, Collins and the King James Bible. Some interesting sidelights on Jefferson's preferences develop. For example, he considered blank verse far superior to rhyme. The latter he equated with mere jingles, and he considered that "the fondness for the jingle leaves us with that for the rattles and baubles of childhood." Nevertheless, he managed to give a good, plain, nontechnical account of English verse from which a foreign student might well profit.[17]

During the summer of 1785, a request came to Jefferson from Virginia that must have thrilled him to the core. His native state was now ready to build a new Capitol to glorify the otherwise dingy town of Richmond. Even before he had left for Europe, Jefferson had envisaged the hillside of the new capital as the site of a noble series of government buildings that would make Richmond not merely a local state capital, but the architectural center of America. In his mind's eye he saw a stately grouping of a Legislative Building, Halls of Justice to house the courts, and a Governor's Mansion, all in the finest classic style, yet with improvements worked out by himself.

As early as October, 1776, Jefferson had proposed such adornments to a capital not yet in being; in 1779, on the eve of his governorship, the Assembly had acceded so far as to set up a master plan and a board of five—later, nine—Directors of the Public Buildings. Jefferson, during his term of office, became one of the directors.

It was probably then that Jefferson drafted a set of notes and plans for the Capitol building, rectangular in shape and classical in style, with porticoes running full around it. Detailed floor plans covered the first and second stories, with a separate drawing of a rotundaed Governor's house; and he drew a map of the lofty ground to be crowned by the cluster of buildings.[18]

Further activity necessarily was suspended during the last dark days of the war, and did not recommence until the spring of 1784, when the Assembly voted to raise funds for construction by the sale of public property. The Directors, deciding that there was no architect sufficiently competent in America to supervise what they had in mind, thought first of Italy, and then of France. Fortunately, Jefferson was there and could find them the proper man.

Accordingly, they entreated him to consult with an able architect to draft plans for their purpose. Obviously, they were unaware that Jefferson had already drawn a complete set of his own. They had about £10,000 in Virginia currency available for the entire project, which included a Capitol building (housing the courts as well), a Governor's house and a prison. The latter two could wait; but the first required speed, since the beginning of August had been set for starting work on the Capitol. The reason for such haste was the necessity to silence certain stubborn members of the Assembly who viewed Richmond with a jaundiced eye as a permanent capital for Virginia.[19]

Jefferson received the letter on June 14, 1785. It was impossible, of course, to consult an architect, draw plans, and get them back to Virginia by August. But he did what he could; and discovered in Charles Louis Clérisseau, an architect steeped in antiquity, just the man he needed. The fact that he was also the author of the *Monuments de Nîmes* completed the recommendation. For the Maison Carrée at Nîmes, which Jefferson had not yet seen except in drawings, represented to him the ultimate in architectural splendor, and had been the basis of his own drawings for the Capitol.

Clérisseau was an amiable man, and probably recognized that Jefferson was an excellent architect in his own right; for he sank to a subsidiary position in what became a collaboration rather than an independent undertaking as the Virginians had envisaged. Jefferson raced ahead, using the Maison Carrée as a model, but changing the Corinthian entablatures of the original portico to a more graceful Ionic and introducing windows for light and air along the side walls. Clérisseau's suggestions were as often as not rejected, and the final product was essentially Jefferson's. With Gallic courtesy, the Frenchman expressed his satisfaction at having been able to second Jefferson's intentions; his assistants drafted the technical plans; and the collaboration was over.

In the meanwhile, Jefferson was writing to Madison explaining what he had in mind, with the request that nothing be done until his plans arrived. He was sending one, he declared, "taken from the best morsel of ancient architecture now remaining. It has obtained the approbation of fifteen or sixteen centuries, and is therefore preferable to any design which might be newly contrived.[20]

Several weeks later he repeated his enthusiasm for the temple at Nîmes; it was "one of the most beautiful, if not the most beautiful and precious morsel of architecture left us by antiquity." In the interim, however, he had received word that work had already been commenced on another plan. Angrily he demanded that Madison stop it. "How is a taste in this beautiful art to be formed in our countrymen," he exclaimed, "unless we avail ourselves of every occasion when public buildings are to be erected, of presenting to them models for their study and imitation?"

Jefferson called himself "an enthusiast on the subject of the arts," and proud of it, "as its object is to improve the taste of my countrymen, to increase their reputation, to reconcile to them the respect of the world & procure them its praise." [21] That taste, as we have already seen, he considered much in need of improvement. He himself possessed a blind spot for the simple and graceful proportions of Colonial and Georgian architecture; he cared nothing for English Tudor, and he thought the Parisian style "far from chaste." [22] All his admiration was directed toward the ancient forms, notably Roman adaptations of the Greek; yet he had not as yet seen a single original; nor was he ever to see more than a few. His admiration stemmed wholly from the drawings and dimensions in Palladio and other architectural volumes.

Jefferson sent the finished plans to Virginia in January, 1786, with an explanation why he preferred to a new idea in architecture "some model already devised and approved by the general suffrage of the world." The plans being forwarded, he was careful to note, were his own. The only change suggested by Clérisseau was to make the portico two columns deep instead of three, so as not to darken the interior; and Jefferson had consented "to satisfy him." But Jefferson was averse to any such change from the proportions at Nîmes; therefore he recommended that the three columns be restored. Obviously, he thought that Clérisseau would never know of the change, and *everybody* would be happy. To make certain, however, that the workmen would not go astray, Jefferson would build a model in "plaister" and send it later.[23]

And privately, he bragged a little. "I send by this conveiance," he wrote Dr. James Currie, "designs for the Capitol. They are simple & sublime. More cannot be said. They are not the brat of a chimerical conception never before brought to light, but copied from the most perfect model of antient architecture remaining on earth." [24] Self-satisfaction and enthusiasm could go no further.

True to his word, he forwarded in May a plaster model, which had been constructed by an artist under Clérisseau's direction. That model still exists, appropriately displayed within the precincts of the Capitol at Richmond.

The Capitol, as finally completed after many delays, varied somewhat from Jefferson's original plans; and architectural authorities agree with Jefferson that the changes were not for the better. Even so, the building remains one of the finest examples and the first of the classical revival in America; and served as a model for the innumerable Graeco-Roman structures that thereafter began to dot the American landscape. Jefferson had succeeded in changing the American taste, at least in part. Whether it was an improvement or not, whether the imitation of classical forms did not help stifle native architectural originality and ingenuity, is another matter.

Meanwhile, Jefferson was enjoying himself in Paris, though the expenses were mounting and outrunning, not only his Congressional pay, but even his private income. He had moved again in September, 1785, to a house in the Champs-Élysées (belonging to the Count de Langeac), which suited him "in every circumstance but the price, being dearer than the one I am now in. It has a clever garden to it." [25] He had also added Petit, a *valet de chambre*, to his establishment, who did not lessen his expense. But Petit was to prove faithful and invaluable; and after Jefferson returned to America, followed him to enter into his service again. Mazzei, too, became somewhat of a problem. He was constantly effervescing with new schemes for the advancement of the United States—and incidentally his own—and he was just as constantly in need of ready cash. Jefferson kept lending him money when he was in debt himself; though eventually, it seems, the loans were honorably returned.[26]

Nor did his strapped circumstances prevent Jefferson from attending the opera in season, concerts, and visiting the various art galleries, where tips were *de rigueur*. He loved music passionately; and he admired certain types of painting on a more temperate scale. He attended a *Te Deum* at Notre Dame, where the audience attracted his attention far more than the music. "You lost much by not attending . . ." he told young Short humorously. "It bids defiance to description. I will only observe to you in general that there were more judges, ecclesiastics & Grand seigneurs present, than Genl. Washington had of simple souldiers in his army when he took the Hessians at Trenton, beat the British at Princeton, & hemmed up the British army at Brunswick a whole winter." [27]

Jefferson had little use for uniformed pomp, gold braid and lace. Even when the French Court departed for Fontainebleau in the fall, and courtiers and the foreign diplomatic corps hastened there to watch the King hunt, Jefferson did not consider the expense of a continued residence justified. "A very small and indifferent house" in Fontainebleau cost 100 to 150 guineas for the short season; and this represented practically the whole of Jefferson's salary for the period; leaving him, as he told Adams, "nothing to eat." He proposed, therefore, to journey down from Paris on specific occasions, and return the forty miles as soon as possible.[28]

What interested him more than the King's levees and the formal and splendid ritual of the King's hunt were the common people of France. He had thus far met chiefly the aristocracy and the elite and, though he professed himself much pleased with them, because "the roughness of the human mind is so thoroughly rubbed off with them, that it seems as if one might glide through a whole life among them without a jostle," yet their domestic morals, their wretched system of government and the abject poverty of their masses spoilt everything. "Every step that we take towards the adoption of their manners," he was convinced, "is a step to perfect misery." [29]

He had an opportunity to observe that abject poverty and to contrast it with the magnificence of the Court on a walk he took while at Fontainebleau.

He met a woman of the laboring class walking the same way and struck up a conversation with her. The story he heard was simple. Jefferson wrote Madison the next day that "she was a day labourer, at 8. sous or 4 d sterling the day; that she had two children to maintain, & to pay a rent of 30 livres for her house, (which would consume the hire of 75 days) that often she could get no emploiment, and of course was without bread." As they parted—the American minister and the poor Frenchwoman—Jefferson gave her 24 sous; whereupon "she burst into tears of a gratitude which I could perceive was unfeigned, because she was unable to utter a word. She had probably never before received so great an aid."

As Jefferson proceeded solitary on his walk, this short and simple annal of the poor started "a train of reflections on that unequal division of property which occasions the numberless instances of wretchedness which I had observed in this country & is to be observed all over Europe. The property of this country is absolutely concentrated in a very few hands, having revenues of from half a million of guineas a year down wards."

The matter grew in his mind as he trudged along. This woman at least had some work. How about the poor who could find no work at all? "I asked myself what could be the reason that so many should be permitted to beg who are willing to work, in a country where there is a very considerable proportion of uncultivated lands?" In America, he remembered, the presence of unoccupied lands meant opportunities for settlement and use; but not here, where such lands were deliberately kept idle so that game might increase and aristocrats might hunt.

His "train of reflections" began to expand and generalize. What was the solution? "I am conscious," he admitted, "that an equal division of property is impracticable. But the consequences of this enormous inequality producing so much misery to the bulk of mankind, legislators cannot invent too many devices for subdividing property, only taking care to let their subdivisions go hand in hand with the natural affections of the human mind." One of the solutions, therefore, was what he himself had initiated in Virginia—the abolition of entails and the primacy of the eldest male. Another method for lessening inequality was "to exempt all from taxation below a certain point, & to tax the higher portions of property in geometrical progression as they rise." This was indeed a remarkable prevision of the graduated income tax of today.

"Whenever there is in any country, uncultivated lands and unemployed poor," he philosophized, "it is clear that the laws of property have been so far extended as to violate natural right. The earth is given as a common stock for man to labour & live on. If, for the encouragement of industry we allow it to be appropriated, we must take care that other employment be furnished to those excluded from the appropriation. If we do not the fundamental right to labour the earth returns to the unemployed. It is too soon yet in our country to say that every man who cannot find employment but who can find uncultivated land, shall be at liberty to cultivate it, paying a moderate rent. But it is not too soon to provide by every possible means that as few as possible shall be without a little portion of land. The small landholders are the most precious part of a state." [30]

That walk at Fontainebleau had been a most fruitful one, for it enabled Jefferson to bring sharply into focus thoughts that had been brooding inchoately in his mind for a considerable time. He was expressing at once a philosophy and a plan of action. The inequalities of the world disturbed him deeply—whether they were political, social or economic—and nowhere were they more in evidence than in Europe. Subconsciously he was noting the root causes for that vast upheaval known to history as the French Revolution. But his thoughts, as always, reverted to America and the means whereby these inequalities, still faint there and not yet extreme, might be avoided in the future. He was proposing no cataclysmic changes, no revolutionary overthrows or a complete and equal redistribution of property. When the tenets of even the earliest form of communism came to his attention, he expressed his distaste for them and decried their practicability. But any methods by which inequalities could be alleviated and the right to work and a decent livelihood secured, met with his favor. He believed in the rights of property, but not at the expense of human rights. It must be remembered that he had eliminated from the famous Lockian triumvirate of "life, liberty and property" the last-named right and substituted for it "the pursuit of happiness."

Expand his concept of land to include industry, and these propositions become the foundation and precursor of a steady strain in American thought and practice—from Jackson through the Populist movement and Henry George to the "New Deal" of Franklin D. Roosevelt. What is particularly noteworthy—and contradictory of much loose talk today of Jefferson's laissez-faireism in government—is the fact that he did not hesitate to invoke the powers of government in order to limit property rights for the benefit of human rights. It was only when government infringed on *human* rights that he raised his voice in solemn protest.

The more he saw of conditions in Europe, the more he became homesick for his native land. To one correspondent in Virginia who thought to feed him with political details as best calculated to excite his interest, the homesick man pathetically replied: "Of political correspondents I can find enough. But I can persuade nobody to believe that the small facts which they see pressing daily under their eyes are precious to one at this distance; much more interesting to the heart than events of higher rank. Fancy to yourself a being who is withdrawn from his connections of blood, of marriage, of friendship, of acquaintance in all their gradations, who for years should hear nothing of what has passed among them, who returns again to see them & finds the one half dead. This strikes him like a pestilence sweeping off the half of mankind. Events which had they come to him one by one & in detail he would have weathered as other people do, when presented to his mind all at once are over whelming. Continue them to give me facts, little facts, such as you think every one imagines beneath notice, & your letters will be the most precious to me." [31]

True, Jefferson had Patsy with him, but she was in the convent school and only visitable on stated occasions. She was well and happy there, and Jefferson was satisfied with the atmosphere and the instruction. But, as he wrote Mrs. Trist in Philadelphia, he had too little of her company. He was trying to make some arrangements whereby he could see her more often; but, after all, he could not disrupt her studies. He therefore began to give thought to having little Polly, his only other remaining daughter, join him. Unfortunately, the problems of the long passage across the sea for such an infant caused him to waver in mind.[32]

A month later, however, his resolution became fixed, and he wrote to little Polly (formally, Maria) that she was to come over the following summer.[33] But it was not until two summers had passed that all the formidable obstacles, including the small lady's own aversion to quitting her familiar surroundings, were overcome, and Polly was deposited in her father's arms.

CHAPTER 22

The Asbestos Mind

NEVERTHELESS, politics could not long remain out of Jefferson's ken, either in America or in Europe. As American Minister to France, it was his job to be fully acquainted with developments at home and abroad, and to work steadily for the advantage and benefit of his country. Jefferson was no shirker of work, and he performed his duties steadily and well, in spite of certain flights off the handle which fortunately did not show up in his public commitments.

Washington, back home, was financially and otherwise interested in a project for digging canals which would join the western waters with the rivers that flowed through Virginia and Maryland into the Atlantic. It was a tremendous scheme, with inestimable economic advantages to the two states, and bearing far-reaching political consequences in its train. For the western country, confronted with the almost impassable barrier of the Appalachian Mountains, was compelled to ship its produce down the Ohio and Mississippi to New Orleans and the Gulf. Thereby it came under Spanish influence and suffered from the disabilities imposed by the Spaniards on foreign trade. More and more, the western settlers were to look for their salvation, either through juncture or obversely by war, with the Spaniard.

Washington foresaw those consequences plainly, and convinced the legislatures of Maryland and Virginia that the canals he contemplated were both feasible and advantageous. But neither the public treasuries nor private individuals seemed to have funds sufficient to finance the scheme. In desperation he turned to Jefferson for help. Would "the monied men of France, Holland, England or any other Country with which you may have intercourse ... be induced to become Adventurers in the Scheme" and, if so, on what terms? [1]

At this particular moment, American funds and projects were not in repute in Europe. Even the Dutch, the chief investors and moneylenders of the day, were cautious about making further commitments to a country whose finances were in chaotic condition and whose Congress seemed to have little power to levy taxes and duties whereby foreign debts could be paid.

Almost at the same time that Jefferson received Washington's request, the famous Dutch firm of bankers, N. & J. Van Staphorst, was inquiring of him whether American funds were sound. He assured the bankers that the funds which constituted the foreign debt of America were absolutely safe "because no man in America ever entertained a doubt that our foreign debt is to be paid fully; but," he admitted, "some people in America have seriously contended that the certificates & other evidences of our domestic debt ought to be redeemed only at what they have cost the holder." These, however, Jefferson hastened to add, constituted only a small minority and, he continued, "were I the holder of any of them, I should not have the least fear of their full paiment." [2]

This was a remarkable statement from Jefferson, in view of his later stand when that same matter of the domestic debts arose to convulse the new nation. For the very views he now dismissed as those of a small minority became the bulwark of the Republican party which he was to head, and one of the fundamental causes of the split between that party and the Federalists.

In spite of his present assurances, however, the Dutch as well as other European moneylenders tended to hold back from investing their money in America until Hamilton, by a series of brilliant maneuvers, finally placed American finances on a sound basis.

Jefferson did not have too much hope of getting Washington's canals financed abroad. He turned the idea over to Ferdinand Grand, who had good banking connections in France and elsewhere, and who was to act as financial agent for Jefferson and America in the future. Grand did his best but, Jefferson was compelled to report, without any success. He urged on Washington continued efforts to raise the money at home, because he realized the immense importance of connecting the western territory with Virginia by strong economic bonds. "I shall continue uneasy," he added, "till I know that Virginia has assumed her ultimate boundary to the Westward. The late example of the state of Franklin separated from N. Carolina increases my anxieties for Virginia." [3]

Washington later wrote that there was no further need for foreign aid. Subscriptions to his Inland Navigation Co. now totaled £40,300, almost the sum required.[4] But the project never did get much beyond the planning stages.

Jefferson had a sufficiency of headaches closer at hand, however. Two, in particular, aroused his unremitting wrath: the failure of England to come to commercial terms with her erstwhile colonies; and the continued, and seemingly immune, depredations of the Barbary Powers on American commerce.

There was only one effective method of forcing England to come to terms, he informed everyone. Boycott her shipping and her goods. "We must show them we are capable of foregoing commerce with them," he wrote Madison, "before they will be capable of consenting to an equal commerce. We have all the world besides open to supply us with gewgaws, and all the world to buy our tobacco." [5]

Publicly, he spoke of the boycott as a means of building up American shipping and commerce. Actually, he was no friend to either of these. Had he his way, he would have embargoed them also. But he dared not say so openly; only to neutral outsiders like the young Dutch baron he had met in Annapolis, did he venture to betray his secret feelings. "Were I to indulge my own theory," he told van Hogendorp, "I should wish [the United States] to practice neither commerce nor navigation, but to stand with respect to Europe precisely on the footing of China. We should thus avoid wars, and all our citizens would be husbandmen.... But this is theory only, & a theory which the servants of America are not at liberty to follow. Our people have a decided taste for navigation & commerce..." he mournfully admitted, "& their servants are in duty bound to calculate all their measures on this datum." [6]

Somewhat more cautiously, he expressed himself along similar lines to John Jay. The cultivators of the earth were our most valuable citizens; next, he grudgingly added, came the mariners. For mechanics and industrial workers, however, he had no use. "I consider the class of artificers as the panders of vice & the instruments by which the liberties of a country are generally overturned."

Since, however, many Americans preferred the calling of the sea, it was necessary to protect our rights thereon. And since such protection meant the probability of insults and war with competing powers, how can they be prevented? "By putting ourselves in a condition to punish them," he answered. "Weakness provokes insult & injury, while a condition to punish it often prevents it. This reasoning leads to the necessity of some naval force, that being the only weapon with which we can reach an enemy. I think it to our interest to punish the first insult; because an insult unpunished is the parent of many others." [7]

Jefferson was obviously impaled on the horns of a dilemma. Against his private feelings, and through the use of pure logic, he found himself advocating a strong navy and a hair-trigger foreign policy. It was a dilemma which he was never to resolve, and explained a good many of the contradictions which bedeviled his career. Had the American people followed his advice and sat comfortably behind their Chinese wall, he would have been far more happy. But they refused; and Jefferson was compelled alternately to swallow the greatest of insults and avenge much lesser ones.

Just now, he was hot for vengeance against the Barbary States. Here was something tangible and, he thought, need not involve a large or permanently established navy. A half dozen warships, under the command of John Paul Jones—that most individualistic of naval heroes—should be sufficient to sweep them from the seas.

But Congress, it seemed, was not as bellicose as Jefferson. That distant body decided on "an amicable treaty with the Barbary states in the usual way"—the "usual way" being to pay an annual tribute. Perhaps fearing the warlike views of its Minister to France, it appointed Thomas Barclay as special agent to Morocco and John Lamb of Connecticut in a similar capacity to Algiers. At least so the report came to Jefferson. The sum of $80,000 was appropriated to cover the ransoms of enslaved American seamen and for the usual *douceur* to avoid similar "accidents" in the future.

The news of this decision and the consequent bypassing of himself and Adams in dealing with the pirates came as a blow to Jefferson. He grasped at a straw. The news had been unofficial; and Lamb, who was supposed to be on his way with official instructions, had not yet appeared. In the meantime, he and Adams had full powers. Why not go ahead on their own; since nothing had been heard from the elusive, and perhaps mythical, Mr. Lamb? He therefore drafted a treaty in all haste, and sent it along to Adams in London for approval.[8]

There were times when Jefferson was disposed to overlook limitations on powers, and this was one of them. He was ready now to enter into binding agreements with the European naval powers who had suffered at the hands of Morocco and Algiers, for joint naval action and a perpetual patrol. "I know it goes beyond our powers," he acknowledged to Adams, "and beyond the powers of Congress too; but it is so evidently for the good of all the States, that I should not be afraid to risk myself on it, if you are of the same opinion." [9]

But the scheme died in infancy. Spain had already bound herself to a large sum in tribute, and was reluctant to lose the benefits. England stood coldly aloof, conscious of her ability to handle her own affairs. The smaller nations were interested, but feared the attitude of France. Jefferson therefore approached Vergennes, tactfully placing the onus on England. He told him that the smaller countries were apprehensive that England, should they decide to join a coalition against the Barbary States, might throw her weight on the other side. "She dares not do it," retorted Vergennes; and Jefferson felt that was sufficient. So did the small nations. All that remained, then, for a binding alliance was the consent of Congress–and money. But Congress was sending Barclay and Lamb, and wanted no part in any such extended involvement.[10]

The dilatory Mr. Lamb finally showed up in Paris in September, 1785, and, Jefferson delightedly discovered, the earlier reports of his plenary powers had been exaggerated. The instructions which he actually brought gave full power to Jefferson and Adams to appoint persons to negotiate with the Barbary States. Jefferson generously appointed Lamb to Algiers and Barclay to Morocco; particularly as he surmised that such appointments were what Congress wished.[11]

The Emperor of Morocco proved a comparatively easy nut to crack. It was true he had seized an American ship; but he had made the capture merely as a whip handle to force the United States to come to terms. Not only did he treat the crew with liberality, but eventually turned ship, cargo and men over to Spain for release to America.[12] By the end of July, 1786, Barclay had successfully completed negotiations with the Emperor and, at the beginning of 1787, a treaty was signed which removed, at least temporarily, Moroccan interference with American shipping.

Algiers was a much harder nut. They had taken two ships and held twenty-two American citizens in slavery. Their demands were much higher than those of Morocco, and there seemed no present possibility of coming to terms with that impudent nest of pirates.

John Adams, now accredited to the Court of St. James, had worked on a mutual basis of friendship and respect with Jefferson during his stay in Paris; and Abigail Adams, who had preceded Jefferson to Europe, had taken to her husband's colleague immediately. Tart of tongue, plain-visaged but mobile of feature, possessed of a penetrating wit and an indiscriminate pen, she could hate or love with equal facility. Just now she loved.

Jefferson had entertained and charmed her in Paris. At his house she met in a single soiree such notables as the Lafayettes; John Paul Jones, shortly to embark on incredible adventures in Russia; a Mr. Jarvis from America, who had brought Jefferson the exaggerated account of Lamb's supersession; William Short, whom Jefferson was able within a few months to get an official secretaryship; the Chevalier de la Luzerne, and an abundance of French counts and nobles too numerous to mention. There was also present a certain Charles Williamos, a Swiss, whom Jefferson had made a member of his household.[13] Williamos, however, was soon to abuse Jefferson's hospitality. Representing himself as Jefferson's confidential agent and an officer of the United States Government, he managed to fleece a good many people on the strength of his supposed connections. Jefferson heard of it, and threatened to have him jailed unless he reimbursed his victims.[14] Whether the threat forced him to make amends is not known; but he died within a few months thereafter and the incident was closed as far as Jefferson was concerned.

On his arrival in England, Adams had complained of the foul odors of London and the tedium of the Court ceremonials. Abigail was a bit more complaisant. Though she had hated to leave Paris and Jefferson—whom she flatteringly called the only person with whom her husband could associate—she thought that thus far the English seemed courteous and their reception good. How long this enviable situation would last, she knew not. "Nothing as yet has diserved my acrimony," she wrote Jefferson in her inimitable style. "Whilst the Coals are coverd the blaize will not burst, but the first wind which blows them into action will I expect envelop all in flames. If the actors pass the ordeal without being burnt they may be considered in future of the Asbestos mind." [15] Her husband, as she was well aware, had no "asbestos mind."

She was a strong woman, and John relied on her considerably; so that she was expressing her husband's opinions as well as her own when she told a friend back home that "in Mr. Jefferson he has a firm and faithful friend, with whom he can consult and advise; and, as each of them has no object but the good of their country in view, they have unlimited confidence in each other." [16]

The necessity for an "asbestos mind" for Adams became shortly apparent. After the first formal welcomes were over, the London press, government-inspired, entered upon a campaign of unremitting abuse against him and the country which he represented. Jefferson commiserated, but thought Adams could stand it. As for himself, he was thinner-skinned. "I do not love difficulties," he confessed candidly. "I am fond of quiet, willing to do my duty, but irritable by slander & apt to be forced by it to abandon my post." [17] It was an honest self-appraisal. Jefferson knew his own failings as a political figure. He had quit under fire as Governor; he was to quit again as Secretary of State, though only after long steeling of his nerves; and every time the storm of abuse rose too high during his Presidency, he began to think of Monticello with longing.

Adams soon discovered that the British were adamant against entering into any treaty with America whereby they might have to yield any of the rights and privileges they claimed for themselves. The indignant American thereupon veered over to Jefferson's truculent position. "We must not, my Friend," he wrote his colleague, "be the Bubbles of our own Liberal Sentiments. If we cannot obtain reciprocal Liberality, We must adopt reciprocal Prohibitions, Exclusions, Monopolies, and Imposts." [18]

Jefferson, in Paris, agreed to the full. The United States, he replied, must immediately pass a navigation act directed against England, load that country's manufactures with duties, and give preferences to other countries. And the States ought to transfer the power to do these things to Congress at their next sessions.[19]

Even while he was writing this, his own state of Virginia, under Madison's guidance, had granted Congress that authority; and the news led Jefferson to expound his philosophy of the division of powers that ought to be observed between the several States and the Federal Government. From his vantage point in Europe he was able to discern certain necessities more clearly than the people at home. "The politics of Europe," he wrote Madison, "render it indispensably necessary that with respect to everything external we be one nation only, firmly hooped together. Interior government is what each state should keep for itself." [20] He never deviated from this philosophy.

Nor did he deviate from a similar fixed belief that it was the destiny of all the Americas, both North and South, eventually to be peopled and governed by the United States. So sure was he of the inevitability of this process that he was willing to bide his time, "and not press too soon on the Spaniards. Those countries cannot be in better hands"; for this purpose, at least. His sole fear was "that they are too feeble to hold them till our population can be sufficiently advanced to gain it from them piece by piece. The navigation of the Mississippi we must have. This is all we are as yet ready to receive."[21] *Manifest Destiny* was no new doctrine when Henry Clay took it up a full generation later and made it into a war cry.

On February 21, 1786, John Adams sent his secretary and aide, Col. William Stephens Smith, posthaste to Paris with an urgent message that Jefferson come over to London without loss of time. The ostensible reason concerned the treaty with Portugual which, after long delays, now seemed on the verge of immediate completion. But, to Adams, there was another and stronger motive in desiring Jefferson's presence for which the Portuguese affair might serve as a cloak. He dared not even explain the full details in a letter; but he said enough to set Jefferson packing at once. "There is here a Tripolitan Ambassador with whom I have had three Conferences," was all he permitted himself to say. "The substance of what passed Colonel Smith will explain to you. Your Visit here will be imputed to Curiosity, to take a look at England and pay your Respects at Court and to the Corps Diplomatick. There is nothing to be done in Europe, of half the Importance of this, and I dare not communicate to Congress what has passed without your Concurrence. What has been already done and expended will be absolutely thrown away and we shall be involved in a universal and horrible War with these Barbary States, which will continue for many years, unless more is done immediately. I am so impressed and distressed with this affair that I will go to New York or to Algiers or first to one and then to the other, if you think it necessary, rather than it should not be brought to a Conclusion."[22]

Alarmed by the manifest agitation into which Adams had been thrown and by the nature of the disclosures which young Smith conveyed to him, Jefferson sought and obtained a hurried audience with Vergennes and on March 5th posted with Col. Smith and two servants for Calais and the boat crossing to England. On the 11th, after a rough journey, he was in London.

Adams's agitation had not decreased during the enforced wait; quite the contrary. The Portuguese minister was ill, and the negotiation would have to be delayed, he told Jefferson; but that did not much matter. The all-important business was with the gentleman from Tripoli. Jefferson thought differently—at least, so he later wrote to John Jay.[23] He had considered a treaty with Portugal as of prime importance; as for Tripoli or *any* Barbary state, he preferred the mailed fist to further palaver, especially of the kind that Adams now had in mind.

Nevertheless, Adams hurried him into a conference with the mysterious ambassador from Tripoli; and the horrendous details were unfolded. The emissary demanded, in return for a perpetual treaty of protection against piratical assaults by his government on American shipping and citizens, that the sum of 30,000 guineas be paid forthwith for the benefit of his employers and £3,000 as an unblushing bribe for himself. And these staggering sums must be paid on signing, in cash; "no kind of Merchandizes could be accepted." Tunis, he believed, would give a similar guarantee on the same terms; he was not quite sure of Morocco; and he could not answer at all for Algiers.

What would happen if the demands of the smooth-talking ambassador, who sported the name of Abdrahaman, were not met? Abdrahaman proceeded to paint with gusto a horrifying picture, complete with all the gory details, of what their corsairs did when they captured a ship, their invincibility on the sea, and how they treated their slaves.

Adams had already heard the twice-told tale, and had literally gone to pieces. Besides calling Jefferson to his side, he had rushed the story off to Jay. The cost of placating *all* the Barbary Powers, he figured, would come to 120,000 guineas, besides handsome presents to the Ambassadors, and the payment of their incidental charges. "No Man wishes more fervently that the Expense would be less," he concluded his urgent recommendation for acceptance, "but the Fact cannot be altered, and the Truth ought not to be concealed." [24]

But Jefferson did not rate the power of this swarthy blackmailer, or that of his employers, as highly as did Adams. He listened in silence to the demands and the accompanying veiled threats and, at their conclusion, avowed merely that such a sum exceeded their power of treating, and that they must send to Congress for further instructions.

Nevertheless, it was obvious that he too was impressed. In a joint report to Jay, the American ministers declared their willingness, if Congress so authorized, to try to borrow the amounts demanded in Holland. "We are not certain it can be had there—But if Congress should order us to make the best terms we can with Tunis, Tripoli, Algiers & Morocco, and to procure this money ... our best endeavours shall be used to remove this formidable obstacle out of the way, of the prosperity of the United States." [25]

In truth, once considerations of morality and honor were laid aside—as they had been by many nations for a considerable period of time—the proposition of a lump payment of £200,000, as Adams figured the total, to gain perpetual immunity was rather attractive. Spain had paid $3,000,000 for a more limited protection; while the sums paid out by the various European powers were staggering. But, as Jefferson was justly to remark, what guarantee was there that the four blackmailing states would hold to the treaties, once the money was in their hands? "The continuance of this peace," he wrote privately to Monroe, "will depend on their idea of our power to enforce it, and on the life of the particular Dey or other head of government with whom it is contracted. Congress will no doubt weigh these circumstances against the expence & probable success of compelling a peace by arms." [26]

As Jefferson suspected—and half-wished—Congress did not send plenary powers, and the business eventually fell through. It was to take many years, and a war, before the Barbary Powers finally were taught to respect the American flag and refrain from molestation.

The Portuguese affair went through much more smoothly. Once the Chevalier de Pinto, the envoy to England, recovered from his illness, it took only a short time to come to an agreement; though de Pinto predicted that the American insistence on the unrestricted entrance of American flour into Portugal would arouse the wrath of noble and influential flour grinders. Nevertheless, de Pinto inserted the article; and, as he predicted, the interested nobles had sufficient influence at Court to obstruct ratification.

With these two matters out of the way, England herself next drew the attention of the two Ministers. Jefferson had no illusions about any possible success of negotiations with her—he noted at once how thoroughly boorish was their reception when Adams presented him to the King and Queen—but he was willing to do his best, if only to "put an end to all further expectations on our side of the water, and shew that the time is come for doing whatever is to be done by us for counteracting the unjust & greedy designs of this country." [27]

If he had hated England before, the results of this trip were to strengthen that hatred to permanence. "I saw at once," he discoursed to his Autobiography at a time in life when it might be thought that such passions were spent, "that the ulcerations in the narrow mind of that mulish being [George III] left nothing to be expected on the subject of my attendance; and on the first conference with the Marquis of Caermarthen, his Minister of foreign affairs, the distance and disinclination which he betrayed in his conversation, the vagueness & evasions of his answers to us, confirmed me in the belief of their aversion to have anything to do with us." [28]

Adams was more optimistic than his embittered colleague; and they met with Caermarthen again and again, heard the same recriminations about the failure of America to observe the terms of the peace treaty or, if they were lucky, merely cooled their heels in anterooms, until even Adams was compelled to agree to a report home that "there is no party nor individual here in favor of a treaty, but upon the principle that the United States will retaliate if there is not one. All agree that if America will suffer England to *pocket* (that is the expression) all her navigation, England would be unwise not to avail herself of the advantage." [29]

The arrogance of the British continued to infuriate Jefferson; nor were his feelings soothed when, at a dinner party, a certain General Clark informed him with the utmost seriousness that "were America to petition Parliament to be again received on their former footing [as colonies], the petition would be very generally rejected." Indeed, aside from a few liberals and intellectuals like the Marquis of Lansdowne and Dr. Richard Price, there were few in England who were not contemptuously hostile to America.[30]

Jefferson found another feeling prevalent among those in power. Why enter into any equal commercial arrangement, when there was no necessity for giving any *quid pro quo?* It was the Northern States that largely suffered, and the South would never yield sovereignty over commerce to a federal body altruistically to aid them. "It remains for us to shew whether they are true prophets," commented Jefferson.[31]

There was one item, however, in the British case which was unanswerable and to which they kept returning when all others failed. You promised on your faith and honor in the treaty of peace, they asserted, to permit our merchants to collect the debts lawfully due them from your people; yet practically every one of your States, in defiance of all justice, has closed its courts to the means of collection. The ever-repeated argument galled Jefferson. Though he retorted on the British *their* failure to give up the frontier forts and to pay for the slaves they took, privately he admitted the force of the arraignment. Time and again, he urged that Congress propose a general rule covering such payments to which the States would submit. "Whether England gives up the posts or not," he wrote strongly to Monroe, "these debts must be paid, or our character stained with infamy among all nations and to all times. As to the satisfaction for slaves carried off, it is a bagatelle which if not made good before the last instalment becomes due, may be secured out of that."[32]

He urged such an honorable course even though it would have been to his personal interest to hide behind the cloak of legality which Virginia, his own state, had thrown over defaulting debtors. The great debt which he owed to English and Scottish merchants—largely because of the encumbered estate which his wife had inherited—had arisen to plague him again, and was to continue to drive him almost frantic for many years to come. He found himself now in the position of having to pay it twice. During the war, he had paid the sums due into the Virginia treasury, as provided for by special legislation; and, in order to raise the necessary funds, had sold portions of his lands on promissory notes that depreciated rapidly in value as the currency deteriorated.

The English creditors had properly refused to accept the almost worthless Virginia currency in satisfaction of the debts and, under the treaty, now insisted on payment in solid cash and in full. Jefferson admitted the justice of their claims, even though he was badly hurt thereby. But the merchants were not content with face value; they wanted interest on their money for all the years since the debts accrued. Jefferson fought this new claim, both as a public and a private man. He considered it unjust that interest be paid for the war years—at the current rate of interest, this amounted almost to a 50 per cent markup on the original debt.

He agreed with a committee representing English creditors that the courts of Virginia should be opened to their claims; proposing only, that after judgments were rendered, payments should be permitted in equal annual installments running until 1790.[33] But no interest for the war years; on that he was unalterably determined.

Jefferson's own private debts were largely held by two firms—the Scottish Alexander McCaul and the English Farrell and Jones. They had refused his tender of Virginia currency during the war as a dishonorable attempt to pay in almost valueless paper, and were pressing him for payment now. The ethics of some of the original transactions, particularly between Farrell and Jones and Jefferson's father-in-law, John Wayles, relating as they did to a trade in human flesh, might be considered equally doubtful in modern eyes; but it was perfectly legitimate at the time they occurred.[34]

To McCaul, Jefferson explained his position. Given time, he would pay off what he owed him, with interest for the years preceding and subsequent to the war. With some bitterness he delved into the history of the transaction. In 1776, he had sold land for £4,200 to pay McCaul and Jones. "I did not receive the money till it was not worth Oak leaves." Then Cornwallis had devastated his lands, all to his damage in the sum of three or four thousand pounds. Nevertheless, he intended to be honorable. He had left instructions in Virginia to apply all the profits of his estates to the payments; nor would he draw one shilling personally from them until the debts were fully paid. But again, he would pay *no* interest for the war years.[35]

As though the known Wayles' debts were not sufficient to plague him, a woman by the name of Mrs. Necks bobbed up in England during his stay who claimed Wayles had owed her £8/8. She had no written evidence; but Jefferson paid her anyway, and noted in his account book: "If justly, charge it to the estate: if not due, consider it as a charity."[36]

Yet it must not be considered that Jefferson's stay in England was all fruitless trouble and exacerbation of spirits. Disgusted though he was with the English government and English arrogance, he nevertheless managed to enjoy his sojourn immensely in his capacity as a private citizen.

He had barely landed when he went on a buying spree. In France, he had been unable—except at an exorbitant price—to obtain good editions of the classics. "Greek and Roman authors," he had written sarcastically to Madison, "are dearer here than I believe any where else in the world. Nobody here reads them therefore they are not reprinted." [37]

But whatever else Jefferson might say of the British, he could not accuse them of neglecting the great ancients, and editions were plentiful in London. Jefferson bought heavily of these precious items; also maps, a thermometer, a protractor, a globe, a telescope, a solar microscope—and a walking-stick. A little later he added a camp theodolite, a botanical microscope, an air pump complete with apparatus, mathematic instruments of various kinds, spurs and two whips. The total of these expenditures was truly staggering; especially when it is remembered that he was now wholly dependent on his salary, since he had allocated the avails of his estates to the payment of his debts. He also descended to the slightly ridiculous—he paid one shilling to see "the learned pig." [38]

In the middle of their negotiations with the various ministers—English, Portuguese and the blackmailing Tripolitan—Jefferson and Adams decided they needed a vacation. Where could they go? If there was anything in

Collection of the Hon. Charles Francis Adams. Courtesy the Frick Art Reference Library

THOMAS JEFFERSON

Painting by Mather Brown

Collection of Mrs. George R. Balch. Courtesy the John Levy Galleries

MARIA COSWAY

Painting by Richard Cosway

England that Jefferson wanted to see, it was the famous English gardens that had recently been brought to a peak of perfection. He had studied intently the various books available in Virginia which described the theory and practice of that noble art, particularly Thomas Whately's *Observations on Modern Gardening*, and had attempted to follow their precepts in laying out his own gardens at Monticello. Now, however, he had a chance to view the famous originals themselves.

On April 2, 1786, therefore, Jefferson and Adams left London by post chaise—Abigail, for some reason, did not go along—for a grand tour of the English countryside.

Both men were highly practical—scenery was all very well, and so were the noble piles in which the aristocracy of England took their ease and pleasance. But they particularly wanted to know what was transportable to America—methods of cultivation, plants, layouts—and what it would cost. The puritanical strain in John Adams was plainly visible. He enjoyed, indeed, the aristocratic seats, with their luxurious architecture, paintings, statuary and poetry; but, he devoutly hoped, it would be long before "riding parks, pleasure grounds, gardens and ornamented farms grow so much in fashion in America." [39]

Jefferson had no such qualms. He luxuriated in the constant panorama of magnificent gardens, and thought only of how he might make and maintain a garden in the same style. Whately's book was his Bible, and always in his hand. He was amazed, as he compared the originals with their descriptions, to note how accurate and just Whately had been. "I always walked over the gardens with his book in my hand," Jefferson noted, "examined with attention the particular spots he described, found them so justly characterized by him as to be easily recognized, and saw with wonder, that his fine imagination had never been able to seduce him from the truth. My inquiries were directed chiefly to such practical things as might enable me to estimate the expense of making and maintaining a garden in that style." [40]

They journeyed first to Chiswick, owned by the Duke of Devonshire, which Jefferson thought showed "too much art." Then on to Hampton Court, which he considered, for all its magnificence, "old-fashioned." Then to Twickenham, where the Americans paid obeisance to the garden of Alexander Pope; though additions had been made since his time. Jefferson duly copied down the famous inscription on Pope's monument to his mother: *Ah! Editha, matrum optima, mulierum amantissima, Vale.*

Next they visited Esher Place, belonging to Lady Frances Pelham, where Jefferson approved of the fine balance of trees; but he was disappointed in Lord Clive's Claremont, of which he noted that there was "nothing remarkable." At Paynshill, however, though the architecture of the house itself was incorrect, the Doric temple was beautiful, and the grottoes—which Jefferson had thought to emulate in his Gothic youth—had cost £7,000.

They continued on their appointed rounds until they came to Stowe, one of several seats of the Marquis of Buckingham, which was truly fantastic. Thirty-three gardeners ceaselessly tended a lake and basin, a dismantled Egyptian pyramid, temples to Friendship and the more amorous Venus; while a mile-straight approach led to a Corinthian arch and to the great house itself. Jefferson sniffed at the arch which, he felt, had "a very useless appearance"; and he emphatically did not like straight approaches. To him the ideal of beauty was the winding S; he used it wherever possible in walks and gardens and even walls. The most notable example of this favorite line of his is the famous serpentine brick walls that border the walks of the University of Virginia.

Blenheim overpowered and dazzled the ordinary visitor; but Jefferson's gaze was critical. He admitted the 2,500 acres, the 200 people employed on its grounds, the 2,000 deer and 2,000 to 3,000 sheep that grazed its woods and parks; but, aside from the lake and its cascade, the garden to him had "no great beauties."

At Kew, an Archimedes' screw for raising water to a higher level attracted his attention. Here was something that delighted his mechanical mind, and he made sketches of the principle for its possibilities at home.

The two Americans returned to London from their tour with different impressions, in accordance with their different characters. Adams grumbled that "the beauty, convenience and utility of these country seats are not enjoyed by their owners. They are mere ostentation of vanity; races, cocking, gambling, draw away their attention." Even at Stratford-on-Avon, mecca of centuries of awed visitors, he saw only a house "as small and mean as you can conceive"; though, in accordance with custom, both he and Jefferson cut off a chip from Shakespeare's chair in the chimney corner.[41]

Jefferson, on the other hand, though dryly passing over Shakespeare with a noncommittal notation, later described his impressions of England and its gardens to his boyhood friend, John Page. "The gardening in that country," he wrote, "is the article in which it surpasses all the earth. I mean their pleasure gardening. This, indeed, went far beyond my ideas." But as for England as a whole, he had been deeply disappointed. It was true that they knew better than the French how to get the most out of a naturally barren soil by proper manuring (due to their system of longer leaseholds), and the laboring people were not as poor, either. London, too, was handsomer than Paris; but not, he patriotically added, as handsome as Philadelphia. He damned the architecture of both cities as "in the most wretched stile I ever saw." But chiefly he hated the English and they, in turn, from the highest to the lowest, hated us. "I think," he concluded, "their hostility towards us is much more deeply rooted at present than during the war."[42]

On April 26, 1786, with the feeling that his two months in England had been completely futile from the political viewpoint, he quit London, never to return. All his previous prejudices had been confirmed, and he had acquired a flock of new ones.

CHAPTER 23

Head versus Heart

PARIS seemed like home to Jefferson after England, and he viewed with a fresh and keen delight the amiable, civilized people among whom it was his fortune to be resident for so many years. Their smooth, well-rubbed ways, their *politesse* that made even a refusal seem palatable, were contrasted favorably with the insolence and boorishness of even the greatest English lords, not to speak of King George and his consort.

The moment he landed at Calais, he noted the difference, and was happy to present "the successor of Sterne's monk" there with a donation of a franc, 4 sous.[1]

But he was no sooner safely ensconced in Paris than he hankered for certain items that were obtainable only in London. Young Col. William S. Smith, secretary to Adams and shortly to become his son-in-law, sent Jefferson a small traveling copy press he had ordered. It cost five pounds, ten—an outrageous price, Smith admitted, "but I know of no Gentleman better qualified to pass over the disagreables [*sic*] of life than Mr. Jefferson." Smith was slyly giving back some of the advice which Jefferson had been so fond of handing out to the younger generation. "So he makes his calculations for a certain quantity of imposition," Smith continued, "which must be admitted in his intercourse with the world—when it shews itself in high colours—he has only to count ten and he is prepared for the subject—happy state of mind."[2] Jefferson's favorite advice was to count ten when one was angry; if still angry, proceed to a hundred.

Jefferson had also ordered a harpsichord made to his specifications before leaving London. It was to be one of Kirkman's best, "with a double set of keys, and the machine on the top resembling a Venetian blind for giving a swell. The case to be of mahogany, solid not vineered [*sic*], without any inlaid work but deriving all its beauty from the elegance of the wood." To this instrument was to be added a "celestini apparatus." He wanted the harpsichord to be worked by either a weight or a spring, instead of the usual treadle, since "the constant motion of the foot on a treadle diverts the attention & dissipates the delirium both of the player & hearer." He was also in the market for an organ, proper for "a chamber 24 feet square & 18. feet high.[3]

Jefferson's passion for minute details (so strangely opposed to that "delirium" of which he speaks) often got him into trouble; and this was a shining example. His specifications occasioned considerable misunderstanding on the part of the instrument maker, and it took long and vexatious correspondence before the confusion was finally ironed out.

Books, and still more books, poured in from London through the obliging Col. Smith, who was also asked by Jefferson to have his tailor make "a couple of pair of breeches & two waistcoats (Gilets double buttoned) of the same buff cotton which he made for me while in London." [4]

Lafayette must have objected to Jefferson's patronizing of English wares; so that he was forced to explain: "The reason for my importing harness from England is a very obvious one. They are plated, & plated harness is not made at all in France as far as I have learnt. It is not from a love of the English but a love of myself that I sometimes find myself obliged to buy their manufactures." [5]

Jefferson ought to have taken his own explanation to heart. How did he expect ordinary mortals to abide by boycotts and embargoes when he thus candidly confessed his own inability to deny himself English goods?

The scene of Paris brought him back to diplomatic concerns as the American minister to France. The ever-present Barbary problem continued to hound him. Shortly after he arrived, he sought Vergennes' advice on the feasibility of a diplomatic mission to Constantinople, in an attempt to persuade the Porte to call the fierce Algerians to heel. Vergennes dissuaded him from the scheme. It would cost the Americans a great deal of money for presents and bribes, he said, and they would not be able to buy a peace "one penny the cheaper" than at Algiers. The canny French minister said further, Jefferson reported to Adams, "that those people do indeed acknowledge a kind of vassalage to the Porte & avail themselves of it when there is any thing to be claimed; but regard it not at all when it subjects them to a duty. That money & fear are the two only agents at Algiers." [6]

Adams took the same realistic stand. He continued to urge on Jefferson that it was wisest "for Us to negotiate and pay the necessary Sum, without Loss of Time"; that the longer the United States delayed, the more it would cost; and that all the influence and good will of the European powers would not help one jot. To his colleague's warlike stand he interposed the pertinent comment: "If this is your Sentiment, and you can persuade the Southern States into it, I dare answer for it that all from Pensylvania inclusively northward, would not object. It would be a good occasion to begin a Navy." [7]

He knew, and Jefferson knew, that the South could not be persuaded. After all, it was *Northern* trade that was being harassed. But Jefferson also knew, and was too polite to retort, that it would be equally Southern money that went into the payment of any tribute.

John Jay, in distant America, agreed with Jefferson that war was preferable, *if*—and it was a big *if*—the money could be found. America was definitely impaled on the horns of a dilemma. It had no money for either war, tribute or ransoms; and, in the meantime, American captives were languishing in slavery. Congress, in fact, had no money for *anything*, Jay lamented. "Their requisitions [on the States] produce little, and government (if it may be called a government) is so inadequate to its objects, that essential alterations or essential evils must take place." [8]

Jefferson was to hear more and more of these jeremiads from America. David Humphreys, his old secretary of legation, who had returned to the States—thereby giving Jefferson a chance to install William Short in a more respectable, and paying, position—reported that the Federal Government was at a low ebb; it had no funds, paper money was prevalent, and the troops stationed in the West were deserting for lack of pay. "I believe the country is much altered in many respects since we left it," he wrote mournfully. "Govr. Clinton is said to have become an antifederalist.... Many people appear to be uneasy & to prognosticate revolutions they hardly know how or why. A scarcity of money is universally complained of." Yet Humphreys also reported that "to judge by the face of the country; by the appearance of ease & plenty which are to be seen every where, one would believe a greater portion of the poverty & evils complained of, must be imaginary." [9]

In Virginia, Madison wrote, the appetite for paper money as a means of canceling or reducing debts, was growing apace. Its avowed patron was Patrick Henry (Madison wrote his name with transparent dashes —H—n—y). Henry was also opposed to accelerating court proceedings in debt actions and, so Madison feared, wanted either a partition or a total dissolution of the Confederacy of the States.[10]

All this was anathema to Madison, who believed strongly in a true nation. He would deal forcibly with those States who evaded their just quotas for the support of the Federal Government, he had earlier declared in an amazing letter. A single frigate, under Congressional orders, would make the coastal States see the light. And he would find other means for coercing those that were not amenable to naval guns.[11]

And Jefferson, stung by news such as this and his own preoccupations with methods for coercing the Barbary Powers, offered the same solution that Madison was advocating.

"It will be said there is no money in the treasury [to bring the pirates to terms]," he wrote angrily to Monroe, the third point of the triangle. "There never will be money in the treasury till the confederacy shows its teeth. The states must see the rod; perhaps it must be felt by some one of them. I am persuaded all of them would rejoice to see every one obliged to furnish its contributions. It is not the difficulty of furnishing them which beggars the treasury, but the fear that others will not furnish as much. Every rational citizen must wish to see an effective instrument of coercion, & should fear to see it on any other element but the water. A naval force can never endanger our liberties, nor occasion bloodshed; a land force would do both." [12]

Coming from Jefferson, the later apostle of States' Rights and the father of Nullification, this sounds like heresy indeed. But it must be remembered that Jefferson always carefully differentiated between foreign and domestic affairs; and that in the foreign field he had proclaimed from the beginning the supremacy of the Federal Government. The problem was to crop up again, on a larger and more serious scale, during the Presidencies of the two men who were now so forthright about the answers. They both found the actuality much more difficult of solution than they had thought.

Much more heartening was the news that the great statute for establishing religious freedom had finally passed all hurdles in Virginia, and had now become law. The moment the information arrived in France, Jefferson hastened to disseminate copies among the literati, the Court and the diplomatic corps, as an example of the regard for truth and liberty of conscience in America, and as possible propaganda in Europe.

He was much gratified by the favorable reaction. The French incorporated the text in their new Encyclopedia, and the authors of several philosophical volumes quoted it with approval. Even the ministers of several European countries asked Jefferson for copies to forward to their own sovereigns. Jefferson may be excused for believing, in this general atmosphere of enlightenment and good will, that the example of Virginia would "produce considerable good even in these countries where ignorance, superstition, poverty & oppression of body & mind in every form, are so firmly settled on the mass of the people, that their redemption from them can never be hoped." [13]

Jefferson considered himself as a kind of honest broker between the Old World and the New. From the Old, he was constantly sending details of the latest advances in the arts and sciences to the New, together with seeds, plants and animals which might advantageously assist its economy. From the New, he was similarly importing plants and cuttings unknown to Old World soil for the benefit of his friends; but chiefly, it was ideas—political, social and economic—that he imported. His aim was twofold: first, to explain America and its novel Revolution to the French; second, to teach by its great example. No French writer of any standing, who wished to write on America or its institutions, would have dreamed of going ahead with his work until he had discussed it thoroughly with the extraordinarily well-informed and wholly obliging Mr. Jefferson.

Usually Jefferson gave them far more than they had bargained for; just as he had handed the astonished Barbé-Marbois a book-length dissertation on Virginia. This is practically what happened to M. de Meusnier who, while preparing an article on the United States for the *Encyclopédie Politique*, naturally turned to Jefferson as a source of information. The American not only answered his questions at length, but corrected his proofs, pointed out his errors and added innumerable observations.[14]

Here again, as in the more famous *Notes*, Jefferson permitted himself an unrestrained frankness in discussing the most controversial problems that faced the United States. In large part they were duplications of similar observations in the *Notes*, but there were several comments which are worth recording as evidence of Jefferson's current frame of mind.

The Confederacy, he maintained, "is a wonderfully perfect instrument, considering the circumstances under which it was formed." There were certain defects, however, which required changing. The most important was a grant of power to Congress to make full treaties and lay uniform taxes. Only Rhode Island objected, he noted acidly, as it did to every other suggested change. Jefferson believed that geography accounted for her recalcitrance, and proceeded to expound his favorite theorem. "The cultivators of the earth are the most virtuous citizens, and possess most of the *amor patriae*. Merchants are the least virtuous, and possess the least of the *amor patriae*. The latter reside principally in the seaport towns, the former in the interior country ... there is not a single man in Rhode Island who is not a merchant of some sort."

Having thus explained Rhode Island's opposition to his own satisfaction, Jefferson considered the remedy. There were certain theoretical alternatives. Annex Rhode Island to agricultural Connecticut, banish her from the Union, employ force to compel her to submit, or let her go on by herself. He acknowledged that all these alternatives were hazardous.[15]

But he still believed that "when any one state in the American Union refuses obedience to the Confederation by which they [*sic*] have bound themselves, the rest have a natural right to compel them to obedience. Congress would probably exercise long patience before they would recur to force; but if the case ultimately required it, they would use that recurrence." [16]

He defended the indentured-servant system as a means by which the poor of Europe were enabled to get to America and better their condition; and he dismissed the slander that America had been chiefly peopled by convicts with the remark that, of the not more than 2,000 convicts transported, most were men "eaten up with disease," who "married seldom & propagated little." [17]

As always, the question of slavery was put to him and, as always, he replied with complete candor. But this time he added an almost apocalyptic wrath to his regular theme.

"What a stupendous, what an incomprehensible machine is man!" he cried, "who can endure toil, famine, stripes, imprisonment & death itself in vindication of his own liberty, and the next moment be deaf to all those motives whose power supported him thro' his trial, and inflict on his fellow men a bondage, one hour of which is fraught with more misery than ages of that which he rose in rebellion to oppose. But we must await with patience the workings of an overruling providence, & hope that that is preparing the deliverance of these, our suffering brethren. When the measure of their tears shall be full, when their groans shall have involved heaven itself in darkness, doubtless a god of justice will awaken to their distress, and by diffusing light & liberality among their oppressors, or at length by his exterminating thunder, manifest his attention to the things of this world, and that they are not left to the guidance of a blind fatality." [18]

The words seemed to erupt from the white-hot depths of the man as, from distant Europe, he contemplated the shame and anomaly of his native land which, time and again, he was forced to explain to inquiring Europeans.

Jefferson did not like to admit that he was beginning to feel at home in France, and that its intellectual, artistic and social contacts were grateful to his mind and heart. He was forever writing to his American friends how he hated Europe, its miseries and its people; and how he longed to return to the blessings of America. An evening in Philadelphia with Hopkinson, Rittenhouse and Dr. Franklin, he would exclaim, would be worth far more to him than a whole week in Paris.[19]

But, at the time he was relieving himself of sentiments such as these, he was enjoying to the full one of the most brilliant societies in the world, and had surrounded himself with a bevy of as charming, witty and devoted women as any that had flocked around the venerable Benjamin Franklin during the heyday of his popularity at Passy. The great salons of Paris were open to the American author of the Declaration of Independence, and his own house was the scene of many a notable company. It was an era of good feeling for the new republic across the seas; and the aristocracy, even in the highest court circles, toyed delicately with such subversive ideas as liberty and fraternity, if not with equality. Most of them were children of the Enlightenment; had read Voltaire, the Encyclopedists, and even Rousseau; were sceptical in religion and rational in politics; and nodded approvingly at theories from which, when later translated and exaggerated into action, they were to recoil in horror.

It was fortunate that the United States had been represented in their midst by two such men as Franklin and Jefferson. It was from them that the French gained their opinions of America, and from men of their own kind like the Marquis de Lafayette, who had fought and suffered for that country and returned filled with generous enthusiasm and large concepts. America, and all things American, were quite the vogue, and the approving topics of conversation in every fashionable salon.

Jefferson mingled easily and gracefully in these circles, and just as easily—and perhaps more ardently—among the intellectuals, the scientists and the artists. The two areas mixed and mingled—for the intellect, the arts and the sciences were also fashionable; and no salon was complete without its quota of lions.

With Lafayette to guide him, Jefferson was soon an honored guest and a welcome friend in the highest society.[20] He hobnobbed on equal terms with the fabulous Duc de Rochefoucauld and the Marquis de Condorcet; with abbés and papal nuncios; with the Marquis de Chastellux, of course, and with Turgot and Mirabeau; with Diderot and D'Alembert; and, naturally, with the duchesses, marquises and artistic ladies without whom French society was inconceivable. With the men he discussed politics, economics, scientific advances and theories of liberty. With the ladies he spoke of some of these things as well, but also added a surprising charm of person and talent for small discourse which they found delightful.

It is true that Jefferson was never to become the tremendous legend in France that Franklin already was—this must be attributed to the fact that Franklin was there at a most propitious moment, to his remarkable store of apothegms and appropriate anecdotes, and to that simplicity which he affected and which seemed to incarnate to the French their preconceptions of America and a primitive "golden age." Jefferson, with his fine dress, his show of plate and excellent store of wines, might have been himself a Frenchman or, at least, a cosmopolitan European; and therefore did not strike the imagination as forcibly. He himself realized that he was treading in the wake of a great legend when he remarked, on assuming Franklin's position as minister, that no one could replace him, only succeed him.

His friends were divided among the Americans who flocked in a steady stream to Paris and naturally sought out their minister, and the Europeans. He had seen John Paul Jones, poised between France and exotic Russia, and had thought to use him to clean out the pirate nest. John Ledyard, of Connecticut, who had been in the Pacific on Captain Cook's famous expedition, was in Paris seeking to form a fur company to exploit America's western coast. Jefferson suggested to him the exploration of the great Northwest and West, via Russia and Siberia. It was the later Lewis and Clark expedition in reverse and a project that was never far from Jefferson's mind. With the failure of his own plans, and possessed of an itching foot and adventurous turn, Ledyard eagerly agreed. Jefferson sought permission from Catherine of Russia for his protégé to journey through her vast possessions; but the iron curtain was no recent development. She refused, and Ledyard rashly entered Russia to plead his case personally. He found that she had quit St. Petersburg for Siberia, followed her and was duly arrested, sent to Poland and there finally released.[21]

More happy was Jefferson's experience with young John Trumbull, whom he had met in London during his visit there, through the mediation of Abigail Adams. Trumbull had come to England to study painting under the famous Benjamin West, and had visions of himself as the great national American painter, the depicter on canvas of her heroic deeds. Jefferson encouraged these dreams, and invited the young man to Paris.[22]

Trumbull availed himself of the invitation and was given the run of Jefferson's house. He brought with him two of his conceptions of the American scene which he had painted in London—the huge "Battle of Bunker's Hill" and the "Death of Montgomery." Jefferson thought the paintings full of talent, and ascribed their failure to sell in England to the fact that "they are too true to suit the English palate." [23]

The association proved of mutual advantage. Jefferson perhaps suggested to Trumbull his most famous, if not his best heroic painting—the "Signing of the Declaration of Independence," gave him tips as to the characteristic traits of the men who had signed, and sat personally for his own portrait in the ensemble. Together they went to art galleries, churches and other repositories of paintings; though Trumbull does not seem to have been able to improve Jefferson's taste in the art.

Jefferson was never to disclose any such appreciation of the genre as he showed in the kindred field of architecture. He managed later to pass through some of the great collections of Europe and pick out for special accolade only those which were thoroughly third-rate. He diligently collected pictures to adorn eventually the walls of Monticello and chose, with unerring accuracy, the most mediocre and insipid. The general taste of the time, it is true, was not high; running largely to the hugely allegorical, the pseudoclassical and the portrait.

What Jefferson sought in particular, and for the most laudable reasons, were portraits from the life of the great men of the Revolution and of his friends. He purchased, or commissioned, pictures or copies of existing pictures, of Washington, John Adams, Lafayette, and of the early explorers—Columbus, Magellan, Cortez and Americus Vespucius. To these he added, at a later date, pictures of Newton, Locke and Bacon.

But the most important result, perhaps, of this association between Jefferson and Trumbull was Trumbull's service in introducing him to Maria Cosway.

Jefferson had not lacked for female society in France. Abigail Adams, the wife of John, had become his firm friend. It was a thoroughly American type of friendship; comfortable, solid, without any of the overtones that usually accompanied male-and-female friendship among the French. The acquaintance, begun during the stay of the Adamses in France, had ripened when Jefferson came to England.

Some two months after his return to Paris, he wrote with graceful exaggeration to John: "I am meditating what step to take to provoke a letter from Mrs. Adams, from whom my files inform me I have not received one these hundred years." [24]

The whimsical appeal brought results. She sent her reply along with "Mr. Trumble [Trumbull]" and told of keeping Jefferson's portrait (for which, during his London stay, he had sat to Mather Brown, an American painter) in their room; though, she politely added, "it is but a poor substitute for those pleasures which we enjoyed some months past." Her daughter, also named Abigail, had married young Col. Smith since Jefferson had departed. Since she already had three sons, and only one daughter left, she proposed an exchange with Jefferson. "Suppose you give me miss Jefferson [Patsy], and in some [fu]ture day take a son in lieu of her. I am for strengthening [our?] federal union." [25]

To this half-humorous, half-serious proposal, Jefferson retorted that while he should be very glad to have her son, he could not part with his daughter. More seriously, he had heard of an attempt to assassinate the English king. "No man on earth," he declared with bitter irony, "has my prayers for his continuance in life more sincerely than him. . . . Twenty long years has he been labouring to drive us to our good and he labours and will labour still for it if he can be spared." In France, there were no such plots. "Here we have singing, dancing, laugh & merriment, no assassinations, no treasons, rebellions nor other dark deeds. When our king goes out, they fall down and kiss the earth where he has trodden." [26]

If Jefferson was writing this seriously, then he promptly heads the list of the world's poorest prophets. He misread the times completely, and noted none of the premonitory quivers which amplified to later convulsions and upheavals, the like of which the world had not witnessed to that time. And he *was* serious; for, in all his letters of this period, he stressed the utter peace and calm of Europe. He foresaw the possibility of trouble ahead *only* in the event that the elderly king of Prussia, then quite ill, might die.[27]

Among Frenchwomen his first acquaintance, naturally, was with Lafayette's young wife, the vivacious and loyal Marie Adrienne, Marquise de Lafayette. She had helped gain Patsy an entry into the convent school at Panthemont, and the Lafayettes were as often in Jefferson's home as he was in theirs. Somewhat later, and before he had fully entered society, he made the acquaintance of "old Countess d'Hocquetout," visiting her at Saunois. He sedulously furthered the friendship, largely on the ground that it "opened a door of admission for me to the circle of literati with whom she is environed." In that country seat he first heard the nightingale. All poetry to the contrary, it was inferior, he thought, to the American mockingbird and the fox-colored thrush.[28] Jefferson was not one to permit any European *natural* phenomenon to be adjudged superior to its American counterpart.

He also established a going friendship with Madame Lafayette's aunt, the Comtesse Noailles de Tessé, with whom he shared common horticultural and architectural interests, as well as a high republican enthusiasm. It was largely with her that, for many years thereafter, he exchanged seeds and plants for the mutual benefit of their respective gardens and countries.

Each of the women to whom Jefferson thus devoted himself seems to have had some specific qualification that led him to seek her out. Madame de Tott, of Greek descent, painted professionally and could guide him through the mazes of art. He had been to see a picture by Drouais, a pupil of David, whose subject matter was the assassination of Marius. "All Paris is running to see it," he wrote her, "& really it appears to me to have extraordinary merit." He admitted, however, that his judgment was bad and he needed a guide. Would she be that guide? [29]

In return, he was happy to "commence the pleasing office of studying with you the rythm of Homer. For this purpose I have committed to writing the few rules of Greek prosody which must be indispensably known." Besides these rules, he forwarded "the best edition extant of your divine countryman Homer." [30]

Painters seemed to attract him, especially if they were lady painters. Madame de Bréhan, whose husband was an army officer and whose brother-in-law was the Comte de Moustier, of whose relations and of Jefferson's embarrassment thereby more anon, was also an amateur with pencil and brush. Madame de Corny, wife of a member of the learned Académie de Besançon, youthful and sparkling, similarly had a taste for the arts.

But to all of these ladies, old and young, Jefferson was merely a devoted friend. With Maria Hadfield Cosway he was something more.

Maria Louisa Catherine Cecilia Hadfield—to give the full roster of her names—had been born in Florence of an English couple who maintained a boardinghouse for tourists. At the age of four she learned music; a little later she betook herself to drawing. Charles Hadfield, her father, died in 1779; and the widow and daughter departed for England where Angelica Kauffman, herself a portrait painter of note, foresaw a career for Maria.[31]

Maria Hadfield took London by storm. Aged twenty, her beauty enraptured the *haut monde*, while her accomplishments—as well as her beauty—thrilled the artistic world. The extant pictures of her—though done by herself or her husband, and therefore suspect—show a ravishing and ethereal being, complete with a great crown of ringleted, golden hair, an oval, charming face with delicately chiseled features, and wide, large blue eyes. By all accounts, however, there can be no doubt that she was a great beauty; though there were those who thought she languished a bit and was "graceful to affectation." [32]

Richard Cosway, who was famous in his day as a miniaturist and had amassed a large fortune as a result of his popularity in that fashionable art, fell in love with the young girl and married her in 1781. Aside from his fame and his fortune, it is difficult to understand why the talented beauty married him. He was a tiny man, hardly bigger than a dwarf, and his foppish ways and dandyism in dress and accouterments excited only merriment and ridicule.

The summer of 1786 found them in Paris, where the Duke of Orléans had commissioned Cosway to immortalize his duchess and their children on the glazed surface of a miniature. There they met Trumbull and other members of the artist world and, in their company, visited the galleries and art exhibitions.

Jefferson had usually been a member of the group, under Trumbull's tutelage; and it was natural, therefore, that he and Maria should eventually meet. That meeting was fraught with consequences.[33]

He was forty-three, mature, famous, a man of the world and a widower. She was twenty-seven, beautiful, talented, and moving with her dwarfish husband in a fraternity of free and easy ways and gay camaraderie. And the atmosphere of Paris was conducive to gallantry and frank admiration between the sexes—particularly when the lady had a husband to give her a solid social status.

For four years Jefferson had mourned his departed wife, and paid her the tribute of a faithful memory; his female friendships had been largely based on common interests and intellectual pursuits. But he had not yet met with a young woman who combined beauty with vivacity, charm, a talent for music—his lifelong passion—and for sketching and painting—his current hobbies. The pretty Italian accent of her youth lent an added fascination, and her modesty and gentleness of disposition made her irresistible. Within the space of a month he was her devoted *cavalier servi-ente*—in the older, chivalric sense; for there is absolutely no evidence nor reason to believe that the relation became anything else but platonic.

The company of artists and amateurs, under Trumbull's leadership, made almost daily excursions to the galleries and into the surrounding country. Trumbull, it seems, had spoken often to Jefferson of the Cosways, but they did not meet until the group visited the Halle aux Blés, newly erected and surmounted by a dome conceived by the architects Legrand and Molinos. Jefferson, passionately fond of architecture, was induced by Trumbull to come along and, as he later justified the trip, he went with a strictly utilitarian purpose in mind. He wanted to obtain ideas for a public market which was being contemplated for Richmond; and the idea of the noble dome, with its skillful method of bridging and supporting the vast expanse of arch, opened up possibilities of similar uses at home.[34]

But when Trumbull finally introduced him to the Cosways, all architectural ideas—though he admitted the dome was superb—vanished from his mind. There was Maria—and Jefferson was immediately vanquished. The day was not long enough; and every member of the company, including Jefferson, had other engagements for the balance of the day. To prevent their breaking up, and thereby cutting himself off too soon from the fair charmer, Jefferson suggested that they cancel their engagements, and dine together. The suggestion was received with acclamation.

As Jefferson whimsically told it later in the winter of his discontent, "lying messengers were to be despatched into every quarter of the city, with apologies for your breach of engagement. You [Jefferson's *Heart*] particularly had the effrontery to send word to the Dutchess Danville that, on the moment we were setting out to dine with her, despatches came to hand which required immediate attention. You wanted me [Jefferson's *Head*] to invent a more ingenious excuse; but I knew you were getting into a scrape, & I would have nothing to do with it."[35]

The "lying messengers" dispatched, the party went to St. Cloud for dinner; then on to Ruggieri's and Krumfoltz. It was an unforgettable day for Jefferson; and in the evening, after he could hold on no longer to the actuality, he recapitulated each incident in memory.

From then on, for an all too short few weeks, Jefferson contrived to be daily with his Maria. When Trumbull quit Paris on September 9th for Germany, and eventually London, there to work on his "Declaration of Independence," the rambling company was broken up; but Jefferson was now on such a footing with the Cosways that he was able to frequent their house in the Rue Coq-Héron. As was customary, Richard, no doubt, after a few polite words of greeting, excused himself and left the visitor and his wife to enjoy their tête-à-tête.

They went on a sightseeing tour together as well; and it does not appear that the husband was along. They examined the King's library and viewed the château of Madrid; they attended a "concert spirituel"; they watched the rainbows hovering over the machine at Marly as it tossed the river water high into the air; they saw châteaux galore and the "gardes meubles"; and, finally, on September 16th, they went to see the Désert de Retz.[36]

If the meeting at the Halle aux Blés was the first high spot of their acquaintance, this joint adventure was the last. The Désert was a series of ingenious gardens not far from Saint-Germain, complete with all the trappings so dear to the romantic heart—grotto, obelisk, Chinese *orangerie*, a temple of Pan, the replica of a ruined Gothic church, and a fluted broken column with spiral staircase and four stories of rooms inside.

Out of this amazing potpourri, Jefferson chose to exclaim most ardently over the ruined column. How grand was the idea of this ruined column! he exclaimed; how beautiful the spiral staircase!

It was here, though, that Maria saw fit to speak unkindly to her partner; though Jefferson afterwards forgave her. The day "was a little too warm, I think; was it not?"[37] One can only speculate whether he was really referring to the weather; or thus delicately to a different kind of warmth into which, perhaps, the close proximity of several days and the romantic surroundings had tempted him and for which she saw fit to chide him.

At any event, the blissful excursion, even with this final contretemps, was now at an end. The wheels of their carriage rolled them rapidly back to Paris.

Two days later, on September 18th, disaster befell Jefferson. Whether it was the headiness of the past few days, the coltishness of a magically restored youth, or some other reason forever to remain unknown, Jefferson chose to essay leaping over a large kettle that proposed an obstacle to him in the courtyard of his establishment. He tripped and fell heavily on his right wrist.[38] The pain was severe, and the wrist useless.

Two surgeons attended him immediately and pronounced it a dislocation; though, obviously, from the aftereffects it must have been a fracture. They set the wrist; but set it so clumsily that the bones never knit properly and Jefferson suffered from the fall for the rest of his life.

It was a catastrophe of the first magnitude; it was his right hand, and both his duties as minister and his private correspondence required extensive writing which his secretary, Short, could only partially handle for him.

With indomitable courage, therefore, he set himself the task of learning to write with his left hand. The amazing results can be traced in fascinating sequence in his account book and in his correspondence. Painfully, slowly, he composed large, tremulous, wavering letters with fingers unused to the task; each day the writing grew a little better, a trifle more flowing and legible until, on November 10th (or, rather the final item in the account book for November 9th), a new hand suddenly appears—the old, beautiful, copperplate writing which is the hallmark of Jefferson.[39] His right hand had evidently resumed its use, though it was always to remain weak. Yet Jefferson kept practicing with his left so that he could write with either hand in the future with almost equal facility.

If this was catastrophe, fate had what perhaps to him was an even greater blow in store. The Cosways had determined to return to England —Richard's commission for the Duke of Orléans was finished, and other commissions beckoned in the English metropolis.

Maria had heard of the accident and tried to come, but always something intervened. Though her uneasiness—so she said—was greater than she could express, she was compelled to say it by letter late the following night. She had hoped to come that morning, but "my husband killed my project I had proposed to him by burying himself among pictures and forgetting the hours." When they finally did drive out, and were close to Jefferson's house, they remembered that they were already due to dine with the Duchess of Kingston at Saint-Cloud and had to turn around. They tried again that evening, perhaps on their way back from Saint-Cloud; but the noise of their carriage and their knockings on the door disturbed the neighbors and woke up the servants; and they were compelled to depart without seeing Jefferson who, from the context, seems also to have been asleep. But they intended to come again, first thing in the morning, "if nothing happens to prevent it." [40]

Just when Maria finally managed to visit her injured friend is not known; but by Wednesday, October 4th, Jefferson considered himself well enough to go out driving with her. The jaunt had unfortunate consequences: the rattling of the carriage over the cobbled pavements of Paris jarred the badly set wrist and he went home in such pain that the following morning the surgeon was called in again.

The Cosways were supposed to commence their journey this day and Jefferson wrote painfully with his left hand that he must, with infinite regret, "relinquish her charming company for that of the Surgeon. . . . If you do not go today I shall still have the pleasure of seeing you again. If you do, god bless you wherever you go. Present me in the most friendly terms to mr. Cosway, & let me hear of your safe arrival in England. Addio Addio." [41]

Maria sent over a servant immediately with a note blaming herself for the renewed pain; which both attributed to the carriage drive of the preceding day. "Why would you go?" she cried, "& why was I not more friendly to you & less to Myself by preventing your giving me the pleasure of your Company? You repeatedly said it would do you no harm, I felt interested and did not insist." They *were* leaving that day; though "nobody seems redy, but Mr. Cosway seems more dispos'd than I have seen him all this time." [42]

On receipt of this farewell note, Jefferson forgot the pain and the admonitions of his surgeon, and ordered his carriage to drive in all haste to the Rue Coq-Héron. He arrived in time—the Cosways were always dilatory, and their packing had to be completed. Not content with this no doubt all too brief interview, Jefferson and another friend, M. Danquerville, insisted on escorting the departing pair to Saint-Denis.

There, as he wrote the vanished Maria in that utterly charming dialogue which has become known to fame as *My Head and My Heart,* "having performed the last sad office of handing you into your carriage at the pavillon de St. Denis, and seen the wheels get actually into motion, I turned on my heel & walked, more dead than alive, to the opposite door, where my own was awaiting me." Danquerville joined him in the journey back to a suddenly desolate Paris. For a long time they rode in silence; then burst out in mutual exclamations of distress. He let the gentleman out at his home; and then was carried off to his own house.

In the privacy of his chamber, "seated by my fireside, solitary & sad, the following dialogue took place between my Head & my Heart." [43] It was not until a week later that Jefferson sent on to Maria this most moving and most revealing of all his writings. Into it, in the form of a mutually recriminatory dialogue between his reason (the Head) and his emotions (the Heart) he poured the pent-up longings of years of repression and yet, at the same time, the realization of the dangers he had just escaped. He had fallen in love with a young married woman—he knew only too well what had happened to him—and there could be only grief ahead. That was what the rational part told him. But his heart cried out in anguish, and welcomed even the danger. He was forty-three, in the prime of life and in the full vigor of his powers. Why could he not love, and be loved again? The beloved dead—whom he never mentioned—was dead; *he* was alive. Life beckoned. Was he to remain forever immured within the close confinements of memory?

Something like this must have passed through his mind as he sat by the fireside and composed his epistle. He was wrestling with himself, and who knows what might have happened had not the object of his desire departed? That she did not know the state of his feelings is incredible; that she was flattered is patent; but her heart was not as wrought upon as his, and good sense therefore was able to warn her away from the ardor of his fire.

Meanwhile, he suffered—and wrote. The Heart was speaking: "I am indeed the most wretched of all earthly beings. Overwhelmed with grief, every fibre of my frame distended beyond its natural powers to bear, I would willingly meet whatever catastrophe should leave me no more to feel or to fear." Coldly the Head replied: "These are the eternal consequences of your warmth & precipitation. This is one of the scrapes into which you are ever leading us." And, "you will be pleased to remember that when our friend Trumbull used to be telling us of the merits & talents of these good people, I never ceased whispering that we had no occasion for new acquaintance; that the greater their merits & talents, the more dangerous their friendship to our tranquillity, because the regret at parting would be greater."

Spare me these homilies, cried out the Heart in return. Was it not you who dragged us to see the Halle that fatal day? "I never trouble myself with domes nor arches," it added smugly.

But the Head refused to spare the Heart. It admitted that the lady had "qualities & accomplishments belonging to her sex, which might form a chapter apart for her: such as music, modesty, beauty, & that softness of disposition which is the ornament of her sex & charm of ours"; but all that merely helped increase the pangs of eventual separation.

They had promised to be back next year, cried the Heart hopefully. But the Head punctured even that vain hope. Suppose they do, and you see them another two months. What then? Will they follow you to America?

Why not? exclaimed the Heart defiantly. Were there not enough subjects in America to engage the attention of her art—Niagara, the passage of the Potomac, the Natural Bridge; above all, Monticello, with its sublimities of mountains, forests, rivers, storms and sunrise?

Look at the lying character given our America in the London press, jeered the Head. *That* will be enough to scare our friends away. But *we* know America is not like that, objected the Heart. "There is not a country on earth where there is greater tranquillity, where the laws are milder, or better obeyed." Look at our occupations: digging canals, building roads, establishing public schools, protecting religious freedom, abolishing sanguinary punishments—are not these "better evidence of our true state than a London newspaper, hired to lie, & from which no truth can ever be extracted but by reversing everything it says?"

Naturally, the Head could not answer such manifest truisms; therefore it shifted the argument. You tossed all last night with pain, it pointed out; the physical pain of your wrist and the mental pain occasioned by your friends' approaching departure. The surgeon—"an ignoramus"—could not divine the cause; but *you* knew. "This is not a world," it proceeded sternly, "to live at random in as you do. To avoid these eternal distresses, to which you are forever exposing us, you must learn to look forward before you take a step which may interest our peace." Balance the pains and sorrows of every action. Retire within ourselves and "suffice for our own happiness." Derive your pleasures from the intellect, which never cloy. Avoid these passionate friendships which subject you to misfortunes, sorrows and regrets.

This was Stoic philosophy, of course; and the Heart reacted violently. Better tears and sorrow, it cried, as long as there is love and friendship! "If our country, when pressed with wrongs at the point of the bayonet, had been governed by its heads instead of its hearts, where should we have been now? Hanging on a gallows as high as Haman's."

It was, of course, essential that the dialogue, intended for the eyes of Maria, end with a triumphant dissertation by the Heart and the utter rout of the Head; and Jefferson so ended it. In the future, he promised, with an abrupt shift from fancy to plain prose, he would not bore her with such lengthy effusions; but on her part there must be no curtailing. "If your letters are as long as the bible," he assured the absent fair one, "they will appear short to me. Only let them be brimful of affection"; and let them spell out the words "*je t'aime.*"

Barely had this remarkable performance been painfully and awkwardly indited and sealed when a letter arrived from Antwerp, the first stop of the Cosways on their way to London. It was a voluminous affair, promising a feast; but, alas, as Jefferson opened it eagerly, only four lines of it were hers, and in her hand. And even those poor lines were arid and uninformative.[44]

More information came from Trumbull, however, who had met them in Antwerp, and was squiring them back to London. Most of his letter, though, was devoted to an account of his own travels in Germany; but Maria added a small postscript in Italian. English was still a foreign language to her, and her thoughts flowed more smoothly in the Tuscan.[45]

Trumbull became, in a sense, the intermediary through whom the future correspondence passed. Jefferson enclosed his letters to Maria in covering packets to the young painter. To him he wrote wistfully of his travels—"my first wish was to see the places you described; my second to see in preference Italy, Greece &c. but god knows when I may be able to see either, or if ever."[46] He was never to see Greece; and of Italy, only a small and rather unsatisfactory part.

To all his correspondents, Jefferson complained exceedingly of his wrist and the difficulty he had in writing with his left hand. It was late in November before he essayed the right again, and found it stiff and painful.

His first attempt was dedicated to Maria. "But I write with pain & must be short. This is good news to you; for were the hand able to follow the effusions of the heart that would cease to write only when this shall cease to beat." Madame de Corny was going to London; and "I wish," he added, "she could put me into her pocket when she goes, or you when she comes back."[47]

At length, much to his delight, a proper—at least to him—response came from Maria in London. In mingled English and Italian she spoke with awe of the passionate "Head and Heart" effusion, and protested her inability to match in words his master touch. It would take her an hour to consider every word, and to every sentence she could write a volume. "Why do you say so many kind things? Why present so many opportunities for my feeling undeserving of them? Why not leave me a free consolation in admiring a friend?" [48] Safe in London, Maria could afford to be a little more complaisant with her distant admirer; yet, at the same time, hold him off from too much ardor with phrases like these.

Their letters crossed in the mails and thereby became confused. *He* feared that the post offices of both countries, interested in Jefferson's doings, opened all his mail and thereby exposed tender expressions to the blight of cynical and unfeeling officials; *she* sent him a roll of the songs in Italian she had composed and complained that she had not heard from him in a century. But she will punish him. She will use only a small sheet of paper so as to say as little as possible. To which Jefferson, in a rare bit of humor, told Trumbull: "My love to Mrs. Cosway. Tell her I will send her a supply of larger paper." [49]

She was to come again to Paris in the following year, and their acquaintance was to be renewed. Jefferson's interest remained; but some of the vital spark had departed. His letters gradually achieve the formal elements of mere gallantry, instead of the living passion of the earlier ones. And, as too often happens, as he cooled, she kindled. The end, however, as we shall see, was mere friendship, and a memory.

Jefferson, escaped from what might have been a difficult entanglement, was never again to place himself in danger of a similar occurrence. The fires of romance had blazed up strongly in his middle age. From now on, they remained safely banked and under control.

CHAPTER 24

Southern Journey

THE fracture of his wrist and its seeming inability to heal threw obstacles in the way of Jefferson's official duties as well as his romance; but he refused to be deterred from either. For his private affairs, he wrote with his left; for public correspondence, William Short lent him the use of his own uninjured hand; so that he managed to get through his epistolary duties without too much difficulty. He slighted no correspondent; nor any topic of interest.

News came regularly to him from America. His chief informers on the political aspects—aside from official communications—were his friends Madison and Monroe. In return, he delivered himself to them of his own meditations on particular measures and movements, and thereby, through them and others like them, was able to exercise a definite influence on the distant scene.

Reports filtered through to Europe of trouble in America; chiefly in Massachusetts. It was serious enough in actuality—the armed riots and disturbances which have since become known as Shays' Rebellion—and it lost nothing in transmission.

But Jefferson was not alarmed; even though such a usually restrained observer as the Reverend James Madison wrote that it looked like "the Beginnings of a civil War there," which "appear to some as Proofs of ye Instability & Misery inseperable from a Republican Govt. But to others, who I trust judge better, they appear only as ye Symptoms of a strong & healthy Constitution, which, after discharging a few peccant Humours, will be restored to new Vigour." [1]

Abigail Adams, to whom Jefferson had written for information, inclined to the former class. She replied with masculine vigor and atrocious spelling that "I wish I could say that report had exagerated them, It is too true Sir that they have been carried to so allarming a Height as to stop the Courts of Justice in several Counties. Ignorant, [illegible word] desperadoes, without conscience or principals [*sic*] have led a deluded Multitude to follow their standard, under pretence of grievences which have no existance but in their immaginations... instead of that laudible spirit which you approve, which makes a people watchfull over their Liberties and alert in the defence of them, these Mobish insurgents are for sapping the foundation, and distroying the whole fabrick at once." [2]

Jefferson, however, was definitely of that second persuasion which the

Reverend Mr. Madison had described. In letter after letter he adopted a calm, philosophical tone over the disturbances at home.

The most famous of these was his statement to that other James Madison: "I hold it that a little rebellion now and then is a good thing, & as necessary in the political world as storms in the physical. Unsuccessful rebellions indeed generally establish the encroachments on the rights of the people which have produced them. An observation of this truth should render honest republican governors so mild in their punishment of rebellions, as not to discourage them too much. It is a medicine necessary for the sound health of government." He was far more perturbed over reports that the navigation of the Mississippi might be abandoned to Spain. The day that happens, he warned, means the breakup of the Union into a western and an eastern group, the loss of five-eighths of our territory, and the chaining of the public debt—which could only be paid out of the western lands—"on our own necks *in perpetuum*." [3]

He was clarifying in his own mind his concepts of the relation between the governors and the governed. He did not believe in deifying the State, or giving it an abstract life of its own apart from the people who composed it. "The people," he declared, "are the only censors of their governors: and even their errors will tend to keep these to the true principles of their institution. To punish these errors too severely would be to suppress the only safeguard of the public liberty."

Let the people, he insisted, have full information through a free press. "The basis of our governments being the opinion of the people, the very first object should be to keep that right; and were it left to me to decide whether we should have a government without newspapers or newspapers without a government, I should not hesitate a moment to prefer the latter." He had seen enough in Europe to have come to the conviction that once the people "become inattentive to the public affairs, you & I, & Congress & Assemblies, judges & governors shall all become wolves." It seemed to be a law of nature applicable to man alone that he tends to devour his own kind; with "governments preying on the people and the rich on the poor." [4]

He wrote to others in the same vein; and each letter contains apothegms which, placed together, form a fitted mosaic of his theory of revolution and the liberties of the people. To Dr. Stiles of Yale, he wrote that the current commotions in America "are a proof that the people have liberty enough, and I would not wish them less than they have. If the happiness of the mass of the people can be secured at the expence of a little tempest now & then, or even of a little blood, it will be a precious purchase." [5]

And, to David Hartley: "I have no fear that the result of our experiment will be that men may be trusted to govern themselves without a master. Could the contrary of this be proved, I should conclude either that there is no god, or that he is a malevolent being." [6]

He never varied from this belief. Given the true facts—and for this a free press was essential—given literacy and education—for reason must be brought to bear, not ignorant prejudice—and the government of themselves may safely be left in the hands of the people. Jefferson always distrusted excessive government and excessive powers; he would have been the first to approve of Lord Acton's future famous dictum that power tends to corrupt, and absolute power corrupts absolutely. He was forever being confronted with examples of absolutism in Europe and, when the Revolution came, it met with his instant approval. Even the initial blood baths did not perturb him; it was only when Napoleon arose and absolute power, under another form, was vested again in the ruler, that he reluctantly averted his face.

He had not that sense of history which points to the man on the white horse, the Napoleon, as the usual, almost the inevitable end result of violent revolution. The single one in which he had actively participated had been a mild one. It had been largely a war of independence of one nation from another, not a civil war—though there had been overtones of that with respect to the Loyalists; it had been largely political in character—though here, too, there were certain overtones of economic and social conflicts. Yet even in the American Revolution, there were aftereffects. Shays' Rebellion was one, wholly economic in nature and therefore filled with a rancor on both sides far beyond that visible in the earlier political revolution. And, during the period of Federalism, Jefferson himself was to know only too well the bitterness engendered by a social and economic conflict, and to fear, rightly or wrongly, the advent of the man on the white horse.

Perhaps at this moment, too, Shays' Rebellion—the revolt of the desperate debtor against the enforcement of his debts—struck a particularly responsive chord. For his own debts were rising to plague him. It is illuminating to read, around this time, his excoriation of the particular type of creditor with whom he had had, and was still having, humiliating experiences.

"Long experience has proved to us," he wrote to one similarly situated, "that there never was an instance of a man's getting out of debt who was once in the hands of a tobacco merchant, & bound to consign his tobacco to him. It is the most delusive of all snares. The merchant feeds the inclination of his customer to be credited till he gets the burthen of debt so increased that he cannot throw it off at once. He then begins to give him less for his tobacco, & ends with giving him what he pleases for it, which is always so little that let the demands of the customer for necessaries be reduced ever so low in order to get himself out of debt, the merchant lowers his price in the same proportion so as always to keep such a balance against his customer as will oblige him to continue his consignments of tobacco." [7]

The reason for this bitter outburst was plain. All his schemes to pay off his private debts out of the profits of his estate had gone a-glimmering.

Nicholas Lewis, whom he had left in charge of his affairs at home, had sent him a gloomy accounting which disclosed that the entire profits, after expenses, "would be no more than the hire of the few negroes hired out would amount to." Would it not be better, Jefferson asked Lewis in despair, for him to hire out more of his slaves, provided good masters could be found? Perhaps, even, to rent out "the plantations & all, if proper assurance can be provided for the good usage of everything? I am miserable," he burst forth, "till I owe not a shilling: the moment that shall be the case I shall feel myself at liberty to do something for the comfort of my slaves." [8]

Jefferson was compelled to ask his chief creditors for additional time. He had sold some of his slaves to put himself in a position to take care of them, he said; if they agreed to take installments—without interest for the war years, however—he would commence payments on an annual basis.[9]

With the best intentions in the world, Jefferson did not find it easy to rid himself of the incubus of these prewar debts. In the first place, the English firms were unwilling to give up their claim for war-years interest; in the second, Jefferson always overestimated the net income of his lands. It never lived up to expectations. Nor was it the fault of his managers back home; even when he returned and took over personal control, no year yielded what, at the beginning of that year, he was certain it would.[10]

But at least, while insisting on their pound of flesh, the creditors paid tribute to Jefferson's honorable refusal to avail himself of the stay laws still in effect in Virginia which prevented collections. Alexander McCaul, of Glasgow, bewailed to Jefferson the change he noted in the general honesty of the Virginians. "When I first knew that Country," he declared, "I don't beleive there was in general an honester sett of people on the face of the Earth, but wonderfully have they changed of late years, & you will be amazed when I tell you that among the great number of respectable names that owed money to my Partners & myself that not one amongst them have said they would pay their debts except yourself Mr John Rose & Mr John Nicholas." [11]

As though Jefferson had not sufficient of his own troubles, he took upon himself the troubles of others. The worst of these related to the Paradises—John and Lucy Ludwell—whom he had met while in England. Lucy Ludwell had originally been a Virginia girl, the daughter of one of Jefferson's friends, Col. Philip Ludwell of Green Spring. As the heiress to the Ludwell fortune—one of the greatest in Virginia—Lucy was a tremendous catch. She elected to marry a penniless Englishman, John Paradise, and they moved to London. John was something of an intellectual, a Fellow of the Royal Society and the friend of Samuel Johnson. But he had no business ability, secluded himself from company and possessed a fund of neuroses, not the least of which was a pathological fear of lightning.

On the death of Col. Ludwell, the vast estates accrued to the Paradises.

Unfortunately, Jefferson had been the unwitting instrument of their destruction. Paradise was an English subject and the bill which Jefferson drew forfeiting British property in Virginia wiped out the inheritance.

Through the aid of influential Americans, Lucy was able to have the law modified in her favor; but her husband, who should have gone to Virginia to arrange their affairs, shrank from the voyage because of the tremendous thunderstorms that, so he had heard, were usual there. Jefferson assured him that Virginia's storms were no worse than anywhere else, but it took long months before the need for money overcame the fear.

In the meantime, the couple lived on an extravagant scale, in expectation of later recoupment, and both Lucy and her husband pestered Jefferson with requests for funds and mutual complaints against each other. The voluminous correspondence is a case history of two erratic persons—Lucy was eventually to be declared legally insane and John ought to have been —yet Jefferson met demands for money as best he could, harkened to their violence and abject grovelings, and never failed to reply, no matter how rambling the letter, with unfailing courtesy, gentleness and consummate tact. Jefferson was never to show his personal character in a more revealing and endearing light than in his dealings with this pair.[12]

That absurd wrist had never healed, and continued swollen. The bones had not set properly, though Jefferson was assured they had; and it was solemnly agreed by the medical faculty of Paris that the only possibility of cure lay in the mineral waters at Aix, in Provence.[13] He had already been thinking seriously of making a tour through the south of France "as far as the canal of Languedoc which I have a great desire to examine minutely as at some future time it may enable me to give information thereon to such of our states as are engaged in works of that kind."[14] He also thought he would inform himself on the state of French commerce with the United States. Jefferson always liked to have a utilitarian purpose, either for himself or for his country, when he went on travels; so that the thought of combining business with health appealed to him.

Accordingly, he made arrangements for an extended absence from Paris. He attended the French Court at Fontainebleau, settled what business he could in that incongruous atmosphere of mingled intrigue and festivities of the boudoir and the chase, saw Vergennes, on whom the hand of death was already laid (he died in February, 1787), tipped the servants well, visited Patsy for a last farewell and, on February 28, 1787, started his journey to the south to seek both health and instruction.

Health—in the specific sense of his wrist—he did not find. When he finally reached Aix, he found the waters of no help whatever (though he did not remain long enough for an adequate trial); but of instruction and general enlargement of the faculties he found abundance.

Journeying steadily in his own carriage, with changes of post horses, and accompanied by a strange servant hired at Dijon for the purpose (for he wanted no one who knew his station to spy on his inquiries), he reached Champagne on the 3rd of March. He kept a diary of his travels, laconic to the point of distraction in parts, and notably full in others. His travel notes picture, however, the mind and interests of their writer; and therefore possess considerable value of their own. Scenery per se, lovely vistas, did not particularly interest him, and are given scant treatment. But crops, the condition of the soil, methods of agriculture, the plight and means of livelihood of the people, manufactures, machinery, statistics of commerce, canals—these are the things that drew his closest observation and are entered in the fullest detail. No one could be farther from the impractical dreamer of legend than Jefferson. No mountain, however grand, stirred his emotions as much as the sight of a new and improved vegetable that might be transplanted to Virginia and the other States.

From Sens to Vermanton he had noted physiographical details, the soil and the crops. He observed the people and was struck with their poverty and religious superstition. He found "few châteaux; no farm-houses, all the people being gathered in villages. Are they thus collected," he wondered, "by that dogma of their religion, which makes them believe, that to keep the Creator in good humor with His own works, they must mumble a mass every day? Certain it is, that they are less happy and less virtuous in villages, than they would be insulated with their families on the grounds they cultivate." Jefferson never failed to be amazed that people should prefer the gregariousness of towns to the self-communing isolation of the farm.

He saw another sight that also made him wonder: women and children staggering under heavy burdens. "This," he commented, "is an unequivocal indication of extreme poverty. Men, in a civilized country, never expose their wives and children to labor above their force and sex, as long as their own labor can protect them from it." In seeming contradiction of this thesis was the lack of many beggars; but this, he thought, was probably due to rigorous policing.[15]

He went on into Burgundy where the people seemed to be well fed; but he objected to the "ennui" of the interminably straight, tree-lined roads. Winding paths were his delight. He was now coming into the heart of the great wine country—Chalons, Beaujolais, Maison Blanche and the Château de Laye-Epinaye—names that still are odorous with the rich tang of the grape and the beaded beaker winking at the brim. As a lover and collector of the finest in wines, as an agriculturalist who had tried once, and would try again, to transplant to Virginia the vine and the grape, Jefferson was in ecstasies. "This is the richest country I ever beheld," he exclaimed; thick with chateaux and prosperous farm houses; and, to his delight, "the people live separately, and not in villages." He visited the great Château de Laye-Epinaye and received a cordial welcome. And here he saw a marble group—Diana and Endymion—sculptured by one M. A. Slodtz. He promptly went into raptures. "It carried," he wrote in all seriousness, "the perfection of the chisel to a degree of which I had no conception. It is the only thing in sculpture which I have seen in my journey worth notice." But châteaux were not enough—he went into "the houses of the labourers, cellars of the Vignerons, & mixing & conversing with them as much as I could.... Architecture, painting, sculpture, antiquities, agriculture, the condition of the labouring poor fill all my moments." [16]

He came to Lyon on March 11th, and spent four days there. His first view of Roman ruins was unimpressive; he thought these were feeble enough. He was to see much finer ones shortly.

Quitting Lyon, he entered the wide Rhone plain which shortly narrowed into savage, rushing gorges. Emerging, he came to the high spots of his journey; the grandeur that had been Rome and those noble ruins of which the mere drawings had awakened his architectural soul to rapture. Like the vinous names of France, these too evoke another world—Vienne, Orange, the Praetorian Palace, the Pont du Gard—and Nîmes! Above all, Nîmes—where the Maison Carrée reared its battered splendor.

For years Jefferson had pored over drawings and dimensions of the Maison Carrée like a lover examining the picture of his beloved during enforced absence. And now, for the first time, he beheld it—so to speak—in the marble flesh.

The actuality—as is not often the case—far surpassed his dreams. His soul melted and his pen moved in dithyrambs. To Madame de Tessé, a fellow enthusiast, he poured out his love. "Here I am, Madam, gazing whole hours at the Maison Quarrée, like a lover at his mistress. The stocking weavers and silk spinners around it consider me a hypochondriac Englishman, about to write with a pistol the last chapter of his history. This is the second time I have been in love since I left Paris. The first was with a Diana at the Château de Laye-Epinaye in Beaujolois [*sic*], a delicious morsel of sculpture, by M. A. Slodtz.... While in Paris, I was violently smitten with the Hôtel de Salm, and used to go to the Tuileries almost daily, to look at it." And now, beyond all others, the Maison Carrée. "I am immersed in antiquities from morning to night," he wrote enraptured. "For me, the city of Rome is actually existing in all the splendor of its empire." [17]

In later years, he was still to hark back to this, to him, apex of the architecture of the world; at least, in the cubic mold. He agreed that the Pantheon was "the perfection of the Spherical"; though he knew it only from models and drawings. Time drew a veil over his memory then, and he was certain he had been to Nîmes twice, each time for ten days, "and each day stood an hour, morning, noon & night, fixed as a statue to a single spot, and entransed [*sic*] in the beauty of its form and symmetries." [18]

Reluctantly he tore himself away, though not before his more practical instincts had asserted themselves, and he had contemplated with almost equal interest a new-fangled steam engine that was being installed to operate a great mill and take the place of the ancient rites of wind and water.

On March 24th, he was on the road again, proceeding through high hills covered with snow down to Arles. Here were more Roman ruins and a great amphitheater. Meticulously he counted the columns, measured the dimensions of the vaults and arches. By March 26th, he had ended the first stage of his journey. He had come to Aix en Provence, where the healing waters were. It was heaven to the sun-worshiping Virginian after the mists and cold and penetrating rains of Paris. "I am now in the land of corn, vine, oil & sunshine. What more can a man ask of heaven?" he exclaimed to Short in distant Paris. "If I should happen to die at Paris I will beg of you to send me here, and have me exposed to the sun. I am sure it will bring me to life again." [19]

Even the Provence tongue—the tongue of the Troubadours, of the Courts of Love, of Ronsard—was a great delight. It resembled the Italian to him more than the French. "I think it a general misfortune," he observed, "that historical circumstances gave a final prevalence to the French instead of the Provençale Language." [20]

He stayed only four days in Aix, however, "douching" his wrist in the warm mineral waters. In that short space of time he became certain that the effect was nil; and moved on to Marseilles and its commerce. But not before he had gathered certain information which consorts oddly with the ecstasy over sunshine, language and Roman splendors. "Dung," he carefully noted, "costs ten sous the hundred pounds.... An ass sells for from one to three louis; the best mules for thirty louis.... A mule eats half as much as a horse. The allowance to an ass for the day, is a handful of bran mixed with straw." A male laborer gets 150 livres a year; a woman, 60 to 66 livres, with food. "In the morning, they eat bread with an anchovy, or an onion. Their dinner in the middle of the day, is bread, soup, and vegetables. Their supper the same." [21]

At Marseilles, that great seaport town, he remained a week. He had become a seasoned traveler and, as travelers love to do, he expatiated on the joys of the road. "A traveller, sais I," he wrote to the Comtesse de Tott, "retired at night to his chamber in an inn, all his effects contained in a single portmanteau, all his cares circumscribed by the walls of his apartment, unknown to all, unheeded & undisturbed, writes, reads, thinks sleeps just in the moments when nature & the movements of his body & mind require. Charmed with this tranquility, he finds how few are our real wants, how cheap a thing is happiness, how expensive a one pride." He views with pity the "wretch" who is rich and surrounded by harpies. But, alas, there are flies even in Paradise; for suddenly his meditations are interrupted by "4,350 market women (I have counted them) brawling, squabbling, jabbering Patois, 300. asses braying & bewailing to each other, & to the world, their cruel oppressions, 4. files of mule carts passing in constant succession, with as many bells to every mule as can be hung about him, all this in the street under my window, & the weather too hot to shut it." [22]

This is delightful and in Jefferson's happiest vein. But to Lafayette he explained more seriously what his travels meant to him. "I am constantly roving about, to see what I have never seen before, and shall never see again. In the great cities, I go to see what travellers think alone worthy of being seen; but I make a job of it, and generally gulp it all down in a day. On the other hand, I am never satiated with rambling through the fields and farms, examining the culture and cultivators, with a degree of curiosity which makes some to take me to be a fool, and others to be much wiser than I am." To really know a country, he proceeded, "you must be absolutely incognito, you must ferret the people out of their hovels as I have done, look into their kettles, eat their bread, loll on their beds under pretence of resting yourself, but in fact, to find if they are soft." [23] Modern sociologists, economists and roving reporters might well take a lesson from this ferret-eyed eighteenth-century observer.

At Marseilles, Jefferson dutifully collected information that might be of value to American sea-borne commerce; but his real predilections kept irrepressibly cropping out. A friend of Mazzei, whom he discovered there, had promised to introduce him to a well-informed gardener. "From men of that class," he told Mazzei, "I have derived the most satisfactory information in the course of my journey & have sought their acquaintance with as much industry as I have avoided that of others who would have made me waste my time on good dinners & good society." What he particularly was interested in were olives, capers, almonds, rice and other growing things that might flourish "on, or Southward of the Chesapeak." [24] Jefferson was always to be happiest on the soil; cities and the busy haunts of men made him uncomfortable, and he escaped back to the land as soon as he could.

Italy, the seat of Rome, of classical culture, the darling of the poets and the artists, now beckoned. But *not* for any of the reasons enumerated. Jefferson had heard that in the Piedmont they possessed a machine for cleaning rice which brought European rice to the market less broken into fragments than the American product. No one who had seen the machine had been able to explain to Jefferson either its construction or how it worked. Since American rice, though above the European in quality and color, met with less favor in European markets because it came half-crushed by the existing American methods, Jefferson determined to spend the three weeks he figured for the journey in seeing this wonderful machine for himself and, if possible, to copy it for American use.[25]

On April 6th, he quit Marseilles for Italy. He passed through Antibes and Nice and the other show places of the Riviera, and gathered data on capers, oranges and wine, but not a word of the scenic wonders he encountered—except one. You can tell from the shape of a woman's hat, he remarked, exactly what canton or province she came from.[26]

On April 13th, mounted on a mule—since the snow still lay in the passes and his carriage was impracticable—he started to cross the Alps. For the first time he marveled: at the Château di Saorgio, "a scene is presented, the most singular and picturesque I ever saw." Perhaps because it was in the vein of Ossian and the Gothic. "The castle and village seem hanging to a cloud in front. On the right, is a mountain cloven through, to let pass a gurgling stream; on the left, a river, over which is thrown a magnificent bridge. The whole forms a basin, the sides of which are shagged with rocks, olive trees, vines, herds, etc." [27]

On April 16th, he came to Turin; and from there went slowly through the rice country to Milan. This was what he had come for. He spoke to peasants and cultivators; he examined the precious cereal and came to the conclusion that it was a different species from the Carolina rice. He wished to take sufficient to send to South Carolina as seed, but its exportation in the husk was prohibited under heavy penalties. But Jefferson was not to be prevented by restrictive laws from benefiting his country. He filled all the pockets of his several coats to the bulging point; and made an agreement with a muleteer, one Poggio, to smuggle a sack of rough rice from Vercelli to Genoa for him, where he expected to board ship. It meant death for the muleteer if he were caught—so ran the law—but that phase of the bargain seems not to have bothered Jefferson at all.[28]

At Milan, he paid some attention to the alfresco painting of the houses and viewed some salons with approval; but the glorious Cathedral of Milan excited only the rather philistine remark that it was worthy of philosophic contemplation merely as one of "the rarest instances of the misuse of money. On viewing the churches of Italy it is evident without calculation that the same expense would have sufficed to throw the Apennines into the Adriatic and thereby render it terra firma from Leghorn to Constantinople." [29] One is forcibly reminded of Mark Twain's famous *Innocents Abroad.*

But the rice machine, which he had traveled such a considerable distance to see, and which he found at Casino, aroused his diligent attention. It consisted of a beater armed with six pestles and—what made the difference—each pestle was serrated with teeth. It was these teeth, he was assured, that helped clean the rice faster and break it less.[30]

Having accomplished his mission, Jefferson journeyed to Genoa, the port of embarkation; taking note in passing of the way in which Parmesan cheese was made. He boarded ship on April 26th, his pockets still full of rice—though the muleteer seems to have disappointed him—and set sail for Nice. But contrary winds forced him to land at Noli, forty miles up the coast; where he clambered the coastal mountains for two days while waiting for the wind to change.

Now that his utilitarian mission was completed, he could observe the scenery in relaxation. It pleased him wonderfully. Here, he thought, was paradise for him who wished to live solitary and unknown, in the midst of sun, sea and pure air; where song and game birds abounded, where the earth and sea furnished their respective fruits in unlimited quantities and the climate was superb.[31]

But the winds did not co-operate, and Jefferson was compelled to go on into France by mule; back to Nice, Marseilles, and once more to stand enrapt at Nîmes. At Avignon he visited the tomb of Petrarch's Laura and then the fountain of Vaucluse, of which Petrarch had sung. Sitting before that gush of water, he beheld the ruins of Petrarch's château perched high above, while every tree and bush was "filled with nightingales in full chorus." For the first time, he admitted that this fabled songster surpassed any American; this southern variety had a stronger and more varied tone than the one which had disappointed him on the banks of the Seine. Since climate evidently made the difference, patriotism, temporarily crushed to earth, rose again. "What a bird the nightingale would be in the climates of America!" he exclaimed. "We must colonize him hither."

One more reflection flowed from this southern bird. No wonder, he thought, that "there never was a poet north of the Alps and why there never will be one. A poet is as much a creature of climate as an orange or a palm tree." [32] A curious reflection, indeed, when one considers, among scores of possibilities, such poets as Villon, Racine, Corneille, Goethe, Schiller—not to speak of the whole tribe of English songsters, whose name is legion.

He finally came to the great Canal of Languedoc, whereby the great Sun King, Louis XIV, had wedded the waters of the Atlantic and the Mediterranean. It was this canal which Jefferson had earlier proposed to himself as the specific objective of a trip. He hired a bark, some 35 feet in length and drawn by a single horse plodding along the bank, dismounted his carriage and placed it on board.

On this leisurely craft, he voyaged up the long canal, stretching his legs on shore or, seated in the carriage on deck, reading, writing and observing the shifting panorama of fields, farms, orchards and villages. Of all the means of locomotion he had tried, this, he admitted, was the pleasantest. The skies were cloudless above, the waters limpid below and, from either side, the southern nightingale gave full-throated chorus.[33]

But he had not come merely for idyllic reasons. There were canals contemplated in America, and therefore he examined the construction of this particular one, the operation of the locks, and the navigation of the boats.

What filled him constantly with astonishment on his travels in France was the topsy-turvydom of the sexes. Men did women's work, and women did men's. The sight of women working the locks and acting as bargees impelled him to enter in his notebook a long comment. "The encroachments by the men, on the offices proper for the women, is a great derangement in the order of things," he wrote. "Men are shoemakers, tailors, upholsterers, stay-makers, mantua-makers, cooks, house keepers, house-cleaners, bed-makers; they *coiffe* the ladies, and bring them to bed: the women, therefore, to live, are obliged to undertake the offices which they abandon. They become porters, carters, reapers, sailors, lock-keepers, smiters on the anvil, cultivators of the earth, etc. Can we wonder, if such of them as have a little beauty, prefer easier courses to get their livelihood, as long as that beauty lasts? Ladies who employ men in the offices which should have been reserved for their sex, are they not bawds in effect? For every man whom they thus employ, some girl, whose place he has thus taken, is driven to whoredom." [34]

Thus moralized Virginia in the person of Thomas Jefferson.

Having delivered himself on the peculiarities of the French—a favorite topic of foreigners for centuries—Jefferson continued on his own proper business. He noted that the lock system, as worked with a wooden screw, was "excessively slow and laborious," five minutes being lost in each basin. His inventive mind was aroused, and he suggested to M. Pin, the engineer, that they employ "a quadrantal gate, turning on a pivot, and lifted by a lever like a pump handle, aided by a windlass and cord, if necessary." M. Pin was struck by the idea, and promised to try it out.[35]

On May 21st, he came to Toulouse and the canal's end. He had sailed on it for more than a week, right through the heart of France. On to Bordeaux, where he measured the bricks of the old Roman circus in all their dimensions, and found them of a texture like porcelain and much superior to those currently manufactured. He also stopped to make an inquiry concerning that "fact" which he had first found in Voltaire's *Questions Encyclopédiques* and which he had borrowed, with disastrous results, to explain the presence of fossil sea shells on the heights of the Blue Ridge.

The information, it seems, had originally emanated from M. de la Sauvagiere, whose château was close by. M. Gentil, an official of the place, to whom Jefferson applied for confirmation, was well acquainted with the story. Gentil was evidently a diplomat. Sauvagiere, he assured his visitor, "was a man of truth, and might be relied on for whatever facts he stated as of his own observations; but," he continued cautiously, "he was overcharged with imagination, which, in matters of opinion and theory, often led him beyond his facts." Though Gentil himself had not seen shells growing from small to large, as Sauvagiere had, or claimed he had, he thought it quite likely, and that the evidence sounded convincing that "shells are a fruit of the earth, spontaneously produced."

"What are we to conclude?" Jefferson asked himself in perplexity; and furnished his own reply. "That we have not materials enough yet, to form any conclusion." More extensive observations were necessary.[36] Yet he was never to change or modify the thesis which he had set forth in the *Notes on Virginia.*

The long, but fruitful journey was at last approaching an end. Blois and Orléans, and then Paris, from which he started. He arrived on the 10th of June, 1787, after an absence of three months and ten days.

CHAPTER 25

Constitution from Afar

JEFFERSON had barely returned to Paris when his younger daughter, Polly, arrived. On his departure from France he had left Polly and the baby, Lucy Elizabeth, in the charge of his sister-in-law, Elizabeth Eppes, because he thought they were too young to be transplanted. But the shock of Lucy Elizabeth's death made him change his mind. Polly was growing older; she had been six when he quit America—now she was nine. He yearned for her, fearing she might forget him entirely with the passage of the years; and he wanted to reunite what remained to him of immediate family.

It was not easy, however, to accomplish his purpose. The voyage for a small girl was long and arduous, and a proper guardian had to be found to accompany her across the Atlantic; while the threat of capture by piratical corsairs was ever present. Almost two years, indeed, elapsed between the time when the plan first formed in his mind and its final execution.

In August, 1785, he asked Francis Eppes, his brother-in-law, to find some agreeable passenger en route to France to take her in charge; in September his determination almost failed him. "No event of your life," he wrote Mrs. Eppes, "has put it into your power to conceive how I feel when I reflect that such a child, and so dear to me, is to cross the ocean, is to be exposed to all the sufferings and risks, great and small, to which a situation on board a ship exposes everyone. I drop my pen at the thought—but she must come." [1]

But Polly proved unexpectedly stubborn. She was happy enough with her uncle and aunt and playmate cousins; and her memory of her distant father had already dimmed. It took bribes, exhortations and cajoleries to get the willful little miss finally on board ship.

Jefferson had asked that she be sent only in a French or English vessel, since their countries had treaties with the Barbary pirates and were therefore supposedly immune from capture; and gave careful instructions that the ship be sound, "neither new nor old, sailing in the months of April, May, June or July under the care of a trusty person." He added an illuminating footnote: "We all pant for America, as will every American who comes to Europe." [2]

It was the spring of 1787, however, before Polly undertook the long voyage, accompanied by a Negro maid, and under the supervision of Captain Ramsay, the master of the ship. She duly arrived in London in June, where she was met by Abigail Adams. The child, however, had become so attached to the worthy captain during the days on shipboard that Abigail had to employ stratagems to decoy her on shore and into her care.[3]

At first she cried for the departed captain, but Abigail's blandishments finally had their effect and the affections of the little girl were transferred with equal fervor to her.

By the time Jefferson had sent his man, Petit, to London to convey Polly to Paris, the attachment between the pair had grown to such proportions that force had practically to be used to pry Polly away from Mrs. Adams's skirts and place her into the waiting carriage. Abigail, her own children now fully grown, was almost as loath to part with her. "A finer child of her age I never saw," she declared. "So mature an understanding, so womanly a behaviour, and so much sensibility, united, are rarely to be met with. I grew so fond of her, and she was so attached to me, that, when Mr. Jefferson sent for her, they were obliged to force the little creature away.... I regret," she added with Puritan directness, "that such fine spirits must be spent in the wall of a convent." [4]

It was, in fact, Jefferson's intention to place Polly in the convent at Panthemont, together with her older sister, Patsy. He was well satisfied with the care which the nuns had tendered Patsy and, at least at this time, had none of Abigail's fear that proselytism might be intended.

On July 15, 1787, the child reached Paris. To Jefferson's distress she had only the faintest recollection of him and none of Patsy.[5] They had to become acquainted all over again. It did not take long, however, and, within the week, she was safely ensconced in the convent, coming to Paris once or twice a week to visit her father.

Panthemont was, Jefferson assured his sister, Mary Bolling, "a house of education altogether, the best in France, and at which the best masters attend. There are in it as many Protestants as Catholics, and not a word is ever spoken to them on the subject of religion." [6]

The educator and the pedagogue were ever dominant in Jefferson. "I need not tell you," he wrote Patsy in 1786, "what pleasure it gives me to see you improve in every thing agreeable & useful. The more you learn the more I love you, & I rest the happiness of my life on seeing you beloved by all the world." [7]

She had asked him for 15 livres as an anticipation of five weeks' allowance. He accompanied the remittance with a moral essay: "This is a departure from that rule which I wish to see you governed by, thro' your whole life, of never buying any thing which you have not money in your pocket to pay for."[8] Jefferson, however, never followed his own eminently sage advice.

From Aix, he had also exhorted Patsy that "idleness begets ennui, ennui the hypochondria, & that a diseased body. No laborious person was ever yet hysterical." He had heard she was unable to read Livy without her master's aid. "If you always lean on your master, you will never be able to proceed without him," he scolded. "It is a part of the American character to consider nothing as desperate; to surmount every difficulty by resolution & contrivance. In Europe there are shops for every want. Its inhabitants therefore have no idea that their wants can be furnished otherwise. Remote from all other aid, we are obliged to invent & to execute; to find means within ourselves, & not to lean on others." But he softened the blow with pathos. "Retirement from public life will ere long become necessary for me," he reminded her. "To your sister and yourself I look to render the evening of my life serene and contented. Its morning has been clouded by loss after loss, till I have nothing left but you." [9]

Patsy was not the only one to feel the weight of Jefferson's exhortations. He was similarly superintending the education of his nephew, Peter Carr, at long range.

Young Peter had originally been placed by Madison, to whom Jefferson entrusted him, in a grammar school; but he accepted Wythe's invitation in April, 1786, to attend William and Mary and, at the same time, listen to his law lectures. The pupil in Williamsburg and the uncle in Paris kept up a regular correspondence. Peter dutifully wrote of his studies and Jefferson sent books and advice; both by the trunkload.[10]

Peter seems to have had an inquiring turn of mind. For one thing, he disagreed with Jefferson's dictum that no American should go to Europe before he was thirty; *he* had "an invincible inclination to see the world." Similarly, he was troubled about the elderly and very much extolled Mr. Wythe. He was reading privately with him such authors as Herodotus, Sophocles, Cicero and Horace. And Wythe had also placed Lucretius in his hands. Wythe, however, so Peter was given to understand, "is said to be without religion, but to me he appears to possess the most rational part of it." Would Jefferson therefore give him some advice on that same controversial subject of religion, "as I think it time to be fixed on a point which has had so many advocates and opponents, and, still seems to be dubious." [11]

This was the kind of poser that all parents, guardians and educators must eventually meet. Jefferson braced himself, and sat down to write a long reply from which, in spite of necessarily cautious adjustments to an unformed mind, much of his own religious philosophy may be discovered.

After a short discussion of other studies, among which he contemptuously dismissed moral philosophy as a waste of time, he plunged *in medias res.*

"Your reason is now mature enough to examine this object [of religion]," he began. To contemplate it properly one must, on the one hand, eschew all novelty for novelty's sake; on the other, shake off all fears and servile prejudices. "Fix reason firmly in her seat," Jefferson advised, "and call to her tribunal every fact, every opinion. Question with boldness even the existence of a god; because, if there be one, he must more approve of the homage of reason, than that of blindfolded fear.... Read the bible then, as you would read Livy or Tacitus. The facts which are within the ordinary course of nature you will believe on the authority of the writer, as you do those of the same kind in Livy & Tacitus.... But those facts in the bible which contradict the laws of nature, must be examined with more care, and under a variety of faces. Here you must recur to the pretensions of the writer to inspiration from god. Examine upon what evidence his pretensions are founded."

For example, there was the tale of Joshua and the sun which stood still at his command. No one would believe this if Livy or Tacitus had asserted it. Why then believe it merely because it appears in the Bible? You are astronomer enough, Jefferson told his nephew, to know that the earth revolves on its axis; and that such a sudden stoppage of a revolving body would have "prostrated animals, trees, buildings." Peter must therefore consider: "Is this arrest of the earth's motion, or the evidence which affirms it, most within the law of probabilities?" It is obvious where Jefferson's own opinion lay.

With a similar attention to probabilities and reason he discussed the New Testament, which "is the history of a personage called Jesus." On the one hand it was claimed that "he was begotten by god, born of a virgin, suspended & reversed the laws of nature at will, & ascended bodily into heaven"; on the other, that "he was a man of illegitimate birth, of a benevolent heart, enthusiastic mind, who set out without pretensions to divinity, ended in believing them, & was punished capitally for sedition by being gibbeted according to the Roman law." Jefferson did not attempt to resolve the contradiction; but here, again, it is evident that he took the latter view. He was willing to leave the final solution to young Peter; advising him, however, on the manner in which this and other problems ought to be approached.

Examine these questions in books, he wrote, "but keep your reason firmly on the watch in reading them all. Do not be frightened from this inquiry by any fear of its consequences. If it ends in a belief that there is no god, you will find incitements to virtue in the comfort & pleasantness you feel in its exercise, and the love of others which it will procure you. If you find reason to believe there is a god, a consciousness that you are acting under his eye, & that he approves you, will be a vast additional incitement; if that there be a future state, the hope of a happy existence in that increases the appetite to deserve it; if that Jesus was also a god, you will be comforted by a belief of his aid and love. In fine, I repeat that you must lay aside all prejudice on both sides, & neither believe nor reject anything because any other persons, or descriptions of persons have rejected or believed it." [12]

Jefferson himself was never to deviate from the rule of reason which he laid down for his young nephew; and if he left some of the fundamental doctrines of religion thus delicately suspended in mid-air, he was later to enunciate in plain language just what his own private beliefs were. He never, however, attempted to foist them on others and, in turn, demanded a similar reserve on their part with respect to himself.

Jefferson found much to occupy him officially on his return to Paris after his extended jaunt through the south of France and the northern sector of Italy. Both Europe and America were in turmoil; and he was compelled to shift his attention from one to the other with great rapidity and to balance their respective relations with great care.

Naturally, the events at home engrossed his attention the most, even though he was compelled to remain, by reason of distance from the scene, a mere spectator of the new revolution through which his beloved country was passing. He was not entirely a spectator, however; for, through influential friends at home like Madison, Monroe, Joseph Jones, Edward Carrington and others who sought his comments and advice, if they did not always follow them, he was able to add his weight to one side of the fight then raging.

It had long been realized by many sensible men—and Jefferson had been among them—that the Articles of Confederation under which the several States had been acting were inadequate for a solid and enduring union. Jefferson's experiences in Europe had only strengthened the conviction at which he had arrived as a member of Congress, that, until teeth were put into the compact, particularly in the raising of money and in foreign relations, America would never command the respect of the rest of the world or be able to enforce its own proper demands. He had even gone so far on occasion to express a wish that Congress be empowered to use force against recalcitrant States.

Among those at home who were convinced that the time had come for action were Madison and Alexander Hamilton. Of the brilliant, young and cocksure Hamilton, Jefferson knew very little at this time. They had probably met at some of the sessions of Congress, though there is no mention of any personal relationship in any of their discussions of Congressional events. Hamilton, illegitimately born in the West Indies, had come as a boy to study on the mainland, and had early made his mark as an orator, pamphleteer, soldier, lawyer and strong nationalist.

Infuriated with the squabbles of the States, alarmed by the portent of Shays' Rebellion—which Jefferson from his vantage point in Paris had viewed with considerable complacency—and determined to mold a strong, centralized government along English lines which would respect property rights at home and assume a powerful position abroad, Hamilton issued a call in 1786 for a Convention at Annapolis to discuss, as he put it, certain more binding commercial arrangements among the States. Actually, he hoped under this cover to come to a binding agreement on political questions as well.

Madison knew of the real reason for the Convention and so informed Jefferson. "Many Gentlemen both within & without Congress," he wrote, "wish to make this Meeting subservient to a plenipotentiary Convention for amending the Confederation. Tho' my wishes are in favor of such an event; yet I despair so much of its accomplishment at the present crisis that

I do not extend my views beyond a commercial Reform. To speak the truth I almost despair even of this." [13]

The Annapolis Convention was so poorly attended that it did not attempt to function; but Hamilton cannily caused the delegates present to issue a bold call for another meeting at which amendments to the Articles of Confederation themselves would be discussed. After much agitation and shilly-shallying such a Convention was called, this time to meet in Philadelphia in May, 1787.

Washington and Madison both strongly approved of the call, and wrote Jefferson to tell him so. "That something is necessary," remarked Washington, "none will deny; for the situation of the general government, if it can be called a government, is shaken to its foundation, and liable to be overturned by every blast. In a word, it is at an end; and, unless a remedy is soon applied, anarchy and confusion will inevitably ensue." [14]

Madison had now come around from despair to hope. "The names of the members will satisfy you that the States have been serious in this business. The attendance of Genl. Washington is a proof of the light in which he regards it. The whole Community is big with expectation. And there can be no doubt but that the result will in some way or other have a powerful effect on our destiny." [15]

At this point in his career Madison was as strong a nationalist as Washington and almost as strong a one as Hamilton. He was willing to go so far even as "to arm the federal head with a negative *in all cases whatsoever* on the local Legislatures." [16] Such a veto power went far beyond anything Jefferson had ever contemplated; and he so retorted, with the result that Madison never again adverted to it. Jefferson also insisted that the Executive power be separated from the Legislative, and that the Judiciary be independent of both.[17]

"To make us one nation as to foreign concerns, & keep us distinct in Domestic ones, gives the outline of the proper division of power between the general & particular governments." He had already written this to Madison as the *sine qua non* of a proper and just union among the States.[18]

As reports of proceedings moved their slow way across the Atlantic to him, Jefferson must have felt that helplessness which comes to a man keenly interested in the event, yet so far removed from it that he can do nothing but watch and pray, and hope that some suggestion of his might reach America in time to help modify or strengthen a decision already in the making.

One of the first decisions of the infant Convention—that of secret sessions—moved him to anger. "I am sorry," he wrote John Adams in London, "they began their deliberations by so abominable a precedent as that of tying up the tongues of their members. Nothing can justify their example but the innocence of their intentions, and ignorance of the value of public discussions." He took the edge off his criticism, however, by expressing his assurance "that all their other measures will be good and wise. It is really an assembly of demigods." [19]

The assembly of demigods worked through the long summer months of 1787 to hammer out a new frame of government that would at once be workable and at the same time satisfy the diverse interests of the several States and of the various classes of society of which they were composed. Their deliberations were secret; but rumors fled abroad, and Jefferson was kept as well informed as was possible at that distance of the issues involved by some of the participating delegates.

The story of the Constitution-making has been told many times, and it is unnecessary to repeat it here. What interests us particularly are Jefferson's varying reactions to the reports he received, and the nature of his suggestions during the process.

Reports had filtered through that there were those in America who thought a kingly government was the only one that could avoid anarchy and chaos. Jefferson denied this vehemently. He advised the advocates of a monarchy to read the fable of the frogs and King Stork. "If that does not put them to rights," he added, "send them to Europe to see something of the trappings of monarchy, and I will undertake that every man shall go back thoroughly cured." [20]

He still believed that Congress was not as helpless to enforce its decisions on the States under the old Articles of Confederation as was pretended, particularly in the collection of money levies. Even though no such power was expressly mentioned in the Articles, "they have it by the law of nature," he argued. "When two parties make a compact, there results to each a power of compelling the other to execute it. Compulsion was never so easy as in our case, where a single frigate would soon levy on the commerce of any state the deficiency of its contributions." [21]

He had reverted to this idea of compulsion on several occasions; and it furnishes a clue to some of the seeming inconsistencies in Jefferson's philosophy of government. How, for example, reconcile this assertion of the power of the central government to employ force, if necessary, to compel State obedience to its decrees with the later doctrine of the Kentucky Resolution that the States were sovereign entities who could declare an act of Congress null and void? The answer lies in Jefferson's reiterated distinction between foreign and domestic affairs. In foreign matters—for which the contributions were intended—Congress was supreme and representative of a unity. In domestic matters, on the other hand—even under the Constitution—the States were supreme and Congress representative of a federated group of sovereign powers.

At length the deliberations of the Constitutional Convention were over; the great debate was ended; and the final document was turned over to the States for ratification or rejection. A new debate commenced—this time in the open; parties emerged and passions grew high. The Constitution had necessarily been a thing of many compromises, and both extremes inveighed against it. The chief objections, however, came from the members of what, in modern terms, might be called the left—the democrats, the radicals, the upholders of States' rights. If Hamilton, though supporting the Constitution, thought it a poor thing and a baseless fabric which was too weak to last, the members of the left shouted that it was monarchical in essence, a powerful instrument to subvert the States, and an economic weapon in the hands of the rich and the merchants to crush the farmer and the poor.

William S. Smith, John Adams's son-in-law, sent a copy of the new Constitution to Jefferson from London. It beat the copy that Madison forwarded from Philadelphia by some three weeks. Jefferson's first reaction was mixed. "There are very good articles in it; & very bad," he told Smith. "I do not know which preponderate." He particularly did not like the idea of "a chief magistrate eligible for a long duration." In every constitution which he himself had drafted he had insisted on a short term for the Chief Executive and his ineligibility for re-election. More than anything else he feared the possibility that a strong executive, so eligible, would use the power of his office to perpetuate himself in that office and thereby set up a life tenure which might have hereditary overtones.

He wanted the article, which he believed to have been inserted because of the revolt in Massachusetts, eliminated from the final document. That revolt—Shays' Rebellion—did not mean that anarchy existed in America, he declared with some heat. "Can history produce an instance of rebellion so honourably conducted?" he demanded. Its motives "were founded in ignorance, not wickedness. God forbid we should ever be 20 years without such a rebellion.... what country can preserve its liberties if their rulers are not warned from time to time that their people preserve the spirit of resistance? Let them take arms. The remedy is to set them right as to facts, pardon & pacify them. What signifies a few lives lost in a century or two? The tree of liberty must be refreshed from time to time with the blood of patriots & tyrants. It is its natural manure." [22]

This is perhaps one of the most famous outbursts ever penned by Jefferson, and the most widely quoted of his sayings with the exception of certain passages in the Declaration of Independence. Resistance to tyranny was a right of nature—whether that tyranny was political, social, economic, religious or mental. Later on, he was to swear on the altar of Almighty God to fight tyranny in every form; nor was he ever to deviate from his fixed belief in the right of the people to defend their liberty and their natural rights with arms in their hands. Even a misguided revolution—provided it stemmed from generous convictions—was preferable to none at all. He ever viewed with suspicion the rulers of mankind and considered them eternally eager to grasp at absolute power unless checked by a wholesome fear of resistance and revolt. He also believed—somewhat naïvely—that the mass of people, once acquainted with the facts, would act rationally and be guided in all their relations by them; that wicked men could instigate revolutions among the people only if the true facts and their rational consequences had been completely withheld from them.

The delayed copy of the Constitution forwarded by Madison with his extended analysis of its provisions reached Jefferson by the middle of December. Since Madison had been its foremost advocate and philosophical father, it was only natural that his comments should be on the whole favorable, though he was careful to point out the defects of the completed instrument as well as its merits. There would be difficulty in getting it adopted in Virginia, he warned. Only three of the Virginia delegates had subscribed their names to the instrument; Edmund Randolph, now Governor, and George Mason had refused. Mason considered "the want of a Bill of Rights as a fatal objection."[23]

With Madison's informed comments at hand, Jefferson studied the document afresh. There were certain things that he liked: the fact of a general government "without needing continual recurrence to the state legislatures"; the division into three co-ordinate departments; the power of the Legislature to levy taxes, "and for that reason [I] solely approve of the greater house [House of Representatives] being chosen by the people directly." He went on to explain this somewhat startling statement—though it must be remembered that he had similarly expressed his distrust of direct elections at an earlier date. "For," he said, "tho' I think a house chosen by them will be very ill qualified to legislate for the Union, for foreign nations &c. yet this evil does not weigh against the good of preserving inviolate the fundamental principle that the people are not to be taxed but by representatives chosen immediately by themselves."

He also liked the series of compromises between the large and small States whereby their interests were mutually protected; and he approved the qualified veto power given the President over Congress, though he would have preferred to have had the Supreme Court associated in that power, or given "a similar and separate power." Had such a veto been given to the Court as Jefferson suggested, subject to being overridden by a two-thirds vote of Congress, it would have prevented *ab initio* the long struggle between the Supreme Court and the other branches of government over the right of the Court to declare an act of Congress unconstitutional.

Having thus disposed of the things he liked, Jefferson took up those to which he definitely objected. First and foremost was the omission from the document of a Bill of Rights—such restraints on the Federal Government against abuses of the rights of the people as had been incorporated in the constitution of Virginia. Provision must be made, he insisted, "clearly & without the aid of sophisms for freedom of religion, freedom of the press, protection against standing armies, restriction against monopolies, the eternal & unremitting force of the habeas corpus laws, and trials by jury in all matters of fact triable by the laws of the land & not by the law of nations." He refused to listen to the argument that such might be inferred from the reservations in the document. "A bill of rights," he declared, "is what the people are entitled to against every government on earth, general or particular, & what no just government should refuse, or rest on inferences."

He also disliked most heartily the abandonment of the principles of rotation in office and ineligibility for re-election, which he now discussed with equal vehemence and at equal length as in his letter to Col. Smith. It was a sore spot with him.

These, then, were his two main objections to the Constitution—the lack of a Bill of Rights and the failure to prohibit re-election to office.

The practical issue therefore arose—how keep the good things, and eliminate the bad? Should it be done by adopting the present instrument now and moving for future amendments, or by recalling the Convention into session and amending immediately? There were objections to both courses, and Jefferson left the matter open for Madison's consideration.

He owned, however, that he was "not a friend to a very energetic government. It is always oppressive." He also believed "that the will of the majority should always prevail"; and if the people decided to adopt the Constitution as it stood, he would cheerfully concur, merely hoping that in the future they would choose to amend those parts which were proved to be wrong.

He concluded his lengthy letter with another of his pet topics. He expected the governments in America to remain virtuous for many centuries; *provided* they were chiefly agricultural and there were vacant lands for the poor to occupy. But, should "they get piled upon one another in large cities, as in Europe, they will become corrupt as in Europe. Above all things I hope the education of the common people will be attended to; convinced that on their good sense we may rely with the most security for the preservation of a due degree of liberty."[24] On this note he ended.

As the long struggle over ratification unfolded, Jefferson moved gradually from his earliest position of neutrality through various stages toward an advocacy of adoption. By February, 1788, he was declaring to William S. Smith that "were I in America, I would advocate [the Constitution] warmly till nine [the number of States necessary for ratification] should have adopted & then as warmly take the other side to convince the remaining four that they ought not to come into it till the declaration of rights is annexed to it." By this time he was willing, albeit reluctantly, to yield on the principle of re-eligibility for office; since no one else in America seemed to fear it as much as he did.[25]

By June, he had veered wholly over, and was now convinced that the best plan was to adopt the Constitution as it was, and amend it later.[26]

In his earliest stage he had inquired of John Adams how he liked the proposed Constitution and indicated his own objections, going so far as to suggest that perhaps it might be best to incorporate its good parts into three or four articles "to be added to the good, old and venerable fabric" of the

Articles of Confederation, "which should have been preserved even as a religious relique." [27]

That sturdy gentleman replied that he too had objections, but they were not Jefferson's. "You are afraid of the one—I, of the few. We agree perfectly that the many should have a full fair and perfect Representation.—You are Apprehensive of Monarchy; I, of Aristocracy.—I would therefore have given more Power to the President and less to the Senate." He had no fear of the President being chosen again and again. "So much the better," he exclaimed. "Elections, my dear sir, Elections to Offices which are great objects of ambition, I look at with terror." [28]

Madison, watching from afar the slow evolution of Jefferson's thought, noted that he was steadily becoming more and more a friend to the Constitution, though he never wavered in his insistence on a Bill of Rights, at least as a future amendment, nor in his fears on the principle of re-eligibility.[29]

Even when Madison sent him the *Federalist Papers*—that tremendous series of pamphlets which Madison, Hamilton and Jay had dashed off in the heat of controversy to help swing the tide toward ratification—Jefferson read, was impressed, yet stuck to his guns on these two issues. He thought that Jay had nothing to do with the *Papers*, that Hamilton "not a great deal," and that Madison, the third, had written the most of them. "It does the highest honor to the third," he praised warmly, "as being, in my opinion, the best commentary on the principles of government which was ever written." [30] Aside from his belittlement of Hamilton's share and his cavalier dismissal of Jay, his estimate of the *Papers* was remarkably accurate.

The matter of the Bill of Rights was shortly thereafter rectified by appropriate amendments; the other objection was never legally remedied. What Jefferson had seen firsthand of the kings of Europe made him almost pathologically fearful of the institution taking root in America. "I was much an enemy to monarchy before I came to Europe," he told Washington. "I am ten thousand times more so since I have seen what they are." He could safely say that "there is not a crowned head in Europe whose talents or merits would entitle him to be elected a vestryman by the people of any parish in America." [31]

In later years he finally agreed that perhaps the idea of two terms of four years each for the President, with the privilege of rejecting him for the second term, was better than his original idea of a single term of seven years. Though never formally written into law, Jefferson believed that the example which Washington and he had set of retiring after two terms would be faithfully followed in the future; and, if not, that the people would decisively reject the ambitious aspirant.[32] He was correct for over a hundred years; until Franklin D. Roosevelt upset all traditions and was nominated and elected for four consecutive terms.

CHAPTER 26

Public Debts and Rhine Journey

WHILE events in America were thus pressing rapidly toward a beneficent conclusion, events in Europe were moving with equal rapidity toward a series of tremendous cataclysms whereby the revolutions of which Jefferson spoke were encompassed on a scale beyond anything he had ever imagined, and his tree of liberty was to be manured with so much blood of patriots and tyrants and of those who were neither that the tree itself eventually became choked in the process.

As a neutral diplomat in Paris, the heart of ensuing convulsion, Jefferson became both a favored spectator and almost a participant. Yet he could not lay claim to any prophetic vision. True, he had correctly assayed the misery of the people, the cruelty of the institutions and the heartless pomp of the courts; but he did not see the revolution moving up with seven-league boots, and it came upon him full force almost before he was aware that it had begun.

He was more interested for the moment in gaining from France certain advantageous commercial arrangements for America and in settling the complicated American debts with foreign creditors. The Comte de Vergennes, with whom he had been able to discuss, if not to settle, their points of dispute in the friendliest fashion, had died; and the Comte de Montmorin had taken his place as Minister of Foreign Affairs. Montmorin was an equally pleasant, though not an equally able individual.

Lafayette's ardent co-operation in everything that affected his second country proved of the utmost value. By the end of 1786, Jefferson was able to report home that he had overcome some of the hurdles which American commerce faced in French ports, and he hoped eventually to gain entry into the French colonies as well, especially for fish and flour.[1] He was also trying to get Honfleur declared a free port of deposit for American goods and he envisioned it as a vast storage depot for American whale oil, rice, tobacco and furs; from which sales could be made to all parts of France and to neighboring countries.[2]

In July, 1787, he made a determined effort to come to an agreement with Montmorin on all moot points. The first, and sorest, point was the famous tobacco contract with Robert Morris. Jefferson recapitulated the history of this "double" monopoly and the decision of the French government not to renew the contract on its expiration date. Furthermore, Vergennes had ordered the farmers-general to purchase of others, on an equal basis with Morris, twelve to fifteen thousand hogsheads a year. Jefferson suspected that the order had not been obeyed, and requested an investigation. He also pressed urgently for complete, unrestricted trade in all categories between the United States and France.[3]

With the new ministry friendly, Jefferson believed that he could successfully accomplish these aims; but the unpaid debts which America owed to the King, the officers and the farmers-general of Europe were a constant source of irritation. He wrote to Adams to see if it was possible to hypothecate these debts by transferring them into private Dutch hands. True, they would not have been paid; but the French would be out of the picture and the renegotiation would furnish a breathing spell to the United States.[4]

A little later, Jefferson was writing home to Madison that he had heard Adams had managed to raise some money in Holland. If this was so, then Congress must borrow sufficient to pay off *all* the French debt. Matters had taken such a turn that France was on the verge of bankruptcy. For the first time he noted the possibility of a convulsion. "Such a spirit has risen within a few weeks as could not have been believed," he declared. Revenues were deficient, Parlement had refused to register any new taxes, demanding instead the convocation of a States-General; the king had taken to drink, the queen is detested; "and an explosion of some sort is not impossible." [5]

Less than a month and a half before, Jefferson had written that "the King loves business, economy, order & justice, and wishes sincerely the good of his people"; though admitting that he was rude, bigoted and limited in understanding.[6]

The payment of debts was more than a mere general problem to Jefferson; it was deeply personal as well. In spite of all his own promises, he had been unable to clear away even a part of the accumulated and long-outstanding accounts of the British merchants. His scheme to pay annual installments out of the profits of his estates had backfired; there were little or no profits. He found that the keep of his slaves ate up the avails of his tobacco, and that it was far more profitable to hire them out to other planters than to use them to farm his own lands. He had once thought of selling his lands, but now he decided against it; preferring rather to hire out both land and slaves to perhaps more fortunate or able cultivators.

"I cannot decide to sell my lands," he wrote his agent in Virginia. "I have sold too much of them already, and they are the only sure provision for my children, nor would I willingly sell the slaves as long as there remains any prospect of paying my debts with their labor." Would the agent therefore try to rent both land and slaves in small parcels. He realized that "we cannot guard the negroes perfectly against the [ill?] usuage, but in a question between hiring & selling them (one of which is necessary) the hiring will be temporary only, and will end in their happiness; whereas if we sell them, they will be subject to equal ill usuage, without a prospect of change." [7] Slavery, to a humane master, was evidently a good deal of a burden.

To cap his misfortunes, Jefferson's personal finances were exhausted, and the French agent, M. Grand, had advanced so much for Jefferson and Short that he refused any further requests. In desperation, Jefferson wrote to Adams to arrange for funds to come to him from Holland. Adams complied.[8]

With personal debts troubling him, with official debts irritating the French, with a revolution in the offing, Jefferson nevertheless managed to win a resounding victory—at least on paper—for his country. The French government finally yielded to his persistent, unrelenting campaign for better terms for American trade and, on December 29, 1789, issued an order in Council "for the encouragement of the commerce of France with the United States of America."

That order provided that American whale oil and spermaceti might be brought to France in either American or French ships, subject to a duty only of 7 livres, 10 sols the barrel. Other American fish oils, as well as dried and salted fish, were to pay no greater duties than those paid by the Hanseatic towns or other most favored nations. Agricultural products, potash, skins, furs and timber were to be subject to a ⅛ per cent duty. Vessels built in the United States and sold to Frenchmen were to be wholly exempt. Turpentine, tar and pitch were to pay 2½ per cent duty. American goods were to be permitted an entrepôt for six months in "all the ports of France open to the commerce of her colonies." All nonspecified merchandise was to enter France under the same privileges as that belonging to French subjects. The United States was to receive most-favored-nations privileges in the French colonies in America.[9]

Jefferson had finally cracked the solid wall of French mercantilism, and had gained substantial advantages for his country. Unfortunately, they had barely been achieved when most of the foreseeable gains were dissipated by the fast-approaching revolution and the onrush of more formal wars.

France had been moving headlong toward bankruptcy—a condition to which corruption, the extravagant expenditures of the Court, a tax system which rested lightly on the privileged classes and the rich and weighed heavily on the poor, the long and costly war that stemmed from the American Revolution, all contributed. Jacques Necker, the Swiss banker, as Director General of Finances, had tried with half-hearted measures to stem the tide and failed; M. de Calonne, who succeeded him with the title of Comptroller General, did no better. Slowly it dawned on all concerned that unless drastic reforms were instituted in the tax systems and in the administration of the country, France was ruined. To institute such reforms, yet at the same time gain possession of an instrument amenable to the royal will, Calonne hit upon the expedient of convoking an Assembly of the Notables—an aristocratic grouping of grandees who had met infrequently in the past and had obeyed the royal commands with submission and dispatch.

The Assembly of Notables opened on February 22, 1787, at Versailles—

and Jefferson watched the proceedings with attentive interest. Calonne made his speech and offered his proposals; but, to his surprise, the Assembly refused to submit or to obey. Instead, it launched a counterattack that drove Calonne from power, spread the abuses complained of publicly over the land, and almost turned on the King himself.

To add to the immeasurable confusion Europe, hitherto peaceful, burst into conflagration during the summer of 1787. The war came from quarters wholly unexpected to Jefferson who, not long before, had seen no cloud on the horizon except what might possibly eventuate from the death of the King of Prussia.

England had attacked the Netherlands whose Stadtholder, the Prince of Orange, was secretly in league with the enemy. A party of republican patriots attempted his overthrow, and in the ensuing civil war, all Europe was on the verge of being engulfed. Prussia attempted to intervene on the side of the Prince of Orange, France was ready to aid the Patriots, and war between England and France seemed inevitable.

The expected opening of a new and general European war posed serious problems for the United States. Would it be drawn into the vortex, or could it remain safely on the side lines? The question was thrown squarely into Jefferson's lap by the English ambassador to France. "What," he inquired, "would be the effect of the American treaty with France in the event of a war between England and France?" Jefferson answered with complete frankness that the United States would remain neutral; but, at the same time, called the Englishman's attention to the treaty clause which committed American aid if the French West Indian islands were attacked. The ambassador replied with equal frankness: "Then it will be war, for they will assuredly be attacked." [10]

If Jefferson was taken aback by this bold statement, he gave no sign. Rather, he seemed confident that the United States could remain neutral and that it was much to her advantage to be so. He weighed the possibilities in several letters home. "A war between these two powers would, at first blush," he wrote Wilson Miles Cary, "promise advantage to us. But it might perhaps do us more injury on the whole by diverting us from agriculture, our wisest pursuit, by turning us to privateering, plunging us into the vortex of speculation, engaging us to overtrade ourselves, & injuring our morals & in the end our fortunes. A steady application to agriculture with just trade enough to take off its superfluities is our wisest course." [11]

But to William Carmichael, Chargé d'Affaires in Spain, he indulged in much more realistic discourse. "Neutrality should be our plan," he avowed: "because no nation should without urgent necessity begin a second war while the debts of the former remain unpaid. The accumulation of debts is a most fearful evil." Nevertheless, he was afraid that England, though it was to her advantage not to involve us, would do just that, by harassing and seizing our ships. Such a course on their part, averred Jefferson with most engaging aplomb, would compel us to seize Canada and Nova Scotia, "which it is not our interest to possess." [12]

The war scare passed over, however, and America was given a breathing space in which to consider the reorganization of her own form of government without being compelled to take Canada and Nova Scotia.

While Jefferson was thus engaged with problems of war, diplomacy and revolution, he did not permit his intellectual, social or even emotional life to atrophy. He kept up a varied correspondence with learned men and savants all over the world, and was ready to discuss with equal enthusiasm a new invention or a new theory of the beginning of the world.

To Charles Thomson in Philadelphia, he described the use of steam power he had witnessed in the mills of London, and predicted a glowing future for the new engine. But he was much more unfortunate in his theories concerning the formation of the earth. He cast aside with contempt the suggestion that the earth had once been hot and fluid, and that mountains and valleys were the result of upthrusts from within. Jefferson thought that any such theory cast doubt on the abilities and resourcefulness of the Creator, since it required two special creations from him instead of one: the first, for the world; the second, after waiting ages for his first handiwork to cool and compose itself, for the fashioning of plants, animals and men to inhabit it. How did he then account for the observed strata and distortions in rocks? "It is now generally agreed that rock grows, and it seems that it grows in layers in every direction, as the branches of trees grow in all directions. Why seek further the solution of this phenomenon?" [13] Why, indeed!

He was happier in his attribution of a remote antiquity to the settlement of America, and to the close relationship between the American Indians and the inhabitants of eastern Asia. He argued the antiquity from the vast variety and complete disparity of the current Indian tongues. "The time necessary for the generation of so many languages must be immense," he thought.[14]

Jefferson's interest in every new scientific theory of the age was insatiable; but, as has already been noted, he did not always apply to them the cool logic and analytical training of the true scientist. A letter which he wrote to the Reverend James Madison contains as many fallacious observations on current theories and discoveries as it is possible for a single missive to contain. He ridiculed, for example, the discovery by the great English astronomer, Sir John Herschel, of mountains and dead volcanoes on the moon. With a fine scorn he placed Herschel's observations "among the other vagaries of a head, which seems not organized for sound deduction. The wildness of the theories hitherto proposed by him, on his own discoveries, seems to authorize us to consider his merit as that of a good optician only."

He treated with a similar contempt the theory of Dr. Ingenhouse that light promoted the growth of vegetation. He did indeed suppose that sunlight might affect colors; but that living bodies received "*nutriment* from that fluid, must be permitted to be doubted of, till better confirmed by observation. It is always better to have no ideas, than false ones; to believe nothing, than to believe what is wrong."

Even on the great experiments in chemistry conducted at the time by Lavoisier, he managed to go wrong. True, he disagreed with Buffon, who considered chemistry as just so much cookery, while Jefferson thought it "among the most useful of sciences, and big with future discoveries for the utility and safety of the human race." But he considered Lavoisier's attempt to reform the ancient and outmoded system of chemical nomenclature as premature, and was wholly blind to the implications of his work as the beginning of modern chemistry.[15]

Jefferson's circle of friends—that which had involved him so emotionally and had departed for England—was now beginning to return to Paris. The harbinger was the young painter John Trumbull, who was expected in time for the Salon exhibition. While still on his tour of France, Jefferson wrote him cordially: "Your apartment here will expect you, & that you become a part of our family again. Tell mrs Cosway she is an inconstant. She was to have been in Paris long ago, but she has deceived us. The first evening that I find myself seated in a comfortable inn, warm, solitary, & pensive, I [will?] invite her to sup, and will commit our conversation to writing. It will be a very scolding one on my part. In the mean time lay all my affections at her feet, desire her to write to me to comfort me on my journey." [16] The old leaven was beginning to work again.

It was August 28, 1787, when the fair charmer finally arrived in Paris, this time without her husband, to remain for four months. Trumbull followed her shortly, both to see the exhibition and to paint his battle picture of the Siege of Yorktown. It seemed like old times again. The trio once more made the rounds of salons and ateliers, and shared a mutual admiration for the work of Jacques-Louis David. Maria Cosway, herself a talented artist, was ecstatic over him; and Jefferson caught something of her enthusiasm. "I do not feel an interest in any pencil but that of David," he was to write.[17]

But it was not quite like old times. Perhaps the absence of the essential husband compelled them both to be more circumspect; perhaps Maria's ambition to make her way in her art required the adjunct of a great salon thronged by potential customers. In any event, Jefferson saw her, as he put it, only "by scraps." [18]

By December, Maria was returning to London. She was to leave on a Saturday, and she invited Jefferson to breakfast with her before she took coach. But when he arrived, he found that the bird had flown at five in the morning. A note was all that remained, scribbled the night before. "I cannot breakfast with you tomorrow; to bid you adieu once, is sufficiently painful, for I leave you with very melancholy ideas. You have given my dear sir all your commissions to Mr Trumbell [*sic*], and I have the reflection that I cannot be useful to you; who have rendered me so many civilities." [19]

The flight was essential; who knew what spark might have kindled from the solitary tête-à-tête? Safe in London again, Maria repeated her regrets and her misery at leaving Paris. But she offered him a substitute. "Have you seen yet the lovely Mrs. Church? . . . If I did not love her so much I would fear her rivalship. But no, I give you free permission to love her with all your heart and I shall be happy if you keep me in a little corner of it, when you admit her even to reign queen." [20]

Yes, Jefferson had met "the lovely Mrs. Church," and had been duly conquered. Concealing his mortification over Maria's erratic action, he reported: "I never saw her before: but I find in her all the good the world has given her credit for. I do not wonder at your fondness for each other." [21]

This new entry upon the scene of Jefferson's circle of fair women was a most interesting one. Born Angelica Schuyler, the daughter of General Philip Schuyler, she had eloped from her Albany home during the Revolution with an Englishman whose real name was John Barker Church, but who, for reasons of his own, had masqueraded in America under the name of John Carter. Having made his fortune in the United States, he and Angelica went to England to live in lavish style, and Church eventually entered Parliament, where his abilities proved most modest. Angelica's sister, Elizabeth, shortly thereafter married the youthful Alexander Hamilton.

Angelica Church, witty, charming, intelligent, enamored of the social world and a trifle flighty, passionately adored her brilliant brother-in-law even after the waters of the Atlantic had separated them; and there were those who placed a darker construction on their intimacy when she eventually returned to America to meet Hamilton in the flesh. By contrast her husband, shrewd enough and unscrupulous enough as a business man, appeared stodgy and lumpish.[22]

This was the lady whom Jefferson now met in Paris. She, too, had come without her husband, but attended by her little daughter Kitty, whom she placed in the same school at Panthemont as Jefferson's Patsy and Polly. Of approximately the same age as Polly, the two little girls became great friends. So did their respective parents. But there was a difference in tone between Jefferson's relationship with the lively Angelica Church and that with Maria Cosway. The former was a very gallant one, indeed, and the letters they exchanged were full of the usual terms of endearment and occasional light-hearted reproaches; but the overtones and the latent emotional depths of the latter were missing.

Angelica returned to London in February, 1788, and Jefferson rode with her to Saint-Denis to speed her on the way; later spending the evening with

Madame de Corny "where we talked over our woes." Kitty had been left behind, and Jefferson solaced himself for the absence of the new charmer by visiting Kitty and his own daughters at Panthemont.[23]

He kept up an extended correspondence with her, quite gallant in the accepted mode and bantering in tone. He had Kitty, Patsy and Polly to Sunday dinner, he wrote Angelica, and wished her presence, too. After being "worn down every morning with writing on business, I sally at 12. o'clock into the bois de Boulogne, and unbend my labours by thinking on my friends." When, somewhat later, he contemplated returning to America, and heard that she was similarly situated, why should they not, he asked, go together? "Think of it then, my friend, and let us begin a negociation on the subject. You shall find in me all the spirit of accomodation with which Yoric began his with the fair Piedmontese." [24] Bantering though the tone might be, to anyone who has read the history of that "negociation" in Sterne, this proposition is one of the most curious that Jefferson had ever permitted himself in writing to any woman.

Jefferson had some curious notions on the subject of women generally. At a time when Angelica was following with passionate attention the fortunes of the American Constitution in New York, where her beloved Hamilton was laboring mightily for ratification, Jefferson adverted to the struggle in New York only to dismiss it with the remark: "But that need not agitate you. The tender breasts of ladies were not formed for political convulsion; and the French ladies miscalculate much their own happiness when they wander from the field of their influence into that of politicks." [25]

Meanwhile Maria Cosway, having run away from Jefferson, was now angry that she had received only one short note from him. "Will you give Mr. Trumbull leave," she reopened the correspondence, "to make a Coppy of a certain portrait [of Jefferson] he painted at Paris? It is a person who hates you that requests this favor." [26]

In the same mail, however, came an explanation from Trumbull. "She is angry yet she teases me every day for a copy of your little portrait.—that she may scold *it* no doubt." Trumbull did not think much of the portrait himself.[27]

Trumbull finally got around to copying the picture, though Maria in her impatience accused him of being extremely dilatory. He made one also for Angelica Church, who thought he had done a better job for her friend.[28] All of which, no doubt, gratified Jefferson exceedingly.

He had one more lady on his hands—Madame de Brehan—but she left for America under strange circumstances. She had found her way into Jefferson's acquaintance in the company of other amateur artists, when her brother-in-law, the Comte de Moustier, was appointed in 1787 as the French Minister to the United States. Though she had a husband, an obscure army officer, and a child, she decided to accompany the unattached Moustier to America with her young son, but without her husband.

This was strange enough; but the conduct of the pair when they finally arrived in America was stranger still—at least to the untutored sensibilities of the Americans. Brother and sister-in-law lived together in a single ménage, and the strong suspicion arose that the unity in housing extended to other unities not strictly classical in nature. John Jay wrote to Jefferson that "appearances (whether well or ill founded is not important) have created and diffused an opinion that an improper Connection subsists between [Moustier] and the Marchioness. You can easily concieve the Influence of such an opinion on the minds and feelings of such a People as ours —For my part I regret it—she seems to be an amiable woman." [29]

Jefferson regretted it, too. He had lived long enough in France to understand, if not to admire, such *ménages à deux.* But his patience and understanding were to be sorely tested. Both Moustier and his companion grew disgruntled with America, though for different reasons; and they both complained bitterly to Jefferson of the savage land in which they found themselves. Moustier was discommoded by matters of etiquette, in which he fancied that his dignity as a Count and as a Minister was being slighted. Jefferson retorted with some asperity: "These disputes are the most insusceptible of determination, because they have no foundation in reason. Arbitrary and senseless in their nature, they are arbitrarily decided by every nation for itself." It would have been better, he added, for a new country like the United States to have excluded etiquette altogether.[30]

Madame de Brehan's plaint was different. The ladies and gentlemen of America were not fond of the "candor, simplicity and goodness" she offered them. They kept track of visits; and refused to visit again unless their former calls had been returned. "They have been too exigents [*sic*] for my health, I am not able to spend my life in paying visits; it is not possible." Madison, indeed, kept calling.[31] It seems that in spite of Jefferson's warnings, she had imagined she was going to Arcadia, where everything was simple in the style of French court ladies playing at shepherdesses; and the reality sent her into a furious displeasure.[32] Eventually the disillusioned pair returned to France, their mission having added nothing to the friendship between the two countries.

The tangled finances of the United States with relation to European debtors and the personal finances of her ministers abroad reached a climax at the beginning of 1788. As a result of defaults in payment, the credit of America was never at a lower ebb; and John Adams determined, before he quit England for his native land, as he shortly expected to do, to make a last herculean effort to clean up the mess. Holland, as the *situs* of most of the privately held debt, was his destination. Abigail apprised Jefferson of her husband's projected journey, and that he would have been delighted to meet Jefferson there; but time pressed and allowed only of a flying visit. Then, wifelike, Abigail unburdened herself of their private financial difficulties. "You have resided long enough abroad," she said, "to feel & experience how inadequate our allowence is to our decent expences. And that it is wholly impossible for any thing to be saved from it. This our countrymen in general will neither know or feel." [33]

Jefferson read the public and private parts of the letter with considerable attention. On the private end, he could sympathize most sincerely. If the Adamses, frugal and unostentatious, could not live on the ministerial salary, what about himself? His account books disclose a continuing lavish scale of expenditures which would have appalled the Adamses. Jefferson was keeping up an elaborate establishment, paying expensive fees for the education of his two daughters, providing them with lessons on the harpsichord and guitar—he had purchased a harpsichord and rented a pianoforte for his own quarters as well. He bought books wherever he could find them—Paris, London, Amsterdam; he was continually reaching into his pocket to help stranded American sailors and others; and no scientific instrument was extant of which he did not try to obtain a specimen.[34] He was anticipating both his regular salary and his private income; and neither was inexhaustible.

But it was the public debts that concerned him most. Not only the principal, but the interest payments could not be met; and Jefferson, as well as Adams, realized that a default would spell catastrophe to all future financing. He therefore seized the opportunity of Adams's hurried trip to The Hague to join him there on the same mission. Jefferson had no illusions concerning his own dexterity in financial bargaining and was glad to avail himself of his colleague's greater experience in that field.[35]

On March 4, 1788, therefore, Jefferson set out in his carriage for The Hague. He reached that ancient town on the 9th, and was fortunate enough to find Adams still there. The next morning, both diplomats started for Amsterdam where, as Jefferson told Short, "if we fail in the principal object, I shall at least have the solace of easing my own shoulders of the burthen." [36]

In Amsterdam the two men did not quite see eye to eye on what was to be done. Adams considered the whole affair as a "Plott" of the Amsterdam moneylenders, and in particular of the great banking firm of Willinks & Van Staphorst, who "have been purchasing immense Quantities of American Paper, and they now want to have it acknowledged and paid in Europe." Never! declared Adams violently. We two cannot agree to it, nor will Congress. It would be better to stop borrowing from them altogether than to establish a precedent of paying anywhere but in America. Since Adams was going home to assume his new duties as Vice-President of the United States, Jefferson would have to handle the matter himself. "I pity you, in your Situation," Adams sympathized, "dunned and teazed as you will be, all your Philosophy will be wanting to support you." But do not let them frighten you, he warned. "Depend upon it, the Amsterdammers love Money too well, to execute their Threats. They admit to gain too much by American Credit to destroy it." [37]

Jefferson was not as certain as Adams that the Dutch bankers did not mean business; and he felt, perhaps rightly, that it was better to yield the point of the place of payment for the present and obtain a new loan in order to make the payment than to insist on their rights. By so doing, the credit of the new nation would be preserved for two years longer; at the end of which time he believed that, under the new form of government, the United States would have collected sufficient taxes to meet all further obligations.

Adams grumbled and at first refused to exercise his authority to negotiate the loan; but Jefferson insisted and, as Adams put it, "would take no denial." Reluctantly at length, Adams yielded. The Dutch bankers furnished enough to pay all calls on the American debt until the end of the year, and a plan was arranged, subject to Congressional approval, for a sufficient supply to last until 1790.[38]

Adams departed, somewhat disgruntled, on March 21st; but Jefferson remained on until the 30th, completing the final negotiations. He had reason to be well satisfied with himself. For a man who knew little about the intricacies of finance, as he himself was the first to acknowledge, he had done much to clear up a festering sore in American-European relations.

With this load off his mind, Jefferson considered that he was entitled to a vacation. He wanted to see things "what I have not yet seen"; and this included the famous Rhine and parts of Germany. The jaunt would also give him a chance to renew old acquaintances with certain of the German officers who had been his Convention prisoners in Virginia. Among them were the Barons de Geismar and de Unger.[39]

As in his former tour, Jefferson kept a journal, in which he noted down those things which interested him.[40] In Amsterdam, for example, in the midst of weighty financial dealings, he had found time to enter profuse notes on how houses and windows were put together, the method of fixing the flagstaff on the mast of a vessel, a machine for drawing empty boats over a dam, types of wind sawmills, the street-door lanterns, the music of the West Church chimes, swivel canal bridges, aviaries, Dutch wheel barrows—all with sketches and designs. Nothing escaped his questing eye that might some day prove useful at home.[41]

On the 30th, he started on his travels. As he crossed the line from Holland into Prussia he was struck by the sudden transition "from ease and opulence to extreme poverty." Why was this? he wondered. The soil and climate were the same. The answer, of course, was the difference in the governments: the former, liberal and semirepublican; the latter, an absolute monarchy. He imagined he saw the visible signs of slavish fear in the faces of the Prussians, as well as their poverty.[42]

On April 2nd, he reached Düsseldorf, where he visited the art gallery and thought it "sublime, particularly the room of Vanderwerff." In his later description to Maria Cosway of this particular gallery, Jefferson unwittingly disclosed his limitations as a discriminating critic of painting. He waxed enthusiastic about such third-rate artists as Van der Werff and

Carlo Dolci, preferring them "to the old faded red things of Rubens. I am but a son of nature," he added disarmingly, "loving what I see & feel, without being able to give a reason, nor caring much whether there be one." [43] It was the old cry: "I don't know much about art; but I know what I like."

More interesting to him, perhaps, and concerning a subject on which he *could* give reasons, were the hogs from which came the famous Westphalian hams. He noted with indulgence that the people of Westphalia thought they were the only ones who smoked their bacon for curing. "They do not know that we do it." [44]

On the 4th, he was in Cologne. He had no words for the magnificent cathedral; but he did observe that the town's trade was in the hands of Protestants who, however, were "extremely restricted in their operations, and otherwise oppressed in every form by the government, which is Catholic, and excessively intolerant." [45]

But fair-mindedness compelled Jefferson to admit that in Frankfort, which he reached in rain, hail and snow on April 6th, and where the prevailing government was Lutheran, an equal intolerance was displayed against the Catholic and Calvinist minorities.[46]

Here he met his old friend, Baron de Geismar, to whom he had written in advance; and at neighboring Hanau, he visited with many other German officers, acquaintances of that idyllic stay of the Convention prisoners in Albemarle. The reunions were joyous and were doubtless celebrated in stirrup cups of the famous wines in whose culture and preparation Jefferson took such a keen interest. Hanau, a garrison town, was filled with "the silence and quiet of the mansions of the dead." The streets were "cleaner than a German floor, because nobody passes them"; and "the drum and fife are all that is heard." [47]

The surrounding country struck Jefferson as being a "second mother country" to America. For it was from this palatinate on the Rhine "that those swarms of Germans have gone, who, next to the descendants of the English, form the greatest body of our people. I have been continually amused by seeing here the origin of whatever is not English among us. I have fancied myself often in the upper parts of Maryland & Pennsylvania." [48]

In the great wine country of Hochheim and Rüdesheim, Jefferson purchased 100 vine shoots which he carried back to Paris with him and planted in his garden. They grew luxuriantly, and Jefferson expected to take them eventually to America. "If you ever revisit Monticello," he wrote Geismar with anticipatory satisfaction, "I shall be able to give you there a glass of Hock or Rüdesheim of my own making." [49]

At length Jefferson reluctantly tore himself away from old friends and old wines, and took boat to sail down the Rhine, sketching towers, floor plans of castles and crossed cruets along the way, as well as making meticulous entries of the various vintages he encountered. On April 14th, he paused at storied Heidelberg to measure its famous tun in all its dimensions; but alas, "there is no wine in it now." He did like, however, the noble ruin of a château, and the climate that was soft like that of Italy; though he thought the gardens at Schwetzingen tasteless and ugly for such an expenditure of money.[50]

On April 16th, he was in Strassburg, where he bought books, recrossed the Rhine and was in France again for the homeward journey. Here he was on fairly familiar ground and he quickened his steps. But he paused long enough in his journey to make a most important observation. The French peasants were ploughing with a clumsily shaped wooden moldboard which turned up the sod with difficulty and considerable inefficiency. The sight caused Jefferson to reflect: would not a different shape do the job better? His mechanical turn of mind was aroused; and he jotted down in his journal both his consideration of the problem and its solution. "The awkward figure of their mould-board," he wrote, "leads one to consider what should be its form. The offices of the mould-board are to receive the sod after the share has cut under it, to raise it gradually, and to reverse it. The fore-end of it, then, should be horizontal to enter under the sod, and the hind end perpendicular to throw it over; the intermediate surface changing gradually from the horizontal to the perpendicular. It should be as wide as the furrow, and of a length suited to the construction of the plough." [51]

Having thus lucidly stated the theory, Jefferson proceeded with a detailed description of just how such a moldboard might be constructed. He had hit upon something that was, for its time, to revolutionize the ploughing of fields.

On his return to America, he constructed a model of his new moldboard from a single block of wood, and showed it to his friend David Rittenhouse, who enthusiastically approved of it. Thus encouraged, he tested it at Monticello, found it excellently efficient, and demonstrated its operation to an English visitor, who in turn reported on it to the Board of Agriculture of England. Sir John Sinclair, the President of the Board, asked Jefferson for further details and in due time received a comprehensive account of the principle and a working model. Another model eventually found its way to France. On March 13, 1798, Jefferson published the account he had sent Sinclair in the Transactions of the American Philosophical Society under the title, "A Mouldboard of the least resistance and of the easiest and most certain construction." [52] He had done for the agriculture of his day what Benjamin Franklin had done, with his new-type stove, for the interior heating of houses.

On his way to Paris he was struck once more with the employment of women; here, as in Germany, for the heaviest types of labor. Again it aroused him to indignant reflections. "Women are formed by nature for attentions, not for hard labor," he wrote in his journal. "While one considers them as useful and rational companions, one cannot forget that they are also objects of our pleasures." [53]

On April 23rd, he reached Paris and journey's end.

He brought back with him a philosophy of travel, especially for Americans. These, like John Rutledge, Jr., John Mason and Thomas Lee Shippen, avid to make the best of their European tours, were constantly availing themselves of Jefferson's good offices and advice. For the benefit of young Rutledge and Shippen, recently arrived, he expatiated at length on that philosophy.

"On arriving at a town," he advised, "the first thing is to buy the plan of the town, and the book noting its curiosities. Walk round the ramparts when there are any, go to the top of a steeple to have a view of the town and its environs." Remember that you may never be back, so see as much as possible; but do not, he warned, permit porters or guides to burden you with trifling details.

Ask only for the *vin du pays;* and realize that "the people you will naturally see the most of will be tavern keepers, *valets de place*, and postilions. These are the hackneyed rascals of every country. Of course they must never be considered when we calculate the national character."

Americans should pay particular attention to everything connected with agriculture, and whatever might be transported home. They should also obtain hints from those heavier mechanical articles, like forges, quarries, boats, bridges, etc., which, though not transportable, might offer useful duplications at home. But as for other forms of manufacture, "circumstances rendering it impossible that America should become a manufacturing country during the time of any man now living, it would be a waste of attention to examine them minutely."

Gardens and architecture deserve special attention; the latter is "among the most important arts; and it is desirable to introduce taste into an art which shows so much."

Painting and statuary, however, are "too expensive for the state of wealth among us. It would be useless, therefore, and preposterous, for us to make ourselves connoisseurs in those arts. They are worth seeing, but not studying."

But politics are certainly worth careful study. "Examine their influence on the happiness of the people. Take every possible occasion for entering into the houses of the laborers, and especially at the moments of their repast; see what they eat, how they are clothed, whether they are obliged to work too hard; whether the government or their landlord takes from them an unjust proportion of their labor; on what footing stands the property they call their own, their personal liberty, etc., etc."

As for the royal courts, they should be seen "as you would see the tower of London or menagerie of Versailles with their lions, tigers, hyenas, and other beast of prey, standing in the same relation to their fellows. A slight acquaintance with them will suffice to show you that, under the most imposing exterior, they are the weakest and worst part of mankind." [54]

Whether the two young men to whom these didactic observations were directed profited by them is doubtful; but they cast an illuminating beam on Jefferson's own tastes, predilections, and general outlook.

One further statement, made by Jefferson at about this time, rounds out the general picture of his beliefs. He had been asked by a Virginia neighbor, J. Peter de Rieux, to stand as godfather to his child. He refused the honor in significant language: "The person who becomes sponsor for a child, according to the ritual of the church in which I was educated [Episcopalian] makes a solemn profession, before god & the world, of faith in articles, which I had never sense enough to comprehend, and it has always appeared to me that comprehension must precede assent. The difficulty of reconciling the ideas of Unity & Trinity, have, from a very early part of my life, excluded me from the office of sponsorship, often proposed to me by my friends, who could have trusted, for the faithful discharge of it, to morality alone, instead of which the church requires [word heavily inked out] faith." [55]

CHAPTER 27

Time to Return

JEFFERSON found Paris on his return in an even greater state of fermentation than when he had left. During his absence, after the surprising resistance of the Assembly of Notables, the government had dismissed it and sought to register various reform measures with the Parlement. Some were duly registered; but others, notably tax decrees, were turned down on the ground that a States-General was alone competent to authorize them. This, to the Court as well as to the Parisian judges who proposed it, seemed a bold, nay, a revolutionary step; for the States-General, composed of the three great orders of the realm—nobility, clergy and bourgeoisie, sitting separately—had last been convoked in 1614. But to the excited French people, it appeared only in the light of a delaying action and a reference to an obsolete and unenlightened body. They now clamored for a fixed constitution, with specific guarantees and limitations on the crown. In fact, hopeful eyes were already being directed toward the various American documents cast in that form. To avoid the greater evil, the King finally agreed to call the States-General, setting the date for May 1, 1789.

Jefferson hailed these various events as evidence that a vast and peaceful revolution was already in progress. In his eyes, public opinion had become the new power, and had forced the King, most absolute of monarchs, to retrace his steps.[1] Even Lafayette's disgrace—his deposition from command of the French troops in the south, significant evidence of the royal displeasure with his libertarian sentiments—was considered by Jefferson as a stroke of good fortune for his old friend. Under the present regime, he commented, Lafayette had nothing to expect; the degradation now established him in the national favor and would eventually serve him with any succeeding regime.[2]

While society was thus fermenting, and the shadow of things to come was casting a baleful gloom for those who had eyes to see, Jefferson quietly picked up the various threads of his life. He kept his friends at home informed of European affairs, though, as he acknowledged, he did not think they excited much interest there. "I know too," he admitted, "that it is a maxim with us, and I think it a wise one, not to entangle ourselves with the affairs of Europe. Still, I think, we should know them." [3] But, strangely, most of the news that flowed from his pen related to such distant matters as the Turks, the Austrians and the Russians and, as yet, related but little to the great revolution that was burgeoning under his very eyes. Not until it actually burst in all its fury did he wake up to its true significance.

At the moment, indeed, he was more vitally concerned with the progress of ratification of the American constitution. He rejoiced when the nine States necessary for ratification finally signified their consent. By and large it was a good document, he thought, though not perfect. He kept insisting in all his letters, however, that the two fundamentals of a Bill of Rights and an amendment prohibiting re-election to office be added. A man "once chosen," he was certain, "will be always chosen, he is a king for life." [4]

The funding of the foreign debt similarly engrossed his attention. He sent for Madison's consideration two observations on the subject, one by himself and the other "by a gentleman infinitely better acquainted with the subject." Together, the plans proposed to consolidate the whole foreign debt of the United States and to borrow 21,000,000 florins in Holland whereby the entire amount currently due in France and elsewhere could be paid off, and the new debt placed in Dutch hands. To ensure payment of this sum and accrued interest by the year 1802, he suggested that Congress levy an impost of 5 per cent ad valorem on all imports and such other additional duties as would bring in an annual income of $1,000,000; the amount calculated to pay the installments of principal and interest.[5]

Two official items required Jefferson's constant attention: the procurement of a satisfactory consular convention with France; and the improvement of trade relations with that country and its colonies. On the first he was fairly successful. In 1784, Benjamin Franklin had negotiated a convention, but it was so weighted against the United States that Congress refused to ratify, and sent it back to Jefferson, who had in the meantime taken over the diplomatic post, to get the objectionable features expunged. This involved a long, toilsome negotiation that did not terminate until November 14, 1788, when the French ministry rather unwillingly yielded on most of the objectionable points, and the new convention was signed; later to be ratified by Congress as the first of its kind ever made by the United States.[6]

The other was not as easy of solution. It was true that Jefferson had pushed through a trade agreement which John Jay considered as bearing "marks of wisdom and liberality and cannot fail of being acceptable." But Jay—and Jefferson also—would have liked to obtain a completely reciprocal agreement whereby the nationals of each country would receive in the other the full privileges of its native citizens. Jay, however, was sceptical of achieving that result—to this day still a utopian concept. "Toleration in commerce," he remarked, "like toleration in religion gains ground, it is true; but I am not sanguine in my expectations that either will soon take place in their due extent." [7]

Indeed, Jefferson was hard put to it to hold on to the gains he had already achieved. He tried to talk with the ministers on the all-important question of opening the French West Indies to American trade, but "on this head," he ruefully explained to Washington, "the ministers are invincibly mute." Accordingly, "I have laid my shoulder to the opening the markets of this country to our produce, and rendering its transportation a nursery for our seamen. A maritime force is the only one by which we can act on Europe." [8]

Even here he had trouble, in spite of agreements and assurances. The French government, afflicted with the clamors of French merchants who wished for no competitors, nibbled constantly at the plain intent of the agreements, and Jefferson was forced in turn to take up the complaints he received from American ship captains and their agents in France, and obtain redress in each specific case.

One such instance, had it been allowed to stand, would have struck a mortal blow at the New England trade. On September 28, 1788, France issued an *Arrêt*, prohibiting the introduction of foreign whale oils. Ostensibly directed against England, the decree in the first stages made an exception in favor of American oils; but in its last stage that exception was withdrawn suddenly and without warning. Jefferson promptly protested in a formal note to the Comte de Montmorin and followed it up with a conference at which the indefatigable Lafayette attended. Montmorin finally agreed to permit American oils to enter, but demanded rigorous assurances that such oils were in fact of American origin, and not English oils from Halifax under the cover of our flag.[9]

During his ministry in France—perhaps because of the special vantage point from which he could contemplate all of America—Jefferson was far more continentally minded than he was ever again to be. He was advocating and laboring diligently for measures that later tended to become anathema to him. He concerned himself with the interests of New England equally with those of the South; he demanded a powerful navy; he insisted on building up the merchant marine of the United States, even though it was now, and for the foreseeable future would continue to be, in the hands of New Englanders and nonagriculturalists. There are extant certain unpublished notes of his dating from this period in which he urged the importance of encouraging American shipping, and declaring that its increase would benefit not merely the carrying States, but all the others as well. Ingeniously he proved that the charges imposed by the British for the use of their ships were in fact a tax on American agriculture and, by raising their rates during their interminable wars, they were in effect making us pay for the cost of those wars.[10]

It was not until he returned to the United States, and became involved in party politics and sectional disputes, that he tended to look once more on the shipbuilding and carrying interests as sources of danger and subversive of true agricultural prosperity.

Some time in July, 1788, Jefferson found himself involved in a transaction which had all the trappings of an international spy story. A Monsieur Foullay appeared one day at his house with two tattered manuscript volumes under his arm. He was, he declared, a friend of Silas Deane, who had been one of the American commissioners, together with Benjamin Franklin and Arthur Lee, representing America in France during the Revolution. Deane, now in England, had turned over to him his account book and letter book of those highly important and most secret proceedings, so Foullay averred, in payment of a debt of 120 guineas. He was willing, he said, to sell them to the United States government; should Jefferson refuse to purchase, he intended to offer them to the British Ministry in London.

Somewhat taken aback, Jefferson asked that they be left with him for a day so that he might examine them and determine if they had the value claimed. Foullay assented. For the rest of the day and through the night Jefferson went through the books, and as he read, his anger and apprehension mounted. Here were the secret financial accounts of the Revolutionary period from 1778 to 1781, and the secret letter file of five months in 1777. They involved payments and dealings that it would not be wise to spread before the world, and most of all, before the British government.

He carefully copied out the accounts and a list of the letters, and posted them to the Treasury Office and to John Jay. He was troubled. He felt that the books ought not to fall into the hands of the British, yet he did not feel authorized to expend government monies for their purchase. When Foullay appeared the next day, he so informed that gentleman, but said he would write home for instructions. Foullay took the books and departed for London, breathing vague threats.[11]

It took more than three months for Jay to reply, and an additional two months for Jefferson to receive the answer. By all means purchase, urged Jay. He had no doubt Congress would ratify the item.[12]

Thus armed, Jefferson wrote at once to Foullay, who fortunately had not yet gone to the British with his treasure. Foullay returned with the books, the price was arranged at twenty-five louis, and Jefferson breathed a sigh of relief. What was his horror then to hear, as Foullay smilingly pocketed the money, that Deane had six to eight more volumes on hand and that he, Foullay, was now on his way to London to get them. They, too, would be offered for sale and, intimated Foullay, the price would come high.

In this dilemma, Jefferson turned in all innocence for help to Dr. Edward Bancroft in London. Bancroft had been the secretary to Benjamin Franklin during the negotiations in Paris and therefore knew Deane well. But what Jefferson did not know was that Bancroft had in fact been a spy in the pay of England and that, while Franklin, Deane and Lee had been working at cross-purposes with England and France—and incidentally with one another—all their most secret intentions were being fully disclosed to English agents in France and relayed to the ministry in London.

Jefferson related the story of Foullay and the secret letter books to Bancroft. "You are sensible of the impropriety of letting such books get into hands which might make an unfriendly use of them," he wrote with unconscious irony. "You are sensible of the immorality of an ex minister's selling his secrets for money." Would Bancroft, therefore, see Deane and try to get the remaining books from him before Foullay managed to do so; by purchase, if necessary.[13]

Bancroft must have enjoyed this communication immensely. He had already, years before, transmitted most of what was in the books to the British. But he wrote back gravely that he would do what he could, and unfolded a sordid tale of the degradation to which Deane had descended since his days of glory.

"That unhappy man," he narrated, "two or three years ago became very much attached to a woman here in the line of Prostitution, and was mislead [*sic*] by her" to buy a house for her in Rathbone Place and furnish it completely. Deane also went security for her additional purchases. She pretended to let out lodgings, though Bancroft hinted it was actually a bawdy-house. Deane lived on the second floor of this unsavory dwelling, and spent all the money he had and all he could borrow on the infamous woman.

She failed to pay for the furniture and Deane, as her security, was arrested on the debt. During the period of his incarceration she stole his watch and personal possessions; and, when Deane emerged from debtor's gaol, he plunged into "inebrity" which brought about "a total loss of the Powers of his body & mind." While in this helpless condition, the woman warned Bancroft, who had been—so he said—aiding Deane out of compassion, that she would throw him out into the gutter if Bancroft did not promptly remove him. Bancroft found a lodging for Deane and carried him off. When Deane's trunks arrived, he discovered them almost empty; all the clothes and other property had been stolen. Bancroft queried the woman about the missing effects. Her story was that a Frenchman named Foullay, who masqueraded as her husband, had been the villain of the piece. It was he who had stolen Deane's possessions and run off with them to France. Included in the theft were the letter books. Bancroft absolved Deane of complicity in the attempted sale of the documents; he had a combination, so Bancroft asserted, of "Dropsy, Palsey & Idiotism," and was now subsisting on a charitable subscription by his friends.[14]

On receipt of this amazing relation Jefferson, who had authorized Bancroft to go as high as fifty guineas to get the missing volumes from the "crapulous" Deane, now wrote Jay that Deane did not have them, that Foullay had failed to show up, and he hoped that the business was finished.[15]

Somehow or other, Deane managed to retrieve some of the missing books and Jefferson again tried to get them; but Deane, having recovered "the use of his bodily faculties & in a considerable degree of his mental also," was shortly embarking for Boston, having determined to end his days in his native land. He knew nothing of what had taken place or of Jefferson's inquiries; and Bancroft was determined to keep him in that state of innocence.[16]

Private matters, including the affairs of his family and of his friends, engrossed much of Jefferson's time. From America came the pleasing information that his sister, Anna Scott Jefferson, had married a Mr. Hasting Marks whom, though a near neighbor of Jefferson, he knew only slightly.[17] The news was all the more pleasing because Anna Scott had never been a bright girl; in fact, her mentality was somewhat substandard. The same held good for Jefferson's brother Randolph, in spite of the attempt to educate him at William and Mary. Jefferson was always to treat these two unfortunates with the greatest consideration, kindness and patience, and only on rare occasions did he permit himself the slightest reference to their afflictions. Perhaps the only example—and it is delicate enough—may be found in a letter which he sent his brother Randolph in January, 1789. "The occurrences of this part of the globe," he wrote, "are of a nature to interest you so little that I have never made them the subject of a letter to you." But, he hastened to add, "I have not the less continued to entertain for you the same sincere affection, the same wishes for your health and that of your family, and almost an envy of your quiet and retirement."[18]

Jefferson's friend Mazzei, who had plagued him in the last days in America, now that they both were in Paris, had been reinstated in his confidence and regard. Good fortune had finally befallen him. After constant borrowings from Jefferson, he had managed to obtain a lucrative sinecure as the Parisian correspondent of the King of Poland at 8,000 livres a year. He fell heir to still another stroke of fortune. His termagant wife, who had remained behind in Virginia, had died and, as Jefferson put it with rather macabre humor, "this last event has given him three quarters of the globe elbow-room, which he had ceded to her, on condition she would leave him quiet in the fourth. Their partition of the next world will be more difficult, if it be divided only into two parts, according to the Protestant faith."[19]

Other news, however, that came from the United States could not similarly excite Jefferson's risibilities. James Madison, his faithful friend, had been defeated in the Virginia Assembly for the United States Senate by a mere two or three votes. "This was owing entirely to Mr Patrick Henry," his informant wrote, "who openly opposed his election, & who carries every measures [*sic*] he espouses, in the Assembly. In throwing the State into Districts for the choice of Representatives to Congress, it is said he has taken particular pains to prevent Mr Madison from being chosen."[20]

Madison's defeat could not but be a severe blow to Jefferson. One of his staunchest co-workers and supporters was no longer in government; and it meant that parties were crystallizing back home on the basis of adherence or nonadherence to the Constitution. It was shortly after the receipt of this unwelcome news that Jefferson penned his memorable protest: "I am not a Federalist, because I never submitted the whole system of my opinions to the creed of any party of men whatever in religion, in philosophy, in politics, or in anything else where I was capable of thinking for myself. Such an addiction is the last degradation of a free and moral agent. If I could not go to heaven but with a party, I would not go there at all." But he was even further removed from the anti-Federalists. He was of neither party, "nor yet a trimmer between parties." Nevertheless, though he never had an opinion in politics or religion which he was afraid to avow, he owned frankly that "my great wish is to go on in a strict but silent performance of my duty; to avoid attracting notice & to keep my name out of newspapers, because I find the pain of a little censure, even when it is unfounded, is more acute than the pleasure of much praise." [21]

Thomas Paine, the famous radical pamphleteer and deist, whose *Common Sense* and *The American Crisis* had aroused the American people from the slough of despair in the early days of the Revolution, and whose *Rights of Man* and *Age of Reason* were to bring from them later a storm of obloquy, was now in London, busying himself with projects for iron bridges and waiting for the oncoming French Revolution to afford him another opportunity for striking huge blows in favor of human rights and liberties. Jefferson had, before he left America, tried to get Paine a grant of 2,000 guineas from the Virginia Assembly in recognition of his services to the Revolution; but had failed. Now he corresponded with him on engineering and scientific problems, mingled with some politics, and suggested to Paine the use of a catenary arch to carry the structure of his proposed bridge.[22]

Jefferson was also ordering books from London, in huge quantities, and laid down some interesting rules for the bookseller's guidance in furnishing them. "When I name a particular edition of a book, send me that edition and no other. . . . When I do not name the edition, never send me a folio or quarto if there exists an 8vo. or smaller edition. I like books of a handy size. . . . I disclaim all pompous editions and all typographical luxury; but I like a fine white paper, neat type, and neat binding, gilt & lettered in the modern stile." [23]

To Trumbull he was giving different orders. He wanted a carriage made in London, and his insistence on certain specifications almost drove Trumbull crazy. "I would wish it to be 3 feet 2 inches wide within," he wrote, "a strapontin to unship & ship as may be wanting, the steps to shut within, a box to take in & out, coachman's seat to ship & unship readily, mortise locks, venetian blinds, spring curtains & vallons, a large oval backlight of 2 feet diameter lengthwise to let down & up, crane neck. I would wish a mantle painted in front, flanks &c, without either arms or cypher. The carriage to be hung half way between the old fashion & the new, that is to say lower than the new, and somewhat high for the old fashion. It is intended for America, where you know our roads do not admit a high carriage with safety." All for £105. And, as an afterthought, "Kneel to mrs Cosway for me, & lay my soul in her lap." [24]

A long correspondence followed on this immense project, with Trumbull doing his best, but protesting that certain items would add considerably to the cost, while he did not find the word "vallons" in the dictionary, and "the Coachmaker knows as little as I do." Did he mean, perhaps, "festoon Curtains?" Jefferson did; and later added a new request; get him a "good harmonica, the glasses fixed on an axis, to comprehend 3 octaves, if they ever comprehend as much, in a plain mahogany case." [25]

As though poor Trumbull had not a sufficiency of commissions to carry out, Jefferson now asked for painted reproductions of Bacon, Locke and Newton. To him these three men represented the trinity of humankind, and he wanted them depicted in that form. "As I consider them as the three greatest men that have ever lived," he explained to Trumbull, "without any exception, and as having laid the foundation of those superstructures which have been raised in the Physical & Moral sciences, I would wish to form them into a knot on the same canvas, that they may not be confounded at all with the herd of other great men. To do this I suppose we need only desire the copyist to draw the three busts in three ovals all contained in a large oval..." Jefferson drew a diagram to show what he meant, with Bacon at the apex, and Locke and Newton underneath.[26]

Trumbull did not think that particular arrangement would look well; and he abandoned the scheme, authorizing, instead, separate pictures of the three great men.[27]

For some time Jefferson had been anxious to get back to Virginia; not, indeed, as a resignation of his ministerial functions, but as an intermission. He had several excellent reasons for this desire: the condition of his estates, which had failed to provide that margin of profit by which he had hoped to pay off his long-outstanding debts, caused him a great deal of anxiety; he wanted to resume "the tone of mind of my constituents, which is lost by long absence, and can only be recovered by mixing with them"; and, above all, he considered it was time to take his daughters back to their own country.[28]

The last was the most cogent reason of all. To his dismay, Jefferson had discovered that Abigail Adams's scepticism about the atmosphere of Panthemont had unfortunately been soundly based. An astonishing letter from Patsy came into her father's hands. It requested his permission to remain in the convent and dedicate herself to a religious life. Jefferson did not waste a moment. He called for his carriage, went forthwith to the Abbaye and obtained a private interview with the Abbess. What the nature of that interview was is not known; but when he emerged, he placed both daughters in his carriage and took them away forever. Thereafter Patsy presided over his establishment, while Polly received private lessons.[29] France, he was now convinced, was no place for susceptible young American girls.

In almost every official—and nonofficial—letter home he wrote of his desire to obtain a leave of absence for some five or six months, preferably during the spring and summer season, to avoid the storms and cold of the Atlantic. He commenced his requests early in 1787 and they increased in urgency as the months rolled by and no reply came from Jay or Congress.

He was too conscientious to pack up and leave without proper authority; even though he was certain that young William Short would be able to handle the legation's affairs during his absence.

Further to complicate matters, both his daughters took sick at the end of 1788; Patsy running a fever for a fortnight and Polly down with a nervous fever and "in considerable danger" for two months. By the end of January, 1789, they were both out of danger, but still convalescent.[30] The weather added to his misery; it had never been so cold before and, Jefferson wryly told Maria Cosway, "to me who am an animal of a warm climate, a mere Oran-ootan, it has been a severe trial." [31]

He thought that both his charming female friends, Maria and Angelica Church, would accompany him to America. Of Angelica he still had hopes; but alas, Maria had expressed a sudden determination to go to Italy. He wrote her mournfully to change her mind. "The one or the other of us goes the wrong way, for the way will ever be wrong which leads us farther apart. Mine is a journey of duty and of affection. I must deposit my daughters in the bosom of their friends & country. This done, I shall return to my station. . . . But why go to Italy? You have seen it, all the world has seen it, and ransacked it thousands of times. Rather join our good friend Mrs. Church in her trip to America. There you will find original scenes, scenes worthy of your pencil, as the Natural bridge, or the Falls of Niagara. Or participate with Trumbull the historical events of that country. . . . Think of this, my dear friend, mature the project with Mrs. Church, & let us all embark together at Havre." [32]

But Maria was adamant. She was going to Italy. Nevertheless, she could not avoid exercising some female wiles. In introducing a dramatist (female) to his attention, she cried out: "how I envy her & every body that can converse with you. Pray write, pray write, pray write, & dont go to America without coming to England. God bless You & believe me Your Most affte. friend M. C." [33]

It was not, however, until June, 1789, that word finally came from America that a leave of absence had been granted to Jefferson. In the meantime, he was caught up in the first rush of the exploding French Revolution.

CHAPTER 28

French Revolution

THE French Revolution was now well under way. With notable reluctance the King had issued a writ convoking the States-General and, from February through May, 1789, all France was engrossed in a complicated system of voting. The composition of the Nobles and the Clergy was pretty well fixed; what attracted the most excitement was the Third Estate —the representatives of the *people* of France.

While the balloting was still going on, Jefferson expressed his satisfaction with the way the revolution was progressing. He was certain that it would be peaceful and that a fairly good constitution would result from the deliberations of the forthcoming States-General. True, he thought that the assemblage of 1,200 was entirely too numerous for a proper job of legislating, and that they "have indeed a miserable old canvas to work on, covered with daubings which it will be difficult to efface"; but he believed that "some they will efface, & some soften, so as to make a tolerable thing of it, perhaps a good one." [1]

In fine, to Jefferson the revolution was already accomplished—merely by the force of public opinion—and nothing remained but to put the results into writing.

The States-General opened at Versailles on May 5, 1789, with considerable pomp and ceremony, and Jefferson journeyed daily from Paris to witness its proceedings. Though his interest was largely, by reason of his principles, concentrated on the Third Estate, he knew far more intimately many of the representatives of the Nobles. Among them were Lafayette, now thirty-two; his brother-in-law, the Vicomte de Noailles, similarly known to Jefferson from American days; the Duc de la Rochefoucauld, and others whom he had met in the Parisian salons. Among the Clergy he knew the Abbé Maury and had doubtless met the most famous of them all, the brilliant, unscrupulous Talleyrand, Bishop of Autun, though no one in the world could have been less properly cast in the role of an ecclesiastic than he. Among the representatives who crowded the benches of the Third Estate was a group of scientists and scholars with whom Jefferson was acquainted—notably Bailly and Volney. He did *not* know a small, precise, pallid lawyer who came inconspicuously from the provincial town of Arras —one Maximilien Robespierre—and it was doubtful that he had yet encountered the dissipated nobleman Mirabeau who, rejected by his own Order, had triumphantly been returned to the States General by the Third Estate.

Jefferson harkened to the speeches in the *Salle des Menus Plaisirs* and thought the King spoke well, the Chancellor could not be heard, and that Necker painted a consoling and plausible picture, though he did not dwell enough on those great constitutional reforms which Jefferson had expected. But he hoped they had been described in the inaudible speech of the Chancellor "which, like the Revelations of St. John, were no revelations at all." [2]

Seated close to Jefferson as an interested observer of the pageant was another American, the one-legged, cynical young Gouverneur Morris, who had recently arrived in Paris to adjust the tobacco contracts of Robert Morris (no relation) with the farmers-general. *Bon vivant*, gallant, irresistible with the ladies in spite of his wooden leg, aristocratic and royalist in tone, Morris viewed the Revolution with much different spectacles than Jefferson and later, as himself Minister to France, established policies which infuriated his predecessor. At the moment, however, the two Americans were friendly enough and Jefferson even introduced him to Maria Cosway when Morris went to England. Maria was delighted with him. "I am quite in Love with Mr. Morris," she wrote Jefferson. "Are all americans so enjoying as those I know? pray take me to that Country." [3]

Morris rode with Jefferson in the Bois de Boulogne and had the Bridge of Neuilly pointed out to him as the handsomest in the world. He also found that Jefferson "commands very much Respect in this Country and which is merited by good Sense and good Intentions"; though, at another time, Morris considered that he had "too sanguine Expectation of a downright republican Form of Government." Much more to his taste was the fact that Jefferson lived well, kept a good table and good wines, which he distributed freely, and that his house was hospitably open to all Americans in Paris.[4]

But everyone, including Jefferson, was disappointed when they came to read the speeches in the States-General, with their vague optimism and lack of precise proposals; nor was the situation remedied by the struggle which immediately arose over the system of voting. The Nobles and the Clergy naturally clung to the old method of voting by Orders, which gave them the whip hand; the Third Estate, just as naturally, by reason of the preponderance of their numbers, demanded a unitary session.

The quarrel grew so great that all other proceedings were suspended; and it was despaired that they would ever actually get under way. But Jefferson saw nothing to fear as yet. "The nation is in a movement that cannot be stopped," he explained to the Chevalier de Moustier in America. "I think that in the end the Nobles will be obliged to yeild [*sic*] to the vote by persons, because the Tiers are more unanimous, more inflexible, and more formidable." [5]

He was incapable of sitting on the side lines in these stirring times. As the notable representative of an already successful revolution was he not able to offer sound advice in the management of this new one? He thought so, and so did a goodly number of liberal French delegates. The logical liaison between the American Minister and the French delegates was, of course, Lafayette. It never entered Jefferson's mind that, as the diplomatic representative of a foreign power, it was morally and politically his duty to exercise a strict neutrality in the domestic affairs of the French. But neither, it must be confessed, did it occur to the French themselves. Nationalist lines were not as strictly drawn then as now; the watchwords of natural rights, of liberty and freedom, were universal; and all men, in a sense, were citizens of the world as well as of their own country.

The day after the opening of the States-General, Jefferson was advising Lafayette to quit allegiance to the Nobles and go over to the Third Estate; because, he said, "it will be impossible for you to live in a constant sacrifice of your own sentiments to the prejudices of the Noblesse." But Lafayette ought not to wait too long to do so. If he did, he would be received by his new allies "coldly and without confidence." The time to do so is now, urged Jefferson. "This will win their hearts forever, be approved by the world which marks and honours you as the man of the people, and will be an eternal consolation to yourself." [6]

Under the leadership of the Abbé Siéyès, the Third Estate finally determined to cut the Gordian knot and inform the other two Estates that, unless they acquiesced, the Third Estate would organize itself without them. On June 10th, Siéyès made a great speech to that effect; on June 12th, not having heard officially from the others, the Third Estate commenced its own registration. Gradually, a few members of the Clergy drifted in to be registered, amid the wild acclamations of the commons, who saw in it the beginning of their final triumph. No Noble came, however; nor did Lafayette as yet, in spite of Jefferson's advice.

Now calling themselves the National Assembly—a bold and revolutionary step—the Third Estate, with these few accessions, began to consider the state of the country and to legislate.

On June 2nd, Jefferson was in the company of Short, Lafayette and Rabaut de St. Etienne, a Protestant who later acted a leading role in the Revolution. They discussed what could be done to break the impasse. St. Etienne left early, but the other three remained to continue the discussion. Someone—very likely Jefferson—proposed that the King, in a *séance royale*, should offer a Charter of Rights for France, which would be signed by him and by every member of the three Orders. Lafayette was impressed with the idea and Jefferson, after he went home, considered it afresh. With the weight of the royal influence thus placed behind it, with a series of reforms thus imperishably embodied in a written document to which all the parties could agree, the Revolution might well be resolved with resounding success.

Excited by these thoughts—and perhaps by the consideration that thereby he might be the architect of this second revolution in which he found himself, as of the first—Jefferson sat down at his writing desk and drew up "A Charter of Rights, solemnly established by the King and Nation."

1. The States-General shall be elected triennially and meet annually without limitation.

2. The States-General alone shall levy money on the nation, and shall appropriate it.

3. Laws shall be made by the States-General only, with the consent of the King.

4. No person shall be restrained of his liberty except by due process of law, and the right of habeas corpus shall be instituted.

5. The military shall be subordinate to the civil authority.

6. The press shall be free and unrestricted.

7. All pecuniary privileges and exemptions shall be abolished.

8. Debts already contracted by the King shall be made the debts of the nation.

9. Eighty million livres now granted to the King shall be raised by a loan.

10. The States-General shall adjourn until November 1st.

The Charter which, in substance, Jefferson thus formulated was indeed only modestly liberal and reformist, and might well have received the plaudits of all Orders, with certain exceptions. The Nobles and Clergy did not wish their traditional privileges and exemptions taken away; the King was not prepared to have his money-raising power thus ruthlessly removed; and the Third Estate would have felt that the reforms did not strike at any economic roots. It certainly was not as radical as Jefferson's own draft constitution for Virginia, nor did it go as far even as the Federal Constitution of the United States.

The next morning, Jefferson made fair copies of his proposals and sent one to Lafayette and the other to St. Etienne.[7]

Nothing came of it, but Lafayette was incorporating some of the provisions, together with others taken from the American Bill of Rights, with an obeisance to the Declaration of Independence, in a Declaration of the Rights of Man of his own, which he was to offer the Convention in the following month.[8]

In the meantime, however, the Assembly (in reality the Third Estate), by a series of bold enactments, was attempting to transfer jurisdiction over finances to itself. The Court, outraged over these ostensibly illegal acts, overbore the protests of Necker and other liberal members of the Ministry, and persuaded the King to act with decision before all his prerogatives were cut off.

On a memorable June 20th, therefore, the deputies on their way to attend a session of the Assembly, found the doors closed, soldiers barring their path, and the information that further sessions were suspended on royal order.

After a few minutes of milling confusion, the suggestion was made and received with acclamation that the deputies go in a body to the bare hall of the nearby indoor tennis court and resume their interrupted deliberations. There, packed and uncomfortably standing, the assembled delegates, with but one vote dissenting, swore a solemn compact never to separate until a constitution had been established. The compact has since become known to history as the "Tennis Court Oath." The real Revolution had begun.

By this time, the Clergy had come over to the new Assembly practically in a body, and more Nobles were wandering in. Lafayette was still not one of their number, considering himself bound by the instructions of his election; but he wrote to his constituents either to change his instructions or accept his resignation.[9]

Faced with this open defiance, the King hesitated and postponed his forthcoming *séance royale;* while the rage of the Court party burst about the ears of Necker, now the popular idol, and whom the courtiers considered the author of all their ills. He offered to resign, but he was peremptorily told he would be held as a hostage instead.

On June 23rd, the King held his Royal Session under circumstances deliberately intended to humiliate the obstreperous Third Estate. But the program misfired. With solemn ceremony the King declared all the proceedings of June 17th and after null and void, and that the States-General *must* meet in their separate Orders, each voting as a unit. His speech met with applause from the Nobles and those of the upper Clergy who had not seceded; but with sullen silence from the Third Estate and those lower Clergy who had joined with them. With a final command to disband, the King left, followed by the upper Orders. But the Third Estate and their allies remained.

The King's Master of Ceremonies returned. "Gentlemen," he said, "you have heard the King's orders. His Majesty requests the deputies of the Third Estate to withdraw." At one bound Mirabeau leaped into national fame. He pushed his way forward. "Go," he cried, "tell those who sent you that we are here by the will of the people and that we shall not leave except at the point of the bayonet." And the Assembly remained, defiantly to reaffirm all the measures which the King had just solemnly proclaimed to be null and void.

The disobedience proved successful. More of the Clergy and Nobles joined and, by June 27th, Louis the Sixteenth was bowing to the inevitable and himself requesting the remainder to participate in the Assembly.

But the Court party refused to bend or compromise. Secretly they were mobilizing the foreign regiments of France to regain by force what they had lost in the States-General and, on July 11th, persuaded the King to dismiss Necker and order him to leave France. The rumor of the fall of this idolized minister, added to the alarm already felt at the gathering of the troops, drove the Parisian populace to madness. A citizens' National Guard was formed to defend the Revolution and, on July 14th, by a single uncontrollable impulse, the Bastille, dreaded fortress of lifelong prisoners and *lettres de cachet*, was stormed amid scenes of indescribable enthusiasm and mob cruelty.

Jefferson happened at the time to be at the house of Madame de Corny, and it was from her husband, an eye-witness of the dramatic events, that he heard the story of this Lexington of the French Revolution.[10]

He was shocked. In vain he had told members of the Assembly, whose confidence he possessed, that they should offer the King an immediate compromise, "to secure what the government was now ready to yield, and trust to future occasions for what might still be wanting." But the radicals were flushed with success and wanted the Revolution to proceed until their most extreme demands were granted. Years after, Jefferson meditated on "their lamentable error." After thirty years of frightful war, "they have obtained no more, nor even that securely."

He thought then, and later, that the King, if left to himself, might have yielded sufficiently to have avoided the excesses and evils of the Revolution, "but he had a Queen of absolute sway over his weak mind, and timid virtue; and of a character the reverse of his in all points.... I have ever believed that had there been no queen, there would have been no revolution."

When the grim denouement came, Jefferson refused either to approve or condemn of the double royal execution; though he personally would have shut the Queen up in a convent and retained the King with severely limited powers. Thereby, he reflected, "no void would have been created, courting the usurpation of a military adventurer [Napoleon], nor occasion given for those enormities which demoralized the nations of the world, and destroyed, and is yet to destroy millions and millions of its inhabitants." [11] But all this was at yet in the limbo of inchoate time.

In the midst of these tremendous events, Jefferson's house was three times broken into and robbed. The third time he was really annoyed, for the thieves took a brace of candlesticks which were his special pride. He searched every shop in Paris in a vain attempt to replace them, and finally was compelled to call on the ever-obliging Trumbull in London for help. To make certain he got what he wanted, he accompanied description with drawing. They were plated, he wrote, and in the form of "a fluted Corinthian column, with the capital of its order, & the bottom of the candlestick was of the form in the margin," referring to his drawing. "I think," he added, "no form is so handsome as that of the column."

Since, with the troublous times and the breakdown of police vigilance, there might be more robberies, Jefferson formally demanded on his own behalf and that of the other inhabitants of the quarter an adequate police guard from the Comte de Montmorin.[12]

The dismissal of Necker and the fall of the Bastille stirred all France and, within a few weeks, the revolution which had commenced in Paris was imitated and extended in every city, town and rural district of the provinces. The *ancien régime*—seemingly immutable—had crumbled in a single giant blow, never to recover.

But before Necker left office, he had become involved in an incident which hit Jefferson directly and caused him endless embarrassment.

Mirabeau, the renegade Noble, had far-reaching ambitions. He sought control of the National Assembly and, through it, of all France. But this presupposed a calculated course of violence and ever more radical proposals. Necker stood in his way, with his suggestions of moderate reforms. It was necessary to discredit him in the eyes of the people, to whom he was still idol, if the yeast were to ferment and himself be thrown on top by the resulting forces.

During the preceding winter, the unprecedented cold had ruined crops and caused much suffering among the poor. Bread was scarce. Mirabeau saw his chance. He rose in the Assembly and accused Necker of having turned down the offer of Mr. Jefferson, the American Minister, to have shipped from America a quantity of corn and flour to relieve their necessities. Mirabeau could not have chosen a better method of causing Necker's stock with the populace to drop precipitately. Did it mean, they must ask, that the plausible Necker was secretly in league with the Court party and was attempting to starve the people into submission?

But Jefferson, when he heard of the attack, was both mortified and indignant. He wrote to Lafayette at once to correct Mirabeau and to placate Necker. "I do not know how Monsieur Mirabeau has been led into this error," he exclaimed. "I never in my life made any proposition to Mr. Necker on the subject; I never said I had made such a proposition." [13]

Lafayette had already taken action, even before he received Jefferson's angry disavowal. He obtained from Mirabeau not only an engagement to retract publicly his remarks, but an agreement to read Jefferson's letter to the assemblage as soon as it came to his hands. By this handsome *amende* Mirabeau prevented a long debate that might have caused the whole affair to rebound on him. As a matter of fact, his enemies seized upon Jefferson's communication with glee and distorted its contents to Mirabeau's discredit in the telling; so that Jefferson felt impelled to print the real letter in the *Journal de Paris*.[14]

On July 11, 1789, Lafayette rose in the Assembly to bring up his long-prepared Declaration of Rights, on which both Jefferson and Madison had offered suggestions. For some time Lafayette had feared for his own safety, because he had supported an Assembly motion protesting the gathering of the royal troops. The Court party was furious against this noble renegade, and visions of a *lettre de cachet* flitted before his uneasy vision. This was before the storming of the Bastille. In hot haste he had written to Jefferson: "If they take me up you must claim me as an American citizen." [15] But the crisis passed, and Jefferson, who doubtless would have complied, was spared an exceedingly embarrassing situation.

If he was thus, by miraculous interventions, spared from participating too publicly in the affairs of another nation, Jefferson was shortly faced with another embarrassing assault on his supposed neutrality. The Assembly had appointed a committee of which the Archbishop of Bordeaux, the Abbé Siéyès, Talleyrand and other notables were members, to submit a draft constitution. The committee, through the Archbishop, politely requested an interview with Jefferson in order "to make use to the profit of France of the lights of your reason and experience.... There are no foreigners any more in our opinion," they added, "when the happiness of man is at stake." [16]

This was all very well, and perhaps good philosophic doctrine; but the worthy Archbishop should have understood that Jefferson was not merely a foreigner, but the representative of a foreign nation and that, in such capacity, it was his duty not to meddle, even when requested.

Jefferson's first reaction, indeed, was along these lines. He regretted to the Archbishop that he was completely tied up at the moment with dispatches from America; and hinted it was not correct for him to participate in discussions, "where there might be a question of abridging the powers of the Chief Magistrate, and of changing fundamentally the form of the government." [17]

This was a sound position, and it is a pity that Jefferson did not see fit to hold to it. Matters were fast approaching another crisis. The King in alarm had sent a messenger to Switzerland to recall Necker; but it proved too late. On August 4th, under the impulse of the Vicomte de Noailles and a small group of young Nobles, a most amazing scene took place in the Assembly. Like self-flagellants, they proposed despoiling themselves of all their old privileges. In a wave of generous enthusiasm others followed suit, including the clergy, who insisted on renouncing their tithes and fees. In a mass hysteria, cities and provinces followed with *their* privileges, until the entire feudal regime seemed to have split asunder and the millenium arrived.

For days after this extraordinary outburst the Assembly was busy passing laws to implement the voluntary sacrifices and to legislate into being the Declaration of the Rights of Man which Lafayette had initiated. With this as preamble, they turned again their attention to the Constitution.

On August 25th, Jefferson received an agitated note from Lafayette: "My dear Friend, I beg for liberty's sake you will break every engagement to give us a dinner to morrow wenesday [*sic*].—We shall be some members of the National Assembly—eight of us whom I want to coalize [*sic*] as being the only means to prevent a total dissolution and a civil war.—The difficulty between us is the King's veto.... If they don't agree in a few days, we shall have no great majority in a favor of any plan, and it must end in a war.... Those gentlemen wish to consult you and me; they will dine to morrow at your house, as mine is always full.—I depend on you to receive us." [18]

The request again put Jefferson in an embarrassing situation. Since he had already refused the semiofficial invitation of the Archbishop of Bordeaux—made with the knowledge and consent of the Assembly—to participate in the drafting of a constitution, it was even more his duty to turn down this semiconspiratorial gathering of certain factions of the Assembly. This would be no open and aboveboard meeting of an Assembly committee to consider the constitution, but a secret session of two groups in a violently divided body which, according to Jefferson's own description, had already assumed "a fearful aspect."

Nevertheless, Jefferson assented; perhaps because it was Lafayette who made the demand, perhaps because he could not resist the opportunity to take a hand in forming the course of this new revolution.

Lafayette appeared on the afternoon of the 26th with seven other deputies—Duport, Barnave, Alexander Lameth, Blacon, Mounier, Maubourd and Dagout. Jefferson referred to them as the leading patriots of the Assembly. Perhaps they were; but what he meant was that their politics agreed to a large extent with his own. They were the representatives of two parties—the moderate Royalists who wished to set up a limited monarchy somewhat on the lines of the British; and the equally moderate Republicans who, preferring to abolish the kingship, were nevertheless willing to consider a sort of hereditary presidency. It was Lafayette's desire to bring these two together, to effect some compromise on the points of difference, and to present with them a solid front against the extreme factions to the right and left. Should that fail, as Jefferson later remarked to Jay, Lafayette's influence, backed as it was by his command of 35,000 armed militia and regulars, could bring one faction up and force the other down.

Jefferson served dinner—and his dinners were justly famous. Then, the cloth being removed and the wine set out, the guests proceeded to the business at hand. Jefferson's account of the occurrence in his Autobiography is disingenuous, to say the least. He skillfully gives the impression that he had not known in advance what the purport of this dinner party was, and having discovered it, he remained a silent and a neutral witness.[19] This, of course, was not true. Lafayette's letter was sufficiently explicit and, when Jefferson described the meeting in a confidential letter to Jay, he made no bones of his intense interest in the proceedings, of his knowledge of the entire situation and just what was intended.[20]

The discussion and plans for union against the party of the Nobles went on into the night. According to Jefferson, it was accompanied by "logical reasoning, and chaste eloquence, disfigured by no gaudy tinsel of rhetoric or declamation, and truly worthy of being placed in parallel with the finest dialogues of antiquity." That Jefferson took no part, as he intimates, is most improbable.

The two groups finally came to an understanding—to permit the king a suspensive veto, and to propose a unicameral legislature, chosen by direct vote of the people. Thus in agreement, they were later able to force through a constitution against the protests of the Court party and the nobility, as well as of the more radical members, which in effect made of France a limited monarchy, with chief power in a popularly elected Assembly.

The next morning, however, Jefferson felt impelled to visit the Comte de Montmorin and explain what had happened. Such a meeting at his home of prominent members of the Assembly, he realized, could not have been unknown to the agents of the government. He was correct in his surmise. After the American Minister had explained how he had been taken by surprise at this political gathering, Montmorin interrupted to assure him that he already knew all about the gathering and its deliberations, that he wished Jefferson would continue to assist with the benefit of his advice and, by moderating the hotheads, promote "a wholesome and practicable reformation only." Whereupon Jefferson demurely pleaded his duties as a neutral, and avowed he would "persevere with care in the character of a neutral and passive spectator."[21]

Or so, at least, he was to write for public consumption many years later. But nothing of this appears in the contemporary account which he forwarded to John Jay of the entire incident.

Jefferson felt pretty optimistic about the eventual outcome of the Revolution, in spite of the ominous excesses which had accompanied the storming of Bastille, and in spite of the fact that what he called "the lees and dregs of the patriotic party" were swinging over to the Duc d'Orléans, a prince of the royal blood who saw a chance of fishing in troubled waters. Jefferson appraised the Duke as "a man of moderate understanding, of no principle, absorbed in low vice, and incapable of abstracting himself from the filth of that to direct anything else." He was also aware that Orléans was the dupe of Mirabeau, brilliant, unprincipled and unscrupulous, who was hiding behind the royal duke's name in order to gain power for himself. But Jefferson was certain that the two conspirators would have only temporary success, if at all; that "the King, the mass of the substantial people of the whole country, the army, and the influential part of the clergy, form a firm phalanx which must prevail."[22]

If Jefferson miscalculated, it was because he had left out of consideration the swarming mob of Paris and of the other cities of France—that congested proletariat of the town which he was always to view with a certain horror and shrinking of the flesh.

But Jefferson was already on the verge of quitting France forever, so that he could follow only from a distance the long and bloody course of the Revolution which he now thought was proceeding in such orderly and satisfactory fashion, and which was to produce convulsions in both the Old and New Worlds for a generation to come, the repercussions of which have continued to echo down to the present day.

It had been Jefferson's intention, when he assumed the diplomatic mission, to remain only two years in France. But Franklin's departure had compelled a longer stay. He came to love France and the French—at least some of them; his duties were absorbing and at the same time not onerous; and he was willing to continue for some years more in office; though, as he told Trumbull, "I do not propose to be very long in any office."

But his secretary, William Short, did not feel the same way about remaining. He was young, ambitious, and he saw no future in his present position. He wanted "something permanent, independant, in his own country, and which may admit him to marry." For some time he had proposed returning, and only Jefferson's request had held him on. By June, however, he made up his mind and Jefferson was compelled reluctantly to agree to his departure. The post being vacant, he offered it to Trumbull.[23] But that worthy, himself ambitious and engrossed in his series of huge historical paintings, refused the sinecure.[24]

For some time Jefferson had been trying to obtain from America permission for a five to six months' leave of absence. He had many matters, as has already been indicated, that imperiously called for his presence in Virginia: the safe placement of his daughters, the rejuvenation of his political and social contacts, and the examination of his private affairs and attempted settlement of his debts.

And now, at long last, toward the end of August, the much belated permission arrived. Jefferson promptly commenced getting his affairs in order. He expected to return. Had he known it was a permanent good-by, he would have departed with considerable reluctance and sadness. Great events were in the making, and he would not be there to watch and help direct them. He had made a host of friends, both male and female, most of whom he would never see again. And there was France herself, *la belle France*, even in the course of a revolution pre-eminent among the nations of the earth, with a people warm, devoted and benevolent, eminent in science, in politeness, in the ease and vivacity of their conversation. Of all the countries of the world France would remain his second choice after America.[25]

He went to see Montmorin to make final arrangements between the two countries. He obtained assurances that the ports of the French West Indies would remain open to American trade at least until February. He also proposed to the French Minister that, in view of the shortage of bread in Paris, it would be to France's advantage to permit the entry of American salt beef, which could be sold to the populace at moderate prices. Montmorin was at first reluctant, but finally agreed that Jefferson might take it up with Necker, now triumphantly returned. After some delay, Jefferson incorporated his proposition in a letter, which Short was to deliver to Necker after Jefferson had sailed.[26] But nothing ever came of it.

There were good-bys to be said, outfits to be purchased for himself and his daughters, his servants to be paid off, books, furniture and all the instruments, paintings, statuary and bric-a-brac he had bought so freely to be packed for transport. It made up to an enormous bulk—86 large packing cases; so enormous, indeed, that when they finally arrived at the docks of Havre for lading on board ship, the revolutionary mob suspected that it could only be the effects of a fleeing aristocrat, and insisted on unpacking the boxes under the supervision of the National Guard. Luckily, nothing was harmed; and the precious articles were repacked, and safely placed on board.

Fifteen of the cases contained books; and among much more were 6 sofas, 44 chairs encrusted with gold leaf, tables, beds, commodes, mirrors, chiffoniers, curtains, drapery, bell pulls, paintings, statuary, wines, seeds, plants and scientific instruments.[27]

Yet in the midst of the hurry and scurry of these preparations, Jefferson found time to write out and send to Madison a long, theoretical argument directed against the right of any one generation to saddle succeeding generations with a load of debts. This philosophical principle of finance was to preoccupy him for many years to come; and it always remained a cardinal base for his own political operations. It was fundamental to his conflict with Hamilton, to his career as President, and he adverted to it again and again after he quit the Presidency.

His argument ran something as follows. An individual occupies a portion of earth only during his lifetime. On his death, it no longer is his; and reverts to society, either in the large or in the persons of his heirs. No man, therefore, has a natural right to saddle that land with his own debts; otherwise, during his lifetime, he could eat up the usufruct for generations to come, so that "the lands would belong to the dead, and not to the living." And what was true for an individual, was equally true for society collectively.

"The earth," he declared, "belongs always to the living generation." And that generation, he figured—employing actuarial tables of doubtful validity—consisted only of nineteen years, representative of the shift from a majority of one generation to a majority of another. From this calculation he concluded that, to establish his principle, all contracts, debts, constitutions and laws should be limited in binding effect to that period only. In other words, even the Constitutions of the United States and of Virginia should cease after nineteen years, and the new generation then alive have the right to form new ones in their stead.[28]

This was doctrinaire theory with a vengeance. Aside from the convulsions and dislocations of society inevitable on the repeated extinctions of laws and societies after set terms of years, he overlooked the fact that many debts, individual as well as communal, are entered into to pay for long-range improvements, whose benefits accrue not so much to the current generation as to posterity. Such items as the planting of orchards that take years to mature and bear fruit, the building of canals, roads and harbors, come instantly to mind. If Jefferson's sacred principle of pay-as-you-go were rigidly to be applied, no one generation would ever do anything for the future, but would busy itself only with short-range projects of which it could selfishly exhaust the avails during its own life.

Finally, all arrangements were made. Young Short, who had been the first to propose going home, remained with the temporary title of Chargé d'Affaires until Jefferson's expected return. The bulky baggage was left for transportation by Short, and Jefferson, with Patsy and Polly, started out on September 26, 1789.

They arrived in Havre on the 28th to find their troubles only begun. The axle tree of Jefferson's phaeton had broken on the way, as well as the tire of his chariot. Both of these vehicles were to accompany him to America. And, the day after his arrival, the elements broke loose with a fury he had never before witnessed. The storm continued without abatement until the 4th of October, during which time it was impossible for any ship to leave the harbor.

On that day the wind began to drop, and Jefferson hurriedly put his baggage on board the packet *Anna,* hoping to start. But the storm rose again, and it was not until the 8th that sail was set for England. During the interim, on the 6th, in a furious tempest of wind and rain, Jefferson determined to seek out a pair of shepherd dogs for importation to America. He walked ten miles in the dirty weather, clambering cliffs in quest of shepherds who might sell him the animals, but finding none foolhardy enough to brave the storm as he did. On his way back, he came across the body of a man who had just that moment shot himself. The corpse was still warm, though already sodden with rain; and its face was so shredded and torn that identification was practically impossible.[29]

Though shepherd dogs were lacking, he had already managed to obtain some bulldogs, which duly arrived with him in Virginia, and became the ancestors of a numerous progeny.[30]

On the 8th the gale dropped, and the packet stood out of Havre for Cowes, in England, where Jefferson was to transship to an English boat. No French vessel, it seems, was then leaving direct for an American port.

Contrary winds lengthened the usually short run, and it was not until the 17th that it arrived at its destination. Trumbull had made arrangements for Jefferson to sail from Cowes on the English ship, *Clermont;* but here again contrary winds intervened until the 22nd. Jefferson beguiled his impatience with various matters. He still hoped that Angelica Church might change her mind and travel down from London to join him; and he wanted to hear the results of James Rumsey's much-heralded experiments with steam navigation, the trial of which was shortly scheduled to take place.[31] But the wind veered on October 22nd, and the *Clermont* left Cowes before he received any word. The experiment proved unsuccessful;

but Jefferson's intense interest in steam navigation was to continue until Robert Fulton and John Fitch finally made it practicable.

The voyage home was accompanied by favoring winds and fine weather, and was accomplished in the remarkable time of twenty-six days; plus three days of beating about the Chesapeake Capes in a heavy fog, and a final run for Norfolk in a strong wind that carried away the top sails. Barely had Jefferson and the other passengers landed at the dock when fire broke out in the "middle steerage" of the vessel and destroyed the cabin before it was extinguished. Fortunately, Jefferson's immense baggage, still on board, was unharmed, and thereafter promptly evacuated.[32]

On November 23, 1789, amid these exciting circumstances, Jefferson stepped foot on American soil, after an absence of more than five years.

CHAPTER 29

Home Again

IN a sense, it was strange soil on which Jefferson now set foot. For five and a half years he had heard the French tongue almost exclusively, and had been submerged in the warm sea of French manners, customs, civilization. He had witnessed the beginning of a great revolution; but a revolution far different in inception and in method from the one he had earlier quitted on American soil.

Nor had America remained static in the interim. He had left a loosely bound aggregation of independent States, and was returning to a nation with a fixed constitution and a government with carefully defined powers. George Washington, his fellow Virginian, was President of the new nation; and John Adams, his former fellow commissioner, had returned from his post in England to become Vice-President. Europe, for so many years the head and center of his own affairs, was but a mere geographical term to most of his countrymen; their interests were concentered in this vigorous continent of their own. Jefferson required time to renew his old identity, to become neighbor and intimate once more with these cruder, more alive, more raucous people whose manners had not yet been so rubbed down by time that they slid easily and frictionlessly down the stranger's gullet.

But the people of his native Virginia sought to make the transition smooth for the returned exile. His old accomplishments were remembered and had grown into a legend; his failures had been tempered by the passage of time and were forgotten. He was as yet untouched by the party passions and vehement politics of the transition years. All, therefore, could join sincerely to honor the distinguished elder statesman.

Norfolk turned out officially to welcome Jefferson. The mayor, the aldermen and the recorder offered their addresses, and Jefferson obliged with a graceful response. Dr. James Currie of Eastwood placed his carriage and horses at his disposal for transport to Monticello.[1]

But Jefferson's first destination was Eppington, the home of his brother-in-law, Francis Eppes. He had much private business to discuss—the condition of his estates, his debts and certain family matters; one of which related particularly to the future of Patsy.

Therefore, as soon as he could decently escape from the congratulations of his fellow citizens, he set out with Patsy and Polly for Eppington, noted with a vast satisfaction the partially constructed capitol building, the visible embodiment of his architectural dream. When finished, he wrote Short, it "will be worthy of being exhibited along side the most celebrated remains of antiquity." Charlottesville had grown considerably during his absence, and held such old friends as Monroe, John Nicholas, Dr. Gilmer and Colonel Bell.

His greatest eagerness, however, on reaching Eppington was to get all the local news—the marriages, births and deaths in Virginia during his absence. His next was to acquaint himself with the local political situation. That was not too good. "Anti-federalism is not yet dead in this country," he told Short with some indignation. "The Gentlemen who opposed [the Constitution] retain a good deal of malevolence towards the new Government: Henry is its avowed foe. He stands higher in public estimation than he ever did, yet he was so often in the minority in the present assembly that he has quitted it, never more to return, unless an opportunity offers to overturn the new constitution." [2]

If Patrick Henry had come to be, in Jefferson's mind, both his personal and political enemy, the Virginia Assembly had no such feelings about their returned compatriot. Momentarily freed from Henry's domination, they were eager to let bygones be bygones, and to overcome the bad taste of that ancient investigation by present fulsome honors. On December 7th, they formally congratulated their distinguished citizen on his return from Europe; and Jefferson, with mixed feelings and unpleasant memories, replied. It was evidently one of the most difficult tasks of writing he ever had in his life. The draft of his reply is a veritable maze of erasures, crossings-out and insertions that again were eliminated. The ordinarily facile molder of phrases stumbled and halted. He could not make up his mind exactly what to say to this Assembly of his peers who had once submitted him to the most painful mortification of his life, but who were now glad to do him honor.

His first drafts were effusive. "My faculties, such as they are," he wrote, "too poor indeed to be offered, are devoted to the public [service?] & their approbation is my supreme reward"; with ensuing expressions such as "their will is my law." But that too was crossed out; and his final draft was much lower-toned in key and quite formal in content. "I shall hope to merit a continuance of their goodness," he now wrote, "by obeying the impulse of a Zeal of which the public good is the first object, and public esteem the highest reward." [3]

He was confronted with the same dilemma when his neighbors of Albemarle County addressed him, even though the memorial was signed by such good friends as Monroe, George Gilmer, Nicholas Lewis, W. C. Nicholas, John Breckinridge and a host of others. His draft of a reply was similarly crisscrossed with corrections, and eventually shifted from plain-spoken warnings about the necessity for vigilance in government to a series of genial platitudes perhaps more appropriate to the occasion.[4]

But a more important matter was at hand; one on which Jefferson's ultimate decision was calculated to change the whole course of his life. As early as May, 1789, Madison had written to Jefferson in Paris to sound him out on the possibility of his accepting an appointment at home in the new Federal Government.[5]

Jefferson had then declined any American office; in fact, he had come to America fully determined, after settling his daughters in Virginia, eventually to resume his duties in France.

But the very day he had landed in Norfolk, he found himself reported in the newspapers as having been nominated by George Washington to the new office of Secretary of State.[6] And, at Eppington, a more official notification, dated October 13th, awaited him from Washington.

Jefferson was in a dilemma. He wanted to return to Paris. He had been happy there; he had made many friends; and, above all, he ardently desired to witness firsthand the course of that glorious revolution which he was certain would end happily and bloodlessly within a year. After that, it was his intention to yield his post, return once more, this time for good, to Monticello, retire from politics and live the life of a student and a country gentleman.[7]

But another cause for hesitation peeped through his reply to Washington; one which disclosed his morbid sensitivity to criticism and the unhealed quality of the wound which had been inflicted on him by the Virginia inquiry into his governorship. He would prefer, he told Washington, to return to France, rather than accept an office where he foresaw "the possibility that this may end disagreeably for me," with "the criticisms and censures of a public, just indeed in their intentions, but sometimes misinformed and misled." However, he did not interpose a positive and unequivocal refusal. If Washington, after due deliberation, still insisted, he would obey. He ended on a rather pathetic note: "My chief comfort will be to work under your eye, my only shelter the authority of your name, and the wisdom of measures to be dictated by you and implicitly executed by me." [8]

In other words, Jefferson shrank from assuming primary responsibility; naïvely believing that thereby he could avoid that involvement with political passions and public scrutiny which he most dreaded. He was to be sadly disillusioned.

Washington did insist and, on February 14, 1790, Jefferson reluctantly and with grave misgivings, signified his assent.[9]

It seemed as if everyone else had known about Washington's desire to bring Jefferson into the government before he did. William Short, back in Paris, had heard about it late in November from the Comte de Moustier and a Mr. McCartey, just arrived from the United States. Moustier, mercifully unwitting that Jefferson had requested Lafayette to arrange for his recall as Minister, told Short, so the latter wrote, that Washington had so set his heart on Jefferson's accepting the post of Secretary of State "as will induce him to press, sollicit & beg it of you—they add that his sollicitations & intreaties are so seldom given that they cannot be given in vain." Which brought Short to his own affairs. Since Jefferson would not return, what was going to happen to him? Both Cyrus Griffin and Gouverneur Morris wanted Jefferson's old post. But so did Short; clearly intimating that Jefferson ought to get it for him.[10]

Short obviously knew whereof he spoke. Even before Jefferson quite knew what his own plans were, Griffin was soliciting his recommendation for his post as Minister to France.[11] Once Jefferson had made up his mind, however, he exerted all his influence in favor of his "son" Short. He tried hard to get him the legation; or any other honorable and lucrative post within the purviews of the government. His efforts failed—Washington and Congress did not view this inexperienced and untried young man with the fond eyes of a Jefferson.

But far more important to him at the moment was an event which was to take place in his own family. During the summer of 1788 young Thomas Mann Randolph, Jr., the eldest son of Col. Thomas Mann Randolph of Tuckahoe and a second cousin and childhood playmate of Patsy Jefferson, had arrived in Paris. He had been studying at the University of Edinburgh and, during vacation, sought the opportunity of paying his respects to his relatives. He and Patsy—or Martha, as perhaps from this point on she ought more dignifiedly to be called—met again, renewed old recollections, and achieved warmer ones. Whether young Randolph proposed then, or waited, after his return to Virginia, for Martha's appearance there, is unknown; but it is probable that the knowledge of forthcoming events quickened Jefferson's anxiety to bring Martha once more to Monticello.

At any event, no sooner had the young couple been reunited on Virginia soil than plans were arranged for speedy marriage. The paternal parents on both sides—the mothers were dead—cordially approved of this additional union between their families. Col. Randolph, to whom all information points as being singularly testy and abrupt in his dealings, nevertheless wrote Jefferson of his "real and singular pleasure" in the proposed marriage; and signified his intention to give the newlyweds immediate possession of his estate at Varina.[12]

Jefferson was similarly overjoyed at the approaching marriage of his eldest daughter. His fears that she might marry a Frenchman and a Catholic or, in the alternative, a Virginia "blockhead," now vanished. He knew young Randolph, knew his antecedents and capabilities, and thought highly of both. After the event, he was to write to a friend in Paris: "My daughter is married agreeably to my most sanguine wishes. The talents, temper, family & fortune of the young gentleman are all I could have desired." [13]

The date for the wedding was set for February 23, 1790. Immersed in preparations, Jefferson was unable to leave Monticello as speedily as Washington had hoped to assume his new duties in New York, the temporary capital of the United States. He had already told Washington it would be impossible; and he now wrote to Madison to explain to him the particular reason. Col. Randolph was coming to Monticello only a few days before the ceremony to arrange with him the essential financial and other provisions they expected to make for the youthful couple. "Thus you see," he ended, "that the happiness of a Child, for life, would be hazarded were I to go away before this arrangement is made." [14]

The arrangements were duly concluded and, on the appointed date, the wedding took place at Monticello. Immediately following the ceremony, Jefferson handed his daughter a most curious document—a series of memoranda he had jotted down on what constituted good wifely conduct. It is difficult to say whether the aphorisms were original with him—certain expressions indicate they might have been written by a woman—but obviously they expressed his sentiments and met with his full approval. "Sweetness of temper, affection to a husband, attention to his interests, constitute the duties of wife & form the basis of matrimonial felicity," was one. Another declared that "marriage, be a husband what he may, reverses the prerogative of sex; his will expect to be pleased, and ours [?] must be sedulous to please." It was the wife's fault, asserted still another, if the husband sought company and pleasure elsewhere than in her company.[15]

Jefferson would have much preferred that the new bride and groom settle down at Edgehill, near Monticello, instead of at distant Varina, which Col. Randolph had given them. "No circumstance," he wrote mournfully to Martha, "ever made me feel so strongly the thralldom of Mr. Wayles's debt. Were I liberated from that, I should not fear but that Colonel Randolph and myself, by making it a joint contribution, could effect the fixing you there, without interfering with what he otherwise proposes to give Mr. Randolph." [16]

It was with perhaps that in mind that, two months earlier, he had written to his Dutch banker friends, the Staphorsts, asking for a cash loan of one or two thousand dollars.[17] To such a low ebb had his physical fortunes fallen.

Five months after the marriage, Martha wrote in considerable agitation to her father. Old Col. Randolph, from whom financially such high hopes had been anticipated, had decided to shed his lonely state and remarry—with a young girl no older than his new daughter-in-law.

Doubtless Jefferson was at first taken aback. But when the initial shock was over, he sent his daughter some sound advice, particularly as it seemed she was openly showing her disapproval to her father-in-law of his approaching blissful state. "Col. Randolph's marriage was to be expected," he soothed. "All his amusements depending on society, he cannot live alone. The settlement spoken of [with his new wife] may be liable to objections in point of prudence and justice. However, I hope it will not be the cause of any diminution of affection between him and Mr. Randolph and yourself. That cannot remedy the evil, and may make it a great deal worse." He concluded with practical suggestions for their keeping good relations with the Colonel and his expected lady.[18] The marriage did take place; and, obviously, Martha hid her resentment in accordance with her father's instructions; for no breach followed between the two families.

With his private affairs thus placed in some sort of order, and his daughter safely married, Jefferson departed from Monticello by phaeton on March 1, 1790, bound for New York and the newly created office of Secretary of State.

He paused first in Richmond, however, to see his old friends and to acquaint himself with the political ideas of his native state before he entered upon the larger field of Federal affairs. On March 8th, he was on the road again; on March 11th, he arrived in Alexandria. From there he shipped to the Comtesse de Tessé in Paris a box of native American plants for her garden, in accordance with the "botanical commission" she had imposed on him before his leaving France.[19]

He also wrote to Short to wind up his affairs in Paris, terminate the lease and give notice to the staff of servants; but to continue their salaries until they found other places or he advised to the contrary. "I exempt from this Petit," he added, "whom I very much wish to have with me at New York in the same capacity of housekeeper." Let Petit sell Jefferson's horse, chariot, cabriolet and paper press for whatever they would bring; and pack carefully his papers, philosophical instruments, books and pictures; then invoice and ship them.[20]

A deep fall of snow at Alexandria forced Jefferson to change his mode of travel. He sent his phaeton to New York by boat; and, having his horses led, decided to "bump it myself in the stage to my journey's end." [21]

His next stop was Philadelphia, where he visited "the venerable and beloved Franklin," then in his last illness. Franklin inquired after all his friends in France, and Jefferson gave him the latest news. Before he left, never to see the elder statesman again, Jefferson was given by the dying man a copy of his narrative of the negotiations with Lord North. Jefferson later turned it over to Franklin's grandson, William Temple Franklin, who published it many years later with certain excisions which Jefferson marked and deprecated.[22]

On March 21, 1790, Jefferson arrived in New York. His first task was to seek living quarters. He found them at No. 57 Maiden Lane, which he leased from the owners, Robert and Peter Bruce, for £100 per annum.[23]

The task of setting up house remained. Petit was sorely needed. He sent another letter, this time urgent, to Short. "Petit must be prevailed on to come at all events.... I find I cannot do without him here. I shall not attempt to commence housekeeping till he arrives with my furniture." When Petit did come, he was to bring "a stock of Maccaroni, Parmesan cheese, figs of Marseilles, Brugnoles, raisins, almonds, mustard, Vinaigre d'Estragon, other good vinegar, oil"; in fine, all those products of Europe whose acquaintance Jefferson had made and loved, and which could not be had without great difficulty in America.

There were also commissions for Short himself to handle. He was to have a clock made for Jefferson, in place of the one stolen from his Parisian residence. It was to consist of two obelisks, connected by a chain from which a round-faced clock depended. He also wanted a copying press, books, some rolls of "plain sky blue paper for papering a room," festoons and cornice paper. And the servants were now to be paid off.[24]

Jefferson was not too happy about his new quarters; but he had not been able to find a decent house on Broadway, which would have been closer to the seat of government. Until the last moment, he hoped that a better one might appear on the market by the time his furniture arrived. It did not; and on June 1st, for lack of a better, he moved into the Maiden Lane establishment.[25]

It was only then that he was able to renew his weather observations—at least in the climate of New York; for he had been diligently taking readings at Monticello, with Madison's father similarly occupied in Orange. Jefferson urged his son-in-law, Thomas Mann Randolph, to do the same; approving in the process of young Randolph's decision to study law. It is, he declared, "the most certain stepping stone to preferment in the political line."

As always, Jefferson was more than willing to map out a course of studies. Adam Smith's *Wealth of Nations* was the best for political economy. Montesquieu's *Spirit of Laws* was generally recommended for the science of government; but Jefferson cautioned against its uncritical use. "It contains indeed a great number of political truths; but also an equal number of heresies; so that the reader must be constantly on his guard." Locke's little volume on government was "perfect as far it goes." And, in the practical field, "there is no better book than the *Federalist*." [26]

Jefferson also received a letter from Europe that touched him deeply and awakened memories. It gives me, he assured the writer, Maria Cosway, "a foretaste of the sensations we are to feel in the next world, on the arrival of any new-comer from the circle of friends we have left behind." If only she would bring her pencil and harp to the United States! The circle would then be complete. For Trumbull was now in Philadelphia, busy with his painting; and Angelica Church, whom he had unfortunately missed both at Philadelphia and New York, was at least close at hand. Jefferson did not then realize that he would never see either Maria or Angelica in the flesh again. Upon Angelica he was urging that she bring her husband to America, where he might enter Congress and continue his career of politics.[27] When John Barker Church finally did come, however, it was to engage in insurance underwriting, a far more lucrative profession for him than politics.

With his private affairs thus arranged, and with engaging personalities out of the way, Jefferson entered upon his new political duties.

CHAPTER 30

A Stranger to the Scene

JEFFERSON was only a month short of his forty-seventh birthday when he assumed his duties as Secretary of State. Dr. Benjamin Rush, with whom he had visited at Philadelphia on his way to New York, thought that he dressed plainly and that his manners had not changed as a result of his European experience. Much to the eminent doctor's satisfaction, Jefferson still considered himself a republican and deplored John Adams's alleged shift in opinion to a more aristocratical idea, even though he spoke of him with respect and affection as a great and upright man.[1] What brought about this new view of Adams were the stories that assiduously circulated of his attempt to introduce monarchical salutations and courtly protocol into the business of government.

A more detailed—and more critical—description of the new Secretary of State at this time has come to us from the pen of William Maclay, backwoods Pennsylvania radical and United States Senator. To this fierce egalitarian, all Virginia gentlemen were suspect as essential aristocrats, and Jefferson's much-touted republicanism seemed but a pale simulacrum of the real thing.

He met Jefferson for the first time in May, 1790, and that night set down his impressions of the author of the Declaration of Independence. "Jefferson is a slender man," he wrote; "has rather the air of stiffness in his manner; his clothes seem too small for him; he sits in a lounging manner, on one hip commonly, and with one of his shoulders elevated much above the other; his face has a sunny aspect; his whole figure has a loose, shackling air. He had a rambling, vacant look, and nothing of that firm, collected deportment which I expected would dignify the presence of a secretary or minister. I looked for gravity, but a laxity of manner seemed shed about him. He spoke almost without ceasing. But even his discourse partook of his personal demeanor. It was loose and rambling, and yet he scattered information wherever he went, and some even brilliant sentiments sparkled from him. The information which he gave us respecting foreign ministers, etc., was all high-spiced. He had been long enough abroad to catch the tone of European folly." [2]

Maclay's somewhat caustic description has been too readily accepted as standard for the Jefferson of this period. Yet Maclay himself contradicted this alleged loose-shackledness of posture and behavior, this lack of collected deportment and gravity, by his own comment of only a month later. *Then*, while dismissing Hamilton as a "skite" and possessed of a "very boyish, giddy manner," he thought that Jefferson transgressed on the other extreme of a stiff gentility and a lofty gravity.[3] As against his acid reaction to Jefferson's anecdotes of the French court we have Rush's testimony that he had found his friend unchanged by his experience abroad. Nor does the lounging, loose-jointed figure comport with the description left by Jefferson's overseer, Edmund Bacon, who specifically mentions his master's frame—six feet, two and a half inches in height—as "straight as a gun-barrel," without an ounce of surplus flesh upon it. And in place of the rambling, vacant look that Maclay noted, Bacon speaks of a mild, pleasant and unruffled countenance—a description that sits much more readily with every portrait that has come down to us.[4]

The business of government was already well under way when Jefferson entered office at the end of March, 1790. Washington had been inaugurated on April 30th of the year before; Congress had been elected and begun its functions; and the other government departments had been organized and their chiefs installed. Only the Department of State had awaited Jefferson's acceptance and arrival.

The most important of the administrative branches, aside from State, had been the Treasury; and Washington had chosen Alexander Hamilton for that difficult post. Young, short in stature and surmounting his lack of inches by an erect and vigorous carriage, brilliantly opinionated and ready with his pen, knowing exactly what he wanted and hewing a straight line toward sharply defined goals, exponent of a strong, centralized government, Hamilton had deemed the Constitution a weak, watered-down, mere shilly-shally affair, yet had accepted it as the best that could be attained under the circumstances. He had entered the Treasury with considerable hesitation; but, once in office, he was determined, though the heavens fell, to place the nation's finances on a sound, impregnable basis and thereby forge a unity in place of the loose-jointed confederation of independent sovereignties he had always despised. No one more antithetical in character, in philosophy and in ultimate goals to his new colleague, Jefferson, could possibly have been chosen.

The Department of War went to Henry Knox of Massachusetts, a mountain of a man in body and sluggish in mind. Knox had been a general in the Revolution; and his services, if undistinguished, had not fallen below the average. Conservative in temperament, he betrayed no originality in office, and was content generally to follow the leadership of his more brilliant associate, Hamilton.

Edmund Randolph, Jefferson's erstwhile disciple and, during his friend's absence in Europe, the governor of Virginia, was given the office of Attorney General. Randolph had ability and had been decidedly republican in sentiment. But he too seemed to require someone of bolder initiative to follow; yet, at the same time, he was extremely sensitive to the idea that pressure might be applied to him and was liable unpredictably to kick over the traces. He was to cause Jefferson considerable annoyance with his on-the-fence, off-one-side-and-over-the-other attitude during Cabinet sessions.

Washington had been faced with a dilemma when it came to choosing the head of the State Department. There were very few men in public life who knew much about Europe or the tangled web of foreign relations that confronted the newborn republic. Benjamin Franklin would have been the ideal choice for the position—but Franklin was coming to the end of a long and fruitful life. John Adams was ensconced in the Vice-Presidency, and John Jay, who had handled foreign affairs during the last stages of the Confederacy and would therefore have been the logical choice, was slated for the chief position in the newly erected Supreme Court. That left Jefferson as the only man with a sufficient knowledge of European diplomacy and personalities, and a background in diplomatic techniques. It was for that reason that Washington had been so urgent that he accept, and that he had been so willing to wait patiently for his arrival.

But Jefferson's first introduction to government had but little to do, except indirectly, with the proper functions of his department. In truth, neither its duties nor those of the other departments had as yet been sharply defined. There was considerable overlapping—a condition which led to much mutual raiding and sharp conflicts among the Secretaries—and the Department of State, in particular, was a sort of catchall. Aside from foreign affairs, its special domain, it included many domestic functions that today have been separated into other divisions. Indian affairs, weights and measures, the mint, lighthouses, patents, internal improvements and other internal matters were deposited in the Department.

But Washington did not expect, nor was it intended at first, that the several Secretaries be confined to their own duties. Washington, feeling his way in this novel and untried government, consulted with all of them, either as a group or individually, on the general questions that arose from time to time. Whether it was a problem of war or peace, of a treaty with a foreign power, of intricate matters of finance, of a Constitutional question—entirely within the purview of a single Department or not—he called for the opinions of all the Secretaries before coming to a final decision. And, generally, he permitted himself to be guided by the majority opinion; casting a deciding ballot, as it were, only when there was a deadlock among his appointees.

The first matter on which Washington asked Jefferson's opinion was a procedural one: "How shall communications from the several states to Congress through the channel of the President be made?" Madison, now a member of the House of Representatives from Virginia, suggested that they be delivered to Congress in person by the Secretary of State if the communications required any recommendations by the President; if not, by Tobias Lear, Washington's private secretary. Jefferson transmitted Madison's advice without other comment than that Washington might order what he thought best; that it did not much matter at present, since the government was still young and changes could be made later, if desirable.[5]

Another matter concerned a proposition by Virginia to establish a woolen manufactory within the state, with a subsidy to the promoter and aid in the importation under contract of skilled workmen from England. Jefferson wrote an opinion in favor of Washington's intervention in the project and outlined the terms for a possible contract; but, after he had written it, second thought prevailed, and he endorsed on the back of his memorandum: "N. B. After this report was given in the Secy of State thought upon farther considerations that the President had better not have any further agency in the business." [6]

Far more urgent business, however, was on tap; and Jefferson had come to New York and assumed his office in the very middle of it. Hamilton had set in motion his wide-ranging propositions for placing the financial house of the United States in order and had thereby aroused animosities and passions that threatened to wreck the youthful nation even before it had commenced to get under way.

On the surface, the propositions seemed logical, desirable, and even inevitable. The outstanding debt of the nation, both Federal and State, amounted with accrued interest to a total of $85,000,000. This was a staggering sum, considering the largely agricultural economy of the country and the fact that the Federal Government, as such, had not yet devised a proper system of taxes to take care of its day-to-day functions, much less the service of a national debt.

Hamilton proposed to levy an internal excise tax on distilled liquors and an impost on imported articles for the benefit of the national government. This was not too vehemently opposed; though, later, the excise tax gave rise to what was known as the Whisky Rebellion.

On the Federal debt, the evidences of which were held by foreign and domestic creditors, Hamilton held that *both* were primary obligations of the government which must, in honor and in sound business practice, be paid in full. No one disputed the first section, relating to the foreign obligations; but a storm arose over the second, concerning domestic creditors.

No sooner had Hamilton's famous "First Report on the Public Credit" been submitted to Congress than the domestic proposition met with furious opposition. For much had happened to that portion of the debt since it had been originally contracted during the Revolution. The holders—soldiers and small merchants chiefly—had for the most part long since given up any real prospect of being paid, and had parted with the paper evidences to more speculative gentry with a sufficient backlog of money at fractions of the face value, ranging as low as twelve cents on the dollar.

Was it fair, asked the opposition, for these original holders now to be taxed so that payment in full might be given to mere speculators who had taken advantage of their necessities and had neither rendered services nor parted with substantial goods? Would it not be more just either to pay the current holders what they had actually given for the certificates and allot the difference to the dispossessed original holders—or pay *all* the certificates at a fixed discount? To this, Hamilton retorted that neither law nor equity supported such a contention; that the certificates had been made negotiable and were therefore subject to the ordinary practices of trade; and that the shaky national credit could only be bolstered by payment in full to those in whose name the certificates were currently registered.

He proposed, therefore, to fund the entire debt, to issue new interest-bearing certificates of indebtedness for the full amount and to use the proceeds for payment of the old certificates. He also intimated that such a new funded debt, to run for a lengthy period, might properly be considered as advantageous to the government and be, in effect, "a national blessing." For thereby the influential propertied classes, necessarily the largest purchasers of the new certificates, would find it to their interest to bolster and make permanent the government from whose coffers both principal and interest must in the future flow.

Hamilton submitted his report to Congress on January 14, 1790, and the fight was joined. The opposition, chiefly from the agricultural states in which the money classes—and, therefore, the present and future holders of certificates—were not numerous, shouted denunciations of what they conceived to be a piece of class legislation. They spoke openly of corruption as well; for, in anticipation of the Report and even before its terms became generally known to the public, northern financial interests had secretly and in haste purchased old certificates still in the hands of the unwitting public and stood to reap a harvest should Hamilton's proposals be adopted. The corruption—and the leakage of information—could be traced to Hamilton's own Assistant Secretary of Treasury, William Duer, private banker and prince of speculators.[7]

Madison had, up to this point, seen eye to eye with Hamilton on the necessity for a strong central government and had even approved, though cautiously and with certain reservations, the main tenets of Hamilton's proposals. Jefferson, while still in France, had assured the Dutch bankers that there would be no discrimination between foreign and domestic debtors, and that only a small minority wished to pay the domestic debt other than in full.

But now Madison swung away from co-operation with Hamilton, and became his most formidable opponent. To him, as to others, the speculative activities of the coterie surrounding Hamilton proved the last straw; and he offered in Congress a counterproposal that the current holders be paid at the highest prevailing market price of the securities, and the balance go to the original holders.

The debate in Congress was furious and the beginnings of parties were visible; but, toward the end of February, Madison's motion was voted down, and Hamilton's plan passed *in toto*.

All this was past history by the time of Jefferson's arrival on the public scene; but he appeared in time to be caught in the middle of an even more acrimonious debate on the next step in Hamilton's vast scheme of reorganization. This was the assumption by the Federal Government and the similar funding of the debts which the states themselves had accumulated during the Revolutionary period.

It might have been thought that the states would be only too happy to unload their burdens on the national government. But there were several hidden elements involved which sent several of the states—in particular, Virginia—into a veritable frenzy of opposition.

It was Hamilton's openly avowed purpose, by thus having the central government assume the obligations of the states, to bind them as a matter of self-interest to the continued existence of the nation. For, should the nation fail, the load of debt might return to the shoulders of the states from which it had been shifted. Also, as in the case of the funding of the national debt, the monied men who would purchase would have additional reasons to seek the success of the nation to whom they looked for eventual repayment.

But these same reasons were precisely the ones that caused certain of the states vehemently to oppose assumption. As jealous guardians of their own sovereignties they did *not* wish to create a strong federal government that would encroach on their independence; and, as primary agricultural communities, they feared that with the shift in ownership of the debt to absentee money men in the more industrialized states, the power to influence the decisions of the national government must inevitably shift as well. Furthermore, as in the case of the national debt, the first inklings that Hamilton was going to propose assumption of the state debts sent fast ships, couriers and special agents of northern capitalists rushing south to remote and backwoods sections to buy at heavy discounts the state securities still in the hands of small farmers and petty merchants.

Another potent reason for states like Virginia to oppose assumption was the fact that they had already, by tremendous efforts, paid off portions of their debts; while the northern states had done so sparingly or not at all. Why, therefore, argued the former, should *their* citizens be compelled through taxation to pay again for the benefit of the citizens of the latter states what they had already paid before? Should not credit at least be given by the government to those states which had liquidated their debt in whole or in part?

The debate was raging heavily in Congress on Jefferson's arrival. Madison, though fearing the consequent concentration of wealth in northern hands, would have been willing to settle on the basis of a mutual settlement of accounts between the states and the national government so that those who had paid the greater part of their debts would not be burdened with payment for the debts of those who had not.[8]

But before it ended, Jefferson was involved in a deal that became notorious, and from the consequences of which he tried desperately in later years to dissociate himself, on the plea that he had been a mere late arrival and an innocent, who had been taken in by the machinations of Hamilton and his cohorts. "I was most ignorantly and innocently made to hold the candle," he complained. He had arrived in the midst of the struggle, he said, and "but a stranger to the ground, a stranger to the actors on it, so long absent as to have lost all familiarity with the subject, and as yet unaware of its object, I took no concern in it." [9]

The disingenuous plea cannot stand up in the cold light of the facts. Years before, both Jefferson and his native state had considered with a degree of favor this very proposition for the assumption of state debts by the confederated government. This, of course, was before Virginia had paid off the major portion of her own. Nor was he a "stranger" to the scene. There was Madison—and others—fully acquainted with every twist and turn of the great debate, able and willing to present him with the complete background. And, in truth, Jefferson was watching the course of that debate with an intelligent and interested eye.

When, in the first test, the Hamiltonian forces went down to defeat in the House of Representatives by a vote of 31 to 28, Jefferson reported to his son-in-law, Thomas Mann Randolph, that the measure would be brought up again in another form. "It appears to me," he wrote, "one of those questions which present great inconveniences whichever way it is decided: so that it offers only a choice of evils." [10]

Jefferson knew perfectly well what the choice consisted of; and he committed his thoughts to paper for the benefit of correspondents. No other business could be transacted by Congress, he declared, until the twin questions of assumption and the choice of a permanent capital for the United States were resolved. It was essential, therefore, for the peace and continuance of the Union, that a compromise be arrived at. He saw the necessity for funding the public debts, and that a failure to do so would mean "the end of government." Assumption, he agreed, "must be admitted, but in so qualified a form as to divest it of its injustice. This may be done by assuring to the creditors of every state, a sum exactly proportioned to the contribution [in taxes] of the state: so that the state will on the whole neither gain nor lose. There will remain against the measure only the objection that Congress must lay taxes for these debts which might better be laid & collected by the states." [11]

He also saw clearly that assumption and the question of the Federal capital were intimately tied together. The struggle over the location of the capital was just as severe, and had aroused as many passions, as that over assumption. That struggle was divided into two parts: the eventual placement of the permanent site; and the temporary site until the permanent capital should be built.

The Southern States insisted that the *permanent* capital be awarded to them, and offered the banks of the Potomac for its locus. The Northern

States demanded it within their own territory, and were willing to consider either New York or Pennsylvania. The choice was further complicated by the internecine struggle between New York and Pennsylvania for the *temporary* capital, since it would be ten to fifteen years before any permanent one could be readied for occupancy.

Fisher Ames of Massachusetts, leader of the pro-assumption forces in Congress, noted with alarm and disgust the sidetracking of his pet measure by the controversy over the temporary capital. Votes for and against assumption were being frankly traded by the Pennsylvania and New York delegations in an effort to gain adherents for their respective claims. Ames called it "this despicable grogshop contest, whether the taverns of New York or Philadelphia shall get the custom of Congress." [12]

To his realistic sense, assumption and funding, with all that their financial structure entailed, were far more vital than the vanity or temporary gain involved in the placement of the capital.

But he was quick to see the possibility of advantage for his own cause in the struggle. The Pennsylvania delegation, led by Robert Morris, was negotiating with the southern members: let us have the temporary capital for fifteen years, said the Pennsylvanians, and we shall throw your way the necessary votes for putting the permanent capital on the banks of the Potomac.

As Ames righteously put it, "to do this, and at the same time reject the assumption, is such an outrage upon the feelings of the eastern people, as I persuade myself they dare not commit;—and as our claim of justice has been expressed in a loud tone, and our approaches [*sic*] and resentments have been reiterated since it was denied us, they have become afraid of consequences; and . . . I think I see strong indications of an assent to assumption." [13]

Ames read the signs and portents correctly. And so did Jefferson. As a Virginian, he wanted the capital on the borders of his own state as intensely as any other of his compatriots. As a national figure, he saw the advantages of the assumption of the state debts by the Federal Government and their funding, *provided* Virginia was not harmed thereby. Therefore, if he could get the capital for the South, he would be willing to offer a modified assumption in return. He said as much to his son-in-law: "On the question of residence, the compromise proposed is to give it to Philadelphia for 15. years, & then permanently to Georgetown by the same act. This is the best arrangement we have now any prospect of, & therefore the one to which all our wishes are at present pointed. If this does not take place, something much worse will; to wit an unqualified assumption & the permanent seat on the Delaware." [14]

To Monroe he argued that, should no funding bill be agreed upon, "our credit (raised by late prospects to be the first on the exchange at Amsterdam, where our paper is above par) will burst and vanish, and the states separate to take care every one of itself." [15] Nor did the fact that Monroe promptly retorted with a warning that Virginia was so irreconcilably opposed to assumption that even the *immediate* removal of the capital to the Potomac would not reconcile them to it, change Jefferson's opinion on the subject.[16]

It is therefore impossible, in the light of these and other letters to the same effect, to accept Jefferson's naïve innocence and strangeness to the scene as the explanation of his famous negotiation with Hamilton.

The Secretary of the Treasury had been staggered by the storm of resistance raised by his proposal for assumption and by its initial defeat in Congress. To him, as to Ames, the contest over the capital was a side issue; nor did he care particularly where it would be placed. But he grasped the potentialities of the situation. All that he needed for the passage of assumption was one additional vote in the Senate, and five in the House. Since Pennsylvania was so hot for the capital, let them have it, if they would furnish those extra votes for assumption. Senator William Maclay, to whom he sent an emissary, would have none of the scheme; but Robert Morris found nothing morally wrong in the proposal. He agreed to consult with the other members of his delegation. But before he could do so, Hamilton had been unexpectedly successful in another quarter, and called the Pennsylvania deal off.[17] He had met with Jefferson.

Jefferson, so he was later to tell the story, was stopped by Hamilton in the street as he was going to the President's quarters. Hamilton seemed in despair, and walked him up and down before Washington's door for half an hour, painting for his benefit a pathetic picture of legislative confusion, the disgust of the creditor states, and the danger of their secession. "The members of the administration ought to act in concert" in this grave emergency, he said; and Jefferson had it in his power, by appealing to his friends to vote for assumption, to save the Union. Jefferson was impressed by these arguments; and invited Hamilton to join him and a few of his friends for dinner the following day, where they could discuss the matter as "reasonable men."

The dinner took place and, writes Jefferson, he took no part in the ensuing discussion. It was agreed, however, by the southern members present that some of them should change their votes; "but it was observed that this pill would be peculiarly bitter to the Southern States, and that some concomitant measure should be adopted to sweeten it a little to them." That sweetener, of course, was to present the permanent capital to Georgetown in Virginia, after a temporary residence in Philadelphia for ten years. The bargain was quickly made. Alexander White and Richard Bland Lee, both Virginia members, agreed to vote for assumption; while Hamilton undertook to get his followers to vote for Georgetown. White, noted Jefferson, entered the pact "with a revulsion of stomach almost convulsive." Since he noted no similar phenomenon in Lee, evidently that worthy's stomach was of a stronger and harder mold. And so, ended Jefferson, "the assumption

Courtesy the New-York Historical Society, New York City

THOMAS JEFFERSON

Plaster bust by Jean Antoine Houdon

Collection of Arthur M. DuBois. Courtesy the Frick Art Reference Library

JOHN JAY

Painting by Gilbert Stuart

was passed, and 20. millions of stock divided among the favored states, and thrown in as a pabulum to the stock-jobbing herd." [18]

But this was definitely hindsight; after Jefferson had awakened to Hamilton's full intentions. At the moment he was well satisfied. The federal capital had gone to Virginia; and the original assumption bill had been modified so that Virginia would pay out exactly what she would receive, and therefore not lose a jot in the transaction.[19]

Washington considered himself extremely fortunate in his choice of a Cabinet. "By having Mr. Jefferson at the Head of the Department of State," he wrote Lafayette, "Mr. Jay of the Judiciary, Hamilton of the Treasury and Knox of that of War, I feel myself supported by able Coadjutors, who harmonize extremely well together." [20] Their ability, with the possible exception of Knox, was undoubted; but the harmonious cooperation Washington envisaged was another matter. However, Washington could not at the moment peer into the mists of time.

The grandiloquently named Department of State—as all of the Departments—was a mere embryo of things to come. The entire staff consisted of Jefferson, two chief clerks whose salaries were $800 and $500 respectively, two assistant clerks at $500 each, and a translator at $250.[21] This modest establishment put an unending round of drudgery upon the head, with even the most routine details coming within his province and without any possible delegation of authority to subordinates. The salary attached was $3,000 a year.

Jefferson found himself almost immediately *in medias res.* Both the foreign and the domestic scene required his vigilant attention. Even the battle over assumption and funding, in which he had participated and of which it might have been considered that it was not his proper business, held implications that spilled over into his Department. One was the tie with the seat of government; another was the repercussion on foreign credit.

Both the President and Congress called on Jefferson—and on the other members of the Cabinet—to answer the host of questions that kept thronging up. It was a brand new government, unlike any that had yet appeared on the face of the earth, and it had to be put into immediate operation. Many of the problems that confronted it were novel, and could not be decided from precedents. Others, if not wholly new, required prompt resolution if the government were not to burst open at the seams and the component states fly centrifugally into independent orbits.

Jefferson had barely been installed in office when the questions began to fly at him thick and fast. Perhaps the rate at which they came exacerbated an old condition of his—for his migraine headaches returned with such force that for over a month he was almost wholly incapacitated from sustained thought. Nor did Washington's siege of pneumonia, which occurred at about the same time and which brought him perilously close to death, help him in his own ailment.[22] Nevertheless, Jefferson conscientiously attended to his manifold duties.

Congress had asked him to submit a plan for establishing uniformity in the coinage, weights and measures of the United States. That such uniformity was vital to the success of the national economy no one knew better than Jefferson. He had submitted to the Continental Congress a simple plan for decimal coinage before he had sailed for France; but nothing had come of it at the time. The complications arising from the vast number of foreign coins in circulation, and the varying rates of their exchange, had set almost insurmountable barriers to interstate trade.

Insofar as the coinage was concerned, Jefferson had simply to take out his old report and bring it up to date. But the problem of weights and measures was another matter. As he told his scientific friend, David Rittenhouse, "five and twenty years ago I should have undertaken such a task with pleasure, because the [bases?] on which it rests were then familiar to my mind and the delight of it." But he was now rusty in mathematics and his books and papers, from which he might have derived assistance, were either in Paris or in Virginia. New York, it seemed, "yeilds fewer resources in the way of books than could have been imagined."[23]

In spite of the lack of essential materials, in spite of blinding headaches, Jefferson hacked grimly away at the arid task. He finished the report on May 20th, but held it in his hands for corrections and polishing. On June 12th, he sent it along to Rittenhouse, with a request that he look it over for possible errors, before the "world at large" should do so. On June 15th, there came into his hands from Paris a printed proposition on weights and measures which Talleyrand had submitted to the French Assembly; and three days later he found reported in the press a speech in the British House of Commons covering the same subject. Both these plans were carefully scanned for possible suggestions, Rittenhouse's advice had to be awaited—so that it was July 4, 1790, before Jefferson was finally able to submit his plan.[24]

For a supposed novice and amateur, the report was remarkably logical and soundly based. It was a scientific dissertation on the standards to be employed; a recommendation of the decimal system in weights and measures as well as in coinage, instead of "the present complicated and difficult ratios." He proposed, for example, 10 inches to the foot, 10 feet to a decad, 10 decads to a rood, 10 roods to a furlong, and 10 furlongs to the mile.[25]

Had these suggestions been adopted—somewhat similar to the metric system later accepted by the French and most of the civilized world—the infuriating difficulties that have plagued commerce and generations of schoolboys would have been avoided and the American system of weights and measures been integrated into that to which all but a few nations now adhere.

The report was submitted to the House on July 13th, but inasmuch as Jefferson himself advised that a final decision be put over to the next session in order to find out how France and England were handling the same problem, nothing was then done on it. Eventually, Congress did put into effect the sensible decimal coinage; but the matter of decimal weights and measures was allowed to drop.

But if Congress was not unduly impressed by the report, Jefferson's scientific friends made up for it with a stout chorus of praise. Benjamin Vaughan wrote enthusiastically from London that "I believe you are the first nation that ever produced statesmen who were natural philosophers"; while Ezra Stiles used it as a text for his senior students at Yale, and began a one-man campaign for Jefferson's election to the Presidency when Washington, "that best of Men ... shall be translated to the World of Light." [26]

Another important question that was troubling the Administration was what to do about the so-called "Yazoo Land Grants" made by the State of Georgia. The state legislature, under circumstances of almost unbelievable corruption and outright bribery, had granted to a private company an immense tract of Indian lands within its chartered limits, but of which the state had never acquired legal title from the Indian owners. The repercussions were immediate, and were to bedevil national affairs for many years to come, including Jefferson's own administrations.

At this moment, Jefferson maintained that the grant was void, inasmuch as the Indian title could be acquired only by conquest or by treaty. Since Georgia had ceded to the United States, through the Constitution, her rights of making war and negotiating treaties, only the Federal Government could extinguish the Indian title. Yet, in deference to the sensibilities of Georgia, Jefferson did not advise the stern proclamation that Washington intended; but rather to seek an amicable settlement with that recalcitrant state.[27]

It is interesting to note that Jefferson was standing firmly under the Constitution for the general as against the state government in this clash of sovereignty. Yet, when the matter arose again during his own Presidency, he quietly forgot his constitutional qualms and sided then with Georgia. His decision to do so helped cost him the support of John Randolph of Roanoke, who thundered against the iniquities of the sudden change of front.

Congress had dutifully, in accordance with behind-the-scene maneuvers on the matter, passed a bill shifting the temporary capital to Philadelphia by the 1st of December, 1790, and, after ten years, to set it permanently on the Potomac.

This meant that Jefferson had to move again. He asked William Temple Franklin to find him a house in Philadelphia. Franklin replied that very few were suitable, but suggested several for Jefferson's consideration. Jefferson thought that the one owned by Thomas Leiper was the best suited for his purposes. But it would require extensive alterations. The room over the kitchen he would use for himself; but another room would have to be built as an extension, to be supported above the ground by pillars. This room was to be 14 feet wide and as long as the lot itself. The two lower rooms were to be divided into an antechamber and a dining room. Stables were also to be built to accommodate five horses, with additional room for three carriages. But, he warned, there must be "no seats at the street door to collect lounging servants." Since these specifications would manifestly stagger any landlord, Jefferson added the assurance that "I can say with truth I never had a pin to cavil with a landlord in my life on quitting a house. I take care of it myself, & exact rigorous care from my servants." [28]

Leiper, who was to become a good Republican and a faithful follower of Jefferson, at first balked at these extensive alterations to his premises, but at length, on Jefferson's agreement to stand most of the expense, agreed to the tenancy. Before the protracted negotiations came to a final conclusion, Jefferson was already in Philadelphia, without a house as yet and with the enormous boxes of his furniture, just arrived from Paris, still unpacked.[29]

As late as July, 1790, Short was reporting from Paris that the furniture was still in the process of packing and that Petit, the major-domo, was still obstinate in his refusal to go to America. His chief objection, it seemed, was that the wages Jefferson offered were "infinitely too low." Jefferson had to increase his offer, and a frantic series of letters journeyed back and forth over the Atlantic until finally, toward the end of July, 1791—a full year later—the indispensable Frenchman arrived in Philadelphia, nonchalant and smiling assurance "that he was come pour rester toujours avec moi." [30] If not forever, at least for many years.

As if Jefferson did not have enough trouble over Petit's obstinacy, William Short posed other headaches for him. The moment Jefferson had taken office he had tried to obtain a permanent appointment for his young ward as Chargé d'Affaires. It proved impossible, and he so notified Short in cipher, much to that gentleman's mortification. Jefferson thereupon sought to soothe his angry "son." Since a minister was soon to be appointed to the French post, and Short would thereby be relieved of his duties, "make up your mind," he wrote, "to come & enter sturdily on the public stage. I now know the characters on it, and assure you candidly you may be anything you please at home or abroad as soon as you shall make yourself known and possess yourself of American affairs. We are extremely puzzled to find characters fit for the offices which need them." [31] But young Short was not to be mollified thus easily by the flattery of the older man; and kept up a running series of demands and complaints from his European post with which Jefferson, though sometimes at his wit's end, tried hard to comply.

CHAPTER 31

Secretary of State

TO Jefferson the chief importance of his department, nay, even the chief importance of the United States, lay in the field of foreign relations. Had there been no other nations in the world, had there been no compulsion to present a solid front before them so as to win respect and freedom from aggression, Jefferson would have been well content, practically as well as philosophically, for the liberated Colonies to have continued as independent, self-contained sovereignties.

But the world in which he lived was an aggressor world, in which naked power was the touchstone of morality and big fishes tended to swallow little ones. The Colonies had won their liberty only because they had been united—loose as that unity may have been; and they could obtain their just demands now only by the irresistible power that came from union. He had been long enough in Europe to understand the failure of reason and logic to gain concessions from the nations of the earth unless backed by such power. That was why Jefferson had insisted on his seeming paradox—autonomy and separatism at home, and subordination to a federal unity in all dealings abroad.

Of the problems that confronted the new government in its foreign relations, he had long been aware. Five years in the courts of Europe had given him an unrivaled perspective. Europe was a vast cockpit of rival and suspicious powers, each seeking aggrandizement at the expense of the others. Jefferson would have wanted nothing better than to have sealed off the United States from involvement in Old World affairs, and to erect a Chinese wall behind which the New World could continue under the happiest of auspices to work out its own salvation. But that, he found reluctantly, could not be. The ocean, instead of the vast barrier and Chinese wall he had contemplated, was rather, a broad highway on which the two worlds met and clashed.

A stringent tobacco monopoly in France might mean disaster to Virginia; mercantilist restrictions on fish, whale oil and salt meats brought storms of protest from a suffering New England; closure of the Mississippi to the free shipment of Western produce might mean the eventual separation of the West from the East. Nor was the Old World as far away as at first blush it seemed. Through Canada, Louisiana, the Floridas, Mexico and the West Indies, the nations of Europe parked on our very doorsteps, and constituted an ever-present threat to national independence and expansion.

And, in the more impalpable, though no less real, realm of ideas, Europe exerted unremitting pressure.

Jefferson had returned to America fresh from the initial stages of the great French Revolution, the harbinger of Utopia and a new deal for the oppressed peoples of the earth. He had left America shortly after its own revolution had been consummated, while the great revolutionary phrases were still bright and untainted. He had witnessed in France the stirrings of a great people, and had drunk of the heady wine of revolutionary ardor. He now came back to America with his republican principles new-burnished and whetted from constant use; only to find, to his horror, that something had happened in America during his absence—at least in the circles to which he necessarily gravitated. A weariness and a cynicism had set in, a distrust of the very principles of the great revolution they had only recently accomplished, a hankering for the tyrannical system of England they had just been at such great pains to discard, a positive fear and dread of the similar revolution now rearing its head in France.

"When I arrived at New York in 1790, to take a part in the administration," Jefferson was to recall with contemporary vividness in almost the last year of his life, "being fresh from the French revolution, while in its first and pure stage, and consequently somewhat whetted up in my own republican principles, I found a state of things, in the general society of the place, which I could not have supposed possible. Being a stranger there, I was feasted from table to table, at large set dinners, the parties generally from twenty to thirty. The revolution I had left, and that we had just gone through in the recent change of our own government, being the common topics of conversation, I was astonished to find the general prevalence of monarchical sentiments, insomuch that in maintaining those of republicanism, I had always the whole company on my hands, never scarcely finding among them a single co-advocate in that argument, unless some old member of Congress happened to be present." [1]

While it was true that New York even then was not America, nor was Philadelphia—and that republican principles still held their charm elsewhere—Jefferson realized that this society at the seats of government possessed an influence far beyond its numerical weight. He therefore began to suspect that similar monarchical principles motivated the measures that Hamilton and his associates were advocating and enacting into law.

To find that England—the great enemy and Jefferson's particular bête noire—was now the admired and the emulated, while France—the ally and current republican—was feared and hated, was a shock from which Jefferson never got over. He began to seek sinister meanings in even casual conversation, and discovered monarchical plots in the most innocent acts. The term "monocrat"—meaning a believer in monarchy—became the most opprobrious item in his arsenal of epithets. Inevitably, by virtue of this distrust of all things English, he gravitated to a trust in all things French even when the course of revolution there shifted away from the purity and generous enthusiasm of its beginning. To the end of his days, he was firmly convinced that Hamilton and his friends were intent on establishing an English-type monarch, aristocracy and English-type institutions in this country; and that it was only because of the unremitting efforts of himself and *his* friends that that intent had not been translated into action.

But, for all his philosophical and personal preconceptions, Jefferson followed in his handling of foreign relations a strictly American attitude. The test to him, as to Washington and—in spite of Jefferson's belief to the contrary, to Hamilton also—was the advantage and benefit of the United States.

Even when Jefferson discoursed enthusiastically of the French Revolution, he invariably ended with some observation on how it would benefit the United States. All goes well there, he told his son-in-law shortly after he took office; but the single definite opinion that he expressed was that it might lead to opening the French West Indies to the sale of our goods. "It is impossible," he added, "the world should continue long insensible to so evident a truth as that the right to have commerce & intercourse with our neighbors is a natural right. To suppress this neighborly intercourse is an exercise of force, which we shall have a just right to remove when the superior force" lapses.[2]

Spain and England were at this time on the verge of war, and Jefferson was certain that France must inevitably be involved in it. Yet he saw in the oncoming conflagration only the advantage to the United States. "In that case," he declared, "I hope the new world will fatten on the follies of the old. If we can but establish the principles of the armed neutrality for ourselves, we must become the carriers for all parties as far as we can raise vessels."[3]

A little later, he was writing along similar lines to Monroe, praising that very funding of the debt against which he was afterwards to inveigh in unmeasured terms. It had established our credit at Amsterdam, he avowed, and "our business is to have great credit and to use it little. Whatever enables us to go to war, secures our peace. At present it is essential to let both Spain & England see that we are in a condition for war.... Our object is to feed & theirs to fight. If we are not forced by England, we shall have a gainful time of it."[4]

Nothing could be more remote from the truth than the general portrait of Jefferson as the philosophical idealist who permitted a vague humanitarianism and pacifism to sway his dealings with the world. He could be as hard-boiled, as practical and as cynical, if you will, when the occasion arose, as any veteran diplomat of the Old World.

He expected the war in Europe to become universal, and he took steps in his own private affairs to make the utmost profit out of it. Wheat, he foresaw, would be at a premium in Europe. He therefore ordered his agent in Virginia, Nicholas Lewis, to plant as much wheat as possible, and to drop the culture of tobacco. He was to grow and manufacture hemp, flax, cotton and wool—all the items ordinarily imported from Europe and the flow of which would now be impeded. "*If we may decide from past experience, we may safely say that war and domestic manufacture are more gainful than peace and store supplies.*" [5] The italics, needless to say, are not Jefferson's.

The European war to which Jefferson referred had not actually commenced, though it seemed ready to burst forth any moment. Curiously enough, its roots were to be found on the savage shores of the American Northwest. Spanish influence had been moved steadily northward along the Pacific coast from Spain's possessions in California, and English power had impinged in the form of a trading post on Nootka Sound, in what is now British Columbia. Spain, indignant at what she deemed an encroachment on her rightful sphere of interest, sent an armed ship to seize the post and captured a British vessel in the process. The outraged British demanded reparations and prepared for war.

Since the seat of the controversy was on the American continent, it was rightly believed that any war between the opposing powers in Europe must inevitably spread to the New World. Above all else, Washington feared that spread. Any attempt by England to seize Spanish possessions in America, and especially Louisiana and the Floridas, must necessarily be of the greatest moment to the United States. Neither he nor his Cabinet advisers could view with equanimity their possession by a powerful Great Britain instead of a comparatively weak Spain. But what could the youthful government of this country do about it? The opinions of the Cabinet were solicited.

Jefferson saw the full import of a possible English seizure of the Spanish possessions. It would mean our complete encirclement—on the one side by the English fleet; on the other by English posts and allied Indians. England would thereby gain control of the Mississippi and ruin for the western territory that precious outlet for their produce.

But, he queried realistically, "would the prevention of this be worth a War?" And what were the chances of winning that war, should we decide to go in? None, he was compelled to confess; *unless* France came in on our side. However, he added optimistically, there was "no need to take a part in the war as yet—we may chuse our own time. Delay gives us many chances to avoid it altogether." Eventually, he was also compelled to admit, if England *did* take and continue to hold Louisiana and the Floridas, "we should have to re-take them." Just how that was to be done, he did not say.

The problem was—what was to be done now? He suggested that we propose to Spain that since she could not save her possessions, she declare them independent, and that we join her in guaranteeing their independence. Let us, he added, also enter into an amicable treaty with England providing for our strict neutrality in the war; specifying, however, that "we should view with extreme uneasiness any attempt of either power to seize the possessions of the other on our frontier, as we consider our own safety interested in a due balance between our neighbors." [6]

Nothing was done at the moment along the lines of Jefferson's rather naïve suggestions. But shortly thereafter, Hamilton came to Washington with disturbing information. A Major Beckwith had approached him unofficially as the representative of Lord Dorchester, the British Governor of Canada, to sound out the prospects of the United States granting permission to British troops to march from Canada across United States territory to attack the Spanish possessions. On the memoranda which Hamilton made of his conversations with Beckwith, he added a notation that "Mr. Jefferson was privy to this transaction." [7] Jefferson was later to deny that he had known anything of the transaction; and the facts seem to bear him out.

Why Beckwith should have gone to Hamilton in the first place with a matter that was definitely in the purlieus of the State Department is a matter of extraordinary interest, and affords an illuminating insight into the rapidly unfolding split between Hamilton and Jefferson. To the English, the matter was simple. Hamilton was definitely British-oriented—at least on the international scene—and they felt they would find a more sympathetic listener in him than in Jefferson, of whose adverse sentiments they had no doubt. To the claim that thereby they were guilty of a profound breach of protocol, they could interpose a ready answer. They had no official minister to the United States, through whom such communications would necessarily have had to pass to the State Department. Beckwith had no official status; his conversations and intimations were purely private and could be disavowed if necessary.

But if England's position was understandable, how about Washington's? On receipt of the information from Hamilton, he should have promptly submitted it to Jefferson for his attention. Instead, he first discussed the matter at length with Hamilton and John Jay (Chief Justice of the Supreme Court and not in the Cabinet at all) and said nothing of it to Jefferson.

On the basis of that secret discussion, Hamilton went back to Beckwith for additional conversations. *Then,* and then only, Washington brought the whole matter formally before his Cabinet and, incidentally, to Jefferson's attention.

What, asked Washington, should be the answer of the President of the United States to Lord Dorchester, should he apply for permission to march his troops across American territory? If, as was most probable, such a move should be made without our leave, what notice ought to be taken of the encroachment? [8]

The business, as Washington put it, was wholly hypothetical; nor was there any intimation of Hamilton's private talks with Beckwith, nor of Washington's consideration of them with Hamilton and Jay.

It is true that the constitution of the Cabinet, the separation of its duties and the relation of its individual members to the President were as yet in a state of flux and had not yet attained that rigid demarcation they were later to possess; nevertheless, there was a grave breach of domestic protocol in this cavalier overlooking of the head of the Department of State, to which the management of foreign relations peculiarly adhered. Jefferson would have been well within his rights to have resented his exclusion from a business of such prime importance. Fortunately, he was unaware of the circumstances at the time. When he *did* discover them, his wrath centered chiefly on Hamilton, whom he considered as having intruded on his own domain. The intrusions expanded rather than decreased, and became one of the major issues over which the two men eventually split. While Jefferson never said so openly, it also marked that first doubt concerning Washington's attitude and policy which gradually separated the two men —once so close together—farther and farther apart.

Jefferson's reply to Washington's queries was the first to be submitted from the Cabinet. He reiterated his former opinion that if the only means of preventing England from seizing the Spanish possessions was to enter the general war, we should do so. But this, he added, should only be a last resort, the dread necessity of which ought to be avoided as long as possible.

It was generally agreed, he wrote, that neutrals have the right to grant or refuse permission for belligerent troops to pass through their territory, provided the same treatment was impartially afforded to *all* the belligerents. But, should the United States refuse permission to the British, and they pass notwithstanding, of which course, Jefferson remarked, "there can be little doubt, we shall stand committed. For either we must enter immediately into the war, or pocket an acknowledged insult in the face of the world; and one insult pocketed soon produces another."

Jefferson therefore proposed a middle course: "To avoid giving any answer. They will proceed notwithstanding, but to do this under our silence, will admit of palliation, and produce apologies, from military necessity; and will leave us free to pass it over without dishonor, or to make it a handle of quarrel hereafter, if we should have use for it as such." Should, however, England press us officially in such fashion that we cannot avoid an answer, then, most reluctantly we must grant permission, since we are not ready for an immediate entry into the war.[9]

He had learned much during his stay in France, and from masters of the diplomatic craft. The direct, shirt-sleeve diplomacy of which he had boasted in his first dealings with Vergennes had vanished, and a more subtle, complex variety had taken its place. The edges had been rubbed off his mind, and it had received a smooth, high polish.

Whatever else may be said of Hamilton, subtlety and indirection were not qualities that can be claimed for him. He attacked the same problem with vigorous forthrightness. He agreed with Jefferson that we were in no position to wage war with England, and that neutrality was our best policy; but he disagreed with Jefferson on the method of handling the instant case. Particularly did he oppose Jefferson's suggestion of giving either no answer or an evasive one. That, he declared, was neither dignified nor politic. We should, once the request was officially made, grant permission. If, however, it was decided to refuse, and the British *should* march, then we must resist forcibly, even to the extent of open war. And if, as seemed likely, the British marched first without asking our approval, then we should be content with mere remonstrances.[10] In effect, Hamilton's practical conclusions were similar to Jefferson's though the reasoning by which they were respectively arrived at was wholly dissimilar.

American neutrality, fortunately, was not to be put to this acid test. Dorchester neither asked official permission nor did he march; and the controversy over Nootka Sound was shortly thereafter settled between the contending parties without a resort to war.

The dissipation of the war clouds had an unexpected effect on Jefferson's private fortunes. In expectation of a European conflict, he had ordered his farm lands to be converted to wheat, and had sent some white wheat for planting, which Washington had assured him was the best he had ever seen. Jefferson considered him "so excellent a farmer that I place full confidence in his recommendation." [11]

But now the bonanza seemed at an end. The price of wheat was still high; but that, he thought, was due to the farmers "being exalted by last years high prices," and holding back for still higher. They would, he predicted, be forced to dump their holdings by the spring of 1791; and he did not want his own crops to be caught by the slump. He therefore sent instructions that his wheat be sold in a hurry at current market prices.[12]

Land values had also gone up as a result of the higher prices for both wheat and tobacco; and Jefferson availed himself of the opportunity for bettering his cash position by selling a parcel of 750 acres in Cumberland County and smaller tracts elsewhere for the lump sum of 1,076 pounds sterling.[13] If, at the same time, he purchased a new riding horse named Brimmer for his stables, his satisfaction over the steed's performance doubtless compensated him for the outlay.

Jefferson was definitely disappointed at the sudden collapse of the war scare in Europe. While it was true that the onset of hostilities between England and Spain might have led to an invasion of American neutrality by British troops, the consequences of which were unforeseeable, Jefferson thought that, at the same time, a beleaguered Spain could be forced to yield concessions she was otherwise indisposed to grant.

As a citizen of Virginia, whose territory extended over the mountain barrier into the vague stretches of the West, he had always watched with intense interest the rapid expansion of settlements along the Ohio and toward the Mississippi. With prophetic vision he predicted the irresistible course of empire to the west and southwest, and its eventual bursting of the Spanish boundaries of containment. But he also realized that, unless the Federal Government could obtain for these far-flung settlements the right to the navigation of the Mississippi, they must inevitably seek their economic and territorial salvation apart from the union of the Eastern States. To avoid such a disastrous cleavage called for his utmost diplomacy.

In August, 1790, while the clouds of war were gathered most ominously over Europe, Jefferson set his diplomatic machinery in motion. To the representatives of the United States at the three Courts of Europe most affected by the controversy, he sent long and confidential instructions.

William Carmichael, well-meaning but rather incompetent, was Chargé d'Affaires at Madrid, the heart and center of the matter. Jefferson drafted a series of heads of consideration on the navigation of the Mississippi for Carmichael's use in his discussions with the Spanish foreign office.

We have both the right and a necessity for the navigation of that vital stream, he instructed. The West was clamoring for it and would take it by force, if Spanish obstructions continued. Let Carmichael suggest, therefore, that it would be wiser for Spain to cede peacefully to us all the territory on our side of the Mississippi, on condition that we guarantee to her all her possessions on the other side. After all, Jefferson argued, it was much better for Spain that *we* hold the territories contiguous to her trans-Mississippi possessions than England. "Conquest," he declared, was "not in our principles: inconsistent with our government." We never intended to cross the Mississippi and Spain could feel entirely safe in her western empire. "In fine," Jefferson ended with a flourish, "for a narrow slip of barren, detached and expensive country"—meaning thereby the isle of New Orleans, key to the Mississippi—"Spain secures the rest of her territory, and makes an ally where she might have a dangerous enemy." [14]

These were maximum proposals, of course. It must have been evident to Jefferson that Spain would never submit voluntarily to the loss of the valuable Floridas *and* the strategic port of New Orleans except under overwhelming force or the direst necessity. What he really wanted at the moment, and hoped by frightening Spain with impossible demands to yield as the lesser evil, was the opening of the Mississippi to the unrestricted use of our western territories, and the removal of Spanish barriers to trade at the mouth. These minimal demands were incorporated in a separate letter to Carmichael for his own instructions. Here he spoke plainly and to the point. Impress on the Spaniards, he wrote, that we shall not resume negotiations with them unless they are willing, as a basis, to give us full and immediate rights to the use of the Mississippi. And that meant the right to a port at the entrance to the Gulf of Mexico, where ocean and river vessels could meet and exchange loads without interference. If they agree, let them send a negotiator to the United States at once. Warn them, he added sharply, that time is of the essence. At any moment our western people might take the matter into their own hands; and if they did, "neither themselves nor their rights will ever be abandoned by us." [15]

This was menacing language, of the kind that is usually not employed unless the user is ready to back up language by force of arms. Jefferson had no intention of going to war—and certainly the United States was in no position to do so at the time—but he was so certain that Spain would shortly be involved in a death struggle with far more powerful enemies that he felt safe in employing what was tantamount to an ultimatum.

So certain, indeed, was he of that war that he sent to William Short, now Chargé d'Affaires in France, a set of very confidential communications to be shown to Lafayette as soon as hostilities between England and Spain were commenced. You and he, Jefferson told Short, will then consider the advisability of imparting their contents to Montmorin, the French Minister. France, so Jefferson believed, would enter that war on the side of Spain and would therefore, as her ally, be in a position to bring pressure on her to grant our demands. We *did* want New Orleans; but, if that idea was too "obnoxious" to Spain, let her give us some other port near the mouth of the river, with sufficient surrounding territory to support it properly.[16]

At the same time, Jefferson did not overlook what we might be able to extract from England in the impending crisis. Advise her, he wrote Gouverneur Morris, who was then at London as an informal American agent, "in delicate and friendly terms" that "we wish to be neutral, and will be so, *if they execute the treaty* [of peace] and *attempt no conquests adjoining us*." What he meant by a fair execution of the treaty was the giving up of the trading posts and forts which England still held on our northern and northwestern frontiers. For those, Jefferson added flatly, we will in no case accept any equivalent.[17]

As if these widespread written instructions were not sufficient, Washington and Jefferson sent Col. David Humphreys, the former Secretary of Legation in Paris, to Europe as a secret agent. He was to make the rounds of London, Lisbon and Madrid in the guise of a mere private traveler, and to meet with the American representatives, particularly with Carmichael, and give them a full picture of American affairs that could not safely be committed to paper.[18]

Perhaps Jefferson's audacity might have paid some dividends had the threatened European war actually flamed forth; but the rapid dissipation of the ominous clouds spiked all his schemes, and years of vicissitude were to pass before they came to unexpected fruition.

The single part of the negotiations that had necessarily to continue related to England and her unwarranted retention of the posts. Morris had been directed to discuss *all* the matters of the peace treaty that were still in dispute—the posts, indemnity for the Negro slaves carried off during the Revolution; a commercial treaty; and the exchange of ministers between the two countries so that their relations could be placed on a regular, official basis.

But Morris's reports home were discouraging, and Jefferson summarized them for Washington's benefit. Great Britain did *not* intend to surrender the posts, using as a pretext the claim that even though our courts were now open to British debt actions, so much time had elapsed that even if judgments were granted, no recoveries were possible. On the question of indemnification for the slaves, they demanded such legal proof of British kidnaping in each individual case as was practically impossible to furnish. With respect to a commercial treaty, "they equivocate on every proposal," unless we agree to drop relations with France and bind ourselves to an alliance with *them*. On the question of exchanging ministers, nothing definite could be extracted. Jefferson concluded that "it would be dishonorable to the United States, useless and even injurious, to renew the propositions for a treaty of commerce, or for the exchange of a minister," and that we cease our demands for the posts and the Negroes "till we are in readiness to do ourselves the justice which may be refused." [19]

Thus, during the first year of his term of office as Secretary of State, all of Jefferson's attempts to settle our relations with England and Spain met with defeat. Neither threats nor gentle persuasions were effective; and the force that might have backed them up was unavailable. On that point, both Hamilton and Jefferson, though for widely differing reasons, were in agreement.

On August 15, 1790, President Washington, accompanied by Jefferson, Governor George Clinton of New York, Congressman William Loughton Smith of South Carolina, and other notables, boarded a vessel on Long Island Sound and set sail for Rhode Island. The occasion of the journey was to honor that stubborn and cross-grained little state's final decision to accept the Constitution and enter into the United States of America.

Jefferson had joined the party partly because it was diplomatic to do so, and partly in the hope that a water voyage might dissipate the severe headaches to which he was constantly a martyr. They arrived on the 17th at Newport, where the Presidential party was welcomed with a salute of guns, memorials, set speeches, banquets and a final tour of the town. The next day they embarked for Providence where the same formalities were observed. To the parade of troops and the thudding of drums, the party moved slowly down the main thoroughfare with Washington, Governor Arthur Fenner of Rhode Island, and a senator majestically in front; while all the rest, Jefferson included, made an indistinguishable group behind. On the 19th, protocol satisfied, the party boarded ship once more and returned to New York, arriving on August 21st.[20]

Ten days later, Jefferson quit New York again in the company of Washington; this time not on official business, but headed for Virginia and their own affairs.

Jefferson stopped in Philadelphia for some days to make arrangements for the additions and alterations he contemplated in the house he was renting when the capital was shifted to that town. He also wrote to Short in Paris commissioning him to forward an extensive wine list for Washington and himself. As against Washington's demands, Jefferson's were comparatively moderate. Jefferson's total came to a mere 550 livres; while Washington's totaled 3,000, including 40 dozen of champagne, 30 dozen of sauterne, 20 dozen of Bordeaux and 10 dozen of Frontignan.[21] It must be remembered, however, that Jefferson had already shipped an ample supply for himself.

He arrived in Monticello on September 20th, and was joyfully received by family and servants alike. Martha was now a sedate married woman, on the way shortly to have her first child; and Polly was rapidly growing up.

For a month and a half, Jefferson reveled in domestic felicities; at the same time, however, informing himself as to the political situation in his native state. That was not encouraging. Both Virginia and North Carolina had been bitterly opposed to the assumption of their debts under Hamilton's scheme, and their dissatisfaction must have been decidedly embarrassing to Jefferson, who had been the chief architect of the deal whereby assumption was finally passed.

It may have been wishful thinking on his part to cover up that embarrassment, but he believed, so he told Gouverneur Morris, that the constant harping on assumption was a cloak "to mask their disaffection to the government on other grounds. Its great foe in Virginia is an implacable one"—Patrick Henry. "He avows it himself, but does not avow all his motives for it. The measures and tone of the government threaten abortion to some of his speculations; most particularly to that of the Yazoo territory." [22] Henry had already embarked on the pursuit of riches and, though now opposed to Hamiltonian policies while engaged in the pursuit, once he had achieved them, discovered that those policies were best fitted to secure and enlarge his fortune. He thereafter turned into the staunchest of Federalists.

While at Monticello, Jefferson was confronted with a bill that must have aroused melancholy memories. A Williamsburg dressmaker named Jane Charlton had submitted to Edmund Randolph to forward to Jefferson a statement of account. It showed a balance for goods sold to Martha, Jefferson's wife, in May, 1777. Randolph, at Jefferson's request, paid the bill—more than thirteen years late—and that chapter of his life was once more closed.[23]

CHAPTER 32

War with Hamilton

ON November 8, 1790, Jefferson left Monticello for Philadelphia and the resumption of his duties. During his absence the capital had been moved thence in accordance with the bargain over assumption. Arriving on November 21st, his first days were occupied with getting his new house into order. The place he had rented from Thomas Leiper was situated at 274 High Street (now known as Market); while his office was a short distance away on the same street.

To his dismay, the workmen had been exceedingly dilatory about the remodeling job and, on December 7th, it still was not ready for occupancy, except for one room which they promised for the end of the week. That room, wrote Jefferson ruefully, "will be my bed-room, study, dining-room, and parlor."[1] To add to his discomfort, his French furniture and belongings, amounting in all to 86 packing cases, had only just arrived and, besides the staggering freight bill of $544.53 which he had to pay, there was no place as yet to unpack them.

But all things, even house alterations, finally come to an end, and Jefferson duly ensconced himself in his new quarters, spread his prized French possessions around, and found himself quite comfortable. It was here that he first installed, in a recess between the library and breakfast room, his bed worked by pulleys so that it could be hoisted into the ceiling during the day and let down into position at night. That feature, later duplicated at Monticello, never fails to evoke the exclamations of visitors.

During the interim between sessions of Congress, and of the vacation of the principal officers of government, the climate of opinion had definitely shifted. The discontent with Hamilton's policies had deepened, and Virginia had uttered defiance, much to Jefferson's embarrassment. He had thus far worked with some semblance of amicability with Hamilton; but from now on they were to diverge more and more until the gap became unbridgeable, and the future of America became involved in the struggle.

The definitive break came with Hamilton's historic report to Congress, submitted on December 14, 1790, advocating the establishment of a National Bank. The bank was to be both public and private; public in the sense that the government would subscribe to twenty per cent of the stock and have the right to borrow up to the full amount of its investment; private in that it would be controlled by the votes of the private stockholders and would perform the normal functions of a bank to the community at large.

To Hamilton, this represented the capstone of his system. By permitting certificates of the public debt to be used in payment for bank stock, by granting the bank the power to issue interest-bearing demand notes that would be negotiable and legal tender for all obligations of the United States, Hamilton foresaw such a commingling of governmental and private interest as to place the United States forever on a secure foundation. The moneyed men and the merchants, as themselves holders of governmental securities, as shareholders in a bank bottomed on those securities and whose very existence must necessarily depend on their market strength and the solidity of the nation that emitted them, would, he was convinced, become the strongest supporters of government. Make it the selfish interest of the rich and the well-born to uphold the United States, so ran his reiterated thesis, and you have assured its continued existence.

But those who were *not* rich and well-born—and their representatives in Congress—viewed the matter from an entirely different angle. To them the bank was the last nail that Hamilton was hammering into the coffin of the agriculturalist, the small farmer and those who lived by the toil of their hands and the sweat of their brows. They had witnessed with alarm the step-by-step procedures by which Hamilton had reared his system of finance, his setting up of a public debt to bind unborn generations, his hand-in-glove partnership with those whom, rightly or wrongly, they had always conceived to be their oppressors. The outburst of speculation and stock manipulations that had greeted each of Hamilton's measures and was now, with the announcement of the Bank Bill, doubled and redoubled into a veritable frenzy, only confirmed their suspicions. It was *they*—the people—who would have to pay the piper in the form of increased taxes, while the speculators and the moneyed men would reap all the profits.

There was an immediate rush to buy up the public funds, with consequent increases in their price of sixteen and seventeen shillings to the pound. Not merely American moneyed men rushed to buy, but canny Dutch financiers as well. For the certificates could be used, up to three-quarters of the price, in the purchase of bank stock. The subscribers could both have their cake and eat it—receiving at one and the same time the continued interest on their securities and sharing in the profits of the bank.

These economic and class distinctions were the true motivation for the vehement opposition to the Bank Bill, and were frankly so avowed. But it was realized that, on this basis, there would be little chance to defeat the measure, inasmuch as the Congressmen themselves were hastening to participate in the speculation. Another objection was therefore found and put into effect—there was nothing in the Constitution which permitted the Federal Government to establish a national bank. It was on this objection that the whole fight was thereafter centered.

The constitutional objection was not interposed insincerely. It dug into fundamentals. The proponents had believed, when the Constitution was first adopted, that it was a severely limited instrument, that the general government had no other powers than those which were specified therein, and that all other sovereignties resided in the States. Since there was no mention in the Constitution of any power to erect a bank, *ergo*, the government did not have that power. Any other construction, they argued, would leave the door wide open to ever-increasing encroachments by the general government on the sovereignties of the States—a course that must inevitably end in monarchy and tyranny.

The great debate in the House of Representatives, which began belatedly on February 1, 1791, had all the elements of intense drama. Parties had definitely formed in a nation which had assumed, curiously enough, that parties were impossible, that organized opposition was factious and could only lead to disruption and anarchy. True, Patrick Henry—through the Virginia legislature—had already shouted that the Assumption Bill was unconstitutional; but this was the first time that Congress itself was divided into two mutually opposing parties on the question.

If the strict constructionists—as those who would limit the powers of government to those plainly written into the Constitution were called—were victorious, then, according to the followers of Hamilton, the nation could not go about its proper business and must dissolve. On the other hand, the strict constructionists alleged that if the Hamiltonian thesis that there were powers implied in the Constitution which were not visible on the surface won the day, then the States might as well shut up shop and submit to unrelieved tyranny.

What made the debate more ominous was that not only economic lines were sharply drawn, but geographic as well. By and large, it was the agricultural South arrayed against the mercantile and financial North; and such contradictory pockets as existed in either section could be traced readily to the economic division. Madison of Virginia spearheaded the strict constructionists; while Fisher Ames of Massachusetts led the advocates of implied powers.

On February 8, 1791, the Hamiltonian forces won a crushing victory in the House and, since the Bank Bill had already passed the Senate, it came to President Washington for signature.

But Washington had been shaken by the loud cries of unconstitutionality. He called on Edmund Randolph, the Attorney General, for an opinion. Randolph unhesitatingly declared the bill unconstitutional. He turned next to Jefferson for his opinion.

Up to this point, Jefferson had gone along with Hamilton in his measures, even though his closest and most respected friend, Madison, had fought them bitterly. He had agreed with Hamilton that it was essential for the new government to have a firm financial base if it was to survive. He had viewed with approval the sudden reversal of the position of American securities on the exchanges of the world—from the bottom to the top of the heap. He had greeted Patrick Henry's animadversions on assumption with suspicion, and sought the private motive which lay behind them. But now he turned aside. He and Hamilton had come to the parting of the ways.

He had watched with considerable uneasiness the outburst of speculation which had accompanied the passage of the first two of Hamilton's measures. He had noted, with even more uneasiness, that the chief speculators and holders of the stock were the moneyed men of the Northern States.[2] That meant that all the profits would go to the North; and the South, as usual, would pay the bill in the form of interest on inflated values, increased taxes, and lower prices for her own commodities.

But more important, perhaps, than all other reasons, was the deep-rooted suspicion which he, in common with the planters of the South, had for those who dealt solely with evidences of money. These were mere parasites on the economy of a country, spinning not and toiling not, creating nothing solid from the fruits of the earth, but battening solely on the labor of others and lying in wait to take away from them by chicanery and manipulation the products they had created. A private bank was bad enough; but a bank that exercised semigovernmental functions would be an engine to suck irresistibly the lifeblood of the toiling agriculturalist and keep him in eternal bondage to a small group of financiers in the large cities of the North. Through their fortunate position at the seat of government, they must inevitably corrupt the government and the legislators for their private advantage, and seek for greater and greater centralized powers to that government in order to coerce the States in which they were weak.

Even before the Bank Bill was passed, Jefferson was pessimistic about the prospect. "All will pass—" he wrote gloomily, "the excise will pass—the bank will pass." The only way, he thought, to correct "what is corrupt in our present form of government" was to enlarge the House of Representatives "so as to get a more agricultural representation, which may put that interest above that of the stockjobbers."[3]

But he pinned his faith in Washington who, after all, was a Virginian and sympathetic to the needs and wishes of his fellow countrymen. "Government being founded on opinion," he remarked, "the opinion of the public, even when it is wrong, ought to be respected to a certain degree. The prudence of the President is an anchor of safety to us."[4]

The confidence which he reposed in the President seemed justified when Washington called on him for his opinion as to the constitutionality of the proposed bank. He sat down at once and formulated his opinion with all the care and learning of which he was capable.

He first attacked the corporate character of the bank. Such an indefinite corporation, he declared, with the powers which had been granted it, violated every principle of the great laws governing mortmain, alienage, descents, forfeitures and escheats, distribution and monopoly. Since, in many states, these laws were already in effect, the corporation must necessarily be paramount to the laws of those states and not subject to their jurisdiction.

But, argued Jefferson, the fundamental basis of the Constitution was the Tenth Amendment, which specifically provided that "all powers not delegated to the United States, by the Constitution, nor prohibited by it to the States, are reserved to the States or to the people." A single step taken "beyond the boundaries thus especially drawn around the powers of Congress, is to take possession of a boundless field of power, no longer susceptible of any definition."

This was the heart of the argument of the strict constructionists. The Federal Government was the creature of the States, with specific granted powers and no others. In every other field, the States were sovereign and limited only by the will of their respective peoples. Should these delegated powers be made flexible and the subject of interpretations beyond their plain, common-sense meanings, then there was nothing to prevent the Federal Government from encroaching further and further on the sovereignties of the States, until the latter became but mere adjuncts of an all-powerful central tyranny that differed from monarchy only in form and not in substance.

The next step, by this process of reasoning, was to prove that the incorporation of a national bank did not come within the powers delegated to the United States by the Constitution. Congress had been given the power to lay taxes and to borrow money. But "this bill neither borrows money nor ensures the borrowing of it. The proprietors of the bank will be just as free as any other money holders, to lend or not to lend their money to the public." Neither does it regulate commerce, nor lay taxes to provide for the general welfare. "For the laying of taxes is the *power*, and the general welfare the *purpose* for which the power is to be exercised." This was Jefferson's reasoned argument to those who were pointing to the magical words "the general welfare" as the cover-all for Congressional jurisdiction.

Nor did the proceedings of the Convention at which the Constitution was drafted justify the exercise of any power to incorporate a bank. In fact, a proposition to authorize Congress to incorporate canal companies had been voted down on the very basis that such a grant would leave the way open to incorporate *banks* as well.

Jefferson next turned his attention to that other phrase in the Constitution on which the proponents of the bank relied most strongly: "To make all laws necessary and proper for carrying into execution the enumerated powers." But the enumerated powers, he insisted, "can all be carried into execution without a bank." Therefore a bank could not be considered as *necessary*. Even if, as the other side argued, a bank might be *convenient* for the collection of taxes, that did not make it *necessary*, in any sense of the word. Nor, if the truth were known, he pursued, was a bank a convenient method for collection. Stick to the Constitution, he ended with an admonitory finger at Congress, and do not attempt to prostitute our laws and system of jurisprudence on the basis of any interpretive shadings of convenience.[5]

Washington now had two opinions against the bank—Randolph's and Jefferson's. But the other two members of the Cabinet—Knox and Hamilton—were to be heard from. Knox usually followed Hamilton in Cabinet discussions, and ventured a short, formal statement without much amplification that the bill was constitutional. Hamilton's opinion, however, was a different matter.

There was no question as to whether he would defend the constitutionality of the bill—after all, it was his own measure. The interest lay in the arguments he could summon up to defend it against the onslaughts of its enemies.

The opinion which he wrote at breakneck speed, staying up all night to finish it, was one of his greatest efforts and perhaps his most notable production. Certainly, its influence on the course of American history has been immeasurable. It was directly on Hamilton's opinion, and sometimes in Hamilton's phraseology, that John Marshall later based his own epoch-making interpretations of the powers inherent in the Constitution of the United States.

The heart of the matter for Hamilton lay in the nature of government itself. Impatiently, he brushed aside what he considered as mere pettifogging arguments on the other side. There could be no such limitations on the powers of government as they pretended. "This *general principle* is *inherent* in the very *definition* of government, and *essential* to every step of the progress to be made by that of the United States, namely: That every power vested in a government is in its nature *sovereign*, and includes, by *force* of the *term*, a right to employ all the *means* requisite and fairly applicable to the attainment of the *ends* of such power, and which are not precluded by restrictions and exceptions specified in the Constitution, or not immoral, or not contrary to the *essential ends* of political society."

He differed sharply with Jefferson in his construction of the words "necessary and proper." To him, "necessary" meant *needful*, *requisite*, *incidental*, *useful* or *conducive to*. And it was well within the province of Congress to decide what bills were incidental or conducive to the carrying out of their specified powers.

With great dexterity he turned the test of the constitutionality of a measure completely around. It was not to be discovered, he asserted, by examining the specific powers granted in the Constitution; rather, "Does the proposed measure abridge a pre-existing right of any State or of any individual? If it does not, there is a strong presumption of its constitutionality."[6]

With his Cabinet thus split, Washington decided in favor of Hamilton's thesis, and signed the Bank Bill.

From a legalistic point of view, perhaps, Jefferson, Randolph, Madison and their followers had the best of the argument. But, had they won, and the principle of strict construction become the accepted law of the land, the Constitution could never have proved the flexible instrument it later became nor would it have been able to last until the present day. It is true, as Jefferson pointed out, that there was the power of amendment; but amendment is a cumbersome process, subject to the veto of any determined minority (witness the fate of the Child Labor amendment) and could never keep pace with the multitudinous needs of a growing nation. Jefferson was himself to be faced with this dilemma during his Presidency; and deliberately avoided the process of amendment when it came to the purchase of Louisiana.

Nor was he to find the Bank the terrible engine of corruption and the void instrument he had envisaged when it later came within the purviews of his office. He accepted it, utilized its functions, and left it for Andrew Jackson considerably later to abolish.

The controversy over the Bank, however, was infinitely important in another respect. More than any other one cause, it hastened the formation of the two parties—Federalist and Republican—and helped create those issues on which the fate of the nation was to be decided. And, to Jefferson's regret, Washington, his fellow Virginian, was from now on more and more definitely committed to Federalist principles and Hamiltonian operations, and thereby threw the power of his name and the prestige of his office into the camp of the enemy.

As though it were not enough for the two definitely hardening groups to split on domestic issues, foreign affairs added another sharp line of cleavage.

The French Revolution, which Jefferson had hailed as the beacon of the world and the hope of mankind, had shifted during the year from its pristine idyllic innocence to a rougher, more brutal phase. More and more, moderate republicans like Lafayette were being pushed aside and men like Danton, Robespierre and Marat coming to the fore. More and more, the mobs of the big cities were becoming the true ruling power, classes of society were being arrayed sharply one against the other, and the king whom, in Jefferson's words, the people had once worshiped, was beginning to move with accelerating speed along the dismal road that led ultimately to the guillotine.

The first flush of the Revolution had met with general approval among Americans. Here was another great people treading the path along which they themselves had come; an ally whose services in their own Revolution were still remembered with gratitude. Washington had viewed the early days with benevolent interest, and even Hamilton had awarded it the accolade of his neutrality. But the ever-increasing excesses, the radical nature of the attacks on personal and property rights, alarmed the property men of America, the merchants, traders and financiers. To them it was Shays' Rebellion on a more cosmic scale.

Already turned toward England on the basis of commercial trade and the moderateness of her constitution, these conservatives recoiled more and more from radical France. But, as the Federalists recoiled, the Republicans (though it must be remembered that neither party had as yet hardened into fixity) eagerly embraced the Revolution across the sea. There might perhaps be a little bloodletting; but blood, as Jefferson had observed, was a necessary manure for the tree of liberty. They could well understand the problems that faced the revolutionaries of France. Had they not been confronted with similar ones, first in the way of Tories, and now with the Hamiltonians who, to their mind, were seeking to rob them of the fruits of the Revolution and fasten on them once more the chains of monarchy and English institutions?

Jefferson not only approved of the course of the French Revolution, but tied up its success with the success of the American experiment. "I consider the establishment and success of their government," he wrote, "as necessary to stay up our own, and to prevent it from falling back to that kind of Half-way house, the English constitution." There were those among Americans—and he meant the Hamiltonians—who considered the latter "to contain whatever is perfect in human institutions"; but as for himself, "I still rely that the great mass of our community is untainted with these heresies, as is its head." This was just before Washington shook his confidence by signing the Bank Bill. "On this I build my hope that we have not laboured in vain, and that our experiment will still prove that men can be governed by reason." [7]

It was therefore logical for Jefferson to uphold the arms of France, just as it was equally logical for Hamilton to support Great Britain. Yet one point must never be forgotten—*both* men sincerely pursued their respective courses not for the benefit of the foreign nation whose side they took, but for what they conceived to be the best advantage of the United States.

Nor was there any sharp divergence of opinion between them on the necessity for a flourishing overseas trade; even though, theoretically, Jefferson would have preferred a sole agricultural economy.

On December 28, 1790, at the request of the House of Representatives, Jefferson reported to them on the state of the Mediterranean trade. Our navigation in those waters had been of prime interest to him all through his ministry in France, and no one could have been more indignant than he, or more belligerent in reaction to the interferences with that trade by the Barbary pirates.

Recapitulating his old dispatches to John Jay, he inveighed in his Report against the pirates and their impudent demands for large bribes as the price of peace. He weighed the possible approaches to the problem: one was to give them their bribes, for which, he commented acidly, "we have the Example of rich and Powerful Nations, in this Instance counting their Interest more than their Honor." Or—and it is obvious that such a course met with Jefferson's approval—"repel Force by Force." Should Congress decide on this alternative, then it would be prudent to raise a naval armament equal to the whole of that belonging to all the Barbary powers. "What that equal Force would be," he added, "will belong to another Department [War] to say." [8]

He also advised Washington against paying ransoms for the enslaved American captives at Algiers until Congress had had an opportunity to decide which of these courses it would adopt. "The liberation of our citizens," he declared, "has an intimate connection with the liberation of our commerce in the Mediterranean, now under the consideration of Congress. The distresses of both proceed from the same cause, & the measures which shall be adopted for the relief of the one, may very probably involve the relief of the other." [9]

Congress did not adopt the alternative which Jefferson had hoped it would; the navy was not increased nor the pirates chastised. After long negotiations, the unfortunate captives were eventually freed; ransoms and *douceurs* were intermittently paid by the United States until Jefferson had the power, during his own administration, to pursue the policy he had ardently advocated from the beginning and thereby put an end to the Mediterranean depredations.

He also reported to the House on the state of the cod and whale fisheries—an industry which vitally concerned the northern coastal states and not at all, as many naïvely believed to be an economic truth, the South. The fishing interests were clamoring for government subsidies in order to meet foreign competition; but Jefferson firmly opposed the demand. What *was* required, he wrote, were free markets for their products. These markets might possibly be obtained, he advised, by "friendly arrangements towards those nations whose arrangements are friendly to us, and the residue be compensated by giving to the seamen thrown out of business the certainty of employment in another branch of which we have the sole disposal." [10]

What Jefferson meant by this cautiously impersonal language was of the utmost importance to his views on foreign relations. It was the obverse side of the coin on which had been imprinted the domestic financial policies of Hamilton, and with which foreign policy was intimately interrelated.

Hamilton wanted above all peace and trade with Great Britain. As by far our best customer, any rift in relations would deal a mortal body blow to his whole delicately balanced financial system, and bring it toppling into ruins. He was therefore willing to swallow slights—even insults—to accept restrictions and the lack of a reciprocal commercial treaty, as long as that trade could continue.

Jefferson, on the other hand, did not see any necessity for accepting England's galling assumption of superiority or for swallowing insults. Nor were there any such compensations to the Southern States for the restrictions imposed on their exportable products as were available to the shipping interests of the North. And he was a firm believer in the thesis that the American trade was all-important to the English; that any threat to cut it off would bring that proud nation humbly to her knees.

What he insisted on in every relation with foreign nations, therefore, was the principle of complete reciprocity, buttressed by commercial treaties in which that principle was firmly and openly established. He would have preferred to have no shackles whatsoever on the trade between nations; but if, in this imperfect world, such a utopian arrangement was impossible, then he refused to admit any superiority on the part of one nation over another, and demanded the *quid pro quo* of equality of restrictions on both sides of the fence.

His philosophy of trade is nowhere more plainly visible than in the report which he submitted to Congress on "the nature & extent of the privileges & restrictions of the commercial intercourse of the U.S. with foreign nations."

After a lengthy analysis of the duties, restrictions and downright prohibitions on our native products imposed by the several foreign nations, he discussed the methods by which they might be removed. Of course, he declared in the best free-trade tradition, a friendly arrangement with the offending countries would be best, to the extent of banishing *all* restrictions. "Instead of embarrassing Commerce under piles of regulating laws, duties & prohibitions, could it be relieved of all its shackles in all parts of the world, could every country be employed in producing that which nature has best fitted it to produce, & each be free to exchange with others mutual surpluses for mutual wants, the greatest mass possible would then be produced of those things which contribute to human life & human happiness; the numbers of mankind could be increased, & their condition bettered." To which he added in the manuscript draft, and then eliminated, his pet thesis: "In such a state of things Agriculture would be doubly eligible to us."

He was willing to enter into such a reciprocal relation of free trade with even one nation; hoping that, gradually, others would follow suit. He was willing, also, if complete freedom could not be had, to allow import duties for revenue only, or a mutual system of favors.

But what about recalcitrant countries who refused to meet us on this reciprocal basis? Retaliate, insisted Jefferson, with the same counterprohibitions, duties and regulations against their goods as they have instituted against ours. We must, he sternly declared, adopt the "principles of those who thus put us on the defensive."

Where a nation, he wrote, puts high duties on or prohibits our products, do the same to theirs. But here the practical statesman triumphed over the doctrinaire. Jefferson would select only those articles for retaliatory measures which we could either get elsewhere or, by recruiting skilled artisans from abroad, manufacture at home under a system of subsidies. Jefferson was anticipating by a good nine months Hamilton's famous Report on Manufactures.

A similar retaliation would apply to the carrying trade. Any nation that limited our vessels to cargoes of our own produce would find the same prohibition clamped on *their* ships; and such a prohibition would be extended to the trade of the mother country even where the restrictions on ours only related to their colonies.[11]

Madison had already attempted to put his friend's theories into effect in the first tariff and tonnage bill of 1789, and had actually pushed it through the House; but the Senate emasculated the reprisals by removing all differentials and discriminations from the bill. Theoretically, and from the point of view of even-handed justice, Jefferson's thesis was sound; and his distant successor, Secretary of State Cordell Hull, was able to negotiate reciprocity agreements with brilliant success. But *then* the United States was in a different position vis-à-vis other nations and could throw her weight around. In these earlier years, the United States was in no shape—financial, commercial or military—to engage in a commercial war with Great Britain, the prime target for contemplated retaliations. At this point, such a war, spilling over in all likelihood into a military one, would have spelled disaster to a small nation faced with problems enough as it was.

Curiously enough, Jefferson's great antagonist, Hamilton, agreed with the theory. He also wanted reciprocal trade agreements wherever possible, and avowed to Jefferson that, as he put it, "my commercial system turns very much on giving a free course to Trade and cultivating good humour with all the world." But he refused to be drawn into a course of commercial warfare, feeling with some justice that any ex-parte exemptions and preferences to one nation as against another would be regarded by that other as unfriendly and liable to lead to "a worse kind of warfare."[12]

The basis for these animadversions was a dispute, not with England, but with France. The Acts of Congress relating to import and tonnage duties had differentiated between American and foreign vessels to the benefit of the former. M. Otto, the French Chargé d'Affaires, had protested vigorously against French ships being placed on the same scale of disadvantage with British, claiming exemption on the basis of Article 5 of the treaty of commerce between France and the United States.

Jefferson sent the protest to Hamilton with a note that "this matter will become serious, and though I am pointedly against admitting the French construction of the treaty; yet I think it essential to cook up some favor which may ensure the continuance of the good dispositions they have towards us. A nation which takes one third of our Tobacco, more than half our fish oil, and two thirds of our fish . . . and a great deal of Rice; and from whom we take nothing in return but hard money to carry directly over and pour into the coffers of their enemies, such a customer I say, deserves some menagemens [*sic*]."[13]

With Hamilton's disinclination to grant ex-parte favors to France before him, Jefferson reported publicly to Congress that the article of the treaty to which M. Otto adverted, did not apply; and later wrote privately to the same effect to the French Chargé. But in the private letter he permitted himself to hint, in spite of Hamilton, that the ensuing session of Congress *might* do something of advantage to their mutual intercourse.[14]

Jefferson fully expected that Congress would put into effect his theory of retaliation as set forth in his report of March 15th. In fact, the day his report was submitted to the House, he wrote Short in France. "The measure," he declared, "is just, perfectly innocent as to all other nations, and will effectually defeat the navigation Act of Great Britain, and reduce her power on the ocean within safer limits." He also expressed satisfaction at the news that the French arrêt of 1787, which he had negotiated, stood a chance of being continued in effect. This arrêt had granted a free importation of American salted meats into France and provisions of all kinds into her colonies. "It is in truth," he averred, "the sheet anchor of our connection with France, which will be much loosened when that is lost." [15] He might also have added that the withdrawal of the arrêt would knock the props from under his proposed retaliations against Great Britain.

By his public stand against the French protest, however, Jefferson almost lost the adherence of some of the more radical members in Congress. Senator Maclay noted in his diary his mingled anger and astonishment. "There certainly is a design of quarreling with France, and that Jefferson should seem to countenance this! What can this mean? I am really astonished at all this. I think I must be mistaken, and yet to think so is to disbelieve my senses." [16]

There were those, already, to whom France could do no wrong; just as there were those who expressed similar sentiments with respect to England.

What Maclay did not know was that Jefferson was secretly trying to get through Congress at its next session special favors for France and a Navigation Act directed specifically against Great Britain. In fact, the Act had already been drafted, and Jefferson sent a copy to Carmichael in Spain asking him to sound out that country, while Col. Humphreys and Short similarly sounded out Portugal and France, whether they would not join the United States with like measures to ensure that "the freedom of the ocean be better secured to all the world." [17]

It was not a particularly propitious moment to approach Spain, considering that only a few days earlier Jefferson had instructed both Carmichael and Short to demand the release of an American citizen seized by the Spaniards on the east bank of the Mississippi. With this demand was coupled a threat that if Spain did not definitely acknowledge the American right of navigation on the Mississippi, and as a result the western border folk flamed into action, "we are involved beyond recall by the eternal principles of justice to our citizens, which we will never abandon." [18]

To Harry Innes of Kentucky, one of the borderers to whom he referred, he wrote privately of the steps he had taken to ensure that navigation. "Nothing short of absolute rupture is omitted," he informed him. "What its effect will be, we cannot yet foretell; but we should not stop even here, were a favorable conjuncture to arise. The move we have now made must bring the matter to issue." [19]

But Spain brushed aside the threats, because she had settled her difficulties with England and therefore no longer feared an American attack on her flank while engaged in a major war.

Her governor in Florida, however, had committed the blunder of inviting foreigners to settle in the unpeopled lands of that territory. To Jefferson this was a heaven-sent opportunity. "I wish a hundred thousand of our inhabitants would accept the invitation," he exclaimed. "It will be the means of delivering to us peaceably, what may otherwise cost us a war." But he cannily added: "In the meantime we may complain of this seduction of our inhabitants just enough to make them believe we think it very wise policy for them, & confirm them in it." [20]

Jefferson, in his old age, was to witness the first steps in a similar infiltration of Texas, with exactly the end results he now contemplated.

While he was thus adopting a belligerent tone toward Spain, he was observing the same truculence—though not as publicly underlined—toward British encroachments to the northeast and northwest. The British claimed the Passamaquoddy area on the ill-defined northern border of Maine and certain sections on the northern border of New York; enforcing their pretensions by moving into the disputed territories.

Jefferson was perplexed as to what course of action to pursue. It was useless, he felt, to attempt any adjustment with London. Diplomacy would, in the present temper of the British, inevitably fail. But suppose the two invaded areas—Maine and New York—demanded redress. In that case, he advised the use of force by their citizens to oppose British force; if necessary, with the aid of the militia from the neighboring states. Such direct action by the border citizens, he thought, would be sufficient to bring the British to the council table, and at the same time, keep the Federal Government from involvement. Meanwhile, Col. Beckwith, England's unofficial agent, was to be warned of such impending clashes if she persisted in her present course.[21]

Washington, who had quit Philadelphia for Mount Vernon, and was poised for a tour of the Southern States, approved of Jefferson's method for handling the border disputes, and asked him, in addition, to convey to the Governor of Canada, either directly or indirectly, a warning against British aid or supplies to the Indians of the Northwest who were then at war with the United States.[22]

Since Washington suggested Beckwith as the indirect channel to be employed in getting to the Canadian governor, Jefferson turned to Hamilton as the natural channel for getting to *Beckwith*. But he had been forestalled. The Secretary of Treasury had already spoken to him, and had been assured that the British had merely given the Indians their regular annual present of arms and ammunition. Somewhat mortified that such a conversation—which was wholly within the province of his own Department—had taken place behind his back, Jefferson proposed to Madison, who lived in the same house with Beckwith, that he represent to the British agent that such presents ought not to be repeated, since they constituted a violation of neutrality which the United States would resent.[23]

Jefferson could be a stickler for forms when he wished; and this was one of the occasions when he so wished. He resented England's refusal to accredit a regular minister to the United States, and he regarded as an insult to American dignity the presence of the protean Col. Beckwith, unofficially official and officially unofficial, as British advantage warranted. He resented also the constant intimate communications between Beckwith and Hamilton, of which he learned, if at all, only by sheerest accident.

Jefferson was extremely busy these days; so busy, in fact, that he was compelled to apologize to correspondents for his delay in answering their letters. But he was never too busy to partake in a scientific discussion. As he told one correspondent who had sent him a report of the discovery of prehistoric fortifications in the Western country, politics was a duty with him, but the pursuit of natural history a passion.[24]

To his son-in-law he recommended an investigation of "the great question relative to the Opossum. The proper season is now coming on, and you can so easily procure them in any number you please. If you can obtain satisfactory evidence of the whole process of gestation & parturition it would be an acceptable thing to the philosophical society here to recieve a paper from you on the subject." [25]

Amazing as it may seem, the life cycle of the opossum was still shrouded in obscurity; and Thomas Mann Randolph's observations, which seemed to indicate that the pouch in which the opossum carried its young disappeared after weaning, struck Jefferson as inconclusive. He remembered that as a boy, he had amused himself with trying to open the pouch when the opossum carried no young, and that the pouch had been difficult to find and more difficult to open. Therefore, he now supposed, the solution of the mystery might well be that the pouch, after weaning, contracted rather than disappeared.[26]

Jefferson was very proud of his connection with the Philosophical Society, of which he had just been elected Vice-President, and attended its meetings regularly whenever he was in Philadelphia. In spite of his onerous duties as Secretary of State, he accepted a committee appointment to study the natural history of the Hessian fly, which was playing havoc with crops, and to discover ways and means to prevent or destroy it. He called several meetings of the committee, of which Charles Thomson and Dr. Benjamin Barton were also members; and when he set out on his famous botanical expedition with Madison a little later, he hoped to gather material that might be of material assistance to the project.[27]

Of a more official nature were his investigations into a method claimed by one Jacob Isaacs of Newport for distilling fresh water from salt by the use of "the common iron caboose." Since such a process would prove of inestimable value to ships at sea and castaway seamen, Congress referred Isaac's application to Jefferson for study.

The reason for this seemingly strange addition to the duties of a Secretary of State was the presence, on the Congressional desks, of a bill which Jefferson himself had drafted, proposing a system of patenting inventions and new and useful arts, by depositing pertinent descriptions and models in the office of the Secretary of State whereby, after certain formalities, the inventor would gain their exclusive use for fourteen years.[28] The bill, however, was not passed until the following session.

On receipt of the request, Jefferson called on his fellow members for assistance in checking on the validity of the proposed process. On March 21 and 24, 1791, the scientists gravely gathered in Jefferson's office, where Isaacs had erected his apparatus for demonstration with the use of his mixture; and a control distillation without the mixture was likewise set up.

The results, it was finally agreed, favored straight distillation as against the mixture; but the general process seems to have been successful; and Jefferson so reported to Congress in a carefully drawn scientific paper.[29]

He was busy also with his various protégés, among whom the chief was William Short. Young Short resented his indeterminate position in France as Chargé d'Affaires, and kept prodding Jefferson with considerable impatience to get him a full ministerial post, either in France or in Holland. Jefferson assured him, in cipher, that he was actively promoting his interests; but warned him that it was better not to press Washington too hard on the subject. "To overdo a thing with him," he remarked, "is to undo it. I am steering the best I can for you."

Jefferson was also handling Short's rather considerable financial affairs for him. Much of his fortune was invested in the public funds. But Jefferson feared that the funds would soon "tumble precipitately," and, surprisingly enough, advised that Short's money be taken out of the funds and placed in bank stock, instead. Coming from Jefferson, the most ardent political opponent of the bank, this was a testimonial to the soundness of Hamilton's institution as a commercial venture. However, he continued, "very particular reasons prohibit me from acting for you in this way: by no means appoint any body of the treasury."[30] The reasons were obviously political; it would not do for Hamilton to get wind that Jefferson, or Jefferson's "adopted son," was actually investing in the bank both supposedly abhorred.

Short was to continue to abuse his favored position with Jefferson, and to complain vehemently against what he considered his foster-father's inaction in his behalf. Jefferson always replied with a certain pathetic dignity.

To one such especially vehement complaint, he replied that "had you been here, there should have been no silence or reserve, and I long for the moment when I can unbosom to you all that past on that occasion. But to have trusted such communications to writing & across the Atlantic would have been an indiscretion which nothing could have excused. I dropt you such short and pregnant sentences from time to time as, duly pondered, would have suggested to you such material circumstances as I knew.[31]

Besides handling Short's finances, Jefferson was trying to straighten out his own tangled affairs. He gave instructions to sell one of his chief estates, Elk Hill, in order to obtain ready cash; but ordered that the advertisement omit his name as owner, "which as long as I am in public I would wish to keep out of view in every thing of a private nature." He also tried an experiment: since the price of tobacco was low in Virginia and high in Philadelphia, he ordered twenty hogsheads shipped by water to the latter city for sale. If it was salable at the price he hoped, he would have the rest of the crop forwarded as well.[32]

Yet, as always, while feeling the pinch of ready cash, Jefferson did not hesitate to order expensive things abroad, such as a complete set of Piranesi's drawings of the Pantheon, or a clock that cost 15 guineas. Nor did he object when Short informed him that Petit had finally capitulated and would come to America at a salary of $100 a month, besides board and lodging—a fantastic wage for those days.[33]

He also took this particular period to refurbish his wardrobe in the finest style. If "a superfine French cloth, of the very dark blue which you know I wear," could be found, he commissioned his tailor to make him a coat; as well as one pair of black silk and one of black satin breeches. A little later he added to his order a "gilah & pr of breeches of buff casimir, a very little buff, not a yellow one." [34]

CHAPTER 33

A Newspaper Is Born

WITH the coming of the spring in 1791, Jefferson's thoughts moved more and more to flight from the brick walls and paved streets of Philadelphia, which he despised, into the sights and sounds of the open country that he loved. He disliked also the hurly-burly of politics and the personal passions it aroused. His sensitive mind shrank from criticism and harsh words, and he hated every controversy that was not conducted on abstract and philosophical levels. And more and more he was discovering that the level of politics on a national scale was, if anything, lower than that under which he had writhed in anguish during the last days of his governorship in Virginia. He sincerely, and without mental reservations, wanted to get away from it all and return to the pursuits he truly loved.

When he wrote to his daughter Maria that the frogs had begun their first spring-song, that the blue birds had flourished their first salute, and the weeping willow, the lilac and the gooseberry had uncurled their tender leaves in the strengthening sun,[1] he was not writing down to her or merely for effect—these were the things that meant more to him than a sharp rejoinder to Hamilton or a British agent.

"Watch," he begged her elder sister, "for the annular eclipse of the sun, which is to happen on Sunday se'nnight to begin about sunrise. It will be such a one as is rarely to be seen twice in one life." [2] One may be sure that Jefferson himself was up long before that morning dawn to view the event and take its measurements.

With similar avidity he had called on his son-in-law to observe the opossum's strangely elusive pouch, and now required of him a report on the natural history of the "weavil of Virginia" for the Philosophical Society. "I long," he added with desperate sincerity, "to be free for pursuits of this kind instead of the detestable ones in which I am now labouring without pleasure to myself, or profit to others." [3]

Already he was beginning to propose to himself release from public affairs; this time forever. "I am in an office of infinite labour," he told Mazzei, "& as disagreeable to me as it is laborious. I came into it utterly against my will, and under the cogency of arguments derived from the novelty of the government, the necessity of its setting out well &c. But I pant after Monticello & my family. I cannot let it be long before I join them." [4]

What added mightily to his disgust with Philadelphia and all its works

Collection of the Albany Institute and Historical and Art Society. Courtesy the Frick Art Reference Library

CITIZEN GENÊT

Painting by Ezra Ames

Photograph by Dementi Studio

CAPITOL OF VIRGINIA

was the sudden quarrel which threatened to endanger his ancient friendship with John Adams.

Tom Paine had published in England his famous pamphlet on *The Rights of Man*, a bold defense of the French Revolution and its principles against Burke's equally famous attack. The pamphlet created a tremendous storm; but it was a full year before the British government took steps to suppress it and indict the author for treason. Before the trial, however, Paine escaped to France where he was enthusiastically received, made a citizen and, characteristically, ran into trouble again.

The Rights of Man reached America by the first boat across and created a similar, if lesser, storm on this side of the Atlantic. The conservatives considered its tenets subversive; the radicals and sympathizers with the French cause hailed it with delight.

John Beckley, radical Virginian politician, lent his copy to Madison who passed it on to Jefferson together with Beckley's request that after he had finished reading it, he transmit it to one Jonathan B. Smith, whose brother wanted to reprint it in an American edition.

Jefferson did so with a note that he was "extremely pleased to find it will be re-printed here, and that something is at length to be publicly said against the political heresies which have sprung up among us. He has no doubt our citizens will rally a second time round the standard of Common sense." [5]

This approving and seemingly innocuous message was shortly to raise a veritable tempest in a teacup. For Smith's brother brought out his American edition of *The Rights of Man* with Jefferson's animadversions on political heresies prominently displayed as a masthead. In hot retort, a series of articles appeared in the *Gazette of the United States*, semiofficial newspaper of the government, and signed with the classical pseudonym "Publicola." In turn, a host of republican champions rose to defend Paine, refute "Publicola," and anathematize him as the advocate of an aristocratic and monarchical system.

When Jefferson saw his private letter thus publicly displayed, without so much as a by-your-leave, he knew he was in for it. For everyone knew—or thought they knew—that the pseudonymous "Publicola" was none other than the redoubtable John Adams, Vice-President of the United States. Actually he was not, though the miss was not by much. "Publicola" in fact was his young and brilliant son, John Quincy Adams, who was thus fleshing his weapons for a future political career. But this half-truth did not become known until later.

Jefferson saw at once the implications of this unauthorized publication of his letter. When he had spoken of "political heresies" he had actually had in mind, among others, the views expressed by John Adams in his earlier *Discourses on Davila*, a reasoned, philosophical and moral statement of principles of government that did not sit well with democracy as Jefferson and his friends envisaged it. Ever since their return to the United States from the European scene, the two old friends had gradually diverged politically, and the intimacy of former days, though not completely gone, had nevertheless suffered considerable impairment.

In some alarm, Jefferson considered what he should do. He realized that his unfortunate phrase, as "Publicola" and others soon evidenced, would be taken as a direct assault on Adams. Yet he could not disavow the letter; he had actually written it. Nor could he disavow his approbation of Paine; he was "fully in sentiment with it." He therefore thought it wisest to keep a discreet silence. Even when "Publicola" sprang furiously to the attack, and the republicans rose in counterattack, he "determined to let them write and wrangle as they please without intermeddling in word or deed." [6]

But he soon found it impossible to keep to this sensible course. The original pamphlets of Paine and Burke were almost forgotten by the controversialists in this much juicier—for their purposes—antagonism between Jefferson and Adams. Garbled reports of Jefferson's stand were being transmitted to Adams, vacationing at his home in Braintree, Massachusetts, and to Washington, similarly engaged at Mount Vernon in Virginia.

In considerable perturbation as to what course he should pursue, Jefferson turned to Madison for advice. Madison was inclined to treat the business philosophically, and to consider that Adams had received only his just deserts. "Mr. Adams can least of all complain," he replied. "Under a mock defence of the Republican Constitutions of his Country, he attacked them with all the force he possessed, and this in a book with his name to it whilst he was the Representative of his Country at a foreign Court. Since he has been the 2d Magistrate in the new Republic, his pen has constantly been at work in the same cause; and tho' his name has not been prefixed to his anti republican discourses, the author has been as well known as if that formality had been observed. Surely if it be innocent & decent in one servant of the public thus to write attacks agst its Government, it cannot be very criminal or indecent in another to patronize a written defence of the principles on which that Govt. is founded." [7]

But Jefferson had already deemed it prudent to notify Washington of the circumstances under which his letter had come to be published. "I certainly never made a secret of my being anti-monarchical, & anti-aristocratical; but I am sincerely mortified to be thus brought forward on the public stage, where to remain, to advance or to retire, will be equally against my love of silence & quiet, & my abhorrence of dispute." [8]

For a man who thus loved silence and quiet, and abhorred dispute, Jefferson was to get himself into more acrimonious quarrels than any other man in history; and, though he was loudly and bitterly to complain of the unauthorized publication of his letters on controversial topics, he continued to write them under circumstances which made their recipients feel only too often impelled to publish them to the world, with most unfortunate results to their writer.

There still remained Adams to placate; and, in spite of Madison's advice,

Jefferson finally wrote that injured sage to explain the contretemps. "That you and I differ in our ideas of government," he ended, "is well known to us both: but we have differed as friends should do, respecting the purity of each other's motives, & confining our difference of opinion to private conversation." [9]

This was rather disingenuous, for hardly was the ink dry on this avowal before Jefferson was writing his pleasure at the sentiments contained in his pamphlet to Paine, without a word of regret that his own letter had been published at its head. As for the attacks which it had elicited against Adams, "I thank God," he exclaimed, "that [the people] appear firm in their republicanism, notwithstanding the contrary hopes & assertions of a sect here, high in names, but small in numbers. These had flattered themselves that the silence of the people under the *Defence* and *Davila* [both by Adams] was a symptom of their conversion to the doctrine of king, lords & commons. They are checked at least by your pamphlet, & the people confirmed in their good old faith." [10]

Adams accepted the explanation; and denied on his part that he was "Publicola"; though he failed to disclose the fact that "Publicola" was his son. He objected, however, to Jefferson's final statement concerning their differences in philosophy. He did *not* know that they differed as radically as Jefferson pretended. "I know not what your idea is of the best form of government," he retorted. "You and I have never had a serious conversation together, that I can recollect, concerning the nature of government.... If you suppose that I have, or ever had, a design or desire of attempting to introduce a government of King, Lords, and Commons, or in other words, an hereditary executive, or an hereditary senate, either into the government of the United States or that of any individual State, you are wholly mistaken." [11]

Jefferson was never to be convinced by this denial; going so far as to write in his *Anas* toward the end of his life that Adams *was* at this period a monarchist, and citing as proof a conversation at Jefferson's dinner table at which the members of the Cabinet were present. Adams had remarked that, were the British constitution purged of its corruptions, and equality of representation given to the House of Commons, "it would be the most perfect constitution ever devised by the wit of man." To which Hamilton had retorted that it would then be wholly impracticable; that, in its present form, *with* corruption and inequality, it was the most perfect that had ever existed.[12]

This sudden explosion of personal dispute, plus his desire to get away from Philadelphia, impelled Jefferson to join with his friend Madison on an extended "botanizing tour" through the Northern States during the spring and early summer of 1791.

Much has been written concerning this famous "botanizing" expedition, and many deep political schemes have been claimed as the true, as against the ostensible, basis for it. It was, so it has been declared again and again, deliberately contrived to bring together into a political party all of the leaders in the North who, for whatever reasons, were opposed to the Hamiltons, the Adamses and the policies of the emergent Federalists. The thesis has the elements of plausibility and conforms to contemporary conjecture as to the purpose of the jaunt. Then, as now, no political figure could be expected to be interested in the flowers of nature when there were political nosegays to be plucked.

Sir John Temple, the British Consul at New York, was certain that he knew what Jefferson and Madison intended, and so reported to his government. "I am sorry to inform Your Grace," he wrote gloomily to the Duke of Leeds, "that the Secretary of State's Party and Politicks gains ground here, and I fear will have influence enough to cause acts and resolves which may be unfriendly to Great Britain, to be passed early in the next session of Congress. The Secretary of State, together with Mr. Madison ... are now ... gone to the Eastern States, there to proselyte as far as they are able to a commercial war with Great Britain."[13]

It is interesting to note that Jefferson was already being acknowledged as the head of a party; and it is true that Temple had every reason to believe that he understood the purpose of the journey undertaken by the two friends. But a careful examination of their itinerary, of the brief time they spent in those places where political missionary work might indeed be indicated, and of the inordinate periods they spent in places where by no possible chance was there a politician within miles, must put an end to the hitherto regnant belief. If that is insufficient, then a further examination of Jefferson's diary of the trip, among his papers in the Library of Congress, and of his Account Book, on deposit in the New York Public Library, will clinch the matter.[14]

Madison was in New York and had intended journeying with Beckley to Boston; but he readily agreed to a far different route first with Jefferson. "Health recreation & curiosity being my objects," he wrote significantly, "I can never be out of my way."[15]

Jefferson set out from Philadelphia on May 17, 1791, to join his friend in New York. He traveled in a carriage equipped with an odometer, so that he could calculate his daily mileage. As he left the bricks and pavements of the city he breathed the fresher air with delight and noted the whippoorwill's first harsh cry of the season. It was the evening of the 19th when he was ferried across to New York and put up at Madison's establishment.

He remained only a day and a half in that teeming city of republican politicians—just long enough for Madison to ready himself for the journey—and then they betook themselves on their way up the Hudson. The moment they quit New York, Jefferson began to take notes of the flowers and trees they encountered, with their botanical names and attributes, their structures and mode of growth. He also observed the fish in the streams and lakes, the birds, the animals, and full topographic details; as well as the quality of the soil, types of forestration, etc. Little escaped his observant eye, particularly when he was confronted with species of wild life and of vegetation strange to his native Virginia.[16]

At Poughkeepsie, their carriage was placed on board boat, and they sailed up the river to Albany, arriving on May 26th. In this capital of New York, there was again a sufficiency of politicians, including the redoubtable Governor, George Clinton, one of the later stalwarts of the Republican party. But obviously the two travelers had little, if any, time to discuss the national situation with him and with other good republicans in the old Dutch town; for, after a single day's stay for provisioning, their carriage jolted over level country roads into Fort George, at the head of the lake, on the 29th.

From this lovely vantage point they confronted primeval wilderness. The carriage was left behind, and they took boat up Lake George, portaged the narrow spit that separated it from Champlain, took another boat and sailed twenty-five miles up the lake until head winds and high seas forced them to turn back to Ticonderoga.[17]

Jefferson's observations of the land contours and the streams led him to conclude that a canal connecting Lake George with Champlain on the north and with the Hudson on the south, was a perfectly feasible undertaking; a prophecy that was not to be realized for many years to come.

He thought Lake George, over which they now retraced their course, "without comparison, the most beautiful water I ever saw." Champlain, though much larger, "is a far less pleasant water ... muddy, turbulent." But he found both of them hot and humid, and patriotically declared that there was "nothing anywhere else, in point of climate, which Virginia need envy to any part of the world." [18]

On June 4th and 5th, the travelers visited the battlefields around Bennington and Saratoga, and duly mused on the bloody scenes that had played so vital a role in American history. But Jefferson confessed himself "more pleased however with the botanical objects which continually presented themselves"; listing those which were either unknown or rare in Virginia, and examining the cataracts and strata of rocks. It was Saturday evening when they completed their battlefield inspection at Bennington in Vermont; but they were compelled to remain in the village all the next day, for the laws of Vermont were strict against Sunday travel, even for men of their eminence.[19]

Once it was lawful to ride again, they made their way steadily down the peaceful Connecticut valley, arriving in Hartford on June 8th. There they rested for two days and went on to Guilford and the shore of the Sound, taking boat across to the tip of Long Island. Here, for the first time, they met with someone who might conceivably be called politically minded—General Floyd. On June 14th, they breakfasted and dined with him; then went to visit the tribe of Unquachog Indians.

Coming down the length of the Island, with Jefferson inquiring along the way as to the life habits and ravages of the Hessian fly, they finally reached New York and journey's end on the 16th. The entire tour had taken one month, had covered five states, and they had traversed 256 miles by water, with the odometer clicking off 664 miles by land.

At New York, the two friends parted. The insatiable Madison had intended starting out again with Beckley for Boston, but his own illness and that of his horse prevented it. Beckley went alone, and came back with reports that Adams was highly unpopular in his own territory and that "Publicola" was probably his son, but that the materials for his diatribe had been furnished by the father.[20]

Jefferson went back alone to Philadelphia to resume his official duties, much rested and rid finally of the headache that had plagued him during the previous winter and spring. He had been compelled to borrow money on the trip from Madison, and he now sent him the amount he owed; filling the balance of his letter with a discussion of the plants and trees they had observed together en route, and begging Madison, on his further trip toward Boston and Portsmouth, to continue inquiries concerning the Hessian fly. Not a word of politics or of political characters.[21]

But if the trip had been dedicated primarily to health, sightseeing and scientific curiosity, politics caught up with Jefferson the moment he set foot again in Philadelphia. The campaign against him, based on that appellation of "heretic" which he had applied to Adams, was now in full swing. Hamilton, he wrote bitterly, was making public capital of it by asserting that it "marks my opposition to the government. Thus endeavoring to turn [upon] the government itself those censures I meant for the enemies of the government, to wit those who want to change it into a monarchy." [22]

Oddly enough, in a private conversation between the two antagonists which Jefferson claimed he copied down immediately after it took place, Hamilton condemned the writings of Adams, particularly the *Discourses on Davila*, as having themselves a tendency to weaken the government. Then he went on to unfold his own views with remarkable frankness. "I own it is my own opinion," he declared, "though I do not publish it in Dan or Bersheba, that the present government is not that which will answer the ends of society, by giving stability and protection to its rights, and that it will probably be found expedient to go into the British form. However, since we have undertaken the experiment, I am for giving it a fair course, whatever my expectations may be." So far, he admitted, its success had been greater than he had anticipated, and he felt that all methods should be tried before definitely giving up republicanism altogether; "for that mind must be really depraved, which would not prefer the equality of political rights, which is the foundation of pure republicanism, if it can be obtained consistently with order." [23] Jefferson, as he diligently wrote down the heads of the conversation that night, felt that this last disclaimer had been hastily added by Hamilton to take the edge off the earlier and franker statements.

The two great representatives of the rapidly coalescing parties were still on speaking terms and employed courteous language in the presence of each other, though privately to their friends and political affiliates their language was sharply different. Each tried to throw on the other the onus of being in opposition to the government; and each defined the government in the light of his own philosophy. To both, Washington stood above the battle as the visible embodiment of that government; though, as Washington veered more and more to the ideas of Hamilton, he swayed more and more on the pedestal so far as Jefferson was concerned; though he never fully tumbled into the dust.

Long after, during his own Presidency, Jefferson gave his opinion of Washington and of his fellow Cabinet members during these days to his private secretary, William A. Burwell; and Burwell recorded the gist of the conversation in a hitherto unpublished memoir.[24]

Jefferson, so Burwell noted, always spoke respectfully of Washington, though he did not believe the latter had full confidence in the form of government established in the United States. Jefferson admitted, however, that Washington had been determined to give it a fair trial. If his affections eventually became alienated, Jefferson attributed it to the artifices of Hamilton and his party. Washington, he added, was a man of strong passions. Turning to the portrait of the late President by Gilbert Stuart which then hung in the White House, Jefferson asked Burwell to note "the remarkable compression of the skin immediately over the nose between the Eye brows, which had been produced by a continual struggle to control his feelings."

Then Jefferson discoursed on the members of the Cabinet. General Knox he overlooked as a nonentity, who slavishly followed Hamilton. The latter, of course, was his personal enemy and had labored long and with final success to prejudice Washington against him. But he reserved his heaviest fire for Edmund Randolph. Hamilton, he insisted, had been able to win the ascendancy only because of "the irresolute, timid conduct of E. R. upon whose cooperation it was impossible to rely . . . & he [Jefferson] often had the mortification to find himself abandoned by a man whose weight would have prevented the introduction & arrested the career of a system of corruption which defrauded the poor, debased the rich, & changed the morals of a nation."

What made the alleged betrayal, of course, more galling to Jefferson was the memory of his earlier close personal and political friendship with Randolph. It was then, so he told Burwell, that he determined to collect all the materials necessary for his own future vindication, and which eventually were incorporated into his *Anas*. Any close study of this remarkable collection must, therefore, always bear in mind the deliberate purpose for which it was painstakingly amassed.

No party system had been contemplated in the Constitution or in the ideas of its draughtsmen. It had been believed that men might differ on individual measures; but the concept of organized and disciplined groups, inspired by differing philosophies of government, voting together as a unit on political enactments, and striving for power in the government in order to put their philosophy into effect, was abhorrent to all concerned. The term "faction," not "party," was applied to those who differed in viewpoint, and was considered both by the applier and the applicant as the most galling and opprobrious term that could have been used.

Since the Hamiltonian forces at this juncture had gained control of Congress, the Cabinet and—to some extent—of Washington, they felt justified in applying the hateful word to Jefferson and *his* followers. The latter were thrown into a frenzy by the hateful appellation, retorting with the more classical—and therefore weaker—expression of "phalanx." A mutilated letter from Jefferson to Madison is in existence in which the former denounces Hamilton as "daring to call [the Republicans] a *faction*."

In the same letter the ominous shadow of things to come is clearly marked. Hamilton, so Jefferson had learned, had expressed a wish to see John Marshall of Virginia in the Congress of the United States; and Marshall had expressed half a mind to come. Jefferson concluded that "Hamilton has plyed him well with flattery, & sollicitation, and I think nothing better could be done than to make him a judge." [25] Had Jefferson been able to peer into the future, he would have thought twice before suggesting that Marshall be given a judgeship in order to keep him out of Congress.

But the logic of events inevitably tended toward the formation of two parties, the Federalist and the Republican. In every department of government, in every attitude on domestic and foreign affairs, the line of cleavage was daily becoming more marked. Since the Federalists were generally in control and, by virtue of their belief in a strong national government, compelled to propose measures that would add to its powers, they necessarily took positive steps. By the same token, the first role of the Republicans was generally negative, and devoted to opposition rather than to positive measures of their own. But the philosophy in back of their opposition was in its way just as positive as that which motivated the Federalists. Both were delving into fundamentals which to this day have not been wholly resolved.

Jefferson and Madison had for some time been troubled by a great gap in the armory of their weapons. By and large, the newspapers of the country were in the hands of Federalist sympathizers and all news, all political reporting, were slanted toward the Federalist point of view, while the leading articles inveighed venomously against the persons and principles of the Republicans. The worst of the lot, from their standpoint, was *The Gazette of the United States*, edited by John Fenno, which had achieved a semiofficial status as a government organ and was wholly devoted to Hamilton and his policies.

True, there were a few newspapers which took the Republican side, but they had neither the financial backing nor the range and volume of readership of the Federalist organs. The chief of these was *The Philadelphia General Advertiser*, later to become more famous under the name of the *Aurora*. It was published in Philadelphia under the editorship of Benjamin Franklin Bache, a nephew of the inimitable Ben, and himself an ardent radical.

Jefferson turned his attention to this paper as a possible vehicle for expansion into what he contemplated—a powerful newspaper weapon for combatting the heresies of Fenno and his fellows. He wrote a careful letter to Bache, ostensibly to congratulate him on the improvement of his paper, but actually to offer him advice on how to make it a better one for Republican purposes. Using the third person, he told Bache: "He still wishes some means could be found of making it a paper of general distribution, thro' the states. The advertisements, perfectly useless there, occupying one half of the paper, renders the transportation too embarrassing." This was before the days of second and third class postal rates. Might not the advertisements, Jefferson suggested, be placed in the back section, which could be "torn off or omitted for distant customers. Mr. Bache will be so good as to excuse these officious hints, which proceed from a wish to serve him, & from a desire of seeing a purely republican vehicle of news established between the seat of government & all its parts." [26]

Bache found the advice impracticable from a mechanical viewpoint, and Jefferson was compelled to look elsewhere for that organ of national circulation which he envisaged, and which could stand up to Fenno's paper "of pure Toryism, disseminating the doctrines of monarchy, aristocracy, & the exclusion of the influence of the people." [27]

But Jefferson and Madison had already placed an iron in the fire. On February 28, 1791, Jefferson had written a letter to Philip Freneau in New York: "The clerkship for foreign languages in my office is vacant. The salary, indeed, is very low, being but two hundred and fifty dollars a year; but also, it gives so little to do, as not to interfere with any other calling the person may choose, which would not absent him from the seat of government." [28]

On the face of it, this was merely an offer of a minor job. Actually, it was something much more, and hid within its cautious language an arrangement that had already been discussed between Madison and Freneau. Madison was in New York at the time and was well acquainted with Freneau. They had been classmates at Princeton together, and then their paths had diverged. Freneau, short, thin, muscular, with dark gray eyes and a countenance seamed with the winds of ocean and of doctrine, had written stirring, vehement poetry for the Revolutionary cause and sailed the seas as a trading captain. Possessed of a caustic tongue, a trenchant invective and a facile pen, and burning with impetuous republicanism, he was now a writer for the *N. Y. Daily Advertiser;* but he sought a paper of his own for the advancement of his fortunes and the better purveyance of his political beliefs. In their dilemma, Madison and Jefferson had fixed on him as the ideal man for their purposes.

Madison thought the stage was set for Freneau's acceptance; but Freneau, on receipt of Jefferson's offer, had a change of heart. In language equally as careful as that in which Jefferson's had been couched, he replied: "Having been for some time past engaged in endeavouring to establish a Weekly Gazette in Monmouth County, East Jersey, and having at present a prospect of succeeding in a tolerable subscription, I find myself under the necessity of declining the acceptance of your generous *unsollicited* proposal." [29]

The declination filled Jefferson with consternation, and it is unquestionable that he sought Madison's services in getting the recalcitrant journalist to reconsider. Madison did so, and thought he succeeded. He wrote to Jefferson that Freneau was actually on the way. But the latter failed to appear in Philadelphia. After waiting almost a week, Jefferson wrote to Madison in New York: "Your favor of the 1st came to hand on the 3rd. Mr. Freneau has not followed it: I suppose therefore he has changed his mind back again, for which I am really sorry." [30]

There the matter rested for several months, while Jefferson sought to convert Bache's paper from a local to a national distribution. That scheme failing, he returned to the attack. "I am sincerely sorry," he wrote Madison again, "that Freneau has declined coming here. Tho' the printing business be sufficiently full here, yet I think he would have set out on such advantageous ground as to have been sure of success. His own genius in the first place is so superior to that of his competitors. I should have given him the perusal of all my letters of foreign intelligence & all foreign newspapers; the publication of all proclamations & other public notices within my department, & the printing of the laws, which added to his salary would have been a considerable aid. Besides this, Fenno', being the only weekly or half weekly paper, & under general condemnation for its toryism & its incessant efforts to overturn the government, Freneau would have found that ground as good as unoccupied." [31]

All pretense had been cast aside, and the proposition put in its most naked form. If Freneau would set up a paper that would advocate Republican doctrine as Fenno followed Federalist, he would be subsidized by the Secretary of State with a government salary and official advertising, and given access to all information, confidential or otherwise, within the purviews of the State Department.

This put a much more attractive aspect on the hitherto somewhat vague proposition. Madison used it and the services of Henry Lee, another ardent republican and classmate of Freneau, to press the matter once again on the poet-journalist. This time he was able to overcome Freneau's objections, which had been chiefly financial.[32]

Freneau announced to Jefferson that he was now ready to come to

Philadelphia and set up a newspaper. He had written a Proposal for it, which "I shall request the favor of you to glance your eye over, previous to its being printed." [33]

On August 16, 1791, he was officially appointed by Jefferson as "clerk of foreign languages"; [34] and, within a short period, the *National Gazette* was launched on its short but turbulent career.

The new organ promptly proved its worth to its sponsors. It plunged at once into the fray, attacking with a fine abandon Hamilton, Adams, the Federalists in Congress, the Bank Bill, the later report on manufactures, Fenno's *Gazette of the United States*, Great Britain, monarchists, aristocrats and even—though by indirection—taking an occasional sideswipe at Washington. On the other hand, everything Jeffersonian was upheld on this side of the Atlantic and everything French on the other side. Freneau's pen was mordant and savage, and his phrases cut to the quick. By comparison, Fenno was weak and pallid.

Madison's later characterization of Freneau as "a poet and man of literary and retired tastes, knowing nothing of the world," has a slightly ridiculous air about it. Madison himself wrote articles for the paper under the usual classical disguises, and other republican advocates added their squibs, which even Madison was to admit were sometimes "actuated by overheated zeal, and some, perhaps, by malignity." [35]

Jefferson was delighted with Freneau's efforts, and diligently sought subscribers for the semiweekly paper. He considered it far superior to Bache's daily, writing to his daughter Martha that "Freneau's two papers [a week] contain more good matter than Bache's six." [36] He also engaged Rittenhouse to furnish the *National Gazette* with meteorological observations.[37]

The sudden apparition of this new and powerful anti-Federalist—and therefore, in its current phase, anti-Administration—organ, edited by Jefferson's newly appointed translator and recipient of official advertising, raised an angry storm. Hamilton, the particular target, took it as a personal affront and counterattacked.

On July 25, 1792, there appeared in the columns of Fenno's *Gazette of the United States* a portentous inquiry:

> The editor of the *National Gazette* receives a salary from government. *Quere.*—Whether this salary is paid him for *translations*, or for publications, the design of which is to vilify those to whom the voice of the people has committed the administration of our public affairs.... In common life it is thought ungrateful for a man to bite the hand that puts bread in his mouth; but if the man is hired to do it, the case is altered.[38]

The signature to the bitter question was merely "T. L.," but everyone knew, or was soon to know, that the author was Hamilton. As if in response, a signatory "An American"—again Hamilton—responded in a series of three letters attacking Freneau and Jefferson, this time by name, and tracing with remarkable accuracy the negotiations between the pair. Jefferson was specifically told to resign, if he disapproved of the government, but not to hide behind sneak attacks in the name of another.[39]

The fat was in the fire. The smoldering hostility between the two men had burst into open flames, and even outward courtesy was henceforth completely abandoned.

But, in the meantime, Jefferson was placed on the defensive. Instead of open avowal and justification of his course—he might have retorted that Fenno's sheet was equally a party organ, subsidized with official Treasury advertising—he resorted to subterfuge, equivocation and evasion.

On August 6, 1792, two days after the first blast of "An American" appeared, Freneau sent his solemn affidavit to the *Gazette*, averring "that no negociation was ever opened with him by *Thomas Jefferson*, Secretary of State, for the establishment or institution of the *National Gazette;* that the deponent's coming to the City of Philadelphia, as publisher of a Newspaper was at no time urged, advised or influenced by the above officer, but that it was his own voluntary act; and that the said Gazette, nor the Editor thereof, was ever either directed, controuled, or attempted to be influenced, in any manner, either by the Secretary of State, or any of his friends. . . ."[40]

The second part of the affidavit was perhaps technically true: Freneau required no influence or control to follow the correct line; and even the first half might fit legalistic requirements. No communication from Jefferson to Freneau direct mentioned the fatal word "newspaper." But, as "An American" was quick to point out, that while in a literal sense Jefferson may not have *personally* negotiated with Freneau, "yet it may be very certain, that a negotiation was opened with him, directly or circuitously, by a *particular friend* of that officer, and expectation given of his patronage and encouragement."[41]

The open attack on him required something more from Jefferson than Freneau's affidavit. Washington had said nothing to him, but it was evident that his anger had been mounting at the steady sniping against him and his administration in Freneau's paper. Now, however, that the dissensions in his Cabinet had thus been thrust violently into the open, he felt called upon to intervene. He wrote both participants to the quarrel, gently chiding them for the bitterness of their disputes, and asking them for the sake of the country and its fortunes, to exercise more charity and mutual forbearance; otherwise, he gravely declared, both government and country might well be torn asunder.[42]

Neither party receded, and both defended their conduct. Jefferson attacked Hamilton's policies, his intrigues and corrupting influence on Congress, and his high-handed interference in the affairs of Jefferson's own department. If Hamilton, under the guise of "An American," could charge Freneau as evidence of Jefferson's underhanded conduct, what about the way Hamilton had staffed the Treasury with his friends and henchmen, and "the dealing out of Treasury-secrets among his friends in what time & measure he pleases."

As to Freneau, he was wholly disingenuous. Freneau, according to Jefferson, had asked for a clerkship while the seat of government was in New York. There had been no vacancy then; as soon as one arose in Philadelphia, he offered it. Whether Freneau had talked about a newspaper at the time of offering, or later, Jefferson had absolutely no recollection. But when it *was* broached, so he blandly asserted, "I considered it as a circumstance of some value, as it might enable me to do, what I had long wished to have done, that is, to have the material parts of the Leyden gazette brought under your eye & that of the public, in order to possess yourself and them of a juster view of the affairs of Europe than could be obtained from any other public source."

And, on a note of unprecedented bitterness, he ended: "I will not suffer my retirement to be clouded by the slanders of a man whose history, from the moment at which history can stoop to notice him, is a tissue of machinations against the liberty of the country which not only has received and given him bread, but heaped its honors on his head." [43] It was not history that was stooping at the moment; but Jefferson himself.

Barely four days after, however, Jefferson was giving a completely different picture of the transaction to his fellow Cabinet member, Edmund Randolph. To him he admitted that he had wished and advised Freneau to establish his paper in Philadelphia, and that he hoped it would be an "antidote to the doctrines & discourses circulated in favour of Monarchy and Aristocracy...." This, he amazingly added, "is a truth which I never could be tempted to conceal, or wish to be concealed." [44]

Nor, in spite of Washington's intervention, did the controversy end at that point. Others, like "Aristides," who was probably Dr. George Logan of Pennsylvania, rushed to Jefferson's defense; and Hamilton, under the belief that "Aristides" was Jefferson, promptly retorted as "Catullus" in an extended series of articles. It was not to end until both Hamilton and Jefferson had finally retired from Washington's official family; and not even then.

In the midst of the hullabaloo over Freneau, Hamilton issued another Report which to Jefferson only proved his own wisdom in setting up a public vehicle for attacking his antagonist's measures. This was the famous Report on Manufactures. Coming as it did on the heels of the Bank Bill, it strengthened Jefferson's belief that Hamilton, unless checked, was definitely and deliberately attempting to subvert the principles on which the government was based, and was trying, by every means in his power, to create another and even more corrupt Great Britain on these shores.

Though Jefferson had earlier, and was again later, to nibble at the idea of encouraging some form of manufacture in the United States, he recoiled at this thoroughgoing proposition to create a vast, industrialized nation in what, to him, was the ideal setting for an agricultural utopia. He shrank from such arguments as the one that an increase in manufactures would bring a large immigration of factory workers into this country, or that women and children of tender age could be employed in the factories. He viewed with the greatest alarm the proposal that these new industries be protected by prohibitive tariffs and supported by government subsidies. The Report, he clearly realized, would fasten forever on this nation a way of life and a system of economy that presupposed everything to which he was passionately opposed.

Jefferson promptly told Washington that he considered protective duties and government subsidies for manufacturers unconstitutional, as giving to Congress powers far beyond those enumerated in that document;[45] and alerted his friends in Congress on the subject.

For the first, and only, time he was successful in defeating a Hamiltonian project. The House, to whom the Report was rendered on December 5, 1791, failed to act; and the nation proceeded, at least so Jefferson thought, along the accustomed grooves of an agricultural economy. But the inexorable forces of the industrial revolution eventually brought Hamilton's plan to fruition and left the Jeffersonian philosophy in this particular respect an outworn memory. For good or ill, it was Hamilton rather than Jefferson who had anticipated the future.

CHAPTER 34

City Planning and Foreign Disputes

PART of the deal between Jefferson and Hamilton over assumption had been the eventual transfer of the capital of the United States to the banks of the Potomac. As was natural under the circumstances, and because it came within the duties of his Department, Jefferson took an active interest in the project from the very beginning.

Congress had passed a Residence Act authorizing the acquisition of land for the capital; and Jefferson made a series of notes for proceedings to be had under that Act. He estimated the eventual size of the Federal territory as 100 square miles, and called for the appointment of three commissioners to purchase or accept by gift such present quantities of land as the President deemed proper. He thought that one square should be allotted for the Capitol and offices of government, one for a Market, and nine for public walks. He proposed that the streets be laid out at right angles as in Philadelphia, but that they should be wide, straight and spacious; and not in any event to be narrower than 100 feet, with footways of 15 feet for pedestrians. The commissioners, he characteristically insisted, even though they would be subject to the President's direction, "should have some taste in architecture."

As he went along with the plans, his own architectural enthusiasm kindled. "I doubt much," he declared, "whether the obligation to build the houses at a given distance from the street, contributes to its beauty. It produces a disgusting monotony. All persons make this complaint against Philadelphia. The contrary practice varies the appearance, & is much more convenient to the inhabitants." [1]

On February 2, 1791, Major Andrew Ellicott was designated to lay out and survey the new city; while Thomas Johnson, David Stuart and Daniel Carroll were appointed Commissioners. The next month, Major Peter Charles L'Enfant was directed to assist Ellicott, particularly with reference to the site of the town itself and its buildings. Interestingly enough, Jefferson made another appointment to the survey, which the *Georgetown Weekly Ledger* commented on in the following language. That on-the-spot southern newspaper announced the arrival of Major Ellicott, "attended by Benjamin Banniker [*sic*], an Ethopian, whose abilities as a Surveyor and Astronomer clearly prove that Mr. Jefferson's concluding that race of men were void of mental endowments was without foundation." [2] The sarcastic reference was, of course, to Jefferson's animadversions in the *Notes on Virginia.*

Benjamin Banneker was indeed a good mathematician and something of an astronomer. A free Negro of Philadelphia, he had achieved the cooperation and respect of Jefferson's friends in the Philosophical Society, and they had doubtless recommended him for the post. A few months later, he sent Jefferson a copy of the astronomical Almanac he had compiled, and received a kindly acknowledgment in return. "Nobody wishes more than I do," wrote Jefferson, "to see such proofs as you exhibit, that nature has given to our black brethren, talents equal to those of the other colors of men, and that the appearance of a want of them is owing merely to the degraded condition of their existence, both in Africa & America."[3]

Nevertheless, in spite of this polite exchange, Jefferson was never to become fully convinced of these "proofs."

As always, Jefferson was not satisfied with mere supervision when there were ground planning and architectural schemes afoot. He drafted a sketch map of what he conceived the new city should look like. He proposed that the Capitol building and the residential area should front on the juncture of the Potomac with Tyler Creek; that the balance should extend to Rock Creek on the north and to the south along the river.[4]

For the Capitol building itself, which would naturally be the focal point of the entire development, Jefferson used almost the identical language to Major L'Enfant that he had employed years before in connection with the Virginia capitol. "I should prefer," he wrote, "the adoption of some one of the models of antiquity, which have had the approbation of thousands of years; and for the President's House I should prefer the celebrated fronts of modern buildings, which have already received the approbation of all good judges. Such are the Galerie du Louvre, the Garde Meubles, and two fronts of the Hotel de Salm." He also sent L'Enfant the plans of the various cities in Europe he had picked up on his travels for study in connection with laying out the city proper.[5]

It is notable that Jefferson still looked to Europe and to antiquity for his models; that he failed to grasp the boundless possibilities for a new architecture, as he had for a new ethic and way of life, in the new country he had helped build. In fact, he hoped that the private residents of the Federal city would follow suit when they came to build their own dwelling houses, and was willing to engrave copies of his drawing of Parisian buildings and distribute them gratis among the inhabitants, so that they "might decide the taste of the new town."[6]

But matters did not proceed as Jefferson would have wished. L'Enfant's plan, as finally accepted, and which is the basis of the modern city of Washington, followed Jefferson's rectangular idea only partially, superimposing on the monotonous regular squares a series of spaced circles, in the chief of which towered the Capitol building, and from which radiated broad avenues like the spokes of a wheel.

L'Enfant proved an opinionated and arrogant man. Secure in the knowledge of his own abilities, he shrugged off advice and criticism, and resented even the supervision of his official superiors. Without consulting the Commissioners, he proceeded to demolish the home of Charles Carroll of Duddington, on the ground that it protruded into one of the streets he had laid out; nor did the fact that Charles Carroll was the nephew of Daniel Carroll, one of the Commissioners, deter him in the slightest.

Daniel Carroll and his fellow Commissioners were properly outraged at these high-handed proceedings and protested vigorously; at the same time, however, a little afraid that the Major might take umbrage and quit.[7] Washington turned the business over to Jefferson to handle. He, too, felt that L'Enfant had gone too far, yet was equally afraid that the impetuous Frenchman might, if spoken to sharply, drop the project. "At the same time," he added with some exasperation, "*he must know*, there is a line beyond which he will not be suffered to go... or we shall have no Commissioners." [8]

Jefferson determined on a showdown. He wrote sharply to L'Enfant that he had laid himself open to the laws by demolishing Carroll's house without authority. "I wished you to be employed in the arrangements of the federal city. I still wish it: but only on condition that you can conduct yourself in subordination to the authority of the Commissioners, to the laws of the land, & to the rights of its citizens." [9]

But L'Enfant heeded neither reprimands nor commands, and went his own way regardless of Commissioners, Secretary of State and President. The comedy lasted for several months, with threats and blandishments alternating in swift succession, until Jefferson, faced finally with L'Enfant's flat refusal to submit to the Commissioners' "will and caprice," put an end to his employment and placed Ellicott in charge.[10]

As both Washington and Jefferson had been afraid, however, there was a great outcry over L'Enfant's dismissal from the property owners in the new city, but Jefferson was adamant and Washington backed him up. The Frenchman's re-employment, wrote Jefferson to one of the protestants, can "never more be thought of... that the success of the enterprise depended on his employment is impossible to believe." [11]

But he was soon to find out that he had got rid of one prima donna only to have two others on his hands. Thomas Johnson, one of the Commissioners, and Andrew Ellicott, the new engineer for the city, became involved in violent quarrels and recriminations over the plans; and Ellicott also was dismissed.

Nevertheless, the work managed somehow to go ahead; haltingly and with many gaps, it is true, until at least the skeleton of a city was ready for occupancy by 1799. All through Jefferson's own administrations, the work progressed, particularly on the Capitol and the President's House; and Jefferson busied himself with the architectural details with perhaps more gusto than with the regular duties of his office.

In the meantime, however, Jefferson kept a diligent watch on the proceedings and participated in every step of the plans. He was fertile with suggestions and ideas; sometimes, no doubt, much to the dismay of the working architects and engineers. He disliked angular buildings at the commencement of avenues as "offensive to the eye, if not well managed." He suggested, instead, bow windows and semicircular porticoes; and proposed long rows of trees as borders for the streets and avenues. Eventually he got the trees on Pennsylvania Avenue. He preferred brick to stone for construction; remembering with enthusiasm the Roman bricks in the south of France, of which the grain was as fine as the best earthenware.[12]

Nor was he content with mere suggestions. The Commissioners had announced a competition for the best design of a Capitol building. Jefferson made a free-hand sketch based on his beloved Pantheon; with a huge central dome and balancing wings, each surmounted by a lesser dome. But Dr. William Thornton, a self-taught architect, won the competition with his design, and Jefferson generously approved of it as "simple, noble, beautiful, excellently distributed, and moderate in size." [13]

Jefferson had not officially entered his sketch of the Capitol; but when a competition for the President's House was announced, he could not resist the temptation. He drafted two sets of plans and submitted one anonymously to the judges. The plan of the house, as he conceived it, was Palladio's famous Villa Rotunda with modifications.[14] His submission was rejected; but his pride was salved by the knowledge that all the other entries had been similarly discarded.

More and more, the foreign relations of the United States were looming ominously on the horizon. France, England and Spain—these were the three great European powers which impinged vitally on the fortunes of the infant republic. Themselves engaged in a triangular life-and-death struggle, and changing partners with lightninglike rapidity, every move they made, every policy intended to damage the antagonist of the moment, wrought even greater havoc on the supposedly neutral and distant nation across the Atlantic.

The careful jockeying for position by the three Powers, in anticipation of the eventual world conflict which all knew was inevitable, caused as many by-blows to fall on America as on one another. But the meaning of the blows was variously interpreted by Americans, depending on the particular party to which they adhered. On one of the impending contestants, however, there was no dispute, except perhaps from a few secret pensioners in the West. That was Spain. All agreed in damning her and all her measures; and looked forward to the day when they could strip her of her American possessions.

On France and England, however, there was not only no unanimity, but a definite cleavage of opinion. Each party attached itself for better or worse to its favorite nation overseas; the Federalists to Great Britain, and the Republicans to France. Each lauded the institutions and policies of its choice, and damned those of the other. The same measures which, when enforced by one, aroused bitter denunciation and demands for countermeasures *à l'outrance*, met with palliative excuses and justifications when put into effect by the other. Small wonder, then, that each party saw with terrible clarity the illogical mote in the other's eye, and indignantly repudiated the retort of the beam in its own.

It is true that, for the first few years of Washington's administration, the chief provocations came from England; and Jefferson was properly indignant over the British ruling which refused to admit a ship sailing under the American flag as American unless it had actually been built in an American shipyard. This means, he fumed, that in the case of a European war in which we are neutral, "they put it out of our power to benefit ourselves of our neutrality, by increasing suddenly by purchase & naturalization our means of carriage." [15]

Jefferson was the chief protagonist of retaliatory measures; but the Federalists refused to harken, and he despaired of success. Some of the Southern States even, much to his amazement, were also opposed. He sought, through his friend Edward Rutledge, to bring the recalcitrants to a reasonable view. "I have little hope," he wrote, "that the result will be any thing more than to turn the left cheek to him who has smitten the right. We have to encounter not only the prejudices in favor of England, but those against the Eastern states whose ships in the opinion of some will overrun our land. I have been sorry to see that your state [South Carolina] has been over-jealous of the measures proposed on this subject." Would Rutledge, therefore, try to convert the dissidents? [16]

But the French, at about the same time, were beginning to harass American shipping with even more severe restrictions than the British. They placed a discriminatory duty on American tobacco imported in American ships as against French bottoms. Jefferson called on Short to get Lafayette to intervene. It is, he declared, "such an act of hostility against our navigation as was not to have been expected from the Friendship of that Nation." Even the British Navigation Act, "so much and so justly complained of, leaves to all nations the carriage of their own commodities free." But in *this* case, Jefferson never considered the idea of retaliation. "We presume," he told the French representative, "the National Assembly must have been hurried into the measure, without being allowed time to reflect on its consequences." [17]

In spite of his indignation, moreover, Jefferson believed the French Revolution to be fundamental to the happiness of the world. When he heard of the flight of the king and his recapture, his chief concern was that it might rest in the power of one man to defeat "the issue of so beautiful a revolution. I hope and trust it is not, and that, for the good of suffering humanity all over the earth, that revolution will be established and spread through the whole world." He was also convinced that the American and the French Revolutions were closely interrelated, and that any failure abroad would seriously lessen the permanence of our own; and that it would be employed as a powerful argument for eventual failure at home.[18]

Fortunately, France had just appointed a regular Minister to the United States—Jean Baptiste Ternant, who arrived in Philadelphia in August, 1791. Shortly after, England followed suit, terminating the highly irregular and galling unofficial agency of Col. Beckwith in favor of the properly accredited George Hammond. With these two ministers on the spot, Jefferson was better able to conduct direct negotiations than formerly, and to keep the several strings firmly in hand.

If he thought, however, that the presence of official representatives would put an end to Hamilton's interpositions, he was mistaken. Hamilton took up with Hammond exactly where he had left off with Beckwith; and even, astonishingly enough, seized the occasion to discuss foreign affairs with Ternant.

Much to Jefferson's discomfiture, Ternant had not brought with him any instructions authorizing the discussion of a commercial treaty between France and the United States nor, as he frankly expressed it, did he expect any. Discussions looking toward a treaty must, therefore, take place in Paris. Jefferson, for obvious reasons, preferred that they be pursued in Philadelphia.[19]

But here Hamilton stepped into the picture. In a private conversation with Ternant, he suggested that Ternant discuss terms with Jefferson on a "volunteer" basis; that, after conditions had been arranged between them, they be sent to France for confirmation or rejection. He also broached the idea to Washington, who liked it and passed it on to Jefferson. The latter, however, objected on the ground that while such an arrangement would be binding on us, the French were free to refuse; and, in the meantime, had found out exactly how far we were willing to go.[20]

Jefferson's appraisal of the situation was sound; but Washington, under Hamilton's prodding, insisted. With considerable reluctance, therefore, Jefferson drafted a set of proposed clauses for a treaty, the heart of which consisted in a mutual agreement that the citizens of each country, their ships, produce and manufactures, receive the same treatment from the other as their own citizens and effects; and that the import duties laid by both remain at current maximums, with the proviso that if either country lowered its duties, then the other must reduce its own by an equivalent amount.[21]

Hamilton, on the other hand, had prepared his own proposals, which differed sharply from Jefferson's in that he incorporated a higher schedule of duties, from which America would not recede no matter what France might do.[22]

Ternant also refused to go along with Jefferson in the matter of the duties. Instead of freezing the maxima at the current levels, he demanded the right to increase French duties on American goods by as much as 50 per cent. This put an end to further discussions.

But Hamilton now came up with his trump card. Since France refused to negotiate, he argued, why should not a similar proposition be put to Hammond—equally in the role of a "volunteer"?

A great light burst on Jefferson. This, then, was what Hamilton had really been angling for. While pretending to negotiate with Ternant and sabotaging any possibility of success by his insistence on higher duties, he actually had in mind the negotiation of a treaty with Great Britain on terms so favorable to the latter that we would be attached forever to her commercial orbit.[23]

This trap, as he labeled it, Jefferson fought with the greatest determination. He had been persuaded against his better judgment into a negotiation with Ternant, where there might have been a chance of success. With England, he was convinced, there was none. He had enough controversial matters to discuss with Hammond without being bypassed into fruitless conversations over a commercial treaty. Had not the old treaty, specific enough in its terms, been breached in its most important sections by the British? It was on these he would press compliance on Hammond, and discuss nothing else until satisfaction had been received; always, however, with the proviso that, should Hammond ever obtain full powers to negotiate a treaty of commerce, he would be willing then to take it up.

On November 29, 1791, Jefferson called for sharp clarification from Hammond. He pointed to Article VII of the Peace Treaty which had forbidden the destruction or carrying away of American property—including Negroes—and a complete British withdrawal from American territory. "I need not observe to you," he added dryly, "that this article still remains in a state of inexecution." Was Hammond, he inquired, authorized to present any explanations on the execution of that article? [24]

Hammond promptly countered with an attack on the American position. With equal dryness he retorted: "It is scarcely necessary for me to remark to you, Sir, that the king my master was induced to suspend the execution of that article on his part, in consequence of the non-compliance, on the part of the United States, with the engagements, contained in the fourth, fifth, and sixth articles of the same treaty. These two objects are therefore so materially connected with each other, as not to admit of separation." He would be glad, however, to discuss *all* questions of non-compliance by both parties.[25]

Jefferson was in a spot; and knew it. He could not afford to associate a discussion of *American* breaches of the treaty with those of the English; for that meant interminable and fruitless talks. It was in vain that he had pointed out in the past that the Federal Government had no power to coerce the States into permitting British actions on debts in their courts or into restoration of confiscated Loyalist property. Privately, he saw the justice of the British position; officially, he could only seek for means to evade the point and obtain as a minimum the evacuation of the posts still held by England on American soil.

He therefore sought delay in answering the unanswerable by a pretense that there had been a delay in copying certain documents relating to the treaty, and seized upon an expression in Hammond's letter indicating that the British government might be ready to discuss a commercial treaty. Did this mean, artfully inquired Jefferson, that Hammond himself had no power to do so? [26]

Hammond fell into the trap. He *did* have such powers, he admitted. Then present your credentials, retorted Jefferson.[27] He had won his point with Hamilton; by steadfastly refusing to treat with Hammond as a *volunteer*, he had forced him to show his hand. Now he could return to the matter of the treaty violations.

On December 15, 1791, he replied to Hammond's letter of November 30th. He had drafted the communication with great care. The United States, he wrote, wished "to lessen difficulties, by passing over whatever is of smaller concern, and insisting on those matters only which either justice to individuals, or public policy render indispensable." Such, to his mind, were the refusal to quit the border posts and the carrying away of Negroes. Let Hammond, he proposed, list in like fashion *his* specific and substantial complaints.[28]

Hammond took his good time about it, but when he finally submitted his "abstract of such particular Acts of the United States, as appear to me infractions on their part of the definitive treaty of peace," it was voluminous, carefully detailed, and went into the minutest infractions in every state of the Union.[29]

Washington, to whom it was submitted, was staggered at its length; but inquired of Jefferson whether the whole might not be balanced by the loss to the United States of the Indian trade and the expenses of the Indian war, both of which, so ran the American argument, were direct results of the continued British holding of the frontier posts.[30]

But Jefferson realized that Hammond's schedule of indictments could not be thus cavalierly dismissed. He drafted an extended reply; but before he sent it to Hammond, he submitted it to Madison, Edmund Randolph and Hamilton for criticism and comment. Hamilton's chief objection was that Jefferson should merely have extenuated the obstacles which the States had placed in the way of British debt collections, instead of seeking to justify them; but this time Washington backed up Jefferson, and the justifying arguments were permitted to stand.

On May 29, 1792, the revised document was forwarded to Hammond. Jefferson's justifications were voluminous, running, in the printing, to ninety-five solid pages of type.[31]

It was a masterpiece of forensic argument and legal marshaling of points. In diplomacy, so Jefferson had learnt, one must never apologize or extenuate, as Hamilton had wished. One must justify—and again justify; yielding no admission of wrongdoing on even the smallest point. Item by item, he took up Hammond's complaints and replied to them. With one sweep of legal citations he brushed aside all instances of objectionable acts on the part of the States *prior* to the peace treaty. The signing of the latter, he insisted, wiped the slate clean.

The two chief items, of course, were based on Article V of the treaty, wherein provisions were made for the restitution of Loyalist property confiscated during the war, and for the collection of prewar debts. On the first, Jefferson pointed to the exact wording of the Article—it called merely for a *recommendation* by Congress to the States that the property be restored. This Congress had done in good faith; it could do no more. The British Commissioners were well aware at the time of negotiation that Congress had no power of enforcement; and the matter had even been adverted to in the debates in Parliament over the pending treaty.

Thus far, Jefferson was on good arguable ground. But when he came to the debt collections, it was another matter. The language of the Article had been positive and without reservations; and the States to the south—including Virginia—had passed stay laws in open defiance of the treaty. Therefore Jefferson had to employ the argument *ad hominem*—you also have violated the treaty, and you did it first.

Disregarding Article V for the moment, he concentrated his attention on Article VII, in which the British had agreed to give up the frontier posts and withdraw without carrying off any American property. They had *not* yielded the posts, in spite of repeated demands, and they *had* carried off numerous slaves. By clinging to the posts, they had hampered our fur trade and made it difficult for us to pursue and punish marauding Indians who periodically swooped down on our frontier settlements. Since these treaty violations came *first* from the British side, and had continued to the present day, how, inquired Jefferson, can the Americans be expected to adhere rigidly to their side of the bargain? Even so, he added, many States had so adhered, and their courts were open to British suits.

Thunderstruck at what he conceived to be the denials, irrelevant matter and "the general acrimonious stile and manner of this letter," Hammond went promptly to Hamilton to complain "of this extraordinary performance." He had been in the habit of going to Hamilton on all occasions when he wanted confidential information of what was actually going on behind the façade of American diplomacy, and Hamilton had never failed him. Nor did he fail him now.

"This Gentleman," Hammond reported to his superior in London, "treated me, (as he has done upon every occasion), with the strictest confidence and candour. After lamenting the intemperate violence of his colleague, Mr. Hamilton assured me that this letter was very far from meeting his approbation, or from containing a faithful exposition of the sentiments of this Government." Furthermore, so Hamilton continued, Washington was just returned from Virginia and had not read the communication, but had relied on Jefferson's assurances that it represented the opinions of all the members of the Cabinet.[32]

This was an amazing situation. A responsible member of government was, in effect, informing the representative of a foreign power that an official communication to that power from another responsible member of government, and purporting to speak for that government, did not in fact do so, and might therefore be safely ignored. Nor was this the first time that Hamilton had sabotaged, with his "strictest confidence and candour," the policies of the Department of State. The confidential correspondence of the British Minister with his home government is most illuminating on this point.

Jefferson wrote only the bare truth when he noted bitterly in his *Anas* that at Cabinet meetings, Hamilton "had constantly ready something which Mr. Hammond had communicated to him, which suited the subject, and proved the intimacy of their communications; insomuch that I believe he communicated to Hammond all our views & knew from him in return the views of the British Court." [33] But even Jefferson, willing as he was to believe the worst of Hamilton, did not suspect the entire truth.

It is no wonder then that Jefferson found himself unable to make any real headway with Hammond, in spite of a conversation he had with the British Minister several days after he had submitted his defense of the American position. Hammond had then seemed quite agreeable and willing to explore the entire situation; and had left Jefferson with high hopes of an early solution.[34]

But if Jefferson's hopes were to be dashed, so were Hammond's. The latter's satisfaction over the evidence of a rift in the American Cabinet was considerably dampened when he returned to Hamilton with a proposal that the English act as mediators in the dispute between the United States and the Indian tribes along the border. Hamilton had been willing enough to disclose State secrets to the British Minister when he personally disagreed with the course under consideration; but this was a different matter. For the first time he was quite sharp with his good friend, Hammond. If the Indians, he declared, would not yield to "persuasion and gentle means, it would be indispensably necessary to complete their subjection by the terror and success of the American arms. He added that the mediation or intervention of any foreign power would degrade the United States in the estimation of the Indians, and would sow the seeds of future dissension."

He was even more abrupt in his dismissal of Hammond's suggestion that a buffer Indian state be erected between the English and the Americans. He refused to enter into any discussion of the plan, "but replied briefly and coldly, that he wished me to understand that any plan, which comprehended any thing like a cession of territory or right, or the allowance of any other power to interfere in the disputes of the Indians, would be considered by this government as absolutely impracticable and inadmissible." [35] Hammond retired to meditate on the obvious fact that there was a point beyond which even such a good friend to England and himself as Hamilton could not be pushed.

Meanwhile, unknowing of what was going on behind his back, Jefferson was sending instructions to the newly appointed American Minister to England, Thomas Pinckney, to seek an immediate solution of two points in dispute: the lifting of restrictions on our commerce with the British dominions, but "most especially in the West Indies"; and the impressment of our seamen into British service, on which the thesis must be established that seamen on board an American vessel are prima facie American citizens.[36]

The United States had finally appointed ministers to the various courts of Europe. Thomas Pinckney of South Carolina had gone to London; Gouverneur Morris, over considerable protests, had been accredited to Paris. The latter was, in truth, a "most unfortunate" appointment, as Tom Paine angrily declared when he heard of it.[37] By instinct, training and prepossessions, Morris was opposed to the French Revolution and all its works; certainly he was not a fit ambassador in a place where tact, discretion and a decently sympathetic attitude were required. Jefferson had hoped to gain the post for his protégé, William Short; but Washington had preferred Morris, and Short was compelled to settle for the Ministry to The Hague.

Jefferson resented the overriding of his wishes, but managed to obtain for Short an interim appointment as a special commissioner, with William Carmichael, for the negotiation of a treaty with Madrid. Communicating these facts to Short, Jefferson also spoke of "the determination I have unalterably fixed for retiring from my office at the close of our first Federal cycle, which will be first of March, 1793. All this is confided sacredly to your secrecy, being known to no living mortal but the President, Madison, and yourself."[38]

Carmichael, the other member of the commission, had been Chargé d'Affaires in Spain for a considerable period, but length of service had not added to his qualifications. It was of him that Washington was finally to explode: "I believe we are never to hear *from* Mr. Carmichael; nor *of him* but through the medium of a third person. His —— I really do not know with what epithet to fill the blank, is, to me, amongst the most unaccountable of all the unaccountable things! I wish much to hear of the arrival of Mr. Short at Madrid, and the result of their joint negotiations at that Court."

There was indeed much to hear about, and Carmichael had been the most dilatory of correspondents with his home government. Relations with Spain, always bad enough, had considerably worsened. There had been trouble with the powerful Indian tribe of the Creeks, strategically located between Spanish possessions in the south and the United States, and Washington justly suspected the Spaniards of offering aid and comfort to the disaffected Indians. "If Spain is really intrieguing [*sic*] with the Southern Indians..." declared Washington, "I shall entertain strong suspicions that there is a very clear understanding in all this business between the Courts of London and Madrid; and that it is calculated to check, as far as they can, the rapid encrease, extension and consequence of this Country." [39]

This was, however, only one of the items in dispute. Back in June, 1791, Spain had sent Don Joseph Jaudenes to join with Don Joseph Viar in Philadelphia as special commissioners to discuss these items, but Jefferson had found that their powers were insufficient for a full negotiation, and he had advised the mission in Europe. On March 18, 1792, he outlined the three main headings of dispute between the two countries, and issued instructions to Carmichael and Short how they should be handled in the negotiations at Madrid.[40]

The first involved the boundary between Georgia and Spanish Florida. Spain claimed a sizable section of southern Georgia on the ground that she had seized it from England during the late war. Jefferson countered that Spain had been our ally at the time; and that by her final treaty with England she had bound herself to restore all conquered territories with certain exceptions, of which this was not one.

The second was of much greater importance—the ever-troublesome question of our right to navigate the lower Mississippi. This right Jefferson placed on several grounds—some legalistic and one that invoked the famous laws of Nature and of Nations. "It is written in the heart of man..." he declared with perfect gravity, "that the Ocean is free to all men, & the Rivers to all their inhabitants.... When their rivers enter the limits of another society, if the right of the upper inhabitants to descend the stream is in any case obstructed, it is an act of force by a stronger society against a weaker, condemned by the judgement of mankind." The appeal to natural rights was the weakest of all arguments. There is no case on record that it ever impressed the other side sufficiently to grant the point in question. Furthermore, Jefferson had given Spain an opportunity to make an unfortunate inference—that *she* was the stronger society, and *we* the weaker.

The third matter at issue was the proper basis for a commercial treaty. Jefferson proposed two leading principles—the same as those he had proposed to France: that the citizens of each nation possess all the rights of the other, and that most favored nation privileges be extended, in all the possessions of each country. In contradistinction to Hamilton's policy, he refused to have the treaty specify any fixed scale of tariffs which either nation might apply to the goods of the other.

The instructions ended with the usual threat that unless Spain acceded, the American West would take direct action.

Privately, Jefferson exhorted Short to consider this the most important mission of his career, and "to meditate the matter day and night." [41] It was to be completed before any idea got abroad that Jefferson intended to resign; otherwise Spain might delay in hopes of a change of policy. It is obvious that he feared his successor would be a member of the Hamiltonian faction.

The matter of the turbulent Creeks, however, was too exigent to wait for negotiations in distant Madrid; and Jefferson took it up directly with Jaudenes and Viar. On July 9, 1792, armed with information that a Spanish agent had gone among the Creeks to stir them up again, he sent a sharp protest to the Spanish commissioners. This time the threat was naked and unadorned. "It is not to a nation whose dominions are circumstanced as those of Spain in our neighborhood," he wrote pointedly, "that we need develop the inconveniences of permitting reciprocally the unlicensed mission of Agents into the territories of each other." [42]

There the matter rested until the end of October, when Jefferson, convinced that he was getting nowhere with the Spaniards, proposed laying all the correspondence before Congress and letting that body decide whether we should wage war against the Creeks or the Spaniards or both.

Hamilton, however, was for peace; and his reasons were consistent with his leading philosophy. "War," he argued, "would derange our affairs, greatly, throw us back many years in the march towards prosperity.... A year, even, was a great gain to a nation strengthening as we were." Equally consistent was his belief that, in view of the future inevitability of war, we should prepare for it by seeking an alliance with England. Whereupon Washington remarked that Hamilton's "remedy would be worse than the disease." [43]

It was finally decided not to lay the business before Congress, so that, in effect, Hamilton won his point.

Jefferson, however, was happy to find support from Washington in his fixed belief that it was to France we must turn for aid and alliance, and not to Great Britain. He returned to this theme time and again. No matter what convulsions took place in France, no matter how cantankerous the National Assembly sometimes seemed to be, he never wavered in his faith in the eventual success of the French Revolution and of future cordial relations with its government.

Even when he was instructing Gouverneur Morris to press upon the National Assembly the advisability of repealing their "very obnoxious laws respecting our commerce," and to hint that it would be impossible, if this were not done, to keep the next Congress from invoking retaliatory measures, he did it with every manifestation of a friendly spirit.[44]

He was angered by "the general abuse of the Jacobins" that prevailed in this country. That extreme radical faction had seized power in France, with consequent expropriations, violence and tremendous social changes. Those who had viewed the whole revolution with suspicion from the beginning now felt justified by the new shift in power. But Jefferson accepted the rise of the Jacobins without any reservations; in fact, he told Madison, "I begin to consider them as representing the true revolution—spirit of the whole nation, and as carrying the nation with them. The only things wanting with them is more experience in business, and a little more conformity to the established style of communication with foreign powers."[45]

A little bloodletting, as long as it was in a cause he believed in, did not unduly alarm Jefferson; and he was willing to lay to inexperience the truly arrogant attitude which the Jacobins were adopting in their foreign diplomacy.

Probably what threw him so far to the left when it came to any consideration of France was the fact that the Federalists looked upon that nation as the beast described in the Apocalypse. To Joel Barlow, American poet and pamphleteer, who had thrown himself enthusiastically into the Revolution, he breathed a prayer: "God send that all the nations who join in attacking the liberties of France may end in the attainment of their own."[46] To Tom Paine, similarly engaged, who had sent him a sheaf of his pamphlets, he exclaimed: "Would you believe it possible that in this country there should be high & important characters who need your lessons in republicanism, & who do not heed them?"[47]

And to Lafayette, then in command of the French troops opposing the allies, though already tottering on the verge of dismissal and disgrace, he wrote even more specifically: "While you are exterminating the monster aristocracy, & pulling out the teeth & fangs of its associate monarchy, a contrary tendency is discovered in some here. A sect has shown itself among us, who declare they espoused our new constitution, not as a good & sufficient thing itself, but only as a step to an English constitution, the only thing good & sufficient in itself, in their eye."[48]

Nor did the excesses, the proscription of rivals and the September massacres shake his stand; not even the eventual execution of the king and queen. "We surely cannot deny to any nation," he wrote Morris, who was justifiably uneasy about his own personal safety in Paris, "that right whereon our own government is founded, that every one may govern itself under what forms it pleases, and change these forms at its own will, and that it may transact its business with foreign nations through whatever organ it thinks proper." Since, therefore, a legal Convention had been established—this was late in 1792—he wanted Morris to resume payments on the American debt which had been suspended during the earlier upheaval, and convince the ruling Convention "how cordially we desire the closest union with them."[49]

Just before he sent this letter, Jefferson recorded a remarkable conversation with Washington. The President, so Jefferson noted, told him he thought "it was time to endeavor to effect a stricter connection with France, and that G. Morris should be written to on this subject." Our relations with England and Spain were strained, pursued Washington, "and there was no nation on whom we could rely at all times but France." If we did not prepare an alliance with her in advance of rupture with the others, we should be guilty of criminal negligence. Jefferson was delighted at this sudden unfolding. "It was the very doctrine," he noted, "which had been my polar star, and I did not need the successes of the Republican arms in France lately announced to us, to bring me to these sentiments." Obviously, he attributed to that news the change in Washington's position. Aloud, however, he suggested that the debt payments, suspended on Hamilton's argument that there was no longer any *king* to receive them, be resumed. To this Washington agreed.[50]

Inasmuch as Jefferson's official letter to Morris followed immediately, as well as a similar communication to Pinckney in London, his notes of the conversation with Washington must be accepted as accurate. But the "aberration" on Washington's part from Federalist thinking can only be considered as temporary. Events were soon to shape up which shifted him violently in the opposite direction.

CHAPTER 35

Federalist and Republican

JEFFERSON had come into his office with the greatest reluctance; and the longer he remained the greater became his anxiety to get out. He hated the political passions that had been aroused and which spilled over into private relations; he loathed the constant strife with Hamilton, the Federalists in Congress and their massed cohorts; he was unutterably weary of battling unsuccessfully and in vain against measures he was certain were tending to ruin the country.

It was true he was not alone in the struggle. A substantial party was gradually building up around him and looking to him for leadership; but as yet he did not view it as a party, nor do anything to solidify it as a workable instrument, as a tool in the struggle for power. That would come later.

In the meantime, he wished merely to be rid of it all; to retire to his tents in Monticello and bask in the bosom of his family. Every letter, every utterance, breathes the desperate sincerity of this longing. He panted, he exclaimed to his daughter Martha, to exchange "labor, envy, and malice for ease, domestic occupation, and domestic love and society; where I may once more be happy with you, with Mr. Randolph and dear little Anne [his granddaughter], with whom even Socrates might ride on a stick without being ridiculous." [1]

He had a sufficient sense of his obligations, however, to realize that it would be unfair to resign until at least the end of the Presidential term, and he very early made his wishes confidentially known to Washington. The President had attempted to dissuade him; but his resolve was fixed, he said, and unalterable. This was at the beginning of 1792; but already he was looking forward to the day of his release. "The ensuing year," he told Martha, "will be the longest of my life, and the last of such hateful labors; the next we will sow our cabbages together." [2]

If Washington had tried to dissuade him, it was not because he was not sympathetic. In fact, Washington himself was looking forward to the end of his term as the last of his adventures in public office. Just as Monticello beckoned to Jefferson, so did Mount Vernon possess irresistible attractions for Washington. Barely had Jefferson made clear his own determination when Washington informed him that he too intended to retire.

Jefferson let it pass at the moment but, as domestic and foreign affairs took a turn for the worse, he became convinced that the one man who might be able to ride out the storm, hold the contending factions together and save the Union from total disruption was Washington. He therefore marshaled all the arguments for Washington's accepting a second term as President when, as was certain, it would be offered to him in the elections at the end of 1792.

In a lengthy letter, he listed all the causes, "real or imaginary," for the current discontents. The public debt, he said, had become so staggering that the ordinary sources of revenue were insufficient for its servicing. The impost, as a result, had been raised to a point where armed force might be necessary to collect it. High as it was, it still was not enough, and excise taxes were being employed as a means of adding to the government income. Such taxes, asserted Jefferson, were even more odious than the impost, and resistance against any coercion even more probable on the part of an enraged citizenry.

The paper money of the national bank, with its 10 to 12 per cent annual profit to the lenders "taken out of the pockets of the people," was driving out solid coin, and leading to barren gambling instead of productive commerce and agriculture. The bank and the stock issues, so Jefferson believed, had given rise to a "corrupt squadron" in Congress who were seeking to get rid of constitutional limitations, with the ultimate object of changing the "present republican form of government, to that of a monarchy, of which the English constitution is to be the model."

This corruption of the legislature, to Jefferson, was the greatest evil that stemmed from the banking and paper system. From that, he predicted, a host of other evils must inevitably flow. The only hope that he saw was in the forthcoming Congressional election, when there might be a change in the present complexion of the House.

But even here there was grave danger. For the division of interest and sentiment had unfortunately assumed a sectional and geographical tinge, and might, he feared, lead to the eventual breaking up of the Union. If that happened, the fault would not lie in the South. For the present government had always "sacrificed" Southern prejudices, and "soothed" those of the North. All the debtors were in the South; all the creditors in the North.

This situation strengthened those who had fought ratification of the Constitution, and who now could point to the fulfillment of their predictions. There was grave danger, too, that those republicans who had originally favored the Constitution might join with their former opponents. "And this is an event at which I tremble," Jefferson concluded, "& to prevent which I consider your continuance at the head of affairs as of the last importance." Washington alone could prevent disruption and the end of the Union.[3]

There can be no question that Jefferson was wholly sincere in his insistence that Washington continue in the Presidency for another term; but the letter was far more than that. It was a skillful presentation to the President of all the things which he conceived wrong with the conduct of the Administration and the legislature, and against which he had been conducting a losing rearguard battle. Jefferson hoped by this plain statement to gain, even at this last date, the immeasurable influence of Washington's position and authority against what he honestly believed to be the deliberate purpose of Hamilton and his followers—the setting up of a monarchical system in the United States.

The fear of this haunted Jefferson continually and became almost pathological in its manifestations. He would jot down carefully every casual phrase which Hamilton let drop that might be construed as pointing to such an eventuality. Hamilton had spoken of the British constitution, bottomed on corruption, as the most perfect instrument devised by man; Hamilton had declared our own Constitution to be "a frail and worthless fabric"; Hamilton had avowed the imminent expedience of going over to the British form; Gouverneur Morris was "a high-flying monarchy man"; etc., etc. And assumption, the bank, the stock issues, the imposts, the excise taxes, were all engines deliberately designed to bring about that final consummation.

Washington had been vacationing in Mount Vernon when Jefferson penned this passionate appeal; but it missed him there and followed him back to Philadelphia. On July 10, 1792, the two men had a long and confidential conversation over its contents. Washington was still determined to retire; he was afraid that the people might consider that "his former professions had been mere affectation, & that he was like other men, when once in office he could not quit it." He spoke also with some pathos of his increased difficulty in hearing, and he feared that his other faculties might similarly decay without his being aware of it.

But he attempted to soothe Jefferson's uneasiness over the so-called "monarchist party." He did not believe that more than a few—and they were concentrated in the large eastern cities—wished for a monarchy. The great body of people, he was certain, were definitely opposed.

Then he shifted the discussion to complaints against recent newspaper pieces, particularly in Freneau's paper, which he considered as personal assaults upon himself. "He must be a fool indeed," he continued sternly, "to swallow the little sugar plumbs here & there thrown out to him." In condemning the Administration they were condemning him, "for if they thought there were measures pursued contrary to his sentiments, they must conceive him too careless to attend to them or too stupid to understand them. That tho indeed he had signed many acts which he did not approve in all their parts, yet he had never put his name to one which he did not think on the whole was eligible."

Having thus turned the flank of Jefferson's charges against the Hamiltonian influence in the Administration—for both men knew they were exactly that, just as both men knew that Jefferson approved of, and in a sense was responsible for, the newspaper assaults on Washington—the President proceeded to less embarrassing topics. On the matter of the bank, he said, "a difference of opinion must be tolerated." He himself, on his recent journey through the South, had found no evidences of discontent with it; and he intimated that such discontent was being artificially manufactured by certain politicians in Philadelphia.

Jefferson defended himself with the assertion that there *were* general complaints, and that they were based on the unnecessary increase in the national debt, and the means which it had furnished for the corruption of Congress. Washington took no notice of the charge of corruption, but insisted that the assumption measures had not increased the actual debt, and that the excise law was correct in principle and justifiable in practice.

Jefferson was defeated, and he realized it. "Finding him really approving the treasury system," he noted sadly, "I avoided entering into argument with him on these points." [4]

If the conversation hardened his determination to resign, it strengthened at the same time his determination to fight during his continuance in office all the things of which he had complained. Now that he knew definitely there was no hope of swinging Washington to the side of "republicanism," he began for the first time to consider the possibilities of gaining allies and forming a regular opposition party. Events had shaped themselves in such fashion that, despite Washington's political diagnosis, he was certain that there was a large body of discontent waiting for a leader.

The funding of the debt, based chiefly on assumption and the erection of the national bank, had led to an orgy of speculation, stock-market jobbing and corruption in high places. The operations had sent a scramble of northern financiers *and* members of Congress to the hinterlands of the South, where the reports of higher prices had not yet penetrated, to buy up the still-extant evidences of debt at tremendous discounts. The announcement of the bank also furnished a fruitful field for speculation. The moment subscriptions were opened, there was a mad rush by the monied men of the great eastern cities to buy the stock; and the price soared to extravagant heights even before the shares were actually issued.

Jefferson commented that many were "left in the lurch, among these Robt. Morris & Fitzsimmons." The plight of this particular pair furnished him a certain sardonic satisfaction; for they were members of Congress and in the inner Federalist circle. "They accuse," he wrote, "the Directors of a misdeal, & the former proposes to sue them, the latter to haul them up before Congress." [5]

Madison was indignant for other reasons. Everyone admitted, he fumed, that the plan of the bank gave a moral certainty of gain. "The subscriptions are consequently a mere scramble for so much public plunder which will be engrossed by those already loaded with the spoils of individuals. ... It pretty clearly appears also in what proportions the public debt lies in the Country. What sort of hands hold it, and by whom the people of the U. S. are to be governed. Of all the shameful circumstances of this business, it is among the greatest to see the members of the Legislature who were most active in pushing this Job openly grasping its emoluments. The Coffee-House is in an eternal buzz with the Gamblers." [6]

Jefferson was convinced that Hamilton had deliberately fostered this "delirium of speculation" which, he declared, was abstracting capital from useful pursuits which would have helped build up the country.[7]

There was a measure of truth in the accusation. Hamilton was viewing the traffic in stocks with complacency, to say the least. It helped promote that union between government and the interests of the monied men without which, he was convinced, no government could long continue.

But he almost overreached himself. His complacency had extended too far. He had permitted one of the most egregious speculators of all—his Assistant in the Treasury, William Duer of New York—to utilize his inside position to promote his own speculative fortunes and those of his friends. Duer's underhanded machinations and almost criminal manipulations are too complex to be explored here; [8] but even after he was compelled to resign from the Treasury, he continued his activities on an unexampled scale.

Hamilton defended him stoutly to the end, and there is evidence that he used the power of his office to help relieve Duer of the final consequences of his pyramiding. But there was a limit beyond which he could not, and would not go; and the whole top-heavy structure collapsed with a resounding crash. In March, 1792, Duer went bankrupt and, as if by magic, the boom was over. With him went, like a pack of cards, other speculative financiers; and panic swept the country. Ruin came, not only to Duer and his fellows, but to hundreds of small folk who had become infected with the craze for easy money and had sought to ride to fortune on the coattails of their betters.

Jefferson viewed this triumphant vindication of his predictions with philosophic meditation. "No man of reflection," he wrote, "who had ever attended to the South sea bubble, in England, or that of Law in France, and who applied the lessons of the past to the present time, could fail to foresee the issue tho' he might not calculate the moment at which it would happen. The evidences of the public debt are solid & sacred things. I presume there is not a man in the U. S. who would not part with his last shilling to pay them. But all that stuff called scrip, of whatever description, was folly or roguery, and yet, under a resemblance to genuine public paper, it buoyed itself up to a par with that. It has been a severe lesson: yet such is the public cullability [*sic*] in the hands of cunning & unprincipled men, that it is doomed by nature to receive these lessons once in an age at least." [9]

But in one thing he was destined to disappointment. He had hoped that public reaction would tumble "its authors headlong from their heights." [10] It was true that for a while Hamilton rocked unsteadily on his seat, but he managed to weather the storm, and continued in office more boldly than ever.

Undeterred by the disaster, those whom Jefferson contemptuously called the "Treasuro-bankites" intended to establish a branch of the Bank of the United States in Richmond. The proposal sent Jefferson into a frenzy of alarm. His beloved state was being invaded by the forces of evil, by those who had caused ruin and destruction elsewhere. His first reaction was to fight fire with fire—to set up a "counter-bank" that, under state auspices, would "befriend the agricultural man by letting him have money on a deposit of tob[acc]o notes, or even wheat, for *a short time*." [11]

But the more he reflected on it, the more he was opposed to any form of bank. So that, when Governor Lee of Virginia proposed a State bank to the Virginia Assembly to counterbalance the Federal branch, though along the sames lines, Jefferson had whipped himself into such a state that he wrote his friend Madison one of the most amazing letters of his long career. This letter, hitherto unpublished, deserves quotation in full.

> I have reflected on Govr. Lee's plan of opposing the Federal bank by setting up a state one, and find it not only inadequate, but objectionable highly & unworthy of the Virginia assembly. I think they should not adopt such a milk & water measure, which rather recognizes than prevents the planting among them a source of poison & corruption to sap their catholicism, and to annihilate that power, which is now one, by dividing it into two which shall counterbalance each other. The assembly should reason thus. The power of erecting banks & corporations was not given to the general government it remains then with the state itself. For any person to recognize a foreign [i.e., the Federal] legislature in a case belonging to the state itself, is an act of *treason* against the state, and whosoever shall do any act under colour of the authority of a foreign legislature whether by signing notes, issuing or passing them, acting as director, cashier or in any other office relating to it shall be adjudged guilty of high treason & suffer death accordingly, by the judgment of the state court. This is the only opposition worthy of our state, and the only kind which can be effectual. If N. Carolina could be brought into a like measure, it would bring the general government to respect the counter-rights of the states. The example would probably be followed by some other states. I really wish that this or nothing should be done. A bank of opposition, while it is a recognition of the one opposed, will absolutely fail in Virginia.[12]

This is so amazing in context—the assumption that the national government was a "foreign" one; the thesis that obedience to a national law which a state deemed unconstitutional could be considered as treason to the state; the advocacy of the death penalty for those who dared follow the Federal government on a constitutional issue—that it might plausibly be set down as a momentary aberration on Jefferson's part. Unfortunately, this cannot be done; for, as will be shown in its proper place, Jefferson at a much later time of stress claimed somewhat similar vigilante powers against those with whom he politically disagreed, and upheld for his state a degree of governmental compulsion against which, in general theory, he was forever fulminating.

Madison, wisely enough, never replied to this letter.

As the time approached for Jefferson's intended return to Virginia as a private citizen, his thoughts veered more and more to the local politics of his state.

He had never been satisfied with the constitution of 1776, and had attempted time and again to substitute a new one closer to his heart's desire. By the end of 1791, he detected signs that this might now be possible; but it was essential, before any steps were taken, to see if some agreement could not be reached with Patrick Henry. Otherwise, he told his Albemarle neighbor, Archibald Stuart, "I consider his talents and influence such as that, were it decided that we should call a Convention for the purpose of amending, I should fear he might induce that convention either to fix the thing as at present, or change it for the worse." Jefferson had a healthy respect for Henry's ability to sway any assemblage.

In the interim, he formulated once more the basic principles of the intended constitution, and sent them to his political friends for use in the forthcoming discussions. They represented his consistent views on the nature of powers and their careful separation. Most of all, he was intent on accentuating the line drawn by the Federal Constitution between the National and the State government. He did not fear a grant of powers to the State, because he believed the State responsive to the will of its people and, if anything, tended "to an excess of liberty." But the Federal Government "will tend to monarchy," and must therefore be kept within stringent bounds. The only way to do it was to strengthen the State. This could be accomplished, in his view, by making certain changes in its various branches—cut down the number of representatives and lengthen their term of office; make the executive more independent of the legislature, lengthen his term and declare him forever ineligible for re-election; abolish the old executive council that hampered the governor; and increase the power and importance of the judiciary.[13] Jefferson was a strong believer in a system of checks and balances.

It was nearly a year later that he came to the conclusion that the people of Virginia were ripe for the change in constitutions; and he was more optimistic now that the redoubtable Patrick Henry would go along. "He has been the great obstacle to it hitherto," he wrote Short; "but you know he is always alive to catch the first sensation of the popular breeze, that he may take the lead of that which in truth leads him."[14] This may have been an excellent analysis of Henry; or indeed of any popular demagogue; but Jefferson had miscalculated the strength of the ground swell he thought he had detected, and Virginia was to continue under its makeshift constitution for a considerable period thereafter.

It was characteristic of Jefferson that at the same time he proposed a traitor's death for those who disagreed with him on the political question of a federal bank in Virginia, he could, without any sense of inconsistency, lament to Angelica Church, his charming companion of Parisian days, that in his own case political antagonisms had spilled over into personal relations. "Party animosities here," he complained, "have raised a wall of separation between those who differ in political sentiments. They must love misery indeed who would rather at the sight of an honest man feel the torment of hatred & aversion than the benign spasms of benevolence & esteem." [15]

During this period, Jefferson's private affairs grew increasingly entangled. The debts he had undertaken as the accompaniment of his wife's estate had mounted, with accumulated interest, to an unbearable load. And his creditors were understandably becoming impatient. Twenty years had come and gone, and still there seemed no sign of ultimate payment. Jefferson was forever proposing new schemes to satisfy the debts, based on anticipated tobacco yields which never seemed to eventuate; and one of the creditors, through his American representative, became very sharp about it.

"I may say with truth," Jefferson retorted with some heat, "that no man on earth has been readier to do every think [*sic*] possible to discharge that debt, of a portion of which you are become the representative. The first year after the death of mr Wayles who contracted it, I sold 5000 pounds worth of land and tendered the bonds to mr Jones's agent who refused to receive them. There was not then a shilling of paper money in circulation; but before payment was received, it was not worth receiving. At the close of the war I delivered my whole estate into the hands of two of the best men on earth, and have not now for seven years drawn one shilling of its profits for my own use: and finding that this has not answered, I again sold property enough to pay the whole debt. Not having the power of creating money, I know not what more I could have done." [16]

In desperation, and much against every humanitarian impulse, Jefferson was forced to sell a considerable number of slaves to meet the claims against him. His son-in-law, Thomas Mann Randolph, attended to the details; but the results were disappointing. They averaged only £45 apiece —there had been a time when a good Negro worker brought in £200— and Jefferson received barely enough to pay the installments on one account alone for two years, with £1,500 still to go in three annual installments. Unless, therefore, he found a customer for his Elk Hill property, which had previously been advertised for sale without any takers, he would be compelled to sell more Negroes in the fall.[17]

He tried to obtain a purchaser for his lands among the French refugees from the Revolution who, he said, were "coming to this country in quest of quiet." [18] But that prospect also failed; and he was compelled to throw more slaves on the market. They were not to be sold, he ordered, in the immediate neighborhood, nor was his name to be mentioned as the owner. "I do not (while in public life)," he explained to his agent, "like to have my name annexed in the public papers to the sale of property." He also wished family groups to be sold as a unit. One family, however, he was compelled to break up; the adult male was too essential. He asked his brother Randolph to buy the wife and children; failing that, to sell them to some good master in the vicinity so that they might remain near their husband and father.[19] Even in the hands of the best and kindest of masters, the lot of slaves was miserable enough.

To add to his financial difficulties, every one of Jefferson's relations and friends considered him an inexhaustible cornucopia from which gifts, loans and endorsements endlessly flowed. His nephew Peter Carr, for whose support Jefferson had obligated himself, complained bitterly that his uncle had not paid his substantial Williamsburg debts as promised. Peter's mother—and Jefferson's sister—similarly demanded some eighty pounds; "my having a Daughter Married & to fix off for Kentucky after which it is hardly probable that I shall ever see her agane has put me to some unusal expence this together with my bad management." And another nephew, John Garland Jefferson, who had gone to Philadelphia ostensibly to study, also wrote constantly for money.[20]

As though family obligations were not enough, one of his earliest friends, John Page, now called on him to endorse his note for $630. Jefferson could not refuse; but, he warned Page, "at the same time ingenuously must say that were the payment to fall on me, it would be impossible for me to make it, & consequently I should be liable to a process which would distress me in the extreme."[21]

Though Page managed later to shift endorsers on this particular note, he was compelled to come, "unhappy & ashamed," for further endorsements to his friend.[22]

As usual, however, Jefferson did not permit his own unhappy financial situation to stand in the way of the most lavish personal expenditures. When his wine cellar ran low, he ordered from France 500 bottles of "the best vin rouge of Bordeaux, such as is drunk at the best tables there."[23] In Philadelphia, his heart had yearned for an expensive equatorial instrument; but he had barely enough in his pocket to get him home to Monticello, and he departed without it. On his arrival, however, he found a note for $238.50 waiting. Without losing a moment, he rushed it off to Rittenhouse in Philadelphia, begging him to put it up as security for the eventual possession of the precious instrument. But, he hastened to add, the note was not to be put in a bank for collection. Jefferson was always afraid that his enemies might distort any banking transaction in which he was involved. In addition to the equatorial, he ordered from London a "manual orrery & planetarium," price not given.[24]

In the full expectation that he was retiring shortly from office, Jefferson resumed extensive building operations at Monticello. These were endless: buildings to be demolished and others erected that were more in harmony with his evolving ideas. He ordered materials on a grandiose scale and hired a skilled mason to set the pace for his slaves. He wanted his interiors decorated with fresco paintings. When in New York, a man named Schneider had done a series of panels for the house which Jefferson had occupied, and they had caught his fancy. He wrote now to his friend Henry Remsen, asking him to check on the panels for durability and permanence of color. If his investigation was satisfactory, would he inquire of Schneider whether he was willing to come down to Monticello to do the frescoes? [25]

Remsen followed instructions; the colors were fast and still vivid. Schneider agreed to go to Virginia; but he demanded the "extravagant" sum of two dollars a day. Jefferson was taken aback; he was willing, he wrote back, to pay six guineas a month, with board and lodging.[26]

An examination of Jefferson's accounts for the year 1792 furnish plain evidence of the reason for Jefferson's continued financial distress. His salary as Secretary of State—on which it was presumed he could live—was $3,000. His expenses, in Philadelphia alone, came to $5,240.03.[27]

However, Jefferson was not to retire as he had anticipated. Much was happening which, coupled with Washington's pleas, held him in office for many an arduous month.

As he had predicted, the excise taxes which Hamilton had maneuvered through Congress were now reaping their harvest of protest and even forcible resistance. In order to meet the heavy debt load occasioned by his funding operations, Hamilton had placed a tax on the domestic manufacture of whisky. No other tax could possibly have raised as much of a storm as this one. For it struck directly at the farmers and frontiersmen of western Pennsylvania, Virginia and North Carolina, where whisky was the current coin of the realm in place of the almost nonexistent gold and silver; and where conversion into easily portable whisky was the only disposition possible for their grain. Since the tax was payable in hard cash, it proved an intolerable burden on these moneyless folk; and, at the same time, invaded a field in which the advocates of States' rights held that the Federal Government had no jurisdiction.

Both as taxpayers and as vindicators of state sovereignty, therefore, the western farmers protested, and backed their protests with force. Taxes were refused, and tax-collectors were met with coats of tar and feathers, with the additional warning of worse to come if they did not clear out forthwith. Sheriffs, judges and other law-enforcement officers were similarly threatened; and liberty poles, dread symbols of revolutionary defiance, dotted the scene.

Hamilton welcomed the challenge; it gave him an opportunity to prove, once for all, that the Federal Government was supreme. He urged on

Washington the necessity, if the nation was not to crumble, to meet force with force, with every power of the government, including the military, "in case a refractory spirit should continue to render the ordinary and more desirable means ineffectual."[28]

Washington, with the example of the French revolutionary mobs ever before him, finally agreed; and Hamilton lost no time in drafting a proclamation addressed to the alleged rebels. Thus confronted with immediate action, Washington hesitated and asked for the advice of his Cabinet. Both Knox and Randolph upheld Hamilton's contention that the proclamation be issued. Jefferson, however, was at Monticello, and Washington insisted on getting his opinion before any further steps were taken.

In spite of Hamilton's protests over the delay involved, Washington sent the draft proclamation down to Jefferson, with a note: "I have no doubt," he said, "but that the measure I am about to take, will be severely criticised, but I shall disregard any animadversion upon my conduct when I am called upon by the nature of my Office to discharge what I conceive to be a duty—and none in my opinion is more important, than to carry the Laws of the United States into effect."[29]

The reasoning was impeccable; but Jefferson was confronted with a ticklish situation. He sympathized with the embattled frontiersmen; he, too, had vehemently opposed the excise tax, considering it a dangerous usurpation of States' rights and bearing hardest on the farmer and the poor; and, the so-called rebels were the very backbone of the republican party. Nevertheless, as an officer of government, he could not openly countenance armed rebellion.

Accordingly, with a few unimportant verbal changes, he signed the proclamation and returned it to Washington with a letter which covertly conveyed his feelings in the matter: "I am sincerely sorry to learn that such proceedings have taken place: and I hope the proclamation will lead the persons concerned into a regular line of application which may end either in an amendment of the law, if it needs it, or in their conviction that it is right."[30]

Fortunately for Jefferson's standing with the western republicans, by the time Washington was ready to issue the proclamation, reports came in that the rebellion had collapsed. The only one who was disappointed was Hamilton; he had to wait a full two years before resistance to the excise rose again, and he was able to employ overwhelming military force in suppression and thereby establish the readiness and power of the central government to enforce its decrees.

Meanwhile, slowly but surely, the Republicans were building their strength for an eventual life-and-death struggle with the Federalists for control of the government. The prime areas of conflict were in the states; since the state legislatures appointed the Senators, and local elections determined the complexion of the House of Representatives. The South, by and large, was Republican; New England, just as overwhelmingly, was Federalist. That gave the Middle Atlantic States—notably New York and Pennsylvania—a pivotal position.

Particularly important was the situation in New York, where the durable George Clinton had held the governorship ever since the beginning of the Revolution, and Aaron Burr was coming along fast with a political machine of modern design. But New York also happened to be Hamilton's special bailiwick, and the Federalists put forth all their efforts to unseat Clinton in the gubernatorial election of 1791, nominating John Jay as their candidate.

The election was bitterly contested and the final result close; and there is no question that Jay was actually elected. But the Clintonians, who controled the state electoral machinery, pretended to discover certain technical irregularities in the returns from three counties and, by rejecting their votes *en masse*, declared the incumbent Governor re-elected.

The Federalists rose in wrath, as was natural, and some of them even proposed illegal means to subvert an illegal result. But Hamilton himself warned against this, rightly considering that illegality was a two-edged weapon, and the precedent dangerous.

On the other hand Jefferson, who had been following the proceedings with the keenest interest, deplored the methods employed by the members of his own party. "Upon the whole," he wrote privately to Monroe, "it seems probable that Mr. Jay had a majority of the qualified voters, and I think not only that Clinton would have honored himself by declining to accept, and agreeing to take another fair start, but that probably such a conduct would have ensured him a majority on a new election. To retain the office when it is probable the majority was against him is dishonorable." [31] But Clinton had no such qualms, and willingly accepted the office thus thrust upon him.

Of more importance, in Jefferson's view, were the forthcoming Congressional elections at the end of 1792; for they would afford the first real test of the country's reaction to Hamiltonian policies. John Beckley, one of the most active of Republican politicians, thought that everything was "fast verging to the issue of a contest between the Treasury department and the people, whose interest shall preponderate in the next Congress." He recognized Jefferson as titular head of the Republican party; and asserted that the Federalists, similarly recognizing him as such, were concentrating their attacks on him in order to influence the popular mind in the ensuing voting.[32]

The elections, late in the fall, renewed Jefferson's faith in the sound instincts and common sense of the plain people. A majority of Republican Congressmen were returned to the House and, for the first time, Jefferson and Madison had a workable instrument in the legislature to counterbalance Hamilton's influence. The victory was not total, however; since the Senate, by virtue of its staggered system of elections and its restricted method of choice by the state legislatures, still remained in the Federalist column.

Nevertheless, Jefferson was content. "I think we may consider," he wrote Thomas Pinckney in London, "the tide of this government as now at the fullest, and that it will, from the commencement of the next session of Congress, retire and subside into the true principles of the Constitution." The "monocrats" had sought to befog the issue by pretending that the Republicans were opposed to payment of the public debt, and had attempted to equate republicanism with the "ghost of antifederalism," and both with Jacobinism; but had failed.[33]

But more was at stake in 1792 than the composition of Congress. It was a presidential year as well. As to the Presidency there was no contest. Everyone—Republicans as well as Federalists—was unanimous in determination to continue Washington in the chair of State; even those who had inveighed most bitterly against his seeming subserviency to Hamilton. It was universally realized that he was the only man alive who could keep the contending factions from flying at each other's throat, and the Union from bursting into its former parts. Both Jefferson and Hamilton appealed to Washington to reconsider his decision to retire; and such was the pressure that he reluctantly consented to stand again.

As to the Vice-Presidency, however, there was no such unanimity. Here politics reared its ugly head. John Adams had offended the Republicans with his forthright views, his alleged aristocratical principles and his love of ceremony and display. He had also given offense to many Federalists with his incorrigible honesty, stubbornness and occasional deviations from the strict party line. But there was no one they dared substitute in his place; and even Hamilton, who would have liked to see him superseded, backed him for re-election.

The Republicans, however—or some of them, at least—were in a different position. Governor Clinton of New York, flushed with his recent questionable triumph in his home state, announced his candidacy. And there was talk that Aaron Burr, similarly of New York, might throw his hat into the ring; though this eventually proved but a rumor.

Jefferson at this time was not too well affected toward Clinton: there was the matter of the disputed election, for one; for another, Clinton had been the mainspring of the opposition to the Constitution and was visible proof of the Federalist thesis that antifederalism and republicanism were synonymous. Jefferson was therefore fearful that "the cause of republicanism will suffer and its votaries be thrown into schism by embarking it in support of this man, and for what? to draw over the antifederalists who are not numerous enough to be worth drawing over."[34]

Accordingly, he privately supported Adams and so advised his confidential friends in Virginia. In spite of Jefferson, however, Virginia cast its votes for Clinton. Even Archibald Stuart, bound by neighborly and commercial ties, disregarded his advice, though apologizing for so doing. "I must confess," he wrote, "tho I disapprove of Mr. A's political creed yet from ye character you gave me of him as a man of Wisdom & honesty and who had rendered essential services to our country at a critical period I felt great reluctance in voting against him. I have ever thought the desertion of old servants a blemish on the character of Republics but on the other hand I conceive it dangerous & inconsistent to retain in so important an office however worthy in other respects a man not entirely devoted to the republican cause."[35]

Adams won over Clinton; but the latter's vote was heavy. The final count in electoral votes was 77 to 50. Jefferson, who had not been a candidate, received 10 complimentary votes from the new state of Kentucky; while Burr was given a lone vote in South Carolina.

Jefferson was in Monticello during the initial phases of the election, preparing his affairs for eventual retirement as soon as Washington commenced his second term. The articles written by Hamilton under the transparent pseudonym of "An American" were currently appearing in Fenno's paper, and Jefferson was moved to bitter protest. "I have preserved through life," he wrote Edmund Randolph, "a resolution never to write in a public paper without subscribing my name, and to engage openly an adversary who does not let himself be seen, is staking all against nothing. The indecency too of newspaper squabbling between two public ministers, besides my own sense of it, has drawn something like an injunction from another quarter." This was a reference to Washington. "Every fact alleged under the signature of 'an American' as to myself is false, and can be proved so; and perhaps will be some day. But for the present, lying and scribbling must be free to those mean enough to deal in them, and in the dark."[36]

Five days after he wrote this letter, Jefferson started back for Philadelphia, pausing on the way at Mount Vernon to meet Washington. They spent the morning of October 1st together in earnest conversation. Once more Washington tried to dissuade Jefferson from his avowed intention to resign. "Where," he asked, "could he find such another character to fill the office?" He himself, he told his caller, was still undecided about accepting another term; but, if necessary to the nation, he would make the sacrifice.

Jefferson assured him that the South had "but one voice, which was for his continuance." Then the conversation turned to the differences between Jefferson and Hamilton, over which Washington expressed keen regret. He had been aware, he said, of *political* differences; but not that they had ended in a *personal* dispute. He wished to act as mediator between them; and, so Jefferson noted in his *Anas*, "he thought it important to preserve the check of my opinions in the administration in order to keep things in their proper channel & prevent them from going too far."[37]

Nevertheless, the interview ended indecisively; for Jefferson made no promises on either point under discussion. The matter was too deep-seated, and the cleavage too fundamental for any compromise.

CHAPTER 36

Proclamation of Neutrality

SEEMINGLY, Washington had labored in vain to dissuade Jefferson from resignation; in fact, at the beginning of the new year the newspapers were reporting that he had already done so.

General Gates, now in retirement and pleased to call himself "the Hermit of Rose Hill," read the item and hastened to add his protest to the swelling Republican chorus. He peered into his own "prophetic Soul" and discovered that Jefferson's supposed action "Augurs no Benefit to the State by such a Sacrafice [*sic*]; If the best Seamen abandon the Ship in a Storm, she must Founder, and if all Human means are neglected, Providence will not for The Vessel, She must Perish!" [1]

The premature publication discommoded Jefferson considerably. For Hamilton's bitter public attacks on him under the guise of "An American," plus a concerted campaign of vilification in the Federalist press, had just preceded the notice and were steadily rising in fury, going so far as to demand an investigation of his conduct in office. The juxtaposition and sequence of the two gave rise, therefore, even in the minds of some of his best friends, to the thought that the one had led to the other, and that Jefferson was retiring in the face of the storm and, perhaps, even to avoid the threatened investigation.

Nothing could have been better calculated to give Jefferson pause. Even greater than his abnormal sensitivity to public criticism was his passionate desire for public approbation. To escape from the former would inevitably lead to the loss of the latter. "The only reward I ever wished on my retirement," he wrote in considerable agitation to Martha, "was to carry with me nothing like a disapprobation of the public. These representations have, for some weeks passed shaken a determination which I had thought the whole world could not have shaken." [2]

He had already begun to pack, sold some of his furniture and found a tenant for his Philadelphia house. At Monticello, he had hired workers and laid in materials for extensive building operations, which included the construction of a canal at the base so that his produce could be floated safely into the main river. All these projects were at sixes and sevens; though he had asked his son-in-law to attend to the canal, which was to be six feet wide at the bottom, "and to slope at the sides so as to permit grass to grow on them." [3]

Under the circumstances, however, Jefferson felt he owed it to his honor and public repute not to appear to have resigned under fire. On February 7,

1793, he informed the President that he would stay in his post until the summer or autumn of the year. Washington expressed his delight and again urged that he and Hamilton "coalesce in the measures of government." Hamilton, he said, had already agreed to this. But Jefferson bluntly refused. "If by that," he declared, "was meant that either was to sacrifice his general system to the other, it was impossible. We had both no doubt formed our conclusions after the most mature consideration and principles conscientiously adopted could not be given up on either side." [4] What Jefferson meant, without openly saying so, was that the compromise would have to be wholly on his part.

With a heavy heart, Jefferson took a small house outside Philadelphia on the banks of the Schuylkill and returned to his duties. These almost immediately assumed a more ominous aspect than ever before. The war which had long overshadowed Europe now took a turn which for the first time brought it close to the United States and, for many months, threatened to involve her in its coils. On February 1, 1793, France declared war on England; and thenceforth, not only the land mass of Europe, but the seven seas and the distant colonies, blazed with conflict.

Though the official news did not reach America until the end of March, the rumors of strife preceded it on seven-league boots.

Jefferson's first reaction to the impending conflagration was singularly detached; almost gleeful, in fact. He saw in it only an advantage to the United States; an advantage from which he was cynically willing to profit. "The more you fight," he pointed out to a commercial friend in England, "the more you will eat & waste, & the less you will make. Fight on then; leave us at peace, & let us feed you while you clothe us."

He was the more ready to cry "Lay on, McDuff!" because the United States was then in the middle of a financial panic. Ready cash had vanished from sight, the banks had stopped discounts, and the public securities were being thrown on the market at steadily falling prices. But this did not mean, Jefferson was quick to add, that foreign holders of the paper need worry. "There is not upon earth a more solid property; and tho' one party here affect to charge the other with unfriendly dispositions towards the public debt, yet I believe there is not a man scarcely in the United States who is not sacredly determined to pay it; & the only difference which I can see between the two parties is that the republican one wish it could be paid tomorrow, the fiscal [Hamiltonian] party wish it to be perpetual, because they find in it an engine for corrupting the legislature. Bank property stands on very different ground; as that institution is strongly conceived to be unauthorized by the constitution, it may therefore be liable to shocks." [5]

But if Jefferson was thus offhandedly minimizing the differences between the parties for the benefit of an anxious English holder of paper, the cleavage at home was as deep as a well and as wide as a barn door. For too long a period Jefferson had been under attack without publicly striking back.

Now he and his friends determined to counterattack, hitting directly at the head and front of the enemy—Alexander Hamilton.

On February 27, 1793, William B. Giles, Congressman from Virginia and closely allied to Jefferson and Madison, moved a series of nine resolutions in the House. They accused Hamilton of dereliction in office; of applying appropriated funds to purposes not authorized by laws; of deviating from instructions in the transfer of funds; of borrowing money from the Bank at five per cent when public funds lay idle; of withholding information from the House even after a request.

In preparation for this grand assault, Giles had previously moved for a general accounting by Hamilton. Working at top speed, Hamilton submitted a full report, complete with documents and vouchers; which left but little for Giles and his fellow Republicans to carp at except technicalities. Nevertheless, these were seized on in the Congressional debate over the resolutions. One by one the charges were taken up, and in spite of Republican efforts, went down to crashing defeat. The result was a triumphant vindication for the Secretary of the Treasury.

Jefferson hid his mortification over the result with the comment that it was only to be expected in a House composed of bank directors, stockholders, stockjobbers, ignoramuses and those who were either too good-natured or too lazy to bother about the facts.[6]

He was all the more mortified because he had been the secret prime mover of the Giles resolutions. They had actually been drafted by him, and he had even added a tenth which Giles, with commendable caution, had refused to introduce. The omitted tenth purported to declare that "the Secretary of the Treasury has been guilty of maladministration in the duties of his office, and should, in the opinion of Congress, be removed from his office by the President of the United States." [7]

During the preparation of his defense, Hamilton had asked Jefferson for a statement setting forth the Cabinet discussion in 1790 dealing with Washington's instructions concerning the allocation of the European loan. Almost a month after the question had become academic, Jefferson responded with a masterpiece of evasion. The matter, he said, had really gone "out of my mind altogether, till the late enquiries brought it forward again." However, he believed that the President's instructions had not sanctioned Hamilton's course. "I did not take it up then as a Volunteer," he ended, "nor should now have taken the trouble of recurring to it, but at your request; as it is one in which I am not particularly concerned, which I never had either the time or inclination to investigate, & on which my opinion is of no importance." [8]

A truly amazing statement from the author of the Giles resolutions!

Obviously, Washington had failed completely in his repeated attempts to heal the schism. Inasmuch as Jefferson had been compelled almost against his will to remain in office, he was determined to employ every weapon that might ensure the triumph of republican principles. Hitherto, there had been no party in the true sense of the word. Men had been elected to office on general principles which expressed themselves chiefly in opposition to Hamilton's operations, and in denunciation of "monarchists" and "monocrats"—the latter rapidly overcoming the former in the arsenal of epithets. And even in Congress, the Republican contingent had chiefly expressed itself in opposition rather than in constructive program.

Jefferson sought now to remedy this defect, and jotted down some heads for a definite agenda to be followed by the House Republicans. Among them were the slogans of the future.

> Agenda—Divide the Treasury department. Abolish the bank. Repeal the Excise law & let states raise the money. Lower impost, Treasurer to pay and receive cash not bills. Repeal irredeemable quality and borrow at 4. pr. cent. Exclude paper holders [from Congress?]. Condemn report of [Hamilton's report of Jan. 3, 1793 on foreign loans?] [9]

The content of this program may seem unduly narrow, relating as it does exclusively to finances; but it was precisely on these that the two parties were violently opposed. And it must be remembered that every other governmental policy—foreign as well as domestic—hinged on the financial structure of the United States.

Why divide the Treasury? To break up what Jefferson conceived to be and was in fact a vast concentration of powers which overshadowed all other departments of government. By abolishing the bank—aside from the constitutional issues involved—Jefferson hoped to end the double stranglehold of the monied class over Congress and over the landowner and the farmer. By formally prohibiting holders of securities in Congress, he thought to remove the incentive for vested-interest legislation. By repealing the excise tax, he sought two ends: a removal of an unconscionable and discriminatory burden on the remote farming communities; and a vindication of the principle of State sovereignty.

In this short platform was the best possibility for a popular appeal and a successful bid for power.

When Washington, vacationing at Mount Vernon, heard of the outbreak of war between England and France, he returned with all possible speed to Philadelphia. He was under no illusions as to what it meant in terms of the future of the United States. While Jefferson was anticipating with satisfaction the prospect of a better market for American farmers, Washington saw clearly that the very existence of the nation might be endangered in the forthcoming clash. Neither of the great antagonists had been particularly noted for its concern over neutral rights and neutral trade in time of peace; now certainly, when their existences were at stake, a ruthless disregard for the rights of others was to be expected.

There can be no question on which side Jefferson's sympathies lay. The French Revolution to him was the greatest fact on earth, and the one most fraught with beneficent consequences for the future of the human race. Not so long before he had passionately defended the excesses of the Jacobins against the strictures of his protégé, William Short. The latter, on the spot, had witnessed enough to have lost much of his earlier enthusiasm for the revolutionary cause. Jefferson chided him for his about-face. True, he admitted, "many guilty persons fell without the forms of trial, and with them some innocent. These I deplore as much as any body, & shall deplore some of them to the day of my death. But I deplore them as I should have done had they fallen in battle." For "the liberty of the whole earth was depending on the issue of the contest, and was ever such a prize won with so little innocent blood? My own affections have been deeply wounded by some of the martyrs to this cause, but rather than it should have failed, I would have seen half the earth desolated. Were there but an Adam & Eve left in every country, & left free, it would be better than as it now is."

Even Washington had been offended, so Jefferson asserted, by the acrimonious tone of Short's dispatches and had directed him to write that "you should consider yourself as the representative of your country and that what you say might be imputed to your constituents." France, so the President had remarked, was "the sheet anchor of this country and its friendship . . . a first object." [10]

There is a curiously modern ring to this exposition of the doctrine of revolution—the words might well have been taken verbatim from the writings of the first liberal upholders of the Russian Revolution. Short, however, was unimpressed. He had seen the revolution at work; and he later returned to America shorn considerably of his ideals to become what today might be termed a "conservative democrat."

But Jefferson remained steadfast. Neither the guillotining of Louis the Sixteenth nor the imprisonment of Lafayette shook his abiding faith in the Revolution. The first, indeed, met with his approval, as subjecting a monarch to punishment like any other criminal.[11] The second, naturally, did not; for Lafayette was one of those friends and martyrs for whom his heart had bled; and he requested Gouverneur Morris in Paris, and Thomas Pinckney in London, to use "all prudent efforts" to accomplish his release. This was at a time when he knew that Morris was *persona non grata* in France, and that the French Ministry had shut its doors to him.[12]

What committed Jefferson so deeply to the cause of France was his profound belief that the fates of the two great revolutions were inextricably intertwined. He was certain—and said so over and over again—that the collapse of the French Revolution meant not only the loss of freedom in all Europe, but in the United States as well. The monarchists here, he was convinced, were waiting only for the collapse abroad to ride the tide of universal reaction and proclaim a monarchy at home.

He was alarmed also by the activities of the French minister to this country, Jean Baptiste Ternant, who had gone publicly into mourning on the news of the king's execution, and who had become strangely confidential with Hamilton. But he consoled himself with the thought that Ternant was being recalled by his home government, and a new envoy was soon to arrive—one Citizen Edmond Charles Genêt—"with full powers to give us all the privileges we can desire in their countries, & particularly in the W. Indies." Or so ran the reports.

In recalling Ternant, however, the French demanded a similar treatment for the hostile Morris. Would Jefferson be willing to replace him? asked Washington. Not at all, replied the latter. He had no intention of continuing in public life.[13]

Washington arrived in Philadelphia on April 17, 1793. The following day he submitted thirteen questions to his Cabinet, "with a view to forming a general plan of conduct for the executive" in the face of the war in Europe.

The questions were sweepingly comprehensive. What should be the American policy in the impending crisis? Should a proclamation of neutrality be issued? Should the new French Minister—Genêt—be received when he arrived? Should the treaties of alliance with France, dating from the Revolutionary War, and binding the United States to defend the French West Indies in case of attack, be considered as still in effect? If so, should they be suspended or openly renounced? Should Congress, now in recess, be reconvened?[14]

Each member of the Cabinet received a copy of the queries and was asked to consider them before an official meeting was held. The moment Jefferson glanced over his copy he was certain that, though the handwriting was Washington's, the composition was Hamilton's. "The style, their ingenious tissue and suite," their "prepared chain of argument," their "language"—in short, everything about them pointed to Hamilton as the sole author. Edmund Randolph agreed with Jefferson, telling him that the day before they were delivered, Hamilton had gone over with him "the whole chain of reasoning of which these questions are the skeleton, & that he recognized them the moment he saw them."[15]

It is fairly certain that Hamilton had prepared at least the leading ideas for the questions; yet his participation did not militate against their relevancy or the necessity for arriving at definite answers on the points at issue.

The first, and perhaps most important question, concerned the advisability of issuing a proclamation of neutrality. While still at Mount Vernon, Washington had decided that "it behoves the Government of this Country to use every means in its power to prevent the citizens thereof from embroiling us with either of these powers, by endeavouring to maintain a strict neutrality." He had then requested both Jefferson and Hamilton to lay the groundwork for effectuating this purpose.[16]

But how to do so was no simple task. It is true there was no dissent from the proposition that the United States ought to remain neutral. Neither Jefferson nor Hamilton, whatever their private predilections as to the outcome, wanted this country to enter the struggle. There was, however, a sharp divergence on the wisdom of proclaiming the *fact* to the word.

Hamilton argued strongly for a public proclamation. Jefferson thought it unwise at the moment. He interposed two objections. The first was technical: a declaration, he pointed out, was in essence a statement that the United States would not go to war; and that was the province of Congress, not of the Executive. The others acknowledged the force of the reasoning, and Randolph, who as the law officer of the government would be entrusted with the drafting, was instructed to avoid the word "neutrality."

The second objection was substantive. Would it not be better, he inquired, "to hold back the declaration of neutrality, as a thing worth something to the powers at war, that they would bid for it, & we might reasonably ask a price, the *broadest privileges* of neutral nations?"[17]

There was much to be said for this point of view. The rights of neutral nations which were supposedly to be respected by the combatants, were tenuous in the extreme. Ostensibly, there was a law of nations to which appeal might be made, as set forth in the writings of the jurisconsults. Actually, these pronunciamentos had no legal or binding status; and the only rights of neutrals which were in practice respected were those which they were strong enough to enforce, or which it was to the advantage of a particular belligerent to observe.

Great Britain had cavalierly overruled Jefferson's protests against her unilateral trade restrictions in time of peace. How could she be expected to relax them in time of war—especially when she received gratuitous notification in advance that the United States would not go to war? Here then, argued Jefferson, was a golden opportunity to extract substantial concessions: first, commercial; second, a specific definition of neutral rights.

He was unaware, however, that Hamilton had already eliminated this opportunity by his private assurances to the British Minister that we would maintain a strict neutrality, and that we would refuse to honor any treaty obligations with France that might conflict with it. It is no wonder that Hammond was doubly determined to cultivate this most valuable gentleman and to have "very little interference [*sic*]" with Jefferson, "except in cases of necessity."[18]

Since the rest of the Cabinet followed Hamilton's lead in favor of a proclamation, Jefferson reluctantly gave his consent. He was the more disposed to do so because he feared that continued opposition on neutrality might prejudice the consideration of the next question in the series: should Genêt be received as the French Minister? Jefferson was furious at the very broaching of the question; he termed it "the boldest & greatest that ever was hazarded, and which would have called for extremities, had it prevailed."[19] For a denial of recognition to Genêt could only be predicated on a denial of recognition to the National Assembly as the constituted government of France; which would place us most unneutrally on the side of the monarchical governments of Europe.

If it is true, as has been hinted, that Hamilton deliberately posed this question as a bargaining point to gain Jefferson's acquiescence on the other queries, then he was notably successful. Yet Jefferson ought to have known that the question of Genêt's reception had already been disposed of. On March 12th, he had sent official instructions, with Washington's approval, to Gouverneur Morris to recognize the National Assembly as the duly constituted government of France.

"We surely cannot deny to any nation," he had then written, "that right whereon our own government is founded, that every one may govern itself according to whatever form it pleases, & change these forms at its own will; & that it may transact its business with foreign nations through whatever organ it thinks proper, whether king, convention, assembly, committee, president or anything else it may chuse. The will of the nation is the only thing essential to be regarded." [20]

Hamilton merely interposed some *pro forma* regrets that the appointment of Genêt had made it necessary for us to take action that constituted a recognition of the Assembly; nevertheless, he raised no serious objections, and Genêt's reception was agreed on unanimously. What was left in the air, however, was a curious problem as to whether he should be received absolutely, or with qualifications.

This, again, was Hamilton's phrasing. He feared that an unqualified reception might preclude any determination of the third question—should the treaty with France be deemed void, suspended or still in effect?

On this question, Jefferson was adamant. He was certain that Hamilton had in mind a declaration that the treaty had lapsed, since it had been entered into with the *king* of France, and the kingship was no longer in existence. Actually, all that Hamilton asked was to have Genêt informed that the United States reserved "to future consideration and discussion the question—whether the operation of the treaties . . . ought not to be deemed temporarily and provisionally suspended." [21]

The continued existence of the treaty, as a matter of fact, constituted a Damoclean sword over the United States. The pact had been made during the American Revolution when both countries were allies against the common foe, England, and called for active intervention by the United States in the event of an English attack on the French West Indies. It was difficult to conceive that England, mistress of the seas, would withhold seizing these rich prizes merely because of the treaty obligations of the United States. In such an event, once we conceded that the treaty was binding on us, we would be compelled to enter the war.

On the other hand, any unilateral denunciation of the treaty as null and void, or even as temporarily suspended, would rightly be viewed not only as a gratuitous insult to France, but as a faithless breach of a solemn and binding agreement.

The debate in the Cabinet was superheated. Hamilton developed his points at length and perhaps overstated them in the heat of discussion, thereby leading Jefferson to the belief that he advocated nullification. General Knox, for whom Jefferson had the greatest contempt, followed suit, "acknoleging, at the same time, like a fool that he is, that he knew nothing about it." Jefferson was firm that the treaty was valid; that the change in government did not render it void; and Randolph agreed with him. But Hamilton offered to prove his point on the authority of Vattel, the great Dutch jurisconsult, and Randolph asked for an adjournment of the question until he had a chance to look into the authorities.[22]

On the last question—should Congress be called into session?—there was no dispute. All were unanimous that it should not.

This left only the question of the French treaty still in doubt; and written opinions were called for. Hamilton, always a facile writer, gave his first; Jefferson's followed on April 28th; Randolph submitted his on May 6th, concurring with Jefferson; while Knox rendered none at all. His opinion, according to Jefferson, "was never thought worth offering or asking for."

Jefferson put a great deal of work into his opinion; and it constitutes one of his great State Papers. He reiterated the position he had taken in his instructions to Morris, and which was fundamental to his political philosophy. "I consider," he wrote, "the people who constitute a society or nation as the source of all authority in that nation, as free to transact their common concerns by any agents they think proper, to change these agents individually, or the organization of them in form or function whenever they please: that all the acts done by those agents under the authority of the nation, are the acts of the nation, are obligatory on them, & enure to their use, & can in no wise be annulled or affected by any change in the form of the government, or of the persons administering it." [23]

Consequently, the treaty had not been between Louis Capet, who then happened to be the King of France, and the United States, but between the two nations as such, and was therefore unaffected by the fact that France had since become a republic.

It was true, he admitted, that there were cases which justified withdrawal from the terms of a treaty obligation, but those cases must obey the same moral laws as applied to obligations between individuals. (This was a dig at Hamilton, who insisted that different rules of morality applied to nations.) Contracts could only be abrogated, he continued, when performance was impossible or self-destructive; but not, as Hamilton implied, when merely useless or disagreeable; or even fraught with possible—though not clear and present—danger.

That danger, of course, was the possibility of war with England over the West Indies islands. But Jefferson argued that the guarantee might never be invoked; that even if invoked, we could then consider the question *de novo*. Certainly we should not, for fear of *possibilities*, insult in advance an old ally and a comrade republic, by declaring at an end a treaty which, when entered into, had been all in our favor.

With the Cabinet deadlocked on the question, Washington made the final decision himself. It was in accord with Jefferson's opinion. Privately he told Jefferson that he had never had any doubts that the treaty was valid.[24]

Jefferson might well be satisfied with the outcome. He had won substantial victories on two of the three questions in dispute; and had not actually opposed the third on a matter of principle, only on tactical grounds. In fact, he won a partial victory here too; in deference to his technical objection the word "neutrality" was omitted from the proclamation. Time, however, has taken its revenge. The outlawed term, if not a part of the text, has since been universally associated in the title.

On April 22, 1793, the Proclamation of "Neutrality" was duly issued under the signature of the President. Considering its tremendous importance and the vital role it has since played in the diplomatic thinking of America, the Proclamation is remarkably terse and succinct. Taking cognizance of the general war, it declared it to be the duty and interest of the United States to "adopt and pursue a conduct friendly and impartial toward the belligerent Powers"; and warned American citizens "carefully to avoid all acts and proceedings whatsoever, which may in any manner tend to contravene such disposition."

Warning was given that the United States would not attempt to protect those of its citizens who might incur punishment or forfeiture because of hostile acts against any of the belligerents, or (and this was the crux of the Proclamation) "by carrying to any of them those articles which are deemed contraband by the *modern* usage of nations." In fact, the United States would itself prosecute and punish any of its citizens who, within the jurisdiction of its courts, violated the law of nations in these respects.[25]

Two items are worthy of note. The first is the use of the italicized word "*modern*" in characterizing that usage of nations which made certain goods contraband. On this alone there had been, and would continue to be, pregnant opportunities for dispute between Great Britain and the United States. According to American understanding, the "modern usage" narrowed sharply the definition of contraband to those enemy goods which aided their war effort. Thus enunciated, all other enemy goods carried in neutral ships were immune from seizure. Great Britain never agreed to this principle, nor, later on, did France; and it became the major element of dispute and eventual war with both countries.

The other notable item is the curious fact that it was Edmund Randolph, as Attorney General, and not Thomas Jefferson, as Secretary of State, who drafted the Proclamation. Perhaps Jefferson was willing enough for Randolph to have the authorship. He had disagreed with the timing of its issuance, and preferred not to have his name associated with it when, as happened, it met with considerable Republican criticism.

It was one thing, however, to pronounce neutrality by fiat; another to enforce it. Woodrow Wilson was to discover that when he attempted a similar proclamation during World War I; particularly when he attached to it the impossible proviso of neutrality in thought as well as in deed.

The Republicans in the United States were definitely not neutral in thought; and all too often, not in deed. They openly favored France, and made no secret of their ardent partisanship. They wore the famous French cockade; they cheered her victories and wept over her defeats; they formed Jacobin clubs in imitation of the revolutionary parent in Paris and democratic clubs which, as Washington came to believe, were birds of the same feather; and they made of Genêt's journey from Charleston to Philadelphia, when he finally arrived, a literal march of triumph.

Neither did Jefferson seek to veil his partisanship; in private, at any rate. Washington, much to his exasperation, had remarked that while Genêt ought to be received, he should not be greeted "with too much warmth or cordiality, so only as to be satisfactory to him." [26]

Jefferson complained to Madison: "We expect Mr. Genest [*sic*] here within a few days. It seems as if his arrival would furnish occasion for the *people* to testify their affections without respect to the cold caution of their government. Would you suppose it possible that it should have been seriously proposed to declare our treaties with France void on the authority of an ill understood scrap in Vattel?" [27]

When, a little later, a French frigate sent a captured British prize to Philadelphia, Jefferson noted with obvious approval that "thousands & thousands of the *yeomanry* of the city crowded & covered the wharves. Never before was such a crowd seen there, and when the British colours were seen *reversed*, & the French flying above them they burst into peals of exultation." Then, as if remembering that he was an officer of a neutral government, he added primly: "I wish we may be able to repress the spirit of the people within the limits of a fair neutrality." [28]

Nor was it neutrality in thought when, hearing that 400 "aristocrats & monocrats" from the insurrectionary island of St. Domingo were seeking refuge in Philadelphia, he wished they could be distributed among the Indians, "who would teach them lessons of liberty & equality." [29]

But the coming of Citizen Genêt, anticipated with so much relish by Jefferson and those whom he called the "people" and "yeomanry" of Philadelphia, was to precipitate a crisis in which neutrality and its solemn affirmations almost went by the board, and sent the United States trembling on the verge of war.

Of all the envoys whom revolutionary France might have accredited to an overwhelmingly sympathetic America, Edmond Charles Genêt was the worst possible choice that could have been made. In his favor were youth, vivacity, good looks and experience in diplomacy from a surprisingly early age. On the debit side were his conceit, flightiness, inability to take advice and a contempt for any people not having the good fortune to be born French. In all fairness, however, it must be said that the Assembly which had chosen him for the mission was similarly obsessed, and misjudged completely the essential temper of the American people and its government.

Genêt's secret instructions prove the point. He was to demand the enforcement of existing treaties; "to prevent any arming of privateers in American ports except on behalf of the French nation"; and prevent entry into American ports of any prizes "except those captured by the Republic." He was also to negotiate a new treaty, a "national pact in which the two nations should amalgamate their commercial and political interests, and establish an intimate cooperation in order to assist in every way the extension of the Kingdom of Liberty, guarantee the sovereignty of nations, and punish the Powers that still cling to an exclusive colonial system."

This was a large order which, if successfully consummated, would have torn American neutrality to shreds and made her just another satellite in the revolutionary orbit of France. In fact, still another instruction made it Genêt's business to bring the United States definitely into the war against England and Spain.

France, as a nation fighting for her life, had a right to seek military aid from the United States; but she went about it the wrong way. Since the Assembly was convinced that only Washington and the Senate stood in the path of the American people's alleged eagerness to precipitate themselves into the war, one more secret instruction filled Genêt's pouch. He was ordered "to make your representations more effective to direct opinion by means of anonymous publications. The Boston and Baltimore gazettes will be the best ones to use for distributing such publications in order to turn aside suspicion of authorship from you; but the more you contrive to influence public opinion indirectly, the more your official discussions with the President and with the Senate must be kept secret so as not to arouse alarm and give them time to cabal against you." [30]

Of Jefferson, however, Genêt's informants—chiefly Moustier and Otto, the ministers to the United States who had preceded Ternant—were lavish in their praise. He was the man France had most desired at the head of the State Department; he had always taken the liveliest interest in the success of the French Revolution and had never ceased to expose the "prejudices, the pride and the vainglory of England as well as her hatred of Americans." He was, indeed, the man "more likely than any other to succeed" Washington in the Presidency.[31]

These extravagant instructions must be taken into account in any final estimate of Genêt's mission; though it must be confessed that a more moderate and level-headed man would have understood, once he had appraised the American scene, that it would have been more to the advantage of France to have prudently toned down or altogether forgotten some of them. However, France was in revolution and quick to suspect treachery in her envoys and generals; and any deviation from instructions might have led straight to the guillotine. It must also be confessed that the mission was congenial to Genêt's own temperament.

Genêt sailed on the French frigate *Embuscade* and landed in Charleston on April 8, 1793. This distant landing from the capital may have been due to the danger of falling in with the British fleet; it may also have been deliberately planned as the opening gun in Genêt's appeal to the American people.

His first experiences on American soil bolstered every preconception with which he had come. Governor Moultrie of South Carolina welcomed him with effusive cordiality, and the populace treated him like a hero returned from the wars. He was feted and banqueted; there were speeches, processions, salvos of artillery and vinous toasts. Moultrie, so Genêt reported to his home government, "gave me all the assistance within his power." He "allowed me immediately to arm some privateers, while taking certain precautions in order still for a while to safeguard the neutrality of the United States."

What these "precautions" were is somewhat hazy; for the end result was that the Federal Government, including Jefferson, was at once confronted with a first-class headache and a major international incident. Genêt had been granted every facility to arm, equip and man four privateers—the *Republican*, *Sans Culotte*, *Anti George* and *Patriot*. American citizens had been recruited to sail the vessels, while Moultrie obligingly shut his eyes. They went out to sea in the company of the *Embuscade* and played havoc with British merchantmen, sending their prizes back to Charleston and Philadelphia for safekeeping and for sale.

Once these arrangements were made to Genêt's complete satisfaction—and others which included the distribution of French commissions to American citizens for service against the Spanish possessions in Florida and Louisiana—he decided to proceed to Philadelphia, where he was officially accredited. But he was in no hurry. He traveled at a snail's pace overland, basking in the popular assemblages that stopped him only too easily along the way, and making hay for the glorious French Revolution. What he did not realize was that he was traversing stanch Republican territory; that had he landed in Boston, and proceeded southward through New England, his passage would have taken on a far different aspect.

CHAPTER 37

Citizen Genêt

THE reports which came to Philadelphia of Genêt's exceedingly dilatory, yet triumphant progress through the Southland filled all good Federalists with apprehension and made Washington simmer with tightly repressed anger. Hamilton felt that his premonitions had been vindicated; and Knox followed suit. Even Edmund Randolph, republican though he was, veered irresolutely from this forthcoming apparition of the revolution.

But Jefferson found nothing untoward in the curious actions of the new minister. He beamed approval over the manifestations of republican and Francophile sentiment; and he hoped they would strengthen his hand in what was rapidly becoming a solitary position in the councils of the Cabinet. Hamilton, he wrote venomously to Monroe, "is panic-struck if we refuse our breach to every kick which Gr Brit. may chuse to give it. He is for proclaiming at once the most abject principles, such as would invite & merit habitual insults. And indeed every inch of ground must be fought in our councils to desperation in order to hold up the face of even a sneaking neutrality, for our votes are generally 2½ against 1½."[1] The fractional votes constituted Jefferson's mathematical estimate of Randolph's wavering between the two camps.

On May 17, 1793, more than five weeks after he had landed in Charleston, the new French plenipotentiary finally arrived in Philadelphia and was greeted by the same vast outpouring of cheering republicans as had attended him all along the way. He presented his credentials to Jefferson, who welcomed him cordially and took him to the President. There, for the first time, a decided chill became manifest in the atmosphere. Washington met him with formal politeness and spoke merely of American friendship toward France, but nothing of her Revolution.[2]

If Washington was chilly, the "yeomanry" of Philadelphia made up for it. It was a repetition of Charleston and the triumphal march, with banquets, toasts, and parades of the new Democratic society. Jefferson took the Frenchman promptly under his wing, and became as confidential and unbuttoned with him as Hamilton had ever been with the Englishman, Hammond.

Genêt was later to acknowledge Jefferson's assistance in orienting him to his strange surroundings and warning him against Hamilton and Senator Robert Morris who, so Jefferson told him, were attached to the interests of Great Britain and exercised the strongest influence on the President—an influence which Jefferson could hardly counterbalance.[3]

At almost the same time Hamilton was similarly warning Hammond against Jefferson and assuring him that "*he* shall exert his influence to defeat the success of any proposition on the part of France, which, tempting as it might appear, might ultimately render it necessary for this government to depart from the observance of as strict a neutrality as is compatible with its present engagements, and which is so essential to its real interests." [4]

It was a strange sight—this of the two chief Cabinet officers of the United States, hobnobbing each with a representative of a foreign power and giving him aid and comfort against the other.

Whatever one proposed, the other almost automatically opposed. Hamilton had drafted a letter to the customs officers, instructing them to be on the alert for any infractions of neutrality by American citizens and to notify him of the event. The more Jefferson reflected on the proposed letter, the more it seemed objectionable to him. It made the customs collectors "an established corps of spies or informers against their fellow citizens" and gave them a chance to vent personal spites. He also resented Hamilton's calm arrogation of additional powers to "a department already amply provided with business, patronage, & influence." [5]

When Hamilton's circular letter came up for Cabinet discussion, Jefferson objected strenuously. But, as he told Madison, "the Anglophobia [*sic*] has seized violently on three members of our council"; and he was voted down. All his wrath thereupon vented itself on the backslider, Randolph. "Everything, my dear sir," he exploded, "now hangs on the opinion of a single person, and that the most indecisive one I ever had to do business with. He always contrives to agree in principle with one but in conclusion with the other." Only Washington and "the ardent spirit of our constituents" prevented "a merely English neutrality" instead of a "manly" one. This, however, did Randolph an injustice; for he had notified Jefferson in advance that he was standing with Hamilton on this particular issue because of principle.[6]

What constituted true neutrality became an immediate problem. When Jefferson benevolently watched the wild scenes of rejoicing which greeted the arrival of the captured English ship, the *Grange*, in Philadelphia, he had not realized that this would become the first test of American policy.

Fortunately, it was a comparatively simple test. The *Grange*, according to Hammond, had been seized by the French frigate in American territorial waters. Jefferson assured him that if this were so, adequate steps would be taken to detain both ship and cargo, and to prevent further violations of American sovereignty.[7]

The second was almost equally simple. Another British vessel had been sent to Charleston as a French prize, and been condemned and offered for sale by the French consul. Again Hammond protested. Jefferson agreed with him that if the stated facts were true, the entire proceeding had been illegal and the consul guilty of "an act of disrespect towards the United

States."[8] But, in passing on the complaint to Ternant, still Minister at the time, he softened it down to "an error in judgment in that particular officer," and asked him to prevent similar "errors" in the future.[9]

Thus far, Jefferson was acting with rigorous impartiality. The *Grange*, after inquiry had established the correctness of Hammond's contention, was restored to the British; and the overzealous French consul in Charleston had been duly called to account. Jefferson was honestly trying to walk the tightrope of neutrality under provocations from both warring powers, and with but little in the way of precedents to guide him. "We shall be a little embarrassed occasionally," he wrote his old law teacher, George Wythe, "till we feel ourselves firmly seated in the saddle of neutrality."[10] And he was well aware that "a fair neutrality will prove a disagreeable pill to our friends, tho' necessary to keep out of the calamities of war."[11]

The embarrassments and the disagreeableness were not long in coming. The privateers which Genêt had outfitted in Charleston with enthusiastic American support and with American sailors and supplies were literally coming home to roost. Not content with playing havoc with English shipping on the high seas, they flaunted their prizes in American ports. In hot indignation, Hammond voiced a series of vigorous protests, documenting all the outrages involved in these violations of neutrality.

The matter came up for Cabinet discussion on May 20, 1793 in the form of a question: "Shall the Privateer fitted out at Charleston & her prizes be ordered out of the ports of the U. S.?"

At this point Jefferson balked, and haled out the old French treaty in defense of Genêt. That treaty, he maintained, by specifically prohibiting the *enemies* of France from outfitting privateers in American ports conversely implied that it was lawful for the French to do so. He cited still another article which permitted French ships to enter our ports with their prizes; though he admitted that it made no mention of a right to condemn and sell them. As to the complaint that sailors had been recruited in Charleston and elsewhere to man the privateers, French citizens had a legal right to defend their country by sea or land, to purchase ships and man them, as long as they committed no acts of hostility within American limits. "Are we playing y' part England plaid?" he demanded heatedly; and thereby "force France to attack us?"[12] That some of the "French" citizens were in fact Americans, whom Genêt had conveniently converted into Frenchmen by a hasty scrawl of citizenship, did not alter Jefferson's conviction of the legality of the transaction.

Hamilton and Knox, however, demanded that either the prize be yielded or the privateer ordered away. Randolph, the "indecisive one," came up with a third proposal—that the prize be allowed to remain, and only the privateer be ordered out of port. For the nonce, Washington agreed with Randolph.

By this time friction had developed between Jefferson and Washington; concealed under the forms of politeness, but there nonetheless. Jefferson sneered at what he called "the pusillanimity" of the Proclamation of Neutrality and found in it "a fear lest any affection should be discovered" toward France. "This base fear," he exclaimed to Madison, "will produce the very evil they wish to avoid. For our constituents seeing that the government does not express their mind, perhaps rather leans the other way, are coming forward to express it themselves." [13]

On the other hand, Washington had reached the end of his temper and patience with Freneau's continued attacks on him. Well aware of the charge that Freneau was Jefferson's creature, he made the occasion for a private talk with the latter. He despised the attacks on himself, he said; but, he went on with great heat, "there never had been an act of the government . . . which that paper had not abused." He left Jefferson with the impression that he expected him to put a stop to Freneau's diatribes, either by personal intervention or by dismissing him as translation clerk. "But I will not do it," Jefferson confided to his *Anas*. "His paper has saved our constitution which was galloping fast into monarchy, & has been checked by no means so powerfully as by that paper." [14]

In public, Jefferson walked the rigid line of neutrality; in private, he lamented his obligation to give official sanction to a theory of neutrality to which he was opposed. With due formality he issued the proper instructions and forwarded the correct complaints to Genêt; in private communications to that gentleman, however, he disavowed any active agency and asked to be considered "only as the passive instrument of the President." [15]

Genêt's instructions had called for a political and commercial alliance with the United States. But he chose to open negotiations in such grandiloquent tones as seem inevitably to be associated with the standard-bearers of revolution.

"Sir:" he informed Jefferson, "Single, against innumerable hordes of tyrants and slaves, who menace her rising liberty, the French nation would have a right to reclaim the obligations imposed on the United States, by the treaties she had contracted with them, and which she has cemented with her blood; but strong in the greatness of her means, and of the power of her principles, not less redoubtable to her enemies than the victorious arm which she opposes to their rage, she comes, in the very time when the emissaries of our common enemies are making useless efforts to neutralize the gratitude—to damp the zeal—to weaken or cloud the view of your fellow-citizens; she comes, I say—that generous nation—that faithful friend —to labor still to increase the prosperity, and add to the happiness which she is pleased to see them enjoy."

Having thus granted—that generous nation—*everything* to the United States, she "has charged me to propose to your government to establish, in a true family pact, that is, in a national compact, the liberal and fraternal basis, on which she wishes to see raised the commercial and political system of two People, all whose interests are confounded [*sic*]." [16] Modern

Freudians might possibly have a field day with Genêt's technical use of that final expression.

There was small possibility that such an alliance—even though stripped of excessive verbiage and removed from its plane of condescension—could be consummated. It would have meant war with England; it would have irrevocably tied the United States to the revolutionary chariot of France; and it would have precipitated this country into that very whirlpool of disaster which everyone—Washington, Jefferson and Hamilton—was determined to avoid.

But Genêt had no time to pursue his instructions further. Almost immediately he found himself immersed in a flood of complaints emanating from the indefatigable Hammond, and duly passed along—sometimes with reluctance, and increasingly with annoyance—by Jefferson.

As instance after instance piled up of flagrant French violations of the position of the United States as a neutral nation, of the arrogance of French officers and representatives—from the Minister himself down to the lowliest consul—Jefferson's attempts to strike a balance between "a fair neutrality" and his private predilections became more and more difficult.

The complaints came in one by one—the incident of the *Grange;* the seizure of the British ship *Catharine* two and a half miles off the American shore (in which the United States eventually laid down the famous rule that sovereignty extends three miles out to sea); the privateers out of Charleston and from other ports; the recruitment on American soil of men for the French service. In each case, Genêt either defied the right of the American authorities to intervene or, if compelled to yield, did it with angry expostulations and a sullen mien.

But gradually Jefferson was hammering out—with considerable proddings from the other members of the Cabinet and the President—a workable set of doctrines and rules to govern neutrality that laid the basic foundations for American policy in the future.

His explosive reaction in the Cabinet meeting of May 20th—in which he had denounced any attempts to hamstring French activities on American soil—was reconsidered in a calmer moment and reversed. When the case of the *Little Sarah*—to be discussed later—came up for consideration, he expressed a wholly different attitude in a formal opinion. He now construed the pertinent article of the treaty with France to mean that, since we could not permit the enemies of France to outfit privateers in our ports, "we ought not therefore to permit France to do it, the treaty leaving us free to refuse, & the refusal being necessary to preserve a fair and secure neutrality." [17]

When Genêt, in highhanded language, demanded the immediate release of two "French" officers—with the significant names of Gideon Henfield and John Singletary—who had been taken from the privateer, *Citizen Genêt*, while lying at anchor off Philadelphia, Jefferson replied politely that they were in the hands of the civil authorities, over whom the Executive had no control.[18] This became a formula which Jefferson was to use with increasing frequency in cases of alleged violations—both to Genêt and Hammond. It afforded him a welcome respite from harassment; and allowed the matters to be adjudged in the law courts.

Henfield and Singletary—actually American citizens—had been among those recruited by Genêt at Charleston; and the Philadelphia authorities arrested them on the ground that, under the Proclamation of Neutrality, they had violated the law. The question posed to the courts, therefore, was whether the Proclamation, an executive order and not an Act of Congress, constituted the law of the land. The prosecution based its case on the theory that, by violating the terms of certain treaties with some of the nations at war with France, the accused had been guilty of a breach of the peace. Thereby, any inquiry into the validity of the executive proclamation was avoided.[19]

Yet, though the reasoning seemed impeccable, the Philadelphia jury, wholly sympathetic to the French, brought in a verdict of "not guilty."

Meanwhile, Jefferson kept gently prodding Genêt on the particularly thorny problem of the Charleston privateers. His first complaint had been to Ternant; when Genêt superseded him, he went to his home to discuss it. Genêt adopted the position that the whole business had been carried through by overzealous French residents of Charleston; that when he had asked Governor Moultrie's opinion, the latter had said "he knew no law to the contrary, but begged that whatever was to be done, might be done without consulting him; that he must know nothing of it, etc." However, Genêt added with some reluctance, though he felt himself justified, he would submit to the President's decision.[20]

Washington did decide—that armed vessels of this description be ordered out of American ports. Whereupon Genêt, in spite of his oral professions, entered a written protest; to which Jefferson retorted coldly that the decision must stand.[21]

It was not until more than a month later that Genêt called on Jefferson and agreed to abandon *further* arming of ships in American ports; refusing, however, to give up those already outfitted.[22]

Meanwhile, Governor Clinton of New York had seized under the Proclamation the sloop *Polly* which, rebaptized the *Republican,* was being outfitted and armed in New York harbor as a privateer against the British. It was Hammond who had called this flagrant case to the attention of the government, as well as the presence of the British brigantine *Catharine* as a French prize of war in New York. Jefferson wrote at once to the United States District Attorney in New York directing him to prosecute both citizens and aliens involved in either incident; [23] and received as a result an indignant protest from Genêt, contending that the *Republican* had been armed only for defense, and not for aggression. Jefferson retorted that the French consul at New York had himself admitted the contrary; and cited the usual Vattel, Wolf and the law of nature to prove that the course he was following was one of true neutrality.[24]

Genêt lost his temper and for once spoke plain and unadorned English. "Discussions are short," he replied sharply, "when matters are taken upon their true principles. Let us explain ourselves as republicans. Let us not lower ourselves to the level of ancient politics by diplomatic subtleties." Jefferson's reasonings might be extremely ingenious; "but I do not hesitate to tell you, that they rest on a basis which I cannot admit." And—in final exasperation—to his just complaints Jefferson had interposed the "aphorisms of Vattel." [25] The honeymoon was coming to an end.

In spite of the growing coolness with Genêt, Jefferson still clung to his sympathies with France and hoped for the success of her arms abroad and a cordial compact with her at home. He was afraid that any French reverses on the European battlefields would give "wonderful vigor to our monocrats, and unquestionably affect the tone of administering our government. Indeed, I fear that if this summer should prove disastrous to the French, it will damp that energy of republicanism in our new Congress, from which I had hoped so much reformation." [26]

The times, he thought, were "pregnant of events." He committed to paper for the benefit of Monroe just what those pregnancies were. He had taken at face value, for example, the offer of political and commercial cooperation which Genêt had brought with him. This he considered most generous; seizing particularly on the assertion, insofar as it could be disentangled from the verbiage, that France did not intend to call on the United States for the execution of its guarantee. England, by contrast, was sullen and reserved. She made demands where *her* interests were involved; and interposed delays when ours were. Spain's attitude was most mysterious; should France be overthrown, Jefferson was certain that Spain would become truculent on the Mississippi.

But the situation at home was even more disturbing. "Parties seem to have taken a very well defined form in this quarter. The old tories, joined by our merchants who trade on British capital, paper dealers, and the idle rich of the great commercial towns, are with the kings. All other descriptions with the French. The war has kindled & brought forward the two parties with an ardour which our own interests merely, could never excite." [27]

With England, as a matter of fact, all negotiations over the vital frontier posts had come to a halt. Hammond was pretending to wait for instructions from home; but they were unaccountably slow in coming. Either the British Ministry was on a long week end when the packet sailed, or engrossed in other matters, or preparing for war, or engaged in unfathomable affairs, so Jefferson complained, "the stack of which is inexhaustible, and can therefore never fail those who desire nothing but that things should rest as they are." [28] When it came to French privateers, however, both

Hammond and his home government were alert, prompt and quick to action.

It was therefore with understandable satisfaction that Jefferson was finally able to turn the tables on the British. Even as Hammond was protesting strongly against *French* violations, word came of the capture of an American ship, the *Snow Suckey*, by a *British* privateer. Jefferson protested immediately to Hammond and called on the American Minister in London to seek restitution and punishment of the offenders.[29]

At about the same time word was received that the Governor of Georgia had seized a British privateer outfitting in a Georgia port; and Jefferson was happy to inform Genêt to that effect. Genêt was equally happy to hear of it, but he could not resist a sarcastic aside: "It is to be wished, sir, that the same watchfulness and firmness may be employed in all the States of the Union." According to him, armed British ships had the run of Charleston, Baltimore, Philadelphia, and New York. *There*, British vessels were treated tenderly, while the French were "pursued with rigor." [30]

Genêt's ill-repressed anger was shortly to explode, and with the eruption came his downfall and a dangerous turn in Franco-American relations.

The inciting spark was a small English merchant vessel called the *Little Sarah*. Sailing out of Philadelphia, it had fallen in with a French frigate, been captured, and sent back to Philadelphia in May as a prize of war. There it remained quietly, while Hammond demanded restitution.

On July 6, 1793, Hamilton, who had doubtless received the information from Hammond, informed Jefferson and Knox that the *Little Sarah*, renamed the *Little Democrat*, was being secretly outfitted by the French as a privateer. He suggested that they have Governor Thomas Mifflin of Pennsylvania conduct an immediate inquiry.

At Jefferson's request, Mifflin investigated and found enough to cause him to send a midnight representative to Genêt to demand that the ship, scheduled to sail the following day, be held in port. Genêt flew into a passion and refused to make any such commitment. Whereupon Mifflin rushed all the details to Jefferson the following morning of the 7th.

The news posed something of a crisis. Washington was away at Mount Vernon, and Randolph was also out of town. Yet, should the *Little Sarah* sail from under their very noses, Hammond would have strong grounds for his contention that the United States was allowing Genêt to violate its neutrality with impunity.

Jefferson hurried over to Genêt's home and asked him to hold the alleged privateer at least until inquiry could be made whether she really had been armed in contravention of the President's proclamation. This was Sunday; Washington was due to arrive in Philadelphia on Wednesday, July 10th, and the matter could then be laid before him.

But Genêt flew into the same passion with his friend, Jefferson, that he had exhibited to Dallas, Mifflin's emissary. He poured forth such an endless stream of tirade and complaint that the astounded Jefferson found it impossible to get a word in edgewise. The United States, ranted Genêt, had violated its treaties, suffered her flag to be insulted by the British and permitted them to seize French goods from her ships. If the Americans could not protect their rights, then the French would have to take over the job. The French, he shouted, had shown entirely too much tenderness for American neutrality in the past. The name of Washington excited him into even greater frenzy. He, Genêt, had come with the friendliest instructions, yet the President had treated him coldly and refused to convene Congress in order to discuss them. He would certainly demand from Washington now, he screamed, that Congress be immediately called into session.

At this point the storming Minister paused for breath, and Jefferson seized the opportunity to intervene. Such matters, he explained, belonged under the Constitution to the Executive alone. Then, deftly, he turned the talk into its original channel—that the *Little Sarah* remain in port pending an investigation.

Genêt, now somewhat quieted, made no definite promise, but said something vaguely to the effect that the ship was not ready, and therefore could not possibly sail that day. Jefferson persisted; but only received in reply certain Gallic shrugs and gestures which he construed to mean that the ship would not depart until Washington's arrival; or, at the least, would drop no further than a little down the river. With the remark that he was taking this for granted, and meeting with eloquent silence, Jefferson left.

Laboring under the disastrous impression that he had elicited, if not a formal, at least a gentleman's promise from Genêt, Jefferson hastened to Mifflin and expressed his conviction that the boat would not sail. Thereupon the Governor, who had in the meantime ordered out the militia to use force, if necessary, to detain the *Little Sarah*, countermanded his orders. He then told Jefferson of an interesting portion of Dallas's conversation of the previous night with Genêt. The latter had asserted that he intended "to appeal from the President to the people." [31]

Content that he had staved off any immediate emergency, Jefferson met with Hamilton and Knox at Mifflin's office on the following day. Hamilton did not share Jefferson's confidence in Genêt's honorable intentions, and demanded that a battery of artillery be stationed at Mud Island, further down the river, with orders to fire on the *Little Sarah* if she attempted to pass. Knox concurred with Hamilton; but Jefferson dissented strongly, and put down in writing a formal statement of the reasons for his dissent.

He was satisfied, he said, that the brigantine would not depart pending Washington's arrival. On the other hand, the erection of a battery might hasten rather than retard her departure; and in the event she should attempt the passage, bloodshed must follow. As a result, a strong French fleet, shortly expected up the river, might intervene. Such an open outbreak of hostilities had too serious consequences for subordinate officials of the government to shoulder. It would be inconsistent, he commented, for the

United States, which had borne patiently for ten years "the grossest insults & injuries from their late enemies [Great Britain], to rise at a feather against their friends and benefactors [the French]." He would not, he proceeded, "gratify the combination of kings with the spectacle of the two only republics on earth destroying each other for two cannon; nor would I, for infinitely greater cause, add this country to that combination, turn the scale of contest, & let it be at our hands that the hopes of man received their last stab." [32]

This was not the language of calm deliberation; something of Genêt's own declamation, and even turn of phrase, had crept into Jefferson's Cabinet pronouncement.

The President rode into Philadelphia to find everything at sixes and sevens. A first-class international incident was in the making, and his Cabinet were at loggerheads. His own reaction—based on the reports rendered him by Hamilton and Mifflin—was immediate. An indignant note from him was on its way to Jefferson even before he had a chance to read the latter's statement.

"What is to be done in the case of the Little Sarah, now at Chester?" he demanded hotly. "Is the Minister of the French Republic to set the acts of this Government at defiance, *with impunity?*—and then threaten the Executive with an appeal to the people? What must the world think of such conduct—& of the Government of the U States in submitting to it?" [33]

Jefferson promptly forwarded in answer the remarkable defense of his position he had drafted several days before, with an explanation that he would wait on the President early the next morning, though he had been feverish the two nights past.[34] The recent events, indeed, had been enough to put any man into a fever.

But by the time the opinions of the several Cabinet members were in Washington's hands, and before he had a chance to digest them, it was too late to do anything. The *Little Sarah* had dropped quietly to a point down the river at which it would be impossible to get batteries in position in time to stop her, if she decided to make a dash for it. All that could be done, therefore, was to send another note to Genêt professing the understanding that he would not permit the *Little Sarah* and other ships in similar standing to sail pending a formal decision.[35]

In order to make a proper decision, Washington posed a series of questions to his Cabinet.

Did the treaty with France leave the United States free to prohibit her from arming vessels in our ports? The unanimous answer was that it did.

How far would such a prohibition be retroactive as to the vessels armed at Charleston; and what about the prizes they had brought into American harbors? Jefferson held that the prohibition was *not* retroactive, and that the French could legally dispose of the prizes. Hamilton and Knox were of the opinion that the prizes ought to be given up, and the privateers suppressed. Randolph, now back in Philadelphia, compromised. The prizes might be sold, but the privateers ought to be ordered away.

Are American citizens who join in hostilities against nations at peace with us punishable by law? The Cabinet was unanimous in the affirmative.[36]

But while they were thus gravely debating the law, word came that the *Little Sarah*, in defiance of orders and in spite of Jefferson's wishful thinking about Genêt's intentions, had slipped down the river and stood out to sea. The bird in dispute had flown.

It appeared to Jefferson that Washington regretted the ship had not been stopped by gunfire. Hamilton, in a white fury, moved that the French government be notified to recall Genêt and that, in the meantime, he be suspended from his functions as Minister. To this, Jefferson countered with a milder proposal: that the correspondence with Genêt be communicated to France with some "friendly observations" thereon. He noted, however, that the President maintained complete silence all through the furious debate.[37]

The escape of the *Little Sarah* furnished Hammond with a clear-cut case of the secret connivance of the United States in breaches of its own neutrality, or at best, its utter inefficiency. Surprisingly, he made no use of the weapon thus providentially placed in his hands; and merely wrote home that the government, "from the want of having any cannon or military in readiness, was compelled to submit to the indignity." [38]

But there was another, and from a local point of view, far more important repercussion. Genêt's threat to appeal to the American people over the head of their President, and the contents of a long and insulting communication to Washington along the same lines, had leaked out. Hammond heard of it through Hamilton; and the Federalists were gleefully spreading the news through the nation. This is what happens, they jeered, from republican hobnobbing with the French revolutionaries. We are subjected to threats and insults, and the Republicans (meaning Jefferson) turn the other cheek.

Even before the matter broke in the public press, Jefferson had realized all the implications. It might well be, he feared, that in the inevitable public reaction to Genêt, the Republicans would be discredited and the nation thrown into the arms of Hamilton and the Federalists.

Hamilton had already started the ball rolling with powerful attacks on Jefferson and on France under the pseudonym of "Pacificus." Writhing under the repeated sledgehammer blows, Jefferson called, as in the past, on Madison to champion the republican cause. His plea was almost frantic: "Nobody answers him, & his doctrines will therefore be taken for confessed. For god's sake, my dear Sir, take up your pen, select the most striking heresies and cut him to pieces in the face of the public. There is nobody else who can & will enter the lists against him." [39]

Madison was tired of this continued jousting with the indestructible Hamilton; nevertheless he yielded to the urgent solicitation and replied to "Pacificus" in the guise of "Helvidius." But, as he told Jefferson in some exasperation, the task was "the most grating one I have ever experienced...."

One thing that particularly vexes me is that I foreknow from the prolixity & pertinacity of [Hamilton], that the business will not be terminated by a single fire, and of course that I must return to the charge in order to prevent a triumph without a victory." [40]

If Hamilton had been able to strike such blows *before* the fracas with Genêt, he was able to redouble them after in a new series entitled "No Jacobin," in which the entire controversy was aired for public delectation.

It is no wonder then that Jefferson decided it was time to scuttle Genêt before the association sank himself and his party. When Monroe, therefore, who was more violently Francophile than even Jefferson, denounced to him the prosecutions under the Proclamation of Neutrality as "both unconstitutional & impolitick," [41] he replied with considerable asperity. He defended the course of the Administration, pointing out in the process that the obnoxious word "neutrality" had not been used. Arming vessels in our ports to attack another nation, he asserted, is "punishable, & that, if found otherwise [by the courts] Congress ought to make it so, or we shall be parties in every maritime war in which the piratical spirit of the banditti in our ports can engage.

"I fear," he continued, "the disgust of France is inevitable. We shall be to blame in part. But the new Minister much more so. His conduct is indefensible by the most furious Jacobin. I only wish our countrymen may distinguish between him & his nation, and if the case should ever be laid before them, may not suffer their affection to the nation to be diminished. H[amilton], sensible of the advantage they have got, is urging a full appeal by the government to the people. Such an explosion would manifestly endanger a dissolution [*sic*] of the friendship between the two nations, and ought therefore to be deprecated by every friend to our liberty." [42]

He wrote in similar vein to Madison, and that he must see him before Congress met. Genêt, he said, "is so evidently in the wrong that those are pressing for an appeal to the people who never looked towards that tribunal before." [43]

Heartsick with the knowledge that because of Genêt the tide was running strongly against everything in which he believed, Jefferson tendered his resignation on July 31st to Washington, to take effect the end of September. He intended, he said, to retire from those scenes "which I am every day more & more convinced that neither my talents, tone of mind, nor time of life fit me." [44] Almost two months before, he had opened his heart to Madison. He had labored long enough for his fellow citizens—twenty-four years all told. He wanted tranquillity, his home, family, neighbors, books and plantation more than anything else in the world. What was his present existence? he asked with pathos. "Worn down with labours from morning to night, & day to day; knowing them as fruitless to others as they are vexatious to myself, committed singly in desperate & eternal contest against a host who are systematically undermining the public liberty & prosperity, even the rare hours of relaxation sacrificed to the society of persons in the same intentions, of whose hatred I am conscious even in those moments of conviviality when the heart wishes most to open itself to the effusions of friendship & confidence, cut off from my family & friends, my affairs abandoned to chaos & derangement, in short giving everything I love, in exchange for everything I hate, and all this without a single gratification in possession or prospect, in present enjoyment or future wish." [45]

There is much to stir the emotion in this cry from the heart, and much from which to gain an insight into Jefferson's true concerns. Yet there is also a trace of self-pitying exaggeration. He was not as alone in his solitary combat with the forces of evil (such as they were) as he seemed to think. Even in the Cabinet, Randolph agreed with his position as often as he accepted Hamilton's, and in many cases intervened with a sensible compromise. But Jefferson considered those not wholly on his side as against him, and perpetually poured the vials of his wrath on that unfortunate Virginian's head. When Randolph proposed to go home for a vacation, Jefferson tipped off Madison in advance to see to it that the errant Attorney General fell into such hands as Wilson Cary Nicholas, and to impress on Nicholas "the necessity of giving him a strong & perfect understanding of the public mind." Meaning, of course, the republican mind. Perhaps, continued Jefferson, the journey "may strengthen his nerves, and dispose him more favorably to the propositions of a treaty between the two republics," such as Genêt had proposed.[46]

Nor was Philadelphia exactly an undivided stronghold of Federalism and unremitting hatred for Jefferson. The "yeomanry" were all republican and all for France; and so were the intellectuals of the Philosophical Society with whom Jefferson consorted.

On July 17, 1793, in fact, some of the Society's members joined with a group of others to publish the constitution of a newly organized Democratic Society, announcing that "with a view . . . to cultivate a just knowledge of rational liberty, to facilitate the enjoyments and exercise of our civil rights, and to transmit, unimpaired, to posterity, the glorious inheritance of a free Republican Government, the Democratic Society of Pennsylvania is constituted and established." [47]

David Rittenhouse and such political stalwarts as Charles Biddle, Alexander J. Dallas, Michael Leib, Israel Israel and Peter St. Duponceau publicly affixed their names. To Federalists such as Hamilton, and even to Washington, this new society was a radical, revolutionary club of Jacobins whose purpose, they were convinced, was to overthrow the existing form of government in the United States and substitute in blood and gore the anarchy of France.

If Jefferson, then, met only with people who hated him and loathed his principles, it was his own fault. Not many months before, Benjamin Smith Barton, another Philadelphia member of the Philosophical Society, had renamed a species of plant the *Jeffersonia Diphylla*, in honor of a beloved leader and an inquiring botanist.[48]

Washington was dismayed to receive Jefferson's formal note of resignation. His Cabinet was crumbling about him; only a little before, Hamilton had expressed a similar determination to retire. He therefore personally called at Jefferson's house, just outside the city, in an attempt to dissuade him. He himself, he said, ought to have resigned, inasmuch as those on whom he had counted were deserting him. Jefferson repeated his fervent wish to go home. Washington suggested that he could take a leave of absence to attend to his private affairs; but that he should hold off resigning until the end of the year, when the pressing matters now in trend would very likely have been straightened out. To this, although with the greatest reluctance, Jefferson finally agreed.[49]

CHAPTER 38

Last Days in Office

ON August 1, 1793, the day after Jefferson had attempted to resign, the Cabinet met to discuss what course of action to take on Genêt. This time there was no essential disagreement; even the most passionate adherents of France had by this time come to the sorrowful conclusion that Genêt must go.

It was unanimously agreed that a full statement of his conduct and correspondence be sent to Gouverneur Morris to lay before the French government, and that his recall be required; though Jefferson wanted the request to be couched "with great delicacy." Knox, roused from his wonted sluggishness, proposed to send Genêt packing immediately; but the others voted him down. But what was carried over Jefferson's objection was a resolution to notify Genêt immediately that a demand for his recall had been made.

Perhaps the most important problem of all, and the one most fraught with political consequences, now reared its head. Should the complete story of the affair be published to the people? The two antagonists on the question, strangely enough, were Randolph and Hamilton. For once, Jefferson sat quietly on the sidelines, and allowed Randolph to carry the burden. Hamilton, of course, wanted the story to be spread before the nation. Randolph did not.

It was only when Hamilton, according to Jefferson, went into an inflammatory harangue against the Democratic Society, as though he were addressing a courtroom jury, that Jefferson decided to take a hand. The Society, he countered, was a local political organization only. If left alone, it would quietly expire after the coming gubernatorial election in Pennsylvania. Should it be proscribed, however, as Hamilton hinted it should, it would gain a new lease of life and "multitudes would join it merely to assert the right of voluntary associations."

Having thus broken the ice, Jefferson now added his arguments to those of Randolph in opposition to any publicizing of the Genêt affair. He pointed out that this would give Genêt just the opportunity he wanted—a chance to appeal to the American people on his own; and that thereby the whole business would degenerate into an undignified contest between the President of the United States and Genêt.

Washington, however, was not impressed by this consideration and inclined toward publication. There the Cabinet meeting might have ended, had not Knox, with what Jefferson called "a foolish incoherent sort of speech," displayed a printed pasquinade which was being circulated around

Philadelphia, in which Washington was displayed as King, with his head under the guillotine. The implication was only too obvious.

Jefferson was both embarrassed and furious at Knox for bringing the broadside to Washington's attention; for what he most dreaded did occur. Washington went into one of those rare passions in which his usual iron control broke down. He was tired, he stormed, of all the personal abuse that was being heaped on him; he repented every moment of the day and night that he had not resigned; and by God, he'd rather be in his grave than in his present situation. He'd rather be back on his farm than be Emperor of the World; yet every rascal accused him of wanting to be King. As Jefferson squirmed in silence, the raging President turned his attack on "that rascal Freneau" who dared send him his papers every day, in a manifest design to insult him.[1]

When Washington finally expended his passion, there was a long silence; then the question of the appeal was raised again and left hanging. All in all, it was a thoroughly uncomfortable meeting for Jefferson. The barbs directed against Genêt might have passed him by; but the pasquinade (Republican in origin) and the attack on Freneau, his protégé, were shafts aimed directly at his heart.

Yet it was a bare few days after this unpleasant experience that Washington pleaded with Jefferson to delay his resignation. Five days later, on August 11th, Jefferson sent Madison a long, important letter as far removed from the lamentation and self-pity of his earlier one of June 9th as two letters could possibly be. This one was a cool and searching analysis of what his conversation with Washington portended, and what it meant in terms of future Republican strategy. This was the skilled political leader speaking, the careful strategist planning a campaign. Forgotten for the moment was the retired hermit of Monticello, the panter after privacy in the bosom of one's family, and forgetfulness of the world. There were two Jeffersons, and they alternated with some degree of regularity. Whichever situation he happened to be in, he yearned for the other. An understanding of both is essential for a true understanding of the totality of the man.

The letter deserves quoting *in extenso.*

I write a second letter to-day, because going by a private conveyance I can venture in it a paper [notes of his conversation on August 6th with Washington] which never could have been hazarded by the post. Timely information of its contents (which must be sacredly kept to yourself unless you have an opportunity of communicating them to Monroe) may enable you to shape your plan for the state of things which is actually to take place. It would be the moment for dividing the Treasury between two equal chiefs of the Customs, and Internal Taxes, if the Senate were not so unsound. A declaration of the true sense of the Const[itution] on the question of the bank, will suffice to divorce that from the government, tho' made by a single house. Censures or censurable things clearly confessed in the reports etc.—With respect to the

Proclamation, as the facts it declared were true, and the desire of neutrality is universal, it would place the republicans in a very unfav[ora]ble point of view with the people to be cavilling about small points of propriety; & would betray a wish to find fault with the President in an instance where he will be approved by the great body of the people who consider the substance of the measure only, & not the smaller criticisms to which it is liable. The conduct of Genet too is transpiring & exciting the indignation it is calculated to excite.

The towns are beginning generally to make known their disapprobation of any such opposition to their gov[ernment] by a foreigner, and declaring their firm adherence to their President, & the Proclamation is made the groundwork of their Declarations. [This was happening in New York and to the north; and even Philadelphia was quitting Genêt, though] its popular leaders have not the good sense to go over with them. They will go without them, & be thus transferred to the other party.—So in Congress. I believe that it will be true wisdom in the Republican party to approve unequivocally of a state of neutrality, to avoid little cavils about who shall declare it, to abandon G[enêt] entirely, with expressions of strong friendship & adherence to his nation & confidence that he has acted against their sense. In this way we shall keep the people on our side by keeping ourselves in the right.—

I have been myself under a cruel dilemma with him. I adhered to him as long as I could have a hope of getting him right, because I knew what weight we should derive to our scale by keeping in it the love of the people for the French cause & nation, and how important it was to ward off from that cause & nation any just grounds of alienation. Finding at length that the man was absolutely incorrigible, I saw the necessity of quitting a wreck which could not but sink all who should cling to it.—It is determined to insist on his recall, and I am preparing a statement of his conduct to be laid before the Executive council. Hamilton & Knox have pressed an appeal to the people with an eagerness I never before saw in them. They made the establishment of the democratic society here the ground for sounding an alarm that this society . . . was put into motion by mr G. and would by their corresponding societies in all the state draw the mass of the people, by dint of misinformation, into their vortex & overset the governmt.

The Pres[ident] was strongly impressed by this picture, drawn by H. in three speeches of ¾ of an hour length each. I opposed it totally, told the President plainly in their presence, that the intention was to dismount him from being the head of the nation, & make him the head of a party; that this would be the effect of making him in an appeal to the people declare war against the Republican party. R[andolph] according to his half-way system between wrong & right urged the *putting off* the appeal. [Washington liked Randolph's idea, and the matter was postponed.]

If the demonstrations of popular adherence to him [Washington] become as general & warm as I believe they will, I think he will never again bring on the question: if there is any appearance of their supporting Genet, he will probably make the appeal.—

I can by this confidential conveyance speak more freely of R[andolph]. He is the poorest Cameleon I ever saw having no colour of his own, & reflecting that nearest him. When he is with me he is a whig, when with H[amilton] he is a tory, when with the P[resident] he is that he thinks will please him. The last is his strongest hue, tho' the 2d. tinges him very strongly. The first is what I think he would prefer in his heart if he were in the woods where he could see nobody, or in a society of *all whigs*. [Randolph's] opinion always makes the majority, & that the President acquiesces *always* in the majority; consequently that the government is now solely directed by him. . . . I have kept on terms of strict friendship with him hitherto, that I might make some good out of him, & because he has really some good private qualities. But he is in a station infinitely too important for his understanding, his firmness, or his circumstances.[2]

Confronted with this complete exposition of the political scene and blueprint for Republican strategy in the future, Madison lost no time in consulting with Monroe; and then informed Jefferson of the result of their joint lucubrations. As they analyzed the information furnished by their chief, Washington's anxiety to retain him in office meant that he needed him as a shield against republican attacks, and that Jefferson ought to make the most of his strategic value to the President, making "as few concessions as possible that might embarrass the free pursuit of measures which may be dictated by Repub[lican] principles & required by the public good."[3]

The advice was unnecessary. Jefferson had no intention of compromising. When he threw Genêt overboard, it was only after a cool appraisal of the consequences; and a knowledge that he would sink the republican cause if he were retained.

Accordingly, he was particularly careful about the official letter destined to Gouverneur Morris for submission to the French government. He marshaled the facts concerning Genêt with skill and mastery, all the more damning for the restraint with which they were set forth, and made a detailed legal and diplomatic analysis of the points in dispute.[4]

When Jefferson sent the letter he did not know that the *Gironde*—the party to which Genêt belonged—had been ousted from power in France; and that the *Mountain*, with Robespierre at the helm, was now in control. As a matter of fact, even before Jefferson's demand for Genêt's recall was penned, the new French Foreign Minister had written to Genêt, excoriating his activities in America, his arming of privateers and enlistment of volunteers "before even having been recognized by the American Government, and before having received its assent to a measure of such importance." He even charged Genêt with having disregarded his old instructions and subjecting them to a "strange interpretation." This was unfair, to say the least. "You are ordered," he ended peremptorily, "to treat with the Government and not with a portion of the people, to be the mouthpiece of the French Republic before Congress, and not the leader of an American party. . . . We must not, we cannot recognize in America any legitimate authority other than that of the President and of the Congress." And "it seems, Citizen, that since your arrival at Charleston, you have been surrounded by ignorant or very ill intentioned people. . . . Dazzled by a false popularity, you have alienated the one man [Washington] who must be for us the mouthpiece of the American people." [5]

Even the most ardent American Federalist could go no further than that. Obviously, the new French government, though further to the left than the one it had superseded, was willing to throw Genêt to the wolves and withdraw from what had become an untenable position.

Without knowledge of this new and favorable turn of events, the American Cabinet decided on August 23rd to send an official demand for Genêt's recall.[6] But that volatile and jaunty gentleman—in spite of the tongue lashing he had just received from France—refused to trim his sails. On September 18th, he was still arrogantly on the offensive. He demanded from Jefferson the right to appear before Congress. "It is in the name of the French people," he declared shamelessly, concealing the recent change in his instructions, "that I am sent to their brethren—to free and sovereign men: it is then for the representatives of the American People, and not for a single man [Washington] to exhibit against me an act of accusation, if I have merited it. A despot may singly permit himself to demand from another despot the recall of his representative, and to order his expulsion in case of refusal. . . . But in a free State it cannot be so, unless order be entirely subverted." [7]

It was fortunate for Genêt that this insulting communication was forwarded to Virginia during Jefferson's sojourn at Monticello, where it missed him, and did not catch up with him again in Philadelphia until December 2nd; by which time it had become academic.

As though the turmoils of the political scene were not enough, Nature now took a hand. The dreaded yellow fever, whose origin none knew and whose incidence of mortality was appalling, appeared in Philadelphia and made that once bustling city a place of lamentation and death.

First appearing at the end of August, by September 1st hundreds were already stricken and seventy had died. Jefferson hurriedly sent his daughter Polly out of town to his country house on the banks of the Schuylkill, and spent his nights there. But the business of government compelled him to return daily to the half-deserted town.[8]

As the days went on, the fever spread with alarming rapidity, and the ominous carts of death became an only too familiar sight on the cobblestoned streets. The hegira increased its momentum. Even the doctors fled; and of those few who remained, many succumbed to the disease.

In this crisis, Dr. Benjamin Rush rose to heroic proportions. He had shocked and angered the people of Philadelphia by attributing the infection to the bad sanitation of the town; but now he labored night and day to treat the patients abandoned by his fainthearted confreres. His regimen included mercurial doses, cleanliness, avoidance of drafts, rest and a temperate diet. Triumphantly he pointed to the case of an opposition physician who, after dining copiously with Mr. Jefferson in the open air, had come down with the dread disease.[9] That Jefferson, similarly exposed, had not become infected, was overlooked by the thesis-ridden doctor.

The officers of government also took alarm, particularly when Hamilton took ill—so ill, indeed, that for some days his life was despaired of. Washington left for Mount Vernon on September 10th; but he had decided on this before the advent of the plague; and Jefferson found no fault with his going. When Knox decided to go, however, he called it flight. As for Hamilton, he was by this time so embittered that he lost all semblance of his usual humanity. He pooh-poohed the condition of his great enemy, insinuating that he had brought on the fever by his excessive alarm. "A man as timid as he is on the water," he sneered, "as timid on horseback, as timid in sickness, would be a phaenomenon if his courage of which he has the reputation in military occasions were genuine." As for himself, said Jefferson, he would really like to leave; but pride forbade. He had announced that he would not go until the beginning of October, and, he continued, "I do not like to exhibit the appearance of panic." [10]

Nevertheless, he prudently moved his office to his country house, so as not to have to enter the infested town.[11] And, on September 12th, prudence became tinged with that panic he had previously deprecated. The staccato phrases he penned to Madison breathe his urgency. "The fever spreads faster. Deaths are now about 30. a day. It is in every square of the city. All flying who can. Most of the offices are shut or shutting. The banks shut up this day. All my clerks have left me but one: so that I cannot go on with business. I shall therefore set out in 3. or 4. days." [12]

Indeed, he would have quit earlier; but he was "money-bound." He was compelled to obtain from the Bank of the United States a loan of $100 for his traveling expenses.[13] On September 17th he too had quit the plague-stricken city.

He had, however, worked conscientiously up to the very last moment; and left no unfinished business behind. He assured Hammond that if the United States would be unable to obtain compensation from the French for illegally captured British ships, we would assume the burden ourselves.[14] He sent a circular letter to the French consuls warning them that any further violations of our laws and neutrality would be met with revocation of their credentials and criminal prosecutions.[15] He had lost all patience with the French representatives; though careful to "distinguish between the conduct of their nation, which is replete with affection to us, & that of those gentlemen themselves, to which it is difficult to give a proper & yet temperate appellation." [16]

As for Genêt, the head and fount of all the trouble, and blithely persistent in his defiance, Jefferson informed him sternly that a complete account of his illegal proceedings had been forwarded to his government; and that, pending his expected replacement, he would be permitted to continue only so long as his actions "shall be restrained within the limits of the law as heretofore announced to you." [17]

With similar finality, he told the Spanish envoys, Jaudenes and Viar, that their constant complaints about alleged American violations of the frontier were so remarkably worded and their tone so insolent that "the President thought it was high time to come to an eclaircissement [*sic*] with your Government directly, and has taken the measure of sending a courier to Madrid for this purpose." [18]

The situation with respect to the Spanish domains in America had completely changed. When Jefferson proposed that the American envoys abroad offer Spain a guarantee of Louisiana in exchange for the cession of the Floridas, Spain had been on the verge of war with England. Now, however, England and Spain were acting in concert against France; and there were intimations that a strong French fleet had put to sea to assist the Spanish colonies in gaining their independence and would look benevolently on American seizure of the Floridas. Jefferson, therefore, now wrote to Carmichael and Short: "You should not, by any clause of treaty, bind us to guarantee any of the Spanish colonies against their own independance. Nor indeed against any other nation." The coveted plums, he was certain now, would shortly fall into our lap without "our risking the involving ourselves in a war for them." [19]

Jefferson was glad to quit Philadelphia for his beloved Monticello; and the plague was but one of several reasons. He was tired of his job; and had hoped that his vacation would be permanent instead of mere interlude.

As far back as April he had complained to his son-in-law that "I go on like a horse under whip & spur from the start to the poll, without time to look to the right or left, my mind eternally forbidden to turn even for a moment, to any thing agreeable or useful to myself or family." The simile came to him naturally because his stable was much in his mind at the moment. Brimmer had been sold, and Matchless killed in a runaway. Tarquin must also be sold, because his hooves were too tender for the rugged roads of Monticello. That left Jefferson with only a single pair; and he required three. But Philadelphia horseflesh was not up to Virginia standards; would Randolph therefore find him a good mount? [20]

While engaged with matters of state in Philadelphia, his thoughts managed to turn a lot to Monticello. He had hoped to be able to build at least one wing of his house that fall; but now he knew it would have to wait to the following year. He might, he told Randolph, be able to "devote this season to my canal. It is a great object, & enters materially into my plan of renting my estate." Until that was done, he would be unable to start his "pot-ash plan which I have also at heart as a resource for money subsidiary to the farm." [21]

Jefferson had finally become alarmed over the condition of his finances. His lands were not paying their way, though the Randolphs lived most of the year at Monticello and helped manage them in his frequent absences. Plans for improving his crops filled Jefferson's thoughts and his correspondence. A proper rotation that would restore the exhausted soil seemed the answer; but he was diffident over his own judgment in such matters. He therefore appealed to Washington, Madison and his own son-in-law for advice; having a high regard for their practical knowledge of farming.[22]

He also sought information in Pennsylvania and met up with Dr. George Logan, of whom much more will be said in another connection. Logan, it seems, was well versed in the theory and practice of crop rotation, and suggested sowing fields with red clover instead of letting them lie fallow. Jefferson had already known about clover, but thought it kept the land too long out of production. But when he saw the rich fertility of the soil where it had been employed, he became an enthusiastic convert. "For a Virginia table," he explained to Randolph, "it will certainly give unbounded plenty of meats, milk, butter, horse-food, instead of being eternally on the scramble for them as we are in Virginia for the want of winter & summer food." So immersed was he in this pleasant prospect that he rambled on and on until he brought himself short with an apology: "You see how much my mind is gone over to the business of a farmer, for I never know when to finish, if once I begin on the subject." [23]

Yet he found time to make inquiries about that charmed European circle whose memory was already remote and belonged to a fabulous age of innocence. "What is become of Madame de Corny?" he queried Angelica Church, once more back in London. "Where is Mrs. Cosway? I have heard she was become a mother; but is the new object to absorb all her affections?" [24]

To which Angelica mournfully replied: "How changed are the fortunes of those we loved at Paris, and whose welfare were dear to us. Lafayette is in a prison at Magdeburg... Madame de Corney is a widow with a very limited fortune & retired to Rouen. Mrs. Cosway gone into a convent at Genoa. Monsieur de Condorcet under accusation but fortunately escaped & concealed in France." Would Jefferson and Washington do what they could to free Lafayette from prison? [25]

The French Revolution, while convulsing the earth, had also scattered forever that brilliant coterie in whose company Jefferson had taken such delight.

With a sad and heavy heart, Jefferson replied to the tragic budget of news. The influence of the United States had already been employed on behalf of Lafayette; but alas, "that distance & difference of principle give little hold to Genl. Washington on the jailors of Lafayette." As for poor Madame Corny: "Sad times indeed! and much lamented victim! ... and Madame Cosway in a convent! I know that to much goodness of heart, she joined enthusiasm & religion: but I thought that very enthusiasm would have prevented her from shutting up her adoration of the god of the Universe within the walls of a cloyster; that she would rather have sought the *mountain-top*. How happy should I be that it were *mine* that you, she & Mde. de Corny would seek."[26]

But even as he wrote thus wistfully, he must have known that the past could no longer be recaptured; that the dream he envisioned could never come to pass.

Jefferson reached Monticello on September 22, 1793; but he found it impossible to leave the world behind as he had hoped. Mingled with his farming operations were affairs of state that followed him to his retreat. For one thing, Duplaine, the French Consul in Boston, had violated the terms of Jefferson's warning circular; and Jefferson promptly revoked his exequatur, as an example to keep the others within bounds.

For another, Genêt demanded to know what *were* the territorial limits of the United States at sea, within which French captures would be considered as violations of neutrality. This raised an extremely important question that had never been fully and officially decided. With a full awareness of the far-reaching consequences of any decision he might make, Jefferson would have preferred to extend territorial sovereignty as far out to sea as possible; even though such an extension would mean that we would have to pay heavy damages to Great Britain for those of her ships which had been seized within those limits. Up until then, a three-mile limit had been loosely fixed in international practice, as representing the traditional range of coastal artillery. But Jefferson proposed, instead, a distance of three leagues (approximately nine miles); and was willing to compensate Great Britain for seizures within that range, *provided* she would accede to the definition. He was not certain that France would be amenable; but he was prepared, in return, to yield to her the ships already captured, and pay England for them out of American funds.[27]

Unfortunately, none of the great Powers saw eye to eye with Jefferson in this enlargement of the bounds of sovereignty; with the result that, even today, when coastal guns have a range of more than twenty miles, the sacred three-mile limit still applies, with consequent disputes in every naval war.[28]

It was October 25th when Jefferson reluctantly left Monticello to return to official duties. Yet he consoled himself with the knowledge that, within a bare two months, he would retrace his steps; this time, he sincerely believed, forever.

During his absence, both Congress and the seat of government had moved to Germantown, not far from Philadelphia, but far enough from the stricken capital to avoid the plague. Meeting Washington at Baltimore, similarly returning from Mount Vernon, the pair journeyed through extremes of heat, cold, dust and rain. It was good news on arrival to hear that the plague was slackening; but bad news—at least for Jefferson—that Freneau had been compelled to discontinue his controversial *National Gazette*. He had run out of funds; but expressed his willingness to Jefferson to resume publication, if only his subscribers paid up what they owed him. The news was a blow to Jefferson, who had expected the paper to mold public opinion during the forthcoming session of Congress; and he took it upon himself to bring the laggards to life in Albemarle and to obtain new subscriptions.[29]

Jefferson was in a bad temper. The journey had been most wearisome. From Baltimore there had been no stage to Philadelphia available; and he had been "fleeced of seventy odd dollars" by the rapacious owner of a private conveyance to complete his trip. Nor did Germantown help his mood. That small community was jammed to the bursting point with refugees from Philadelphia and rooms were at a premium. As a special favor he was granted a bed in the corner of the public room of the King of Prussia tavern; and he was faced with the prospect of such public sleeping until some of the Philadelphians decided it was safe for them to go home again. Even then, he said angrily, "we must give from 4 to 6 or 8 dollars a week for cuddies [cubicles?] without a bed, and sometimes without a chair or table. There is not a single lodging-house in the place." [30]

But it turned out not so bad after all. He finally managed to obtain decent quarters, not only for himself, but also for Madison and Monroe, both of whom were on their way to attend the session of Congress. While others could not find even "half beds," he was able to get a good room with a fireplace and two beds, with breakfast to boot, though other meals would have to be taken at the tavern across the street.[31]

With all these difficulties, the business of government had to go on. Once again there was a full Cabinet—the vacationers and the escapists had returned; and Hamilton was now fully recovered. Some question was raised as to whether Congress had a legal right on its own to change their place of meeting; but it was decided to let it pass. There was more serious business on tap; notably, the perennial case of Genêt.

That by now thoroughly discredited Minister had been busying himself with a voluminous correspondence, through which he hoped, with not too great finesse, to sway Congress against the President. Jefferson read some of the communications at the Cabinet meeting of November 8th. Washington, thoroughly aroused, put the question whether Genêt should not be summarily expelled from the country without waiting for his recall. As was to be expected, Hamilton and Knox spoke in the affirmative. Randolph, however, did not favor such drastic action; and Jefferson let him carry the argument for the negative.

Unable to come to a conclusion, the matter was adjourned until Washington, scheduled to go to Reading and Lancaster, could return. On November 18th, the Cabinet reconvened. Jefferson now added his weight to Randolph, arguing that an answer was hourly expected from France; and that such a hasty slap in the face might even lead to war. With the Cabinet thus sharply and evenly divided, Washington decided to drop the business.[32]

Next on the agenda was the President's message for the opening of Congress; particularly in relation to the delicate question of Washington's right to proclaim neutrality without the consent of Congress. There was reason, indeed, to fear that Genêt's incessant propaganda on this point might have induced a dangerous attitude on the part of the lawmakers.

Randolph had prepared a statement on the subject for Washington to communicate to Congress but Hamilton attacked it as straddling the issue. He insisted that, though not binding on Congress, the President had a legal right to issue such a proclamation. Both Jefferson and Randolph, however, though discreetly silent as to the *past* proclamation, opposed any further presidential declaration as to a *future* course of neutrality. Jefferson, as a matter of fact, wanted no statements to be issued at all, preferring to keep the warring Powers "doubtful & to come & bid for our neutrality." Washington intervened to deny that he had any intentions of binding Congress, or that his proposed additional proclamation looked beyond the first day of its meeting. Yet, when it came to drafting this all-important section of his message, he asked Hamilton, rather than Jefferson, to do it.[33]

It was finally decided that Randolph should prepare the opening speech, and Jefferson the section on foreign affairs. As might have been expected, Jefferson was strong enough in his denunciation of Genêt, but took great pains to placate France with friendly phrases. He was under no such inhibitions when it came to England, adverting in sharp terms to her restraints on American trade and her spoliations of American ships and commerce.[34]

As might equally have been expected, Hamilton opposed the message "*in toto*." He denied that we were under obligations to France and averred that the contrast in tone between the paragraphs on France and on England was tantamount to a declaration of war on the latter. "In complaisance to him," Jefferson wrote later, he struck out some of the harsher expressions and modified others; without, however, modifying Hamilton's intransigence in the least. Knox obediently followed his master's voice; and even Randolph, though agreeing with Jefferson on the main issue, thought that the documents which Jefferson had wished to append for the information of Congress ought to be kept secret. For once, Washington sided vehemently with Jefferson. *All* the papers, he insisted, must be made public.[35]

By December 2, 1793, the opening date of Congress, the plague had subsided so much that it was deemed safe to return to Philadelphia; and Jefferson left Germantown on November 30th, a few days in advance.

Before he left, he transacted some private business. He ordered a new threshing machine from England—one for which it was claimed that it could thresh 150 bushels of wheat in 8 hours, using 6 horses and 5 men. The inventor had accompanied the machine to New York; and Jefferson asked him to go on to Richmond, both to exhibit it and to manufacture others. The machine, so Jefferson believed, would be "most precious to my future occupation as a farmer."

He had also ordered a telescope and an orrery from London; and was willing to have Giuseppe Ceracchi, the portrait sculptor, make a bust of him. The bust, when completed, became the standard delineation of Jefferson in stone.[36]

Jefferson was ever on the lookout for new and improved machines, especially in the field of agriculture. Perhaps the most important invention ever to be placed before him was Eli Whitney's cotton gin. Whitney wanted to patent it and Jefferson, in his official capacity, supplied him with the requisite information. As a private citizen, he submitted a series of searching questions to the inventor. "Has the machine been thoroughly tried in the ginning of cotton, or is it as yet but a machine of theory? What quantity of cotton has it cleaned on an average of several days, & worked by hand, & by how many hands? What will be the cost of one of them made to be worked by hand? Favorable answers to these questions would induce me to engage one of them to be forwarded to Richmond for me." [37]

Alert as he was, Jefferson could not foresee *all* the potentialities of this revolutionary invention. He thought of it primarily as an aid to the private ginning of cotton; had he envisaged what it would do to the economy of the South, the shift to a single crop and enormous plantations, the irrevocable fastening of the institution of slavery on the land—with their consequent termination in a bloody civil war—he might well have proposed then and there that the infernal machine be dumped into the deepest recesses of the sea.

Jefferson found comfortable quarters for his final month's sojourn in Philadelphia, at the corner of 7th and Market Streets. He noted with sorrow that Freneau's paper was "put down forever"; but the regret was tempered by the knowledge that John Fenno's *Gazette of the United States* had met with a similar fate.[38]

In spite of the demise of these two controversial sheets, there seemed no lack of others to fill the void, as Jefferson immediately learned to his cost. Two days after his arrival in Philadelphia, the New York *Daily Advertiser* commenced a series of articles that brought his name once more embarrassingly before the public. John Jay and Rufus King, with the advice and consent of Hamilton, had decided to publish the story of Genêt.

This was bad enough, considering that the government had not yet come to a decision to make public the facts; what made it worse—from Jefferson's point of view—was that the articles quoted *him* as the source of their information concerning Genêt's famous remark that he would appeal from the President to the People.[39]

Thus put in the invidious position of aiding and abetting the Federalists, Jefferson faced both denials and attacks from his own party. Dallas was particularly furious, since the articles quoted him on the Genêt episode once removed, with Jefferson again as the reporter.

Dallas promptly wrote to Jefferson, citing the offending article, and demanding to know "how far it was authorized by you." [40] Jefferson maintained a discreet silence; though trying at the same time to give the impression that he had been misquoted and that Genêt had never made the remark. Dallas himself, eying warily the repercussions to the republican cause in Pennsylvania, issued a flat denial to the newspapers. What Genêt had actually said, Dallas asserted, was that he would submit his case to *Congress*, as the "only constituted body" of the American people.[41]

This would have been all very well had not Jefferson some months before written flatly to Madison: "You will see much said & again said, about [Genêt's] threat to appeal to the people. I can assure you it is a fact." [42]

But the saga of Genêt was fast coming to a close. France was already sending a replacement in the person of M. Fauchet, with instructions to disavow Genêt's conduct and send him back under arrest. He emitted one last gasp, however, before Fauchet arrived. On December 20th, he forwarded to Jefferson a translation of the instructions he had originally received from France, and demanded that the President officially lay them before Congress. Jefferson sent the communication along to Washington, who replied with considerable vexation: "Every day, more & more, discovers the intention of this Agent to perplex this Government, & to scatter thick & wide the seeds of dissention." [43]

Thus armed, and on the very last day of his official life, Jefferson returned the documents to Genêt with a cold rebuke: "Your functions as the missionary of a foreign nation here, are confined to the transactions of the affairs of your nation with the Executive of the United States . . . and that the President must be left to judge for himself what matters his duty or the public good may require him to propose to the deliberations of Congress." [44]

Genêt was extremely fortunate that Washington was not vindictive. When Fauchet shortly thereafter arrived, with instructions for Genêt's arrest, Washington refused to honor them. Genêt married Cornelia Clinton, the daughter of Governor Clinton of New York, and prudently decided to remain in the country he had flouted, rather than face the chance of the guillotine in France. He even took up farming; emerging from obscurity but once in 1797 to denounce Jefferson as "the real author of all my ills" and the man who, while pretending aid and friendship, had secretly sabotaged all his efforts.[45]

The Congress which convened in Philadelphia during the final days of Jefferson's office was, according to him, "a fuller & more equal representation of the people, and likely I think, to approach nearer to the sentiments of the people in the demonstration of their own." [46] What he meant was that the Republican party had gained appreciably in strength in the new Congress.

As the last day of the year approached, Jefferson began to pack his personal effects and wind up his affairs, both personal and official. Washington made one final attempt to change his mind, but Jefferson was immovable. On December 23rd, he placed on board a sloop bound for Richmond some fifty to sixty packages of books and furniture not already shipped; and ordered his horses to meet him at Fredericksburg on January 12th.[47]

But the vessel was dilatory in sailing and became icebound in the river; with the result that Jefferson had to wait until the following spring for the receipt of his possessions at Monticello.[48]

In like manner he wound up his affairs in the State Department, turning over a statement of his accounts and all unfinished business to Washington, together with a formal letter of resignation.[49]

His statement of accounts is of particular interest. The *domestic* expense of the State Department, including his own salary of $3,500, office salaries, rent, firewood, newspapers, stationery, and a sizable item for the advertisement and printing of the laws of Congress, came to the staggering total of $8,151.67. The cost of the *foreign* service was considerably greater—since it included the salaries and expenses of the ministers, agents and other diplomatic representatives at a number of expensive courts. This ran to $57,847.82.[50]

On January 5, 1794, Jefferson bade good-by to his friends and colleagues, packed Washington's gracious letter of regret over his resignation into his bags, and clattered out of Philadelphia—to the best of his knowledge and belief, forever.[51]

Jefferson departed with a feeling of futility and a profound sense of defeat. His approximate four years in office had been distasteful to him—compounded of long hours at his desk, arid endeavors and constant personal and political bickerings. He had watched with the extremes of anguish and alarm the steady advancement of Alexander Hamilton to a position of commanding importance in the Administration; he had noted the corruption of Congress and the rise of an era of unrestrained speculation; he had seen what he thought to be the subversion of the original principles of the Revolution in favor of a despotical, monarchical-trending State; he had witnessed what he also thought was the succumbing of such once impregnable bastions of liberty as Washington and Adams to the prevailing trend; he had traced the conversion of the Constitution to an instrument for the suppression of the States and of the agricultural interest; and even the glorious Revolution in France had shifted, during his term of office, to something which he was more and more compelled to admit was not the simon-pure article of its nascent days.

For a man as sensitive as he was to public criticism, and who had never forgotten the abortive attempt to criticize his administration as Governor of Virginia, he had now been subjected to such a barrage of abuse and twistings of every act and motive as to make that other seem kindly praise in comparison. He panted for home and the anonymity of the private citizen. He was finished with public affairs and public squabbles.

In reality, he had been a truly great Secretary of State. Coming into a novel office and at the most trying of times, he had forged an instrument, and laid down lines of policy which were to stand the new nation in good stead for all the years to come. In spite of constant Cabinet quarrels, in spite of seemingly irreconcilable doctrines, he and Hamilton had not been as far apart as either thought on matters of foreign relations. Nor had Washington, as to his heated imagination it sometimes appeared, been invariably on the other side of the fence. Washington had handled with surpassing skill the team of spirited and strongly individualistic men who had made up his Cabinet; and extracted from them those policies and measures which best fitted the country in its dangerous and unprotected situation in a world at war.

Neutrality—whether called by that name or not—was no mere dogma proclaimed as an eternal principle; it was a special doctrine for a special occasion; and both Jefferson and Hamilton were agreed upon the fact, if not the public utterance. One false step, and the experiment that was America might well have vanished from the earth; and Jefferson, for all his personal hatred of England and friendliness toward France, saw to it in his formal relations that we did not take that false step. He pressed his points against England with vigor and dignity, yielding nothing of our rights, yet refraining from the last resort of war. Even with Spain, where his intransigence peeped through the diplomatic façade on several occasions, he managed to withdraw in time when the tide of world affairs made it inadvisable to proceed to extremes. With France, he never feared the outbreak of hostilities; and if his fixed approval of her Revolution sometimes led him into embarrassing situations, here again he was able to extricate himself before it was too late.

What the United States required more than anything else was peace. Jefferson realized it and so did Hamilton. But it is possible that, with a more belligerent and less subtle individual at the head of the State Department, we might have been precipitated, without quite knowing how we got there, into a state of war with some great European power, or combination of powers. The results would have been catastrophic.

But of all this Jefferson took no heed as he drove steadily toward Monticello. In his heart was bitterness at what lay behind; and joy at what beckoned ahead.

Notes, Chapters 1-38

CHAPTER 1

1 Jefferson to Thomas Adams, Feb. 20, 1771; *Works*, Ford, II, 5. The allusion, of course, is to Lawrence Sterne's *Tristram Shandy*.
2 Autobiography, *Works*, Ford, I, 3.
3 *Va. Mag.*, II, 61.
4 *Va. Mag.*, XV, 134.
5 *Va. Mag.*, XXIII, 19.
6 Will of Christopher Branch, dated June 20, 1678, and probated Feb. 20, 1681-82, in which a bequest was made to his granddaughter, Mary, as wife of Thomas Jefferson, and appointing Jefferson as one of his executors; *Va. Mag.*, XXIII, 173.
7 Henrico Co. Records, Va. State Lib., 1677-92, Bks. 1-5.
8 Henrico Co. Records, Va. State Lib., 1677-92, p. 214.
9 *Va. Mag.*, I, 208-11. The inventory was dated Dec. 22, 1697, and the exact sum was £97, 16s, 6½d.
10 *Tyler's Quarterly*, VII, 119.
11 *Va. Mag.*, XXIII, 173-5 n.
12 Autobiography, *Works*, Ford, I, 4.
13 *Secret Diary of Wm. Byrd*, I, 410, 414.
14 Henrico Co. Records, Bk. X, 378.
15 *Va. Mag.*, II, 5.
16 Executive Journals, Va. Council, III, 470, 500.
17 Meade, *Old Churches, Ministers and Families of Va.*, I, 125, 137, 440.
18 Journals, House of Burgesses, 1712-26, p. 293.
19 *Va. Mag.*, II, 296-8.
20 *Va. Mag.*, XXXVII, 163-4.
21 *Tyler's Quarterly*, VII, 121.
22 Henrico Co. Records, 1725-37, p. 293.
23 Jefferson, in his Autobiography, *Works*, Ford, I, 4, speaks of Fields's "numerous descendants."
24 *Vestry Book of Henrico Parish, 1725-37;* entries of Oct. 11, 1731, Oct. 13, 1732, Oct. 12, 1733; pp. 7, 10, 15.
25 Randall, *Life of Jefferson*, I, 13.
26 Autobiography, *Works*, Ford, I, 4.
27 Inventory of Peter Jefferson's Estate, filed Aug. 17, 1757; Albemarle Co. Will Book, No. 2, p. 41.
28 Peter Jefferson's MS. Acct. Bk.; entry under year, 1728; Huntington Lib.
29 *Ibid*, 1731-2.
30 Autobiography, *Works*, Ford, I, 4.
31 MS. Will, Va. State Lib.
32 Chastellux, *Travels in North America* (London, 1787), II, 151.
33 *Secret Diary of Wm. Byrd*, I, 153.
34 Henrico Co. Records, 1710-14; Pt. 1, pp. 215-18.
35 Executive Journals, Va. Council, IV, 429.
36 Wm. Darlington, *Memorials of John Bartram and Humphry Marshall*, p. 88.
37 Bond dated Sept. 20, 1737; Goochland Deed Bk., No. 3, Pt. 1, p. 58.
38 Aug. 5, 1737; *Va. Mag.*, XIV, 6-7.
39 Dec. 19, 1738; *Va. Mag.*, XIV, 239.
40 May 5, 1741; *Va. Mag.*, XV, 120-1.
41 Goochland Deed Bk., No. 16, p. 60.

[42] Mar. 30, 1751; Jefferson Papers, U. of Va On the same day the Council also granted this group 1.790 acres on Tomahawk and Rock Castle Creeks; *ibid.*

[43] Goochland Deed Bk., No. 2, p. 222 See also *Wm. & Mary Quarterly*, Ser. I, v. 5, p. 112.

[44] Goochland Deed Bk., No. 3, Pt. 2, p. 535.

[45] Land roll, 1794, in MS. Farm Book, Mass. Hist. Soc. Actual acreage disclosed is 4,650 acres.

[46] Marriage bond dated Oct. 3, 1739; Goochland Co. Court House.

[47] The promise to pay is recited in Isham Randolph's will, dated Apr. 6, 1741; *Va. Mag.*, XIV, 226.

CHAPTER 2

[1] Autobiography, *Works*, Ford, I, 4-5.

[2] Sept., 1744; *Hening's Statutes*, V, 266.

[3] In 1745 the actual count was 106 whites, 177 Negroes and one lone Indian, doubtless also a slave; Alexander Brown, *The Cabells and Their Kin*, p. 53.

[4] E. Woods, *Albemarle County in Virginia*, p. 8.

[5] Albemarle Co. Order Bk., 1744-48, pp. 1-2, 7-8; *Va. Mag.*, XXIII, 75, 173-5.

[6] Goochland Deed Bk., No. 5, pp. 73 ff.

[7] Randall, *Jefferson*, I, 11.

[8] Thomas Anburey, *Travels through ... America*, II, 318-19.

[9] Peter Jefferson's MS. Account Book, 1743-56; Huntington Lib.

[10] *Ibid.* See also Randall, *Jefferson*, I, 11.

[11] See the terms of the grant to Peter Jefferson and others of 50,000 acres, described on p. 8 herein (Chap. I, note 38).

[12] Peter Jefferson's Acct. Bk., Huntington Lib.

[13] For an account of his life, see P. Slaughter, *Memoir of Col. Joshua Fry.*

[14] *The Fairfax Line: Thomas Lewis's Journal of 1746* (John W. Wayland, ed.).

[15] *Ibid*, 8.

[16] *Ibid*, 17.

[17] *Ibid*, 18, 20. Punctuation has been added.

[18] *Ibid*, 24.

[19] *Ibid*, 29-30, 31.

[20] *Ibid*, 73.

[21] S. N. Randolph, *Domestic Life*, 19-20; Dec. 13, 1749, Exec. Journals, Va. Council, V, 310.

[22] July 2, 1749; *ibid*, V, 296-7.

[23] Oct. 15, 1751; *ibid*, V, 354.

[24] Peter Jefferson's Acct. Bk., Huntington Lib.

[25] P. Slaughter, *Joshua Fry*, 35-7.

[26] Peter Jefferson's Acct. Bks., Huntington Lib.

[27] A full account of the excavations is in Marie Kimball, *Jefferson, The Road to Glory*, 21-3.

[28] *Va. Mag.*, IV, 324.

[29] Indenture between Peter Jefferson and Matthew Jordan, as Churchwardens, with William Cabell, dated Apr. 10, 1755, binding out two poor children to him; Emmet Coll., N. Y. Pub. Lib.

[30] Journals, House of Burgesses, 1752-1758, pp. 214, 235. He received £28 for 46 days attendance and 10 days travel; Peter Jefferson's Acct. Bks., Huntington Lib.

[31] Randall, *Jefferson*, I, 18.

[32] *The Douglas Register*, 1750-97 (Wm. Jones, ed.), 5.

[33] Peter Jefferson's Acct. Bks., 1754; Huntington Lib.

[34] Jefferson to Adams, June 11, 1812; *Works*, Ford, XI, 250-5.

CHAPTER 3

[1] Inventory dated Apr. 13, 1758; Albemarle Co. Will Bk., No. 2, pp. 41-7.

[2] Will dated July 13, 1757; probated Oct. 13, 1757; Albemarle Co. Will Bk., No. 2, 32-4.

[3] Dr. Walker practiced medicine only intermittently. By his marriage to a wealthy

widow in 1741 he had found himself in possession of 15,000 acres in Albemarle, on which he built Castle Hill. He took part in Braddock's expedition and later became active in politics, entering the Va. House of Burgesses and the Council of State, and joining in the revolutionary agitation as a member of the Convention of 1775 and the Committee of Safety. He died in 1794, aged 79. For an account of his life see Natalie J. Disbrow, "Thomas Walker of Albemarle," in the *Papers of the Albemarle Co. Hist. Soc.*, I (1940-41). John Harvie had come to Virginia from Scotland in 1730 and obtained an estate of 2,500 acres near the Randolphs, on which he built Belmont. He was one of the first to practice law in Albemarle, but his chief activities were mercantile and land-speculative. He died in 1767. See Woods, *Albemarle Co. in Va.*, 224-5. Harvie's accounts as executor, extending from 1757 to 1765, are in his Acct. Bk. on deposit in the Huntington Lib. The most interesting item involves the sale of "3 harps," evidently purchased originally for the musical education of Peter Jefferson's daughters. Court settlements of the estate in 1760 may be found in Albemarle Co. Will Bk., No. 2, 83-7 and, from 1759 to 1761, in manuscript form in the Mass. H. S. Dr. Walker's accounts are in the Rives Coll., LC.

[4] John Harvie's Acct. Bk., Huntington Lib.

[5] Jefferson to T. J. Randolph, Nov. 24, 1808; *Writings*, Mont., XII, 196.

[6] Hening's *Statutes*, VI, 568; VII, 240.

[7] The story of the "Parson's Cause" is adequately given in H. J. Eckenrode, *Separation of Church and State in Virginia.* For the details of Maury's career, see J. Fontaine and A. Maury, *Memoirs of a Huguenot Family*, and "A Dissertation on Education..." (H. D. Bullock, ed.) in *Papers of the Albemarle Co. Hist. Soc.*, II (1941-42). More data may be found in the unpublished papers of the Maury Deposit at U. of Va. His obituary, laudatory in tone, appeared in the *Va. Gazette* of Aug. 24, 1769.

[8] Fontaine and Maury, *supra*, 342. Jefferson devoted a whole section of his *Notes on Va.* to the subject, and numerous discussions in his correspondence disclose his abiding interest in the matter.

[9] Maury to Robert Jackson, July 17, 1762; edited by H. D. Bullock as "A Dissertation on Education..." See Note 7, *supra*. The MS. letter is in U. of Va.

[10] Maury to Elizabeth Herndon, June 1, 1827; *Intimate Virginiana* (A. F. Maury, ed.), 13.

[11] There is a short biographical notice of Dabney Carr in *Va. Mag.*, II, 225-6.

[12] Anne Maury's Diary, Oct. 25, 1831; *Intimate Virginiana*, 18. Jefferson considered this period as the happiest of his life; Jefferson to James Maury, Jr., Apr. 25, 1812; *Works*, Ford, XI, 239-44; also same to same, July 20, 1804: "I have found in my progress through life that the friendships of our earliest years are those which are the deepest seated..."; Jefferson Papers, LC., v. 142, p. 24638.

[13] John Harvie's Acct. Bk. for Peter Jefferson's Estate; Huntington Lib. Entries of Feb. 28, 1759 and Aug. 29, 1760.

[14] *Ibid*; entry of Oct. 24, 1759: "for teaching 5 Children 6 Mo. to dance"—£7, 10. See also the settlement of Harvie's accounts with the Estate (1759-63) in the Jefferson Papers, Mass. H. S.

[15] Jefferson to Wm. Wirt, Aug. 5, 1815; *Works*, Ford, XI, 415 n. See also *Private Correspondence of Daniel Webster*, I, 364 ff. But Jefferson's memory failed him when he told Webster in 1824 that he was only fifteen at the time, and that he was already on his way to college when he met Henry at the Christmas party.

[16] Jefferson to Harvie, Jan. 14, 1760; *Works, Ford*, I, 433-4.

[17] *Priv. Corresp. of Daniel Webster*, I, 364 ff. Also *Wm. & Mary Quart.*, ser. 2, I, 27-42. Tuition and board cost $75 a year; John Harvie's Accounts, Albemarle Will Bk., No. 2, 83-7.

[18] *Notes on Va.*, Query XV; *Works*, Ford, IV, 70.

[19] *Ibid.*

[20] *Ibid.*

[21] *Wm. & Mary Quart.*, ser. 1, III-V, IX, XVI, XIX, *passim*. See also R. Goodwin, *A Brief & True Report concerning Williamsburg; Historical Collections...* (W. S. Perry, ed.), I, 517; H. B. Adams, *The College of William and Mary.*

[22] Autobiography, *Works*, Ford, I, 5-6. Jefferson erroneously dates Small's departure for England as 1762. See also Jefferson to L. H. Girardin, Jan. 15, 1815; *Writings*, Mont., XIV, 231-2.

[23] *An Island in the Moon* is in the Nonesuch edition of Blake's *Works*. See also Bernard

Blackstone, *English Blake* (Cambridge, 1949) for an account of the Lunar Society. For further information on Small, see "Memoir of John Page," in *Va. Hist. Register*, III, 150, referring to him as "the great Dr. Small, of Birmingham, the darling friend of Darwin"; *Tyler's Quarterly*, II, 287; Stephen to Edward Hawtrey, Mar. 26, 1765, in Wm. & Mary College Papers, Folder 12.

[24] Jefferson Papers, LC., v. 1. The political portion only is in *Works*, Ford, II, 99-100. The original has recently been discovered in Birmingham, and is printed in *Wm. & Mary Quart.*, ser. 3, IV, 508-11.

[25] "Memoir of John Page," in *Va. Hist. Register*, III, 151.

[26] *Ibid*, 147.

[27] L. G. Tyler, *The Letters and Times of the Tylers*, I, 55. For additional stories of Jefferson's close application to his books see T. J. Randolph's MS. Memoirs, U. of Va. and R. B. Davis, *Francis Walker Gilmer*, 350.

[28] Jefferson to J. C. Cabell, Jan. 24, 1816; *Writings*, Mont., XIV, 413.

[29] Jefferson to Rev. Jason Chamberlayne, July 1, 1814; Jefferson Papers, LC., v. 201, p. 35818. To the same effect see his letter to John Smith, May 5, 1802; *ibid*, v. 123, p. 21201; to John Brazier, Aug. 24, 1819; *Writings*, Mont. XV, 208-9.

CHAPTER 4

[1] Autobiography, *Works*, Ford, I, 6.

[2] Jefferson to John Sanderson, Aug. 31, 1820; Jefferson Papers, LC., v. 218, pp. 38932-4. See also his letter to L. H. Girardin, Jan. 15, 1815; *Writings*, Mont., XIV, 231-2.

[3] A. Burnaby, *Travels through North America*, 53.

[4] Jefferson to Sanderson, *supra*, gives a short biographical sketch of Wythe. For estimates see Burnaby, *supra; Works*, Ford, I, 6; *ibid*, XI, 158-9; Jefferson to Wm. Duval, June 14, 1806; Jefferson Papers, LC., v. 159, p. 27898.

[5] Jefferson to Duval, *supra*. Duval to Jefferson, June 19, 1806; Jefferson Papers, LC., v. 159, p. 27915. The Jefferson Papers has also a copy of Wythe's will, and notice of its probate; v. 159, pp. 27971-2.

[6] Jefferson to Thomas Turpin, Feb. 5, 1769; *Two Letters from Thomas Jefferson to his Relatives, the Turpins*... (Marie Dickore, ed.), 8-9. Thomas Turpin had married Mary Jefferson, Jefferson's aunt. Turpin had written Jefferson to place his son, Philip, in his office. Jefferson refused for the reason stated and because he had no room. Whether it was because of this refusal or not, Philip gave up the idea of studying law, and took up medicine instead.

[7] R. B. Davis, *Francis Walker Gilmer*, 350.

[8] Schedule for Bernard Moore, enclosed in letter from Jefferson to John Minor, Aug. 30, 1814; *Works*, Ford, XI, 420-1.

[9] Feb. 10, 1814; *Writings*, Mont., XIV, 85. One commonplace book is in the Library of Congress, and has been published and edited by Gilbert Chinard; another, consisting of 2018 items, is in the Huntington Library. Other law notes and cases may be found in Jefferson Papers, LC., v. 233, *passim*.

[10] Jefferson to John Page, Dec. 25, 1762; *Works*, Ford, I, 436.

[11] The MS. draft of the "Bill for proportioning crimes and punishments" is in Jefferson Papers, LC., v. 232, pp. 42052-8, and contains notes based on Coke. For his later estimate of Coke see Jefferson to Peter Carr, May 8, 1791; Jefferson Papers, U. of Va.

[12] Jefferson to Horatio G. Spafford, Mar. 17, 1814; *Writings*, Mont., XIV, 118-20.

[13] See A. F. Tytler, *Life of Lord Kames* (2 v., 1807) for details of his career.

[14] Jefferson to Peter Carr, June 22, 1792; *Writings*, Mont., VIII, 384.

[15] Jeffersons *Commonplace Book* (Chinard, ed.), 107-8.

[16] *Ibid*, 116-17. Jefferson's constitutional aversion to entails received additional nourishment from his readings in Sir John Dalrymple, *An Essay towards a General History of Feudal Property in Great Britain*, London, 1757; *ibid*, 135-50. In this volume may also be traced some of the roots of Jefferson's lifelong belief that all ills in England were attributable to the Norman Conquest.

[17] Jefferson to W. Taylor, Feb. 13, 1821; MS., N.Y.H.S. *Wm & Mary Quart.*, ser. I, v. 20, p. 146; v. 25, p. 161. Jefferson to Thomas McCauley, June 14, 1819; copy in Jefferson Papers, LC., v. 215, p. 38450; original in Jefferson-Short Papers, Wm. & Mary College.

[18] Jefferson to John Walker, Sept. 3, 1769; Franklin Papers, Yale Univ.

[19] For accounts of Fauquier see Fairfax Harrison in *Fauquier Hist. Soc. Bull.*, No. 4, 343-50; John Burk, *Hist. of Va.*, III, 333-4.

[20] Jefferson to L. H. Girardin, Jan. 15, 1815; *Writings*, Mont., XIV, 231-2. The date of the introduction must be taken as 1762 or later, since Jefferson specifically declares that Wythe also was one of his sponsors. In his Autobiography (*Works*, Ford, I, 6) Jefferson mentions only Small, but by that time his memory was weaker.

[21] Jefferson to Girardin, *supra*.

[22] MS. Memoirs of T. J. Randolph; Edgehill Randolph Papers, U. of Va.

[23] Jeff. to Dr. Thomas Walker, Jan. 18, 1790; Jefferson Papers, LC., v. 53, pp. 9067-70.

[24] Burk, *Hist. of Va.*, III, 140-1.

[25] R. A. Brock, *Virginia and Virginians*, 58-9.

[26] Bishop Meade, *Old Churches... of Va.*, I, 99.

[27] Dec. 25, 1762; *Works*, Ford, I, 434-9.

[28] Jan. 20, 1763; *ibid*, I, 439-41; but not sent until two months later, with postscripts.

[29] Postscripts to above of Jan. 20, 1763, dated Feb. 12th and Mar. 11th, 1763; Franklin Papers, Yale Univ.

[30] *Works*, Ford, I, 441-4.

[31] Jefferson to Wm. Fleming [Sept.], 1763; *ibid*, I, 444-6.

[32] Oct. 7, 1763; *ibid*, I, 446-7.

[33] Jan. 19, 1764; *ibid*, I, 447-8; original in Franklin Papers, Yale Univ.

[34] Mar. 20, 1764; *ibid*, I, 450-2. A curious error has crept into many of the biographies of Jefferson to the effect that he had been invited to attend Rebecca Burwell's wedding as best man (see, for example, Chinard's *Jefferson*, 17). The error is based on a wrong reading of Jefferson's letter to Page, Apr. 9, 1764 (*Works*, Ford, I, 452-3) in which he tells the story of his becoming "bridesman" at the wedding of "B——y" and "B——d." But these cryptic names are in fact "Betsey" Yates and William "Bland" (see references to this marriage in the letter to Fleming, Mar. 20, 1764; here cited).

[35] Apr. 9, 1764; Franklin Papers, Yale Univ.

[36] Jefferson's Literary Commonplace Book, LC.; printed by Gilbert Chinard as *The Literary Bible of Thomas Jefferson.*

CHAPTER 5

[1] See his letter to John Minor, Aug. 30, 1814, cited in chap. 4, note 8.

[2] For the pertinent literary quotations made by Jefferson in his commonplace book, see Chinard's edition under the title of *The Literary Bible of Thomas Jefferson, passim.*

[3] Chinard, *supra*, 75.

[4] Jefferson purchased an Italian-English dictionary and volumes in Italian on Feb. 4, 1764; *Va. Gazette*, Day Books.

[5] *Works*, Ford, I, 71-2.

[6] MS., U. of Va.

[7] Jefferson to Herbert Croft, Oct. 30, 1798; *Writings*, Mont., XVIII, 361-4. The *Essay* itself is printed in *ibid*, XVIII, 365-411.

[8] His *Commonplace Book* is full of illustrations taken from his readings. Of especial interest is a quotation from Robert Moleworth's *An Account of Denmark:* "All Europe was beholden to the Northern nations for introducing or restoring a constitution of government far excelling all others that we know in the world. It is to the antient inhabitants of these countries, with other neighboring provinces that we owe the original of parliaments, formerly so common, but lost within this last age in all kingdoms but those of Poland, Great Britain and Ireland." (Chinard, *The Commonplace Book of Thomas Jefferson*, 212).

[9] See Jefferson's approving quotations from Sir Henry Spelman, *Glossarium Archaiologicum*, and others in his *Commonplace Book*, and his sharp comments on authors like F. S. Sullivan, who claimed that feudalism had first come to England with the *Saxons* (Chinard, *supra, passim*).

[10] Jefferson to John Cartwright, June 5, 1824; *Writings*, Mont., XVI, 43-4.

[11] Jefferson to Nathaniel Burwell, Mar. 14, 1818; *Works*, Ford, XII, 91.

[12] Feb. 25, 1773; *ibid*, II, 36-7. Certain errors in the printed text have been corrected from Jefferson's duplicate copy in the Jefferson papers, LC.

[13] Aug. 7, 1773; Jefferson Papers, LC., v. 1, p. 81. The MS. is mutilated. It was sent to Jefferson by Charles McPherson with a note of regret and the information that there were no books, dictionaries or grammars in the Gaelic tongue. All that he could send were a Gaelic New Testament and a vocabulary; Aug. 12, 1773; Jefferson Papers, LC., v. 1, p. 82.

[14] Chastellux, *Voyages dans L'Amérique*, II, 40-8.

[15] *Literary Bible*, 40-71.

[16] Jefferson to Wm. Short, Oct. 31, 1819; *Works*, Ford, XII, 140-4. See also "The Morals of Jesus," *Writings*, Mont., XX, Appendix.

[17] Jefferson to Francis Eppes, Jan. 19, 1821; *Writings*, Mont., XV, 305-6. See also John Bernard, *Retrospections of America*, 238.

[18] Fauquier to Board of Trade, June 5, 1765; *Journals of the House of Burgesses, 1761-65*, lxvii-viii.

[19] Fauquier to Board of Trade, *supra;* and *Journals, 1761-65*, p. 358.

[20] W. W. Henry, *Patrick Henry*, I, 80-1, 91-2.

[21] Jefferson was never to modify essentially his estimate of Patrick Henry. See Jefferson to Wm. Wirt, Aug. 5, 1815; *Works*, Ford, XI, 415n.

[22] Autobiography, *Works*, Ford, I, 8.

[23] *Private Correspondence of Daniel Webster*, I, 364 ff. By the time that Jefferson came to put down his impressions of Patrick Henry he had broken with him politically, and this fact, in addition to the usual errors due to failing memory, must be taken into account.

[24] Burk, *Hist. of Va.*, III, 309; Wirt, *Patrick Henry*, 65, on Tyler and Jefferson's accounts to Wirt. Jefferson's statement, dated Aug. 4, 1805, when Wirt was gathering materials for his biography, includes his general estimate of Henry. After admitting that "he was certainly the man who gave the first impulse to the ball of revolution," and agreeing to his good humor, oratorical qualities, and "knowledge of the human heart," Jefferson declared that Henry's "judgment in other matters was inaccurate. In matters of law it was not worth a copper. He was avaritious & rotten hearted. His two great passions were the love of money & of fame: but when these came into competition the former predominated." (MS., Jefferson Papers, LC., v. 151, p. 26461.)

[25] Randolph's Essay on the Revolution in Va. is published in *Va. Mag.*, commencing v. 43, pp. 113-38, *et seq.* The original MS. is in Va. Hist. Soc. The account of the French traveler is in *Am. Hist. Rev.*, v. 26, p. 727 *et seq.* Gov. Fauquier, in his detailed report of the proceedings to his home government, discreetly refers merely to Henry's "very indecent language."

[26] Jefferson to Sanderson, Aug. 31, 1820; Jefferson Papers, LC., v. 218, pp. 38932-4. According to Fauquier, in his report to the Board of Trade, *supra*, "the most strenuous opposers of this rash heat were the late Speaker, the king's attorney and Mr. Wythe; but they were overpowered by the young, hot and giddy members."

[27] Fauquier to Board of Trade, *supra.*

[28] Jefferson to Wirt, Aug. 14, 1814; *Works*, Ford, XI, 400-10. In an earlier account to Wirt, dated Apr. 12, 1812, Jefferson says Randolph offered 500 guineas; *ibid*, XI, 226 ff.

[29] Fauquier, *supra;* also Jefferson to Wirt, *supra.* The *Journal* of the House carries under date of May 30, 1765, only the passage of the four resolutions; no mention is made of the fifth. Pursuant to the action taken on the 31st it had been expunged (1761-65, p. 360).

[30] Maury to John Fontaine, Dec. 31, 1765; Fontaine & Maury, *Memoirs of a Huguenot Family*, 424.

[31] Fauquier to Board of Trade, *supra.*

[32] Fauquier to Board of Trade, Nov. 3, 1765; *Journals, House of Burgesses*, lxviii-xxi.

[33] Gov. Bernard to Earl of Halifax, Aug. 15, 1765; cited in Channing, *Hist. of the U. S.*, III, 55.

[34] Randall's *Jefferson* gives the traditional account.

[35] He took with him a letter from Dr. George Gilmer addressed to Dr. John Morgan, dated May 11, 1766; Gratz Coll., Pa. Hist. Soc.

[36] Jefferson to John Page, May 25, 1766; Jefferson Papers, Box 1, N. Y. Pub. Lib.

[37] *Ibid.* The *Virginia Gazette* had announced the repeal on May 2nd, and gleefully chanted that "*Britons never will be slaves.*" And Governor Fauquier watched benignly an illumination and ball at the Capitol building to celebrate the event; *Virginia Gazette*, June 20, 1766.

[38] Jefferson to Francis Willis, July 23, 1766; privately owned; photostat in the Jefferson Project at Princeton Univ.

[39] Randall, *Jefferson*, I, 46.

[40] Jefferson to Elbridge Gerry, June 11, 1812; Franklin Papers, Yale Univ. Jefferson gives the date of their meeting in N. Y. as 1764, but this is wrong.

CHAPTER 6

[1] *Jefferson's Garden Book* (E. M. Betts, ed.), 1.

[2] *Ibid*, 4, 7.

[3] Jefferson's Case Book and Fee Books, Huntington Lib.; also Memorandum Books, 1767-1770; LC. Other legal data may be found in Mass. H. S.

[4] Memo. Bks., 1767-1770; LC.

[5] *Ibid.*

[6] Pocket Acct. Bk., 1771; Mass. H. S.; Fee Bk., Huntington Lib.

[7] *Va. Gazette*, Sept. 13, 1770.

[8] *Va. Gazette*, May 20, 1773; printed in *Works*, Ford, II, 38-40.

[9] *Works*, Ford, I, 470-81.

[10] Randall's *Jefferson*, I, 50; based on Madison's and Wirt's reminiscences.

[11] *Va. Mag.*, XLIII, 123.

[12] Jeff's acct. books for these years, 1767-70, are in LC.

[13] *Ibid.*

[14] N. P. Trist's Memoranda; Randall's *Jefferson*, I, 131.

[15] The best study of Jefferson as architect is Fiske Kimball, *Thomas Jefferson, Architect.* See also Lambeth and Manning, *Thomas Jefferson as an Architect and Designer of Landscapes;* and I. T. Frary, *Thomas Jefferson, Architect and Builder.*

[16] *Garden Book*, Aug. 1, 1767.

[17] Memo. Bks., 1767-1770; LC. In his last entry for 1770, Jefferson wrote down "Hermitage," then crossed it out and substituted "Monticello" again.

[18] Fiske Kimball, *supra*, 23, points out Palladio's enthusiasm for the Roman villa; and K. Lehmann, *Thomas Jefferson, American Humanist*, amplifies on the theme. Quotation from Palladio is in Bk. II, Chap. 12 of Leoni's translation.

[19] Memo. Bks., 1767-70, LC., *passim.* He actually ordered the clavichord in 1771; Jefferson to Thomas Adams, Feb. 20, 1771; *Works*, Ford, II, 5.

[20] Memo. Bks., 1767-70, LC.; *Garden Bk.*, entries for 1769.

CHAPTER 7

[1] W. S. Johnson to W. Pitkin, Feb. 12, 1767; *Mass. H. S. Colls.*, 5th ser., IX, 215.

[2] Acct. Bks., 1767-1770; LC.

[3] *Journals, House of Burgesses*, 1766-69, p. 189.

[4] Jefferson to Wm. Wirt, Aug. 15, 1815; *Works*, Ford, XI, 414n.

[5] *Ibid*, I, 7. No slave might be set free "upon any pretence whatsoever, except for some meritorious services, to be adjudged and allowed by the Governor and Council." Acts of the Assembly, 1769.

[6] Jefferson to Wirt, Aug. 14, 1814; *Works*, Ford, XI, 407.

[7] *Journals, House of Burgesses*, 1766-69, p. 215.

[8] *Ibid*, p. 218.

[9] K. M. Rowland, *George Mason*, I, 136-40.

[10] Burk's *Virginia*, III, 345-9, n.; *Va. Gazette*, May 25, 1769.

[11] Lee to Theodorick Bland, Aug. 21, 1770; *The Bland Papers*, I, 29. But the northern colonies seemed to be able to enforce the Associations much more effectively.

[12] Acct. Bks., 1767-1770; LC.

[13] Earl of Hillsborough to Botetourt, May 13, 1769; *Journals, House of Burgesses*, 1766-69, p. 227.

[14] *Journals, House of Burgesses, ibid*, p. 233.

[15] Autobiography, *Works*, Ford, I, 9.

[16] *Journals, House of Burgesses*, 1766-69, p. 310.

[17] Invoice of books purchased from T. Cadell, London; Va. H. S.

[18] *Commonplace Book*, 175-6.

[19] *Ibid*, 181.

[20] *Ibid*, 182-5.

[21] Jefferson Papers, LC., v. 1, p. 1; undated.

[22] *Commonplace Book*, Art. 754.

[23] *Ibid*, Art. 775-802.

[24] Jefferson to Thomas Mann Randolph, May 30, 1790, *Works*, Ford, VI, 61-5; Jefferson to Wm. Duane, Sept. 16, 1810; *Writings*, Mont., XII, 413-17.

[25] T. J. Randolph MS., Edgehill-Randolph Papers, U. of Va., *Va. Gazette*, Feb. 22, 1770: "We hear from Albemarle that about a fortnight ago the house of Thomas Jefferson, Esq.; in that county, was burnt to the ground, together with all his furniture, books, papers, &c. by which that Gentleman sustains a very great loss. He was from home when the accident happened."

[26] Feb. 21, 1770; original MS. in Franklin Papers, Yale Univ., printed in *Works*, Ford, I, 467-70.

[27] Thomas Nelson, Jr., to Jefferson, Mar. 6, 1770; Jefferson Papers, Mass. H. S. See also John Page to Jefferson, Mar. 6, 1770; *ibid*. George Wythe helped out by sending grape vines, nectarine and apricot grafts for planting; Mar. 9, 1770; *ibid*.

[28] Jefferson to James Ogilvie, Feb. 20, 1771; *Works*, Ford, II, 5-7. The original is in Jefferson Papers, Mass. H. S. The date of his removal to Monticello is given in his Acct. Bk. for 1770, LC.

[29] Jefferson Papers, LC., v. 1, pp. 53, 54.

[30] Jefferson's Acct. Bk., 1770, LC.

[31] Autobiography, *Works*, Ford, I, 8.

[32] John Wayles to Jefferson, Oct. 20, 1772; Jefferson Papers, Mass. H. S.

[33] *Wm. & Mary Quart.*, ser. II, v. 1, p. 39.

[34] Randall's *Jefferson*, I, 63. Martha's housewifely accounts are entered in Jefferson's case book, on blank pages in the back; LC. Aside from two short notes of invitation, this is the only sample of Martha's hand that has survived.

[35] Jefferson to Ogilvie, Feb. 20, 1771; Jefferson Papers, Mass. H. S., and *Works*, Ford, II, 5-7.

[36] Jefferson to Thomas Adams, Feb. 20, 1771; *Works*, Ford, II, 3-5. See also Mrs. Drummond to Jefferson, Mar. 12 [1771]; Jefferson Papers, Mass. H. S., for an old lady's quaint encouragement of Jefferson's suit.

[37] There is an extensive collection of Jefferson's architectural drawings for Monticello in existence. The main body is in Mass. H. S., with additions in U. of Va. and Huntington Lib. The most important of these are reproduced, with illuminating comments, in Fiske Kimball's *Thomas Jefferson, Architect*.

[38] Fiske Kimball, *supra*, figs. 23 and 32.

[39] Jefferson's Acct. Bk., 1771; Mass. H. S. His Gothic landscapes were in line with the prevailing rage in England.

[40] *Garden Book*, 23, dated Sept. 7, 11, 1771.

[41] Agreement dated Apr. 11, 1771, recorded in the General Court Apr. 12th; *Works*, Ford, II, 8-9. Ford gives the sum to be paid by Jefferson's estate as £800, but this is an error.

[42] Aug. 25, 1775; Jefferson Papers, LC., v. 1, p. 162. This section is omitted from the letter printed in *Works*, Ford, II, 133-7.

[43] Acct. Bk., 1775, under date of Aug. 17th; Huntington Lib.

[44] Acct. Bk., 1771, Mass. H. S.

[45] The marriage bond is in Va. State Lib. The other items are in Jefferson's Acct. Bk., 1771; Mass. H. S.

[46] The various items of expense are listed in Acct. Bk., 1772; Mass. H. S.

[47] Randall's *Jefferson*, I, 64. The next day, Jan. 26, 1772, Jefferson recorded in his *Garden Book* that the snow lay three feet deep in Albemarle, "the deepest snow we have ever seen."

CHAPTER 8

[1] Jefferson's Fee Book, Huntington Lib., shows undated entries under the heading, "John Skelton, son of Bathurst, in acct. with Th. Jefferson, his guardian in right of Martha, his wife." On Feb. 26, 1772, there is an entry of "goods imported for Mrs. Jefferson & J. Skelton from Cary & Co." This evidence of the child's continued existence at the time of

Jefferson's marriage must overweigh the authority of a memorandum in a notebook in the Edgehill-Randolph Papers, U. of Va., made at a much later date, to the effect that young John had died on June 10, 1771.

[2] John Wayles' will, dated Apr. 15, 1760, and proved July 7, 1773; *Va. Mag.*, XXIII, 86.

[3] Autobiography, *Works*, Ford, I, 8.

[4] "List of Mr. Wayles's lands" in Acct. Bk., 1773, LC.

[5] For the various items of the Wayles' estate, see Jefferson's Acct. Bk., 1764-79, Huntington Lib.; his Acct. Bk., 1773, LC.; his Farm Bk., 1774, Mass. H. S.; and Randall's *Jefferson*, I, 65 where, however, the estimate of the estate is considerably exaggerated.

[6] Jefferson to Alexander McCaul, Jan. 4, 1789; to William Jones, Jan. 5, 1789; *Works*, Ford, V, 241-4, 244-50.

[7] Acct. Bk., 1764-79; Huntington Lib.

[8] *Wm. & Mary Quart.*, ser. 2, v. 1, p. 122. Randolph's first term of residence was from Oct. 14, 1771 to Sept. 10, 1772.

[9] See Randolph Jefferson's illiterate, pathetically rambling letters in the Univ. of Va. collections (printed as *Thomas Jefferson and his unknown brother, Randolph,* Bernard Mayo, ed.).

[10] Mar. 30, 1772; Acct. Bk., Mass. H. S., and Jan. 8-11, 1773; Acct. Bk., LC. Also the Farm Bk., 1774, Mass. H. S.; Mar. 31, 1776; Acct. Bk., Mass. H. S.; and Acct. Bk., 1764-69; Huntington Lib.

[11] S. N. Randolph, *Domestic Life of Thomas Jefferson,* 26; also *Garden Bk.*, 40.

[12] Feb. 21, 22, Mar. 1, 1774; Acct. Bk., Mass. H. S.

[13] Mar. 7, 1774; *ibid.*

[14] MS. Reminiscences of Isaac Jefferson; McGregor Coll., U. of Va.

[15] In 1784 Mazzei lamented that "Monticello was a sad place for me, because I often remembered the angelic deceased wife of Jefferson. She vivified that home"; *Wm. & Mary Quart.*, Ser. 2, v. 10, p. 11.

[16] *Private Corresp. of Daniel Webster*, I, 364 ff.

[17] Jefferson to Thomas Adams, Feb. 20, 1771; *Works,* Ford, II, 3-4. The New York merchants had officially abandoned the boycott.

[18] Jefferson to Thomas Adams, June 1, 1771; *Works*, Ford, II, 11-12.

[19] *Journals, House of Burgesses*, 1770-72, pp. 101-2.

[20] MS., Huntington Lib.

[21] Acct. Bk., 1773; LC.

[22] Jefferson to St. George Tucker, May 9, 1798; Coleman-Tucker Coll., Colonial Williamsburg Archives.

[23] Jefferson to Robert Skipwith, Aug. 3, 1771; *Works,* Ford, II, 12-16.

[24] Jefferson to Nathaniel Burwell, Mar. 14, 1818; *Writings,* Mont.

[25] Autobiography, *Works*, Ford, I, 9.

[26] *Ibid*, I, 10.

[27] *Journals, House of Burgesses*, 1773-76, p. 28.

[28] Minutes of the Comm. of Correspondence; *ibid*, pp. 41-64.

[29] Acct. Bk., 1774; Mass. H. S.

[30] Acct. Bks., May 14, Sept. 13, 1772, Mar. 14, 1774; Mass. H. S.

[31] *Wm. & Mary Quart.*, ser. I, v. 14, p. 29.

[32] Acct. Bk., 1773; LC.

[33] The list of slave occupations is taken from Jefferson's Farm Bk., Mass. H. S.

[34] The names and roll of slave occupations are in the Farm Bk. The sale of Sandy to Col. Chas. Lewis is in Acct. Bk., Jan. 29, 1773; LC. The transactions for 1774-78 are in Acct. Bk., 1764-79; Huntington Lib.

[35] *Journals, House of Burgesses*, 1773-76, p. 116. Hening's *Statutes*, VIII, 450.

[36] Autobiography, *Works*, Ford, I, 12. Randolph's Essay; *Va Mag.*, v. 43, pp. 214-15. Randolph names Charles Lee as Jefferson's coadjutor, but it was very likely R. H. Lee.

[37] Autobiography, *Works*, Ford, I, 12.

[38] Randolph's Essay; *Va. Mag.*, v. 43, pp. 214-15.

[39] Autobiography, *Works*, Ford, I, 12.

[40] *Ibid.* But see *Journals, House of Burgesses*, 1773-76, p. 124, where Edmund Pendleton is given the credit for bringing in the bill. Randolph, however, backs up Jefferson's account with his accustomed cynicism; Essay, *Va. Mag.*, v. 43, p. 215.

[41] Jefferson's Memorandum, "On the instructions given to the 1st delegation of Virginia

to Congress in August 1774"; Jefferson Papers, LC., v. 1, pp. 111-12. See also Autobiography, *Works*, Ford, I, 13.

[42] Jefferson's Memo; *ibid.* Autobiography, *ibid.* For text of the resolution see *Journals, Va. Council*, v. 3, pp. 1588-89.

[43] Acct. Bk., May 28, 1774; Mass. H. S.

[44] Autobiography, *Works*, Ford, I, 13. For St. Anne's Parish, however, it seems that Jefferson and Dr. Walker proclaimed June 23rd as the fast day; *ibid*, II, 41-2. The account given in Webster, I, 364 ff., based on an interview with Jefferson in old age is garbled; it speaks of "Bottetourt" as the Governor involved.

[45] Jefferson's Memo., Jefferson Papers, LC., v. 1, pp. 111-12.

[46] *Works*, Ford, II, 42-5.

[47] Jefferson's Memo., Jefferson Papers, LC., v. 1, pp. 111-12. Sections of this memorandum appear in *Works*, Ford, II, as a footnote to the "Summary View."

[48] Randolph's Essay, *Va. Mag.*, v. 43, p. 131.

[49] "A Summary View," *Works*, Ford, II, 63-89.

CHAPTER 9

[1] Autobiography, *Works*, Ford, I, 14-15; and *ibid*, II, 50. It is interesting to note that Jefferson's MS. Memo. on this period (Jefferson Papers, LC., v. 1, pp. 111-12), written at an earlier period than the Autobiography, makes no mention of Henry's possible inattention to the "Summary View" because of laziness.

[2] Edmund Randolph's Essay; *Va. Mag.*, v. 43, p. 216.

[3] Jefferson's MS. Memo., *supra; Works*, Ford, II, 50. See also Jefferson to Meriwether Jones, Oct. 19, 1804, Jefferson Papers, LC., v. 144, p. 25017, in which he declares that Peyton Randolph laid the "Remonstrance"—as Jefferson termed it—"on the table of the convention for the perusal of the members, and by them justly deemed ahead of the sentiments of the times." In other words, it was never formally submitted for adoption.

[4] *Works*, Ford, II, 50, 53. The two English editions were printed by G. Kearsley, 1774.

[5] Girardin's continuation to Burk's *Hist. of Va.*, IV, 6-7.

[6] "Defects in the associations" [Oct. 1774]; *Works*, Ford, II, 93-4.

[7] Jefferson to Archibald Cary and Benjamin Harrison, Dec. 9, 1774; *ibid*, II, 94-6.

[8] Entry in Acct. Bk., Huntington Lib. for Aug. 11, 1775: "pd James Buchanan freight of my window frames from Norfolk, 18/."

[9] Of 15 candidates, Jefferson received the greatest number of votes—211; Acct. Bk. for 1775, Huntington Lib.

[10] Dunmore to Dartmouth, Dec. 24, 1774; Force, *Archives*, 4 ser., I, 1062.

[11] Acct. Bk., 1775, Huntington Lib.

[12] The entire proceedings of the Richmond Convention are reported in the *Va. Gazette*, Apr. 1, 1775.

[13] There is no contemporary account of Henry's speech. The one that has come down to us is found in Wirt's *Life of Patrick Henry*, 121-3.

[14] Randolph's Essay, *Va. Mag.*, v. 43, p. 223.

[15] *Works*, Ford, II, 96-7.

[16] Acct. Bk., Apr. 7, 1775; Huntington Lib. Garden Bk., 66.

[17] Garden Bk., 47-9, 52-4.

[18] *Memoirs of Philip Mazzei* (trans. by Howard R. Marrano), 193. The *Memoirs* are lively, but must be used with caution. Mazzei tended to exaggeration and self-adulation. A more sober and accurate account of his life is Garlick's *Philip Mazzei, Friend of Jefferson.* More information may be obtained from his papers in the Pisan Archives, recently discovered, and the Jefferson Papers, LC.

[19] Garden Bk., 47-55.

[20] Burk's *Hist. of Va.*, IV, 2-3, 14.

[21] The battles were fought on Apr. 22nd; the news was published in the *Va. Gazette* of Apr. 29th.

[22] Autobiography, *Works*, Ford, I, 17.

[23] *Works*, Ford, II, 101-6; *Journals, House of Burgesses*, 1773-76, pp. 219-21. There is some confusion over Jefferson's authorship, but there seems no reason to deny it.

[24] Autobiography, *Works*, Ford, I, 17.

[25] Acct. Bk., 1775; Huntington Lib.

[26] The trip route and expenses are noted in Acct. Bk., 1775, Huntington Lib.

[27] George Reade to Mrs. Reade, May 18, 1775; *Letters, Members of the Cont. Cong.* (E. C. Burnett, ed.), I, 92.

[28] *Journals of the Cont. Cong.* (W. C. Ford & J. C. Fitzpatrick, eds.), II, 101.

[29] John Adams to Abigail Adams, Sept. 25, 1774, Oct. 9, 1774: *Letters of John Adams to his Wife* (C. F. Adams, ed.), I, 29, 34.

[30] R. H. Lee to Wm. Lee, May 10, 1775; *Letters, Members of the Cont. Cong.*, I, 89-90. See also Silas Deane to Mrs. Deane. June 3, 1775; *Colls. of Conn. Hist. Soc.*, II, 252-3.

[31] Acct. Bk., June 27, 1775; Huntington Lib.

[32] J. Adams to T. Pickering, Aug. 6, 1822; Adams, *Works*, II, 514n.

[33] *Journals, Cont. Cong.*, II, *passim.* Autobiography, *Works*, Ford, I, 18-19.

[34] *Works*, Ford, II, 110-25.

[35] For Dickinson's role, see Autobiography, *Works*, Ford, I, 18-19, and endorsement on draft. For Livingston's comment, see Livingston to Lord Stirling, July 4, 1775; quoted in *Works*, Ford, II, 111n.

[36] For an extended consideration of the several drafts see *Papers of Jefferson* (Boyd *et al.*, eds.), I, 187-219.

[37] Autobiography, *Works*, Ford, I, 19.

[38] *Journals, Cont. Cong.*, II, 202, 224; Autobiography, *Works*, Ford, I, 19-20; II, 125-33.

[39] Acct. Bk., 1775; Huntington Lib.

[40] *Journals, Cont. Cong.*, II, 242-3.

[41] Jefferson Papers, LC., v. 1, p. 168.

[42] This section is in *Works*, Ford, II, 133-7. The complete letter is in Jefferson Papers, LC., v. 1, p. 162.

[43] Aug. 31, 1775; Jefferson Papers, LC., v. 1, p. 165.

[44] *Journals, Cont. Cong.*, III, 297, 427, 430-1.

[45] Jefferson to John Page, Oct. 31, 1775; Myers Coll., N. Y. Pub. Lib. Printed in *Works*, Ford, II, 140-1.

[46] Jefferson to Francis Eppes, Nov. 7, 1775; photostat, Misc. Jefferson Papers, LC. The printed version in *Works*, Ford, II, 141-2, contains some minor errors of transcription.

[47] The letter is not extant, but is referred to in Jefferson to Francis Eppes, Nov. 21, 1775; *Works*, Ford, II, 142-3.

[48] Acct. Bk., 1776; Mass. H. S.

[49] Acct. Bk., Jan. 25, 1776; Mass. H. S.; Farm Bk., May, 1775; Mass. H. S.

[50] Jefferson Papers, LC., v. 6, p. 1063.

[51] Acct. Bk., 1776; Mass. H. S.

[52] Jefferson to Thomas Nelson, Jr., May 16, 1776; *Works*, Ford, II, 151.

CHAPTER 10

[1] Page to Jefferson, Apr. 6, 1776; Jefferson Papers, LC., v. 2, p. 215. Jefferson did not receive this letter until May 14th, when he found it in Philadelphia.

[2] *Journals, Cont. Cong.*, IV, 134-6.

[3] R. H. Lee to Patrick Henry, Apr. 20, 1776; *Letters of R. H. Lee* (J. C. Ballagh, ed.), I, 176.

[4] Jefferson to Thomas Nelson, May 16, 19, 1776; *Works*, Ford, II, 151-4.

[5] Jefferson to Dr. James Mease, Sept. 16, 1825, with postscripts and addenda; Jefferson Papers, LC., v. 230, p. 41156. The body of the letter, without the postscripts, is printed in *Works*, Ford, XII, 413-14, but misdated there as Sept. 26th. See also Donaldson, *The House in Which Jefferson Wrote the Declaration* . . . and Acct. Bk., May 23, June 9, 1776; Mass. H. S.

[6] Acct. Bk., May 24, May 31, June 1, 1776; Mass. H. S.

[7] Jefferson Papers, LC., v. 2, p. 225.

[8] Randolph's Essay, *Va. Mag.*, v. 44, p. 43.

[9] *Ibid.* See also Jefferson's *Notes on Va.*, *Works*, Ford, IV, 17-22, for his later considered objections.

[10] Both are printed in *Works*, Ford, II, 158-183.

[11] Among the Jefferson Papers, LC. (v. 234, p. 4193) are some Notes for Va. Const.,

dated June, 1776, which indicate that Jefferson originally intended to throw open the suffrage to "every male citizen of the commonwealth liable to taxes or to militia duty in any county." The regular drafts do not contain this outright declaration for able-bodied, manhood suffrage; but Jefferson was to return at later stages of his life to this earlier concept.

[12] Jefferson to August B. Woodward, Apr. 3, 1825; *Works*, Ford, XII, 407-8. Jefferson bases his recollections on a letter addressed to him by Pendleton which, however, cannot now be found. See also Wythe to Jefferson, July 27, 1776; Jefferson Papers, LC., v. 2, p. 284. Wythe declared that "the system agreed to in my opinion requires reformation. In October I hope you will effect it."

[13] Hening's *Statutes*, IX, 112-19.

[14] Pendleton to Jefferson, Aug. 1, 1776; Jefferson MSS., American Philosophical Soc. Jefferson to Pendleton, Aug. 26, 1776; Washburn Papers, Mass. H. S. (italics added).

[15] The *Declaration of Rights* as finally enacted is in Hening's *Statutes*, IX, 109-12. Mason's first draft is in K. M. Rowland's *George Mason*, I, 240 (facsimile).

[16] Rowland's *Mason*, I, 240.

[17] Rives, *Madison*, I, 142.

[18] *Journals, Cont. Cong.*, V, 425.

[19] Autobiography, *Works*, Ford, I, 23-4; Rutledge to John Jay; *Correspondence... of John Jay* (H. P. Johnston, ed.), I, 66.

[20] Autobiography, *Works*, Ford, I, 24 ff.

[21] Elbridge Gerry to Warren, June 11, 1776; Jas. T. Austin, *Life of Gerry*, I, 191-2.

[22] Adams to Pickering, Aug. 6, 1822; Pickering Papers, Mass. H. S.

[23] Autobiography, Feb. 29, 1776; Adams, *Works*, II, 510-15.

[24] Adams, *Works*, III, 52; II, 510-15. Adams to Pickering, Aug. 22, 1822; *ibid*, II, 514. See also John H. Hazelton, *The Declaration of Independence*, for a discussion of the whole episode.

[25] Autobiography, Adams, *Works*, II, 512. Adams to Pickering, Aug. 22, 1822; *ibid*, II, 514. Jefferson to Madison, Aug. 30, 1823; *Works*, Ford, XII, 306-9. Jefferson to Joseph Delaplaine, Apr. 12, 1817; Jefferson Papers, LC., v. 209, p. 37363. The genesis of the Declaration is painstakingly studied in Carl Becker's *Declaration of Independence;* J. H. Hazelton's *Declaration of Independence;* J. C. Fitzpatrick in *Daughters of the Amer. Revol. Mag.*, v. 55, pp. 363 ff.; and more recently in Julian P. Boyd's important *The Declaration of Independence*, with additional material in Boyd's article in *N. Y. Times*, Apr. 13, 1947.

[26] This highly dramatic description of the scene comes from the letter to Pickering, *supra;* but it is based in all essentials on the chaster version in the Autobiography, *supra.*

[27] Adams, *Works*, III, 21. The fifth member was R. R. Livingston, *not* Harrison. Mr. R., of course, is Edward Rutledge.

[28] Franklin's then domicile is disclosed in a letter from him to Dr. Rush, June 26, 1776, discovered by Lyman H. Butterfield in the Lib. of Cong. and mentioned in the *N. Y. Times* article by J. P. Boyd, *supra.*

[29] Jefferson to Madison, Aug. 30, 1823; *supra.* The appropriate texts of the several drafts of the Declaration are printed in parallel columns in *Works*, Ford, II, 199 ff., with facsimiles. To these must be added what Boyd thinks is a fragment of an even earlier draft; *N. Y. Times*, Apr. 13, 1947; *supra.*

[30] Jefferson to Henry Lee, May 8, 1825; *Works*, Ford, XII, 408-9.

[31] Adams to Pickering, Aug. 22, 1822; Adams, *Works*, II, 514.

[32] For example, Wilson declared: "All men are, by nature, equal and free: no one has a right to any authority over another without his consent: all lawful government is founded in the consent of those who are subject to it: such consent was given with a view to ensure and to increase the happiness of the governed, above what they would enjoy in an independent and unconnected state of nature. The consequence is, that the happiness of the society is the first law of every government."

[33] The quotations are from the Declaration of Independence as finally adopted.

[34] *Journals, Cont. Cong.*, V, 491.

[35] *Journals, Cont. Cong.*, V, 504.

[36] Adams, *Works*, III, 54; Adams to Samuel Chase, July 1, 1776; *ibid*, IX, 415.

[37] Autobiography, *Works*, Ford, I, 32; Adams to Chase, *supra; Journals, Cont. Cong.*, V, 504-5.

[38] Adams to Abigail Adams, July 3, 1776; *Letters of John Adams to his Wife*, I, 124.

[39] Autobiography, *Works*, Ford, I, 32.
[40] Jefferson to Robert Walsh, Dec. 4, 1818; *Writings*, Mont., XV, 175.
[41] Autobiography, *Works*, Ford, I, 32-3; Jefferson to Robert Walsh, *supra*.
[42] Peter Force, *Archives*, 5th ser., I, 119; Charles Biddle, *Autobiography*, 86.
[43] Force, *Archives*, 5th ser., I, 119-20, 174; *Va. Gazette*, July 29, 1776.

CHAPTER 11

[1] Jefferson's Memo. Bk., *Record of the Weather*, 1776-1820, is on deposit in LC. Other notebooks of *Weather Observations*, 1784-1794, 1802-1816, are in Mass. H. S.
[2] Acct. Bk., 1776-78; Mass. H. S.
[3] Pendleton to Jefferson, Aug. 1, 1776; Jefferson MSS., American Philos. Soc.
[4] R. H. Lee to Jefferson, July 21, 1776; *Letters of R. H. Lee*, I, 210. The original is in Jefferson Papers, LC., v. 2, p. 276. Jefferson had written to Lee on July 8, 1776, enclosing both copies. "You will judge whether it is the better or worse for the critics." *Works*, Ford, II, 217.
[5] John Page to Jefferson, July 20, 1776; Jefferson Papers, LC., v. 2, p. 275.
[6] Wm. Fleming to Jefferson, June 22, 1776; "Some Jefferson Correspondence" (W. C. Ford, ed.), in *N. E. Hist. and Genealogical Register* (1901-1902).
[7] Jefferson to Fleming, July 1, 1776; *Works*, Ford, II, 198-9.
[8] Edmund Randolph to Jefferson, June 23, 1776; Jefferson Papers, LC., v. 2, p. 260.
[9] Fleming to Jefferson, July 27, 1776; Jefferson Papers, LC., v. 2, p. 283. Jefferson's dark forebodings of machinations against him were baseless; the reduction of the delegation to Congress had nothing to do with his personal popularity.
[10] Jefferson to Francis Eppes, July 15, 1776; *Works*, Ford, II, 221-3.
[11] Jefferson to Pendleton [July, 1776]; *ibid*, II, 219-20.
[12] Jefferson to R. H. Lee, July 8, 1776; Jefferson Papers, LC., v. 2, p. 169. In all the published versions of this letter, the reading is: "... I shall hope to see you, and *not* Wythe, in convention ..." (Italics added). But the manuscript in LC. discloses the mistake, because of a tear in the paper. It reads: "I shall hope to see you & M [tear] Wythe ..." Obviously an "r" is missing after the "M". It is incredible, in the light of all the circumstances, that Jefferson would have indicated a hope that Wythe would not be present. The reading is confirmed by Jefferson's similar statement to Page, July 20, 1776; *Works*, Ford, II, 231.
[13] Jefferson to John Page, July 20, 1776; *Works*, Ford, II, 229-31.
[14] Pendleton to Jefferson, July 22, 1776; Jefferson Papers, LC., v. 2, p. 277.
[15] Pendleton to Jefferson, Aug. 10, 1776; Jefferson Papers, LC., v. 2, p. 289.
[16] On term of office, see Draft Suggestions, July, 1776; Jefferson Papers, LC., v. 2, p. 201. On seals, see Acct. Bk., 1774; Mass. H. S., and John Adams, Aug. 4, 1776; *Familiar Letters*, 211. On coins, Jefferson was added to the committee on July 24, 1776. He wrote the report which, when presented to Congress on Sept. 2, 1776, was ordered "to lie on the table"; *Journals, Cont. Cong.*, V, 608, 724-8.
[17] Adams' *Diary*, July 25, Aug. 2, 1776; *Works*, II, 492, 493, 502.
[18] Jefferson to [Pendleton], Aug. 13, 1776; *Works*, Ford, II, 239-40.
[19] Jefferson to R. H. Lee, July 29, 1776; *Letters, Members of Cont. Cong.*, II, 28.
[20] Jefferson to Page, Aug. 5, 1776; *Works*, Ford, II, 234.
[21] Jefferson to Pendleton, Aug. 13, 1776; *ibid*, II, 241.
[22] Jefferson to Page, Aug. 5, 1776; *ibid*, II, 233.
[23] Autobiography, *ibid*, I, 57.
[24] Acct. Bk., 1776; Mass. H. S.
[25] Acct. Bk., 1776; Mass. H. S.; Weather Bk., 1776; LC.
[26] *Journals, Cont. Cong.*, V, 827.
[27] *Letters of R. H. Lee*, I, 218.
[28] Jefferson to John Hancock, Oct. 11, 1776; *Works*, Ford, II, 251-2; *Journals, Cont. Cong.*, Oct. 27, 1776, VI, 897.
[29] *Letters of R. H. Lee*, I, 222-5.
[30] Wythe to Jefferson, Nov. 18, 1776; Jefferson Papers, LC., v. 2, pp. 313-14; Acct. Bk., 1776; Mass. H. S.
[31] The *Commonplace Book* discloses the minuteness and variety of his readings on this

point. When he came across an author who indicated that feudalism was a *German*, not a Norman, introduction, Jefferson argued his findings and abused his learning. See his animadversions on Francis S. Sullivan's *An Historical Treatise on the Feudal Laws and the Constitution and Laws of England* in the *Commonplace Book*, Arts. 759-74.

[32] *Commonplace Book*, Art. 767. See also his comment, "Nothing but free argument, raillery and even ridicule will preserve the purity of religion," to a citation from Shaftesbury; *ibid*, p. 389.

[33] Autobiography, *Works*, Ford, I, 78.

[34] *Ibid*, I, 77.

[35] *Journals, House of Delegates*, Oct. 11, 1776.

[36] *Journals, House of Delegates*, 1776-8, *passim; Hening's Statutes*, IX, *passim; Works*, Ford, I, 57n. Jefferson, in his Autobiography, *ibid*, I, 57, seems to indicate that *all* the bills were passed in regular course and without trouble.

[37] *Journals, House of Delegates*, Oct. 12, 1776.

[38] *Ibid*, Oct. 14, 1776.

[39] *Works*, Ford, I, 58-9; II, 268-70; *Hening's Statutes*, IX, 226.

[40] *Works*, Ford, I, 59.

[41] Landon Carter to George Washington, Oct. 31, 1776; Force, *Archives*, 5th ser., II, 1304-7.

CHAPTER 12

[1] *Journal, House of Delegates*, Oct. 17, Oct. 26, 1776.

[2] Hening, *Statutes*, IX, 175-6.

[3] *Works*, Ford, I, 66-7.

[4] *Commonplace Book*, 226. Jefferson to Wythe, Nov. 1, 1778; *Works*, Ford, II, 393-4n.

[5] Autobiography, *Works*, Ford, I, 67-8. Jefferson to Skelton Jones, July 28, 1809; *Writings*, Mont., XI, 298-9.

[6] Autobiography, *Works*, Ford, I, 69.

[7] Jefferson to Wythe, Nov. 1, 1778; *supra*.

[8] Pendleton to Jefferson, Aug. 10, 1776; Jefferson Papers, LC., v. 2, p. 289. Abbreviations written out, and some changes in punctuation.

[9] *Commonplace Book*, Arts. 806-31.

[10] Jefferson to Pendleton, Aug. 26, 1776; Washburn Papers, Mass. H. S.

[11] Autobiography, *Works*, Ford, I, 69-70.

[12] Jefferson to Wythe, Nov. 1, 1778; *supra*.

[13] *Works*, Ford, II, 393-414.

[14] Autobiography, *ibid*, I, 74.

[15] Jefferson and Wythe to General Assembly, June 18, 1779; *ibid*, II, 384-5.

[16] Madison to Samuel H. Smith, Nov. 4, 1826; Madison, *Writings* (Hunt, ed.), IX, 257-8.

[17] *Works*, Ford, II, 390-2. Jefferson thought it was his own bill which became law in 1778; actually, it was a bill by one Richard Kello; Hening, *Statutes*, IX, 471-2.

[18] Autobiography, *Works*, Ford, I, 77.

[19] See also the author's "Church, State and Education," in the *American Jewish Year Book*, v. 49 (1947-48), pp. 1-48.

[20] Notes on Va., *Works*, Ford, IV, 77-9.

[21] *Journal, House of Delegates*, 1776, p. 7.

[22] *Ibid*, Oct. 11, 1776.

[23] *Ibid*, Nov. 8, 1776.

[24] *Ibid*, Nov. 6, 9, 1776.

[25] *Ibid*, Nov. 19, 1776.

[26] *Ibid*, Nov. 19, 1776.

[27] *Ibid*, Dec. 5, 9, 1776; Hening, *Statutes*, IX, 164-7.

[28] *Works*, Ford, II, 252-68.

[29] Hening, *Statutes*, X, 197-8.

[30] *Works*, Ford, II, 438-41.

[31] See the petition of the Virginia Baptist Association, Dec. 25, 1776; Jefferson Papers, LC., v. 2, pp. 317-8.

[32] MS., Va. State Lib.; quoted in Eckenrode, *Separation of Church and State in Va.*, 58-61.

[33] Jefferson Papers, Mass. H. S.

[34] John Todd to Jefferson, Aug. 16, 1779; Jefferson Papers, Missouri H. S.

[35] Hening, *Statutes*, XII, 84-6. The bill was signed on Jan. 19, 1786. See also *Journal, House of Delegates, passim*, for the various steps in the struggle, and Eckenrode, *supra*, for a detailed account. For the efforts of Patrick Henry and R. H. Lee to force through multiple establishments, see Edmund Randolph to Jefferson, May 15, 1784; Conway's *Randolph*, 56 and Lee's *R. H. Lee*, II, 51.

[36] Jefferson to Wythe, Aug. 13, 1786; *Works*, Ford, V, 151-5.

[37] Preamble to Jefferson's Bill; *ibid*, II, 414-26.

[38] "A Bill for Amending the Constitution of the College of William and Mary"; *ibid*, II, 426-36.

[39] *Ibid*, II, 436-8.

CHAPTER 13

[1] Autobiography, *Works*, Ford, I, 64. The bill itself is in *ibid*, II, 271-6.

[2] *Journal, House of Delegates*, 1776, p. 51. Hening, *Statutes*, X, 85.

[3] Dec. 6, 1776; *Works*, Ford, II, 294-5.

[4] Jefferson's Weather Book, 1777; LC. and *Garden Book*, 70.

[5] Jefferson was appointed Justice of the Peace on Mar. 5, 1777; *Council Journals*, I, 359. For allotments of funds to him for militia supplies and for "the highland Prisoners," see *ibid*, I, 224, 359.

[6] Thomas Nelson to Jefferson, Jan. 2, 1777; Jefferson Papers, LC., v. 3, p. 354.

[7] Acct. Bk., Apr. 29, May 4, 1777; Mass. H. S.

[8] Acct. Bk., *supra*. *Journal, House of Delegates*, 1777; pp. 3-4.

[9] The text is in *Works*, Ford, II, 295-302.

[10] *Ibid*, II, 302-4. For Jefferson's abortive attempt to write a similar principle into the resolutions of Congress during July, 1776, see *ibid*, II, 220. John Banister, who personally disliked R. H. Lee, nevertheless condemned the measure "as a most flagrant act of injustice, and as a precedent dangerous in its nature." To Theodorick Bland, June 10, 1777; *Bland Papers*, I, 57.

[11] *Journal, House of Delegates*, May 20, 1777.

[12] Acct. Bk., 1777; Mass. H. S.

[13] R. H. Lee to Jefferson, Aug. 25, 1777; Jefferson Papers, LC., v. 3, p. 387.

[14] Jefferson to Adams, May 16, 1777; *Works*, Ford, II, 304-6.

[15] Adams to Jefferson, May 26, 1777; Jefferson Papers, LC., v. 3, p. 370a. Printed, with slight variations, in Adams, *Works*, IX, 467.

[16] Jefferson to Franklin, Aug. 13, 1777; *Works*, Ford, II, 306-7.

[17] Jefferson to Adams, Aug. 21, 1777; *ibid*, II, 308-10.

[18] *Journal, House of Delegates*, Oct. 10, 20, Dec. 15, 1777.

[19] *Works*, Ford, II, 387-90. The bill was introduced on Jan. 17, 1778, and was passed on Jan. 22nd.

[20] Acct. Bk., Jan. 12, Jan. 17, 1778; Mass. H. S.

[21] Weather Book, 1778; LC.

[22] Acct. Bk., Feb. 7, 1778; Mass. H. S.; *Garden Book*, 77-8.

[23] *Journal, House of Delegates*, May 12, 1778.

[24] The letter is dated June 8, 1778, and is addressed to Paris without giving the recipient's name. There is sufficient evidence to attribute it to Fabbroni. The original is now on deposit in the Clinton Papers, Clements Library. The draft copy is in Jefferson Papers, LC., v. 3, p. 419, and is printed in *Works*, Ford, II, 338-42.

[25] Jefferson to Samuel Henley, June 9, 1778; *Works*, Ford, II, 343-4.

[26] Jefferson to Rittenhouse, July 19, 1778; *ibid*, II, 344-7. The original is in Barton Papers, Pa. H. S.

[27] Acct. Book, 1776-78; Mass. H. S.

[28] Jefferson to R. H. Lee, Aug. 30, 1778; Lee Papers, Va. H. S.

[29] Jefferson to John Hancock, Oct. 19, 1778; facsimile, Sabin Coll., N. Y. Public Library.

[30] *Journal, House of Delegates*, Oct. 7, Nov. 23, Nov. 30, Dec. 12, Dec. 14, 1778.

[31] *Ibid*, Nov. 12, 1778.

[32] Washington to Harrison, Dec. 30, 1778; Washington, *Writings* (J. C. Fitzpatrick, ed.), XIII, 467.

[33] *Memoirs, etc. of Major General Riedesel*, II, 69-70.

[34] *Letters and Journals. by Mrs. General Riedesel*, 154-60.

[35] *Ibid.* See also Mazzei's *Memoirs.*

[36] Gen. Phillips to Jefferson, June 18, 1779; Jefferson Papers, Mo. H. S. *Letters, etc. of Mrs. Gen. Riedesel*, II, 157-8.

[37] Jefferson to R. H. Lee, Apr. 21, 1779; *Works*, Ford, II, 363-4.

[38] Translated and enclosed in letter from Jacob Rübsamer to Jefferson, Jan. 1, 1780; Jefferson Papers, LC., v. 6, p. 994.

[39] Jefferson to Patrick Henry, Mar. 27, 1779; *Works*, Ford, II, 350-63.

[40] Apr. 5, 1779; *Journals, Council of State*, II, 254-5.

[41] Pendleton to Jefferson, May 11, 1779; Pendleton Letters, May's Coll., LC.

[42] *Journal, House of Delegates*, June 1, 1779.

[43] John Page to Jefferson, June 2, 1779; Jefferson Papers, LC., v. 3, p. 493; Jefferson to Page [June, 1779], *Works*, Ford, II, 372-3.

CHAPTER 14

[1] *Works*, Ford, II, 170-2.

[2] Hening's *Statutes*, IX, 223; X, 31, 165.

[3] Acct. Bks., 1779-80; Feb. 25, July 22, 26, Sept. 27, 1779; Apr. 6, Aug. 28, Sept. 7, 28, Nov. 25, 1780; LC.

[4] R. H. Lee to Jefferson, May 22, 1779; Jefferson MSS., Amer. Philos. Soc.

[5] Jefferson to Wm. Fleming, June 8, 1779; *Works*, Ford, II, 373-5.

[6] Letter dated Jan. 3, 1778; *Ill. Colls.*, VIII, 37-8. See also Jefferson to Oliver Pollock, Dec. 31, 1811; Jefferson Papers, LC., v. 194, p. 34541.

[7] Act of June 22, 1779; Hening's *Statutes*, X, 50-65.

[8] T. P. Abernethy, *Western Lands and the American Revolution*, chap. 15.

[9] Council Minutes, June 18, 1779; *Off. Letters of the Govs.*, II, 9-11. Jefferson to Theodorick Bland, Jr., June 18, 1779; *Works*, Ford, II, 379-80. Same to same, June 8, 1779; *ibid*, II, 376-7.

[10] Washington to Jefferson, July 10, 1779; Washington, *Writings*, XV, 401.

[11] Jefferson to Washington, July 17, 1779; *Works*, Ford, II, 452-4. To Sir Guy Carleton, July 22, 1779; *ibid*, II, 454-62, in which Jefferson widened the justification to a discourse on the general British treatment of American prisoners.

[12] Washington to Jefferson, Aug. 10, 1779; Washington, *Writings*, XVI, 68-9.

[13] Jefferson to Washington, Oct. 1, 1779; *Works*, Ford, II, 464-5.

[14] Washington to Jefferson, Sept. 13, 1779; Washington, *Writings*, XVI, 272.

[15] Jefferson to Washington, Oct. 2, 1779; *Works*, Ford, II, 465-6.

[16] Jefferson to Washington, Oct. 25, 1780; *ibid*, III, 66.

[17] Jefferson to Wm. Fleming, June 8, 1779; *Off. Letters of the Govs.*, II, 4-5.

[18] Jefferson to R. H. Lee, June 17, 1779; *Life of R. H. Lee* (Ballagh), II, 189.

[19] Jefferson to Benjamin Harrison, Oct. 22, 1779; *Works*, Ford, II, 470-2.

[20] Jefferson to Jay, June 19, 1779; *ibid*, II, 447-8.

[21] Nov. 30, 1779; *Off. Letters of the Govs.*, II, 72; Hening's *Statutes*, X, 140, 149-50.

[22] Jefferson to the Pres. of Cong., Dec. 16, 1779; *Works*, Ford, II, 492-6.

[23] Jefferson to Benjamin Harrison, Dec. 23, 1779; *ibid*, II, 498-9. The original is in the Franklin Papers, Yale Univ. The warning had come from Washington, Dec. 11, 1779; Washington, *Writings*, XVII, 246; but on Dec. 25, 1779, he wrote again that the warning had been premature; *ibid*, XVII, 317.

[24] Hening's *Statutes*, X, 309-14.

[25] Jefferson to [R. H. Lee], Sept. 13, 1780; Lee Papers, Va. H. S.

[26] Jefferson to Col. James Wood, May 17, 1780; Emmet Coll., N. Y. Pub. Lib.

[27] Jefferson to Joseph Martin, Jan. 24, 1780; *Ill. St. Hist. Lib. Colls.*, VIII, *Va. Ser.*, III, 385-6.

[28] Jefferson to Clark, Jan. 29, 1780; *Off. Letters of the Govs.*, II, 90-4.

[29] Jefferson to Pres. of Congress, Feb. 9, 1780; *ibid*, II, 97-100. Hening's *Statutes*, X, 159-62.

[30] *Cal. of Va. State Papers*, I, 363-4.

[31] Jefferson to Washington, Feb. 10, 1780; *Works*, Ford, III, 9-10; Washington to Jefferson, Mar. 5, 1780; Washington, *Writings*, XVIII, 74-5.

[32] In fact, as early as Mar. 19, 1780, Jefferson was reluctantly writing Washington that "the want of men, want of money, and difficulty of procuring provisions, with some other reasons more cogent if possible, and which cannot be confided to a letter, have obliged

to decline that object." *Jefferson Correspondence, from the Bixby Coll.* (W. C. Ford, ed.), p. 2. However, he shortly reversed himself and plans to subdue Detroit continued.

[33] Jefferson to Steuben, Feb. 15, 1780; Steuben Papers, N. Y. H. S.

[34] Jefferson to Wm. Campbell, July 3, 1780; Franklin Papers, Yale Univ. Printed, with slight variations, in *Off. Letters of the Govs.*, II, 138.

[35] Jefferson to Chas. Lynch, Aug. 1, 1780; *Off. Letters of the Govs.*, II, 147-8.

[36] Jefferson to Wm. Campbell, Aug. 9, 1780; *ibid*, II, 158. Campbell's first name is wrongly printed as *Arthur.*

[37] Hening's *Statutes*, X, 221-6, 244-54, 257-62, 279-86, 291-2, 309-14.

[38] Washington to Jefferson, July 18, 1780; Washington, *Writings*, XIX, 195.

[39] Washington to Jefferson, Aug. 14, 1780; *ibid*, XIX, 374.

[40] Gates to Jefferson, July 19, 1780; Jefferson Papers, LC., v. 5, pp. 747-8.

[41] Gates to Jefferson, July 20, 1780; *ibid*, v. 5, p. 752.

[42] Gates to Jefferson, Aug. 3, 1780; Gates Papers, N. Y. H. S. For others in similar vein see Jefferson Papers, LC., v. 5, *passim.*

[43] Jefferson to Samuel Huntington, June 9, 1780; *Works*, Ford, III, 15-19. To Washington, July 2, 1780; *ibid*, III, 27-8.

[44] Jefferson to Madison, July 26, 1780; *ibid*, III, 31-3.

[45] Jefferson to Gates, Sept. 3, 1780; Jefferson Papers, LC., v. 6, p. 895. Gates to Jefferson, Oct. 6, 1780; *ibid*, v. 5, p. 801.

[46] Jefferson's Notes of emergency measures [Sept. 1780]; Jefferson Papers, LC., v. 6, p. 925.

[47] Jefferson to Members of the Council, Aug. 28, 1780; *Off. Letters of the Govs.*, II, 170. To Washington, Sept. 3, 1780; *Works*, Ford, III, 43-4. To Huntington, Sept. 14, 1780; *ibid*, III, 52-3.

[48] Jefferson to Luzerne, Aug. 31, 1780; *Off. Letters of the Govs.*, II, 175-6. To Chevalier d'Anmours, Sept. 9, 1780; *ibid*, II, 198-9.

[49] Gates to Jefferson, Sept. 9, 1780; Gates Papers, N. Y. H. S. Washington to Jefferson, Sept. 11, Oct. 10, 1780; Washington, *Writings*, XX, 29-31, 147.

CHAPTER 15

[1] Jefferson to R. H. Lee, Jan. 2, 1780; Lee Papers, U. of Va. July 1, 1780; *Journals of the Council*, II, 264.

[2] The story of this abortive invasion is well-documented in Jefferson's letters of the period. See *Works*, Ford, III; *Off. Letters of the Govs.*, II; and Jefferson Papers, LC., *passim.*

[3] Jefferson to Speaker of the House of Delegates, Nov. 24, Dec. 11, 1780; *Off. Letters of the Govs.*, II, 236-7, 240.

[4] Oct., 1780; Hening's *Statutes*, X, 326-7, 338-43, 344-6, 347-50. See also R. H. Lee to Theodoric Bland, Dec. 15, 1780; *Bland Papers*, II, 40.

[5] Greene to Jefferson, Nov. 20, 1780; Steuben Papers, N. Y. H. S.

[6] Mazzei to Jefferson, May 19, 1780; Franklin Papers, Yale Univ.

[7] Jefferson to Chevalier d'Anmours, Nov. 30, 1780; Jefferson Papers, LC., v. 6, p. 993.

[8] John Page to Jefferson, Dec. 9, 1780; Jefferson Papers, LC., v. 6, p. 996.

[9] Acct. Bk., Nov. 3, 1780; LC.

[10] Greene to Jefferson, Nov. 20, 1780; Steuben Papers, N. Y. H. S.

[11] Jefferson to Steuben, Dec. 1, 1780; Steuben Papers, N. Y. H. S. Steuben to Jefferson, Dec. 3, 1780; *ibid.* Jefferson to Steuben, Dec. 4, 1780; *ibid.*

[12] Washington to Jefferson, Jan. 2, 1781; Washington, *Writings*, XXI, 51-2.

[13] *Reminiscences of Isaac Jefferson;* McGregor Coll., U. of Va.

[14] The source material for Arnold's invasion of Virginia is voluminous. Jefferson claims that he kept a day-to-day diary of events, but only copies of that diary, made by him at a much later date and varying somewhat from one another, are extant. These might be classed as self-serving, inasmuch as they were written and, some of them, published to clear his name of later imputations of cowardice and neglect; yet, in the main, they check fairly accurately with what we know of the events from other sources. Henry Lee, Jefferson's enemy, also published an account in his *Memoirs of the War in the Southern Department of the U. S.*, which is quite severe on Jefferson; but Jefferson denied his charges and pointed out to Lee's son (May 15, 1826, printed as a note to the *Memoirs*,

315-18) that his father had no personal knowledge of the facts he adduced. The *Journals of the Council* furnish valuable firsthand material; as do the *Off. Letters of the Govs.*; and the multitude of letters of the numerous participants, published and unpublished. More suspect is the mass of affidavits which Jefferson collected from friends and subordinates many years later when he was under political attack. Some of these have been printed; others are still in the Jefferson Papers, LC.

[15] Wm. Tatham to Wm. A. Burwell, June 13, 1805; copy by Jefferson in Jefferson Papers, LC., v. 150, pp. 26215-6. One of the reasons, perhaps, for Jefferson's reluctance to call the militia now was that only a week before he had ordered out the militia of two counties to join Clark's proposed expedition against Detroit; Jefferson to Co. Lts. of Hampshire and Berkeley, Dec. 24, 1780; *Works*, Ford, III, 94-5.

[16] Jefferson to Steuben, Dec. 31, 1780; *Works*, Ford, III, 104-5.

[17] *Journals of the Council*, II, 269.

[18] Jefferson's Diary, *Works*, Ford, III, 105; variant version in Jefferson Papers, LC., v. 6, pp. 1012 ff. *Journals of the Council*, II, 269-70.

[19] Jefferson to Thomas Nelson, Jan. 2, 1781; *Off. Letters of the Govs.*, II, 260. To Washington and Samuel Huntington, Jan. 10, 1781; *Works*, Ford, III. To Jacob Wray, Jan. 15, 1781; *ibid*, III, 130-1.

[20] *Journals of the Council*, II, 271-2. Jefferson's Diary, *supra.*

[21] Jefferson's Diary; Jefferson Papers, LC., *supra.*

[22] *Isaac Jefferson's Reminiscences*, McGregor Coll., U. of Va. For example, he declared that Jefferson was in Richmond at the time of the British arrival, and rode off only when cannon shots fell in the town.

[23] *Isaac Jefferson's Reminiscences, supra.*

[24] Henry Lee, *Memoirs*, 302. This is the solitary commendation of Jefferson's activities in the entire volume. His strictures otherwise are exceedingly severe. Henry Lee was politically and personally opposed to Jefferson when he wrote the book.

[25] Deposition of Daniel Hylton, Oct. 12, 1796; Jefferson Papers, LC., v. 100, p. 17225. Jefferson's Diary, *supra.* Jefferson to Steuben, Jan. 7, 1781; Steuben Papers, N. Y. H. S.

[26] Jefferson to Washington and Huntington, Jan. 10, 1781; *supra.*

[27] *Journals of the Council*, II, 274-5. The Proclamation is in *Works*, Ford, III, 144-6.

[28] Jefferson to the Pres. of Cong., Jan. 17, 1781; *Off. Letters of the Govs.*, II, 284-5.

[29] Jefferson to Members of Gen. Assembly, Jan. 23, 1781; *ibid*, II, 298-9.

[30] Jefferson to [Gen. Muhlenburg], Jan. 31, 1781; *Off. Letters of the Gov.*, II, 312-13. This section is also in *Works*, Ford, III, 158-9, where, however, the name of the addressee is given as George Rogers Clarke.

[31] The complete draft of the above letter, with the hitherto unpublished deletions, is in Jefferson Papers, LC., v. 7, p. 1085.

[32] Washington to Jefferson, Feb. 6, 1781; Washington, *Writings*, XXI, 191-2.

[33] Gates to Jefferson, Feb. 2, 1781; Jefferson Papers, LC., v. 7, p. 1086. Jefferson replied that "I have been knocking at the door of Congress for aids of all kinds ... since the middle of summer. The Speaker Harrison is gone to be heard on that subject." Feb. 17, 1781; *Works*, Ford, III, 175-6.

[34] Steuben to Jefferson, Feb. 11, 1781; Steuben Papers, N. Y. H. S. Jefferson to Steuben, Feb. 12, 1781; *ibid.*

[35] Feb. 15, 1781; *Journals of the Council*, II, 293. Jefferson to Steuben, Feb. 16, 1781; Steuben Papers, N. Y. H. S.

[36] Feb. 27, 1781; *Journals of the Council*, II, 300. Jefferson to Chevalier d'Anmours, Nov. 30, 1780; Jefferson Papers, LC. v. 6, p. 993.

[37] Washington to Jefferson, Feb. 21, 1781; Washington, *Writings*, XXI, 270-1.

[38] Jefferson to Co. Lts., Feb. 15, 1781; *Works*, Ford, III, 168-9.

[39] Jefferson to R. H. Lee, Speaker of the House, Mar. 1, 1781; *Off. Letters of the Govs.*, II, 377-80. To same, Mar. 9, 1781; *Works*, Ford, III, 208-9.

[40] Jefferson to Lafayette, Mar. 10, 1781; *Works*, Ford, III, 213-14.

[41] Jefferson to Lafayette, Mar. 12, 1781; *ibid*, III, 216-17.

[42] Jefferson to Steuben, Feb. 24, 1781; Steuben Papers, N. Y. H. S.

[43] Col. James Jones to Steuben, Mar. 5, 1781; photostat of original, *ibid.* John Page wrote along similar lines to Steuben on Mar. 7, 1781; *ibid.*

[44] Steuben to Jefferson, Mar. 9, 1781; *ibid.*

[45] Mar. 29, 1781; *Journals of the Council*, II, 322.

[46] Apr. 12, 1781; *ibid*, II, 333.
[47] Jefferson to Steuben, Mar. 10, 1781; *Off. Letters of the Govs.*, II, 399.
[48] Jefferson to Rev. James Madison and Robert Andrews, Mar. 31, 1781; *Works*, Ford, III, 235-6. To Madison, Apr. 8, 1781; *ibid*, III, 244-5.
[49] Lafayette to Jefferson, Mar. 17, 1781; *Va. Mag.*, V, 374-5.
[50] Jefferson to Steuben, Mar. 10, 1781; *supra.*
[51] Jefferson to Greene, Apr. 1, 1781; Jefferson Papers, LC., v. 7, p. 1119.
[52] Greene to Steuben, Apr. 6, 1781; Steuben Papers, N. Y. H. S.
[53] *Journals of the Council*, II, 337-9. *Off. Letters of the Govs.*, II, 485.
[54] Jefferson to Col. James Innes, Apr. 21, 1781; *Off. Letters of the Govs.*, II, 490.
[55] Apr. 25, 1781; *Journals of the Council*, II, 341.
[56] Jefferson to Steuben, Apr. 27, 1781; Steuben Papers, N. Y. H. S. Printed in *Works*, Ford, III, 264-5.
[57] Jefferson to Col. Abraham Penn, May 4, 1781; *Works*, Ford, III, 268-70.
[58] Jefferson to Col. Vanmeter, Apr. 27, 1781; *ibid*, III, 263-4.
[59] Hening's *Statutes*, X, 413-18.
[60] *Journals of the Council*, II, 345-8.

CHAPTER 16

[1] Jefferson to Lafayette, May 14, 1781; *Off. Letters of the Govs.*, II, 515. To Benjamin Harrison, May 28, 1781; *ibid*, II, 523-4.
[2] Jefferson to Washington, May 28, 1781; *Works*, Ford, III, 283-5. Washington to Jefferson, June 8, 1781; Washington, *Writings*, XXII, 189-90.
[3] The story of the joint raids is told, from the British point of view, in the memoirs of the participants: Tarleton's *A History of the Campaigns of 1780 and 1781* and Simcoe's *A History of ... the Queen's Rangers.*
[4] Jefferson's account of the raid is in Randall's *Jefferson*, I, 336-9, and in his Papers, LC., v. 207, pp. 36977-80.
[5] Tarleton's *History*, 295-7.
[6] Jefferson's account, *supra.* Tarleton, *supra.* Deposition of Christopher Hudson, July 26, 1805; Jefferson Papers, LC., v. 151, p. 26426. Jefferson to Dr. William Gordon, July 16, 1788; *Works*, Ford, V, 417-21.
[7] Jefferson's Papers, LC., v. 207, p. 36980.
[8] Eliza J. Ambler to Mildred Dudley, 1781; *Va. Mag.*, XXXVIII, 167-8.
[9] Jefferson to Dr. Wm. Gordon, July 16, 1788; *supra.*
[10] Farm Bk., 1781; Mass. H. S.
[11] R. H. Lee to Washington, June 12, 1781; *Letters of R. H. Lee*, II, 234.
[12] *Journal, House of Delegates*, June 12, 1781.
[13] Randolph's *Essay; Va. Mag.*, XLIV, 320-1.
[14] Archibald Cary to Jefferson, June 19, 1781; Jefferson Papers, LC., v. 7, p. 1138.
[15] Jefferson to Lafayette, Aug. 4, 1781; *Works*, Ford, III, 290-1. Lafayette had forwarded to him the notice of his appointment to the peace mission, and Jefferson, while declaring his mortification at losing an opportunity "of seeing countries whose improvements in science, in arts, & in civilization it has been my misfortune to admire at a distance but never to see," insisted he must remain where his efforts "have not been such as to give satisfaction to some of my countrymen." For the later tale of his fall, see Richmond *Enquirer*, Aug. 23, 1805.
[16] Jefferson to George Nicholas, July 28, 1781; Jefferson Papers, LC., v. 7, p. 1145.
[17] George Nicholas to Jefferson, July 31, 1781; *ibid*, v. 7, pp. 1146-7.
[18] *Heads of charges ... with the heads of answers; ibid*, v. 6, p. 1011.
[19] Jefferson to Edmund Randolph, Sept. 16, 1781; *Works*, Ford, III, 291-3. Randolph to Jefferson, Oct. 9, 1781; Jefferson Papers, LC., v. 7, p. 1162.
[20] *Journal, House of Delegates*, Nov. 26, 1781.
[21] *Ibid*, Dec. 12, 1781.
[22] Hening's *Statutes*, X, 568-9; and Jefferson Papers, LC., v. 6, p. 1013.
[23] John Harvie to Jefferson, Nov. 27, 1781; Jefferson Papers, LC., v. 7, p. 1181.
[24] Jefferson to Isaac Zane, Dec. 24 [1781]; Misc. MSS., Pa. H. S.

CHAPTER 17

[1] Jefferson's election as delegate to Congress took place Nov. 30, 1781, even before his vindication; Jefferson Papers, LC., v. 7, pp. 1133-4. He resigned from the House on Dec. 19, 1781; *Journal, House of Delegates*, under that date.

[2] George Wythe to Jefferson, Dec. 31, 1781; Jefferson Papers, LC., v. 7, pp. 1191-2.

[3] Chastellux, *Voyages*, II, 40-8.

[4] Jefferson's plans, etc. are scattered in half a dozen repositories, but the chief mass are in U. of Va., Mass. H. S. and the Huntington Lib.

[5] Jefferson to Marbois, Mar. 4, 1781; *Works*, Ford, III, 314.

[6] Jefferson to Marbois, Dec. 20, 1781; *Am. Hist. Rev.*, XII, 76.

[7] Jefferson to Marbois, Mar. 24, 1782; Jefferson Papers, LC., v. 8, p. 1227.

[8] Autobiography, *Works*, Ford, I, 94.

[9] Jefferson was made a member on Jan. 21, 1780.

[10] *Works*, Ford, III, 358.

[11] *Ibid*, III, 372.

[12] *Ibid*, III, 381.

[13] *Ibid*, III, 392.

[14] *Ibid*, III, 427.

[15] *Ibid*, III, 444.

[16] *Ibid*, III, 445-6.

[17] The general facts of the controversy are contained in Brantz Mayer, *Tah-Gah-Jute; or Logan and Cresap* (1867) and in *Works*, Ford, III, 446 ff. The matter has been freshly re-examined by Irving Brant, *Madison*, I, 281-91, who discovered the confirmation of Jefferson's original account in Force's *American Archives*, I, 285.

[18] *Works*, Ford, III, 458-60.

[19] *Ibid*, III, 487-8.

[20] *Ibid*, IV, 85-6.

[21] Jefferson to Lithgow, Jan. 4, 1805; *Works*, Ford, IV, 86-8n.

[22] *Works*, Ford, III, 491; IV, 48-59.

[23] *Ibid*, III, 496, 504-8.

[24] *Ibid*, III, 511.

[25] *Ibid*, IV, 17-20.

[26] *Ibid*, IV, 64.

[27] *Ibid*, IV, 79-80.

[28] *Ibid*, IV, 99-100.

[29] Jefferson to Chas. Thomson, May 21, 1784; *Works*, Ford, IV, 362. To Madison, May 25, 1784, *ibid*, IV, 363-4.

CHAPTER 18

[1] Jefferson to Speaker of the House of Delegates, May 6, 1782; Jefferson Papers, LC., v. 8, p. 1232.

[2] Monroe to Jefferson, Sept. 7, 1780; Monroe, *Writings*, I, 8-11.

[3] Jefferson to Monroe, May 20, 1782; *Works*, Ford, III, 298-302.

[4] Edmund Randolph to Madison, June 1, 1782; Madison Papers, LC.

[5] Madison to Randolph, June 11, 1782; Madison, *Writings*, I, 207-8.

[6] *Garden Bk.*, 94. Acct. Bk., May 3, 1782; LC. Lucy Elizabeth died two and a half years later.

[7] Monroe to Jefferson, June 28, 1782; Jefferson Papers, LC., v. 8, p. 1245.

[8] Acct. Bk., LC.

[9] Randall, *Jefferson*, I, 382.

[10] *Garden Bk.*, Sept. 11, 1782.

[11] Debates of Congress; Madison, *Writings*, I, 259-60.

[12] Jefferson to Benjamin Harrison, Sept. 22, 1782; *Works*, Ford, III, 303. To R. R. Livingston, Nov. 26, 1782; *ibid*, III, 303-4. Autobiography, *ibid*, I, 80.

[13] Jefferson to Chastellux, Nov. 26, 1782; *ibid*, III, 306-8.

[14] Advertisement in *Va. Gazette*, Dec. 28, 1782. Acct. Bk., entry of Dec. 19, 1782; LC.

[15] Acct. Bk., items of Jan., 1783; Mass. H. S.

[16] Acct. Bk., Jan. 31, 1783; Mass. H. S.

[17] Jefferson to R. R. Livingston, Feb. 7, 1783; *Rev. Diplomatic Correspond. of U. S.* (F. Wharton, ed.), VI, 247. To Madison, Feb. 7, 1783; *Works*, Ford, IV, 127-31.

[18] Jefferson to Madison, Feb. 14, 1783; *Works*, Ford, IV, 136-40. Madison replied in cipher: "Your portrait of yr Amanuensis is I conceive drawn to the life. For all unconfidential services he [can?] be a convenient instrument. For any thing farther negutor ultra a crepidam"; Feb. 18, 1783; Madison Papers, LC. This section is omitted from his printed *Writings*, I, 372.

[19] Jefferson to Edmund Randolph, Feb. 15, 1783; photostat at Princeton Univ., *Papers of Thomas Jefferson;* also printed excerpts in Maggs Bros. Catalogue, London, Spring, 1921.

[20] R. R. Livingston to Jefferson, Feb. 14, 1783; *Rev. Diplom. Corresp.*, VI, 252. *Journals, Cont. Cong.*, XXIV, 132; XXV, 898-9.

[21] Jefferson to Francis Eppes, Feb. 15, 1783; McGregor MSS., U. of Va.

[22] Jefferson to Gov. Abner Nash, Mar. 11, 1783; Jefferson Papers, LC., v. 9, p. 1444.

[23] Jefferson to Madison, Nov. 11, 1784; *Works*, Ford, IV, 368-70.

[24] R. R. Livingston to Jefferson, Apr. 4, 1783; *Rev. Diplom. Corresp.*, VI, 357-8. *Journals, Cont. Cong.*, XXIV, 226.

[25] Dec. 31, 1782; *Wm. & Mary Quart.*, ser. I, v. 16, p. 73.

[26] *Works*, Ford, IV, 147-66.

[27] Jefferson to Madison, May 7, 1783; *Works*, Ford, IV, 144-6.

[28] Jefferson to Madison, June 1, 1783; *ibid*, IV, 147.

[29] Jefferson to Madison, June 17, 1783; *ibid*, IV, 166-8.

[30] Madison to E. Randolph, May 27, 1783; Madison, *Writings*, I, 474n. Autobiography, *Works*, Ford, I, 81. *Journals, Cont. Cong.*, XXV, 969.

[31] Catalogue of Books; Jefferson Papers, Mass. H. S.

[32] Jefferson to Charles Carter, Oct. 12, 1783; *Works*, Ford, IV, 172-3.

CHAPTER 19

[1] Acct. Bk., Nov. 3, 19, 20, 1783; Mass. H. S.

[2] *Ibid*, Jan. 1, 1784. Jefferson to Martha Jefferson, Nov. 28, 1783; *Works*, Ford, IV, 178-9.

[3] Jefferson to Marbois, Dec. 5, 1783; *Am. Hist. Rev.*, XII, 76-7.

[4] Jefferson to Francis Eppes, Nov. 10, 1783; Franklin Papers, Yale Univ.

[5] Jefferson to Madison, Dec. 11, 1783; *Works*, Ford, IV, 180-1.

[6] Jefferson to——, n.d.; Dreer Coll., Pa. H. S.

[7] Jefferson to Benjamin Harrison, Dec. 24, 1783; *Works*, Ford, IV, 203-4. The original is in the Dreer Coll., Pa. H. S.

[8] *Works*, Ford, IV, 212-15. Jefferson to Madison, Feb. 20, 1784; *ibid*, IV, 239-41; also *ibid*, I, 84-9.

[9] *Journals, Cont. Cong.*, XXVI, 22-9. On the expresses sent out by Congress, see Jefferson to Madison, Jan. 1, 1784; *Works*, Ford, IV, 209-12. Even in the midst of these anxieties, Jefferson could not resist discussing Buffon's "central heat" hypothesis—that the earth was once in a state of hot fusion and was now cooling off.

[10] Jefferson to Harrison, Jan. 16, 1784; *Works*, Ford, IV, 219-21. To same effect, Jefferson to E. Pendleton, Jan. 18, 1784; photostat, U. of Va.

[11] Jefferson to Madison, Feb. 20, 1784; *supra.*

[12] Jefferson to Chastellux, Jan. 16, 1784; Jefferson Papers, Mo. H. S.

[13] Charles Thomson to Jefferson, May 19, 1784; Jefferson Papers, Mo. H. S.

[14] Autobiography, *Works*, Ford, I, 89-91.

[15] Hening's *Statutes*, XI, 326-8.

[16] *Journals, Cont. Cong.*, XXVI, 113-16.

[17] *Works*, Ford, IV, 275-80.

[18] A copy of a map embodying the boundaries and the names is in the Wm. L. Clements Lib.

[19] *Journals, Cont. Cong.*, XXVI, 246-7. Jefferson to Madison, Apr. 25, 1784; *Works*, Ford, IV, 329-33.

[20] *Journals, Cont. Cong.*, XXVI, 277.

[21] Jefferson to Madison, Feb. 20, 1784; *Works*, Ford, IV, 243-6. To Washington, Mar. 15, 1784; *ibid*, IV, 266-70.

[22] "Notes on the Establishment of a Money Unit, and of a Coinage for the U. S.," Apr.,

1784; *Works*, Ford, IV., 297-308. "Supplementary Explanations," May 9, 1784, *ibid*, IV, 308-13. Autobiography, *ibid*, I, 82-3.

[23] *Works*, Ford, IV, 229-34, 235-6.

[24] Autobiography, *ibid*, I, 84.

[25] *Journals, Cont. Cong.*, XXVI, 356.

[26] Washington to Jefferson, Apr. 8, 1784; Jefferson Papers, LC., v. 10, p. 1667. Jefferson to Washington, Apr. 16, 1784; *Works*, Ford, IV, 323-9.

[27] E. Randolph to Jefferson, Apr. 24, 1784; Jefferson Papers, LC., v. 10, p. 1674. See also Jefferson to Horatio Gates, May 7, 1784; Emmet Coll., N. Y. Public Library.

[28] Jefferson to Madison, May 8, 1784; W. C. Rives Papers, LC.

[29] Madison to Jefferson, May 15, 1784; July 3, 1784; Madison, *Writings*, II, 51, 62. Jefferson also expounded his views on constitutional changes in a letter to Edmund Pendleton, May 25, 1784; Jefferson Papers, Box 1, N. Y. Pub. Lib. Here he repeated his firm conviction of the necessity of an Executive and a Judiciary independent of the Legislature, and a Constitution supreme over all, which had infused his draft Constitution for Virginia.

[30] Madison to Jefferson, Apr. 25, 1784; Madison, *Writings*, II, 47-8.

[31] Jefferson to Madison, Mar. 16, 1784; *Works*, Ford, IV, 270-2.

[32] Jefferson to Patsy Jefferson, Jan. 15, Feb. 18, Mar. 13, 1784; Jefferson Papers, Morgan Lib. Some of these have been printed, wholly or in part, in S. N. Randolph, *Domestic Life*.

[33] Peyton Short to William Short, Oct. 31, 1783; Short Papers, Wm. & Mary College.

[34] Jefferson to Madison, Feb. 20, 1784; *Works*, Ford, IV, 246, 249.

[35] Jefferson to Short, undated; *Wm. & Mary Quart.*, ser. 2, v. 11, pp. 242-3. The date, however, is May 7, 1784; as may be gathered from Short's acceptance note of May 14, 1784; Jefferson Papers, LC., v. 10, p. 1697.

[36] Short to Jefferson, May 14, 1784 (2nd letter); Jefferson Papers, LC., v. 10, pp. 1700-1.

[37] Hogendorp to Jefferson [May] 1784; Jefferson Papers, LC., v. 11, p. 1908-9. Hogendorp later expanded his estimate of Jefferson in a volume he published abroad, *Brieven en Gedenkschriften*, the pertinent section of which is quoted by Kimball, *Jefferson*, II, 326.

[38] Jefferson to Hogendorp, May 4, 1784; Jefferson Papers, LC., v. 10, p. 1680.

[39] Jefferson to Philip Turpin, Apr. 28, 1784; *Two Letters from Jefferson to ... the Turpins* (M. Dickore, ed.), 13-16. This Philip Turpin, now a physician, was that same "Phill" whom, as a boy, Jefferson had refused to accept as an apprentice attorney.

[40] Jefferson to Clark, Nov. 26, 1782; Dec. 4, 1783; *Ill. State Hist. Lib. Colls.*, v. 19, *Va. Series*, v. 4, pp. 155-6, 250-1.

[41] Acct. Bk., May 20, 1784; Mass. H. S.

[42] Jefferson to Charles Thomson, May 21, 1784; *Works*, Ford, IV, 362-3.

[43] Autobiography, *Works*, Ford, I, 93.

[44] *Draft Instructions*, *ibid*, IV, 353-8.

[45] Acct. Bk., June 5, 1784; Mass. H. S. *Memoirs, J. Q. Adams*, I, 317.

[46] *The Literary Diary of Ezra Stiles* (F. B. Dexter, ed.), III, 124-6, 239. Jefferson to Ezra Stiles, June 10, 1784; privately owned, photostat in Jefferson Papers, Box 1, N. Y. Pub. Lib.

[47] Acct. Bk.; Mass. H. S.

[48] *Memoranda*, July, 1784; Jefferson Papers, LC., v. 11, pp. 1805-10. Autobiography, *Works*, Ford, I, 93.

[49] Jefferson to Elbridge Gerry, July 2, 1784; Franklin Papers, Yale Univ.

CHAPTER 20

[1] Acct. Bk., July 5-26, 1784; Mass. H. S. Patsy Jefferson to Elizabeth Trist; Edgehill Randolph Papers, U. of Va.

[2] Acct. Bk., July 26-August 6, 1784; Mass. H. S.

[3] Letters of Patsy Jefferson to Mrs. Trist; Edgehill Randolph Papers, U. of Va.

[4] Acct. Bk., August 6-16, 1784; Mass. H. S.

[5] *Ibid*, August 10-September 1, 1784.

[6] *Ibid*, August 26, 1784.

[7] *Ibid*, September 4, 1784 to March 15, 1785.

[8] Jefferson to Franklin, August 18, 1784; Jefferson MSS., American Philos. Soc. Patsy noted the same thing of her father's halting French on their arrival.

[9] Jefferson to Chastellux, June 7, 1785; *Works*, Ford, III, 318-19. See also Jefferson to

Madison, May 11, 1785; *ibid,* IV, 412-13, and Autobiography, *ibid,* I, 94. The *Notes* were printed by La Marche for 1245 francs; Acct. Bk., Sept. 13, Oct. 15, 1784; Mass. H. S.

[10] Madison to Jefferson, Nov. 15, 1785; also Jan. 22, 1786; Madison, *Writings,* II, 214-15n., 215.

[11] Jefferson to Thomson, June 21, 1785; Thomson to Jefferson, Nov. 2, 1786; *N. Y. Hist. Soc. Colls., Publication Fund Ser.,* XI, 201-2, 214.

[12] A good account of his career may be found in L. R. Hawley, *Charles Thomson.*

[13] Autobiography, *Works,* Ford, I, 94-5.

[14] "Notes on Errors in translation"; Jefferson Papers, LC., v. 27, pp. 4717-23. Jefferson to John Stockdale, Feb. 1, 1787; *ibid,* v. 28, p. 4781. To Francis Hopkinson, August 14, 1786; *Works,* Ford, V, 155.

[15] Jefferson to Stockdale, Feb. 27, 1787; Jefferson Papers, LC., v. 28, p. 4876.

[16] Jefferson to Alexander Donald, Sept. 17, 1787; *ibid,* v. 33, pp. 5622-3.

[17] Benjamin Vaughan to Jefferson, Jan. 26, 1787; *ibid,* v. 28, pp. 4744-8. Rittenhouse to Jefferson, September 28, 1785; *ibid,* v. 25, p. 2566.

[18] Elizabeth Eppes to Jefferson, Oct. 13, 1784; S. N. Randolph, *Domestic Life,* 102.

[19] *Letters of Mrs. Adams,* p. 216. Jefferson to Monroe, March 18, 1785; *Works,* Ford, IV, 404-8.

[20] Weather Bk., 1776-1820; LC.

[21] Official Cipher Codes; Jefferson MSS., U. of Va.

[22] Jefferson to Madison, Dec. 8, 1784; *Works,* Ford, IV, 381-5.

[23] Jefferson to Patrick Henry, Jan. 12, 1785; *ibid,* IV, 392-5.

[24] Jefferson to Va. Delegates, July 12, 1785; *ibid,* IV, 437-40.

[25] Jefferson to Washington, Aug. 14, 1787, *Writings,* Mont., VI, 274-5.

[26] Bellini to Jefferson, Apr. 8, 1782; *Wm. & Mary Quart.,* ser. II, v. 5, pp. 1-3.

[27] Jefferson to Bellini, Sept. 30, 1785; *Writings,* Mont., V, 151-4.

[28] Jefferson to Monroe, June 17, 1785; *Works,* Ford, IV, 424.

[29] Jefferson to John Bannister, Jr., Oct. 15, 1785; *Writings,* Mont., V, 185-8. See also his remarks to Charles Thomson, almost a year earlier; Nov. 11, 1784; *Works,* Ford, IV, 381.

[30] Jefferson to David S. Franks, June 17, 1785; Jefferson Papers, LC., v. 13, p. 2177. The letter was a reply to Frank's request of June 17, 1785; *ibid,* v. 13, p. 2176. Jefferson felt that he could never make good his debt, "were I to stay here seven years," and he asked his friends at home to try and get Congress to reimburse him for the cost of his outfit; Jefferson to Monroe, *Works,* Ford, IV, 377-8.

[31] Autobiography, *Works,* Ford, I, 95-6.

[32] Jefferson to Nathanael Greene, Jan. 12, 1785; *ibid,* IV, 391-2. The original is in the Dreer Coll., Pa. H. S.

[33] Jefferson to Monroe, Dec. 10, 1784; *ibid,* IV, 385-9.

[34] Jefferson to Monroe, Nov. 11, 1784; *ibid,* IV, 370-9.

[35] Jefferson to Monroe, Nov. 11, 1784; *supra* (italics added). To same effect to Horatio Gates, Dec. 13, 1784; *ibid,* IV, 390-1.

[36] Jefferson to Nathanael Greene, Jan. 12, 1785; *supra.*

[37] Jefferson to Monroe [Feb., 1785]; *Works,* Ford, IV, 395-400.

[38] Adams, Franklin and Jefferson to Vergennes, Mar. 28, 1785; Paris, Affaires Étrangères (Steven's and Doysies' transcripts), LC., v. 29, fols. 144-5.

[39] Jefferson to Madison, Jan. 30, 1787; *Writings,* Mont., VI, 70.

[40] *Journals, Cont. Cong.,* XXVIII, 134. John Jay sent Jefferson his notification by letter dated Mar. 15, 1785, which was received on May 2nd.

[41] *Diplomatic Correspondence of U. S.,* I, 532-3.

[42] Jefferson to John Jay, June 17, 1785; *Writings,* Mont., V, 9.

[43] Paris, Affaires Etrangeres (S. & D. transcripts), Mar. 29, 1784; LC., v. 27, fols. 224-36.

[44] "Notes on T.J.'s early Diplomatic Service in Paris," Mazzei Papers, LC.

[45] *Ibid.*

[46] Autobiography, *Works,* Ford, I, 98.

[47] *Ibid,* I, 99.

[48] Jefferson to Vergennes, Aug. 15, 1785; *Writings,* Mont., V, 68-76.

[49] "Record of Conversations with Vergennes"; Jefferson Papers, LC., v. 17, pp. 2982-3029.

[50] *Ibid.* See also Jefferson to Adams, Dec. 10, 1785; *Writings,* Mont., V, 229-31.

[51] Jefferson to Vergennes, Nov. 20, 1785; *Writings,* Mont., V, 220-1.

[52] "Record of Conversations"; *supra.*

[53] Jefferson to James Ross, May 8, 1786; *Works*, Ford, V, 101-5. *Diplomatic Correspondence*, I, 760-3.

[54] Jefferson to Gov. of Va., Jan. 24, 1786; *Writings*, Mont., V, 254.

[55] Lafayette to Jefferson, Mar. 18, 1786; *Letters of Lafayette and Jefferson* (G. Chinard, ed.), 92-3.

[56] Jefferson to Jay, Apr. 23, 1786; *Writings*, Mont., V, 295-7.

[57] Vergennes to Jefferson, May 30, 1786; *Diplomatic Correspondence*, I, 764.

[58] Jefferson to Jay, May 27, 1786; *Works*, Ford, V, 116-23.

CHAPTER 21

[1] Autobiography, *Works*, Ford, I, 96.

[2] Jefferson to Thomson, Nov. 11, 1784; *ibid*, IV, 380-1. To Madison, Nov. 11, 1784; Jefferson Papers, LC., v. 5, p. 28 (this section omitted from the published letter in *Works*, Ford, IV, 380).

[3] Jefferson to Madison, Sept. 1, 1785; Madison Papers, LC., v. 6, p. 1 (published in *Writings*, Mont., V, 110).

[4] Jefferson to Thomson, Oct. 8, 1785; Dreer Coll., Pa. H. S. He also described the disaster to two balloonists who had tried to cross the Channel. Their balloon had burst in mid-air and the unfortunate occupants "were crushed to atoms." He feared that the tragedy "will probably damp the ardor with which aërial navigation has been pursued." (To Joseph Jones, June 19, 1785; *Writings*, Mont., V, 22-4.)

[5] Jefferson to Hopkinson, July 6, 1785; Jefferson Papers, LC., v. 13, p. 2222. The sad tidings of the English duplicate was sent May 9, 1786; *ibid*, v. 20, p. 3501.

[6] Webster, I, 364 ff.

[7] Jefferson to Archibald Cary, Jan. 7, 1786; *Writings*, Mont., V, 244-6. He also wrote to Hopkinson in Philadelphia for stuffed specimens of American grouse and pheasant for presentation to Buffon's museum; Jan. 3, 1786; *ibid*, V, 238-44.

[8] Gov. John Sullivan to Jefferson, Apr. 16, 1787; Jefferson Papers, LC., v. 29, pp. 4955-7.

[9] Jefferson to Wm. S. Smith, Aug. 31, 1787; *ibid*, v. 32, pp. 5553-4. See also same to same, Sept. 28, 1787; *Writings*, Mont., VI, 323-5.

[10] Jefferson to Sullivan, Oct. 5, 1787; *Writings*, Mont., VI, 328-30.

[11] Jefferson to Buffon, Oct. 1, 1787; *Works*, Ford, V, 352-4 (wrongly dated in Mont. as Oct. 3. The letterpress copy is in Jefferson Papers, LC., v. 33, pp. 5716-7). See also Webster, *supra*.

[12] Jefferson to Ezra Stiles, July 17, 1785; *Writings*, Mont., V, 35-9.

[13] Acct. Bk., Aug. 8, 1785; Mass. H. S.

[14] Peter Carr to Jefferson, Apr. 20, 1785; Jefferson MSS., U. of Va.

[15] Jefferson to Peter Carr, Aug. 19, 1785; *Writings*, Mont., V, 82-7.

[16] He paid the balance of his account for the set on Oct. 13, 1785; Acct. Bk., Mass. H. S.

[17] "Thoughts on English Prosody" [1786]; *Writings*, Mont., XVIII, 415 ff., where the date is wrongly given as 1789. By that time Chastellux was dead.

[18] The drawings, notes and plans are in the Huntington Lib. See the *Huntington Lib. Quart.*, XII, 303-10, for Fiske Kimball's discussion and dating.

[19] James Buchanan and William Hay to Jefferson, Mar., 1785; quoted in Fiske Kimball, *First Monument of the Classical Revival in America*, 11-12.

[20] Jefferson to Madison, Sept. 1, 1785; *Writings*, Mont., V, 110.

[21] Jefferson to Madison, Sept. 20, 1785; *ibid*, V, 134-7; original in Madison Papers, LC., v. 6, p. 3. To same effect, on same day, to Edmund Randolph; *ibid*, V, 137-40.

[22] For his estimate of Parisian architecture, see Jefferson to Buchanan & Hay, Aug. 13, 1785; Jefferson Papers, LC., v. 14, pp. 2350-3.

[23] Jefferson to Buchanan & Hay, Jan. 26, 1786; *ibid*, v. 18, pp. 3202-5.

[24] Jefferson to James Currie, Jan. 28, 1786; *ibid*, v. 18, pp. 3223-5.

[25] Jefferson to Abigail Adams, Sept. 4, 1785; *ibid*, v. 14, pp. 2468-9.

[26] Acct. Bk., May 22, Sept. 8, Oct. 24, Nov. 18, 1785; Mass. H. S.

[27] Jefferson to Short, Apr. 2, 1785; Jefferson-Short Papers, Wm. & Mary College.

[28] Jefferson to Adams, Aug. 10, 1785; *Writings*, Mont., V, 58-60.

[29] Jefferson to Mrs. Trist, Aug. 18, 1785; *ibid*, V, 80-2.

[30] Jefferson to Madison, Oct. 28, 1785; Madison Papers, LC., v. 6, p. 11. He wrote the

same day to the same effect to Madison's cousin, Rev. James Madison; Jefferson Papers, LC., v. 232, p. 41504-5.

[31] Jefferson to James Currie, Sept. 27, 1785; Jefferson Papers, LC., v. 15, pp. 2562-5.

[32] Jefferson to Mrs. Trist, Aug. 18, 1785; *ibid*, v. 14, p. 2391 (this section omitted from the published letter in *Writings*, Mont., V, 80-2).

[33] Jefferson to Maria Jefferson, Sept. 20, 1785; *Works*, Ford, IV, 461-3.

CHAPTER 22

[1] Washington to Jefferson, Feb. 25, 1785; Washington, *Writings*, XXVIII, 77-81.

[2] Jefferson to N. & J. Van Staphorst, July 30, 1785; *Works*, Ford, IV, 442-4.

[3] Jefferson to Washington, July 10, 1785; Jefferson Papers, LC., v. 13, pp. 2232-3. The independent State of Franklin was, however, a short-lived affair.

[4] Washington to Jefferson, Sept. 26, 1785; Washington, *Writings*, XXVIII, 278-81.

[5] Jefferson to Madison, Mar. 18, 1785; *Works*, Ford, IV, 400-4. For Jefferson's plan to use such a boycott to force open the West Indian colonial trade, see his letter to Monroe, June 17, 1785; *ibid*, IV, 415-25.

[6] Jefferson to Hogendorp, Oct. 13, 1785; *ibid*, IV, 469.

[7] Jefferson to Jay, Aug. 23, 1785; *ibid*, IV, 449-52.

[8] Jefferson to Adams, Aug. 6, 1785; *Writings*, Mont., V, 54-5. See also Jefferson to Wm. Carmichael, June 22, 1785; Jefferson Papers, LC., v. 13, pp. 2207-8.

[9] Jefferson to Adams, July 28, 1785; *Writings*, Mont., V, 42.

[10] Autobiography, *Works*, Ford, I, 99-103.

[11] Jefferson to Adams, Sept. 19, 1785; Jefferson Papers, LC., v. 14, p. 2528. See also Jefferson to Jay, Oct. 11, 1785; *Writings*, Mont., V, 171-5.

[12] Jefferson to Francis Eppes, Dec. 11, 1785; *ibid*, v. 16, p. 2835.

[13] Abigail Adams to Lucy Cranch, May 7, 1785; *Letters of Mrs. Adams* (C. F. Adams, ed.), II, 85-90.

[14] Jefferson to Chas. Williamos, July 7, 1785; Jefferson Papers, LC., v. 13, p. 2227.

[15] John Adams to Jefferson, June 7, 1785; Jefferson Papers, LC., v. 12, p. 2138. Abigail Adams to Jefferson, June 6, 1785; *ibid*, v. 12, p. 2136.

[16] Abigail Adams to Lucy Cranch, Oct. 1, 1785; *Letters of Mrs. Adams*, II, 122-3.

[17] Jefferson to Abigail Adams, Sept. 25, 1785; *Works*, Ford, IV, 463-6.

[18] Adams to Jefferson, Sept. 4, 1785; Jefferson Papers, LC., v. 14, p. 2470.

[19] Jefferson to Adams, Nov. 19, 1785; *Writings*, Mont., V, 213-19.

[20] Jefferson to Madison, Feb. 8, 1786; *Works*, Ford, V, 78-83.

[21] Jefferson to Archibald Stuart, Jan. 25, 1786; *ibid*, V, 73-6.

[22] Adams to Jefferson, Feb. 21, 1786; Jefferson Papers, LC., v. 19, p. 3284.

[23] Jefferson to Jay, Mar. 12, 1786; *Works*, Ford, V, 85-7.

[24] Adams to Jay, Feb. 26, 1786; extract in Jefferson Papers, LC., v. 19, pp. 3288-90.

[25] Jefferson & Adams to Jay, Mar. 28, 1786; Jefferson Papers, LC., v. 19, pp. 3329-30.

[26] Jefferson to Monroe, May 10, 1786; Monroe Papers, N. Y. Pub. Lib.

[27] Jefferson to Jay, Mar. 12, 1786; *Works*, Ford, V, 86.

[28] Autobiography, *ibid*, I, 97.

[29] *Diplomatic Correspondence*, I, 601.

[30] Jefferson to R. H. Lee, Apr. 22, 1786; *Works*, Ford, V, 92-4.

[31] Jefferson to Nicholas Lewis, Apr. 22, 1786; Jefferson Papers, LC., v. 20, p. 3418. See also Jefferson to Wm. Carmichael, May 5, 1786; *Writings*, Mont., V, 306-9.

[32] Jefferson to Monroe; May 10, 1786; Monroe Papers, N. Y. Pub. Lib.

[33] Jefferson to Madison, Apr. 25, 1786; Madison Papers, LC., v. 6, p. 53.

[34] See Farrell and Jones to Jefferson, July 30, 1773, in which the English firm express their sorrow at the death of "our worthy Friend Mr. Wayles," and hope to establish similarly friendly relations with his executor, Mr. Jefferson. They had procured insurance for Wayles and his partner, Richard Randolph, covering the voyage of their African slave ship during the preceding year; Microfilm of MSS. in Va. Archives, collected by Dr. Robert D. Meade; on deposit in LC.

[35] Jefferson to Alexander McCaul, Apr. 19, 1786; *Works*, Ford, V, 88-91.

[36] Acct. Bk., Apr. 26, 1786; Mass. H. S. See also Jefferson to Francis Eppes, Apr. 22, 1786; Jefferson Papers, Mass. H. S.

[37] Jefferson to Madison, Sept. 1, 1785; Madison Papers, LC., v. 6, p. 1.
[38] Acct. Bk., Mar. 11-Apr. 26, 1786; Mass. H. S.
[39] Diary; Adams, *Works*, III, 394.
[40] "Memorandums made on a tour to some of the gardens in England"; *Writings*, Mont., XVII, 236-44.
[41] Diary; Adams, *Works*, III, 394-7.
[42] Jefferson to John Page, May 4, 1786; *Works*, Ford, V, 98-101.

CHAPTER 23

[1] Acct. Bk., Apr. 28, 1786; Mass. H. S.
[2] Wm. S. Smith to Jefferson, May 21, 1786; Jefferson Papers, LC., v. 20, p. 3571.
[3] Jefferson to John Paradise, May 25, 1786; to Dr. Charles Burney, July 10, 1786; Jefferson Papers, LC., v. 21 pp. 3608, 3610-12.
[4] Jefferson to Wm. S. Smith, Sept. 13, 1786; *Bulletin of the Boston Public Library*, Apr., 1943.
[5] Nov. 3, 1786; *Letters of Lafayette and Jefferson* (G. Chinard, ed.), 108.
[6] Jefferson to Adams, May 30, 1786; Jefferson Papers, LC., v. 21, p. 3639.
[7] Adams to Jefferson, July 3, 1786; *ibid*, v. 22, p. 3787-8.
[8] Jay to Jefferson, Dec. 14, 1786; Jay, *Correspondence and Public Papers*, III, 222-4.
[9] David Humphreys to Jefferson, June 5, 1786; Jefferson Papers, LC., v. 21, pp. 3657-8. See also Franklin to Richard Price, Aug. 16, 1784; Franklin, *Writings*, IX, 256. It was on reports such as these that the late Charles Beard based his famous thesis that the troubles prior to the Constitution were grossly exaggerated. He failed to realize that outward prosperity may sometimes cloak explosive subterranean forces (*vide* the recent example of 1927-33) and that continued abuses, such as other observers noted, would inevitably have ended in such an explosion.
[10] Madison to Jefferson, June 6, 1787; Madison Papers, LC., v. 7, p. 88.
[11] Madison to Jefferson, Oct. 3, 1785; Madison, *Writings*, II, 179-80.
[12] Jefferson to Monroe, Aug. 11, 1786; *Works*, Ford, V, 147-50.
[13] Jefferson to Wythe, Aug. 13, 1786; *ibid*, V, 151-5. See also to Madison, Dec. 16, 1786; *ibid*, V, 228.
[14] *Works*, Ford, V, 3-71.
[15] *Ibid*, V, 8-12.
[16] *Ibid*, V, 16.
[17] *Ibid*, V, 32-4.
[18] *Ibid*, V, 71-2.
[19] Jefferson to Francis Hopkinson, Aug. 14, 1786; *Works*, Ford, V, 156.
[20] "Words cannot express to you how much I am pleased with Mr. Jefferson's conduct. He unites every ability that can recommend him with the ministers and at the same time possesses accomplishments of the mind and of the heart which cannot but give him many friends"; Lafayette to Washington, 1786; Lafayette, *Memoirs*, I, 129-30.
[21] Autobiography, *Works*, Ford, I, 103-4.
[22] John Trumbull's *Autobiography* gives most of the pertinent details.
[23] Jefferson to Hopkinson, *supra*.
[24] Jefferson to John Adams, July 9, 1786; *Works*, Ford, V, 138.
[25] Abigail Adams to Jefferson, July 23, 1786; Jefferson Papers, LC., v. 23, p. 3901.
[26] Jefferson to Abigail Adams, Aug. 9, 1786; *Works*, Ford, 145-7.
[27] See, for example, Jefferson to Monroe, Aug. 11, 1786; *ibid*, V, 148.
[28] Jefferson to Abigail Adams, June 21 [1785]; *ibid*, IV, 428.
[29] Jefferson to Mme. de Tott, Feb. 28, 1787; Jefferson Papers, Mo. H. S. Mme. de Tott duly went to see the picture, and reported to Jefferson that it was indeed admirable, but that she did not think it was a portrait of Marius; Mar. 4, 1787; *ibid*.
[30] Jefferson to Mme. de Tott, Nov. 28, 1786; *ibid*.
[31] For extended studies of Maria Cosway and her husband, see G. C. Williamson, *Richard Cosway*, and H. D. Bullock, *My Head and My Heart*.
[32] Williamson, *Richard Cosway*, 27.
[33] Trumbull, *Autobiography*, 118.
[34] Jefferson to Maria Cosway, Oct. 12, 1786; *Works*, Ford, V, 202-4. It is amazing that

no one of the numerous commentators on the Jefferson-Maria episode has noted that *this* was the first meeting between the two. But the language of the letter which describes it is plain and unmistakable. "*Heart.* Accordingly, Sir, this acquaintance was not the consequence of my doings. It was one of your projects which threw us in the way of it. It was you [the *Head* of the dialogue], remember & not I, who desired the meeting at Legrand & Molinos. I never trouble myself with domes nor arches," etc.

[35] *Ibid*, 204.

[36] Acct. Bk., Sept. 5-16, 1786; Mass. H. S. Jefferson was manifestly too busy on this jaunt to enter these items daily, as was his custom. He therefore wrote them in *after* his hand was fractured, when he had time to contemplate the departed glories.

[37] Jefferson to Maria Cosway, Oct. 12, 1786; *supra.*

[38] The details–and even the date–of this accident have been clouded in uncertainty. His daughter, Martha, when an old lady, told Randall, Jefferson's first biographer, that he fractured his wrist while walking in the country with a friend; and that it occurred on September 4th. Randall accepted the date, because it tallied with the sudden change in Jefferson's handwriting in the Acct. Bk. as of that day; Randall's *Jefferson*, I, 456. But it has since been pointed out that these items were written in later, and letters exist after that date in his normal hand. L. H. Butterfield and H. C. Rice ("Jefferson's Earliest Note to Maria Cosway," in *Wm. & Mary Quart.*, 3rd ser., V, 26-33) believe that the accident might have happened on Sept. 16th, the day of the visit to the Desert. But the controversy is definitely concluded, as to date, place and circumstance, by the contemporary account of M. Le Veillard to Wm. Temple Franklin, Sept. 20, 1786 (Franklin Papers, Amer. Philos. Soc., v. 107, p. 15). Marie Kimball, in her *Jefferson: The Scene of Europe*, 168, has seen the same letter and arrived at the same conclusion.

[39] The progress of his writing may be studied to best advantage in the Acct. Bk., Mass. H. S., under the appropriate dates.

[40] Maria Cosway to Jefferson, undated; original in Jefferson Papers, Mass. H. S. Printed in S. N. Randolph, *Domestic Life*, 59. Though undated, the surrounding circumstances indicate it was written late at night of the day following the accident–Sept. 19th–and sent by servant on Sept. 20th.

[41] Jefferson to Maria Cosway, Thursday; cited in Butterfield & Rice, *supra.* They date this letter Oct. 5th and I agree. Mrs. Kimball's thesis that it should be dated Sept. 21st seems implausible (*Jefferson: The Scene of Europe*, 332, note 33). It makes the date of Jefferson's ride with Maria too soon after the accident; and it was quite possible (as the contents of the various letters indicate) for Jefferson to have sent a note by servant to her, received one in reply, also by servant, the same morning; and then to have decided to drive out to see her off.

[42] S. N. Randolph, *Domestic Life*, 59-60. The original is in Jefferson Papers, Mass. H. S.

[43] Jefferson to Maria Cosway, Oct. 12, 1786; *Works*, Ford, V, 201-17.

[44] Jefferson to Maria Cosway, Oct. 13, 1786; *ibid*, V, 217-18.

[45] Trumbull to Jefferson, Oct. 9, 1786; Jefferson Papers, LC., v. 25, pp. 4230-1.

[46] Jefferson to Trumbull, Oct. 13, 1786; *ibid*, v. 25, p. 4249.

[47] Jefferson to Maria Cosway, Nov. 19, 1786; MS., U. of Va.

[48] Maria Cosway to Jefferson; Jefferson Papers, Mass. H. S.

[49] Jefferson to Maria Cosway, Nov. 29, 1786; MS., U. of Va. Maria to Jefferson, July 9, 1787; *ibid*. Jefferson to Trumbull, July 16, 1787; Jefferson Papers, LC. Much of their correspondence appears, in whole or in part, in H. D. Bullock, *My Head and My Heart.* The manuscripts are chiefly in LC., U. of Va. and Mass. H. S.

CHAPTER 24

[1] Rev. James Madison to Jefferson [1786]; Jefferson Papers, LC., v. 27, p. 4570.

[2] Abigail Adams to Jefferson, Jan. 29, 1787; *ibid*, v. 28, pp. 4761-2.

[3] Jefferson to Madison, Jan. 30, 1787; *Works*, Ford, V, 254-62.

[4] Jefferson to Edward Carrington, Jan. 16, 1787; *ibid*, V, 252-4.

[5] Jefferson to Ezra Stiles, Dec. 24, 1786; Jefferson Papers, Box 1, N. Y. Pub. Lib. Printed in *Writings*, Mont., VI, 25.

[6] Jefferson to David Hartley, July 2, 1787; Franklin Papers, Yale Univ. Printed in *Writings*, Mont., VI, 150-2.

[7] Jefferson to Lucy Paradise, Aug. 27, 1786; Jefferson Papers, LC., v. 24, p. 4078. Printed in *Works*, Ford, V, 172-4.

[8] Jefferson to Nicholas Lewis, Dec. 19, 1786; *Works*, Ford, V, 234-8.

[9] Jefferson to Alexander McCaul, Jan. 4, 1787; *ibid*, V, 241-4. To Wm. Jones, Jan. 5, 1787; *ibid*, V, 244-50.

[10] The correspondence relating to these debts is voluminous. See Jefferson Papers, LC., particularly v. 40, pp. 6928-31; v. 41, pp. 6938-45, 6955-6.

[11] A. McCaul to Jefferson, Aug. 14, 1788; Jefferson Papers, LC., v. 42, p. 7164.

[12] The entire correspondence is contained in the Jefferson Papers, LC. See also A. B. Shepperson, *John Paradise and Lucy Ludwell.*

[13] Jefferson to Madison, Dec. 16, 1786; *Works*, Ford, V, 225. To Trumbull, Nov. 28, 1786; Jefferson Papers, LC., v. 26, p. 4462.

[14] Jefferson to Wm. S. Smith, Sept. 13, 1786; Jefferson Papers, LC., v. 24, pp. 4143-4.

[15] "Memoranda taken on a Journey . . . 1787"; *Writings*, Mont., XVII, 154.

[16] *Ibid*, XVII, 154-62. Jefferson to Short, Mar. 15, 1787; *Wm. & Mary Quart.*, ser. 2, v. 11, pp. 244-5.

[17] Jefferson to Madame de Tessé, Mar. 20, 1787; *Writings*, Mont., VI, 102-6.

[18] Jefferson to James Sloan, Jr., June 15, 1818; Jefferson Papers, LC., v. 213, p. 38006.

[19] *Writings*, Mont., XVII, 170-1. Jefferson to Short, Mar. 27, 1787; *Wm. & Mary Quart.*, ser. 2, v. 11, pp. 245-7.

[20] Jefferson to Short, Mar. 29, 1787; *Wm. & Mary Quart.*, ser. 2, v. 11, pp. 247-8.

[21] *Writings*, Mont., XVII, 174-5.

[22] Jefferson to Comtesse de Tott, Apr. 5, 1787; Jefferson Papers, LC., v. 29, pp. 4931-2.

[23] Jefferson to Lafayette, Apr. 11, 1787; *Writings*, Mont., VI, 106-10.

[24] Jefferson to Mazzei, Apr. 4, 1787; *Va. Mag.*, v. 51, 113 ff.

[25] Jefferson to Jay, May 4, 1787; *Works*, Ford, V, 270-1.

[26] *Writings*, Mont., XVII, 180-3.

[27] *Ibid*, XVII, 185.

[28] Jefferson to Edward Rutledge, July 14, 1787; *Works*, Ford, V, 302-4. "Memoranda, etc.," *Writings*, Mont., XVII, 192.

[29] "Travelling Notes for Mr. Rutledge and Mr. Shippen," June 3, 1788; *Writings*, Mont., XVII, 290-3.

[30] *Writings*, Mont., XVII, 195.

[31] *Ibid*, XVII, 202.

[32] Jefferson to Martha Jefferson, May 21, 1787; *Works*, Ford, V, 281-3.

[33] *Ibid*. Also Jefferson to Short, May 21, 1787; *Wm. & Mary Quart.*, ser. 2, v. 11, pp. 336-42.

[34] *Writings*, Mont., XVII, 211-12.

[35] *Ibid*, XVII, 215-16.

[36] *Ibid*, XVII, 232-4.

CHAPTER 25

[1] Jefferson to Francis Eppes, Aug. 30, 1785; S. N. Randolph, *Domestic Life*, 77-9. Jefferson to Elizabeth Eppes, Sept. 22, 1785; *ibid*, 76.

[2] Jefferson to Francis Eppes, Dec. 11, 1785; Jefferson Papers, LC., v. 16, p. 2835.

[3] Jefferson to Mrs. Bolling, July 23, 1787; Jefferson Papers, Mass. H. S.

[4] Abigail Adams to Lucy Cranch, July 16, 1787; *Letters of Mrs. Adams*, II, 179-80. See also the correspondence between Abigail Adams and Jefferson concerning Polly in the Jefferson Papers, LC.; especially v. 30, pp. 5150, 5168, 5217-8, 5239, 5240.

[5] Jefferson to Abigail Adams; July 16, 1787; Jefferson Papers, LC., v. 31, p. 5270.

[6] Jefferson to Mary Bolling, July 23, 1787; *Works*, Ford, V, 305-7.

[7] Jefferson to Patsy Jefferson, Mar. 6, 1786; Jefferson MSS., Morgan Lib. Partly printed in S. N. Randolph, *Domestic Life*, 80-1.

[8] Jefferson to Patsy Jefferson, June 14, 1787; Jefferson MSS., Morgan Lib.

[9] Jefferson to Patsy Jefferson, Mar. 28, 1787; Jefferson MSS., Morgan Lib. There are textual errors in the printed version in *Domestic Life*, 115-17.

[10] Peter Carr to Jefferson, Dec. 30, 1786; Jefferson Papers, U. of Va. Much of their correspondence can be found in this collection.

[11] Peter Carr to Jefferson, Apr. 18, 1787; *ibid*.

[12] Jefferson to Peter Carr, Aug. 10, 1787; *Works*, Ford, V, 322-8. The original is in Jefferson Papers, LC., v. 32, pp. 5471-77, where a reading list is appended.
[13] Madison to Jefferson, Aug. 12, 1786; Madison, *Writings*, II, 262.
[14] Washington to Jefferson, May 30, 1787; *Records of the Federal Convention* (M. Farrand, ed.), I, 31.
[15] Madison to Jefferson, June 6, 1787; *ibid*, I, 35-6.
[16] Madison to Jefferson, Mar. 19 [18], 1787; Madison, *Writings*, II, 326.
[17] Jefferson to Madison, June 20, 1787; *Works*, Ford, V, 284.
[18] Jefferson to Madison, Dec. 16, 1786; *ibid*, V, 226-7.
[19] Jefferson to Adams, Aug. 30, 1787; *Writings*, Mont., VI, 285-9.
[20] Jefferson to Benjamin Hawkins, Aug. 4, 1787; *Works*, Ford, V, 320-1.
[21] Jefferson to Edward Carrington, Aug. 4, 1787; *ibid*, V, 318-9.
[22] Jefferson to Wm. S. Smith, Nov. 13, 1787; *ibid*, V, 360-3.
[23] Madison to Jefferson, Oct. 24, 1787; Madison, *Writings*, V, 17-41.
[24] Jefferson to Madison, Dec. 20, 1787; *Works*, Ford, V, 368-75.
[25] Jefferson to Wm. S. Smith, Feb. 2, 1788; *ibid*, V, 384-5.
[26] Jefferson to Wm. Carmichael, June 3, 1788; *ibid*, V, 406.
[27] Jefferson to Adams, Nov. 13, 1787; *Writings*, Mont., VI, 368-71.
[28] Adams to Jefferson, Dec. 6, 1787; Jefferson Papers, LC., v. 35, p. 5981.
[29] Madison to E. Randolph, July 2, 1788; Madison, *Writings*, V, 235.
[30] Jefferson to Madison, Nov. 18, 1788; *Works*, Ford, V, 433-4.
[31] Jefferson to Washington, May 2, 1788; *ibid*, V, 388-90.
[32] Autobiography, *ibid*, I, 120.

CHAPTER 26

[1] Jefferson to Madison, Dec. 16, 1786; *Works*, Ford, V, 226.
[2] Jefferson to Adams, Feb. 20, 1787; Adams, *Works*, VIII, 431-2.
[3] Jefferson to Montmorin, July 23, 1787; *Writings*, Mont., VI, 180-7.
[4] Jefferson to Adams, July 1, 1787; *Works*, Ford, V, 289-92.
[5] Jefferson to Madison, Aug. 2, 1787; *ibid*, V, 314-18.
[6] Jefferson to Madison, June 20, 1787; *ibid*, V, 286.
[7] Jefferson to Nicholas Lewis, July 29, 1787; *ibid*, V, 309-14. See also to Francis Eppes, July 30, 1787; MSS., Huntington Lib.
[8] Jefferson to Adams, July 23, 1787; Jefferson Papers, LC., v. 31, pp. 5320-1. Adams to Jefferson, Aug. 25, 1787; *ibid*, v. 32, pp. 5533-4.
[9] *Amer. State Papers: Foreign Relations*, I, 113-14.
[10] Autobiography, *Works*, Ford, I, 114.
[11] Jefferson to W. M. Cary, Aug. 12, 1787; Jefferson Papers, LC., v. 32, pp. 5490-1.
[12] Jefferson to Wm. Carmichael, Sept. 25, 1787; *Works*, Ford, V, 348.
[13] Jefferson to Charles Thomson, Dec. 17, 1786, Sept. 20, 1787; *ibid*, V, 231-4, 342-4.
[14] Jefferson to Ezra Stiles, Sept. 1, 1786; privately owned, photostat in Jefferson Papers, Box 1, N. Y. Pub. Lib.
[15] Jefferson to Rev. James Madison, July 19, 1788; *Writings*, Mont., VII, 73-9.
[16] Jefferson to Trumbull, Feb. 23, 1787; Jefferson Papers, LC., v. 28, p. 4868.
[17] Jefferson to Mme. de Brehan, Mar. 14, 1789; *Works*, Ford, V, 460.
[18] Jefferson to Maria Cosway, Apr. 24, 1788; MSS., U. of Va. See also his letter of Jan. 14, 1788; Jefferson Papers, Mass. H. S.
[19] Maria Cosway to Jefferson, Friday night, Dec., 1787; Jefferson Papers, LC., v. 36, p. 6202.
[20] Maria Cosway to Jefferson, Christmas Day [1787]; Jefferson Papers, Mass. H. S.
[21] Jefferson to Maria Cosway [Jan., 1788]; *ibid*.
[22] For an extended account of Angelica Church, see Schachner, *Alexander Hamilton, passim.*
[23] Jefferson to Angelica Church, Feb. 17, 1788; *Mo. Hist. Soc.: Glimpses of the Past*, 77-8.
[24] Jefferson to Angelica Church, July 27, 1788; Aug. 17, 1788; MSS., Huntington Lib.
[25] Jefferson to Angelica Church, Sept. 21, 1788; *Correspondence of Jefferson* (W. C. Ford, ed.), 35.
[26] Maria Cosway to Jefferson, Mar. 6 [1788]; Jefferson Papers, Mass. H. S.
[27] Trumbull to Jefferson, Mar. 6, 1788; Jefferson Papers, LC., v. 38, p. 6498.

[28] Maria Cosway to Jefferson, Apr. 29 [1788]; MSS., U. of Va. Angelica Church to Jefferson, July 21, 1788; Jefferson Papers, LC.

[29] Jay to Jefferson, Nov. 25, 1788; Jefferson Papers, LC., v. 44, pp. 7591-2.

[30] Jefferson to Moustier, May, 1788; *Writings*, Mont., VII, 12.

[31] Mme. de Brehan to Jefferson, Dec. 29, 1788; Jefferson Papers, LC., v. 46, pp. 7762-3.

[32] Jefferson to Maria Cosway, Jan. 14, 1789; Jefferson MSS., U. of Va.

[33] Abigail Adams to Jefferson, Feb. 26, 1788; Jefferson Papers, LC., v. 38, pp. 6472-3.

[34] Acct. Bk. for 1788; Mass. H. S.

[35] *Diplomatic Corresp.*, II, 135.

[36] Jefferson to Short, Mar. 10, 1788; Jefferson Papers, LC., v. 38, p. 6508.

[37] Adams to Jefferson, Feb. 12, 1788; *ibid*, v. 37, pp. 6425-6.

[38] *Letters of John Adams to his Wife*, II, 111-12. Jefferson to Wm. Carmichael, June 3, 1788; Jefferson Papers, LC., v. 40, pp. 6791-99. This section is omitted from the printed version in *Works*, Ford, V, 403.

[39] Jefferson to Geismar, Mar. 18, 1788; Jefferson Papers, LC., v. 38, p. 6534. To Trumbull, Mar. 27, 1788; *ibid*, v. 38, p. 6546. To Unger, Feb. 16, 1788; *ibid*, v. 37, p. 6441.

[40] *Writings*, Mont., XVII, 244-90. See also Jefferson Papers, LC., v. 233, p. 41789.

[41] *Ibid*, XVII, 244-8.

[42] *Ibid*, XVII, 252.

[43] *Ibid*, XVII, 254. Jefferson to Maria Cosway, Apr. 24, 1788; Jefferson MSS., U. of Va.

[44] *Writings*, Mont., XVII, 254-5.

[45] *Ibid*, XVII, 255.

[46] *Ibid*, XVII, 260.

[47] *Ibid*, XVII, 260.

[48] Jefferson to Short, Apr. 9, 1788; *Wm. & Mary Quart.*, ser. 2, XI, 341-2.

[49] Jefferson to Geismar, July 13, 1788; Jefferson Papers, LC., v. 41, p. 6960.

[50] *Writings*, Mont., XVII, 263-73.

[51] *Ibid*, XVII, 278-9.

[52] Jefferson's draft of this article is in Jefferson Papers, LC., v. 234, pp. 41813-16.

[53] *Writings*, Mont., XVII, 279-80.

[54] "Travelling Notes for Mr. Rutledge and Mr. Shippen," June 3, 1788; *Writings*, Mont., XVII, 290-3.

[55] Jefferson to J. Peter de Rieux, July 25, 1788; Jefferson Papers, LC., v. 41, p. 7036. This confession of Jefferson's doubts has never been published.

CHAPTER 27

[1] Jefferson to Jay; *Diplomatic Corresp.*, II, 90-1.

[2] Jefferson to Madison, July 31, 1788; *Works*, Ford, V, 424.

[3] Jefferson to E. Carrington, Dec. 21, 1787; *ibid*, V, 377.

[4] Jefferson to Monroe, Aug. 9, 1788; Jefferson Papers, LC., v. 42, pp. 7135-8. Omitted from printed version in *Writings*, Mont., VII, 112.

[5] Jefferson to Madison, Nov. 18, 1788; *Works*, Ford, V, 436. The plans for funding, however, are omitted, and are to be found in Jefferson Papers, LC., v. 44, pp. 7518-26.

[6] The documents relating to the negotiations are in *Affaires Étrangères*, Stevens Transcripts, LC. The draft convention is in *ibid*, v. 33, fols. 356-63.

[7] Jay to Jefferson, Apr. 24, 1788; Jay, *Correspondence*, III, 326-7.

[8] Jefferson to Washington, Dec. 14, 1788; *Works*, Ford, V, 438-9.

[9] Jefferson to Montmorin, Oct. 23, 1788; *Writings*, Mont., VII, 156-9; to Jay, Nov. 19, 1788; *ibid*, VII, 189-220.

[10] "Notes on Importance of U. S. Carrying Trade," [May, 1789]; Jefferson Papers, LC., v. 53, p. 9035.

[11] Jefferson to Jay, Aug. 3, 1788; "The Deane Papers," in *N. Y. Hist. Soc. Colls., Pub. Fund Ser.*, v. 5, pp. 485-6.

[12] Jay to Jefferson, Nov. 25, 1788; *ibid*, v. 5, pp. 504-5.

[13] Jefferson to Dr. Edward Bancroft, Mar. 12, 1789; Jefferson Papers, LC., v. 47, pp. 8040-1. Printed in "The Deane Papers," v. 5, pp. 512-13.

[14] Bancroft to Jefferson, Mar. 10, 1789; Jefferson Papers, LC., v. 47, pp. 8068-70.

[15] Jefferson to Jay, Mar. 12, Mar. 15, 1789; "The Deane Papers," v. 5, pp. 513, 514.

[16] Jefferson to Bancroft, Apr. 9, 1789; Jefferson Papers, LC., v. 48, p. 8220. Bancroft to

Jefferson, Aug. 21, 1789; *ibid,* v. 51, pp. 8649-50. Bancroft's remarkable tale is corroborated in the private letters from Silas Deane to his brother, Barnabas; particularly those of Aug. 10, 1788 and Nov. 10, 1788; "The Deane Papers," v. 5, pp. 489, 495.

[17] Jefferson to Anna Scott Marks, July 12, 1788; S. N. Randolph, *Domestic Life,* 135-6.

[18] Jefferson to Randolph Jefferson, Jan. 11, 1789; *ibid,* 136-7.

[19] Jefferson to Bellini, July 25, 1788; *Writings,* Mont., VII, 88-90.

[20] David Humphreys to Jefferson, Nov. 29, 1788; Jefferson Papers, LC., v. 45, pp. 7603-9.

[21] Jefferson to Francis Hopkinson, Mar. 13, 1789; *Works,* Ford, V, 456-9.

[22] Jefferson to Charles Thomson, May 21, 1784; *ibid,* IV, 362; to Thomas Paine, Dec. 23, 1788; *Writings,* Mont., VII, 241-4.

[23] Jefferson to Mr. Payne, Oct. 2, 1788; Jefferson Papers, Mo. H. S.

[24] Jefferson to Trumbull, Aug. 24, 1788; Jefferson Papers, LC., v. 42, p. 7191.

[25] Trumbull to Jefferson, Sept. 2, 1788; *ibid,* v. 42, pp. 7245. Jefferson to Trumbull, Sept. 10, 1788; Oct. 11, 1788; *ibid,* v. 43, pp. 7284, 7373.

[26] Jefferson to Trumbull, Feb. 15, 1789; *ibid,* v. 47, p. 7988.

[27] Trumbull to Jefferson, Mar. 10, 1789; *ibid,* v. 47, pp. 8064-5. Jefferson to Trumbull, Mar. 15, 1789; *ibid,* v. 47, p. 8117.

[28] Jefferson to Madison, Nov. 18, 1788; *Works,* Ford, V, 435-6. Jefferson to Francis Eppes, Dec. 15, 1788; Jefferson MSS., Huntington Lib. He wrote to David Humphries a little later in the same vein: He wished "to possess myself anew, by conversation with my countrymen, of their spirits & their ideas. I know only the Americans of the year 1784. They tell me this is to be much a stranger to those of 1789." Mar. 18, 1789; *Works,* Ford, V, 467-71.

[29] Randall, *Jefferson,* I, 538.

[30] Jefferson to Short, Jan. 22, 1789; Jefferson Papers, LC., v. 46, pp. 7908-10.

[31] Jefferson to Maria Cosway, Jan. 14, 1789; Jefferson MSS., U. of Va.

[32] Jefferson to Maria Cosway, Sept. 26, 1788; *ibid.*

[33] Maria Cosway to Jefferson, Dec. 23 [1788]; *ibid.*

CHAPTER 28

[1] Jefferson to Wm. Carmichael, Mar. 4, 1789; *Works,* Ford, V, 454. To Madame de Brehan, Mar. 14, 1789; *ibid,* V, 459.

[2] *Writings,* Mont., VII, 337-8.

[3] Jefferson to Maria Cosway, July 25, 1789; Jefferson MSS., U. of Va. Maria Cosway to Jefferson, Aug. 19 [1789]; *ibid.*

[4] Gouverneur Morris, *A Diary of the French Revolution* (B. C. Davenport, ed.), I, 83, 104, 159n.

[5] Jefferson to Moustier, May 20, 1789; Jefferson MSS., Morgan Lib.

[6] Jefferson to Lafayette, May 6, 1789; *Works,* Ford, V, 472-3.

[7] Jefferson to Lafayette, June 3, 1789; *ibid,* V, 479. To St. Etienne, June 3, 1789; *ibid,* V, 479-81. "A Charter of Rights," *ibid,* V, 481-3.

[8] A MS. copy of Lafayette's "Declaration of the Rights of Man" is in Jefferson Papers, LC.

[9] Jefferson to Jay; *Diplomatic Correspondence,* II, 299-300.

[10] Jefferson to Jay, July 19, 1789; *Writings,* Mont., VII, 409-22.

[11] Autobiography, *Works,* Ford, I, 139, 149-50.

[12] Jefferson to Trumbull, Aug. 5, 1789; Jefferson Papers, LC., v. 51, pp. 8614-5. Jefferson to Montmorin, July 8, 1789; *Works,* Ford, V, 402-3.

[13] *Writings,* Mont., VII, 400-1.

[14] See the exchange of letters in *Lafayette and Jefferson* (G. Chinard, ed.), 132-3; also *Writings,* Mont., VII, 401-2, 405.

[15] Lafayette to Jefferson, undated; *Lafayette and Jefferson,* 134-5.

[16] Archbishop of Bordeaux to Jefferson, July 20, 1789; *ibid,* 143-4.

[17] Jefferson to the Archbishop, July 22, 1789; *ibid,* 144-5. In French; translation mine.

[18] Lafayette to Jefferson, Aug. 25, 1789; Jefferson Papers, LC., v. 51, p. 8626.

[19] Autobiography, *Works,* Ford, I, 154.

[20] Jefferson to Jay, Sept. 19, 1789; *Writings,* Mont., VII, 474-5.

[21] Autobiography, *Works,* Ford, I, 155.

[22] Jefferson to Madison, Aug. 28, 1789; *Works,* Ford, V, 490.

[23] Jefferson to Trumbull, June 1, 1789; Franklin Papers, Yale Univ. See also Jefferson to Short, Mar. 24, 1789; Jefferson Papers, LC., v. 48, pp. 8163-8.

[24] Trumbull to Jefferson, June 11, 1789; Trumbull, *Autobiography*, 157-62.
[25] Autobiography, *Works*, Ford, I, 157.
[26] Jefferson to Jay, Sept. 30, 1789; *ibid*, VI, 16-19.
[27] *Antiques*, XV, 128. See also E. Dumbauld, *Thomas Jefferson, American Tourist*, 160.
[28] Jefferson to Madison, Sept. 6, 1789; *Works*, Ford, VI, 3-11. Madison's reply contains reasoned objections to Jefferson's theory; Feb. 4, 1790; Jefferson Papers, LC., v. 53, pp. 9089-91.
[29] Jefferson to Short, Oct. 4, 1789; Jefferson Papers, LC., v. 52, pp. 8878-9. To Short, Oct. 7, 1789; *ibid*, v. 52, pp. 8884-5.
[30] "Reminiscences of Isaac Jefferson"; Jefferson Papers, U. of Va.
[31] Jefferson to James Rumsey, Oct. 14, 1789; *Works*, Ford, VI, 19. To Daniel Parker, Oct. 20, 1789; Jefferson Papers, Mo. H. S.
[32] Jefferson to Trumbull, Nov. 23, 1789; Jefferson Papers, LC., v. 52, p. 8921. Randall's *Jefferson*, I, 551-2.

CHAPTER 29

[1] "Address of Welcome by Mayor of Norfolk and Jefferson's Response," November 25, 1789; Jefferson Papers, LC., v. 52, p. 8930. Dr. James Currie to Jefferson, Nov. 27, 1789; *ibid*, v. 52, p. 8931.
[2] Jefferson to Short, Dec. 14, 1789; *Works*, Ford, VI, 22-7.
[3] Va. House of Delegates to Jefferson, Dec. 7, 1789; Jefferson Papers, LC., v. 53, p. 8937. Jefferson to House of Delegates, undated, *ibid*, v. 53, p. 8938.
[4] Citizens of Albemarle Co. to Jefferson, Dec. 24, 1789; *ibid*, v. 53, p. 9021. Jefferson's draft reply; Dec. 24, 1789; *ibid*, v. 53, p. 9023.
[5] Madison to Jefferson, May 27, 1789; Madison, *Writings*, V, 317n.
[6] Jefferson to Short, Dec. 14, 1789; *supra*.
[7] Washington to Jefferson, Oct. 13, 1789; Washington, *Writings*, v. 30, pp. 446-7. Autobiography, *Works*, Ford, I, 158.
[8] Jefferson to Washington, Dec. 15, 1789; *Works*, Ford, VI, 27-9.
[9] Jefferson to Washington, Feb. 14, 1790 (replying to Washington's letter of Jan. 21, 1790); *ibid*, VI, 30-1.
[10] Short to Jefferson, Nov. 30, 1789; Jefferson Papers, LC., v. 53, pp. 8935-6.
[11] Cyrus Griffin to Jefferson, Dec. 11, 1789; *ibid*, v. 53, pp. 8951-2.
[12] Col. Thomas Mann Randolph to Jefferson, Jan. 30, 1790; Jefferson Papers, Mass. H. S.
[13] Jefferson to Dr. Gem, Apr. 4, 1790; Jefferson MSS., Huntington Lib.
[14] Jefferson to Madison, Feb. 14, 1790; Jefferson Papers, LC., v. 53, pp. 9102-3.
[15] "Notes on Wifely Conduct," Feb. 23, 1790; *ibid*, v. 234, p. 41985.
[16] Jefferson to Martha Jefferson Randolph, Apr. 26, 1790; Randall, *Jefferson*, I, 623.
[17] Jefferson to N. & J. Staphorst and Hubbard, Feb. 28, 1790; *Works*, Ford, VI, 32-4.
[18] Jefferson to Martha J. Randolph, July 17, 1790; Randall, *Jefferson*, I, 625-6.
[19] Jefferson to Comtesse de Tessé, Mar. 17, 1790; Jefferson Papers, LC., v. 53, pp. 9114-5.
[20] Jefferson to Short, Mar. 12, 1790; *ibid*, v. 54, pp. 9150-2.
[21] Jefferson to Mr. Fitzhugh, Mar. 11, 1790; Jefferson Papers, Mass. H. S.
[22] Autobiography, *Works*, Ford, I, 161.
[23] Acct. Bk., Mar. 29, 1790; Mass. H. S. Agreement of lease, Mar. 29, 1790; Jefferson Papers, LC., v. 54, p. 9149.
[24] Jefferson to Short, Apr. 6, 1790; Jefferson Papers, LC., v. 54, pp. 9196-9203.
[25] Jefferson to Martha J. Randolph, Apr. 4, 1790; Jefferson MSS., Morgan Lib. Acct. Bk., June 1, 1790; Mass. H. S.
[26] Jefferson to T. M. Randolph, May 30, 1790; *Works*, Ford, VI, 61-3.
[27] Jefferson to Maria Cosway, June 23, 1790; Jefferson Papers, LC., v. 55, p. 9482. To Angelica Church, June 23, 1790; *ibid*, v. 55, p. 9477.

CHAPTER 30

[1] *Autobiography of Benjamin Rush* (G. W. Corner, ed.), 93, 181.
[2] *Journal of William Maclay*, 265-6.
[3] *Ibid*, 302.
[4] H. W. Pierson, *Jefferson at Monticello*, 70-1. Pierson had taken down Bacon's reminiscences.

[5] Jefferson to Washington, Apr. 1, 1790; *Works*, Ford, VI, 38-9.
[6] Memorandum, undated and unsigned; Misc. Records, Dept. of State; National Archives.
[7] For a more detailed account of Hamilton's Reports and of the speculation in the funds, see Schachner, *Alexander Hamilton, passim.*
[8] *Annals of Congress*, II, pp. 1387-9.
[9] So Jefferson was to write in his Anas; *Works*, Ford, I, 173. The famous *Anas* were memoranda made, as Jefferson put it, on loose scraps of paper which, as they accumulated, he later had bound, just as they were, into volumes. Twenty-five years after the events they described, Jefferson looked them over, eliminated some and copied the rest in a fair hand, after which the originals were destroyed. Some were undoubtedly left untouched; others, from internal evidence, seem to have been modified to conform to later views and possible hindsights. The whole mass, filled as it is with second and third-hand reports, rumors and mere gossip-mongering, must be treated with the greatest caution by the historian. The item on Jefferson's role in the assumption deal is definitely, as he acknowledged, hindsight and not based on any contemporary memorandum.
[10] Jefferson to T. M. Randolph, Apr. 18, 1790; *Works*, Ford, VI, 47.
[11] Jefferson to T. M. Randolph, June 20, 1790; *ibid*, VI, 76-7. He wrote to the same effect to Francis Eppes, July 4, 1790; *ibid*, VI, 84-5.
[12] Fisher Ames to Thomas Dwight, June 11, 1790; Ames, *Works*, I, 79-81.
[13] Ames to Minot, June 23, 1790; *ibid*, I, 81-3.
[14] Jefferson to T. M. Randolph, June 20, 1790; *supra*.
[15] Jefferson to Monroe, June 20, 1790; *Works*, Ford, VI, 78-81.
[16] Monroe to Jefferson, July 3, 1790; Jefferson Papers, LC., v. 56, pp. 9544-5.
[17] Maclay, *Journal*, 291-3.
[18] Anas, *Works*, Ford, I, 173-7.
[19] Jefferson to T. M. Randolph, July 25, 1790; MSS., Huntington Lib.
[20] Washington to Lafayette, June 3, 1790; Washington, *Writings*, XXXI, 46.
[21] Jefferson to Bellini, June 13, 1790; *Wm. & Mary Quart.*, ser. 2, v. 5, p. 10.
[22] Jefferson to Short, May 27, 1790; *Works*, Ford, VI, 58. To Martha J. Randolph, June 6, 1790; Jefferson Papers, Morgan Lib.
[23] Jefferson to Rittenhouse, June 12, 1790; Jefferson Papers, LC., v. 55, pp. 9371-3.
[24] Jefferson to Speaker of the House of Representatives, July 4, 1790; *ibid*, v. 56, p. 9554.
[25] "Plan for establishing uniformity in the Coinage, Weights and Measures of the United States," July 4, 1790; *Writings*, Mont., III, 26-57.
[26] Benjamin Vaughan to Jefferson, Oct. 21, 1790; Jefferson Papers, LC., v. 57, pp. 9856-7. Ezra Stiles to Jefferson, Aug. 27, 1790; Franklin Papers, Yale Univ.
[27] "Opinion on the Validity of the Yazoo Land Grants by Georgia," May 3, 1790; *Works*, Ford, VI, 55-7.
[28] Wm. Temple Franklin to Jefferson, July 20, 1790; Misc. Letters, Dept. of State, Nat. Archives. Jefferson to [Wm. T. Franklin], July 25, 1790; copy in Edgehill–Randolph Coll., U. of Va. The name of the recipient is not given in the letter, but it is obvious that it is Franklin.
[29] Jefferson to Martha J. Randolph, Dec. 23, 1790; Jefferson Papers, Morgan Lib. This section is omitted from the printed letter in S. N. Randolph, *Domestic Life*, 191-2.
[30] Short to Jefferson, June 14, July 7, 1790; Jefferson Papers, LC., v. 55, pp. 9389-9404, 9566-7. Jefferson to Martha J. Randolph, July 24, 1791; Jefferson Papers, Mass. H. S.
[31] Short to Jefferson, June 14, 1790; *supra*. Jefferson to Short, July 26, 1790; Jefferson Papers, LC., v. 56, p. 9673.

CHAPTER 31

[1] Jefferson to Short, Jan. 8, 1825; *Works*, Ford, XII, 395.
[2] Jefferson to T. M. Randolph, May 30, 1790; *ibid*, VI, 64.
[3] Jefferson to Edward Rutledge, July 4, 1790; *ibid*, VI, 88.
[4] Jefferson to Monroe, July 11, 1790; *ibid*, VI, 88-90.
[5] Jefferson to Col. N. Lewis, July 4, 1790; *Writings*, Mont., VIII, 57-9.
[6] *Cabinet Opinion*, July 12, 1790; *Works*, Ford, VI, 90-5.
[7] Hamilton, *Works* (H. C. Lodge, ed.), II, 302.
[8] "Queries to Heads of the Dept.," Aug. 27, 1790; Washington, *Writings*, XXXI, 102-3.
[9] *Cabinet Opinion*, Aug. 28, 1790; *Works*, Ford, VI, 141-3.

[10] *Cabinet Opinion*, Sept. 15, 1790; Hamilton, *Works*, IV, 313-42.
[11] Jefferson to T. M. Randolph, Nov. 12, 1790; Jefferson Papers, LC., v. 58, p. 9886.
[12] Jefferson to T. M. Randolph, Nov. 23, 1790; *ibid*, v. 58, p. 9895.
[13] Deed from Jefferson and Nicholas Lewis to William Ronald, Oct. 17, 1790; Deed Bk. No. 7, Cumberland Co. Court House.
[14] "Heads of Consideration," Aug. 22, 1790; *Works*, Ford, VI, 123-31.
[15] Jefferson to Carmichael, Aug. 2, 1790; *ibid*, VI, 111-14.
[16] Jefferson to Short, Aug. 10, 1790; *ibid*, VI, 114-18.
[17] Jefferson to Gouverneur Morris, Aug. 12, 1790; *ibid*, VI, 123.
[18] Jefferson to David Humphreys, Aug. 11, 1790; *ibid*, VI, 118-20.
[19] "Report on British Negotiations," Dec. 15, 1790; *ibid*, VI, 167-70.
[20] "Journal of William Loughton Smith," in *Mass. H. S. Proc.*, v. 51, pp. 35-9. Jefferson to Martha J. Randolph, Aug. 22, 1790; Jefferson MSS., Morgan Lib.
[21] Jefferson to Short, Sept. 6, 1790; *Works*, Ford, VI, 145-7.
[22] Jefferson to Gouverneur Morris, Nov. 26, 1790; *ibid*, VI, 153-5. When Hamilton was confronted with the protesting resolutions engineered by Henry through the Virginia House of Delegates, he remarked grimly that "this is the first symptom of a spirit which must either be killed, or it will kill the Constitution of the United States." Hamilton to Jay, Nov. 13, 1790; Hamilton, *Works*, IX, 473-4.
[23] Jane Charlton to Edmund Randolph, June 26, 1790; Jefferson Papers, LC., v. 58, p. 9912. On the statement is a memorandum by Randolph showing payment on Nov. 25, 1790.

CHAPTER 32

[1] Jefferson to Maria Jefferson, Dec. 7, 1790; S. N. Randolph, *Domestic Life*, 191.
[2] Fisher Ames later admitted frankly that "the stock of the bank is chiefly held in New York and Massachusetts." To Thomas Dwight, Oct. 30, 1791; Ames, *Works*, I, 99-100.
[3] Jefferson to George Mason, Feb. 4, 1791; *Works*, Ford, VI, 186.
[4] Jefferson to Nicholas Lewis, Feb. 9, 1791; *ibid*, VI, 194.
[5] *Cabinet Opinion*, Feb. 15, 1791; *ibid*, VI, 197-204.
[6] *Cabinet Opinion*, Feb. 23, 1791; Hamilton, *Works*, III, 445-93.
[7] Jefferson to George Mason, Feb. 4, 1791; *Works*, Ford, VI, 185-6.
[8] "Report on the Mediterranean trade," Dec. 28, 1790; Misc. Letters, Dept. of State, National Archives.
[9] Jefferson to Washington, Dec. 28, 1790; Jefferson Papers, LC., v. 59, pp. 10057-60.
[10] "Report on Cod and Whale Fisheries," Feb. 1, 1791; *ibid*, v. 60, pp. 10412-63.
[11] "Report to House of Representatives," Mar. 15, 1791; *ibid*, v. 69, pp. 11914-26.
[12] Hamilton to Jefferson, Jan. 13, 1791; *ibid*, v. 59, p. 10228.
[13] Jefferson to Hamilton, Jan. 1, 1791; American Letters, State Dept., Nat. Arch. Jefferson evidently meant "*ménagement*" (consideration or tenderness).
[14] "Report on Tonnage Law" [Jan. 18, 1791]; *Works*, Ford, VI, 175-84. Jefferson to M. Otto, Mar. 29, 1791; American Letters, State Dept., Nat. Arch.
[15] Jefferson to Wm. Short, Mar. 15, 1791; U. S. Instructions to Ministers, Nat. Arch.
[16] Maclay's *Journal*, Feb. 7, 1791; p. 375.
[17] Jefferson to Carmichael, Mar. 17, 1791; *Works*, Ford, VI, 220-2.
[18] Jefferson to Carmichael, Mar. 12, 1791; also to Short, same date; *ibid*, VI, 213-5, 215-6.
[19] Jefferson to Harry Innes, Mar. 7, 1791; *ibid*, VI, 210-11.
[20] Jefferson to Washington, Apr. 2, 1791; *ibid*, VI, 239.
[21] Jefferson to Washington, Mar. 27, 1791; Misc. Letters, Dept. of State, Nat. Arch.
[22] Washington to Jefferson, Apr. 1, 3, 1791; *ibid*.
[23] Jefferson to Washington, Apr. 17, 1791; *Works*, Ford, VI, 243-7. For the general feeling about Beckwith, see Sir John Temple to the Duke of Leeds, May 23, 1791 (Hammond Transcripts, by W. C. Ford; N. Y. Pub. Lib.), that Beckwith's presence has disgusted even those who heretofore had leaned toward Great Britain and that "he can be considered in no other light than as a petty Spy."
[24] Jefferson to Harry Innes, Mar. 7, 1791; *supra*.
[25] Jefferson to T. M. Randolph, Feb. 24, 1791; Jefferson Papers, LC., v. 61, pp. 10595-6.
[26] Jefferson to David Rittenhouse, May 8, 1791; *ibid*, v. 63, p. 11002.
[27] Jefferson to Chas. Thomson, Apr. 20, 1791; *ibid*, v. 63, p. 10924. To Benjamin Barton, May 12, 1791; *Bull. of Boston Pub. Lib.*, Apr., 1943, pp. 156-7.

[28] "Bill to Promote the Useful Arts," Feb. 7, 1791; *Works*, Ford, VI, 189-93.

[29] Jefferson to James Hutchinson, Mar. 12, 1791; Jefferson Papers, LC., v. 62, p. 10674. To Washington, Mar. 27, 1791; Misc. Letters, Dept. of State, Nat. Arch. "Report on the methods for obtaining Fresh Water from Salt"; *Writings*, Mont., III, 1-8.

[30] Jefferson to Short, Mar. 16, 1791; *Wm. & Mary Quart.*, ser. 2, v. 13, p. 102.

[31] Jefferson to Short, Oct. 16, 1792; *ibid*, ser. 2, v. 13, pp. 114-15.

[32] Jefferson to Nicholas Lewis, Feb. 9, 1791; Jefferson Papers, LC., v. 61, p. 10514.

[33] Jefferson to Short, Mar. 16, 1791; *supra*. Short to Jefferson, Apr. 26, 1791; Jefferson Papers, LC., v. 63, p. 10946.

[34] Jefferson to Christian Baehr, Aug. 14, 29, 1791; copies in Edgehill-Randolph Papers, U. of Va.

CHAPTER 33

[1] Jefferson to Maria Jefferson, Mar. 31, 1791; *Works*, Ford, VI, 234-5.

[2] Jefferson to Martha J. Randolph, Mar. 24, 1791; *ibid*, VI, 225.

[3] Jefferson to T. M. Randolph, May 1, 1791; *ibid*, VI, 250-1.

[4] Jefferson to Mazzei, Aug. 2, 1791; copy in Edgehill-Randolph Papers, U. of Va.

[5] Jefferson to Jonathan B. Smith, Apr. 26, 1791; Hanley-Smith Papers, LC.

[6] Jefferson to T. M. Randolph, July 3, 1791; *Writings*, Mont., XIX, 76-8.

[7] Madison to Jefferson, May 12, 1791; Madison, *Writings*, VI, 50-1, n.

[8] Jefferson to Washington, May 8, 1791; *Works*, Ford, VI, 254-7.

[9] Jefferson to Adams, July 17, 1791; *ibid*, VI, 282-5.

[10] Jefferson to Paine, July 29, 1791; *ibid*, VI, 297-9. To same effect, among others, Jefferson to Lewis Littlepage, July 29, 1791; Jefferson Papers, LC., v. 65, p. 11364.

[11] Adams to Jefferson, July 29, 1791; Adams, *Works*, VIII, 506-9.

[12] Anas, *Works*, Ford, I, 179-80.

[13] Temple to Leeds, May 23, 1791; quoted in S. F. Bemis, *Jay's Treaty*, 84 n.

[14] "Notes on Trip," May 22-June 3, 1791; Jefferson Papers, LC., v. 69, p. 11910. Acct. Bk., May 17-June 19, 1791; N. Y. Pub. Lib.

[15] Madison to Jefferson, May 12, 1791; Madison, *Writings*, VI, 51 n.

[16] Jefferson to T. M. Randolph, June 5, 1791; *Works*, Ford, VI, 268-70.

[17] Jefferson to Washington, June 5, 1791; *ibid*, VI, 266-8.

[18] Jefferson to Martha J. Randolph, May 31, 1791; *ibid*, VI, 264-6.

[19] Jefferson to Martha J. Randolph, June 5, 1791; Jefferson Papers, Morgan Lib.

[20] Madison to Jefferson, July 13, 1791; Madison, *Writings*, VI, 56-7, n.

[21] Jefferson to Madison, June 21, 1791; *Works*, Ford, VI, 271-2. To Martha J. Randolph, June 23, 1791; Randall, *Jefferson*, II, 21.

[22] Jefferson to Madison, May 9, 1791; Jefferson Papers, LC., v. 64, p. 11107. Published in *Works*, Ford, VI, 257-9; but with an error in transcription. The quoted word "marks" is given as "makes."

[23] Anas, Aug. 13, 1791; *Works*, Ford, I, 184 (Text modernized).

[24] MS. Memoir of Wm. A. Burwell; LC.

[25] Jefferson to [Madison], June [28], 1791; Jefferson Papers, LC., v. 232, p. 41484. Published in *Works*, Ford, VII, 130, under the date of June 29, 1792.

[26] Jefferson to B. F. Bache, Apr. 22, 1791; privately owned; copy in U. of Va.

[27] Jefferson to T. M. Randolph, May 15, 1791; *Works*, Ford, VI, 263-4.

[28] Jefferson to Freneau, Feb. 28, 1791; *Writings*, Mont., VIII, 133.

[29] Freneau to Jefferson, Mar. 5, 1791; Jefferson Papers, LC., v. 61, p. 10650. Italics added.

[30] Jefferson to Madison, May 9, 1791; *Works*, Ford, VI, 257.

[31] Jefferson to Madison, July 21, 1791; Madison Papers, LC., v. 14, p. 28. Letterpress copy in Jefferson Papers, LC., v. 65, p. 11314-6.

[32] "Trist's Memoranda of conversation with Madison," May 25, 1827; Randall, *Jefferson*, II, 74-5.

[33] Freneau to Jefferson, Aug. 4, 1791; Jefferson Papers, LC., v. 66, p. 11396.

[34] Jefferson Papers, LC., v. 66, p. 11423.

[35] "Trist's Memoranda"; *supra*.

[36] Jefferson to Martha J. Randolph, Nov. 13, 1791; Jefferson Papers, Morgan Lib. See also to T. M. Randolph, Nov. 20, 1791; Jefferson Papers, LC., v. 67, p. 11656. In his Acct. Bk., under date of July 8, 1792, Jefferson transmitted to Freneau $21 for the subscriptions of 14 of his Charlottesville neighbors; N. Y. Pub. Lib.

[37] Jefferson to T. M. Randolph, Nov. 27, 1791; copy in Edgehill-Randolph Papers, U. of Va.
[38] Hamilton, *Works*, VII, 229.
[39] "An American"; *Gazette of the U. S.*, Aug. 4, 11, 18, 1792.
[40] *Gazette of the U. S.*, Aug. 8, 1792.
[41] *Ibid*, Aug. 11, 1792.
[42] Washington to Jefferson, Aug. 23, 1792; Washington, *Writings*, XXXII, 130-1. A somewhat similar letter went to Hamilton, Aug. 26, 1792; *ibid*, XXXII, 132-4.
[43] Jefferson to Washington, Sept. 9, 1792; *Works*, Ford, VII, 136-49. Hamilton replied to Washington, Sept. 9, 1792; Hamilton, *Works*, VII, 303-6.
[44] Jefferson to Edmund Randolph, Sept. 13, 1792; Madison, *Writings*, VI, 117 n.
[45] Anas, Feb. 29, 1792; *Works*, Ford, I, 196 ff.

CHAPTER 34

[1] Notes on "Proceedings to be had under the Residence Act," Nov. 29, 1790; quoted in S. Padover, *Jefferson and the National Capital*, 30-6.
[2] *Georgetown Weekly Ledger*, Mar. 12, 1791.
[3] Jefferson to Banneker, Aug. 30, 1791; *Works*, Ford, VI, 309-10.
[4] "Plan for the Federal City," Mar., 1791; Jefferson Papers, LC.
[5] Jefferson to L'Enfant, Apr. 10, 1791; American Letters, State Dept., Nat. Arch.
[6] Jefferson to Washington, Apr. 10, 1791; Misc. Letters, State Dept., Nat. Arch.
[7] Commissioners to Washington, Nov. 25, 1791; Commissioners' Letter Bk., I, 40-1, Nat. Arch.
[8] Washington to Jefferson, Nov. 30, 1791; Washington, *Writings.*
[9] Jefferson to L'Enfant, Dec. 1, 1791; to Washington, Dec. 1, 1791; Jefferson Papers, LC., v. 67, p. 11709. The entire negotiations are reported in detail in Padover, *Jefferson and the National Capital.*
[10] L'Enfant to Jefferson, Feb. 26, 1792; Jefferson to L'Enfant, Feb. 27, 1792; E. S. Kite, *L'Enfant and Washington*, 145-50, 151-2.
[11] George Walker to Jefferson, Mar. 9, 1792; Jefferson to Walker, Mar. 14, 1792; *ibid*, 167-8, 173.
[12] Jefferson to Thomas Johnson, Mar. 8, 1792; Jefferson Papers, LC., v. 71, pp. 12423-6.
[13] Jefferson's freehand sketch is reproduced in F. Kimball, *Thomas Jefferson—Architect*, fig. 132. Jefferson to Daniel Carroll, Feb. 1, 1793; Jefferson, *Writings* (H. E. Washington, ed.), III, 508.
[14] One set of plans is in the Md. Hist. Soc. The design is reproduced in Kimball, *supra*, fig. 129.
[15] Jefferson to Washington, Apr. 17, 1791; *Works*, Ford, VI, 243-7.
[16] Jefferson to Edward Rutledge, Aug. 25, 1791; Rutledge Papers, Pa. H. S. Printed in *Works*, Ford, VI, 307-9 under the erroneous date of Aug. 29th.
[17] Jefferson to Short, July 28, 1791; *Works*, Ford, VI, 292-7. To M. la Motte, Aug. 30, 1791; *Writings*, Mont., VIII, 238-40.
[18] Jefferson to Sir John Sinclair, Aug. 24, 1791; *Writings*, Mont., VIII, 230-1. To Edward Rutledge, *supra.*
[19] Jefferson to Short, Nov. 24, 1791; *Works*, Ford, VI, 329-34.
[20] Anas, *Works*, Ford, I, 207-9.
[21] "Clauses for Treaty of Commerce with France" [Nov., 1791]; *Works*, Ford, VI, 335-7.
[22] *Ibid*, VI, 336 n.
[23] Anas, *Works*, Ford, I, 209.
[24] Jefferson to Hammond, Nov. 29, 1791; *Works*, Ford, VI, 338-9.
[25] Hammond to Jefferson, Nov. 30, 1791; Jefferson Papers, LC., v. 67, pp. 11704-6.
[26] Jefferson to Hammond, Dec. 5, 1791; *Works*, Ford, VI, 341-2.
[27] Jefferson to Hammond, Dec. 13, 1791; *ibid*, VI, 344-5.
[28] Jefferson to Hammond, Dec. 15, 1791; Jefferson Papers, LC., v. 68, pp. 11780-3.
[29] Hammond to Jefferson, Mar. 5, 1792; *ibid*, v. 71, pp. 12321-86.
[30] Washington to Jefferson, Mar. 6, 1792; *ibid*, v. 71, p. 12393.
[31] Jefferson to Hammond, May 29, 1792; *American State Papers: For. Rel.*, I, 201-16. The Rough Draft is in *Works*, Ford, VII, 3-98.
[32] Hammond to Grenville, June 8, 1792; Hammond Transcripts, N. Y. Pub. Lib.

[33] Anas, Mar. 11, 1792; *Works*, Ford, I, 209.
[34] *Ibid*, June 3, 1792; *ibid*, I, 219-27. Jefferson to Madison, June 4, 1792; *ibid*, VII, 100-2.
[35] Hammond to Grenville, July 3, 1792; Hammond Transcripts, N. Y. Pub. Lib.
[36] Jefferson to Thomas Pinckney, June 11, 1792; *Works*, Ford, VII, 104-9.
[37] Thomas Paine to Jefferson, Feb. 13, 1792; Jefferson Papers, LC., v. 70, p. 12242.
[38] Jefferson to Short, Jan. 28, 1792; *Works*, Ford, VI, 380-2. Also letter of Jan. 23, 1792; *ibid*, VI, 369.
[39] Washington to Jefferson, Aug. 23, 1792; Washington, *Writings*, XXXII, 128-30.
[40] "Report on Negotiations with Spain," Mar. 18, 1792; *Works*, Ford, VI, 414-45.
[41] Jefferson to Short, Mar. 18, 1792; *ibid*, VI, 411-14.
[42] Jefferson to Jaudenes and Viar, July 9, 1792; *ibid*, VII, 133-4.
[43] Anas, Oct. 31, 1792; *ibid*, I, 237-40.
[44] Jefferson to Gouverneur Morris, Apr. 28, 1792; *ibid*, VI, 484-5.
[45] Jefferson to [Madison], June 1, 1792; Jefferson Papers, LC., v. 232, p. 41494.
[46] Jefferson to Joel Barlow, June 20, 1792; *Works*, Ford, VII, 122-3.
[47] Jefferson to Thomas Paine, June 19, 1792; *ibid*, VII, 121-2.
[48] Jefferson to Lafayette, June 16, 1792; *ibid*, VII, 109-11.
[49] Jefferson to Gouverneur Morris, Dec. 30, 1792; *ibid*, VII, 198-201.
[50] Anas, Dec. 29, 1792; *ibid*, I, 247-9.

CHAPTER 35

[1] Jefferson to Martha J. Randolph, Jan. 15, 1792; *Works*, Ford, VI, 365-6.
[2] Jefferson to Martha J. Randolph, Mar. 22, 1792; *ibid*, VI, 453-4.
[3] Jefferson to Washington, May 23, 1792; *ibid*, VI, 487-95.
[4] Anas, July 10, 1792; *ibid*, I, 227-31.
[5] Jefferson to Madison, July 6, 1791; *ibid*, VI, 277-8.
[6] Madison to Jefferson, July 10, 1791; Madison, *Writings*, VI, 54-6 n.
[7] Jefferson to Edmund Pendleton, July 24, 1791; *Mass. Hist. Soc. Colls.*, 7th ser., v. 1, pp. 37-8.
[8] See Schachner, *Hamilton* and Brant, *Madison*, v. 3, for the full details.
[9] Jefferson to Henry Remsen, Apr. 14, 1792; Jefferson MSS., U. of Va. Remsen's reply gives an extremely valuable account of Duer's crash and imprisonment, Apr. 23, 1792; Jefferson Papers, LC., v. 73, pp. 12722-8.
[10] Jefferson to Short, Mar. 18, 1792; *Works*, Ford, VI, 413.
[11] Jefferson to Madison, July 3, 1792; *ibid*, VII, 131-3.
[12] Jefferson to Madison, Oct. 1, 1792; Wm. C. Rives Papers, LC.
[13] Jefferson to Archibald Stuart, Dec. 31, 1791; *Works*, Ford, VI, 349-52.
[14] Jefferson to Short, Oct. 16, 1792; *ibid*, VII, 164.
[15] Jefferson to Angelica Church, Oct., 1792; *ibid*, VII, 154-6. Abbreviations written out.
[16] Jefferson to Dobson, Jan. 1, 1792; Jefferson Papers, Mass. H. S.
[17] Jefferson to Francis Eppes, Mar. 11, 1792; Jefferson Papers, LC., v. 72, pp. 12450-1.
[18] Jefferson to de Barth, Mar. 17, 1792; *ibid*, v. 72, p. 12487.
[19] Jefferson to Bolling Clarke, Sept. 21, 1792; *ibid*, v. 77, p. 13389. To Randolph Jefferson, Sept. 25, 1792; *ibid*, v. 77, p. 13391.
[20] Jefferson to Peter Carr, May 8, 1791; Jefferson MSS., U. of Va. Mrs. Martha Carr to Jefferson, Dec. 15, 1792; *ibid*. It is true, however, that Jefferson had money from her husband's estate in his hands, and which he had used in part for his own purposes (Jefferson to Peter Carr, Nov. 10, 1793; *ibid*). The extended correspondence between Jefferson and John Garland Jefferson is in the Carr-Cary Papers, U. of Va.
[21] John Page to Jefferson, Jan. 11, 1792; Jefferson Papers, Mass. H. S. Jefferson to Page, Jan. 12, 1792; *ibid*.
[22] John Page to Jefferson, Nov. 19, 1792; *ibid*.
[23] Jefferson to Joseph Fenwick, Oct. 10, 1792; Jefferson Papers, LC., v. 77, p. 13413.
[24] Jefferson to David Rittenhouse, Aug. 12, 1792; *ibid*, v. 77, p. 13305. To John Jones, Dec. 26, 1792; *ibid*, v. 79, p. 13790.
[25] Jefferson to Stephen Willis, Nov. 12, 1792; Jefferson Papers, Mass. H. S. To Henry Remsen, Nov. 13, 1792; Jefferson Papers, LC., v. 79, p. 13623.
[26] Henry Remsen to Jefferson, Nov. 19, 1792; Jefferson Papers, LC., v. 79, pp. 13664-5. Jefferson to Remsen, Nov. 25, 1792; *ibid*, v. 79, p. 13701.

[27] Acct. Bk., 1792; N. Y. Pub. Lib.

[28] Hamilton to Washington, Aug. 10, 1792; Hamilton, *Works*, X, 11.

[29] Washington to Jefferson, Sept. 15, 1792; Misc. Letters, Dept. of State, Nat. Arch.

[30] Jefferson to Washington, Sept. 18, 1792; *ibid.* Also printed in *Works*, Ford, VII, 153.

[31] Jefferson to Monroe, June 23, 1792; *Works*, Ford, VII, 127-9. The original is in Monroe Papers, N. Y. Pub. Lib.

[32] John Beckley to Madison, Sept. 2, 1792; Madison Papers, N. Y. Pub. Lib.

[33] Jefferson to Thomas Pinckney, Dec. 3, 1792; *Works*, Ford, VII, 191-2.

[34] Jefferson to Madison, June 21, 1792; *ibid*, VII, 123-5.

[35] Archibald Stuart to Jefferson, Dec. 6, 1792; *Mo. Hist. Soc.*, *Glimpses of the Past*, 80.

[36] Jefferson to Edmund Randolph, Sept. 17, 1792; *Works*, Ford, VII, 151-2.

[37] Anas, Oct. 1, 1792; *ibid*, I, 233-7. Washington followed this up with a letter to Jefferson, renewing his plea for an accommodation between the two Cabinet officers. "A Measure of this sort," he wrote, "would produce harmony, and consequent good in our public Councils; the contrary will, inevitably, introduce confusion, and serious mischiefs; and for what? because mankind cannot think alike, but would adopt different means to attend the same end." Washington, *Writings*, Oct. 18, 1792; XXXII, 185-6.

CHAPTER 36

[1] Horatio Gates to Jefferson, Jan. 5, 1793; Jefferson Papers, LC., v. 80, p. 13960.

[2] Jefferson to Martha Jefferson Randolph, Jan. 26, 1793; *Works*, Ford, VII, 214-16.

[3] Jefferson to T. M. Randolph, Feb. 3, 1793; Jefferson Papers, LC., v. 81, pp. 14088-9.

[4] Anas, *Works*, Ford, I, 250-1.

[5] Jefferson to Alexander Donald, Mar. 5, 1793; Jefferson Papers, LC., v. 82, pp. 14243-4.

[6] Anas, Mar. 2, 1793; *Works*, Ford, I, 262. See also Jefferson to T. M. Randolph, Mar. 3, 1793; *ibid*, VII, 252-4.

[7] "Draft Resolutions"; *ibid*, VII, 220-3.

[8] Jefferson to Hamilton, Mar. 27, 1793; *ibid*, VII, 270-2. In my *Hamilton*, 310-14, where the resolutions are discussed in detail, I had assumed—as have all other historians—that this letter had actually been sent to Hamilton. But on the letterpress copy in the Jefferson Papers, LC., v. 83, pp. 14413-5, Jefferson wrote: "*Not Sent.*" The only other copy extant is the original draft in the Madison Papers, LC., which Jefferson had forwarded to Madison with an accompanying note that Hamilton "will not find my letter to answer his purpose"; Mar. 31, 1793; *Works*, Ford, VII, 272-3.

[9] "Agenda"; *Works*, Ford, VII, 223-4.

[10] Jefferson to Short, Jan. 3, 1793; *ibid*, VII, 202-6.

[11] Jefferson to ——, Mar. 18, 1793; *Writings*, Mont., IX, 45.

[12] Jefferson to Gouverneur Morris, Mar. 15, 1793; *Works*, Ford, VII, 263-4. Anas, Feb. 20, 1793; *ibid*, I, 253.

[13] Anas, Feb. 20, 1793; *supra.*

[14] "Cabinet Questions"; Apr. 18, 1793; Washington, *Writings*, XXXII, 419-20.

[15] Anas, Apr. 18, 1793; *Works*, Ford, I, 267-9.

[16] Washington to Jefferson, Apr. 12, 1793; Washington, *Writings*, XXXII, 415-16. To Hamilton, same date; *ibid*, XXXII, 416.

[17] Jefferson to Madison, June 23, 1793; *Works*, Ford, VII, 407-8.

[18] Hammond to Grenville, Apr. 2, 1793; Hammond Correspondence, N. Y. Pub. Lib.

[19] Jefferson to Madison, June 23, 1793; *supra.*

[20] Jefferson to Gouverneur Morris, Mar. 12, 1793; *Works*, Ford, VII, 259.

[21] Hamilton to Washington, Apr., 1793; Hamilton, *Works*, IV, 369-96.

[22] Anas, Apr. 18, 1793; *Works*, Ford, I, 268.

[23] Cabinet Opinion; *ibid*, VII, 283-301.

[24] Anas; *ibid*, I, 268.

[25] *Amer. State Papers: For. Rel.*, I, 140.

[26] Anas, Mar. 30, 1793; *Works*, Ford, I, 264.

[27] Jefferson to Madison, Apr. 28, 1793; *ibid*, VII, 301-2.

[28] Jefferson to Monroe, May 5, 1793; *ibid*, VII, 308-11.

[29] Jefferson to Martha J. Randolph, May 26, 1793; Jefferson Papers, Morgan Lib.

[30] The pertinent documents may be found in Meade Minnigerode's *Jefferson, Friend of France*, 145 ff. The title is a misnomer; it is really a biography of Genêt, valuable for its

source materials, but to be used with great caution for interpretation and value judgments

[31] *Ibid*, 154.

CHAPTER 37

[1] Jefferson to Monroe, May 5, 1793; *Works*, Ford, VII, 309.

[2] Genêt to Jefferson, Sept. 18, 1793; *Amer. State Papers: For. Rel.*, I, 172-4.

[3] Genêt to French Minister of Foreign Affairs, Oct. 7, 1794; *Annual Reports, Amer. Hist. Assoc.* (1903), II, 245.

[4] Hammond to Grenville, Mar. 7, 1793; Hammond Correspondence, N. Y. Pub. Lib.

[5] Jefferson to Edmund Randolph, May 8, 1793; *Works*, Ford, VII, 315-19.

[6] Jefferson to Madison, May 12, 1793; *ibid*, VII, 323-5. Randolph to Jefferson, May 9, 1793; Jefferson Papers, LC., v. 85, pp. 14757-8.

[7] Jefferson to Hammond, May 3, 1793; *Works*, Ford, VII, 306. To Ternant, May 3, 1793; *ibid*, VII, 307.

[8] Jefferson to Hammond, May 15, 1793; *ibid*, VII, 325-8.

[9] Jefferson to Ternant, May 15, 1793; *ibid*, VII, 328-32.

[10] Jefferson to Wythe, Apr. 27, 1793; *ibid*, VII, 282.

[11] Jefferson to Madison, Apr. 28, 1793; *ibid*, VII, 301-2.

[12] Anas, May 20, 1793; *ibid*, I, 271-3.

[13] Jefferson to Madison, May 19, 1793; *ibid*, VII, 336.

[14] Anas, May 23, 1793; *ibid*, I, 274.

[15] Genêt to Minister of Foreign Affairs, Oct. 7, 1793; *ibid*, I, 273 n.

[16] Genêt to Jefferson, May 23, 1793; *Amer. State Papers: For. Rel.*, I, 147.

[17] Cabinet Opinion [May 16, 1793]; *Works*, Ford, VII, 333.

[18] Genêt to Jefferson, June 1, 1793; *Amer. State Papers: For. Rel.*, I, 151. Jefferson to Genêt, June 1, 1793; *ibid*, I, 151.

[19] Randolph to Jefferson, May 30, 1793; Jefferson Papers, LC., v. 86, p. 14984.

[20] "Note given to the President relative to Genêt," undated; *Writings*, Mont., XVII, 340-3.

[21] Jefferson to Genêt, June 5, 1793; *Works*, Ford, VII, 362-4.

[22] See Note 20.

[23] Jefferson to Richard Harrison, June 12, 1793; *Works*, Ford, VII, 380-2.

[24] Genêt to Jefferson, June 14, 1793; Jefferson to Genêt, June 17, 1793; *Amer. State Papers: For. Rel.*, I, 152, 154-5.

[25] Genêt to Jefferson, June 22, 1793; *ibid*, I, 155-6.

[26] Jefferson to T. M. Randolph, June 2, 1793; Jefferson Papers, LC., v. 87, pp. 15031-2. Printed in *Writings*, Mont., IX, 107-9; but there the addressee is wrongly given as *Edmund* Randolph.

[27] Jefferson to Monroe, June 4, 1793; *Works*, Ford, VII, 360-2. The original is in Monroe Papers, N. Y. Pub. Lib.

[28] Jefferson to Thomas Pinckney, Apr. 20, 1793; U. S. Instructions to Ministers, State Dept., Nat. Arch.

[29] Jefferson to Hammond, June 26, 1793; *Works*, Ford, VII, 412-13. To Thomas Pinckney, June 26, 1793; Jefferson Papers, LC., v. 89, p. 15307.

[30] Jefferson to Genêt, June 23, 1793; *Amer. State Papers: For. Rel.*, I, 159. Genêt to Jefferson, June 25, 1793; *ibid*, I, 159.

[31] Anas, July 10, 1793; *Works*, Ford, I, 282-8.

[32] *Works*, Ford, VII, 439-43.

[33] Washington to Jefferson, July 11, 1793; Communications with State Dept., Nat. Arch.

[34] Jefferson to Washington [July 11, 1793]; *Works*, Ford, VII, 438-9 n.

[35] Jefferson to Genêt, July 12, 1793; *ibid*, VII, 445-6.

[36] Anas; *ibid*, I, 290.

[37] *Ibid*, I, 291.

[38] Hammond to Grenville, Aug. 18, 1793; Hammond Correspondence, N. Y. Pub. Lib.

[39] Jefferson to Madison, July 7, 1793; *Works*, Ford, VII, 436.

[40] Madison to Jefferson, July 30, 1793; Madison Papers, LC.

[41] Monroe to Jefferson, June 27, 1793; Jefferson Papers, LC., v. 89, pp. 15316-7.

[42] Jefferson to Monroe, July 14, 1793; *Works*, Ford, VII, 446-50.

[43] Jefferson to Madison, July 14, 1793; Jefferson Papers, LC., v. 90, p. 15508.

[44] Jefferson to Washington, July 31, 1793; *Works*, Ford, VII, 462-3.

45 Jefferson to Madison, June 9, 1793; *ibid*, VII, 373-7.
46 Jefferson to Madison, June 2, 1793; *ibid*, VII, 357-9.
47 *Gazette of the U. S.*, July 17, 1793.
48 *Trans. Amer. Philos. Soc.* (1793), III, 334-47.
49 Anas, Aug. 6, 1793; *Works*, Ford, I, 310-15. Washington to Jefferson, Aug. 12, 1793, Washington, *Writings*, XXXIII, 45.

CHAPTER 38

1 Anas, Aug. 1, 1793; *Works*, Ford, I, 305-8.
2 Jefferson to Madison, Aug. 11, 1793. The original is in Madison Papers, LC., v. 16, p. 55. A badly blurred and mutilated press copy is in Jefferson Papers, LC., v. 91, pp. 15692-5. M. C. Conway, in his *Omitted Chapters of History*, 190-1, quotes only that section which deals with Randolph's character.
3 Madison to Jefferson, Sept. 2, 1793; Madison, *Writings*, VI, 190-7. Monroe wrote along similar lines, Sept. 3, 1793; Monroe, *Writings*, I, 273-6.
4 Jefferson to Gouverneur Morris, Aug. 16, 1793; *Works*, Ford, VII, 475-507.
5 Deforgues to Genêt, July 30, 1793; quoted in Minnigerode, *Jefferson, Friend of France*, 278-80.
6 Cabinet Opinion, Aug. 23, 1793; *Works*, Ford, VIII, 5-6.
7 Genêt to Jefferson, Sept. 18, 1793; *Amer. State Papers: For. Rel.*, I, 172-4.
8 Jefferson to Madison, Sept. 1, 1793; *Works*, Ford, VIII, 11-14.
9 *Old Family Letters, Series B*, 15-18.
10 Jefferson to Madison, Sept. 8, 1793; *Works*, Ford, VIII, 32-4.
11 Jefferson to Martha J. Randolph, Sept. 8, 1793; Jefferson MSS., Morgan Lib.
12 Jefferson to Madison, Sept. 12, 1793; Jefferson Papers, LC., v. 93, p. 15965. He also notified Washington of his decision to leave "as soon as I could clear my own letter files"; Sept. 15, 1793; *Works*, Ford, VIII, 45-6.
13 Jefferson to John Ross, Sept. 13, 1793; Misc. MSS., Pa. H. S. Printed in *Works*, Ford, VIII, 44.
14 Jefferson to Hammond, Sept. 5, 1793; *Works*, Ford, VIII, 18-21.
15 Jefferson to the French Consuls, Sept. 7, 1793; *ibid*, VIII, 31.
16 Jefferson to Gov. Lee of Md., Sept. 13, 1793; Misc. Letters, Mo. H. S.
17 Jefferson to Genêt [Sept. 15, 1793]; *Works*, Ford, VIII, 46-7.
18 Jefferson to Jaudenes and Viar, July 14, 1793; *Amer. State Papers: For. Rel.*, I, 268-9.
19 Jefferson to Carmichael and Short, Mar. 23, 1793; *Works*, Ford, VII, 267-8.
20 Jefferson to T. M. Randolph, Apr. 21, 1793; Jefferson Papers, LC., v. 84, p. 14594.
21 Jefferson to T. M. Randolph, May 19, 1793; *ibid*, v. 86, pp. 14864-5.
22 Jefferson to Madison, June 29, 1793; *ibid*, v. 89, pp. 15341-4. To T. M. Randolph, June 30, 1793; *ibid*, v. 89, pp. 15381-2.
23 Jefferson to T. M. Randolph, July 28, 1793; *ibid*, v. 91, pp. 15598-601.
24 Jefferson to Angelica Church, June 7, 1793; Jefferson Papers, LC.
25 Angelica Church to Jefferson, Aug. 19, 1793; *ibid*, v. 91, p. 15752.
26 Jefferson to Angelica Church, Nov. 27, 1793; *ibid*, v. 95, p. 16269.
27 Jefferson to Washington, Oct. 3, 1793; Misc. Letters, State Dept., Nat. Arch.
28 Jefferson to Genêt, Hammond *et al.*, Nov. 8, 1793; *Works*, Ford, VIII, 60-3.
29 Jefferson to T. M. Randolph, Nov. 2, 1793; *ibid*, VIII, 56-8.
30 Jefferson to Madison, Nov. 2, 1793; *ibid*, VIII, 58-9.
31 Jefferson to Madison, Nov. 17, 1793; *ibid*, VIII, 72-3.
32 Anas; *ibid*, I, 324-8.
33 *Ibid.*
34 Draft Message [Nov., 1793]; *Works*, Ford, VIII, 79-83.
35 Anas, Nov. 28, 1793; *ibid*, I, 331-4.
36 Jefferson to Madison, Sept. 1, 1793; *Jefferson's Germantown Letters* (C. F. Jenkins, ed.), 50 n. To Henry Remsen, Nov. 9, 1793; *ibid*, 49-51. To Mr. Newbern, Nov. 14, 1793; *ibid*, 72. To Patrick Hart, Nov. 14, 1793; *ibid*, 74. To Ceracchi, Nov. 14, 1793; *ibid*, 75-6.
37 Jefferson to Eli Whitney, Nov. 16, 1793; *Works*, Ford, VIII, 70-1.
38 Jefferson to Martha J. Randolph, Dec. 1, 1793; Jefferson MSS., Morgan Lib.
39 *N. Y. Daily Advertiser*, Dec. 2, 1793. See also *Rufus King* (C. R. King, ed.), I, 458-69.
40 A. J. Dallas to Jefferson, Dec. 4, 1793; Jefferson Papers, LC., v. 95, p. 16304.

[41] *Phila. American Daily Advertiser*, Dec. 9, 1793.

[42] Jefferson to Madison, Sept. 1, 1793; *Works*, Ford, VIII, 12.

[43] Washington to Jefferson [rec. Dec 28, 1793]; Jefferson Papers, LC., v. 96, p. 16417.

[44] Jefferson to Genêt, Dec. 31, 1793; *Works*, Ford, VIII, 135-6.

[45] Genêt to Jefferson, July 4, 1797, Minnigerode, *Jefferson, Friend of France*, 413-25.

[46] Jefferson to Enoch Edwards, Dec. 30, 1793; *Works*, Ford, VIII, 134-5.

[47] Jefferson to Martha J. Randolph, Dec. 22, 1793; *ibid*, VIII, 124-5. To Robert Gamble, Dec. 22, 1793; Jefferson Papers, LC., v. 96, p. 16395.

[48] Jefferson to T. M. Randolph, Dec. 30, 1793; Jefferson Papers, LC., v. 96, p. 16425.

[49] Jefferson to Washington *et al.*, Dec. 31, 1793; *ibid*, v. 96, pp. 16441-50.

[50] "Estimated expenses for State Dept. for yr. 1793"; Domestic Letters, Dept. of State, Nat. Arch.

[51] Washington to Jefferson, Jan. 1, 1794; Washington, *Writings*, XXXIII, 231.

Courtesy the New-York Historical Society, New York City

THOMAS JEFFERSON

Watercolor on cardboard by Robert Field

CHAPTER 39

Antediluvian Patriarch

JEFFERSON'S retirement from public life caused his enemies to rejoice and his friends to view the future with foreboding. General Gates, who liked to think of himself as a Roman warrior retired to his Sabine farm, shook his head gloomily over the prospect. "His prophetic soul," he lamented, "augurs no benefit to the States by such a Sacrifice! If the best Seamen Abandon the Ship in a Storm, she must Founder." [1]

Ezra Stiles of Yale noted in his diary the "inconcealable disgust" with which Jefferson had retired; and his vow never to touch a newspaper again or meddle further with politics. Stiles narrated how Jefferson had unburdened himself to a mutual friend—the patriots of 1775 were neglected; the coterie surrounding Washington was disposing of patronage with a view to gaining a majority in Congress; and a "system of *omnia venalia*" was rapidly approaching.[2]

But the laments of his friends and followers could not shake Jefferson's resolve. He reached Monticello on January 16, 1794; and the first glimpse of his beloved home, of his family and familiar servants, filled him with delight. He breathed the pure air and noted eagerly the recurring drama of the seasons: the advent of the bluebirds, the later arrival of the strident blackbirds, the first bloom of his almond trees, and the reiterated clamor of the whippoorwill.[3] These were the sights and sounds that expanded his soul.

Gates had invited him to share his solitude at Rose Hill. Jefferson declined with thanks. "The length of my tether," he responded, "is now fixed from Monticello to Richmond. My private business can never call me elsewhere, and certainly politics will not, which I have ever hated both in theory & practice. I thought myself conscientiously called from those studies which were my delight by the political crisis of my country, & by those events *quorum pars, magna fuisti*. In storms like those all hands must be aloft. But calm is now restored, & I leave the bark with joy to those who love the sea. I am but a landsman, forced from my element by accident, regaining it with transport, and wishing to recollect nothing of what I have seen, but my friendships." [4]

He tried hard to dissociate himself from politics, refusing even to read the newspapers. He claimed to agree with Montaigne that ignorance was the softest pillow on which a man could rest his head; and every letter he wrote during this period proclaimed his determination to pay no further heed to the state of the nation.[5] Perhaps he protested too much. Madison, who of all his friends knew him best, ignored the heated disclaimers and sent him three regular letters a week, filled with politics and personalities from Philadelphia; so that Jefferson's ostentatious avoidance of the press did not deprive him of the slightest detail of the political scene. Eventually, he forgot his self-imposed hermitage and returned pointed comments and political advice, just as Madison no doubt had cannily foreseen.

For the first months, however, Jefferson held strictly to his seclusion. His daughter Martha, with her husband Thomas Mann Randolph and their two children, spent at least as much time at Monticello as on their own estates of Edgehill and Varina. Maria, the younger daughter, was still unmarried and busied herself with domestic affairs. Monticello itself and the far-flung properties required unremitting attention.

Jefferson had 10,647 acres of farm, plantation and undeveloped land scattered over central and western Virginia, not to mention some town plots in Beverly and Richmond. To work these numerous establishments required the services of 154 slaves and an animal population of 34 horses, 5 mules, 249 head of cattle, 390 hogs and 3 sheep. A total of 7,240 pounds of hog meat was required annually to feed family, visitors and slaves.[6]

The management of such a vast and sprawling community required sound business practices, and Jefferson filled his various notebooks with innumerable calculations: what, for example, it cost to feed and clothe a ploughman and maintain a plough horse. He estimated their keep at £2/13 the acre.[7]

Naturally, the plantations had not been properly run during Jefferson's extended absences abroad and in Philadelphia, and he was now determined to bring them as soon as possible to a peak of efficiency. His plans for their improvement and for increased building at Monticello were vast and carefully mapped. He was never able to achieve the full measure of his desires; but the actuality was impressive enough. During this first year, for example, he set out 2,400 cuttings of weeping willow to border the lower paths and those circumjacent to the spring.[8] He instituted a rotation of crops to restore the fertility of his lands which, he sadly discovered, had been almost wholly exhausted by previous ill usage.[9] He envisaged for the "terrasses" below his garden wall concentric levels of fig trees, walks, strawberry beds, a vineyard and an abundance of trees.[10] He also decided to commence a manufactory of nails, using iron rods shipped by boat from the north and employing the labor of his slaves. The manufactory started off auspiciously—by the autumn of 1794, he calculated that he had cleared £209 on the project.[11]

Not everything was smooth sailing, however. He had trouble in finding a satisfactory overseer. He had hired two on his arrival at Monticello; one never showed up, and the other proved so inefficient that he despaired of being able to go ahead with his plans for the next year.[12] The search for a good overseer continued to plague him until he finally installed his French major-domo, Petit, in the position.[13]

Yet, in spite of difficulties and retrogressions, this was what Jefferson supremely desired. "I return to farming," he wrote John Adams, "with an ardor which I scarcely knew in my youth, and which has got the better entirely of my love of study. Instead of writing 10. or 12. letters a day, which I have been in the habit of doing as a thing of course, I put off answering my letters now, farmer-like, till a rainy day." [14]

His unwonted outdoor activity, however, was probably responsible for a severe attack of rheumatism which laid him up from the beginning of September until the end of November, and kept him confined to his quarters. As a result, his overseers neglected the ploughing and allowed everything to go to ruin.[15] Planting, in fact, was not begun until the middle of November, by which time Jefferson was able to hobble around again and painfully mount his horse.

He was particularly anxious to find substitutes for the inevitable corn and bacon; both of which, he thought, contributed to the exhaustion of the soil. He proposed in their place potatoes, clover and sheep; "the two former to feed every animal on the farm except my negroes, and the latter to feed them, diversified with rations of salted fish and molasses, both of them wholesome, agreeable, and cheap articles of food." [16] It is obvious that Jefferson saw nothing unusual in his classification of Negroes.

Try as hard as he would, and protest as vociferously as he did, it was inevitable that Jefferson could remain for only a little time the complete recluse and abstainer from the political scene. For this there were several reasons: the faithful reports from his friends, his own ineradicable instincts, and the explosion of events in Philadelphia.

Just as France, because of her ineffable envoy, Genêt, had concentrated the public indignation during 1793, now England became the target for attack. Immersed in a life-and-death struggle with France, she had sought to cripple her great enemy by cutting off all neutral trade. In a series of Orders in Council, the French West Indies were made forbidden territory to American commerce, and hundreds of American ships that refused to obey were seized and confiscated.

While still in office, Jefferson had protested the restrictions repeatedly; but Hammond, fortified with Hamilton's confidential assurances that the United States would not go to war in defense of her rights, evaded or ignored the protests. Almost Jefferson's last official act was to lay before Congress his long-delayed report on the privileges and restrictions of the commerce of the United States with foreign countries.[17]

Armed with the irrefutable evidence contained in the report of England's interference with American trade, and supported by Jefferson's recommendations of retaliation in kind, Madison rose on January 3, 1794, in the House to propose once again his Resolutions of 1791 for levying such discriminatory duties on English goods and vessels as virtually to exclude her from all further commercial intercourse with the United States.

The Resolutions found the country for once united and in a fighting mood. Even Hamilton swung into line. For they had barely been introduced when the news arrived of a new and even harsher Order in Council promulgated as of the November 6th preceding.

Though Hamilton was now aroused and angry at his favorite country, he wanted no war. In the present temper of the people, however, and with the seemingly certain passage of Madison's Resolutions, war appeared inevitable. The leading Federalists therefore met in conclave and agreed that the only chance to avoid overt conflict was to send a special envoy to England with full powers to treat on all the matters at issue between the two nations.

Meanwhile, the triumphant Republicans were pressing for the passage of the Resolutions, with the Federalists fighting a desperate rear-guard action. So critical was the situation that Richard Peters, in sending to Jefferson a proposal for a State Society of Agriculture, appended some ominous observations. "You can do much," he wrote the retired statesman, "if Leisure is allowed you, in these plans, which are among the Arts of Peace. But I fear we shall have other Arts to practice, as our Situation seems very critical. You are like many of the good Things in this World of which the Value is not either known or properly estimated 'till it is lost. If we get into the Bustle of War, which I hope more than think we shall avoid, you will be drawn out of your Recesses." [18]

Peters did not know that Jefferson had already been drawn from his "Recesses," at least for advice and assistance. William Smith of South Carolina had made an extraordinary speech in the House in opposition to Madison's Resolutions; a speech which no one believed that the ordinarily pedestrian Smith could possibly have written. "I am at no loss to ascribe Smith's speech to its true father," Jefferson asserted to Madison, forgetting his resolve to meddle no longer with politics. "Every tittle of it is Hamilton's except the introduction." Which, indeed, was the fact. Having taken the first step into the sea of politics, Jefferson plunged deeper. The people of Albemarle, he reported, were not averse to sating "their ancient hatred" against Great Britain by a war, even though it meant the loss of trade. Nor did he doubt that, when the time came, we would confirm our guarantee of the French islands and "declare both to England & France that these islands are to rest with France, and that we will make a common cause with the latter for that object." [19]

Such was the temper of Congress that in spite of Smith's (or Hamilton's) speech, in spite of the hurried closing of Federalist ranks, it rushed through a temporary Embargo Act to last a single month, which was later renewed for another month, and failed by only a little of passing the whole of Madison's Resolutions. Certain provisions in fact passed the House and were defeated in the Senate only by the casting vote of Vice-President Adams.

So fraught with dangerous possibilities was the situation that the Federalist leaders redoubled their efforts for an envoy extraordinary to England. The idea was privately conveyed to Washington; and even more privately it was suggested that Hamilton was the man for the post.

Jefferson heard of it through Madison, his regular grapevine into the secrets of Philadelphia, and exploded with wrath. "A more degrading measure," he stormed, "could not have been proposed: and why is Pinckney to be recalled? For it is impossible he should remain there after such a testimony that he is not confided in. I suppose they think him not thorough fraud enough." The fact that Hamilton was to be the "missionary" only added fuel to the fire.[20]

But Hamilton was not chosen. John Jay, Chief Justice of the Supreme Court, was picked for the delicate mission; though there were those who suggested Jefferson himself for the post.

At first blush, Jay seemed an excellent choice. He was a good, though moderate Federalist, and therefore favorably disposed toward England. He occupied a judicial position, and might be relied on not to be intemperate in his dealings. He was already familiar with diplomatic procedures and techniques through his handling of foreign affairs in the days of the Confederation.

Yet the Republicans passionately, though in vain, opposed his nomination; and Monroe and others rose in the Senate to denounce his as pro-British and the worst emissary, with the possible exception of Hamilton, that could have been sent.

John Adams wrote privately to his old friend, Jefferson, that while he had "no great Faith in any very brilliant Success," he hoped Jay would be able to keep the United States out of war. "Another war would add two or three hundred Millions of Dollars to our Debt; rouse up a many headed and many bellied Monster of an Army to tyrannise over Us; totally disadjust our present Government, and accellerate the Advent of Monarchy and Aristocracy, by at least fifty years."[21]

One wonders whether Jefferson savored the full irony of this communication. For the allegedly monarchical author of the *Discourses on Davila* was using almost verbatim the arguments of the Republicans against war and its probable effects; only—the Republicans had employed them to counter a war against France, while Adams was opposing a war with England.

Jefferson fully agreed with Adams in not wanting war. "I am anxious," he wrote Tench Coxe, "that we should give the world still another useful lesson, by showing to them other modes of punishing injuries than by war, which is as much a punishment to the punisher as to the sufferer." He preferred "cutting off all communication with the nation [England] which has conducted itself so atrociously. This, you will say, may bring on war. If it does, we will meet it like men; but it may not bring on war, & then the experiment will have been a happy one."[22]

The defeat of the Nonintercourse Resolution, therefore, was a severe blow to him; and he waxed indignant against the Senate, in which the defeat had been administered. "This body," he exclaimed, "was intended as a check on the will of the Representatives when too hasty. They are not only that, but completely so on the will of the people also.... I have never known a measure more universally desired by the people than the passage of that bill." [23]

Jefferson found other causes for indignation in his rural retirement. Instigated by Hamilton, Washington had finally determined to suppress by force of arms the resistance of the western Pennsylvania farmers to the tax on whisky. A great army was gathered, a proclamation to the alleged rebels issued, and the troops were set in motion.

From his eyrie in Monticello, Jefferson viewed the proceedings with acute alarm. How could such "an armament against people at their ploughs" be ordered by Washington, he demanded of Madison, "and an appeal to arms justified before that to the law had been tried and *proved* ineffectual." [24]

The question was never answered. The army marched with pomp and banners to a rather ridiculous anticlimax. No resistance was encountered; a few stills were destroyed and some liberty poles cut down; a few alleged ringleaders were arrested and charged with treason.

It was the more levelheaded among the Republicans who were responsible for the collapse of the "Whisky Rebellion" and its anticlimax. The Democratic Society of Pennsylvania, for example, had at the first sign of trouble hastened to publish a resolution to the effect that, while conceiving "excise systems to be oppressive, hostile to the liberties of this country, and a nursery of vice and sycophancy, we, notwithstanding, highly disapprove of every opposition to them, not warranted by that frame of government, which has received the sanction of the people of the United States." Other democratic and republican societies disavowed rebellion in similar vein.[25]

Jefferson also advised nonresistance. "Make friends with the trans-Alleganians," he significantly suggested to William B. Giles, one of the leading Republicans in the House. "They are gone if you do not. Do not let false pride make a tea-act of your excise-law." [26]

In spite of the hasty dissociation of the democratic clubs from the "Whisky Rebellion," they were not saved thereby from Washington's denunciation. In turn, Jefferson denounced the denunciation. "It is wonderful indeed," he exclaimed, "that the President should have permitted himself to be the organ of such an attack on the freedom of discussion, the freedom of writing, printing & publishing." [27]

Jefferson never attacked Washington directly; he always insisted that the President was being hoodwinked by the small group of "monocrats" who surrounded him. It is doubtful whether the circumlocution was not more offensive to Washington than a direct assault.

Actually, some of Jefferson's sentiments on another occasion concerning him had been retailed to Washington by willing tongues. Washington refused to believe the reports. "There could not be the trace of doubt on his mind," he replied to Governor Henry Lee, one of the talebearers, "of predilection in mine, towards G. Britain or her politics, unless (which I do not believe) he has set me down as one of the most deceitful, and uncandid men living." [28]

Testifying his faith in his alleged traducer, the President offered Jefferson two days later the post of special envoy to Spain to seek a similar accommodation of differences with her as motivated Jay's mission to England.[29] Jefferson turned it down with the flat statement that "nothing will ever more tempt me to engage in anything public." [30]

As if to prove his point, he wrote shortly thereafter to a correspondent that he was so immersed in farming and the manufacture of nails "that politicks are entirely banished from my mind." Only the success of the French Revolution still mattered; and he hoped "that the execution of Robespierre and his bloodthirsty satellites is a proof of their return to that moderation which their best friends had feared had not always been observed." [31]

To his ancient law teacher, George Wythe, he was even more bucolic and, as befitted the recipient, scholarly. He sent Wythe a little treatise "on the use of the middle voice in Greek.... If it gives you half the pleasure it did me, mine will be doubled still." He allowed himself a little pardonable bragging about his collection of books, "now certainly the best in America." And his figs had yielded an enormous crop. Unfortunately, his building operations had not progressed. "We are now living in a brick kiln," he reported sadly, "for my house, in its present state, is nothing better." [32]

The winter of 1794-95 was one of extraordinary severity and deep snows, so that ploughing operations were held up until the month of March. But his nailery kept Jefferson busy, with the boats carrying the nail rod penetrating up the rivers to the base of Monticello even in the dead of winter.[33] He hoped to be able to realize enough from the sale of his nails to clear up his ancient debts; but this, like all other projects intended to achieve that happy result, failed to fulfill his expectations. His tobacco crop too fell short, and he was compelled once again to beg for extensions to meet his annual installment.[34]

The work of farming and manufacturing was strenuous, but Jefferson was happy in it, penning lyrical apostrophes on the life bucolic to all and sundry. He assumed personal charge of the nailery, where his work force consisted of a dozen small slaves ranging from ten to sixteen years old; and he rode over his plantations from early morning until dark.[35]

He described his activities in tones reminiscent of an Eclogue of Vergil. "Have you become a farmer?" he inquired of General Knox, his former Cabinet associate who had similarly retired. "Is it not pleasanter than to be shut up within 4. walls and delving eternally with the pen? I am become the most ardent farmer in the state. I live on my horse from morning to night almost. Intervals are filled up with attentions to a nailery I carry on. I rarely look into a book, and more rarely take up a pen. I have proscribed newspapers, not taking a single one, nor scarcely ever looking into one. My next reformation will be to allow neither pen, ink, nor paper to be kept on the farm. When I have accomplished this I shall be in a fair way of indemnifying myself for the drudgery in which I have passed my life." [36]

He even sent the glad tidings across the sea to Maria Cosway and Madame de Tessé. Maria, alas, was shortly thereafter to yield to despair over husband and child and enter a religious retreat in Italy.[37]

The suspicion might arise that Jefferson was pulling a long bow for the benefit of his correspondents; and certainly his claimed disinterest in the news of the world and in politics was a good deal put on. But of his contentment with the life he led, there is external evidence. The Duc de la Rochefoucauld-Liancourt, forced on his travels by the French Revolution, visited Jefferson at Monticello and later published his impressions.

The noble visitor was particularly enthusiastic about the house itself, even in its unfinished state, hailing it as "infinitely superior to all other houses in America." He was convinced that when completed it would rank "with the most pleasant mansions in France and England." As for the view from the mountaintop, superlatives were insufficient. As a matter of fact, every European traveler exclaimed over the majestic prospect.

The soil, left for so many years to the indifferent care of overseers, was exhausted; a condition which the duke attributed to crude methods of culture. It was Jefferson's chief employment to rehabilitate his land. He diligently studied the books on the subject and sought advice from competent persons; in which latter class the noble lord modestly placed himself. He had divided his lands into four farms, and was employing a seven-year rotation of crops: the first year, wheat; the second, Indian corn; the third, peas or potatoes; the fourth, vetches; the fifth, again wheat; and the sixth and seventh, clover.

Each farm was worked by an overseer, eight Negroes, four oxen and four horses. Instead of the traditional Virginia method of trodding out the grain under horses' hooves, Jefferson installed a recently invented threshing machine which accounted for 120 to 150 bushels a day.

The duke, however. did find some matters for criticism. Not enough manure was used; and Jefferson cut his clover only twice a season and left it on the fields, instead of gathering it for fodder. For he had the curious idea that "the heat of the sun destroys, or at least dries up in a great measure, the nutritious juices of the earth," and therefore insisted on protecting the ground from the lethal rays.

However, in his system of crop rotation, Jefferson was decidedly an innovator in his native state; and his neighbors watched his methods with censorious eye.

As for his private life, the Frenchman wrote that "Mr. Jefferson displays a mild, easy and obliging temper, though he is somewhat cold and reserved. His conversation is of the most agreeable kind, and he possesses a stock of information not inferior to that of any other man. In Europe he would hold a distinguished rank among men of letters, and as such he has already appeared there; at present he is employed with activity and perseverance in the management of his farms and buildings; and he orders, directs and pursues in the minutest detail every branch of business relative to them. I found him in the midst of the harvest, from which the scorching heat of the sun does not prevent his attendance. His negroes are nourished, clothed, and treated as well as white servants could be. As he cannot expect any assistance from the two small neighboring towns, every article is made on his farm; his negroes are cabinet-makers, carpenters, masons, bricklayers, smiths, etc. The children he employs in a nail factory, which yields already a considerable profit. The young and old negresses spin for the clothing of the rest. He animates them by rewards and distinctions; in fine, his superior mind directs the management of his domestic concerns with the same abilities, activity and regularity which he evinced in the conduct of public affairs, and which he is calculated to display in every situation of life." His daughter, Martha, and Maria, "handsome, modest, and amiable women," superintended the domestic household; while Thomas Mann Randolph was like a son to him.[38]

The picture thus presented is idyllic, and showed the Virginia plantation at its best. In fact, most of the great Virginians devoted more thought and energy to their agricultural pursuits than to affairs of state. Madison was constantly on the lookout for new ideas; while Washington was esteemed one of the best farmers in the land. One needs only read those letters in which the latter expands on agricultural topics to note the difference; the cold, formal sentences of his political style are gone, and in their place are warmth, eagerness and almost garrulity.

Yet Jefferson did not banish pen and paper from his life as he constantly threatened. Somehow, in the midst of his manifold duties, he managed to put one to the other. Perhaps, as his horse jogged from one field to another, he brooded over problems that extended beyond the confines of his plantations.

One of these dealt with education. Jefferson believed profoundly in the virtues of knowledge. Let the people *know*, was his constant thesis, and there need be no fear for the future of America. From his earliest days he had steadfastly advocated free educational opportunities for all—at least in the lower branches, and free advanced studies for those capable of their absorption. As soon as the Revolution had commenced, he had sought to place Virginia in the vanguard of educational progress; and had failed.

But he was not discouraged; and now that there was a federal government, he transferred his ideas to the national scene. Through Madison's mediation, he now proposed to Washington and Edmund Randolph, his successor in the State Department, a plan for a national academy, devoted to practical scientific studies, and staffed with eminent scientists from Europe. Madison duly forwarded the plan, though privately sceptical of its feasibility.[39]

Washington thought the scheme in the main good; and had, in fact, proposed on his own account to endow with his stock in the Potomac River Company both a federal university and seminary in Virginia. With such institutions, he said, it would be unnecessary to send American youth abroad, where they imbibed antirepublican principles. At the same time, by creating a locus for the youth of the entire nation, local prejudices and jealousies might gradually be eliminated.[40] Unfortunately, neither Washington's nor Jefferson's plan went beyond the talking stage; particularly as the Potomac shares did not appreciate in value as the promoters had expected. But the basic idea was never far from Jefferson's mind, and burst into clear flame in the final years of his life.

Jefferson managed also to use a request for information from a German scholar, Christopher Daniel Ebeling, as a springboard for some searching comments on the American scene, its scholars and intellectuals, its history and politics. Ebeling was writing a *Biography and History of North America* and had already been in communication with certain learned Americans for his facts. At the last moment he wondered about his correspondents, and turned to Jefferson for advice. Were they really authorities in their respective fields, he asked.

As usual, Jefferson went far beyond the expectations of his interrogator. He wrote a substantial treatise. Of the so-called "authorities," all from the northern states, he disposed in short, sharp sentences. Ezra Stiles of Yale was an excellent and learned man, "but remarkable for his credulity." Others, like Barton, the botanist, and Joel Barlow, the poet, were worthy of confidence. Jedidiah Morse and Noah Webster—he of the later Dictionary—were limited in their knowledge to the eastern states. When they spoke of the South, they were "worse than none at all."

Jefferson's local pride was severely irritated by their attempt to discuss the South on the basis of a single journey. "To pass once along a public road thro' a country," he exclaimed, "& in one direction only, to put up at its taverns, and get into conversation with the idle, drunken individuals who pass their time lounging in these taverns is not the way to know a country, its inhabitants or manners. To generalize a whole nation from these specimens is not the sort of information which Professor Ebeling would wish to compose his work from."

Having thus efficiently polished off Ebeling's northern informants, Jefferson proceeded with his own discourse on America. The "monocrats," he declared, had tried hard to model the Constitution on the British form; but the new Congress "will be able to defeat the plan of sliding us into monarchy, & to keep the Executive within republican bounds."

He made a detailed analysis of the two parties in the country which throws much more light on the workings of Jefferson's own mind than on the parties themselves. "They embrace respectively," he wrote, "the following descriptions of persons—The Anti-republicans consist of 1. The old refugees & tories. 2. British merchants residing among us, & composing the main body of merchants. 3. American merchants trading on British capital. Another great portion. 4. Speculators & Holders in the banks & public funds. 5. Officers of the federal government with some exceptions. 6. Office-hunters, willing to give up principles for places. A numerous & noisy tribe. 7. Nervous persons, whose languid fibres have more analogy with a passive than active state of things."

The Republicans, naturally, were of a different order. They were "1. The entire body of landholders throughout the United States. 2. The body of labourers, not being landholders, whether in husbandry or the arts." The Republicans outnumbered the Antirepublicans in the ratio of 500 to 1; "but their wealth is not as disproportionate, tho' it is also greatly superior, and is in truth the foundation of that of their antagonists." Unfortunately, Jefferson lamented, the urban concentration of the Antis and their control of the press enabled them to exercise an undue influence in government which the Republicans, scattered on their farms and remote from one another, found it difficult to match.[41]

One wonders what the bewildered German professor thought of this "objective" analysis of the state of parties in the United States.

There had been a series of radical changes in the Cabinet since Jefferson's retirement. Edmund Randolph, the "trimmer," had taken over the State Department; and his old job of Attorney General had gone to William Bradford. Randolph's tenure was comparatively short. The British government obligingly turned over to Washington certain letters which had passed between Randolph and Genêt's successor, Fauchet, and which they had discovered on a captured French ship. Randolph resigned under dark suspicions of bribery and treason, though vigorously protesting his innocence. Timothy Pickering, most extreme and fanatical of Federalists, took his place. General Henry Knox resigned from the War Department shortly after Jefferson, and James McHenry of Maryland stepped into the vacancy. But the major event was the final exit of Alexander Hamilton from the scene—over a year after his great antagonist; and Oliver Wolcott of Connecticut, his former assistant, was placed in charge.

It was the twilight of the gods. The two giants who had towered over the political landscape, and whose clashing personalities and philosophies had struck such sparks between them as to enkindle a new nation, were gone. Those who remained, and those who substituted, were pygmies by comparison. John Adams, contemplating the final event, wrote mournfully of the past: "The offices are once more full. But how differently filled than when Jefferson, Hamilton, Jay, &c., were here!" [42]

John Jay, for all his admitted qualifications and inflexible integrity, proved unfitted for the desperate mission on which he had embarked. He was no match for the worldly wise Lord Grenville in diplomatic fencing; while the flatteries with which the British enveloped the American softened his defenses and made him an easy prey. The world situation had suddenly changed during Jay's preparations and embarking, and England found herself confronted with the threat of a concert of neutral powers in arms against her arrogance; but of all this Jay knew nothing. Nor did the unsolicited and amazing disclosure at home by Hamilton to Hammond that the United States intended to remain aloof from the contemplated association of European neutrals help his mission, either.[43]

The treaty with England to which Jay affixed his signature on November 14, 1794, has been a subject of major controversy ever since. It did obtain for the United States one vital concession—an agreement to evacuate the border posts. Yet even this all-important clause merely reiterated the old treaty and left the date of evacuation unspecified. Practically every other matter in dispute remained in *status quo*, with the exception that an exceedingly limited right was granted American ships to trade with the West Indies. This right, moreover, was so hedged in with restrictions as to render it almost valueless; and in return, the British were granted for *their* ships full and unrestricted trading rights between the Islands and the United States. This one-sided arrangement was written into Article XII of the treaty, and created more of a furore in America than any other clause. Freedom of the seas, impressment of American sailors, the instigation of Indian raids—all the galling matters at issue—were conspicuous by their absence.

When the terms of the treaty leaked out, the Republicans rose in arms. The United States, they shouted, had been betrayed. Even the Federalists were at first dismayed; and only after considerable hesitation made it a party measure and pressed for ratification. While the Senate debated angrily, the populace of New York and elsewhere displayed their indignation in mass meetings and riots.

Jefferson, from his eyrie on Monticello, watched the storm with immense interest. He saw at once the potentialities of the hated treaty as a weapon with which to destroy the Federalists. He delved into his books and traced in a series of notes the entire history of the negotiations with England from the days of the Revolution to the time of Jay.[44] What use he intended to make of his assembled data is unclear; it is possible that he proposed to turn the facts and arguments over to Madison as the basis of a speech in Congress.

Hamilton, after his initial shock, had determined to make the best of the treaty. If it did nothing else, at least it assured the United States of an indefinite period of peace; and peace was the all-important, all-essential consideration to Hamilton. As usual, he betook himself to pen and paper, and wrote a series of articles over the signature of "Camillus" which presented the most favorable aspects of the treaty in powerful argument and skilled forensic terms.

It was a dazzling performance. Jefferson read it in great alarm. Unless Hamilton was properly answered, the Federalists whom he had considered crushed, would rise again. There was one man, and one man only, competent to reply. In hot haste he wrote to Madison: "Hamilton is really a colossus to the anti-republican party. Without numbers, he is a host within himself. They have got themselves into a defile, where they might be finished; but too much security on the republican part will give time to his talents & indefatigableness to extricate them. We have had only middling performances to oppose to him. In truth, when he comes forward, there is nobody but yourself who can meet him.... For god's sake take up your pen, and give a fundamental reply to Curtius [Noah Webster] and Camillus." [45]

Madison read the frantic appeal with dismay. He was weary of answering Hamilton. What could one do with an antagonist who refused to accept defeat, or end a controversy, and whose pen seemed to flow inexhaustible fountains of ink? Nevertheless, once more and with many misgivings, he obediently set himself to the abhorred task.

It was all in vain, for the Senate finally ratified the treaty, though with one significant reservation. Even the Federalists had gagged at the terms of Article XII, and Hamilton himself admitted publicly that there was justification for refusing to accept the humiliating article. Yet, in spite of its omission, the Republicans were dissatisfied; and the struggle passed over to the House where they tried, and almost succeeded, in refusing the appropriations necessary to put the treaty into effect.

Jefferson approved of this backdoor method of getting around the Constitution, which had placed the treaty-making power solely in the hands of the Executive and the Senate. He believed the true theory rather to be that "the representatives are as free as the President & Senate were to consider whether the national interests requires or forbids [*sic*] their giving the forms & force of law to the articles over which they have a power." [46]

Edmund Randolph had evolved this convenient theory; but Randolph was by then on his way out of the State Department over the Fauchet incident. He asserted his innocence on the charge of bribery in a long pamphlet, which Jefferson hailed as impregnable. Yet, while thus politically defending his former co-worker, he took the opportunity to present still another of his many estimates of Randolph's character.

"The fact is," he told Giles, "that he [Randolph] has generally given his principles to the one party & his practice to the other; the oyster to one, the shell to the other. Unfortunately the shell was generally the lot of his friends the French and republicans & the oyster of their antagonists. Had he been firm to the principles he professes in the year 1793, the President would have been kept from a habitual concert with the British & Anti-republican party. But at that time I do not know which R. feared most, a British fleet, or French disorganizers.... Where the principle of difference is as substantial and as strongly pronounced as between the republicans & the Monocrats of our country I hold it as honorable to take a firm & decided part, and as immoral to pursue a middle line, as between the parties of Honest men, & Rogues, into which every country is divided." [47] Jefferson had no doubts as to who constituted the honest men and who the rogues in the United States.

During all this political intervention and activity, Jefferson still kept up his pretense of never reading the newspapers or paying any attention to politics. He was, he insisted, "in a retirement I doat on, living like an Antediluvian patriarch among my children & grand children, and tilling my soil." [48]

CHAPTER 40

The "Mazzei" Letter and Return to Politics

THE role of an "Antediluvian patriarch" was not all one long idyl. The spring of 1796 brought in its train a sufficiency of domestic problems and troubles. There had been a continued and unexampled drought, and the seeds that should long before have sprouted, showed no evidences of life as late as the end of April.[1] There was also the lengthy and unexplained illness of his son-in-law, Thomas Mann Randolph. He had gone to Warm Springs and even as far as New York seeking medical opinions and relief, but without success. A seated melancholy set in; the first significant symptom of an ailment that was to burst forth at a later date and end in tragic denouement.[2]

Jefferson's nailery was also running into difficulties. He had hoped that the local merchants would give their neighbor's product the preference over the imported article; but he ran into a situation which, perhaps naïvely, he had not anticipated. The regular importers resented the domestic competition and compelled the merchants, if they wished to obtain other items for their stock, to purchase the imported nails as well. Jefferson countered by selling direct to the retail storekeeper. He was turning out a ton of nails a month, and expected shortly to step up his production to a ton and a half.[3]

He set for himself at the same time a more public and disinterested task. The laws of Virginia had never been arranged or codified and, in their scattered manuscript state, were subject to mildew, fire and irretrievable loss. Jefferson had a strong historical sense and an understanding of the value of archival material. Too many precious Virginia documents had already been lost to posterity, and he took upon himself the task of collecting what manuscripts remained, in order, he said, "that when the day should come in which the public should advert to the magnitude of their loss in these precious monuments of our property, and our history, a part of their regret might be spared by information that a portion has been saved from the wreck." Much of the material was in the hands of private individuals with a too careless sense of its importance, and Jefferson enlisted Wythe's services in ferreting it out. He had already made a collection of laws and other pertinent documents covering the period from 1624 to 1783, and he sought now to bring his collection up to date. Nor would he rest until the entire mass was properly printed at the public expense, and copies deposited in public offices and libraries.[4] It was largely due to Jefferson's indefatigable efforts that as many irreplaceable Virginia documents have come down to us as did.

He also received the ultimate recognition from the American Philosophical Society. On the death of David Rittenhouse, its president, in 1796, the Society elected Jefferson to the chair and retained him in it, in spite of polite protests on his part, for almost twenty years. The honor pleased Jefferson as much, if not more, than most of his political offices, and he hastened to present a scientific paper on the fossil leg bones and joints of a hitherto unknown quadruped that had been discovered in western Virginia.[5] These bones (from the giant sloth) were so immense that he exultantly offered them as one more proof of the falsity of Buffon's theory of "the pretended degeneracy of animal nature in our continent," and urged further explorations to uncover other remains.[6]

But his chief interest was the remodeling of his home. From its very inception, Monticello had been in a constant state of turmoil, with old structures being torn down and new ones being erected on an ever more magnificent architectural scale and in conformity with newer and more grandiose ideas. This year of 1796 stands out particularly as the high-water mark of activity.

Early in the spring he began the demolition of the upper portion of the house in which he lived. It had never really been completed, what with war and absences; and it had fallen into decay. So much so, indeed, that Jefferson found the interior timbers rotten and shaky. The brick walls, however, proved solid; and his seven workmen were unable to pry loose more than three to four thousand bricks a day. The resultant noise, confusion and danger from falling bricks—one laborer was hit and injured—were indescribable. During the alterations and rebuilding, Jefferson and his family camped out "under the tent of heaven." It was a matter, he wrote ruefully to Volney, an expected guest, that "will require all our philosophy & patience"; but he was welcome nevertheless.[7]

What Jefferson had in mind was to remove the second-story attic and spread all of the rooms on a single ground floor. In place of the attic he proposed an octagonal dome, with a mezzanine balcony around the interior, thus providing privacy for bedrooms and toilet facilities. In his own suite, located on the ground floor, he provided a bed alcove between his dressing room and study, accessible to both, and with a clear passage between the two formed by ingeniously drawing the bed up into the recessed ceiling during the day. So determined was he to keep the great central room unencumbered beneath the vault of the dome that he paid little heed to the problem of getting up to the mezzanine rooms. Almost as an afterthought he built narrow tortuous stairs in the galleries leading to the wings. He devoted much more time to the planning of noble proportions, to decorating the main rooms with classic friezes and mantels, with mythologic griffins and oxheads, with urns and Wedgwood inserts influenced by the style of Louis the Sixteenth and the brothers Adams.[8] He was fascinated by the oxhead motif which stemmed from Vespasian, and used it again in the University of Virginia.

Jefferson had expected to be finished by the end of the summer; but the undertaking was vaster than he had anticipated, and an early autumnal frost halted all proceedings. The next year his Vice-Presidency intervened; and the following spring found Monticello still roofless and forlorn.[9] As late as 1799 he was writing despondingly: "Scarcely a stroke has been done towards covering the house since I went away, so that it has remained open at the north end another winter. It seems as if I should never get it habitable."[10] The complete habitation, in fact, was not finished, if then, until after he had retired from the Presidency.

Early in 1796 Jefferson dropped his former pretense that he had no interest in politics. It was a presidential year and Washington had definitely made it plain that he was retiring at the end of his current term. That left the field wide open; and the political atmosphere grew thick with tension as party lines tightened and candidates were being groomed for the high office. By now, there was no question that official parties existed: the Federalist (or Antirepublican, as their opponents preferred to call them) and the Republican (or Democratic, as *their* adversaries derisively labeled them, a name which eventually they themselves accepted).

The opening gun was the struggle over the Jay Treaty. Jefferson was quick to see its value as campaign material. He exhorted his followers to keep pressing the treaty as an issue in the House of Representatives and insisted that the future construction of the Constitution depended on their action.[11] He lost patience with "the incomprehensible acquiescence of the only honest man [Washington] who has assented to it"; and so far forgot his usual caution to add: "I wish that his honesty and his political errors may not furnish a second occasion to exclaim, 'curse on his virtues, the[y]'ve undone his country.'"[12]

In fact, Jefferson had become heartily tired of Washington and the constant exaltation of his virtues; so much so that he committed one of the worst mistakes of his entire career. He unbosomed himself in a long letter to Phillip Mazzei. He felt himself safe in so doing, because Mazzei was in Italy and far removed from the American scene. But he failed to reckon with the effervescent enthusiasm and unthinking volubility of his distant friend.

Filled with indignation and exasperation over Washington's advocacy and signing of the Jay Treaty, Jefferson wrote on April 24, 1796, what has become known to history as the "Mazzei" letter.

The aspect of our politics [he penned] has wonderfully changed since you left us. In place of that noble love of liberty, & republican government which carried us triumphantly thro' the war, an Anglican, monarchical, & aristocratical party has sprung up, whose avowed object is to draw over us the substance as they have already done the forms of the British government. The main body of our citizens however remain true to their republican principles, the whole landed interest is republican, and so is a great mass of talents. Against us are the Executive, the Judiciary, two out of three branches of the legislature, all the officers of the government, all who want to be officers, all timid men who prefer the calm of despotism to the boisterous sea of liberty, British merchants & Americans trading on British capitals, speculators and holders in the banks & public funds, a contrivance invented for the purposes of corruption, & for assimilating us in all things to the rotten as well as the sound parts of the British model.

Thus far, though intemperate enough, Jefferson was merely paraphrasing what he had said in his notes to Professor Ebeling and on innumerable other occasions. But this time he touched the untouchable, continuing:

It would give you a fever were I to name to you the apostates who have gone over to these heresies, men who were Samsons in the field & Solomons in the council, but who have had their heads shorn by the harlot England. In short we are likely to preserve the liberty we have obtained only by unremitting labors & perils. But we shall preserve them, and our mass of weight & wealth on the good side is so great, as to leave no danger that force will ever be attempted against us. We have only to wake and snap the Lilliputian cords with which they have been entangling us during the first sleep which succeeded our labors.[13]

There was no question whom Jefferson meant by "the Samsons in the field & Solomons in the council" whose heads had been shorn by "the harlot England." Thus generically he referred to the single Washington. That he believed his appellations sincerely, there can also be no question; but that he put them into cold ink may be attributed to the condition of his health at the time. It was such, he told Mazzei, that he did not believe he had much longer to live.

The letter took months to travel to Italy; but when it arrived, Mazzei waxed so enthusiastic over this inestimable political exposé by his friend, Jefferson, that he translated it into Italian and had it published in a Florentine newspaper. There it might have rested, had not the Paris *Moniteur* picked it up, translated it into French, added some inimitable Gallic touches of its own, and republished it on January 25, 1797.

From there it was only a question of time when the American newspapers would get hold of it. *The Minerva* obtained a copy, diligently completed the circle by retranslation into English, and published the much-traveled letter on May 14, 1797, with some appropriate editorial comments of its own. "The foregoing letter," remarked *The Minerva*, "wears all the external marks of authenticity. And yet it seems hardly possible an American could be capable of writing such a letter. As the letter is circulating in Europe, we deem it just, if a forgery, to give Mr. Jefferson an opportunity to disavow it."

An examination of the translation, despite the vicissitudes of language through which the original passed, discloses a remarkable fidelity to the original text. For example, the published version called England "whore" instead of "harlot"; and spoke of the "form" of the British government, instead of the "forms."

The only substantial difference was not the fault of *The Minerva;* it lay in an additional sentence which the *Moniteur* had thoughtfully tacked to the original piece, and which had not appeared in the Italian. "It suffices," it made Jefferson say, "that we arrest the progress of that system of ingratitude and injustice towards France, from which they would alienate us, to bring us under British influence, &c." [14]

With the publication in America, the fat was in the fire. Jefferson had either to deny or admit, as had happened to him before, and was to continue to happen in spite of former horrible examples. To admit was suicidal; though fortunately the publication came *after* the election and he was safely ensconced in the Vice-Presidency. For Washington, in spite of attacks, was still the idol of the nation, and could not be directly assaulted without arousing an indignation which the Federalists would have been only too happy to exacerbate. Yet how could he deny?

What made the whole business particularly delicate at this time was the fact that in the preceding year, and little more than a month after Jefferson had actually written the Mazzei letter, there appeared in Bache's *Aurora* of June 9, 1796, a full copy of the highly confidential questions on France which Washington had submitted to his Cabinet on April 18, 1793.

Published for partisan purposes in the current election, it was obvious that Bache could only have received the document from a highly placed member of government and a Republican. Jefferson had foreseen the finger of suspicion inevitably pointing to *him*, and had hastened to swear to Washington that he had nothing to do with the leak.[15]

Washington accepted his explanation and the additional protestation that someone was trying to "sow tares between you & me, by representing me as still engaged in the bustle of politics, & in turbulence & intrigue against the government." Jefferson left unmentioned the name of "this miserable tergiversator," but in the margin of his own copy he wrote the name of General Henry Lee.

As long as the subject was brought up, however, Washington admitted he had heard talk that Jefferson had spoken of him in derogatory terms; adding that he had always shut the mouths of the accusers. Filled with a sense of his own grievances, the President burst forth: "Until within the last year or two ago, I had no conception that Parties would, or even could go, the length I have been witness to," or "that every act of my administration would be tortured, and the grossest, and most insidious mis-representations of them be made (by giving one side *only* of a subject, and that too in such exaggerated and indecent terms as could scarcely be applied to a Nero; a notorious defaulter; or even to a common pickpocket)." [16]

With this exchange in the past, it is obvious that Jefferson was now, with the publication of the Mazzei letter (which seemed to prove everything he had previously denied) impaled on the horns of a particularly sharp dilemma. He therefore took refuge in his usual resource of silence, to which he was also urged by the friends he consulted. To Madison he sought to explain the subtle distinction between his original reference to the *forms* of the British government, and the published translation as the singular *form*. The former, he said, referred merely to such items as birthdays, levees, processions to parliament and inauguration pomposities; the latter, so he maintained, made him appear hostile to the *form* of the government itself, and therefore to the Constitution.[17] It is an ingenious distinction, but singularly unconvincing. On the reference to Samsons and Solomons, he was discreetly silent.

Madison agreed with him that it would be unwise to issue a public statement; though he forwarded without comment Monroe's belief that "honest men would be encouraged by your owning & justifying the letter to Mazzei." [18]

The Federalist press naturally fell upon the letter with unholy glee; while Washington, in the face of Jefferson's silence, took the alleged reference to himself much to heart.

As if to add fuel to Washington's unhappiness, a curious incident now occurred. He received a letter from Warren, in Albemarle County, Virginia, purporting to be signed by one John Langhorne, which referred indignantly to personal attacks on the President. Washington dismissed it with a brief note of thanks; but a month later came another letter, this time from John Nicholas of Charlottesville, with a fantastic story. Langhorne, so Nicholas wrote, was a pseudonym for Jefferson's favorite nephew, Peter Carr. The whole business, declared Nicholas, was a trick to get Washington to express sentiments in his reply that could be used publicly against him. With the letter came seemingly unimpeachable evidence of Langhorne's true identity.[19]

This time Washington was convinced of Jefferson's treachery. With stately anger he answered Nicholas: "Nothing short of the Evidence you have adduced, corroborative of intimations which I had received long before, through another channel, could have shaken my belief in the sincerity of a friendship, which I had *conceived* was possessed for me, *by the person* to whom you allude [Jefferson]. But attempts to injure those who are supposed to stand well in the estimation of the People, and are stumbling blocks in their way (by misrepresenting their political tenets) thereby to destroy all confidence in them; is one of the means by which the Government is to be assailed, and the Constitution destroyed." [20]

Thereafter Washington broke off all relations with Jefferson, and never spoke to him again for the brief year that still remained to him of life.

What induced young Peter Carr to write this mysterious letter can only be the subject of conjecture. John Nicholas, the informant, was a Federalist and no friend to Jefferson; and he may well have put a sinister meaning on an innocent note. Yet the question arises why Carr took such elaborate precautions to conceal his identity, even to the extent of arranging to pick up Washington's reply to the mythical Langhorne at the post office. Perhaps, in his resentment against the Federalist attacks on his uncle, he hoped to lay hands on some unguarded expression of Washington that would prove the correctness of Jefferson's estimate in the Mazzei letter. But there is absolutely no reason to believe that Jefferson knew anything of the affair; either then or later.

That Jefferson in 1796 considered Washington as the great stumbling block in the path of a Republican triumph is unquestionable. After Congress had adjourned, and the Jay Treaty became the supreme law of the land, he wrote bitterly to Monroe: "You will have seen by their proceedings the truth of what I always observed to you, that one man [Washington] outweighs them all in influence over the people who have supported his judgment against their own & that of their representatives. Republicanism must lie on its oars, resign the vessel to its pilot, and themselves to the course he thinks best for them." [21]

The Republicans were particularly incensed against Washington because they had hoped in this presidential year to use the Treaty as a means of gaining power; and Washington's prestige had apparently lulled the storm. Madison was quite frank about it. "The name of the President," he wrote Jefferson, "& the alarm of war, have had a greater effect, than were apprehended on our side, or expected on the other. A crisis which ought to have been so managed as to fortify the Republican cause, has left it in a very crippled condition." In eloquent testimony were the results of the local elections in New York and elsewhere, where victory had perched on the Federalist banner.[22] This was all the more disastrous, since it was the state legislatures that in most instances chose the presidential electors. Hence the choice of the next President might well be determined by the local balloting in the spring and early summer of 1796.

Inasmuch as Washington had definitely refused re-election, many of the Federalists turned to John Adams as his logical successor. But Hamilton, though retired, was still the leader of his party and the man to whom Washington's new Cabinet turned for advice. He was not favorably disposed toward Adams and would have preferred Thomas Pinckney of South Carolina, recently returned from his ministry to England.

In this instance, however, the New England Federalists refused to follow his leadership; and the specters of Jefferson and Burr assumed such threatening proportions that Hamilton finally acceded to the candidacies of

Adams for President and Pinckney for Vice-President. The resentful New Englanders, however, feared treachery and privately determined to "waste" some votes in order to ensure that Pinckney would not run ahead of Adams.

On the Republican side, there was even more backing and filling. Jefferson was head and shoulders above all other possible choices, even though he had previously avowed that he was finished with public office. But the Republicans considered him as the only candidate they could put forward who had any chance of success; and the prospect of four more years of Federalism filled them with alarm.

At a very late date Jefferson suggested Madison; but Madison could not swing the pivotal Middle Atlantic States and himself urged Jefferson to run. New York and Pennsylvania, it was generally acknowledged, would prove decisive. New England could be counted on to vote pretty solidly for the Federalist slate; though as early as June, John Beckley was cynically reporting that Massachusetts would cast half its ballots for Jefferson while giving *all* to Adams, "on the true Yankee ground, that the former will make an unexceptionable Vice President." [23] To understand the curious mathematics, it must be remembered that under the Constitutional provision presidential electors were chosen in accordance with local state law, and that each elector cast his ballot for *two* presidential candidates. When the total ballots were counted, the candidate receiving the most votes became President, and the runner-up Vice-President.

The South would wind up largely in the Republican column; but New York and Pennsylvania were in the doubtful column and the scene of fierce local contests and feuds. In New York, Hamilton reigned supreme among the Federalists; but the Republicans followed two rapidly diverging banners. One faction was controlled by former Governor Clinton and his nephew, De Witt Clinton; the other by Aaron Burr. Both were ambitious men, though Burr was by far the more able, and was building up a strong political machine in the form of the Tammany Society in New York City. After much secret negotiation and some chicanery, it was finally decided to run Burr for the Vice-Presidency on a ticket headed by Jefferson.

During this period of indecision and hunt for likely candidates, Jefferson remained quietly at Monticello, writing very few letters and saying nothing at all about the rising agitation that he become the Republican standard-bearer. He duly read in the September 13th issue of Bache's *Aurora* that "it requires no talent at divination to decide who will be the candidates for the chair. THOMAS JEFFERSON & JOHN ADAMS will be the men, & whether we shall have at the head of our executive a steadfast friend to the Rights of the People, or an advocate for hereditary power and distinctions, the people of the United States are soon to decide."

But not even this public announcement of his candidacy brought any response from the recluse of Monticello. He diligently avoided the topic in those letters which did come from his pen during this period, confining himself largely to neutral matters or to political generalizations unrelated to any specific candidate. He was seemingly more interested in surveying and computing the height of the neighboring Blue Ridge Mountains and in perfecting his moldboard for ultimate communication to the Philosophical Society.[24]

This was no mere pretense; yet it is equally true that had he definitely and publicly repudiated all claims to the nomination at this stage, Burr, Clinton and others would have been only too happy to come forward for the highest office. But he held his silence until it was too late; and even then, it was only privately and to close friends that he disavowed any intention to run.

As autumn came and waned, the various states held their elections, at times fixed by themselves and by methods in accordance with their own laws. In some instances, the legislatures chose the electors by joint ballot; in others, there was a measure of popular voting. Where there *was* popular balloting, but few of the inhabitants held the right of suffrage. Most states had strict property qualifications; it has been estimated that barely a sixth of the white, adult male population were permitted at the polls. It must also be understood that though, in most instances, it was known for which two men the electoral candidates would vote if chosen, they were bound neither by law nor custom to do so.

Beckley, who with Burr represented a new breed of practical politician, still felt as late as October that Hamilton was intriguing to place Pinckney rather than Adams in the chair of "old Automatous [Washington]"; but that the election would be close, with Pennsylvania decisive in the final result.[25]

In fact, as reports and rumors came filtering in from the several states, it became increasingly evident that such would be the case. Since the Pennsylvania election was one of the last to be held, all eyes turned toward that pivotal state. Governor Thomas McKean was himself Republican, and it was hoped that he would be able to swing his state into the proper column.

But Jefferson had his doubts. He countered his son-in-law's confident predictions with the assertion that "the preponderance of the McKain [*sic*] interest in the Western counties of Pensylvania is by no means as great as is there supposed. Few will believe," he complained, "the true dispositions of my mind on that subject. It is not the less true however that I do sincerely wish to be the second on that vote rather than the first. The considerations which induce this preference are solid, whether viewed with relation to interest, happiness, or reputation. Ambition is long since dead in my mind. Yet even a well-weighed ambition would take the same side." [26]

What may have added to his reluctance to return to office at this time was the state of his finances. They had always been in bad shape, but a crisis now impended. He was the owner of 150 slaves, but they were heavily mortgaged. Now, in consideration of a loan of $2,000 from the Dutch banking firm of the Van Staphorsts and Hubbard, he conveyed to them the equity of redemption as an additional mortgage.[27] The rebuilding and expansion of Monticello was plunging him deeper and deeper into debt.

News of the election came with maddening slowness to the watchers in Virginia. At that distance the prospect seemed indeed black. On December 5th, Madison was writing cautiously to Jefferson that it was too soon to know the result; that it was even possible that Pinckney might win, as there were secret forces opposed to Adams because of his enmity to "banks & funding systems which is now become public, and by an apprehension that he is too headstrong to be a fit puppet for the intriguers behind the skreen." [28]

Five days later, though he pretended a tiny flicker of hope, Madison was certain that Pinckney was the next President, with Adams taking second place. "You *must* reconcile yourself," he nevertheless urged on Jefferson, "to the secondary as well as the primary station; if that should be your lot." [29] Even by Christmas Day, when the results were already well known in Pennsylvania, Madison thought that his friend was out of the running; though this time he gave the precedence to Adams over Pinckney.[30]

The week before, however, Jefferson was in such a state of jitters that he wanted Madison to take the Republican electoral votes; if that were impossible, then he prayed for himself to be either second or third. Even if there were a tie, and the election should thereby be thrown into the House of Representatives, he authorized Madison "to solicit on my behalf that mr. Adams may be preferred. He has always been my senior from the commencement of my public life, and the expression of the public will being equal, this circumstance ought to give him the preference." [31]

Now that the issue was in the balance, the prospect of becoming President seemingly terrified him. He assured Edward Rutledge that his name had been brought forward "without concert or expectation on my part; (on my salvation I declare it.) . . . On principles of public respect I should not have refused; but I protest before my god, that I shall, from the bottom of my heart, rejoice at escaping. I know well that no man will ever bring out of that office the reputation which carries him into it. . . . I have no ambition to govern men; no passion which would lead me to delight to ride in a storm." [32]

He need not have worried. By now the results from Pennsylvania were pretty clear. On December 2nd, Governor McKean had publicly declared that 13 of the 15 Pennsylvania electors would vote for Jefferson and Burr, and 2 for Adams and Pinckney.[33] On December 7th, the electors met and cast 14 votes for Jefferson, 13 for Burr, 2 for Pinckney and 1 for Adams.[34]

Since the results from the other states were now all in, it was definite that Adams had been elected President with 71 electoral votes, and Jefferson Vice-President with 68 votes. Pinckney and Burr trailed with 59 and 30 respectively.

Both Pinckney and Burr had reason to suspect treachery. New England

Federalists had cast away votes from Pinckney in order to ensure Adams's election, and thereby deprived him of the Vice-Presidency. Burr noted that the solidly Republican state of Virginia—Jefferson's private bailiwick—had cast a unanimous vote for Jefferson, but only a single vote for his running mate.

A curious dispute, moreover, arose in Pennsylvania. It seemed that two Jeffersonians had actually been elected in western Greene County, but the official returns were not submitted to the state authorities in time. Meanwhile, two Federalists had presented themselves, claiming election, and had been admitted. One of them, as might be expected, cast his ballot for Adams; but the other most surprisingly voted for Jefferson!

This contretemps created a tremendous mix-up, the repercussions of which have not died down to the present day. The Republican press raised an outcry then, insisting that Jefferson had in fact been elected; and as late as 1948 an article appeared in the *New York Times* repeating the allegation.[35]

The claim was based on the assumption that the votes of the two rejected Republican electors would have gone to Jefferson, which is correct; and that both ballots cast by the usurping Federalists went to Adams, which is untrue. One of the Federalists—a man named Powell—voted for Pinckney and Jefferson, and omitted Adams. Therefore, even had both votes been thrown out, and Republican votes for Jefferson and Burr substituted in their place, Adams would still be in the lead with 70 votes; while Jefferson's total would have risen to 69, just one short of a tie.

Jefferson was well aware of the truth, and explained the tangle at length to his son-in-law. When a Republican publication attempted to revive the controversy during the election of 1800, he amplified the details in a private memorandum, frankly admitting that he had been previously fairly defeated.[36]

Jefferson was sincerely happy that he was second to Adams. Even Madison grew reconciled, expressing the hope to Jefferson that the closeness of the vote would "lessen the evil of such an ostensible protest by this country agst Republicanism. Your acceptance of a share in the administration will not fail to aid this tendency."[37]

Fearing, indeed, that his friend might refuse the Vice-Presidency, Madison kept urging him and painted a picture of the influence he could exercise over Adams in the field of foreign affairs, adding artfully that Adams "is said to speak of you now in friendly terms and will no doubt be soothed by your acceptance of a place subordinate to him."[38]

This last brushstroke touched Jefferson. He composed an effusive letter to Adams:

DEAR SIR,—The public & the papers have been much occupied lately in placing us in a point of opposition to each other. I trust with confidence that less of it has been felt by ourselves personally. In the retired canton where I am, I learn little of what is passing; pamphlets I see never; papers but a few; and the fewer the happier.... I have never one single moment expected a different issue [of the election]; & tho' I know I shall not be believed, yet it is not the less true that I have never wished it. My neighbors as my compurgators could aver that fact, because they see my occupations & my attachment to them. Indeed it is impossible [*sic* for *possible*] that you may be cheated of your succession by a trick worthy the subtlety of your arch-friend of New York [Hamilton] who has been able to make of your real friends tools to defeat their and your just wishes. Most probably he will be disappointed as to you; and my inclinations place me out of his reach. I leave to others the sublime delights of riding in the storm, better pleased with sound sleep and a warm birth [*sic*] below, with the society of neighbors, friends & fellow-laborers of the earth, than of spies & sycophants.... I have no ambition to govern men. It is a painful and thankless office. Since the day too on which you signed the treaty of Paris our horizon was never so overcast. I devoutly wish you may be able to shun for us this war by which our agriculture, commerce & credit will be destroyed. If you are, the glory will be all your own; and that your administration may be filled with glory, and happiness to yourself and advantage to us is the sincere wish of one who tho' in the course of our own voyage thro' life, various little incidents have happened or been contrived to separate us, retains still for you the solid esteem of the moments when we were working for our independence, and sentiments of respect and affectionate attachment.[39]

After rereading what he had written, Jefferson hesitated. Should he send it or should he not? He sought Madison's reliable advice, sending him the letter and placing the decision with him. "If mr. Adams," he said, "can be induced to administer the government on its true principles, & to relinquish his bias to an English constitution, it is to be considered whether it would not be on the whole for the public good to come to a good understanding with him as to his future elections. He is perhaps the only sure barrier against Hamilton getting in." [40]

But Madison thought it unwise to forward Jefferson's letter, and told him so. Adams, he wrote back, was already aware that Jefferson felt warmly toward him, and the effusive nature of the communication might give rise to suspicions of ulterior motives. The new President was also sufficiently aware of Hamilton's machinations and, Madison added dryly, "there may be a danger of his suspecting in mementos on that subject, a wish to make his resentment an instrument for avenging that of others." [41]

Jefferson acknowledged the force of his friend's reasoning, and the letter was never sent.[42] Nevertheless, word of his new Vice-President's declarations of regard filtered through unofficially to Adams, and pleased him immensely. Ironically enough, Adams believed that Jefferson was himself being flattered by the Francophiles for purposes of their own, and that *he* could hold him steady. He set down his belief in a hitherto unpublished letter that throws considerable light on the tangled maneuverings on both sides.

"Mr Jeffersons Letters and Declarations," he confided to a political friend, "are no Surprise to me. We laboured together in high friendship in Congress in 1776 and have lived and dined together very frequently since that time. His Talent and Information I know very well, and have ever believed in his honour, Integrity, his Love of his Country and his friends. I may say to you that his Patronage of Paine and Freneau, and his Entanglements with Characters and Politicks which have been pernicious, are and have long been a Source of Inquietude and Anxiety to me, as they must have been to you. But I hope and believe that his Advancement and his Situation in the Senate, an excellent School, will correct him. He will have too many French Friends about him to flatter him: but I hope, we can keep him Steady. This is entre nous." [43]

Thus, in the open, everything seemed sweetness and light, with the savage personalities of the campaign forgotten. Jefferson testified to his esteem for Adams, and Adams countered with similar protestations. Just as Jefferson's pronouncements had come to Adams, so Jefferson in turn heard that Adams "speaks of me with great friendship, and with satisfaction in the prospect of administering the government in concurrence with me." Though glad to hear of it, he would refuse, so he declared, the offer of a Cabinet position, if one were made. "I cannot have a wish," he wrote Madison with retrospective shudder, "to see the scenes of 93. revived as to myself, & to descend daily into the arena like a gladiator, to suffer martyrdom in every conflict." [44]

Remembering the ironic laughter that greeted Adams's attempted "monarchical" trappings when he was inducted into the Vice-Presidency, Jefferson wanted his own ceremony to be as simple and informal as possible. He asked both Madison and Henry Tazewell for advice. He would have liked to remain at Monticello and receive the official notice of his election by mail; but then he feared that he might be considered as sulking in his tents over his failure to win the Presidency. Therefore he would go to Philadelphia. But, he warned, he wished for no official welcome, and would try to "escape into the city as covertly as possible." [45]

These were perhaps trifles, but they gave Jefferson considerable trouble. He believed that *forms* were important, as symbolizing the inner content to the public. Ceremony was an essential trapping of monarchy; a republic ought to manifest itself in simplicity and modest behavior. He therefore remained at Monticello until the twentieth of February; then rode for Philadelphia, arriving on March 2, 1797—only two days before he was due to be sworn in as Vice-President of the United States.

CHAPTER 41

Vice-President Jefferson

THE administration of John Adams commenced under inauspicious circumstances. If relations with England were somewhat better because of Jay's treaty—inadequate as it was—those with France were considerably worse. A steady succession of French ministers had managed to keep the pot boiling furiously; first Genêt, then Fauchet, and now M. Adet, the last of a curious trio.

France, flushed with a series of victories over England and her allies, was pushing revolution into every nook and cranny of the Continent, and was not disposed to treat as an equal with the futile little republic across the seas. She dismissed American neutral rights as contemptuously as ever the British had done, and paid no heed to any protests. It was now the Federalists who breathed fiery demands for war against the transgressor. Hamilton, ill at ease in his retirement, joined the fray with a series of public papers, in which he demanded Adet's recall and roused the people against supineness in the face of French aggression.[1]

Jefferson was greatly alarmed over the situation. War even with England had been far from his thoughts; war with France was unthinkable. Yet the clamor grew; every eastern merchant, every shipowner and moneyed man joined in public meetings and memorials. And Hamilton had added his powerful pen.

However, Jefferson hoped that war could be avoided. "I do not believe," he had written Madison, "mr. A[dams] wishes war with France; nor do I believe he will truckle to England as servilely as has been done. If he assumes this front at once, and shews that he means to attend to self-respect & national dignity with both the nations, perhaps the depredations of both on our commerce may be amicably arrested. I think we should begin first with those who first begin with us, and, by an example on them, acquire a right to re-demand the respect from which the other party has departed." [2] In other words, France had merely been following England's example; and if the United States was to become "tough," let it be with England first.

He was inclined at this time to blame everything on Washington, whom he sarcastically described as "fortunate to get off just as the bubble is bursting, leaving others to hold the bag." Any trouble that might arise would be attributed to the new administration; and Washington would have his "usual good fortune of reaping credit from the good acts of others, and leaving to them that of his errors." [3]

In fact, Jefferson's letters of this period are extremely bitter against his former chief. Not long before, he had composed the "Mazzei" letter; he wrote another one now that, had it ever been made public, would have raised a storm to which the former would have been mere polite afternoon tea. For here there was no opportunity to claim mistranslations or wrong interpretations. It was specific, detailed, enlightening.

Addressing Archibald Stuart, his business agent and friend, Jefferson unbuttoned himself. "I shall speak explicitly," he wrote, "because I know I may do it safely to you. Such is the popularity of the President [Washington] that the people will support him in whatever he will do or will not do, without appealing to their own reason or to anything but their feelings toward him. His mind has been so long used to unlimited applause that it could not brook contradiction, or even advice offered unasked. To advice, when asked, he is very open. I have long thought therefore it was best for the republican interest to soothe him by flattering where they could approve his measures, & to be silent where they disapprove, that they may not render him desperate as to their affections, & entirely indifferent to their wishes, in short to lie on their oars while he remains at the helm, and let the bark drift as his will and a superintending providence shall direct." [4]

The new President, Adams, however, was a different matter. Jefferson was certain that he too would be amenable to flattery, but that no such circumspection in handling him was required as with Washington. And Hamilton's influence and policies, so potent in the preceding administration, would no longer have any effect. In this he was mistaken, but for reasons which neither he nor Adams understood at the time.

Jefferson's conception of the Vice-Presidency was most modest. The Constitution had been singularly vague concerning the duties of the second highest officer of the land, mentioning specifically only his right to preside over the Senate and his contingent succession to the Presidency in case of the incumbent's death, resignation or removal.

The first to hold the office, Adams, had fumed over his own futility; though occasionally Washington called on him for advice. But Jefferson, at the very beginning, hastened to disavow any part in Cabinet proceedings. The Vice-Presidency, to him, was limited strictly to the Constitutional provision of a presiding officer in the Senate, and he wanted it to remain as such.[5] The results were unfortunate, both during his own term, and ever after. For the office, because of this interpretation. became a haven for mediocrities and a plum for the payment of political debts.

Jefferson had slipped into town almost unnoticed on March 2nd, via the anonymity of the stagecoach. He put up at Madison's lodgings, and then called on Adams. The next day Adams returned the call, closed the door, and plunged into the situation with France. So alarming was it that he proposed an immediate mission to the ruling Directory. He would have preferred to send Jefferson, he declared, but that he was needed at home. Therefore he intended to send Madison and Elbridge Gerry. Would Jefferson sound out Madison? Jefferson did so, and Madison declined; much to Adams's relief, for the Federalist leaders when they heard of it raised strong objections. This, according to Jefferson, was the first and last time that Adams ever consulted him on measures of government; a fact which he atrributed to the private expostulations of the members of the Cabinet.[6]

This may well have been. For the Cabinet was an inheritance from Washington's administration, and contained extreme Federalists and Hamilton's personal henchmen: Timothy Pickering in the State Department, Oliver Wolcott in the Treasury, and James McHenry in the Department of War. Unknown to Adams, they secretly imparted to their distant leader complete information of Cabinet discussions and proposed measures, and did nothing of major importance, or even rendered an opinion, until Hamilton in New York had first advised them what to do.

No wonder Hamilton wrote sarcastically to his friend, Rufus King, now minister to England, concerning the new heads of government: "Mr. Adams is President, Mr. Jefferson Vice President. Our Jacobins say they are well pleased, and that the *Lion* & the *Lamb* are to lie down together. Mr. Adams' PERSONAL friends talk a little in the same way. Mr. *Jefferson* is not half so ill a man as we have been accustomed to think him. There is to be a united and vigorous administration. Sceptics like me quietly look forward to the event, willing to hope, but not prepared to believe." [7]

Hamilton's scepticism was justified, for he had much to do with the ensuing disunity and confusion. Adams was in office a bare two days when he first fell into the toils of the cabal. He inquired of the Cabinet—in accordance with the precedent established by Washington—what course should be pursued with France. But the members, before replying, forwarded the questions to Hamilton with an inquiry as to *his* opinion. To each, Hamilton replied in similar vein: let a mission go, composed of Pinckney, an opposition leader like Jefferson or Madison, and a "safe" man like George Cabot or Jay. Pending the result, let an immediate embargo be placed against France—a procedure he had repudiated in former days when aimed at England; increase the navy and raise a provisional army.[8]

McHenry meekly turned in Hamilton's report almost verbatim to Adams; but Pickering and Wolcott—more extreme in their views than Hamilton himself—balked. *They* thought the proposed procedure too placating of France on the one hand, and of the Republicans on the other. But their rebellion proved abortive; for the balance of Adams's administration they faithfully followed Hamilton's direction, and bedeviled and sabotaged their titular head at every step. It was an amazing situation that led to ultimate explosion, and was in large part responsible for the Federalists being swept out of office at the next election.

Jefferson, in accordance with his own view of the duties of his office, was a complete outsider. He busied himself with his private affairs and presided discreetly over the Senate when that body was in session. A week or so after induction into office, he went to view an elephant and some elks on exhibition; and sought to purchase at 3,000 livres a bust of himself by the sculptor Ceracchi.[9]

After his first inconclusive interview with Adams—and the extended silence thereafter—Jefferson decided that the President had returned to his former Federalist party views and that further co-operation would be impossible. All that could be done now must be done through the Republican members in Congress and through incessant education of the people. Meticulously he put down in his private notes every bit of gossip he could collect concerning the aristocratic, nonrepublican views of Adams, and of the decided monarchical sentiments of the leading Federalists. He continued this self-imposed chore all through his Vice-Presidency.[10]

Indeed, he took his official duties so lightly that he quit his post ten days after his inauguration, and returned to Monticello. On March 20th, he rode up the beloved mountain, his heart gladdened with the sight of his peach and cherry trees in full blossom. Three days later, asparagus and spinach from his own garden appeared fresh on his table, and he expanded blissfully in the warmth and geniality of the days, after the frosts and snows he had left behind.[11]

Politics were also left behind. He examined his building operations afresh. He disapproved heartily of the custom which had been imported from European cities, where land was scarce, of raising homes to heights of two, three and even four stories. Though the custom had already disappeared in Europe, it was still being slavishly copied in America. In Paris, as a matter of fact, new houses were of a single story only, with high-ceiled rooms devoted to entertainment, and the bedrooms relegated to two tiers whose total height matched the one story of the public rooms. The upper tier was reached by a small, private staircase. "By these means," wrote Jefferson, "great staircases are avoided, which are expensive & occupy a space which would made a good room in every story." [12] This hitherto unpublished comment throws a new light on what has always puzzled commentators on Monticello—the narrow, steeply pitched and inconvenient stairs. They were not original with Jefferson, but a copy of what he had seen in Paris during his ministry.

As usual, scientific pursuits continued to fascinate him. He toyed once more with an old idea of his to have correspondents in every county of Virginia take daily temperature readings and forward their observations to him. He believed there was a direct correlation between temperature and wind direction, and he hoped to prove his thesis by charting both variables on a series of maps. In time, he proposed to cover the entire United States.[13]

A gift of bread-tree seeds from France evoked a characteristic response. "One service of this kind rendered to a nation," he exclaimed, "is worth more to them than all the victories of the most splendid pages of their history, and becomes a source of exalted pleasure to those who have been instrumental to it." [14]

He also listened with approval to Dr. Rush's analogy between the former animal tyrants who had roamed the ancient American forests—and of whom only fossil bones remained—and the human kings and tyrants of Europe. Just as the gigantic animals of yore had been extirpated by a confederacy of smaller beasts, may we not hope, asked the optimistic doctor, "that kings will be extirpated from the face of the earth by a general insurrection of the reason and virtue of man, and that the exhibition of crowns, sceptres and maces, like the claws & bones of extinct animals, shall be necessary to prove to posterity, that such canibals ever existed upon our globe?"

But whether Jefferson equally approved of a paper which Rush announced in preparation is not known. This, declared the doctor, was intended to prove "that the black Color (as it is called) of the Negroes is the effect of a disease in the Skin of the Leprous kind." [15]

Jefferson had hoped to be able to roof in his building during a summer's stay at Monticello. He was suffering from a rheumatic attack and, he told the French scientist Volney, "as far as my indisposition & solitude could permit I have been in the enjoiment of our delicious spring. The soft genial temperature of the season, just above the want of fire, enlivened by the reanimation of birds, flowers, the fields, forests & gardens, has been truly delightful." In short, he was residing in the Eden of America.[16]

Alas, he was now compelled to leave his Eden. A summons had come from Philadelphia. Congress was meeting on the 15th of May, and he was required to preside over the Senate. He was reluctant to go, both because of his rheumatic condition and because he dreaded a convocation of Congress at this particular time. If peace with France had been decided on, there would have been no need for a meeting of Congress. Its summoning, therefore, had an ominous ring.[17]

It was with grim forebodings that he girded himself for the journey; comforting himself with the knowledge that, traveling by stage, he would have "an opportunity of plunging into the mixed characters of my country, the most useful school we can enter into, and one which nothing else can supply the want of. I once intimately knew," he told Volney, "all the specimens of character which compose the aggregate mass of my fellow-citizens. But age, office, & literature have too long insulated me from them. I find that either their features or my optics have considerably changed in twenty years." [18]

He had barely entered Philadelphia, however, when the publication of his "Mazzei" letter rocked the nation. The repercussions were felt even in Europe. Young John Quincy Adams, stationed in London, read it with considerable dismay and wrote his mother, Abigail, that the letter "shows a mind full of error or an heart full of falsehood. I cannot yet believe this last to be the case. My old sentiments of respect veneration and attachment still hang about me with regard to that man." [19]

Courtesy the New York State Historical Association

THOMAS JEFFERSON

Original plaster life mask by Bowere, 1825

Courtesy the New-York Historical Society, New York City

ALBERT GALLATIN

Painting by William H. Powell

At home his parents, though somewhat shaken, similarly clung to their old attachment to Jefferson. The final break did not come until Jefferson was President; and *then* only because of this very son who now avowed his allegiance.

Jefferson was now fifty-four; and a description of him at this time has come down to us, penned by an avowed enemy and put on paper at a much later date with the frank acknowledgment that it was not "offered with confidence."

The author, William Sullivan, described him as long-limbed and loose-jointed, with a sandy complexion, hair of reddish hue, combed loosely over his forehead and tied behind in a queue. His forehead was high and broad, his eyebrows long and straight over eyes of blue. His cheekbones were high, his chin long and his mouth large. His dress was ordinarily a black coat with light-colored underclothes. His manners were unpolished, but his deportment was simple, sober, quiet and unobtrusive. He spoke calmly and deliberately, without any gestures. The expression on his countenance was thoughtful and observant, but neither open nor frank, and his eyes were evasive.[20] Taking into consideration that this was the appraisal of a political foe, it was fair enough.

Congress opened its session in an inflamed atmosphere both at home and abroad. French seizures of American ships had far outdistanced the worst spoliations of the British in previous years; and all demands for restitution were met with arrogant refusals. Monroe, the Minister to France during the closing years of Washington's administration, had conducted himself in such fashion that he had been recalled, much to his own anger and that of his friends.

The question before the new Congress, just as Jefferson had dreaded, was one of peace or war. Adams's opening message, according to his Vice-President, was of a sufficiently warlike nature to cause a drift in the direction of war among the members.[21]

Actually, the speech was nothing of the sort. It pointed out, as the President had a right to do, the serious nature of the situation and stated the facts—that the French government had refused to receive the new American minister sent to replace Monroe, that fresh decrees had been issued which added to the ravages on our commerce, and that a permanent system of naval defense was essential.[22]

What Jefferson had feared most of all—the establishment of an embargo on France—appeared neither in the message nor in Congressional debate. The Virginia tobacco exporters, who would have been hardest hit, could be tranquil on that subject, Jefferson reported to his son-in-law. But a week later, much to his dismay, the ominous subject had suddenly reared its head. Jefferson's own interests were involved. He had withheld his tobacco from the market in the expectation of a rise in prices. But if an embargo were laid and foreign sale thereby became impossible, the price would drop precipitously.[23]

It was with a peculiarly helpless feeling that he watched the march of events. For Virginia had betrayed the Republican cause in the recent elections, with the result that, instead of the expected majority in the House, the two parties were so evenly balanced that measures were decided on utterly fortuitous grounds.[24] The Senate, over which Jefferson personally presided, was strongly Federalist. His role was solely that of arbiter of the rules; he could neither participate in the business before the Senate nor cast a vote.

Little is known of his conduct in the chair, except that he conscientiously prepared himself for the task. As soon as his election had been confirmed, he began a careful study of the parliamentary rules of procedure, reading all the books on the subject on which he could lay hands, and calling on Wythe for assistance. Unfortunately, Wythe proved of little help; he had lost his old notes and his memory had failed him.[25] Undeterred, from his books and his inquiries Jefferson was able to compile a set of rules of procedure that still possess considerable value for legislative use.

The Senate's reply to the Presidential address, so Jefferson thought, was fully as "high toned" as the address itself; but fortunately, the news of the failure of the Bank of England cooled down the war fever. Even the most extreme Federalist, in the face of that surprising debacle and its attendant train of American bankruptcies, thought twice before entering on a major war at this moment. The high talk died down to a whisper—of arming American ships for defense against French aggression.[26]

Nevertheless, Jefferson lost none of his pessimism over the outcome. Nothing but the desperate condition of England had prevented the Fedralists from joining openly with that country. His vivid imagination conjured up the horrors yet to come. "When I contemplate the spirit which is driving us on here," he wrote gloomily to Thomas Pinckney, recently returned from England, "& that beyond the water which will view us as but a mouthful the more, I have little hope of peace. I anticipate the burning of our sea ports, havoc of our frontiers, household insurgency, with a long train of et ceteras, which is enough for a man to have met once in his life."[27]

He was particularly alarmed over the cession of Louisiana by Spain to France; thereby placing the latter, in case of war, on our most vulnerable flank. "War," he declared firmly, reverting to his pet thesis, "is not the best engine for us to resort to, nature has given us one *in our commerce*, which, if properly managed, will be a better instrument for obliging the interested nations of Europe to treat us with justice." If only that potent weapon had been employed at an earlier stage (against England), "we should at this moment have been standing on such an eminence of safety & respect as ages can never recover."[28]

In thus harking back to his old idea of an embargo against England, he failed to note the inconsistency of his passionate objection to an embargo against *France*, the current despoiler of American commerce.

Adams, in spite of Jefferson's apprehensions, was no warmonger. He ardently desired peace if it could be obtained without loss of honor, and he was willing to go to substantial lengths to find a *modus vivendi* with the victory-swollen rulers of France. When Jefferson had first arrived in Philadelphia, he had sounded him out as one of a proposed triumvirate of special plenipotentiaries to France. Jefferson had refused; so had Madison. Undeterred, Adams persisted. He wanted no renewal of the partisan uproar over the Jay mission, and sought to balance his appointments so that all factions might be satisfied. He finally determined on John Marshall of Virginia and Charles Cotesworth Pinckney of South Carolina (not to be confused with Charles Pinckney, a cousin), both Federalists, and Elbridge Gerry of Massachusetts who, if still technically a Federalist, already showed Republican leanings.

Jefferson's first reaction was one of suspicion. He did not believe it disclosed any real conversion of Adams to the cause of peace.[29] But nothing of this appeared in his letter of congratulation to Gerry. Urging him to accept the post, Jefferson sought skillfully to guide him in the task ahead.

> Peace [he asserted] is undoubtedly at present the first object of our nation. Interest & honor are also national considerations. But interest, duly weighed, is in favor of peace even at the expence of spoliations past & future; & honor cannot now be an object. The insults & injuries committed on us by both the belligerent parties from the beginning of 1793, to this day, & still continuing by both, cannot now be wiped off by engaging in war with one of them. ... Our countrymen have divided themselves by such strong affections to the French & the English, that nothing will secure us internally but a divorce from both nations ... but for this peace is necessary. Be assured of this, my dear Sir, that if we engage in a war during our present passions & our present weakness in some quarters, that our union runs the greatest risk of not coming out of that war in the shape in which it enters it.[30]

The passions of which Jefferson spoke so earnestly had indeed risen to an unprecedented degree. "Men who have been intimate all their lives," he noted, "cross the streets to avoid meeting, & turn their heads another way, lest they should be obliged to touch their hats. This may do for young men," he added plaintively, "with whom passion is enjoyment. But it is afflicting to peaceable minds."[31]

Congress was similarly a battleground, with the Federalists ruling the Senate and a wavering balance in the House. The bills which were pushed through both Houses in the first rush of excitement excited Jefferson's utmost apprehension. All of them, including pending bills for fortifications along the coast and for manning three frigates, were to him aggressively warlike measures.[32]

With Congress thus taking the bit in its mouth, Jefferson began to think seriously of mending political fences. The sudden reversal in Virginia had alarmed him, and he looked to New York for aid, where Aaron Burr at the moment seemed the dominant political figure. He wrote Burr a careful letter which at once recalled himself to that gentleman's memory and sought by indirection his services in swinging New York and other eastern states over to the Republican camp.[33] It was the beginning of an alliance that was to have portentous results in the lives of both men and in the fortunes of the nation.

But Jefferson's worst fears were not realized. When Congress finally rose, war had not been declared and instead, a mission had been chosen to seek for a peaceable solution of the difficulties with France. It was therefore with a lighter heart that, on July 6, 1797, Jefferson quit the arid atmosphere of Philadelphia for the mountain breezes of Monticello.

His normal eagerness for home was enhanced by news that had come a month earlier. Maria—his affectionate Polly—had fallen in love. Her young affections had centered on John Wayles Eppes, one of her innumerable cousins, with whose family Jefferson was on the most cordial terms. He hailed the information with considerable satisfaction. Since Martha's marriage his single anxiety had been to see Maria follow suit. The choice she had made could not have been more to his wishes and, he happily prophesied, "I now see our fireside formed into a groupe, no one member of which can ever produce any jarring or jealousies among us. No irregular passions, no dangerous bias, which may render problematical the future fortunes & happiness of our descendants." He would, he avowed, present to them the plantation on Pantops, a lower elevation directly opposite Monticello.[34]

There was much to keep him busy: he had to prepare for the impending wedding, hasten his constructions and live gypsylike elsewhere during the confusion, and entertain his visitors, Madison and Monroe, in the midst of turmoil and disorder. But politics invaded even this domestic scene.

Monroe, furious at his recall and smarting under the abuse which the Federalist press had heaped upon his ministry in France, intended to defend himself in a pamphlet which at the same time would attack the whole basis of Washington's foreign policy. He undoubtedly showed the manuscript to Jefferson and sought his aid in choosing a title for it.[35] The assault on Washington was slashing and intemperate; and the Federalists, when it finally appeared, retorted in kind, drawing from Madison the remark that the counterattacks seemed to be officially inspired and proved that Monroe's pamphlet had hit its mark.[36] Washington was no longer sacrosanct to the embattled Republicans.

The latter were now definitely on the offensive; and Monroe's pamphlet had barely reached the press when another publication appeared which preferred the most serious charges against Alexander Hamilton.

One James Thomson Callender, a Republican hack pamphleteer, had undertaken a long-winded *History of the United States for the Year 1796* in which history became a Roman holiday and a justification of Republican principles. In this praiseworthy task he received moral encouragement and more-welcome financial aid from a group of Republican leaders. At this stage Jefferson's contribution was modest, amounting only to a subscription of $15.14 for the initial installments.[37] Later on, however, he gave Callender more substantial contributions.

In the fifth installment of his History, Callender accused Hamilton of bribery, corruption and financial malfeasance in the conduct of the Treasury during the years 1792-93, buttressed with what seemed damning and unimpeachable evidence. This evidence was probably furnished Callender by Monroe or John Beckley, or both. Thus faced with the possibility of the ruin of his political honor, Hamilton chose rather to destroy his private reputation, and wrote an amazing response that unfolded a sordid tale of adultery and blackmail which has become known in history as "the Mrs. Reynold's affair." He also charged that Monroe had personally known the true facts—which he had—and that he had instigated Callender's current assault. A duel almost resulted, and was only prevented by the intermediary offices of Aaron Burr.

Though he knew the inside story, Jefferson nevertheless was not too unhappy over the predicament in which Hamilton found himself. He sneered at the latter's defense and declared that, "finding the strait between Scylla and Charybdis too narrow for his steerage, he has preferred running plump on one of them. In truth, it seems to work very hard with him; and his willingness to plead guilty as to the adultery seems rather to have strengthened than weakened the suspicions that he was in truth guilty of the speculations." [38] Jefferson was always willing to believe the worst of his great antagonist.

He also continued to sponsor Callender. That worthy appealed to him for some financial assistance in the progress of his History, and suggested the modest sum of five or ten dollars. The check, however, was to be made out in the name of a designated third party. Jefferson obliged somewhat later with purchases of his pamphlets and several donations of $50 each.[39] All of which elicited from the still modest Callender the thankful response that "if I could find any 4th person to do what Mr. D[allas], or ½ of what L[eiper] or Mr. Jefferson have already done, I would make myself heard very distinctly for a considerable distance." [40] But Jefferson was to find out to his cost that appetite grows with what it is fed, and gratitude diminishes in inverse proportion.

Politics also penetrated his mountain fastness in the guise of a grand jury indictment for criminal libel issued under the benign auspices of a Federalist judge against a Virginia Congressman, Samuel Jordan Cabell, who, in the language of the indictment, wrote letters to his constituents "endeavoring, at a time of real public danger, to disseminate unfounded calumnies against the happy government of the United States, and thereby to separate the people therefrom."

Jefferson was quick to see the dangers inherent in the indictment—dangers which eventually led to the Sedition Act—and drafted a petition to the Virginia House of Delegates, signed by citizens of the four neighboring counties, which denounced on constitutional grounds both the indictment and its judicial sponsorship, and demanded that the House impeach the offenders.[41] The petition was not acted on.

On October 13, 1797, Jefferson saw Maria satisfactorily married to young John Wayles Eppes; on December 4th, he departed for Philadelphia, arriving there on the 12th to resume his meager duties as Vice-President of the United States.

The simmer of the last session had quieted down. Both Congress and the Administration were marking time waiting for news to come from the envoys in France; though Fauchet, the departing French Minister in America, was doing his best to muddy beyond retrieving the already sufficiently roiled waters of international amity by writing a pamphlet which boldly accused Adams of being the enemy of France.[42] Jefferson privately agreed with the accusation, writing Monroe that it merely reinforced what the latter had already said in his own published pamphlet.[43]

He was bitter over the compulsion that kept him in Philadelphia. "We are lounging our time away," he complained to his daughter, Martha, "doing nothing, & having nothing to do. It gives me great regret to be passing my time so uselessly when it could have been so importantly employed at home.... Nor are we relieved by the pleasures of society here. For partly from bankruptcies partly from party dissensions society is torn up by the roots. I envy those who stay at home, enjoying the society of their friendly neighbors, blessed with their firesides, and employed in doing something every day which looks usefully to futurity." [44]

The old urge was manifesting itself once more; but the period of dull activity and seemingly senseless waiting was shortly to be exploded by news from France.

CHAPTER 42

Cold War with France

NEWS from France, however, was slow in coming. January and February of 1798 passed, and the packet boats brought nothing. The three plenipotentiaries seemed to have been swallowed up in the maelstrom of Europe, leaving no trace of their whereabouts.

Jefferson feared, not so much war from the Directory, as a refusal to come to terms and a continuance of depredations "according to the English example." If only, he mused, France would invade and "republicanize" England; then "all will be safe with us, whatever mortifying things we may suffer in the meantime." [1] He was certain that all our troubles with France stemmed from the exigencies of her struggle to the death with England. Once France had conquered, she would cease her arrogance and disregard for American rights.

As the weeks passed, and still no news came, his hopes rose. "This long silence (if they have been silent) proves things are not going on roughly," he wrote Madison. "If they have not been silent, it proves their information, if made public, would check the disposition to arm." [2]

This comment of his raises several interesting points. For one, it throws a significant light on the relations between Jefferson, the Vice-President of the United States, and the administration of John Adams. Though ostensibly the second officer of the nation, he was *persona non grata*, neither consulted nor consulting, and knowing as little of administration affairs as the meanest citizen in the streets. For another, it discloses the steadfast belief of the Republicans that Adams was hot for war; and that news of a probable settlement would be withheld deliberately from the people.

Monroe considered the breach irremediable. Indignantly he exclaimed to Jefferson: "You did everything in your power to unite the people under his administration, & to give him in negotiation the aid of the republican character & interest to support the pretensions of our country & not without hazard to yourself. But this he spurned with a degree of wantonness of which there is no example. He would have none of his ranks but tried men, whose political creed corresponded with his own." [3]

Monroe's diatribe against Adams does not accord with the known facts. If Jefferson was the outsider, it was because he had voluntarily assumed that position. It is true that, in the first flush of election, he had offered cooperation to Adams; but Madison never forwarded the letter. When Adams consulted with him on relations with France, and offered to send either Jefferson or Madison to accompany Gerry, both gentlemen had declined.

Thereby Adams was thrown perforce into the arms of his inherited Cabinet, who cabaled with Hamilton against him behind his back.

But Jefferson, instead of seeking that *modus vivendi* which Monroe thought had been rudely refused, was philosophizing about the future of the American scene, a blessed utopia in which the States, revolving around the central government "like the planets revolving round their common sun, acted & acted upon according to their respective weights and distances, will produce that beautiful equilibrium on which our Constitution is founded, and which I believe it will exhibit to the world in a degree of perfection, unexampled but in the planetary system itself." [4]

This was a noble vision, but little in consonance with the current facts. At no time in our history, with the exception of the period during the convulsions of the Civil War, was there as sharp a cleavage and as furious a hatred among the component parts as in these years.

The Boston *Federal Gazette*, for example, contributed this editorial masterpiece to the cause of mutual amity: "The period has at length arrived, when hellish Jacobins and Demo's must sink to their native shade—and the motto of *Amor Patriae* shine only on the standard of *Federalism.* France, imperious France, refuses our friendship, and insults our ministers—The price of amity with them must be our national infamy!" [5]

In Baltimore, assembled Federalists drank toasts hardly dripping with fellowship: "A halter of strong hemp in the place of a French pension to Bache, Printer of the Aurora" and "Gallatin, Jefferson, Monroe, Livingston, Tazewell, Mason, Burr, etc. etc. . . . the universal contempt and detestation of their fellow citizens." [6]

Bache's *Aurora* retorted in kind. "People begin to see their madness," it exclaimed, "in preferring John *Adams* and a *French war* to *Thomas Jefferson with a French peace*." But it was Hamilton, rather than Adams, who was the special target of Republican insults. He was, proclaimed the *Aurora*, "the son of an IRISH CAMP GIRL," and "a *confessed adulterer* and an *avowed monarchist*." [7]

Jefferson had believed that the public lack of news from the envoys in France was good news: either negotiations were proceeding smoothly and the envoys had not wished to write pending final determination; or they *had* written, and Adams was withholding the communications because they would have forced his warlike preparations to a halt.

But his optimism suffered its first rude shock when, at the beginning of March, the long silence was broken; and letters came in announcing a new French decree which made neutral ships carrying enemy goods subject to confiscation. This faced up to the worst of the British Orders in Council and struck consternation into the hearts of American merchants. Even Jefferson was thunderstruck, realizing that American ships must be driven wholly out of the lucrative British and Continental trade in favor of British bottoms.[8]

If the merchants were in consternation, Congress—at least the Federalist members—was furious. President Adams sent what Jefferson called an "insane message" to Congress, setting forth the consequences of the French decree and declaring his withdrawal of the Executive prohibition against the arming of private vessels. The Federalists in Congress drove immediately for measures of their own, both for the arming of ships and for troops and munitions.

Jefferson hoped that the Republican majority in the House was sufficient to halt the drive toward war; though he feared Adams's message might have cut it to the danger point. He proposed to his party a delaying procedure: first, call for all the documents in the case; second, pass a Congressional prohibition of armed ships; third, adjourn and consult with the people on the current crisis.[9]

In the present temper of Congress, this was easier proposed than done; but the Republican members followed Jefferson's advice as far as was practicable. They could not muster sufficient strength for adjournment, but they did bring forward, in a committee on the state of the union, a resolution that "it is inexpedient to resort to war against the French republic." It was promptly and heavily assaulted by the Federalists, and Jefferson was gloomy about the outcome. "The question of war & peace," he commented, "depends now on a toss of cross & pile. If we could but gain this season, we should be saved. The affairs of Europe would of themselves relieve us."[10] Meaning, that France would have won the war by then.

The current two or three weeks, he acknowledged, "is the most eventful ever known since that of 1775. and will decide whether the principles established by that contest are to prevail, or give way to those they subvert." The tories, he believed, were trying to ride the whirlwind and direct the storm, and both Congress and the President were their willing tools. He pinned his faith, however, in an aroused populace, and saw with profound satisfaction remonstrances against war coming in from Massachusetts town meetings. Whig printing presses were being set up in Connecticut and elsewhere; and every technique of propaganda was being employed. He banked everything on delay; if only the Congressional debate could continue for some time, the weight of public remonstrance would make itself felt, and events in Europe somehow ease themselves.[11]

But against all Republican countermeasures rose the indomitable specter of Hamilton. Under the pseudonym of "Marcellus" he was writing a series of articles in the *Gazette of the United States* that, to Jefferson, promised "much mischief." As always, he appealed to Madison "to take up your pen against this champion. You know the ingenuity of his talents; & there is not a person but yourself who can foil him. For heaven's sake, then take up your pen, and do not desert the public cause altogether."[12]

But it was too late, even for the much wearied Madison. Word had come again from the envoys—incredible news. Talleyrand, the "fox" of Europe and Minister of Foreign Affairs under the Directory, had proposed insulting terms to the Americans through three henchmen whom the envoys prudently designated in their dispatches as Messrs. X, Y and Z. These gentlemen hinted that a substantial bribe for Talleyrand's private pocket, and an even more substantial loan to France—repayment indefinite—might possibly lead to favorable terms and a gracious condescension. The surprised envoys turned the offer down with indignation. Thomas Pinckney cried out: "No! No! Not a sixpence! (which later was distorted to the ringing: "Millions for defence, but not a cent for tribute!"), and Marshall and Pinckney packed for home. Gerry stayed on, hoping against hope that he still might come to honorable terms.

President Adams published the reports early in April, and created a furore. The war spirit rose enormously; all mass meetings and remonstrances were now on the other side; and the Federalists in Congress and out rode high on the tide of public indignation. The navy was at once strengthened and all ships of war outfitted for active duty, merchantmen were armed and ordered to capture French armed ships wherever found, and an army of vast dimensions—at least on paper—was authorized. The cold war was fast approaching the realities of a shooting war.

Much against his wishes and his better judgment, Adams was being pushed into these warlike preparations; first, by the logic of events, and second, by the urgings of his Cabinet who, unknown to him, took orders from Hamilton.

But Jefferson gave Adams no credit for inner doubts. He believed him eager for war and doing his best to force the country into it. Like everyone else, the first reports had stunned him, though he thought them confused and possibly erroneous. He did not put it beyond the Federalists—and Adams—to manufacture the story out of whole cloth. But even if true, he still did not think it sufficient to justify a war; though he realized that many Republicans, fearful of having their patriotism impugned, "will go over to the war measures so furiously pushed by the other party." [13]

The Federalists indeed pushed their advantage hard. They introduced an Alien Bill, giving the government power to deport or arrest all aliens in the United States. And a Sedition Bill was in the offing, which would make any attacks on the government, its officers and policies, criminal libels under Federal jurisdiction, and subject to prosecution in the Federal Courts. Jefferson saw the Alien Bill aimed specifically at such men as Albert Gallatin, Swiss-born and leader of the Republicans in Congress, and Volney, the French *philosophe* residing in Philadelphia. The proposed Sedition Bill he saw as a bludgeon to destroy the Republican press, and particularly the *Aurora*, under Benjamin Franklin Bache's vigorous editorship.[14]

A great light burst on Jefferson and his friends. These measures, intended seemingly to destroy the Constitution and the Republican party, had been deliberately planned. Was it not possible then that the so-called "XYZ" affair had been just as deliberately planned? So at least thought Madison.

He called the story absurd, improbable and a libel on the French Government; while Monroe believed it "a swindling experiment." [15]

Whatever the Republican leaders thought, the whole country was in a turmoil. In Philadelphia, the young men of both factions appeared in foreign cockades—the Federalists in black English headgear and the Republicans in the French tricolor (though Jefferson afterwards claimed it was really the cockade of our own Revolution). The inevitable happened; there was a riot and fighting in the streets; the light horse troops were called out; and Adams was certain there had been a plot to burn the city. The timorous packed their belongings and poised for flight.[16]

In this time of stress and excitement, Jefferson sought desperately to avoid the seemingly inevitable war; though fearing that, because of Adams's bellicose address to Congress, the French themselves might commence hostilities. Should war come, however, as true patriots, "we shall defend ourselves as one man. When our house is on fire, it matters little whether fired from without or within, or both. The first object is to extinguish it." [17]

His own private affairs were also affected by the war fever. He had intended to hold his tobacco for an expected rise in values, but now he ordered it sold, "contrary to what I had determined on if the madness of our government was not hastening as it is to ruin our private fortunes as well as the public interests."

The French, too, were quitting Philadelphia by the shipload, he wrote to his son-in-law. Volney, whom Jefferson believed to be the chief object of the Alien Bill, was preparing to depart. "It suffices for a man to be a philosopher," he exclaimed bitterly, "and to believe that human affairs are susceptible of improvement, & to look forward, rather than back to the Gothic ages, for perfection, to mark him as an anarchist, disorganizer, atheist & enemy of the government."

Jefferson was thinking of himself as well as of the soon to be proscribed Volney. For all of these epithets had been applied to him in the past, and were to increase in volume in the future. If only his house at Monticello were roofed in, "and that we shall not be long without a shelter to write under. 'Oh! welcome hour whenever!' " [18] There is a strangely modern ring to all this—the epithets, the witch hunts, the repressive legislation.

One after another the repressive measures were passed and became the law of the land. The Alien Act, the Sedition Act, the Naturalization Act—which increased the term of residence required for citizenry to fourteen years—and the Logan Act.

All were attributable to the impending war, to the fear that foreign agents and their native adherents were engaged in plotting the overthrow of the government and were only awaiting an invasion by French troops to rise in arms to join them. Jefferson blamed their passage on weak-kneed Republicans in Congress, who prudently remained away from sessions while the voting went on. Some of those who remained in their seats, indeed, favored the Naturalization Act; fearing that should France invade England, our shores would be flooded with fleeing English aristocrats.[19]

The Logan Act had a curious history. Dr. George Logan of Stenton, Pennsylvania, was a man of many enthusiasms. Aside from his medical practice, he found time to organize an agricultural society and to throw himself enthusiastically into the cause of the French Revolution. Genêt had been a frequent visitor to his Philadelphia house; so had Jefferson when Secretary of State and many of the Republican leaders.

In this crisis of affairs, he conceived the remarkable plan of going to France and persuading, single-handed, its rulers "to alter the tone of their conduct towards the United States." (Here, again, modernism creeps in—and recent practices disclose their roots in early American tradition.) But it was not to the official channels that Logan turned for "passports" to the French; it was rather to Thomas Jefferson and to Thomas McKean, Chief Justice of the Supreme Court of Pennsylvania. They obligingly furnished him with credentials of good citizenship—though Jefferson later rued his participation, and denied that he knew the purposes of Logan's journey.[20]

He sailed secretly on June 12, 1798; but the secret soon leaked out, and there was a great to-do. Brown's *Philadelphia Gazette*, a Federalist sheet, declared that Logan was conveying dangerous information to the French and proposing to come back with a French army to destroy American "*lives, property, liberty and holy religion.*"[21]

Logan found the French almost as suspicious of his designs as the Federalists at home, and it was only Lafayette's intervention that gained him admission and an audience with Talleyrand and his associates. Amazingly enough, he convinced them of the necessity of raising the embargo imposed on American ships in French ports and of liberating American seamen imprisoned in French jails. He joyfully shipped the order to America and followed suit in the last vessel to clear Bordeaux.[22]

His reception in the United States was not the effusive welcome he had anticipated. Adams received him politely; but responded to his startling information that France was now ready to receive an accredited minister from the United States with the cold remark: "Yes, I suppose if I were to send Mr. Madison or Mr. Giles or Dr. Logan they would receive either of *them.*" Timothy Pickering, to whom he next turned, was much more brutal. "Sir," said the Secretary of State with considerable asperity, "it is my duty to inform you that the government does not thank you for what you have done."[23]

The fury of the Federalists over this one-man mission knew no bounds, and became crystallized in the notorious Logan Act, approved on January 30, 1799. It declared that any citizen of the United States who "shall, without the permission or authority of the government of the United States, directly or indirectly, commence, or carry on, any verbal or written correspondence with any foreign government, or any officer or agent thereof, with an intent to influence the measures or conduct of any foreign government, or of any officer or agent thereof, in relation to any disputes or controversies with the United States, or to defeat the measures of the government of the United States . . . shall be guilty of a high misdemeanor." That law still stands unrepealed on the statute books.

But it was the bill authorizing the capture of French armed vessels off our coast that represented to Jefferson the touchstone of "war without a declaration." So certain was he of its passage and a later open conflict that he urged his elder son-in-law, Randolph, to lay out a course of agriculture, the products of which could be stored without deterioration to the end of such a war.[24]

All his resentment burned against the New England states. The southern states, he avowed, "are completely under the saddle of Massachusetts and Connecticut, and . . . they ride us very hard, cruelly insulting our feelings, as well as exhausting our strength and subsistence." These were the leaders, but the other three eastern states followed obediently. This unfortunate situation was due, he added, though carefully attributing the statement to certain vaguely designated Republicans, to "the irresistible influence and popularity of General Washington played off by the cunning of Hamilton, which turned the government over to anti-republican hands"; and which has since continued under Adams.

In spite of this release of resentment, he repudiated a suggestion by John Taylor of Caroline, that perhaps it was time for Virginia and North Carolina to consider secession as a means of ending their troubles. No! Jefferson retorted. "In every free and deliberating society, there must, from the nature of man, be opposite parties, and violent dissensions and discords; and one of these, for the most part, must prevail over the other for a longer or shorter time. . . . But if on a temporary superiority of the one party, the other is to resort to a scission of the Union, no federal government can ever exist. If to rid ourselves of the present rule of Massachusetts and Connecticut, we break the Union, will the evil stop there?" Of course not. "Are we not men still to the south of that, and with all the passions of men? Would not a Pennsylvania and a Virginia party at once arise," and the public mind "be distracted with the same party spirit?" Even should the secession be of Virginia and North Carolina alone, the same thing would happen. It is better, he concluded, to have "a little patience, and we shall see the reign of witches pass over, their spells dissolved, and the people recovering their true sight."[25]

This was reasoned eloquence of the highest order; and particularly interesting as disclosing that at this time Jefferson had no thought of the concepts which were to appear only a few short months later in the Kentucky Resolutions.

On June 23, 1798, Jefferson paid a call on John Marshall at O'Eller's Hotel in Philadelphia, where the returned envoy was stopping. Unfortunately, Marshall was out, and Jefferson left his card with a note: "Thomas Jefferson presents his compliments to General Marshall. He had the honor of calling at his lodgings twice this morning, but was so unlucky as to find that he was out on both occasions. He wished to have expressed in person his regret that a pre-engagement for to-day which could not be dispensed with, would prevent him the satisfaction of dining in company with General Marshall, and therefore begs leave to place here the expressions of that respect which in company with his fellow citizens he bears him." [26]

The object of the visit was doubtless to seek firsthand information as to the results of the mission; the interesting thing was the slip of the pen (which moderns would call Freudian) by which Jefferson first wrote "lucky" and then hastily inserted the qualifying "un." Years later, when the pair had become the deadliest of enemies, Marshall sardonically referred to the slip as one time, at least, when Jefferson came near telling the truth.[27]

This was a period of terrible anxiety for Jefferson, with rumors flying thick and fast—of invasion by France of England, of Marshall seeming less hot for war than Hamilton, of suppressions of truth by Adams, of Dr. Logan returning with a French army to seize Philadelphia—so that he was hard put to it to ponder one before a hundred others clamored for instant attention. He had intended leaving for Monticello early in June, but the exacerbated state of public nerves, the gusts of panic that blew through the streets, decided him to remain awhile. On June 27th, however, he felt it was safe for him to go; and he shook the turmoil and hysteria of Philadelphia from him with a vast feeling of relief.[28]

Jefferson left the scene while the Alien and Sedition bills were still before Congress. He quit his post as presiding officer of the Senate while it was still in session, and found himself on the road home when the Sedition Bill passed the Senate on July 4th—a most "unauspicious" date for a law of this character, as Henry Tazewell, Congressman from Virginia, was to remark. Washington was unanimously nominated as Commander-in-Chief of the new army being raised to meet the rumored French invasion; and there were hotheads among the Federalists who clamored for an immediate declaration of war on our part.[29]

Jefferson reached Monticello on July 9th. It is difficult to unravel the particular reasons that motivated his departure from the scene at a time when, in his own belief, the fate of the nation was trembling in the balance. On July 6th, while he was still jogging toward Monticello, the Alien Bill finally passed; and on July 14th, five days after he reached home, the hated Sedition Act was approved by the House.

Any reasons that might be adduced for this seeming desertion can only be conjectural; but it is probable that he was already revolving in his mind those countermeasures which were to culminate in the Virginia and Kentucky Resolutions. There was nothing more he could do in Philadelphia; he had no vote in the Senate unless there was a tie, and he was certain the bills would pass by substantial Federalist majorities. The atmosphere was superheated, and blind panic both in government and in the street prevented reasoned consideration. In Virginia, however, he expected to find a wholly different climate of opinion, more in consonance with his own. There, too, were his friends and political allies; with whom a strategy might be worked out to bring the people and the Federal Government back to their senses.

In Philadelphia, too, whether rightly or wrongly, he considered himself under constant surveillance by Federalist "spies." He had slunk along back streets to shake them off when he visited Deborah Logan, the Doctor's wife; and when the Philadelphia papers accused him of being "closeted" with Bache and others, soon to be charged under the Sedition Act, he was the more convinced that "all my motions at Philadelphia, here, and everywhere, are watched and recorded."

Why shouldn't he visit with friends? he demanded wrathfully. He was ashamed neither of them nor of his principles. "On the contrary," he informed Samuel Smith of Maryland, "I wish them known, & therefore willingly express them to every one. They are the same I have acted on from the year 75. to this day, and are the same, I am sure, with those of the great body of the American people. I only wish the real principles of those who censure mine were also known. But, warring against those of the people, the delusion of the people is necessary to the dominant party. I see the extent to which that delusion has been already carried, and I see there is no length to which it may not be pushed by a party in possession of the revenues & the legal authorities of the US. for a short time indeed, but yet long enough to admit much particular mischief. There is no event therefore, however atrocious, which may not be expected. I have contemplated every event which the Maratists of the day can perpetrate, and am prepared to meet every one in such a way as shall not be derogatory either to the public liberty or my own personal honor." This sounds very much as though Jefferson was prepared for the possibility that he himself, though Vice-President of the United States, might be charged with sedition.

As for his own position, he was quite ready to declare it again: he was for peace with *both* France and England; though both had given, and continued daily to give, sufficient cause for war. Since, however, he was certain the two belligerents would be at peace by the end of winter, he believed it best to bear injuries a while longer and *then*, in the hour of peace, claim indemnification from both.

He ended this remarkable letter with a warning that it was not for newspaper publication. "At a very early period of my life," he remarked, "I determined never to put a sentence into any newspaper. I have religiously adhered to the resolution through my life, and have great reason to be contented with it." [30]

It is no wonder then that he felt more at ease and freer to express his opinions in Virginia, where he was happy to find that "the deep rooted disgust produced in this state by the Alien & Sedition acts is beyond any thing ever seen since the days of the Stamp act." He had written this in the first draft of his letter to Smith, but later crossed it out and omitted it from the final copy.[31] Perhaps he felt that the language, ominous in its connotations, might, if the letter ever fell into hostile hands, be seized upon as evidence of meditated revolt.

Evidences of opposition were mounting. From Kentucky came word that the people of that state were "almost unanimous" against war with France, and considered the obnoxious Acts unconstitutional. "Crowded meetings" at every Court House were adopting resolutions "deprecating war, & denouncing the Alien & Sedition laws in the strongest terms." And George Nicholas, a Virginian who had gone to Kentucky, issued a pamphlet attacking their constitutionality and professed himself ready to face prosecution for it.[32]

At the same time, news poured in—exaggerated in the telling—of a reign of terror already instigated by the triumphant Federalists against honest Republicans under the new laws. Benjamin Franklin Bache, editor of the Philadelphia *Aurora*, the most noted of the Republican papers, had been indicted even before the passage of the Sedition Act under the old common law for alleged libelous publications concerning John Adams. Prosecutions under the law itself were commenced against the editors of the Richmond *Examiner*, the New York *Argus*, the Boston *Independent Chronicle*, the New York *Time Piece* and the New London *Bee*.

Nor were national and local Republican leaders immune from the attentions of the law. The most notorious case involved Matthew Lyon, the fiery Congressman from Vermont; but Dr. Thomas Cooper, a notable educator and Jefferson's friend, and Jedediah Peck of the New York Legislature, also fell into the toils. John D. Burk, a native of Ireland, and the radical editor of the New York *Time Piece*, who later wrote the first good history of Virginia with Jefferson's asistance, escaped prosecution only by agreeing to depart for his former country. Dr. Joseph Priestley, perhaps the greatest scientist of his day and the discoverer of oxygen, had been an English radical and a member of a revolutionary group with William Blake, William Godwin, Tom Paine, Dr. Price and others. Forced to leave England, he arrived in Philadelphia in time to be greeted with bitter attack and threatened deportation under the terms of the Alien Act. William Duane, another radical with a checkered career in America, India and Great Britain, was also almost deported, but instead was indicted for sedition. When Bache died, late in 1798, Duane took over the *Aurora* and made it the most powerful organ of the Jeffersonian party and a constant thorn in the side of the Federalists.[33]

To cap the climax, Jefferson received a frightened letter from James Callender, the hack writer whose *History of the United States* had forced into the open the Hamilton scandal. He was in hiding in Virginia, he said, fleeing probable arrest in Philadelphia. He was sick even of the Republicans. They had used him dishonestly and cheated him so often he wanted to get out of the country and go back to his native Scotland. "I engaged in American controversies," he whined, "not from choice, but necessity; for I dislike to make enemies, and in this country the stile of writing is commonly so gross, that I do not think the majority of such a public worth addressing." [34]

Jefferson forwarded a draft of $50 for the account of the frightened hack, which bucked up his spirits so much that he decided to remain and even to commence a newspaper in the congenial climate of Richmond.[35] Jefferson would have been well advised to have speeded Callender on his way back to Scotland. Callender was eventually convicted in a famous sedition trial, sent to jail, and later pardoned by Jefferson as one of the first acts of his Presidency. The scribbler, however, untouched by any considerations of gratitude, literally blackmailed his benefactor and, when blackmail proved ineffective, spilled a nauseous mixture of semitruths and downright lies into the public press which caused Jefferson endless embarrassment.

With every post thus bringing its almost daily evidence of Federalist fury and, at the same time, more heartening evidence of rising popular opposition in Virginia and Kentucky, Jefferson set in careful motion one of the most crucial schemes of his long and varied career. The United States, the nation he had helped build, stood at the crossroads. What happened within the next few months might well decide whether it was to remain republican and free, or subvert into monarchy and despotism under the bludgeonings of the Federalists. A Constitution had been adopted, intended to preserve the liberties of the people and the States; would it cavalierly be set aside by the blatant misinterpretations of a power-mad federal administration? A stand had to be taken by the true apostles of liberty before it was too late. But how?

Only a few months before, John Taylor of Caroline had intimated that secession might be the answer, and Jefferson had repudiated the suggestion with a ringing affirmation. But now he was not quite so sure. The perils which Taylor had foreseen had come to pass. True republicans were being persecuted and clapped into jail by partisan judges and packed juries. Secession, however, was an ultimate weapon and not lightly to be employed. Before that, another affirmation must be made—and by those most competent to make it, the States—of the essential principles of the Constitution and of the division of powers that had been worked into its very fabric.

CHAPTER 43

Kentucky Resolutions

SOME time in September, 1798, ensconced in his eyrie at Monticello, Jefferson commenced work on a series of resolutions which he intended to have submitted to a sympathetic state legislature for consideration and passage. He worked in the strictest secrecy and enveloped the entire proceedings in such an extraordinary veil of mystery that the exact details have furnished a fruitful field for historical dispute down to the present day.[1]

For the secrecy and mystery there was good and sufficient reason. Jefferson was Vice-President of the United States; the resolutions were an appeal from the authority of the Federal Government to the authority of the States. They proclaimed boldly the right and duty of the States to declare measures of the national government unconstitutional and void; and hinted even at the last resort of secession from that government. At *any* time, such a pronouncement would have created an immense furore; in the current state of exacerbation and superheated tempers, it might well have been considered as treason; and particularly so when penned by the second in command in the nation.

Therefore Jefferson took no one into his confidence except for one man. Strangely enough, that man was not Madison, his bosom friend and stoutest political ally. At least not in the beginning.[2] Perhaps he feared that, with the connection between them so well known to the outer world, some hint of what impended might filter through, and the origin of the explosive resolutions be eventually traced. The man to whom he entrusted the perilous secret was Wilson Cary Nicholas of Virginia, an old friend and enthusiastic Republican, but not as intimately associated in the public mind with Jefferson as Madison would have been, or Monroe.

What made Nicholas particularly well equipped to act as Jefferson's intermediary and emissary was the fact that his private and business affairs took him out of Virginia into the neighboring states, and his journeyings and meetings with the political leaders of those states would not occasion undue comment or be connected with Jefferson.

The Resolutions, as Jefferson shaped them into final form, expounded a theory of the federal compact which made the several States the final arbiters of Constitutional construction and the sole guardians of their own absolute powers against the delegated powers of the national government. The Alien and Sedition Acts were the springboard for this assertion of powers; but the Resolutions went far beyond the particular occasion to enunciate broad and sweeping affirmations on the true residence of sovereignty that were to have reverberations and almost fatal results in the long years to come. Nor can it be claimed that Jefferson did not fully understand all of the implications of his doctrine of nullification. It was in line with his deepest convictions, expressed many times before, and on numerous occasions thereafter. This was no mere indignant reaction to a particular situation; it was a carefully conceived statement of a philosophical position that went to the roots of the American federal system and was not finally overthrown until the land was drenched with blood and agony.

Jefferson drafted a series of nine resolves.[3] The first declared "that the several States composing the United States of America, are not united on the principle of unlimited submission to their general government"; but only through the compact of a Constitution which granted that government specific powers and reserved all the rest to themselves. From this general statement Jefferson drew as a logical conclusion: "That whensoever the general government assumes undelegated powers, its acts are unauthorative, void, and of no force." That it had not been made by the Constitution "the exclusive or final judge of the extent of the powers delegated to itself," but that "each party has an equal right to judge for itself, as well of infractions as of the mode and measure of address."

Having thus laid down the general theory of the relation of powers, Jefferson proceeded to the particulars of the Alien and Sedition Acts, the prime motivators of the Resolutions. The second resolve asserted that those two Congressional enactments did not come within the purviews of the specific grants to punish specific crimes, and were therefore "altogether void, and of no force."

The third resolve denounced the Sedition Act as an infringement of the First Amendment to the Constitution, since it purported to abridge the freedom of the press.

The next three resolves paid their respects to the Alien Act, setting forth the proposition that "alien friends are under the jurisdiction and protection of the laws of the State wherein they are: that no power over them has been delegated to the United States."

The seventh resolve was perhaps the most significant of all. It went beyond the current Acts to examine the whole course of events since the beginning of the national government; and attacked the Hamiltonian thesis which both the Executive and Congress had accepted, that the Constitution was to be broadly construed; and under which the Bank had been established and excise taxes levied. If any section of the Resolutions should have indicated their authorship, it would have been this one.

The construction by the general government of certain Constitutional clauses, declared Jefferson, "goes to the destruction of all limits prescribed to their power by the Constitution." Then, significantly: "the proceedings of the General Government under color of these articles, will be a fit and necessary subject of revisal and correction, at a time of greater tranquility, while those specified in the preceding resolutions call for immediate redress."

The eighth resolve had ominous revolutionary overtones. It recalled to the public mind the procedures which initiated the original revolution against Great Britain. It demanded the appointment of a "committee of conference and correspondence" to communicate the entire body of Resolutions to the other states. It asserted that while the ratifying state sincerely believed in the Union as specified in the Constitution, it was determined to submit "to undelegated, and consequently unlimited powers in no man, or body of men on earth," and "a nullification of the act is the rightful remedy." Every State, it proceeded, had a natural right "to nullify of their own authority all assumptions of power by others within their limits"; that the States were the sole makers and judges of the compact, "Congress being not a party, but merely the creature of the compact, and subject as to its assumptions of power to the final judgement of those by whom, and for whose use itself and its powers were all created and modified." The doctrine of nullification could not have been more frankly or boldly stated.

But the resolve went even further, warning that such arrogated assumption of undelegated powers by the general government would, "unless arrested at the threshold, necessarily drive these States into revolution and blood." Wherefore, the ratifying state called on its sister states for a similar expression of sentiments on the acts complained of, a concurrence in declaring them void, and the adoption of measures seeing to it "that neither these acts, nor any others of the General Government not plainly and intentionally authorized by the Constitution, shall be exercised within their respective territories."

The ninth resolve authorized the committee of correspondence to consult with those that might thereafter be appointed by the other states.

Not even in his *Summary View* and other precursors of the Revolution had Jefferson spoken so plainly of resistance and, if need be, of eventual "revolution and blood." It is true that he hoped and expected that the passage of these Resolutions by a given state and their later passage in other states would give the Federalists in the national government pause, and compel them not only to a recession from the Alien and Sedition Acts, but to a reformation of the entire scheme of government. But he must have realized that the Federalists were not an unorganized body; that they too had the authority of a group of states—notably in New England—to back them up; and that they would not yield readily to the ukase of the Republican states. In that event, Jefferson was seemingly quite prepared to resist enforcement by force; a thesis which, logically developed, must mean the dissolution of the Union.

Wilson Cary Nicholas was at Warren, Virginia; and Jefferson sent him the Resolutions, intending that Nicholas take them up with a member of the North Carolina legislature for introduction in that state.

But a series of fortuitous circumstances decided Nicholas to exercise his own judgment. For one thing, he feared that Jefferson's ties with the person indicated in North Carolina were too well known, and might lead to the discovery of Jefferson's prime authorship. "Sir," he wrote Jefferson, "my chief inducement was to shield you from the invective, that I feared you might be exposed to if I had pursued a different course." That is, from the one he finally took.

The other, and deciding circumstance was the arrival of John Breckinridge of Kentucky at Nicholas's home in Warren. Breckinridge, Virginia-born, had been a member of the Virginia House of Delegates, had studied law and removed to Albemarle County to practice during Jefferson's absence in Europe. On the latter's return, the two men became friendly and found their political beliefs mutually satisfactory. In 1793, Breckinridge was elected to Congress, but never took his seat, having migrated in the interim to the newly erected State of Kentucky to further his fortunes. His rise there was rapid; he became a leader both at the bar and in politics, entering the legislature and becoming its Speaker within a few months of the period with which we are now concerned. Nicholas's brother George had also gone to Kentucky, where he joined Breckinridge in some land speculations. It was doubtless in connection with these speculations that Breckinridge now appeared in Warren to see Wilson Cary Nicholas.

Nicholas seized the opportunity as heaven-sent. He knew Breckinridge's influence in Kentucky and confided both in his political views and his discretion. Kentucky was almost unanimously in arms against the Alien and Sedition Acts and had expressed its attitude in unmistakable language. Kentucky was ripe for resolutions even as bold as these—his brother George had gone almost as far in a pamphlet of his own and was facing prosecution by the federal authorities—and, best of all, no suspicion of complicity would fall on Jefferson.

He therefore showed a copy of the Resolutions to Breckinridge. The latter readily agreed to submit them to the forthcoming session of the Kentucky legislature and expressed his confidence that they would be adopted. Under seal of secrecy, Nicholas disclosed the name of the author to Breckinridge, who was eager at first to journey to Monticello to pay his respects to Jefferson and, probably, discuss the Resolutions further. But sober second thought prevailed. It was agreed by Nicholas and Breckinridge both that such a meeting would be unwise, and might give later rise to suspicion as to its true meaning. Breckinridge therefore forewent the opportunity, and returned to Kentucky with the precious manuscript, assuring Nicholas that Kentucky would have taken action by the time of the opening of the Virginia Assembly.[4]

Jefferson agreed to the change in the original plan, and assured the apologetic Nicholas that he had done the correct thing; particularly since there had been recent changes in the composition of the North Carolina legislature that made passage of the Resolutions there somewhat doubtful. He also asked Nicholas to see Madison. "You know of course I have no secrets from him. I wish him therefore to be consulted as to these resolutions." [5]

Nicholas did not see Madison, because he took ill shortly after Breckinridge departed. On October 10th, from his sick bed, he wrote Breckinridge to inform him of what had happened in the interval. "I have had a letter from our friend [Jefferson], he approves what I have done, he says you possess his confidence entirely, that he thinks the business had better commence in your state.... he suggest [*sic*] nothing further upon the subject, indeed I think every thing is said that can be, in the paper that you have. I shall be impatient to hear from you." [6]

So, no doubt, was Jefferson. He was perforce compelled to possess his soul in patience, awaiting the hoped-for news. Three people now knew of the Resolutions, and the part he had played in them—Nicholas, Breckinridge and himself. But seemingly not Madison. And it was vital for more reasons than one that Madison be made aware of what impended; not merely because he was entitled to the knowledge, but because something similar ought to be introduced into the Virginia legislature as soon as it opened its session.

Just when the two friends finally met is difficult to ascertain. A letter from Jefferson to Madison, dated October 26th, indicates that it took place only a few days before at Monticello, to which Madison had come. Momentous projects were obviously discussed, and decisions arrived at.

One of these related to special tactics, and involved two documents to be laid before the Virginia legislature. The first sought to obviate the disastrous consequences of prosecutions by a partisan Federal judiciary under the Sedition Act in the state of Virginia. Immediately after Madison left, Jefferson drafted a petition to the General Assembly which, declaring that "the people themselves are the safest deposit of power," demanded that the choice of jurors, now under control of "officers dependant on the executive and judiciary bodies" and therefore "pliable to the will and designs of power," should thereafter be chosen by the people by school districts.[7] This novel procedure of electing jurors was designed to ensure the failure of future prosecutions under the obnoxious Acts. What Jefferson failed to realize was that thereby he made *all* court actions subject to popular pressures and passions in much greater degree than under the old system.

When he finished the draft, Jefferson was not entirely satisfied with it, and sent it to Madison for corrections.[8] These were later incorporated, but the petition never emerged to the light of day in the Assembly.

The second was a curious bill "for the relief of sufferers under certain illegal prosecutions." This was intended to give damages to those Virginians who had suffered prosecutions, fines and imprisonments under color of the Sedition Act; an Act which. asserted the text, was "unauthorized & null by the constitution," and "in violation of rights never placed under the controul of the General government." [9] This too was eventually swallowed up in the larger proposition.

That proposition, of course, was to put Virginia on record in the same fashion as Kentucky. Evidently, though, it had been agreed to let Kentucky be the bellwether rather than Virginia. This was a question of tactics; it was felt, perhaps, that it might be easier to push comparable resolutions through the Assembly once another state had acted.

During the waiting period, Jefferson cautiously felt out influential Virginians, dropping certain hints. "The alien & sedition laws are working hard," he wrote Stephens Thompson Mason. "I fancy that some of the State legislatures will take strong ground on this occasion. For my own part, I consider those laws as merely an experiment on the American mind, to see how far it will bear an avowed violation of the constitution. If this goes down we shall immediately see attempted another act of Congress, declaring that the President shall continue in office during life, reserving to another occasion the transfer of the succession to his heirs, and the establishment of the Senate for life." [10]

The Kentucky legislature assembled at Frankfort, the state capital, on November 7, 1798. Governor James Garrard struck the keynote in his opening address, inviting the lawmakers to enter "your protest against all unconstitutional laws and impolitic proceedings." [11]

Breckinridge was placed on a committee of three to make formal reply, and promptly served notice that he would move resolutions in the House in accordance with that particular part of the Governor's address. On November 8th, the House went into a committee of the whole, and Breckinridge introduced the first eight of Jefferson's nine resolutions.

But Breckinridge proved to be no mere messenger boy, doing Jefferson's bidding. He had taken it upon himself to make certain changes in the document handed him; and these changes were all in the direction of softening and toning down some of the bolder and more vigorous expressions.

The first seven were followed word for word; though an amendment from the floor made a slight change in the sixth. The eighth resolution, however, was radically changed. Since this was the one in which Jefferson had specified action, to which all the others were mere preamble, the changes were of the utmost importance.

Jefferson had called for a committee of correspondence to treat with other states in manner reminiscent of the Revolution; the revised resolution merely directed that copies of the Resolves be sent to the Kentucky representatives in Congress, with the request that they do their best to obtain a repeal of "the aforesaid unconstitutional and obnoxious acts." Much of the rest of Jefferson's lengthy verbiage was transferred to a ninth resolution, including the ringing declarations about not submitting to undelegated powers in any man or body of men on earth, and that acts based on such power were void and of no force. *But*, instead of Jefferson's key clause "that every State has a natural right in cases not within the compact . . . to nullify of their own authority all assumptions of power by others within their limits," the resolution ended tamely with the proposition that the other states would be invited to unite with Kentucky in requesting the repeal of the Alien and Sedition Acts at the next session of Congress.[12]

Through these significant changes, all talk of forcible resistance was eliminated, and a theoretic, unimplemented statement of Constitutional voidness substituted for the active and danger-fraught "nullification."

The House passed the modified Resolutions on the 10th, after three days of debate. Only one voice was raised in opposition—William Murray of Franklin County. Breckinridge rose in reply, and made one remark that throws a flood of light on his intentions. "If, upon representations of the States from whom they derive their powers, they [Congress] should nevertheless attempt to enforce them [the Alien and Sedition Laws], I hesitate not to declare it as my opinion that it is then the right and duty of the several States to nullify those acts, and to protect their citizens from their operation."[13]

In other words, Breckinridge had eliminated Jefferson's demand for immediate nullification, not because he disbelieved in the power of the state or in its use, but because he wished first to offer Congress a chance to withdraw from its position.

The Kentucky Senate passed the Resolutions unanimously on the 13th; and the Governor signed them on the 16th. A thousand copies were printed, and sent to Congress and the Governors of the other states.

That Breckinridge knew exactly what he was doing, and that he preferred to exhaust all constitutional means before embarking on a course that might destroy the Union, is evidenced by a hitherto unpublished letter he wrote a friend to accompany a copy of the Resolutions. "I trust they will silence alll calumnies, with respect to our disposition towards disorganization or disunion. I think the ground we have taken cannot be shaken; that no just exception can be made to the firm but decent language in which we have expressed ourselves. I assure you with confidence, we have but one object, & that is, to preserve the constitution inviolate, & that by constitutional efforts.—No people in Am[erica] are more sensible of the necessity of the union; or more alive to unconstitutional strides of power by those in authority, than the people of Kent[ucky]."[14]

Jefferson also received copies. What his thoughts were when he saw that his key propositions had been emasculated, is not known. He evinced no outward disappointment; and it may be that second considerations convinced him that Breckinridge had been right.

In any event, such was the attitude he adopted when he sent a copy along to Madison. By now, Madison was engaged in formulating a similar set for introduction into the Virginia legislature, and Jefferson told him: "I think we should distinctly affirm all the important principles they contain, so as to hold to that ground in future, and leave the matter in such a train as that we may not be committed absolutely to push the matter to extremities, & yet may be free to push as far as events will render prudent." [15]

It is probable that Madison had not seen Jefferson's original draft, but had been working independently on the basis of his conversation with Jefferson.[16]

Madison's Resolutions were much more compact than Jefferson's and, at the same time, more general and moderate. After the usual preamble setting forth the nature of the federal compact, they declared that the States have the right and duty to interpose "for maintaining within their respective limits the authorities, rights and liberties appertaining to them."

A discussion of the abuses complained of followed, ending naturally with the Alien and Sedition Acts. The remedy proposed in the seventh resolution was one merely of protest and eventual co-operation with other states. It called on the States to "concur with this Commonwealth in declaring, as it does hereby declare, that the acts aforesaid are unconstitutional; and that the necessary and proper measures will be taken by each for co-operating with this State, in maintaining unimpaired the authorities, rights, and liberties reserved to the States respectively, or to the people." Copies were to be sent by the Governor to the other states and to Virginia's representatives in Congress.[17]

Not a word about nullification, committees of correspondence, or resistance. Compared to Jefferson's proposals, or even to the Resolutions actually passed in Kentucky, these were moderate in language and cautious in final action.

Jefferson was not satisfied with Madison's draft. He addressed himself to Nicholas, asking him to pass on his observations to Madison. "The more I have reflected on the phrase in the paper you shewed me, the more strongly I think it should be altered. Suppose you were instead of the invitation to cooperate in the annulment of the acts, to make it an invitation 'to concur with this commonwealth in declaring, as it does hereby declare, that the said acts are, and were *ab initio*, null, void and of no force, or effect.' I should like it better." [18]

But Madison had no liking for Jefferson's revision, either. He did not believe that a state legislature had the power to declare a federal law void and of no effect. Scorning intermediaries, he wrote direct to Jefferson: "Have you ever considered thoroughly the distinction between the power of the *State*, & that of the *Legislature*, on questions relating to the federal pact. On the supposition that the former is clearly the ultimate Judge of infractions, it does not follow that the latter is the legitimate organ, especially as a convention was the organ by which the compact was made. This was a reason of great weight for using general expressions that would leave to other States a choice of the modes possible of concurring in the substance, and would shield the Genl. Assembly agst. the charge of usurpation in the very act of protesting the usurpations of Congress." [19]

Just as Jefferson had hidden his authorship in the Kentucky Resolutions, so Madison hid his in those submitted in Virginia. John Taylor, the radical and forthright philosopher of both state and agrarian rights, was chosen to present them. To him, Jefferson addressed himself and said he would be content for the present to have the Resolves declare the Alien and Sedition laws "to be against the constitution & merely void, and for addressing the other States to obtain similar declarations." [20]

Taylor followed Jefferson rather than Madison, and inserted an approximation of the language Jefferson had originally suggested to Nicholas, including the two dread words, "null" and "void."

But the Resolutions ran into rough going in the Assembly. While Taylor, Nicholas and Giles argued strenuously in their behalf, an equally formidable group that included Mercer and General Lee were opposed. Madison's qualms proved triumphant, and the offending language was stricken out and Madison's weaker words restored. In that form, the Resolutions were finally passed on December 21st, after a full week of debate, by a vote of 100 to 63. The Senate concurred on December 24th, and the Resolutions were signed by the Governor.

If, to Jefferson's mind, both sets of resolutions were drastically emasculated, the Federalists all over the country were convinced that they represented anarchy, treason and bloody revolution; and so shouted in newspapers, mass meetings and in Congress. As for the Republicans, it was their job to pass similar resolutions in those states which they controlled.

But the Federalists got the jump. In February, 1799, Delaware formally asserted that the Kentucky Resolutions were "a very unjustifiable interference with the general government and constituted authorities of the United States, and of dangerous tendencies, and therefore not a fit subject for the further consideration of the General Assembly." [21] Every other Federalist-controlled state followed suit. From New York, Aaron Burr wrote gloomily to Jefferson that the Resolutions of Virginia and Kentucky had been laid before the legislature, but had not been acted on as yet. If they were, he expected them to be defeated. "Under circumstances so inauspicious, I have not thought it discreet to urge a determination in either house." [22]

But New York eventually acted, and *against* the Resolutions. So did Rhode Island, Massachusetts, Connecticut, New Hampshire and Vermont. Maryland, New Jersey and Pennsylvania, while avoiding direct replies, placed themselves on record against the principles of the Resolutions. Even the southern states held a painful silence.

Jefferson had completely misread the temper of the people. While they were on the whole opposed to the Alien and Sedition Acts, they were not prepared to adopt the extreme position that any state, or combination of states, had the right or power to declare acts of Congress void and of no effect. They also rightly read into the language, toned down though it had been, the proposition that separation and disunion might be the end result; and they recoiled from any threat, no matter how veiled, that the Union might be dissolved.

CHAPTER 44

Specter of Nullification

IN December, 1798, Jefferson returned to his official duties in Philadelphia, arriving on Christmas Day. He had private worries, as well as public. His finances, as always, were in a desperate state. He had pinned his hopes for hard cash on his nail factory, but the results of a half year's unremitting work had yielded painfully little; so little, in fact, that he was unable to meet even small obligations.[1]

A cold caught on the road laid him up for two days in Philadelphia, so that he did not enter the Senate to preside until December 27th. He sought political gossip eagerly, and was assured by his Republican friends that the public was fast coming round to their standard.[2]

He was further gratified by a serenade, complete with band and lusty song, put on for his benefit on New Year's Day by the faithful Republicans. They sang:

> "Bless'd with genius, with talents, with virtue divine,
> Still Columbia thy boast is that *Jefferson's* thine." [3]

All this, of course, was heartening; but the national picture still presented a most ominous aspect. An undeclared war, real enough in all conscience, was in progress with France. Privateers and ships of war roamed the seas and fought on sight. Congress had authorized the raising of an army, Washington had been called out of retirement to head it, and Hamilton, ostensibly second in command, was chief in fact and dreaming dreams of glory. Adams's opening address to Congress breathed military fire to Jefferson, who thought it had been written for him "by the military conclave, & particularly Hamilton." He was also certain that Gerry's correspondence with Talleyrand, which Adams had refused to publish, would "shew France in a very conciliatory attitude, and . . . contradict some executive assertions." [4]

Jefferson's alarm grew stronger with every day. Unless some herculean effort was made—and soon—the Federalists would be able to jam an official declaration of war through Congress. As a last resort he begged Madison to publish the secret debates of the Constitutional Convention, of which he had taken such voluminous notes. Perhaps the knowledge of what actually took place might throw sufficient light on the true nature of that instrument as to be decisive with the public.[5] But Madison made no move to do so.

Elbridge Gerry, now returned to the United States, was shocked at the way his mission had been distorted. Jefferson replied that he too had been "a constant butt for every shaft of calumny which malice & falsehood could form, & the presses, public speakers, or private letters disseminate." Particularly had his relations with Dr. Logan been made the subject of forgery and abuse. To make his position clear, therefore, Jefferson set forth the tenets of his political creed to Gerry, hoping thereby to win that moderate Federalist over to Republican principles.

He wanted "an inviolable preservation of our present federal constitution, according to the true sense in which it was adopted by the States."

He was for a government "rigorously frugal & simple, applying all the possible savings of the public revenue to the discharge of the national debt."

He relied for internal defense "on our militia solely, till actual invasion, and for such a naval force only as may protect our coasts and harbors from such depredations as we have experienced; and not for a standing army in time of peace, which may overawe the public sentiment."

He was "for free commerce with all nations; political connection with none; & little or no diplomatic establishment."

He was opposed to "linking ourselves by new treaties with the quarrels of Europe."

He was for "freedom of religion, & against all maneuvres to bring about a legal ascendancy of one sect over another." He was for complete freedom of the press, and believed in the progress of science, philosophy and the human race.

As for his attitude on the French Revolution, that had subtly changed. He still wished sincerely for its success and hoped "it may end in the establishment of a free & well-ordered republic; but I have not been insensible under the atrocious depredations they have committed on our commerce. The first object of my heart is my own country. In that is embarked my family, my fortune & my own existence. I have not one farthing of interest, nor one fibre of attachment out of it, nor a single motive of preference of any one nation to another, but in proportion as they are more or less friendly to us.

"These, my friend," he concluded this important affirmation, "are my principles; they are unquestionably the principles of the great body of our fellow-citizens."[6]

These might have been the principles of the general public, but Jefferson realized that unless they were galvanized into activity, the nation might be precipitated into a full-panoplied war from which there would be no retreating. He had already distributed on a large scale the anonymous pamphlets written by George Nicholas in Kentucky opposing the Alien and Sedition Acts. Now he asked Edmund Pendleton to write a short handbill exposing the true nature of "the X. Y. Z. dish cooked up by Marshall" and "the wicked use" of the French negotiation by the government. If Pendleton would do the job, Jefferson would print ten to twenty thousand handbills and have them distributed throughout the country by the Republican members of Congress.[7]

As the weeks passed, Jefferson's agitation increased. He welcomed eagerly every petition which came in from citizens of the surrounding states denouncing the abhorred laws (the state legislatures had not yet acted to dash his hopes). In Pennsylvania, in fact, "we fear that the ill designing may produce insurrection." But he set his face sternly against riots. "Nothing could be so fatal," he asserted. "Anything like force would check the progress of the public opinion & rally them round the government. This is not the kind of opposition the American people will permit." [8]

He placed all his faith in education of the public. But this required money. "Systematic energies & sacrifices" were called for. "The engine is the press. Every man must lay his purse & his pen under contribution." [9]

But another matter rose to agitate him even more strongly; one that evidences his deep-seated aversion to any additional contacts with the Negro race. A bill had been introduced into Congress offering limited recognition of Toussaint L'Ouverture and Haitian independence from France. By the terms of the bill, the President was authorized to admit the Haitian blacks to free commerce with American ports. "We may expect therefore black crews," Jefferson wrote in great alarm, "& supercargoes & missionaries thence into the southern states; & when the leven begins to work, I would gladly compound with a great part of our northern country, if they would honestly stand neuter. If this combustion can be introduced among us under any veil whatever, we have to fear it." [10]

John Adams, second President of the United States, had not been master in his own house. An invisible puppetmaster pulled the strings, and all the figures with whom he was surrounded and on whom he relied for aid and comfort danced to a tune not of his making. The members of his Cabinet were not his men. They took his policies elsewhere for consideration, and brought them back mangled and distorted beyond all recognition. The Federalists in Congress followed him not; and even in the new army, of which constitutionally he was commander-in-chief, he had been compelled against his will to nominate an inspector general he hated.

The puppetmaster, the backstairs power, the inspector general were all one—and that one was Alexander Hamilton. It is incredible that Adams, normally suspicious enough, could have continued so long in a state of innocence as to the nature of his frustrations; but when his eyes were finally opened—as now they were—he acted with speed and courage.

To glorify a clique of Federalists, to raise Hamilton to the heights of military and political power, he had been steadily pushed toward a shooting war with France. With one bold stroke he burst out of the enveloping net. On February 18, 1799, without prior consultation with either Cabinet or Federalist leaders, he announced the nomination of William Vans Murray as a new plenipotentiary to France.

The news stunned the war party. For Murray, stationed at The Hague, had informed Adams he had received assurances through Talleyrand's emissary at the Dutch capital that, should the United States send a fresh envoy to France, he would be received with all the respect due the representative of a free, independent and powerful nation, and that all differences between the two nations could be satisfactorily settled.

If the dismayed Federalists thereby saw their greatest issue summarily taken from them, the nomination caused the widest rejoicing among the battered Republicans. Jefferson hailed it as great news, and even the violent *Aurora* wrote editorially: "Whatever sentiments men may entertain of the President's attachments to English modes of government or to English connections, every one must applaud his appointment of Mr. *Murray* to go to Paris." [11]

Hamilton and his cohorts promptly rallied from their first dismay, and sought through their power in the Senate to hamstring Adams by attaching two sound Federalists to the mission. Even Jefferson, after the first exultation, sought hidden motives in Adams's sudden move. The latter had known of Talleyrand's gesture right along, Jefferson wrote; yet only now, in the face of exposure, had he made it public. He had attached conditions which forced France to a public humiliation and, in fact, hoped secretly that the Senate would reject.[12]

This, of course, was untrue. Adams sincerely wanted no war, and he hewed to the line in spite of clamor from the right and the left. He was forced by the Senate to add to other envoys, but the mission was eventually, if reluctantly, confirmed. He also cleaned his own house by summarily dismissing Hamilton's men from his Cabinet, and thereby gained the latter's mortal hatred.

But the crisis was over, and the war fever rapidly subsided. Jefferson, viewing the scene, gave the credit not to Adams, but to the American people. "The spirit of 1776 is not dead," he philosophized. "It has only been slumbering. The body of the American people is substantially republican. But their virtuous feelings have been played on by some fact with more fiction; they have been the dupes of artful manoeuvres, & made for a moment to be willing instruments in forging chains for themselves. But time & truth have dissipated the delusion, & opened their eyes." [13]

It was unfortunate, he thought, that with the rising tide of republicanism, there were still two more years of Adams "to go through." He feared particularly the standing army that was being raised, and of which Washington was the titular, but Hamilton the real head. Could such an army be disbanded? he wondered. And would it not be employed by Hamilton and his group to subvert the liberties of America? His only hope was that it would consist only of officers; that the plain folk would never enlist.[14]

Jefferson was now in Monticello, tending to his own affairs and keeping at the same time a finger on the public pulse. Before he left Philadelphia he had tried to set in motion another Republican newspaper, and had collected money from all his friends. The amount he collected was disappointing; yet he hoped by the coming summer to be able to get one started. Remembering, however, his unfortunate experience with Freneau, he tried to cover his tracks as skillfully as possible.[15]

The modern publicist might consider such efforts to reach the public in the nature of propaganda, but Jefferson sincerely believed that the Republican press furnished only the truth and thereby educated the people.

He had an abiding faith in the power of the human mind to know the truth when it was offered, and to dissociate it from error; and he foresaw indefinite advance for the human race. To a young student at William and Mary who had queried him on the subject, he wrote eloquently:

> I join with you ... in branding as cowardly the idea that the human mind is incapable of further advances. This is precisely the doctrine which the present despots of the earth are inculcating, and their friends here re-echoing; and applying especially to religion and politics.... But thank heaven the American mind is already too much opened, to listen to these impostures, and while the art of printing is left to us, science can never be retrograde.... To preserve the freedom of the human mind then and freedom of the press, every spirit should be ready to devote itself to martyrdom; for as long as we may think as we will, and speak as we think the condition of man will proceed in improvement.[16]

Yet while thus envisaging the wonderful future, Jefferson did not overlook the mundane present. The closure by Congress of trade with France had played hob with tobacco prices; and his last year's crop, amounting to some 90,000 pounds, was still lying idle in his storehouses. He stood to lose $3,000 on it at the current prices. But hope sprang up when a printed list of prices current in New York fell into his hands. He wrote promptly for information. If he could be sure of getting $11 a hogshead there, as quoted, he would ship his tobacco. He waxed lyrical about its quality. It was the best in Virginia, truly extraordinary; and "if there ever was a better hogshead of tobacco bought or sold in New York I may give it to the purchaser." [17] Salesmanship could go no further.

Eventually he sent ten hogsheads as a trial balloon; but alas, his New York correspondent by that time could only get $6 a barrel. Jefferson at first angrily refused to sell; but the renewal of the nonintercourse act directed against France made him fearful that the price would tumble still further, and with the greatest reluctance he let his prized tobacco go at this disaster figure.[18]

He was also watching the local elections with great care. In the Congressional elections, at least five Federalists had been victorious; but Jefferson comforted himself with the Republican victories in the legislature. Patrick Henry had come out openly as a Federalist; but Jefferson no longer feared him, though still showing a certain respect for his undoubted

Courtesy the New-York Historical Society, New York City

JOHN RANDOLPH OF ROANOKE

Painting by John Wesley Jarvis

Courtesy the Massachusetts Historical Society

JEFFERSON'S ARCHITECTURAL SKETCH OF MONTICELLO, FRONT ELEVATION

Wide World Photo

MONTICELLO

powers. "Our legislature," he asserted, "is filled with too great a mass of talents & principle to be swayed by him. He will experience mortification to which he has been hitherto a stranger. Still I fear something from his intriguing & cajoling talents, for which he is still more remarkable than for his eloquence. As to the effect of his name among the people, I have found it crumble like a dried leaf, the moment they become satisfied of his apostacy." [19]

By this time, however, the replies of the states to the Virginia and Kentucky Resolutions had finally come in, and the results were not good. The tremendous backfire which Jefferson had hoped to build against federal encroachments had sputtered and seemingly gone out.

Though tremendously disappointed, Jefferson and his friends rallied their forces for another try at it. Perhaps a reaffirmation by both states of the fundamental principles involved, coupled with the waning of the war hysteria during the intervening period, might bolster the timid and bring at least the Republican states into the fold.

It was Wilson Cary Nicholas who started the ball rolling. In a hitherto unpublished letter to Jefferson, dated August 20, 1799, Nicholas advised that "a most unfortunate and melancholy event, makes it necessary that I shou'd go in a few days to Kentucky. I believe you think it proper that the legislature of these two states, should defend the ground they have taken. If that is still your opinion, and you will put upon paper what you think the Kentucky assembly ought to say, I will place it in safe hands. They now require aid more than ever. I flatter myself that assurances of proper caution, in the use of any paper that I may receive from you are not necessary." [20]

With this communication in hand, Jefferson promptly wrote to Madison to concert a common plan of action. "It is so advantageous," he declared, "that Virginia & Kentucky should pursue the same tract [*sic*] on this occasion, & a difference of plan would give such advantage to the Consolidationers that I would immediately see you at your own house, but we have a stranger lying ill here, whose state has been very critical, & who would suffer in spirits at least if not substantially by my absence."

Who this stranger was is unknown; but we ought perhaps to be thankful to him; since thereby Jefferson placed himself on record on certain most important principles.

He was going to invite Nicholas to Monticello a week from Sunday, he continued. Would Madison "take a ride" a few days before, pick Nicholas up on the way and bring him along,

> . . . and let us consider a little together what is to be done. Not that I should prepare any thing, but the opportunity is certainly a valuable one of producing a concert of action. I will in the mean time give you my ideas to reflect on.

That the principles already advanced by Virginia and Kentucky are not to be yielded in silence, I presume we all agree. I should propose a declaration or Resolution by their legislatures on this plan. 1st. Answer the reasonings of such of the states as have ventured into the field of reason, & that of the Comm[itt]ee of Congress. Here they have given us all the advantage we could wish. Take some notice of those states who have either not answered at all, or answered without reasoning.

2. Make a firm *protestation* against the principle & the precedent; and a *reservation* of the rights resulting to us from these palpable violations of the constitutional compact by the Federal government, and the approbation or acquiescence of the several co-states; so that we may hereafter do, what we might now rightfully do, whenever repetitions of these and other violations shall make it evident that the Federal government, disregarding the limitations of the federal compact, mean to exercise powers over us to which we have never assented.

3. Express in affectionate & conciliatory language our warm attachment to union with our sister-states, and to the instrument & principles by which we are united; that we are willing to sacrifice to this every thing except those rights of self government the securing of which was the object of that compact; that not at all disposed to make every measure of error or wrong a cause of scission, we are willing to view with indulgence to wait with patience till those passions & delusions shall have passed over which the federal government have artfully & successfully excited to cover its own abuses & to conceal its designs; fully confident that the good sense of the American people and their attachment to those very rights which we are now indicating will before it shall be too late, rally with us round the true principles of our federal compact; but determined, were we to be disappointed in this, to sever ourselves from that union we so much value, rather than give up the rights of self government which we have reserved, & in which alone we see liberty, safety & happiness.[21]

In that last section, the dread word "secession" had finally appeared, openly and frankly stated. "Nullification" had yielded to its logical and inevitable successor. In later years, and after Jefferson's death, when another group of nullifiers (in South Carolina) used the revered departed's name in defense of their own contentions, Madison waxed virtuously indignant. "It is remarkable," he then exclaimed, "how closely the nullifiers who make the name of Mr Jefferson the pedestal for their colossal heresy, shut their eyes and lips, whenever his authority is ever so clearly and emphatically against them."[22]

At the time that Madison received this communication, however, with its startling conclusion, the "colossal heresy" was patent to his own eyes. Jefferson, he felt, had gone too far. Himself an ardent nationalist, he was prepared neither to acquiesce in any such doctrine of secession, nor permit Jefferson to place himself on record to that effect.

In great anxiety and alarm he made his way to the appointed destination of Monticello; but alone.[23] Nicholas, hurrying to Kentucky to attend the funeral of a brother, was unable to come. Madison expostulated most strongly about that last fatal section and doubtless pointed out the consequences that might ensue. He won Jefferson around at least partially to his way of thinking, not only, as Jefferson was to put it to Nicholas, "in deference to his judgment, but because as we should never think of separation but for repeated and enormous violations, so these, when they occur, will be cause enough of themselves." In other words, Jefferson still clung to the right of the States to secede, should the proper occasion arise.

Repeating in briefer form to Nicholas what he had already proposed to Madison, Jefferson nevertheless declined his invitation to draft the necessary resolutions for Kentucky, "to avoid suspicions (which were pretty strong in some quarters on the last occasion), and because there remains still . . . a mass of talents in Kentucky sufficient for every purpose. The only object of the present communication is to procure a concert in the general plan of action." [24]

It is obvious then that, aside from general instructions, Jefferson had no draughtsman's hand in the second series of resolutions that came out of Kentucky. These were introduced on November 14, 1799, in the House at a time when John Breckinridge presided as Speaker, and were passed without a dissenting vote. Seemingly it had been intended, when the legislature opened its session, not to do anything, but it was then felt—and Jefferson's letter to Nicholas was undoubtedly the inducing cause—that silence might be misconstrued. In the Senate, however, the new Resolutions met with considerable opposition, particularly on the significant sentence which declared that "a nullification of those acts by the States to be the rightful remedy." After a bitter debate, the Senate finally concurred with the House, leaving the offending sentence intact. Breckinridge, sending the resolutions to Jefferson, commented that the opposition had come from whatever federal influence still existed in the state, "concentred in the Senate"; but that "the great mass of the people are uncontaminated and firm." [25]

The Kentucky Resolutions of 1799 were vigorous and plain-spoken. They retorted to the general condemnation of the first set by the other states with a ringing affirmation of their original stand. While Kentucky, they declared, "will be among the last to seek [the Union's] dissolution," nevertheless, the several States who had formed the Constitution, "being sovereign and independent, have the unquestionable right to judge of its infraction; and that a nullification by those sovereignties of all unauthorized acts done under color of that instrument, is the rightful remedy." [26]

It is to be noted that, whereas Breckinridge had omitted from the first set the ominous word "nullification" as specified by Jefferson, it now appeared in the second set; even though Jefferson, in his general instructions, had yielded to Madison's entreaty and removed it.

But Breckinridge, who had drafted the second set, was neither inconsistent nor illogical. He had openly avowed during the debate on the first set that should Congress continue to enforce the Alien and Sedition Acts, it would then be the "right and duty of the several States to nullify those acts, and to protect their citizens from their operation." [27] Congress *had* continued prosecutions; and Breckinridge acted on his original warning.

It has recently been stated that Breckinridge could not have been the author of the second set, just *because* it used the word "nullification"; but among his papers in the Library of Congress is the original draft of the resolutions in his handwriting, which contains the following paragraph: "That in cases of abuse of the delegated powers, the members of the Genl. Govt. being chosen by the people, a change by the people would be the constitutional remedy; but where powers have been assumed which have not been delegated, a nullification of the act is the rightful remedy: that every State has a natural right in cases not within the compact to nullify of their own authority all assumptions of power by others within their limits." [28]

Jefferson had hoped to meet Madison and join with him in drafting the second set of resolutions for the Virginia Legislature; but Monroe, visiting at Monticello, advised against it as subjecting both men to public suspicion, and Jefferson reluctantly agreed.[29]

As a substitute, Jefferson put down on paper for Madison's consideration an extended outline of what he conceived the Republican strategy should be.

Our objects, according to my ideas, should be these. 1. peace even with Great Britain. 2. a sincere cultivation of the Union. 3. the disbanding of the army on principles of economy and safety. 4. protestations against violations of the true principles of our constitution, merely to save them, and prevent precedent and acquiescence from being pleaded against them; but nothing to be said or done which shall look or lead to force, and give any pretext for keeping up the army. If we find the monarchical party really split into pure Monocrats & Anglo-monocrats, we should leave to them alone to manage all those points of difference which they may chuse to take between themselves, only arbitrating between them by our votes, but doing nothing which may hoop them together.[30]

Jefferson had once again become the statesman and party leader; dropping the intransigence and heat of his earlier resolves. No longer did he cry "nullification" or "secession"; and he was particularly careful to disavow force on his own side or even those actions which might cause force on the other. As for the distinction which he raised between "pure Monocrats & Anglo-monocrats"—the first were those who, in his estimation, wanted a straight monarchy here; while the second favored the principles embodied in the British constitution—he cried a plague on both their houses, hoping that they would destroy one another in internecine struggle.

Another portion of this letter is extremely significant in illuminating his future policy on the right to public office. "I suppose it is thought time," he wrote, "that the republicans should know that offices are to be given exclusively to their opponents by their friends no longer. It is advantage enough to the Feds to possess the exclusive patronage of the administration; and so long as they go on the exclusive principle, we should do the same." The occasion was his recommendation of William Wirt, a Republican, for the clerkship of the Virginia House of Delegates.

Jefferson was now definitely pointing to the next presidential election in 1800, and preparing strategy, slogans and a method of attack. He armed himself in still another way, by abjuring the writing of any political letters that would have to pass through the mails. "I cease from this time during the ensuing twelvemonth," he told John Taylor, "to write political letters, knowing that a campaign of slander is now to open upon me, & believing that the postmasters will lend their inquisitorial aid to fish out any new matter of slander they can to gratify the powers that be. I hope my friends will understand & approve the motives of my silence." [31]

The Virginia Resolutions, in which Jefferson had no hand except for general advice, were drafted and sponsored by Madison, now a member of the legislature, in the form of a Report. The Report, in line with Madison's fixed belief in the sanctity of the Union, denounced the accusation that the earlier Resolutions had upheld the right of a state to nullify Congressional enactments or advocated disunion. The Resolutions, he now expressly declared, had been promulgated to arouse public discussion and opinion "by exciting reflection." [32] Nevertheless, the Report met with strong opposition; but passed the House by 60 to 40, and the Senate by 15 to 6.

The Virginia Report was much weaker than the Kentucky Resolutions; and certainly far removed from Jefferson's original intentions. But Jefferson had finally come around to the position, in view of the expressed opposition of the other states and of the impending presidential election, that caution was indicated. It was enough to have Kentucky pronounce the fundamental principles; but Virginia, politically the bellwether, must be careful to do nothing to antagonize the moderates.

The campaign of 1800 was already under way when the Report was approved; and Jefferson, now back in Philadelphia, demanded from Monroe and received with seeming satisfaction a copy of it. He promptly had copies struck off and circulated them in Pennsylvania and the other states.[33]

He was pointing for the future. "It is too early to think of a declaratory act as yet," he believed in April, 1800, "but the time is approaching & not distant. Two elections more will give us a solid majority in the H. of R. and a sufficient one in the Senate. As soon as it can be depended on, we must have 'a Declaration of the principles of the constitution' in nature of a Declaration of rights, in all the points in which it has been violated.

The people in the middle states are almost rallied to Virginia already; & the eastern states are recommencing the vibration which had been checked by X. Y. Z. North Carolina is at present the most dangerous state. . . . The medicine for that State must be very mild & secretly administered. But nothing should be spared to give them true information." [34]

He had learned to make haste slowly.

CHAPTER 45

Second Revolution

JEFFERSON quit Monticello on December 21, 1799, and arrived in Philadelphia a week later to resume his duties as Vice-President. This was perhaps the first time in his career that he departed from his home with some willingness and without undue bemoaning of his fate. For this was the first time that he had good reason to feel optimistic about the cause of republicanism in America. The Federalists had overreached themselves. The Alien and Sedition Acts had roused the lovers of liberty and rallied them to the Republican standard. Though the response to the Kentucky and Virginia Resolutions had been discouraging, nevertheless a theoretic platform had been solidly built for future political construction. The war hysteria, thanks to Adams's unexpected move, was on the wane and dissension pervaded the Federalist ranks. All in all, the prospects were bright.

The Republican leaders were beginning to gather around Jefferson. The year 1800 was a presidential year, and all strategy was pointed toward the glittering prize. Without question–in spite of the machinations of disgruntled Federalists like Hamilton, Pickering and others–Adams was going to run again. And, without question, it was now generally conceded by the Republicans that Jefferson was to be their standard-bearer in the ensuing election.

But, to ensure victory on the national scene, the local elections in the states were all-important. In many of them, it was the legislature that selected the presidential electors; and even where general elections were held, the peculiar complexion of the local scene determined the choice. Aaron Burr, firmly ensconced as Republican leader in New York City and disputing with old Governor Clinton and his rising young nephew, De Witt Clinton, for the supremacy in the state, paid a flying visit to Jefferson in Philadelphia. The two men discussed the situation in New York. The Republicans there, Burr was convinced, were in the majority, but needed a skillful leader to rally them against the organized Federalists under Hamilton. He did not say so outright; but he believed that *he* was that leader. He also had a finger in the political pie of New Jersey and Pennsylvania; and outlined a general strategy for the forthcoming local elections in April.

Jefferson listened attentively; though with some qualms over the frankness of the discussion. As a candidate, he did not quite know how to act. Should he not remain aloof from the sordid details of political maneuvering, leaving them to his more robust aides; and, while avowing his desire for private life, consent to stand only in order to "see this government brought back to its republican principles?" [1] But he was realist enough to know that, while such an attitude might do for public consumption, there was hard day-by-day work to be done; and the politicians of the states were essential if success was to be achieved.

Of the Republican leaders, Aaron Burr was perhaps the most important. Slight of frame, standing barely five feet, four on tiptoe, but erect and soldierly in carriage, Burr had rapidly come to the fore. Brilliant of intellect, subtle in thought and complex in character, he had gone through the Revolution with gallantry and distinction, and become one of the ablest lawyers of the day, disputing pre-eminence in New York with the great Hamilton himself. Entering on the tangled scene of New York politics, he had forged the Society of Tammany—an outgrowth from the original Sons of Liberty—into an irresistible political machine that idolized him and followed him to the death. He was the only man who could outmaneuver Hamilton for the suffrages of the New York voters, thereby gaining his mortal enmity. He refused to brook the dynasty of Clintons in his own party, and was able to obtain a balance-of-power position in the pivotal state. He had been a Senator of the United States; and his restless ambition sought still higher honors. Just now, he was aiming to the second place on the Republican ticket, under Jefferson.

It was essential, therefore, for eventual national victory, that Jefferson deal with him confidentially and at length. But Jefferson, confronted with this new phenomenon—a man of talents and of breeding who nevertheless descended into the hustings and welded a machine of artisans and mechanics—always felt uneasy in his presence and subconsciously suspected his motives. Yet a political compact had to be forged—between the yeomanry of whom Jefferson was representative, and this new group of city mechanics—if the Republicans were to win. Thereby the third apex of the fatal triangle was conjoined—Jefferson, Burr and Hamilton. A strange triangle, in which two men were now joined against the third—Jefferson and Burr against Hamilton; but, within a short space of time, a disjointure in which each man became the enemy of the other two, and whose mutual antipathies profoundly influenced the course of American history.

But if Jefferson was thus laying the foundations for the forthcoming battle of the giants, he did not set aside his more congenial pursuits. No matter how heated the political fray, he always had time for the things of the intellect.

The bloody ground of Europe was gradually yielding to America a group of political and intellectual refugees whom Jefferson hailed with delight. Joseph Priestley had quit his native England in 1794, and was established in Pennsylvania. He was at once a great scientist and a political and religious radical. His discovery of phlogiston (oxygen) and his experiments with gases and electricity had won him world renown. But his bold pronouncements in politics and religion had forced him to seek more congenial soil. He had hailed the French Revolution and witnessed a mob burn his Birmingham home down for his pains. He had denied the divinity of Christ and written a *History of the Corruptions of Christianity* that brought another storm about his ears. At the age of sixty, therefore, he sought the sanctuary of the New World, and became an ardent republican here and a friend of Jefferson's. But the persecution that had dogged his steps in England followed him to America, and the Federalist pamphleteers screamed "atheist" and "Jacobin" at him with the same abandon they had hitherto reserved for Jefferson.

"You have sinned against church & king," Jefferson remarked dryly, "and can therefore never be forgiven."

It was to Priestley that Jefferson now turned for assistance in an old scheme of his that he had been compelled to put temporarily aside, but had never forgotten. This was to reform the educational system of Virginia.

During his famous revisal of the laws, he had proposed a comprehensive, graded plan; but none of it had gone through at the time. Eventually, however, though with considerable emasculation, the legislature had enacted that part of his bill which set up "English" or elementary schools; but made them optional on the counties instead of obligatory. Jefferson was hopefully expecting similar action on his "middle" or high schools.

But the apex of his plan, on which his energies had most been concentrated, was a public institution of higher learning, centrally located, and preferably in Albemarle. It was his idea to utilize the existing—and somewhat moribund—William and Mary College for that purpose, transplanting it to the desired location and modernizing it. But the dissenting sects, fearing the Episcopal tone of the institution, had objected, and nothing had come of it at the time. Now he wanted to try again. Could Priestley therefore recommend a course of instruction in the sciences, so that he could attract the best professors from Europe to teach the subjects?

Priestley as well as Jefferson believed in the "indefinite perfectibility of man"; and to him Jefferson could speak freely. "The Gothic idea," he avowed, "that we are to look backwards instead of forwards for the improvement of the human mind, and to recur to the annals of our ancestors for what is most perfect in government, in religion & in learning, is worthy of those bigots in religion & government, by whom it has been recommended, & whose purposes it would answer." [2] It was obvious what kind of instruction Jefferson intended in his proposed new seat of higher learning.

Priestley was only too happy to oblige, and enclosed for Jefferson's perusal certain "Hints Concerning Public Education" that he had already written on the basis of his experience abroad. But alas, he ruefully added, "if I be rightly informed, my poor *Letters* have done more harm than good." [3]

To this Jefferson retorted sympathetically that "if they are not turned to useful account for posterity, it will be from the insensibility of others to the importance of good education. As soon as we can ripen the public disposition we shall bring forward our propositions." [4]

But Jefferson did not rely on Priestley alone for ideas. Another distinguished refugee had just come to these shores; this one from France—Pierre Samuel du Pont de Nemours. Jefferson greeted the newcomer with the profoundest satisfaction. He had met Dupont during his Ministry in France, and had then hailed him as a fellow spirit. He had received invaluable assistance from him during the course of his extended negotiations—Dupont had been an official under the old government—assistance which Dupont modestly called to his attention now that he intended to emigrate. "During your embassy," he wrote Jefferson, "you saw me struggle on behalf of your country, and for principles of liberality, of sincere friendship between the two nations, and against every financial and commercial prejudice which our government had at that time."

A member of the physiocratic school, which held that land was the true source of wealth, his liberal opinions had proved too conservative for the eventual course of the Revolution, and he barely escaped the guillotine. Now only partially restored to favor, he seized the opportunity afforded him by a commission from the Institut de France to report on the condition of scientific research in America, to "prolong the trip to the end of my life. I wish to die in a country," he declared with great fervor, "in which liberty does not exist only in the laws, always more or less well, more or less badly, carried out, but chiefly in the fixed habits of the nation." [5]

Dupont arrived with his family on January 1, 1800, and Jefferson welcomed him cordially. He had always considered him, so he told his son-in-law Thomas Mann Randolph, "the ablest man in France." [6] As soon as he heard Dupont had landed, Jefferson hastened to write him, at the same time warning him that America had its imperfections as well as Europe. "The present agonizing state of commerce, and the swarms of speculators in money and in land, would induce me to beseech you to trust no-body, in whatever form they may approach you till you are fully informed; but your son [who had preceded the father to the United States], I am sure, is able to guard you from those who in this as in every other country consider the stranger as lawful prey, & watch & surround him on his first arrival." [7]

Dupont eventually settled in Virginia, where his son instituted a gunpowder manufactory; and Jefferson sought his advice as well as Priestley's on the subject of the university. He particularly wanted advice as to the subject matter of the sciences; since, with the limited resources at hand, it would be best to leave the so-called liberal studies to the private schools.[8]

The Frenchman was enthusiastic about the scheme; and agreed with Jefferson's views as expressed in the *Notes on Virginia* as to the nature and efficacy of education. But though Jefferson had been careful to postulate a short sketch from Dupont, what he eventually received was a heavy treatise, some two to three hundred pages in length, and headed by the formidable title of *National Education in the United States.*[9] For once, Jefferson was paid back in his own coin.

It was in truth a staggering work, and filled with excellent theoretical considerations; but, as might have been expected, of little value in connection with the peculiar needs of the American scene.

Nor were Jefferson's interests confined to the university. He welcomed an offer from William Dunbar of Natchez, Mississippi, to correspond with him on such matters as meteorological observations and the vocabularies of the Indian tribes in the Indian tongues, and heard for the first time of the sign language by which the various western tribes communicated with one another.[10]

The comparative study of languages fascinated him; and he was one of the first to realize their importance for tracing historical connections; though he tended to exaggerate their utility in blood relationships. He was ardently engaged in collecting as many Indian vocabularies as he could, in order to trace those connections, and he sought them far and wide. "I have long believed," he wrote Benjamin Hawkins, who was on the Creek frontier and might therefore be able to supply him with data, "we can never get any information of the antient history of the Indians, of their descent & filiation, but from a knowledge & comparative view of their languages. I have, therefore, never failed to avail myself of any opportunity which offered of getting their vocabularies." He already had a large collection, and hoped shortly to print them for the benefit of science.[11]

He was also interested in his job of presiding over the Senate. He had found, much to his surprise, that there was no handy manual to which he might turn for rules of procedure and standard parliamentary practice. Some time before, he had queried Wythe on the subject; and now again, after he had set down what he remembered from his own reading and found in his commonplace books, he called on Wythe, "the only spark of parliamentary science now remaining to us," to check his data for him.[12] He intended to spend the ensuing summer in writing a Parliamentary Manual, "which I shall deposit with the Senate of the US. and may thence possibly get into the public possession.... It may do good by presenting to the different legislative bodies a chaste Praxis to which they may by degrees conform their several inconsistent & embarrassing modes of proceeding." [13]

Wythe, after several disclaimers, finally corrected Jefferson's manuscript insofar as he was able; and so did Edmund Pendleton, to whom it was also submitted.[14] The Manual, as finally published, is a remarkable production, and still has its value as a guide to the principles of conducting a legislative body.

Jefferson had always complained of his essential loneliness in Philadelphia, and of the hatred that pursued him in those places in which he had foregathered. Now, sensibly, he did something about it. "I have changed my circle here according to my wish," he told his daughter, Martha, "abandoning the rich and declining their dinners and parties, and associating entirely with the class of science, of whom there is a valuable society here." [15]

The wonder is, with these multifarious and distracting interests, that Jefferson was able to devote any attention to the increasingly strident politics of the period. For a while, with the sudden death of Washington in the closing days of 1799, there had been a lull. All parties joined to mourn the passing of a great man, who had done more than anyone else to pilot the struggling young country through its formative years. There were, it is true, some unholy mutterings from the more intransigent Republicans; but Jefferson, for all his coldness toward Washington in the later years, sincerely mourned him with the rest. Some of the more extravagant tributes, however, revolted him as seeming to border on impiety, particularly those which emanated from the Federalist press. Washington himself, he thought, would similarly have been revolted.[16] An era had come to an end; and a new one, of which Jefferson was to be the chief architect, had begun.

But at the moment, the outlook was darkening again, both at home and abroad. He watched with painful interest and an incredulous horror the looming apparition of Napoleon Bonaparte as it cast its lengthening shadow over France and all Europe. Must we repeat again the history of Robespierre and of Julius Caesar? he asked plaintively. Or is this a "new phaenomenon of an usurpation of the government for the purpose of making it free?" There was a lesson in this rise of dictatorship, however, for our citizens at home. "They should see in it a necessity to rally firmly & in close bands round their constitution; never to suffer an iota of it to be infringed; to inculcate on minorities the duties of acquiescence in the will of the majority, and on majorities a respect for the rights of the minority; to beware of a military force even of citizens; and to beware of too much confidence in any man. The confidence of the French people in Buonaparte, has enabled him to kick down their constitution, & instead of that to leave them dependent on his will & his life. I have never seen so awful a moment as the present." [17]

This was ripe wisdom, and is as appropriate to the present age as to the time of which Jefferson wrote. The French Revolution had gone into its final stage, in which, through a *coup d'état*, Napoleon had ruthlessly overthrown the generous ideals—attenuated as they had become—of the earlier Revolution and substituted a naked dictatorship, days of *la gloire*, and eventual catastrophe.

What is particularly interesting about this remarkable *aperçu* of Jefferson, addressed in a hitherto unpublished letter to a comparatively obscure neighbor in Albemarle, is the frankness with which he expressed his forebodings as against the cautious optimism of his communication on the same event with his leading political companions. To John Breckinridge, for example, he expressed the wish that Bonaparte might be spared "as, according to his protestations, he is for liberty, equality & representative government, and he is more able to keep the nation together, & to ride out the storm than any other." [18]

His views were mixed on the portent, and he alternated between hope that it might turn out all right in the end, and fears—only too justified—that it might turn out dreadfully. Certainly, he wanted no Napoleon to grasp the reins in America.[19]

The object lesson against a standing army was uppermost in his mind. And that was exactly what America now had. "It would seem," he told Martha, "as if the army themselves were to hew down whoever shall propose to reduce them. The non-intercourse law is to be renewed, but whether only for the tobacco states, or for all, is a question. Were it not for the prospect of its expiring by the effects of a treaty [with France], our state would do better to drop the culture of tob[acc]o altogether." [20]

Politics at home were indeed beginning to boil. The Federalists, Jefferson noted with satisfaction, were getting seriously alarmed about the results of the forthcoming presidential election. For this alarm there was considerable justification. Aside from the repercussions of the Alien and Sedition Acts—much exaggerated in the aftertelling by historians—a feud had sprung up among the Federalists themselves that threatened their continued lease of power.

Hamilton had never been too kindly disposed toward Adams, the titular head of the party, and Adams had retorted in kind. But now the latent quarrel had burst into the open, and became an irrevocable split that sundered the foundations of the party. Adams's reluctance to grant top military command to Hamilton and his explosive ousting of Hamilton's henchmen from his Cabinet had touched off the fuse. Thenceforth, Hamilton was determined to keep Adams from a second term, and began negotiations to replace him with Charles Cotesworth Pinckney of South Carolina, a safe, conservative Federalist.

But before he could come into the open, Hamilton had to make certain of his control of the pivotal state of New York. Everyone recognized the fact that the pending national elections would be close; and whoever won New York, had an excellent chance of winning the nation. Since, according to its laws, the state legislature chose the presidential electors, it was essential to gain control of that vital body in the local elections of April, 1800.

There was formidable Republican opposition in New York, however. Burr had worked skillfully and tirelessly to build up a solid party machine, particularly in the key city of New York. He breathed confidence to Jefferson of the results; and Jefferson echoed that confidence.[21]

Hamilton worked hard but, in his anxiety to have a pliable group of legislators, put up a mediocre slate. Burr, more politically astute, entered a list of nationally known figures headed by himself. With the eyes of the nation focused on the city of New York, the electorate went to the polls.

As the great day approached, Jefferson lost some of his earlier optimism. "I am of opinion," he told Monroe, "the republicans here have been much too sanguine as to the issue of this last"; referring to the contest in New York.[22] This in the face of Edward Livingston's assurance from that beleaguered town that Burr's activities were so enormous that nothing but success could be expected.[23]

Livingston's confidence was justified. The careful spadework of Burr paid off. When the votes were counted, the Republican ticket was found to have swept the city, and thereby gained control of both houses of the New York Legislature. The national election was in effect already decided.

Jefferson, though not yet quite understanding the full extent of the victory, exulted to his son-in-law: "The federalists do not conceal their despair on this event. They held a caucus on Saturday night and have determined on some hocus-pocus maneuvres by running Genl. Charles C. Pinckney with mr Adams to draw off South Carolina, and to make impression on N. Carolina." [24]

The triumph in New York ensured Burr's place on the national ticket; and it was now universally acknowledged that the Republican slate would consist of Jefferson for President, and Burr for Vice-President.

No such unanimity, however, existed in the Federalist ranks. Desperate with his unexpected defeat, Hamilton proposed extralegal means to keep that "atheist in religion, and a fanatic in politics [Jefferson], from getting possession of the helm of state." In an astonishing letter to John Jay, the Federalist Governor of New York, he demanded that the old method of choosing the New York electors be shifted from the legislature to direct popular vote, where he might have a second chance. "In times like these in which we live," he asserted, "it will not do to be over-scrupulous. It is easy to sacrifice the substantial interests of society by a strict adherence to ordinary rules." [25]

Fortunately, Jay was possessed of more rigid ethical standards than Hamilton. He wrote merely on the back of the letter: "Proposing a measure for party purposes, which I think it would not become me to adopt." [26] He did not even bother to answer Hamilton.

Thus thwarted, Hamilton hurried from extravagance to extravagance. To him, the national elections as they now stood were between Tweedledum and Tweedledee. Both Jefferson and Adams were anathema. Perhaps, if the truth were known, he now hated Adams more than Jefferson; particularly after Adams ousted Pickering and McHenry—Hamilton's obedient followers—from the Cabinet. It was a declaration of war *à l'outrance.*

"For my individual part my mind is made up," he wrote Theodore Sedgwick, Federalist leader in Massachusetts. "I will never more be responsible for him [Adams] by my direct support, even though the consequence should be the election of *Jefferson.* If we must have an *enemy* at the head of the government, let it be one whom we can oppose, and for whom we are not responsible, who will not involve our party in the disgrace of his foolish and bad measures. Under *Adams,* as under *Jefferson,* the government will sink. The party in the hands of whose chief it shall sink, will sink with it, and the advantage will be on the side of his adversaries." Therefore, he intended to arrange matters so that Charles Cotesworth Pinckney might be elected.[27]

In order to gain this laudable end, Hamilton wrote a pamphlet intended for confidential circulation among the party leaders, in which he explained his position. The pamphlet, entitled *The Public Conduct and Character of John Adams, Esq., President of the United States,* was a bitter and passionate attack on the personal as well as the political character of Adams, in which Hamilton threw caution and restraint to the winds. Invective and hate jostled one another on every page.

The leaders who received it were dismayed; but their dismay turned to a sense of catastrophe when the carefully guarded document suddenly turned up in the hands of the Republicans and was published, amid waves of laughter and jeers, to an incredulous world. Aaron Burr, through devious ways, had managed to lay hands on a copy fresh from the printer and hastened it to the general press.

The bombshell stirred up a literal tempest. Faithful Federalists, still loyal to Adams, rushed to reply; while the Republicans stood on the sidelines, joyously egging the contestants on. If anything more were needed to ensure a Republican triumph, this pamphlet was it.

The *Aurora* expressed the general opinion: "*Alexander Hamilton* and the New York *Feds* have split upon the *Adamantine* rock;—he says that John *Adams* must not be President, they say that John Adams must—so says the proverb where thieves fall out honest men may come by their own." [28]

Jefferson was at first content to let the Federalists rip their own ranks asunder by bitter factional fights, while the Republicans relied "solely on the slow but sure progress of good sense & attachment to republicanism, & build our fabric on a basis which can never give way."

He was leaving for Monticello on May 15th and deliberately chose the route along the eastern shore; first, because he had never been that way before, and second, because he could travel practically incognito and avoid ceremonial displays and addresses to the Republican candidate. He shrank from all public shows, particularly when he himself was involved; and he resented "being the mannequin of a ceremony." [29]

He held deep convictions on the whole matter of pomp and display. "I never doubted the impropriety," he told Monroe, now Virginia's Governor, "of our adopting as a system that of pomp and fulsome attentions by our citizens to their functionaries. I am decidedly against it as degrading the citizen in his own eye, exalting his functionary, & creating a distance between them which does not tend to aid the morals of either. I think it a practice which we ought to destroy & must destroy, & therefore must not adopt as a general thing, even for a short time." [30] When Jefferson became President, he did not forget his own admonitions.

But if he thus thought to seclude himself from newspaper comment from his own side, he could do nothing about the attentions he was receiving from the Federalist press. Hamilton had set the tone with that epithet of "atheist." It was an epithet, with appropriate additional ones, that the Federalists were coming to employ more and more about their great antagonist. Jefferson's frank remarks in his *Notes on Virginia* were now coming home to roost. So was his well-known admiration for the French.

A Boston Federalist sheet was comparatively restrained. It cited five reasons why Jefferson should not be elected: 1—he is a deist; 2—he has uniformly opposed measures of government; 3—he is head of a party "whose object is opposition to the laws, subversion of order, and destruction of religious principles"; 4—his abilities as a legislator are suspect; 5—"his household is *French*—his language, his dress, his manners, his associates are *French*—and his library and Philosophy are French." [31]

But this was mild. The charge of atheism, and all that it connoted to the religious mind, was reiterated in a hundred different ways, and a thousand changes rung upon it. Sometimes it seems, indeed, as if the entire Federalist campaign was conducted on that single issue. What they were seeking to stir up was the fear and horror of every religious individual in the country, and they succeeded in obtaining the effective co-operation of the New England divines. Those ministers of the gospel, dedicated theoretically to the gentle teachings of Christ and the brotherhood of man, outdid one another in objurgations and embittered hate for the self-confessed deist. There have been elections since that perhaps equaled this one in unrestrained invective; but never as openly on the subject of a man's religion.

The divines thundered against him from the pulpits and in pamphlets, conjuring up for the delectation of their horrified auditors pictures of hell-fire and damnation, seduction and rape.

"I do not believe," shuddered one Connecticut minister in the privacy of his diary, "that the Most High will permit a howling atheist to sit at the head of this nation." [32]

Others were not so private. The Reverend John M. Mason issued "The Voice of Warning, to Christians, on the ensuing Election of a President of the United States." This election, he cried, is not merely a choice between individuals or policy "but, what is infinitely more, of national regard or disregard to the religion of Jesus Christ." Will the people choose "a confirmed infidel"? Read in his infamous *Notes on Virginia*, he exhorted, his disbelief in the Deluge, in the story of Adam and Eve, his "profane babbling" on the subject of God's chosen people, as well as "the ten thousand impieties and mischiefs" of that famous paragraph which declares that "it does me no injury for my neighbors to say there are twenty Gods or no God."

Christians! warned the outraged divine, as you value eternity, vote against this infidel! By voting *for* him, "you will do more to destroy a regard for the gospel of Jesus, than the whole fraternity of infidels with all their arts, their industry and their intrigues." [33]

The Reverend Dr. Linn was somewhat more restrained, though he too fished in the inexhaustible pond of the *Notes* for data. But he managed to add one delicious anecdote, which he admitted getting third-hand. Mazzei and Jefferson had been out riding. Mazzei expressed his surprise at the poor condition and general decay of the churches they passed. "'It is good enough,' rejoined Mr. Jefferson, 'for him that was born in a manger.'" [34]

Perhaps the worst of all appeared in a Massachusetts newspaper for the edification of its horror-struck readers. "Should the infidel Jefferson be elected to the Presidency," thundered the *New-England Palladium*, "the *seal of death* is that moment set on our holy religion, our churches will be prostrated, and some infamous prostitute, under the title of the Goddess of Reason, will preside in the Sanctuaries now devoted to the worship of the Most High." [35]

Even some good Republicans were shaken by this barrage. One such anxiously wrote Jefferson "to answer me (if you think fit) only these two Questions—first do you believe there was a Deluge and do you believe that Mankind Originally Sprang from one pair." [36]

Jefferson refused to answer these and similar queries about his alleged atheism. He was used to calumny, he told Monroe, and it was impossible to contradict all the lies directed against him.[37]

But other Republicans sprang to his defense; and the battle of the pamphlets raged unabated. John Beckley of Virginia, in particular, rivaled the Federalists in sustained invective: "Read, ye fanatics, bigots, and religious hypocrites," he shouted, "of whatsoever clime or country ye be—and you, base calumniators, whose efforts to traduce are the involuntary tribute of envy to a character more pure and perfect than your own, read, learn, and practice the *Religion of Jefferson*, as displayed in the sublime truths and inspired language of *his* ever memorable 'Act for establishing religious freedom!'" [38]

In spite of Jefferson's seeming sangfroid under fire, the accusations, the calumnies and the abuse got under his easily penetrable skin. "Differences of political opinions," he wrote Gen. Knox, who certainly differed politically from him, "excited in me no unfriendliness more than a difference of feature. It is not thus that I view or value man.... I never deserted a friend for difference of opinion in politics, in religion, in physics; for I place all these differences on a footing. But great numbers have deserted me." [39]

To one person only at this time did he state his real position—Benjamin Rush, medical doctor, member of the American Philosophical Society and, like him, a deist. In private conversation Jefferson denied the charges of antireligion to Rush. He said "he believed in the divine mission of the Saviour of the World, but he did not believe that he was the Son of God in the way in which many Christians believed it.... He believed likewise in the resurrection, and a future state of rewards and punishments."[40]

Rush urged him to set his thoughts down in writing, and Jefferson promised to do so; then reconsidered the matter, and decided against it. But the letter in which he announced his decision to Rush is famous on several counts.

The first related to the yellow fever epidemic which had some time before again swept Philadelphia, and which was now raging elsewhere. "Providence," he philosophized, "has in fact so established the order of things as that most evils are the means of producing some good. The yellow fever will discourage the growth of great cities in our nation; & I view great cities as pestilential to the morals, the health and the liberties of man. True, they nourish some of the elegant arts; but the useful ones can thrive elsewhere, and less perfection in the others with more health virtue & freedom would be my choice."

The second spoke of Christianity. "I have a view of the subject which ought to displease neither the rational Christian or Deist; & would reconcile many to a character they have too hastily rejected. I do not know however that it would reconcile the *genus irritabile vatum* [the Calvinist ministers], who are all in arms against me. Their hostility is on too interesting ground to be softened. The delusions into which the XYZ plot shewed it possible to push the people, the successful experiment made under the prevalence of that delusion, on the clause of the constitution which while it secured the freedom of the press, covered also the freedom of religion, had given to the clergy a very favorite hope of an establishment of a particular form of Christianity thro' the US. and as every sect believes its own form the true one, every one perhaps hoped for its own; but especially the Episcopalians & Congregationalists. The returning good sense of our country threatens abortion to their hopes, & they believe that any portion of power confided to me will be exerted in opposition to their schemes. And they believe truly, *for I have sworn upon the altar of god eternal hostility against every form of tyranny over the mind of man.*" [41]

As though the cry of atheism was not enough, the Mazzei letter again turned up to plague him; and the Federalists added this to their arsenal of weapons. So too did private worries. Thomas Mann Randolph, Martha's husband, though an excellent farmer, had run into debt and called on his father-in-law for help. Sorrowfully Jefferson was compelled to reply that he was in no position to do so. The profits of his Bedford estate were being used to pay off the old Wayles' debts and the new ones he had incurred to meet them; while "the unprofitable state of Albemarle has kept me in a constant struggle." [42]

In addition, he found in balancing his accounts with young William Short that he owed him far more than he had thought. While in Europe, Short had turned over the management of his private fortune to Jefferson. Jefferson had used part of it in 1794 to finance his nailery, and had then executed a chattel mortgage on eighty of his slaves as security. He now discovered that what he actually owed Short was $9,000 with accrued interest, and that the old mortgage was insufficient. He therefore added still another mortgage, covering 1,000 acres of Bedford land.[43] Jefferson was sinking deeper and deeper into the morass.

He took a census of his "family" during his stay at Monticello. There were 11 free whites, and 93 slaves; quite a comedown from former years. His last year's crop of tobacco totaled 43,433 pounds—not enough, at current prices, to keep his head above water.[44] He leased out most of his lands across the river, and was devoting all his time to his nailery and to building a mill, which he hoped also to rent out.[45]

Meanwhile the campaign was proceeding apace. With Burr's great victory in New York promising success in the coming election,[46] Jefferson deemed it time to set down on paper what a Republican Congress ought to do. It should, he said, be dedicated to the preservation of states' rights, freedom of religion and of the press, trial by jury, economy in government, opposition to standing armies, paper systems, war, and all connection, except by commerce, with other nations. He thought the United States too large to have all its affairs directed by a single government—shades of Montesquieu!—and therefore demanded that the general government concern itself with foreign affairs only, and leave all other matters to the states. He also vehemently opposed the idea that the federal government could employ the common law in its courts—that, he insisted, would make it "the most corrupt government on earth." [47]

What aroused his particular animosity against the common law was the fact that the Federalists were using the English rule on libel, as well as the statutory Sedition Act, to indict and prosecute Republican editors. William Duane, the new editor of the Philadelphia *Aurora*, bellwether of the Republican press, was one such. Callender was another who, after a farcical trial before Judge William Chase, had been incarcerated in Richmond Jail. Seated in his cell, Callender kept writing his notorious *Prospect Before*

Us, and sending sheets to Jefferson with not too subtle hints for money. He would, he said, like to set up a press to publish it, but the cost was about two to three hundred dollars.[48] Jefferson had already given him $100; now he sent him another $50.[49] The volume—a scurrilous attack on Adams, Washington and the administration of the government—appeared at the end of 1800, with the preface dated "Richmond Jail, Nov. 4th, 1800."

Jefferson treated Callender so tenderly because he considered the prosecutions as designed "to cripple & suppress the republican efforts during the campaign which is coming on. In the meantime their [the Federalists'] own batteries are opened, and teeming with every falsehood they can invent by defamation. Our campaign will be as hot as that of Europe. But happily we deal in ink only; they in blood." [50]

In the midst of these national concerns, Governor Monroe wrote in considerable alarm that a plot for a Negro insurrection had just been discovered in Richmond. Thirty Negroes had already been arrested; and more were being hunted.[51] A week later, he had more news. The conspiracy was "unquestionably the most serious and formidable . . . we have ever known of the kind." Ten of the ringleaders had been condemned and swiftly executed; and some forty more awaited trial, "of whose guilt no doubt is entertained." While Monroe felt that the hand of the executioner should not be stayed, he would like nevertheless to have Jefferson's opinion.[52]

Jefferson replied cautiously that though those citizens who had escaped from murder and rapine might well feel that *all* involved should be executed, yet "the other states & the world at large will forever condemn us if we indulge a principle of revenge, or go one step beyond absolute necessity." While he agreed that the Negroes ought not to be permitted at large, yet might they not be confined in some fort, where rescue would be precluded?[53]

Jefferson's calmer counsels prevailed, and those unfortunates who had not already been hurried to execution were closely confined. But the problem of what to do with them remained. More than a year later, a resolution was introduced in the Virginia legislature to purchase lands in the western territory on which to settle the condemned conspirators; but Jefferson protested that some day those lands must be incorporated into the Union. Better send them, he advised, to the West Indies, among people of their own color; or, as a last resort, to Africa.[54] The resolution was dropped; but the Negro problem was to plague Virginia for some years to come.

Scattered local election returns were slowly coming in. Baltimore had gone Republican, and Jefferson hastened to congratulate Gen. Samuel Smith, the local Republican stalwart, on the result. "The spirit of 76. had never left the people of our country," he wrote. "But artificial panics of raw head & bloody bones had put it to sleep for a while. We owe to our political opponents the exciting it again by their bold strokes. Whatever may be the event of the Executive election, the Legislative one will give us a majority in the H. of R. and all but that in the Senate. The former alone will keep the government from running wild, while a reformation in our state legislatures will be working and preparing a compleat one in the Senate. A President can then do little mischief." [55]

It may seem strange to modern observers that Jefferson could thus, in the heat of the conflict, keep quietly to his mountaintop at Monticello and conduct a "front-porch" campaign through the medium of letters. But no other type of campaign was then indicated. The states could best be left to local politicians, communications from one to the others were difficult, and a candidate must stay in his own bailiwick and possess his soul in patience.

Jefferson remained at Monticello from the end of May until the end of November. He would have gone on earlier to the new capital of the United States—the city of Washington, to which it had been removed in June—had he not decided on a bit of strategy. He explained it to Madison: "I think it possible that mr Adams may put some foolish things into his speech on the possibility of its being his valedictory one; and that this may give the Senate an opportunity again of shewing their own malice. I propose therefore to give time for the speech & answer to be over before I arrive there." [56]

On November 22, 1800, therefore, Jefferson rode to Washington to assume his final duties as Vice-President of the United States, and to await the slow-gathering returns that would decide whether he had become President, or was permanently retired to Monticello.

CHAPTER 46

Jefferson—or Burr?

JEFFERSON arrived in the city of Washington on the evening of November 27, 1800, and took lodgings in the boardinghouse of Conrad and McMunn on New Jersey Avenue, Southeast, and about two hundred paces from the Capitol building.[1]

Coming thus late, he was fortunate to find any lodgings at all, and he modestly took his place at the end of the crowded table during meals, even though it was farthest from the fireplace and therefore bitterly cold.[2]

The capital city could hardly be called a city. It was a place of magnificent distances interspersed with a few scattered buildings; a quagmire of mud when the sun shone and a sea of frozen ruts during the winter nights. The Capitol building rose still gaunt and skeletonized on the brow of the hill; surrounding it and making the sum total of the Federal city were seven or eight boardinghouses, a tailor shop, a shoemaker, a printer, a washerwoman, a grocer, a stationer, a dry-goods establishment and an oyster house. Swamps on all sides emitted the putrid odors of decay and from them rose at breeding seasons the clouds of mosquitoes responsible for the fevers that periodically swept the town.

The President's house, "a very elegant building," stood on the road to Georgetown; and strung along that road were a cluster of public offices and new residences in various stages of completion. Since these were at some distance from the Capitol where Congress met, most of the legislators crowded into the boardinghouses within the "federal city."

Conrad & McMunn's seemed the most popular. Albert Gallatin of Pennsylvania, Republican leader in the House, shared a room with another Congressman and found the charges high. For room, board, firewood, candles, and liquors, he paid $15 a week. The beef, he complained, was "not very good; mutton and poultry good"; and there were "hardly any vegetables."

Some thirty boarders crowded the establishment—practically all men, and members of Congress—and, were it not for two women in the group, they looked to Gallatin like a refectory of monks.[3] This was the place in which Jefferson, accustomed to the spaciousness and lavish foods and wines of Monticello, now found himself.

The campaign of calumny against him had risen to shrill heights during his long vacation in Virginia, and there were those among the Federalists in Washington who stared at the newcomer as though they expected to see literal horns and tail sprouting in the proper places from his tall, lank form. Even Margaret Bayard Smith, married to Samuel Harrison Smith, the Republican editor of the newly established *National Intelligencer*, was prepared to meet a bold profligate, coarse and vulgar in his manners. For, though she had married a good Republican, her father, Col. John Bayard, was a fiery Federalist. But, to her great surprise, this infidel and limb of Satan turned out to be "so meek and mild, yet dignified in his manners, with a voice so soft and low, with a countenance so benignant and intelligent," that her heart went out to him, and ever after she enrolled herself in the list of his ardent worshipers.[4]

The first two weeks of December were weeks of anxious waiting as the results, and rumors of results, from the various states came gradually by letter and by messenger to the crowded capital. John Adams, ensconced in the President's House, was firmly convinced of his re-election, and believed that the machinations of Hamilton would prove of no avail. He thought too that Jefferson might well nose out Pinckney for the Vice-Presidency; and "such was the gullibility of this old gent," wrote John Randolph of Roanoke sarcastically in his private diary, "& such the *address* of his competitor that he could not be made to believe, until it was too late, that Mr. J. was his rival. He said he had such assurances from his friend J. that he could not doubt them & quarreled with his Federal adherents for wishing to put him (J) out of the V. presidency—believing that their support of Pinkney [*sic*] for that office was only a covert design of elevating him to the first place in the government."[5]

In truth, the election was touch and go during that crucial fortnight. The results from New York were definitely known; that state had gone Republican. So had Virginia, of course. The New England states, just as firmly, had chosen Federalist electors. But the picture was clouded and full of forebodings in states like Pennsylvania, South Carolina and Rhode Island; and more and more it became clear that the final result was to depend on these doubtful states.

The situation became worse confounded because of the number of cross-currents and secret knifings in both parties. Among the Federalists it was practically in the open; among the Republicans there was a certain degree of stealth.

So bitter by this time had become the feud between Hamilton and Adams that Hamilton would have been willing, if he could not elect Pinckney to the Presidency, to see even the "atheist" and "fanatic" Jefferson in the chair rather than the hated Adams. But a new fear rose to befog his mind and render him frantic. That was the steadily lengthening specter of Aaron Burr. If Hamilton hated Adams, he was literally beside himself when Burr's name was mentioned. For Burr had broken his hold on New York State; Burr had fought him in the law courts and in politics and had beaten him with too great regularity; if Burr was up, then he, Hamilton, must inevitably go down.

When the possibility first dawned on the Federalists that neither Adams nor Pinckney might be elected; and that the choice might be between Jefferson and Burr, there was much correspondence among them as to their course in such an eventuality. Hamilton tried to put a stop to any talk of Burr. "Burr," he exclaimed, "will certainly attempt to reform the government *à la Buonaparte*. He is as unprincipled and dangerous a man as any country can boast—as true a Cataline as ever met in midnight conclave."[6]

But not all the Federalists took Hamilton's diatribes seriously. They understood the personal animus that drove him, and that eventually brought him to his death on the dueling field. George Cabot of Massachusetts, high in the Federalist councils, considered the matter coolly. "The question has been asked," he wrote Hamilton, "whether if the federalists cannot carry their first points, they would not do as well to turn the election from Jefferson to Burr? They conceive Burr to be less likely to look to France for support than Jefferson, provided he would be supported at home. They consider Burr as actuated by ordinary ambition, Jefferson by that and the pride of the Jacobinic philosophy. The former may be satisfied by power and property, the latter must see the roots of our society pulled up and a new course of cultivation substituted."[7]

In the meantime, the Federalists in New England, well aware that Hamilton was banking on certain votes going to Pinckney in South Carolina that would not be similarly cast for Adams, determined not to listen to his siren pleas to have equal votes for both candidates cast in their own bailiwicks, and provided for a few to be dropped from Pinckney.

In the Republican camp there were similar fears. Burr claimed he had been double-crossed by Virginia in the election of 1796; and was apprehensive that Virginia might throw away votes from him to insure Jefferson's election.[8] On the other hand, there were rumors that Burr was seeking to do the same on his own account in New York and Rhode Island. No wonder then that never in the history of the United States has there been any election as complicated from every point of view as the presidential election of 1800.

Even in Rhode Island there was trouble. Its governor was a Republican, and some arrangement had been made to give Jefferson a full complement of votes and drop one or two from Burr in order to make certain that Jefferson would be President, and Burr take the second post.[9] But something went wrong, and it seemed that Rhode Island might go Federalist altogether.

Alexander J. Dallas of Pennsylvania counted up the votes as they then stood on the national scene, and found to his alarm that *without* Pennsylvania, the electoral ballots seemed to indicate that Pinckney would top Jefferson by a single vote, with Adams trailing by seven votes. He proposed to Governor McKean, therefore, that Pennsylvania should attempt so to arrange its choice that Jefferson and Burr would tie, and throw the election into Congress. Otherwise, he feared that the Federalists would get in.[10]

The difficulty in Pennsylvania was that the Senate was Federalist and the House Republican. In previous elections, presidential electors had been chosen by the general voters; but now the legislature changed the rules, and placed the appointment in its own hands. The House demanded a joint ballot, in which their Republican numbers would outvote the smaller Federalist Senate; but the Senate refused to fall into the trap. A compromise was finally arranged whereby eight Republicans and seven Federalists were chosen as electors. When Jefferson heard of the arrangement, he considered that it clinched the national election; that "the vessel of the Union will be put on her republican tack, and shew us how she works on that."[11]

He based his optimism on the news from South Carolina, Pinckney's home state. There the Hamiltonians had attempted to persuade Pinckney to ditch Adams and permit the state's electoral ballots to be cast for Pinckney and Jefferson. But Pinckney honorably refused to have any part in the plot, declaring that the votes must be all for Adams and himself, or he would retire from the contest.[12] As a result of Pinckney's stand, the contemplated deal with the Jeffersonian forces became impossible; and, in revenge, South Carolina went unanimously for Jefferson and Burr. It is therefore patent that Burr had sound reasons for his mistrust. Had the deal gone through in its original form, he would have trailed all the other candidates.

By December 20th, however, the results were pretty well known. The electoral votes read: Jefferson—73, Burr—73, Adams—65, Pinckney—64, John Jay—1.

The Republicans had swept the Federalists out of office and broken their power irrevocably. From its inception the government had been in the latter's hands. They had established a Union and pushed through measures of tremendous importance which set the United States on a course from which there might be deviations, but no fundamental about-face. Yet, in the end, their arrogance defeated them. They had ridden roughshod over the rights of the States, and had contemptuously overlooked the mass of the people. They had attempted to set aside the safeguards with which freedom was hedged, and had favored the old enemy, England, too much. In their pride, they thought that the rich, the wellborn and the professional intellectuals were the only safe repositories of power. Therefore they had fallen.

But the general thesis that the people had swept them out of office, that a vast popular outpouring of indignant small farmers and city artisans had created a revolution, does not hold water. Because of property qualifications, the percentage of legal voters to the total population was lamentably low. Nor, even among the qualified few, had there been any great upheaval. Jefferson had failed of the preceding election by inches; nor even now, had there been no mortal feuds among the Federalists themselves, would the Republicans have been elected. Hamilton's secret and overt machinations; the votes dropped from Pinckney in New England, and the votes dropped from Adams in the South; the general disgust with the name-calling among themselves—to all these factors may be attributed the Federalist downfall.

A strange situation, however, now arose. The Republicans had won; but their two candidates had come to the finish line in a dead heat. For this the Constitution of the United States was responsible. It had never contemplated the growth of parties, each with its slate of candidates for the Presidency and the Vice-Presidency. It had been intended that each elector would cast the two votes granted him for individuals, on their individual merits; that the one with the greatest number of total votes would become President, and the runner-up would take the Vice-Presidential chair.

There had been no difficulty in the three preceding elections; but now, for the first time, the fatal flaw showed itself. Jefferson and Burr were tied. Which was to be President, and which Vice-President? The Constitution, it is true, made provision for such an unlikely contingency. Such an indecisive election must go into the House of Representatives for choice between the pair.

Some inklings of this anomalous situation had already troubled certain Republicans. Jefferson thought the necessary arrangements had been made to ensure that he would have more votes than Burr. He told Thomas Mann Randolph that "it was intended that one vote should be thrown away [in South Carolina] from Colo. Burr. It is believed Georgia will withhold from him one or two. The votes will stand probably T. J. 73, Burr about 70, Mr. Adams 65." [13]

But word came shortly from South Carolina that, in the confusion of the negotiations with Pinckney, something had gone wrong. The vote which was supposed to be dropped from Burr and go instead to George Clinton of New York, had not been switched.[14] Burr had not been notified of this plan, and *he* had arranged with Governor Fenner of Rhode Island to drop a vote there from him. This, too, had failed of consummation.

Here was a situation which Jefferson realized could lead to considerable trouble.[15] The election was now thrown into the House of Representatives. Had it been the newly elected Congress, there would have been no difficulty, for that body had gone strongly Republican. But his fate was in the hands of the old, lame-duck House, and *that* was still Federalist. Furthermore, the voting would be by States, and not by individuals, so that party decisions would bind the casting ballot against individual revolt.

The Federalists, indeed, were beginning to awaken from the first despair of their defeat, and were studying the picture with a dawning hope. With the House under their control, might it not be possible still to wrest victory out of defeat? They could, of course, choose either Jefferson or Burr; and make a bargain in return for the coveted plum. The sole problem here was the pliability and amenability of the two men. Hamilton plumped for Jefferson; but a goodly number of Federalists would have preferred Burr. In their calculations, no one brought up the point that it had really been the intention of the electors, and of the people and legislatures that had voted for them, to place Jefferson in the first position, and Burr in the second.

But there was an extreme group of Federalists who wanted to push beyond this point. Why not, they argued, seize the heaven-sent opportunity, and retain control of the government in spite of the mandate of the people and the ethics of the occasion? Suppose, they insinuated, a decisive choice between the pair be avoided altogether, and a good Federalist be named President of the Senate *pro tem*, to assume the reins until another election could be held. Such a course, according to them, said Jefferson bitterly, "would only be a *stretch* of the constitution." [16]

Cooler and wiser heads prevailed, however. Threats from alarmed Republicans had been heard that in such a case the militia of the Republican states might decide to march on Washington. In spite of Hamilton's outraged cries, in spite of the plain intent of the electors, the Federalist leaders in Congress decided to throw their strength behind Burr. "It seems to be the general opinion," Gouverneur Morris wrote in his diary, "that Colonel Burr will be chosen President by the House of Representatives. Many of them think it highly dangerous that Mr. Jefferson should, in the present crisis, be placed in that office. They consider him as a theoretic man, who would bring the National Government back to something like the old Confederation. Mr. Nicholay comes today, and to him I state it as the opinion, not of light and fanciful but of serious and considerable men, that Burr must be preferred to Jefferson." [17]

In all this turmoil Jefferson kept his head. He sought ways and means by which the expressed purposes of the Federalists might be defeated. The first, and most obvious method, was to come to an agreement with Aaron Burr.

On December 15th, before the final votes of some of the states were known, he wrote a very careful letter to Burr in New York. After going into the details of what had been planned in the way of dropping a vote here and there to avoid parity between the two Republican candidates, he acknowledged that

> ... it was badly managed not to have arranged with certainty what seems to have been left to hazard. It was the more material, because I understand several of the high-flying federalists have expressed their hope that the two republican tickets may be equal, & their determination in that case to prevent a choice by the H of R. (which they are strong enough to do), and let the government devolve on a President of the Senate. Decency required that I should be so entirely passive during the late contest that I never once asked whether ar-

rangements had been made to prevent so many from dropping votes intentionally, as might frustrate half the republican wish; nor did I doubt, till lately, that such had been made.

While I must congratulate you, my dear Sir, on the issue of this contest, because it is more honorable, and doubtless more grateful to you than any station within the competence of the chief magistrate, yet for myself, and for the substantial service of the public, I feel most sensibly the loss we sustain of your aid in our new administration. It leaves a chasm in my arrangements, which cannot be adequately filled up. I had endeavored to compose an administration whose talents, integrity, names, and dispositions should at once inspire unbounded confidence in the public mind, and insure a perfect harmony in the conduct of the public business. I lose you from the list, & am not sure of all the others. Should the gentlemen who possess the public confidence decline taking a part in their affairs, and force us to take persons unknown to the people, the evil genius of this country [Hamilton] may realize his avowal that "he will beat down the administration." [18]

Not a word about the possibility that they might be rivals for the great office. Also a contradiction between this detailed discussion of the attempts to drop votes from Burr and Jefferson's later disavowal of knowledge that any such arrangement had been made.

What he was trying to do was to convince Burr that in the event he had failed of the Vice-Presidency, Jefferson had earmarked him for a Cabinet position; and the bait was now temptingly dangled that, should Burr prefer such a position to the comparative obscurity of the Vice-Presidential post, a hint to that effect might still get it for him. The exact Department might then become a matter of bargaining.

Burr's reply, on its face, sounded perfectly frank, open and aboveboard. He spoke of the arrangement with Fenner of Rhode Island that had misfired, and continued: "I do not however apprehend any embarrassment even in Case the Votes should come out alike for us—my personal friends are perfectly informed of my wishes on the subject and can never think of diverting a single Vote from you—on the Contrary, they will be found among your most zealous adherents. I see no reason to doubt of your having at least nine States if the business shall come before the H. of Reps."

To the second part of Jefferson's letter, he was equally frank. While he did not doubt that there was a sufficiency of Republican talent to fill all offices, nevertheless, "as to myself, I will chearfully abandon the office of V. P. if it shall be thought that I can be more useful in any Active Station. In short, my whole time and attention shall be unceasingly employed to render your Administration grateful and honorable to our Country and to yourself." [19]

It is curious that Jefferson, having tempted Burr to offer for a Cabinet position, never took up the offer when it was made. But by the time he received the letter, he was beginning to suspect that Burr was in secret negotiations with the Federalists to oust him from the first position; and after the contest was over, he had worked himself into such a state of resentment that he preferred to keep Burr in the obscurity and empty honor of the Vice-Presidency.

The lame-duck Congress was scheduled to convene in February, 1801. But the intervening period was filled with alarums and excursions, with plot and counterplot, with frantic conferences and even more frantic letters, with racing rumors and denials that never caught up.

The Federalists in Congress had decided to back Burr. To Hamilton, however, this was anathema. In letters that grew ever more reckless in phrase he denounced Burr as a "voluptuary by system," a man "without probity," a cynical bankrupt who would not hesitate to sell his country for foreign gold. He even threatened to withdraw from the party if its leaders failed to take his advice.[20]

In one of the few letters in which he was sufficiently calm to be logical, he actually made out a case—at least from the Federalist point of view. If the Federalist plan to elect Burr succeeded, he warned, "it will have done nothing more or less, than place in that station a man who will possess the boldness and daring necessary to give success to the Jacobin system, instead of one, who for want of that quality, will be less fitted to promote it." He felt reasonably certain that, in exchange for their votes, assurances could be obtained from Jefferson on issues vital to the Federalists: the preservation of Hamilton's fiscal system; continued neutrality in Europe; an increased navy; and the continuance of Federalists in all public offices except for department heads.[21]

But the very recklessness of his invective weakened still further his already waning influence with his party, and its leaders sought privately to gain Burr over to their views. They failed. In spite of suspicions then, open accusations later, and the dutiful recording of every bit of unsupported gossip in Jefferson's *Anas*, there is no evidence that Burr connived at or entered into any deal with the Federalists to place himself in the Presidency.

As soon as it seemed probable that there would be a tie, he wrote an open letter to General Samuel Smith, Jefferson's campaign whip, to the effect that "if such should be the result, every man who knows me ought to know that I would utterly disclaim all competition. Be assured that the federal party can entertain no wish for such an exchange. As to my friends, they would dishonour my views and insult my feelings by a suspicion that I would submit to be instrumental in counteracting the wishes and expectations of the United States. And I now constitute you my proxy to declare these sentiments if the occasion should require."[22] At the appointed time, Smith hastened to publish this forthright disclaimer.

The Federalists sent an emissary, David A. Ogden, to treat with Burr. He received such replies that he reported in disgust to the leaders that they had better "acquiesce in the election of Mr. Jefferson, as the less dangerous man of the two." [23] To the New York delegation in Washington, however, Ogden insinuated that he was in Burr's confidence, and that it would be to their interest to join with the Federalists in electing him.[24]

The Republicans by this time were at fever pitch. They still believed that the real intention of the Federalists was to create a stalemate which would give them an excuse to continue themselves in power. In that case, some of the hotheads were ready to use force. Republican troops would march, they threatened. "Virginia would instantly proclaim herself out of the Union," warned Joseph H. Nicholson.[25]

Even Monroe, in his official capacity as Governor of Virginia, declared his intention to keep the Assembly in constant session to meet with the crisis, and to install a chain of expresses between Washington and Richmond to get word as quickly as possible of any Federalist action. While clinging to the belief that the Eastern States were only bluffing, he was ready for eventualities. "If the union could be broken," he avowed, such a Federalist coup would do it.[26]

But there was not the slightest hint that, should the Federalists succeed in their announced intention of electing Burr, there would be any convulsion on the part of the Republicans, no matter how bitter their disappointment. Even Jefferson, after the event of his own election, declared that he would have acquiesced. "Had it terminated in the elevation of mr Burr," he then told McKean, "every republican would I am sure have acquiesced in a moment; because, however it might have been variant from the intentions of the voters, yet it would have been agreeable to the constitution. No man would more chearfully have submitted than myself, because I am sure the administration would have been republican, and the chair of the Senate permitting me to be at home 8. months in the year, would on that account have been much more consonant to my real satisfaction. But in the event of an usurpation I was decidedly with those who were determined not to permit it." [27]

During the struggle itself, the one thing that Jefferson mourned was the want of their foresight in not having made an arrangement sufficient to have avoided a tie. "The contrivance in the Constitution for marking the votes works badly," he exclaimed, "because it does not enounce precisely the true expression of the public will." The Republican strategy in the current situation was to press for an election by the House. If that failed, then it was decided to have Jefferson and Burr issue a joint proclamation allocating the offices between them.[28] Madison suggested instead that the two candidates issue a joint proclamation calling the newly elected Congress into session, in order that it might decide the issue rather than this lame-duck one. He acknowledged that such a procedure might not be "strictly regular" under the Constitution, but "the irregularity will be less in form than any other adequate to the emergency." [29]

Albert Gallatin, Republican leader in the House, opposed both these plans as "an assumption of power not strictly warranted by the forms and substance of our constitutions." As a good general, he formulated his own plan to meet every possible contingency. The attempt to elect Burr, he felt, could be defeated by the firmness of the Republicans in Congress. Any attempt to order a new election would end in futility for the Federalists. Adams would merely be licked again. Should they seek to assume executive power during an interregnum, such "usurpation must be resisted by free men whenever they have the power of resisting." How could that be done? First, the Republican states would refuse to recognize or obey the usurper. Second, they must try to defeat any proposed law to that effect in Congress, and failing that, prevail on Adams to veto it, and have the legislatures of the states meet to determine their course.[30]

Hugh Henry Brackenridge of Pittsburg, as became a frontiersman, advocated a bold and decisive stroke. He advised Jefferson to proclaim himself President on March 4th, get Burr's consent in writing to the proclamation, and have "the legitimate authorities" instantly ratify the act. "In a case of this nature," he asserted, "all depends on the decision and rapidity of the movement, the hadrepebelon or fortunate boldness of the Greeks, the coup de main of military men." [31]

In the midst of all this excitement, Jefferson was still able to direct his attention to other matters. He duly transmitted to the American Philosophical Society certain communications on the steam engine from Robert R. Livingston, former Chancellor of New York. He asked Livingston to get him some large bones, supposed to be mammoth, which had been discovered not far from his residence. Almost as an afterthought, he offered Livingston the post of Secretary of Navy in his forthcoming Cabinet.[32]

He was also keeping a careful eye on his affairs at home. He told his son-in-law to speak sharply to the overseer "as to the treatment of the nailers. It would destroy their value in my estimation to degrade them in their own eyes by the whip. This therefore must not be resorted to but in extremities. As they will be again under my government I would chuse they should retain the stimulus of character." [33] And on February 3rd, a week before Congress opened, he found time to purchase a bay horse for $300, though payment would have to wait until May 1st.[34]

In spite of his seeming insouciance, however, the atmosphere of Washington clouded his sensitive nature. He was worn down, he complained, with distasteful pursuits, and "surrounded by enemies & spies, catching & perverting every word which falls from my lips or flows from my pen, and inventing where facts fail them." He was in an enemy's country. "It is an unpleasant circumstance, if I am destined to stay here, that the great proportion of those of the place who figure, are federalists, and most of them of the violent kind. Some have been so personally bitter that they can never forgive me, tho' I do them with sincerity. Perhaps in time they will get tamed." [35]

But there were also Federalists who were fighting valiantly for Jefferson, and these included his former great enemy, Hamilton. John Adams, still licking his wounds in defeat, stood aloof with a kind of "a plague on both your houses" attitude. "I know no more danger of a political convulsion," he wrote privately, "if a President, *pro tempore*, of the Senate, or a Secretary of State, or Speaker of the House, should be made President by Congress than if Mr. Jefferson or Mr. Burr is declared such. The President would be as legal in one case as in either of the others, and the people as well satisfied." But what good would it do to follow the first course? he inquired. There would have to be another election, and Jefferson would again be chosen. "We shall be tossed, at any rate," he ended mournfully, "in the tempestuous sea of liberty for years to come, and where the bark can land but in a political convulsion, I cannot see." [36]

On February 11, 1801, Congress convened. The atmosphere was electric with tension; and the dreary city was blanketed with snow. Every available accommodation was taken, with newcomers clamoring for even a board to sleep on. Intrigue was everywhere, and men foregathered to speak in whispers and with a sidelong glance to see if they were overheard. Bargains, deals, corrupt promises were in the air; and rumor multiplied them manyfold.

The first order of business was to count the electoral votes. This was the joint business of both Houses, and Jefferson sat in the President's chair with immobile face while the counting proceeded. There were no surprises. Jefferson and Burr were tied for the lead.

The next step was the crucial one. Under the Constitution, an indecisive election was thrown into the House of Representatives. The balloting was to be done by States, and there were sixteen States.

Jefferson estimated his chances. He was certain of eight States; the Federalists were equally certain of six; and two seemed equally divided, thereby losing their votes. Nine—a majority—was necessary to win. If any one of six individuals, all of "moderate disposition," would switch his vote to Jefferson, he would provide that all-essential ninth State.[37]

The first ballot proved the accuracy of the prediction. Eight States—New York, New Jersey, Pennsylvania, Virginia, North Carolina, Kentucky, Georgia and Tennessee—voted for Jefferson. Six States—New Hampshire, Massachusetts, Rhode Island, Connecticut, Delaware and South Carolina—cast ballots for Burr. Two States—Vermont and Maryland, their own delegations deadlocked—cast blanks. In actual individual votes cast, however, Burr had a majority of 55 to 51.[38]

With a snowstorm raging outside, and the House chamber bare, draughty and unheated, the balloting proceeded, roll call after roll call. From one in the afternoon, all through the night, until eight o'clock the next morning, twenty-seven ballots were taken, with the same monotonous result. Not a vote had shifted; not a State had budged. The tired and shivering members agreed then to suspend until noon; and they staggered out to eat and catch some sleep. Promptly at the appointed hour they were back again, and tried another ballot. Still the same.[39] The members "looked banged badly," observed one of them.[40]

There were cases of heroism. Joseph Nicholson of Maryland was ill with a high fever, but he trudged determinedly through the snow and lay on a cot in the draughty chamber through every ballot, voting for Jefferson. Had he not done so, Maryland's blank vote would have gone to Burr. Even Harrison Gray Otis, Boston Federalist and working for Burr, could not forbear admiration. "It is a chance that this kills him," he wrote his wife. "I would not thus expose myself for any President on Earth." [41]

Since there was, according to Gallatin, a possibility that another member of the Maryland delegation might be induced to come over to Jefferson, it was even more vital that Nicholson attend.

A few more test votes and the House lay over to the following morning. By February 14th, thirty-three ballots had been taken; and the lines still remained firm. Further voting was therefore adjourned until Monday. Gallatin fumed at the impudence of the Federalists in continuing the struggle so long. We ourselves shall never yield, he asserted vehemently.[42]

But that Saturday came the first ray of hope. James A. Bayard, lone Representative from Delaware, and leader of the Federalist coalition for Burr, had privately stated that he intended to shift his vote to Jefferson.[43] Nevertheless, Saturday passed without any sign.

On February 15th, Jefferson was writing to Monroe that the signs pointed toward a break on Monday. He analyzed the Federalist position as follows: if they could have passed a law placing the government in the hands of a president pro tem, they would have done so. But the Republicans had told them plainly that the day such an act was passed, the Middle States would arm to oppose the usurpation. Furthermore, a convention would be called to reörganize the government and amend the Constitution. These affirmations, Jefferson was convinced, shook the Federalist will to proceed to extremes. He added one bit of interesting information. "Many attempts," he said, "have been made to obtain terms & promises from me. I have declared to them unequivocally, that I would not receive the government on capitulation, that I would not go into it with my hands tied." [44]

By this time Jefferson was convinced that Burr was intriguing with the Federalists for the post. He crammed his *Anas* with all sorts of rumors to that effect, most of them third and even fourth hand. For example, he heard and carefully preserved for posterity that Bayard had approached Samuel Smith, Edward Livingston and Dr. Linn of New Jersey, offering them Cabinet posts and other appointments if they switched to Burr; and claimed, in one instance at least, that Burr had authorized the offer.[45]

But Bayard had a wholly different story to tell. He was disgusted with Burr. All efforts to gain his co-operation in his own behalf had failed; Burr, attending the session of the New York Assembly in Albany and busy with his daughter's wedding, had steadfastly refused to yield to Federalist blandishments. "The means existed of electing Burr," Bayard declared to

Hamilton, "but this required his co-operation. By deceiving one man (a great blockhead), and tempting two (not incorruptible), he might have secured a majority of the States. He will never have another chance of being President of the United States; and the little use he has made of the one which has occurred, gives me but an humble opinion of the talents of an unprincipled man." [46] The last appellation can only be considered as the epithet of a disgruntled Federalist.

In another direction, however, Bayard was more successful; at least, so he was to testify at a later date. Realizing at length that they could expect nothing from Burr, the Federalists decided to attempt to obtain from Jefferson those assurances which Hamilton had laid down as essential. Bayard of Delaware, Baer and Craik of Maryland, and Morris of Vermont, had agreed to vote together. Now, with deadlock unending and Burr recalcitrant, they applied to Nicholas of Virginia as an intermediary to obtain terms from Jefferson. Their terms—and Hamilton's—were that the public credit be left untouched, the navy increased, and subordinate Federalist officials left in office. Nicholas refused to act, whereupon they turned to General Samuel Smith of Maryland. Smith agreed to see Jefferson and to obtain his answer. The following morning he returned to the four Congressmen with the information that he had laid their proposition before Jefferson, who authorized him to say that the points "corresponded with his views and intentions, and that we might confide in him accordingly." [47]

Jefferson was to deny most vigorously and emphatically that he had made any such bargain. But Smith, interrogated in the same proceedings with Bayard, was compelled unwillingly to admit that he *had* acted as intermediary, and that Jefferson had at least stated, in connection with a friend of Bayard in political office, that "Mr. Bayard might rest assured . . . that Mr. Jefferson would conduct, as to those points, agreeably to the opinions I have stated as his." [48]

Whether or not there was a misunderstanding on Jefferson's part of the true nature of General Smith's inquiries, can naturally never be determined. But the effect was immediate. When the House reconvened on February 17th, on the thirty-sixth ballot, the Federalist forces broke their hitherto solid ranks. The members from Vermont and Maryland who had hitherto voted for Burr, now cast blank ballots, and those States went to Jefferson. Bayard of Delaware refrained from voting, and so did the entire South Carolina delegation. Only four New England States refused to be parties to a deal, and went down fighting to the last. When the final results were announced, ten States were for Jefferson, four for Burr, and two did not vote.

The long and most bitterly contested election in American history was over. Jefferson was President, and Burr Vice-President.

"Thus," Gallatin wrote the epitaph, "has ended the most wicked and absurd attempt ever tried by the Federalists." [49]

CHAPTER 47

President Jefferson

AS the sun rose on March 4, 1801, over the new capital of the United States, there was a decided unanimity of opinion that the events of the day would seal and make permanent the Second American Revolution. Both Federalists and Republicans were convinced that an era had ended, and a new and different one was about to begin. Naturally, the event was viewed with sharply diverse feelings.

On the one hand, the more bitter Federalists foresaw the end of the world, the subversion of orderly government and the trampling of the breechless mob through the streets of the cities; while their even more embittered adherents among the New England clergy prophesied the reign of Antichrist and the death of all religion. The Republicans, however, intoxicated with the wine of victory, hailed the dawn of a new and more glorious era, in which the will of the people would be mighty and prevail, and dark days would vanish forever from the earth.

Jefferson himself was optimistic. "The storm through which we have passed," he wrote, "has been tremendous indeed. The tough sides of our Argosie have been thoroughly tried. Her strength has stood the waves into which she was steered, with a view to sink her. We shall put her on her republican tack, & she will now show by the beauty of her motion the skill of her builders." [1]

John Marshall, however, whom Adams had appointed Chief Justice of the Supreme Court in the closing days of his administration, viewed the future in gloomier vein. "Today the new political year commences," he wrote on the morning of the inauguration. "The new order of things begins. . . . There are some appearances which surprize me. I wish however more than I hope that the public prosperity & happiness may sustain no diminution under democratic guidance. The democrats are divided into speculative theorists & absolute terrorists. With the latter I am not disposed to class Mr Jefferson. If he arranges himself with them it is not difficult to foresee that much calamity is in store for our country—if he does not they will soon become his enemies & calumniators." [2]

But the plain people had no such fears. They saw only the advent of heaven on earth—in which it was bliss to be alive. Lustily they sang the new song struck off for the occasion. Entitled "The People's Friend," the tune rose high:

No more to subtle arts a prey,
Which, fearful of the eye of day,

A Nation's ruin planned:
Now entering on th' auspicious morn,
In which a people's hopes are born,
What joy o'erspreads the land...

Devoted to his country's cause,
The Rights of Men and equal Laws,
His hallow'd pen was given:
And now those Rights and Laws to save,
From sinking to an early grave,
He comes, employ'd by Heaven.

What joyful prospects rise before!
Peace, Arts and Science hail our shore,
And thro' the country spread:
Long may these blessings be preserv'd,
And by a virtuous land deserv'd,
With JEFFERSON our head.[3]

Washington was crowded with spectators come to attend the inauguration. But there were two significant absentees. One was John Adams, the outgoing President; the other was Theodore Sedgwick, the Federalist Speaker of the House of Representatives. Both had quit Washington early in the morning, to avoid seeing the death of all their hopes.

Adams's abstention was by far the more important. As still President—until the oath was given to the new incumbent—it was his duty to be present. As one who had once been friendly with Jefferson, it was only the merest of courtesies to have graced the occasion with his presence. But Adams, in those last dark days of the campaign, had come to feel himself mortally aggrieved. As John Randolph of Roanoke sarcastically observed, he had with touching naïvete believed almost until the end that Jefferson had had no further ambition than again to be Vice-President under himself. When his eyes were opened, the disillusionment was too much; and for the first time, he harkened eagerly to all the calumnies which his more extreme followers were industriously promulgating against the incoming candidate. Forgotten were the days of friendship and of trust in Europe; remembered now only were the dedication at the masthead of Tom Paine's pernicious volume, the secret maneuvers of the Jeffersonians against his administration and the foul insults of the Republican press.

He now sincerely believed that calamity had fallen upon the nation; and he spent his last days in office in a desperate endeavor to build bulwarks against the tide of anarchy he was certain was scheduled to crash upon the land. Grimly and furiously he bent to the task. He placed the Virginian John Marshall, whom Jefferson detested and by whom he was in turn detested, in the high office of Chief Justice of the Supreme Court. He co-operated gladly with the Federalists in the lame-duck Congress to push through a Judiciary Act which enlarged the Federal judiciary and created new judgeships. These he promptly filled with sound Federalists for terms limited only by "good behavior." It was this measure that Jefferson dreaded more than any other, "because appointments in the nature of freehold render it difficult to undo what is done." [4]

Adams remained at his desk signing commissions to Federal offices as fast as they could be laid before him, working until the very last moment of his stay in office. These were the famous "midnight appointments" which have since given rise to the legend that Adams sat in his lonely chamber through the wee, sma' hours of March 3rd and March 4th racing with facile pen over the mountainous sheaf of appointments.[5]

No wonder then that enmity sprang up between the two men; though Jefferson, as late as December 19th, had expected to be able to arrive "at a candid understanding with Mr. A[dams]. I do not expect," he then said, "that either his feelings or his views of interest will oppose it. I hope to induce in him dispositions liberal and accommodating." [6]

The great day of March 4th was ushered in by a parade of artillery and riflemen before the President-elect's lodgings at Conrad & McMunn's, accompanied by a salvo of guns and cannon. At noon, dressed plainly and without ostentation, Jefferson walked on foot in the company of Benjamin Stoddert, Secretary of Navy, and Samuel Dexter, Secretary of Treasury, together with a group of Republican members of Congress and an anonymous following of citizenry, from the boardinghouse to the Capitol. A company of Maryland artillery, dragging their cannon, paraded with them.

Only the north wing of the Capitol building was completed, and this was occupied by the Senate, the courts and the library. The center was still unfinished; while the south wing consisted of a temporary oval brick structure, irreverently called the "Oven," where the House of Representatives sat in great discomfort.

As Jefferson mounted the steps of the north wing to the Senate chamber, the militia fired their cannon and then dispersed. Assembled and waiting in the chamber were the members of both Houses, with Aaron Burr, recently arrived from New York, erect and dignified in the Senate chair. The members rose, Burr vacated the central seat and motioned Jefferson to assume it. Burr sat down on his right hand, and John Marshall sat down on the left. There ensued a few minutes of silence, then Jefferson rose again, with a manuscript in his hand, and commenced reading his Inaugural Address in what all those present agreed was a low-pitched, inaudible voice.[7]

Jefferson had taken a great deal of care in the preparation of his Inaugural Address. He knew that the country was waiting eagerly, though with varying emotions, to ascertain his intentions, to determine whether in fact a revolution had taken place, and if so, to what extremes it would go.

There had been considerable dispute among the Republicans themselves over the course to be plotted. Monroe, from his gubernatorial chair in Richmond, had expressed the view that any compromise with the Federalists would ruin the Republican cause. "There is no political error more to be avoided," he told Jefferson, "than a step [which] gives cause to suspect an accommodation with that party, or coloring to an opinion it is feared or respected. . . . Be assured, with the leaders of the royalist party you will never have a friend. With principles so opposite, it is impossible you [should]. The way is to drive off the mass of the people by a wise, firm, yet moderate course, from those leaders, and leave them to the ignominy they merit." [8]

This was exactly what Jefferson had intended, long before he received Monroe's exhortation. He wanted an administration that would proceed as smoothly as possible, and that would be supported by the overwhelming majority of the people. Though the election had ended in victory, the actual returns had been uncomfortably close. But he believed that the mass of the Federalists who had voted against him were misled by their leaders; if he could assure them that no anarchy was intended, that bloody revenge was not to follow, that no monster of infamy had come into office, they would, he thought, desert the fanatic "royalists" and enter the Republican fold. In the words of a later President, his mission was "to bind up the wounds" and to bring peace and harmony to a distracted country.

He explained his strategy to his friends and followers. "On the whole," he wrote General Gates, "I hope we shall make up an administration which will unite a great mass of confidence, and bid defiance to the plans of opposition meditated by leaders, who are now almost destitute of followers. If we can hit on the true line of conduct which may conciliate the honest part of those who were called federalists, & yet do justice to those who have so long been excluded from [the government], I should hope to be able to obliterate, or rather to unite the names of federalist & republican. The way to effect it is to preserve principle, but to treat tenderly those who have been estranged from us, & dispose their minds to view our proceedings with candour. This will end in approbation." [9]

It is with this strategy in mind that the Inaugural Address must be considered; and, in spite of the later sneers of certain commentators, the strategy proved a brilliant success.

After the usual expression of thanks for his election, and with some oratorical flourishes concerning the destiny of America, Jefferson settled down to the business at hand. The election, turbulent though it was, had been conducted according to the rules of the Constitution, and "all will, of course," he took it for granted, "arrange themselves under the will of the law, and unite in common efforts for the common good." In order to accomplish this, "all, too, will bear in mind this sacred principle, that though the will of the majority is in all cases to prevail, that will to be rightful must be reasonable; that the minority possess their equal rights, which equal law must protect, and to violate would be oppression. Let us, then, fellow-citizens, unite with one heart and one mind. Let us restore to social intercourse that harmony and affection without which liberty and even life itself are but dreary things. And let us reflect that, having banished from our land that religious intolerance under which mankind so long bled and suffered, we have yet gained little if we countenance a political intolerance as despotic, as wicked, and capable of as bitter and bloody persecutions."

These were sweet words and reasonable, calculated to soothe and placate; yet with an undertone of meaning to indicate that there *had* been intolerance, persecution and social ostracism under the Federalists.

"Every difference of opinion," he continued in similar vein, "is not a difference of principle. We have called by different names brethren of the same principle. We are all Republicans, we are all Federalists." With this famous phrase, Jefferson deftly turned the flank of the opposition; though at the same time creating some grumblings within his own ranks. It was the olive branch he held out to the generalty of the Federalists; the subtle implication that though arrayed under different banners the aims and objectives of honest Federalists and Republicans were the same; the unmistakable invitation for the defeated to come and partake at the common table.

"Let us, then," he proceeded, "with courage and confidence pursue our own Federal and Republican principles, our attachment to union and representative government" in a chosen land, "kindly separated by nature and a wide ocean from the exterminating havoc of one quarter of the globe; too highminded to endure the degradations of the others"; enlightened "by a benign religion" and "acknowledging and adoring an overruling Providence"; and under "a wise and frugal Government, which shall restrain men from injuring one another, shall leave them otherwise free to regulate their own pursuits of industry and improvement, and shall not take from the mouth of labor the bread it has earned. This is the sum of good government, and this is necessary to close the circle of our felicities."

Not enough attention has been paid to the skill and dexterity with which Jefferson managed in short compass to quiet the fears of the Federalists and build up an entirely different picture of himself in their minds from that to which they had been accustomed in their campaign literature. At one and the same time he disavowed any entanglements with France, put across the point that he, the alleged "atheist," was in fact a humbly religious man, and denied any intention to interfere with the sacred rights of property.

This accomplished, he was now able to propose his positive program in short, pithy sentences:

Equal and exact justice to all men ... peace, commerce, and honest friendship with all nations, entangling alliances with none; the support of the State governments in all their rights ... the preservation of the General Government in its whole constitutional vigor, as the sheet anchor of our peace at home and safety abroad; a jealous care of the right of election by the people ... absolute acquiescence in the decisions of the majority ... a well-disciplined militia ... the supremacy of the civil over the military authority; economy in the public expense ... the honest payment of our debts and sacred preservation of the public faith; encouragement of agriculture, and of commerce as its handmaid; the diffusion of information and arraignment of all abuses at the bar of public reason; freedom of religion; freedom of the press, and freedom of person under the protection of the habeas corpus, and trial by juries impartially selected.[10]

In these succinct phrases was ample fare for everyone; for Federalists as well as Republicans. Peace, freedom, prosperity, have always been magical terms. If some Federalists might have quarreled over the insistence on States' rights, there was sufficient genuflection in the direction of the General Government; no one could quarrel with the restatement of the Bill of Rights, though all knew it held implicit an attack on the abuses of those rights during the preceding years; commerce was mentioned as well as agriculture, though the farmer could take comfort in the subtle hierarchy of their placement; while both Francophiles and Anglophiles could unite in the ringing "entangling alliances with none" taken verbatim from the lamented Washington's Farewell Address. The Inaugural was all things to all people, and was intended as such.

Unfortunately, though the auditors in the crowded Senate chamber strained to hear, Jefferson's words were almost inaudible, and they had to wait for their appearance in newsprint to weigh and digest the sentiments expressed. In the meantime, the ceremony proceeded unimpeded. John Marshall, as became his office, administered the oath of office, first to Jefferson, and then to Burr.

The Inaugural ended, the combined session adjourned, and Jefferson repaired, still on foot, to his boardinghouse. That evening, at dinner, he found every accustomed seat in the dining room taken. No man present rose to offer the President of the United States his seat, until the wife of John Brown, the Senator from Kentucky, offered to yield hers at the more desirable end of the table. But Jefferson declined, and quietly sat down in his regular place at the bottom, far removed from the cheerful warmth of the fire.[11]

He remained at Conrad's until March 19th, when he moved into the President's House. He found that mansion, from which the Adamses had removed their private possessions, plainly and scantily furnished. The East Room, famous to later generations, was still unfinished. For the next few years Jefferson busied himself with furnishing the bare bones, particularly the cabinet room, which became his study. He placed a long table inside in the drawers of which he kept his garden and carpentry tools. He adorned the walls with maps and charts, and set his globes and books in all the corners. In the window recesses he placed potted plants, roses and geraniums; and suspended the cage of his pet mockingbird, whose singing comforted him in hours of trial. He loved to open the cage and let the bird fly at liberty in the room and come finally to a perch on his shoulder, taking food from between his lips.[12]

The first reaction to Jefferson's Inaugural came from John Marshall who, seated as he was immediately alongside the speaker, had a chance to hear that which was temporarily denied the others. At 4 P.M., he scribbled an addendum to his letter to Pinckney: "I have administered the oath to the President. You will before this reaches you see his inauguration speech. It is in the general well judgd & conciliatory. It is in direct terms giving the lie to the violent party declamation which has elected him, but it is strongly characteristic of the general cast of his political theory." [13]

If Marshall, one of the most perspicacious of the Federalist leaders, thus had his direst fears relieved, it may well be understood that the common mass of the Federalists were only too happy to find that the fire-breathing monster they had anticipated was cooing like a suckling dove.

The Rev. Manasseh Cutler, perhaps more known to fame as a land speculator on a gigantic scale than for his prowess in the pulpit, was somewhat perplexed; yet he was able to note the implications. "Jefferson's speech," he wrote a friend, "though a mixed medley of Jacobinism, Republicanism, and Federalism, of religion and atheism, of sentiments consistent and inconsistent with the constitution of an energetic government, yet it is extremely smooth, and must be highly popular with the people at large. There is a fair opening, and I think a hope, that he may prove a prudent man, and, though the next Congress will have a majority of Jacobins, the administration may not be greatly changed." [14]

George Cabot, one of the more temperate leaders of the tight little Junto of Massachusetts Federalists, agreed that the speech "is so conciliatory that much hope is derived from it by the Federalists; it certainly contains *some foolish* & *some pernicious* as well as *many good* ideas. On the whole however its temper entitles it to respect & whatever may be the sincerity of its professions, good policy requires that they be trusted till contradicted by actions." [15]

The Chevalier d'Yrujo, the Spanish Minister to the United States, wrote Jefferson enthusiastically from Philadelphia that "in my way I have convers'd with tyrians and troyans, high and low; and all to a man consider your exaltation as the triumph of merit and vertu; your speech, which could not easely be heard in the room of the Senate, is making great noise and many conversions without doors." [16]

Not every Federalist, however, was placated. Hamilton, to whom Jefferson's speech ought to have been a triumphant vindication of his earlier diagnosis, nevertheless muttered gloomily in his retreat that nothing but ruin would develop and serious commotions.[17] And Theodore Dwight, the great Calvinist divine, minced no words in a warning oration at New Haven.

"The great object of Jacobinism," he thundered, "both in its political and moral revolution, is to destroy every trace of civilization in the world, and to force mankind back into a savage state.... We have now reached the consummation of democratic blessedness. We have a country governed by blockheads and knaves; the ties of marriage with all its felicities are severed and destroyed; our wives and daughters are thrown into the stews; our children are cast into the world from the breast and forgotten; filial piety is extinguished, and our surnames, the only mark of distinction among families, are abolished. Can the imagination paint anything more dreadful on this side hell?"[18] It was indeed fortunate for his audience that Dr. Dwight's imagination faltered at this point.

But Jefferson had anticipated that he would never win over the die-hard leaders of Federalism, particularly those who were gentlemen of the cloth. There would be, he recognized, eternal war between himself and the clergy. He hated what he called their obscurantism, and they despised what they termed his atheistic infidelity. Between such antagonists there could be no quarter. "The Eastern States," wrote Jefferson, "will be the last to come over [to republicanism], on account of the dominion of the clergy, who had got a smell of union between Church and State, and began to indulge reveries which can never be realized in the present state of science."[19]

On the other hand, the reception of the Inaugural by the Republicans was mixed. There were those who were taken aback. Had they fought the good fight and won their resounding victory merely to be told that there was little difference between Federalism and Republicanism? Had they sustained persecution and abuse for the sake of extending the hand of comradeship to their persecutors? Were the Federalists snug in office to remain there while faithful Republicans, parched with years of deprivation, had their thirst for public funds unslaked? These were the murmurings that shortly rose to audible growls and angry shouts.

In the meantime they were muted, though keen students of the popular mind like Monroe could detect their presence. From Richmond he voiced a warning. Though the speech had been approved in Virginia, "still there are dangers in yr. way which it is necessary to shun." The Federalists, in power for twelve long years, had abused their trust, and the people had driven them out. "Honest" Federalists had deserted their leaders and become converted. But there was the rub. For many of the converts held public offices or panted for it. Certainly, Monroe avowed, "these new converts should be cherished, but it should be done with care so as not to wound the feelings of those who have deserv'd better of their country

& of mankind. I am persuaded that any marked attention from you as yet, by which I mean advancement to office, of any of these persons, would be impolitick as it might lessen the confidence of the republicans in your administration." [20]

Monroe's plain-spoken warning gave Jefferson due notice that the plan he had thought to adopt in apportioning offices so as to attach as many erstwhile Federalists as possible to his policies was going to run into trouble with the members of his own party. He had hoped, by giving vacant offices only to Republicans, and permitting Federal officeholders to remain, that he would be able to wean the latter from their die-hard leaders. Some dismissals, he acknowledged, had to be made, but "they must be as few as possible, done gradually, and bottomed on some malversation or inherent disqualification." [21]

The more immediate problem before Jefferson, however, was to fill certain offices of which there would be no question that they belonged wholly to the Republicans. These were the Cabinet positions. Pending his own appointments, he had asked Adams's Cabinet to remain temporarily, and they had agreed.

There were now five Departments—a Secretary of Navy had been added to the State, Treasury, War and Attorney General of earlier days. Jefferson, as a former Cabinet officer himself, was keenly aware of the necessity of obtaining first-rate men who, at the same time, could work harmoniously together and be in essential agreement on the fundamental policies of the Administration. He wished for no recurrence of the guerilla warfare that had existed between Hamilton and himself; and certainly he did not want men who would acknowledge an outsider as their leader, as had happened in Adams's Cabinet.

As soon, therefore, as he had known that he was elected, he tried to pick his men. It was not as easy as he had thought.

For the most important post—the State Department—there was no hesitation. That place had been earmarked for James Madison; he was nominated and confirmed by the Senate. But it would be some time before Madison could arrive at Washington to assume his new duties.

For the Treasury, there was similarly but one man fitted in all respects for the job—that was Albert Gallatin. He had been the only one in Congress who could untangle the maze of Hamiltonian finances and find the soft spots for the Republicans to attack. It was feared, though, that the Senate might refuse to confirm him, and it was decided not to place his name in nomination until the next session of Congress; though in the meantime, he would discharge the duties of the Treasury on a temporary basis. Yet even here, Gallatin insisted on time to return to Pennsylvania, wind up his affairs, and move his family to Washington.

Nor did he have any trouble with the office of Attorney General. That went to a New Englander, Levi Lincoln, a Massachusetts lawyer who had recently been elected to Congress. Lincoln also doubled as Secretary of State until Madison arrived.

The War Department went to Henry Dearborn of Maine; while Samuel Dexter, the Secretary of Treasury under Adams, expressed his willingness to stay on until Gallatin completed his personal arrangements and appeared in Washington.

But the Secretary of Navy proved the most difficult of all to find. It was a comparatively new post and one that went counter to every Republican principle. For the position had been erected to take care of an enlarged navy, and it was Republican dogma that an enlarged navy had but one purpose—to fight a naval war with France in defense of New England's commercial interests. Jefferson had forgotten by this time his earlier insistence on a navy—but that had been to harry the Barbary pirates and force England to respect American rights.

He first offered the post to Robert R. Livingston, Chancellor of New York, after Livingston had turned down the Ministry to France. But the New Yorker, interested though he was in steam navigation and a co-worker with Robert Fulton, refused this post also. Jefferson next tried General Samuel Smith of Maryland, begging him to accept, since there were few Republicans—and he was one—who had any knowledge of naval matters.[22] Smith's title of General—though official enough—did not presuppose any actual knowledge of army tactics. As for his naval knowledge, that came merely from his career as a merchant in Baltimore. But he had been in Congress, and had helped lead the Republican forces.

Smith, in spite of the doubtful compliment, rejected the bid and Jefferson turned in despair first to John Langdon of New Hampshire, and then to William Jones of Philadelphia. But it seemed that no one wanted the unloved post; and Jefferson, now thoroughly desperate, offered it again to Smith. He was willing, if Smith would only agree to take it at some future date, to make a complicated series of temporary appointments in the interim.[23]

According to a Congressional enactment, certain ships of the little navy were supposed to be sold, others laid up and still others equipped for sea; and Jefferson was at a complete loss what the next steps were. "As to what is to be done," he confessed to Smith, "when everything shall be disposed of according to law . . . oppresses me by night & by day: for I do not see my way out of the difficulty. It is the department I understand the least, & therefore need a person whose compleat competence will justify the most entire confidence & resignation." That person, obviously, was Smith.[24]

Smith yielded to this final plea, especially since Benjamin Stoddert, the holdover from the previous administration, had now decided to resign. But he made it clear that he would fill the post only until another Secretary could be found. His own brother, Robert Smith, a lawyer who had no qualifications whatever, at length graciously consented to relieve the general on July 15th. But Jefferson, who had spent the month of April at

Monticello, was only too happy to get his administration moving somehow, in the hope that later on it would pick up speed and smoothness of operation.

The Cabinet, as finally chosen, was a mixed one. It had two top-notch men in the most important posts—Madison in the State Department, and Gallatin in the Treasury. These two could compare in some degree with the two stalwarts of Washington's administration—Jefferson and Hamilton. Lincoln was a good lawyer, though not as well known as Edmund Randolph had been. Dearborn was a good business man, if not particularly strong for his post in the War Department; but certainly he could fill it at least as well as his predecessor, General Knox. Jefferson trusted him; though, when Dearborn during Madison's term was faced with the problems of the War of 1812, his former chief turned on him with excoriating language. Robert Smith was the weakest link; but then Jefferson's interest in the Navy was at a low ebb. His final appointment—the post of private secretary to himself—went to Lt. Meriwether Lewis, a young Virginia neighbor who was now on duty in Gen. James Wilkinson's command.[25]

Thus armed and accoutered, Jefferson returned from Monticello on April 29th to assume his duties of President of the United States, and to attempt to steer the ship of state on the new course he intended.

There were a good many problems awaiting his consideration. The first—and the one that was to plague him the most—was the question of what to do with the incumbent officeholders. The Federalists insisted that they had struck a bargain with him whereby none of them in purely administrative—as against executive and policy-making—positions should be ousted. Jefferson denied he had entered into any bargain, but had merely replied to a query concerning a specific case—that of Allan McLane of Delaware in the Customs.

Jefferson made his position clear in letters to his two sons-in-law. To Thomas Mann Randolph he declared that "a few removals from office will be indispensable. They will be chiefly for real mal-conduct, & mostly in the offices connected with the administration of justice. I shall do as little in that way as possible. This may occasion some outcry; but it must be met." [26]

To John W. Eppes he posed the problem more carefully. "That all former officers should be removed, no man thinks; that some should, all agree. But no two draw the same line. Mr. Adams's last appointments, made just as he was going out of office, are treated by me as nullities (except the judges). I appoint others instead of them generally. Marshals & attorneys who have packed juries or committed other legal oppression on our citizens are under a course of removal. Officers in every line who have been guilty of misconduct & abuse of office, will be removed. But for mere difference of principle, I am not disposed to disturb any man. This is exactly what we have complained of in the former administration." [27]

This was a reasonable, yet cautious course. Certainly those who had been guilty of maladministration and oppression should be dismissed from office. The difficulty consisted, however, in deciding who came under that heading. To the Republicans, every marshal and federal attorney who had had anything to do with the prosecution of the cases under the Sedition Act, was manifestly guilty of such practices. The federal judges whom Adams had appointed under the terms of the Judiciary Law could not be touched; but all other appointments which he had made during the period after he knew he had been defeated for re-election, were anathema to the Republicans.

Jefferson rightly felt that, aside from a few, they had not been made in the regular and ordinary course of administration, but had been intended to pack the federal government with party officeholders against his own entry into office. On these he was adamant. Furthermore, something had to be done for the Republicans who had been excluded from office during the final days of Washington and all through the term of Adams. "They have a reasonable claim to vacancies," he declared, "till they occupy their due share. My hope however," he added, "is that the distinction will be soon lost, or at most that it will be only of republican & monarchist." [28] Thus early, in February, even before taking office, did he announce the famous doctrine that to the victor belongs at least half the spoils.

John Adams, who had ungraciously quit Washington at dawn to avoid seeing his rival installed in office, now, under the stress of personal tragedy, sought to make amends. One of his sons had drowned at sea under mysterious circumstances, and he wrote Jefferson about it. "It is not possible," he said, alluding to the fact that Jefferson had no son, "that any thing of the kind should happen to you, and I sincerely wish you may never experience any thing in any degree resembling it." Massachusetts, he added, "is in a State of perfect Tranquility, and I see nothing to obscure your prospect of a quiet and prosperous Administration, which I heartily wish you." [29]

The olive branch thus held out was seemingly ignored by Jefferson. At least there is no evidence of a reply. And the chance of reconciliation was definitely aborted when Adams's son, young John Quincy Adams, with whom Jefferson had been friendly enough in Europe, was ousted from one of those "midnight" appointments and a good Republican installed in his place. Jefferson was always to avow vigorously that he had not known of it; but Abigail Adams never forgave him for it, and John took many, many years to overcome his sense of wrong.

With grim determination, Jefferson set about the tedious task of weeding out the "midnight" appointments. He carefully defined them as those which had been "made by mr Adams *after* Dec. 12. 1800. when the event of the S. C. election which decided the Presidential election was known at Washington and until Midnight of Mar. 3. 1801." These were to be "considered as Null." [30]

He drew up several lists of such appointees, dividing them into those who had already received their signed commissions and those who had not. Against each name he placed some personal comment, and the name of his replacement. They were chiefly United States attorneys, marshals, surveyors, collectors, supervisors, port officers and commissioners of loans. John Quincy Adams had come under the last category. Against the name of the United States Attorney in Vermont, for example, Jefferson entered the damning comment that he had been "the oppressor of Lyon," the Vermont Congressman whose trial and conviction under the Sedition Act had been the most notorious of all. Harrison of New York was dismissed as "a revolutionary refugee" or Tory; and the post of Attorney given instead to Edward Livingston, who had done yeoman service for Jefferson during the fateful balloting in Congress. In New Jersey, Jefferson reminded himself to "turn out the Tory collector, an atrocious appointment"; and the Maine marshal was "to be removed by and by, a very violent & influential & industrious fed. put in not very fairly."

The first list which Jefferson drew up after coming into the Presidency ended with the comment: "The above 24. cases are the whole of the removals which have been made in order to give some participation in office to the Republicans, previous to the close of the session of Congress." Another eight had been removed for cause: "malversation," nonattendance to duty, drink, delinquency in accounts, "profligacy" and "brutal & odious deportment generally." [31]

The matter still bothered him in 1803, and he made up a second and retrospective list. From June 5, 1801, until May 10, 1803, he asserted, he had removed only 14 officeholders in order to replace them by deserving Republicans; and 12 of them were for cause, while only two were for being what he called "a revolutionary Tory." [32]

In pursuance of his course, Jefferson sent a general circular to all of the "midnight" appointees:

SIR,

The late President, mr Adams, having not long before his retirement from office, made several appointments to *civil* offices, holden *during the will* of the President, when so restricted in time as not to admit sufficient enquiry & consideration, the present President deems it proper that those appointments should be a subject of reconsideration & further enquiry. He considers it as of palpable justice that the officers who are to begin their course as agents of his administration should be persons on whom he has personal reliance for a faithful execution of his views. You will therefore be pleased to consider the appointment you have received as if never made, of which this early notice is given to prevent any derangements which that appointment might produce.[33]

The Judiciary Act, approved in haste by the outgoing Congress on February 13, 1801, was the great bone that stuck in the Republican craw. For, by adding a substantial number of federal judges to those already established, the Federalists sought to provide a secure refuge for many of their adherents in a department of government that, under the Constitution, might prove an adequate counterbalance to any radical moves by the Republicans in Congress and the Executive. Since such appointments were for life, nothing could be done to dislodge them.

Nothing was calculated to make Jefferson more furious. His eyes were already opened to the power of the Judiciary, and he sought ways and means to blast out this last intrenchment of the Federalists. Adams had filled every last office available, including forty-two Justices of the Peace for five-year terms in the District of Columbia. Many of these, however, had been appointed so late that they had not had time to take their oath of office before Adams's term expired. Even though they had been confirmed by the Senate in a last-minute sweep on March 3rd, their commissions still reposed on the table of the Secretary of State when Jefferson moved in. These he treated as null and void, and thrust them unceremoniously from the public trough. As a result of his direct action, a suit came later before the Supreme Court which gave John Marshall, similarly shifted to the Chief Justiceship in the final moment, a chance to lay down memorable law. Of this famous case of Marbury v. Madison there will be more to say.

In addition, Jefferson bent his best energies to securing a repealer of the Judiciary Act; and he was happy to put his signature to that repealer when it came to his desk on March 8, 1802.

Yet, in spite of these direct actions, and stern circulars, Jefferson was unable to satisfy his own followers. The removals were pitifully few, and the mouths to be fed many and ardent. Jefferson knew that he was offending many of his friends by refusing to make a clean sweep and, as he admitted to his old friend Rush, "that torrent has been pressing me heavily, & will require all my force to bear up against; but my maxim is '*fiat justitia, ruat coelum.*'"[34] This was noble and magnificent, but before the heavens actually fell, Jefferson was forced to reconsider his position.

CHAPTER 48

To the Victor the Spoils

JEFFERSON had barely seated himself in his office when the Republican clamor for the political fleshpots rose to overwhelming proportions. Some importunity came from Delaware, particularly at the seemingly inexplicable retention in office of Allan McLane. How could the faithful be expected to know that Jefferson had assured Congressman Bayard that McLane would not be disturbed? New Jersey similarly resented the fact that so many good Federalists remained snug in their stations. In Pennsylvania, Governor McKean was doing his own house cleaning; but in the process stirred up a factional fight among the victors. New York posed the biggest headache of all; for the Republican party there was split into three irreconcilable groups who hated one another more than they hated the defeated Federalists. These were the Clintonians, the powerful middle group of the Livingstons, and the followers of Burr. Here, for reasons which will be made clear later, Jefferson was determined to yield but little to the pressure for removals, and to favor two of the groups against the third. Only in Connecticut did he consider the local situation to require a general sweep of all Federalists. "Their legislature now sitting are removing every republican even from the commissions of the peace and the lowest offices. There then we will retaliate," he remarked grimly.[1]

The opportunity came very soon. David Austin, the Collector of New Haven, had died in the waning days of Adams's administration. The outgoing President promptly appointed one Elizur Goodrich, a zealous Federalist, in his place. The Republicans called on Jefferson to rectify the injustice; and he obliged by removing Goodrich and replacing him with Samuel Bishop, an equally zealous Republican.

But Bishop was old—seventy-seven, in fact—feeble in mind and body, and possessed of no qualifications for the position that the merchants of New Haven could discern. Whereupon they drafted a Remonstrance, addressed to Jefferson, in which they used strong language about the removal of Goodrich and the elevation of the incompetent Bishop. In the course of their argument, they pointed to the assurances contained in Jefferson's Inaugural that there would be no removals on political grounds alone, and inquired whether those assurances had been meant to be observed.

The New Haven Remonstrance gave Jefferson the opportunity for which he had been eagerly waiting. The soothing phrases of the Inaugural had, on the one hand, aroused certain Federalist hopes that could not possibly be met; and on the other, created dismay and dissension in the Republican ranks. The whole unfortunate situation was due to a misconception of what he actually meant—at least, so Jefferson now felt—and he welcomed the chance to issue a statement that would set them both right, and placate his own party.[2]

The time, indeed, was almost overripe. Levi Lincoln, his Attorney General, was reporting from Massachusetts that he had found the subject of removals "every where the most common political topic of conversation, connected with that of appointments; vague reports and individual clamours had clothed the subject with many false circumstances, & ascribed to it principles & motives which never existed."[3]

The situation had become so bad, indeed, that Jefferson was compelled to write to Republican leaders in Delaware and Pennsylvania imploring them to stop the bickerings among the rank and file over removals and appointments. "How can federalists coalesce with those," he asked plaintively, "who will not coalesce with each other?"[4]

So that Jefferson's reply to the merchants of New Haven was meant not only for them, but for the country at large. It was at once an interpretation of the Inaugural and a statement of policy for the future.

He seized upon the language of the protest "that a change in the administration must produce a change in the subordinate officers" to make his own point clear. The words of his Inaugural had been misconstrued, he declared, into assurances that there would be no removals. During the previous administration, had not every Republican been excluded from office? "Was it to be imagined that this monopoly of office was still to be continued in the hands of the minority?" Has the majority no right to a proportionate share? And, "if a due participation of office is a matter of right, how are vacancies to be obtained? Those by death are few; by resignation, none. Can any other mode than that of removal be proposed? This is a painful office; but it is made my duty, and I meet it as such." Once, however, a just proportion was obtained, Jefferson would "return with joy to that state of things, when the only questions concerning a candidate shall be, is he honest? Is he capable? Is he faithful to the Constitution?"[5]

Though the Federalists jeered at both the questions Jefferson thus put, and the answers he gave himself, the reply managed to soothe some of the injured feelings of the Republicans, though most would have preferred no nonsense about "due participation" and would have been more happy had the President thrown all "the rascals" out, and divided the spoils solely among the faithful.

In New York, moreover, the tangled situation could not be unwound by mere words. There the scramble for offices exceeded all bounds; and the internecine quarrel had burst into the open.

Aaron Burr felt, with some justice, that his immense contribution to the ultimate national victory entitled him to a degree of patronage in New York. His position as Vice-President could only add to his claims. He had seen the clan of Livingstons well rewarded—Edward Livingston had been appointed United States District Attorney for New York, and the Chancellor Robert R. Livingston had been given the refusal of the embassy to France and a seat in the Cabinet. Therefore, in conjunction with a group of New York senators and representatives, Burr made up a list which included four of his own followers as well as members of the other factions.[6] On the whole, it was a moderate list; and the candidates whom Burr personally offered were surprisingly few in number.

But Jefferson was by now determined to destroy Burr. He had been thankful enough to him when the results of the New York election were announced; and he had considered Burr's conduct during the first days of the electoral struggle in Congress as "honorable and decisive." [7] Then, as the struggle increased in intensity, he harkened to the inevitable gossip and the rumors, and came finally to the conclusion that Burr's conduct was Machiavellian rather than honorable, and that secretly he was seeking the presidential prize for himself.

He was now saddled with Burr as Vice-President, but he had no intention of increasing his power by granting him patronage rights. He had not consulted Burr in making his Cabinet appointments, and word came to him that Burr had expressed resentment over the slight. Worse, Monroe reported a conversation between Burr and Henry Lee, now one of Jefferson's bitterest enemies. Lee had slyly told Burr that had he "come forward & pursued the views of those who supported him in the House of Representatives [the Federalists] he might have produc'd a different state of things." [8]

The very thought that such an idea, deftly insinuated, might cause Burr to rectify the "error" in the future, made it only the more imperative to cripple his power to do harm. Jefferson had no love for the Clintons—the aging Governor and his young, ambitious and unscrupulous nephew, De Witt Clinton. But they were far less dangerous on the national scene to Jefferson and his Virginia friends than Burr. Accordingly, he sent a copy of Burr's patronage list to Governor Clinton. Objections had been raised to Burr's choices, he wrote, though by whom he did not say. Since he, Jefferson, was not acquainted with the New York candidates and therefore forced to rely on the opinions of others, "there is no one whose opinion would command with me greater respect than yours." Would Clinton advise him accordingly, with the assurance that his information would be treated as confidential? [9]

Clinton was only too happy to oblige; and as a result, Burr found himself in the embarrassing position of not being able to reward his faithful followers, while at the same time noting that the requests of the Clintons and the Livingstons were being honored to the hilt.

One appointment in particular, Burr had set his heart on obtaining—the post of Supervisor for his personal lieutenant, Matthew L. Davis. He wrote angrily to Albert Gallatin, with whom he was friendly: "Strange reports are here in circulation respecting secret machinations against Davis. . . . The opposition to him, if any, must proceed from improper motives, as no man dare openly avow an opinion hostile to the measure." [10] The curious thing was that the Vice-President of the United States felt compelled to seek an intermediary to gain the ear of the President.

Gallatin did his best; but it was not enough. Davis, sick at long deferment, finally journeyed to Monticello to see Jefferson himself. Gallatin tried to dissuade him; but failing, gave him a letter to present to the vacationing President. The Secretary of Treasury spoke frankly of his disgust with "the general spirit of persecution which, in that State particularly, disgraces our cause and sinks us on a level with our predecessors." [11] For De Witt Clinton, in control of the appointive power, had labored under no such scruples as had actuated Jefferson on the national scene. The Federalists were rooted out ruthlessly, no matter how inoffensive or competent, and their places filled with Clintonians only. Burrites need not apply.

As soon, however, as Davis was on his way, Gallatin wrote another letter to Jefferson that laid bare the whole texture of the treatment accorded to Burr. In remarkably plain language, he demanded to know if it was the intention of the Republicans to support Burr again for the Vice-Presidency at the next election; and to consider him as Jefferson's successor when the latter retired. After a discussion of the possibilities, he shifted to the local situation in New York. He personally disliked supporting the Clintonians and the Livingstons against Burr, who, after all, had the support of the majority of the Republicans. And he warned Jefferson that should Davis be turned down, Burr would consider it a declaration of war.[12]

But Jefferson disregarded his Secretary of Treasury's advice. He knew that through Burr's own error, the Clintons had gained control of the state machinery and had hamstrung Burr's ability to do him harm. He knew also that a leader without patronage was bound to find his followers deserting to those who could take care of their justifiable claims. He never answered Gallatin's private letter—Jefferson always feared the mails. To the public one he merely said: "Mr. Davis is now with me. He has not opened himself. When he does, I shall inform him that nothing is decided nor can be till we get together at Washington." [13] Davis might just as well have saved himself the long and weary pilgrimage to Monticello.

When Burr, in final desperation, addressed himself directly to Jefferson, the latter deigned to answer only the last of three letters. It was chilling in its formality. "These letters all relating to office," declared Jefferson with amazing sangfroid, "fall within the general rule . . . of not answering letters on office specifically, but leaving the answer to be found in what is done or not done on them." [14] It must have been apparent to a duller wit than Burr's that he had nothing further to expect from Jefferson or from the Republican party as long as he was in control.

One of the major issues of the campaign had been the Alien and Sedition Acts. Kentucky had declared them a nullity, and Virginia had gone almost as far. Several good Republicans were languishing in jail, and the threat of prosecution still hung formidably over the heads of others. It was necessary, therefore, pending Congressional action, for Jefferson to exercise his presidential powers in order to extricate the hapless victims.

The first of these was the notorious Callender. Incarcerated in the Richmond jail, he had bombarded Jefferson with frantic pleas even before the latter's induction into office. His term was shortly up, but he could not quit the jail until a fine of $200 had been paid. Would Jefferson remit the fine? [15]

Confusion arose. Jefferson remitted the unexpired sentence, but *not* the fine, which Callender had in the meantime paid. The liberated editor was furious. He complained to the heavens and to all who would listen that Jefferson had faithfully promised the return of the money. "I now begin to know what Ingratitude is," he cried to Madison, and hinted at reprisals. Did Jefferson pause to reflect "how his numerous and implacable enemies would exult in being masters of this piece of small history?" He demanded a *quid pro quo*—the postmastership of Richmond; and ended with an overt threat: "And surely, sir, many syllogisms cannot be necessary to convince Mr. Jefferson that, putting feelings and principles out of the question, it is not proper for him to create a quarrel with me." [16]

In a measure, Callender was right. Jefferson had promised to remit the fine, and had actually entered a notation to do so in his *Anas*.[17] But something went wrong, and Samuel Smith had written Callender somewhat peremptorily that the fine had *not* been remitted.[18]

Jefferson now made a mistake. Knowing of Callender's threats, he decided to raise privately the amount of the fine, and gave his private secretary, Meriwether Lewis, the sum of $50 to turn over to the disgruntled editor. In his account book he listed it as "charity." [19] Thereby he laid himself open to the implication that he had yielded to blackmail. Callender, who had come to Washington, used exactly that language to Jefferson's emissary. He intimated "that he was in possession of things which he could and would make use of in a certain case: that he received the 50.D. not as a charity but a due, in fact as hush money; that I knew what he expected, viz. a certain office, and more to this effect." When Lewis reported the conversation to Jefferson, the latter determined to break off completely with Callender. He had treated him, he told Monroe somewhat disingenuously, "as a man of genius suffering from persecution, and not as a writer in our politics. It is long since I wished he would cease writing on them, as doing more harm than good." [20] This, of course, does not jibe with the facts of Jefferson's gifts and subscriptions to Callender's reckless writings during the recent campaign.

Monroe had a sharper eye to the possibilities than his friend. He expressed concern that Jefferson had given the editor any money, and advised that it would be well "to get all letters however unimportant from him. Meriwether Jones [a mutual friend] is or will be by the time this reaches you at Washington. He has that ascendancy over the wretch to make him do what is right, and he will be happy to do it for you. Confide in him without reserve as a man of honor.... Your resolution to terminate all communication with him is wise, yet it will be well to prevent even a serpent doing one an injury." [21]

It has usually been considered that Callender's threats were based merely on an exposure of Jefferson's connection with him politically. But the recent discovery of the so-called "Walker Correspondence" throws a more sinister light on his reference to "a certain case." It is now obvious that what Callender was referring to was no mere political secret, but a private one that touched Jefferson's personal honor to the quick. It is also obvious that Monroe knew something of the matter as well, since his exhortation to Jefferson to confide in Meriwether Jones as "a man of honor" would ordinarily be out of place in mere political matters. And, in fact, Callender made good on his threat eventually, as will be shown in its proper setting.

This interpretation is buttressed by intermediate events in 1802. Callender published in a Richmond paper a purely *political* attack on Jefferson, claiming that he had in fact been in the latter's employ as a writer in penning his scurrilous attacks on Washington and Adams. Jefferson expressed himself as "mortified at the base ingratitude" and its presentation of "human nature in a hideous form." He defended himself against the charge in a series of letters to Monroe; and the latter, with manifest relief, decided that Callender's attack was "a harmless thing" that ought not to be answered, since the answer might give the Federalists reason to believe that there were stronger motives behind Jefferson's "charitable" gifts.[22]

The Federalists, nevertheless, did so suspect; and Callender was to furnish them secretly with the unsavory Walker story to break in the public press with most unfortunate results.

Another Republican editor who had fallen afoul of the Sedition Act and whom Jefferson tried to help proved almost as ungrateful as Callender. This was William Duane, who had taken over the Philadelphia *Aurora* on Bache's death and had promptly been subjected to several indictments and a term in jail for contempt in connection with his attacks on Adams and the Government.

Duane's situation, however, was complicated by the fact that he had been prosecuted not only under the Sedition Act, but by special order of the United States Senate; and Jefferson sought advice on the legal tangle from Robert R. Livingston, the former Chancellor of New York.

Avowing that his own legal knowledge was rusty after thirty years, Jefferson put two questions to him. Under the Constitutional provision of freedom of the press, could the printing of the *truth* be considered a libel, no matter what the common law of England held? Could not the President pardon a Senate contempt conviction, as well as all other offenses with the exception of impeachments? [23]

He had already discontinued all prosecutions against Duane under the Sedition Law, but he hesitated to act in the case of the Senate contempt proceedings; and finally left that to die of its own weight.[24]

Duane, penniless, came to Washington seeking government patronage for a national newspaper he intended to publish but, to his extreme mortification, found the field already pre-empted by Samuel Harrison Smith's *National Intelligencer.* He thereupon set up a clamor to Jefferson of ingratitude, coupled with demands for some office that might compensate him for his trials and tribulations. Jefferson and Gallatin helped him open a printing and stationer's establishment; but the business was not successful, and he later turned on Gallatin, Madison and Monroe, though maintaining an uneasy relationship with Jefferson.

From France also came a call for help. Tom Paine, as only too many other radicals, had found France not the heaven that had been contemplated, and cast longing eyes across the Atlantic. On October 1, 1800, he had written to Jefferson, then Vice-President, wondering if any American frigate might perchance put into a French port which would offer him passage back to the United States.[25]

By the time Jefferson received the request and succeeding letters from Paine, he was already installed as President. He accordingly wrote back cordially that the American warship *Maryland* had been given orders to take Paine on board, if he were ready to sail when the ship did. "I am in hopes," he added, "you will find us returned generally to sentiments worthy of former times. In these it will be your glory to have steadily laboured and with as much effect as any man living." [26]

But the exchange leaked out, and the unreconstructed Federalists promptly raised the cry that Jefferson had sent the warship to France solely to pick up that anarchical atheist, Tom Paine. The hubbub penetrated to France, and Paine decided it was wise to decline; coming over later in more modest fashion and landing in Baltimore on October 30, 1802.[27]

A good many problems faced Jefferson at the beginning of his administration, though fortunately the question of war and peace had been satisfactorily terminated before he took up the duties of his office. There were other great advantages that bespoke optimism for the future. Congress was overwhelmingly Republican in the House, and safely so in the Senate. Though there were schisms in the ranks in New York and Pennsylvania, there was nothing as yet to threaten Jefferson's leadership either on the national or local scene. He had two staunch and able supporters in the most vital Cabinet positions—State and Treasury; and the Federalists were still routed and disorganized from their recent defeat.

Only the die-hard ministers of New England continued their pulpit attacks against the "atheist" in office, and gloomily, though with a certain joy, prophesied dire and terrible things for a country subject to such a leader. Jefferson returned their hatred with cordial interest. Connecticut seemed their particular locus; and Jefferson, while optimistic that most of New England would eventually turn Republican, thought that Connecticut presented a special case. He told Pierpont Edwards of that state that "the nature of your government being a subordination of the civil to the Ecclesiastical power, I consider it as desperate for long years to come. Their steady habits exclude the advances of information & they seem exactly where they were when they separated from the Saints of Oliver Cromwell. And there your clergy will always keep them if they can. You will follow the bark of liberty only by the help of a tow-rope." [28]

To the English-born Joseph Priestley, now come to the United States, who had similarly felt the stings of the clergy, he sent congratulations on his recovery from a long illness and heartening words. "What an effort, my dear Sir, of bigotry in Politics & Religion have we gone through!" he exclaimed. "The barbarians really flattered themselves they should be able to bring back the times of Vandalism, when ignorance put everything into the hands of power & priestcraft. All advances in science were proscribed as innovations. They pretended to praise and encourage education, but it was to be the education of our ancestors.... This was the real ground of all the attacks on you. Those who live by mystery & *charlatanerie*, fearing you would render them useless by simplifying the Christian philosophy,—the most sublime & benevolent, but most perverted system that ever shone on man,—endeavored to crush your well-earnt & well-deserved fame. But it was the Lilliputians upon Gulliver." [29] Jefferson was thinking of himself as well as Priestley when he penned this exordium.

The libels of the clergy, however, were but pinpricks to some others that were industriously circulated concerning Jefferson. One such roused him to the extremes of indignation. Madison had brought his recent bride, the lively and charming Dolly Madison, to Washington with him. Space was at a premium in the congested quarter around the Capitol, and Jefferson graciously put them up at the President's House until, toward the end of May, they were able to set up housekeeping in a residence outside the town proper. But a rumor spread through Virginia that Jefferson's interest in boarding them had stemmed from an undue familiarity with Dolly. Who it was that circulated the slander is not known, though suspicion might well point to Callender, the source and fount of many a malignant canard for some years to come. Jefferson repelled the base allegation with dignity: "I thought my age & ordinary demeanor would have prevented any suggestions in that form, from the improbability of their obtaining belief . . ." he wrote his informant. "I believe all the persons concerned are too conscious of innocence to feel the burden." [30]

But dignified silence did not save him from an even more malignant attack; this time openly in the Federalist press. There appeared in *The Portfolio*, supposedly dedicated to literature and belles-lettres, "A SONG, supposed to have been written by the SAGE OF MONTICELLO," to be sung to the tune of Yankee Doodle. Nothing quite so vile was ever to appear in print:

Of all the damsels on the green,
On mountain, or in valley,
A lass so luscious ne'er was seen
As Monticellian Sally.

Yankee doodle, who's the noodle?
What wife were half so handy?
To breed a flock, of slaves for stock,
A blackamoor's the dandy. . . .

When press'd by load of state affairs,
I seek to sport and dally,
The sweetest solace of my cares
Is in the lap of Sally.

Yankee doodle, (etc.) . . .

What though she by the glands secretes;
Must I stand shil-I-shall-I?
Tuck'd up between a pair of sheets
There's no perfume like Sally.

Yankee doodle, (etc.) [31]

Albert Gallatin was the first member of the Cabinet to start on his duties, though from a distance. On March 14, 1801, from Philadelphia, Gallatin sent his chief what he called some rough sketches of the financial situation. He was well qualified for the office, having been the brains of the Republican party in Congress in the interminable struggles with Hamilton. His survey of the situation, however, paid unwilling homage to the financial structure of that great antagonist. For he estimated, though with some reservations, that the fiscal year would show a net surplus of $2,000,000 that could be applied to the reduction of the public debt. Since the Republican party, however, had made a campaign issue of the repeal of the internal duties, such as the excise on whisky, he proposed substantial cuts in the army and navy to meet the loss of revenue involved.[32] Thereby several Republican birds would be killed with one shot—the unpopular excise could safely be abolished, the Federalist navy (in spite of Jefferson's alleged pledge to Bayard) reduced, and government expenditures cut. It is noteworthy, though, that in spite of their major thesis that the Bank of the United States was unconstitutional and a monarchical haven, nothing was suggested by Gallatin or proposed by Jefferson to hamstring its powers or curtail its functions.

Jefferson agreed with Gallatin on all points, particularly that the navy must be reduced in size; though Benjamin Stoddert, the holdover in the Navy Department, was understandably not happy over the prospect. He ordered all of the naval vessels sold with the exception of the thirteen frigates established by Congressional enactment, and therefore temporarily at least untouchable. Seven of these he had brought to Washington, to be laid up in what modern parlance would call "mothballs." The expense of the fleet would thereby, he estimated, be reduced to about half a million annually; and he expected that sum to be met for 1801 by the proceeds from those that were to be sold.[33]

He did this in spite of the fact that Europe was still engaged in a desperate struggle, and that insults and prohibitions on American commerce continued. Nor did the fact that he had once insisted that a strong navy was the only hope for forcing the belligerent powers to treat the United States with respect disconcert him in the least. He had swung around once more to a wholly isolationist standpoint, and a retreat behind that Chinese wall he had once envisaged. Even when Dr. George Logan, who had made the journey to the French, now proposed our joining in an armed confederacy to repel interferences with commerce, Jefferson chided him for his "heresy." While agreeing in principle on "the necessity of restoring freedom to the ocean," he declared that "it ought to be the very first object of our pursuits to have nothing to do with the European interests and politics. Let them be free or slaves at will, navigators or agricultural, swallowed into one government or divided into a thousand, we have nothing to fear from them in any form. Our commerce," he added almost as an afterthought, "is so valuable to them that they will be glad to purchase it when the only price we ask is to do us justice."[34] Now that the Republicans were in power, he no longer feared that a failure of French arms in Europe would imperil the democratic experiment in America. And by this time he had lost his stubborn belief that the French Revolution meant the enfranchisement of all mankind. The image of Napoleon Bonaparte did not lend itself readily to the idea.

The subject of economy in government had become an overmastering passion with him. He looked everywhere for methods of reducing expense. "We are about to dismiss all the Marines," he told Thomas Mann Randolph, "except a number sufficient for the half dozen ships which Congress obliged us to keep armed; though three of them would have been quite enough. The summer will be pretty closely employed in procuring the information necessary to enable Congress to reduce the Government to a reasonable scale of expence. We are hunting out & abolishing multitudes of useless offices, striking off jobs &c &c. Never were such scenes of favoritism, dissipation of treasure, and disregard of legal appropriations seen.

Provided they [the previous administration] did not spend more than all the appropriations amounted to, they overspent some & neglected others without regard to the legislative will." [35]

Yet, while thus in effect reducing the navy to utter helplessness, he raged against the Barbary pirates and the British admiralty courts in confiscating American ships. "I am an enemy to all these douceurs, tributes & humiliations..." he exclaimed to Madison. "I know that nothing will stop the eternal increase of demands from these pirates but the presence of an armed force, and it will be more economical & more honorable to use the same means at once for suppressing their insolencies."

Similarly, he wanted a factual basis for "the enormities" of the British admiralty courts. "I am persuaded it must be the ground work of a demand on our part of stipulations from that country entirely novel in their nature, and which nothing but the disgrace of their proceedings can extort from them. But they are indispensably necessary for us. We are surely never more to submit to such ruinous degradations again." [36] Just how Jefferson expected to exert armed pressure on the Barbary Powers and force Great Britain to yield, when he had practically done away with the navy and the marine corps, he did not say.

Gallatin was busy reorganizing the Treasury Department in the interests of economy and centralization of power. He was particularly incensed at the laxity of the collectors of the internal revenue, and proposed a tightening of supervision over them. He also drafted a circular letter to the collectors, informing them that while appointments in the future would be made solely on the basis of merit, nevertheless they must not use their official positions to restrain or influence the political beliefs of others.[37]

Jefferson wholeheartedly approved of the proposed circular; in fact, he had intended to issue a proclamation to that effect, but Madison and he had finally agreed to hold it back until the public had had a chance to digest his reply to the New Haven remonstrants.[38]

Yet he and Gallatin did not quite see eye to eye on the root question of appointments. Gallatin advised caution, and hoped that only a few more removals were to be made.[39] Jefferson evaded this point, insisting that "we must be inflexible against appointing federalists till there be a due portion of republicans introduced into office. It gives just offence to those who have been excluded heretofore, to be still excluded by those who have been brought in to convert the system." While his New Haven letter gave mortal offense to the "Monarchical federalists," he was not worried about their reaction. He did fear, however, that it had raised unjustified hopes among "the *Sweeping* republicans." He hoped, nevertheless, that he would be able to placate them. While gathering "all the republican federalists possible" into the fold, "we must not, even for this object," he added significantly, "absolutely revolt our tried friends. It would be a poor maneuvre to exchange them now for new converts." [40]

But if both Jefferson and Gallatin wished to proceed cautiously, John

Taylor of Caroline, the great agrarian theorist, foresaw a revolution that would be radical and thoroughgoing. In rapturous, if rather vague language, he voiced his anticipation of great things from Jefferson; but at the same time tendered an unmistakable warning if the President did not live up to expectations.

"You are warm for some constitutional reform," he wrote the sceptical Wilson Cary Nicholas, "and yet you ask me, what can Mr. Jefferson do towards it? What can he not do? Has he complained of the power of the executive, in weak and passionate hands, to do evil; & can he deny its power, guided by consummate talents, to do good? . . . How often has Mr. J. contemplated in raptures the idea of a patriot king! Let him realize that idea, and not utterly astound the philosophers of the world, by the sight of the head of their body, at the head of a great nation, without doing any thing material for human happiness."[41]

But this vision of Taylor's has a family resemblance to Plato's philosopher-king, with all its authoritarian implications. Certainly it did not follow the usual republican doctrine of a weak executive, hedged with limitations; nor does his reference to Jefferson's "raptures" over the idea of a "patriot king" find confirmation anywhere else in the vast body of Jefferson's writings. It sounds more like the figment of Taylor's own superheated imagination.

CHAPTER 49

Making Haste Slowly

IT was May, 1801, before the roster of Jefferson's Cabinet was complete and in good working order. He made one more major appointment, outside the Cabinet—Gideon Granger of Connecticut as Postmaster General. Granger was very much the politician, and knew the New England situation thoroughly. He made many trips through the eastern states and consistently reported to Jefferson on men, personalities and political conditions. The idea that there is some inherent connection between carrying the mails and the management of political campaigns seems to be of ancient vintage.

It was Gallatin's special province to take care of financial affairs, and such was the recognition of his knowledge and skill in this difficult department that none of the others ventured suggestions to him on anything but leading principles. Foreign affairs, however, even though Madison was the titular head, was considered the department of government in which everyone had sufficient knowledge for his opinion to matter. Jefferson followed Washington's course in the handling of his Cabinet—he would lay before its members questions in writing for them to answer; and he sought as much as possible to follow the majority decision.

One of the first matters that engaged his attention in the foreign field was the renewed piratical activities of the Bashaw of Tripoli. He had strong and definite ideas on the proper method of treating with the Barbary Powers. Whatever caution he exercised in dealing with other Powers, this was one group against whom he advocated the most abrupt and forcible measures.

On May 15, 1801, he posed two questions to the newly assembled Cabinet: "Shall the squadron now at Norfolk be ordered to cruise in the Mediterranean?" and "What shall be the object of the cruise?" The very tenor of the questions indicated precisely what answers Jefferson expected.

While all agreed that the cruise should be made and that it would be manifestly directed against Tripoli, there was some divergence of opinion as to what the exact function of the belligerent gesture ought to be. Levi Lincoln thought the warships should be used to repel attacks on American shipping, but not to take the offensive. Gallatin agreed, hewing to the constitutional line that any other course would constitute war, which only Congress had the power to declare. Dearborn and Madison demanded that the purpose of the voyage be openly declared to the nation and the world

—the protection of our commerce with whatever force required to effectuate it.[1]

Accordingly, Madison wrote to William Eaton, the American Consul at Tunis, to apprise him of the course on which the government had determined. Three frigates and a sloop of war were sailing to the Mediterranean, under the command of Commodore Dale. If, by the time they arrived, Tripoli had already commenced hostilities, the squadron would go immediately into action to protect American commerce. Should Tunis and Algiers join Tripoli in depredations, their piratical craft were equally to be repelled and punished. "The present moment," Madison concluded, "is peculiarly favorable for the experiment, not only as it is a provision against an immediate danger, but as we are now at peace and amity with all the rest of the world, and as the force employed would, if at home, be at nearly the same expense, with less advantage to our mariners." [2]

The tiny squadron sailed on June 1st to reinforce the few ships already cruising the troubled waters. Jefferson was resolved that the piratical states must be confronted boldly. Tripoli, with whom the United States had a treaty, was now pretending that the money it had received had been merely for *making* peace at the time; it demanded more for *keeping* it. Algiers had a more legitimate claim. Under its treaty, we had engaged to pay them $30,000 a year. But the tribute was three years in arrears, and Jefferson, though convinced that "it is money thrown away," reluctantly obeyed the mandate of the law by sending one year's tribute in cash and one more in an equivalent amount of goods. "There is no end to the demand of these powers," he asserted angrily, "nor any security in their promises." He wanted Congress to decide as soon as possible on a course of action: whether to abandon the Mediterranean altogether, or to rotate cruises of fleets with other interested powers in those waters to put a stop to all depredations.[3] He would have much preferred the latter course, though how he was going to obtain concerted action from the European nations, in view of all his former unsuccessful attempts in that direction, is another matter.

Surprisingly enough, the little squadron of American vessels managed to do an effective job, and actually captured a Tripolitan cruiser in the process; but was compelled to release it because, as Jefferson later put it, Congress had not officially proclaimed a state of war.

Madison had made the statement in his letter to Eaton that we were "at peace and amity with all the rest of the world." This was not quite true; at peace we were, but not at amity.

At a time when Jefferson was cutting our diplomatic establishment abroad to the bone—in conformity with pre-election campaign promises—and discontinuing American representation in Holland, Portugal and Prussia, our relations with Great Britain, France and Spain followed the old monotonous routine. The same problems that had vexed the administrations of Washington and Adams were inherited by Jefferson. If open war was no longer directly in the offing, certainly the same materials that had threatened to touch it off in the past were still present.

With Spain there were the old questions of the navigation of the Mississippi and the acquisition of a port at its mouth, exacerbated by the more recent use of her ports by French privateers who sallied forth to raid American shipping and brought the captured vessels back for condemnation and sale.

But a new note now appeared in this ancient picture, though as yet only, so far as the United States was concerned, in the initial stage of rumor. Reports filtered through to Jefferson that a deal was pending, or had already been consummated, between Spain and France whereby some part of the Spanish possessions in America, including New Orleans and the mouth of the Mississippi, was to be transferred to France.[4] If this were so, it must be of the utmost importance to the United States, which had long looked with considerable apprehension on the possibility that, instead of a weak Spain, she might have a more powerful France or England directly on her western and southern borders.

Neither Jefferson nor Madison was as yet aware of the full picture, nor of the vast and incredible cession that was already in its final stages. As far back as 1798, in the arrogant heyday of the Directory, Talleyrand sought to recapture the old dominion of Louisiana, which France had ceded to Spain in 1763 as compensation for her losses to victorious England in the war just ended. "There are," he then remarked, "no other means of putting an end to the ambition of the Americans than that of shutting them up within the limits which Nature seems to have traced for them; but Spain is not in a condition to do this great work alone. She cannot, therefore, hasten too quickly to engage the aid of a preponderating Power, yielding to it a small part of her immense domains in order to preserve the rest."[5] It was only natural, of course, that Talleyrand should propose France as the sacrificial assumer of this white man's burden.

He failed in his great scheme at the moment; but one more powerful than he was now ready to take up the good work again—Napoleon Bonaparte.

The vague rumors of impending events made Jefferson uneasy. Besides alerting our representatives abroad, he confidentially advised William C. C. Claiborne, the newly appointed Governor of the Mississippi Territory, to be especially accommodating and even affectionate to the Spanish authorities in the adjacent Spanish possessions. It was best for our interests, he stated, that Spain continue to hold that country rather than France.[6]

But more immediate problems required attention. The mighty world struggle between Napoleonic France and England, flanked by her allies, was at its peak. As a neutral nation, the United States was being slowly ground between them. Barely was one issue determined, when another would rise to harry Jefferson and his Cabinet.

Jefferson, however, was spending the summer at Monticello; and had to handle the most delicate matters from that distant and secluded spot. Each year he fled the "two bilious months" of August and September from Washington, and he retorted to any possible grumbling over his absences by pointing to Adams's *eight* months of annual vacation.[7]

He had a measure of justification for his summer absences. The climate or waters of tidewater Washington had upset his system, and he suffered from a debilitating diarrhea that was to plague him for several years. Dr. Rush later prescribed for him on the basis of Jefferson's description of his symptoms. One item in the recommended treatment is of particular interest. Jefferson had made a practice of washing his feet in cold water every morning—no mention is made of other parts of the body; and Rush thought he was now too old for such Spartan measures, and suggested warm water instead.[8]

A treaty with France had been pending for some time which attempted to settle the matters of dispute between the two nations; notably on the question of neutral rights. But the undue delays of the French in ratifying led Jefferson to suspect that perhaps they wanted to obtain in it an express renunciation of the American demand for indemnities for the prior confiscation of her ships and cargoes.

William Vans Murray, a holdover from Adams's administration, was handling the negotiations. But Jefferson decided to replace him, and offered the post of Minister to France to Robert R. Livingston. The unexpected delay in ratification made Jefferson all the more anxious to send Livingston off at once, with detailed instructions.[9] He even thought that it might be better to let the proposed treaty lapse altogether. Such a consummation, he remarked, "will only begin the work of placing us clear of treaty with all nations."[10]

Jefferson never changed his original opinion that the ideal for the United States was to isolate herself from the rest of the world and steer clear of any treaties that might somehow involve her in European affairs. He stated his views on the future of the United States very forcibly to William Short. "Peace," he averred, "is our most important interest, and a recovery from debt. We feel ourselves strong, & daily growing stronger." The population of the country was increasing rapidly; and "if we can delay but for a few years the necessity of vindicating the laws of nature on the ocean, we shall be more sure of doing it with effect. The day is within my time as well as yours, when we may say by what laws other nations shall treat us on the sea. And we will say it. In the meantime, we wish to let every treaty drop off without renewal."[11]

There were two important questions to be considered in the meantime. One related to the old problem of admitting foreign prizes into American ports. The question was much simpler than it had been in Washington's administration, when the French treaty complicated matters and Genêt added to the complications. Robert Smith, who had taken over the Navy

Courtesy the New-York Historical Society, New York City

GENERAL JAMES WILKINSON

Mezzotint by Charles W. Peale

Courtesy the New-York Historical Society, New York City

AARON BURR

Painting by John Vanderlyn

from his brother, to whom Jefferson posed the question, agreed with his analysis of the situation. "I consider," wrote the President, "that we are free to recieve, or to refuse the prizes of both nations, & that our best policy will be to reject both: treating them with exact equality." [12]

But Gallatin interposed an unexpected objection to the second part of the thesis. "I do not understand," he wrote his chief with some asperity, "on what ground you think that we are free to exclude the prizes of both French & English. That it is our policy cannot be doubted; but it seems to me that we are prevented from pursuing it by our treaties with both nations." [13]

Jefferson patiently sent him a historical discussion of the doctrine he advocated. The treaties, he said, gave both nations the right to enter our ports with their prizes for limited purposes only, and to depart as speedily as possible *with* the prizes. Before the treaty with England, France had been permitted to sell her prizes in American ports as a favor, not as a right. Now, we were free even of that favor; and we ought to bar both in order "to throw difficulties in the way of the depredations committed on commerce, & chiefly our own commerce." [14] It cannot be said that Gallatin was satisfied with this explanation, but as a loyal subordinate he submitted to the President's judgment.

Livingston was scheduled to sail on the warship *Boston* as soon as it could be outfitted for departure. Jefferson drafted for him a careful set of instructions, of which his original memoranda display the texture of his thought with greater clarity than the final document. "When two nations chuse to go to war," he declared, "it should in no wise affect those who remain in the ordinary relations of social & moral intercourse with them & with one another. The rights then of commerce & navigation remain unaltered by the war of others." What were these rights of neutrals? "That a nation may avail itself of an opportunity of enlarging its commerce at all times, whether that opportunity occurs while others are at war, or in peace. That nothing is contraband in war more than in peace. That of course there can be no right of search. That free bottoms make free goods, because the bottom cannot be searched." It was time, he insisted, that prior usurpations of these fundamental neutral rights by strong naval nations be brought to an end; and it was time for neutrals to turn their attention to "first principles" and "of establishing the true principles which ought to have been at first established, & would have been, but for the accidental history of the times." [15]

This was strong meat; which Jefferson had to tone down considerably in his final instructions. There he admitted the right of blockade, as standing on a different ground, and fleshed the bare bones of his "principles" with conciliatory language. He expressly avowed that they were not worth going to war for in the present state of things, nor that war was the best method of enforcing them. What he cautiously pointed to were "those peaceable coercions which are in the power of every nation, if undertaken in concert & in time of peace." In other words, let Livingston seek the aid of other neutrals in imposing possible future retaliations and embargoes on those who would refuse to subscribe to such a convention on neutral rights; but the concert must only go into effect after the current war was over.[16]

Somewhat earlier, Madison had instructed Charles Pinckney, the newly appointed Minister to Spain, to take up the question of French spoliations from Spanish bases, and to propose a joint international tribunal to investigate American claims for damages.[17]

These were mounting to tremendous proportions. All through the latter part of 1801, the State Department was flooded with memorials from American merchants, chambers of commerce and insurance companies protesting Spanish and French seizures of American shipping. By the time Jefferson finally placed the whole mass before Congress on April 20, 1802, there were verified figures of 174 ships seized by the French and 118 by the Spaniards since October 1, 1796, with losses ranging in the many millions.[18]

It was during this critical juncture that the Cabinet agreed to reduce the number of navy captains from fifteen to nine, and proposed the sale of those American galleys which had survived the first slash in armament.[19]

Jefferson found life in Washington rather lonely. It can not be said that there was much society there as yet—many of the Congressmen preferred to leave their wives at home rather than submit them to the rawness and rigors of the new capital. And the President was essentially a family man.

During the few weeks that Dolly Madison stayed at the President's House, that barnlike cavity held a certain warmth and gaiety; but when she departed with her husband to more permanent quarters, Jefferson and his secretary, Meriwether Lewis, felt lugubriously like "two mice in a church." During Dolly's short sojourn, some of the official ladies had tentatively come to dinner, but with her passage, the situation became awkward again. He hoped that either of his daughters might be able to come to Washington and act the hostess; but they had husbands, children and cares of their own. For the while it was impossible.[20]

The diarrhea he had caught almost immediately from the waters of Washington and which remained with him for several years, so weakened and debilitated him that, by the end of the year, he sincerely believed he had not much longer to live.[21] In spite of his secret fear, however, he held to a Spartan regimen in his duties, spending from ten to thirteen hours a day at his desk, and allowing himself a bare four hours a day for riding, dining and "a little unbending." [22]

His interest in methods of combating the smallpox continued unabated. When he heard from a Dr. Benjamin Waterhouse of Boston that a new process was being experimented with—inoculation with smallpox matter taken directly from human patients afflicted with the disease, his scientific curiosity was instantly aroused. A long correspondence ensued; and Waterhouse sent him batches of the material under the crudest and most difficult of conditions. Jefferson in turn forwarded the pustulant mass to Monticello for use, first on his own people, then for distribution to doctors for inoculations throughout Virginia. As reports came to him, he forwarded them to Waterhouse; finally, after some disheartening failures, being able to announce that it seemed to be a success.[23] Jefferson did more than any layman, and more than most doctors, to ensure the final success and wide acceptance of vaccination.

But if his interest continued thus unwearied in all matters scientific, the same could not be said for leisured communings with the aesthetic. To a hopeful poet who sent him a copy of his epic, he professed his present state: "Of all men living I am the last who should undertake to decide as to the merits of poetry. In earlier life I was fond of it, and easily pleased. But as age and cares advanced the powers of fancy have declined.... So much has my relish for poetry deserted me that at present I cannot read even Virgil with pleasure.... The very feelings to which it is addressed are among those I have lost." [24]

His love of horseflesh, however, remained. He was unable to resist the sight of fine, spirited animals, and considered the price, no matter how high, as justified. He purchased also, for his use in Washington, a "new plain, well-furnished Chariot, with plated Harness for 4 Horses, and 2 postillion Saddles" for the modest sum of $1,200, and expressed himself as well satisfied with his bargain.[25]

It might have seemed that, with his new presidential salary of $25,000 a year, he ought for the first time in his life to make ends meet. But such a happy condition was impossible for Jefferson. Whatever his income, he managed to spend more. His private accounts in Washington alone, chiefly on credit through the merchant John Barnes, disclose amazing sums slipping through his fingers. For the six-month period from May to November, 1801, his expenses amounted to $8515.20; not including a wine bill for a cellar laid down the preceding April, with some sundries, in the amount of $957.58.[26] And this was at a time when his dinner parties, for which he became famous, were as yet few and far between.

Yet he firmly believed in simplicity and complete absence of ostentation. He considered the system of "levees" or morning receptions which Washington had instituted and Adams continued, as mere mimicries of European courts. When he entered the Presidency, diplomats and Congressmen assumed that the custom would be kept up; but Jefferson significantly hinted to the contrary by arising early on the mornings usually set aside for levees and going out riding. He would return at a late hour and, with the utmost politeness, ask the disconcerted guests who had milled around waiting for him, to stay for dinner. The dinners, however, were substantial; and a splendid array of pies, puffs, preserves and custards would cover the table, while excellent French wines were served. He stressed moderation in drinking, and seldom took more than one or two glasses after the meal.[27]

Jefferson was well satisfied with the course of events as 1801 gradually waned. On the domestic scene, the initial flurry of protests over his policy of removals from and appointments to office—both from Federalists and Republicans—was slowly abating. He had organized his Cabinet into a fairly efficient machine, and reinstituted the procedures which had been followed during Washington's administration and which he claimed had been ignored by Adams. Any letters addressed to department heads that required an answer were to be forwarded to the President, with the proposed answer. If he believed the answer should be modified, he indicated it by an appended note. If an important doubt arose, the question was submitted to a conference of the Cabinet. Thereby, declared Jefferson, Washington had been able to know exactly what was going on, formed "a central point," preserved amity among the departments, and assumed final responsibility for all decisions. He, Jefferson, intended to do the same.[28] The procedure was sensible; one wonders, though, how Jefferson could aver with a straight face that there had been amity in the halcyon days of Washington.

The autumn elections, also, proved eminently satisfying. The Republicans won sweeping victories everywhere, invading even some hitherto sacrosanct Federalist strongholds in New England. The Congress was heavily Republican, with the Federalists weak, disgruntled and unable to exercise any really effective opposition. Even in the inner sanctum of the Senate, the Republican majority was sufficiently safe. Jefferson was delighted. His soothing policies, as exemplified in his Inaugural Address, had paid excellent dividends in spite of the sneers and headshakings at the time. There might be some little ill temper from the recalcitrant and mortified minority, he admitted, and the die-hard Federalist press continued to season its invectives from the "pepper pots"; but, if only he would be permitted to make the removals demanded by the Republicans at a gradual pace and thereby not alarm "the well meaning citizens who are coming over to us in a steady [stream?]," he expected soon to consolidate the nation completely, "excepting always the Royalists & Priests." [29]

To effectuate this great aim, and to oppose the "phalanx" of Federalist hard core, he sought a similar phalanx of Republicans, collected in a mass around the Administration and comprising "all the abilities, & the respectability to which the offices exercised here can give employ." Good principles, he insisted, "wisely & honestly administered cannot fail to attach our fellow citizens to the order of things which we espouse." [30]

The one fly in the ointment was this ever-present matter of office seekers. Jefferson was confronted with a dilemma. He wished to placate the moderate Federalists by making no removals except for cause; and when he did, he hoped by not making new appointments except in essential positions, eventually to reduce the total of government positions by a full half. Economy was his talisman, and he felt nothing but contempt for most officeholders. They were, he said frankly, chiefly people who had trouble in making a living in private life and sought relief at government expense. But he hoped, by abolishing useless offices and thereby affording a means of reducing taxes, that these misfits would be able to find private employment "from services rendered to others." [31]

Gallatin thoroughly agreed with him on the necessity of reducing taxes. "If this Administration shall not reduce taxes," he warned, "they never will be permanently reduced. To strike at the root of the evil and avert the danger of increasing taxes, encroaching government, temptations to offensive wars, &c., nothing can be more effectual than a repeal of *all* internal taxes, but let them all go, and not one remain on which sister taxes may be hereafter engrafted. I agree with you fully," he told Jefferson, "that pretended tax-preparations, treasury-preparations, and army-preparations against contingent wars tend only to encourage wars." [32]

Even abroad, the skies seemed to have cleared. The war-weary nations had made an uneasy peace, which was in fact only to be an armed truce. But Jefferson was thankful for the respite. It was, he wrote joyfully, "the most fortunate thing which could have happened to place the present administration on advantageous ground. The only rock we feared was war: and it did not depend on ourselves but others whether we should keep out of it. We hope Great Britain will have so much to do at home that she will not have time to intrigue and plot against this country." [33]

If the matter of Aaron Burr, Vice-President of the United States, still was a sore spot, it had not as yet grown to the ominous proportions it did later. Its present quiescence was no fault, however, of the Clintonians in New York. They did their best to irritate the sore, and demanded of Jefferson that he eliminate their hated rival completely. James Cheetham, their editor-henchman, kept sending Jefferson long, confused and wholly garbled accounts of Burr's former activities in seeking to supplant him in the Presidency, which Jefferson silently filed for future reference and reprisal.[34]

The time was now approaching when Congress would meet in session, and a Presidential Message to the assembled lawmakers was indicated. Jefferson started his draft early in November, and sent copies around to his Cabinet officers for suggestions, revisions and additions. Both Washington and Adams had delivered their addresses in person, but Jefferson had made such a fiasco of his Inaugural—when no one could hear him—that he was determined to break with precedent and submit a written message to be read by the Clerk.

He did not place the change in procedure on its true ground, however. He officially informed the Senate that he was doing it principally out of "regard to the convenience of the Legislature, to the economy of their time, to their relief from the embarrassment of immediate answers, on subjects not yet fully before them, and to the benefits thence resulting to the public affairs." [35]

This was amplified somewhat in a private explanation to his friend, Dr.

Rush. There he claimed that he had "prevented the bloody conflict to which the making of an answer would have committed them. They consequently were able to set into real business at once." [36]

Whatever his reason, he thus set a tradition which was to continue for more than a century, until Woodrow Wilson broke it by appearing once again in the halls of Congress. The Federalists could be depended on to sneer at the innovation and to speculate on its real reason. The arch-Federalist *Gazette of the United States* jeered that perhaps the President was unable to keep track of his own policies and feared to be caught tripping if he appeared in person. It also reacted violently to his use of what it called "the French style of address" when Jefferson referred to his auditors as "Fellow Citizens." This, the newspaper considered, was mere leveling and an appeal to the mob. Were not the Federalists "Gentlemen" and should they not be addressed as such? Let the Republicans be called "Citizens," but not the Federalists.[37]

Several important things are to be noted in the Message as originally drafted, and as it was finally delivered. The intent of the annual message was to review the accomplishments of the preceding year, and to present to Congress a program and recommendations for its consideration as to the future.

But Jefferson had learned a lesson from the results of his Inaugural. The more soothing and noncontroversial the substance, the greater the chance for harmony and the blunting of the opposition fangs. In his first draft he almost forgot this important principle, and inserted a long passage on the Sedition Act. After much meditation and consultation with his advisers, he struck it out, and commented on the margin of the draft: "This whole paragraph was omitted as capable of being chicaned, and furnishing something to the opposition to make a handle of. It was thought better that the message should be clear of everything which the public might be made to misunderstand."

Yet so important is this censored passage for an understanding of Jefferson's own thought and philosophy of government that it must be considered in detail.

Our country has thought proper [he wrote] to distribute the powers of its government among three equal & independent authorities, constituting each a check on one or both of the others, in all attempts to impair its constitution. To make each an effectual check, it must have a right in cases which arise within the line of its proper functions, where, equally with the others, it acts in the last resort & without appeal, to decide on the validity of an act according to its own judgment, & uncontrouled by the opinions of any other department. We have accordingly, in more than one instance, seen the opinions of different departments in opposition to each other, & no ill ensue. The constitution moreover, as a further security for itself, against violation even by a concurrence of all the departments, has provided for its own reintegration by a change of the persons exercising the functions of those departments. Succeeding functionaries have the same right to judge of the conformity or non-conformity of an act within the constitution, as their predecessors who past it.

Realizing that this doctrine might lead to a perpetual uneasiness in the law, Jefferson qualified it with the admission that long usage, and ratification by repeated officeholders and elections "would so strengthen a construction as to render highly responsible a departure from it."

On his accession to the Presidency, he had received petitions claiming protection against the operation of the Sedition Act. "Called on by the position in which the nation had placed me, to exercise in their behalf my free & independent judgment," Jefferson examined the Act carefully, and now declared "that I hold that act to be in palpable & unqualified contradiction to the constitution. Considering it then as a nullity, I have relieved from oppression under it those of my fellow citizens who were within the reach of the functions confided to me. In recalling our footsteps within the limits of the Constitution, I have been actuated by a zealous devotion to that instrument. It is the ligament which binds us into one nation. It is, to the national government, the law of its existence, with which it began, and with which it is to end." [38]

This Jeffersonian doctrine held implications, not all of which he realized. In effect, it set up *four* constitutional censors. The first, Congress itself, could only act by refusing to pass a law. Once that was done, the other three—the President, the Supreme Court, and the state legislatures, might consider the law as null and void. Of these three, the Supreme Court held the weakest position, for *its* nullification could only be put into effect by the positive action of the other two. It was therefore in the President on the national scene, and in the state legislatures within their own boundaries, that true censorship on Constitutional grounds resided. What happened then to Jefferson's theory of *equal* departments? And what happened to the stability of the laws in the case of conflicting opinions—a moot case which Jefferson himself realized and tried lamely to answer?

Jefferson sent the completed draft, minus this all-important section, to Madison, Gallatin and others. From Madison he asked "serious revisal, not only as to matter" but to grammar. As to the latter, he had become sensitive of criticism, particularly since the Federalist press had sneered at the construction of his Inaugural and, in one instance at least, had gone back to the Declaration of Independence to tear it apart.[39] As long as the sense was not changed, he advised Madison, "it should be attended to in complaisance to the purists of New England, but where by small grammatical negligences, the energy of an idea is condensed, or a word stand for a sentence, I hold grammatical rigor in contempt." [40]

It was Gallatin, however, rather than Madison, who gave the document a thorough going over. He sent a detailed list of corrections and amendments, chiefly in his own department of finance. One item, in particular, he was anxious to have added—a recommendation to Congress to guard against misapplications of public monies by making only specific appropriations for specific purposes, where practicable, and to limit discretionary powers in public officials in the administration of such funds. He wanted no further shifts of moneys from their original purpose to other purposes as had obtained in the previous administrations.[41]

After all the soul-searching and careful preparation, the actual Message, as finally delivered, proved to be a most innocuous document. Jefferson devoted but little space to foreign affairs, and that little presented nothing but pious platitudes. He was gratified, he wrote, to be "able to announce to them . . . that the wars and troubles which have for so many years afflicted our sister nations have at length come to an end." He was especially thankful that the United States had been spared the horrors of war, and that "a cessation of the irregularities which had affected the commerce of neutral nations, and of the irritations and injuries produced by them," would afford an opportunity of reviewing the wrongs done and of obtaining indemnities for the past.

With this cavalier dismissal of foreign affairs, he turned to a consideration of the Indians, where also everything was peaceful. He noted with approval the shift in the Indian economy from a hunting and fishing existence to one based on farming and the household arts.

There was only one unfortunate exception, however, to this blessed condition of peace, and that was Tripoli. He spoke of their insolent demands, and of the squadron he had sent to the Mediterranean; for defense only, he hastened to add, since Congress had never declared war. Since that important function was "confided by the Constitution to the Legislature exclusively," he said primly, he left it to them to decide whether or not the "defensive" war should be changed to one of offense.

He next turned, and with more enthusiasm, to a consideration of the population statistics as disclosed by the recent census. The rate of increase, he was happy to report, promised the doubling of the population within twenty-two years. "We contemplate this rapid growth," he said, "and the prospect it holds up to us, not with a view to the injuries it may enable us to do to others in some future day, but to the settlement of the extensive country still remaining vacant within our limits, to the multiplications of men susceptible of happiness, educated in the love of order, habituated to self-government, and valuing its blessings above all price."

If this was somewhat over the heads of the people for whom it was intended, Jefferson promptly brought it down to earth again by declaring that, as a result, "we may now safely dispense with all the internal taxes, comprehending excise, stamps, auctions, licenses, carriages, and refined sugars," as well as postage on newspapers. This, of course, completely overthrew the Hamiltonian system, justified the Whisky Rebellion and turned those potent sources of income over to the treasuries of the states.

Obviously, with this curtailment of the national income, the expenses of government, including the army and navy, required drastic revision. Harking back to his fundamental thesis that the federal government was charged only with foreign relations and the mutual relations of the states, Jefferson pondered aloud his doubt "whether our organization is not too complicated, too expensive; whether offices and officers have not been multiplied unnecessarily and sometimes injuriously to the service they were meant to promote."

Here he came cautiously to a matter close to his heart. He had, he said, reduced substantially those offices within the purviews of the Executive; but unfortunately, most had been established by law, and could therefore only be abolished by law. He would, he affirmed, be happy to furnish them with information as to those he intended. What he had in mind, without openly saying so at the moment, were the judgeships which had been added in the last days of Adams's administration.

Next he recommended the provisions for specific appropriations, which Gallatin had suggested to him, as a means of reducing expenditures; and offered, in place of the internal taxes, the revenues from the sale of public lands as a means for reducing the public debt.

The army establishment was entirely too large, he pronounced. "For defense against invasion their number is as nothing; nor is it conceived needful or safe that a standing army should be kept up in time of peace for that purpose." There was always the militia. Jefferson had a perfect horror of a professional army, seeing in it a method of government to subvert the liberties of the people. Nor had his experience with the militia during the Revolution done anything to change his reliance on an outpouring of free men to oppose an invader.

As for the navy, only a small force was required for Mediterranean service against the Barbary pirates; the rest—what there remained of it—could be laid up against emergencies. He had also, pending Congressional approval, "suspended or slackened" work on certain naval yards.

His next section could be approved *in toto* by the most conservative of modern industrialists. "Agriculture, manufactures, commerce, and navigation, the four pillars of our prosperity," he asserted, "are then most thriving when left most free to individual enterprise. Protection from casual embarrassments, however, may sometimes be seasonably interposed."

But the judiciary, "especially that portion of it recently erected," aroused his greatest wrath. He had received from the United States District Attorneys a complete list of all the cases that had come before the federal courts from 1792 to the present day,[42] and he offered it as evidence that there was not enough business for the number of judges. He also wanted Congress to consider whether juries had been impartially selected in those states where the marshals were court appointees.

His final recommendation was for a shortening of the term of naturalization from the requirement of fourteen years residence which had been passed during the hysteria over "aliens." "Shall we refuse to the unhappy fugitives from distress," he demanded eloquently, "that hospitality which the savages of the wilderness extended to our fathers arriving in this land? Shall oppressed humanity find no asylum on this globe?"[43]

Such was the Message Jefferson laid before Congress. To his old friend, Mazzei, he was much more forthright.

> You cannot imagine [he exclaimed] what progress republican principles have made here. Business is conducted calmly, and with unanimous consent in both Chambers. The Tories are generally either converted or silenced by rational evidence or by prudence.
>
> All the excess expenditures which were turning the ship of state toward monarchy are being rapidly abolished, and the fundamental principles of 1775, once more assert themselves vigorously. Briefly, there is every proof that people are enjoying life, although none have exclusive privileges, nor are there proscriptions for any except those guilty of infamous conduct.
>
> Our country will be a haven for the oppressed, without fourteen years being necessary for qualification, and we have found a way of carrying on affairs without any need for an Act of Sedition. The appointments made by Mr. Adams to the District Courts, will, necessarily, have to be abandoned, the taxes on press and other things will be abolished; the '94 [laws] are suppressed; and, finally, all that is oppressive will be removed, and every encouragement will be given to naturalization, to commerce, to industry and to right conduct.[44]

In short, the millennium.

CHAPTER 50

Triumphant Republicanism

THE year of 1802 dawned on a tranquil nation. So soothing had been the uttered words of the new President, so gradual and nibbling had been the changes in government, so still intact was the fundamental structure, so quietly and serenely had this alleged atheist and wild-eyed anarchist comported himself that the rank-and-file Federalists found nothing to arouse their fears and even the leaders were hard put to it to discover issues on which the tocsin might be sounded.

It has often been said that Jefferson was merely drifting. But he knew exactly what he was doing. He had to rid the country of the fear that a French type of revolution impended and to sever the Federalist leaders from their electoral support. He had to make haste slowly in bringing about the millennium. Yet he kept the eventual goal ever clearly in mind.

He realized that the Hamiltonian financial system had become so deeply imbedded and interpenetrated with the very structure of the government that it was now impossible to excise it. Willy-nilly, and in spite of theory, it had to be continued. He made his guiding principles clear to Dupont de Nemours, who had thought his Message too big for the nation, yet exhorted him to continue on his course like Socrates, Cato, Confucius, Marcus Aurelius—and Turgot.[1]

Jefferson explained his strategy to the enthusiastic French expatriate. "When this government was first established," he wrote, "it was possible to have kept it going on true principles, but the contracted, English, half-lettered ideas of Hamilton, destroyed that hope in the bud. We can pay off his debt in 15. years: but we can never get rid of his financial system. It mortifies me to be strengthening principles which I deem radically vicious, but this vice is entailed on us by the first error. In other parts of our government I hope we shall be able by degrees to introduce sound principles and make them habitual. What is practicable must often controul what is pure theory: and the habits of the governed determine in a great degree what is practicable." [2] So spoke the man who was supposed by his opponents to be a pure theoretician and dreamer.

Though he disliked the financial system—and particularly the Bank—he knew at least that he could in a measure control them, and make good out of evil. But the federal judiciary was another matter. Here was the stronghold into which federalism had retired; an entrenched position over which, by virtue of the Constitution, he had no power. "There," he remarked bitterly, "the remnants of federalism are to be preserved and fed from the treasury, and from that battery all the works of republicanism are to be beaten down and erased. By a fraudulent use of the Constitution, which had made judges irremovable, they have multiplied useless judges merely to strengthen their phalanx." [3]

This was one area in which he believed that gradualism would prove ineffective and that he was compelled to declare open and immediate war. As the event was to disclose, he might have done better to have held to his original doctrine.

On New Year's Day, in spite of the fact that the President had abolished the traditional levee, a group of Federalist Congressmen came in coaches to present him with the compliments of the season. Jefferson received them with due politeness and offered them cake and wine. Then he displayed to them a "mammoth" cheese that had come to him that morning from the Republican farmers of Cheshire, Massachusetts. It was indeed a mammoth offering, weighing 1230 pounds, and measuring over four feet in diameter and fifteen inches in thickness.

It had been made, so the President informed the amused Federalists, from a day's milk supply from all the "Republican cows" in the community, pressed out with prayer and hymn-singing, and driven by sleigh all the way to Washington.[4]

Dr. Samuel Latham Mitchill, a Republican Congressman from New York, was seeing the leader of his party for the first time; and he regaled his wife with a complete description of the hero. He found Jefferson "tall in stature and rather spare in flesh. His dress and manners are very plain; he is grave, or rather sedate, but without any tincture of pomp, ostentation, or pride, and occasionally can smile, and both hear and relate humorous stories as well as any other man of social feelings." Being himself a bookish man, Dr. Mitchill surveyed the little group of books on the mantelpiece with considerable interest. There was a volume of the French Encyclopedia, a volume of Tacitus with facing texts of Latin and Spanish translation, and an elegant copy of Plato. The presence of the Plato is interesting; for Jefferson always expressed the heartiest contempt for the great Greek philosopher.

The worthy medical Congressman found a common interest with the President in the subject of smallpox. Jefferson told him that he had inoculated many persons with his own hand, and he talked about the subject "with the intelligence of a physician, so ardent is his philanthropy and such is his zeal to extirpate the small-pox." [5]

Much more curious was another conversation Mitchill had with Jefferson. He had read the *Notes on Virginia* and asked the President just where he had stood to view the cleft of the Potomac from which he had drawn his famous description. Jefferson gravely told him the spot no longer existed; that during Adams's administration a company of Federalist troops had blasted the rock with gunpowder so as to make Jefferson's account sound fallacious to other travelers who would attempt to duplicate the view. "What shameful, what vandalic revenge is this?" exclaimed the simple doctor.[6]

But if Jefferson was perhaps pulling the worthy Congressman's leg with this account of Federalist revenge, he was deadly in earnest about his reply to a memorial from the members of a Baptist congregation. They had asked him to proclaim a day of fasting and of thanksgiving; and he determined, much as he disliked to answer memorials, to utilize the occasion for putting on record certain deep-seated convictions. It gave him the chance, he wrote his Attorney General, Levi Lincoln, to make public "a condemnation of the alliance between Church and State, under the authority of the Constitution. It furnishes an occasion, too, which I have long wished to find, of saying why I do not proclaim fastings & thanksgivings, as my predecessors did.... I know it will give great offence to the New England clergy; but the advocate of religious freedom is to expect neither peace nor forgiveness from them."[7]

The question of the exact nature of the separation of Church and State under the Constitution had become again in modern times a matter of dispute and heated controversy; but to Jefferson it meant but one thing—*complete* separation in every possible phase of activity. Yet it was Jefferson who, with tongue in cheek, had proposed and seen carried through in the days of the Revolution just such a day of fasting in order to arouse the people.

Levi Lincoln, himself a New Englander, advised against it. Not merely the Federalists, but even the Republicans in New England, he declared, might be offended. Nevertheless, Jefferson went through with his plan and sent the Baptists a ringing explanation of his reasons why he could not accede to their request, and used that famous phrase of the "wall of separation" which has since been repeatedly quoted, even in decisions of the Supreme Court.[8]

Congress had listened quietly to the report on the state of the nation and on Jefferson's recommendations for the future. There had been no immediate repercussions. If there were many things in the message that the Federalists disliked, they were couched in such general terms and placating language that sensibilities were not too violently lacerated.

The Republican majority in the House was substantial—sixty-nine to thirty-six. The influential Republicans were almost all from the South—William B. Giles of Virginia, the elongated, brilliant and erratic John Randolph of Roanoke, also from Virginia, Samuel Smith and Joseph H. Nicholson of Maryland. The Speaker was an honest but not too able Carolinian, Nathaniel Macon. Opposed to them was an experienced and skilled coterie of Federalists, including James Bayard of Delaware, Roger Griswold and Samuel Dana of Connecticut.

In the Senate, the parties were much more evenly divided, though the

Republicans held a precarious edge which absenteeism sometimes brought to the vanishing point. Here the Republicans had John Breckinridge of Kentucky, the putative father of the famous Kentucky Resolutions; somewhat later, De Witt Clinton of New York, able and unscrupulous; and James Jackson of Georgia. Facing them from the Federalist benches were Gouverneur Morris of New York, Jeremiah Mason of Massachusetts, James Hillhouse and Uriah Tracy of Connecticut.

The first order of business from the Republican point of view—and the one next Jefferson's heart—was the repeal of the Judiciary Bill that had been pushed through in the closing days of the previous administration. It was this bill, adding a considerable number of judges and other judicial officers to the existing establishment, that Jefferson had described in bitter terms as the last stronghold of federalism.

On January 6, 1802, John Breckinridge rose on the Senate floor and moved "that the act passed last session respecting the Judiciary Establishment of the United States be repealed." Two days later he led off the debate. The law, he argued, had been unnecessary and improper. The number of cases before the federal courts did not require such an extension; they had been created for political purposes and constituted a heavy charge on the strained finances of the country. What then was to be done with the present incumbents? Since Congress had the power to abolish the courts, he declared, the Constitution could not be tortured to mean that a judge must continue in an office that no longer existed.[9]

Jeremiah Mason and Gouverneur Morris promptly sprang to the defense. Mason waxed sarcastic over the ingenuity displayed in removing the office in order to remove the man, while Morris warned rhetorically: "We are now about to violate the Constitution. Once touch it with unhallowed hands; sacrifice but one of its provisions, and we are gone." It was "the vile love of popularity," he declaimed, that had ruined every republic in history. "Why are we here?" he demanded. "To save the people from their most dangerous enemy; to save them from themselves." [10]

Morris's extravagant language was not calculated to win friends among the Republicans; but Mason's more temperate argument gave some of them pause. They had disapproved of the additional offices; but they felt the force of the Constitutional argument anent cutting the job from under a judge whom the Constitution had plainly meant to hold office for life. Even Jackson, the Georgia firebrand, acceded to the argument and said so from the floor.

On January 15th, in the midst of the turbulent debate, Aaron Burr appeared to assume his seat as President of the Senate. At the sight of his dignified, erect figure, and under his calm, even voice the Senate straightened perceptibly from its usual slouch and surreptitiously pocketed the apples it had been accustomed to munch.

The issue was much in doubt as the debate proceeded. Both sides marshaled their forces. The Federalists sent urgent messages to two of their absentees, Ross of Pennsylvania and Ogden of New Jersey, to come forthwith. Republican Senator Bradley of Vermont, who had gone home because of family illness, promised to return after the shortest decent interval. So evenly were the two parties divided, in fact, that Bayard believed Burr, as presiding officer, would be forced to give a casting vote. He professed a great deal of satisfaction over the dilemma in which the Vice-President would thus be placed.[11]

The bill was reported out of committee on January 22nd. Jefferson, watching the proceedings with intense interest, expressed his doubts as to the final result. "Our friends [in Congress]," he reported gloomily, "have not yet learned to draw well together, and there has been some danger of a small section of them, aided by the feds, carrying a question against the larger section. They have seen however that this practice would end in enabling the feds to carry every thing as they please, by joining whichever section of Republicans they chose; and they will avoid this rock." [12] Jefferson had made the passage of this bill an administration measure, and expected—in spite of his usual disclaimers of executive interference with the legislature—that the Senators would heed the crack of the whip.

What behind-the-scenes maneuvering was employed is unknown, but Jackson of Georgia was finally made to see the light; and when the bill came up for vote on February 3rd, it passed by a bare 16 to 15. Actually, however, it was the outcast Burr who saved the day for the Republicans. For, on January 26th, when the bill was moved for its third reading, the vote was tied at 15 to 15, and Burr's casting vote passed it over the unexpected hurdle. Gouverneur Morris was disgusted. He had hoped Burr, in view of his treatment at Jefferson's hands, would have thrown in his fortunes with the Federalists. "There was a moment," he recorded, "when the Vice-President might have arrested the measure by his vote, and that vote would, I believe, have made him President at the next election; but there is a tide in the affairs of men which he suffered to go by." [13]

Yet his aid was wholly overlooked by the Republicans in their resentment against his action on the following day, when Jonathan Dayton of New Jersey moved to recommit the bill for further consideration with the explanation that the *entire* judiciary system ought to be revised. Once again, a strict party vote brought on a tie, but this time Burr, thinking perhaps that a conciliatory move now might win over the Federalists to the measure, cast his vote with them. The respite was temporary, however, for Breckinridge called the bill up again on February 2nd, and the following day it was passed.[14]

The bill went now to the House, where John Randolph took over its management on the floor. Here the Republican majority was so overwhelming that, in spite of a desperate rear-guard action by the Federalists, it was pushed through on March 3rd by a strong majority of 59 to 32. But not before Jefferson, impatient for immediate passage, had received something of a scare. "The H. of R.," he complained on February 21st, "have now been a week debating the judiciary law, and scarcely seem to be yet on the threshold of it. I begin to apprehend a long session: however," he added optimistically, "I believe all material matters recommended in the first day's message will prevail. The majority begins to draw better together than at first. Still there are some wayward freaks which now & then disturb the operations." [15]

The first test on the recommendations made by Jefferson had proved successful, although there had been hard sledding and several near catastrophes. But Burr had now irretrievably lost whatever small chance there was for regaining favor. His first pro-Republican vote was forgotten in the furore over the second. And he made a final mistake that damned him forever. The Federalist chiefs invited him to attend the annual birthday party for their departed leader, George Washington. It was a trap, deliberately baited to cause an irremediable schism among the Republicans, and Burr fell into it. Appearing dramatically before the astonished rank and file, who had not been taken into the secret, he proposed a toast: "*The union of all honest men!*" That meant only one thing—a bid for union between the Federalists and himself; and Hamilton, in retirement, gleefully saw in it an opportunity to destroy the Republican party.[16] From this fatal step there was no retreating.

Immersed in national affairs, Jefferson was nevertheless always willing to heed the call of duty from Virginia. The Virginia legislature, still suffering from the shock of the abortive Negro conspiracy, had sought once more to find a place outside their state to which they could deport all Negroes guilty either of enumerated crimes or, though innocent of wicked intentions, free or thereafter emancipated. For the first class, they proposed deportation to Africa or South America; for the second, the place of asylum could be chosen by the Negroes themselves, so long as they quit the state.[17]

Jefferson, to whom Virginia appealed for advice through Governor Monroe, saw nothing morally wrong in this sudden wrenching from their homes of free Negroes untainted by misconduct. He suggested Sierra Leone in Africa as a fit place for *both* categories, and promised to propose the scheme to the British, the rulers of that colony. He actually did write to Rufus King, the American Minister to England, to lay the proposition before them.[18]

The scheme did not appeal to Monroe. Sierra Leone, he had heard, forbade slavery, and he did not wish the culprits to be set free. It was better, he said, to seek some place in South America where they could be treated and sold as slaves.[19] All plans, however, eventually fell through; neither the state nor federal government could find a place that would accept the deportees.

Jefferson's interest in Virginia affairs remained constant. He still held to his old idea that the state ought to be laid out in "hundreds" or "captaincies," and he prodded his son-in-law, John Wayles Eppes, who was preparing to enter local politics, to put the plan into effect. "There can be no other basis of republican energy," he insisted. "Police, justice, elections, musters, schools, and many other essential things can have no other effectual bottom. There is not a single political measure for our state which I have so much at heart. The captain or head borough would be there what the Sergeants are in an army: the finger of execution." [20]

Perhaps one other plan for Virginia was just as much at his heart: a "general university... on the most extensive & liberal scale that our circumstances would call for & our faculties meet." [21]

He also favored his Virginia friends for federal posts. One in particular—John Page, the comrade of his youth—exercised his ingenuity for years. Page had fallen on evil days financially, and Jefferson sought unweariedly to place him in a comfortable berth. Admitting that Virginia already had more than her due proportion of appointments, Jefferson nevertheless offered to remove the Federalist collector of customs at Petersburg and turn the office over to Page. Page refused it because the emoluments had been curtailed, but Jefferson kept trying to find him another situation. Fortunately, Page's election to the governorship of Virginia at the end of the year solved the problem temporarily; but on the termination of that office Page, still indigent and encumbered with a large family, was thrown back into the market place.[22] But the story of his friend's further attempts to find him an easy niche at the government's expense must await its proper place.

Domestic problems burdened him as well—a strange retiring from society of his younger daughter, Maria. To combat it he urged her to come to him in Washington, or at least to visit with Martha. The troubled state of his daughter brought up tragic memories. For your own happiness, he urged, mix with the world; or you will suffer for it. "I can speak from experience on this subject," he wrote feelingly. "From 1793. to 1797. I remained closely at home, saw none but those who came there, and at length became very sensible of the ill effect it had upon my mind, and of its direct & irresistible tendency to render me unfit for society, & uneasy when necessarily engaged in it. I felt enough of the effect of withdrawing from the world then, to see that it led to an anti-social & misanthropic state of mind, which severely punishes him who gives into it: and it will be a lesson I shall never forget as to myself." [23]

His elder daughter's husband also required his attention. Thomas Mann Randolph, plagued with ill health and financial worries, proposed to quit Virginia and seek new fortune in a cotton plantation at Natchez. Jefferson dissuaded him from the attempt, though he agreed that cotton culture was proving profitable. But Natchez, he argued, was unhealthy and exposed to the Spaniards and Indians. Why not try Georgia, which was healthier, closer and safer, and already peopled with many Virginians? "In fact," he ended in a glow of enthusiasm, "I should be delighted to own a cotton estate in Georgia, & go and pass every winter under the orange trees of that country." [24]

Neither father nor son-in-law ever went to Georgia; and Jefferson, from Washington, busied himself rather in making more permanent and magnificent the buildings at Monticello. He sent detailed instructions with appropriate sketches—brick pilasters, the flanking northwest building to hold his coaches, and an underground icehouse, solid and circular.[25]

While thus inquiring into Georgia cotton plantations and engaging in expensive building at Monticello, Jefferson was running headlong into debt. His expenses far outstripped his income. For his first year in office, his expenditures totaled the amazing sum of $33,624.84. To meet them, he had his presidential salary of $25,000, while the sale of his tobacco and his nailery profits netted $3,507.33. His deficit for the year therefore amounted to $5,117.51. Lest this be thought an unusual year, his accounts for all succeeding years in office disclose the same enormous expenses and the same steady deficits. He was compelled to go into debt to his factor, John Barnes, who advanced him monies monthly and charged interest on the account. By the time he was ready to retire from the Presidency, he was so deeply involved that he had to borrow $8,000 from a wealthy female neighbor, Mrs. Tabb of Amelia, to pay off some of his Washington debts.[26]

What caused this lavish expenditure, particularly when it is taken into account that the regular levees had been abolished, the former trappings of office done away with, and Jefferson's personal habiliments were plain to the point of embarrassment? Monticello, of course, was a bottomless drain; and Jefferson's dinners and wines, for all their simplicity, were justly famous among Washington political figures. Even the Federalists thought it a treat to be invited to one of his meals. His passion for fine horses, fine books, fine scientific instruments and fine wines was insatiable, and he never reckoned expense when any of these items swam into his view.

With the repeal of the judiciary law successfully encompassed, the Jeffersonian forces in Congress now moved to the other items which their leader had proposed in his annual message.

The repeal of the internal taxes had been a major issue with the Republicans, and they sought to make their promises good as soon as the drastic slashes in government expense rendered it feasible. On March 8, 1802, John Randolph of Roanoke moved in the House to repeal the hated taxes and, in spite of all attempts by interested parties to retain individual items of the excise, the bill passed on March 22nd by the comfortable majority of sixty-one to twenty-four.[27] The Senate assented on March 31st with some slight changes, to which the House agreed on April 2nd.[28] The Republican majority, Jefferson noted with considerable satisfaction, was now working much more harmoniously; and his program was moving with smoothness and dispatch.

Gallatin had been diligently at work examining the operations of the sinking fund, which Hamilton had started and which every Republican insisted was so involved that no mortal but Hamilton himself could understand it. Jefferson warmly approved of Gallatin's report for its recasting. "I think it an object of great importance..." he wrote his Secretary of Treasury, "to simplify our system of finance, and bring it within the comprehension of every member of Congress. Hamilton set out on a different plan. In order that he might have the entire government of his machine, he determined so to complicate it as that neither the President or Congress should be able to understand it, or to control him. He succeeded in doing this, not only beyond their reach, but so that he at length could not unravel it himself." What Jefferson wanted was an accounting system whereby it would be possible at the end of each year, at a glance, to determine the exact surplus or deficit, and whether current taxes were too high or too little.[29]

It was essential to watch income and outgo closely; first, because of the curtailment of revenue due to the repeal of the excise taxes, and second, because the long controversy with Great Britain over the damages due her from the failure of her merchants to collect their pre-Revolutionary debts had finally been settled by a lump sum convention of £600,000, payable in three annual installments.

The Federalists waxed sarcastic over this gratuitous unloading of the private debts of the Southern States—Virginia in particular—onto the federal government; but Jefferson rightly pointed out that the assumption had been not of their doing, but of the Federalists themselves as a result of Jay's Treaty. As a matter of fact, he took credit for scaling down an original claim of twenty-odd millions to a mere three million dollars. "If the bargain be hard," he spoke of the Federalists with some asperity, "it is their work. That it is not more hard has been the effect of our measures. If this be given up it can never be settled but by war." [30]

Another matter that had to be settled—and settled before the next presidential election—was the method of choosing the President and Vice-President. The old method had not only proved unworkable, but had led the nation almost to the brink of civil war. The Constitution makers had not envisaged political parties when they set up their machinery; but parties had come into being and were obviously there to stay. On April 12, 1802, De Witt Clinton introduced a proposed amendment to the Constitution in the Senate "that in all elections of President and Vice President, the persons voted for shall be particularly designated, by declaring which is voted for as President, and which as Vice President." The House passed a similar resolution on May 1st; but the solid opposition of the Federalists caused it to fail by a single vote of the required two-thirds in the Senate on May 3rd.[31] Perhaps they dreamed, as a minority party, of a similar contretemps to that of 1801 when they might again hold the balance of power in selecting a President.

It was not until the end of 1803 that the amendment was proposed again, and this time, in a slightly different form, passed and later ratified by the States as the Twelfth Amendment to the Constitution.

Jefferson watched the spring elections in the various states carefully, and sent his Postmaster General, Gideon Granger, on a tour of the northern states to report on the results. They were disappointing.

The first accounts from the pivotal state of New York, in fact, were alarming; but later reports disclosed that it was still safely Republican, though the Federalists had gained several Congressional seats. Vermont was safe; but Massachusetts showed few gains, while rock-ribbed Connecticut gave the Federalists an almost two to one majority over their opponents.[32]

With the South solidly Republican, there was no fear of overthrow, but Jefferson had an almost pathetic yearning to see the last strongholds of federalism turn to him for aid and comfort. Unanimity was what he wanted, a solid backing of approval for his policies and an end to sniping and criticism of himself as man and President. He was like the princess in the fairy tale—the tiniest pea underneath the sevenfold featherbeds was sufficient to disturb his slumbers and harass his thoughts.

Yet he refused to despair. He attributed the still extant evidences of dissent to a few Tory leaders, but chiefly to a priesthood with whom he would eternally be at war. He winced whenever he read an attack on himself or on the government in the Federalist press, yet he wanted to "see the experiment tried of getting along without public prosecution for *libels*. I believe we can do it," he added.[33]

He expanded on the theme to Volney in France. The Federalists hated him, and like Nero, would have concentrated all their hatred of republicanism on his devoted head so that one sweeping blow would eliminate the whole. But, he continued self-righteously, "I shall protect them in the right of lying and calumniating, and still go on to merit the continuance of it, by pursuing steadily my object of proving that a people, easy in their circumstances as ours are, are capable of conducting themselves under a government founded not in the fears & follies of man, but on his reason, on the predominance of his social over his dissocial passions, so far as to restrain him in no moral right, and so firm as to protect him from every moral wrong..." He admitted he was too old to do more than start on the road to the millennium; but hoped that his successors would eventually reach the goal.[34]

He took in the Federalist papers with a kind of self-flagellant desire to see what they had to say about him, but he refused to support them by direct purchase; and evolved a most complicated system whereby the price would go to Republican papers instead.[35]

But, while thus voicing noble sentiments, he was at the same time practical enough to realize that the "lies" and "calumnies" must be met; just as in the days of Freneau. Therefore he cautiously acceded to the idea that the Philadelphia *Aurora* be subsidized in order to stand up against the many Federalist papers in that town. "I am satisfied," he declared, "that truth & reason can maintain themselves, without the aid of coercion, if left free to defend themselves. But then they must defend themselves." [36]

He considered himself not only as President of the United States, but as the national head of the Republican party. He kept a vigilant eye on the various elections; and his wrath was particularly aroused by James A. Bayard, the solitary representative of Delaware in the House. Bayard, ironically, had been the Federalist who had finally ensured Jefferson's election; but he was now his most active opponent and leader of the minority in Congress. For God's sake, run for Congress against him, Jefferson urged Caesar A. Rodney, the Delaware Republican. Bayard's "long speeches and wicked workings at this session have added at least 30 days to its length, cost us 30,000 D. and filled the union with falsehoods and misrepresentations." [37] Unfortunately, it was impossible to dislodge Bayard, and he remained to embarrass Jefferson with later accounts of the negotiations whereby Jefferson had been chosen and Burr defeated.

In the main, however, the President was satisfied with the work of Congress as it closed the session. Practically all of his recommendations had been enacted into law; and those few which had not were merely laid over for want of time. He characterized the minority as "the bitterest cup of the remains of Federalism rendered desperate and furious by despair." But even *they* were compelled to acknowledge that their party would never more raise its head.

Yet while thus contemplating the demise of the Federalists, Jefferson was politically perceptive enough to realize that it was not in the nature of man to be long in unanimous agreement. What would happen then? "We [the Republicans]," he foresaw, "shall now be so strong that we shall certainly split again; for free men thinking differently and speaking and acting as they think, will form into classes of sentiment, but it must be under another name, that of federalism is to become so scouted that no party can rise under it." He thought the division would come as Whig and Tory, as in England, since that division "is founded in the nature of man." [38]

There spoke the philosopher; but when the actuality came, under the guise of John Randolph and his "Quids," the man quivered under the blow and attacked the faction with all the invective at his command.

He never could get over his morbid sensitivity in the face of opposition. He excused himself to Madame de Corny for not having written her these many years with the complaint: "Born, as unfortunately I was, in an age of revolutionary storm; the sweet sensations & affections of domestic society have been exchanged with me for the bitter and deadly feuds of party." He never saw Angelica Church, though she was close enough in New York. "In our party divisions too it happened that her nearest friends were my bitterest opponents; and altho' that could not affect our mutual esteem, it tended to suppress the demonstrations of it." [39]

As if to prove Jefferson's prophecy of an eventual split among the triumphant Republicans, he received frequent reports of factional quarrels in Pennsylvania and New York. The situation in Pennsylvania was bad enough, with every Republican politician hostile to every other; [40] and Jefferson was sorely distressed, seeking always to pour oil over the troubled waters. But the far more deadly war to the knife that raged in New York met with a surprising degree of philosophic fortitude. For here it was the forces of De Witt Clinton and of Aaron Burr that were locked in mortal combat; and Jefferson's sympathies, for all his public protestations, were with the Clintonians. Bolstered by federal patronage, De Witt Clinton was remorselessly weeding out every Burrite in office he could find, and driving the Vice-President from the seats of power into the very arms of the Federalists.

Gallatin did not share Jefferson's Olympian calm. He took a serious view of the faction-torn state, and sought to alert his chief to the dangers implicit in the situation and to call off the ravening Clinton; going so far as to submit to him a copy of a letter by Burr denying that he had secretly intrigued with the Federalists against Jefferson in the late election.[41] But Jefferson quietly ignored his subordinate's pleas; though rendering lip service that "there can be no harm in wishing for forbearance," and promptly vitiating the faint remark by adding: "It is not for me to meddle in this matter." [42] He was quite willing to see Burr destroyed and removed forever from his path.

The irrepressible Barbary States now began to act up again. Hardly had the Tripolitans been treated with a show of force when relations with Algiers and Morocco worsened. Algiers thus far had done nothing but mutter some threats, and Jefferson was willing enough to comply with Madison's suggestion that a *douceur* of another $30,000 might pacify them temporarily. But Morocco had taken an insolent stand, going so far as to order the American consul out of the realm.

Jefferson was puzzled what to write the emperor of Morocco, complaining that "when one has nothing to write about it is difficult to find the end to begin with." [43] But he found plenty to commune over with his Cabinet in the crisis. It was obvious that Morocco either intended war now, or later in conjunction with the other Barbary Powers. He therefore thought it wise to recall any instructions to our Mediterranean fleet about their return to American waters, and to hold them there against eventualities.[44]

But Gallatin, who would be responsible for raising the money to carry on a war, was willing to swallow national pride. "I consider it a mere matter of calculation," he advised the President, "whether the purchase of peace is not cheaper than the expense of a war, which shall not even give us the free use of the Mediterranean trade.... Eight years hence we shall, I trust, be able to assume a different tone; but our exertions at present consume the seeds of our greatness and retard to an indefinite time the epoch of our strength." [45] The eight-year period to which Gallatin alluded related to the time set for the final extinction of the public debt.

These were the very arguments that Jefferson himself always employed when the question of conflict with any other power arose; but the impudence of the Barbary States had consistently made him lose sight of his cardinal principle. Disregarding Gallatin's cautious advice, he countermanded a cargo of gun carriages destined for Morocco as tribute, and ordered two frigates to be made ready to sail to reinforce the Mediterranean fleet. "These, with those already there, & the Swedes [similarly at odds with the piratical States], are surely sufficient for the enemies at present opposed to us." [46]

Difficulties arose. The frigate *New York* was in any event due to sail for France; but Gallatin insisted that there was no money left in the naval appropriation for outfitting the *John Adams*. Jefferson was home in Monticello, trying to conduct the business of the United States through the mails. He sought Madison's advice; who thought the frigate ought to go. So did Robert Smith, Secretary of the Navy. But Jefferson yielded, albeit unhappily, to the financial argument. After all, had he not made it a cardinal article of faith that appropriations be made for specific purposes, and that one fund must not be commingled with another? Had he not sought Hamilton's dismissal and even criminal prosecution for doing just that? Yet—could not some way be found later to include the expense as a "debt incurred?" [47]

Fortunately, the embarrassing situation resolved itself without the necessity of any subterfuge. By the time Jefferson returned to Washington on October 7th, news had arrived that peace had been made with Morocco, and that there never had been any danger of rupture with either Tunis or Algiers.[48] A Cabinet meeting was held on October 21st and it was decided that up to $20,000 might be offered the Emperor of Morocco for "a firm establishment of a state of peace." [49]

The scare taught Jefferson a lesson. He realized now that a navy must always be in "a state of perfect preservation, so that at the beginning of a subsequent war it shall be as sound as at the end of the preceding one when laid up, and the lessening the expence of repairs, perpetually necessary while they lie in water, are objects of the first importance to a nation which to a certain degree must be maritime." His inventive mind therefore became active. The European dry docks were below water, but could only be used at high tide. "If the dry dock were above the level of the tide water," Jefferson proposed, "and there be any means of raising the vessels up into them, and of covering the dock with a roof, thus withdrawn from the wet and sun, they would last as long as the interior timbers, doors & floors of a house." In order to float the ships into the dock, a canal type of lock might be employed. He sent the idea to Benjamin H. Latrobe, the architect, and asked him to prepare the necessary drawings for such a plan.[50]

Gallatin, however, with his passion for economy, opposed the ingenious idea. In fact, anything that smacked of additional expense could be counted on to meet with his disapproval.[51]

For once, however, Jefferson overrode his penurious Secretary of Treasury, and when Latrobe submitted specifications and an estimated expense of $417,276 for the entire operation, he laid the matter before Congress on December 27th for its consideration.[52] There it died.

There was some reason, however, for Gallatin's frugality. The peace in Europe—short and illusory as it was—nevertheless cut heavily into the American carrying trade and therefore reduced revenues. Jefferson had hoped to be able to drop the duties on sugar and salt, and substitute for them increased duties on luxury imports chiefly affecting the rich. But he was afraid now that all the forms of revenue would have to be kept intact, and that even the already minimum expenses of the navy must be further reduced.[53]

The navy was particularly in his mind at this time. When, therefore, it was proposed in Congress to build a series of piers in the Delaware River, and he had to conform to his views of the Constitution to declare that, or any other internal improvement unconstitutional, he found in that same navy a method of getting around the difficulty. Employing an argument perilously close to that which he had anathematized when Hamilton used it, he now said that "a power to provide and maintain a navy, is a power to provide receptacles for it, and places to cover & preserve it." If, therefore, these same unconstitutional piers could be placed where ships of war would be able to lie at them, they would then become constitutional.[54]

CHAPTER 51

Dreams of Empire

THUS far, except for the solitary incident of the Barbary Powers, the attention of the United States had been devoted almost exclusively to domestic problems. The undeclared war with France and the repercussions of the XYZ affair that had kept the last years of Adams's administration in a turmoil had been satisfactorily settled. Napoleon, after his seizure of power through the *coup d'état* of the 18th Brumaire (November 9, 1799), and faced with the combined might of Europe, had determined to settle affairs with this strange new republic across the sea. A treaty was negotiated whereby, in return for an extinguishment of American claims for damages over confiscated cargoes and ships, or so the French were to claim, the embarrassing guarantee of the United States to protect French possessions in the western hemisphere was similarly withdrawn. Jefferson submitted the treaty to the Senate, and it was duly ratified on December 19, 1801. Seemingly, there were no further points of contact between the two nations at which friction could develop.

But on July 22, 1800, shortly after his overwhelming victory over the Austrians at Marengo, Napoleon felt himself once more in a position to cast a speculative eye on America. The dreams of a vast American empire, made familiar by earlier unsuccessful moves of Talleyrand, stirred again. The great trans-Mississippian West, granted to Spain as a *douceur* for losses elsewhere, loomed in Napoleon's mind both as an extension of his own world power and as a containment for the youthful, but aggressive United States. Spain, weak and dying, could not be depended on to hold the line. Therefore, Spain must return what she could not hold.

Napoleon sent a courier in secrecy and haste to the French Minister at Madrid. Obtain a treaty, he ordered, whereby Spain would return, or retrocede, Louisiana to France at a fixed future date; and, to sweeten the pill, offer her the Duchy of Parma in Italy.

Since Spain lay in the shadow of the great First Consul's power, she could not help but obey. A preliminary *projet* was quickly drawn on August 28, 1800, in which Spain pledged herself "to retrocede to the French Republic the colony of Louisiana, with the same extent it actually had in the hands of Spain, and such as it should be according to the treaties subsequently passed between Spain and other States." But more was obtained than had even at first been intended. "Spain," continued the *projet*, "shall further join to this cession that of the two Floridas, eastern and western, with their actual limits." [1] Talleyrand, who had been recalled to the Foreign Ministry, could now feel himself vindicated.

The final Treaty of San Ildefonso was signed on October 1, 1800; but, while following the *projet* as to Louisiana, it omitted mention of the Floridas. It was, however, orally agreed that certain sections of *West* Florida would be ceded after a general peace, on the special demand of Napoleon.

Spain repented of its one-sided bargain almost as soon as the ink had dried on the document; and called back to power Don Manuel Godoy, who bore the strange title of Principe de la Paz (Prince of the Peace), given him in recognition of his services in arranging a former peace with France. Bitterly anti-French, he had been forced out of his primary position at the Court of Spain in 1798; now he was back.

On July 27, 1801, Napoleon demanded possession; but Godoy evaded on the ground that Parma had not been turned over in accordance with the understanding. Napoleon, in a rage, determined to seize Louisiana without further ado. Making peace with England, the last major antagonist in his path, he first turned his attention to the French island of St. Domingo, where the remarkable Toussaint L'Ouverture was heading a great Negro revolt to drive the French into the sea. A vast army eventually crushed the Negro leader and his desperate followers, and St. Domingo came once more under French dominion.

With the Caribbean island as a vantage point, Louisiana was next. "My intention," wrote Napoleon, "is to take possession of Louisiana with the shortest delay, and that this expedition be made in the utmost secrecy, under the appearance of being directed on St. Domingo." [2] But Talleyrand, who always preferred the uses of tortuous diplomacy to naked force, managed eventually to overcome Godoy's evasions by a specific pledge that France would neither sell Louisiana nor alienate it in any manner once it came into her possession. What Spain feared more than anything else—and what eventually did happen—was the placing of this huge territory into the hands of the United States. Spain sensed the insatiable expansive drive of the Americans. Once they possessed Louisiana, what could prevent them from pushing on to the Pacific in the west, and south into Mexico and even further?

All these negotiations, treaties, cessions and countercessions had been conducted in such secrecy that the nation most interested—the United States—remained in blankest ignorance of the proceedings. Jefferson had been in the Presidency for several months before the first faint rumors of the Treaty of Ildefonso, completed more than eight months before, began to trickle through and to raise a vague uneasiness. On May 29, 1801, Jefferson voiced his first definite alarm to Monroe; on June 9th, Madison, as Secretary of State, issued the first of a series of instructions to the American Ministers in Europe to investigate the matter.[3]

The dread confirmations reached America early in 1802 from both

England and France. Rufus King forwarded certain pertinent documents from England; while Robert R. Livingston, not long before arrived in France, was able to enclose a copy of the actual treaty. "It is a transaction," he reported, "of pretty long standing." [4]

The alarming news galvanized Jefferson into immediate activity. More than almost anyone else he realized the implications of having a powerful and aggressive neighbor like Napoleon Bonaparte on the very doorstep of the United States. He had already had a foretaste of what it would mean. The victorious French in St. Domingo had seized American goods on the island, and imprisoned American merchants and ship captains. Madison had protested to Pichon, the French Minister to the United States, who obligingly remonstrated with Leclerc, the French commander responsible; and was himself summarily superseded for his pains. Jefferson's unofficial observer in St. Domingo, Tobias Lear—the former private secretary of President Washington—was expelled from the island with brutal dispatch.

On April 13, 1802, by a happy accident, Dupont de Nemours informed Jefferson that he intended going to France for commercial reasons, but primarily to attempt, à la Dr. Logan, to cement good relations between the two countries; and offered his services.[5] Jefferson promptly seized the heaven-sent opportunity and urged him to come to Washington. "I believe," he wrote, "that the destinies of great countries depend on it, such is the crisis now existing. I shall say to you much which I cannot commit to paper." [6]

But Dupont found it impossible to go to Washington. He was sailing from Philadelphia on May 5th. He had heard, however, that Jefferson had the idea of purchasing Louisiana; if so, he approved of it heartily.[7]

Before this astonishing bit of news reached Jefferson, he had already drafted a lengthy and confidential letter to Livingston to be entrusted to Dupont for safe carriage.

"The cession of Louisiana and the Floridas by Spain to France works most sorely on the U. S.," he wrote. "It compleatly reverses all the political relations of the U. S. and will form a new epoch in our political course." Even yet, however, Jefferson did not grasp the full implications, in spite of Dupont's clairvoyance. It was New Orleans, rather than the vast expanse of Louisiana, that engaged his attention. "There is on the globe," he said, "one single spot, the possessor of which is our natural and habitual enemy," and that is New Orleans! "France placing herself in that door assumes to us the attitude of defiance. Spain might have retained it quietly for years."

He gave the reasons. Spain was feeble and exercised no real threat; but France was energetic and powerful, as was the United States. "The day that France takes possession of N. Orleans," he warned, "fixes the sentence which is to restrain her forever within her low water mark. It seals the union of two nations who in conjunction can maintain exclusive possession of the ocean. From that moment we must marry ourselves to the

British fleet and nation. We must turn all our attentions to a maritime force, for which our resources place us on very high grounds: and having formed and cemented together a power which may render reinforcement of her settlements here impossible to France, make the first cannon, which shall be fired in Europe the signal for tearing up any settlement she may have made, and for holding the two continents of America in sequestration for the common purposes of the united British and American nations." This, Jefferson added, we neither seek nor desire, but it will be forced on us by France. Let these considerations be imparted to France, not as a threat "but as consequences not controulable by us, but inevitable from the course of things."

Even if France should consider the acquisition of Louisiana essential, let her at least cede New Orleans and the Floridas to us, an action which would "in a great degree remove the causes of jarring and irritation between us." [8]

This was a remarkable letter, for several reasons. In the first place, it discloses the fact that Jefferson's attention was so fixed on the immediate vicinage of New Orleans and the Floridas that he failed to recognize the great significance of Louisiana. Or, recognizing it, he was willing to leave the great West to the future, in the hope and belief that France, deprived of control of the Mississippi by the cession of New Orleans, would be unable to build an empire there sufficiently strong to withstand the determined encroachments of an expanding America.

In the second place, the advent of Napoleon and the present threat had so alarmed him that all his former hatred of England could not stand in the way of a willingness now to seek an alliance with her to withstand the French. That he meant sincerely the striking phrase—"from that moment we must marry ourselves to the British fleet and nation"—may be open to doubt. It was excellent strategy thus to play on the fears of the French; yet he must have seen that eventually the logic of history would drive him, willy-nilly, into the strange alliance.

But the rumor which had reached Dupont concerning his alleged intentions on Louisiana filled him equally with alarm, and he sought hastily to disabuse him.[9] Forwarding to him the letter to Livingston, as well as letters of a private nature to friends abroad, he gave him leave to read the official communication, so that "you may be able to impress on the government of France the inevitable consequences of their taking possession of Louisiana; and tho', as I here mention, the cession of N. Orleans & the Floridas to us would be a palliative; yet I believe it would be no more; and that this measure will cost France, & perhaps not very long hence, a war which will annihilate her on the ocean, and place that element under the despotism of two nations, which I am not reconciled to the more because my own would be one of them." This, of course, was not disavowal, except insofar as it related to current negotiations.

He sought also to employ Dupont to placate Talleyrand. Dupont was to assure the latter that the XYZ imbroglio had been an artifice of the Federalists to consolidate their power; that they had since been dismissed, and that Jefferson and the Republicans, now in the seats of government, had always disbelieved the story.[10] Talleyrand must have smiled sardonically when Dupont faithfully relayed this disavowal. After all, who better than he knew that the story had been true?

Dupont expressed doubts over these instructions. While he had approved of an amicable attempt to purchase Louisiana, he felt strongly that these fire-breathing threats would merely alienate Napoleon. Why not, he inquired, seek merely a freedom of passage through New Orleans and the mouth of the Mississippi? And, if the United States still insisted on a foothold on the west bank, offer a *quid pro quo*—aid to France in regaining Canada from the British.[11] But he could not convince Jefferson, and was compelled to sail in May with the original instructions.[12]

Even before Dupont arrived in Paris and revealed what Jefferson wished, Livingston had been engaged in negotiations on his own. He hinted to the French that we might be willing to purchase West Florida and make the payment to their American creditors; but the hint was blandly ignored. As he dejectedly informed Rufus King, the American Minister in England, "no argument we can use will be of the least use on the subject."[13] What made the stone wall even more insurmountable was the infuriating pretense of the French that they neither had New Orleans, nor had made any treaty with Spain concerning it.[14]

Livingston, confronted with contradictory reports and isolated from his home government by many weeks of tedious communication, groped rather blindly toward a solution. While the French continued to deny—though an authentic copy of the treaty was in his hands—Rufus King from his listening post in London wrote that "according to my creed" New Orleans and the Floridas "must and will ultimately belong to us; if so every step we take should have a reference to this acquisition."[15]

At the same time, Charles Pinckney, even closer to the scene in Madrid, insisted that the Floridas were *not* included in the cession from Spain to France; and the Spanish Ambassador in France told him the same thing. This was most extraordinary, as Livingston himself was certain that they *were*.[16] The confusion, of course, arose from the equivocal wording of the final treaty as opposed to the *projet*—West Florida was to be conveyed after a general peace and then only on specific demand.

By the time Dupont arrived, bearing Jefferson's instructions, the harried American Minister had a somewhat clearer picture of events. The French Ministry now readily acknowledged the cession of Louisiana and New Orleans, and frankly countered Livingston's proposals with the grim statement that they intended to take possession first, before entering into any consideration of his offers. The Floridas, Livingston also learned, were not included in the deal, and would remain with Spain. "There never was a Government," he wrote home angrily, "in which less could be done by negotiation than here. There is no people, no Legislature, no counsellors. One man [Napoleon] is every thing. He seldom asks advice, and never hears it unasked. His ministers are mere clerks; and his Legislature and counsellors parade officers."[17] Which is an excellent description of a dictatorship.

Even Dupont, who as a Frenchman had come with the full belief that he could act as an honest broker between the two nations he loved, was compelled to report in discouragement that the atmosphere of the country of his birth was thick with suspicion of the motives of the country of his adoption. Yet he refused to be daunted by rebuffs and proposed that New Orleans and the Floridas be purchased by the United States for the sum of $6,000,000.[18]

The situation at home, however, had changed in the interim for the worse. Ominous news came from New Orleans that the Spanish Intendant, Don Juan Ventura Morales, had imposed harsh restrictions on American commerce passing on the river.[19] Jefferson was furious, particularly when he could obtain no satisfaction from the Spanish Minister in Washington, to whom he complained. "I wish," he wrote bitterly to Madison, "we could once get the European powers to give to their diplomatic representatives here such provisional authorities as would enable them to [control?] the conduct of their governors in whatever relates to us. We are too far from Europe to dance across the ocean for attendance at their levees whenever these pigmy kings in their colonies think proper to injure or insult us."[20]

What Jefferson thought was the irresponsible action of the Intendant at New Orleans, however, had become the considered policy of the Spanish government. On July 14, 1802, the Intendant received official instructions from his King to close the port entirely to American goods except by express permission from Madrid. In order to avoid an open break, though, the order was cannily worded so to throw the onus on the Intendant himself, as having examined the Spanish-American treaty of 1795 and discovered that the right of American deposit had been limited to three years, a term long since expired.[21]

It was the French who had pressed this bold move on Spain; preferring to take over New Orleans with the prohibition against the Americans already a *fait accompli*. Tennessee and Kentucky, the chief sufferers, set up a clamor in Washington for war against the Spaniards. The Spanish Minister, Don Carlos Martinez de Yrujo, eventually sought to smooth over American ruffled feathers by assuring Madison that the act of Morales had been entirely unauthorized and, in fact, sent him a sharp note denouncing him for it.[22]

Nor was the news coming from Livingston and Dupont in Paris of better omen. Jefferson was goaded to an outburst that "we stand, compleatly corrected of the error, that either the government or the nation of France has any remains of friendship for us. On the contrary, it appears evident, that an unfriendly spirit prevails in the most important individuals of the government, towards us." The long honeymoon was over. No longer did Jefferson intend to favor France in any altercation with England; hereafter, he asserted, we shall observe a strict neutrality, and take sides with either only when forced to it by the provocations of the other.[23]

Pichon, the French Minister, appraised the new attitude that Jefferson was adopting toward France. "However timid Mr. Jefferson may be," he reported to Talleyrand, "and whatever price he may put on his pacific policy, one cannot foresee precisely what his answer will be. . . . I find in general a bad temper as regards us; and I cannot help seeing that there is a tendency toward adopting an irrevocably hostile system. This circumstance will be decisive for Mr. Jefferson. If he acts feebly, he is lost among his partisans; it will be then the time for Mr. Burr to show himself to advantage."[24]

The specter of the thrust-aside Vice-President of the United States indeed lay heavy in the consciousness of the President, as the perceptive Frenchman had noted. Among the most ardent partisans of the Republican party were the turbulent frontiersmen of Kentucky and Tennessee. They loved Jefferson, but Burr was almost equally popular with them. If their grievances against Spain and her inheritor France were disregarded by Jefferson, their love would suffer a decided sea change; and Burr's star would rise as the symbol of a gallant soldier who would take no nonsense from Don or Monsieur.

Nothing of these violent behind-the-scenes proceedings appeared in Jefferson's Second Annual Message to Congress. Rather, he sought deftly to play them down and avoid having his hand forced too prematurely. He tried, indeed, to concentrate all attention on the domestic scene.

He asked Madison to get him a docket of the cases before the federal courts during the preceding year, in order to show Congress and all men "how little is to be done by the federal judiciary, and will effectually crush the clamour still raised on the suppression of the new judges." But Madison advised him to let sleeping dogs lie, and Jefferson yielded.[25]

From Gallatin he sought subjects for recommendation to Congress. He himself could think of but two, he said: a militia law, and the reformation of the civil list.[26] Gallatin replied with a similar naïvete when a draft was finally placed before him: "I hope that your administration will afford but few materials to historians; and we have already a favorable symptom in the difficulty under which we are to collect materials for a message."[27] Nowhere, even in these confidential interchanges between the President and the members of his Cabinet, was there the faintest mention of Louisiana and of the grave problems it had raised. Everything was sweetness and light.

Jefferson diligently sought to give that impression to everyone. These were halcyon days, and the function of government was to meddle neither with the affairs of other nations nor with the affairs of its own citizens. *Laissez faire* was the motto; and the slogan for Congress: "Let things alone." [28]

The President, indeed, seemed far more interested in other matters; such as, for example, the establishment of a Library of Congress. This had been near his heart and when, at his instigation, an appropriation was made to purchase books, he took the task eagerly upon himself. He sent to London and Paris for books in "good editions but not pompous ones; neat bindings but not splendid"; to be purchased with the same degree of "vigorous economy as that of an individual." [29]

Tom Paine, the stormy petrel of two worlds, had come to Washington, and Jefferson made much of him, though he was warned by such a fellow radical as the printer, William Duane, that Paine was again exercising his unequaled talent for getting into trouble. Duane had seen the first numbers of the famous *Age of Reason* and begged Paine not to publish it. Such an attack on revealed religion, he said, would cause even the Republicans to desert him, and all his political influence be destroyed. But Paine refused to listen.[30]

Dr. Mitchill, the New York Republican, who met the "celebrated Thomas Paine" for the first time at Gallatin's house, has left an interesting account of his appearance. "He has a red and rugged face," Mitchill wrote his wife, "which looks as if it had been much hackneyed in the service of the world. His eyes are black and lively, his nose somewhat aquiline and pointing downward. It corresponds in color with the fiery appearance of his cheeks.... He is fond of talking, and very full of anecdote." [31]

There had been considerable outcry over Jefferson's patronage of the "atheist" Paine even before the *Age of Reason* was published; and the outcry was redoubled after it appeared. But Jefferson refused to desert his friend, and went out of the way to show his respect for him in the most open fashion. It was, he felt, his duty to do so and to defy the raging priesthood and "federal calumny." [32] He deemed it all the more necessary because Paine had accused him of avoiding him in deference to public opinion. He had, he complained, come to Washington to show the President some models he had made of iron bridges, and to talk to him about France and Louisiana; and he thought he was being deliberately slighted.[33]

Newly arrived Congressmen were just as curious to see the President as the notorious infidel Paine. Those who were Federalists lumped them both in the same category, and may have expected certain outward physical manifestations of inner corruption. One of these was the newly elected Senator from New Hampshire, William Plumer, whose careful notes on the Washington scene give invaluable, if somewhat partisan, information on day-to-day proceedings.

Plumer arrived on December 2, 1802; on the following day he was intro-

Collection of Henry Cabot Lodge, Jr. Courtesy the Frick Art Reference Library

ALEXANDER HAMILTON

Painting by John Trumbull

Collection of Washington and Lee University. Courtesy the Frick Art Reference Library

JOHN MARSHALL

Painting by Chester Harding

duced to the President by a colleague, General Varnum of Massachusetts. The pair waited in the reception room of the President's House, and in a few minutes "a tall highboned man came into the room; he was drest, or rather undrest, with an old brown coat, red waistcoat, old corduroy small clothes, much soild—woolen hose—& slippers without heels. I thought this man was a servant; but Genl Varnum surprized me by announcing that it was the President.... I tarried about twenty minutes—he is easy of access, & conversed with great ease & freedom." [34]

All through his Presidency, every visitor remarked on Jefferson's negligent, somewhat shabby dress in the privacy of his home, and even when he appeared at levees or entertained foreign diplomats. There seems to have been something of deliberate attitudinizing in this careful disarray and the threadworn quality of his garments. He thereby sought to convey his sense of republican equality with the mass of plain Americans and his contempt for the forms and conventional finery of court levees. The people loved it, just as later they loved the tales of humble origins and log cabins; and clever politicians always stressed rough speech and negligent grammar. It was held against Martin Van Buren that he dressed with care and in fashion; and Lincoln's loose-fitting, rusty clothes helped create a myth. Jefferson could dress as expensively and as well as any high-flown Federalist; he had ruffled it with the aristocrats in France, and even during his Presidency, he ordered from his tailors the finest cloth available for his personal garments. But they were for private wear, and not for these occasions when he was plain Mr. President, and not His Excellency.

The Federalists hated and feared him, but they attended his dinners, which had become famous for their lavishness of food and wines; and they found him, even though they sneered at his dress, "very social." Both daughters, Martha Randolph and Maria Eppes, came to Washington at the end of 1802 for an extended stay, and graced his table. "They appeared well-accomplished women—very delicate and tolerably handsome," remarked that arch-Federalist and land speculator extraordinary, the Reverend Manasseh Cutler.[35]

Congress met in session on December 15, 1802, and listened to the reading of Jefferson's Message. It was low-keyed in tone, soothing, and optimistic. There was little in it to exacerbate the tenderest sensibilities of the most fiery Federalist; there were few recommendations; and as far as Jefferson was concerned, Congress might just as well have packed up and gone home. "God's in his heaven; all's right with the world," was the general tenor.

The opening sentence set the tone: "Another year has come around, and finds us still blessed with peace and friendship abroad; law, order, and religion, at home; good affection and harmony with our Indian neighbors; our burdens lightened, yet our income sufficient for the public wants, and the produce of the year great beyond example."

If here and there a minor flaw existed, it could easily be corrected. There were, he admitted, some European discriminations against our carrying trade; but he believed a little "friendly discussion" would obtain reciprocity; if not, it would be for Congress to decide whether to provide "countervailing inequalities at home."

He dismissed the all-important retrocession of Louisiana to France with a few words. It might, he admitted cautiously, if carried into effect, make "a change in the aspect of our foreign relations." That was all.

He touched on the uneventfulness of the undeclared war with Tripoli, on the settlement of boundaries with the Indians. He was more profuse on the pleasing subject of finances. "It is with pleasure I inform you that the receipts of external duties for the last twelve months have exceeded those of any former year." All expenses of government had been met, the public debt was reduced by $5,500,000, and there was a neat surplus in the Treasury.

He dwelt with satisfaction on the economical course of government, its paring of expenses, and the fact that the "moral canker," the public debt, was well on the way to extinguishment.

Though he had privately insisted on a militia on a national scale to replace any standing army, he now merely suggested that Congress review the institution of a militia, without offering a single specific recommendation. As for the navy, which had already been cut to the bone, he spoke only of the possibility of a few small vessels to be added; declaring that any further expense in this department should go "to the saving of what we already possess." He suggested, therefore, his pet plan for a naval dry dock, with locks to lift the ships to "a dry and sheltered bed." [36]

To listen to or to read this soporific Message, the innocent bystander might well have taken it for granted that not a cloud remained to trouble the national horizon. Louisiana was completely played down; and as for the sudden closure of the Mississippi that had roused the Western States to such a veritable frenzy, not a word.

This gentle calm did serve some useful purpose, however—it helped placate the Federalists, who cared not for Louisiana or the Mississippi, and were happy to have peaceful relations, even an alliance, with England. Plumer thought the Message "an excellent one" and "calculated to soothe the angry passions, & quiet the fears of the people"; yet he continued to doubt Jefferson's integrity, and wrote sourly that "it was with an ill grace he boasted of the fulness of the treasury, when at the same time he condemned those federal laws by which the money was collected." [37]

But Jefferson's fellow Republicans were not to be thus easily put off. John Randolph of Roanoke, eccentric, brilliant and a hater of shams, spilled Jefferson's carefully prepared apple cart by rising in the House two days after the Message and moving that all the documents relating to the right of American deposit at New Orleans and the present closure be submitted by the government to Congress.

John Randolph is one of the most interesting and peculiar figures in American history. Related by a complex series of cousinships with Jefferson on the one side and John Marshall on the other, he was at once passionately republican and personally aristocratic. Tall, willowy, with a small, smooth baby face perched on an elongated body, voice shrill and effeminate, given to sudden passions, famed for his oratorical outbursts and feared for his savage satire and biting sarcasm, he nevertheless, as Plumer justly noted, "was destitute of that prudence & sound judgment, that patience of entering into details, & those habits of business, which are requisite for the leader of a party." [38]

By this sudden move he practically announced to the world that he had broken with the President, and that an important, if not too large, section of Republicans who followed his banner would reserve for themselves the right to examine Jefferson's activities with a critical eye.

Inasmuch as the main body of the Federalists in Congress were largely unreconstructed, in spite of Jefferson's continual gestures in their direction, this new Republican faction which now began to form around the figure of Randolph boded ill for Jefferson's subtle policies.

Congress, as Plumer noticed, was sharply divided into two party camps. They boarded in separate establishments, and rarely visited or mingled socially with each other. Plumer, who had a more open and inquiring mind, was the only Federalist who sought out Republicans and partook with them in friendly converse. It is true that Jefferson regularly invited the Federalists, with but few recalcitrant exceptions like Uriah Tracy of Connecticut, to dine with him. But he was careful never to mix them with Republicans, a procedure which Plumer thought an error that tended "to mark & perpetuate party." [39] Jefferson might just as well have saved his assiduous attentions, for he never converted—except for a very few—the Federalist leaders he wooed with food, drink and flattering conversation.

On December 22, 1802, Jefferson sent the required documents to the House. By a happy stroke of fortune, a letter came from Governor Claiborne of the Mississippi Territory stating that Salcedo, the Spanish Governor, denied responsibility for the act of the Intendant in closing the port, and declared it to be wholly unauthorized.[40]

This new letter, which Jefferson promptly submitted to the House on December 30th, turned the tide. The House debated the matter of the closure in secret session until the 7th of January, when it opened its doors to announce the passage of a resolution on the subject by a vote of 50 to 25. The resolution was a complete victory for Jefferson. While expressing the House's "unalterable determination to maintain the boundaries and the rights of navigation and commerce through the river Mississippi, as established by existing treaties," nevertheless, "relying, with perfect confidence, on the vigilance and wisdom of the Executive, they will wait the issue of such measures as that department of the Government shall have pursued for asserting the rights and vindicating the injuries of the United States." [41]

The Senate, after a long debate, passed a much stronger and more positive set of resolutions on February 25, 1803. While similarly upholding the President, the Senate put weapons into his hands in the event the Intendant's "unauthorized" closure continued. Jefferson was empowered, in his discretion, to call on the States to muster, equip and have ready to march 80,000 militia; and a sum of money was appropriated, the amount later to be decided, for paying the militia during actual service, and for such other expenses, during Congressional recess, as the President "may deem necessary for the security of the territory of the United States." [42] This was indeed granting Jefferson a blank check.

If Congress thus obediently responded to the wishes of the President, the western legislatures were not as amenable. Closer to the situation, and with their most vital interests involved, they passed fiery resolutions demanding that troops be forthwith dispatched to Natchez and that New Orleans be seized at the first attempt by the French to take it over from the Spaniards.

Roger Griswold, Federalist Congressman from Connecticut, took advantage of this western Republican clamor to embarrass Jefferson. He called in the House for a similar submission of all the documents relating to Louisiana before them as John Randolph had successfully demanded for the Mississippi closure. This was a far more serious move than Randolph's, since it would have exposed to public gaze negotiations much too delicate for such rude handling; and the Administration forces rallied to lay the resolution on the table by a vote of 51 to 35.[43]

On the same day that the Federalist assault was thus successfully met—January 11, 1803—Samuel Smith of Maryland, to whom Jefferson looked more and more for Republican leadership in the House, countered with a surprise resolution behind closed doors. "*Resolved*," it read, "That a sum of two millions of dollars, in addition to the provision heretofore made, be appropriated to defray any expenses which may be incurred in relation to the intercourse between the United States and foreign nations ... to be applied under the direction of the President of the United States, who, if necessary, is hereby authorized to borrow the whole or any part thereof; an account whereof, as soon as may be, shall be laid before Congress." [44]

This amazing resolution, far more sweeping than the one which the Senate was later to consider, and seeking to deliver $2,000,000 into the President's hands without any strings attached, was an essential part of a preconceived and carefully dovetailed strategy which Jefferson had worked out with Smith and a few Republican leaders in his confidence.

The West, he realized, could not be held much longer in line with mere pious resolutions and vague promises of future action; something dramatic would have to be done to keep them temporarily quiet. That something, he decided, was to send Monroe on an extraordinary mission to

France, to work with or to supersede Livingston in negotiating for a final settlement of the Mississippi question. It was obvious that nothing could be gained by talking with Spain, since France was the equitable, if not already the legal, owner, and Spanish moves were dictated from Paris.

On January 10th, he had written to Monroe offering him the mission which, he explained, was necessitated by "the fever into which the western mind is thrown by the affair at N. Orleans stimulated by the mercantile, and generally the federal interest threatens to overbear our peace."[45] It suited Jefferson to place the blame on the Federalists rather than the western Republicans.

On January 11th, the nomination was submitted to the Senate; and simultaneously Smith came forward in the House with *his* resolution. The resolution was referred to a committee headed by Joseph H. Nicholson, another Republican stalwart; and they were privately informed of the real purpose of the appropriation—to seek the purchase of New Orleans and the two Floridas from France. On that basis, they recommended its adoption.[46]

The Senate approved Monroe's nomination without much debate and Jefferson immediately urged Monroe to accept, amplifying on the reasons which had induced him to take this step. "The agitation of the public mind on occasion of the late suspension of our right of deposit at N. Orleans is extreme," he wrote. "In the western country it is natural and grounded on honest motives. In the seaports it proceeds from a desire for war which increases the mercantile lottery; in the federalists generally and especially those of Congress the object is to force us into war if possible, in order to derange our finances, or if this cannot be done, to attach the western country to them, as their best friends, and thus get again into power. Remonstrances memorials &c. are now circulating through the whole western country and signing by the body of people. The measures we have been pursuing being invisible, do not satisfy their minds. Something sensible therefore was become necessary; and indeed our object of purchasing N. Orleans and the Floridas is a measure liable to assume so many shapes, that no instructions could be squared to fit them; therefore a minister extraordinary, with discretionary powers, was essential."[47]

Thus, by a bold move reminiscent of Adams's sudden dispatch of Vans Murray on a mission to France during a time of crisis, Jefferson effectively silenced his critics in both parties, and thought to put off the day of judgment. Actually, he anticipated no results from the mission. A year later, he confided to Priestley that "I did not expect he [Napoleon] would yield until a war took place between France and England; and my hope was to palliate and endure, if Messrs. Ross, Morris, etc. [Federalist Congressmen] did not force a premature rupture, until that event."[48]

At the same time, he was uneasy about his Constitutional powers to purchase territory for addition to the United States. Gallatin stoutly assured him that he had that right, quoting chapter and verse; and then, himself unconvinced, suggested that the matter be further examined.[49] The Attorney General, Levi Lincoln, however, expressed doubts as to the constitutionality of acquisition; but Jefferson preferred to accept Gallatin's main thesis that territory could be acquired. "Whether," he added, "when acquired, it may be taken into the Union by the Constitution as it now stands, will become a question of expediency. I think it will be safer not to permit the enlargement of the Union but by amendment of the Constitution." [50] He was to change his mind on this vital point later on.

Under Jefferson's urgings, Monroe finally, if reluctantly, accepted the mission; and set sail for France on March 8, 1803.

CHAPTER 52

Louisiana Purchase

MONROE'S mission afforded Jefferson well-grounded cause for self-congratulation. "This measure," he wrote happily to his son-in-law, "has suppressed all further inflammatory proceedings meditated by the Federalists for instigating the Western country to force on a war between us & the owners of New Orleans. Their confidence in Monroe will tranquilise them on the subject. In the mean time we have the best grounded presumptions that the suspension of the right of deposit will be immediately removed." [1]

He had dexterously outwitted the opposition and at the same time placated his friends. He felt securely optimistic that somehow the French, if not the Spanish, could be made to see the light; and in the meantime, he had a breathing space to attend to certain matters closer at home. These were both public and personal.

Monroe's sailing turned his attention to those pitiful few of his old friends who were still alive in Europe. A sheaf of letters went in Monroe's bag, addressed to Maria Cosway, Madame de Tessé, Madame de Corny, Volney, Cathalan and others. They had fallen on evil days; and others, equally regarded, were dead. "Twenty seven years of revolutions and counter revolutions," mused Jefferson mournfully, "have swept off the whole of my friends & acquaintances in Paris, Madame de Corny & Mons. de la Fayette excepted." Madame de Corny, it was true, was alive, but she had been crippled by a fall and lived retired from the world of which she had once been such a gay ornament.[2] Madame de Tessé was still his botanical correspondent par excellence, and to her he confided his intention when he finally retired—that ever receding date—to become a florist and plant flowers at Monticello, though his prior passion had been for trees.[3]

Maria Cosway, who once had been the unwitting cause of a famous struggle between Jefferson's head and heart, had finally emerged from her religious retirement and was back in Paris making etchings of paintings in the Louvre. A prospectus of them came to her old friend, the President of the United States. At the same time, she expressed concern over the treatment of the Catholic faith in America. Jefferson dutifully subscribed to the etchings, and reassured her about American Catholics. "All religions here are equally free," he replied, "and equally protected by the laws, and left to be supported by their own respective votaries. In some places the

Catholic is better off than other sects, as they possess valuable endowments of land." [4]

He was thinking a good deal these days about the broader aspects of religion and of the nature of man and his destiny. The fashionable patter about "man in a state of nature" disgusted him. Locke and Hobbes had first brought it into popularity, but at least with logical limitations. Rousseau, however, had glorified the "natural" man and set him up as a noble ideal which civilization had subverted and deteriorated. Jefferson vented his feelings to a French savant via that same capacious bag which Monroe took with him.

"I have long been fatigued," he avowed, "with the eternal repetition of the term '*man in the state of nature*,' by which is meant man in his savage and stupid state, with his faculties entirely undeveloped. If this be his natural state, then the foetus in embryo exhibits it in its utmost perfection. As if the improvement of the senses of man, the strengthening and developing his reasoning faculties, any more than the growth of his body, rendered him an unnatural being, and placed him beyond the limits of his nature!" [5]

The idea of Rousseau's "noble savage" clashed irreconcilably with Jefferson's conception of the indefinite perfectibility of man. Whatever romantic strain there might have been in Jefferson—as evidenced by his earlier passion for Ossian—had long since been dissipated by the rational inheritor of the Enlightenment.

Perhaps Maria Cosway's anxious inquiry about the treatment of Catholics in this country brought up the subject again, perhaps it was the immeasurable abuse that poured upon his devoted head from the Calvinist preachers of New England; in any event, Jefferson's thoughts reverted to certain long evening conversations that had taken place between Benjamin Rush and himself during the winter of 1798-99. The Christian religion had been a major topic for these two veteran rationalists; and Jefferson had then promised that some day he would put his views of Christianity down on paper for Rush to read.

Now, in the spring of 1803, in the midst of his duties as President of the United States, the final spark came from a small book he received from Joseph Priestley, entitled *Socrates and Jesus compared.* It came to him just as he was leaving Monticello for return to Washington; and he reflected on its contents as he jogged along the road. The result of his lucubrations was a syllabus or outline of the comparative merits of Christianity and other religions, which he proposed to Rush for expansion into a regular volume.

"They are the result," he told Rush, "of a life of enquiry & reflection, and very different from that Anti-Christian system imputed to me by those who know nothing of my opinions. I am indeed opposed; but not to the genuine precepts of Jesus himself. I am a Christian, in the only sense in which he wished any one to be; sincerely attached to his doctrines, in preference to all others; ascribing to himself every *human* excellence; & believing he never claimed any other."

In confiding his Syllabus to Rush, Jefferson trusted it would "not be exposed to the malignant perversions of those who make every word from me a text for new misrepresentations & calumnies. I am moreover averse," he added with a noble dignity, "to the communication of my religious tenets to the public; because it would countenance the presumption of those who have endeavored to draw them before that tribunal, & to seduce public opinion to erect itself into that inquisition over the rights of conscience which the laws have so justly proscribed. It behoves every man, who values liberty of conscience for himself, to resist invasions of it in the case of others; or their case may by change of circumstances, become his own. It behoves him too in his own case, to give no example of concession, betraying the common right of independant opinion, by answering questions of faith, which the laws have left between god and himself." [6]

The Syllabus which he enclosed was, unfortunately, only the barest outline of his deep-seated convictions on the subject. He compared the teachings of the great philosophers of antiquity—Pythagoras, Socrates, Epicurus, Cicero, Epictetus, Seneca, Marcus Antoninus—and discovered that while they were profound and inspiring in their personal precepts and in their rules for the government of individual passions, "in developing our duties to others, they were short and defective," particularly in inculcating "peace, charity & love to our fellow men."

The ancient Jews, it was true, believed in one God, "but their ideas of him & his attributes were degrading & injurious," and "their Ethics were not only imperfect, but often irreconcilable with the sound dictates of reason & morality, as they respect intercourse with those around us; & repulsive & anti-social, as respecting other nations."

Jesus, therefore, came to reform them. "His parentage was obscure; his condition poor; his education null; his natural endowments great; his life correct and innocent: he was meek, benevolent, patient, firm, disinterested, & of the sublimest eloquence."

Like Socrates and Epictetus, he wrote nothing himself; unlike them, he had no learned men to write for him. The learned, indeed, opposed him as seeking to undermine their advantages. The task of committing his life and doctrines to writing, therefore, "fell on the most unlettered & ignorant men; who wrote, too, from memory, & not till long after the transactions had passed."

The death of Jesus at an early age prevented him from "developing a complete system of morals"; hence his doctrines "were defective as a whole, and fragments only of what he did deliver have come to us mutilated, misstated, & often unintelligible." Then the "corruptions of schismatising followers, who have found an interest in sophisticating & perverting the simple doctrines he taught by engrafting on them the mysticisms of a Grecian sophist [Plato?], frittering them into subtleties, & obscuring them with jargon, until they have caused good men to reject the whole in disgust, & to view Jesus himself as an impostor."

Nevertheless, Jefferson continued, "a system of morals is presented to us, which, if filled up in the true style and spirit of the rich fragments he left us, would be the most perfect and sublime that has ever been taught by man."

Jefferson avoided any direct discussion of the alleged Godhead of Jesus, or of his supernatural inspiration; deeming rightly that it would be pounced upon to his detriment, and all other parts of his thesis ignored. It is obvious, however, from his accompanying letter to Rush and elsewhere that he did not believe in either.

To Jefferson, the peculiar superiority of the system of Jesus lay in its inculcation of a universal philanthropy which extended "not only to kindred and friends, to neighbors and countrymen, but to all mankind, gathering all into one family, under the bonds of love, charity, peace, common wants and common aids." The others, so Jefferson believed, were interested in actions only, while Jesus "pushed his scrutinies into the heart of man," and his doctrine of a future state became "an important incentive" to moral conduct.[7]

Jefferson sent copies of his Syllabus to a selected group of friends, as well as to members of his own family, swearing them all to secrecy in the process. This was his religious creed, and he was profoundly satisfied to have placed it on paper for them to see. The statement would, he felt, enable them to "estimate the libels published against me on this, as on every other possible subject."[8] He gladly acknowledged his indebtedness to Priestley, though admitting that they differed on one or two points in their estimate of Jesus. One of these, as Priestley was quick to retort, was on the question whether Jesus had ever claimed divinity for himself. Jefferson thought he had not; Priestley was sure that he had.[9]

Jefferson was well aware of the dangers involved in thus sending out so many copies of the Syllabus. Should one of them fall into unfriendly hands, a storm of abuse, fraught with the gravest political consequences, would have descended on his head. Yet, in spite of former horrible examples, he could never resist the itch to communicate with his fellows and literally place his life and fortunes in their hands. To one such, however, he gave vent to one of his noblest utterances, and embalmed his hatred of snoopers and meddling busybodies in imperishable words.

"I never will," he avowed proudly, "by any word or act, bow to the shrine of intolerance, or admit a right of enquiry into the religious opinions of others. On the contrary we are bound, you, I, & every one, to make common cause, even with error itself, to maintain the common right of freedom of conscience. We ought with one heart and one hand to hew down the daring and dangerous efforts of those who would seduce the public opinion to substitute itself into that tyranny over religious faith which the laws have so justly abdicated."[10]

If he hated those who sought to control the opinions of men, he evinced an equal hatred for those who attempted to enslave their flesh. There was nothing he could do about those unfortunates already in bondage, but he was determined to enforce to the fullest rigor the laws against further traffic. One Nathaniel Ingraham had been convicted and heavily fined for engaging in the slave trade. Since he was unable to pay the fine, he was clapped into jail, and powerful influences were brought to bear on Jefferson to obtain his pardon. He denied the petition at the moment, writing sharply that Ingraham's "situation, as far as respects himself, merits no commiseration: that of his wife, children & mother, suffering for want of his aid, does: so also does the condition of the unhappy human beings whom he forcibly brought away from their native country, & whose wives, children & parents are now suffering for want of their aid & comfort." Let him remain two years in prison, he declared; and then let the matter be examined again.[11]

With the whole question of the western and southwestern boundaries of the United States brought sharply to his attention by the negotiations with France and Spain, Jefferson turned his thoughts to several interrelated projects that had been in the back of his mind for years. One was the problem of how to deal with the Indian tribes who inhabited the fringes of American territory; the other, the exploration of the great and unknown reaches beyond.

From early boyhood, Jefferson had professed a vast admiration for the noble red man and, in his *Notes on Virginia* and elsewhere, had compared him favorably with the other races of mankind. But this theoretical admiration did not prevent him from viewing with a cold and practical eye the consequences of the continued existence of the Indian tribes within the confines of the United States.

In a series of letters to his Secretary of War and the Governor of the Western Territory, he laid down a policy for the eventual removal of the tribes across the Mississippi; peacefully and by purchase, if possible; by pressure and eventual force, if not. While paying lip service to peace, justice and friendship, Jefferson's graduated steps for dealing with the Indians envisaged a cynical and effective procedure for getting rid of them that held little of these abstract principles and had only expediency to commend it.

He outlined his confidential views to Governor William Henry Harrison. While "our system is to live in perpetual peace with the Indians," he commenced righteously enough, and to be just and liberal with them, and protect them from wrongs at the hands of the white man, nevertheless it must be our policy to "draw them to agriculture, to spinning and weaving," and to induce them to give up their immemorial hunting of game.

Why should this be done? So that "they will perceive how useless to them are their extensive forests, and will be willing to pare them off from time to time in exchange for necessaries for their farms and families. To promote this disposition to exchange lands, which they have to spare and we want, for necessaries, which we have and they want, we shall push our trading uses, and be glad to see the good and influential individuals among them run in debt, because we observe that when these debts get beyond what the individuals can pay, they become willing to lop them off by a cession of lands.... In this way our settlements will gradually circumscribe and approach the Indians, and they will in time either incorporate with us as citizens of the United States, or remove beyond the Mississippi."

Of course, he added, "should any tribe be foolhardy enough to take up the hatchet at any time, the seizing the whole country of that tribe, and driving them across the Mississippi, as the only condition of peace, would be an example to others, and a furtherance of our final consolidation." It was most essential, he concluded cynically, that what was happening to them be not "understood by the Indians. For their interests and their tranquility it is best they should see only the present age of their history." [12]

Jefferson was determined to present a solid front along the entire length of the Mississippi. To do this required on the one hand, the cession of New Orleans and the Floridas from their current owners; on the other, a steady and relentless pressure on the Indians to force them over to the west bank, and to fill the vacuum with a line of settlements that could provide their own protection against any assault from the other side.[13]

But Jefferson was peering also into the future. If, at the moment, he was content to push the frontiers of the United States solidly up to the line of the Mississippi and entrench there, he had a restless and active interest as well concerning what lay beyond. He foresaw that some day the empty spaces on this side of the great dividing river would be filled up with a spawning, ever-expanding citizenry. Could that self-imposed border continue to hold for generations to come against the irresistible pressures of Americans seeking new lands and further horizons? After all, was not the truly natural boundary the far-distant Pacific?

What lay, therefore, beyond the Mississippi? There were reports and rumors, and the careless talk of trappers and fur hunters who had penetrated the vastness. But much more must be known, as to habitability, natural resources, climate, etc., before the future might be envisaged and plans laid for eventual occupation.

Ten years before, when Jefferson was Secretary of State, the idea of exploring the great Louisiana region had already interested him. A Frenchman, André Michaux, had broached the possibility to the Philosophical Society, and sought subscriptions to finance the journey. Jefferson aided him in every way, and asked him to seek the shortest and most convenient route between the Mississippi and the Pacific, to report on the inhabitants, geography, flora and fauna; and particularly to determine whether any mammoths still roamed the uncharted spaces.[14] The proposed expedition, however, never eventuated.

Perhaps that perennial interest in the possibility of live mammoths, indigenous llamas similar to those of Peru, mountains of pure salt, and other natural wonders, motivated Jefferson as much as the dream of future imperial expansion. In any event, he had nurtured the seed throughout the years, and now that he was President, proposed it formally again.

Taking advantage of the current preoccupation with the peripheries of the United States, Jefferson sent a confidential message to Congress on January 18, 1803, months before Monroe sailed on his mission to France. He cloaked his real aims under the cover of the continuance of an act establishing government trading posts with the Indians. Since private traders, thus forced out of business, were resentfully exciting discontent among the Indians, why not, he asked, divert their hopes of profit in the direction of the Missouri River? Thereby two birds could be killed with one stone. The government traders would be left in undisputed possession on this side of the Mississippi, with the aim of bringing the Indians eventually into debt and forcing the sale of their lands; while the dispossessed private traders could open up a new territory for trade that now went exclusively to Great Britain.

"An intelligent officer," he proposed, "with ten or twelve chosen men . . . might explore the whole line, even to the Western Ocean," and return in two summers with valuable information.

Great Britain, naturally, might object to our invasion of their hitherto exclusive domain. Remembering how he had once fumed over an earlier British proposal to explore this same territory under the guise of philosophical benefits, Jefferson now intended neatly to turn the tables. Let us, he told Congress, announce the venture "as a literary pursuit"; while the necessary appropriation for expenses could be hidden under the guise of "extending the external commerce of the United States." [15]

Congress agreed, and Jefferson immediately acted. The first, and most important, job was to find the right leader or leaders. The qualifications were difficult: he must join daring, prudence, familiarity with existence in the woods and the Indian character with a perfect knowledge of botany, natural history, mineralogy and astronomy. Fortunately, he had just the right man close at hand—Meriwether Lewis, his own private secretary. That young man had seen service in the West and Southwest under General Wilkinson, and he had, under Jefferson's guidance, trained himself in the methods of fixing latitude and longitude. The President felt, however, that a co-leader was essential, in case of the death or disablement of one, and he gave Lewis permission to pick his confrere.[16] Lewis chose young William Clark, also from Albemarle, who had been in the army and seen Indian fighting. William's qualifications gained greatly in Jefferson's estimation from the fact that his older brother was none other than the famous George Rogers Clark.

Jefferson wasted no time in getting the expedition started. He promptly released Lewis from his duties as private secretary, and appointed another young neighbor from Albemarle, Lewis Harvie, in his stead.[17] He managed to obtain permission for the journey from the interested governments of Spain, France and England on the plea that it was purely scientific and "literary" in intention.[18] He issued detailed instructions to young Lewis. He was to explore the Missouri River, and such headwaters as might connect with the Pacific; to take careful notes of his course, landmarks and portages; to study the native Indian tribes, their customs, languages, possibilities of trade, etc.; to report on soil, animals, minerals and climate; and to keep a full journal of everything he did and saw. Should he manage to reach the Pacific, he was to determine whether furs from that area might not be shipped back to the United States on the Missouri River. If, in his judgment, returning by land would prove unsafe, then the expedition was to take boat and come back by the long sea voyage.[19]

All of these preparations, it must be remembered, were made before Louisiana, the territory to be traversed, had come within the jurisdiction of the United States. Jefferson had hoodwinked the countries involved into granting passports, but it is extremely doubtful that they would have been honored had the true purposes of the expedition been known. Certainly, England would not have watched with a benign eye her fur trade snatched from her grasp; and Napoleon would have instantly understood the precise meaning of this "literary" exploration of his territories. Fortunately, before Lewis and Clark finally got under way, and plunged into the forbidden unknown, the whole matter was neatly solved by events in Europe.

James Monroe sailed for France on March 8, 1803. Jefferson primed Robert R. Livingston, already on the ground, in advance of Monroe's coming and of Dupont's unofficial mission. They were all to work together, said the President, since "the future destinies of our country hang on the event of this negotiation." [20]

He was even franker with Dupont. "Our circumstances," he instructed the Frenchman, "are so imperious as to admit of no delay as to our course; and the use of the Mississippi so indispensable, that we cannot hesitate one moment to hazard our existence for its maintenance. If we fail in this effort to put it beyond the reach of accident, we see the destinies we have to run, and prepare at once for them." [21] This was the language of war; or at least they were skillful phrases to be dropped deftly into the minds of the French without, however, any commitment to back them up.

The fact that Livingston might feel resentful over having Monroe thus summarily conjoined with him, if not indeed superseding him, did not bother Jefferson or Madison one whit. Madison was thoroughly critical of Livingston, complaining sharply to Jefferson of his unsatisfactory letters. They were "enigmas" and remarkable for their paucity of facts; yet they undertook to "prescribe measures, without hinting even the reasons for them." And certainly Livingston showed considerable naïveté in entrusting *unciphered* dispatches to a British minister for transmission to Madison.[22]

Livingston, on the other hand, bitterly resented the appearance of Monroe on the scene. "I cannot wish, sir," he wrote back to Madison as soon as he heard of the proposed mission, "that my fellow-citizens should not [*sic*] be led to believe, from Mr. Monroe's appointment, that I had been negligent of their interests, or too delicate on any of the great points entrusted to my care. I trust that a communication of my notes to some of them would show that I had gone as far as it was possible for me to go, and perhaps further than my instructions would justify." [23]

He was the more uneasy because Talleyrand was using the new appointment as a lever for delaying further negotiations with him, and hinting slyly that he had been displaced in the negotiations.[24] To which Livingston, in hot resentment and seeking to bring matters to a head *before* Monroe arrived, pressed for an immediate answer from the wily French minister, retorting with some asperity that he had *not* been superseded.[25]

As a matter of fact, Livingston had been doing a good job under extraordinary handicaps. He properly complained that full instructions had not been sent him from home (Jefferson's letter of February 3, 1803, did not reach him until after Monroe arrived) and that energetic measures by the home government were essential to strengthen his hand in dealing with the shifty and evasive French court.[26]

Back home, the government was moving slowly but surely toward a definite policy. On March 2nd, Madison issued a new and precise set of instructions for Livingston and Monroe to follow. After an argumentative history of past events designed to convince France that it was to her best interests to come to terms with the United States, he offered the following plan: 1) France to cede all territories *east* of the Mississippi, including the island of New Orleans and the two Floridas, and to keep the territories *west* of the river; 2) the navigation of the Mississippi "in its whole breadth from its source to the ocean" to be equally free to France and the United States; 3) the United States to pay (amount left blank) millions of *livres tournois* for the cession; 4) the inhabitants of the ceded territories to be incorporated as citizens of the United States on an equal footing and without unnecessary delay and, in the meantime, to be secure in their persons, property and religion; 5) the envoys were confidentially advised that Jefferson had made up his mind to go as high as fifty million livres "rather than lose the main object. Every struggle, however, is to be made against such an augmentation of the price, that will consist with an ultimate acquiescence." As a matter of fact, declared Madison, weakening the instructions still further, the United States was ready to take even a *part* of the island of New Orleans, and omit the Floridas altogether, provided it received rights of deposit and free navigation of the rivers emptying into the Gulf of Mexico through that territory.[27]

To such a whittling down of the original aims, couched by Jefferson in bold and menacing language, had the American government finally descended. In truth, Jefferson was correct in his later statement to the British: "Peace is our passion, and wrongs might drive us from it. We prefer trying every other just principle, right and safety, before we recur to war."[28]

Yet, though peace was Jefferson's "passion," he played his cards skillfully at home; frightening the French Minister, Pichon, with what seemed to be furious negotiations with the British. Actually, the alleged negotiations had not proceeded beyond certain winks and nods. It is true that the Cabinet had decided to instruct Livingston and Monroe, in the event that no arrangement could be made with France, "to use all possible procrastinations with them and in the meantime enter into conferences with the British Govmt. thro' their ambassador at Paris to fix principles of alliance, and leave us in peace till congress meets, & prevent war till next spring."[29]

But this was mere shadowboxing; anything to hold off the day of judgment. A month later, the Cabinet was debating another question: in the event of war between England and France, should the United States issue a proclamation of neutrality? It was 1793 all over again, but with a situation completely different. Nevertheless, Jefferson and his Cabinet took a position not far removed from that which Jefferson had advocated on the former occasion. The United States ought not to assure anyone of her neutrality without receiving a price for it. There was indeed some opinion that the outbreak of such a war would give us an opportunity to obtain New Orleans; but in the event direct negotiation failed, then the Cabinet became exceedingly vague. Should we take it by force? Should we encourage a declaration of independence on the part of the citizenry and enter into an alliance with the new State? The Cabinet shilly-shallied, finally agreeing to leave the point for future consideration and not to enter into any binding convention with France that would not give us either the whole of New Orleans, or a sufficient part of the island on which to erect a town of our own.[30]

Even at this late date, Jefferson was not very sanguine of getting New Orleans, much less the Floridas. He was sufficiently satisfied that Spain had disavowed the summary action of her Intendant in closing that vital port to the deposit in transit of American goods. Thus, he exclaimed exultantly, "by a reasonable and peaceable process, we have obtained in 4. months what would have cost us 7. years of war, 100,000 human lives, 100 millions of additional debt."[31] In his enthusiasm, he exaggerated somewhat.

If Jefferson's desires had thus been scaled down to an exceedingly modest level, in France, all unknown to him, matters were moving swiftly to a surprising denouement. Almost overnight, the hostile climate in which Livingston had found himself enveloped had subtly changed.

The grand expedition which Napoleon had intended for New Orleans to occupy it and the rest of his new possessions had, by force of circumstances, been diverted to the turbulent island of St. Domingo. There the proud French veterans met with defeat and disaster. The news traveled all too speedily back to France, and Napoleon, early in January, was forced to reconsider all his grandiose plans for a new and greater empire across the seas. If St. Domingo were lost—and with it a secure base in the Caribbean—of what use would Louisiana be to him? Almost overnight he determined to let the barren wilderness in North America go, and devote his full attention instead to the continent of Europe and northern Africa.

Pichon, too, was sending dismal news from the United States. "It is impossible," he wrote Talleyrand, "to be more bitter than this Government is at the present posture of affairs and at the humiliating attitude in which our silence about Louisiana places them.... Mr. Jefferson will be forced to yield to necessity his pretensions and scruples against a British alliance. I noticed at his table that he redoubled his civilities and attentions to the British *chargé*." Jefferson was putting on an excellent show for the benefit of the Frenchman.

Since Napoleon now planned a fresh war with England, Louisiana was a liability rather than an asset to him. What would prevent that nation, in command of the seas, from seizing it? On April 10, 1803, therefore, he informed his Finance Minister, Barbé Marbois, that he was thinking of ceding Louisiana to the United States. "I can scarcely say that I cede it to them," he added, "for it is not yet in our possession. If, however, I leave the least time to our enemies, I shall only transmit an empty title to those republicans whose friendship I seek. They ask of me only one town in Louisiana; but I already consider the colony as entirely lost; and it appears to me that in the hands of this growing Power it will be more useful to the policy, and even the commerce, of France than if I should attempt to keep it." [32]

The next day he made it specific. "I renounce Louisiana," he exclaimed to Marbois. "It is not only New Orleans that I cede; it is the whole colony, without reserve.... I direct you to negotiate the affair. Have an interview this very day with Mr. Livingston." [33]

Meanwhile, Livingston had been assiduously if somewhat hopelessly bombarding Talleyrand, Napoleon, every French official to whom he could obtain access, with memorials, letters, protests and increasingly plain talk. Some of the significance of the disaster at St. Domingo penetrated his mind, and he redoubled his efforts to obtain some sort of settlement before Monroe came and thereby shared in or even monopolized the glory of success.

But he was not prepared for the breath-taking query that Talleyrand, in the course of Livingston's usual demands, suddenly fired at him on April 11th. "Would the United States," asked Talleyrand, "wish to have the whole of Louisiana?"

Livingston, absorbed in his own line of thought, did not at once catch the full significance of what seemed a casual and offhand remark. "No," he replied. All that we wished was New Orleans and the Floridas. Perhaps, though, he added cautiously, we might be able to use the country above the Arkansas River. But Talleyrand brushed half measures aside. Without New Orleans, he asserted, the rest of Louisiana was of little value to them. "What would we give for the whole?" Somewhat flabbergasted, and still not certain he was not being hoaxed, Livingston suggested tentatively 20,000,000 livres, *provided* the spoliation claims were met out of the fund. Too low, retorted Talleyrand. Think it over by tomorrow.

But Monroe had already landed in France, and was due in Paris by the 13th of April, two days after this momentous conversation. Livingston said he would have to consult with the newly arrived envoy before making any further offer.[34]

When Livingston retired to his own chamber to digest the sudden turn of events, he realized he had made a fool of himself. Here was a vast and glittering project dropped suddenly in his lap, and he was going to wait for Monroe to come and cheat him of the prize! The next day, April 12th, he awoke and hastened to Talleyrand to clinch the deal immediately. Yet he dared not increase his offer without Monroe's consent; and the wily French minister persisted in shrugging the whole idea off as merely a passing thought of his own without authority.

When the American returned to his own house that evening, he found a note from Monroe. The new envoy was already in Paris, and wanted to talk over the entire situation the following morning with Livingston. On April 13th, the two men met at Livingston's apartment. They passed the day exchanging information and examining documents. By a remarkable coincidence, Marbois *happened* to be taking the air in Livingston's garden at the particular moment when the American envoys left their paper work and sat down to dinner. Naturally, Livingston invited Marbois in. Then the two men, much to Monroe's inner fury, strolled into another room and left Monroe fuming helplessly over the remains of the dinner. By this time Monroe knew that Livingston was not too happy over his arrival, "since it took from him the credit of having brought everything to a proper conclusion without [Monroe's] aid."

The next thing Monroe heard was that Livingston and Marbois had arranged another *private* interview at Marbois's house; again leaving Monroe out in the cold.

That conference took place at eleven at night; and for the first time Livingston was told what he had suspected all along, that the proposition had come from Napoleon himself. The price for Louisiana was 100,000,000 francs, and the United States was to take care of the spoliation claims to its own citizens (amounting to about 25,000,000 francs). Livingston put a surprised look on his face, and retorted that the sum was out of the question; that anyway all that we wanted was New Orleans and the Floridas for 10,000,000 francs. Marbois pressed for an offer on the whole, hinting that 60,000,000 francs plus the claims might be considered. With that, Livingston went home to confer with the impatient Monroe.[35]

Monroe was in a dilemma. He felt that Livingston was trying to steal the show from him, yet he dared not refuse to allow his fellow envoy to proceed on the path so providentially opened; or he might be charged afterwards, in the event of failure, with having sabotaged the negotiations because of personal pique. Therefore, while insisting that Livingston make no official offer, he permitted him to *suggest* to Marbois that we would buy Louisiana for the price already offered for the territory *east* of the Mississippi alone; provided that France would relinquish all pretensions to the Floridas and support our claims to them against the Spaniards.[36]

The calm impudence of such an offer is truly amazing. But by this time, the Americans had correctly gauged the frantic desire of Napoleon to rid himself of this burden before the British grabbed it, and were negotiating accordingly.

They almost overreached themselves, however. A week of fruitless bargaining ensued, with the French attitude abruptly stiffening. In fact, Napoleon almost changed his mind; and his brothers, Lucien and Joseph, hearing of the contemplated sale, hastened to upbraid him violently for his treachery to France. They caught their famous brother in his bath, and berated him in audacious language.[37] Perhaps it was his anger at being harangued that determined Napoleon's waverings, and made him stubbornly decide to go through with the deal.

Monroe meanwhile had taken ill, and most of the burden fell on Livingston. Both were in a curious position. Nothing in their official instructions authorized them to discuss Louisiana; indeed, they were limited strictly to New Orleans and the Floridas. Yet months must necessarily elapse before letters requesting and granting the requisite authorizations could travel over the Atlantic, and in that time a thousand accidents might arise to banish the chance forever. For once, therefore, Livingston was happy to share the responsibility of proceeding without power.[38]

On April 27th, the impasse broke. Marbois, in company with Livingston, came to the ailing Monroe. Marbois had two proposed treaties in his pocket. One was official, reiterating the original terms of 100,000,000 francs and 20,000,000 for the spoliations. But he himself disarmingly admitted that they were harsh and unreasonable, and thereupon pulled out of his pocket a *second* proposal which, so he said, was his own—calling for a total of 80,000,000 francs, *including* the spoliations.

After the meeting, Livingston drafted a counterproposal which Monroe sourly reported as "very loosely drawn." This differentiated between the two sums—the Americans feared that if they were lumped, and so paid over to Napoleon, that worthy might *forget* to pay the American spoliation claims out of it—and offered 50,000,000 on the purchase, and an additional 20,000,000 which the United States would pay its citizens.

On April 29th, Monroe having recovered somewhat, the two envoys went to Marbois with their counteroffer. Marbois insisted on the original terms, and the Americans finally agreed. On May 1st, Monroe was presented for the first time to Napoleon, who graciously told him that "our affairs should be settled." On May 2nd, a French-language treaty was signed for the cession of Louisiana to the United States for 60,000,000 francs; copies in English were signed several days later. And, some days after, a convention was signed whereby, on the basis of 20,000,000 francs, the United States agreed to settle its spoliation claims against France and make payment to its own citizens.[39] The total sum, therefore, that was paid for Louisiana, New Orleans and an inchoate claim against the Floridas came to $16,000,000 in American money. Since, however, the spoliation claims had amounted to considerably more than the sum agreed on for taking care of them, the American government found itself in endless difficulties later with its own citizens in settling the accounts.

It was a great triumph, nevertheless; the greatest in the entire history of American diplomacy. A vast new territory had come unexpectedly into American hands; one that doubled the size of the nation. The history of this country, of the world, and of the generations to come, would have been unpredictably different had not Napoleon suddenly decided to throw Louisiana into the bargain. The historian can only cautiously speculate on possibilities. Had the sale not been consummated, and Great Britain seized the territory in the ensuing war, the United States might well have been confined to the east bank of the Mississippi and become a second-class power. Or, as was more probable, the irresistible pressure of population would have forced her into a series of devastating wars with Great Britain which, no matter how they ended, would have set a pattern of relations between the two English-speaking powers that would have had the most far-reaching and incalculable consequences on the course of world history.

Livingston truly said, in his triumphant cry to Rufus King—allowing understandably for his dismissal of whatever part Monroe played in the proceedings: "You may congratulate me upon having obtained by the most unwearied exertion a treaty which whether well or ill-rec'd I am content to be charged with to my latest posterity."[40]

CHAPTER 53

Sub Silentio

THE treaty for the purchase of Louisiana was sent with some inner trepidation by the envoys to America. "An acquisition of so great an extent was," they acknowledged, "we well know, not contemplated by our appointment; but we are persuaded that the circumstances and considerations which induced us to make it, will justify us in the measure to our Government and country." [1]

According to the terms of the treaty, Louisiana was transferred "with the same extent that is now in the hands of Spain and that it had when France possessed it, and such as it should be after the treaties subsequently entered into between Spain and other States." The Americans tried hard to find out just what was this pig in the poke which they had purchased, but were met with smiling evasions from the French. Napoleon must have chuckled as he told Marbois: "If an obscurity did not already exist, it would perhaps be good policy to put one there."[2] Livingston asked Talleyrand in vain what were its eastern boundaries, and what the French had actually intended to take from Spain. All that he received was a monotonous: "I do not know." A light burst on the American. "Then you mean that we shall construe it our own way?" he inquired. Talleyrand shrugged. "I can give you no direction. You have made a noble bargain for yourselves, and I suppose you will make the most of it." All that he was ready to say was that the Floridas were not included; though Napoleon had indicated orally—refusing to incorporate it in writing—that he would support the United States in negotiating for them with Spain.[3]

Livingston, considering the matter in the privacy of his own chamber, determined for himself that at least West Florida—the Gulf Coast between the Mississippi and East Florida (approximately what is now known as Florida)—came within the purchase. He wrote to Madison: "Now, sir, the sum of the business is, to recommend to you, in the strongest terms, after having obtained the possession, that the French commissary will give you, to insist upon this as a part of your right; and to take possession, at all events, to the river Perdido. I pledge myself that your right is good; and, after the explanations that have been given here, you need apprehend nothing from a decisive measure." [4] And later Monroe joined him in a similar assurance that it was "incontrovertible that West Florida is comprised in the cession of Louisiana." [5]

Actually, it was nothing of the sort, and went directly counter to what Talleyrand had expressly told them. But the envoys, uneasy over the fact that they had not followed their instructions, which called for the acquisition of the Floridas—even though they had acquired New Orleans in the larger purchase of Louisiana—sought to bluster it out and were willing to accept the consequences of possible war with Spain by advocating a forcible seizure.

Another matter rose to plague the envoys. Barely was the ink dry on the treaty and a form of ratification for the Government of the United States drafted, than Napoleon repented of the bargain. He asserted that the whole of the spoliations amounted to no more than 4,000,000 francs, and that the United States had received 20,000,000 to pay them; that the ratification by France should not have been delivered to the American envoys but should have been sent to Pichon to hold until it could be exchanged for the American ratification; and that unless the stock called for on the spoliations was delivered within the prescribed period, the entire treaty was void. In great alarm, Livingston wrote directly to Jefferson that "we must as far as possible soothe the youthful Conqueror whose will knows no resistance," and that the President must guard against any delays or even the slightest change in the form of the ratification; "for be assured," he concluded, "that the slightest pretence will be seized to undo the work." [6]

There was good reason for Napoleon's change of heart. The moment Spain heard of the treaty which had been pushed through secretly and in such haste she entered the strongest possible formal protest against the intended sale. For one thing, she had not yet transferred Louisiana to French sovereignty; for another, the sale or *any* form of alienation had been expressly prohibited to France by the terms of the treaty of retrocession.

It is true that Spain, living in the shadow of the great conqueror, and an unwilling ally to him, had been in a sense compelled to retrocede Louisiana; but what had made the compulsion somewhat more palatable was the consideration that France would be better able to hold the territory against an aggressive United States. By thus creating a buffer state between the imperial-minded Americans and their own precious possessions in Mexico, Central and South America, the Spaniards had congratulated themselves that at least the latter had been made safe for the indefinite future. What was their horror, therefore, to find out that France had double-crossed them, and that the terrible Americans had actually been placed squarely on the borders of Mexico and California.

"This alienation," wrote the Spanish Minister in France angrily to Talleyrand, "not only deranges from top to bottom the whole colonial system of Spain, and even of Europe, but is directly opposed to the compacts and formal stipulations agreed upon between France and Spain." He therefore "hoped" that the arrangement would be revoked. [7]

Thus harried both in Paris and in Madrid, Napoleon sought to throw the blame on Spain, resorting to barefaced prevarication in the process. He had done what he did, he retorted, because Spain had first broken her own pledges. She had promised him, so he said, to sustain the Intendant at New Orleans in his prohibition of American deposits; and she had since reversed him and weakly granted that inestimable right to the Americans. Thereby, he claimed, the entire colony had become less valuable to the French.[8] All of which was made up of whole cloth, but gave Napoleon a sense of being in the right.

At home, while waiting for news of the final negotiations from France, Jefferson found himself confronted with a series of domestic problems; some personal and some political.

He had been suffering from a diarrhea almost from the moment he had entered the Presidency, a condition which he attributed to some tainted fish he had eaten. He kept experimenting with diets, and finally concluded that fish brought on further attacks, though oysters and crabs did not. He found that riding helped—a form of treatment that was thoroughly agreeable to such an ardent horseman as Jefferson.[9]

He was also entering on a long, tangled and acrimonious litigation with Henderson, a neighbor whose land adjoined his Albemarle properties. His agent had purchased the rights to the Henderson property, proposing to take title in his own name so that Jefferson would not be known in the transaction. But Jefferson found difficulty in meeting the payments. Henderson, according to the agent, Craven Peyton, had commenced a lawsuit with "fraudulent intentions." In retaliation, Peyton wanted to tear down a dam which Henderson had placed on the stream feeding Jefferson's mill, thereby rendering it useless. Not content with thus straddling Jefferson's land, Henderson had also built "an excellent canal" to divert further the waters from his hated neighbor; but Peyton triumphantly reported that he had obtained a restraining order. Henderson's land to which the whole dispute attached, amounted to only four acres; and Jefferson was willing to purchase it as well as his mill; but indignantly refused to pay an excessive price for it.[10] The litigation was further complicated by the fact that Henderson's wife, possessing dower rights, lived in Kentucky and cannily put obstacles in the way, unless she received what she conceived to be a good price for a waiver. The quarrel and the court proceedings were to drag on in bitterness and recriminations for long, weary months.

More to Jefferson's taste was the formal entry of both his sons-in-law into politics. Young John W. Eppes had offered for Congress in place of the old Republican stalwart, William Branch Giles, and had been elected. Giles had been ailing for some time; and though Jefferson regretted his loss, he was happy to see Eppes take his seat; the more so since it meant that both he and Maria would necessarily come to Washington.[11]

Thomas Mann Randolph had also been elected, though after a disagreeable campaign which almost made him wish he had not, and by such a small majority that there was talk of a recount. He had finally given up his project to emigrate to Georgia and raise cotton, but his private affairs were in very bad shape. Jefferson optimistically offered to help, once he cleared off his own pressing debts. Perhaps, he wrote, by the end of this second term in office, "(which will certainly be my last) I can see all of us out of debt and my mill & farms in such a state as to supply the expences of living to which the [termination?] of my political life will expose me, I fear unavoidably." [12]

An even more pleasant election was that of John Page, who had become Governor of Virginia. Jefferson was thereby relieved, at least temporarily, of the weight of supplying Page with public office to keep him from actual starvation; a delicate enough business which Page sufficiently appreciated, though it had aroused sarcastic comments from others not thus fortunately fortified by the President of the United States. But Jefferson stuck to his indigent friend through all hostile criticism; and even after Page's governorship lapsed—and with it his income—sought further federal perquisites for him. "We were affectionate friends & inseparable companions in youth," Jefferson wrote warmly, "and have always preserved our feelings with mutual fidelity to each other through the stormy times into which we were thrown." [13]

Jefferson was certain he was climbing out of debt, yet his own figures belied him. For the year ending March 4, 1803, he estimated his expenses at $27,720.92. His income for the same period, including presidential salary, profits from tobacco, rents and the nailery, amounted in all to $26,446.99; and this happened to be one of his better years.[14]

All that one has to do is to note the reckless stocks of wine that flowed and vanished in the President's House—he estimated that from 415 to 500 bottles of champagne alone were used every year—as well as the lavish purchases of books and scientific instruments, to understand that Jefferson would never be able to balance his personal budget, whatever was the fate of the national one.[15]

As the titular head of the Republican party, as well as the President of the United States, Jefferson kept a close watch on local politics and elections. The results in Pennsylvania were most gratifying. Both Senators and eighteen Representatives were triumphantly Republican; and Governor McKean hastened to assure him that he could vouch for their orthodox politics personally, though admitting, somewhat ruefully, he would have been happier "if some of them had a little more learning & knowledge, or a little more diffidence than what is attributed to them." He also wanted to prosecute certain Federalist editors in the state for libel; and asked Jefferson's advice.[16]

The President congratulated him on the political victory; and, with reservations, approved of *State* prosecutions for libel. What he had to say on this ticklish subject is intensely interesting. "The Federalists," he wrote confidentially, "having failed in destroying the freedom of the press by their gag-law, seem to have attacked it in an opposite form, that is by pushing its licentiousness and its lying to such a degree of prostitution as to deprive it of all credit.... This is a dangerous state of things, and the press ought to be restored to its credibility, if possible. The restraints provided by the laws of the states are sufficient for this if applied: and I have therefore long thought that a few prosecutions of the most eminent offenders would have a wholesome effect in restoring the integrity of the presses. Not a general prosecution, for that would look like persecution: but a selected one." In fact, Jefferson had an editor already in mind, and sent along a copy of one of his articles on which a prosecution might be predicated.[17]

In the same letter, he complained of the ever-increasing patronage pressure upon himself, and delivered himself of some choice remarks on the itch for public offic. "Office," he observed, "began to be looked to as a resource for every man whose affairs were getting into derangement, or who was too indolent to pursue his profession, and for young men just entering into life. In short it was poisoning the very source of industry, by presenting an easier resource for a livelihood, and was corrupting the principles of the great mass of those who cast a wishful eye on office."

Jefferson thought of the business of government essentially as requiring little or no professional skills, and was convinced that any intelligent man of affairs, versed in the ordinary business of life, could assume administration during interludes from his proper affairs, and carry it through successfully. This concept of government as an avocation rather than a permanent profession became a part of the American scene; and even the advent of civil service and tenure has done little to change it.

He was always to be peculiarly sensitive to the charge that he was deliberately replacing Federalists with Republicans in office. When the New York *Post* adverted to it editorially, he broke his lifelong rule against answering charges by composing a reply which he anonymously sought to have printed in a Massachusetts paper under the pseudonym of "Fair Play." He went to extreme lengths to hide his identity, sending it to his Attorney General, Levi Lincoln, and asking him to recopy it so that his handwriting would not be detected. The article was written in the best name-calling tradition of the day.[18]

The news that the American envoys had purchased all the vastness of Louisiana as well as New Orleans hit Jefferson and his administration with the force of a thunderbolt. Jefferson had instructed Livingston and Monroe to seek New Orleans and the Floridas, for which he was willing to pay up to $2,000,000. But he had had no real hope of success even in this limited area. He would have been willing to settle for New Orleans alone; or even for a strip of contiguous land on which to build a port for deposit and transshipment, so long as the Mississippi would be open to navigation.

Now there was dumped into his hands an empire—huge, unknown, unpeopled except for wandering Indian tribes, and stretching vaguely to the distant western ocean. But he was *not* certain that he had the Floridas, which were as important to the Southern States as New Orleans and the Mississippi to the Western. It is true that the envoys insisted that the Floridas were included, but their interpretation was farfetched and would certainly lead to trouble with Spain.

Other serious considerations were involved. The amount to which the envoys had bound themselves was $16,000,000—a staggering sum to an administration dedicated to parsimony in government, and besides, unauthorized by Congress. What about the Constitution? Could any clause be found therein permitting the acquisition of an external empire, parts of which, according to the terms of purchase, were eventually to become equal States in the Union? Would not such an interpretation, even if desirable, contradict utterly the fixed Republican dogma and the trumpeted tenets of the Kentucky and Virginia Resolutions?

The great news broke in the United States at the end of June, 1803, and created a sensation. The Republicans hailed it with tremendous rejoicings, and the Federalists with forebodings that the end of the world had come. The reactions were strictly along party lines, with positions strangely reversed: the Republicans now forgetting or dismissing Constitutional qualms, and the Federalists heatedly calling attention to them. For the new territories, if ever incorporated into the Union, would obviously be Republican in character; and Federalism, already in the minority, would suffer a mortal blow from which it would never recover.

Jefferson's first reaction was that the opportunity to double the territory of the United States should not be refused; his second, that the Constitutional power to receive it was extremely doubtful. It was true that Gallatin had already argued that the United States had the power to assume new lands, but Jefferson, though admitting the doctrine in part, thought it safer to seek an amendment to the Constitution permitting the transaction.[19]

He drew up two drafts of such an amendment, specifically permitting the incorporation of Louisiana into the United States, and investing the federal government with jurisdictional powers somewhat similar to those it had possessed over the Northwest Territory.[20]

These he sent to members of his Cabinet for consideration. Gallatin did not reply, considering perhaps that his earlier letter had stated his position adequately. Robert Smith, Secretary of the Navy, believed that Jefferson had engrafted too many restrictions on the powers of the government, and proposed a more general enabling amendment.[21]

The Cabinet met to consider the whole question on July 16th. It was agreed that the purchase should be made, and that Congress be convened on October 17th to ratify the transaction. It was also agreed that Monroe (no mention was made of Livingston) should be instructed to purchase, if possible, both Floridas at the price already agreed upon; if he could not, to seek full rights in all the rivers rising within the United States and flowing into the Gulf of Mexico and the ocean. At this time, obviously the Cabinet did not see eye to eye with Livingston that the Floridas had been included in the original idea. "We are more indifferent about pressing the purchase of the Floridas," was their remarkable conclusion, "because of the money we have to provide for Louisiana, & because we think they cannot fail to fall into our hands." [22]

Jefferson insisted on playing up Monroe's role in the proceedings because the Federalists, though grumbling at the result, were just as eager to give the credit to Livingston. Jefferson also declared that he had foreseen this eventuality as long before as 1801, and had accurately forecast the progress of the European war which had made the acquisition possible. He considered it a triumphant vindication of his thesis that European wars were America's opportunity; and that if this country only waited long enough, the nations of Europe would bid for the price of its neutrality.[23]

But what were the actual boundaries of Louisiana? Napoleon had left them purposely vague. Livingston had convinced Monroe that they included the Floridas. Jefferson cautiously avoided that point for the moment. But his interest in the matter was naturally intense; as it remained throughout his life on this noble accession which became the high spot of his administration. He diligently studied all the old maps, charters and books on the subject, and set forth their contents and his conclusions in a series of detailed memoranda. Later on, he drafted personally most of the measures for Congress to consider in the government of Louisiana and for its future destiny.[24]

His researches convinced him that it included all the headwaters of the Mississippi and Missouri rivers; he thought we might claim along the Gulf westwardly to the Rio Norte or Bravo, and eastwardly perhaps to the Rio Perdido, which flowed into the Gulf between Mobile and Pensacola. But these claims, he significantly added, "will be a subject of negociation with Spain, and if, as soon as she is at war, we push them strongly with one hand, holding out a price in the other, we shall certainly obtain the Floridas, and all in good time. In the mean while, without waiting for permission, we shall enter into the exercise of the natural right we have always insisted on with Spain; to wit that of a nation holding the upper part of streams, having a right of innocent passage thro' them to the ocean. We shall prepare her to see us practice on this, & she will not oppose it by force." [25]

As for Louisiana itself, he continued, though the Constitution revealed nothing to justify its acquisition, Congress *must* ratify the purchase, "casting behind them Metaphysical subtleties" and throw themselves upon the country for approval. Using the analogy of a guardian and his ward, the deed must first be done, saying: "I pretend no right to bind you. You may disavow me, and I must get out of the scrape as I can." But, declared Jefferson, reverting to himself in *propria persona*, "we shall not be disavowed by the nation, and their act of indemnity will confirm & not weaken the constitution, by more strongly marking out its lines."

At this moment, it was his intention to ratify, but to go to the country with his Constitutional amendment to make the purchase legal ex post facto. Then alarming news came from France which compelled him to change his mind, and drop all idea of an amendment, at least for the present. This was the letter from Livingston on June 2nd, and a similar one from Monroe, to the effect that Napoleon regretted the sale and would seize any pretext to undo it. If Jefferson therefore placed before Congress his Constitutional amendment, thereby acknowledging his doubts, to say the least, of their authority to enter into the transaction, he might furnish sufficient ammunition to the Federalists for influencing wavering members, and see the coveted prize slip from his grasp altogether.

He therefore shifted his tactics. No longer must Congress be apprized of those doubts, no longer must the analogy of the guardian and ward be produced for their attention. Ratification must be slipped through smoothly and swiftly, without a murmur of Constitution or misgivings. He thereupon notified all his stalwarts in Congress and in the Cabinet of the new role they must play, and the line they must adopt.

Let Congress do what it has to do, he exhorted his followers, "*sub silentio*" and "with as little debate as possible, & particularly so far as respects the constitutional difficulty." The less said about it the better. Let not a day's delay intervene, lest the day for ratification pass and France thus be given the right to void the sale.[26] Haste and silence were the watchwords.

His followers, however, did not share his qualms as to the alleged Constitutional difficulty. In fact, they showed a marked distaste for bringing it up. Ironically, the two men most involved in the ringing phrases of the Kentucky Resolutions—John C. Breckinridge and Wilson Cary Nicholas—evinced not the slightest concern over a constitutional question far more fundamental than the Federalist encroachments against which they had inveighed. Nicholas thought his chief a little strait-laced about the whole affair and his conscience too tender. In the very best Federalist vein, he somewhat tartly informed Jefferson that *his* examination of the Constitution disclosed a sufficiency of power not only to make such a treaty, but to admit new states from the acquired territory as well.[27]

Jefferson was willing enough to be pushed into a position he secretly favored, yet such an open avowal of "Federalist" doctrine compelled him, at least theoretically, to defend his thesis. "I had rather," he replied to Nicholas, "ask an enlargement of power from the nation, where it is found necessary, than to assume it by a construction which would make our powers boundless. Our peculiar security is in possession of a written Constitution. Let us not make it a blank paper by construction." Having thus salved his own conscience, Jefferson ruined his position by adding: "If, however, our friends shall think differently, certainly I shall acquiesce with satisfaction, confiding that the good sense of our country will correct the evil of construction when it shall produce ill effects."[28] But he had never allowed the Federalists the luxury he was now willing to permit himself.

Gallatin, the strictest of strict constructionists, agreed in principle with Nicholas. He even pooh-poohed the idea that France would try to back out of the agreement. Jefferson had asked him to prepare a bill ratifying the treaty, and for the issuance of stock to cover the purchase price, so that it might be submitted to Congress on the first or second day of the session. If the matter could be attended to by the legislators "without talking" and without delay, an armed ship would be ready to take both ratification and stock to France on October 31st. To which Gallatin retorted that a bill was being prepared to put the treaty into effect, but that Jefferson could not expect that "the house will take up the subject before a ratification or decide without much debate & opposition." [29]

But if Gallatin was inclined to dismiss the idea that time was of the essence, the envoys took a far more serious view. Monroe, fearing that Napoleon would seize upon any delay in the financial end of the arrangements as a reason for abrogation, offered to guarantee payment through the English banking firm of Hope and Baring. Livingston objected strongly to such a guarantee as going beyond their powers; but Monroe insisted that his instructions *had* given him the power.[30]

Spain, naturally, looked upon the entire proceedings with mingled anger and dismay. She had been deliberately double-crossed by Napoleon and had entered her formal protest; yet dared not go too far because she lay helpless under the mighty paw of her supposed ally. She entered her formal protest as well to the United States; but felt her helpless position in that direction almost as keenly.

Yrujo, Spain's Minister to the United States, called Madison's attention to the fact that France had disregarded her most solemn engagements not to alienate Louisiana, and insisted that France had no right to sell, nor the United States to buy.[31] Madison dismissed the protest cavalierly, expressing surprise at Spain's surprise; and was fortified in his position by a statement from Pichon, the French Minister, that France *did* have the right to cede and that the Spanish claims were "specious reasonings." [32]

Jefferson drafted his annual message for presentation to Congress with extreme care. The most important matter before the special session, of course, was Louisiana. There was need for secrecy, silence, haste and avoidance of controversy. He feared, however, that objections might arise over the cost of the acquisition, particularly if new taxes had to be raised to meet the interest on the stock (bonds) to be tendered in payment. Should such taxes be necessary, there might be sufficient defections from Republican ranks in the Senate to defeat ratification. Therefore he sought ways and means of cutting government expenses so as to avoid them.

As usual, it was the unfortunate navy that first caught his eye. Gallatin at the beginning of the year had raised his voice in protest that the navy wanted entirely too much money.[33] But Robert Smith, its Secretary, had then been adamant. Jefferson now sought to put pressure on him in the name of Louisiana. Could not Smith reduce his estimate of expenditures for the forthcoming year by $170,000? After all, both the State and War Departments had managed to lop off $100,000 each.[34]

Congress convened in obedience to the summons for a special session and, on October 17th, heard the Presidential Message. He had called them earlier, said Jefferson, because of "matters of great public concernment." After an extended history of American interest in New Orleans and the navigation of the Mississippi, he laid the new windfall of Louisiana squarely in their laps. It was up to the Senate, he declared, to exercise its Constitutional power of treaty ratification, and to the House for providing the requisite funds. On both rested the duty of taking the necessary measures for occupying and governing the newly acquired territory.

Not a word did he say about possible Constitutional difficulties. Silence, in this case, was golden!

He adverted to other topics: a cession of lands by the Kaskaskia Indians (discreetly failing to mention the means that had been employed to obtain them), a renewal of the naval blockade of Tripoli, the convention with Great Britain fixing the northern boundary, and the state of the finances. He acknowledged that $13,000,000 would have to be added to the public debt because of Louisiana, but insisted that the increasing wealth and population of the United States would take care of interest and eventual principal without the necessity for adding new taxes. As for the war in Europe, he avowed gratitude that we were not involved, and that it was essential, through existing or new legislation, to safeguard our neutrality.[35]

Privately, he had hailed the European convulsion with even profounder satisfaction. "Tremendous times in Europe!" he exclaimed. "How mighty this battle of lions & tygers! With what sensations should the common herd of cattle look on it? With no partialities, certainly. If they can so far worry one another as to destroy their power of tyrannizing, the one over the earth [France], the other the waters [England], the world may perhaps enjoy peace, till they recruit again."[36]

The two Houses separated after the message was delivered, and proceeded to business.

In the matter of the Louisiana treaty, the Senate naturally had to move first. In spite of Jefferson's urgency that the issue of constitutionality be held "*sub silentio*," it persisted in raising its ugly head. The Federalists promptly brought it forward, and the Republican Senators frankly avowed that the treaty was unconstitutional. But while Federalists like William Plumer of New Hampshire feared that the accession of such a vast territory would eventually dissolve the Union, John Taylor of Virginia—no less—boldly declared: "I have no doubt our envoys had no authority to make such a treaty, & that it is a violation of the constitution; but I will, like an attorney who exceeds the authority delegated to him by his client, vote to ratify it, & then throw myself on the people for pardon." [37] Who can doubt that the phraseology stemmed directly from Jefferson!

On October 20th, the Senate ratified the treaty by the overwhelming vote of 24 to 7; every Federalist present, except Jonathan Dayton of New Jersey, voting against it. Plumer was to complain that they took "less time to deliberate on this important treaty, than they allowed themselves on the most trivial Indian contract." [38]

The Republicans were in firm control of the Senate, and went ahead with speed and dispatch. On October 22nd, Breckinridge moved that the President be authorized to take possession of the territories ceded by France and to direct and supervise them until Congress provided for their permanent government. Another bill provided for the issuance of bonds—then called stocks—in the sum of $11,250,000 to carry the treaty into effect.[39]

The House, where the Republican majority was larger, was more dilatory. Debate did not start until October 24th, with the Federalists seizing the initiative. Gaylord Griswold of New York moved to have the President lay before the House all the documents "tending to ascertain whether the United States have, in fact, acquired any title to the province of Louisiana by the treaties with France." It was his contention that the title was defective, and that the country was buying a pig in a poke.[40]

John Randolph of Roanoke was managing the Republican majority and, in spite of sound Republican tradition that Congress was always entitled to call for documents from the Executive, exercised all his skill and ingenuity to defeat the motion. He succeeded, but by an uncomfortably close margin of 59 to 57. Many Republicans, remembering their former role when the positions had been reversed, broke from his leadership. Even Joseph H. Nicholson, staunchest of stalwarts, after taunting the Federalists with their *volte-face* and reminding them how *they* had refused to permit a similar motion to pass when the Jay treaty was involved, nevertheless stood by his principles and voted for the resolution. So did men like Caesar A. Rodney of Delaware and the fiery Matthew Lyon, now representing Kentucky.[41]

Republican chickens were indeed coming home to roost. The precedents they had established in connection with the Jay treaty were now being employed with telling effect by the Federalists. Though, constitutionally, the Senate had sole jurisdiction over treaties, the House Republicans had *then* claimed—with Jefferson's complete approval—that they would refuse to effectuate them by withholding the necessary funds.

The debate on the treaty itself and the means for carrying it into effect commenced on October 25th and raged for three days. Griswold led off again with a strongly expressed doubt that the provision calling for eventual citizenship for the inhabitants was constitutional. John Randolph countered with biting sarcasm that we had been ready enough to seize New Orleans by force, and reminded Griswold that he had been among the first to advocate such violent measures. "Can a nation acquire by force that which she cannot acquire by treaty?" he ironically inquired.[42]

It was now the Federalists who were attempting narrowly to limit the Constitution and the Republicans who were pressing for broad interpretations. The former fought valiantly, throwing the old Republican arguments into the teeth of their opponents, whereupon the latter retorted with ancient *Federalist* dogma. And, since they had the overwhelming numbers, sheer voting power took the place of reasoned argument. One by one, they pushed their resolutions through.

But *one* motion, coming from the Senate floor, which granted the President authority to take possession of Louisiana, to employ the armed forces for that purpose, and to direct the civil, judicial and military government of the territory until Congress made other provisions, ran into unexpected opposition from John Randolph himself. He had labored mightily for a theory of broad construction and for powers to the central government that went against every principle he had formerly professed—but this was too much.

"If we give this power out of our hands," he exclaimed in his shrill, high, penetrating voice, referring to the Presidential authority over the territory, "it may be irrevocable until Congress shall have made legislative provision; that is, a single branch of the Government, the Executive branch, with a small minority of either House, may prevent its resumption." He demanded, instead, that such authority be limited to the end of the current session, or prior Congressional action.

Whereupon the Federalists joyfully moved to strike out the grant altogether; to which the fledgling member, John W. Eppes, Jefferson's son-in-law, countered with an inquiry as to the vacuum which must then ensue. Submerged Republican principles rose again in the veterans. Jackson of Georgia retorted to Eppes that he would rather have an interregnum "to doing anything which should militate against the Constitution, or principles that have been long respected."[43]

Jefferson was following the proceeding with the keenest interest and anxiety. Overtly, he could do nothing; but he tried to hold the sagging lines intact, and sought indirectly to bolster the faithful and overcome the recalcitrants. Politely he sent the French originals of the treaty to John Randolph. There had been some dispute, he heard, about the meaning of the English translation. Randolph rebuffed him with the curt rejoinder that he had no need for them; "the constitutionality is the theme of the opposition."[44]

The debate was finally resolved with Randolph and his dissidents compelled to bow to their fellow Republicans; though salving their defeat by the insertion of a qualifying amendment that the powers vested in the President were "for maintaining and protecting the inhabitants of Louisiana in the full enjoyment of their liberty, property, and religion."[45]

Jefferson had won a resounding victory, and hastened to put it into effect. He had been angered and alarmed by the strong protests from Spain over the cession. Curiously enough, he had thought that Spain would meekly accept the complete subversion of her compact with France and allow the United States to become heir to a princely domain adjacent to her most treasured possessions without a murmur. But Yrujo's fierce opposition here, and the reports from the envoys abroad, soon disabused him.

If Spain thinks she can give us New Orleans and refuse Louisiana, he fumed to Madison, she is mistaken. We shall use force to obtain what belongs to us.[46] He discussed the matter with his Cabinet even before Congress met. New Orleans must be occupied the moment Congress authorized it.[47]

On October 28th, Congress had duly granted the power. On the following day, Jefferson set the machinery in motion. Orders were to be sent to Governor Claiborne of the Mississippi Territory and to General James Wilkinson, in command of the troops along the border, to march 500 regulars from Fort Adams and 1,000 volunteers from the Territory. Tennessee and Kentucky were to be called on for 6,000 volunteers. Arrangements were to be made with Daniel Clark, an American merchant in New Orleans, to promote a simultaneous insurrection among the populace. Laussat, the French Commissioner, who was supposed to receive sovereignty from Spain in the name of France (before turning it over to the United States) was to co-operate.[48] Jefferson could act decisively and with the utmost speed when he wanted to. This was one of the occasions he wanted to; another related to all dealings with the Barbary States. His indecisions, delays, subtleties and indirections—so prominently in evidence when it came to dealings with France and England—fell from him like a masking cloak to reveal the steel beneath when it came to the American frontier and pirates.

In the midst of these hurried preparations, he could nevertheless find time to discuss another matter close to his heart—the gradual elimination of sovereign Indian lands from the limits of the United States. He congratulated General Dearborn on the news that the Choctaws had agreed to sell their possessions on the Mississippi. Buy whatever they will sell, he told the Secretary of War. But don't, he warned, pay high prices. "They are poor, and will probably sell beyond what will pay their debts, so as to be entitled to an annual pension, which," he cannily remarked, "is one of the best holds we can have on them." [49]

Fortunately, the use of force was not necessary. Spain, faced with the determined show of it on the part of the United States, and the displeasure of the French, was compelled to yield to the inevitable. With a bad grace, she formally turned over New Orleans and Louisiana to Laussat on behalf of France; and on December 20, 1803, Laussat in turn lowered the French flag and Claiborne raised the American Stars and Stripes over New Orleans in token of final sovereignty.

The greatest expansion of the United States in all her history—perhaps the greatest single expansion of territory of any nation in the world—had taken place without a single shot or a single armed soldier. From now on, the destinies of America were firmly fixed, and the march to the Pacific made inevitable.

Jefferson properly exulted over this mighty achievement of his administration. "Tho' we shall be only the 2nd of the civilized nations in [mere?] *extent* of territory," he exclaimed, "we shall be the first in that which is cultivable." [50]

CHAPTER 54

Pell-Mell

THE formal cession, however, left some matters of the highest importance undetermined. What, for example, were the exact boundaries of the territory thus delivered to the United States? This was a matter of the greatest interest to the South. The West was well taken care of by the accession of New Orleans and the uninterrupted navigation of the Mississippi along its whole length to the open sea. New England looked sourly on the whole business and feared that the collapse of her early predominance would now become permanent. But New England was largely Federalist and the Republicans were not concerned over her misgivings. The South was another matter. All the rivers that flowed southward into the Gulf were useless unless the Floridas—and particularly West Florida, comprising the littoral of what are now the states of Mississippi and Alabama—belonged to the United States.

In Europe, Livingston and Monroe insisted that West Florida was a part of the bargain and advised sudden seizure, on the theory that possession made good title. Jefferson and Madison toyed with the idea, but preferred first to see if Spain could not be induced to yield. Unfortunately, they ran into an unexpected snag.

Livingston had originally believed that France would support American pretensions to the Floridas; but the strong reaction from Madrid caused Napoleon to think twice. The envoy was now told by Talleyrand that he was willing to aid in negotiations to *purchase* East Florida; but he kept a discreet silence about West Florida. However, Livingston confidentially insisted to Madison that "the moment is so favorable for taking possession of that country, that I hope it has not been neglected, even though a little force should be necessary to effect it. Your minister must find the means to justify it." [1]

Livingston's advocacy of violent measures stemmed from a complex of causes. But the hidden motive lay in his resentment over the way in which Monroe had taken the lion's share of the glory, and his belief that, should his advice be followed in this particular, he could recapture what had been rightfully his from the beginning.

Several significant items militated against his position. For one thing Laussat, in formally turning over Louisiana, had "confidentially signified that it did not comprehend any part of West Florida"; though he did admit that it extended westward to the Rio Bravo, sometimes called the Rio Norte.[2] For a second, Talleyrand positively assured the Spaniards that he had given the United States no more than what France had originally held —and that this included only the territory west of the Mississippi and the river Iberville. Thereby he flatly denied that any part of West Florida was involved.[3]

The American government was willing enough at this stage of the proceedings to concede that *East Florida* was still Spanish territory, and sought to negotiate its purchase under the original authority received from Congress. But it held stubbornly to the belief that West Florida had been transferred. Nevertheless, in view of Spanish resistance and in the knowledge that its pretensions would not be supported by the French at the time of taking title, it wisely determined not to make an issue of it then, but to leave the solution to future and possibly more favorable circumstances.[4]

But Congress, under the determined drive of the southern Republicans, had no such qualms. They proceeded on the bland assumption that West Florida was an integral part of the United States and legislated on that basis.

The first and most pressing need, however, was to organize the newly received territory. Jefferson mapped out a program for legislative consideration. Louisiana was to be divided into Lower and Upper Louisiana. In the lower section, the President was to appoint a governor and three judges, with initiating legislative powers in the judges and the right of veto in the Governor and in Congress. Otherwise, the rights and freedoms of the American Constitution were to be introduced; and a mandate given to the judges to mold the laws in general to the American pattern as gradually as possible, without exciting the discontent of the inhabitants, accustomed as they were to the French civil code. Upper Louisiana, sparsely settled and exposed to foreign invasion, was to continue under its current territorial rule, subject directly to the national government.[5]

This was a surprising program to come from Jefferson, the philosopher of libertarianism and the consistent exponent of the rights of all people to govern themselves. While no quarrel can be had with the organization of Upper Louisiana, a wilderness with hardly a settlement and requiring a superimposed government, the same considerations did not apply to the comparatively well populated and highly civilized New Orleans and its environs. In fact, whatever rights they had previously had in the way of self-government were ruthlessly taken away from them. They were to be ruled by a governor and board of judges appointed from above, without their consent and without any right of appeal except to a distant and alien Congress.

The Senate, though seemingly only after an extended debate, passed a somewhat different bill from that which Jefferson had advocated, by a vote of 20 to 5.[6] But it had harder sledding in the House. The Senate bill called for a government consisting of a governor and secretary to be appointed by the President, and a legislative council of thirteen similarly to be appointed by him. The judicial officers were also under his control. If anything, this measure granted even more absolute powers to the President than Jefferson had originally proposed. All lines of authority converged solely to his hands. And his creature, the Governor, could at will convene and prorogue the council—supposedly drawn from the inhabitants—who were also the creatures of the President.

Some of Jefferson's most faithful followers gagged at this arbitrary legislation, and joined in protest with many of the Federalists. Michael Leib of Pennsylvania opposed in particular the right of the Governor to prorogue the Council. It made the latter, he argued, "the most dependent thing of its nature in the United States." He might well have added that it resembled that old power of the Royal Governors which had led directly to the Revolution. Varnum of Massachusetts demanded a legislature elected by the people; and the radical Matthew Lyon witheringly compared Jefferson to Napoleon.

Under such heated attacks, the supporters of Jefferson were compelled to give some ground if they wished to save the whole, and an amendment providing for an elective Council after a first year's appointed Council, was adopted on March 16, 1804 by a vote of 58 to 42. With some other changes, notably the removal of limitations on the right of jury trial and fixing the term of the Act at two years, the bill was sent to the Senate for reconsideration. But the Senate refused all the amendments except that which limited the term of the Act—as a concession, reducing that to a single year. Thus confronted with Senatorial obstinacy, the House unwillingly receded from its attempt to liberalize the government, and both Houses repassed the bill on March 23rd. Jefferson signed it on March 26th, and it became law.[7]

At least the governance of Louisiana was a legitimate concern for Congress. But it did not stop there; it assumed to legislate for West Florida as well. On November 30, 1803, John Randolph introduced a bill which directed that the ceded territories, "and also all the navigable waters, rivers, creeks, bays, and inlets lying within the United States, which empty into the Gulf of Mexico east of the River Mississippi, shall be annexed to the Mississippi district." It also authorized the President to set up the bay and river of Mobile, and all waters entering the Gulf of Mexico east of Mobile, into a separate district.

This was a direct slap in the face of Spain, and indirectly of France. For it pronounced to be a part of the United States and therefore subject to its sole control the territory of West Florida which both these countries had decisively declared was *not* a part of the sale. Yet Congress passed the bill and Jefferson, fully cognizant of its meaning, signed it on February 24, 1804.

Yrujo entered a vehement protest to Madison; but Jefferson calmly issued a proclamation on May 30th setting up a collection district for what he was pleased to call "the shores, waters, inlets, creeks, and rivers, lying *within the boundaries of the United States.*"[8]

In all the stress and turmoil of the acquisition of Louisiana and of grave domestic problems, Jefferson was never too busy to resist a chance for philosophical and scientific interchanges.

He seized the opportunity to laud his favorite pursuit of agriculture as a profession even for college graduates. "In every College and University," he declared, "a professorship of agriculture, and the class of its students, might be honored as the first." And the charitable schools, "instead of storing their pupils with a lore which the present state of society does not call for," should be converted to schools of agriculture. He was vehemently opposed to the trend, even then evident, from the country to the towns. "The general desire of men to live by their heads rather than their hands," he said bitterly, "and the strong allurements of great cities to those who have any turn for dissipation, threaten to make them here, as in Europe, the sinks of voluntary misery." [9]

What particularly focused his attention on the advance of agriculture at this time were his contemporary readings in Malthus's gloomy and seemingly logically impeccable theories of a growth of population far outrunning the available food supply. But Jefferson, though ready enough to agree with the general thesis so far as Europe was concerned, did not believe it applied to America. There, he explained, "the immense extent of uncultivated and fertile lands enables every one who will labor, to marry young, and to raise a family of any size. Our food, then, may increase geometrically with our laborers, and our births, however multiplied, become effective." [10] He did not note the fallacy in his reasoning—that such an immense multiplication of births as he envisaged must eventually bring even the vast extent of America within the iron bounds of Malthusian doctrine.

He contemplated leisurely the scene in France, with whose philosophers, scientists and economists he maintained a prodigious correspondence. "There are in France," he admitted, "more real [natural] philosophers than in any country on earth: but there are also a greater proportion of pseudo-philosophers there." What had aroused this last was the report of a rain of stones, attested to by men of respectable learning. "The reason is that the exuberant imagination of a Frenchman gives him a greater facility of writing, & runs away with his judgment unless he has a good stock of it. It even creates facts for him which never happened, and he tells them with good faith." [11]

The unfinished city of Washington also engaged his close attention. His architectural sense was annoyed at the gap between the original grandiose intentions and the palpable fact. In 1803, he called Benjamin H. Latrobe, who had studied architecture and engineering in London, to come from Philadelphia to Washington as Surveyor of Public Buildings. Latrobe had established a reputation through his design of the Richmond Penitentiary and the Greek-classical Bank of Pennsylvania. But the new architect found defects in the unfinished plans of William Thornton, whom he considered totally ignorant of architecture, though possessing some brilliant ideas. He declined therefore to undertake the job unless he was given carte blanche, to which Jefferson agreed.

Latrobe commenced building the south wing of the Capitol and the navy yard, but ran into the usual collisions with the politicians of Congress, who demanded that he adhere rigidly to the plan first approved by Washington. Once more the fiery young architect tendered his resignation; and once more Jefferson refused to accept it. The President respected his talents, but found him difficult to work with; and the construction of the buildings proceeded at a jerky pace, interlarded with numerous quarrels.[12]

When, on February 22, 1804, Jefferson wrote out his report to Congress on the state of the public buildings, and detailed his plans for remodeling and new construction, he noted with a great deal of pride in his letter record that it had been "copied with the double pen of Hawkins." This represents his first recorded use of his famous polygraph, recently invented by the Englishman, John Isaac Hawkins. Possessed as he was of a sense of history and a justified belief that whatever he wrote would some day prove of immense value to historians, Jefferson had from his first entry into public life sought diligently for some method of making copies that would be clean, legible, exact and not too time-wasting.

The usual procedure, of course, had first been to make laborious copies by hand. The second, saving considerably in time, but infuriating to the later researcher, was the letter press, whereby the original with the ink barely dry was placed in contact with a damp second sheet, and an impression squeezed in a press. Naturally, the impression was faint, the combination of damp and ink made the impression spread and blur, with the result that the copy became in many instances partially or wholly illegible with the passage of years.

When Jefferson heard of this new invention called the polygraph, he exerted every effort to obtain a sample. The polygraph, indeed, was a tremendous advance; and in a way, better than the carbons of modern practice. It corresponds to the modern architect's pantograph, and consists of two pens connected by an ingenious series of levers whereby whatever is written manually with one pen on one sheet of paper is simultaneously traced by the other pen on an adjoining sheet.

The first instrument that Jefferson used was comparatively crude, and he experimented with improvements of his own and with new models made to his specifications, until finally he was satisfied. He eventually had two of them, as well as a small traveling set. He was overjoyed at the invention, and so is the modern student who works to any extent with Jefferson's papers. "I only lament," he wrote, "it had not been invented 30. years sooner. I lament nothing more than the not having been able to preserve copies of my letters during the war, which to me would now have been a consoling possession."[13]

As though Jefferson had not enough troubles as President, he now became engaged in an *opéra-bouffe* imbroglio with the diplomatic corps, particularly with the representatives of England and Spain. A curious transformation had come over him since his return from France. There he had ruffed it with the best in fine garments and lavish displays. But the moment he set foot in America again he molted to a more sober plumage and dressed plainly and sedately. When he became President, he went even further. Though he still ordered some expensive garments, and did not hesitate to dress well in the privacy of Monticello, he made it a point at Washington, in his public capacity, to dress with what can only be described—and has been—as an amazing degree of sloppiness and deshabille.

There is no doubt that this was deliberate planning. It expressed to him a reaction from the ruffles and gold lace of an aristocratic court; and it opposed a republican simplicity of plain farmer and artisan against the fine feathers of the Federalists. He had also become imbued with a fixed conviction that pomp, state and ceremonial were indispensable adjuncts of absolutism, and that in a republic there ought not to be, and must not be, any hierarchical classes or orders of precedence—in short, anything that would make one man seem a step higher or better than another. One of his bitterest complaints against the former administrations related to their lavish use of ceremonial and levees, which Jefferson considered a servile imitation of the English court.

The change in dress, the moment he assumed the Presidency, has already been noted, and the astonishment of visitors meeting him for the first time in the President's House. This was bad enough; but Jefferson went further, and thereby became embroiled with the diplomatic corps.

Anthony Merry had been named by the British Foreign Office as Minister to the United States, and he came to Washington with his wife and with every intention of being amiable. Rufus King, indeed, thought him "a plain, unassuming, and amiable man." [14]

He landed in Norfolk, Virginia, and traveled to Washington, to appear on November 29, 1803, at the President's House in full emblazonment of uniform to present his credentials to the President of the United States. To his mortification and anger, he was received by Jefferson in that state of slippered undress of which Plumer had so feelingly written. He could only conceive it as a carefully planned insult to the nation which he represented.

Jefferson *was* following a plan; but it was a plan which was general. As he later defended himself, from the moment of his inauguration he had "buried levees, birthdays, royal parades, and the arrogation of precedence in society by certain self-stiled friends of order, but truly stiled friends of privileged orders." At his numerous dinners—which all admitted to be lavish in food and wines—and at all functions, social or official, he eschewed every semblance of formal etiquette. "In social circles," he insisted, "all are equal, whether in, or out, of office, foreign or domestic; & the same equality exists among ladies and among gentlemen . . . 'pell-mell' and 'next the door' form the basis of etiquette in the societies of this country." [15]

This "republican simplicity" did not sit well with diplomats trained to the formal rules and rigid precedence of European courts. The Marquis d'Yrujo of Spain had resented it but said little; Merry, however, made it a *cause célèbre.*

The explosion came at a dinner given in the President's House on December 2, 1803. The diplomatic corps was present—the Merrys, the Yrujos, the Pichons—as well as the Madisons and a miscellaneous crew of Congressmen and *their* wives. What happened at this famous dinner was made the subject of an indignant letter from Merry to his home government.

On the announcement that dinner was ready, Jefferson gave his hand to Dolly Madison and sat her on his right. Madame Yrujo was placed on his left. Next to Dolly sat Yrujo, and Mrs. Merry had to be content with the station *below* him. Already seething at this seeming slight on the majesty of the British nation, Merry was left to his own resources to find what place at the table he could. He started for the seat below Madame Yrujo, but was forestalled by a lowly Congressman, who rushed by him and seized the coveted place for himself. In a blind fury, Merry finally found an unoccupied chair among the hoi polloi, while Jefferson placidly continued his attentions to the ladies by whom he was flanked. What made it all the worse was the fact that the Pichons were present, with whose nation the English were at war.[16]

Yrujo, who had been favored in the seating arrangement over the Merrys, observed the extreme agitation of the British Minister, and himself acknowledged that the whole affair seemed to be a studied business on Jefferson's part.[17]

As though this were not enough, the same diplomatic representatives with their wives were three days later invited to a party by Madison. This time the Yrujos were made to feel the weight of "pell-mell" as well as the Merrys. The Cabinet officers had usually granted the courtesies of precedence to the foreign diplomats which they were denied by Jefferson; but this time Madison, without warning, copied the practice of his chief. He offered his arm suddenly to Mrs. Gallatin, and left Madame Yrujo, Mrs. Merry and Madame Pichon standing openmouthed. In the resulting confusion, *no one* offered his arm to Mrs. Merry, and she was compelled to stand helplessly by until her husband, white with indignation, himself took her in to the table. Even Pichon, though pleased enough to see the Merrys humbled, was somewhat scandalized at this strange procedure.[18]

All this may sound like a comic opera script, which indeed it was. But social slights penetrate deeper than much more important insults; and the histories of nations have been altered by lesser matters.

Every diplomatic representative by this time was writing to his government about the situation. Merry declared the situation degrading to Great Britain and intolerable to himself. Even Yrujo, at first favored, and then rebuffed, changed his tune, and now allied himself with Merry, his public enemy. Their respective wives created a furious social war of their own, and a deep-laid scheme of reprisal was planned. It was agreed between them that when *they* gave dinners, the ministers would hand in their own wives and let the wives of the Cabinet officers scramble as best they might. They went further, refusing all invitations from the offending Cabinet members, and a meeting of the Cabinet was formally devoted to the impasse. It was there resolved that the President should hand in whatever lady happened to be nearest him, and that there should be no precedence.

The controversy convulsed all Washington, and overshadowed the public business. But Jefferson was adamant. He called Mrs. Merry "a virago" and, when Congress gave a formal dinner to celebrate the acquisition of Louisiana, he invited no foreign ministers in order to avoid the battle of the etiquette. Much as he regretted the absence of his daughter, Martha, to head his table, he rejoiced now that she did not have to bear the brunt of the social war and the butchery of the Federalist papers.[19]

With a stubbornness worthy of a better cause, he refused to yield. "The principle of society with us," he wrote, "as well as of our political constitution, is the equal rights of all; and if there be an occasion where this equality ought to prevail preeminently, it is in social circles collected for conviviality. Nobody shall be above you, nor you above anybody, pele-mele is our law."

While he was thus simplifying society, he was also simplifying diplomacy. "I have ever considered diplomacy," he remarked in the same context, "as the pest of the peace of the world, as the workshop in which nearly all the wars of Europe are manufactured." Therefore he had dismissed one-half of the European legations and would like to dismiss the rest. "Consuls," he thought, "would do all the business we ought to have there, quite as well as ministers."[20]

But diplomacy, either at home or abroad, was not as simple as he would have liked to have it. No consul could have purchased Louisiana; while his "pell-mell" at home created a situation in which international relations worsened and sent both Merry and Yrujo into secret negotiations with the opposition—the Federalists of New England and Burr of New York. Even the new French Minister, Louis Marie Turreau, who replaced Pichon, resented the arrangement. As Spain's ally, he tried to reconcile Yrujo with Madison, but failed because, as he informed his government, Madison "is dry, spiteful, passionate; and his private resentments, still more than political difference, will long keep him apart from M d'Yrujo."[21]

In the midst of these ignominious quarrels, a scandal was gathering that attacked Jefferson's personal reputation and perhaps gave him more heartsick moments than any other incident of his entire career.

The first notice of impending trouble came from the ineffable Callender. Smarting under what he considered the ingratitude of the President of the

United States for services rendered, he methodically collected every scrap of gossip and scandal deleterious to Jefferson. In most instances, his information was political. In two cases, however, it hit Jefferson in his most sensitive spot, his personal behavior. One was comparatively innocuous—an accusation of cowardice during the British raids in Virginia. Yet Jefferson took it seriously enough to gather eye-witness affidavits and to quote from his Journal during that hectic period. The other, however, could not be as easily handled.

The story went back to Jefferson's youth—to the year 1768, in fact. Jack Walker, one of Jefferson's boyhood companions and the son of Dr. Thomas Walker, his guardian, had married Betsey Moore and gone to live at Belvoir, a short distance from Shadwell. The two young men naturally continued their acquaintance, and young Jefferson was a frequent and welcome visitor at Belvoir.

Then something happened. As Jack Walker later reported it in an astounding document intended for political purposes, he had gone with a Virginia Commission to Fort Stanwix to formulate a treaty with the Indians. In his absence, he asked Jefferson to watch over his wife and infant daughter. But Jefferson seized the opportunity to make advances to Betsey, not only in her own home, but later at Shadwell and during a visit at the house of a neighbor, Col. Coles. And, even after his own marriage, Jefferson resumed his importunities.

Young Betsey, while repulsing the offers of illicit love with indignation, nevertheless kept the various attempts from her unwitting husband. It was only after Jefferson left for Europe—sixteen years later—that she spoke to her husband; or at least, so Walker asserted. It seems that Walker had named Jefferson in his will as his executor, and Betsey kept importuning her husband to remove him from the office. Walker finally obtained the story from her, after his steadfast refusals to do so. Whereupon, so he afterwards alleged, he promptly wrote to Jefferson in Paris, berating him for the betrayal of their friendship and demanding certain vague satisfactions.[22]

Here the matter rested for many years. But, in the meantime, Jack Walker had turned Federalist and, obviously, Jefferson's deadly enemy. Henry Lee, known to fame as Light Horse Harry Lee, another personal and political enemy of Jefferson, married a niece of Betsey Walker's and thus gained knowledge of the incident. Yet, during the years, not a word was publicly said until *after* Jefferson became President, when Callender was entrusted with the ancient tale. With great glee he published it in *The Recorder*, the newspaper he had initiated in Richmond and which he had hoped would be subsidized by Jefferson.

The story descended on Jefferson with overwhelming force. That youthful indiscretion of his had long been suspended over his head like the legendary sword of Damocles. He told his private secretary, William Burwell, that Hamilton had known of it and had threatened to use it against him during the period of his own notorious trouble with Mrs. Reynolds.

Jefferson did not attempt to deny the single fact that he had tried to make love to Mrs. Walker; but he insisted that the tale as it eventually came out was grossly exaggerated. It had consisted only of a *single* attempt, prior to his own marriage; and, he solemnly swore, it had been "without premeditation & produced by an accidental visit." [23]

There are certain inherent contradictions in the long, rambling tale that Jack Walker wove in 1805 for the use of Henry Lee. It is incredible that Betsey could have submitted to so many assaults on her virtue over a period of years without telling her husband, or ceasing to afford Jefferson opportunities to molest her. In all fairness, however, the Walkers' side of the story must be told. Her silence was due, so Jack averred, to her fear that the revelation might lead to a challenge and a duel.

But Walker places the date of his knowledge to the immediate period after they heard that Jefferson had sailed for France. That took place on July 5, 1784. Allowing time for the news to travel to Virginia, certainly it was known to the Walkers by September 1st. Yet on February 4, 1786, at least a year and a half later, Walker was writing the friendliest of letters to the man who had sought to break up his home. "My Dear Friend," he called him, spoke of domestic and political matters with every evidence of warmth, and hoped that soon Jefferson would be able "to return to your Country & your Friends. For believe me Sir, they both require you." And he ended with the postcript that "Mrs. Walker . . . begs to be affectionately remembered to you & Miss Patsy." [24]

Certainly this is not the kind of letter than an aggrieved husband would write, and the denunciatory epistle which he later claimed he did write, was never received by Jefferson. It is probable, then, that Jefferson's statement of a *single* attempt was correct and that Mrs. Walker did not deem it then of sufficient significance to report to her husband. It is quite likely that the matter was not mentioned until political enmities had intervened, skillfully agitated by her nephew-in-law, Henry Lee. It may well be that *then* she happened to mention it casually, and that Lee blew it up, realizing its possibilities as a future political weapon, and bided his time for its most effective employment.

When the affair saw the light of day in Callender's scandal-mongering sheet, Walker deemed it incumbent on himself to place further negotiations in Lee's hands. Some obscure interviews ensued, of which the full purport is not known. As a matter of fact, the reason for *all* the negotiations that followed cannot now be determined; the participants wrapping them in a determined fog of vagueness. But Walker now wrote to Jefferson—April 4, 1803—enclosing a copy of that letter which he claimed to have sent to Europe, and which was dated May 15, 1788. Seemingly he as well as Jefferson was alarmed over the sudden burst of publicity, inasmuch as it had traveled far beyond its original source, Callender, and had been taken up with shouts of satisfaction by almost every Federalist newspaper in the land.

Walker's letter of April 4th has vanished, but it must have proposed methods for silencing the newspapers. For Jefferson's response weighed the possibilities of such an action, and found them "difficult if not desperate." "These people," he wrote bitterly, "slander for their bread, & as long as customers can be found who will read & relish & pay for their lies, they will fabricate them for the market." While he had made it a policy never to meddle with the opposition press, he admitted that the occasion justified the use of friends to see what discreetly could be done. He thought that one of his friends could effectively silence the editor of the *Bee;* he was optimistic of a similar success with the *Aurora* (a Republican paper!) and certain others. "My best endeavours," he concluded, "shall be used by these & all other means to consign this unfortunate matter to all the oblivion of which it is susceptible." [25]

But the scandal was not thus easily consigned to oblivion. The Federalist press kept it alive. At the end of 1804, an obscene squib appeared in the *Port Folio,* pretending to be a diary of Jefferson:

> February 21, 1804. Passed a very uneasy night—dream't that Colonel Walker pursued me with a horsewhip—waked in a fright, and found myself on my knees in the middle of the floor:—got Sally [the 'black Sally' of earlier obscenities] to change my linnen, and went to sleep.[26]

Thus kept simmering, the pot boiled over again with a rehash of every charge against Jefferson in the *New England Palladium* of January 18, 1805. He was there accused of atheism, of cowardice during the British invasion, of having "taken to his bosom a sable damsel," and of "having assaulted the domestic happiness of Mr. Walker." Had it ended there, it might have been overlooked; but the publishers of the *Palladium* were the official printers to the Massachusetts legislature, and some of Jefferson's partisans unwisely sought to dismiss them from that lucrative business. The whole affair, therefore, became a matter of public debate on the floor of the legislature. It could no longer be ignored.

To protect himself and his wife—there were those, evidently, who whispered that Mrs. Walker had not viewed Jefferson's advances unkindly —Walker now placed in Henry Lee's hands the rambling and circumstantial account of the incident previously mentioned. A series of letters, signed "Tom Turner," replete with further gory and lurid details, appeared in the *Repertory*. It was necessary for Jefferson, at this stage, to break his silence. His private secretary, young Burwell, was given the task of replying, and responded to "Tom Turner" through the friendly columns of the *Richmond Enquirer.*[27]

Jack Walker, confronted with this new outburst, was heartily sorry he had ever permitted the scandal to leak out. Yet it seems he had been to blame even for this last ebullition, through a private letter to a Mr. Kinloch. Meanwhile, he had been diligently seeking "satisfaction" from Jefferson—probably in the way of a written acknowledgment that Betsey had repulsed him—and he now feared that the latter would use the Massachusetts flare-up as an excuse for refusing it. He was ready, therefore, if need be, to publish the entire interchange of letters between them.[28]

On his own side, Jefferson placed a letter in the hands of his former Attorney General, Levi Lincoln (resigned March 2, 1805) in which he stated that "I plead guilty to one of their charges, that when young and single I offered love to a handsome lady. I acknolege its incorrectness. It is the only one founded in truth among all their allegations against me." [29]

The affair dragged its sordid way for at least a year longer, with Henry Lee insisting that Jefferson accede to Walker's demands for a letter of disavowal that could be published. Jefferson was ready to furnish the letter, but utterly refused to permit its publication, even after he retired from office.[30]

The final act came in 1809, shortly after Jefferson quit the Presidency. Walker was dying of an incurable disease, and Betsey was also "very feeble & low." Regrets gnawed them at the part they had played in the whole unsavory mess, and they intimated, through Monroe, that they would consider a visit to them in their current state an act of kindness. Jefferson could not bring himself to meet face to face those who had brought on him such unhappiness, but he sent a present of figs. It was received gratefully; [31] but he never saw them again. The hurt had been too deep.

Fate, however, had still another and more lasting blow for him. On April 12, 1804, Jefferson wrote simply and poignantly in his account book: "This morning between 8. & 9. oclock my dear daughter Maria Eppes died." [32]

She had been taken ill early in March, and her husband, John W. Eppes, had rushed from Washington to Edgehill to be at her side. The first news he sent the anxious father was good; but then she sank again and quietly passed away.[33]

The President was prostrated with grief. Family and domesticity meant more to him than all the glories of the world. He had never truly recovered from the death of his wife. Now his younger daughter was gone; and only the single thread of his elder daughter, Martha, remained to him for comfort. Thus he poured out his grief to the friends who hastened to offer condolence.[34]

One unexpected letter came to him—from Abigail Adams, that strong-minded lady whom once he had numbered among his dearest friends, and who had fallen away into injured silence since that March day when her husband had silently departed from the President's House and Jefferson had taken his place.

Remembering the little girl who had clung to her skirts in tears in those early days in London and who now was no more, Abigail took up her pen and wrote the bereaved father. It was for her a difficult task; and she wrote in secrecy, without the knowledge of her husband.

"Had you been no other than the private inhabitant of Montecello, I should e'er this time have addrest you, with that sympathy, which a recent event has awakend in my Bosom. but reasons of various kinds withheld my pen. untill the powerful feelings of my heart, have burst through the restraint. and called upon me to shed the tear of sorrow over the departed remains of your beloved and deserving daughter." And, through the blur of tears, she ended: "who once took pleasure in Subscribing Herself your Friend Abigail Adams."[35]

No letter that he received touched Jefferson more than this unwilling cry from the heart of the stern old woman. He sent it proudly to the son-in-law who had shared the bitter loss with him. His esteem and friendship for the Adamses were still unbroken, he avowed, and he was happy that this renewal of communication enabled him to declare it to them. He added a codicil, however. "I shall do it with a frank declaration that one act of his [John's] life, and never but one, gave me personal displeasure, his midnight appointments. If respect for him will not permit me to ascribe that altogether to the influence of others, it will leave something for friendship to forgive."[36]

He would have done better at the moment to have forgotten this bit of ancient history. For, in an otherwise grateful letter of thanks to Abigail, he persisted in harping on this one sore topic, though ending with a magnanimous gesture of forgiveness.[37]

Jefferson might have known that the animadversion would only stir up the latent fires in Abigail, as indeed it did. She retorted on him his sponsorship of Callender in his vicious attacks on John, and adverted by indirection to the dismissal of her son, John Quincy Adams, from his post in Boston.[38]

Now the fires of controversy were enkindled, and the original condolences forgotten in the heat of old resentments. Jefferson sought to soothe them over, renouncing Callender and attempting explanations of their connection. But incautiously he inquired as to the nature of that final hint in her previous letter.[39]

This opened the floodgates. Abigail let pass the matter of Callender, though not without a side dig at Jefferson's claim that the Sedition Law was unconstitutional, and concentrated on the treatment accorded her son. She accused Jefferson of having deliberately removed him from the nonpolitical post of a commissioner in bankruptcy.[40] Jefferson swore that he had not known her son was one of the commissioners when he appointed another, and with a stubborn persistence, argued the reference to the Sedition Act. That law, he insisted, was definitely unconstitutional, and he set forth his views on the right of government to suppress dissent. "I tolerate with the utmost latitude," he declared, "the right of others to differ from me in opinion without imputing to them criminality. I know too well the weakness & uncertainty of human reason to wonder at its different results." Both political parties sought the public good, but their ideas of arriving at it were different. "One fears most the ignorance of the people: the other the selfishness of rulers independant of them. Which is right, time & experience will prove. We think the one side of the experiment has been long enough tried, and proved not to promote the good of the many." [41]

The indomitable old lady was willing to accept his protestations of innocence in connection with her husband and her son, but she could not abide his insistence that the national government could not constitutionally defend its magistrates from scurrilous libel. With a tartness all her own, she ended flatly: "I will not Sir any further intrude upon your time, but close this correspondence." [42] More years were to roll by before the husband, unaware of this correspondence of his wife's, was to pick up *his* pen and finally heal the breach.

Meanwhile Jefferson, lonely in Washington, sought consolation from his bitter sorrow in the cheerful notes of a mockingbird, named Dick, that he had purchased the previous autumn and set up in a cage in his writing room.[43]

CHAPTER 55

Struggle with the Judiciary

ON January 26, 1804, Jefferson received a surprise visit from the Vice-President of the United States, Aaron Burr. The two men, so different in every respect, had gone their separate ways ever since their joint inauguration into office, and their relations had been placed on the most formal basis.

It was a strange visit, and Jefferson, immediately after it was over, set down his version of it in his private *Anas*. Burr's version was never similarly immortalized.

According to Jefferson, Burr commenced with the story of his life; how he had come to New York "a stranger" and found the state in control of the Livingstons and the Clintons. In the crisis of 1800, they had asked his aid to help them to the seats of power and he had given it. He had accepted the vice-presidential nomination only to promote Jefferson's "fame and advancement, and from a desire to be with me, whose company and conversation had always been fascinating to him." Then the Livingstons and the Clintons had become hostile, and "excited the calumnies which I had seen published." His attachment to Jefferson was as strong and sincere as ever; nevertheless, "attachments must be reciprocal or cease to exist."

He was willing, Burr continued, to retire at the end of his term for the good of the Republican cause, in order to avoid a schism. (A presidential election was due in the fall of 1804.) But he did not intend to retire under fire; his enemies were using Jefferson's name to destroy him; and "some mark of favor from me" was essential "which would declare to the world that he retired with my confidence."

Jefferson replied coldly that he had never interfered in any election in the past, and would not do so in the impending one. Then he turned the conversation to "indifferent subjects" and bowed Burr out.

Barely had the discomfited Vice-President quit the room when Jefferson hastened to his desk to record sarcastically that Burr had thought to placate him with strong doses of flattery; but that he, Jefferson, had always distrusted him, and that Burr seemed to be always "at market" for any job anywhere.[1]

Jefferson was not as naïve as he sounded. He knew very well the object of the visit. Burr was fighting for his political life in New York, and matters were coming to a head. For much of Burr's difficulties Jefferson was directly responsible. Ever since the first days of the administration when he had turned a deaf ear to all Burr's requests for patronage, and filled almost every request of the Clintons and the Livingstons, he had been steadily undermining Burr's position.

In the forthcoming presidential election, there was no question that Jefferson would receive the nomination again by acclamation; nor did he fear the result. The Federalists were discredited and divided, and their platform was merely one of negation. Many of their followers had deserted to the Republican camp, and it was Jefferson's strategy to keep them there. The one threat to his future ascendancy, however, and to the ascendancy of the little Virginia dynasty he was grooming to take over after his retirement—notably Madison and Monroe—came from Aaron Burr. As long as Burr could control the forces of New York he might, with the aid and comfort of the unreconstructed Federalists, hold the balance of power and even eventually topple the Virginians from their supremacy. Therefore, wherever possible, Jefferson hewed away at the foundations of that power. From the Clintons and the Livingstons he foresaw no serious competition. The tempting bait dangled before the aging and enfeebled Governor Clinton was the Vice-Presidency; and so well had Jefferson labored, that Burr knew already that he was out in the cold.

Only a month before this fateful interview, De Witt Clinton had written to Jefferson disclosing that Burr had plans for running for the governorship of New York; that the only sure candidate who could defeat him was his uncle, the current Governor; but the latter had refused to run again. A letter from Jefferson might induce him to change his mind.[2]

Jefferson replied with a certain caution. He acknowledged that it would be "a serious misfortune should a change in the administration of your government be hazarded before its present principles be well established through all its parts. Yet, on reflection, you will be sensible that the delicacy of my situation, considering who may be competitors, forbids my intermeddling, even so far as to write the letter you suggest. I can therefore only brood in silence over my secret wishes."[3]

But those secret wishes were present for all, including George Clinton, to see. And they were made more positive when, immediately after the conversation with Burr, Jefferson sent an emissary, Erastus Granger, to warn De Witt Clinton that Burr was definitely going to run for Governor. In fact, he had a spy in the Burr camp—Gideon Granger who, pretending to be a Burrite, was sending daily confidential reports of Burr's plans to his chief in Washington.[4]

Burr hastened back to New York after the failure of his last desperate attempt to neutralize Jefferson and proceeded nevertheless with his plans. The Republicans in the state were split and he commanded one of the factions. But the Federalists, who could not hope to win an election with a candidate of their own, rallied to his banner. In alarm, the other faction of the Republicans, after discovering that their former war horse, George Clinton, preferred the Vice-Presidency to another term in New York, turned finally to Morgan Lewis, Chief Justice of the State and a Livingstonian, to oppose him.

A campaign of unexampled bitterness ensued, in which Burr might have won had not the ghost of Alexander Hamilton arisen to block his path. With every resource of eloquence and influence at his command, he exhorted his erstwhile followers to oppose the dangerous Aaron Burr. But most of them were weary of his leadership, through which they had suffered so many recent defeats. In desperation, Hamilton permitted himself the use of certain opprobrious epithets against his long-hated rival at a Federalist meeting which one of his followers, with more enthusiasm than wisdom, later adverted to in the public press.

Meanwhile, the Federalist leaders of other states were watching the approaching election with considerable interest. They, too, were desperate at their long deprivation from the fleshpots; they hated Jefferson with a consuming hatred; and believed that their only chance for salvation was to split the Union, form a confederacy of the New England States with New York and New Jersey, and go their separate ways. To them, Aaron Burr held the keys to the situation. With him in the saddle of New York, that pivotal state might follow them in their secession and form a powerful industrial and commercial union in the face of whose resources the Republican South must eventually wither and decay.

Already, these leaders—Timothy Pickering, James Hillhouse, Roger Griswold, Uriah Tracy and others—had held secret meetings to discuss their conspiratorial plans. The old-line Federalists of the Essex Junto were cold to the idea, and Hamilton was vehemently opposed; but the hotheads proceeded on their own.

Since Burr was essential to their success, they sought to pin him down, but their emissaries were compelled to report that Burr was proving a slippery customer and, while welcoming their aid in his own campaign, refused to tie himself in with their own secret wishes.[5]

But the conspirators, since they had no other course, were compelled to continue their support and hope for the best. "Shall we sit still," demanded Pickering, "until this system [Jefferson's] shall universally triumph? until even in the Eastern States the principles of genuine Federalism shall be overwhelmed? Mr. Jefferson's plan of destruction has been gradually advancing," and "the principles of our Revolution point to the remedy—a separation." [6]

The most furious of the Federalists, he later allowed himself even more intemperate language. "I am disgusted with the men who now rule," he told Rufus King, "and with their measures.... The cowardly wretch at their head, while, like a Parisian revolutionary monster, prating about humanity, would feel an infernal pleasure in the utter destruction of his opponents." Lashing himself into rage, he cried further: "Without a separation, can those States ever rid themselves of negro Presidents and negro Congresses, and regain their just weight in the political balance?" [7]

Jefferson was not unaware of the formidable conspiracy that was gathering head against him. But he took it calmly, relying on the good sense of the people and the unremitting efforts of the Republicans. The Federalists, he declared, knew that by themselves they were "gone forever. Their object, therefore, is, how to return into power under some other form." Their only means was to divide the Union, and joining the minority of misled Republicans under Burr and other dissidents, seek the cloak of their name under which to rule.[8]

It was because of them, he lamented, that he had felt obliged to run for office again. Otherwise he would have retired to the privacy of Monticello, and lived out his life in peace and quiet.[9]

But, for all his calm, like a good politician he was feeling the pulse of the country and tightening his lines. In Pennsylvania there was a serious split in the Republican ranks, with William Duane, angered at the Administration for failing to grant him the perquisites he considered his just reward, lashing out in his *Aurora* at such administration supporters as Gallatin, Madison, Governor McKean and Alexander J. Dallas. And, in his own Virginia, John Randolph was developing signs of restiveness that resulted eventually in an irreconcilable break. Since Virginia represented the heart of his power, Jefferson sought from his good friend, Littleton W. Tazewell, some insight into the opinion of its mercantile community on "the present order of things." The generalty of the planters and all of the yeomen, he knew, would continue to follow his banner; but would the merchants make common cause with their brethren to the north?

Tazewell's answer was not encouraging. They have no settled political opinions, he said. "They approve today, what tomorrow they will revile; and Interest seems to be the only tenet in their political faith which remains long unchanged.... Their whole attention is absorbed by calculations of pecuniary profit and loss, and reflections of any other kind are rarely permitted to disturb this chain of arithmetrical reasoning—Interest makes them insatiable in their desire of governmental advantage and when any act is done improving their situation, the Government is extolled to the skies, but when a burden is imposed on them in common with their fellow Citizens, they murmur and complain." Even now, in fact, they were complaining over the acquisition of Louisiana, "because it may bring into the West India market competitors in their trade." [10] The pages of history disclose human nature to be pretty much of a constant.

Burr went down to defeat in New York before the assaults of his enemies —a strange combination in which De Witt Clinton, Alexander Hamilton and Thomas Jefferson marched side by side. Even the Federalists, who had banked their all on his chances, now slunk away, leaving him deserted and alone, except for the small band of devoted "Burrites" who still flaunted the banner in the City of New York.

Embittered, disgraced, cast out from the ranks of his own party, and unsuccessful in his efforts to enlist the full roster of the Federalists, Burr stared at Hamilton's language concerning him as it appeared in the public prints. He had long been aware of Hamilton's private impugnments of his personal honor, but this was the first time they had been emblazoned for the public eye. He wrote Hamilton a letter which, by a fatal chain of circumstances, ended in a challenge.

The duel was fought on the heights of Weehawken on July 11, 1804. Hamilton fell mortally wounded at the first fire, and expired shortly thereafter. The nation rocked to its heels at the disaster. The Federalists, to the majority of whom Hamilton had been a discredited leader, now enshrined him and burst out furiously at the "murderer." The Republicans, already alienated, viewed the event with mixed feelings. Indictments for murder were drawn against Burr, and he was compelled to flee south for sanctuary. He had immortalized Hamilton and doomed himself.

Jefferson's sensations at the untoward event were never committed to paper. But he must have felt secretly pleased. At one fell swoop two of his most formidable enemies had been removed from his path—Hamilton and Burr. And the secession conspiracy had been brought to an abrupt end. He could now afford, when Burr ultimately returned to resume his official place as Vice-President for the few remaining months, to treat him with certain signs of favor he had not dared to show before. For now a situation had arisen in which Burr, as President of the Senate, could help make or mar certain plans of his. He even, as evidence of his good will, appointed Burr's stepson a Judge of the Superior Court at New Orleans, and his brother-in-law the Secretary of the Louisiana Territory. All this to the mystification of the Federalists, until a great light dawned upon them.

If two points of conflict between Jefferson and the previous administrations could be singled out from the great mass as decisive, they were the banking system and the judiciary.

But, incensed as he was against the Bank of the United States, there was little that Jefferson could do about it when he assumed office. Its charter had many years still to run; and he did not dare annul it on his old thesis of unconstitutionality as he had attempted with the Alien and Sedition Acts. For one thing, the issue was not as plain for the mass of the people to agree on; for another, much to his astonishment, both he and Gallatin discovered that the Bank had certain necessary functions and was a convenient instrument in the financial dispositions of the United States. His old fury, when he had been ready to hang as a traitor any Virginian who advocated the establishment of a branch in his home state, had spent itself.

Nevertheless, he still feared and hated the Bank, and sought to clip its wings in favor of State Banks that would be more amenable to Republican influence. In 1803, he had tried to work out a scheme whereby all of the State Banks could be shifted to Republican doctrine by sharing the government deposits among them "in proportion to the dispositions they show....

It is material to the safety of Republicanism to detach the mercantile interests from its enemies and incorporate them into the body of its friends." [11]

Five months later, he returned to the attack, spurred to it by the report that the Bank of the United States was considering a branch in New Orleans. "This institution," he insisted, "is one of the most deadly hostility existing, against the principles & form of our Constitution." Should public confidence ever wane, it might be able, through its branches in every part of the Union, and "acting by command & in a phalanx," upset the government. How then emasculate its power for evil? By reducing them to an equal footing with the State Banks in government favors; and by making government deposits a kind of bank on its own, against which government drafts would be honored.[12]

But Gallatin, as a financier and in charge of the Treasury, did not quite see eye to eye with Jefferson on the Bank. Though opposed to its general principles, he recognized its advantages, and continued to employ it. It was not until the Presidency of Andrew Jackson that the Bank of the United States, after a Homeric struggle, finally ended its influential career.

Jefferson had truly told the wife of John Adams that the one act of her husband which had most offended him was his "midnight appointments." These had largely been to the judiciary, and particularly to those judgeships which were for life and therefore irremovable during "good behavior." Nothing had infuriated the Republicans more than this packing of the courts with bitter-end Federalists. What profited their control of Congress and the Executive if the third co-ordinate branch of government was firmly in the hands of their enemies as a stronghold from which they could with impunity sabotage the will of the people?

The first countermeasure had been to repeal the hateful Judiciary Act, and to treat as nullities those appointments which had technically not been completed. But John Marshall ruled the Supreme Court; Samuel Chase of Maryland used the powers of the court to harry and persecute good Republicans; and John Pickering, district judge of New Hampshire, had appeared on the bench intoxicated, bullied witnesses and comported himself generally in a most disgraceful manner.

Jefferson determined to make the complaints against Pickering the first test of the claimed "sanctity" of the courts against interference by the other branches of government. The Constitution had specified that federal judges were to hold office "during good behaviour." The Federalists construed that to mean for life. But the Republicans concentrated on the qualification, *during good behaviour*. Obviously, by another provision of the Constitution, Congress had the power of impeachment and therefore, in their eyes, had the right to determine what "good behaviour" was.

Pickering's case seemed the clearest on which to start. The evidence was overwhelming and undeniable. He had, on many occasions, appeared on the bench in the last stages of intoxication. He had sworn at and grossly insulted witnesses before him. He had, in the specific case of the trial of a forfeiture of a ship and its cargo for smuggling, arbitrarily and against all the law and the evidence, ordered the return of the ship to its owners. He had refused to hear witnesses, had used foul language on the bench, and refused even the legal right of appeal. What better test could have been presented for impeachment under the "good behaviour" clause? Or so Jefferson thought.

On February 4, 1803, acting on the complaints before him, Jefferson sent a message to the House of Representatives, submitting to them the complaints and the accompanying affidavits, as the body "to whom the Constitution has confided a power of instituting proceedings of redress if they shall be of opinion that the case calls for them."

The House referred the matter to a committee and, after due consideration, a resolution of impeachment against John Pickering "for high crimes and misdemeanors" was passed on February 18th by a vote of 45 to 8. Joseph Nicholson and John Randolph, the two pillars of republicanism, were appointed to place the impeachment before the Senate for trial. This they did on March 3rd.[13]

Since Congress was on the eve of adjournment the matter thus rested until the fall reconvening.

But in the interim Chief Justice John Marshall, in the name of the Supreme Court, rendered a decision which infuriated Jefferson and his fellow Republicans beyond all bounds, and made them more than ever determined to clip the wings of the judiciary. This was the famous case of *Marbury v. Madison.*

William Marbury had been appointed by Adams a Justice of the Peace for the District of Columbia under the obnoxious Judiciary Act. The nomination went in haste to the Senate on March 2, 1801—two days before Adams's term of office and the current session of the Senate expired. In equal haste the dying Senate approved the nomination on the following day, the commission was quickly signed by Adams, countersigned by John Marshall as acting Secretary of State, sealed, and placed on the desk of the State Department. But before it could be actually delivered to Marbury, the Old Guard were out, and Jefferson was President of the United States.

Jefferson, treating these "midnight appointments" as a nullity, refused to deliver the commission and its office to Marbury. The aggrieved Federalist moved in the December term of the Supreme Court for a mandamus against Madison, the incumbent Secretary of State, to compel delivery.

On February 24, 1803, John Marshall delivered his opinion. It displayed the Chief Justice at the height of his powers. Through a canny and masterful use of *obiter dicta*, he was able dexterously to extract victory from defeat. Regretfully, he was compelled to admit that the Court had no original jurisdiction under the Constitution to issue a mandamus, and therefore dismissed the motion. By every rule of procedure, this should have been final, and the opinion should have ended there.

But Marshall was determined to seize this heaven-sent opportunity to lay down a precedent for the future, and to resolve once and for all the power of the Court to declare an act of Congress unconstitutional and therefore void. Accordingly, he entered into an extended consideration of the case on its merits, just as if it had not already been dismissed on the technical ground.

The commission, he declared, had been valid. Once signed and sealed, manual delivery was not essential for its completion. Marbury, therefore, was entitled to his five-year statutory term of office, and it could not be revoked by either Congress or the Executive.

But he was able to make Marbury's personal defeat and the consequent limitation on the power of the Supreme Court into a weapon for gaining more far-reaching powers for his Court. For Marbury had moved his writ under an act of Congress—section 13 of the Judiciary Act of 1789—which had purported to give the Supreme Court just such original jurisdiction in cases of mandamus. Marshall, however, virtuously denied the right of Congress to grant a jurisdiction which had not been contemplated in the Constitution.

In other words, he declared an act of Congress unconstitutional, and proclaimed the right of the Supreme Court so to find it. "A legislative act contrary to the Constitution is not law ..." he enunciated. "It is emphatically the province and duty of the judicial department to say what the law is.... The particular phraseology of the Constitution of the United States confirms and strengthens the principle, supposed to be essential to all written constitutions, that a law repugnant to the Constitution is void; and that *courts,* as well as other departments, are bound by that instrument." [14]

Jefferson in his Kentucky Resolution had asserted that a *State* had the right to declare an act of Congress unconstitutional; now Marshall laid down the rule that the Federal Judiciary had that right also. Jefferson's rule never achieved success, but Marshall's did. By skillfully employing a double-edged weapon, Marshall was able to aver at one and the same time that the tenures of judges were fixed and irrevocable, and that the courts could deal with the constitutionality of all measures, legislative and administrative. The consequences have reverberated down the pages of American history.

Baffled by a decision which affirmed a rule particularly obnoxious to himself and which nevertheless, by reason of its peculiar circumstances, gave him no handle for an official trial of strength, Jefferson now moved with accelerating pace against specific members of the court.

On October 20, 1803, the House appointed a committee to draw up articles of impeachment against Pickering. The Federalists fought the articles on the ground that Pickering was in fact insane, and therefore not subject to trial under legal procedures for acts committed in that state. Nicholson retorted that the insanity "proceeded from constant and habitual intoxication," and the articles were finally agreed to without a division. Eleven managers were chosen to conduct the prosecution before the bar of the Senate, including Nicholson, Randolph, Caesar Rodney, Samuel L. Mitchill and others.[15]

On March 2, 1804, the impeachment proceedings opened. The House managers appeared to present the charges against Pickering. They were damning enough, and no attempt was made by Pickering's defenders to deny the facts. Pickering himself did not appear; but his son submitted a petition to the effect that his father was legally insane, and therefore not amenable to the jurisdiction of Congress. His petition was backed by Robert G. Harper, who nevertheless disavowed he was appearing as counsel. A long wrangle ensued and, over Nicholson's vehement protests, Burr, in the President's chair, finally ruled that Harper could appear in support of the petition without a formal entry in the case as counsel.

The managers withdrew to consult this unusual procedure with their own House, but finally returned to hear lengthy testimony, backed up by the Federalist senators from New Hampshire, that Pickering was definitely insane.[16]

On March 12th, the Senate voted (19 to 7) that Pickering was guilty of the acts as charged; and (20 to 6) that he should be removed from office.[17] The Republicans had won an overwhelming victory.

Later commentators have decried the verdict, insisting that the evidence of insanity was sufficiently plain to have obviated the accusation of "high crimes and misdemeanors." They insist that an insane judge, no matter how incompetent to continue on the bench, may not be removed by the Constitutional procedure of impeachment. But there is no other method of removal permitted under the Constitution, and the anomalous situation would exist that an insane judge, for the rest of his natural life, would be empowered to dispose of the lives and fortunes of litigants, and lay down law as precedents in further actions.

Jefferson did not wait for the final verdict to institute proceedings against another member of the Federal Judiciary—this time a member of the Supreme Court itself. He would have liked exceedingly to have proceeded against the head and front—John Marshall himself—but he had no legal grounds. Against Samuel Chase of Maryland, however, he considered he had an impeccable case. He would also have preferred some other method of removing judges, finding impeachment "*a bungling way*"; but the Constitution unfortunately had not provided another.[18]

Chase, whom Hamilton had once accused of feathering his own nest during the Revolution, was a man of violent Federalist principles, harsh, intemperate and overbearing in manner, bullying on the bench and loud in his denunciations of republicanism as the quintessence of anarchy, atheism and the devil. He had taken it upon himself to be a one-man scourge of all that he hated, and he gleefully utilized the Sedition Act as an instrument for that purpose. In the cases of Fries and Callender, he had employed every means to obtain convictions, going far outside the usual province of a presiding judge.

On May 2, 1803, he had seized the occasion of an address to a grand jury in Baltimore to deliver himself of a tirade against democracy and the local and national governments. He denounced the repeal of the Judiciary Act, and insisted that "mobocracy" was already on the way. "The modern doctrines by our late reformers," he warned, "that all men in a state of society are entitled to enjoy equal liberty and equal rights, have brought this mighty mischief upon us; and I fear that it will rapidly progress until peace and order, freedom and property, shall be destroyed." [19]

When Jefferson read the account of the charge in the newspapers, he was incensed. He wrote at once to Nicholson, the chief manager of the Pickering impeachment: "Ought this seditious and official attack on the principles of our Constitution, and on the proceedings of a State, to go unpunished? and to whom so pointedly as yourself will the public look for the necessary measures? I ask these questions for your consideration, for myself it is better that I should not interfere." [20]

It did not require any great perspicacity on Nicholson's part to determine his chief's meaning–Chase should be impeached. But, after thinking it over and seeking advice from friends, he decided not to act.[21]

But another champion arose–John Randolph. On January 5, 1804, he offered a resolution in the House for an inquiry into Chase's judicial conduct. In response to demands from the Federalist group, the cases of Fries and Callender were adduced, as well as the Baltimore charge. On January 7th, the resolution for a committee of inquiry was passed; on March 12th, the report of the committee recommending impeachment was approved by a vote of 73 to 32; and the requisite impeachment articles were drafted.[22]

Practically the same group of managers, spearheaded by Randolph, Rodney and Nicholson, was appointed by the House. On December 10, 1804, the Senate issued a summons for Chase to appear and answer; and constituted itself as a court of trial on January 2, 1805. Aaron Burr, returned from his flight after the death of Hamilton, presided. The Federalists viewed him with horror as the slayer of their idol; but the Republicans suddenly discovered the good points of their erstwhile outlawed Vice-President. Jefferson made it a point to invite him cordially to his house, Gallatin consorted with him, Madison paid him marked attentions, and Giles circulated a petition to quash the indictment in New Jersey against him.[23] And his relatives were given lucrative offices in the Territories.

Burr was quite aware why these attentions were being showered on him. As presiding officer of the court, he had it in his power to make the path of the impeachment smooth or difficult, and the Jeffersonian forces were determined to spare no means of attaining a conviction. This was the test case in their struggle to subordinate the Judiciary, far more than the Pickering trial. For here were no private elements; Chase had thrown down the gauntlet to an entire philosophy, while hovering in the background was the mighty John Marshall. Let but Chase be condemned, and the groundwork could be laid against Marshall as well; and the whole structure of the Judiciary, in which the Federalists had sought refuge as a final stronghold, would be brought crashing about them in ruins.

The actual trial opened on February 4, 1805, in an atmosphere of drama and tension. The eyes of the nation were focused in this last gigantic struggle. With a flair for the spectacular, Burr dressed the Senate chamber in trappings reminiscent of the great English trial of Warren Hastings, and the galleries were crowded with spectators from beginning to end. In spite of initial revulsions against Burr, all were finally compelled to admit that the Vice-President conducted the trial with rigid impartiality, dignity and correctness; going so far even as to refuse to permit the Senators their time-honored custom of munching apples and cakes in the chamber.

John Randolph was the chief counsel for the prosecution. For Chase appeared a mighty array of Federalist brains and abilities, headed by Robert G. Harper and Luther Martin, "the bulldog of Federalism." Randolph found himself out of his depth and miscast. He was no lawyer, and his piercing eloquence that had proved so effective in the House was no match for the legal agility of his adversaries or the thunderings of Luther Martin.

Chase denied all the charges, and particularly that his address to the Baltimore grand jury had been "intemperate and inflammatory." Ever since the Revolution, he claimed, it had been the custom of judges to express political opinions in such cases; nor was there any law against it.

Randolph opened for the prosecution on February 7th with a weak and rambling general indictment; apologizing in a way for what he himself realized was an inadequate treatment by alluding to his illness and short preparation. Then followed a parade of witnesses to substantiate the articles of impeachment, giving chapter and verse for Chase's prejudiced and prejudicial handling of defendants, counsel and witnesses in the cases of Fries and Callender. Then came the matter of the Baltimore address. Closing speeches began on February 20th, and final arguments ended on the 27th.

There had been eight articles in the impeachment, and the Senate—requiring a two-thirds vote to convict—brought in verdict of "not guilty" on all eight, though on three of the articles a numerical majority was mustered for "guilty." [24]

The adverse verdict was a stunning blow to Jefferson. All his plans for forcing the Judiciary into a subsidiary position, for curtailing its powers and clipping its wings, had failed. John Marshall, who had followed the proceedings with intense anxiety, and knowing well that he would be the next victim if Chase were convicted, took heart and proceeded to fix firmly in American jurisprudence the supremacy of the Supreme Court in all matters relating to the Constitution. And, in a series of powerful decisions, he brought all property rights (including contracts) under the protective aegis of that Constitution, so that radical measures later beat in vain against the bulwarks he erected, until the Constitution itself was amended to achieve specific reforms. Jefferson was never to get over the blow, keeping a discreet silence now, but later fulminating against the power of the Judiciary and assiduously trying new, and unsuccessful measures, to overcome it.

While thus engaged in a duel with the Judiciary, Jefferson kept a watchful eye on foreign relations. The purchase of Louisiana required implementation and did not settle the matters in dispute with England and Spain.

England, for example, continued to disregard American neutral rights, or at least as America conceived them. The search of ships sailing under the American flag by British warships, and the seizure and forcible impressment of seamen claimed by the British as their subjects, became more and more a matter of vigorous complaint. England, engaged in a world war, and desperately in need of sailors for her navy, did not always differentiate too carefully between Englishmen and Americans in the process.

Madison ordered Monroe, then in England, to enter strong protests against the practice;[25] and Jefferson instructed him, as soon as possible, to hurry on to Madrid to seek a settlement of the boundaries of Louisiana, offering him at the same time, the governorship of that territory. "We scarcely expect," he wryly remarked, "any liberal or just settlement with Spain, and are perfectly determined to obtain or to take our just limits." As for West Florida, Jefferson expected the inhabitants of certain sections to ask voluntarily for joinder with the United States, while acquisition of the other areas must await a favorable opportunity. Should Spain continue to refuse access to our vessels through the mouths of the rivers feeding the interior, once Spain was at war, he added significantly, "the crisis there will be speedy."

He wished to supersede Charles Pinckney as Minister to Spain, and asked Monroe to "avail yourself of his vanity, his expectations, his fears, and whatever will weigh with him to induce him to ask leave to return." [26]

It was also decided in a Cabinet meeting that Monroe should negotiate with Spain for an extension of our territory east to the Perdido river and to include all of East Florida. In return, we would relinquish our claims from the Mexican to the Rio Bravo rivers, stipulate that a buffer country would be established and left unsettled for a term of years, and pay a million dollars.[27]

Jefferson had made the Cabinet into a component arm of the Executive. About this time he laid down certain rules guiding the relationship of the President and the Secretaries. The head of a department and the President, he said, are "mutual Counsellors. If the case is difficult, usage establishes the practise of a general consultation. There never has arisen a case and I am persuaded never will, where the respect we mutually entertain for the opinions of one another will not produce an accommodation of opinion."[28] This was all very well; but he knew, and his Secretaries knew, that the final authority rested in the President.

Meanwhile, a desultory, undeclared war was in progress with Tripoli. An American squadron under Commodore Preble was cruising up and down the Mediterranean, offering protection to American merchantmen against the sudden raids of the corsairs, and blockading the ports so that the pirates found it difficult to slip out. He had a sizable number of ships under his command, including the forty-four-gun *Constitution* and the thirty-eight-gun *Philadelphia*. Morocco, which had thought to obtain its share of booty, was brought to terms and forced to disgorge its prisoners and resume the old treaty; but disaster befell the *Philadelphia* when she ran aground under the guns of the Tripolitan forts and was compelled to surrender. Captain Bainbridge and some three hundred members of her crew were made captive and set to hard labor. The only bright spot in the tragic episode was the ensuing exploit of young Stephen Decatur who, with a tiny vessel and crew, sneaked boldly into the harbor at night, drove the Tripolitan crew headlong over the sides and burned the *Philadelphia* to the water line under the blazing guns of the forts.

The capture of the ill-fated frigate had occurred in October, 1803; and Jefferson sent the bad news to Congress on March 20, 1804, with a request for additional funds and an increase of the Mediterranean squadron. The news had filled him with a burning anger and a determination for immediate retribution. Diplomacy and negotiations were all right with the other powers, but naked force was the only answer he ever desired for any of the Barbary States. He went along ordinarily with Gallatin as the exponent of a "little navy"; but the prospect of a clash with the pirates would convert him over night—at least until the crisis had passed—into a "big navy" man, touchy on the subject of national honor and breathing revenge against these desecrators of the peace.

But there were Bainbridge and the three hundred American captives to consider. Had it been left to Jefferson, he would have outfitted and sent a mightier squadron, no matter what the cost, to rescue the prisoners, lay the offending city of Tripoli in ruins, and break the power of the corsairs to do any further mischief for all time to come.

He was temporarily forestalled, however, and in a way that drove him to blazing wrath. Robert R. Livingston in France, and the American envoy to Russia, alarmed over the tales of Tripolitan severities to the American prisoners, had made representations to the respective courts to interpose their good offices in behalf of the captives, and received favorable responses.

When Jefferson heard of it, he was both furious and mortified. It was most humiliating, he thought, for the United States to go humbly, hat in hand, to the European nations and beg their intervention. His letters to the members of his Cabinet breathe his agitation and disgust. "I have never been so mortified," he exclaimed to Robert Smith, his Secretary of Navy, "as at the conduct of our foreign functionaries on the loss of the *Philadelphia*. They appear to have supposed that we were all lost now, & without resource: and they have hawked us in *forma pauperis* begging alms at every court in Europe. This self-degradation is the more unpardonable as, uninstructed & unauthorized, they have taken measures which commit us by moral obligations which cannot be disavowed."

What he feared most was that the prompt intervention of France and Russia would cause the release of the prisoners before the American squadron would arrive and thereby "our just desires of vengeance disappointed, and our honor prostrated." Therefore it was essential, he urged on Smith, to send the squadron to sea at once.[29]

He wrote in similar vein to Madison, calling the unauthorized commitment of the American ministers abroad "the most serious one which has happened to the present administration" and "a national stain." His great hope, he fumed to the Secretary of State, was that Tripoli would be blind enough not to heed promptly the request of Alexander of Russia, and that our squadron would arrive *before* the prisoners were released and be able to beat "their town about their ears." And Mr. Harris, our envoy in St. Petersburg, must be given a sharp rap on the knuckles.[30]

Here we are confronted with a curious dichotomy in the character of Jefferson that requires investigation. He hated war, and he could be long-suffering under intense provocation—so much so that the legend of his extreme pacifism has arisen; and yet, on occasion, he could disclose himself suddenly as a fire-breathing warrior, giving vent to such terms as "revenge" and "national honor," and repudiating all attempts at compromise or mediation. Perhaps his own description of Washington as a man of strong passions eternally repressed might apply in some degree to himself. His own passions significantly crack through the placid exterior at times and hint at what lies beneath. Such was the case in his treatment of the British General Hamilton when he was Governor; such were his unpleasant characterizations of that other Hamilton during Washington's administration; such was the case in his every dealing with the Barbary Powers. To France and England, *because* they were great powers and the United States was unable to deal with them adequately, he interposed a meekness and long-suffering patience. To Spain, however, he blew hot and cold, depending on the situation and the probability of success. He could be arrogant and intransigent in tone on one occasion, and assume the mask of diplomacy on another. But he always felt capable of handling the pirates of the Mediterranean and therefore preferred war to diplomacy. And, in this particular instance, he feared that the well-intentioned but ill-advised supplications of his emissaries abroad would lower the prestige of the United States in Europe and ruin his diplomacy in other directions.

His aversion to Livingston was further hardened when he read the correspondence between that unlucky gentleman and the Paris Commissioners.

"A more disgusting correspondence between men of sense," he exploded, "I have never read.... All of them deserved to be immediately superseded for having mingled their old-woman's quarrels with their official communications, & suffered them to influence their public duties. The quarrelsome disposition of Livingston is a trait in his character unknown before to me. He has quarreled with every public agent with whom he had any thing to do... and his letters to the department of State have been rising in the arrogance of their style, till... had he not been coming away, would have justified our informing him that we should make no further use of his services." [31]

It was therefore with considerable celerity that Jefferson accepted Livingston's resignation and offered the post in France to General John Armstrong, former Senator from New York.[32]

Fortunately for Jefferson's pride, Tripoli disclosed no haste in releasing the American captives; and Commodore Preble, with a force spear-headed by the famous *Constitution*, penetrated boldly into Tripoli harbor and bombarded that town almost at will all through the summer of 1804. He was shortly reinforced by one of the mightiest squadrons that the United States had ever put to sea; but Commodore Barron, its commander, overranking Preble, did less with the combined flotilla than Preble had done with lesser forces. After six months of inconclusive warfare, he retired on the plea of ill-health, and young John Rodgers took command. Between Rodgers' bolder strokes and the amazing overland expedition of William Eaton, a flamboyant adventurer, the Pasha of Tripoli finally yielded and sued for peace.

The single overt war of Jefferson's administration had ended triumphantly; the power of the Barbary States had been broken and was never more to threaten American ships. American prestige in Europe rose to new heights, and that navy which Jefferson and Gallatin had sought to hamstring had covered itself with glory.

CHAPTER 56

Re-election

PERSONAL matters were also engrossing Jefferson's attention. He was still engaged in the unfortunate and acrimonious litigation with a neighbor over a plot of ground abutting the Rivanna, on which he had built a dam and a mill, which interfered with his own navigation of the river, and which his agent, Craven Peyton, had bought on his behalf.[1] As usual, the Federalists sought to make political capital of Jefferson's private misadventures, and he was goaded to an anonymous defense of his position (as "A Bystander") in the public press.[2]

In a pleasanter frame of mind he received, through the good offices of Lafayette, copies of works published in France. One was a treatise on Political Economy by Jean Baptiste Say, and the other a volume entitled *Idéologie* by De Stutt Tracy, whose daughter had married Lafayette's son. Both volumes, but particularly Tracy's, profoundly influenced Jefferson's future thinking. He indeed hailed Tracy's work as one of the greatest ever written, and later translated it himself for American consumption. He remembered his good friend Lafayette with gratitude, and was assiduously trying to get for him a Congressional grant of land in the vicinity of New Orleans, where he believed values would rise with great rapidity. Indeed, had Lafayette then been in America, Jefferson would have offered him the governorship of that territory.[3]

The great naturalist and geologist, Baron Humboldt, came to America in 1804 and, as was the case with every European scientist on arrival in the New World, he sought out Jefferson as an intellectual equal and as the foremost exponent in this country of their mutual interests. Jefferson's newly appointed secretary, William A. Burwell, found Humboldt "about thirty, of small figure, well made, agreable Physiognomy, simple unaffected manners, remarkably sprightly, vehement in conversation & sometimes eloquent."

Jefferson welcomed him with the greatest cordiality and listened eagerly to the "treasures of information" which Humboldt was enabled to impart from his own vast stores of knowledge. One morning, while they were at breakfast, Jefferson came down to the company with a newspaper clipping in his hand. It was, he remarked, filled with the grossest personal abuse of himself. He was presenting it, he said, to Humboldt with the request that he deposit it in a European museum, as evidence "how little mischief flow'd from the freedom of the Press. That notwithstanding innumerable pieces of similar nature issued daily from the Press his administration had never been more popular." Burwell, the Boswell of the occasion, thought that Humboldt actually placed the offending document in a museum.[4]

While in France, Jefferson had sought to transfer the culture of the olive tree to America, but the experiment had then failed because of the indifference of the American cultivators. But the project had never lapsed in Jefferson's mind, and now he tried it again, having obtained the consent of a Sea Island Georgian to make the experiment.[5] Unfortunately, the olive tree never took kindly to the eastern seaboard, and had to wait for the advent of California to become acclimated.

Jefferson's indefatigable mind never rested. He pondered the idea of digesting the moral doctrines of Jesus, as given in his own words, and omitting myths, legends and personal history. He actually sent to Philadelphia for two Greek and two English Testaments, from which he expected to cut out the pertinent sections and paste them into a separate volume. He was compelled by pressure of other work to abandon the idea for the time being, and urged it instead on Priestley.[6] But in later years he returned to the scheme, and his beautifully bound volume of printed extracts from these volumes is one of the precious treasures on deposit in the Library of Congress.

He recurred again and again to this theme of differentiating between the pure doctrines of Jesus and the excrescences which had later enveloped them. The latter, he thought, had been deliberately added. "I consider the doctrines of Jesus as delivered by himself," he remarked, "to contain the outlines of the sublimest system of morality that has ever been taught but I hold in the most profound detestation and execration the corruptions of it which have been invested by priestcraft and established by kingcraft constituting a conspiracy of church and state against the civil and religious liberties of mankind."[7]

But above all, the vast new expanse of Louisiana and New Orleans fired Jefferson's enthusiasm. His earlier dreams of expansion to the west had been realized, and he was particularly anxious to bind the new territories to the United States with indissoluble bands.

The great expedition of exploration under the leadership of Lewis and Clark was now under way. He had dreamed of it, planned every detail, raised funds and followed its long germination with a mounting excitement. Barely had the American flag been raised over St. Louis than the expedition shoved off in boats into the Missouri River to move upstream into the uncharted wilderness. For two years and four months the pioneers toiled and marched, never knowing when the Indians they met would prove hostile or peaceful, seeing for the first time the gigantic and dangerous grizzly bear, collecting Indian vocabularies, botanical and mineralogical specimens, making topographical maps, seeking fossil remains, doing all the things on which Jefferson had carefully briefed them. Up dangerous rivers, across savage mountains, over desert and plain, until finally they reached the mouth of the Columbia River and the blue Pacific. Then, the long trek back to St. Louis.

On January 10, 1807, Lewis appeared at the President's House with his glittering tales, his specimens and, as a side show, "the King and Queen of the Mandans." Jefferson tendered him a reception, welcomed the Indian royalty, and later tried to plant at Monticello the seeds and specimens which Lewis had brought for him. He knew the value of what he had purchased, and he knew that Lewis and Clark were but the precursors of a later and more stable migration of pioneers who would settle and hold the land.

New Orleans also engaged his closest attention. Here, too, he realized that rapid and easy communication was the surest way of keeping the land firmly bound to the United States. He proposed, accordingly, the construction of a thousand-mile-long post road stretching from Washington to New Orleans, along which postriders could make as much as a hundred miles a day. He was sending the Surveyor General, Isaac Briggs, on horseback along the proposed route to take survey bearings and asked Bishop Madison to lend him his pocket quadrant for the purpose.[8]

This would, of course, be a government project. But Jefferson was averse generally to putting the government into any business which private companies could handle. He was an ardent exponent of the theory and practice of private enterprise. When an iron manufacturer offered to sell his ironworks to the government, Jefferson laid down the principle that "it is better for the public to procure at the common market whatever the market can supply: because there it is by competition kept up in its quality, and reduced to its minimum price. The public can buy there silver guns cheaper than they can make iron ones. As therefore private individuals can furnish cannon, shot etc. we shall never attempt to make them, nor consequently meddle with mines, forges, or any thing of that kind, to the superintendance of which the public functionaries are incompetent, even if they had leisure from more important affairs." [9] Whether this economic philosophy would have remained intact under modern industrial life must remain a moot question.

He appointed William C. C. Claiborne as the governor of New Orleans, and suggested to him that he place on his Legislative Council seven Americans and six Frenchmen, proportioned among the merchant and planter classes, and with a due regard for geographical distribution. He was particularly insistent that corruption be rooted out with "distinguished severity." [10]

He had also been impressed with the sarcastic animadversions on his "republicanism" when he organized New Orleans into a government directly from Washington, and he sought now to remedy the situation; urging that Congress at its next session give the territory an elective legislature. Any evils that might arise, he told Madison significantly, "will not be so serious as leaving them the pretext of calling in a foreign umpire between them & us." He meant France; and was willing even to make the inhabitants full citizens in order to avoid the danger of such an intervention.[11]

The dangers implicit in the New Orleans situation were obvious to him. Spain was resentful of the treatment which both France and the United States had accorded her, and France herself regretted what she had done. American rule was not popular among the proud Creoles of New Orleans, and they were particularly incensed at the subsidiary position into which they had been pushed. Already a ferment existed which was eventually to grow to conspiratorial proportions, and to tie in obscurely with the mysterious venture of Aaron Burr. It was therefore essential that an agreement be reached with Spain on these and other matters, so that there would be no fishing in troubled waters.

But it was not easy to placate Spain. The Marquis d'Yrujo, her Minister at Washington, who had married a daughter of Governor McKean of Pennsylvania, and who was personally friendly to the United States, was nevertheless pushed by force of circumstances from a position of benevolence to one of fierce antagonism to Jefferson.

The reasons were partly political and partly social. He, as well as Merry, the British minister, had resented Jefferson's "pell-mell" at diplomatic functions. And, after attempting to persuade his home government to accept the cession of Louisiana without a struggle, he had watched with alarm and mounting anger the determination of the American government to include the Floridas as well; by force if necessary. Swinging into the opposition, he listened with a ready ear to the Federalist conspiracy for the secession of New England, and took the controversy against Jefferson's policies anonymously into the American press. He went so far, though he later denied it, as to seem to offer money to a Federalist editor to oppose American policy toward Spain. The editor virtuously repudiated the alleged bribe and made an affidavit on the incident.

Yrujo was on a visit to Monticello when the scandal broke; yet his host received him courteously and without a word of the contretemps. Yrujo and his wife had been with him, Jefferson wrote privately to Madison. "He has opened his budget which we have smoothed off."[12]

But it was not as easy to "smooth off" as Jefferson thought. For Charles Pinckney in Spain was having rough going with an angry Court, and Monroe was sent posthaste from England to see what he could do. Monroe, from London, had already suggested that it might be wise to shut off Louisiana west of the Mississippi to settlement. He feared that the rush of emigration might depopulate the old states and eventually lead to a separation.[13]

Pinckney, however, had adopted a strong tone in Madrid, going so far as to lay down a virtual ultimatum. If he did not receive an immediate answer on the right of Americans to ply the rivers passing through West Florida, he would, he threatened, order all Americans out of Spain and communicate with the American fleet in the Mediterranean.[14] This could only mean bombardment of Spanish ports—and war.

Spain properly refused to be intimidated by threats, and in turn threatened to have no further dealings with him. Thereupon Pinckney lost his head and issued a circular letter to Americans in Spain advising them to leave forthwith, and proposed to ask for his passports. Cevallos, the Spanish Foreign Minister, was unmoved by Pinckney's bellicose actions and merely demanded that he be recalled.[15]

When Madison heard of the scrape into which Pinckney's blunders had led him, he sought to ease the tension with a conciliatory letter to Yrujo, ordered Monroe to Spain to pick up the pieces, and gave Pinckney "leave" to return to America. "I suspect he will not return in a good humor," Madison told Monroe grimly. "I could not permit myself to flatter him, and truth would not permit me to praise him. He is well off in escaping reproof, for his agency has been very faulty as well as feeble." [16]

Nor were relations with England on any better footing. British warships were standing boldly off New York harbor in what was tantamount to an actual blockade, forcing American ships as they sailed in and out to the indignity of a search for contraband and an impressment of seamen on the pretense that they were British subjects.

One particularly flagrant case, it is true, was rectified after protest; which led Jefferson to the outburst that England was "a living example that no nation however powerful, any more than any individual, can be unjust with impunity"; and to the dark hint that public opinion, "an instrument merely moral in the beginning, will find occasion physically to inflict its sentence on the unjust." [17]

What he meant by the "sentence" to be inflicted by public opinion was a twofold course of action. The first would authorize limitations on or cessations of intercourse with the offending nation; the second would offer means of defense.

But defense did not include the use of the navy. Jefferson realized that the American navy could never hope to cope with the mighty British armaments on the high seas, though he did not sufficiently understand the importance of fast commerce raiders to be employed against British shipping in the event of hostilities. To him defense, as always, meant isolation. Remove your own commerce from the seas, refuse all intercourse with the offender, and protect your harbors from outrage. These outrages had been unfortunately only too numerous, with British warships coming and going at will within American harbors and demanding water, provisions and shore privileges under threat of their guns.

To avoid this humiliating spectacle, Jefferson conceived his pet idea of a vast armada of gunboats. These were merely flatboats or platforms, on which heavy guns could be mounted, and which would take up positions of defense in harbors and the mouths of rivers. In effect, they were floating forts, unable to put to sea or to be used except for defense purposes. To Jefferson they were the ultimate answer to his problem. A mobile navy was expensive and encouraged merchants to clamor for protection on the high seas. Gunboats presupposed no commerce, were comparatively cheap, and performed their proper duty of protecting American soil from invasion. That they were unwieldly, helpless in rough weather, unmaneuverable, and might be cut out like sitting ducks by raiding parties, did not change his mind in the slightest. Even after they became the laughingstock of his enemies and the source of secret headshakings by his friends, he clung stubbornly to the myth of their essential efficacy and invulnerability.

On February 28, 1803, Congress had authorized the building of a number of gunboats. A year and a half later, barely a handful of the unwieldly monsters were ready; and Jefferson thought that, had there been more of them, he would have sent every one to New York to clean out the impudent British squadron that sailed in and out with impunity.[18] Just how these ungainly flatboats would have been towed through the seas in the face of weather and the British fleet he failed to discuss.

Yet little of this appeared in his Annual Message of November 8, 1804. The matters that really bothered him, as evidenced in his personal correspondence with the Cabinet officers, were not in the Message at all, or were merely mentioned in passing.

The Message, as usual, was optimistic and tended to soothe and allay alarm. The continued harassments of neutral commerce by the European belligerents were dismissed with the remark that they were less than formerly. Most of the Message was devoted to Spain and the negotiations with her over Mobile and Louisiana. But the tone was so calm and the emphasis so moderate that the country might be presumed to be able to relax and suppose that everything was in a satisfactory train. The Tripolitan "barbarians," Jefferson assured Congress, would shortly sue for peace; another sizable stretch of western country had been ceded by the Indians; and finances were in excellent shape, with a substantial amount of the public debt retired during his term of office.

The only sour note was skillfully skimmed over. Gunboats were building, and it might be wise perhaps, he suggested, to authorize the building of more. Not a word about the practical severance of diplomatic relations with Spain, of the British blockading squadron off New York, and the seizure of men and goods from American ships.[19]

But to his Cabinet and Congressional leaders he was sounding a different note. In order to coerce the belligerent powers into a respect for American sovereignty, he told Gallatin, a nonintercourse law might be necessary. Yet would it not be sufficiently effective, he inquired, meanwhile to forbid the entry of British merchant ships alone? [20]

To gain this limited objective, Jefferson personally drafted a bill which he proposed to John Randolph for Congressional action. All foreign vessels entering American ports, it decreed, must report and submit to harbor regulations. Those who failed to conform were to be ordered away. If they refused to go, they were to receive no supplies and be cut off from intercourse with the shore and other ships in the harbor. All other ships of the same flag were to be refused entry. If these pacific measures failed, then force was to be employed.[21]

In the midst of these various maneuvers one hardly knew that a Presidential election was being held. Remembering the turbulence that accompanied the election of 1800, the howlings of calamity, the threats and counterthreats, the election of 1804 moved toward its climax with barely a ripple.

On the Republican side, it was obvious that Jefferson would be a candidate to succeed himself; and after some decent hesitations and protestations that he would have much preferred to retire, he gracefully acceded. As for the vice-presidential chair, however, it was equally obvious that Aaron Burr had received his dismissal papers, and could expect nothing further from the hands of his old comrades. The prize for having helped beat him down went as a just reward to old Governor Clinton of New York. One spoke of him as old, not because his years were ancient, but because of his long, almost mythical service in his native state, and because he was rapidly deteriorating and giving every physical and mental symptom of innumerable years. Plumer thought him old, and that "time had impaired his mental faculties, & debilitated his corporeal powers." When he later took over the chair in the Senate, he was unable to preserve order, forgot both the business and even the question before the Senate. Yet Plumer acknowledged that the more he saw of Clinton, the more the old man rose in his estimation.[22] What made Clinton acceptable to Jefferson was the knowledge that he would never make a formidable candidate for the presidency, to which Jefferson had already privately chosen his successor.

On the Federalist side, the situation was hopeless. The irreconcilables had long given up any expectation of beating Jefferson for re-election. But some of them had hoped, in conjunction with Burr and his dissident Republicans, to draw off New England, New York and New Jersey into a separate Union of their own which would leave the Republican South and West, largely agricultural in economy, to stew in their own juices. That scheme had failed with Burr's defeat in New York. So that, perforce, they must go through the motions of opposing Jefferson's re-election.

But never in the history of the United States has a rival candidate been so obscure that there were many in the country who did not know who he was. Charles Cotesworth Pinckney had accepted the thankless task of heading a ragged and tattered party, and very sensibly did nothing to disturb the even tenor of the election. So secure, indeed, did Jefferson feel that not once in his correspondence did he mention the approaching election or the name of his supposed rival.

The careful, canny policy of Jefferson for four years bore overwhelming dividends now. The South was his, the Middle States were his, and even rock-bound New England bowed to the torrent. When the election results were announced, Jefferson had won one of the most amazing victories in American history. Only that which accompanied the second term of Franklin D. Roosevelt could be compared with it.

He swept every state except Connecticut and Delaware; and even in Connecticut—that stronghold of Calvinist divines—he lost by a small majority. Massachusetts—the home of the Essex Junto, of the Adamses, of the mercantile and commercial classes—had gone down the line for Jefferson. The electoral vote stood at 162 to 14!

Jefferson took the result modestly and without fanfare. What gladdened him more, perhaps, than anything else, was the triumph in Massachusetts. It was a case, he thought, of the old Biblical adage coming true: that 'this our brother was dead, and is alive again: and was lost, and is found.' With Massachusetts in the fold, he felt certain that Connecticut must eventually follow, "dismount her oligarchy, and fraternize with the great federated family." He foresaw an era of tranquillity and prosperity; and depicted a somewhat utopian state of foreign relations. "With England," he said unblushingly, "we are in cordial friendship: with France in the most perfect understanding; with Spain we shall allways be bickering, but never at war." [23]

He had come around finally to the idea of a presidential term of four years, with *one* privilege of re-election, as against his old firm belief in a single seven-year term and permanent ineligibility thereafter. Accordingly, he advised his friends that he would retire at the end of this second term to which he had been elected; and he hoped that his action and that of Washington would form for the future a sufficient precedent against anyone else attempting more than two terms. Jefferson did, however, allow himself a loophole. There was, he declared, "but one circumstance which could engage my acquiescence in another election, to wit, such a division about a successor as might bring in a Monarchist." [24]

His protégé William Short, now in Philadelphia, reported to him that Federalist hatred of Jefferson had eased off there, and that he himself had actually been made welcome at Federalist tables. Jefferson was happy to hear of it, though somewhat sceptical. He expected the scurrilities in the press against him to continue. "The editors," he remarked, "are but cooks who must consult the palates of their customers." Had the Federalists been co-operative, he added, he would have allowed them "a very moderate participation in office." But they had spurned his overtures; and now "I proceed in all things without caring what they will think, say or do. To me will have fallen the drudgery of putting them out of condition to do mischief; my successor I hope will have smoother seas." [25]

A good many highly placed Federalists, however, were beginning to find in Jefferson, if not yet in Republicanism, less of the horned devil than of old. Senator Plumer of New Hampshire, for example, was willing more and more to dine with the President, though his friends warned him against the contamination. For one thing, he liked the dinners and was enthusiastic about the wines. For another, he was curious about this strange example of heterodoxy. On one occasion, he found Jefferson in an old and threadbare coat, with new and clean scarlet vest, corduroy small clothes and white cotton hose; though the linen, he was sorry to observe, was soiled and the slippers old. A month later, however, Jefferson was resplendent in a new black suit and silk hose, his linen irreproachably spotless and his hair highly powdered.[26]

Another maverick Federalist was also beginning to make Jefferson's acquaintance—or rather, reacquaintance. This was John Quincy Adams, currently Senator from Massachusetts, and willing to resume relations with his ancient friend. He dined with Jefferson, and wrote the results down in his Diary. Jefferson, he observed dryly, loved to tell "tall" stories with a straight face, and to excite the wonder of his auditors. Such, for example, was the one about learning Spanish on his voyage to Europe, using only a copy of Don Quixote as his text. Another was his grave statement that he had been through a six-week period in Paris when the temperature stood constantly at twenty below zero, Fahrenheit.[27]

Both Plumer and Adams were eventually to become Republicans.

Jefferson was very anxious to have the young men of Virginia learn French and Spanish. These two languages, he felt, were essential to anyone who wished to play a part in his country's destiny. From the idea of language study, it was an easy transition to the idea of a University. That had never been far from his thoughts and, hearing now from his friend, Littleton W. Tazewell, that the legislature was likely to consider the project again, all his old enthusiasm revived. "Convinced that the people are the only safe depositories of their own liberty," he wrote, "& that they are not safe unless enlightened to a certain degree, I have looked on our present state of liberty as a short lived possession unless the mass of the people could be informed to a certain degree. This requires two grades of education. First some institution where science in all its branches is taught, and in the highest degree to which the human mind has carried it. This would prepare a few subjects in every state, to whom nature has given minds of the first order. Secondly such a degree of learning given to every member of the society as will enable him to read, to judge & to vote understandingly on what is passing. This would be the object of township schools."

He was fertile with plans and suggestions to be brought to the attention of the legislature, including Priestley's and Dupont's schemes of education. He proposed liberal professorial salaries to attract the finest scholars of Europe, who in turn would attract the youth of all the States to Virginia. Already he had in mind what the University should look like physically.

He hated large buildings as ugly, inconvenient, and exposed to fire hazards. He envisaged plain, small buildings to house the school and lodging of each professor, connected with one another by covered ways, into which the student rooms would open. In short, the University would not be a single structure, but an academic "village."

If the plan went through, he would be happy to bequeath to the University his private library; of which he boasted that, while its financial value was not less than $15,000, "its value is more in the selection, a part of which, that which respects America, is the result of my own personal searches in Paris for 6. or 7. years, & of persons employed by me in England, Holland, Germany and Spain to make similar searches. Such a collection on that subject can never again be made." [28]

Alas, once more the Virginia legislature moved gingerly up to the proposition and then backed away from it. It was twenty years before the plan was consummated, and Jefferson then reminded his old friend, Tazewell, of that earlier proposal of two decades before.[29]

The interim between the end of one term in office and the beginning of another was chiefly devoted to marking time, though Jefferson continued to push his campaign for gunboats as against a navy with vigor and pertinacity. He had calculated mathematically—at least to his own satisfaction—that 240 gunboats at a total cost of a million would adequately defend the fifteen chief harbors of the United States; and that they could be hauled on shore under sheds at a minimum upkeep when not in use. On the other hand, the requisite number of forts would cost $50,000,000 and require from 12,000 to 50,000 men to garrison them. Even then, they would not be nearly as effective.[30]

He never could understand the ridicule that greeted his theory of gunboats, particularly when it came from Republicans. When the merchants of Norfolk joined in opposition, his indignation knew no bounds. "Is it the interest of that place," he demanded wrathfully, "to strengthen the hue and cry against the policy of making the Eastern branch our great naval deposit? Is it their interest that this should be removed to New York or Boston to one of which it must go if it leaves this? Is it their interest to scout a defence by gunboats in which they would share amply, in hopes of a navy which will not be built in our day, & would be no defence if built, or of forts which will never be built or maintained, and would be no defence if built?" [31]

Jefferson's influence was sufficiently strong in Congress, particularly after the impressive evidence of the election, to force through what he wanted. If Congress did not grant the total of gunboats at once, at least it made a good beginning. On March 2, 1805, it authorized the President to build up to twenty-five of these strange new ships of war, and appropriated $60,000 for the operation.[32]

More important, however, was the bill which passed the following day, and which, to Jefferson, embodied the hard core of his theory of dealing with intransigent foreign nations. Under the guise of "An Act for the more effectual preservation of peace in the ports and harbors of the United States, and in the waters under their jurisdiction," it gave Jefferson exactly that power for which he had asked in dealing with England. In the event of any crime committed by a person or persons on a foreign vessel in the waters of the United States, declared the Act, the United States Marshal and the armed forces of the United States were authorized to execute a proper warrant against the guilty parties, even though they were aboard an armed ship of a foreign country. It also gave the President power to interdict, at pleasure, the harbors and waters of the United States to foreign armed vessels and to remove them by force if necessary. Similarly, he could forbid all intercourse with or supplies to such a ship, and arrest any vessel attempting to enter an American port after having committed a trespass against an American ship on the high seas.[33]

These were far-reaching powers, and directed solely, as everyone knew, against Great Britain. Jefferson believed that their exercise, or the threat of their exercise, would shortly bring that proud and arrogant nation to terms; but others were certain that, if enforced, they must inevitably lead to war.

This powerful weapon for good or ill was placed in his hands by an outgoing Congress on the final day of Jefferson's first term as President of the United States. On the following day, his second term of office commenced, and with it, new problems unforeseen and as yet unpredictable.

CHAPTER 57

Trouble with Europe

FOR the second time Thomas Jefferson walked quietly to the Capitol building, accompanied by militia and troops of admiring citizens, and took the oath of office as President of the United States. For a second time he read his Inaugural Address in a voice half-audible and unheard by a large part of his audience.[1]

It was quite a different occasion from that first appearance. Now no one feared he knew not what; everyone felt assured that the re-elected President would proceed along the lines he had already laid down, and that no violent convulsions of nature or of man were to be expected.

Jefferson himself realized the difference, and noted on the draft of his address: "The former one was an exposition of the principles on which I though it my duty to administer the government. The second then should naturally be a *conte rendue*, or a statement of facts, shewing that I have conformed to those principles. The former was *promise:* this is *performance.*" [2]

Therefore, as was fitting for a day of triumph and an era of almost universal good feeling, the address was largely retrospective and an account of a stewardship well done. Nothing was to be permitted to interfere with the harmony of the occasion, or to point to ominous clouds on the horizon.

Abroad, he declared, "we have endeavored to cultivate the friendship of all nations"; at home, "the suppression of unnecessary offices, of useless establishments and expenses, enabled us to discontinue our internal taxes. ... What farmer," he exclaimed, "what mechanic, what laborer, ever sees a tax-gatherer of the United States?" And, when the public debt was finally extinguished, he hoped that a proper Constitutional amendment would permit the revenues thus liberated to be distributed among the States and applied by them "to rivers, canals, roads, arts, manufactures, education, and other great objects within each state." Not, it must be noted, to be employed by the *federal* government for these or any other purpose.

He turned next to the congenial topic of Louisiana, perhaps the most brilliant success of his entire administration. Some had feared its acquisition, he remarked complacently, and thought such an undue extension of territory would endanger the Union. "But who can limit the extent to which the federative principle may operate effectively?" he inquired, with a side glance at Montesquieu's heresy. "The larger our association, the less it will be shaken by local passions."

As for the Indian tribes, Jefferson avowed himself commiserative of their plight in being overwhelmed by the irresistible current of our flowing population. But he was trying, he added virtuously, to accustom them to narrower limits by diverting their attention to agriculture and the domestic arts; though their ignorance, pride and prejudice sometimes hampered his well-meant efforts. What he did not tell his audience was the fantastic number of acres he *had* managed by fair means or foul to transfer from Indian tribal sovereignty to the sovereignty of the United States during the past four years. According to the private report of the Secretary of War, 50,000,000 acres had been thus transferred at a total cost of $142,000.[3] A princely domain, indeed!

The last item on which he spoke was freedom—the freedom of religion and the press. He had, he declared, followed the Constitution faithfully in these respects, even though there had been many abuses of their privilege by the press. He was willing, he said, to leave the offenders to the public indignation.[4]

All in all, the Address skirted every major item, and even made small and unimportant those items which did have intrinsic importance. It was a smooth, superficial performance, giving the people very little insight into the real accomplishments of the preceding administration or any conception of the problems which currently confronted the country. In short, it was a political document that pointed with pride, and placated and glossed over where pride could not be rendered visible.

With the Inaugural out of the way, Jefferson settled down comfortably to the prospect of four more years in office. There were some changes in his Cabinet, though none of major importance. The twin mainstays—Madison and Gallatin—remained steadfastly with him. So did Dearborn in the War Department. But Levi Lincoln resigned as Attorney General, and Robert Smith, tired of a Navy which was obviously the stepchild of the administration, asked to be transferred to the more attractive Attorney-Generalship. Jefferson complied, and offered the Navy post to Jacob Crowninshield of Massachusetts. But Crowninshield refused the position, even after the Senate had confirmed him; and Smith was finally induced to remain in his old post, while John Breckinridge of Kentucky became Attorney General. It made for a technical mix-up; and in the end, it seems that Smith was never officially confirmed in his old post, holding *de facto*.

At about this time, Jefferson made the acquaintance of a curious medical figure, Dr. Benjamin Waterhouse of Massachusetts. It had been through this enthusiast for medical causes that Jefferson had received samples of living virus taken from human smallpox patients for reinoculation into members of his family and a circle of neighbors and friends in Virginia. But Waterhouse had more enthusiasms than the prevention of smallpox. He hated tobacco and liquor as well, and wrote violent tracts against them.

He was a combative person and eventually quarreled with Harvard, tried to set up a rival medical school, and finally, doubtless at Jefferson's instigation, was given a military medical post by Madison in 1813.

With a curious audacity, he now sent his blast against tobacco to Jefferson. After all, Jefferson's livelihood depended on the continued use of the fragrant weed. Yet Jefferson good-humoredly accepted it, and even agreed with its tenets as to the physical, moral and political consequences of tobacco cultivation.[5]

Yet at about the time of this urbane agreement, Jefferson was purchasing a warehouse, in order to bring back to his neighborhood the traffic in tobacco which, for want of proper merchandising, had been going to Columbia, South Carolina.[6]

As usual, he was in want of money, finding it extremely difficult to finance the comparatively moderate cost of the warehouse. But he never undercut the scale of his expenditures. His dinners continued numerous and justly famous. His French maître d'hôtel and his French cook were the envy of all Washington hostesses, and it was universally agreed that no table served such an abundance or variety of rare and costly wines. He had installed in the President's House a set of circular shelves so contrived that, on the touch of a spring, they turned out of the wall laden with dishes from the serving pantry on the other side, and then sprang back into concealment.[7]

He purchased a pair of mockingbirds, one of whom he named Dick, and faithfully noted their days of singing and of silence in his account book. As became his position, he subscribed to numerous charities, churches and educational projects.[8] He also, in spite of his republican simplicity, employed a "Chariot, two Phaetons and one Gig" for his use in Washington, and duly paid the carriage tax therefor.[9]

He was so enthusiastic about the polygraph that Peale had made for him that he pressed its use on all his friends. It was, he averred, "an inestimable invention," to which the old copying press was but a poor thing in comparison.[10]

For all his talk of harmony and sweetness and light domestically, the Republicans, for lack of Federalists to fight, were engaging in bitter civil war among themselves. Though Burr had vanished from the political scene, his followers were still attacking the Clintonians and Jefferson himself with unexampled ferocity; while Burr was laying the groundwork for that expedition, the repercussions of which were to rock Jefferson's second administration. In Pennsylvania, the Republicans were locked in fierce battle, and both sides called on Jefferson for aid. But sensibly, he steered a neutral course, giving aid or comfort to neither as against the other, and fearing rightly that the discomfited minority might make common ground with the Federalists.[11] The revolt of John Randolph of Roanoke was still to come, but the signs and portents were already there. All in all, Jefferson was to have more trouble with his own party than with the defeated Federalists. His prophecy that an overwhelmingly victorious party carried within it the seeds of its own dissensions was coming true.

Foreign relations, in spite of their scanting in his Inaugural Address, continued to hold the center of the stage. Spain, declared Jefferson, "has met our advances with jealousy, secret malice and ill-faith.... And the issue of what is now depending between us will decide whether our relations with her are to be sincerely friendly, or permanently hostile." [12]

Of course, Spain might have retorted with equal or greater justice that protestations of ill faith came with an ill grace from a nation that had relentlessly harried her along every border, taken secretly a vast territory in violation of a French commitment not to give it to her, and now sought more of her territories by claims that were badly founded, to say the least.

Above all, in this delicate state of negotiations, Jefferson feared the dispositions of the people of New Orleans and of Louisiana. He had at first evaded or ignored their protests, through commissioners sent to Washington for the purpose, against the violation of the representative principle in their government. In the last days of the preceding session, however, Congress had been compelled to yield to the growing clamor and had granted New Orleans an elective Assembly, and an offer of admission as a State once it held 60,000 free white inhabitants and formed a proper constitution. Louisiana, as more backward, was still to be ruled by appointed officials.[13]

The trouble did not come so much from Spanish and French Creoles, as it properly might, but from Americans who had sought residence and fortune in the new territories and were determined to be possessed of their inalienable rights. Jefferson, in something of a pet, was particularly incensed at this agitation among those who had been Republicans. "Insubordination and opposition will be tolerated as little in whigs as in tories," he exclaimed sharply. "At the same time it is very afflicting to me to see those who have been useful in restoring the ascendancy of the whig principles of our constitution schismatise on grounds which they cannot honorably explain. We must disarm them of the aid of office in doing mischief, but otherwise treat them with all the indulgence due to separated brethren. With respect to Federalists, whether they are in opposition because hostile to the principles of our constitution or to the measures of its administration legislative & executive, we must not strengthen the effect of their opposition by the weight of office.... Disaffected men ought to be satisfied with the protection of the laws honestly extended to them. They ought not to expect the confidence of a government to which they know themselves hostile." [14]

Monroe had arrived in Madrid on January 2, 1805, to find Charles Pinckney sulking, with bags packed, and ready to quit the country; while the Spaniards were equally ready to break off all diplomatic intercourse.

As usual, the arrival of a new plenipotentiary allowed all parties to save face and start a new deal in the eternal card game of diplomacy. Monroe was fully in agreement with Pinckney as to objectives, though perhaps not as to the abruptness of his methods, and Pinckney agreed to stay on.

The two ministers issued what was in effect another ultimatum to Cevallos, demanding once more the cession of the Floridas, and of Texas as far as the Rio Colorado.[15] Once more Cevallos evaded, and sought French support against these aggressive Americans. Monroe requested Armstrong in Paris to sound out the French position, and received the ominous tidings that in the event of a rupture between Spain and America, France would side with Spain.[16]

Monroe placed a bold face on the situation and demanded his passports, which Cevallos granted with suspicious readiness.[17] His mission, conducted with such political fanfare, had ended in failure; so much so, that an enraged Spain used the frankest and most brutal language to the next representative from the United States, George W. Erving. "You may choose either peace or war," Prince Godoy told him. " 'Tis the same thing to me." [18]

But Jefferson, at home, comforted himself with the thought that the practical certainty of a continental war in Europe would, by involving Spain in its toils, give the United States a chance to bring her "to reason," and without war.[19]

While negotiations with Spain had thus reached an impasse, relations with England were dangerously worsening. All through 1805, British warships were literally blockading New York Harbor, and compelling all ships entering or leaving to submit to search and possible seizure. Seizures were made on the slightest pretext, and meant carriage to Halifax, prize courts, heavy costs and even confiscation. And every seaman, whose American papers were not in apple-pie order, was liable to be seized and impressed forthwith for service in the British navy.

These were humiliations and outrages not to be borne by a sovereign state; yet what was to be done about it? The Federalist merchants of New England and New York, though they grumbled and complained, were eager to swallow their national pride in the face of mounting profits. No matter how they were harried by British practices, the alternative of war was not to be thought of. In spite of harassments, of costs and confiscations, the carrying trade was an extremely profitable one; and those ships which got through unmolested more than made up for the losses on those that did not. War would put an end to all traffic; and ruin, financial if not moral, would stare them in the face.

But the Republicans, the South and Mr. Jefferson were hot against these barefaced invasions of sovereignty. Not having the financial returns to comfort them in their humiliation, they felt all the more keenly the hurt to national pride. Congress, in March, had placed a weapon in Jefferson's hands in the shape of the Interdict. Whether he was to employ it—with the consequence of overt war—rested with him.

Meanwhile, Monroe seemed to be moving from crisis to crisis. Quitting Madrid, he hurried to London, arriving there just as an epochal decision was being handed down (July 23, 1805) by Sir William Scott, sitting on a prize case in the Court of Appeals.

In the case of the seized American ship *Essex*, he reversed a former ruling of the same court whereby American ships had managed to evade the navigation laws. By breaking passage from the French West Indies to England at an American port, they had thereby been able to remove the enemy taint, and to sell French wares as neutral merchandise. But Scott's decision put an end to this practice, and placed the burden of proof on the shipmaster that the original intention had been to bring the goods *permanently* to the United States.

The decision created a storm of indignation when the news of it reached America. The Federalist merchants were for once equally as furious as the Republicans. For it had been just on this ancient rule of the interrupted voyage that they had been able to garner such extraordinary profits.

In fact, Federalist fury now far exceeded the Republican. The latter, indeed, viewed this new development with some complacency. Merry, the British Minister at Washington, reported the results frankly to his home government. "The sensation and clamor excited by this news from England (which has already caused the insurance on such cargoes to be raised to four times the usual premium)," he wrote, "is rendered the greater by such events having been totally unexpected, and by the merchants here having, on the contrary, considered themselves as perfectly secured against them." Yet, to his amazement, Madison had not made a single representation to him about the situation.[20]

Jefferson, indeed, alarmed by the truculence of Spain and the well-grounded belief that her truculence was based on promises of French support, had hoped to be able to come to terms with England. "We should not permit ourselves," he exclaimed to Madison, "to be found off our guard and friendless."[21]

As the news of the break with Spain came in, Jefferson's perturbation increased. So did Madison's. "The more I reflect on the papers from Madrid," wrote the latter, "the more I feel the value of some eventual security for the active friendship of G. B. but the more I see at the same time the difficulty of obtaining it without a like security to her for ours." What that mutual security meant was a military alliance.[22] To such strange bedfellows had the exigencies of the occasion committed these two decriers of all treaties.

So much in earnest were the President and the Secretary of State concerning the necessity of a military alliance with their oldest and most hated enemy that Jefferson actually drew up a set of terms. The treaty, he said, was to be provisional only and come into force in the event of an American clash with either France or Spain during the current European conflict. In such a case, England was not to make peace until Spain acknowledged the boundaries of Louisiana as we conceived them, and paid indemnification for the spoliation claims, for the security of which we would seize the Floridas. Jefferson was convinced that England would be only too happy to agree, so as to have us on her side. With such a treaty, he continued in optimistic vein, "we might await our own convenience for calling up the *casus foederis.*" He expected that Monroe, now in London, would get to work immediately on the treaty.[23]

It is no wonder then that, with these vast schemes in contemplation, Jefferson was averse at the moment to twist the tail of the British lion unduly, and to exercise his powers under the Interdict against the British blockade and impressments, or even to protest too strenuously against Sir William Scott's fateful admiralty decision.

But a variety of circumstances finally caused Jefferson's resolve to weaken, and his plans to vacillate. For one, the clamor of the despoiled merchants, shipowners and the families of impressed seamen rose to new heights. Memorials came pouring in from the merchant groups of New York, Philadelphia, Newburyport, Charleston, Baltimore and Norfolk appealing for relief from the heavy losses sustained as a result of British, French and Spanish seizures, as well as a flood of individual complaints.[24]

Just as ominous was the report now laid on Jefferson's desk, disclosing during a single year a total of 781 applications from American seamen who had been impressed into British service and called on the American legation for relief in their distress.[25]

It was obvious from the nature of the protests and their geographical origin that southern merchants were being hit hard as well as New Englanders.

Nor was Monroe's experience in England in consonance with Jefferson's theoretic belief in the eagerness with which England would welcome an alliance with us. The British, indeed, seemed obtusely indifferent to the advantages thus dangled before them, and callously refused to give up seizures, impressments or Scott's rule for the pleasure of being our military ally. In considerable dudgeon, Monroe wrote Madison that he saw no prospect of coming to terms with England. "On a review of the conduct of this Government towards the United States, from the commencement of the war," he declared wrathfully, "I am inclined to think that the delay which has been so studiously sought, in all these concerns, is the part of a system, and that it is intended, as circumstances favor, to subject our commerce at present and hereafter to every restraint in their power." [26] In fact, he was ready at this moment to pack up and leave for home, convinced that his whole European mission had ended in complete failure.

With these obdurate facts before him, Jefferson refused to abandon his optimistic views. He shifted his tack with agility. Foreseeing that Europe would be shortly embroiled in an extensive war, he now believed that it would be better *not* to be tied up with embarrassing alliances. With all Europe busy with its own problems, an aloof United States would have a breather of perhaps two years to achieve her goals, and even if embroiled, once our aims were achieved, we could retire without asking anyone's leave.[27]

He persisted in blowing hot and cold. There were those, and Monroe had been among them, who insisted that he cut the Gordian knot of Spanish relations by marching American troops into the disputed areas of Texas, seize the Floridas and let events take their course. But Jefferson, who threatened regularly to do just that, as regularly backed away from the use of force each time a showdown seemed imminent. Even now, with his policy seemingly in ruins about his ears, with Spain stubborn, France plainly on her side, and England averse to any consideration of the blessings of an alliance with us, with the warships of all three nations despoiling our commerce at will, Jefferson still clung to the healing uses of time and blandly insisted on his demands.

On November 14, 1805, just as though it had not laid down similar conditions before, the Cabinet reiterated its fading ultimatum. Spain, it decreed, must cede and deliver both Floridas to the United States at once; for which $5,000,000 would be paid. Spain was to agree to the American delineation of the boundaries between their respective territories. Spain was to pay $4,000,000 to the United States as indemnification for her spoliations of American citizens. Spain was to put up the country of the Rio Bravo as security for this payment; and if she did not make good, it was to be forfeited.[28]

Having thus laid down these ironclad conditions, the Cabinet adjourned.

On December 3, 1805, Jefferson went before Congress with his Annual Message. He could no longer content himself, as in his Inaugural, with vague platitudes. We were *not* on terms of harmony and friendship with the nations of Europe, and peace and prosperity did *not* stretch in endless vistas.

Now he was forced to admit that some of the European belligerents were threatening our "peaceable country." Foreign relations had changed considerably for the worse since the last session of Congress. Our coasts were infested with piratical armed vessels, which plundered, captured and sank American shipping. Even the *public* warships of Europe were acting like pirates in our waters, interpolating new principles into the laws of nations (an allusion to Scott's decision) and monopolizing commerce with their own enemies, while denying that commerce to neutrals.

Spain, he complained, had been obdurate. She had refused compensation for spoliations, was obstructing our commerce with Mobile, and had done nothing about settling the boundaries of Louisiana. In fact, she was raiding into Orleans and Mississippi, seized our citizens and plundered their property, necessitating a general alert for our troops on the border.

Such outrages on all sides, declared Jefferson, must be met with force, if no peaceful means of stopping them existed. Hence it was necessary to fortify our seaports, to increase the number of our gunboats, and perhaps to place the militia on a more youthful basis, so as to leave the older men "in the bosom of their families."

He was ready, he averred, if Congress so ordered, to build ships of the line carrying seventy-four guns; and submitted a measure for the immediate prohibition of the export of arms and ammunition. He also suggested that the limits on the number of seamen in peacetime service be raised.

After these alarmist considerations, Jefferson turned to more congenial topics. The war with Tripoli had ended on a most satisfactory basis, the Indians were now sensibly turning to agriculture (and selling their lands to the United States in the process), the Missouri country was being explored, and $4,000,000 more of the public debt had been extinguished.[29]

This was the public message, and it breathed alarm and bellicose threats. It was a clarion call to the country to prepare for war, and advocated all the things that had been anathema to Jefferson before—fixed fortifications and a huge navy. The vacillating Mr. Jefferson, the trimmer and believer in peaceful means, had cast off indecisions and come forth boldly appareled for war. Or so it seemed.

Even some of the Federalists, hard hit as they were by Scott's decision, were impressed with this strange new apparition. The more Senator Plumer considered the message, the more he approved of it. "The sentiments, if I understand them, are more noble, liberal & just than any he ever before avowed."[30]

But Jefferson had no intention of going to war. While thus rattling the saber, he was preparing another and secret message to be delivered to Congress behind closed doors. On December 6, 1805, three days after the public message had gained a measure of applause, came the confidential one.

In this he went into the details of the history of the negotiations with Spain. That nation, he complained, had refused to ratify the convention for the payment of old spoliations, and had refused to draw the boundaries of Louisiana. She had even raided our territories, and Jefferson, while awaiting instructions from Congress, had authorized our border forces to *repel* invasion, but not to pursue into or enter Spanish territory. After some animadversions on the conduct of France, Jefferson declared that the present crisis in Europe was favorable for an immediate pressing for a settlement. "Formal war is not necessary," he avowed. "It is not probable it will follow. But the protection of our citizens, the spirit and honor of our country, require that force should be interposed to a certain degree."

Then came the significant sentences: "But the course to be pursued will require the command of means which it belongs to Congress exclusively to yield or deny.... To their wisdom then I look for the course I am to take, and will pursue with sincere zeal that which they shall approve."[31]

On the face of it, there seemed no reason for sending this second message with all the trappings of secrecy. It went over much of the same ground as the public message; if anything, it was less bellicose. Congress was puzzled. What was the meaning of this seemingly aimless backing and filling? John Randolph of Roanoke, to whose committee the message had been referred, hurried to the President to discover the solution of the mystery. To him Jefferson opened himself cautiously. He wanted Congress, he said, with the same secrecy and dispatch with which it had handled the Louisiana Purchase, to appropriate $2,000,000 and turn it over to the Executive for the purpose of purchasing Florida. To which Randolph retorted—or so he was later to assert—that he would never agree to such a measure; that it should have been asked for officially in the message; that even if it had, he was still opposed on the ground that it sounded like extortion after the failure of all previous negotiations. It would be better, he insisted, to settle with Spain on the basis of an exchange of territories than to offer her cash.[32]

John Randolph was already on the verge of breaking with the administration, and this secret request for money proved the last straw. He had felt that Jefferson and his friends had been unduly tender of the mass of corruption that went under the name of the Yazoo Fraud. That scandal went back to 1795, when the Georgia legislature, under conditions of unbelievable bribery and corruption, had given away to a private company a princely domain on its western borders. When the odor of corruption leaked out, the people of Georgia rose in fury, sent the malefactors packing, and elected a brand new legislature that voided the terms of sale.

The northern purchasers, who by now included innocent holders of title, organized to protest the annulment, and went to Congress and the courts for relief. A Commission of three members of Jefferson's Cabinet—Madison, Gallatin and Levi Lincoln—was appointed to investigate and report on the tangle of claims; while John Marshall, in the pathfinding case of Fletcher v. Peck, laid down the rule that the rescinding act of the second Georgia legislature had attempted to impair an existing contract and was therefore unconstitutional.

All of which, including the suspicious tactics of Jefferson's Commissioners, infuriated Randolph, who denounced the whole business, including the current negotiations, as a complete fraud; and in intemperate language went so far as to imply that Jefferson and his Cabinet were tainted with the spreading corruption.

Now again, it seemed to him that Jefferson was willing to employ dishonorable tactics to gain his ends, and he resolved to have no part of them.

The committee met on December 7th, and Randolph denounced the message and the secret which Jefferson had disclosed to him. Joseph Nicholson, Jefferson's new personal lieutenant in the House, had in his pocket a series of resolutions which Jefferson had drafted and given to him for the recommendation of the committee.

These resolutions were a curious medley. They resolved that Spain must be held to answer for the indemnities, that no armed men of a foreign power must be permitted to enter or remain on territory of the United States, that neither Spain nor the United States, pending negotiations, was to take up new posts or strengthen old ones along the border, that the citizens of each country must be allowed free passage on the Mississippi and on the rivers emptying through West Florida into the Gulf. Jefferson had added another one, which held the meat of the matter: that he be authorized to use any unappropriated moneys in the Treasury in his discretion to carry these resolutions into effect, whether amicably or by force.[33]

But Gallatin had objected to the carte blanche on Treasury funds, and Jefferson yielded insofar as to strike it out. Thereby the resolutions were rendered meaningless; but Nicholson, even so, disapproved of them and returned them the next day without having put them to any use.

Randolph, now determined to break with the administration, gravely pretended that he saw nothing in the message which could be construed as a request for money. (He said nothing about his private interview with Jefferson.) Then, without doing anything, the committee adjourned. Randolph had seen Madison in the interim, and heard from him that the money had to be paid to France as a bribe so as to dissociate her from Spain. The idea, so Randolph said, disgusted him; and he declared unremitting war on the men who could propound such double-dealing bribery.[34]

When Randolph later publicly aired his own virtue and denounced the "backstairs" negotiations for Florida, Jefferson scribbled some indignant notes: "The former appropn for Louisiana approved by J. R. in the same words with that he now argues agt backstairs government. No man [knows] more of this than J. R." [35]

The causes of the split between Randolph and Jefferson have exercised the ingenuity of historians. The Yazoo Fraud has been given its due credit; and even the purported failure of Jefferson to offer Randolph the diplomatic appointment to London. But William Burwell, Jefferson's private secretary at this time, denied the tale of London. He attributed the break to Randolph's determination to oppose the Administration unless he was made the sole government leader in Congress, and that he had become infuriated when it seemed that the coveted post was going to Barnabas Bidwell, a new member from Massachusetts. In any event, the secret message precipitated the quarrel, with dangerous consequences for the future.[36]

The defection of Randolph embarrassed Jefferson mightily. He had received intimations from Armstrong in Paris that Talleyrand would be willing to throw the influence of France into our balance for a considerable sum, and settle the entire matter, including Spain's demands, for a total of

$7,000,000. To which Jefferson thought that $5,000,000 would be ample. But it now seemed that Congress was balking; and the prize, so long eagerly panted for, was slipping out of reach.

On December 14th, the committee reconvened, but refused adamantly any appropriation for Florida, voting instead to raise troops for the defense of the southern frontier "from Spanish inroad and insult, and to chastise the same." On January 3, 1806, this resolution was laid before the House, but the administration forces rallied to defeat it by 72 to 58. Now opposed to Jefferson was a coalition of Federalists and renegade Republicans led by John Randolph, and later known to fame as the "*tertium quids*." In their ranks, on this first measuring of strength, were twelve of Virginia's twenty-two representatives; a body blow to Jefferson's prestige.

At least one perspicacious senator was reading Jefferson's maneuvers aright. This was Plumer, who wrote in his diary: "I am very strongly inclined to think that Mr. Jefferson intends to purchase the Florida's—That he has not been himself deceived as to the eastern boundaries of Louisiana though immediately after the cession, to render that purchase popular he insinuated that it included West Florida. That all the present clamour for warlike preparation, & the publication of supposed aggressions some of which purported to have been committed three years since, are now made to prepare the public mind for the purchase of the Florida's." [37]

Barnabas Bidwell was now the administration whip in Congress. Aside from being a freshman Congressman, he was a man of mediocre abilities, and his deliberate choice to lead the administration forces disclosed the low ebb to which Republican talents had fallen and Jefferson's standing with his own people. Bidwell could not match Randolph in oratory, sarcasm or vituperation, but at least he could deliver the votes, and this was well enough.

Having spent its force in the attempt to push through Randolph's resolution for defense of the Spanish frontier, the opposition could not muster any further energy to defeat Bidwell's counterproposition to appropriate $2,000,000 for extraordinary expenses in foreign relations. The bill passed the House and went to the Senate on January 16th, with a private explanation that the proposed sum was to be used for Florida. The Senate acceded on February 7th, and the bill was triumphantly signed by Jefferson on February 13th. A dispatch was promptly hurried off to Armstrong in Paris to lay before France the proposition to purchase the Floridas and East Texas for $5,000,000. But the situation overseas had changed in the meantime, and France was now unable to deliver.

Of this, however, nothing was as yet known to Jefferson. He had a right to assume that his tortuous diplomacy with respect to France and Spain had been entirely successful, and that the revolt of John Randolph had met with complete failure.

The next step was to come to grips with the British problem. Freed of the shadow of complications on the Continent and on his own borders, he felt more confident in proposing bold measures with respect to British outrages. But he knew that he would have harder sledding in Congress on England than on Spain. Already he had suffered a preliminary defeat on his pet militia measure. He had drafted a bill for making that "people's" army a young men's force, classifying the militia according to age groups and family ties, and differentiating between internal and external state service.[38] Thereby he thought to make it at once a more efficient instrument and a more popular one. If it passed, he confidently expected that not a single regular would have to be raised, except in time of actual war. "A militia of young men," he asserted, "will hold on until regulars can be raised, & will be the nursery which will furnish them. I had rather have that classification established, than any number of regulars which could be voted at this time." [39]

In the midst of these activities he found time also to recommend to Congress a revisal of the laws on citizenship. As always, when dealing with general concepts, he displayed a catholicity of thought and largeness of expression that stamped his every utterance with the intimations of immortality.

"Every man," he said, "has a right to live some where on the earth. And if some where, no one society has a greater right than another to exclude him. Becoming indeed a member of any society, he is bound to conform to the rules formed by the majority. But has the majority a right to subject him to unequal rules, to rules from which they exempt themselves? I hazard these suggestions for the consdn of Congress. The only rightful line is between transient persons & bona fide residents / citizens." [40]

And, by the same token, no country might forcibly hold on to any man who wished to depart from his native land or renounce his connection therewith. "I hold the right of expatriation," he ruled, "to be inherent in every man by the laws of nature, and incapable of being rightfully taken from him even by the united will of every other person in the nation. If the laws have provided no particular mode by which the right of expatriation may be exercised, the individual may do it by any effectual and unequivocal act or declaration." [41]

CHAPTER 58

Monroe's Treaty

ON January 15, 1806, the Senate referred to a committee that section of Jefferson's message which dealt with British seizures and searches. On February 5th, Samuel Smith reported out a series of resolutions which denounced the seizures and recommended prohibitions of British woolens, linens, silks, glassware and other articles as a retaliatory measure.

At almost the same time, a bill was introduced to deal forcibly with British impressments. Any one so impressing an American, it decreed, would be liable to the death penalty as "a pirate and felon," and the President was authorized to retaliate against the offending nation by seizing and punishing vicariously the subjects of that nation and forfeiting their goods as indemnities to the injured seamen.

Such a bill, of course, was so intemperate in its terms and its consequences so assuredly fatal that even though it initially came out of committee in all its pristine crudity, it was later recommitted and quietly postponed to the next session.[1]

In the House, Andrew Gregg of Pennsylvania moved a series of resolutions that were much more stringent and sweeping than Smith's in the Senate. Gregg proposed that "no goods, wares or merchandise, of the growth, product, or manufacture of Great Britain, or of any of the colonies or dependencies thereof, ought to be imported into the United States."[2]

But Joseph Nicholson liked neither Gregg's resolutions nor Smith's. He argued that total prohibitions would hurt the United States much more than England. We would lose some $5,000,000 annually in duties and England would refuse our cotton if she could not sell us her manufactured cloth. *His* solution to the dilemma, therefore, was to select for prohibition only those British manufactures which we could either supply ourselves or import from other countries. He enumerated these as leather goods, tin and brass wares, hemp and flax products, silks, the more expensive woolens, wool hose, window glass, silver ware, paper, nails, hats, ready-made clothes, millinery, playing cards, beer, ale and porter, pictures and prints.[3]

Other members rose to offer their own panaceas. Sloan went even further than Gregg. He would cut off *all* trade with England; while Joseph Clay preferred a milder system which refused trade to ships of those nations which refused similar privileges to our ships.[4]

By common consent, however, Gregg's and Nicholson's resolutions were taken as major and representative of different points of view.

The great debate began on Gregg's sweeping prohibitions on March

5th. John Randolph denounced them immediately as a hidden cloak for war. "If war is necessary—" he thundered, "if we have reached this point—let us have war. But while I have life, I will never consent to these incipient war measures, which, in their commencement breathe nothing but peace, though they plunge at last into war." What carrying trade was being worried about? he demanded. Was it our honest and useful trade? "No, sir. It is that carrying trade which covers enemy's property, and carries the coffee, the sugar, and other West India products, to the mother country. No, sir, if this great agricultural nation is to be governed by Salem and Boston, New York and Philadelphia, and Baltimore and Norfolk and Charleston, let gentlemen come out and say so; and let a committee of public safety be appointed from those towns to carry on the Government. I, for one, will not mortgage my property and my liberty, to carry on this trade."[5]

Randolph's vehement phrases made a profound impression, which administration speakers of considerably less eloquence sought in vain to counter. For he had awakened an echo in the hearts of southern and western agriculturalists. Were they going to fight for a ship trade that benefited solely the seaport merchants, and find the markets for their own raw materials blocked as a result? This was now a struggle between the Northern and Southern wings of the Republicans, with the Federalists standing on the sidelines and cheering the contestants impartially on.

One of the Federalists in the Senate observed the internecine fight with grim satisfaction. "The schism which has taken place between the Northern and Southern Democrats," he wrote, "looks to be of the irreconcilable nature that it never can be healed. J. Randolph and some of his fast friends lead the Southern junto; while Bidwell, General Varnum, Crowninshield and General Thomas appear to manage the Northern Phalanx. In many trials of strength, their force has appeared to be so nearly balanced that the weight of the little Federalist band has given a preponderating turn to the balance."[6]

On March 13th, after almost continuous debate, the House in committee finally refused by a vote of 47 to 70 to consider Gregg's resolution any further, and thereby cleared the way for the others. But Clay withdrew his plan, leaving the field open for Nicholson's resolution.[7]

Once more Randolph rose in opposition, but both he and the administration leaders had exhausted themselves in the preceding debate, and their arguments were comparatively short. Randolph had shot his bolt, and Jefferson's followers now rallied in back of what Jefferson himself wanted. Nicholson's specific prohibitions met with his approval, rather than the total cessation that Gregg envisaged.

The President was following the course of debate with keen interest and considerable anxiety. Should Randolph's revolt prove successful, then his leadership was at an end and his administration ruined. There was more to this than a mere party fight. Randolph had broken irretrievably with

Madison as well as Jefferson, and was seeking to put up Monroe and pull Madison down. But Jefferson had already chosen Madison as his successor, and it was essential to warn Monroe off from joining forces with Randolph.

He therefore wrote Monroe in London a confidential letter. "Some of your new friends [Randolph]," he said carefully, "are attacking your old ones out of friendship to you, but in a way to render you great injury. In a few weeks I shall be able to write less enigmatically. In the mean time be cautious what & to whom you write, that you may not be allied to operations of which you are uninformed. In what is to ensue, my station prescribes to me a sacred neutrality, in which it is in entire unison with my friendships." [8] Jefferson was not being quite frank. He was in fact doing everything in his power to ensure that the Presidential mantle would fall without a struggle on Madison's shoulders; and Monroe was not only to realize it, but to resent it.

At this time, indeed, the whole party seemed at sixes and sevens. William Duane was warning Jefferson that Republicans generally were feeling he had thrown over his southern friends for the benefit of the northeast; that there was treachery within his own Cabinet, with only Madison loyal to him, and that Smith, Gallatin and Dearborn were secretly sabotaging his measures.[9]

His old friend Dr. Logan exhorted his erstwhile idol with stern rectitude. "Your errors in conducting the exterior relations of our country," he wrote sharply, "oppress the minds of your best friends with the most anxious solicitude—you may yet retrieve your character and preserve the confidence of your fellow citizens. Call together your too long neglected Council, take the state of the Union into consideration, submit every subject with frankness to discussion, and united with them, determine on such measures as may preserve the peace and honour of your country. Your own reputation imperiously demands that you should recede from pretensions and projects, which are demonstrably groundless and unjust." [10]

From all sides came warnings, exhortations and threats. Each faction demanded aid and comfort from Jefferson against its enemies, and threatened reprisals if they were refused. Monroe was being undermined abroad, and the charges that Gallatin was working secretly against his chief came thick and fast. Even Joseph Nicholson, it seemed, was being told that Jefferson was trying to throw him over, and the President found it incumbent to write him one of his famous "tares" letters, and another to Nathaniel Macon. To each he wrote along similar lines. "Some enemy, whom we know not, is sowing tares among us. Between you & myself nothing but opportunities of explanation can be necessary to defeat these endeavors.... I must therefore ask a conversation with you."[11] To Nicholson, Jefferson offered a federal judgeship.

He was also compelled to deny the persistent rumors that Gallatin and he were at loggerheads, and that his Cabinet was working secretly against him, insisting that "there never was a more harmonious, a more cordial administration, nor ever a moment when it had been otherwise." [12]

It was obvious therefore that John Randolph must be crushed and Nicholson's resolution passed by an overwhelming majority in the House if the reins of leadership were to remain with the President. Accordingly, he exerted every pressure he could on the members of the House, and did not hesitate to crack the party whip.

On March 17th came the first success—the resolution was adopted by a vote of 87 to 35, with Randolph himself not voting. It was accordingly sent to a committee to bring in a bill. The bill was brought in and triumphantly passed on March 26th by the overwhelming vote of 93 to 32, though Randolph this time firmly voted *nay*.[13]

It was a tremendous victory for Jefferson, and he recognized it as such. "I have never seen a House of Representatives," he wrote exultantly to Monroe, "more solidly united in doing what they believe to be the best for the public interest. There can be no better proof than the fact that so eminent a leader should at once, and almost unanimously, be abandoned." [14] The letter also served as subtle notice to Monroe that he had better not depend on Randolph as an ally to further his Presidential ambitions.

As a matter of fact, Randolph never recovered from the defeat, and eventually lost his powerful position on the Ways and Means Committee. Yet, though his capacity for doing mischief was diminished, there was no one who could stand up to him in debate; and the Jeffersonian forces finally adopted the safe, if ignominious policy of letting his philippics and torrential invective flow unchecked without a single response, except in the voting.[15]

In the Senate, meantime, Smith's resolution never came to a vote; though two others, drawn by John Quincy Adams, denouncing seizures and impressments and demanding indemnities, were passed. But the resolutions contained no means of implementing the denunciations, except that one of them did pave the way toward another negotiation with England. The Federalists voted for this with every intention of embarrassing Jefferson, and of forcing him into a treaty with England which must, they thought, resemble that Jay's Treaty which he had condemned in the past "& branded with odious epithets." [16]

According to Plumer, Jefferson was willing enough to be saddled by the Federalists with a negotiation. He wished himself to appear to be forced by the Senate into a position where he would have to negotiate, though seemingly against his will. And the Federalists, who had thought they were placing him in an embarrassing position, themselves fell into the trap which Jefferson had baited for them.[17]

Thus "urged" by the Senate, Jefferson appointed Monroe as one of the negotiators, and associated William Pinkney of Maryland with him, to the great disgust of Samuel Smith, who had hoped for the appointment himself.

The climate in England had definitely changed in the meantime, and made the prospects of some sort of settlement brighter than they had been for a considerable time. William Pitt, exponent of strong measures on the sea, had died, and Lord Grenville and Charles James Fox had formed a new Ministry. Monroe, who had been ready to return to the United States, now decided to remain. Fox seemed amiable and more sympathetically disposed to America and her envoy; though Monroe warned Madison that not too much reliance ought to be placed on benign appearances. Let Congress, he insisted, not adjourn without adopting coercive measures against England, which ought to be suspended as a Damoclean sword over her until the ensuing negotiations proved either successful or a failure.[18]

A little later, Monroe was able to report that Fox had suited deeds to fair words, and had taken steps to prohibit further seizures and condemnations of American vessels and cargoes.[19] Thus, without a blow, one half—perhaps the greater half—of American grievances against England had been quietly eradicated.

It is curious that just as Fox was displaying a disposition to come to terms, Jefferson was professing himself at the end of his patience. "The love of peace," he asserted, "which we sincerely feel & profess, has begun to produce an opinion in Europe that our government is entirely in Quaker principles, & will turn the left cheek when the right has been smitten. This opinion must be corrected when just occasion arises, or we shall become the plunder of all nations." [20]

Nevertheless, Jefferson was now determined to seek settlements all around. Armstrong and James Bowdoin were in Paris dealing with the Spaniards under the watchful eyes of Napoleon and Talleyrand. But Armstrong was in disfavor with many in the United States, and Jefferson asked Wilson Cary Nicholas to join them as a third plenipotentiary. Nicholas refused, much to Jefferson's disappointment. He feared that Armstrong was so unpopular with the Senate that any treaty he negotiated stood a chance to fail of ratification.[21]

He placed some hope also in Alexander of Russia to champion the rights of neutrality at any forthcoming peace table, and deftly flattered that monarch with fair words and effusive expressions in order to ensure that he would incorporate in the approaching peace treaties "a correct definition of the rights of neutrals on the high seas." [22] But his main reliance was now on England. The change in ministry had been providential, and he wished to strike while Fox was still malleable and friendly to the United States.

Monroe, however, just when England seemed to be in his grasp, heard with astonishment and dismay that Pinkney had been associated with him in the mission. The glory that should have been his was now to be divided, with perhaps the lion's share going to this last-minute interloper. Uneasily, Monroe must have remembered how he himself had come into the negotiations over Louisiana and borne the palm away from Livingston. He did not relish the poetic justice of the same thing happening to him now. Certainly the appointment helped foster in his mind those suspicions of Jefferson and Madison which John Randolph had sedulously attempted to implant.

The unwelcome William Pinkney arrived in London on June 24, 1806, carrying official instructions from home. The two plenipotentiaries, explained Madison, were to treat with England on the maritime wrongs and on the regulation of commerce and navigation. Attention was to be called to the recent act which prohibited certain English manufactures—Nicholson's Act—and the execution of which was being held up pending the result of these negotiations.[23]

Jefferson also sent Monroe a private letter, which offered tempting baits with one hand and a warning with the other. Monroe, said Jefferson, could have his choice of the governorship of Orleans or Louisiana. The latter, he intimated, offered "the finest field in the US for acquiring property." At the same time, he made certain that Monroe was aware that Randolph had passed from the picture as an influential figure, and that he was now a leader with hardly a follower. Eventually, he indicated, Randolph must turn Federalist and thereby become anathema to all true Republicans. As for the situation in England, the accession of Fox insures "a just settlement of our differences," and makes it possible for the two great nations to come to an understanding. We prefer, declared Jefferson, an English ascendancy on the ocean to a French; and there arose in his contemplation the idea that "the whole gulph Stream" came within the sovereignty of the United States, "in which hostilities & cruising are to be frowned on for the present, and prohibited as soon as either consent or force will permit us."[24] This was a grand conception which Jefferson realized only too well was unenforceable at the moment, and which in fact waited for the twentieth century to be made effective.

But Madison's—and Jefferson's—terms as embodied in the instructions were of such a nature that it was incredible that even Fox would assent to them. They demanded as a price for the repeal of the nonimportation act that England abolish impressment, permit the restoration of American trade with the French colonies on the old basis, and pay indemnities for the captures and confiscations under Scott's decision. And, to cap the climax, Fox died on September 13th, bringing the whole structure of fair expectations tumbling to the ground.

In alarm, Monroe and Pinkney asked for a further suspension of nonimportation in order to give their negotiations some chance of succeeding; and later reported that Lord Holland and Lord Auckland, who had taken over the British side of the negotiations, were willing to yield on many points but presented a stone wall on the all-important questions of impressment and trade with the enemy colonies.[25]

As if to add to the troubles of the envoys, Napoleon signed his notorious Berlin Decree on November 21, 1806, which declared England to be in a state of blockade, that all intercourse with her was prohibited, that all British property, public and private, constituted a prize of war, and that all ships sailing from England or her colonies were forbidden entry into any port controlled by Napoleon or his allies. This was in answer to a paper blockade which England had recently placed against the whole French and German coasts; and between them, America seemed cut off at one swoop from all trade with Europe and her colonies.

Under these untoward circumstances the American envoys in England determined to salvage what they could from the wreckage, threw their official instructions into the discard, and signed a treaty with England on December 1, 1806, which omitted all reference to the most important conditions laid down by Madison and Jefferson as conditions precedent.

No mention was made of impressments in the treaty itself—though a separate note promised that care would be taken in the future not to impress Americans. The question of indemnities was dismissed altogether. As for the trade with the French and Spanish West Indies, the stipulation was made that their products must be bona fide property of United States citizens, must first be landed in United States ports, pay custom duty there, and *then* be reshipped to European ports. As for the *British* West Indies, they were to remain closed to American shipping.

As if these terms were not onerous enough, a note was hastily appended on receipt of news of the Berlin Decree that unless the United States, before ratification, gave security that it would refuse to recognize the Berlin Decree, England would in turn refuse to be bound by this treaty.[26] And, England issued its own retaliatory Order in Council on January 7, 1807, which forbade all neutral trade from any one French port, or that of her allies, to another.

No wonder, when this remarkable treaty finally came back to American shores, it aroused a storm to which the ancient Jay's Treaty had been merely a tempest in a teacup.

This was a trying year for Jefferson. Public affairs were not going well, his best friends were squabbling and involving him in the toils, and his party, built up with such infinite pains, was cracking at the seams and appeared ready to burst asunder.

He was also guilty of a grave tactical blunder. By announcing that he was determined not to run again for office, he had lost heavily in influence. Senator Plumer summed up the situation in a few pithy words. "It is letting down his importance. *Most men shun—but all seek the rising sun.*" [27]

Official Washington also remarked that he had aged at least ten years as a result of the squabbles in Congress over his program. The adherents of

Randolph no longer visited him, and the diplomatic corps was at sword's point with him over the rather ridiculous dispute over "pell-mell" and the niceties of etiquette. Only Turreau, the French Minister, still kept up a semifriendly relationship; and Turreau thought he had little "of that audacity which is indispensable in a place so eminent, whatever may be the form of government. The slightest event makes him lose his balance, and he does not even know how to disguise the impression he receives." [28]

Nor were Jefferson's personal affairs in any better state. The calls for money from Monticello were "immense," and he sought desperately from Washington to rehabilitate the nailery and the plantation as the only means for making the estate self-sufficient. He proposed building a new road up the mountain, and fencing in his property from depredations by a fence of thickly planted trees and thorns, sending his overseer a map, materials and full directions. For once his instructions were diligently obeyed, and the road was completed by May 11th.[29]

The controversy with John Randolph also had its impact on his private family life. Both his sons-in-law—Thomas Mann Randolph and John Wayles Eppes—had entered Congress and took the animadversions of the other Randolph on Jefferson very much to heart. So much so that bitter words were bandied back and forth on the floor of the House between Randolph of Roanoke and Randolph of Edgehill and Monticello. The language employed threatened to lead to a duel, and the papers kept the pot boiling furiously with their reporting.

Nothing was calculated to strike greater terror into Jefferson's heart than the thought of an affair of honor which might lead to the widowing of his sole remaining daughter and the orphaning of her brood of children. He penned a moving appeal to his son-in-law to do everything possible, within honor, to avoid the fatal issue of a duel. He begged him not to volunteer anything beyond what the necessities required. "The least expression of passion on the one side," he wrote, "draws forth a little more on the other, & ends at last in the most barbarous of appeals. How different is the stake which you two would bring into the field! On his side, unentangled in the affections of the world, a single life, of no value to himself or others. On yours, yourself, a wife, & a family of children, all depending, for all their happiness & protection in this world on you alone." [30]

Whether it was because of Jefferson's appeal, or calmer considerations on both sides, the matter was allowed finally to drop; but the bitterness persisted to the end of all their lives.

As though Jefferson had not sufficient troubles during this crucial year, two other matters rose to plague him; one of which, in particular, was to lead to what is perhaps the most sensational episode in American history. The other, of lesser importance, related to a filibustering expedition proposed and engineered by one Francesco de Miranda, a native of Venezuela who dreamed of freeing all South America from the yoke of Spain and who had been busy for years seeking aid in England and America for his grandiose plans. England turned him down, but he met with some encouragement in the United States. Hamilton, who had had his own dreams of glory in connection with South America, had listened attentively and was ready to help; but John Adams, then President, would have no part or parcel of the scheme. Miranda, after further years of ineffectual propagandizing in Europe, returned to the more hospitable United States late in 1805 to take advantage of the war clouds that then hung heavily over Spanish-American relations. He found New York ready, eager and willing for the great adventure; particularly the followers of Aaron Burr. Jonathan Dayton, Senator from New Jersey, John Swartwout, United States Marshal, and William S. Smith, Surveyor of the Port of New York, joined in his scheme for outfitting armed ships from New York harbor, raising volunteers and sailing to revolutionize Venezuela as the first step in the liberation of South America.

While a ship he had purchased, the *Leander*, was being outfitted and volunteers recruited, Miranda went to Washington and met with Madison and Jefferson. The tenor of his conferences has been shrouded in a fog of assertions and angry counterassertions. Miranda later claimed that he unfolded his plans to these high officers of the American government and that they had—at least Madison specifically—encouraged him. Both men were to deny anything of the sort. In any event, Miranda returned to New York, announcing that he had been promised American assistance, and a month later the *Leander* sailed publicly out of New York harbor, unmolested by the authorities.

The expedition was a complete failure. The Spaniards, well warned of the filibuster and its destination, captured the vessel on the high seas, and Miranda was hustled off to a Spanish dungeon to languish for years.

But Jefferson was not to escape unscathed. Angry representations over the palpable violation of American neutrality were made by Yrujo to Madison, backed by a mass of incontrovertible evidence.

Very much embarrassed, the government was forced to take action. On February 5th, Jefferson asked that the District Attorney of New York investigate the *Leander* incident and determine how it happened that the duly constituted officers of the port had allowed the vessel to sail without informing the government in Washington.[31] As a result, Smith and Ogden, the owner of the *Leander*, were indicted and brought to trial. Jefferson hesitated whether or not to remove Smith from his office before a final court determination, finally yielding to Gallatin's insistence that he should.[32] It was fortunate he did, for the New York jury, hand-picked by Swartwout, as United States Marshal, triumphantly acquitted Smith of the charge. Only when it was too late did Jefferson also remove Swartwout from his post.[33]

Courtesy the New-York Historical Society, New York City

JAMES MADISON

Painting by Asher B. Durand

Courtesy the New-York Historical Society, New York City

DOLLY MADISON

Painting by Rembrandt Peale

If the Miranda incident embarrassed Jefferson mightily, the second one rocked his administration.

On February 22, 1806, Aaron Burr made a surprise call on Thomas Jefferson, President of the United States. It was almost a full year since he had departed from Washington as Vice-President, and longer than that since his last strange interview with his former chief. This interview was equally as strange, and Jefferson's notations are our sole source of information concerning it.

In the interim between these interviews, Burr had been defeated for the governorship in New York, he had slain Hamilton in a duel, and he had engaged in certain mysterious trips to the western territories and gone as far south as New Orleans. Rumors and reports had reached Washington of curious activities, but nothing which could be substantiated.

In this final interview, Jefferson recorded that Burr spoke of his former services to the common cause, and uttered some veiled threats that he could, if he wished, do Jefferson "much harm"; but that he wished to be on a "different ground." He would, he said, be in Washington for several days, if Jefferson had anything to propose to him. What he meant, of course, was the offer of some honorable position in government.

But Jefferson refused to take the hint and spoke bluntly instead of the lack of confidence which the public had displayed in Burr as evidenced by the preceding election; and said that, furthermore, he feared "no injury which any man could do me."[34] Thus cavalierly rebuffed, Burr departed and Jefferson thought he was finished with him. He was greatly mistaken.

Much had been happening before Burr had decided to make one last effort to come to an honorable accommodation with Jefferson—matters of which the latter had only the vaguest inklings; and the dismissal now proved to Burr that he must go through with his former plans as the only hope for the rehabilitation of his career and his fortunes.

The vast western territories had long inflamed the imagination of ambitious Americans and the opening of the frontier had been the signal for one of the great pioneering and colonizing movements in history. But the pioneers had run into the exasperating stone wall of Spain, whose command of the Mississippi and its outlet to the open sea placed a seemingly insurmountable obstacle in the way of future expansion and, worse still, a closure on the only road by which western products could be profitably traded. As a result, the West clamored for aid from its government, demanding that the intolerable situation be eased; by war, if necessary. Failing to gain the satisfaction they desired at Washington, there were those who proclaimed their readiness to go to war on their own against the hated Dons; while some few dabbled in strange plots with Spain herself, seeking profit for themselves in secret negotiations that looked eventually to juncture with the Spanish dominion.

Burr, as did many other ambitious men whose fortunes had failed them in the East, looked to a brighter future in the West. He had been friendly with James Wilkinson during the Revolution, and Wilkinson had early gone west to commence one of the strangest careers in our history. Through a combination of audacity and secret villainy he had managed to ingratiate himself with both the American government and the Spanish. He became in fact the secret agent of Spain, all unknown to his own government or to his colleagues. So successful had his double-dealing maneuvers been that while he was in Spain's employ as a spy, every American official from the days of Washington and Hamilton down to Jefferson himself considered him a gallant and able officer, a good American and a masterful administrator. The result was that when Louisiana became American soil, Jefferson in all good faith appointed him both civil and military commander of the new territory, and thought that he could not have made a fitter appointment.[35] Thus the fortunes of the United States were placed unwittingly in the hands of an unscrupulous scoundrel who had it in his power to shift the tide between the two nations almost at will, and whose sole touchstone for action was the ensuing profit to himself.

Very probably it was from James Wilkinson that Burr, desperate in his own fortunes, received the first idea of what later became the Burr "conspiracy." As far as can be made out from the available evidence, the two friends, in May, 1804, discussed a dazzling prospect to the west and south waiting for spirits bold enough to seize the opportunity. The United States and Spain were on the verge of war; Mexico was in insurrection against her masters; Wilkinson commanded the American troops on the border; New Orleans, recently ceded to the United States, was discontented; every American in the West was only too eager to participate in an undertaking that would drive Spain out of the Americas. What an opportunity for Burr and Wilkinson to liberate Mexico, perhaps even South America, and carve out an empire for themselves beyond the dreams of either modern or ancient times!

Burr harkened—but money was required, and a certain amount of outside aid. England was the logical source, as already embroiled with Spain and willing enough to lop off the vital limbs of Spanish power. He therefore approached Merry, the British Minister, with an astounding proposition. Since Merry hated Jefferson and everything American, since England was then at odds with the United States and anxious to see her reduced in importance, Burr dangled tempting bait. He was ready, he told the gullible Minister, to offer a separation of the Western States from the East if England would supply funds and ships for his project against Mexico and the Spanish dominions. Merry swallowed the bait whole, and warmly recommended the plan to his home government.[36]

England, however, was cold to the project and preoccupied with the threat of Napoleon's proclaimed invasion of her own shores. Undismayed at the silence from across the sea, Burr audaciously next turned for funds to the very nation whose lands he proposed to revolutionize and seize for himself. He spoke to Yrujo, the Spanish Minister. Naturally he did not disclose his real plans; instead, he filled the disgruntled envoy's ear with vague intimations of a disruption of the United States. But more immediately, he asked for a passport to Mexico. Yrujo, however, was in the possession of secret information—derived perhaps from Wilkinson himself, who was evidently playing both ends against the middle and making certain that, whatever happened, he would come out on top. Yrujo refused the request and wrote in hot haste to the Spanish officials to arrest Burr the moment he should enter any Spanish territory.[37]

In spite of these rebuffs from every side—from Jefferson, England and Yrujo—Burr, shortly after quitting the Vice-Presidency, proceeded west and south on a grand "tour" to examine the terrain and make the necessary connections for a later expedition in force. Traveling by boat down the Ohio, Burr met with an enthusiastic reception all along the way from old army acquaintances and politicians, and from those who welcomed his ideas on an assault against the Spaniard. There were Senator John Smith of Ohio, Jonathan Dayton of New Jersey, Senator John Brown of Kentucky, Senator John Adair of the same state, Matthew Lyon, Congressman, Governor William Henry Harrison of the Indiana Territory, General Andrew Jackson of Tennessee—and of course, General James Wilkinson, Governor of Louisiana. It was an impressive list, comprising the leaders of the West and influential politicians everywhere, who listened to Burr's smooth tongue and were fascinated by his personal gifts and talents, and by the visions of grandeur he unfolded. To none of these, except perhaps to Dayton and Wilkinson, was there the slightest hint of disunion; all the talk was of Mexico and Spain.

But important as these men were, the most valuable acquisition Burr made on this journey was the enthusiastic and devoted support of Harman Blennerhassett, a wealthy and cultivated but eccentric Irishman who had come to America with his young wife, Margaret, to build himself an unusual estate on an island in the Ohio, near Marietta, where he busied himself with chemical experiments and violin playing. Burr, stopping off at the island, promptly dazzled the impressionable pair—particularly Margaret—and enlisted their lives and fortunes in his scheme.

Drifting then down the Mississippi, he met with an equally tumultuous reception at New Orleans, both from the original Creole inhabitants and from such prominent newcomers as the American merchant, Daniel Clark. Well satisfied, Burr returned east; but Wilkinson was cooling in the meantime, due in large part to Yrugo's masterful efforts in spreading rumors concerning Burr's intentions to dismember the Union. In great alarm, Wilkinson foresaw that he might be destroyed in the process if the United States and Spain, his two employers, both turned against Burr, and prudently decided that when the opportunity arose, he would desert and betray the man whom he had initially inspired.[38]

But Yrujo's skill had already produced the effect he desired. Wild rumors began to circulate through the West, and to appear in the public prints, chiefly in Federalist sheets, whose publishers were ready enough to avenge themselves on Burr for Hamilton's death.

The first report that came to Jefferson of Burr's alleged secret intentions was on December 1, 1805, by way of an anonymous, crudely printed note, postmarked Philadelphia. The writer pretended to illiteracy, but some of his information was remarkably exact. Burr, he said, was meditating the overthrow of the Administration and conspiring against the state. "A foreing [*sic*] Agent" in Washington was backing him; and watch his "conexions with Mr. M . . . y [Merry] and you will find him a British Pensioner, and Agent." [39]

The second warning had a name to it—that of Joseph Hamilton Daveiss, the United States District Attorney for Kentucky, and a staunch Federalist. He urged Jefferson to be on his guard against both Burr and Wilkinson. Concerning Wilkinson he also had some remarkably exact information, declaring that he "has been for years, and now is, a pensioner of spain." Daveiss went even further, averring that "a very exalted magistrate of this country, has lately drawn on spain for his pension." He would, if Jefferson so demanded, disclose his name and that of others in the pay of Spain. In case of war with that nation, he ended, "let neither the first nor second in command be appointed out of the western country." [40]

This was detailed, specific—and alarming. The implications went far beyond Burr; they spoke of the West as a hotbed of treason and disunion, and involved its leading characters. Jefferson turned the letter over to Gallatin for his advice. The Secretary of Treasury was inclined to pooh-pooh the direct charge against Wilkinson, though admitting that he had no very exalted opinion of him. "He is extravagant and needy, & would not I think feel much delicacy in speculating in public money or public land. In both those respects he must be closely watched." But he did not believe him capable of betraying his country.[41]

Jefferson nevertheless wrote to Daveiss that "the information is so important that it is my duty to request a full communication of everything known or heard by you relating to it." [42]

But before Jefferson's letter reached him, Daveiss had already sent a damning list. Aside from Wilkinson and Burr, there were John Breckinridge, Senators Adair and John Smith, Judge Sebastian of the Court of Appeals, Judge Harry Innes, Henry Clay, Governor William Henry Harrison and others not as well known to fame.[43] And, *after* Jefferson's request, he reiterated the names, but added specific accusations, with dates and amounts of money passed, to prove Wilkinson's complicity with Spain.[44]

Jefferson must have been aghast on the receipt of these communications. If Daveiss were to be believed, then *every* prominent Republican in the West was deeply involved in a traitorous conspiracy with Spain, the object of which was to break the West away from the United States and come to terms with that foreign power. Included in the charges were some of his staunchest supporters, including his old friend, John Breckinridge, who had co-operated with him so closely in putting through the famous Kentucky Resolutions. And who was the accuser? An unreconstructed Federalist, who doubtless had axes of his own to grind in making these wholesale accusations against good Republicans. It is no wonder then that Jefferson dismissed the whole business as doubtless a Federalist plot to disrupt the Republican party, and did nothing further in the premises.

He was more disturbed at the moment over the possibility that Spain might decide to attack New Orleans and regain that vital port which France had, in defiance of her solemn compact, ceded to the United States. He therefore sought to strengthen the border defenses, put his famous gunboats in commission, and proposed a scheme to Congress whereby 2,000,000 acres of land in the threatened areas, divided into plots of 160 acres each, would be granted in alternate plots to able-bodied colonists, not then residents of the territory, who would agree to live on the land and cultivate the soil for a specified number of years, and render service in the militia. This bill he considered one of the most important before Congress. It would provide, he hoped, a large trained militia composed of men who had a stake in the territory to defend against Spanish attack; especially since he was convinced that a large percentage of the existing inhabitants could not be depended on in case of an invasion. His plan was much better, he told Plumer, than the establishment of a regular standing army. But to Plumer the scheme seemed "to establish a new principle in our government—a partial introduction of the feudal system—a system of military tenures." [45] He might have gone even further back in his analogy —to the Roman military colonies on the borders of empire.

The bill was read in the Senate on April 4th, but was postponed until the next session for further consideration. Jefferson was disheartened. With tears in his eyes he confided that none of his favorite measures had been adopted. The bill for the classification of the militia had been rejected outright, and this bill for defending New Orleans had in effect been turned down. "*The people,*" he exclaimed, "*expect I should provide for their defence, but congress refuse me the means.*" [46]

Both Congress and his own Cabinet were in an unwarlike mood, at a time when Jefferson himself was gravely disturbed over the defenseless condition of the nation. The same difficulty arose over Tripoli. By the terms of a law dated March 25, 1804, once the war with Tripoli was ended and no further hostilities impended, the navy must be reduced to a peacetime establishment. Yet Captain Rodgers urged that the fleet be kept intact in the Mediterranean until the fall, and Jefferson was inclined to agree. But his Cabinet had voted unanimously to obey the law. This posed a dilemma, and Jefferson sought Robert Smith's advice as Secretary of the Navy. Is this a case, he asked, in which it might be better to take the chance of trouble breaking out in the Mediterranean and not give the

Executive discretion which might lead to harm, or "is it one of those cases where the Executive should hazard the doing good against law, and throw himself on his country for justification?" [47] It was a dilemma which Jefferson was never quite able to resolve, even though he had taken the latter course when it came to the purchase of Louisiana.

CHAPTER 59

The Burr Conspiracy

JEFFERSON breathed a sigh of relief when Congress arose and went home in April, 1806. He had lost his major measures, and had been subjected to bitter attacks from the Federalists and even more bitter assaults from those who had borne the mantle of republicanism in the past.

With John Randolph now ranged against him, with even Nicholson to be placated, he sought another leader through whom his policies might be transmitted to the next session. It is difficult to determine just why he picked on Barnabas Bidwell of Massachusetts for the post: a freshman Congressman in the previous session and a gentleman of mediocre attainments. Perhaps his mediocrity made him more amenable to direction; perhaps the fact that he came from a formerly rock-ribbed Federalist state gave him a certain accolade and made him less apt to betrayal than the more volatile and independent Virginians.

In any event, Jefferson proposed to Bidwell that he run again for Congress, remarking flatteringly that "all eyes look to you. It was not perhaps expected from a new member, at his first session, & before the forms & style of doing business were familiar. But it would be a subject of deep regret were you to refuse yourself to the conspicuous part in the business of the house which all assign to you." [1]

Bidwell responded modestly to the flattery that he would run again and do his best if elected, but he feared he would be able to play only a moderate part in the House.[2]

Meanwhile, Jefferson did not forget his old friend, John Page, now out of the governorship of Virginia and again, so to speak, on the dole. He offered him the Loan Office at Richmond just as soon as the current incumbent died, an event very shortly expected. It paid $1,500 a year and commissions and, as Jefferson pointed out, "the office is a perfect sinecure." Page could even put one of his sons in as a clerk to do the job and thereby gain an extra thousand a year. Not only that, but his son would thereby in effect gain a possession of the office, so that, on Page's death, he would have an excellent claim to the succession.[3]

In the matter of the indigent Page, Jefferson forgot all his fine sentiments about the sacredness of office and permitted old friendship to override the public welfare.

This was the first year that Jefferson had remained so far into the summer at Washington, and he hated it. "Absence from you becomes every day more and more insupportable," he wrote his daughter Martha, "and my confinement here more disgusting. I have certainly great reasons for gratitude to my constituents. They have supported me as cordially as I could ever have expected; and if their affairs can preserve as steady a course for two years to come, and I can then carry into retirement the good will they have hitherto bestowed on me, the day of retirement will be the happiest I have now to come." [4]

He later returned to this theme in October, after several months at Monticello. "The lonesomeness of this place," he then complained of Washington, "is more intolerable than I ever found it. My daily rides too are sickening for want of some interest in the scenes I pass over: and indeed I look over the two ensuing years as the most tedious of my life." [5]

Among the matters that held him in Washington during the hot season was the question of Yrujo. That Spanish worthy was made the subject of a Cabinet meeting, particularly with reference to the articles violently attacking the government which it was now known he had suborned editors to publish. Spain had promised to recall him, but had not as yet done so, and it was debated whether he should not be peremptorily told to quit the country. It was finally decided, however, to let such action lie over until October.[6]

At the end of July, Jefferson was able to escape to his beloved Monticello where, amidst the scenes and activities he delighted in, he continued to direct public affairs as best he could. John Randolph had taken his grievances home with him when Congress rose and, under the pseudonym of "Decius," defended his own course and attacked the administration in a series of articles in the Richmond *Examiner*. Jefferson was stung to reply, but not *in propria persona*. He furnished his former secretary, William A. Burwell, with the requisite material for a counterattack, suggesting at the same time that it be published under "the mask of a member of the Legislature" in order to avoid suspicion that Jefferson was the source.[7]

Also, while at Monticello, reports from a variety of scattered sources were coming in of the continued activities of Burr; sources of good Republican character. For the first time Jefferson began to betray uneasiness, and he asked his informants for further confidential particulars of the alleged conspiracy. "A knowledge of the persons who may reject," he advised, "as well as of those who may accept parricide propositions will be peculiarly useful." [8]

On October 4th, Jefferson reluctantly returned to Washington to assume once more the burdens of government. Several serious problems awaited him; one was the rapidly unfolding Burr "conspiracy"; the other, what to do about his friend, James Monroe.

Awaiting him was a letter from Monroe in London, declining Jefferson's offer of the government of Louisiana.[9] The declination, in conjunction with the activities of Monroe's friends at home, meant to Jefferson that Monroe had definitely determined to contest the nomination for the Presidency with Madison in the next election.

An attempt to smoke Monroe out, and to obtain from him, if possible, a disclaimer was made by John Beckley of Virginia. He pretended that John Randolph's activities were without Monroe's knowledge or consent. "Indeed," he proceeded cannily, "the motive to this step was too obvious to admit a doubt that it was a masked friendship to you, to cover the resentment of disappointed ambition *vs* the president & Mr: Madison, for having overlooked *him* in the appointment of Armstrong to succeed Livingston...."

Beckley was Monroe's friend, rather than Madison's; he thought the latter "too timid and indecisive as a statesman, and too liable to a conduct of forbearance to the federal party which may endanger our harmony and political safety." Yet he preferred Jefferson to both of them. Like most politicians, he refused to believe the declarations of an incumbent that he would not be a candidate, and felt that a public demand would be sufficient to make Jefferson run again in order to prevent a schism.[10]

Gallatin also had been placed on a spot. Randolph in a Congressional speech had sought to implicate him in his own split with Jefferson, and the opposition Republican faction in Pennsylvania had on several occasions openly accused him of working secretly at cross-purposes with his chief. Gallatin denied the charges in a letter to Jefferson, and disavowed any collusion with Randolph or any other group. This was in answer to a letter from Jefferson assuring him of his unbounded confidence and his refusal to listen to those who sought to create a split between them.[11]

As a matter of fact, Beckley had been right about the public demand on Jefferson to become a candidate to succeed himself. Whether inspired or not, resolutions, petitions and memorials came in waves from Republican groups all over the country, begging him to stand for a third term.[12] They feared that any other course would lead to an open schism in the Republican ranks, a knockdown fight between Madison and Monroe for the post, and a resulting bitterness that might give the Federalists a chance to sneak back into power. But to all the clamor, Jefferson returned no sign.

Nor did he, in writing to Monroe, give any intimation of the quarrel that was raging at home. He was sorry to hear, he said, of the delay in the negotiations with England because of the death of Fox, whom he greatly admired. "His [Fox's] sound judgment saw that political interest could never be separated in the long run from moral right, & his frank & great mind would have made a short business of a just treaty with you." If a treaty was not concluded by December, however, it could not reach the United States until Congress had risen in March; and ratification would then have to go over to the following December. This would mean that the nonimportation law would have to be in operation for a considerable period, with a consequent "unfavorable influence on the popular temper of both countries."[13] Jefferson was naturally unaware that Monroe and Pinkney had already concluded a treaty just a few days before.

At the end of July, 1806, Burr sent a trusty messenger, young Samuel Swartwout, to General Wilkinson, bearing a cipher message which declared that their mutual plans had now matured; that the protection of England had been assured; that Burr would depart westward on August 1st, accompanied by his famous daughter, Theodosia, "never to return"; that Burr's detachments were rendezvousing on the Ohio; that, with 500 to 1,000 men, the expedition would proceed down the Mississippi to Natchez to meet Wilkinson; and ended on the note that "the gods invite us to glory and fortune; it remains to be seen whether we deserve the boon."[14]

Without waiting for a reply, in August, 1806, Burr commenced that journey from which, so he thought, he "was never to return." His first rendezvous was Pittsburg, where he picked up a handful of adventurers come to join his party—though nothing near the 500 to 1,000 of whom he boasted; his second was at Blennerhassett Island, where his host was expected to be the financier of his expedition. From the island as a center, Burr sought additional recruits and visited with many of the Western leaders, including John Smith, Andrew Jackson and others.

He was more successful in fascinating the leaders than the rank and file, however; particularly as Federalists like Daveiss on the one hand and Yrujo's unwearied exertions on the other were creating a flock of strange rumors that the true purposes of the expedition were not, as he avowed, to revolutionize Mexico, but to tear the West away from the East and create a new nation.

Wilkinson, in the meantime, was having some prudent second thoughts on the course he should adopt. Which way ought he to lean to protect his own best interests? There had been a time when the Spanish advance across the Sabine River boundary between the two nations created an incident from which it seemed inevitable that war must follow. Secretary of War Dearborn had sent him explicit instructions to repel any invasion of American territory by every means in his power.[15] Yet Wilkinson had refused to act, preferring to keep up his secret communications with Spain—in whose files he was known as Agent Number 13. But the activities of Claiborne and Meade, the American Governors of the adjoining territories, forced him into action of his own and, on September 23rd, he sent a stern note to the Spaniards ordering them to evacuate the west bank of the Sabine at once, or face the consequences. At this particular moment Wilkinson, therefore, had decided to throw in his lot with Burr.

To everyone's surprise, including Wilkinson's, the Spaniards obeyed the peremptory demand and moved back over the Sabine. The war which had seemed so imminent now suddenly evaporated. And with it went Wilkinson's impulse, so that once more he could consider the advantages of remaining in Spain's pay.

Accordingly, when young Swartwout appeared in his headquarters at Natchitoches, a concatenation of circumstances had cooled his ardor for Burr and his plans. The cipher letter, breathing war and disclosing that the die had already been cast, alarmed him. He was now placed in an even worse dilemma than before. It was too late to halt his partner, and he no longer saw any advantage for himself in the plot he had helped concoct. Whatever he did might now involve him in ruin. There was only one solution. To employ the cipher letter, with certain discreet changes in translation, as a means for denouncing Burr as a traitor and to pose both to the American government and the Spaniards as their sole savior and conservator.

He acted on this brilliant idea at once. He arrested Swartwout and other emissaries from Burr, and sent off a series of denunciatory letters to Jefferson by special courier.[16]

Having thus accomplished his Judas-like role, he marched to the Sabine and entered into negotiations with the Spaniards. Each, he proposed, was to retire a considerable distance back from the controversial river, and establish a no man's land between, letting the home governments determine the final boundary. To this the Spanish Commandant readily agreed and on November 5, 1806, the pact known as the "Neutral Ground Treaty" was signed.

Spain was elated at this unexpected stroke of fortune. "This treaty," declared the Captain General of Mexico, "insures the integrity of the Spanish dominions along the whole of the great extension of frontier."[17]

The terms of the pact were in direct defiance of Dearborn's orders, yet were unaccountably made good by instructions from Jefferson, written from Washington after the pact had already been signed. Jefferson now wrote that the probability of an early settlement with Spain made it desirable to avoid all hostilities. Let the Sabine therefore be made "a temporary line of separation between the troops of the two nations," and let Wilkinson propose to the Spanish Commandant a convention for the immediate cessation of hostilities, for the holding of current lines without further establishment of military posts, and for the mutual release of citizens of either nation arrested by the other.[18]

What had prompted this sudden retreat by Jefferson was the alarming nature of the reports emanating from the West concerning Burr's expedition, the necessity of dealing with it, and the necessity of proof to Spain that the American government was not involved in the filibuster.

Burr, however, had run into unexpected difficulties of his own. Daveiss, infuriated at Jefferson's inaction, and seeking political capital, had determined to act in his capacity of United States Attorney. Through a subservient press he roused the neighborhood around Blennerhassett's Island to a frenzy of patriotism against the man in their midst who sought to break up the Union. During Burr's absence, a hastily gathered militia raided the island. On November 5th, Daveiss appeared in Frankfort Court and laid formal accusations against Burr. The latter appeared voluntarily in the proceedings, a Grand Jury was impaneled and the charges were quashed. But Daveiss refused to accept defeat and tried again on December 2nd. Again, after a careful investigation, the Grand Jury vindicated Burr and his followers from any intent to destroy the Union; and Daveiss retired in discomfiture to obscurity.

It was now Jefferson's turn to act and make up for the strange inaction of previous months. On October 22nd, 1806, he convened the Cabinet to discuss the situation; and it was decided to write confidential letters to the Governors of Ohio, Indiana, Mississippi and Orleans, to the District Attorneys of Kentucky, Tennessee and Louisiana to have Burr "strictly watched and on his committing any overt act unequivocally, to have him arrested and tried for treason, misdemeanor, or whatever other offence the Act may amount to." As for *Wilkinson*, however, similarly accused with Burr, "consideration adjourned." [19]

Two days later the Cabinet met again, ordered Preble and Decatur to proceed to New Orleans to take command of a naval force to prevent any outbreak there, and sent John Graham as a special investigator into Kentucky "on Burr's trail, with discretionary powers to consult confidentially with the Governors, & to arrest Burr if he has made himself liable." [20]

The following day, however, the crisis seemed at an end; for the mail from the West had just come in and there was "a total silence" on Burr, which obviously proved "he is committing no overt act against law." Therefore, all former actions were countermanded except those relating to Graham's mission.[21]

Thus matters rested until Wilkinson's fatal communications appeared with the force of a bomb in Washington. Nevertheless, Jefferson had during this interim period been fully convinced of Burr's guilt. He told his son-in-law, Randolph, that "Burr is unquestionably very actively engaged in the Westward in preparations to sever that from this part of the Union. ... We give him all the attention our situation admits: as yet we have no legal proof of any overt act which the law can lay hold of." [22]

Almost simultaneously came the explosive news from Wilkinson and letters from Governor Claiborne, whose knowledge was purely secondhand and based on Wilkinson's horrendous disclosures.[23]

Again Jefferson convened his Cabinet. He now had what he thought was the proof for which he had been waiting. A public proclamation was decided on against the alleged treasonable plot, and was accordingly issued. In the proclamation Jefferson warned all who had joined Burr's schemes without knowledge of their true content to withdraw, commanded all others to cease and desist from their activities, and alerted both civil and military authorities to arrest the participants.[24] Curiously enough, the public proclamation was addressed only to Burr's filibuster against the Spaniards; not a word was breathed of the alleged treasonable attempt to destroy the Union. Yet every one knew exactly what lay behind the phrase in the proclamation concerning "criminal enterprises," and from now on Burr was a marked man among those who would have seen no harm in any expedition against the Spaniard.

In December, Congress convened, and Jefferson sent his Annual Message on the state of the Union. He spoke first of the foreign scene. No major problem had been satisfactorily settled during the year. He hoped, however, that before the session was over favorable news would come from England. As for Spain, matters were unchanged, though Wilkinson had proposed the Sabine River as a temporary line of separation between the opposing troops. He mentioned briefly Burr's expedition, without using his name, *as directed against Spanish territories* in contravention of law, and of the proclamation he had issued. (Again, not a word of any threat to the United States itself.) He called attention to the need for more adequate defenses for New Orleans and the necessity for additional gunboats. Though the Barbary States seemed generally peaceful, yet Tunis was uncertain, and he therefore recommended reinforcements for the Mediterranean fleet. He spoke feelingly of the success of the Lewis and Clark expedition (he always spelt it *Clarke*), and of that conducted by Lieutenant Pike, who had ascended to the source of the Mississippi. Freeman's Red River expedition, he admitted, had not been equally successful.

The year 1808, he continued in congratulatory vein, was approaching when Congress would have jurisdiction to prohibit the slave trade, and suggested that legislation looking to that event be now prepared. Another matter of congratulation was the impending extinguishment of the public debt, $23,000,000 of which had already been retired. He recommended the repeal of the salt tax, and the continuation of the Mediterranean fund for a short additional period. Even so, surpluses were adding up in the Treasury and the problem was what to do with them. He thought it unwise to abolish the imposts on foreign luxuries, which would give an advantage to foreign over domestic manufacturers. He would prefer, he said, to apply the surpluses to "public education, roads, rivers, canals, and such other objects of public improvements as it may be thought proper to add to the constitutional enumeration of federal powers." In other words, it would require a Constitutional amendment to make these objects the subject of federal expenditure and supervision. He ended with his usual arguments against a regular army and his belief in the efficacy of a proper militia system.[25]

The next day he sent a special message urging, in view of the pending negotiations with Great Britain, that the nonimportation act be suspended for a further period.[26]

The messages were calm in tone, skimming in their appraisal of events, and were intended, as all Jefferson's messages, to assure the country that all was serene and that the government had the situation well in hand.

He thought that his message had proposed a national university to the attention of Congress (it had not, except perhaps in the most general terms) and he told his friend, Charles Wilson Peale, to whose Museum in Philadelphia he was constantly contributing fossils, bones, skins and live animals received from Lewis and Clark, that he hoped some day to make the Museum into a national establishment.[27]

In spite of his public optimism, privately he expected trouble with Spain, and with Burr; though he was certain that the proclamation on the latter had put an effectual quietus on any possibility that the people would join him.[28] He described Burr's objects confidentially as an attempt to "seise N. Orleans, from thence attack Mexico, place himself on the throne of Montezuma, add Louisiana to his empire, & the Western states from the Alleganey if he can. I do not believe," he added, "he will gain the crown; but neither am I certain the halter will get its due. A few days will let us see whether the Western states suppress themselves this insurrectionary enterprize, or we shall be obliged to make a great national armament for it." [29] The news of Burr's triumphant acquittals had not yet reached Washington.

But obviously Jefferson was ready for all eventualities. He drafted in his own hand a bill "authorizing the employment of the land or naval forces of the US. in cases of insurrection," and giving him power to use the regular army for internal disturbances. He also drafted another bill that would have permitted the arrest of any person on the "suspicion" that he intended to commit a misdemeanor against the United States and bind him over with sureties.

He sent the two bills to John Dawson with the request that "he will be so good as to copy the within & burn this original, as he is very unwilling to meddle personally with the details of the proceedings of the legislature." [30] Which poses a fine distinction, indeed!

The new Congress went to work on several of the recommendations in the Presidential Messages, notably the recommendations to extend the suspension of the nonintercourse act and prohibit the importation of slaves.

On December 4, 1806, John Randolph introduced a resolution for suspension in the House, where it was passed. Similar action was taken by the Senate, and the much suspended law was put over again until July 1, 1807.[31]

The bill to prohibit the slave trade had no difficulty in passing the Senate, but had rougher going in the House. Weakening amendments were attached to the Senate bill, to which that body refused to accede, particularly one which would have removed a clause prohibiting the transportation of slaves from one state to another. The House held firm, however; and a compromise was proposed which merely forbade the transportation of slaves by coastwise vessels of under forty tons and for purposes of sale. But Randolph and others opposed even this; Randolph calling it a future pretext for emancipation. In his high, piercing voice he declaimed that "he had rather lose the bill, he had rather lose all the bills of the session, he had rather lose every bill passed since the establishment of the Government, than agree to the provision contained in this slave bill. It went to blow up the Constitution in ruins." His parting shot was prophetic: "If ever the time of disunion between the States should arrive, the line of severance would be between the slaveholding and the nonslaveholding States." [32]

In spite of his wild language, and the fierce denunciations of other Southerners, the compromise bill was finally adopted on February 26, 1807, by a vote of 63 to 49 in the House, and the Senate agreed. The importation of slaves into the United States was forbidden after January 1, 1808.

If Randolph's bitter-end struggle against the slavery bill was one of personal conviction, his next move was a deliberate attempt to embarrass Jefferson. On January 16, 1807, he slyly rose to discuss that part of the Annual Message which referred to an unauthorized military expedition against the Spaniard. It was a serious matter, he said gravely, *but*—the President had mentioned no names. He therefore called for all the information in Jefferson's possession relating to the expedition and an account of the measures he had taken to suppress it. Since the demand was logical, the House readily passed the resolution.[33]

The resolution, however, forced Jefferson's hand. He had never truly considered Burr's expedition as a serious threat to the United States, and he seemed aware of certain aspects of it unknown to the general public, and of which publicly he made no mention. He did unbosom himself, however, to Wilkinson. Practically the entire flotilla had been seized on the Ohio, he wrote; nor had even 500 persons ever been involved with Burr. And a part of them had joined as innocent settlers for a huge plot of land known as Bastrop's grant in Texas, while many more were engaged "under the express assurance that the projected enterprise was against Mexico, and secretly authorized by this government." [34]

In other words, Jefferson already knew the truth about Burr's expedition and its aims, and had never been taken in by the alarmist reports which he permitted publicly to circulate. For Burr had purchased the title deeds —though they later proved doubtful—to Bastrop's grant and was intending to settle it as part of his plans. He also hoped to strike at Mexico with Wilkinson's aid and the help of the West, and he *had* let it be known by sundry winks and significant nods that the administration was secretly in back of the expedition.

Randolph's resolution, therefore, forced Jefferson into a masterpiece of evasions and double-talk when, in obedience to the call, he laid his *facts* before the House. He admitted the largest part of his information came in the form of letters, "often containing such a mixture of rumors, conjectures, and suspicions, as render it difficult to sift out the real facts, and unadvisable to hazard more than general outlines ..." Therefore he refused to give up any names of participants in the conspiracy except that of the chief actor—Aaron Burr. His delicacy was doubtless motivated by the consideration that had he yielded all the names, they would have included such men as Senators Breckinridge and Smith, General Andrew Jackson and Governor William Henry Harrison, as well as Wilkinson himself, with explosive personal and political connotations.

Against Burr, however, he now for the first time publicly connected a plot against the West with the expedition against Mexico, and dismissed the settlement of the Bastrop grant as a mere blind. He admitted, though, that the plot against the West had been dropped as soon as Burr saw that the fidelity of its people was not to be shaken, and that thereafter his plans envisaged a seizure of New Orleans, a plundering of its bank and naval and military stores, and an assault on Mexico.[35]

He gently pooh-poohed Wilkinson's belief that Burr had an army of 6,000 to 7,000 men with him, telling that fiery general that all that Burr's flotilla consisted of as it went down the Mississippi were 10 boats, 80 to 100 men and 60 oarsmen, "not all of his party."

In the meantime, Wilkinson had instituted a reign of terror in New Orleans, had summarily seized several of Burr's alleged emissaries—including young Swartwout and Erich Bollman, who had helped Lafayette escape from an Austrian prison—and shipped them to Washington without so much as a court order. He had also declared what was tantamount to martial law, was overriding the civil authorities, and ranting about how he would die sword in hand defending the city against the savage hordes whose attack he momentarily expected.

Jefferson cautiously approved of some of the proceedings, but expressed the hope that Wilkinson would not "extend this deportation to persons against whom there is only suspicion, or shades of offence not strongly marked. In that case, I fear the public sentiment would desert you."[36]

Wilkinson paid no attention to these gentle admonitions. He managed to frighten Claiborne into almost abject acquiescence in the illegal measures he was taking, but the people of the city itself refused to take fire. Indeed, they resented vehemently the doughty general and his abrogation of every legal procedure. Habeas corpus writs were granted for some of Wilkinson's victims—Bollman, Swartwout, Peter V. Ogden and a lawyer named James Alexander, whose only offense seems to have been that he had appeared for the other men. The writs were too late to save Bollman and Swartwout; the other pair were freed by the court, but promptly rearrested and hustled on board ship for Washington before the startled judges could act again.

Meanwhile Burr and his little flotilla, all unknowing of the terrific hullaballoo raging ahead, were dropping peacefully down the Mississippi. They passed Fort Massac and dined in friendly fashion with its commander, though an order for their arrest was on its way to the fort. They dropped anchor on January 11th at Bayou Pierre where, to Burr's utter bewilderment, he was confronted by a band of militia. A comic-opera series of negotiations followed; the thousands of armed men in warships turned out to be some 55 men and boys, a few women, children and servants, the boats mere flatboats, and the vast armament consisted of the usual muskets and rifles that were essential baggage in any trip on western waters.

The net result of the extended negotiations, which took on all the portentousness of two sovereign powers engaged in diplomacy, was that Burr agreed to surrender himself to the civil authorities and stand trial for his alleged misdeeds.

While Wilkinson, fuming that his erstwhile friend had thus escaped his tender mercies, offered $5,000 for Burr's kidnapping to his own jurisdiction, a Grand Jury in Mississippi Territory refused to present an indictment against Burr. But the latter, though free, justly feared the illegal efforts directed against him, and decided on flight. In disguise he rode into the wilderness, was recognized by a backwoods lawyer as he sought directions in Washington County, and was seized by a contingent of soldiers from Fort Stoddard. On March 6, 1807, an armed detachment started out overland with their distinguished prisoner; on March 26th, they arrived in Richmond, and Burr was placed in jail to await his fate.

On March 3, 1807, in the evening, a copy of the long awaited treaty which Monroe and Pinkney had negotiated with Great Britain came into Jefferson's hands in Washington. It was even worse than he had feared.

Already adumbrations had come from the ministers in London that the treaty they were fashioning would not prove satisfactory. For all their congratulatory tone, there was a somewhat apologetic air about their letters. To one such in particular—sent before the treaty had actually been put into final form—Madison answered with considerable asperity. Their communication was disappointing to the President, he declared. Jefferson had decided that "it does not comport with his views of the national sentiment or the legislative policy, that any treaty should be entered into with the British Government which, whilst on every other point it is either limited to or short of strict right, would include no article providing for a case which, both in principle and in practice, is so feelingly connected with the honor and the sovereignty of the nation, as well as with its firm interests, and indeed with the peace of both nations." The case referred to was naturally the matter of impressment, which seemingly had been wholly omitted from the proposed written document. If no clear stipulations on impressment could be obtained, Madison continued, "the negotiation should be made to terminate without any formal pact whatever, but with a mutual understanding, founded on friendly and liberal discussions and explanations, that in practice each party will entirely conform to what may be thus informally settled." And they could assure the British that as long as the *practice* was faithfully respected, Jefferson would recommend to Congress to keep the nonimportation act in suspension.[37]

But long before this strict command not to enter into any treaty which did not in plain terms abolish the practice of impressment reached England, the treaty had been signed and was on its way to the United States with a long, explanatory and apologetic letter from the ministers. They were sorry, they wrote, "that this treaty contains no provision against the impressment of our seamen," though they hastened to add that they expected the practice would be "essentially, if not completely abandoned." They also regretted that "no provision has been made by the treaty to indemnify our citizens for their losses by the late seizures, and other violations of the law of nations." Nor could they speak with enthusiasm of the actual clauses embodied in the treaty.[38]

It might then be asked—and both Jefferson and Madison were to ask it with considerable heat—why they had found it necessary to put their signatures to such a treaty at all. If the Jay Treaty, negotiated under much more inauspicious circumstances, had been so roundly denounced by the Republicans, why should their representatives, when no threat of war impended and without even the *quid pro quo* of the western posts that Jay had received, now enter into an arrangement which gave them considerably less?

In later years Monroe defended himself on the ground that the failure of all negotiations with Spain had had an unfavorable effect on his business in England, and that he had thought it wiser "to get out of the general scrape on the best terms we could," and accept private assurances even though not embodied in formal terms. He also admitted that he had felt slighted by Jefferson and Madison because they failed to reply to his letters for an unusual period of time and, though he does not say so, he may well have wanted to wind up affairs and get back to the United States in time for the impending presidential campaign.[39]

The formal document arrived on March 15th, though an unofficial copy had come into Jefferson's hands on March 3rd. His dismay and wrath were boundless, and he expressed both in unmeasured terms to Dr. Mitchill and John Quincy Adams. He was determined, he told the two members of Congress, to send the official document back the moment it arrived, without bothering to submit it to the Senate. But Madison thought it was not as bad as he had feared, and that it ought to be submitted. So did Robert Smith of the Navy.[40]

Samuel Smith likewise thought that Jefferson, sick and distraught, was taking a heavy responsibility on himself in not letting the Senate have the consideration of the document. After all, he said, the Senate had unanimously advised the President to negotiate a treaty, and everyone knew that he had been coerced by that advice into the attempt. By thus summarily sending the treaty back, he was disgracing his own appointees —and Monroe was his friend. The two ministers must, for their own justification, publish the terms, and Smith thought that the people would like them. "The people," he added significantly, "care little or nothing about the seamen." [41]

But, in spite of this heavy pressure from his Cabinet and fellow Republicans, Jefferson for the moment stuck to his guns. Even on the preliminary sketch of terms which Monroe had cautiously sent him, he had informed Madison that he thought the nation would rather go without a treaty than one which failed to settle the matter of impressments definitively. He thought then, however, that perhaps he ought to take the advice of the Senate on the matter.[42]

The more he considered it, the angrier he became. He set down on paper a careful analysis of the provisions, and asserted that, in effect, Monroe's treaty was a worse document than Jay's had been over a decade before.[43] He listed the *essential* alterations that would have to be made before he would consider it: A provision against impressment; the removal of all limitations on our trade between the West Indies and Europe, particularly the insulting provision that voyages between those two termini must first be broken in an American port, and American customs duties paid; a reservation of our claims to indemnification for prior unlawful seizures; and a withdrawal or modification of the rider which made the treaty contingent on our refusal to honor the Berlin Decree of Napoleon.[44]

Most of these alterations he had already managed to get his Cabinet to agree to, even though its members still wished the treaty as a whole to be submitted to the Senate.[45]

For once, Jefferson had taken the bit in his teeth and was refusing to listen to the advice of his closest personal and political friends. And this in spite of the fact, as Samuel Smith had pointed out, that Republicans generally were not too much disturbed over the impressments, arguing that it was essentially a New England and therefore Federalist matter.

He wrote a strong letter to Monroe demanding that he resume negotiations and obtain modifications. "Depend on it, my dear Sir," he warned, "that it will be considered as a hard treaty when it is known. The British commisrs. appear to have screwed every article as far as it would bear, to have taken everything, & yielded nothing." If nothing better could be obtained, then let Monroe back out of the negotiation.

Then, as a placatory measure, and perhaps to get Monroe out of the way in favor of Madison, he once more offered him the governorship of Orleans, claiming it to be "the 2nd. office in the US in importance." [46]

Jefferson's fierce intransigence—so contradictory of his usual caution and willingness to compromise—might perhaps be attributed to certain personal preoccupations at this time. For one thing, he was secretly exacerbated with Monroe because of John Randolph's open advocacy of his candidacy against Madison in the next election, and he probably believed that Monroe was a party to the machinations of his friends.

For another, his son-in-law, Thomas Mann Randolph, now a member of Congress from Virginia, had been quarreling with his other son-in-law, John W. Eppes, similarly in Congress, and had expressed a jealousy over what he thought was Jefferson's preference for Eppes. For a man as closely bound by family ties as Jefferson, this was a grievous accusation. With a heavy heart he sought to reply to the complaint.

> Your letter received this morning [he wrote Randolph] has given me a pang under which I am overwhelmed. I take up my pen to express some of my thoughts, but thousands will remain which are inexpressible. I had for some days percieved in you a gloom which gave me uneasiness. I knew there was a difference between mr Eppes & yourself, but had no idea it was as deep seated as your letter shows it to be. I never knew the cause, nor ever wished to know it. My affections for you both were warm, as well for your respective merits, as for the sake of the dear objects which formed a link between us. I hoped that neither would expect me to take a part between you, or to participate in your feelings towards each other. What acts of mine can have induced you to suppose that I felt or manifested a preference of him, I cannot conceive.

The tone of the whole letter, indeed, was pleading and pathetically eloquent, avowing an affection for Randolph that was as great as for any man on earth.[47]

Randolph's reply cleared up the misunderstanding. The son-in-law had heard that talebearers had brought to Jefferson a report that he, Randolph, had joined with the Federalists in Congress in censuring Jefferson's public conduct, and he had thought he saw in Jefferson's reactions a definite resentment as a result of it. This Jefferson now vehemently denied.[48]

Thomas Mann Randolph was physically ill at this time, suffering from a fever that prostrated him for a considerable period and from which his convalescence was slow and tedious.[49] But his physical ailments did not tell the whole story. He had always been a sensitive, morbidly brooding individual. In spite of the fact that he was considered one of the best scientific farmers in Virginia, he had not made a financial success and had been on many occasions dependent on the bounty of his father-in-law. Even his political career now in Congress and later as Governor of Virginia turned to dust and ashes in his mouth. A deep-seated gloom and a naturally suspicious nature—of which this incident seemed the first public manifestation—lacerated him in increasing measure until, toward the end of his career, they took outward shape in violent eccentricities and an increasing hatred of both Jefferson and his own wife, Martha, that were to end in tragedy for all concerned.

Monroe refused to be kicked upstairs into obscurity, stubbornly maintaining that he had agreed to the best treaty obtainable under the circumstances. And affairs in England took a sudden turn. Toward the end of March the Whig ministry was turned out of office, and the Tories, even more extreme in their views on the United States, entered office.

Meanwhile Congress, about to adjourn, sent a committee to Jefferson to inquire whether the Senate should remain in session to consider the treaty. "Certainly not," replied Jefferson with considerable passion. "The only way," he added, "he could account for our ministers having signed such a treaty under such circumstances was by supposing that in the first panic of the French imperial decree they had supposed a war to be inevitable, and that America must make common cause with England. He should, however, continue amicable relations with England, and continue the suspension of the Non-importation Act."[50] Jefferson had his dates slightly mixed; for the Berlin Decree did not become known until *after* all the terms of the British treaty had been fixed.

When he heard of the change in the British government, Jefferson expressed satisfaction in the hope that the shift would now rid him of the embarrassment of the treaty.[51] His Cabinet, however, did not see eye to eye with him on his inflexible stand. Madison proposed that in exchange for a definite prohibition on impressments, we should offer England to give up all British sailors on American ships who had not been in our employ for two years prior to the ratifications. Gallatin, who estimated that there were 5,000 British sailors who came under the terms of the offer, was nevertheless willing to comply, provided the impressment issue was definitely settled, and other modifications on trade adopted.[52]

This estimate by Gallatin poses an extremely interesting sidelight on the entire controversy. It presents another view of the controversy more favorable to the British than the customary one. England, engaged in a mighty struggle with Napoleon for survival, found her fleet, the sole bulwark of her security, constantly depleted by deserters and mere refugees from her seafaring population who preferred the safety, better wages and working conditions of the American ships to the dreadful life and dangers of the British navy. It was therefore a matter of vital self-preservation for her to attempt to regain them by every means possible.

Madison was impressed by Gallatin's estimate, and drew back a little. He now sought to keep as many British seamen in our service as he could, and Gallatin agreed. Dearborn and Smith, however, were reluctant to make the retention of British subjects a part of the bargaining.[53]

Jefferson was even more impressed than Madison by Gallatin's disclosure. If, in exchange for the abolition of impressments, he would have to give up all British seamen in the American carrying trade, he might well cripple the very thing over which the entire controversy turned. He therefore advised Madison that "Mr. Gallatin's estimate of the number of foreign seamen in our employ renders it prudent, I think, to suspend all propositions respecting our non-emploiment of them. . . . I am more & more convinced that our best course is, to let the negociation take a friendly nap, & endeavor in the meantime to practice on such of its principles as are mutually acceptable." [54]

There the matter rested until May 20th, when Madison informed the two ministers that Jefferson was "constrained to decline any arrangement, formal or informal, which does not comprise a provision against impressments from American vessels on the high seas, and which would, notwithstanding, be proper to adopt for controlling that species of aggression." To this he added such other changes as both he and Monroe knew the British would never consent to.[55]

CHAPTER 60

The *Chesapeake* Outrage

AS though the headaches, physical and mental, which Jefferson suffered as a result of Monroe's ill-advised treaty were not sufficient, news came to Washington of an outrage committed by a British warship on the very doorstep of the United States that, under normal circumstances and in any other hands but Jefferson's, would have touched off an immediate war with Great Britain.

A British squadron had been lying in wait within the Capes of Chesapeake Bay for a French squadron that had taken refuge at Annapolis. On March 7, 1807, a boat's crew of the British sloop *Halifax* landed in Norfolk, claiming asylum as deserters. The indignant captain, receiving information that the deserters, together with three British sailors from the *Melampus*, had enlisted on the American frigate, *Chesapeake*, demanded redress. But Robert Smith, after inquiries, informed the complainant that the *Melampus* men were in fact American citizens who had been previously impressed by the British, and refused to give them up. He said nothing about the *Halifax* deserters.

The British admiral thereupon issued orders on June 1st that in the event any of his ships met up with the *Chesapeake* on the high seas, she was to be boarded and searched. He made no mention of what was to be done if the American warship refused to submit to search.

The *Chesapeake* was at the time being outfitted in the Washington naval yard and at Hampton Roads for service in the Mediterranean. On the morning of June 22nd, with Captain James Barron on board as commodore and Charles Gordon as captain, the American frigate stood out to sea. She carried an armament of twenty-eight eighteen-pounders and twelve thirty-two-pound carronades, but she was still in a state of unpreparedness. As the ship sailed down the Roads, she passed the British fleet and saw the *Leopard*, a frigate of the same class as herself, suddenly hoist sails and stand out to sea.

Wholly unsuspecting, the American warship continued on her way. In midafternoon, when both ships were outside the territorial limits of the United States, the *Leopard* hailed the *Chesapeake* and megaphoned that she had dispatches for Barron. A boat came over, but Barron refused to allow the crew on board, though he was handed the order from the British admiral demanding the right to search for deserters. Only *then*, as the boat sheered off, did Barron become suspicious and give orders to prepare his ship for action.

But it was too late. The *Leopard*, under Captain S. P. Humphries, had maneuvered to a favorable windward position, and promptly hailed the *Chesapeake*. Then, without further warning, she fired two shots across the bow of the American ship. Two minutes later, while the American crew was desperately trying to man the guns and break out ammunition, the *Leopard's* full broadside was poured point-blank into the hapless vessel from a distance of 150 to 200 feet. For fifteen minutes more she blasted the wallowing American, with but a single countering shot. With three of his crew dead, and eighteen more, including himself, wounded, with his masts and rigging in a shambles, Barron ordered the *Chesapeake's* flag to be struck. The British boarded, searched the vessel and took off the three impressed Americans who had deserted from the *Melampus*, as well as a deserter from the *Halifax*.

The *Leopard* then sheered off, and the crippled American limped back to Norfolk in humiliation and disgrace. Barron was later court-martialed for his share in the action, but was acquitted of all charges except the single one that he had failed to prepare for action swiftly enough. For this he was suspended from service for five years.

The news of the outrage shocked the United States as it had never been shocked before. For the first time since the Revolution the nation was wholly united. A mob ran riot in the streets of Norfolk, attacking British sailors on shore and clamoring for war. The town officials decreed an embargo against the British fleet that had been accustomed to land its men and purchase stores. New York held a tumultuous protest meeting, and even Boston, the seat and fount of Federalism, followed suit; though it was to be noted that the members of the Essex Junto were discreetly absent.

Jefferson, on receipt of the news, promptly called his Cabinet into session. Most of its members had already scattered for the summer, and it was not until July 2nd that it could be convened. Jefferson read to his Cabinet a Proclamation he had in readiness, and it was adopted without any parley.

The Proclamation discoursed at length on the prior wanton disregard for our laws, our citizens and our property which England had displayed. Our repeated representations had gone unheeded, nor had a single offense been punished. The *Chesapeake* outrage, "transcending all we have suffered, brings the public sensibility to a serious crisis, and forbearance to a necessary pause."

Therefore, Jefferson proclaimed that all armed vessels of Great Britain in the harbors or waters of the United States were commanded to depart at once, and any further entrance interdicted. Should they fail to do so, then all Americans were forbidden intercourse with or the furnishing of supplies to them; and all who failed to heed the interdict—Americans or English—were to be placed under arrest.[1]

This was as far as Jefferson felt he could go without further powers from Congress, then not in session. "It is our duty," he declared, "not to commit [Congress] by doing anything which would have to be retracted. We may, however, exercise the powers entrusted to us for preventing future insults within our harbors, & claim firmly satisfaction for the past." [2]

He further explained the principles that motivated him in this emergency in a letter to Vice-President Clinton. "1. That the usage of nations requires that we shall give the offender an opportunity of making reparation & avoiding war. 2. That we should give time to our merchants to get in their property & vessels & our seamen now afloat. And 3. That the power of declaring war being with the Legislature, the executive should do nothing, necessarily committing them to decide for war in preference of non-intercourse, which will be preferred by a great many." [3]

It is obvious from this last provision where Jefferson's own preference lay. He did *not* want war, and he thought this was a splendid opportunity to prove the effectiveness of that nonintercourse to which he had been steadfastly loyal since the earliest days of the Republic as a means for bringing recalcitrant nations to their knees. Nor did he take any steps to convene Congress, who alone had the power of declaring war.

The nation, however, was not as restrained as Jefferson seemed to think. Even his own Republicans thought his Proclamation a tame affair, and John Randolph openly declared it to be a mere apology to England for the *Chesapeake* not having submitted to search. Joseph Nicholson, an Old Guard Republican, told Gallatin that "but one feeling pervades the nation; all distinctions of Federalism and Democracy are vanished. The people are ready to submit to any deprivation; and if we withdraw ourselves within our own shell, and turn loose some thousands of privateers, we shall obtain in a little time an absolute renunciation of the right of search for the purposes of impressment. A parley will prove fatal; for the merchants will begin to calculate. They rule us, and we should take them before their resentment is superseded by considerations of profit and loss. I trust in God the 'Revenge' is going out to bring Monroe and Pinkney home." [4]

Nicholson was correct in his estimate of the temper of the people. Had war come over the *Chesapeake* instead of years later during Madison's administration for less obvious causes, there would have been a unity and an enthusiasm behind it that did not then exist, and the whole course of that war would have been considerably different from the actuality.

Even Gallatin, who opposed all war as a setback to his beloved Treasury, was this time compelled to admit that "with you, I believe that war is inevitable." [5] Jefferson, however, thought otherwise.

Only a month before, Jefferson had expressed himself as being merely one member of the Cabinet, and that the government of the United States was in fact a Directory. In a hitherto unpublished letter to Short, he set down his views on the matter:

Our government, altho', in theory, subject to be directed by the unadvised will of the President, is, and from its origin has been, a very different thing in practice.... All matters of importance or difficulty are submitted to all the heads of departments comprising the cabinet; sometimes by the President's consulting them separately & successively as they happen to call on him; but in the gravest cases by calling them together, discussing the subject maturely, and finally taking the vote, on which the President counts himself but as one: so that in all important cases the Executive is, in fact, a Directory, which certainly the President might controul, but of this there was never an example either in the first or the present administration. I have heard indeed that my predecessor sometimes decided things against his council by dashing & trampling his wig on the floor.[6]

At the same meeting of the Cabinet which approved Jefferson's Proclamation, it was determined to recall the Mediterranean fleet to home waters, and to send the *Revenge* with dispatches to England to demand satisfaction for the attack on the *Chesapeake*, including a complete disavowal both of the attack itself and of the principle of searching public armed vessels, a restoration of the seized sailors, and a recall of Admiral Barclay, on whose orders the outrage had been based. It was also determined to send an account of the incident to the Czar of Russia, doubtless to engage his interest and intervention.[7] Three days later, the Cabinet approved a call on the State Governors for 100,000 militia; those on the seacoast to be "ready for any emergency, and for those in the North we may look to a winter expedn against Canada."[8] By July 26th, they were preparing defenses for Norfolk, under threat from the British fleet, and readying an attack on "Upper Canada & the upper part of Lower Canada, as far as the mouth of Richlieu [*sic*] river," and furnishing a complete schedule of plans for defense and offense.[9]

Certainly the Cabinet was ready for war, had Jefferson only given the signal.

Meanwhile, the British fleet was furnishing the American people with new fuel for indignation and warlike fervor. Instead of meekly obeying the President's Proclamation of interdict and withdrawing from American waters, it adopted instead a most arrogant and menacing attitude. It demanded as of right the privilege of landing its parties at Norfolk and of obtaining water and supplies, and it placed what was in effect an actual blockade against the beleaguered port.

So menacing was the British mien, in fact, that Governor William H. Cabell sought to mobilize his militia and sent anguished calls for help to the national government. Jefferson himself admitted that the British had "their foot on the threshold of war," and that "blows may be hourly possible." He therefore dispatched an urgent message to Dearborn, the Secretary of War, to return posthaste to Washington from New York, where he had gone to supervise the defense of that city.[10]

The President even sent a comic-opera spy down to the menaced coast to report on the movements of the British squadron—one William Tatham, an old Virginia neighbor who had supported him only recently with affidavits concerning his ill-fated last days in the Virginia governorship. Tatham bombarded Jefferson from Lynnhaven with a most astounding series of daily expresses. He was sending fishing and whaling boats out to sea to reconnoiter the British, he avowed, and his dispatches, in the best spy-thriller style, were compounded of reports, rumors, facts, alarms and hideous forebodings inextricably mixed together.[11]

In spite of these warlike preparations, Jefferson still sought a *modus vivendi.* If the British warships would give "assurance of immediate departure from our waters," he wrote the Governor of Virginia, "they may have the supplies necessary to carry them to Halifax or the West Indies." He explained this seeming retreat from the uncompromising tone of his Proclamation. "Their retirement would prevent the necessity of a resort to force, and give us time to get in our ships, our property, and our seamen, now under the grasp of our adversary; probably not less than 20,000 of the latter are now exposed on the ocean, whose loss would cripple us in the outset more than the loss of several battles." [12] Actually, Jefferson was playing for time. He was a firm believer in delay. Most matters, he had discovered in the past, were solvable by the mere lapse of time, and he hoped that some measure of satisfaction would eventually be received from the British Ministry and thereby avoid the necessity for a shooting war.[13]

His Republican stalwarts, however, viewed the proceedings with mixed feelings. Joseph H. Nicholson, for example, breathed a warlike ardor. Forbearance, he declared, would be degrading. "The Ministry may probably, and I think will, disavow the late act of their officer; but there are insults and injuries for which neither an individual nor a nation can accept an apology. . . . If Tarquin had begged pardon of Collatinus for ravishing his wife, I think it would not have been granted." [14]

On the other hand, Nathaniel Macon thought that "peace is everything to us," especially in Virginia where the crops were bad, and the planters had been compelled to go into debt. "If the Executive shall put a satisfactory end to the fracas with Great Britain, it will add as much to his reputation as the purchase of Louisiana." [15]

But the Virginia militia was untroubled by qualms. A party from the British ships had come on shore for supplies in defiance of presidential proclamation and congressional enactment. The lusty militia swarmed on them and took them prisoner, thereby adding still another headache to a worried Governor and a harassed President. The Governor, however, was able to dump the problem into the lap of the President. Jefferson replied cautiously that "the relations in which we stand with the British naval force within our waters is so new, that differences of opinion are not to be wondered at respecting the captives, who are the subject of your letter." While he considered them truly as prisoners of war, he nevertheless thought it best to let them go; even though both law and proclamation had rendered their seizure and imprisonment lawful. "Whether we shall do this a second, a third, or a fourth time," he ended lamely, "must still depend on circumstances." [16]

Jefferson himself privately admitted that a voluntary embargo was already in existence, and that American merchants were holding their ships in port, while the insurance companies had stopped their business. He therefore took the last opportunity of a naval vessel setting out to sea to ask the American consul at Leghorn to send him 300 bottles of Montepulciano wine and fifty pounds of "maccaroni." [17] He also admitted, even more privately, that while "my opinion is that we ought never to suffer another armed vessel of any nation to enter our waters," and while he was preparing for war, "I suppose our fate will depend on the successes or reverses of Buonaparte. It is hard," he added wistfully, "to be obliged to wish successes so little consonant with our principles." [18]

With American shipping idle, with memorials and offers of service in war pouring in by every mail from Republican and Federalist alike, Jefferson urged on James Bowdoin, Minister to Spain, that he seek "cordial friendship with France, & peace at least with Spain." The United States, he added, "has never been in such a state of excitement since the battle of Lexington." [19]

Then news came that somewhat eased the mounting tension. The blockading British had retired from Hampton Roads, though Jefferson did not know whether they would be back or not. Nevertheless he seized the opportunity to mobilize his force of sixteen gunboats, while awaiting Captain Decatur's arrival to determine whether "we shall authorize them to use actual force against the British vessels." [20] He still pinned all his faith on the invincibility of these unwieldy monsters.

He continued to blow hot and cold, but always with a single purpose in mind—to unite the nation behind him and, at the same time, delay and delay until the British could be heard from. Though the pressure was heavy on him for an immediate call of Congress into special session,[21] he steadfastly refused to issue the summons, stating as his ostensible reason that he did not want to give "too quick an alarm to the adversary." Yet, in the next breath, he declared that the British "have often enough, God knows, given us cause of war before; but it has been on points which would not have united the nation. But now they have touched a chord which vibrates in every heart. Now then is the time to settle the old and the new." [22]

And, in the very midst of a possible war with England which he sought every avenue to avoid, he was ready and willing to go to war with Spain—or, at least, so he tried to convey to them. For Spain had taken this particular crisis in American affairs to demand satisfaction for the negligence or connivance of the United States in permitting the Miranda expedition to be outfitted in American waters. As always, Jefferson reserved his most violent language and most menacing threats for the Spaniard.

"If anything Thrasonic & foolish from Spain could add to my contempt of that government," he told Madison indignantly, "it would be the demand of satisfaction now made." As soon as we can gather proofs of their western intrigues—by which he meant the Burr "conspiracy"—let us, if Congress approves, "in the same instant make reprisals on the Floridas, until satisfaction for that & the spoliations, and until a settlement of boundary. I had rather have war against Spain than not, if we go to war against England. Our southern defensive force can take the Floridas, volunteers for a Mexican army will flock to our standard, and rich pabulum will be offered to our privateers in the plunder of their commerce & coasts. Probably Cuba would add itself to our confederation." [23] But was not this exactly what Burr had attempted, and for which he was now on trial for his life in Richmond?

At the same time Jefferson considered carefully Robert Fulton's proposition for the use of torpedoes in defending harbors, though he did not agree with the enthusiastic inventor's claim that it was the *only* type of defense required. He was more interested, however, in what Fulton had failed to propose—the use of submarines for attaching the torpedoes to the bottoms of enemy ships. Would not Fulton look into this further? [24]

Years later, when we were actually at war with England and Madison was President, Jefferson still held to his belief that subaqueous guns, torpedoes and submarines might profitably be used to counterbalance the overwhelming surface force of the British.[25]

Thomas Paine also sent an invention to Jefferson—a model of a doubly armed gunboat, with two guns in the bow instead of one. This was even closer to the President's heart than torpedoes or submarines. "Believing, myself," he wrote back, "that gunboats are the only *water* defence which can be useful to us, & protect us from the ruinous folly of a navy, I am pleased with everything which promises to improve them." [26]

Nothing was more calculated to excite Federalist ridicule than Jefferson's firm faith in the efficacy of gunboats over a navy. Even his old friend of the European years—John Trumbull—broke sharply with him on this issue. Trumbull published an attack on Jefferson's theory in a newspaper which, he later confided to his Autobiography, was able "to dissolve that illusion, and to show his admirers, that however great Mr. Jefferson's philosophical and political reputation might be, he was, in the year 1807, no more qualified to lead in naval defense, than he was in warfare on land, in 1781, when, as governor of Virginia, his conduct demonstrated that he possessed no military talents." [27]

In the midst of these alarums and heavy clouds of war, the navy vessel *Revenge* was sailing slowly for England bearing instructions from Madison to Monroe. "This enormity," wrote Madison firmly, "is not a subject for discussion." Monroe must *demand* satisfaction from the British government. "A formal disavowal of the deed, and restoration of the four seamen to the ship from which they were taken, are things of course, and indispensable. As a security for the future, an entire abolition of impressments from vessels under the flag of the United States, if not already arranged, is also to make an indispensable part of the satisfaction." [28]

Monroe viewed these peremptory instructions with dismay. He was already sufficiently resentful over the treatment which he deemed Madison and Jefferson had meted out to him, even though Jefferson had painfully sought to placate him with assurances that he intended to preserve a strict neutrality in the competition of Monroe and Madison for the Presidency.[29] This was somewhat disingenuous. Jefferson was *not* neutral; he was doing his best behind the scenes for Madison; and was later to write Dupont that "there will be no question who is to be my successor. Of this be assured, whatever may be said by newspapers & private correspondencies." [30]

Monroe was not taken in by the pretense, having been well briefed by John Randolph and others. He commenced the draft of a reply to Jefferson which, after much erasings and interlineations, he decided it would be wiser not to send. "At no period of my life," he said bitterly, "was I ever subjected to more inquietude than I have suffered since my return from Spain. I have found myself plac'd in a situation thro' the whole of this interval altogether unexpected & in consideration of the parties to it equally novel." He documented his grievances. He had wished to resign and sail home, but all his requests had met with a blank silence. No instructions had come to him to "mark my course" in the negotiations with England that had been forced upon him; and during this period of "perfect silence" the newspapers had teemed with reports that he was to be replaced. In fact, Pinkney had been foisted on him without warning.[31]

Now, when more than ever he wanted to go home to repair his political fences, this new negotiation, cluttered with impossible restrictions, was placed on his shoulders.

Yet he did his best. The new Foreign Minister of England, George Canning, was an able man. He saw at once the justice of the remark made by his own Minister to Washington that if he rendered a measure of satisfaction for the *Chesapeake* outrage, it would be impossible for Congress to go to war on the other questions in dispute, notably that of impressment.[32] Canning, in fact, had independently come to the same conclusion. Receiving the report of the incident from his own officers before Monroe knew about it, he dropped an oblique note to the latter hinting that something had happened for which, if proven authentic, he might be willing to offer adequate reparations.[33]

The bewildered American Minister first realized what Canning was alluding to when the *Revenge* delivered its packet of papers. He promptly sought out Canning and laid his instructions before him. But the Englishman interposed a masterly delay. He was sending, he told Monroe and Pinkney, a special envoy, William Rose, to Washington to adjust the *Chesapeake* affair. He admitted, however, that Rose would carry no instructions on the vital question of the search of *merchant* vessels and impressments from them.[34]

On being importuned by Monroe for a definite reply on that matter, he coldly retorted that "the nature of Mr. Monroe's instructions [coupling the impressment issue] has unfortunately precluded any settlement" of the *Chesapeake* affair, and that Rose would take it up separately.[35]

Thus completely by-passed, and seething with resentment at his treatment both in London and in Washington, Monroe threw up his commission and sailed for the United States on October 29th, leaving Pinkney in charge. Yet hardly had he quit the English shore when Canning sent an apology at least for the admiral's order that had originally authorized the outrage; though immediately nullifying its effect by issuing one of the most notorious of the British Orders in Council, dated November 11, 1807, which decreed that any American ship, no matter what its cargo, was liable to seizure if it sailed to any European port from which English ships were excluded, *unless* it first stopped at a British port and obtained a license.

In spite of his official distractions in this period of crisis, Jefferson did not forget his private affairs. He had ordered wines from Italy; he also ordered them from France; but he insisted on getting only the soft and silky type (by which he evidently meant a semisweet wine) and not those which were dry and hard. In a previous shipment he had received "artichoke bottoms, mustard de Mailly, vinaigre d'estragon, Maccaroni, Parmesan & Smyrna raisins."

All his French consignments came from Stephen Cathalan, whom he had met when in France. To him he unburdened himself: "My head is well silvered by eight grandchildren. I have one daughter only remaining alive. At the close of my present term I shall retire to their bosoms, & to the enjoiment of my farms and books, a felicity which the times in which my existence has happened to be placed, has never permitted me to know. I have one other great consolation that after 40. years of service to my country I retire poorer than when I entered it. Not that I have any thing to reproach them with. They have always allowed me as much as I thought I deserved myself. But I have believed it my duty to spend, for their credit, whatever they allowed me and something more. No servant ever retired better satisfied with his employers."[36]

He painted a far gloomier picture to his daughter than this serenely Spartan and bucolic view. He was deeply worried over the affairs of her husband, who was in considerable financial difficulties. He had hoped, he wrote Martha, that the perquisites of his Presidency would have enabled him to help Randolph, but "so far otherwise has it turned out that I have now the gloomy prospect of retiring from office loaded with serious debts, which will materially affect the tranquillity of my retirement." And then, for Randolph's benefit, he read her a homily on the necessity for living within one's income! [37]

Before he departed to Monticello for the summer months, he sent directions to his overseer for work to be done on the plantation. The dam was to be finished and the mill repaired; fences were to be built and the fields cleaned up. He issued meticulous instructions for every phase of plantation activity: plant corn, oats and red clover. Cut wood, level the garden and attend to the hogs and sheep. Employ a gang of 17 hands on the farm and for repairs; and 10 hands in the nailery. Employ a smith for superintendence. Store the avails of the mill that had been paid in kind. Issue a good striped blanket every three years to the hands, and give them fish, pork and other products as their food rations. Do all planting horizontally (to prevent soil erosion) "in the manner that mr Randolph does his." [38]

His interest in architecture remained keen and unabated. He had commenced building operations for a second home at Poplar Forest in the form of a regular octagon, which struck his fancy as the most appropriate and graceful of any geometric form. He finally came to the same conclusion for Monticello where, however, he attached supporting wings and a central dome. He hoped to use Poplar Forest as a quiet retreat from the constant turmoil of Monticello, and worked on it at odd intervals. Though it was yet unfinished, he occupied it after quitting the Presidency. He watched the building operations of his friends with avidity, and his hands itched to plan their dwellings. Among some of the houses that he thus designed were the habitations of Madison, Monroe, John H. Cocke at Bremo, Randolph Harrison at Ampthill, his son-in-law and daughter at Edgehill, and others.

Washington was still under construction, and it would have been beyond Jefferson's power to avoid taking an intimate part in the building; though thereby he managed to exasperate and infuriate the professional architect, Benjamin Henry Latrobe.

He himself had appointed Latrobe as Superintendent of Buildings, but he interfered at every step of the proceedings. Their enthusiasms clashed. Latrobe was a Grecian, whereas Jefferson clung to the Roman adaptations, as evidenced by Nîmes, the Pantheon and the Palladian variations. Latrobe wished to place an ornate lantern over the new House of Representatives. Jefferson turned the idea down peremptorily. "You know my reverence for the Graecian & Roman style of architecture," he wrote Latrobe. "I do not recollect ever to have seen in their buildings a single instance of a lanthern, Cupola, or belfry." He considered these the degenerate inventions of the Italians for their churches. He wanted the central part of the Capitol to be done wholly in the style of the Pantheon, without "lantherns" or any such "modern" features.[39]

They clashed on other architectural fine points as well. Jefferson wanted the Corinthian order for the supporting columns, while Latrobe insisted on the simpler Doric. Jefferson demanded glass panels in the ceiling for

Courtesy the Burton Harrison Randall Collection

MARTHA JEFFERSON

Painting by Thomas Sully

Courtesy the James Monroe Law Office and Museum, Fredericksburg, Va.

JAMES MONROE

Painting by Rembrandt Peale

the light to enter, as he had seen in the Halle au Blé in Paris, and Latrobe would have none of them.

Latrobe replied with elaborate sarcasm: "I am very sensible of the honor you do me in discussing with me the merits of the detail of the public building. I know well that *to you* it is my duty to obey implicitly or to resign my office: to myself it is my duty to maintain myself in a situation in which I can provide for my family by all honorable means." Then he proceeded to dispute violently with Jefferson on the merits of his "lanthern" and in opposition to glass panels; pointing out that the times, the nature of their religion, and the climate were different from Greek and Roman days, and therefore buildings must be constructed on different principles.[40]

This was touching Jefferson on his tenderest and most sensitive spot. One might dispute with him calmly and equably on politics, religion, ethics, science and immortality; but *not* on architecture.

He seemingly never answered Latrobe, but he nursed his grievance. The following year he was careful, when transmitting Latrobe's report of work in progress to Congress, to dissociate himself from the excess of the actual cost over the funds officially appropriated. He denied even knowing about the discrepancy until the last moment.

But he wrote an admonitory letter to Latrobe. He intended, he said, to prevent the deficit of a single dollar hereafter. "It was so contrary to the principles of our Government, which make the representatives of the people the sole arbitors of the public expense, and do not permit any work to be forced on them on a larger scale than their judgment deems adapted to the circumstances of the Nation."[41]

It was not until passions had cooled and Jefferson had yielded his responsibility for the Capitol by retirement, that the two great architects were finally reconciled.

Jefferson spent the summer of 1807 as usual at Monticello, in spite of the war clouds that overshadowed relations with England and Spain, and in spite of the sensation of Burr's trial. Returning to Washington in October, he had an accident. While fording the Rapidan in his carriage, his horse Castor slipped and became entangled in the shafts. The water swept into the carriage and Castor almost drowned; but the servants jumped out and cut him loose just in time. Jefferson's funds were also swept away.[42]

As a compensation, however, he found that the war fever in Washington had abated considerably, just as he had expected it would. The members of Congress, come to attend the impending session, he reported, "are extremely disposed for peace: and as there is no doubt Gr. Br. will disavow the act of the Leopard, I am inclined to believe they will be more disposed to combat her practice of impressment by a non-importation law than by arms. I am at the same time not without all hope she may relinquish the pretension to impressment on our agreeing not to employ her seamen, which it is our interest to agree to. If we resort to non-importation, it will end in war & give her the choice of the moment of declaring it." [43]

This was a curious position for Jefferson now to adopt. He had always insisted that nonimportation was the *only* way for bringing England to her knees and avoiding war. Was he, for the moment, hesitating between the alternatives of peace through a further suspension of the old Non-importation Act, and an outright declaration of war? His forthcoming Message to Congress seems to point in the direction of the second alternative, and Gallatin in fact thought of it as such. In any event, this was the first and last time that Jefferson evinced any uneasiness over his oft-repeated doctrine of nonimportation and embargo.

CHAPTER 61

Trial for Treason

AS though Jefferson did not have enough to bedevil him in his foreign relations, the treason trial of Aaron Burr ran like a scarlet thread through the entire year of 1807 and exacerbated his personal emotions to an extent that perhaps exceeded his preoccupation even with the *Chesapeake* affair and its ominous consequences. Just as Hamilton had been the bête noire of his earlier career, so Burr now became the lightning rod on whom he discharged his wrath and frustrations.

It is obvious that at no time had Jefferson considered the alleged "conspiracy," even as magnified by rumor, as a serious threat to the stability of the Union; while there is evidence that he knew more of Burr's real purposes with respect to Mexico and elsewhere than he later pretended. Nor was Burr any longer the political threat to his continued grasp of the Republican—or, as it was now gradually beginning to be called, the Democratic party—that he might have been in the first days of his administration. Nevertheless, Jefferson was determined to crush him and even, if one must judge only from his outer utterances, to hang him. What may well have intensified his current hatred of the man who had helped elect him President was the sudden interest that the Federalists showed in the case, and his fear that the old combination of Burr and New England might still give him serious trouble. And, as Chief Justice Marshall gradually became enmeshed in the proceedings, a new possibility rose to haunt him—that the judiciary he hated might emerge with more sweeping powers than before—powers that must bring the nation back to that monocratic form he saw lurking in every corner.

The true reason for the vindictiveness with which he pursued the fallen man may be found in his comment to Cabell: "This insurrection [Burr's] will probably show that the fault in our constitution is not that the Executive has too little power, but that the Judiciary either has too much, or holds it under too little responsibility." [1] What started out, indeed, as a personal contest between Jefferson and Burr shortly broadened into the more significant contest between Jefferson and the Judiciary, as exemplified in the person of John Marshall.

When he first heard that Burr was being carried a prisoner to Richmond, he gave vent to two inconsistent observations. In one he declared that "Burr has indeed made a most inglorious exhibition of his much overrated talents. He is now on his way to Richmond for trial." [2] The following day he wrote in different vein: "Burr is now on his way to Richmond for trial. No man's history proves better the value of honesty. With that, what might he not have been!"[3]

But his first exultation at the arrest of Burr and his alleged conspirator friends soon passed. It was not enough to make arrests—and General Wilkinson had done so on a wholesale scale; the arrests must be made to stick with legal evidence that a punishable crime had been committed.

In the territories of Orleans and Mississippi, juries and judges had invariably dismissed proceedings against the Burrites whenever the matters were properly brought into court. It was only by highhanded and illegal methods that Wilkinson had whisked most of his victims out of the initial jurisdictions for condemnation up north.

But even within the range of the national government itself, difficulties appeared. Senator John Adair of Kentucky, for example, together with Peter V. Ogden, one of the messengers to Wilkinson, were incontinently freed by no less a respectable member of the Judiciary than Joseph H. Nicholson, whom Jefferson had recently elevated to the bench. Nicholson indeed apologized for his act, but, as he explained to Jefferson, "very much to my surprize and mortification, there was no Proof of any Nature whatsoever ... and I was under the Necessity of discharging the Prisoners." If Jefferson could furnish such proof, however, he would have them promptly re-arrested.[4]

Jefferson therefore determined that the requisite evidence of a crime must be uncovered. To accomplish this end he instituted what was perhaps one of the most amazing dragnets over the nation ever made by any President. He sought witnesses and affidavits from New Orleans to Maine, from Indiana to New Jersey, and constituted himself prosecutor-in-chief, overriding completely the regular machinery of government in dealing with criminal prosecutions. He even sought, through his Congressional lieutenant, William B. Giles, to obtain a suspension of habeas corpus in this particular case, to avoid the wholesale release of prisoners that seemingly impended. The Senate passed the suspension overwhelmingly in secret session, but when a similar procedure was adopted in the House, a reaction set in, the doors were opened to the public and, in a tumultuous debate led by Jefferson's own son-in-law, John W. Eppes, the measure was snowed under by a vote of 113 to 19.[5]

One of those arrested by the indefatigable Wilkinson was Dr. Justus Erich Bollman, the rescuer of Lafayette. Jefferson caused Bollman to be brought to Madison's office for an interrogation at which he also was present. Bollman was ready to talk, and the two high officers of state listened eagerly to his revelations; revelations which, they hoped, would be sufficient to send Burr to his death.

But, alas, for all Bollman's outpouring of words—which, at Jefferson's behest he later reduced to paper—there was no real evidence of treason. The whole conspiracy, it seemed, was directed against the Spaniard and Mexico, though there was mention of an intention to seize shipping in

New Orleans harbor to convey the filibustering force to Vera Cruz. As a matter of fact, Bollman vigorously denied that there was the slightest intent to revolutionize the western areas of the United States or to seize the funds in the banks of New Orleans, as had been charged.[6] All of which was most disappointing to his auditors. Both Bollman and Swartwout were later released by a ruling of John Marshall.

Meanwhile the stage was being set at Richmond for the trial of the "archconspirator." The government had seized on a dictum of Marshall in the matter of Bollman and Swartwout to bring Burr to Richmond for trial. It was not necessary, so Marshall appeared to have said, for a conspirator to be actually present in the flesh at that assemblage of armed men which constituted the crime of treason.[7]

Unfortunately, from the point of view of the prosecution, Richmond lay in Marshall's bailiwick, and the Chief Justice promptly decided to sit personally in the proceedings. And if there was anyone whom Jefferson hated and feared worse than Burr at this moment, it was Marshall. To the President, Marshall was the embodiment of the Judiciary, the rock on which all his visions of a republican form of government might well split, the last bastion and refuge of the irreconcilable Federalists. As if to prove that his fears were not ill-founded, the Federalists made common cause with the prisoner. So did the enemy in his own ranks—John Randolph and his little band of *Quids*. It was all the more necessary, therefore, to convict Burr and break up this new and unholy alliance.

For the government appeared Caesar A. Rodney, the Attorney General, George Hay, United States District Attorney for Virginia, William Wirt, the future biographer of Patrick Henry, and Alexander McRae, Lieutenant Governor of Virginia. For the defense appeared a galaxy of the best legal talents in the country—Burr himself, who had vied with Hamilton as the leading luminary in New York, Edmund Randolph, Jefferson's old political comrade and former Attorney General and Secretary of State, John Wickham, unrivaled in his comprehensive grasp of the law, and the indomitable Luther Martin, whom Jefferson was to term "the bulldog of Federalism," and whose violent tirades against Jefferson in the "Cresap" matter had given the President some most uncomfortable moments. The chief adversaries were to prove Hay on the one side, and Martin and Wickham on the other; with Marshall sitting in lonely majesty, even when associated with a colorless associate judge on the bench.

The first arguments were directed toward holding Burr for trial on a misdemeanor for setting on foot in the jurisdiction of the United States an expedition against the Spanish possessions; and, more serious in its implications, for treason in seeking the dismemberment of the Union. After lengthy argument, Marshall found that a prima facie case had been spelled out on the misdemeanor, and bound Burr over for a grand jury on that. But on the graver charge of treason, he found no such evidence as the

Constitution required: the actual levying of war against the United States, substantiated by the direct testimony of two witnesses.

Jefferson was in a rage when the news was posted to him in Washington. The misdemeanor charge was trifling, and hardly a man in the country considered an action directed against Spain as anything but meritorious. In his fury against Marshall and Burr, he allowed himself some defective legal reasoning that, under more objective circumstances, he would never have agreed to. "Hitherto we have believed our law to be," he wrote James Bowdoin, "that suspicion on probable grounds was sufficient ground to commit a person for trial, allowing time to collect witnesses till the trial. But the judges here have decided, that conclusive evidence of guilt must be ready in the moment of arrest, or they will discharge the malefactor.... The fact is, that the federalists make Burr's cause their own, and exert their whole influence to shield him from punishment, as they did the adherents of Miranda. And it is unfortunate that federalism is still predominant in our judiciary department, which is consequently in opposition to the legislative and executive branches, and is able to baffle their measures often." [8]

He was still complaining bitterly over the decision several weeks later. "All this, however, will work well," he prophesied. "The nation will judge both the offender and judges for themselves. If a member of the executive or legislature does wrong, the day is never far distant when the people will remove him. They will see then and amend the error in our Constitution, which makes any branch independent of the nation." It was on such an amendment that he placed his hopes for curbing the judiciary; for he admitted that "impeachment is a farce which will not be tried again." [9]

Grand jury proceedings on the misdemeanor were to commence May 22nd. At first it was believed that Wilkinson would not come from New Orleans to testify, and the defense took full advantage of the report. Giles warned Jefferson that if Wilkinson was *not* ordered to Richmond, not merely the case itself but the character of the administration would be badly damaged.[10] Accordingly, it was decided to bring the fire-breathing general north.

Just before the trial opened, Jefferson bethought himself of a method for clinching the testimony. While he could not use Bollman's statement to himself—it had been given under a promise that it would remain confidential—he could offer Bollman a pardon if he would testify against Burr. In fact, he sent a sheaf of blank pardons to George Hay, "to be filled up at your discretion, if you should find a defect of evidence, & believe that this would supply it, by avoiding to give them to gross offenders, unless it be visible that the principal will otherwise escape." [11]

Hay, on whom the whole burden of the prosecution rested, complained constantly to Jefferson. Bollman neither accepted nor rejected the offer of a pardon. Wilkinson had not yet appeared and might have perished in the storms raging at sea. Burr was trying every legal trick to harass him. Marshall was in effect an attorney for the defense. In short, Hay was wearied, exhausted and irritable.[12] And, to cap the climax, one of the grand jurymen was no less a personage than John Randolph of Roanoke, whom Marshall promptly and ill-advisedly appointed foreman of the jury.

On the other hand, the long-awaited Wilkinson finally showed up, resplendent in gold lace and swaggering. Hay was so happy to see him that he changed his former judgment of the general; now he was erect, serene, composed, mild and determined—in short, he had been "most grossly calumniated."[13]

Others, however, did not have Hay's special reasons for admiring Wilkinson. General Andrew Jackson was denouncing the noble general "in the coarsest terms in every company";[14] while young Swartwout rudely shouldered him off the sidewalk and offered him the satisfaction of a duel if Wilkinson resented the physical contact. But Wilkinson pocketed the insult in silence.

From the distance of Washington, Jefferson was watching the proceedings intently. He wanted the entire evidence taken down verbatim for later presentation to Congress; and he directed Hay, if no true bill were to be found by the grand jury, to interrogate the witnesses privately. "Go into any expense necessary for this purpose," he ordered, "and meet it from the funds provided by the Attorney General for the other expenses."[15]

In the midst of the proceedings, the dreaded case of Marbury v. Madison was cited—that case in which Marshall had once skillfully set forth the proposition that the courts could declare an act of Congress unconstitutional. Jefferson reacted vehemently. "I think it material," he told Hay, "to stop at the threshold the citing that case as authority, and to have it denied to be law.... On this construction I have hitherto acted; on this I shall ever act, and maintain it with the powers of the government, against any control which may be attempted by the judges, in subversion of the independence of the executive & Senate within their peculiar department.... I have long wished," he continued grimly, "for a proper occasion to have the gratuitous opinion in Marbury v. Madison brought before the public, and denounced as not law; & I think the present a fortunate one, because it occupies such a place in the public attention."[16] Unfortunately, the reference had been made in passing, and Hay never had a chance to make a full dress issue of it.

Then, in the middle of the proceedings, a bombshell burst. The defense demanded that a subpoena *duces tecum* be issued to the President of the United States to produce those letters from Wilkinson and others on which his message to Congress concerning Burr had been predicated. Hay countered angrily that the court had no power to compel the Chief Executive's attendance; and Marshall himself called for argument on the point the following day.

But Hay, fearful that the decision would go against him, sent an express to Jefferson begging him to forward the documents, so that the question of his personal appearance might be avoided.[17]

Jefferson was confronted with a dilemma. He denied any authority in the judiciary over him, yet he too feared a head-on collision with Marshall if the ruling should go against him. He solved the dilemma therefore by expressing his willingness to furnish such papers to the court voluntarily as the public interest permitted to be communicated, but reserving to himself the right to determine what those papers should be.[18] On the question of any *personal* appearance, however, he was adamant, standing on the Constitutional ground that the President could not be withdrawn from his public duties "by any co-ordinate authority."[19]

Marshall, however, prodded by Luther Martin of the defense, issued the subpoena without any strings attached. Jefferson raged at the news and turned all his wrath against the insistent Luther Martin, whom he had private reasons to detest. Something must be done, he fumed to Hay and to Rodney, about this "unprincipled & impudent federal bull-dog." Could not Martin be indicted with Burr as *particeps criminis* in his treason? Could they not "break down the impudent supporters of Burr by shewing to the world that they are his accomplices?"[20] Yet he sent the documents required, and Marshall did not press the issue of his personal appearance. So that this grave constitutional question remained in abeyance.

The prosecution—and Jefferson—heaved a sigh of relief when Wilkinson finally appeared. With him in the witness chair, Burr was as good as convicted. Jefferson hastened to express his public confidence in the general by a congratulatory letter. "You have indeed had a fiery trial at New Orleans," he wrote, "but it was soon apparent that the clamorous were only the criminal, endeavoring to turn the public attention from themselves & their leader upon any other object."[21]

It was essential indeed for Jefferson publicly to bolster Wilkinson; for, should the latter be discredited, his whole administration might go down with him. It was for that reason that Jefferson resolutely shut his ears and eyes to all warnings against Wilkinson, and to plain-spoken allegations that the general had been in the pay of Spain for many years.[22]

But Wilkinson did not make a good impression as a witness. He writhed under the relentless cross-examination of Burr's counsel and of John Randolph as jury foreman, even though his trump card, the cipher letter, could not be evaded. He was even attacked and submitted to indignities for his reign of terror and intimidation of witnesses in New Orleans. It was only by a vote of 9 to 7 that Wilkinson did not find himself in the prisoner's box as well as Burr. Randolph was disgusted at his intended victim's narrow escape. He called him a "villain" and a "finished scoundrel," and through him would have hit at Jefferson.[23]

Nevertheless, in spite of the discrediting of Wilkinson, the cipher letter gave sufficient evidence to hold Burr, as well as Blennerhassett, on charges of treason and misdemeanor, and the Grand Jury so decided.

All was joy in the administration ranks, and the former defeats forgotten. Every nerve was strained to gather such an overwhelming mass of evidence as must convict Burr before a regular jury. The treason trial opened on August 3rd, with a hundred government witnesses rounded up for testimony. They ranged from Wilkinson to General William Eaton, from Colonel George Morgan to a Major Bruff.

But not all of them had a chance to present their testimony. Hardly had General Eaton, as the first witness, taken the stand, when Burr interposed the fundamental objection that before *corroborative* testimony could be adduced, the *overt act* of treason itself must be proven, as required by the Constitution. Marshall overruled him as to the order of testimony, though admitting the basis of the objection. Witness after witness thereupon took the stand to narrate what had happened on Blennerhassett Island, the locus of that overt act on which the prosecution relied.

When they were ended, the defense moved for an arrest of testimony and a dismissal, on the ground that no overt act had been proved; and that, even if proved, Burr was conceded not to have been present on the Island at the time. After some magnificent forensic displays on either side of the motion, Marshall rendered his decision. Under the Constitution and the common law, he declared, the presence of Burr was essential at the site of the overt act for a conviction, and thereupon turned the case over to the jury without further ado. The jury returned forthwith with a Scotch verdict of "not guilty, because not proven guilty." The great treason trial was over, and Burr was acquitted.

George Hay was sick and disheartened; though he was so fed up with the whole business that he believed Marshall's abrupt action had actually saved his life.[24]

But Jefferson was determined not to let Burr escape this easily. Let him at least be convicted on the misdemeanor charge; let the testimony of every witness be taken and preserved so that Congress could make the necessary provisions for the future. "The event has been what was evidently intended from the beginning of the trial . . ." he fumed to Hay. "This criminal is preserved to become the rallying point of all the disaffected and the worthless of the United States, and to be the pivot on which all the intrigues and the conspiracies which foreign governments may wish to disturb us with, are to turn." [25]

Hay wearily followed instructions and sought to commence another treason trial in another jurisdiction, but Marshall ruled that the misdemeanor must first be tried in Richmond. The ensuing trial, however, was an anticlimax, and everyone recognized it as such. Identical evidence was introduced, and Marshall ruled identically. Once again there was an arrest of incompetent testimony, and this time the jury brought in a straight verdict of "not guilty."

Then Hay, still in obedience to orders from Washington, sought further treason indictments based on acts in Ohio, Kentucky and Mississippi; but after interminable evidence, Marshall ruled against him, though holding Burr on bail for a misdemeanor in Ohio.

Burr was never brought to trial, however. Fearing Jefferson's pertinacity in his pursuit, he went into hiding and eventually made his way to Europe, where his schemes and adventures bordered on the fantastic; coming home again during the war with England to spend the remainder of his life in obscurity.

By this time Hay was disgusted with Wilkinson. "My confidence in him is shaken, if not destroyed," he told Jefferson. "I am sorry for it, on his own account, on the public account, and because you have expressed opinions in his favor; but you did not know then what you soon will know."[26]

Jefferson, however, clung to his star witness in spite of all the evidence. "The scenes which have been acted at Richmond are such," he consoled his bedraggled General, "as have never before been exhibited in any country where all regard to public character has not yet been thrown off.... However, they will produce an amendment to the Constitution which, keeping the judges independent of the Executive, will not leave them so, of the nation."[27]

His efforts in the direction of such an amendment proved in vain. He drafted a message to the House embodying some of his conclusions, but seemingly it was never sent.[28] On November 5, 1807, Senator Tiffin of Ohio moved a Constitutional amendment limiting judicial office to a term of years, and providing for the removal of judges by the President on the address of two-thirds of the members of both Houses. It was defeated. Giles sought to redefine treason in a bill which passed the Senate, but failed in the House. On the other hand, John Randolph implacably pursued Wilkinson with a series of investigations of his conduct which eventually ended in a dreary swamp of words, and Wilkinson proceeded to further and just as futile triumphs in the War of 1812 that helped wreck the Canadian invasion. A move was made to expel John Smith of Ohio from his Senate seat because of his alleged complicity with Burr, and that failed by a single vote. Smith bowed to the inevitable, and voluntarily resigned.

Under such discouraging circumstances—from Jefferson's point of view—ended what is perhaps the most sensational and important trial in American history.

Congress assembled October 26, 1807, on the President's call to consider the crisis with England over the *Chesapeake* incident. On the following day it listened to the reading of Jefferson's Message.

"Circumstances, fellow citizens," it commenced solemnly, "which seriously threatened the peace of our country have made it a duty to convene you at an earlier period than usual." After a rapid survey of the unsatisfactory relations with England even before the outrage on the *Chesapeake*, Jefferson narrated the facts of the attack and its aftermath—the perhaps even more serious matter of the decree issued by that nation forbidding neutral trade with all European ports allied with the French.

He then went on to give an account of the defensive measures he had taken—the fortification of New York, Charleston and New Orleans, the mobilization of the gunboats and the tentative call for the militia. The raising of a regular army was discreetly left to the consideration of Congress.

Relations with Spain were touched on lightly. The Burr case was laid before the lawmakers, with the remark that "you will be enabled to judge whether the defect was in the testimony, in the law, or in the administration of the law; and wherever it shall be found, the Legislature alone can apply or originate the remedy."[29]

The message had been considerably emasculated from its original drafts. Jefferson had first inserted a significant phrase in his discussion of relations with England: "and the moment seems approaching when we may owe it to mankind as well as to ourselves to restrain wrong by resistance"; as well as other statements of almost equal vigor.[30]

But Gallatin had taken alarm at the seemingly warlike tone of the draft and entered a strong protest. It appeared to him rather "in the shape of a manifesto issued against Great Britain on the eve of a war," he warned Jefferson, "than such as the existing undecided state of affairs seems to require." To him it was proper rather to *prepare* for war while preserving "that caution of language and action which may give us some more time and is best calculated to preserve the remaining chance of peace . . ."[31] Jefferson yielded to the exhortations of his Secretary of Treasury and excised the offending phrases.

The Republican majority went immediately to work on measures to implement the polite suggestions contained in the Message. With commendable speed it passed over both Federalist and *Quid* opposition appropriations for additional defensive fortifications and for a substantial increase in the number of the President's pet gunboats.

Jefferson was satisfied with the result, and particularly with the failure of John Randolph and his *Quids* to override his program. Some twenty of them had held a caucus to organize an opposition, he wrote his daughter; but they would be unable to "shake the good sense & honest intentions of the mass of real republicans. But I am tired," he added, "of a life of contention, and of being the personal object for the hatred of every man, who hates the present state of things."[32]

At the end of November, however, the disturbing news came from England that Canning had refused to consider the *Chesapeake* incident and the impressment issue as a single unit; that he was sending a special envoy to Washington to discuss the former alone, and that Monroe was quitting his post.[33]

Erskine, the British Minister in Washington, had received his own report of the situation, and hastened to confer with Jefferson. The latter was very much taken aback at Canning's brusk communication to Monroe. He thought it "unfriendly, proud & harsh, and looks little like proposing much more as to the Chesapeake than the disavowal of having ordered the act. It manifests little concern to avoid war. As soon as we recieve the same papers from Monroe," he told Thomas Mann Randolph, "we shall communicate them to Congress, & they will take up the question of whether War, Embargo, or Nothing shall be the course. The middle proposition is most likely." [34] At least this was what Jefferson himself advocated.

The moment the official dispatches arrived, Jefferson laid them before Congress with an accompanying confidential Message; following it later, on receipt of the further double news of the British order for strict impressments from neutral vessels and Napoleon's equally strict order for the enforcement of his Berlin Decree, with another Message which recommended the imposition of an embargo. "I deem it my duty," he informed the lawmakers, "to recommend the subject to the consideration of Congress, who will doubtless perceive all the advantages which may be expected from an inhibition of the departure of our vessels from the ports of the United States." [35]

At long last, he had come to the public advocacy of his secret weapon against offending nations—the imposition of an embargo on all communication and commercial intercourse. No ships were to enter; no ships were to depart. The United States was to retreat within its Chinese wall of exclusion, cut itself off from the world, and live in self-containment. He was certain that neither England nor France—but especially England—could long stand the complete excision of the American trade, and must come to terms within a short time. What would happen to the American economy in the meantime was another matter.

On December 14th, the Nonimportation Act of April 18, 1806, several times suspended, automatically went into effect; though the merchant class protested in the strongest possible terms. Therefore the proposed embargo would be but an extension of a law already in force. Gallatin was inclined to favor his chief's idea of an embargo over the Nonimportation Act, provided it was for a limited period only. He was vehemently opposed to a permanent one. "I prefer war to a permanent embargo," he asserted. However, he was wholly sceptical that the imposition of any restrictive measures would obtain better treatment from England. "Governmental prohibitions," he warned, "do always more mischief than had been calculated; and it is not without much hesitation that a statesman should hazard to regulate the concerns of individuals as if he could do it better than themselves." [36] This was *laissez-faire* with a vengeance.

Jefferson refused to heed the Cassandralike warning of his cautious Secretary, and put the Administration forces in Congress in motion.

In the House, John Randolph, for once not altogether at odds with the President, promptly introduced a resolution "that an embargo be laid on all shipping, the property of citizens of the United States, now in port, or which shall hereafter arrive."

But the resolution held limitations which were unsatisfactory to the Jeffersonian cohorts, and the Senate, dispensing with all rules, hurried through its own more sweeping bill on the very day it received the Message, by a vote of 22 to 6. In the afternoon, so great was Jefferson's haste, the bill was rushed to the House. But Randolph and Jacob Crowninshield, whom Jefferson had coupled with Randolph as a leader of the *Quids*, now turned against the whole idea, and a furious debate raged on the Senate bill. Amendment after amendment was proposed to weaken and emasculate it, but the Jeffersonians steadily beat them down with a few minor exceptions, and the House finally concurred on December 21st by a vote of 82 to 44, with Randolph and his die-hards, together with the Federalists, voting in opposition.[37] Jefferson signed the Act on December 22nd, and his dream of an embargo as an effective and peaceful means of coercion now became the law of the land.

CHAPTER 62

Embargo

JEFFERSON now had his Embargo. The question was, what was he going to do with it, and what would the repercussions be? The law declared that all ships within the jurisdiction of the United States, with the exception of departing *foreign* ships, could not sail for any foreign port; and those which intended only to engage in coastwise trade must give a bond that their destination was actually as stated. This last, incidentally, was to furnish a loophole for evasion which gave the government many a headache.

The law had been rushed through with a minimum of consideration and with practically no debate in the Senate. Those who, like Senator John Quincy Adams, had expressed doubts over its necessity on the strength of the papers submitted by the President, were assured that Jefferson wished it merely as an aid in the forthcoming negotiations with the British special envoy. But Adams, though yielding, suspected other reasons which did not appear on the surface. He was correct; for Jefferson knew—and had not seen fit to disclose it to Congress—of the impending British decree imposing a blockade on all French ports, including those of her colonies and allies.[1]

As time went on, Congress passed supplementary acts to both the Embargo and the Nonimportation Laws, tightening the regulations and increasing the penalties in order to plug loopholes as they appeared. One such, in particular, was the suddenly increased overland trade with Canada; and a law was enacted forbidding exports by land as well as by sea.[2]

Jefferson justified the Embargo Act on the basis of the British order of November 14, 1807. "If we had suffered our vessels, cargoes and seamen to have gone out," he asserted, "all would have been taken by England or its enemies, and we must have gone to war to avenge the wrong. It was certainly a better alternative to discontinue all intercourse with these nations till they shall return again to some sense of moral right." [3]

Yet, oddly enough, the very people he was so assiduously protecting—the shipowners, the merchants and the seamen—protested to the skies against the limitations on their movements and the total destruction of their means of livelihood. They were willing to take their chances with foreign search, blockades, restrictions and even confiscations. It was better to take the risk than to sit supinely back and face inevitable ruin. The profits to be made on any cargo that *did* get through were enormous, and more than counterbalanced the losses on others. Furthermore, the Napoleonic threats against any traffic with England could be dismissed as ineffectual. Provided they submitted to the licensing system of the British, they had the British navy to protect them on the high seas and a secure entry into British ports. The Federalists, largely concentrated in the mercantile and shipping areas, were unwearied in denunciation.

"I fear we are about to plunge the nation into the most dreadful calamities . . ." communicated an anonymous New England Congressman to a Federalist newspaper. "I cannot express to you in terms sufficiently strong my abhorrence of *what* we are doing, and the *manner* in which we are doing it." [4]

The Boston press was particularly violent. Under the headline of *Mr. Jefferson Disgraced*, the *New England Palladium* avowed that "Happily for the country, it will soon be well understood by the world that THE PEOPLE of *America*, do not support Mr. Jefferson in his gallic attachments," and insisted that the embargo laws had been dictated by the President's desire to pacify Bonaparte.[5]

Even in Jefferson's native state the merchants were crying havoc. "This Embargo will ruin this state if it continues long," wailed one of them. "They talk of Locking up the Courts of Justice to save the Country from distruction [*sic*]. In 12 hours after the news of the Embargo, flour fell from 5½$ to 2½. at this place, and Tobacco from 5/2 to 3$ and every thing in proportion & god only knows the result." [6]

The grave Constitutional question, however, seemed to have excited little comment; yet the Embargo stretched that much-stretched instrument far beyond the National Bank or even the purchase of Louisiana. It took out of the hands of individuals, as Gallatin had pointed out, the management of their own affairs and property in time of peace; it clamped on states and private citizens a series of controls, restrictions and regulations for which little justification could be found in the express terms of the Constitution. Yet Jefferson did not even discuss privately—as he had in the case of Louisiana—these considerations which went completely against the grain of his own philosophy of a strict construction.[7]

In the midst of the excitement the Republicans in Congress met in caucus to choose their candidates for the Presidential election in the fall. Until the last moment it had been hoped that Jefferson would consent to run again, and resolutions from Republican state legislatures poured in entreating him to serve for a third term. But Jefferson declared it to be his duty to decline, even though the Constitution was silent on the subject. Otherwise, he said, the office might become one for life and even degenerate "into an inheritance." He wanted, he added, to follow "the sound precedent set by an illustrious predecessor." [8]

Accordingly, and with considerable reluctance, the caucus looked elsewhere. It was well known that Monroe was a candidate, and that John

Randolph and his friends were backing him; but it was equally well known that the President, for all his professed neutrality, had chosen Madison as his successor. So hopeless, therefore, was the case for Monroe, that Randolph absented himself from the meeting. Of the 89 present, Madison received 83 votes, with George Clinton and Monroe trailing far behind with 3 votes apiece. Though there was opposition to Clinton for a continuance in the Vice-Presidency, it was deemed wiser to offer it to him to avoid disgruntlement and a possibility of sabotage in New York against Madison. It was also expected that he would decline the office. But the aging Clinton surprised them—and Jefferson—by accepting.[9]

Monroe came home from the debacle of his negotiations with England in a resentful and embittered mood. He blamed his old friends, Jefferson and Madison, for everything that had happened; and did not hesitate to tell Jefferson at least the subject matter of his complaints. He had never in his whole life been treated so badly, he cried. The administration had foisted Pinkney on him (Monroe conveniently forgot that *he* had been foisted on Livingston in France); the treaty they had fashioned had been cavalierly dismissed; and, while disclaiming any idea of revenge, he demanded justice.[10]

Immediately on Monroe's arrival Jefferson had sought to dissociate himself from the candidacies of Monroe and Madison, alluding to them delicately as the "two principal pillars of my happiness." [11] But he now perceived from Monroe's retort that the matter struck much deeper, and that Monroe must be placated if a dangerous schism were not to develop. He therefore cast the blame for Pinkney's appointment on the insistence of Congress; avowed that the treaty had come to his hands on the day of adjournment; and that he had always been careful to absolve both envoys from any blame.[12]

Monroe harkened to the soothing tale, and expressed satisfaction at having his doubts over Jefferson's friendship thus removed. Nevertheless, uneasy in his own mind over the intended treaty, he launched into a long self-justification.[13] Nor did the memory cease from rankling. Two years later, he agreed with John Taylor that two great errors had marred Jefferson's second administration—one was the Embargo; the other, the rejection of Monroe's treaty.[14]

Jefferson was tired of his post and sincerely anxious for the day when he could quit it for the privacy of Monticello and more congenial pursuits. He no longer was able to goad himself from morning to night in the endless job, as he put it, of cleaning out an Augean stable every night, only to find it filled again in the morning. And, for the entire month of January, 1808, he suffered from an infection of the jaw which confined him indoors.[15]

Yet he roused himself sufficiently, when a New York clergyman politely requested him to declare a day of fasting and prayer in the current emergency, to enunciate once more his unalterable opposition to any commingling of religion with government. "I consider the government of the US.," he repeated firmly, "as interdicted by the Constitution from intermeddling with religious institutions, their doctrines, discipline, or exercises.... Certainly no power to prescribe any religious exercise, or to assume authority in religious discipline, has been delegated to the general government.... Fasting & prayer," he pointed out, "are religious exercises. The enjoining them an act of discipline." To the argument that his predecessors in office had so enjoined them, he retorted that they had labored under a misapprehension of their Constitutional powers.[16]

George Rose, Canning's special envoy, appeared in Washington toward the end of January, 1808, and promptly informed Madison that his instructions expressly precluded him from any negotiations over the *Chesapeake* "as long as the proclamation of the President of the United States of the 2nd of July, 1807, shall be in force." Nor, he continued, did he have the power to discuss *anything* but the *Chesapeake*. Nor could he disclose even what offer he was prepared to make on that, until all other points were cleared up; except to assure Madison that it would prove satisfactory.[17]

This certainly was not the language of diplomacy, and both Madison and Jefferson were correct in refusing to permit any such arrogant attitude. Madison countered with equal coldness and brevity that the American government must decline to accede to these unilateral conditions, that Jefferson was determined not to discuss the *Chesapeake* except in conjunction with the matter of the search of public ships and of impressment; and that any *private* disavowal of the outrage would be no substitute for a formal and public apology. As for Rose's own coupling of the incident with Jefferson's proclamation, Madison dismissed that with icy contempt.[18]

Rose retorted that, under such considerations, he was terminating his mission.[19] One wonders then why he had come in the first place, and what Canning expected to gain by this unnecessary display of arrogance and brutality toward the American government and people.

Perhaps some measure of Rose's curtness at this point was due to the knowledge that a large section of New England Federalists were willing to swallow all insults and to go even to the lengths of treason in their eagerness to trample Jefferson in the mud, rid themselves of embargo and nonintercourse, and tie themselves once more to England at any price.

Senator Timothy Pickering, the unreconstructed firebrand from Massachusetts, waited barely two days after Rose's arrival to get in touch with him. He listened with open approval to Rose's strictures on the American government, and departed convinced in his own mind that England was ready to offer concessions on the *Chesapeake* which, if we refused and went to war with her, would place the fault squarely on the United States.[20]

Nor did he stop with mere conviction. Not long after Madison had informed Rose that his conditions were unacceptable to the American government, Pickering wrote openly to the British envoy: "You know my solicitude to have peace preserved between the two nations, and I have therefore taken the liberty to express to you my opinion of the true point of policy to be observed by your Government toward the United States, in case your mission prove unsuccessful; that is, *to let us alone; to bear patiently the wrongs we do ourselves*.... I also know that in the present unexampled state of the world our own best citizens consider the interests of the United States to be interwoven with those of Great Britain, and that our safety depends on hers." He was certain, he added, that the Embargo would overthrow the administration, and that a new one would alter American policy "in a manner propitious to the continuance of peace." [21] This astonishing intervention emanated from the man who, as Secretary of State in Adams's time, had backed the Logan Act which made it a crime to hold communications with a foreign government in pending controversies!

Nor was this the full extent of Federalist activity. April was an election month in Massachusetts, and both the Republican governor, James Sullivan, and an already wavering Federalist, Senator John Quincy Adams, were up for re-election. Pickering injected himself into the campaign with a letter to Sullivan which he demanded should be laid before the state legislature. It viciously attacked the Embargo and used language that looked unmistakably to a separation of the seaboard States from the Union.[22]

Sullivan naturally refused to lay the seditious communication before the legislature; whereupon the Federalists themselves published it. In the storm that followed, Sullivan barely squeezed through; but the legislature went Federalist, and promptly replaced Adams with one of their own party, James Lloyd. It was the first test of the public reaction to the Embargo, and it proved to be a resounding defeat for Jefferson's policies; though it must be remembered that the Massachusetts shipowners, merchants and seamen had been the most severely affected by the cessation of all foreign intercourse.

But other states were in a not much better position. The journal of a sea captain graphically describes conditions in Pennsylvania and New York. "The embargo has produced dreadful effects. The seaports are all crowded with shipping, the sailors have gone off in search of employment, at least one thousand of them from New York alone, in Halifax the British have given them employment. There is supposed to be at this time in Philadelphia 70 thousand barrels of flour, the greatest part of which must sour. Some persons of information appear to think that a continuance of the embargo beyond the ensuing session of Congress will excite a rebellion, particularly in the eastern states, the dutchmen of Pennsylvania say dey [*sic*] will not vote for Jefferson any more—"[23]

Timothy Pickering and the extreme Federalists found other means besides Rose for entering into communication with the British. A certain John Henry, acting discreetly as unofficial agent for Sir James Craig, the Governor of Lower Canada, was able to mingle in the best Federalist circles of Boston and establish valuable contacts with disaffected Americans. He sent regular reports to Craig, which in turn were transmitted to England. He even managed to attend private meetings of the Federalists where measures were discussed to "rouse the people from their lethargy" and "a firm determination expressed that they will not co-operate in a war against England." Thus encouraged, Henry boldly suggested to them a resolution that "in case of a declaration of war the State of Massachusetts should treat separately for itself, and obtain from Great Britain a guarantee of its integrity." Even the most extreme, however, hesitated over this irrevocable move; though they admitted it might be "a very probable step in the last resort. In fine," Henry concluded his report with a flourish, "every man whose opinion I could ascertain was opposed to a war, and attached to the cause of England." [24]

John Quincy Adams got wind of these private meetings and of John Henry's role in them, and called on Jefferson to warn him to be on his guard against the British intrigue with the disaffected Federalists of New England. The seditious activities he had uncovered shocked the conscience of this son of John Adams, and it was now that he turned wholly to Republicanism. He had been pretty much of an independent for some time, and the suspicions of the Massachusetts Federalists over his orthodoxy, as evidenced by their refusal to reappoint him to the Senate, seemed to them thoroughly justified by his later course.[25]

Madison's firm responses to Rose and the latter's prompt decision to consider his mission at an end should have put a stop to all further negotiations. But Jefferson was aghast. This meant war and, for all his bellicose avowals, Jefferson wanted no war. What followed can only be pieced together from Rose's reports to his home government.

Within a few hours after that last fatal conference between Madison and Rose, Samuel Smith, the Secretary of Navy, found means to communicate to the Englishman that the bone of contention—the withdrawal of Jefferson's Proclamation forbidding American ports to British war vessels—might perhaps be taken care of, if Jefferson could find a way to do it "without exposing himself to the charge of inconsistency and disregard of the national honor, and without compromising his own personal weight in the State." Jefferson therefore "earnestly wished that I [Rose] could make, as it were, a bridge over which he might pass" and "justify him in the course which I required should be taken." In any event, however, Rose was to be assured that no war was intended with England; though of course, if *she* attacked, the United States would defend itself and invade Canada.[26]

If Rose is to be believed—and there is no reason why he should not be, in the essentials at least—Jefferson was placing himself in a most humiliating position. While publicly dealing with England with a firm and unwavering hand, privately he was in effect pleading with her and throwing himself on her mercy. It is not a particularly edifying picture.

Rose listened to Smith's indirect proposals without indicating his own reaction, preferring to wait until, as he put it, "the utmost point to which they would go was ascertained."

Then Smith showed up in person, to assure Rose that Jefferson knew of his communications. The President's difficulty, said Smith, "arose from the sacrifice of public opinion which he apprehended must follow from the abandonment of the proclamation. He said I must be aware how dear to Mr. Jefferson his popularity must be, and especially at the close of his political career . . . and he pressed me earnestly to take such steps as would conciliate the President's wish to give his Majesty satisfaction on the point in question and yet to maintain the possession of what was pre-eminently valuable to him."[27]

All this and more, relating to the Floridas, did Smith narrate to Rose in this amazing interview. Certainly Jefferson could not have been aware of Smith's cynical and slighting references to himself; but the whole affair discloses that Jefferson's old skill in negotiation had deserted him. Perhaps the breakdown of his powers at this point can be attributed to his physical illness. Not only was he confined with an infected and swollen jaw, but those periodical migraine headaches which regularly incapacitated thought were upon him, and were to continue for several months.[28]

Finally Rose acceded, and wrote Madison that if the Proclamation were withdrawn, he was certain the entire business could be settled "amicably and satisfactorily." He was even willing to return to England with a report of Jefferson's difficulty; but Jefferson preferred to settle affairs on the spot. At length Madison was empowered to propose that a formal recall of the Proclamation, signed and sealed, but undated, would be placed in Rose's hands for him to insert the date, when agreement had been simultaneously arrived at on the other points. To this Rose rather reluctantly assented, and Jefferson's honor was saved.

Yet, when negotiations on this basis finally commenced, Madison discovered how little Rose had to offer, and how limited were the reparations for the *Chesapeake* affair which England was willing to make. All the humiliations that Jefferson personally, and the United States as a nation, had undergone had been in vain. Canning's proposals for settlement could not be accepted without arousing a storm to which the furore over the Embargo would be a mere bagatelle. Nothing therefore remained but to swallow the original insults and drop the matter; though Madison left the door discreetly open for a while. Rose, however, shut it with something of a bang; and one of the most discreditable episodes in American history had ended.[29]

With nothing further to be expected from England, with the new Order in Council proposing new outrages on America, with France disclosing an equal determination to trample neutral rights *via* the Berlin and Milan decrees, Jefferson now determined to push the Embargo to the limit. At the same time, on a wave of Congressional indignation against both England and France, the regular army was increased to 10,000 men, and a bill became law which gave Jefferson discretionary powers to suspend the Embargo in whole or in part during the Congressional recess. Then the lawmakers adjourned on April 25th, and Jefferson was left to ride the storm alone as best he might.

He would have preferred to the regular army thus furnished him, a provision for a conscripted militia of young men in the age class from twenty to twenty-six, the number of which he estimated at 250,000; but he had feared to place such a "great innovation" before the current Congress. He had also failed twice in obtaining another measure near his heart —"the immediate settlement, by donation of lands, of such a body of militia, in the territories of Orleans & Missisippi, as will be adequate to the defence of New Orleans." [30]

As for the Embargo itself, he wished to give it a fair trial. It was to him, injurious though he acknowledged it to be to private interests, the only alternative to war. "For a certain length of time," he wrote, "I think the embargo is a less evil than war. But after a certain time it will not be so. If peace should not take place in Europe, & if both France and England should refuse to exempt us from their decrees & orders as we shall very strenuously urge, it will remain for Congress when they meet again to say at what moment it will become preferable for us to meet war rather than a longer continuance of the embargo." [31] What he hoped, of course, was that the Embargo would have brought both England and France to their knees *before* Congress met.

But the people, in spite of Jefferson's optimistic statements that, aside from a few Federalists, they were solidly in back of him, were not disposed to wait until Congress met again. On all fronts the pinch was being felt, and evasions grew more numerous.

Jefferson sought to avoid the inevitable consequences to the nation's economy from a cessation of all foreign trade by proposing an increase in home manufactures. It was about this time probably that he copied out into his commonplace book an extract from Voltaire on manufactures in the "Age of Lewis XIV" with the approving comment: "The above extract is peculiarly appropriate to the present period of American history when the good sense of the Nation has been directed to the encouragement of manufactures in which alone true independence subsists—America possesses within itself all the means of extensive manufactories—all that is necessary to ensure their success is proper encouragement from the Government, without which it is vain to calculate on their permanency to produce any National benefit—The great obstacle hitherto in the prosecution of extensive works has been the want of sufficient Capital; to remove which it is necessary either that several individuals combine their funds, or that proper support be given by the Government."

On the latter, Jefferson suggested "liberal premiums for given quantities and qualities of the different articles manufactured"; the invention of "ingenious and useful machines" for which exclusive patents would be granted; and "Acts of Incorporation to Companies established for the prosecution of Manufactures—by this means the Capital of the country is concentred, and monied men will be secure in their advances without being personally obliged to attend to the details of a concern of which they may be entirely ignorant." [32]

One rubs one's eyes. Can this be Jefferson writing, and not Hamilton? In essence this is a résumé of the proposals and arguments of Hamilton's Report on Manufactures, against which Jefferson had directed some of his bitterest diatribes. He was never again in either public or private utterance to attain this vision of an industrial economy, with its complex system of subsidies and perhaps protective tariffs, with its tenderness for "the monied men" and the safeguarding of their absentee interests. What he publicly advocated was merely a system of *domestic* manufactures, in the home or on the plantation, and not the great industrial corporations that are here envisaged. This private comment, buried in his commonplace book, is essentially what the biologists call a *sport*, never to be repeated.

More in line with his normal opinions was the editorial in the *Richmond Enquirer* which declared that "our women should all learn to spin, card, weave, dye and manufacture. . . . We may not have open markets abroad for years, and our planters will want the aid of manufactures to keep up the price of their produce, and to furnish supplies." [33]

It is interesting to note, however, that the semiofficial *National Intelligencer* hailed with satisfaction certain new manufacturing ventures in Virginia that adumbrated Jefferson's proposed corporate efforts. Such enthusiasm had been engendered in Virginia that Richmond had subscribed $500,000 and Petersburg $25,000. "Britain," crowed the newspaper, "seeing what is already done, will anticipate what will happen if she persist in her injustice; she will see that, five years hence, we shall not need a tenth part of the manufactured goods we now receive from her." [34] Unfortunately the Virginia ventures died a-borning.

As already indicated, the people of New England, New York and Pennsylvania were not willing to wait five years, or any part thereof, for England to yield. Those fortunate shipowners who had vessels abroad at the time the Embargo was proclaimed made no effort to bring them home. Instead, they kept them trading in Europe and England, submitting to risks, licensings and searches in order to reap huge profits. Others, not as fortunate, with their ships already in American ports, sought ingenious methods to slip them out on the pretext of the permitted coastal trade and make a dash for the proscribed West Indies colonies; even at the risk of having their bonds forfeited. Still others turned to a flourishing overland trade across the border with Canada; from which the goods were transshipped to England. Congress eventually tried to plug the loophole in the law which permitted this traffic, but it persisted in defiance of law and of enforcement officers.

These ever-increasing evasions and defiances stirred Jefferson to a pitch of wrath reminiscent of his treatment of the British General Hamilton during the Revolution and of Aaron Burr within recent months. The traffic with Canada, indeed, had risen to insurrectionary proportions. Along the vast, insufficiently guarded border, stretching from the northernmost tip of Maine through Vermont to the upper reaches of New York, the defiant inhabitants conducted smuggling operations on an unexampled scale. Huge rafts were constructed to carry the proscribed goods up Lake Champlain and across the St. Lawrence, accompanied by bands of armed and determined men. The Governors of the states involved called out the militia to put a stop to the traffic; there were some armed clashes; but it continued nevertheless and in increasing volume.

So impotent were the usual law enforcement agencies to halt the smuggling that Jefferson issued a proclamation on April 19, 1808, declaring the Champlain area of Vermont in a state of insurrection, commanding the insurgents to disperse, and invoking the combined civil and military powers for their suppression.[35]

But the same situation existed on the New York side. The spring election in New York had disclosed a decided swing against the administration; though Jefferson refused to attribute it to its proper cause—hostility to his Embargo—preferring rather to blame it on "the old man," George Clinton, his Vice-President, who is, he avowed, "unquestionably hostile in his heart, & it is the doings of that family, & not the embargo that has affected the elections in New York."[36]

Yet New York smuggling reached such a peak that Jefferson seriously considered the issuance of another proclamation declaring *its* people in insurrection, determining finally to let the New York militia be called into service to patrol the border and to have the national government pay all expenses. "I think it so important in example," he wrote the Governor of New York, "to crush these audacious proceedings, and to make the offenders feel the consequences of individuals daring to oppose a law by force, that no effort should be spared to compass this object."[37]

But the "audacious proceedings" were prevalent in upper Maine as well; and Jefferson, now at Monticello on his annual vacation, demanded that Gallatin "spare no pains or expense to bring the rascals of Passamaquoddy to justice, and if more force be necessary, agree on the subject with General Dearborn or Mr. Smith [the Secretaries of War and Navy], as to any aid they can spare, and let it go without waiting to consult me."

Gallatin, however, was openly opposed by now to the continuance of the Embargo, and Jefferson sought to placate him with an agreement "to consider any propositions you may make for mitigating the embargo law of April 25th, but so only as not to defeat the object of the law."[38]

But the Secretary of Treasury, though faithfully administering the law, could see no hope of "mitigation" without complete repeal. He saw clearly that the law was unpopular, that the mass of the people supported the smugglers and not the government, and that even friendly enforcement officers were afraid to act. The situation was so bad on Lake Champlain that he resignedly suggested a company of regulars and two armed gunboats to deal with the smuggling.[39]

By July, Gallatin was in open revolt. He told Jefferson plainly that if the Embargo was to be persisted in, two stringent rules must be adopted: first, that not a single vessel be permitted to move without Jefferson's special permission; second, that the Collectors be empowered to seize property anywhere and to dismantle ships in port sufficiently so that they would be unable to sail, whether there was any suspicion of an attempt or not. "I am sensible," he added morosely, "that such arbitrary powers are equally dangerous & odious. But a restrictive measure of the nature of the embargo applied to a nation under such circumstances as the United States cannot be enforced without the assistance of means as strong as the measure itself."[40]

Jefferson refused to heed the warnings of his plain-spoken Secretary; though he was ready enough to use the army and the navy against his fellow Americans, considering the present as a test of powers that would determine the future. "As I do consider the severe enforcement of the embargo to be of an importance," he wrote his Secretary of Navy, Robert Smith, "not to be measured by money, for our future government as well as present objects, I think it will be advisable that during this summer all the gunboats, actually manned and in commission, should be distributed through as many ports and bays as may be necessary to assist the embargo."[41]

The chief evasions, however, came not so much from the sources listed above as from a new coastwise traffic that had strangely sprung up since the imposition of the Embargo, and which received the blessing of such a good Republican governor as James Sullivan of Massachusetts.

It was discovered suddenly that the people of Massachusetts, for example, were in dire need of grain, flour and other staples that could only be obtained from the southern states. These articles were therefore duly placed on board ship at Charleston, Norfolk, etc., ostensibly bound for Boston, New York or Philadelphia. But always some furious storm arose at sea, or the navigational instruments developed peculiar quirks, and the disabled vessel found itself—altogether by accident—in Halifax or in the West Indies where, naturally, to avoid rot or other loss, the cargo was sold—at a very good profit.

Jefferson sought to put a stop to this traffic by sending a circular letter to the State Governors asking that they detain any suspicious vessel bound *anywhere*, and to consider as suspicious any cargo of domestic goods allegedly bound for another American port which was in demand in the foreign market. Only if the particular Governor found that there was an "extraordinary deficiency in supply" of any such article in his own state, and so certified in writing, would a ship be released for that state with the needful cargo. But, warned Jefferson, no such certificate should be issued that might lead to an evasion of the law.[42]

Unfortunately, the power to issue these certificates of necessity only gave the traffic a new turn and served to corrupt Republican governors like Sullivan of Massachusetts.

On July 15th, Gallatin complained to Jefferson that he had received certificates of necessity from Sullivan covering 49,800 barrels of flour, 99,400 bushels of corn, 560 tierces of rice, 2,000 bushels of rye, together with an additional permission for either 7,450 barrels of flour or 30,000 bushels of corn—all addressed to people in Alexandria and Georgetown, Virginia, who were absolutely unknown to the Governor. Later in the day, more certificates poured in from Sullivan to the amount of 6,200 barrels of flour and 9,000 bushels of corn. Nor was Governor Langdon of New Hampshire far behind his obliging colleague of Massachusetts. *He* called for 4,000 barrels of flour and two full cargoes of rice.[43]

It was obvious to both Gallatin and Jefferson what was taking place. Pressure had been brought to bear on the two Governors to issue these certificates, and the cargoes were heading elsewhere than to the states whose necessities were claimed to be so imperative.

Yet tact had to be employed. Sullivan, for instance, was a Republican and the sole survivor of the debacle in his state. Jefferson therefore wrote him delicately that he felt the proposed shipments of food were far beyond the actual needs of his state. "I have thought it advisable to ask the favour of Your Excellency, after the receipt of this letter, to discontinue issuing any other certificates, that we may not unnecessarily administer facilities to the evasion of the embargo laws." However, if Sullivan would furnish Jefferson with data showing what was actually required over the supplies on hand, the latter would see to it that Massachusetts suffered no hardship.[44]

But Sullivan knew the temper of his state. "You may depend on it," he warned Jefferson in return, "that three weeks after these certificates shall be refused, an artificial and actual scarcity will involve this State in mobs, riots, and convulsions, pretendedly on account of the embargo. Your enemies will have an additional triumph, and your friends suffer new mortifications."[45]

Sullivan's frank warning, together with Gallatin's equally frank speaking and the reports that flooded him from all sides, should have given Jefferson pause. The Embargo could not be enforced in the face of popular disapproval, opposition, evasions and downright revolt any more than the much later Prohibition Amendment could be. Yet he persisted stubbornly in the face of all signs and portents, and wrote angrily to Dearborn, then in Maine, that he was removing recalcitrant collectors, that Sullivan "is not up to the tone of these parricides, and I hope on the first symptom of an open opposition of the law by force you will fly to the scene, and aid in suppressing any commotion."[46]

Jefferson realized only too well, however, that a state of embargo that paralyzed the economy of the nation could not be protracted indefinitely. War would be preferable to such life-in-death inaction. He suggested therefore that the American envoys abroad propose to France and England that they remove American ships from the force of their decrees and to drop discreet hints that, if they did not, war might follow.[47]

But both proposals and implied threats fell on deaf ears. Nor was Pinkney's report from London encouraging. While it was true, he said, that the embargo and the loss of American trade had been deeply felt by the English merchants, neither was "decisive," and he underscored the word so that the home administration would be under no illusions.[48]

Yet Jefferson persisted in his course, clinging to the hope that the nations abroad would yield before disaster struck at home. While memorials, protests and angry mail, including even threats of assassination, continued in unabated flood, he was certain that a party was springing up in his favor in England. "If we can weather war at this crisis," he wrote, "I think we shall enjoy a long career of peace."[49]

There was also revolt in his own Cabinet. Aside from Madison, hardly a member supported him wholeheartedly in this venture. Robert Smith was especially bitter. While obeying instructions like a good lieutenant, he nevertheless exploded to Gallatin: "Most fervently ought we to pray to be relieved from the various embarrassments of this said embargo. Upon it there will in some of the States, in the course of the next two months, assuredly be engendered monsters. Would that we could be placed upon proper ground for calling in this mischief-making busybody"—that is, the embargo.[50]

Limited insurrections broke out in the affected areas, reminiscent of the pre-Revolutionary days and the exploits of the "Sons of Liberty." Only now the shoe was on the other foot. The Canadian border was aflame, with local enforcement officials either in sympathy with the armed smugglers or afraid to combat them with force. Governor Sullivan of Massachusetts persisted in using the certificates of necessity to enable traders to evade the laws, and evoked an angry statement from Gallatin that his certificates ought no longer to be honored.[51] At Newburyport, in spite of gunboats and naval vessels, an armed mob overawed the customs officers and protected the sailing of vessels from that port in defiance of the embargo.[52]

But the more evidence that accumulated of palpable insurrection in New England, the more Jefferson was convinced it was instigated by the extreme Federalists. They were playing a madman's game, he declared bitterly, to prove to England that if she would but hold out, the United States must yield.[53] But if the Federalists were mad, so was Europe. The whole continent, he exclaimed, was "a great mad-house, & in the present deranged state of their moral faculties to be pitied & avoided. There is no bravery in fighting a Maniac." [54]

A British traveler, viewing the port of New York during this period, has left a grim description of the effects of the embargo in a place where it was being strictly enforced:

> The port indeed was full of shipping, but they were dismantled and laid up; their decks were cleared, their hatches fastened down, and scarcely a sailor was to be found on board. Not a box, bale, cask, barrel, or package was to be seen upon the wharves. Many of the counting-houses were shut up, or advertised to be let; and the few solitary merchants, clerks, porters, and laborers that were to be seen were walking about with their hands in their pockets. The coffee-houses were almost empty; the streets, near the water-side, were almost deserted; the grass had begun to grow upon the wharves.[55]

CHAPTER 63

Embargo's End

BY the beginning of August, 1808, Gallatin openly threw up his hands. "The embargo is now defeated..." he exclaimed to Jefferson, "by open violations, by vessels sailing without any clearances whatever; an evil which under the existing law we cannot oppose in any way but by cruisers."[1] Even though Smith was giving orders for the use of the navy, both Gallatin and the Secretary of Navy were equally gloomy over the entire picture. New York harbor might be shut up, but every other port blazed with revolt.

In all the welter of defiance, disobedience and complaints from Federalists and Republicans alike, only a single and unexpected affirmative support came to the harried President. William Plumer of New Hampshire, who had left the Senate to become Governor of his native state, and who was shifting from the Federalist party to the Republican, sent him a heartening message not only of approval for the embargo, but expressing the hope that New Hampshire would return a group of well-wishers to Congress in the next election.[2] But one swallow does not make a summer.

Jefferson was at the time on vacation at Monticello, and was discovering that his beloved Virginia was in almost as great a ferment as Federalist New England. The Embargo had hit the agricultural states as hard as the mercantile ones; an effect he had not anticipated. Tobacco had become practically worthless, and the warehouses were bulging with the year's crop. Wheat had fallen precipitously from a former two dollars a bushel to a mere pittance of seven cents. Land values were being swept away, and those planters who had counted themselves rich now found themselves with useless assets on their hands and a mountainous pile of debts.

Even Wilson Cary Nicholas, most faithful of Jefferson's supporters, was beginning to wonder. "If the embargo could be executed and the people would submit to it," he told Jefferson tactfully, "I have no doubt it is our wisest course; but if the complete execution of it and the support of the people cannot be counted upon, it will neither answer our purpose nor will it be practicable to retain it."[3]

Monroe, still smarting under the insults he fancied had been heaped upon him and ambitious for the Presidency, was practically in the opposition. "We seem now to be approaching a great crisis," he told Nicholson glumly. "Such is the state of our affairs, and such the compromitment of the Administration at home and abroad by its measures, that it seems likely that it will experience a great difficulty in extricating itself.... We are invited with great earnestness to give the incumbents all the support we can,—by which is meant to give them our votes at the approaching election; but it is not certain that we could give effectual support to the person [Madison] in whose favor it is requested, or that it would be advisable in any view to yield it.... After what has passed, it has no right to suppose that we will, by a voluntary sacrifice, consent to bury ourselves in the same tomb with it." [4] In other words, Monroe was a candidate, and ready to avail himself of the administration's mistakes.

To add to Jefferson's difficulties a report came from Baltimore that Robert Smith, his Secretary of Navy, had openly declared that only the President and Madison supported the Embargo in the Cabinet, that all the others were opposed.[5] The fact was true, but Jefferson could not permit such public gossip of dissension in the Cabinet to go unchallenged. He therefore denied the story as a Federalist plot. "The administration was never more unanimous than in the recommendation of the embargo," he asserted, "every member being present & concurring, and no one more cordially than mr Smith." [6] This may have been technically true, but skillfully evaded the real point—that the Cabinet *now* was divided on the subject. When Smith returned from Baltimore, Jefferson evidently had a private talk with him; for, with election in the offing and Congress shortly to be convoked, Smith suddenly changed his tune. He now wrote a letter to the President demanding the immediate recall of our ministers to France and England, and that Congress "suspend all commercial intercourse whatever with the two Belligerents." [7] The letter was obviously destined for public consumption.

Jefferson was truly aghast at the situation in which he found himself; yet he was determined to see it through; straining, if necessary, the Constitution itself to enforce the measure into which he had entered so optimistically. "This embargo law," he wrote Gallatin from Monticello, "is certainly the most embarrassing one we have ever had to execute. I did not expect a crop of so sudden & rank growth of fraud & open opposition by force could have grown up in the US. I am satisfied with you that if orders & decrees [of France and England] are not repealed, and a continuance of the embargo is preferred to war (which sentiment is universal here), Congress must legalize all *means* which may be necessary to obtain its end." [8]

To obtain the repealer from France and England was now his solitary hope for extricating himself. He read an optimism that did not exist into a letter from Pinkney to the effect that he would shortly have a conference with Canning. "If they repeal their orders," Jefferson commented, "we must repeal our embargo. If they make satisfaction for the Chesapeake, we must revoke our proclamation, and generalize its operation by a law. If they keep up impressments, we must adhere to non-intercourse, manufactures & a navigation act." [9]

Canning, however, dashed all these hopes. On the other hand, Napoleon seemed to be offering dulcet words and an alliance to Armstrong in Paris. He even suggested to the American Minister that should the United States make war on England, he would view with benevolent approval the dispatch of our troops into Florida to "aid" Spain in repelling a British attack, and might be willing to intervene with Spain to obtain the cession of the Floridas.[10]

Armstrong, however, had become justifiably sceptical of Napoleon's promises. "With one hand they offer us the blessings of equal alliance against Great Britain," he reported to Madison; "with the other they menace us with war if we do not accept this kindness; and with both they pick our pockets with all imaginable diligence, dexterity, and impudence." Let us select our enemy, he continued plainly, be it either France or England, but "in either case do not suspend a moment the seizure of the Floridas."[11]

Actually, Jefferson required no prodding from Armstrong. His eye was always fixed on the Floridas. By August, in the midst of unimaginable difficulties, he was considering those eventualities in which he might safely occupy Louisiana to the full limits we claimed, and gather up the Floridas in the process. Keep this in mind, he instructed Secretary of War Dearborn, in "stationing our new recruits & our armed vessels so as to be ready, if Congress authorizes it, to strike in a moment."[12]

At that moment, however, we were much more likely to go to war with either France or England than with Spain. In his desperation, Jefferson scanned the European skies for possible allies, and found Russia. He sincerely believed Alexander I to be that strange anomaly, a benevolent and philosophic Emperor. Why not, then, send a secret mission to Alexander for aid against the oppressive Powers?

His protégé, William Short, was now in the United States and at rather loose ends. To Short, therefore, Jefferson offered the mission, but exhorted him to be "secret as the grave" about it. Let him "huddle up" his affairs, and state publicly he was returning to France. He was to go to Russia as soon as Congress approved.[13]

But time was of the essence and perhaps the Senate might not approve. On reconsideration, Jefferson decided to send him before Congress reconvened, and called Madison to Monticello to draft the necessary instructions. The most important object of the mission, however, could not be embodied in the formal documents. This was, he explained to Short, to engage Alexander's services at any future peace table "to patronize our interests there, so as the benefit of the maritime rights which shall then be settled, may be extended to us, & nothing plotted to sacrifice us by France or England, neither of which wish us success."[14]

A letter was drafted, addressed to Alexander, announcing Short's appointment as minister plenipotentiary, and filled with the most fulsome flattery of the "great and good friend and Emperor."[15]

Short wound up his affairs and sailed for France, where he cooled his heels for months seeking some method of getting to Russia. Meanwhile, Congress had met in session, and Jefferson decided to regularize his *fait accompli* by submitting the nomination to the Senate. It was the last of his official communications as President of the United States to that body. The Senate, however, saw no reason for the mission and refused to confirm the appointment, much to Jefferson's dismay. Poor Short was therefore left stranded, and all his travels and mortifications fruitless.[16]

Another of Jefferson's attempts to aid a friend, though this time on a private scale, similarly ended in frustration. This referred to the long-continued case of the indigent John Page. That boyhood friend had been appointed by him to the post of Commissioner of Loans for Virginia; but his health was now failing rapidly and he was unable to take care of even the nominal duties entailed. Jefferson therefore made the astonishing proposal that the office be transferred to Page's son, Francis, "*for your use*, with an understanding that it should afterwards continue with him for the *benefit of the family*. Or would you rather," he inquired of Page, "retain it in your own name, during your own life, with the probability . . . that he will succeed you for the same *family benefit?*"[17]

Page was on what then seemed to be his deathbed, and was duly grateful for the offer of a vested family interest in the office. But there was an unexpected snag. His son, Francis, was *not* as grateful, and refused the office on the proffered terms. Whereupon a friend, one Thomas Taylor of Richmond, came forward with a proposition to accept the post and pay over the full salary to Page's family. Unfortunately, commented Jefferson's informant on these devious maneuvers, Taylor was a *Federalist* and, to make matters worse, had given bail for Aaron Burr during his several trials. If, therefore, Jefferson thought his appointment politically inexpedient, there was Benjamin Harrison, a very young man but a sound Republican, to whom the job could be given. But Taylor, the Federalist, would do the work, and the money would go to the Pages.[18]

Page himself wrote in a quavering hand that he would rather the post went to a friend than to "any *Son* I have." He was extremely bitter against all of them, and accused one in particular, Mann Page, of plotting to claim the family estate on his father's death, and make the rest of the family helplessly dependent on *him*.[19]

Faced with this complicated mess, Jefferson agreed to appoint the very young, but very sound Republican, Benjamin Harrison, to the office on the terms indicated, and so informed Gallatin, to whose Department it pertained.[20] Gallatin rather unwillingly acceded, but pointed out certain patent facts. "I certainly cannot object to B Harrison's appointment if you do not," he replied. "I know nothing of his qualifications, and you understand how far the humane ground of his appointment may be viewed & avowed in Virginia. Will it produce any bad effect at this critical moment?"[21]

Nevertheless, Jefferson insisted on his humane, if decidedly reprehensible endeavor. But Gallatin had truly foreseen the consequences. A "Quid" paper in Virginia, the *Spirit of '76*, got wind of the complicated business and published it to the world with appended "malicious" comments.[22]

These were sufficient, when the nomination finally came before the Senate, to cause it to be negatived; though Jefferson sought by private interviews with a number of Senators to obviate the objections to the "deal." He refused to accept this defeat, and kept up his efforts for Page to the bitter end, yielding finally to the termination of his own tenure in office and then seeking Madison's aid to do what he himself had been unable to do. "If," he suggested to St. George Tucker, the mediator in the negotiations, "you could find any other unexceptionable character, republican, who has the same dispositions with mr Harrison, & the secret can be kept, the blot may yet perhaps be covered." [23] Actually, it never was; for Madison prudently declined to commence his administration with such a shady transaction.

When Congress convened early in November, 1808, it was indeed in a grim mood and with the feeling that Jefferson had unduly extended his powers in many directions. Even among the Senate Republicans, where his sway had been undisputed for so many years, and where there was no John Randolph to stir up trouble, this new tendency was plainly evident. It is true that an outgoing President always loses in political influence; but there was more to it than that. Even in such personal requests as the appointments of Short and Harrison, the Senate kicked over the traces and administered a decided rebuke to the hitherto sacrosanct President. As John Quincy Adams commented in connection with the rejection of Short: "It indicated the termination of that individual personal influence which Mr. Jefferson had erected on the party division of Whig and Tory." [24]

It was more than mere party division, however. The country was in a turmoil and quasi state of insurrection over the Embargo Act, and the politicians, aside from their own private doubts, were peculiarly sensitive to the discontents of their constituents. Such an item as was reported from Richmond by Jefferson's erstwhile secretary, William A. Burwell, disclosed the current state of mind even in Virginia. A Richmond newspaper printed a rumor that the Embargo was about to be lifted, and the price of tobacco promptly skyrocketed from almost nothing to eight dollars. Jefferson's own crop was sold by his agent at that figure. But the price immediately thereafter fell as the rumor proved to be ill-founded. Burwell therefore urged Jefferson, as a matter of political expedience, to release his purchaser from the contract. Jefferson refused to do so.[25]

Both Gallatin and Madison agreed that, "considering the temper of the legislature," it was essential that Jefferson point out to Congress "some precise and distinct course" for them to take. Gallatin could not make up his mind whether that course should be to continue and enforce the Embargo or to go to war. He therefore asked that Jefferson make the final decision.[26]

Madison, now firmly assured of election to the Presidency, adopted a similarly equivocal position; though there were hints that he might be ready, if driven to it, to adopt war as the ultimate solution.

But Jefferson refused to speak up. His policies had come to such an impasse that he was only too happy to seize the excuse of his impending retirement to throw the entire problem into the lap of Congress and of his successor. He was later to offer his ostensible reasons for a "do-nothing" policy to his old friend, Dr. Logan.

> I have thought it right to take no part myself in proposing measures the execution of which will devolve on my successor. I am therefore chiefly an unmeddling listener to what others say.... As the moment of my retirement approaches I become more anxious for its arrival, and to begin at length to pass what yet remains to me of life and health in the bosom of my family and neighbors, and in communication with my friends undisturbed by political concerns or passions.[27]

It was with this readiness to avoid final responsibility that Jefferson drafted his last Annual Message to Congress. He regretted, he said, that he could not tell them that the Embargo had been suspended—as he had been given power to do—because the belligerent Powers had revoked their "unrighteous edicts." Therefore the Embargo had continued. Nor had the *Chesapeake* affair been settled. Some 103 gunboats, he continued, had been built during the year, which he thought were sufficient for defense. But he did hope—and again this was one of his pet measures—that a "well-organized and armed militia" would be instituted.

The situation into which we had been forced by the suspension of commerce, he asserted, "has impelled us to apply a portion of our industry and capital to internal manufactures and improvements. The extent of this conversion is daily increasing, and little doubt remains that the establishments formed and forming will—under the auspices of cheaper materials and subsistence, the freedom of labor from taxation with us, and of protecting duties and prohibitions—become permanent."

Jefferson, in consonance with his steady drift toward a strong stand on domestic manufactures, had been even more positive in his original draft, but had yielded to Gallatin's insistence that it be watered down.[28]

He ended this most unsatisfactory Message on a more agreeable note. Finances were in an excellent condition; the public debt was almost paid off, and revenue surpluses were steadily accumulating. Should not these, he inquired, be applied to the improvement of roads, canals, rivers and education, "under the powers which Congress may already possess, or such an amendment of the constitution as may be approved by the States?"[29]

Not a word of the deplorable economic state of the country, of the armed resistance to the Embargo, of the threat of certain Federalists to break up the Union, of the fact that if there were surpluses in the Treasury, they might shortly have to be put to more ominous and destructive uses than the praiseworthy projects he envisaged.

In the Senate, that portion of the Message which related to the Embargo was placed in the hands of a committee headed by Giles. The following day, one of the committee members, Hillhouse of Connecticut, introduced a motion to repeal it in its entirety. Debate commenced on November 21st and raged for almost three weeks. Hillhouse, one of the little band of extreme Federalists, insisted that the Embargo was of no effect against France and of negligible effect against England. The only harm that was being done was to American citizens. What worse damage could come to us by war, he demanded, than by this embargo which pretends to obviate it?[30]

But Giles defended the Embargo with vehemence. He quoted the Liverpool Prices Current for September to prove that England was already feeling the pinch. That Bible of the traders declared that the grain market was "very dull," prices were high, "good sweet American flour is not to be had in this market," the stock of tobacco on hand was "becoming limited," and cotton speculation was at a new high because "our total imports are inadequate to one-half the usual monthly consumption."[31] It was an extended, powerful speech, bristling with facts and figures, and made a profound impression on the wavering Republicans.

So great, indeed, was the effect of Giles's rebuttal that when the repealer came up for a vote on December 2nd, only 6 votes could be mustered for it, with 25 in the negative. With this overwhelming triumph, Giles was able to report out two bills, one for the better enforcement of the Embargo and the other for placing the navy into active service against violators.

In the House, a somewhat similar procedure was followed. Chittenden offered a repealer, while John G. Jackson called for the counterpart of Giles's enforcement acts. A flood of petitions for repeal poured into both Houses and were solemnly placed on record by the Federalist members. Motions for partial repealers and compromise measures served further to complicate the picture; but finally all were laid over and the Senate bill was approved with some amendments on January 6, 1809, by a vote of 71 to 32.[32]

Then Giles sprang a surprise; introducing a compromise measure to repeal the Embargo against all countries *except* France and England; but adding more stringent provisions against the outlaw two that prohibited all commercial intercourse and the importation of any articles grown or produced by them, and the interdiction of all armed foreign ships in American waters. This was passed in the Senate on February 21, 1809, agreed to in the House, and became law on February 28th.[33]

Giles's surprise move was an attempt at conciliation and, as he acknowledged, represented a great concession on the part of the administration. It purported, by opening the ports to trade with other countries, to find outlets for American shipping and commerce; while at the same time it tightened all controls against the two great offenders. Unfortunately, with England policing the seas, few ships were able to slip through the cordon to gain the benefits of that neutral trade.

Jefferson knew exactly what was going on and, indeed, had been the main architect of Giles's strategy. On November 22nd, he wrote his eldest son-in-law about the situation in Congress, and expressed his opinion that it would be wiser to leave the fundamental question of war or embargo uncommitted as long as possible, so as to weaken the war party by the mere lapse of time. Several weeks later, he outlined the substance of the resolution for partial repealer that Giles introduced almost two months later.[34]

The President's hand can indeed be traced in all the legislation of this period. His views on many matters were changing, not so much as a result of any change in philosophy as of a practical acquiescence in the exigencies of the occasion. One such view had related to the advisability of domestic manufactures. As a necessary corollary, he was now willing to place protective duties on certain articles; and asked Gallatin to draft the requisite bill.[35]

The shift in the President's views evoked a strong protest from John Taylor of Caroline, whose Republican principles were rigid, theoretic and not subject to change. Both nonintercourse and embargo have failed, he insisted. So did "the incitement to a manufacturing spirit" in earlier days. He considered the United States as an agricultural nation, and as such it would grow rich as it had in the past. Protective duties were anathema; they were not only unconstitutional but opposed to every sound republican principle.[36] But Jefferson paid no attention to the jeremiads of the Old Guard Republican and proceeded with his program.

To make a public display of his new devotion to domestic manufactures, Jefferson ordered from a Connecticut tailor a suit of the finest domestically woven cloth, preferably in a deep blue. "Homespun," he wrote, "is become the spirit of the times: I think it an useful one and therefore that it is a duty to encourage it by example." That example he intended to produce at "our new year's day exhibition when we expect every one will endeavor to be in homespun, and I should be sorry to be marked as being in default." In order to get the suit in time, however, he was compelled to accept material of an inferior grade; though even that cost him $4.50 a yard.[37]

If Jefferson was being vindicated in Congress on all major issues, with certain dissident Republicans disclosing their resentment only in minor matters, New England was being prepared for an eventual secession from the Union. Timothy Pickering, the Essex Junto, Uriah Tracy, James Hillhouse and others were working unweariedly to that end.

Pickering was, as usual, the bellwether. Resolutions began to come with suspicious unanimity from certain strong Federalist townships. Bath, in the Maine District, led the way on December 27, 1808, with a series of resolutions calling on the General Court of Massachusetts to take "immediate steps for relieving the people, either by themselves alone, or in concert with other commercial states"; and calling for committees of correspondence to watch over their safety and for defense against any infringement of their "rights" committed "under color and pretence of authority derived from any officer of the United States." [38]

This was revolutionary language, reminiscent of and deliberately intended to imitate the measures preceding the Revolution. Ironically, it was also reminiscent in tone and phraseology of the Kentucky Resolutions and the ensuing proceedings of the *Republicans*.

The Bath resolutions were speedily copied in other New England communities; some in almost identical language, others in more moderate tones. Gloucester, Plymouth, Newburyport, Hampshire County and others followed suit; while a great meeting held in Boston on January 23rd and 24th at Faneuil Hall, cradle of American liberty, passed a resolution that "we will not voluntarily aid or assist in the execution" of the Enforcement Act, and that all who did "ought to be considered as enemies to the Constitution of the United States and of this State, and hostile to the liberties of this people." [39]

When the Massachusetts legislature met, a strong effort was made by the Federalists to confirm these inflammatory resolutions as the general policy of the state. Sullivan had died, and Levi Lincoln, Jefferson's former Attorney General, was now Governor. The legislature itself was Federalist in complexion; yet what finally emerged was much more moderate than the extremists had hoped for, due in large part to the influence of such level-headed Federalist leaders as George Cabot, Samuel Dexter and Harrison Gray Otis. Otis, however, was willing to call a convention of the commercial states, preferably at Hartford, to declare the Embargo and its subsidiary measures unconstitutional, and to obtain "some mode of relief that may not be *inconsistent with the union of these States*, to which we should adhere as long as possible." [40]

In Connecticut, Governor Jonathan Trumbull convened the legislature in special session to follow Massachusetts' lead. To a request from Secretary of War Dearborn for militia aid to the national Collectors, he tartly replied that he considered the Embargo unconstitutional and would therefore decline to assist its enforcement in any way.[41] Which was good Jeffersonian doctrine of an earlier period, and which the Federalists never tired of flinging back into his face.

Jefferson took bitter cognizance of the fact that "the monarchists of the North (who have been for some time fostering the hope of separation) have been able to make so successful use of the embargo as to have federalized the 5. eastern states & to endanger N. York, and they mean now," he added, "to organize their opposition by the regular powers of their state governments." With this in mind, and to save the Union, he set forth his own strategy. "A bill will be brought in tomorrow," he wrote on January 2nd, "for convening Congress about the middle of May. It will be of course that in the debate members will declare the intention to be then to take off the embargo & if the belligerent edicts be not repealed, to issue letters of marque & reprisal. This will let Europe see that our purpose is war, while not expressing it authoritatively. It will not engage their pride to persevere; at the same time it would quiet our own people by letting them see the term when the embargo is to cease." [42]

What is particularly interesting about this important letter is the evidence of Jefferson's active guidance of Congressional measures and even the nature of their debate.

The timing of this program, though not its content, was changed by force of circumstances. On January 30, 1809, Wilson Cary Nicholas moved in the House to repeal the Embargo Act by the 1st of June and to authorize on that day the issuance of letters of marque and reprisal; provided the British and French edicts and orders were still in force.

Jefferson saw no reason why the resolution should not be adopted by a good majority; though he now hinted, to Monroe at least, that he was not in favor of it. He no longer took part in affairs, he proceeded disingenuously, "beyond the expression of an opinion," since he was close to retirement and "I think it fair that my successor should now originate those measures of which he will be charged with the execution and responsibility." [43]

But plans were upset by a sudden revolt in the House, headed, so Jefferson believed, by panicky New England and New York members, which advanced the date of repealer to March 4th.[44] So furious, indeed, was the uprising that even the codicil concerning letters of marque and reprisal was stricken out, leaving a bald, unconditional repealer on the books.

Jefferson forgot now his indisposition to take an active part in affairs, and exercised every ounce that remained of his waning influence. The House Republicans were called into caucus, and the party whip cracked. As a result the measure was reconsidered, and while the repeal date of the general embargo was allowed to stand, a return to nonintercourse with France and England was pushed through in its stead on February 27th, and was signed to become the law of the land on March 1, 1809.

The Embargo, after fifteen months of operation, was dead; but nonintercourse, as defined in the earlier law, remained. The experiment had been made, and was found wanting. Looking back on it, Jefferson was compelled to admit sadly that $50,000,000 of exports had been lost annually and that war would have cost only a third of that, "besides what might be got by reprisal." He saw therefore that war must follow as soon as Congress met in May, *unless* the edicts were repealed before then.[45] It was only in later years that he felt impelled to defend the Embargo unreservedly and to insist that, had it been continued, it must have hit the mark.

Its effects were ruinous in the economic scene and palpable on the political. Madison had no difficulty in obtaining the Presidency; but the great Republican majorities of Jefferson's second election were deeply invaded by the Federalists in the returns for Congress. Nor were all the Republicans, particularly from the North, willing to follow a Presidential lead as submissively as in the past. New England had largely reverted to Federalism, and New York had verged precariously on the abyss. Discontent was rife, insurrection was barely around the corner, and the Constitution had been extended to the bursting point to justify dictatorial powers and measures by the national government as against individuals and even the States.

No wonder that Jefferson, on March 2nd, two days before his term expired, expressed a tremendous eagerness to drop the leaden mantle of responsibility. "Never did a prisoner, released from his chains," he wrote with profound pathos to his friend Dupont, "feel such relief as I shall on shaking off the shackles of power. Nature intended me for the tranquil pursuits of science, by rendering them my supreme delight. But the enormities of the times in which I have lived, have forced me to take a part in resisting them, and to commit myself on the boisterous ocean of political passions. I thank God for the opportunity of retiring from them without censure, and carrying with me the most consoling proofs of public approbation."[46]

That Jefferson's views on the interpretation of the Constitution had undergone a decided change during his term of office may best be indicated by his reactions to a proposal to extend the charter of the Bank of the United States after its expiration date. A petition from the stockholders to that effect had been introduced in the House on March 26, 1808, and was referred to a Committee of the Whole to determine the question of constitutionality *de novo*. A similar memorial to the Senate was referred to the Secretary of Treasury for his opinion. Gallatin's report was a year in the making, but when it was submitted on March 2, 1809, it paid tribute to the Bank's wise and skillful management, "considered as a moneyed institution." He even admitted that the national government had benefited from its operation and that State Banks could not perform a similar service. The only objection he found to renewal did not rest on any constitutional ground, but merely on the amount of stock held by foreigners; and this, he felt, was not serious.[47]

If the strict constructionist, Gallatin, said nothing about constitutionality, Jefferson mentioned it only in passing. In a private letter he declared that the Republican party had always denied the power of Congress to incorporate private institutions, but that the Bank had been incorporated on the theory that it was an incident to the power of raising money. "On this ground it has been acquiesced in, and will probably be again acquiesced in," he added surprisingly, "as subsequently confirmed by public opinion."[48]

To such a tiny squeak had the epic struggle between Jefferson and Hamilton diminished.

Jefferson's thoughts now more and more moved from Washington to Monticello, his private concerns and matters of personal interest as the long awaited day of March 4th approached.

His finances, as always, engrossed a measurable part of his attention. "Nobody," he told his son-in-law with considerable feeling, "was ever more determined than I was to leave this place clear of debt." But alas, he was falling short by $8,000 to $10,000. To raise this sum he sought to sell some of his lands: part of the Henderson tract over which litigation still dragged, the famous Natural Bridge and even a part of his Bedford property.[49]

He had tried to get a bank loan from the Richmond Bank, but availed himself thankfully of a private loan which Abraham Venable offered him, with Venable as the endorser. Madison had also endorsed a note for him at the Bank of the United States, which was still partially unpaid after Madison assumed the Presidency. Nor did Jefferson know, he acknowledged ruefully, when it would be discharged.[50] In the end, he had to borrow a substantial sum from a rich widow to settle his Washington accounts.

What perhaps gave him even more concern was the discovery that a flock of supposed Merino sheep which he had imported at great expense from Spain some fifteen years before through the agency of Robert Morris, were not true Merinos. He had placed high hopes on this flock, as a means of improving the quality of wool in the country, and had offered lambs to his neighbors for similar propagation. Now, for the first time, he had some qualms about the wool, and sent samples to experts in Pennsylvania. The mournful news came back that the wool was inferior and that either the entire flock, or his prize ram, was spurious.[51]

His last days in Washington were clouded with financial difficulties, with the petty barbs directed at him by a resentful Senate, and the knowledge that he was leaving office under a sense of failure. Far better had his *congé* come after the purchase of Louisiana.

On March 4, 1809, James Madison was inaugurated as President of the United States. Jefferson declined to ride with him in a carriage to the Capitol. "I wished," he said, "not to divide with him the honors of the day. It pleased me better to see them all bestowed on him." He therefore quietly rode unattended to the Capitol and, so the story goes, hitched his horse to a post and walked up the stately steps.[52]

On March 11th, after arranging his affairs and packing his bags, he shook the dust of Washington from his feet, never to return.[53] Monticello beckoned, and that privacy for which his soul had panted.

CHAPTER 64

Ex-President Jefferson

IT was cold, blustery March weather as Thomas Jefferson, private citizen, rumbled out of Washington in his coach, piled high with baggage, with an extra horse for riding led by one of his servants. What his thoughts were at this end of an era cannot easily be determined. As the coach bumped along over half-frozen ruts or sank in places into the mud beneath, did they review the long years of service he was leaving behind or fix themselves wholly on the anonymity ahead? From the greatest man in the country—and, by some, the most hated and vilified—he had, in the short space of an hour, receded into the shadows and a new star had risen to become the cynosure of all eyes.

But whatever thoughts might have buzzed and swarmed in his mind, the weather and the excessively bad condition of the roads soon compelled him to concentrate on the journey itself. The coach slogged and slithered in the mud and he shifted to his horse. The skies grew sullen and a blinding snowstorm accompanied him on the last lap of his journey and enveloped his beloved mountain as he toiled up to the summit. Once before, on his wedding day, he had brought his bride home in a heavy snow; but the snow then was clean and his spirits had been young and eager. Now, it was wet and disagreeable, and he was old and alone. Nevertheless, as he reached the welcoming buildings, the blazing hearth and the bosom of his family, he could exult at least that his "*vis vitae*" was still unimpaired.[1]

Of his immediate family, his wife had long been gone, and the death of Maria was still an open wound. Only Martha remained, trailing behind her a brood of active children. Martha's son, Thomas Jefferson Randolph, relieved Jefferson later in life of the general management of his affairs. Maria's legacy was young Francis Eppes, on whose education his grandfather was to take considerable pains.

The first few days in Monticello were devoted to settling himself in what was now to be his permanent abiding place, to receiving the welcome-home addresses of his neighbors and the more distant and more formal, but still gratifying, adulations that poured in from all over the country.[2] The Republicans knew they had lost their greatest leader, and some of them were uneasy over the new chief who had taken his place. It is true the Federalists shed no tears over his passing, but they obtained no satisfaction over the thought of four years or more of Madison.

There were other notes as well. Mingled with sorrow at his passing, and deftly interwoven in the strands, were solicitations that Jefferson exercise his undoubted influence with the new President to place the writers in some warm and comfortable government office with the accompanying perquisites. So enormous was this mail, and so persistent the writers, that Jefferson was compelled to print up a broadside for general distribution, announcing it as a fixed rule that he would not submit applications or make recommendations to the President or a government official on behalf of anyone.[3] He tried to stick to his self-imposed rule, but had to break it on occasion, as the pressure became extreme or old friends were involved.

Jefferson found his personal affairs in considerable disorder. His finances, of course, were in their usual parlous state; and he had to borrow $8,000 from Mrs. Tabb of Amelia on a personal note in order to be able to leave Washington in at least a semisolvent position.

He even had to get an endorsement from Madison for one of his notes, and this now had to be renewed. The balance of his Washington debts was transferred to Virginia, where he optimistically hoped some day to pay them off from the income of his estates. He estimated that Bedford brought him in $2,500 net profit a year; and if only he could limit his expenses at Monticello, that income, in addition to the sale of some outlying lands, might be sufficient to meet his outstanding obligations.[4] Actually, they never did.

He viewed his new management and farming duties with mingled eagerness and hesitation. "My whole life," he acknowledged to his son-in-law, "has been passed in occupations which kept me from any minute attention to them [his farms], and finds me now with only very general ideas of the theory of agriculture, without actual experience." He was therefore only too grateful to Thomas Mann Randolph for his offer of aid and counsel.[5]

Fortunately, he had an excellent overseer on the premises, one Edmund Bacon, who had come to Monticello at the end of 1801 and was to remain with him for twenty years. Even more fortunately, Bacon later reminisced concerning Monticello and its master, and we are indebted to him for many illuminating–though sometimes prejudiced–insights.

Bacon thought that Jefferson's lands, comprising some 10,000 acres, and divided into the four plantations of Tuffton, Lego, Shadwell and Pantops, were not profitable; the ground was too uneven and hard to work. Each plantation had its own Negro quarter and a white overseer to manage it. At Monticello, built underground, were the cisterns, ice house, cellar, kitchen and storerooms. At right angles from the main house were two terraces, underneath which lay on one side the servants' quarters, on the other, the stables. The grounds in front were ornamented with flowers, shrubs and walks; while the rear had been graded and seeded into an open lawn. The gardens, planted with vegetables, grapes and figs, descended in concentric terraces on the sides of the mountain, with roads and paths winding gracefully through.

When Jefferson traveled, it was always with four horses to his carriage, and a fifth one as a mount for himself when he tired of the jouncing enclosure. His favorite horses bore a curious mixture of names—Diomede, Brimmer, Tecumseh, Wellington and Eagle.

Bacon admired his master intensely. He saw him "straight as a gun-barrel," strong and wiry, blue-eyed, and with a clear, pure skin. Jefferson would rise at daybreak or before, take an early morning walk on the terrace, make his own fire in his room, and then ride out at 9 A. M. every day for a tour of his plantations. In spite of the general testimony as to Jefferson's sloppiness of dress at Washington, Bacon declared that at home he dressed neatly and his shoe buckles were always bright and polished. He never used tobacco or played cards; nor did he dance. He preferred the flesh of other animals and of fowl to the almost universal hog meat that was the staple of Virginia households.

Martha Randolph, his daughter, who took over most of the housewifely duties, also elicited the overseer's approval. She was, he said, much like her father; tall, blue-eyed, with a clear, bright complexion and an unruffled temper. Both she and her father regularly hummed a tune as they rode. Of her husband, however, Bacon had considerable reservations. Thomas Mann Randolph was, he reminisced frankly, "a very eccentric man," who was given to sudden wild spurrings of his horse through a harvested wheat field, so that the flying hooves scattered the neat shocks of grain in all directions. Later on, Thomas Mann went insane, and his temper became ungovernable. He would thrash his grown son, Jefferson Randolph, with a cane, and knock down his son-in-law, Charles L. Bankhead, with an iron poker. But Bankhead, admitted Bacon, deserved whatever treatment he got. Married to Anne Randolph, he soon showed himself to be a drunkard, and had once lunged with a knife at his brother-in-law.[6] Of Thomas Mann's mental condition we shall hear more later; he was to become a grievous burden and a trial both to his wife and his father-in-law.

Jefferson himself was proud of his activities. He was "occupied constantly out of doors from an early breakfast to a late dinner every day," he told his Washington factor. "Writing, as with other country farmers is put off to a rainy day. . . . The total change of occupation from the house & writing table to constant emploiment in the garden & farm has added wonderfully to my happiness. It is seldom & with great reluctance I ever take up a pen. I read some, but not much."[7]

To achieve this total absorption in his new-found duties, Jefferson discontinued all newspapers except purely local ones. "I shall give over reading newspapers," he declared to Levi Lincoln. "They are so false & so intemperate that they disturb tranquility, without giving information."[8]

But Jefferson could not cut himself off from the world in which he had played such an enormously important role as easily as he first thought. He was barely installed in Monticello when he was already offering Madison advice in his new office. War must be avoided, he warned, if it is at all possible. "I know no government which would be so embarrassing in war as ours," he added. "This would proceed very much from the lying and licentious character of our papers; but much, also, from the wonderful credulity of the members of Congress in the floating lies of the day." He feared also that with a state of war Congress might decide to remain in permanent session.[9]

A little later he was pondering economic matters with another correspondent. "An equilibrium of agriculture, manufactures, and commerce, is certainly become essential to our independence," he asserted. "Manufactures, sufficient for our own consumption, of what we raise the raw material (and no more). Commerce sufficient to carry the surplus produce of agriculture, beyond our own consumption, to a market for exchanging it for articles we cannot raise (and no more). These are the true limits of manufactures and commerce. To go beyond them is to increase our dependence on foreign nations, and our liability to war."[10]

And still a little later, he was back with more advice to Madison. While expressing pleasure at the news that the clouds of war with England seemed to have rolled safely by, he was not so pleased to hear that an envoy was on the way to attempt a treaty with the United States. His fierce suspicion of England flared once again. "They never made an equal commercial treaty with any nation," he exploded, "& we have no right to expect to be the first." Their method was to try "whipping us into a treaty. They did it in Jay's case; were near it in Monroe's, & on failure of that, have applied the scourge with tenfold vigor, & now come on to try its effect." The form of Jay's treaty, he continued bitterly, "will for ever be a millstone round our necks unless we now rid ourselves of it, once for all."

Then, forgetting his determination to have no more to do with politics, he entered into a long discussion of American relations with France and Spain. Napoleon, no doubt, would give us the Floridas in return for concessions. But we could take them ourselves without strings "in the first moment of the first war." Cuba, he acknowledged, might be a better offer; and Jefferson would "immediately erect a column on the Southermost limit of Cuba & inscribe on it a ne plus ultra as to us in that direction. We should then have only to include the North [Canada] in our confederacy, which would be of course in the first war, and we should have such an empire for liberty as she has never surveyed since the creation." But, he warned, we should never accept any accessions of territory that would require a navy for their defense. Cuba, he felt, could be defended without one.[11] For all Jefferson's disclaimers, this was assuredly an imperial program of expansion and conquest.

Monroe came to visit Jefferson; and the latter was pleased to find him once more "sincerely cordial" and divorced from the "junto" at Richmond headed by John Randolph.[12]

Meanwhile the advice to Madison rolled on. Even though England seems to be changing her policy toward us, wrote Jefferson, let us keep enough of the nonimportation law "to pinch them into a relinquishment of impressments" and "to support those manufacturing establishments which their orders, and our interests, forced us to make." [13] In other words, nonimportation was to be used not merely as a retaliatory weapon, but as a method for protecting infant industries. As a means of protection, nonimportation was naturally much more effective than even the highest tariff.

What Madison thought of this constant stream of advice and exhortations from the retired President is another matter. He listened quietly and respectfully, but usually failed to comment. He had ideas of his own and, as he grew accustomed to his office, went largely his own way. Only on certain great occasions did he seek the advice of the elder statesman of Monticello.

Yet Jefferson continued to offer his views, even when unasked; though loyally upholding the hands of the new administration. He generously gave Madison credit for a share in the policies of his own administration. "Our principles were the same," he said, "and we never differed sensibly in the application of them." [14]

In spite of his vehement protestations that he was living the life of "a country farmer" and had little time for books, intellectual interests or correspondence, Jefferson could no more refrain from these—as well as politics—than from breathing.

He subscribed to Philip Freneau's new book of poems, and sought subscriptions for him in his neighborhood; though he found his neighbors not a reading crowd, especially when it came to poetry.[15] To encourage a taste for literature, he thought of establishing "a small circulating library in every county, to consist of a few well-chosen books, to be lent to the people of the country, under such regulations as would secure their safe return in due time." [16] Nothing, unfortunately, came of the idea.

Most of Jefferson's effects, accumulated during his long years at Washington, had been shipped home by water. In one of the trunks was his great collection of Indian vocabularies, representing thirty years of diligent inquiry. He hoped, by a comparison of the fifty-odd languages, to be able to trace the common ancestry of the Indians and their point of origin. But tragedy befell him. While the boat was sailing up the James, a thief stole the trunk under the impression that its contents were valuable in the monetary sense. On opening it, however, he found that they consisted only of bulky manuscripts. In disappointment and disgust, he threw them into the river. Some few sheets later floated ashore; but they were so caked with mud and sodden with water as to be practically illegible. The thief was eventually caught, and brought to trial. So enraged was Jefferson at this end to his years of assiduous toil and his dreams of a new theory of the Indians that he hoped the culprit would be hanged. "Some such example," he exclaimed, "is much wanting to render property waterborne secure." [17]

Another of Jefferson's aims was also doomed to disappointment—that Virginia would some day build a public university. While that hope still flickered, he intended to bequeath his own library to the institution. With that gone, he proposed instead that Congress establish a university in Washington. Dupont, who had written for him such an elaborate treatise on education, might, so he informed Madison, be willing to become its first president or even a mere professor.[18]

Lafayette, from Paris, sent him news which ought to have excited him greatly. Destutt Tracy, whom Jefferson conceived to be the greatest political and social philosopher of his age, if not indeed of all time, had a plan for publishing some anonymous observations on Montesquieu's famous *Spirit of the Laws*. To further obscure his own identity, however, Tracy wished to ascertain if Jefferson would have his manuscript translated into English and printed by an American press as the work of an American. This in turn would supposedly be retranslated into French, and on that basis published on its native shores.[19] The reason for this devious and circuitous route was Tracy's well-founded fear that the liberal views he expressed in the work might get him into trouble with Napoleon.

Oddly enough, Jefferson did not reply to this request nor did he answer other letters from Lafayette; in the end evoking a bitter reproach from his friend of former years.[20] This time Jefferson broke his long silence with the statement that he had nevertheless been attentive to Lafayette's complicated affairs in New Orleans. "Old men do not easily contract new friendships," he wrote with dignity, "but neither do they forget old ones. Yours & mine commenced in times too awful, has continued thro' times too trying & changeful to be forgotten at the moment when our chief solace is our own recollections."

As an explanation for his silence, he gave the usual excuse that "I am now on horseback among my farms from an early breakfast to a late dinner, with little regard to weather. I find it gives health to body, mind & affairs. I go to my writing table with great reluctance & only for those calls which cannot be put off to morrow." What is the use, he queried, of contemplating the European scene "of murder, rapine, devastation, pyracy, demoralization of national societies & degradation of the instruments of all this evil. If there be a god, & he is just his day will come. He will never abandon the whole race of man to be eaten up by the leviathans and mammoths of a day. I enjoy good health," he ended significantly, "& am happy in contemplating the peace, prosperity, liberty & safety of my country, & especially the wide ocean, the barrier of all these." [21]

Just as he refused to be drawn into the controversies of Europe, so he refused time and again to be drawn into any controversy on religion. To one inquirer as to his views, he wrote back that "reading, reflection & time have convinced me that the interests of society require the observation of those moral precepts only in which all religions agree ... and that we should not intermeddle with the particular dogmas in which all religions differ, and which are totally unconnected with morality. In all of them we see good men, & as many in one as another. The varieties of the structure & action of the human mind as in those of the body, are the work of our creator, against which it cannot be a religious duty to erect the standard of conformity." [22]

Nor were his humanitarian instincts dead, in spite of his avowed washing of hands as far as Europe was concerned. Cuba was in convulsion and refugees were flocking to the territory of Orleans. Jefferson was not convinced they were desirable immigrants, because they tended to retard "the desired epoch of [Orleans'] becoming entirely American in spirit." Yet he insisted that it was "impossible to refuse them, or to withhold any relief they can need. We should be monsters to shut the door against such sufferers." [23]

Yet his charity never extended to England. Here was a country that never lost an opportunity of playing America—or, for that matter, the rest of the world—a dirty trick. The actions of Erskine, the new British envoy, whose coming he had viewed with such scepticism, justified that reproach. Not that he blamed Erskine, but the King, his master, and "the unprincipled rascality of Canning." Great Britain, he lashed out angrily, ought to be banned from the world; "for where is the nation whose internal peace she had not attempted to destroy by the poison of her own corruption? I turn from this disgusting monument of human depravity . . ." [24]

There had also been some depravity at home, of which Gallatin was the victim. Jefferson had stood steadfastly by his Secretary of Treasury during all the complaints of dissatisfied Republicans; but on his retirement, the complaints and secret machinations redoubled and Gallatin, in disgust, contemplated resignation. He had remained on, however, under Madison, but now again he wished to resign.

Jefferson wrote to urge him to stay. "I consider the fortunes of our country as depending in an eminent degree, on the extinguishment of the public debt before we engage in any war." Otherwise "we shall be committed to the English career of debt, corruption and rottenness," and end in revolution. But the discharge of the debt could only be accomplished by Madison and Gallatin working together.[25]

To which Gallatin tartly replied that the reduction of the debt had been the principal reason for first bringing him into office; but that it could only be accomplished by the co-operation of all branches of the government in achieving a balanced budget. Such was not now the case. "I cannot, my dear Sir," he burst out, "consent to act the part of a mere financier, to become a contriver of taxes, a dealer of loans, a seeker of resources for the purpose of supporting useless baubles, of encreasing the number of idle & dissipated members of the community, of fattening contractors, pursers and agents, and of introducing, in all its ramifications, that system of patronage, corruption & rottenness which you so justly execrate." [26] Nevertheless, after relieving himself by this stormy outburst, Gallatin stayed on to struggle with the times and his enemies.

Yet, for all these informed and passionate interventions in politics and the complex of events, Jefferson always kept up the pose that he had no interest in them, and had rid himself of every preoccupation except farming and those sciences on which agriculture was based. Such was the nature of his letter to his old friend and philosophic confidant, Dr. Benjamin Rush. "A retired politician," he said whimsically, "is like a broken down courser, unfit [for the] turf, and good for little else. I am endeavoring to recover the little [I] knew of farming, gardening, &c. and would gladly now exchange [every?] branch of science I possess for the knolege of a common farmer.... I find I am losing sight of the progress of the world of letters. Here we talk but of rains & droughts, of blights & frosts, of our ploughs & cattle; & if the topic changes to politics I meddle little with them. In truth I never had a cordial relish for them, & abhor the contentions and strife they generate. You know what were the times which forced us both from our first loves, the natural sciences." [27]

Monroe had visited Jefferson and been friendly enough, but that did not mean he had forgotten his grievances. Madison sought to draw him back into public service; but did *not* offer him a post in the Cabinet. He would, he hinted, be willing to place him in charge of Orleans or Louisiana. Monroe peremptorily turned them down, and Madison appealed to Jefferson for help.

As soon as he received the letter, Jefferson mounted his horse and rode over to see this Achilles who persisted in sulking in his tents. But Monroe declared he would refuse any office in which "he should be subordinate to any body but the President himself, or which did not place his responsibility substantially with the President and the nation."

Unfortunately, the Cabinet was already filled, and Jefferson hinted at the possibility of a military command. Monroe retorted that "he would sooner be shot than take a command under Wilkinson." His old friend retired somewhat discomfited, to write Madison that night that the only way to heal the breach would be to give him a Cabinet post, an independent military command or perhaps a diplomatic mission.[28] It was not until 1811 that Monroe finally was granted a position compatible with what he conceived his due—the office of Secretary of State.

For all his brave talk of disinterest in politics, Jefferson was watching the rapidly worsening condition of affairs with a vigilant eye and a deep concern. It was not merely that England, after some backing and filling, was back on her old courses again, but that the new administration was torn with dissension from within. The Smiths of Baltimore—Samuel and Robert—were at loggerheads with Gallatin and, as we have seen, Gallatin was kept from resignation only because of Jefferson's urgent plea. But the backbitings continued. In order to smooth over the situation, Jefferson permitted himself some reminiscences of his own troubles in Washington's Cabinet. The current dissensions, he declared, "cannot be greater than between Hamilton and myself, and yet we served together four years in that way. We had indeed no personal dissensions. Each of us, perhaps, thought well of the other as a man, but as politicians it was impossible for two men to be of more opposite principles."[29] Obviously, Jefferson was investing the past with the pathos of distance.

His former private secretary, William A. Burwell, was now in Congress and had introduced a bill to provide convoys for American ships in order to prevent British search and seizure. Though this must have inevitably led to a shooting war, Jefferson approved of it; indeed, he thought it did not go far enough in protecting American rights. Now that he was out of office and without the responsibilities it entailed, he was ready at this time to "force every part of the union to join in the protection at the point of the bayonet."[30] In other words, he advocated that the Federalist states of New England be coerced by the national government, and that the national army be employed for the purpose. It was a far cry from the time of the Kentucky Resolutions.

By now he had convinced himself that the Embargo was repealed too soon. "The embargo," he asserted, "evaded as it was, proved it would have coerced [Great Britain], had it been honestly executed." The wealth which the embargo had brought home to this country, he added bitterly, "has now been thrown back into the laps of our enemies, and our navigation completely crushed."[31]

It is difficult to say which Jefferson hated most—the Federalists at home or Great Britain abroad. He solved the matter neatly by hanging one on the peg of the other. "The toryism with which we struggled in '77," he explained to Governor John Langdon of New Hampshire, "differed but in name from the federalism of '99, with which we struggled also; and the Anglicism of 1808, against which we are now struggling, is but the same thing still in another form. It is a longing for a King, and an English King rather than any other. This is the true source of their sorrows and wailings."

From this preamble he moved logically to a violent assault on perfidious England and on kings in general. "Now, take any race of animals," he exclaimed, "confine them in idleness and inaction, whether in a stye, a stable or a state-room, pamper them with high diet, gratify all their sexual appetites, immerse them in sensualities, nourish their passions, let everything bend before them, and banish whatever might lead them to think, and in a few generations they become all body and no mind.... Such is the regimen in raising kings." No wonder then that most are fools, idiots, hogs or downright insane. No wonder Napoleon beat them so easily. Only Alexander of Russia was an exception. "And so endeth the book of Kings," he concluded sententiously, "from all of whom the Lord deliver us."[32] There is nothing in the writings of Swift that outdoes this savage attack. The sole difference is that Swift generalized it to include *all* men; whereas

Jefferson reserved his innermost hell for kings, the government of England —and Federalists.

With these views of the importance of environment on the characters of men, it is no wonder that Jefferson devoted so much of his time and energies to the problems of education. He began to gather around him a group of young men whose education he directed. These thirsters after knowledge settled themselves in the vicinity of Monticello; they came up the mountain to seek his counsel and guidance, and employed the resources of his library. "In advising the course of their reading," explained their preceptor, "I endeavor to keep their attention fixed on the main objects of all science, the freedom and happiness of man. So that coming to bear a share in the councils and government of their country, they will keep ever in view the sole objects of all legitimate government." [33]

Education was for citizenship, and therefore included ethics and morals, practical science, modern languages, law and government, and history from which lessons might be drawn. There was no room in Jefferson's scheme of tutoring for poetry, literature and the classics per se, science in the abstract, or for such vain pursuits as philosophy and theology.

Chiefly, the young men who came to him wished to study law, and Jefferson encouraged the pursuit as the best road into the "councils and government of their country." His distaste for Blackstone had grown with the years, and he believed that, as a result of the craze for the English compiler, the science of law had degenerated woefully in America. He therefore insisted that his pupils begin with Coke, go on to the Reports, and only after several years of intensive work, end with Blackstone as merely "an elegant digest of what they will then have acquired from the real fountains of the law."

What he was doing on a small scale at Monticello, Jefferson wanted to expand into a general system of education. He had "two great measures at heart," he confessed, "without which no republic can maintain itself in strength. 1. That of general education, to enable every man to judge for himself what will secure or endanger his freedom. 2. To divide every county into hundreds, of such size that all the children of each will be within reach of a central school in it."

He had never receded from this purpose since his struggles with the Virginia Assembly as far back as 1775; and he was never to recede from it for the rest of his life. The older he grew, the more he witnessed the ways of the world and the emotions of man, the more he was convinced that education, provided it was properly directed, was the sole solution for the world's ills. He despised Plato, yet perhaps he had not read sufficiently in him to note that there was at least one thesis on which they could have agreed: that knowledge *is* the good; that ignorance is evil; that those who have knowledge must therefore know the good, and follow it; and that it is only ignorance that makes men prefer the evil.

More and more he became a firm believer in the efficacy of his scheme of the "hundreds," the idea of which he readily admitted was copied from the New England town meeting. Staffed with a justice of the peace, a constable and a captain of militia, each would be an independent corporation "to manage all its concerns, to take care of its roads, its poor, and its police by patrols, etc." Such "little republics," he prophesied, "would be the main strength of the great one. We owe to them the vigor given to our revolution in its commencement in the Eastern States, and by them the Eastern States were enabled to repeal the embargo in opposition to the Middle, Southern and Western States, and their large and lubberly division into counties which can never be assembled. General orders are given out from a centre to the foreman of every hundred, as to the sergeants of an army, and the whole nation is thrown into energetic action, in the same direction in one instant and as one man, and becomes absolutely irresistible. Could I once see this I should consider it as the dawn of the salvation of the republic." [34]

One wonders whether Jefferson quite knew what he was advocating in this final peroration. For he seems to be proposing a nation of hundreds formed on a hierarchical military system, in which each man no longer decides for himself what is good, but receives his orders from the top, and all men move obediently "in the same direction in one instant and as one man." Such a plan contradicted everything for which Jefferson elsewhere stood, and subverted not only the town-meeting idea on which he modeled his plan, but the essence of democracy itself. This is true dictatorship, and contains nothing that a modern totalitarian government would not heartily agree with. It is obvious that Jefferson himself would have recoiled in horror from the logical extension of the plain implications involved in his plan. Sometimes, however, Jefferson disclosed a curious inclination to overlook the nature of the means he was willing to employ in order to achieve what he considered a profound good.

Governor John Tyler of Virginia, to whom Jefferson penned the foregoing views on education and government, was nearing the end of his term of office, and asked Jefferson to intercede with the President to secure for him the position on the Federal bench currently held by Judge Cyrus Griffin, in the event that the latter, who was ailing, should die.[35]

In spite of his resolution not to recommend office-seekers to Madison, Jefferson felt that he ought to make an exception in this case. "We have long enough suffered," he submitted, "under the base prostitution of law to party passions in one judge [Marshall] and the imbecility of another [Griffin]. In the hands of one the law is nothing more than an ambiguous text, to be explained by his sophistry into any meaning which may subserve his personal malice. Nor can any milk-and-water associate maintain his own dependence, and by a firm pursuance of what the law really is, extend its protection to the citizens or the public." [36]

What made Jefferson especially bitter against Griffin was the fact that he had sat with Marshall in the Burr trial and never once intervened in the proceedings, but permitted the Chief Justice to run the case as if he were alone on the bench.

At this moment, too, Jefferson was himself involved in a law suit which might eventually come before the overpowering Marshall or the "cypher," Griffin.

Edward Livingston of New York, who had emigrated to New Orleans under a cloud after the extensive defalcations of a subordinate, rose rapidly to wealth and influence in his new home. Among his holdings was a large tract of land, known as the "Batture," that stretched along the river front and possessed immense potentialities. The title, however, was in dispute and the people of New Orleans insisted it was in the public domain. So, too, did Jefferson during his Presidency; and so did Congress. Livingston brought suit and won his case in the territorial court, but Jefferson directed Madison as Secretary of State to remove Livingston's people forcibly from the disputed tract.

In December, 1807, Livingston brought his grievances to the public view in a lengthy pamphlet; following it with an action against Jefferson, once he had retired to private life, for $100,000 damages for what he claimed were the latter's arbitrary and illegal acts.

Jefferson always viewed any legal proceeding against himself with a strange mixture of rage and panic. In this instance, Livingston had brought his action in Richmond; and Jefferson feared, with Marshall and Griffin on the bench, he would be heavily mulcted in damages. He complained to Madison that Marshall's "twistifications in the case of Marbury, in that of Burr, & the late Yazoo case shew how dexterously he can reconcile law to his personal biasses: and nobody seems to doubt that he is ready prepared to decide that Livingston's right to the batture is unquestionable, and that I am bound to pay for it with my private fortune." [37]

All of Jefferson's energies were engrossed in defeating Livingston's suit and the purpose which he imputed to Marshall. He retained William Wirt and George Hay, two of the most eminent lawyers in Virginia, who had been involved in the prosecution of Burr. He later brought in other counsel, and devoted months of research to seeking out the ancient titles to the property and to an examination of the law, ancient and modern, that might be presumed to govern them. He countered Livingston's pamphlet with a ninety-one page pamphlet of his own, entitled *The Proceedings of the Government of the United States in Maintaining the Public Right Against the Intrusion of Edward Livingston*, which he proffered to his counsel for use in the forthcoming trial. Livingston replied with another pamphlet in which he accused his antagonist of mistranslations and suppressions. Jefferson bombarded government officials for all the material in the possession of the State and Treasury Departments relating to the Batture. He feared that Livingston's intrigues might cause Congress "to take some step which might have an injurious effect on the opinion of a jury"—by which he meant the introduction of a bill which would validate Livingston's title—and therefore he placed his own memorandum in the hands of certain members of Congress in order that they might prevent such "unfavorable interference." He also wanted the Attorney General to intervene since, he argued, his acts had been done as a public officer and for the public benefit.[38]

What he dreaded most of all, however, was the prospective spite of the presiding judges, and a consequent bias that would influence a jury to bring in heavy damages against him. At no time could his fortune have sustained a substantial verdict, but even a lesser one would have been disaster at the moment. So harassed was he by debts that he had welcomed a suggestion of John Barnes, his Washington banker, "like a ray of light beaming on my uneasy mind." General Kosciusko, the Polish hero, had left a substantial sum of money in Jefferson's safekeeping on his departure from America, with instructions to invest it for him and send him the interest. Barnes now proposed that Jefferson himself borrow from this fund—it amounted to $4,500—and the latter eagerly acceded.[39] He later wrote to Kosciusko, informing him what he had done, and asking his permission.[40] Permission was granted; but the fund itself had already been used by Jefferson in paying off a bank loan, and one wonders what would have happened had Kosciusko refused.

A delicate point now arose in the Livingston case. A technical plea to the jurisdiction seemed likely of success, since the subject matter of the dispute related to land, and therefore should have been tried in the district where the land lay—New Orleans.

Jefferson at first hemmed and hawed on the question, but only because he feared that such a special plea would give the judge (Marshall) a chance to vent his spite against him. Nevertheless he felt the plea ought to be used.[41] His counsel Hay, however, urged that no technical plea be entered, but that the case go to trial on its merits. By obtaining a dismissal on technical grounds, he pointed out, the general public might feel suspicious as to the true justice of Jefferson's former actions and of the claims of the United States.[42]

But by this time Jefferson was so much afraid of an adverse verdict that he insisted on the employment of every legal maneuver possible; even to the plea that Livingston, as a citizen of a territory, was not a citizen of a state, and therefore did not come within the jurisdiction of a Federal court on the constitutional ground of diversity of citizenship.[43]

Hay unwillingly acceded, and when the case finally came up for a hearing in the following year, the motion to dismiss for lack of jurisdiction was interposed. By this time, Jefferson's friend, former Governor John Tyler, had been appointed to the court on Jefferson's recommendation (Griffin having conveniently died), and he sat with Marshall to hear the motion. Tyler wrote the opinion granting the motion, with Marshall concurring with obvious regret. The case was therefore thrown out of court and Livingston was unable to bring it to trial again in New Orleans for the very good reason that he could never obtain jurisdiction there over Jefferson's person or property.[44] He did eventually obtain a court decree in New Orleans that he was the rightful owner of the Batture; but the complicated proceedings dragged until 1820, when a compromise was effected. Once angry passions had subsided, the two antagonists, Jefferson and Livingston, became friendly again: and Livingston went on to become Secretary of State during Andrew Jackson's administration.

Meanwhile another death had occurred on the Supreme Court—that of William Cushing, a sturdy Federalist and follower of Marshall. Jefferson rejoiced mightily over the providential death for two reasons: first, that there would be one less Federalist on the bench in the event his case should go up on appeal; second, that it gave Madison a chance to appoint "a successor of unquestionable republican principles." Since Cushing came from New England, Jefferson suggested Levi Lincoln for the place, even though he acknowledged that neither he nor Madison thought very much of Lincoln's legal attainments. But, argued Jefferson with considerable prejudice, *no* lawyer from an Eastern State knew any real law. "Their system of Jurisprudence made up from the Jewish law, a little dash of common law, & a great mass of original notions of their own, is a thing *sui generis*."[45]

To Gallatin, Jefferson wrote even more frankly: "I observe old Cushing is dead. At length, then, we have a chance of getting a Republican majority in the Supreme judiciary. For ten years has that branch braved the spirit and will of the nation.... The event is a fortunate one, and so timed as to be a Godsend to me." What particularly motivated this somewhat unpleasant glee was the pending case with Livingston. For, as he set forth, should the majority still be Federalist, in the event of an appeal, Marshall would dominate it. And he thought that Marshall's "inveteracy is profound, and his mind of that gloomy malignity which will never let him forego the opportunity of satiating it on a victim. His decisions, his instructions to a jury, his allowances & disallowances & garblings of evidence, must all be subjects of appeals. I consider that as my only chance of saving my fortune from entire wreck. And to whom is my appeal? From the judge in Burr's case to himself & his associate judge...."[46]

The same agitated spirit, almost the same vindictiveness, possessed Jefferson in his comparatively minor litigation over the dam and water rights in Albemarle with respect to the Bennett Henderson property. That litigation, in which Craven Peyton was the ostensible plaintiff (though secretly acting as Jefferson's agent), had dragged through the courts since 1804 and a decision was ultimately rendered in the lower court in favor of Henderson's heirs. Peyton took an appeal, and was defeated in the appellate court in 1812. Jefferson moved heaven and earth to gain his point, wrote interminable briefs, harried his own counsel to exasperation, and called on the very heavens to witness the injustices to which he was being subjected.[47]

CHAPTER 65

Sage of Monticello

THE longer Jefferson was away from the Presidency the more he managed to convince himself that the policy of the Embargo had been correct and that, had it been in operation only a few weeks more, England must inevitably have yielded. Its repealer, which he declared had come about through the arts of the Federalists, had been the "most fatal event" since the establishment of independence. Its loss, he prophesied, would eventually be felt by the "authors of the mischief"; but in the meantime it would ruin the "innocent agricultor." Only an immediate return to the Embargo could save the country.[1]

To avoid such ruin, Jefferson sought ways and means to improve the lot of the agriculturist. He had imported at great expense some Merino sheep and, as we have seen, the first reports had been discouraging. But gradually the quality of the wool improved and he had the profound satisfaction of knowing that he had been able to make an important contribution to the American economy. As his flock increased, he generously handed out the progeny to his neighbors on an ever-widening scale, hoping that eventually Virginia would be blanketed with the fleecy animals and a great new industry opened to the struggling farmer.

Unfortunately, some of the farmers to whom he gave young Merinos free or who managed to receive them from other sources, were not as public-spirited as himself. They in turn sold the sheep for fabulous sums and, what infuriated Jefferson, received public praise for their profitable ventures.

"I have been so disgusted with the scandalous extortions lately practiced in the sale of these animals," he wrote indignantly to Madison, "and with the description of patriotism and praise to the sellers, as if the thousands of dollars apiece they have not been ashamed to receive were not reward enough, that I am disposed to consider as right, whatever is the reverse of what they have done. Since fortune has put the occasion upon us, is it not incumbent upon us so to dispense this benefit to the farmers of our country, as to put to shame those who, forgetting their own wealth and the honest simplicity of the farmers, have thought them fit objects of the shaving art, and to excite, by a better example, the condemnation due to theirs? No sentiment is more acknowledged in the family of Agriculturists than that the few who can afford it should incur the risk and expense of all new improvements, and give the benefit freely to the many of more restricted circumstances."[2]

This was *noblesse oblige* in the purest and finest aristocratic sense; and it must be remembered that Jefferson, for all his democracy, had more than a tinge of the benevolent aristocrat about him. He would, he avowed, as his own stock increased, present a full-blooded ram to each county in Virginia for the public servicing of the more common breed of ewes. When one of his friends proposed to publicize the offer, as a counterfoil to those who had basked in the public praise while growing rich on the profits, Jefferson exclaimed: "No, not for the world. This pharisaism would be too much like the pseudo patriotism which I have censured. It would exhibit me as greedy of praise, as they of pence." He wished for no approbation for doing what he considered "a duty incumbent on the richer farmers, to communicate gratis to those less so, any improvements they can introduce." [3]

He was constantly experimenting with new methods of farming, and sought advice from the greatest agriculturists abroad; yet did not refuse to learn from the humblest of his neighbors. His account, garden and farm books are full of notations of bits of lore he had picked up, and of experiments which he conducted himself. He even made intricate calculations of the comparative expense of candles and lamps after experiments which proved to his satisfaction that oil lamps were at least as economical as candles and had the advantage of a steadier light. He sought by actual trial on four-acre plots to determine which produced a better crop of wheat—those on which dung was folded into the soil, or those on which it was merely spread on the surface. He built the dwellings of his slaves close together, so that fewer nurses would be required for the children. These nurses, however, were the children themselves, up to the age of ten. From ten to sixteen, he decreed that the boys go to the nailery, while the girls spin. After sixteen, both sexes were transferred to work in the fields or to apprenticeship in trades.[4]

Now that he was permanently home, Jefferson increased his building operations, eventually making Monticello into the show place of the country. Yet he was never too busy to draw plans for his friends and neighbors when they sought to provide themselves with noble homes. It was his passion to see these architectural creatures of his mind take form and substance throughout Virginia.

Gradually his own cluster of buildings took shape and form on the mountaintop. The precious items he had brought with him from France were installed, and new ones imported. Mirrors, fossil remains, heads of moose and elk, a gallery of portraits, marble busts, onyx tables, a harpsichord, made the premises into something like a museum. But what set it off from every other dwelling in America, and never failed to excite the wonder of his visitors, were the many ingenious inventions Jefferson devised for his own comfort.

Such was the bed that rose on pulleys into the ceiling; the imported Swiss clock run by cannon balls for weights; the interior weather vane connected with the one that flaunted from the topmost roof; the concealed mechanical device that opened the double glass and mahogany doors between the hall and the dining room in a single operation; the turning buffet in the dining-room wall, and the dumb-waiter in the side of the mantelpiece through which wine bottles could be hoisted from the cellar; the adjustable drafting board on which he drew his plans; the folding ladders—these and dozens of other ingenious mechanical devices in which he delighted.

His décor was largely classical, and he plundered Roman motifs from pictures and reproductions for his own purposes. He particularly loved the formalized oxhead design on the frieze that embroidered the temple of Vespasian at Rome. The frieze itself he copied on his mantelpiece, and the oxhead became one of his favorite decorations, even to the extent of using it on the brick walls of the University of Virginia.

Since Monticello *was* a show place, and since Jefferson himself was a great and famous man who gradually assumed, with the gathering years, the position of an elder statesman and sage, visitors rode and drove in ever-increasing numbers up the winding mountain road. Hardly a day passed that at least eight extra plates were not set at the table; and often there were many more, running as high as thirty-two. To all, the known and unknown, those with business and those who were merely curious, Jefferson offered gracious hospitality. His overseer was later to remember that they came in family groups, in carriages and on horseback; that they ate him out of house and home, devouring a whole dressed beef in a day or two. Nor did they come for the day alone; they stayed on for the night and sometimes for a week and more, so that every bed in the house was taken and poor Martha Randolph had to scurry around to find extra beds and equipment.

Yet Jefferson, in the midst of all the hubbub and the drain on his finances, never lost his smile or temper. He pursued the same invariable course. He would either ride out early on his fields or remain in his room, reading and writing, sometimes with twenty-odd books scattered on the floor, dipping from one to the other, and cranking up his private dumb-waiter on which his subterranean servants placed fruit and food for an early morning snack. Only in the late afternoon did he return to the house, or emerge to welcome his guests and partake with them of the evening meal. The hours thereafter until bedtime were devoted to talk and entertainment.[5]

But he managed to solve even this problem and obtain, at least for long periods in each year, that measure of privacy which his body and soul demanded. In the latter days of his Presidency, his thoughts turned to the remoteness of Poplar Forest as a necessary retreat. Slowly, over the years, he commenced building a hermitage there. It took a long time, but he was in no hurry, and was content to spend several months of each late summer and early fall in a makeshift hut on the premises, with no company except a few servants to tend to his personal wants and aid in the construction.

The building as it finally evolved was a single-storied brick dwelling in front, and two stories in the rear where the ground fell away, in his favorite octagon shape and fifty feet in diameter. By the end of 1812, he was ready to plaster the interior; by 1814, he was building a wing of offices similar to that at Monticello. Building to him was never static; he was never satisfied that a structure had been completed; new ideas and more ambitious plans constantly brimmed over. Yet he surveyed the still-unfinished structure with considerable pride, and boasted that it would be "the best dwelling house in the state, except that of Monticello; perhaps preferable to that, as more proportioned to the faculties of a private citizen." By 1814, he had spent $10,000 on Poplar Forest and, he declared, "I am going on." [6]

To this hermitage he retreated, with his beloved books, writing table and polygraph, and took only with him on occasion his granddaughters for comfort in the evenings. Here he loafed, worked and invited his soul, and was able to return refreshed to the noise and bustle of Monticello.

Jefferson's tenderness toward animals was well known. His passion for finely blooded horses ran all through his career and, no matter how strapped he was for money, he never hesitated to buy an expensive new animal and think himself justified. His park was fenced in; but when deer jumped the fence in winter, he would scatter feed for them. When hunters chased them onto his premises, he would pick up his gun and peremptorily order the hunters away. He hunted very little on his own account, preferring to study the habits of living wild creatures in their native habitat.

But dogs were another matter; he never had for them the affection he had for other animals. True, he recognized their necessity and utility on a farm, but it was a strictly practical business and he begrudged their presence. He had brought some dogs with him from France for sheepherding and later imported others through the good offices of Lafayette for breeding and scattering their descendants over the countryside as he had the Merino sheep. He found them faithful and watchful enough, but he believed that, unless well fed, they would destroy sheep and hogs "without a trace." [7]

John Randolph noted in his Diary a conversation he had held with Jefferson on the subject as far back as 1804. Jefferson then said he considered dogs as a pernicious and useless race, and that there ought to be a law for their extirpation. He calculated what a saving that would make in the matter of their food, and declared that hydrophobia would be abolished. Randolph, a mighty hunter and a true Virginian, retorted in amazement that he would shoot anyone who came, law or no law, to destroy his dogs.[8]

In 1811, a bill was proposed in the state legislature to make dog owners liable for any damages they committed, and Jefferson agreed to urge all his friends in the Assembly to vote for it. He was ready to join in any plan, he avowed, to exterminate the whole race. "I consider them as the most afflicting of all the follies for which men tax themselves." [9] And when, several years later, the report came that the Assembly had imposed a tax on more than two dogs on a plantation, he promptly ordered his overseer to kill the surplus number on each of his holdings.[10]

Jefferson was always willing to lend a helping hand to the libertarians who had fled the tyranny of Europe for the hospitable shores of America, and to aid in disseminating their seminal opinions.

One of these had been Thomas Cooper, "a political refugee with Dr. Priestley from the fires & mobs of Birmingham." Cooper had become a judge in his adopted state of Pennsylvania, and sought a correspondent in Virginia with whom to discuss law, chemistry and mineralogy, in all of which pursuits he was famous. He applied to Jefferson, but the latter professed himself a novice in the field of mineralogy and urged a young Albemarle friend, Joseph C. Cabell—of whom more will be heard later—to accept the marvelous chance thus proffered him.[11]

During his Presidency, Jefferson had received the French manuscript of Destutt Tracy's commentary on Montesquieu, with the request that it be translated into English and published anonymously in this country. Now, for the first time, he felt able to attend to the task. He wrote to William Duane, the radical editor of the *Aurora*, offering it to him for translation and publication. Though Montesquieu's great book in many sections contained "much of truth and sound principle," he declared, it also abounded "with inconsistencies, apocryphal facts and false references"; and therefore it was essential to counter the latter with Tracy's critical commentary. This was, Jefferson assured Duane, "the most valuable political work of the present age" and reduced Montesquieu "to his just level, as his predilection for monarchy, and the English monarchy in particular, has done mischief everywhere, and here, too, to a certain degree."

He was all the more anxious to see Tracy's book in print, because it would be a good substitute for Hume's History as well, which every student used as a manual and which he himself had devoured when young. For Hume, so he now thought, was an apologist for the Stuart kings and had instilled a subtle poison in English readers, which "has undermined the free principles of the English government, has persuaded readers of all classes that there were usurpations on the legitimate and salutary rights of the crown, and has spread universal toryism over the land."[12]

Tracy's Commentary, as well as his other works, have long since passed into the limbo of forgotten writings, to be read only by the specialist and the curious student of an era; but in their day they excited the enthusiastic admiration of a select coterie. Jefferson was perhaps his most ardent admirer; but such a keen observer of human affairs as Henri Beyle, better known as Stendhal, similarly came under the spell of Tracy's ideas.

What particularly won Jefferson's approval was Tracy's eloquent exposition of a constitutional government, based on representatives elected by all the citizens, and whose powers were defined and limited to specific areas beyond which they must not trespass. Such a democracy, declared the author in contradistinction to Montesquieu's thesis, could flourish indefinitely and over wide extents of territory. Other assertions similarly followed Jefferson's own thinking. A representative democracy need not fear the truth and, since it is "founded solely on reason and nature, its only enemies are error and prejudice." As a corollary, therefore, a democracy ought to render knowledge universal; prevent the poor from succumbing to ignorance and vice and the rich from becoming insolent; and bring both to "that middle point, at which the love of order, of industry, of justice, and reason, naturally establish themselves." As a further corollary, ideas and their communication must be placed under no restraint; "for it is indisputable, that wherever opinion is left free with reason only to combat it, truth will ultimately prevail." [13]

These were doctrines dear to Jefferson's heart and which he considered, just as much as Tracy, as "indisputable" laws of nature. There was only one pronouncement in the book with which he took issue; and this was Tracy's belief that a plural executive was preferable to a single one. The American experience during the period of the Confederacy had tended to cure him of that fallacy; the sight of the French Directorate had completed the task. Compare, he exclaimed, "the tranquil and steady tenor of our single executive, during a course of twenty-two years of the most tempestuous times the history of the world has ever presented," with the fierce struggles of the Directorate. During Washington's administration, he was convinced, when the Cabinet was so often equally divided, only the fact that a single man was the final arbiter kept the government and the country on an even keel.

Nor did he fear that a single executive might become a dictator like Napoleon, for the state governments were "the true barriers of our liberty in this country" and "the wisest conservative power ever contrived by man." Even if one state were paralyzed by the usurper, there were sixteen others to defend their liberties. In France, he pointed out, "no provincial organizations existed to which the people might rally under authority of the laws . . . and a small force sufficed to turn the legislature out of their chamber, and to salute its leader chief of the nation." [14]

Duane accepted the manuscript, had it translated, and published it later in the year. But he expected a *quid pro quo*. Having violently antagonized the Republicans of his own state, furiously attacked Gallatin and others of the national government, and threatened even President Madison himself, Duane's paper had lost circulation and his personal fortunes were at a low ebb. He therefore appealed to Jefferson for assistance.

The latter gently reproved him for his assaults on Gallatin, who was "of a pure integrity, and as zealously devoted to the liberties and interests of our country as its most affectionate native citizen." Nevertheless, he acknowledged that Duane's zeal and sufferings in the cause of the Revolution entitled him to continued support, and assured him he would seek to raise funds for the *Aurora* among his friends. But, he warned the errant publisher, let not the Republicans, "the last hope of human liberty in this world," break up into quarreling squads. "We ought not to schismatize on either men or measures," he concluded significantly. "Principles alone can justify that." [15]

As usually happens to a mediator, Jefferson suffered rebuffs on either side. William Wirt, to whom Jefferson appealed for funds, replied coldly that Duane had better go to his present allies for help, and that no doubt he intended to attack Madison next. If that were so, Jefferson replied, he would immediately abandon him; "but I still think Duane is more likely to be won by liberality, than to be forced from his direction by persecution." [16]

Wirt's fears were soon justified, for the *Aurora* promptly came out with fierce attacks on Madison. Those few of Jefferson's friends who had reluctantly yielded to his pleas now withdrew their promises of money, and Jefferson wrote a revealing letter to Duane to apprise him of the situation. "An Editor," he admitted, "should be independent, that is, of personal influence, and not be moved from his opinions on the mere authority of any individual. But, with respect to the general opinion of the political section with which he habitually accords, his duty seems very like that of a member of Congress." In other words, Jefferson advocated party discipline. He himself, he avowed, had often voted and acted "on the judgment of others against my own"; otherwise you give victory to the enemy as a consequence of your insistence on your own individuality. He pointed to the example of John Randolph as "a caution to all honest and prudent men, to sacrifice a little of self-confidence, and to go with their friends, although they may sometimes think they are going wrong." [17]

Duane did not take kindly to any of this well-meant advice. He answered neither of Jefferson's letters, and when he finally sent him a copy of the Tracy book, he merely mentioned that they had "excited in my breast very painful feelings," and therefore he had decided on silence.[18]

Jefferson loved to assume in his general correspondence the role of the retired private citizen, of the man who had enough of politics and all its works and now sought only the peace and preoccupations of a devoted farmer. "I am done with politics and have banished all its passions" was his constant refrain.[19]

But to his former political intimates he presented a wholly different face. He followed every twist and turn of the tangled political situation at home and abroad with a passionate interest; he exhorted, advised and even threatened; his language was violent against his former enemies and his words were fiery; and, like all men no longer bound by the inhibitions of total responsibility for the contemplated act, he advocated measures of force and war from which he had shrunk when *he* inhabited the President's House.

"I wish," he exhorted his erstwhile son-in-law, John Wayles Eppes, member of Congress, "you would authorize the President to take possession of East Florida immediately. The seizing West Florida will be a signal to take Pensacola & St. Augustine; and be assured it will be done as soon as the order can return after they hear of our taking Baton Rouge; and we shall never get it from them [Spain] but by a war, which may be prevented by anticipation—there never was a case where the adage was more true, 'in for a penny, in for a pound'; and no more offense will be taken by France & Spain at our seizure of both than of one.... The leading Republican members should come to an understanding, close the doors, and determine not to separate till the vote is carried, and all the secrecy you can enjoin should be aimed at until the measure is executed. The militia of Georgia will do it in a fortnight." [20] This incitement to violent and forcible seizure, with all its unforeseeable consequences, was penned on the very day he breathed that other avowal of retirement from politics and passions.

And, somewhat later, he lashed out with unprecedented bitterness at the Federalists and their new-found ally, John Randolph. The former, he exclaimed, were "bitterer enemies to their country" than any foreigner; they "would be delighted that Great Britain could conquer & reduce us again under her government." Some, indeed, would even prefer French dominion to a Republican administration. As for John Randolph, no epithet was too coarse or unbridled. "With so unprincipled and traitorous an opposition," he declared, "the republican who schismatizes is a traitor indeed, altho' he may not be in intention." But that last grudging qualification referred only to Randolph's followers, not to the leader himself. *He* was "the most envenomed enemy to a democratical republican government which it has ever seen." Eppes, who had thought of retiring from Congress, must run again and defeat that wielder of an "adder tongue." [21]

Madison must be supported and his arm upheld by all good Republicans, he kept on insisting. He was therefore extremely gratified when the breach was finally healed between Madison and Monroe, and the former offered and the latter accepted the post of Secretary of State in the Cabinet. This meant that the Republican ranks were closing again, and that the hated John Randolph had lost his last hope for regaining power. Jefferson wrote warm congratulations to Madison and advised him to treat the returning Monroe "with the cordiality of earlier times. He will feel himself to be at home again in our bosoms, and happy in a separation from those who led him astray. I learn," he added with a touch of satisfaction, "that John Randolph is now open-mouthed against him & Hay." [22]

With this major rift mended, Jefferson could look forward comfortably to a long and uninterrupted session of Virginia administrators in the government. That way, with the proper republican principles, lay the utopia he described to Dupont, and the vision of which exalted him. "Our revenues once liberated by the discharge of the public debt, & its surplus applied to canals, roads, schools, &c., and the farmer will see his government supported, his children educated, & the face of his country made a paradise by the contributions of the rich alone, without his being called on to spare a cent from his earnings."[23] No wonder the Federalists viewed this philosophy of "soaking the rich" for the benefit of the farmer with something less than total approval.

The summer of 1811 found Jefferson laid up with a sharp attack of rheumatism. The moment he thought he was better he set out for his retreat in Poplar Forest. The journey, however, was agonizing; and in his distress he called on the distant Dr. Rush for advice and thought even of a trip to the warm springs for relief.[24]

Rush sent him a list of remedies. Wear a piece of calico on the affected parts, he advised; quilt bruised rolls of sulphur into pieces of muslin and apply; rub the areas with a dry hand or brush; bathe twice a day with a compound of castille soap, camphor, opium and salt in spirits; and take internally spirit of turpentine and sassafras tea.[25]

Even with his rheumatism, however, Jefferson refused to remain idle. He calculated the latitude of Poplar Forest; then, after he had limped back to Monticello, he proposed to go to the top of neighboring Willis's mountain to take its latitude, but only if he could make the grade on horseback. There was an eclipse of the sun on September 17th, and Jefferson got out his instruments to take observations. Unfortunately, he missed the first moments of solar occlusion because he had started to set up the apparatus too late. Nevertheless, he was proud of the fact that, as far as he knew, he had been the only one in Virginia to take observations on the eclipse. He sent his figures to a mathematical friend, William Lambert, for final calculations of the longitude of Monticello. He did not feel up to making them himself; though, as he told Lambert, "I have for some time past been rubbing off the rust of my mathematics contracted during 50. years engrossed by other pursuits, and have found in it a delight and a success beyond my expectations."[26]

Mingled with these scientific pursuits were others of a more mundane and litigious character. He became involved in another of his Homeric lawsuits; this time with the directors of a project for building a canal that would render the Rivanna navigable. Since Jefferson had erected a dam on that section of the river which ran through his land, it was necessary to come to terms with him on the building of a lock in the dam and its maintenance. But the directors and Jefferson did not agree on the terms, and the matter went to court for lengthy litigation, in which Jefferson, as usual, prepared innumerable notes, depositions and vast legal documents for the delectation of his lawyers.[27]

Fortunately, at about the time that this new law action commenced, an old one ended successfully—the claim for damages by Edward Livingston in connection with the Batture. But Jefferson, while rejoicing, felt uneasily that, since it was dismissed on a technicality rather than on the merits, the public might suspect that true justice had not been done and, as Jefferson put it, "their impression produced by Livingston's squalling as if his throat had been cut, will be uncorrected." Therefore, he decided to place his own voluminous exposition of the case in print.[28]

Just as earlier in the year, he had belligerently demanded that force be used to seize the Floridas from Spain, now his wrathful attention turned toward the north. He was thoroughly convinced that Great Britain was determined to permit no commerce on the seas unless it passed through her ports and paid substantial tolls for the privilege. War, therefore, was inevitable, at least as long as King George III still lived. Only the prospect that he might conveniently die in the very near future (an event which would probably lead to a change of policy) deterred Jefferson from demanding the immediate calling of Congress and the seizure of Canada.[29] Having expanded the United States far to the west, Jefferson sought further expansion to the south and north, with the eventual goal of the entire continent, with the possible exception of Mexico, coming under the American flag.

The break between Jefferson and John Adams had continued now for a full decade. Once, as we have seen, on the death of Jefferson's daughter, Abigail Adams had written the bereaved father (without the knowledge of her husband), but the promising overture had ended abruptly after an increasingly acrimonious rehashing of ancient politics. Again there was silence.

The situation troubled old Dr. Rush. He was conducting a cordial correspondence with both parties to the feud, but from neither came so much as a word as to the other. The dispute had gone long enough, he thought, and determined to use his good offices to bring these one-time friends together again. But tact and diplomacy were essential.

He commenced a considered plan of campaign. To each he fired an opening gun. "Your and my old friend Mr Adams," he wrote to Jefferson, "now & then drops me a line from his seat at Quincy. His letters glow with the just Opinions he held and defended in the patriotic years 1774, 1775 & 1776." In fact, added Rush cunningly, he has just expressed his indignation to me against banks that issue paper at interest (an indignation certainly shared by Jefferson). With this mutual indignation definitely established, Rush proceeded to the attack direct. "When I consider," he pleaded eloquently, "your early attachment to Mr Adams, and his—to you— When I consider how much the liberties & Independence of the United States owe to the Concert of your principles and labors, and when I reflect upon the sameness of your opinions at present, upon most of the subjects of Government, and all the subjects of legislation, I have ardently wished a friendly and epistolary intercourse might be revived between you before you take a final leave of the common Object of your Affections. . . . Posterity will revere the friendship of the two Ex presidents that were once opposed to each other. Human nature will be a gainer by it. I am sure," he concluded, "an Advance on your side will be a Cordial to the heart of Mr Adams." [30]

This was eloquent and well-nigh irresistible. Yet Jefferson, flattered though he was, hesitated, remembering the disastrous interlude with Abigail and the still-present resentment over the "midnight appointments." Nevertheless, he assured Rush, the original break had not proceeded from him, and he was willing to renew friendship if, he added cautiously, it were possible.[31]

There the matter rested for almost a year, with Jefferson forwarding to Rush copies of his correspondence with Abigail to prove that renewal was really impossible. He was certain that John had been fully aware of the exchange and had approved of those opinions of his wife which had offended Jefferson so deeply. But two brothers named Cole, Jefferson's neighbors, traveled to Boston late in 1811 and spent a day with Adams at Braintree. They returned to Albemarle to report that Adams had said: "I always loved Jefferson, and still love him."

That simple, unaffected declaration unsealed the frozen springs in Jefferson's heart. "This was enough for me," he wrote immediately to Rush. "I only needed this knowledge to revive towards him all the affections of the most cordial moments of our lives.... I knew him to be always an honest man, often a great one, but sometimes incorrect and precipitate in his judgments.

"I wish, therefore, but for an apposite occasion to express to Mr. Adams my unchanged affections for him. There is an awkwardness which hangs over the resuming a correspondence so long discontinued, unless something could arise which should call for a letter." Could Rush therefore suggest to Adams that *he* start the correspondence? But, added Jefferson sternly, "from this fusion of mutual affections, Mrs. Adams is of course separated. It will only be necessary that I never name her." [32]

Rush, delighted at this break in the log jam, hastened to send selected passages from Jefferson's letter to Adams—discreetly omitting, of course, the references to Abigail and to Adams's "incorrect and precipitate" judgments.[33]

Adams received "the olive branch" with a certain scepticism. "I perceive plainly enough, Rush," he retorted to the intended mediator, "that you have been teasing Jefferson to write to me, as you did me some time ago to write to him." But, he protested, there never had been any war between them, and "where there has been no war, there can be no room for negotiations of peace."

Nevertheless, just as Jefferson had done, he expatiated at length on the points of political dispute between them. The difference was that Adams gave them a humorous light touch. "I held levees once a week," he asserted gravely, "that all my time might not be wasted by idle visits. Jefferson's whole eight years was a levee. . . . I dined a large company once or twice a week. Jefferson dined a dozen every day. . . . Jefferson and Rush were for liberty and straight hair. I thought curled hair was as republican as straight."

But he had always loved Jefferson, he continued in more serious vein, and whatever injury he might have received, he had long since forgiven.

"But why do you make so much ado about nothing?" he asked Rush. "Of what use can it be for Jefferson and me to exchange letters? I have nothing to say to him, but to wish him an easy journey to heaven, when he goes. . . . And he can have nothing to say to me, but to bid me make haste and be ready. Time and chance, however, or possibly design," he ended inconsistently, "may produce ere long a letter between us." [34]

If Rush read between the lines, he might have found ample evidence that he need not despair. The two old men were like coy and reluctant lovers after a quarrel, each refusing to commence overtures, yet secretly waiting for the opening that would enable him to come to terms without loss of face.

Adams was the first to yield. On New Year's Day of 1812, just a week after his retort to Rush, he picked up his pen and instituted, in a large and quavering hand, what is without doubt one of the greatest and most fruitful correspondences in all history.

CHAPTER 66

Reconciliation with Adams

THE beginning of the exchanges between Adams and Jefferson seemed on the surface formal enough. That awkwardness to which Jefferson adverted had first to be broken down. "As you are a Friend to American Manufactures under proper restrictions," wrote Adams, "especially Manufactures of the domestic kind, I take the Liberty of Sending you by the Post a Packett containing two Pieces of Homespun lately produced in this quarter by one who was honoured in his youth with some of your Attention and much of your kindness."

After some news of his family, Adams concluded with ceremonious politeness: "I wish you Sir many happy New Years and that you may enter the next and many Succeeding Years with as animating Prospects for the Public as those at present before Us. I am Sir with a long and Sincere Esteem your Friend and Servant John Adams." [1]

It was formal, it was halting, it was awkward, as if Adams did not quite know where to begin. Or at least so it seemed. But it was enough!

Jefferson replied, himself embarrassed, yet adding just that sufficient touch of warmth which permitted a future gradual unfolding. He thanked Adams for the samples of homespun that had not yet arrived. Still feeling his way, he entered into a long dissertation on the state of manufactures in Virginia. Then the log jam loosened: "A letter from you calls up recollections very dear to my mind. It carries me back to the times when, beset with difficulties and dangers, we were fellow-laborers in the same cause, struggling for what is most valuable to man, his rights of self-government." In spite of all troubles, "so we have gone on, and so we shall go on puzzled and prospering beyond example in the history of man." But the stories of France and England had come out differently. "With all their preëminence in science, the one is a den of robbers, and the other of pirates. And if science," proceeded Jefferson, warming to his theme, "produces no better fruits than tyranny, murder, rapine and destitution of national morality, I would rather wish our country to be ignorant, honest and estimable, as our neighboring savages are." This of course was flying in the face of everything that the Enlightenment—and Jefferson—believed in, and represented nothing more than a temporary revulsion on his part.

But enough of politics. He had given them up, together with newspapers, for Tacitus and Thucydides, Newton and Euclid; and for his memories. Of the signers of the Declaration of Independence, only seven remained alive. "You and I have been wonderfully spared," he concluded. His own health was good and he rode always, though unable to walk much. He heard, however, that Adams was still a good walker, and saluted him "with unchanged affection and respect." [2]

Jefferson sent a copy of the letter to Rush, who had been responsible for the resumption. "To avoid the subject of his family [Abigail], I have written him a rambling, gossiping epistle which gave openings for the expression of sincere feelings, & may furnish him ground of reciprocation, if he merely waited for the first declaration; for so I would construe the reserve of his letter." [3]

He was correct in his interpretation. Adams's reply was substantially more cordial and intimate. "Sitting at My Fireside with my Daughter Smith, on the first of February My Servant brought me a Bundle of Letters." One of them struck his eye. "Reading the Superscription I instantly handed the Letter to Mrs. Smith. Is not that Mr Jeffersons hand? Looking attentively at it, she answered it was very like it."

But he had played a joke on Jefferson. "The Material of the Samples of American Manufacture which I sent you," he chuckled, "was not Wool nor Cotton, nor Silk nor Flax nor Hemp nor Iron nor Wood. They were Spun from the Brain of John Quincy Adams and consist in two Volumes of his Lectures on Rhetorick and oratory, deliv[er]ed when he was Professor of that Science in our University of Cambridge."

In more serious vein, he took up the challenge of some cautious generalizations Jefferson had permitted himself on politics and the future of the country. That future, he asserted gloomily, "will depend on the Union: and how is that Union to be preserved." Already it had several times been in jeopardy; and there was an ever-present danger (with an unmistakable side glance at Napoleon) of a conquering hero against whom civilians like Adams and Jefferson would stand no more chance "than a Swallow or a Sparrow." It was to the *Union*, he declared significantly, that he had sacrificed his popularity in New England and gained no thanks for it in Virginia. (This was a reference to the days when he had withstood the Federalist clamor for war with France.)

He picked up the comment of Jefferson concerning his current interests. "What an Exchange have you made?" he exclaimed. "Of Newspapers for Newton! Rising from the lower deep of the lowest deep of Dulness and Bathos to the Contemplation of the Heavens and the heavens of Heavens. Oh that I had devoted to Newton and his Fellows, that time which I fear has been wasted on Plato and Aristotle," on Bolingbroke, Harrington, Sidney, Hobbes and their fellows.[4]

With the log jam thus completely smashed, Adams hastened in turn to exult to Rush, the mutual confidant. Jefferson's letters, he declared (and Rush faithfully reported the sentiment to Jefferson), "are written with all the elegance, purity and Sweetness of Style of his youth and middle age, and with (what I envy more)—a firmness of finger, and steadiness of chirography, that to me, are lost for ever." [5]

This was very true. Jefferson's style continued impeccable to the last days of his life; so did his finely engraved handwriting. Yet Adams, for all that his hand wavered, was able to express himself, if not with purity and elegance, certainly with a gnarled vigor and crabbed individuality of style and sentiment, a gruff ursine humor and rumbling of epithets, that need fear no comparison with even a Jefferson.

From this point on, until the day of their simultaneous deaths, the two ex-Presidents continued their correspondence, the letters crossing in the mails, the subjects ranging over the entire field of intellectual activities, interspersed with reminiscences and interpretative comments of the mighty events in which they had been such significant actors. Science, natural religion, ethics, morality, politics, history—nothing escaped their insatiable curiosity. The ancient bitterness was gone, old controversial events could now be discussed vigorously and yet with a mutual courtesy and forbearance concerning the role of the other. The sparks of perception kindled between them, and ponderings on the immutable questions of life and death.

When they touched current politics, however, they skimmed them gingerly or left them severely alone. Jefferson later remarked that they corresponded on everything *but* politics. "Where there are so many others on which we agree, why should we introduce the only one on which we differ." [6]

But Adams was wholly at one with Jefferson on the suit for damages which Edward Livingston had instituted. "Good God!" he exclaimed. "Is a President of U. S. to be Subject to a private Action of every Individual?" [7] This was touching a prerogative which he held dear.

War with Great Britain was definitely in the offing as the year of 1812 commenced. The Embargo had failed, the British blockades and forcible searches continued; yet the reasons for war now were much less cogent than they had been at almost any time before. Certainly they were nothing like as urgent as in the days that immediately followed the *Chesapeake* outrage. When it finally came, it was not popular, except with those who either sought aggrandizement in Canada, or had their eyes fixed firmly on the Floridas.

Yet Jefferson found his neighbors at the beginning of the year in full approval of the expected war. A whisky tax was proposed—that same tax which had roused the ire of the Republicans when the *Federalists* had levied it; and Jefferson himself approved of it, though with reservations.[8] He hated whisky as ruinous to the poor and a besotter of the intelligence. He never touched it himself; preferring the light wines even to the fortified ones.

With war coming up fast, Jefferson supported Madison unreservedly. There was relief implicit in his general tone that the die was about to be cast, and that the years of hesitation and shilly-shallying were over. It was another man's responsibility now, and he could indulge himself in the luxury of whole-hearted participation without shouldering the weight.

Now, indeed, he acknowledged that war might in some cases be preferable to the Embargo. The planters and farmers of Virginia, he discovered, had been left with a third of their grain and three-quarters of their tobacco unsold and a dead, unmarketable weight on their hands. Perhaps, he told Madison, with the advent of war commerce might be renewed with Great Britain (under restrictions and licenses, of course) that would prove "mutually advantageous to the individuals, and not to their injury as belligerents. . . . I think a people would go through a war with much less impatience if they could dispose of their produce, and that unless a vent can be provided for them, they will soon become querulous and clamor for peace."[9]

This letter contains certain remarkable sentiments: First, that it is proper to prohibit commerce with another nation in time of peace, but it ought not to be done in time of war. Second, that the pocketbooks of the farmers ought to be tenderly consulted; yet when merchants and traders asked for the same consideration, they were traitors for whom hanging was too good.

Indeed, when the Federalists opposed the proposition of war, Jefferson called for measures against them of a violence and ferocity that comported ill with every profession he had ever made. So inconsistent, indeed, that the editors of his papers have hitherto prudently omitted the passage from the published page.

Congress had declared war in June over the bitter opposition of the Federalists, and Madison had signed the fateful bill on June 18, 1812. Jefferson promptly wrote to the President offering his support and advice. Then he adverted to the Federalists. They, he exclaimed, "indeed are open mouthed against the declaration. But they are poor devils here, not worthy of notice. A barrel of tar to each state South of the Patomac will keep all in order, & that will be freely contributed without troubling government. To the North they will give you more trouble. You may then have to apply the rougher drastics of Govr. Wright, hemp and confiscation."[10]

His advice in the same letter for the conduct of the war was equally remarkable. To make it popular in Virginia, he asserted, it was necessary, first, to put an end to Indian barbarities on the frontier by conquering Canada; second, to furnish markets for the produce of the farmer. To see his crops rot in the barn would soon sicken him of the war; a condition for which, Jefferson remarked with feeling, no wonder or blame ought to attach to him. Let the coastwise trade, therefore, be well protected; and let us wink even at the carriage of that produce in *enemy* ships abroad, as long as face is saved by their employing the subterfuge of a neutral flag.

Perhaps the answer to these strange propositions lies in the state of Jefferson's private affairs. "It is unlucky," he complained to one of his agents, "that the embargo catches me with so much unsold. I expect however that as soon as the merchants have had time to fix on a channel of vent, it will rise again.... The vent of our produce even to our enemies must be desirable; & it would be sound policy during actual war."[11]

He welcomed the war also for other than economic reasons. He believed that "this second weaning from British principles, British attachments, British manners & manufactures will be salutary, & will form an epoch of a spirit of nationalism and of consequent prosperity, which could never have resulted from a continued subordination to the interests & influence of England."[12]

In fact, everything that had ever come from England was tainted to him. Even the common law. He had always vehemently denied that Americans had brought the common law with them to these shores, or that their rights derived from it; though he admitted that arguments based on the common law had been used in the first struggle against England. The truth is, he now insisted, that what actually came over to the New World were "*the rights of men;* of expatriated men." In other words, those rights which, in eighteenth-century parlance, constituted the "natural" rights of mankind. From this chain of reasoning he drew a corollary—that the citing of English authorities *after* the Declaration of Independence, or even after the accession of George III to the throne, ought not to be permitted in American courts of law.[13]

John Adams was much less vehement about the war. He surveyed, indeed, all mankind from a cynical height. "I am weary of contemplating nations," he wrote Jefferson, "from the lowest and most beastly degradations of human life to the highest refinement of civilization. I am weary of philosophers, theologians, politicians, and historians. They are immense masses of absurdities, vices, and lies." Yet he could not refrain from some satiric remarks about the war, and to rise to the defense of the Federalist opposition. "I lament the contumacious spirit that appears about me," he declared, "but I lament the cause that has given too much apology for it, the total neglect and absolute refusal of all maritime protection and defence. Money, mariners, and soldiers would be at the public service, if only a few frigates had been ordered to be built."[14]

The receipt of such critical remarks must have touched Jefferson on a very sensitive spot, for it had been he and none other who had refused to build those frigates. The navy, he admitted, had always been Adams's "hobby-horse," and when the few ships the United States did possess performed the only brilliant exploits of the war and managed to retrieve in part the disasters on land, Jefferson hastened to inform Adams that he had not really differed with him in principle, but only on the question of timing. He defended himself on the ground that a second-class navy was as bad as none at all; or worse, if the expense and burden were considered. Only when the opposition navies would be brought to a balance with the might of England so that *our* navy could turn the scale against her, should we go ahead with a real building program. Until that time, he felt that all we required was a navy sufficiently strong to keep the Barbary States in order; "these being the only smaller powers disposed to quarrel with us." [15]

Jefferson explained the whole strategy of the war to Thaddeus Kosciusko, the Polish hero who had returned to his homeland. The reason we had not long before gone to war with England, wrote Jefferson, was because France had been equally iniquitous, though she did not possess equal power to harm us. England, he thought, would be able to rule the sea; but *we* would rule the American continent and strip her of Canada and her other American possessions. England might be able to burn New York (he did not yet envisage the possibility of Washington); but in that case, he amazingly proposed, "we must burn the city of London by hired incendiaries, of which her starving manufacturers will furnish abundance." [16]

As the war progressed, Jefferson became more and more the advocate of a self-contained manufacturing economy; particularly on the plantation. He himself set the example for his neighbors. By the beginning of 1813 he had in operation thirty-five spindles, a hand carding machine and looms with flying shuttles. "The continuance of the war will fix the habit generally," he was certain, "and out of the evils of impressment and of the orders of council, a great blessing for us will grow. I have not formerly been an advocate for great manufactories," he confessed. "I doubted whether our labor, employed in agriculture, and aided by the spontaneous energies of the earth, would not procure us more than we could make ourselves of other necessaries. But other considerations entering into the question, have settled my doubts." [17] Jefferson's mind was sufficiently flexible to acknowledge an ancient error and to rectify it.

But the war did not take the course he so confidently anticipated. The little navy he had decried as ineffective and a useless expense displayed its valor and fighting qualities in every encounter on the sea. But the army and militia—and particularly the latter, his pet and favorite—were complete fiascoes.

The conquest of Canada as far as Quebec, Jefferson had thought, would be "a mere matter of marching, and will give us experience for the attack of Halifax the next, and the final expulsion of England from the American continent." [18]

An army, it is true, did march, but it did not get very far. General William Hull moved to attack Detroit, the British outpost on the Great Lakes, and from there expected to move into Canada where, it was felt, the mere appearance of an American force would cause the entire territory to surrender. Instead, he fell into a trap; and after an incredible series of disasters, surrendered.

The catastrophe was a staggering blow to American pride; and no one took it harder than Jefferson. It was easier for him to impute the defeat to Hull's incompetence and treason than to the superior fighting power of the British. All his wrath was diverted against the General. Hull, he advised Madison, must be "shot for cowardice & treachery. And will not Van Renslaer be broke for cowardice and incapacity?" [19] The more he thought of it, the more furious he became. It was without doubt treachery, he insisted, because cowardice could not alone account for Hull's actions. "My wonder is," he declared, "that his officers & men permitted themselves to be given up like sheep without even bleating." The only silver lining he could find in the whole discreditable episode was that the public reaction was good, and the spirit of the people high.[20]

He even rejoiced that the intransigeant Percival ministry had been re-established in England, so that there would be no nonsense of "half-way offers" to the United States which would only serve to bolster the Federalists.[21] That minority, however, proved active enough in New England, where the war had been unpopular from its inception. The first mutterings of revolt and separation were already to be heard, and were to culminate in the Hartford Convention during the last dark years of the war.

Yet Jefferson felt that "when the questions of separatism and rebellion shall be nakedly proposed to them, the Gores & the Pickerings will find their levees crowded with silk-stocking gentry, but no yeomanry, an army of officers, without soldiers." [22] This proved true prophecy.

He was by now driven into a position where he was willing to accept a high-duty tariff which would not only provide a revenue but help protect the permanent establishment of American manufactures. It was only by the power of her money, backed by her industrial output, he argued, that England was winning. He was certain that money had been liberally employed at Detroit to induce Hull to surrender, and in Massachusetts to stir up Federalist secession.[23]

In spite of the war disasters, in spite of a tumble from his horse that disabled him for twelve days, in spite of several vexatious law suits in which he now found himself, Jefferson was once again cheerful. His district had gone overwhelmingly Republican in the fall elections; wheat and flour were at their highest price in history; and he expected them to go higher, "if Congress do nothing to prevent exportation which I think it impossible they should do." [24]

His advocacy of the unrestricted exportation of agricultural products, even to the enemy and in enemy ships, was paying excellent personal dividends. By October, 1812, he was able for the first time in many years to contemplate his income with satisfaction. His 10,000 acres and 200 slaves were yielding him well over $10,000 a year; [25] and if prices went higher, he looked forward to making even more. With the Wayles' debt almost paid off, he foresaw the possibility of a comfortable old age.

No wonder then that he kept insisting that this policy be continued. To maintain the popularity of the war in Virginia, he repeated again and again, "you must admit free exportations," without any increase in taxes. "War taxes and a suppression of exports would be to call for bricks without allowing straw. No people," he added significantly, "can stand that." [26]

The war economy only strengthened Jefferson's conviction that science should have a wholly utilitarian purpose. If it could not be directed to useful purposes, to ameliorate the condition of mankind, then it was of no more value than windy philosophy. This was his chief quarrel with the chemists of the time, as not sufficiently attentive to the *applications* of their science. "I have wished to see their science applied to domestic objects," he commented, "to malting, for instance, brewing, making cider, to fermentation and distilling generally, to the making of bread, butter, cheese, soap, to the incubation of eggs, etc." [27] In short, to those arts which would prove most useful to the farmer and plantation owner. What he did not realize, of course, was that no science could ever advance, even for utilitarian purposes, without a background of pure and disinterested research for its own sake. Nor did he note any inconsistency in his own passionate absorption in such "useless" studies as the fossil bones of mammoths and other extinct animals, or the comparative study of Indian dialects in order to trace a common point of origin.

Indeed, he had little opportunity to engage in *any* studies, in spite of the spaciousness of Monticello. "I have living with me," he half-humorously complained, ". . . eight grand children, their parents, & other connections making up a dozen at our daily table, and that number generally enlarged by the successive visits of other friends & relations. Quarters so crowded are illy calculated for the quiet or comfort of the aged or the studious." [28]

Nevertheless, in spite of these disadvantages, he found time to read the work of Cabanis, whose *Rapports du physique et du moral de l'homme* he praised as the "most profound of all human compositions." [29] He enthusiastically agreed with Cabanis's search for a direct relationship between the bodily organs and functions of man and his mental activities, and with his analysis of environmental conditions on human life and conduct.

He also found time to become equally enthusiastic over Destutt Tracy's new manuscript on Political Economy which reviewed the economic ideas of Adam Smith and Say. "As Smith," declared Jefferson, "had corrected some principles of the economists and Say some of Smith's; so Tracy has done as to the whole. He has in my opinion corrected fundamental errors in all of them, and by simplifying principles has brought the subject within a narrow compass." He therefore offered the book to Duane for possible publication, inasmuch as Duane had already marketed Tracy's *Review*.[30] But Duane was not sufficiently impressed at the time, and it took several years before Jefferson was able to place this new text on Political Economy before his countrymen.

He was reading a good deal in ancient history now, professing himself "tired of practical politics, and happier while reading the history of antient, than of modern times." The profligacy and immorality of modern governments, he avowed, "sickens my soul unto death." At least the similar immoralities of ancient days had already received adequate condemnation in the pages of historians and the eyes of succeeding generations; "a solace," he naïvely added, "we cannot have with the Georges and Napoleons, but by anticipation." [31]

It was his readings in ancient history that brought him to the conclusion that universal military training was essential if America was to be safe. Every citizen, he asserted, must be a soldier; just as had been the case with the Greeks and the Romans. "Where there is no oppression," he argued, "there will be no pauper hirelings. We must train and classify the whole of our male citizens, and make military instruction a regular part of collegiate education." [32]

He also thought that the navy should not be scattered in single forays on enemy commerce or against single enemy warships, but ought to be held together in a body in some protected waters, in order to defend the coast and to break blockades. Perhaps he did not altogether realize the implications of his suggestion that the Chesapeake waters (protecting Virginia) would be the ideal place for the fleet. But Monroe, to whom he made the suggestion, and Madison also, disagreed with the strategy thus offered, and Jefferson handsomely admitted that he was wrong.[33] His hidden bias similarly appeared in the next plan he tendered—that a hundred gunboats be built and delegated to the Delaware and the Chesapeake. The coasts and ports to the north, he told Madison, needed no defense against enemy raids, because they were "treated by the enemy as neutrals." [34]

His intense anxiety for naval protection of the Chesapeake—gateway of Virginia—was no doubt motivated by the blockade which cruising British warships had clamped on that length of shore, and their evident determination not to permit that exportation of Virginia products which Jefferson had so eloquently defended. As a result, the prosperity of the preceding year suddenly collapsed. "I am one of those unfortunates," lamented Jefferson, "on whom the blockade came before I had sold a barrel of my flour." Some 500 barrels were lying at Richmond, "the fate of which depends solely on the motions of the blockading squadron." But the British held on grimly, the American gunboats never materialized, so that Jefferson was compelled to sell his flour at a substantial loss. As if this calamity were not enough, the land suffered from a prolonged drought. All in all, it was a bad year for Jefferson. All his optimistic prospects of a few months before went glimmering, and he was thrown back on his usual mournful routine of asking extensions of time to pay his current debts.[35]

With the war proceeding badly, with the several invasions of Canada a complete fiasco, other voices than Jefferson's expressed their indignation and demanded a change in its conduct. There were those who urged that Monroe be shifted from the Cabinet to the command of the northwestern army (though what qualifications he possessed for the post are imperceptible) and that Jefferson be called out of retirement to replace him as Secretary of State.[36] None of the parties directly concerned seem to have considered the proposition with any degree of seriousness.

But the matter of the removal of Robert Smith from the key position of the War Department *was* contemplated; though Madison feared it might offend Wilson C. Nicholas, Smith's political ally. Jefferson suggested that Nicholas might be placated by the promotion of his son, then an army captain, to a majority. The favor to the son, he said, "would have a cordial effect on the mind of the father." [37] He did not worry about the sensibilities of Smith.

The war finally hit home to Jefferson's own family. His son-in-law, Randolph, was, as Jefferson put it ironically, "seised with the military fever" and joined a regiment. Martha and the children remained in Jefferson's care.[38] And death struck among the select group of his relatives and friends. George Jefferson, a cousin, with whom his relations had been personally and financially close, died on a voyage after a nervous breakdown. Dr. Benjamin Rush, his medical adviser, philosopher-friend and correspondent, and the man responsible for the rapprochement with Adams, passed quietly away. So did Jefferson's sister, Anna Scott Marks. The series of deaths within a comparatively short period saddened Jefferson and brought from him acknowledgments of his sorrow. The Old Guard was going, one by one. His brother, Randolph Jefferson, however, still remained.

Twin to the recently deceased Anna Scott, Randolph had managed to farm his land at Snowden, marry twice and have six sons. His mind was limited and his world circumscribed to the narrow confines of his daily routine. His elder brother treated him always with tenderness and respect, and helped him patiently in all the minutiae that troubled the younger man. Randolph would scrawl illiterate little notes to Thomas, in which the loan of a gig loomed larger than the deaths of his sisters, Anna Scott Marks and Mrs. Carr. Thomas would reply simply and kindly, speaking of small, everyday events that were within the scope of Randolph Jefferson's limited understanding. Once only did he suggest that he might undertake the education of one of Randolph's sons who seemed to evince a certain intelligence. Randolph agreed to the proposition with his usual casual brevity, and turned then to more important things like his need for a "spining ginney." [39]

Randolph's second wife, whom he had married without consulting his brother, proved extravagant and a shrew. Poor Randolph fell under her domination, had to sell lands to pay her debts and finally, on his brother's advice, informed the local merchants that she was to receive merchandise only on his written order. Thereupon she forged the orders. Thus harassed, Randolph quietly died in 1815; and a struggle at law for the remaining assets ensued between Randolph's sons by his first marriage and the newly bereaved widow. Jefferson was compelled to interpose with an affidavit on behalf of the sons.[40]

Still another loss in the circle of Jefferson's friends was that of Tom Paine, the fiery radical in whose behalf Jefferson had both struck and received mighty blows. As men like Paine and Rush, who had made some noise in the world, died, the problem of the publication of their papers arose. The prospect proved a considerable source of worry to Jefferson, whose correspondence with them had been confidential and very much unbuttoned. When Rush died, he mingled regrets to the surviving sons with an urgent solicitation for the return of those letters which had dealt with his private religious views.[41] On Paine's death, to a request for permission to publish, he wrote that "while he lived, I thought it a duty, as well as a test of my own political principles to support him against the persecutions of an unprincipled faction." But now that Jefferson was old, "retired from the world, and anxious for tranquility, it is my wish that they should not be published during my life, as they might draw on me renewed molestations from the irreconcilable enemies of republican government." [42]

This matter of the publication of private letters he had written was a constant source of terror to Jefferson, though it never inhibited him from writing more of the same kind. For example, the letter he had addressed to Priestley on religion had fallen into the hands of a scribbler, who published it in his Memoirs. John Adams, to whom he confided his fears over the public exposure of his religious views, dismissed the matter in his usual forthright way, and avowed for himself that he cared not a farthing for his reputation. Generalizing, he defended the theory of checks and balances as a means of avoiding persecutions. "Checks and Ballances, Jefferson, however you and your Party may have ridiculed them, are our only Security, for the progress of Mind, as well as the Security of Body.... Every species of these Christians would persecute Deists, as soon as either Sect would persecute Another, if it had unchecked and unballanced Power. Nay, the Deists would persecute Christians, and Atheists would persecute Deists, with as unrelenting Cruelty, as any Christians would persecute them or one another. Know thyself, human Nature!" [43]

The correspondence between the two old cronies was in full swing again. Adams groaned over the length and complexity of Jefferson's letters. "I cannot write volumes on a single sheet," he exclaimed, "but these letters of yours require volumes from me." Jefferson had animadverted on that old bone of contention—the Alien and Sedition Laws. Adams was stung to a defense of the former. "We were then at war with France," he exploded. "French spies then swarmed in our cities and our country; some of them were, intollerably, turbulent, impudent and Seditious. To check these, was the design of this law. Was there ever a government which had not authority to defend itself against spies in its own bosom—spies of an enemy at war?" Then, in semiapology: "This law was never executed by me in any instance." [44]

Jefferson delved in reply into a philosophical consideration of parties. "Men have differed in opinion, and been divided into parties by these opinions, from the first origin of societies, and in all governments where they have been permitted freely to think and to speak. The same political parties which now agitate the United States, have existed through all time. Whether the power of the people or that of the [*aristoi*] should prevail, were questions which kept the States of Greece and Rome in eternal convulsions, as they now schismatize every people whose minds and mouths are not shut up by the gag of a despot. And in fact, the terms of whig & tory belong to Natural history, as well as civil. They denote the temper and constitution of mind of different individuals."[45]

Occasionally, in the interchanges, particularly when old coals were raked over and the passions of the past relived, the fires burst forth again with renewed vigor. But Jefferson, though constantly pursuing his probing references and thereby bringing on his head the thunders of the enraged old Federalist, always kept his temper and the sputtering volcano subsided into subdued mutterings.

One of the worst eruptions came when Jefferson spoke of "the terrorism of a former day" directed against the Republicans. How about Shay's rebellion? retorted Adams. Or "Mr. Gallatin's insurrection in Pennsylvania?" Or Fries's "most outrageous riot and rescue." Or the terrorism excited by Genêt "when ten thousand people in the streets of Philadelphia, day after day, threatened to drag Washington out of his house." "I have no doubt," he added sarcastically, "you were fast asleep, in philosophical tranquillity, when ten thousand people, and, perhaps, many more, were parading the streets of Philadelphia on the evening of my Fast Day" when, with a few friends, Adams barricaded himself for a desperate defense against the mob.[46]

But Jefferson could turn aside the glowering wrath with some remarks on the Greek tongue and evoke a wry exclamation in response: "Lord! Lord! what can I do with so much Greek?"[47]

Jefferson liked to return again and again to the question of religion in general and the Christian religion in particular. His brand of optimism, derived from the Enlightenment, was in diametric opposition to the dour, cynical, yet half-humorous animadversions of the son of Puritan forebears. In fundamental thinking on the bases for religion, however, they were not so far apart. Jefferson was delighted to find that Adams approved of his outline on religion for Priestley, and hastened to expatiate further on the thesis it contained.

"I very much suspect," he wrote, "that if thinking men would have the courage to think for themselves, and to speak what they think, it would be found they do not differ in religious opinions as much as is supposed.... It is too late in the day for men of sincerity to pretend they believe in the Platonic mysticism that three are one, and one is three; and yet that the one is not three, and the three are not one.... We should all then, like the Quakers, live without an order of priests, moralize for ourselves, follow the oracle of conscience, and say nothing about what no man can understand, nor therefore believe; for I suppose belief to be the assent of the mind to an intelligible proposition."[48] Jefferson had a firm belief in the essential "reasonableness" of men and no patience with any mystical approach to reality.

The break with Abigail had continued to trouble him, and he cautiously appended a conveyance of regards in one of his letters, to which she was only too happy to respond in kind. Thereupon Jefferson replied with a letter directed wholly to herself. But he had learned his lesson and steered carefully away from all controversial topics, exchanging information instead on their respective rheumatisms. Abigail, softened by the death of her own daughter, was willing to forgive and forget. Although political calumny, she wrote, had "for a period interrupted the Friendly intercourse and harmony which subsisted, it is again renewed, purified from the dross." [49]

John Adams had proclaimed the thesis that there was a natural aristocracy among men, and Jefferson agreed with him. But he was careful to differentiate between the natural one based on virtue and talents and the artificial one based on wealth or birth. The former, indeed, he considered "as the most precious gift of nature, for the instruction, the trusts, and government of society.... May we not even say," he inquired, "that that form of government is the best, which provides the most effectually for a pure selection of these natural *aristoi* into the offices of government?" He even toyed with the schemes of Theognis and Plato for a deliberate eugenic breeding of such a race, but discarded them with the comment "that the equal rights of men will rise up against the privileged Solomon and his Harem." Nor did he agree with Adams's plan of placing the artificial or "*pseudo-aristoi*" in a separate Senate of the legislature on the theory that a proper check and balance would follow, and wealth would be protected from the assaults of the have-nots.

You do not have to worry about the wealthy, retorted Jefferson. They can take care of themselves and get into even a unicameral legislature. Nor have the actions of past legislatures proven that an equalization of property is to be feared. He was confident that in general the people, with only an occasional error, "will elect the really wise and good." He adverted to his own proposals in the early days of Virginia. His bills had "laid the ax to the foot of pseudo-aristocracy" and had put down the aristocracy of the clergy. If only his bill for the general diffusion of knowledge had gone through, "our work would have been complete." It was still before the legislature and he hoped it would some day pass and become the "key-stone of the arch of our government."

He was propounding these opinions, he ended cautiously, "not with a view to controversy, for we are both too old to change opinions which are the result of a long life of inquiry and reflection; but on the suggestions of a former letter of yours, that we ought not to die before we have explained ourselves to each other." [50]

Indeed, this remarkable correspondence not only explained the two men to each other, but has helped explain them to posterity.

Jefferson, in fact, employed this great period of his leisure to explain himself to all and sundry. To the ambitious writer of a text on grammar, he avowed that the study had never been one of his favorites. "The scanty foundation, laid in at school, has carried me through a life of much hasty writing, more indebted for style to reading and memory, than to rules of grammar." He believed strongly that usage gave the law to grammar, and not grammar to usage. Certainly so rapidly growing a population as the United States, he thought, "must enlarge their language, to make it answer its purpose of expressing all ideas, the new as well as the old. The new circumstances under which we are placed, call for new words, new phrases, and for the transfer of old words to new objects." An American dialect was in the process of formation, and it would enrich, not adulterate the English language.[51]

He looked to South America and had no doubt that the peoples there would eventually gain their independence. But he was not so sure as to what they would do with it. He had found no example in history "of a priest-ridden people maintaining a free civil government." He foresaw with awful clarity the course that South America would take. "Their people," he claimed, "are immersed in the darkest ignorance, and brutalised by bigotry & superstition. Their priests make of them what they please: and tho' they may have some capable leaders yet nothing but intelligence in the people themselves can keep these faithful to their charge. Their efforts I fear therefore will end in establishing military despotisms in the several provinces. Among these there can be no confederacy. A republic of kings is impossible." Nevertheless he hoped that time, education and the example of the United States would finally qualify them for self-government.[52]

CHAPTER 67

Plan for Education

WHILE Jefferson's mind thus ranged widely in space and time, and even beyond, he did not lose sight of the pressing problems closer at hand.

He was engaged in extensive controversy with the Rivanna Canal Company that was trying to compel him to remove his obstructions to navigation without what he thought was an adequate safeguarding of his rights. The company directors had gone to the legislature to press their claims, and Jefferson countered with pressures of his own. His chief advocate in the Assembly was Joseph Carrington Cabell, a young man of some thirty-five years, who had become an enthusiastic disciple of the Sage of Monticello and was to work valiantly with him in the ensuing years in the promotion of the University of Virginia. "You may rest assured," replied Cabell, "that I shall pay the most pointed attention to this business, and do every thing in my power to guard your rights from invasion." [1]

What mortified Jefferson more than anything else was the fact that the Albemarle delegation—his own neighbors—stood with the Company against himself, and that he had to rely for protection on legislators from other counties. But the latter rallied to his cause and Cabell was able to report triumphantly that he had forced through sufficient amendments to the bill to cause the Company to let it lie over rather than put it to a vote.[2] Thus thwarted in their original plans, the directors eventually came to a compromise agreement with Jefferson and the bill, with amendments, was consented to by both parties.[3]

The conduct of the war continued naturally to engross his attention. Earlier in the year the sky had lightened a trifle, at least to the south where General William Cocke had fought and won some victories over the Creek Indians. Jefferson congratulated him, but expressed his regret that Cocke had not been permitted to seize the whole of Florida, as a measure of redress for our wrongs and before the British moved in. "For this blot," he exclaimed, "left open to be hit by our adversary, we are indebted, it seems, to that Sexennial spirit of the Senate, of which you and I saw so much, which has so often defeated the wisdom and patriotism of their coordinate authorities, and is destined to produce incalculable injury and danger, if not recalled to responsibility at shorter periods." [4]

The more he contemplated the Senate, indeed, the more he was determined to curtail the powers of those "pseudo-aristoi" by shortening their term of office and thereby forcing them to consider the wishes of the people from whom they derived their authority. He was all for "responsibilities at short periods," he wrote, "seeing neither reason nor safety in making public functionaries independent of the nation for life. or even for long term of years." He also advocated a maximum of two terms of four years each for the Presidency, with permanent ineligibility thereafter.[5] Today (1951) that idea of his has been realized by Constitutional amendment.

With banks and banking charters again under consideration, Jefferson repeated his favorite thesis dating as far back as 1789, that "the earth belongs to the living, not to the dead." Once again he brought forward the doubtful statistics which to him proved that a generation changes every nineteen years, and that no man or government has a right to bind the future generations by laws or contracts.

The instant cause of these new reflections was the current series of applications for new bank charters. These meant that more paper money (to which he was unalterably opposed) would be placed in circulation. Let us have banks, he exclaimed, but not banks of discount which offer "anything but cash in exchange for discounted bills." In letter after letter to his former son-in-law, he expounded his theories of money, paper, banks and credit in general, and sought through him to avoid having Virginia fall into the ancient trap.[6]

The war with England was fortunately taking a turn for the better, at least temporarily. Some victories on the Canadian border excited Jefferson's hopes and he told Thomas Mann Randolph, now with the army in northern New York, that with the expected fall of Canada, "the earlier disgraces of the war are now wiped away. This with the execution of Hull, and perhaps the *disgrace* of 3. or 4. more will satisfy all with the state of the war, the Anglomen excepted."[7] He kept insisting that General Hull had been guilty of treachery in surrendering and that therefore he ought to be executed. Fortunately, the rest of the nation was not as vehement for the unfortunate general's blood; and he was merely retired under a cloud.

The indefatigable Dr. Logan, who had once attempted a one-man peace mission to France, was now ready to perform the same "duty" again with England; and sought Jefferson's assistance. But Jefferson was reluctant to interpose his good offices with Madison's administration. As for himself, he thought indispensable to any peace treaty the revocation of the Orders in Council and the discontinuance of impressments. Less indispensable, but advisable, were an indemnity for past damages, and exclusive rights in the Great Lakes to prevent their future passage by the Indians for raiding.[8] Obviously, the current state of the war precluded any possibility that England would submit to anything like these terms.

The war, he reflected, was so difficult to win because the three great classes of "merchants, priests, and lawyers" adhered to England and monarchy rather than to their own country and the Constitution. He could understand the case of the merchants. "Merchants," he wrote bitterly, "have no country. The mere spot they stand on does not constitute so strong an attachment as that from which they draw their gains." As for the class of clericals, "in every country and in every age, the priest has been hostile to liberty. He is always in alliance with the despot, abetting his abuses in return for protection to his own." But he was surprised at the lawyers. With them, he exclaimed, "it is a new thing." He could only ascribe their defection from free principles to the baleful influence of two men—Blackstone and Hume. Their books had sown the seeds of reaction and obscurantism. They "have done more," he was convinced, "towards the suppression of the liberties of man, than all the million of men in arms of Bonaparte and the millions of human lives with the sacrifice of which he will stand loaded before the judgment seat of his Maker." [9]

Time has not mellowed his judgments. Its passage, indeed, seemed rather to sharpen and exacerbate them. He lashed out in a good many directions, and found targets for his wrath in men and institutions everywhere. The years of abuse heaped upon himself, the arrogance of groups and nations, the continuance of the war, had taken their toll.

Christianity, for example, had become "part and parcel of the laws of England" through a fraud originally practiced by King Alfred and later abetted by a series of judges culminating in Sir Matthew Hale.[10]

Even his old friend, John Taylor of Caroline, did not escape the critical tartness that enveloped him at this time. His new book, issued under a transparent veil of anonymity, had some "good things" in it, Jefferson admitted. But they were "so involved in quaint, in far-fetched, affected, mystical conciepts [*sic*], and flimsy theories, that who can take the trouble of getting at them?" [11]

Perhaps the reason for these sudden explosions may be found in the state of his personal finances. His last year's supply of flour was moldering unsold in warehouses; the new year's crop had been destroyed by drought; his notes at the banks and with private individuals were all unpaid. "On the whole," he wrote grimly, "it has been the most calamitous year I have experienced since the year 1755." [12]

It is no wonder then that he reserved some of his most violent excoriations for the banks, to whose issuance of paper money he attributed the current hardships of the planters. "But our whole country," he exclaimed, "is so fascinated by this Jack-lantern wealth, that they will not stop short of its total and fatal explosion." [13]

When the first sign of that explosion occurred some six months later, he hailed it with the satisfaction of a prophet who has seen his foretelling come true. "Providence has now done the work for us," he told Cabell. The banks have declared themselves bankrupt and this is the time to reform the entire system. Congress should issue nationally its own treasury notes based on tax receipts; and Virginia ought to get around the Constitutional provision against the States' issuing "bills of Credit" by an interpretation.

Jefferson's method of evasion was ingenious, to say the least. A state, he asserted, that is unable to pay its debts has the right to issue acknowledgments of the amounts it owes. These can be emitted in small denominations, stating on their face that they would be paid out of the proceeds of a specific tax. Such due bills could then be emitted in turn by the banks in exchange for their own notes, and be employed as legal tender in the payment of taxes. Since the national government owed Virginia $400,000, whenever Congress issued its own treasury notes in payment of that debt, the State notes could then be called in and those of the nation substituted. Thus, Jefferson ended his complicated financial system, the evasion of the Constitution would cease and determine. He was only too well aware that what he advocated, if too long continued, "might lead to new deluges of paper circulation, and to new revolutions and convulsions in private fortunes." [14] What he was *not* aware of was that it is infinitely easier to set an inflationary spiral of paper emissions in motion than to stop it.

Yet even in this time of storm and stress, Jefferson managed to hold on to some of his calmer and more equable pursuits.

Visitors to Monticello were welcomed with the utmost courtesy and hospitality; particularly when their intellectual interests coincided with his own. One such was a Portuguese diplomat, philosopher, intellectual and scientist—Joseph Correa de Serra. The two men found so much in common that a lifelong friendship ensued. Correa was a man of the world, a botanist, traveled and of a quick and nimble mind; and Jefferson would have liked to have kept him forever at Monticello.[15]

From Boston also came two young men eager to meet the Sage of Monticello. They were George Ticknor, aged 23, and at the beginning of a brilliant career; and his companion, Francis Calley Gray. Armed as they were with letters of introduction from John Adams, they had no difficulty in receiving a warm and cordial greeting. Both visitors in later years left accounts of their memorable sojourn at Monticello.

Young Gray described Jefferson as "quite tall, six feet, one or two inches, face streaked and speckled with red, light gray eyes, white hair, dressed in shoes of very thin soft leather with pointed toes and heels ascending in a peak behind, with very short quarters, grey worsted stockings, corduroy small clothes, blue waistcoat and coat, of stiff thick cloth made of the wool of his own merinoes and badly manufactured, the buttons of his coat and small clothes of horn, and an under waistcoat flannel bound with red velvet. His figure bony, long and with broad shoulders, a true Virginian." [16]

The two young men were not particularly struck by the appointments of the famous place, however. One entered the house through a glass folding door into a hall that to their minds was strangely furnished. The chairs were leather-bottomed and stuffed with hair, "but the bottoms were completely worn through and the hair sticking out in all directions." On the walls hung a weird collection of trophies—stuffed heads and horns of elk, deer, buffalo and the bones of a mammoth, as well as other curiosities collected by Lewis and Clark. The paintings were a mixture of good and bad. The prints, Gray thought, were miserable; while Ticknor wondered at the strange juxtaposition of a fine painting of St. Peter with a leather Indian map and the primitive depiction of a bloody battle. There were the copies of paintings which Jefferson had ordered while in France—the Laughing and Weeping Philosophers, Columbus, Americus Vespuccius, Magellan, etc., as well as portraits of Madison, Lafayette and Franklin.

As the young men were themselves booklovers, they studied his library with the greatest interest. On the marble mantelpiece in the entrance hall were Livy, Orosius, the *Edinburgh Review* and Maria Edgeworth; while in the library proper Ticknor observed a most curious collection that ordinarily might have been thought out of place in such a grave and reverend company. This was a privately bound six-volume edition of scandalous memoirs of the courts of France and England, whose covers Jefferson had lettered *The Book of Kings*. "These documents of regal scandal," noted the young visitor, "seemed to be favorites with the philosopher, who pointed them out to me with a satisfaction somewhat inconsistent with the measured gravity he claims in relation to such subjects generally." Ticknor thought that this strange collection was "the most characteristic of the man and expressive of his hatred of royalty." [17]

The family consisted of Jefferson, the Randolphs and their children, and Mrs. Marks, Jefferson's sister. Everything was done with a steady regularity. At eight in the morning, the first bell was rung; at nine, a second summoned the guests to breakfast. After breakfast, one did as one pleased; the children went to their schoolroom, and Jefferson rode out to his mills, returning at noon. At three-thirty, the great bell rang again; at four, it sent out its summons for dining. The meals were excellent and served in the French style; except that the wine came out only after the cloth had been removed. All sat together until six, when the ladies retired, returning however with tea at seven. The remainder of the evening was spent together, with the ladies joining in even the highest intellectual reaches of the conversation. At ten-thirty, the house retired for the night.

It was all very decent and orderly. One anecdote reported by young Ticknor is illuminating. One afternoon, Jefferson returned from his daily survey of his mills to remark in an ordinary tone that his dam had been carried away the night before. From the brevity and casualness of the remark Ticknor thought it was a matter of small consequence. Only later did he discover that the damage done had amounted to about $30,000.[18]

"There is a breathing of notional philosophy in Mr. Jefferson," summed up the perceptive young man, "—in his dress, his house, his conversation." His dress had been made the subject of much laughter "and he might perhaps wisely have dismissed them." His ideas on economics and politics—

such as the "natural" impossibility of one generation binding another, the expediency of vesting all legislative authority in a single House, the executive authority in another, "and leaving them to govern it by joint discretion"—were considered by Ticknor "simply as curious *indicia* of an extraordinary character."[19]

Jefferson's ideas of the normal progression of education were perhaps equally curious, as he expounded them to Benjamin Barton on hearing that many of the Iroquois Indians were able to read. This, he thought, "is beginning at the wrong end." They ought first to be taught the care of domestic animals, agriculture, useful household arts, the acquisition of property and the use of money, with enough arithmetic to manage it and enough writing to note it down. Then, and then only, ought they to be taught to read from books, and last of all, those books which contain "religion as distinguished from morality."[20]

That morality which he unweariedly advocated as against revealed religion did not even consist solely of truth or the love of God, and certainly not of mere egoistic pleasure. "Nature hath implanted in our breasts," he asserted, "a love of others, a sense of duty to them, a moral instinct, in short, which prompts us irresistibly to feel and to succor their distresses.... The Creator would indeed have been a bungling artist, had he intended man for a social animal, without planting in him social dispositions."[21]

This was the crux of Jefferson's belief—that the amelioration of the condition on earth of one's fellow man represented his highest aim and noblest activity. One's religion was a private affair, and a "subject of accountability to God alone. I inquire after no man's, and trouble none with mine; nor is it given to us in this life to know whether yours or mine, our friends or our foes, are exactly the right."[22]

Since reason was the "only oracle which God has given us" and a republican form of government was manifestly the only proper form for man, it is no wonder that he determined to devote the remainder of his life to the furtherance of two great subjects—public education, and the subdivision of state counties into wards or "hundreds." The future of the republic, he was convinced, hung absolutely on "these two hooks."[23]

He now began, therefore, to push with every energy he possessed his scheme for the advancement of education in Virginia; a project to which he devoted almost all the waking hours that remained to him on earth.

His chief instrument for the task was Joseph Carrington Cabell, a fellow Virginian who had traveled in Europe, and was now in the Senate of Virginia. Cabell fell in enthusiastically with his schemes, and worked valiantly alongside to further them. At the end of 1809, he had introduced a bill in the legislature to appropriate certain forfeitures and penalties to the encouragement of learning, which was the beginning of what became known as the "Literary Fund."

But there the matter rested until the proposal to open an academy in Charlottesville, to be known as "Central College," galvanized Jefferson to renewed activity on his favorite topic. He promised the promoters to draft a plan for its building and operation, and he sought advice far and wide among his friends. But, as he informed Dr. Cooper, the college "should comprehend all the sciences useful to us, and none others." This emphasis on the "practical" and "useful" as against the merely ornamental or a delight in learning and cultivation for its own sake, was to grow on him with the passage of the years. If such a college or university were founded—and already his views extended far beyond the local institution to one which would embrace all Virginia—he intended to sell it "on its own terms" his library of some 7,000 to 8,000 volumes. He was extremely proud of that library; calling it "the best chosen collection of its size probably in America, and containing a great mass of what is most rare and valuable, and especially of what relates to America." [24]

But he received the most divergent views from the people to whom he applied for aid and guidance. No two plans were alike, and he was compelled to choose those sections which had application to the specific conditions in Virginia. Dr. Cooper, for example, a radical and freethinker, inveighed against any attempt to incorporate a professorship of theology into the scheme. Jefferson agreed with him wholeheartedly in theory, but realized there would be practical obstacles. "We cannot always do what is absolutely best," he admonished his friend. "Those with whom we act, entertaining different views, have the power and the right of carrying them into practice. Truth," he philosophized, "advances, and error recedes step by step only; and to do to our fellow men the most good in our power, we must lead where we can, follow where we cannot, and still go with them, watching always the favorable moment for helping them to another step." [25]

Jefferson might have been "notional," as Ticknor observed; but he was always a practical politician, and knew something of the psychology of his fellow men. He could never have achieved the success he did had he not possessed both an ideal aim and a practical flexibility for compromise.

When Jefferson came to draft his own plan, he expanded it to take in the entire graded system of education. Every citizen, he insisted, was entitled to an education furnished by the State. But this education ought not, as in modern view, to be equal for all. "The mass of our citizens," he said, "may be divided into two classes, the laboring, & the learned. The laboring will need the first grade of education to qualify them for their pursuits and duties; the learned will need it as a foundation for further acquirements."

After the pupils finished an elementary course of instruction, the two classes would separate. "Those destined for labor will engage in the business of agriculture, or enter into apprenticeships to such handicraft art as may be their choice: their companions destined to the pursuits of science, will proceed to the College." This latter was to be divided into two sections, one comprising a general course and the other the professions. But even the learned could be divided into those who required a profession as a means of livelihood and the wealthy who, possessed of independent fortunes, "may aspire to share in conducting the affairs of the nation, or to live in usefulness & respect in the private ranks of life. Both of these sections will require instruction in all the higher branches of science"; while the "useful" sciences should be taught generally.

The "highest degree" of the sciences was to be reserved for the culmination of his scheme, the strictly professional schools, which would include Fine Arts (architecture, gardening, painting, sculpture and music—for "the Gentlemen"), Military and Naval Architecture and Projectiles, Rural Economy (agriculture, horticulture and veterinary), Technical Philosophy (for mariners, carpenters, clockmakers, opticians, metallurgists, etc.), Medicine, Law and, with an obeisance to prevailing opinion, Theology and Ecclesiastical History.[26]

There is much in this plan to illuminate Jefferson's mind and thought. First, his insistence on *practical* as against *ornamental* knowledge; the latter of which he believed to be the function of "the gentlemen" alone. Second, his belief in the natural inequalities of people on the intellectual level. Higher education for those at the lower level—at the expense of the State—he considered a criminal waste of time. He felt that the poor would necessarily fall into this category; though elsewhere he made provision for a very few of the brilliant among them to obtain the highest education. Third, his idea that the conduct of government was primarily the affair of those with independent fortunes. This was a corollary to his thesis that the administration of public affairs should not be made into a means of livelihood. Here was the aristocrat principle that was as much a part of Jefferson's philosophy as the other and better-known one of his profound belief in the good political sense of the people, *provided* they were able by education to exercise their reason and ascertain the truth. His ideal republic was in a sense both aristocratic and democratic, with those of independent fortune (preferably based on the ownership of land and therefore "gentlemen") possessed of public spirit and administering government; and the mass of the electorate, literate and rational, holding them in rigorous check by the power of the ballot.

He incorporated this scheme in a long letter to Peter Carr, his nephew, now grown to manhood and President of the Board of Trustees of the proposed College. It was published entire in the Richmond *Enquirer*, and so impressed the state legislators that they passed a bill in 1816 incorporating Central College.[27] Riding the crest of the enthusiasm thus created, the legislature further appropriated to the uses of education the entire debt of the United States to Virginia, amounting to $600,000; and ordered the Directors of the Literary Fund previously established to report on a plan of graded schools and universities somewhat along the lines which Jefferson had advocated.[28]

Jefferson's hatred of what he called "innate knowledge," profitless philosophical speculation and mysticism, was constantly cropping up. *Practical* science that would help the world progress was the only true pursuit for youth, and the only one with which education ought to concern itself.[29]

He now read Plato's Republic for the first time and found it, he told Adams, "the heaviest task-work I ever went through. I had occasionally before taken up some of his other works, but scarcely ever had patience to go through a whole dialogue. While wading through the whimsies, the puerilities, and unintelligible jargon of his work, I laid it down often to ask myself how it could have been, that the world should have so long consented to give reputation to such nonsense as this?" He could understand it only by the fact that Plato's "whimsies" had been incorporated into "the body of artificial Christianity." The doctrines of Jesus, he exclaimed, "are within the comprehension of a child; but thousands of volumes have not yet explained the Platonisms engrafted on them." And again he attacked the new fad of "innate" knowledge based on intuition; and the contemptuous rejection of the laborious knowledge accumulated through the ages.[30] To all of which Adams heartily said *amen.*[31]

Two events of importance happened in the outside world during this period, one of which delighted him while the other roused him to a fury of indignation.

The first was the news that Napoleon had finally been overthrown and banished by the conclave of opposing nations to Elba. "The Attila of the age dethroned," Jefferson cried to Adams, "the ruthless destroyer of ten millions of the human race . . . the great oppressor of the rights and liberties of the world, shut up within the circle of a little island in the Mediterranean, and dwindled to the condition of an humble and degraded pensioner on the bounty of those he has most injured. How miserably, how meanly, has he closed his inflated career! What a sample of the bathos will his history present!" Yet mingled with this delight was some fear. The tyrant of the ocean (England) still remained! [32]

What would the Federalists of Massachusetts say to this, he asked, especially if, as had been hinted, a condition of the terms of peace would be the cession of their fisheries to England? Those Federalists he later analyzed into three sections: "1. the Essex junto who are Anglomen, Monarchists, & Separatists. 2. the Hamiltonians, who are Anglomen & Monarchists, but not Separatists. 3. the common mass of federalists who are Anglomen, but neither Monarchists nor Separatists." [33]

He had come so far in his thinking, and the regime of Napoleon had jarred him so mightily from his former preconceptions, that he was now willing to see even the Bourbons restored to France. He believed they were the "only point on which France could be rallied, and that their re-establishment is better for that country than civil wars, whether they should be a peaceable nation under a fool or a warring one under a military despot of genius." [34]

The other event, at once shocking and infuriating, was the burning of

Washington by the British in a sudden and almost unopposed raid. It brought to Jefferson tragic memories of that earlier foray against Richmond during the period of his own governorship. The one particular act that made him cry out was the destruction of the library of Congress.

He had intended giving his own private library to the Central College, but he now offered it as the nucleus for a new and greater Library of Congress. He had spent fifty years in collecting it, he wrote Samuel H. Smith, and had ransacked for its accumulation every bookstore in Paris, and ordered volumes from the major European cities. In his will, he added, he had bequeathed it to the nation (he omitted reference to the recent shift he had contemplated); but in this hour of catastrophe he was ready to present it at once to Congress at its own valuation. He made only one condition—that his collection be kept as a unit.[35]

Eventually, Congress accepted the gracious offer, paying $23,950 for the total;[36] and the current great Library may well be considered as having received its initial impulse from Jefferson's fundamental collection.

CHAPTER 68

The Great Correspondence

WITH the mighty Napoleon smitten to the ground and the long chapter of war in Europe seemingly at an end, the problem for Americans was: would a triumphant England come to an honorable peace with her sole remaining antagonist, or would she now concentrate all the power of her forces to subjugate the republic across the seas?

Jefferson veered in his estimate from day to day. At one time he would be optimistic and, satisfied that peace would come before the winter ended, give instructions to his overseer to get the tobacco and the flour ready and send them down to Richmond with all possible speed. "The great prices will be for that at market the moment peace opens the bay," he wrote.[1]

But other times pessimism would overwhelm him, and he was certain that there must be eternal war with England until she dropped any claim to impressments. Then his warlike vehemence grew out of all bounds, and he urged on Madison, Monroe and members of the Cabinet the most stringent Spartan measures: large loans, heavy taxes, issuance of paper money, a levy *en masse* of militia to render us, like Greece and Rome, "a nation of warriors." In the emergencies of the occasion, some of his cherished doctrines went by the board. He was ready now to see the nation go into debt and throw part of the burdens of the present war upon the "times of peace and commerce." He was willing to see the national government issue paper against specific pledges, and have the people force the merchants to accept it as legal tender. It was a case, indeed, of the lesser of two evils. Rather than have the private banks in "the fatal possession of the whole circulating medium," he preferred it to be in the hands of the government.

Monroe had just taken over the War Department, and Jefferson, with memories of his own, was sorry for it. "Were an angel from Heaven to undertake that office," he wrote feelingly, "all our miscarriages would be ascribed to him.... I speak from experience, when I was Governor of Virginia."[2]

To further complicate matters, the extreme Federalists of New England had finally carried out their long-standing threat to seek open secession from a Union that persisted in war against England. At the notorious Hartford Convention, these bitter-enders met in conclave, ranted and denounced, passed virulent resolutions—and then returned to their homes without putting words into action.

Jefferson likened the leaders to the Marats, Dantons and Robespierres of France as seeking anarchy and in the pay of England. But, he exulted, "the yeomanry of the United States are not the *canaille* of Paris"; and the only ones that would flock to the banner of treason would be "gambling merchants and silk-stocking clerks." In this hour of stress he hymned a paean to the plain people and the indissolubility of the Union. "The cement of this Union," he exclaimed, "is in the heart-blood of every American. I do not believe there is on earth a government established on so immovable a basis. Let them, in any State, even in Massachusetts itself, raise the standard of separation, and its citizens will rise in mass, and do justice themselves on their own incendiaries." [3]

News was slow in coming from Europe. While Federalists plotted treason and the United States girded itself to meet the overwhelming onslaught of a victorious enemy, a peace had already been negotiated at Ghent in Belgium, a peace which Monroe joyfully asserted to be "in all respects honorable to our country. No concession is made of any kind." [4] What he omitted to mention was that nothing had been concluded, either; that all matters in dispute had been discreetly left in *status quo ante bellum,* and that the sorry war might just as well have never been fought.

Jefferson saw this clearly. Though equally rejoicing at war's end, he insisted that England must now enter into a convention for relinquishing the hated impressments. "Without this," he warned, "she must understand that the present is but a truce, determinable on the first act of impressment of an American citizen, committed by any officer of hers." He wanted such a convention wholly divorced from any treaty of commerce. He preferred that the United States enter into no commercial arrangement at all. "We cannot too distinctly detach ourselves from the European system, which is essentially belligerent, nor too sedulously cultivate an American system, essentially pacific." [5]

England never entered into any formal renunciation of the right of impressment; but she never made any move to enforce it again; and the issue ceased to be a further source of conflict between the two nations. The news of the overwhelming victory of General Andrew Jackson at New Orleans against the flower of British veterans, though the battle had been fought after the Treaty of Ghent had been signed, served to soothe injured American feelings and to erase some of the memories of a war hitherto badly conducted and badly fought.

Jefferson refused to remit his deep-seated hatred of England simply because what he conceived to be an uneasy peace had been signed, and continued to sound the tocsin on every possible occasion.

The peace, he told Dupont, was a mere armistice. In the first moment of revival of a European war, we must again go into it. Therefore we must keep on preparing, fortify our seaports, fill our magazines, train our militia, and above all, establish a sound system of finance. This last preoccupied his attention to the exclusion of almost everything else, and he thought that several papers of Dupont on the subject ought to be translated and published for the benefit of Americans.[6]

He was indeed almost sorry that the war had ended so abruptly. Though he acknowledged that "pea [ce] is better than war for everybody . . . we were just getting forward a set of officers, who having already redeemed the honor we lost under the traitors cowards and fools of the first year, would very soon have planted our banners on the walls of Quebec and Halifax." [7]

War *did* return to Europe, though not in the way Jefferson had anticipated. Napoleon escaped from Elba, returned in triumph to Paris, and once more the dogs of war bayed all over the Continent. Some good Americans rejoiced; believing that another chance was thus providentially offered them to even scores with England. But Jefferson, for all his former bellicose pronouncements, viewed the event with sober appraisal. "We stood on good ground before," he wrote, "but now on doubtful. . . . If they have a general war we may be involved in it; if peace, we shall have the hostile and ignorant caprices of Bonaparte to regulate our commerce with that country, instead of its antient and regular course." [8]

Yet, in spite of everything, he loved France. "Were it not for my family and possessions here," he told Short, "I should prefer that residence to any other. Paris is the only place where a man who is not obliged to do anything will always find something amusing to do. Here the man who has nothing to do is the prey of ennui. . . . In this country a family for leisure moments, and a farm or profession for those of employment are indispensable for happiness. These mixed with books, a little letter writing, and neighborly and friendly society constitute a plenum of occupation and of happiness which leaves no wish for the noisy & barren amusements and distractions of a city." [9] Perhaps at this moment Jefferson would have preferred a place where a man need have no fixed occupation and nevertheless manage to enjoy himself.

The one bright spot to Jefferson in the deadly fact of Napoleon's sudden reappearance was the contemplation of the forthcoming debacle of the Pope. "The insult which he [the Pope] and the bigot of Spain have offered to the lights of the nineteenth century by the re-establishment of the Inquisition admits of no forgiveness." [10]

He also hated England and Napoleon as eternal disturbers of the peace of the world, and he prophesied that "not in our day, but at no distant one, we may shake a rod over the heads of all, which may make the stoutest of them tremble." But, he added quickly, "I hope our wisdom will grow with our power, and teach us, that the less we use our power, the greater it will be." [11]

His prejudices, however, veered again when he heard the allies were insisting on the restoration of the Bourbons to the throne in France. Now he was willing to take Napoleon rather than the "antient" dynasty; and avowed that the former "Atilla of the age" was "fighting for the independance of nations, of which his whole life hitherto had been a continued violation, and he has now my prayers as sincerely for success as he had before his overthrow." [12]

While war clouds thus overhung Europe and threatened to cast their shadows once more over America, Jefferson attempted to add up the advantages of the preceding war. The one firm rock of consolation to which he clung was the removal of American commercial dependence on England. He attributed this happy event in the first place to his own embargo and nonimportation measures, but admitted that the war had hastened it even further. "These," he rejoiced, "have permanently planted manufactures among us." It must be remembered, however, that whenever Jefferson spoke of "manufactures," with rare exceptions he meant only the local economy of the family and the farm, and *not* the great industrial factory system of the cities such as modern times are accustomed to. His next sentences make this distinction crystal clear. "The cities, I suppose, will still affect English fashions, & of course English manufactures. But the cities are not the people of America. The country will be clothed in homespun; and what we shall take from England hereafter, will be as nothing to what we took before the embargo. When you come to see us," he told his friend, Caesar Rodney, "you will find our spinning jennies & looms in full activity, never more to be laid aside." Come, he invited, "and see that we are an industrious, plain, hospitable and honest, altho' not a psalm-singing, people." [13] This last was, of course, a sneer at the New England Calvinists.

He was sorry to hear of the second, and this time final, overthrow of Napoleon. It destroyed, he thought, the mutual cancellation and balance of power in Europe against us, and left us once more the possible prey of the victors who hated the example of our republican form of government. (He thus correctly adumbrated the plots of the Holy Alliance, though he miscalculated England's future role.) It was to prepare for such an eventuality that he kept insisting, Cassandralike, on two measures with which adequately to meet the inevitable day. The first was the reform of the military system through his scheme of militia classification. The second was the reform of the financial system, to take the power of emitting paper money from the banks. "The coining of paper money by private authority," he vehemently declared, "is a higher degree of treason than the coining the precious metals." [14]

Negotiations were still continuing in Paris between the American commissioners and England. Both John Quincy Adams and Gallatin were there, and Jefferson was extremely anxious that they settle the matter of impressments, but *not* to enter into a commercial treaty, "*quod deus avertat.*" The first would mean war again, if no settlement could be arrived at. The second would not. "The depredations on our merchants," he avowed, "I would bear with great patience as it is their desire." Besides, they were covered by insurance, largely taken out in *England.*[15]

Yet, for all his bewailments of vicious men abroad and at home—the foreign tyrants and murderers, and the domestic Federalists for whom, "like bawds, religion becomes to them a refuge from the despair of their loathsome vices," and for whom the halter is not good enough, he never once despaired of the future of the human race. Once obtain for it education and a vision of the truth, and "the condition of man may be ameliorated, if not *infinitely*, as enthusiasm alone pretends, yet *indefinitely*, as bigots alone can doubt." [16]

With his library sold to the national government, Jefferson busied himself with arranging and cataloguing the books for shipment; and, at the same time, beginning the foundations for a new library of his own. Young George Ticknor, who had visited him at Monticello, was leaving for a grand tour of Europe, and Jefferson sent him lists of books to purchase abroad for him. Similar lists went also to booksellers and others with European connections. He had kept for himself only a few of his precious volumes, and the great gaps on his shelves were a constant reproach. His grand aim was to gather for a third time a great collection whose wealth and variety would stir the wonder and admiration of the world. "I cannot live without books," he declared.[17]

The task of arrangement and classification was tedious; particularly since his health was beginning to fail, and his limbs did not bear him with the same resiliency as of old, so that he was compelled to avoid the pleasures of riding and resign himself to being driven around in a carriage.[18]

He attributed his increasing feebleness to the lack of wine. In spite of numerous orders, the unsettled condition of Europe had stopped his sources of supply and his cellars were bare. He therefore sent an urgent call to a Spanish factor at Norfolk to please send him some of the best wine he had. "Wine from long habit," he wrote, "has become an indispensable for my health, which is now suffering by its disuse." [19]

Tragic news also came from distant John Adams. Abigail was "in extremis, forbidden to Speak or to be Spoken to." [20] The thought of his indomitable old friend and antagonist thus unable to speak her mind as in more halcyon days must have affected Jefferson deeply. One by one the companions of his youth and vigorous middle age were dropping by the wayside.

He had been keeping up a steady correspondence with John, and Abigail had on occasion asked to be remembered. The two old cronies reminisced continually over the past, avoiding by mutual consent the controversial days of the Nineties, and harking back to the glorious Revolution.

Adams demanded to know who could write the history of that Revolution, and Jefferson retorted: "Who can write it? And who will ever be able to write it? Nobody; except merely its external facts; all its councils, designs and discussions having been conducted by Congress with closed doors, and no members, as far as I know, having ever made notes of them." [21] He was wrong; some, at least, of the members (including himself) had taken notes; though, unfortunately, on a limited scale.

But Adams countered with a profound sense of history that the Revolution was *not* the war, which "was only an effect and consequence of it. The revolution was in the minds of the people, and this was effected from 1760 to 1775, in the course of fifteen years, before a drop of blood was shed at Lexington." [22]

Abigail managed to survive for a while her dangerous illness, but her condition and their own several enfeeblements evoked an interesting discussion between the two aged men. Adams was eighty now, and Jefferson seventy-three. Jefferson propounded the question: Would Adams be willing to live his life all over again? Yes, I would, replied Adams; though not forever and ever. And how about Jefferson? [23]

Jefferson was not so sure. Yes, if it meant only the years from twenty-five to sixty; perhaps even a bit earlier. But *not* later. "For at the latter period, with most of us, the powers of life are sensibly on the wane; sight becomes dim, hearing dull, memory constantly enlarging its frightful blank, and parting with all we have ever seen or known, spirits evaporate, bodily debility creeps on, palsying every limb, and so faculty after faculty quits us, and where, then, is life?" Rather than that, "there is a ripeness of time for death, regarding others as well as ourselves, when it is reasonable we should drop off, and make room for another growth." [24] It was not only with respect to contracts and laws that Jefferson felt that one generation had no right to bind the next.

After years of hesitation, Jefferson now leased out the Natural Bridge tract he owned, though he refused to sell it. He regarded that great natural curiosity as "in some degree a public trust, and would on no consideration permit the bridge to be injured, defaced or masked from the public view." [25] One wonders what he would have thought of its current exploitation; "masked from the public view" except on payment of a substantial fee.

A curious incident aroused some reflections on the nature of human credulity. He had begun another of the numerous remodelings of his house at Poplar Forest in August, 1815, just after the news of Napoleon's second downfall reached America. The number of workmen employed and the activity displayed sent a rumor racing like wildfire through the neighborhood that Jefferson was hastily preparing Poplar Forest as a place of refuge for the defeated ruler of France. "Were there such people only as the believers in this," he exclaimed indignantly, "patriotism would be a ridiculous passion." [26]

In spite of his debility, Jefferson started on September 18, 1815, to undertake a task which he had long contemplated, but which was a feat for youth rather than old age. The elevation of the Peaks of Otter, a remarkable mountain group near Roanoke, had long baffled his curiosity, and he was determined before he died to solve the mystery. Taking along a youthful disciple and worshipper, Francis Walker Gilmer, and the botanist Correa, the trio traveled to the Peaks in a vehicle which young Gilmer profanely described as "a mill hopper." [27] But this was mere youthful exuberance; the young man, son of Jefferson's old friend Dr. Gilmer, was, according to Jefferson, "the best educated young man of our state," and had been delighted to accompany the great man and Correa, whom Jefferson similarly described as "being without exception the most learned man I have ever met in any country." [28]

Carrying a theodolite and other surveyor's instruments, Jefferson measured the Peaks while his two friends busied themselves with exploring the botanical specimens of the wooded mountainsides. The trip took five days, and the calculations five more. Returning, Jefferson left the pair at the Natural Bridge to continue their botanizing, while he went on to Poplar Forest. Later, Correa came to Monticello, where Dupont met him; and both men waited in vain for Jefferson to show up.[29]

The end of the war had touched off the springs of a speculative mania that disclosed itself in a sudden rash of new banks and a concomitant issuance of paper money. As fast as the presses could print, the banks threw the paper on the market, and eager Americans indulged themselves in what seemed an endless inflationary spiral.

To Jefferson these were the days of the Revolution all over again, of the South Sea and the Mississippi bubbles of malodorous memories. He knew the fatal consequences and raised his voice in warning again and again. But his jeremiads fell on unheeding ears. The malady, as always, had to run its course and leave a trail of bankruptcies and ruin in its path. "Like a dropsical man calling out for water, water," he exclaimed bitterly, "our deluded citizens are clamoring for more banks, more banks. The American mind is now in that state of fever which the world has so often seen in the history of other nations.... We are now taught to believe that legerdemain tricks upon paper can produce as solid wealth as hard labor in the earth. It is vain for common sense to urge that *nothing* can produce *nothing*." [30]

If his ideas on the efficacy of paper money had not changed in forty years, some of his other earlier convictions had undergone changes that he was frank enough to admit. Such was his earlier stand on manufactures as set forth in his *Notes on Virginia* and which his adversaries were only too pleased to quote continually against him now. These are new times, he defended himself, and when the *Notes* were written, who could have expected the new courses of England and France? "Experience has taught me," he acknowledged in all candor, "that manufactures are now as necessary to our independence as to our comfort." [31]

All in all, however, his political *theory*, if not always his practice, had remained remarkably consistent during the years. He still firmly believed that "the way to have good and safe government, is not to trust it all to

Courtesy the Pennsylvania Academy of the Fine Arts

DR. BENJAMIN RUSH

Plaster bust by William Rush

Stock of wine on hand Apr. 7. 1787.

1787	bottles	
Apr. 7.	88	Bordeaux. from Bondfeild in 1785 & 1786
	95.	Grave. from Bondfeild in 1786.
		Cayusac.
	29.	Champagne. Chevr. Luzerne.
	100	Gayac.
	183	Madeira. of which 154. is from N. york.
	18.	Setubal
	20.	Port
	19.	Pico
	15.	Calcavallo
		Malvoisie
	10.	Chipre
	8.	Aleatico.

1787.		
May	124	Monrachet. from Parent. de la Tour's. 274 + 65 + 34-10 = 2-4 = 11s = 5s/3-0 the bottle
July 4.	250.	Frontignan. white. Lambert 300 } + 25 + 213
	33	Frontignan. red. Lambert 49-10 } 12-7 / 27-8 / 20-3 } pr. bottle
7.	72	Pacaret. mr. Grand.
13	124.	Meursault de M. Bachey de 1784. goutte d'or. 78 + 48. at Beaune
	126	Caumartin. 126 bottles. 84 en futaille = 13-4 + 48 bottles = 7-8 = 21s the bottle
Aug.	180	Chateau-margaut. from messrs. Feger, Grammont & co. note, I sent 124. bottles of this to A. Donald.
1788		
Feb. 12	248	Meursault de M. Bachey de 1784. goutte d'or 200 + 100 + 66
	123	Voulenaye. 90 + 50 + 33
Apr. 23.	250	Sauterne. du Comte de Lur-Saluce. 312-10 + 28. at Bord. bottles includ. 13 3/4 + 8 1/4 =
1789	248	
Mar. 1	248.	Meursault de 1784. 170 + 102 = 272 is 22s pr. bottle deliv. at Beaune add 66. transportn = 338 is 27 3/4 the bottle

Courtesy the Massachusetts Historical Society

JEFFERSON'S INVENTORY OF WINE AND LIQUOR SUPPLY

one, but to divide it among the many, distributing to every one exactly the functions he is competent to." In other words, the national government should be entrusted with foreign and federal relations and matters of defense. The state governments should handle civil rights, police and their own internal affairs; and the counties and wards matters pertaining to themselves. "It is by dividing and subdividing these republics from the great national one down through all its subordinations, until it ends in the administration of every man's farm by himself; by placing under every one what his own eye may superintend, that all will be done for the best." Liberty could only be destroyed, he was convinced, when *all* power was concentrated in a single man or single body.

After sending these observations off to his friend Cabell, he appended some private addenda to his own copy. They were animadversions on the nature of the Judiciary, a body of which he stood in mortal fear that the autocracy of the future might develop. "Our republic," he now wrote, "is founded on the principle that the people are the source of all powers, & the safest depository of such as they are competent to exercise." He admitted that they were not sufficiently competent to appoint judges of the *law*, but as judges of the *fact* he considered them supreme. Thereby he thought he had found a way to balance the unrestricted authority of the law judges. Let jurors be *elected*, he jotted down, reverting to an earlier idea of his, and be wholly independent of either judges or other branches of the government. The freedom of the jury, he was certain, would counterbalance the power of the judiciary.[32]

But he realized that some of his ideals of government were very likely vain dreams. "A government regulating itself by what is wise and just for the many, uninfluenced by the local and selfish views of the few who direct their affairs," he admitted, "has not been seen perhaps, on earth." [33]

This somewhat gloomy view did not, however, prevent Jefferson from seeking always the best methods of setting up a government that would safeguard the rights of every citizen and be responsive to his control. He understood thoroughly that a "pure" republic was impossible on the scale of the United States (though he had denounced Montesquieu for saying somewhat the same thing) and that a representative government must necessarily be complex, have indirect controls, and adopt a series of checks and balances to arrive approximately at its chief object.

Looking back over the turbulent history of his country and its evolution since the first flush of the Declaration of Independence, he now committed to paper his rounded philosophy of government in one of the most important private letters he ever wrote.

The subject of equal representation had become a burning issue in the politics of Virginia, and a man named Samuel Kercheval sought the opinion of the sage of Monticello on the matter. Jefferson seized the occasion to deliver himself of some of his ripest thinking.

He had always been in favor of equal representation, he replied, and cited in evidence the constitution he had once sought to draft for the benefit of his native state. But the constitution that *had* been adopted, and succeeding ones, "had really no leading principles in them." The matter of representation was a case in point. The House of Delegates, for example, was chosen by less than half the people of the state (and by *people* Jefferson meant free white adult males); the Senate was even more narrowly chosen and for "long terms of irresponsibility"; the Governor, appointed by the Assembly, was altogether independent of the people; and so was his Council. As for the Judiciary, the judges of the higher courts "are dependent on none but themselves"; while the justices of the inferior courts are self-chosen, hold office for life and select their successors.

How amend this undemocratic state of affairs? It was not really as difficult as some pretended, thought Jefferson. "Only lay down true principles," he asserted, "and adhere to them inflexibly. Do not be frightened into their surrender by the alarms of the timid, or the croakings of wealth against the ascendancy of the people." Whereupon he proceeded to lay down those principles as he conceived them.

"The true foundation of republican government," he wrote, "is the equal right of every citizen, in his person and property, and in their management. Try by this, as a tally, every provision of our constitution, and see if it hangs directly on the will of the people. Reduce your legislature to a convenient number for full, but orderly discussion. Let every man who fights or pays, exercise his just and equal right in their election. Submit them to approbation or rejection at short intervals. Let the executive be chosen in the same way, and for the same term, by those whose agent he is to be; and leave no screen of a council behind which to skulk from responsibility." Jefferson was willing, however, to omit *law* judges from this general scheme of direct elections. In their case, he agreed, there might be some doubt as to the competency of the people to decide.

The wards or townships, furthermore, should be granted a large measure of autonomy. They are "the vital principle of their governments, and have proved themselves [in New England] the wisest invention ever devised by the wit of man for the perfect exercise of self-government, and for its preservation." Once again he proposed his division of powers among nation, state and townships; and their cement in the personal participation of the individual citizen.

"I am not among those," he added in all sincerity, "who fear the people. They, and not the rich, are our dependence for continued freedom. And to preserve their independence, we must not let our rulers load us with perpetual debt. We must make our election between *economy and liberty*, or *profusion and servitude*."

Nor were constitutions sacrosanct, "like the arc of the covenant, too sacred to be touched." There had been no superhuman wisdom among the writers of former constitutions. "I knew that age well; I belonged to it, and labored with it," he avowed proudly. "It deserved well of its country";

but it was not different from the current generation, except in one important respect. It had less experience. "Forty years of experience in government," declared Jefferson sweepingly, "is worth a century of book-reading; and this they would say themselves, were they to rise from the dead."

This did not mean, however, that there should be frequent changes in laws and constitutions. Moderate imperfections ought to be borne with and adjusted to. "But I know also," he added, "that laws and institutions must go hand in hand with the progress of the human mind. As that becomes more developed, more enlightened, as new discoveries are made, new truths disclosed, and manners and opinions change with the change of circumstances, institutions must advance also, and keep pace with the times. We might as well require a man to wear still the coat which fitted him when a boy, as civilized society to remain ever under the regimen of their barbarous ancestors."

Here, in short compass, was the crux of Jefferson's philosophy and matured wisdom. Wrapped in its own mantle of thesis—that man grows ever more wise and that the indefinite passage of years brings in its train indefinite progress—is a profound kernel of truth: that each age must find its own institutions and laws appropriate to its own circumstances. The danger, of course, in spite of Jefferson's previous disavowal, lay in a too easy readiness to rid each age of "the regimen of their barbarous ancestors." This tendency becomes explicit in Jefferson's next proposal; based as it is on that ancient fallacy of his, that a generation lasts only nineteen years, and that no generation has a right to bind succeeding ones.

A constitution, he declared, ought to provide for its own revision at stated periods; and that period, he insisted, was nineteen years. Let this new generation, therefore, "choose for itself the form of government it believes most promotive of its own happiness . . . and it is for the peace and good of mankind that a solemn opportunity of doing this every nineteen or twenty years, should be provided by the constitution. . . ." And he pointed out that the *Virginia* constitution had largely been in effect for forty years.

"These, Sir," he ended this famous letter, "are my opinions of the governments we see among men, and of the principles by which alone we may prevent our own from falling into the same dreadful track." [34]

With his usual fear of consequences, he asked that the letter be not published; but, as too often happened, it shortly became a matter of common knowledge and even, so Jefferson heard, was in the hands of a printer for publication in connection with the proposed Constitutional Convention. In great alarm, he wrote to Kercheval beseeching him to recall the letter and all copies. He did not wish, he asserted, to become involved in any partisan politics. If his fellow citizens preferred the present constitution, he was willing to live under it for what little of life remained to him.

"I again throw the quiet of my life on your honor," he ended in much perturbation.[35]

He was, indeed, forever writing letters on controversial issues, beseeching that they be not published, and finding them later, to his dismay, in print and the subject of angry attacks.[36]

He was also beginning to complain bitterly of the multiplicity of his correspondence, and determining to curtail it. "This keeps me," he wrote sadly, "at the drudgery of the writing-table all the prime hours of the day, leaving for the gratification of my appetite for reading, only what I can steal from the hours of sleep." [37] Yet, in spite of his increasing complaints, he never could resist the fascinating, if arduous sessions at his "writing-table"; a deplorable practice for which his biographers must be eternally grateful.

Jefferson's religious beliefs constituted one of the delicate subjects concerning which he lived in constant fear that they might fall into the hands of his enemies. He was willing to avow them fully and frankly to his closest friends; but he avoided any discussion of them with strangers. To his old friend Thomson he felt at ease in declaring that the doctrines of Epicurus constituted "the most rational system remaining of the philosophy of the ancients"; [38] but to most others he presented an impenetrable front. "I have ever thought religion," he declared with almost monotonous regularity, "a concern purely between our god and our consciences, for which we were accountable to him, and not to the priests. I never told my own religion, nor scrutinized that of another. I never attempted to make a convert, nor wished to change another's creed. I have ever judged of the religion of others by their lives . . . for it is in our lives, and not from our words, that our religion must be read. By the same test the world must judge me." [39]

He was similarly reticent about writing his memoirs, as so many urged him to do. Possessed as he was of a sense of history perhaps unexampled in his day, he nevertheless shrank from committing nakedly to the public scrutiny his estimates of men and affairs and the evidences and convictions of his own career. He feared to stir up the sleeping dogs of controversy and to expose himself to the fierce assaults and twisted interpretations of his former opponents. He pleaded his stiffening wrist (the one he had broken in France and which, with increasing age, was to plague him more and more), and he insisted that there was sufficient material for the historian in his public papers as they existed in the public offices.[40] He was willing enough, however—arguing from the meticulousness with which he kept every scrap of paper—to be judged after his death on the basis of his entire correspondence, public and private.

Meanwhile, in spite of his wrist and the numerous calls upon his time and attention, Jefferson took up the various manuscripts that Destutt Tracy had sent him, and sought to bring them to the attention of the world. Tracy's treatise on Political Economy had come into his hands in 1812, and he had then turned it over to Duane for translation and publication. After a two-year interval, Duane declined to publish, though he had had the French translated. Jefferson paid for the alleged translation; but when it came into his hands he found it abominably wretched. Thereupon he undertook the task of revising the English.

He devoted to this labor of love some five hours every day for several months and, when finished, wrote a preface or prospectus to be used anonymously in connection with its publication. The revised translation was sent to a printer in Georgetown, Joseph Milligan, who agreed to publish. But so many delays intervened that he sought another printer and tendered it to Thomas Ritchie, editor of the Richmond *Enquirer*, only to discover to his embarrassment that Milligan was now ready to go ahead with it. In 1817, after much trouble and difficulties, the volume finally appeared, with neither Tracy's nor Jefferson's name attached. Jefferson admitted the trouble, but declared to Dupont that he "would have gone thro' ten times more to procure for the world the publication of this inestimable volume."[41]

Alas, the American people passed the "inestimable volume" unheeding by. Jefferson was never able to infect his friends with his own unbounded enthusiasm for the genius of the Frenchman. It is no wonder then that in his anger he accused his fellow countrymen of a total ignorance of the branch of science known as Political Economy, and sought unweariedly to lighten the darkness in which they were so contentedly swathed.[42]

But Jefferson's own limitations are nowhere better set forth than in the estimate of Tracy's work he tendered to John Adams. He had not been able to read entirely through the basic volumes on Ideology that Tracy had written, since, he acknowledged, "I am not fond of reading what is merely abstract, and unapplied immediately to some useful science."[43]

CHAPTER 69

Triumph of the University

JAMES MADISON served two terms as President and, in accordance with the rule laid down by Jefferson, was ready to retire to private life. He was not too averse to the prospect; his administrations had encompassed an inglorious war and there was general agreement, except among his most loyal followers, that he had not been a great President. The uneasy patience which James Monroe had exhibited over his own discard some eight years before was now vindicated, and the caucus of Republican Congressmen whose mandate was usually accepted as a nomination, chose him as the Republican standard-bearer by a fairly close vote over the rival pretensions of William H. Crawford. Monroe later found it expedient to give Crawford the post of the Treasury in his Cabinet. The nomination, in view of the completely disorganized condition of the Federalists, was tantamount to election; so much so, indeed, that Jefferson hardly found it worth while to refer to the campaign in any of his letters.

He preferred rather to engross himself in general principles and in adopting a world view. The South American colonies had finally erupted into their long threatened revolt against Spain; and Jefferson, in spite of agitation to the contrary, thought it unwise to give them any military assistance *until* we ourselves had gone to war with Spain for other reasons. Surprisingly, however, he hoped that, when victorious, South America would not form a single confederacy, but would split into several groups. The reason he gave is illuminating. "In a single mass," he frankly avowed, "they would be a very formidable neighbor." If divided into three parts, as he thought their geography indicated, the United States might then be "the balancing power." [1]

Yet he viewed their struggles with a sympathetic eye, and when the enthusiastic Dupont drafted a plan of a constitution for the "Equinoctial republics," Jefferson soberly rebuked it as undemocratic. "We both consider the people as our children, and love them with parental affection," he observed. "But you love them as infants whom you are afraid to trust without nurses; and I as adults whom I freely leave to self-government." [2]

But this conception of self-government was strictly as a representative and not a pure democracy. The latter, he believed, could only work usefully in a small town or ward meeting. It was on that basis that he disputed Montesquieu, and insisted that a republican, representative structure could be applied to large areas. In fact, the larger the area, the more solid would be the structure, provided it "was founded, not on conquest, but in principles of compact and equality."[3] Europe, by disobeying these principles, was "returning to Gothic darkness while the mass of ours is advancing in the regions of light."[4]

Because of this, to him, essential difference he also dismissed as useless "almost everything written before on the structure of government." In particular he saw little reason now for reading Aristotle's *Politics*. Aristotle and others of his time "knew no medium between a democracy (the only pure republic, but impracticable beyond the limits of a town) and an abandonment of themselves to an aristocracy, or a tyranny independent of the people." They had no conception of a *representative* "republican, or popular government, of the second grade of purity." That experiment was reserved to the American people.[5]

In this new vision for America, he even lost some of his ancient hatred for the great enemy, England. The Capitol at Washington, burnt to the ground by an English raid, was being rebuilt, and Monroe asked his advice as to an inscription to be carved on its front. Jefferson first suggested: *Founded 1791.—Burnt by a British army 1814.—Restored by Congress 1817.* (After World War I, an inscription of almost similar terrible brevity was placed over the restored library at Louvain.) But, with the Caesarian phrase once coined, Jefferson reconsidered. Why should there be any inscription at all? he inquired. Without it England would suffer a sufficient "immortality of infamy for the barbarity of the act." True, we had "more reason to hate her than any nation on earth." But she was falling from her high estate—or at least so Jefferson thought. He did not wish her to become totally eclipsed, or absorbed into the body politic of another nation, so that their combined strength would constitute an object of dread to all nations, and the United States in particular. Rather, he wrote, let her be on a par, or *nearly* on a par with other nations. Let us therefore, amid these gloomy prospects for England, no longer seek to perpetuate hatred against her; let us "prepare the minds of our citizens . . . by acts of comity towards England rather than by commemoration of hatred."[6]

This magnanimity, based on reports that a powerful European alliance was forming in opposition to England, and of internal discontent, was praiseworthy enough; but the object of pity was soon to dispute all reports of her demise as "greatly exaggerated."

One death, however, had not been exaggerated. Jefferson's "antient friend" Mazzei died in Italy. Jefferson grieved sincerely; but found himself involved in complicated financial difficulties as a result. Mazzei had given him power of attorney over his Virginia holdings before he left for Europe, never to return. Jefferson sold them at a profit but, the War of 1812 intervening, found it impossible to remit the proceeds abroad. As Jefferson was later to narrate it for the benefit of Mazzei's heirs, he considered any bank as an unsafe depository and therefore found a *safer* investment for the fund ($6,342) by lending it to himself. Since 1813, he had been faithfully remitting 6 per cent interest to the heirs; but it seems that they were now demanding the principal. This he could not send, giving as excuse his usual tale of hard luck, bad times and crop failures. As late as 1820 he was still repeating the weary story.[7]

The flood of correspondence that invaded Monticello from friends, politicians and pseudo politicians, aspirant authors, inventors, the seekers after autographs and the merely curious brought continual cries of anguish from Jefferson and finally caused him to explode. "No office I ever was in," he exclaimed to Burwell, "has been so laborious as my supposed state of retirement in Monticello. Unable to bear up longer against it, either in body or mind, I am obliged to declare myself in *a state of insurgency*, and to assume my right to live out the dregs of life at least, without being under the whip & spur from morning to night." [8]

He even authorized one correspondent to publish to the world his plea for mercy from would-be correspondents; but the plea had little effect. The letters continued to roll in; and Jefferson, groaning and complaining, still replied. He had not the temperament or the will power to do what Adams advised him to do: not to answer, or to give "gruff, short, unintelligible misterious, enigmatical, or pedantical answers." But then Adams realized this was impossible for Jefferson, "because it is not in your nature to avail yourself of it." [9]

As a result, Jefferson found little time for any sustained reading, and exclaimed in envy over Adams's proud record of forty-three volumes in a year, "twelve of them quarto!" The results of decades of religious reading ended for Adams in four pithy words: "Be just and good." To which Jefferson, assenting, added: "What all agree in, is probably right. What no two agree in, most probably wrong." [10]

Of the two old philosophers, there is no doubt that Adams was the tougher minded, and Jefferson the more tender. Criticizing Tracy's volume, which Jefferson had sent him, Adams inferentially criticized Jefferson too. "He all along supposes," snorted the sage of Braintree, "that Man are rational and consciencious creatures. I say so too: but I say at the same time that their passions and Interests generally prevail over their Reason and their consciences: and if Society does not contrive some means of controce[p]ting and restrain[in]g the former the World will go on as it has done." [11]

But Jefferson preferred variety and difference to restraint, whether by Society with a capital S, kings or a priesthood. "It is a singular anxiety," he unbosomed himself to another old friend, Charles Thomson, "which some people have we should all think alike. Would the world be more beautiful were all our faces alike? were our tempers, our talents, our tastes, our forms, our wishes, aversions and pursuits cast exactly in the same mould? If no varieties existed in the animal, vegetable or mineral creation, but all move strictly uniform, catholic & orthodox, what a world of physical and moral monotony it would be! These are absurdities into which those run who usurp the throne of God and dictate to Him what He should have done." [12]

He himself had changed his opinion in at least one respect. Whereas in earlier years he had conceived the labor of the agriculturist the only true source of wealth for a nation, and that of the manufacturer as an excrescence operating on dead materials, he now acknowledged that he had seen but half the picture. "The inventions of latter times," he admitted, "by labor-saving machines, do as much now for the manufacturer, as the earth for the cultivator." In one respect, however, he remained unreconstructed. Are dollars and cents, he demanded, "to be weighed in the scale against real independence?" [13]

The election had come and gone, and Monroe assumed the mantle that Jefferson and Madison had worn. Jefferson congratulated him in brief language, and suggested a list of excellent wines for his Presidential table, and the agent, a Mr. Sasserno, from whom he could order them. "By the bye," he added as a carefully casual afterthought, Mr. Sasserno would like to be appointed as Consul at Nice. Monroe promptly consented.[14]

During the first days of Monroe's administration Jefferson did not intrude his advice on the management of government with the same freedom he had employed with Madison. Perhaps he was now longer away from the helm; perhaps he felt under some constraint with Monroe as a result of the long misunderstanding between them. In any event, his suggestions were fewer and Monroe, except on certain notable occasions, did not voluntarily seek his advice. Other times, other problems.

When Monroe vetoed a Congressional bill providing federal aid to canals, roads and education, Jefferson's comments were directed to Gallatin rather than to the President. He approved of the veto; yet he was also happy that Congress had passed the bill and thus brought the whole matter sharply to the attention of the States. The whole difference that now existed between the Federalists and the Republicans, he declared, lay in the interpretation of the "general welfare" clause in the Constitution. The former pretended the clause gave unlimited powers to Congress to provide for the general welfare; the latter insisted that those powers had been specifically enumerated. With the distinction thus again brought into public view, he believed it would be settled once for all.[15]

More and more, however, he was now becoming immersed in what became the consuming interest of his final years and the crowning capstone of a long and fruitful life. The scheme of education on which he had worked and dreamed for over forty years was at last taking shape and form.

To Jefferson the problem of education had two prongs. One related to a state-supported elementary education available to all; the second proposed an institution of higher learning for the capable few, to which poor young men of exceptional ability could be sent at the public expense, while those of means would pay their own way.

Both prongs were equally important to him; but only the second was realized in his lifetime. Nevertheless, in the beginning, the prospects looked bright for the first as well. In 1810, under Jefferson's proddings, Virginia had established a "Literary Fund" chiefly directed to elementary education. Originally limited in its income to forfeitures, escheats and fines, in 1815-16 the debt of the national government to Virginia was added to the Fund; raising the total available by the end of 1817 to the very respectable sum of a million dollars. A board of public officials was designated as the Directors.

At the beginning of 1816, the Assembly asked the Board to submit recommendations for a scheme of public education. Jefferson's plan, as outlined in his letter to Peter Carr, was used with good effect to color the thinking of the Board. Their report, submitted on December 6, 1816, followed Jefferson's ideas pretty closely, with one important exception. Whereas he placed all three branches of his system on an equal footing insofar as state aid was concerned, the Board, with more practical wisdom, created a series of priorities. The fund was to be used first for elementary schools, next for the academies or colleges, and only if there were a residue, was it to be applied to the university.

A bill framed on this epoch-making report actually passed the House of Delegates, but the more conservative Senate defeated it on the grounds that such a vast expenditure of money ought to be submitted for approval to the vote of the people.

Joseph C. Cabell, who had been piloting the various bills through the Assembly, now called on Jefferson to submit a new bill for its consideration on the subject of elementary education. On September 9, 1817, Jefferson completed the task and sent a copy to Cabell with a note of apology for the style in which he had drafted it. But, he declared, "I dislike the verbose and intricate style of the modern English statutes, and in our Revised Code I endeavored to restore it to the simple one of the ancient statutes.... I suppose," he added wryly, "the reformation has not been acceptable, as it has been little followed." [16]

It might have been better, perhaps, had he cloaked his ideas in the usual jargon, and so hidden from too close scrutiny some of the fundamental ideas of his plan. In essence, however, it followed all the various drafts he had been unweariedly making for the past forty years.

The very first clause, indeed, was calculated to rouse the wrath of the larger religious denominations. He provided for the appointment of "three discreet and well-informed persons" in every county to serve as Visitors of the Elementary Schools; but specifically barred "ministers of the gospel of any denomination" from appointment. In spite of an ingenuous footnote that thereby he sought to avoid the jealousy of the sects whose ministers had not been chosen, it was obvious to all that what Jefferson really intended was to keep religion and religious influences altogether out of any scheme of public education.

Each county was to be divided into wards, based on a population sufficient to furnish a company of militia. Indeed, Jefferson intended this system of wards to become the organic element in the administration of government and of the militia of the state.

On an appointed date, all free white male citizens were to meet and vote on the location of the school, the method for erecting it, and whether it should be built by a contribution of money or by joint labor. If by joint labor, those already liable to highway work would be employed on the venture. If by cash, all property owners would contribute in proportion to their regular taxes.

The Visitors were to employ teachers, and the course of instruction included reading, writing, numeral arithmetic and geography.

Free instruction would be furnished to those who had not already had three years of schooling, and thereafter for all from the ages of twelve to fifteen. No one, he decreed, who at the age of fifteen and not mentally disabled, could not "read readily in some tongue, native or acquired," would be considered a citizen of the state.

Once again the question of religion arose, and Jefferson made his intention extremely plain. "No religious reading, instruction or exercise," he wrote, "shall be prescribed or practiced inconsistent with the tenets of any religious sect or denomination." Thereby he rendered any religious instruction impossible, except for possible courses in general morals and ethics.

Having thus disposed of the elementary schools, he next directed his attention to the "colleges"—in modern parlance, high schools. The state was to be divided into nine collegiate districts, each with its own Board of Visitors. Substantial buildings were to be erected, at a cost of not more than $7,500 each.

Two Professors would be attached to each college; one for the classical languages, the other for all other branches of learning. Both the cost of the buildings and the salaries were to be paid out of the Literary Fund.

The University, however, the apex of the pyramid, provided an unusual problem. To placate all parties, Jefferson suggested two alternatives: the first for an independent University to be established as the legislature might decide; the second for its establishment in Charlottesville by a conveyance of the properties and rights of Central College, in whose erection Jefferson had been so deeply concerned. Actually, Jefferson ardently desired the adoption of the second alternative; but he bowed to the known resentment of William and Mary and of other sections of the state to that location.

The University government lay in the hands of a Board of eight Visitors, and Jefferson's plan for choosing exceptionally able poor boys for five years' free education in the University followed the method he had repeatedly set forth in earlier documents. The expense of such scholarships was also to be borne by the Literary Fund.[17]

After the dispatch of this lengthy and carefully formulated plan, Jefferson bethought himself that perhaps it ought not to be known that he had been its chief architect—particularly of those sections which offered his own Central College as the State University. He therefore wrote to Cabell to omit his name in any discussion of it. He did not wish, he added gratuitously, to be considered as meddling in public affairs.[18]

The bill, as Jefferson wrote it then and later expanded, sought to make *elementary* education the charge of the local communities, and only the higher branches were to be state-supported. He feared that any attempt to make the lower schools similarly state-endowed would defeat the entire scheme. The expenses entailed for elementary education—certainly when compounded with the cost of the colleges—would completely exhaust the authorized Literary Fund, and leave his beloved University without a penny for operation. There was much more chance, he rightly believed, of getting the local citizenry to pay for the support of elementary schools than to obtain their funds for the University. "I have always found it best," he told Cabell, "never to permit a rational plan to be marred by botching."[19]

But his scheme of things immediately encountered strong opposition in the Assembly. It was there felt that whatever was to be done ought to be kept wholly within the limits of the moneys available in the Literary Fund, without casting any extra burden on the taxpayers; and, as has been indicated, there was much resentment against the idea of a new University, both from the vested interests of William and Mary and from those who wondered audibly why *Charlottesville* should win the prize.

So close was the division, that Jefferson called on Monroe to add the weight of his name to the plan; while he bombarded Cabell with requests for information as to the progress of the bill. "I have only this single anxiety in this world," he explained with some pathos. "It is a bantling of 40. years birth & nursing, & if I can once see it on its legs, I will sing with sincerity & pleasure my nunc demittas [*sic*]."[20]

Cabell reported that those in Richmond with whom he conferred were unanimous for a university and pretty much in agreement on the colleges, but that there was vehement dispute on the practicability and expediency of the elementary schools. They also advised, as a matter of practical politics, to leave out those prohibitions which involved ministers of religion and religious instruction.[21]

The crosscurrents, therefore, were innumerable and threatened to wreck the entire scheme. As a matter of fact, the bill failed of passage in the lower House on February 11, 1818. Instead, a substitute bill proposed by a delegate from King William County, which restricted the use of the Literary Fund to the education of the poor, and provided that the moneys be distributed by the state to the several counties as a bounty for charity schools, was adopted instead. Cabell commented bitterly that the disposition was merely to lay out a small sum for the charity schools, and use the rest of the Fund to pay the state debts.[22]

With his whole grandiose plan thus toppling about his ears, Jefferson regretted that he had ever meddled with the bill at all, and was thankful that Cabell had managed to keep his name out of the public eye. "There are fanatics both in religion and politics," he declared bitterly, "who without knowing me personally have long been taught to consider me as a rawhead & bloody bones." [23]

Something, however, was salvaged from the wreck. In the Senate, when the substitute bill came up for consideration, a last-minute rally of Cabell and his friends managed to graft onto it a provision for a University which, passing the Senate, was later agreed to by the House. As it stood in the final law, $45,000 a year was subscribed for the education of the poor, and $15,000 for the benefit of a University.[24]

On the face of it the victory was a Pyrrhic one, for not only were the colleges wholly omitted, and the plan for a comprehensive system of elementary education completely ruined, but the amounts actually voted for maintenance were so piddling as to be wholly without effect.

Nevertheless, if the general public schools were irretrievably lost, the mere fact that the *idea* of a University had been graciously accepted was sufficient to furnish the impetus for the final erection of the University of Virginia.

Central College at Charlottesville had occupied Jefferson's best efforts for some time. Originally planned as the Charlottesville Academy, the name had been changed to Central College in 1816, and a distinguished Board of Visitors placed in charge, including Jefferson, Madison, Monroe, Cabell, David Watson and John Hartwell Cocke. Petitions were submitted to the state legislature for funds, but without success.

Jefferson, however, though ostensibly preoccupied with the College as such, secretly intended it as the nucleus for his more ambitious scheme of a State University. It was for that reason he inserted in his bill the proposition that the College's current assets *might* be used for the benefit of the proposed University.

With a University given at least official lip service, the proponents unweariedly continued their exertions. The final decision as to the location of the University was left to a board of twenty-four Commissioners appointed by the Governor and his Council. The Commissioners, of whom Jefferson was one, met at Rockfish Gap from August 1st to 4th, 1818.

Three sites were debated for the location of the new State University —Staunton, Washington College at Lexington, and Central College at Charlottesville. The first two were favored by the western folk as being closer to themselves and because they suspected that the site of the University would also eventually become the capital of the state. Jefferson's old idea of placing the capital at the geographical and population center was coming home to roost. The advocates of William and Mary sought for their own part to throw obstacles in the way of the entire scheme as sealing the doom of that ancient institution.

Jefferson, however, in spite of the fact that he himself was a graduate, had nothing but contempt for William and Mary in its present moribund state. When young Francis Gilmer was offered his choice of either the presidency or a professorship there, Jefferson dissuaded him. "I trust you did not a moment seriously think of putting yourself behind the door of W. & M. College," he wrote. "A more complete cul de sac could not be proposed to you." He advised Gilmer rather to go into the legislature, where his talents were most needed, particularly at the next session when the project of the University would come on the floor again.[25]

Though suffering from a severe attack of rheumatism, Jefferson fought strenuously at Rockfish Gap to convince his fellow Commissioners not only that Charlottesville was the ideal spot for the University, but that it was actually the geographical and population center of the state. At a critical moment in the discussion, he triumphantly spread a map he had prepared across the table, and "proved" by lines he had drawn that everything converged on Charlottesville. He was ready for everything. In his portfolio he had also a complete set of plans for proposed buildings, for courses of instructions and even a system of rules for the governance of the students.

Under such a concentrated assault the Commissioners at length yielded by a vote of 16 to 5, and Central College was chosen. Even Jefferson's plans and rules were adopted. It was a complete victory, and a Report was drawn substantially as Jefferson wrote it, later to be printed in pamphlet form.[26]

The triumph had barely been won when Jefferson hastened to Warm Springs to seek relief from the rheumatism that crippled him throughout the proceedings. Somehow, Jefferson never took kindly to the use of healing waters. Once before, at Aix in France where he sought to mend a broken wrist, he had quit in disgust. Now again, at Warm Springs, after a few days' stay, he left for home, claiming that the company was dull, that the waters had "prostrated" his health, produced "imposthume, eruption with fever, colliquative sweats and extreme debility," as well as boils on his "seat." No wonder, with such a portentous array of symptoms, he found the long, jolting journey home exhausting. The only salve to the whole sorry business was the friendship he struck up at the Springs with Colonel William Alston, who turned out to be the father of Burr's son-in-law![27]

Cabell received the Report of the Commissioners at Richmond on November 20, 1818, immediately printed it and placed copies in the hands of the legislature. It met with much admiration and a bill was promptly introduced on the strength of it. But the proponents of the other sites fought back, both in committee and on the floor, and even sought to cast doubts on Jefferson's map of "centrality." Indeed, they were willing to let the whole idea of a University drop rather than yield the palm to Charlottesville.

Though himself ill, Cabell proved a tower of strength, rallied his forces and, on January 18, 1819, the House voted convincingly by 114 to 69 to utilize Central College. Whereupon a delegate from one of the embittered western counties rose to appeal for unanimity and the sinking of mere local prejudices. So effective was his plea that the bill as a whole passed the following day by an overwhelming vote of 141 to 28; and the Senate followed suit even more overwhelmingly on January 25th with a vote of 21 to 1.

The University was at last an official fact, and Charlottesville was its site.

Jefferson had not waited for the final decision to begin his plans for the University of Virginia. As soon as the more modest scheme for Central College had unfolded early in 1817, his imagination soared and his fingers itched for the drawing board. In his mind's eye he saw not only the College, but the town of Charlottesville itself and the surrounding neighborhood elevated and reformed from their present "barbarous workmanship" to an estate of architectural dignity.[28]

The moment the land for the College was purchased, he personally staked out the grounds, made a survey, and proposed to build immediately a pavilion to house at least the first professorship in languages, so as to be able to begin instruction by the spring of 1818.[29]

The pavilion took shape and form on the drafting board. It was to be a two-storied building, of mixed Tuscan and Doric architecture, with dormitories and a Tuscan colonnade attached on either side. But already Jefferson was planning a whole range of buildings, of eight similar pavilions, with a covered way extending along the entire front, arched and porticoed. He gave exact dimensions, sketched out cornices, frieze, architrave, columns and shafts, all in rough red brick, in a mingled style that combined the Doric, Corinthian and Tuscan orders, and echoed such classical buildings as the Theater of Marcellus, the Fortuna Virilis, the Baths of Diocletian and the Temple of Trajan, as he found them in his architectural Bible, Palladio.

Jefferson was no mere copyist, however. He modified and transmuted to gain new effects. He thought the Attic style in the pilasters of Trajan's Temple entirely too overloaded with ornaments, and therefore simplified the moldings so as "to suit our plainer style, still however retaining nearly their general outlines and proportions."

But as he worked, his enthusiasm soared. He would have a Library, but such a Library as had never been seen before. It would be topped by a Rotunda, the concave ceiling of which would be painted "sky-blue and spangled with gilt stars in their position and magnitude copied exactly from any selected hemisphere of our latitude." It would in fact constitute a planetarium, with an ingenious movable seat swung high, from which an operator could mechanically control the position and location of the painted constellations for the delectation and wonderment of the assembled students. The drawings were architecturally precise, the directions for building meticulous, and the mathematics of the mechanism worked out in detail.[30]

If his plans for the material aspects of the College were ambitious, his ideas for the educational aspects were equally soaring. He did not intend, he avowed, to be content with mediocrity; the professors, both in languages and the sciences, must be "of the first order.... Ours shall be second to none on the continent." [31]

Nor did he rely on his own ability alone. He sought the advice and aid of the best architects in the country, William Thornton and Benjamin F. Latrobe, even though he had quarreled violently with the latter during his Presidency over the operations in Washington.

To Latrobe he explained his purposes in detail. "Instead of building a magnificent house which would exhaust all our funds, we propose to lay off a square, or rather 3. sides of a square about 7. or 800 f. wide, leaving it open at one end to be extended indefinitely. On the closed end, and on the two sides we propose to arrange separate pavilions for each professor & his school. Each pavilion is to have a school-room below, and 2. rooms for the Professor above; and between pavilion and pavilion a range of Dormitories for the students, one story high, giving to each a room 10. f. wide & 14. f. deep. The Pavilions about 36. f. wide in front, & 24. f. in depth.... The whole of the pavilions and dormitories to be united by a colonnade in front, of the height of the lower story of the pavilions & about 8. f. wide under which they may go dry from school to school. The top of the dormitories to be flat.... Now what we wish is that these pavilions... should be models of taste and correct architecture, and of a variety of appearance, no two alike, so as to serve as specimens of 1. orders for the architectural lectures." [32]

Both Latrobe and Thornton responded with sketches and suggestions; but the chief new feature came from Latrobe, who placed the main dome in the center of the group, flanked on each side by the lines of pavilions.[33] Jefferson had already conceived the idea of the domed library, but had not yet decided where to place it, and he accepted Latrobe's idea for its dominating position.

With these additional conceptions on hand, Jefferson proceeded full speed ahead. Unfortunately, his own three copies of the master, Palladio, had gone with his collection of books to the Library of Congress; and he asked Madison in his retirement to lend him his copy for about a year. Madison graciously complied. For all Jefferson's haste, however, the first pavilion which he had hoped to complete for spring occupancy would not be ready in time because of "the sloth and discord of our workmen." [34]

Indeed, trouble arose in several directions. The matter of filling the professorships with first-class men was not as easy as Jefferson had anticipated.

He asked his friend, Dr. Thomas Cooper, to take the chair of chemistry and the physiological sciences and, in addition, to teach the classical languages until a permanent professor could be hired. But Cooper was reluctant, frankly avowing that the demands of his family forced him to go where his financial advantage would be greatest. After a considerable correspondence, during which he intimated that William and Mary College was negotiating with him, he finally accepted and agreed to come to Central College in the midsummer of 1818.[35]

Within two months, however, Jefferson's hopes were dashed. Cooper had changed his mind and thought it likely he would go to the Medical School in Philadelphia, where the chair of chemistry would pay him the enormous sum of $7,000 a year (or so he said), instead of the beggarly $1,000 that Central College could afford. Also, the first enthusiasm for the College had faded, and the stream of subscriptions was rapidly contracting to a mere trickle.

But Jefferson refused to become discouraged. His optimism was as buoyant as ever. Progress was his eternal watchword, and the expansion of the human mind. "I am not of the school," he declared, "which teaches us to look back for wisdom to our forefathers. From the wonderful advances in science and the arts which I have lived to see, I am sure we are wiser than our fathers & that our sons will be wiser than we are."[36]

Cooper's fabulous offer from Philadelphia proved mythical; and he later resumed negotiations with Jefferson, demanding $1,500 but at the same time cannily keeping the door open for the acceptance of the $1,000 pittance originally offered.[37] By this time Jefferson himself was beginning to play coy. It had been decided, he wrote back, to concentrate on finishing the buildings first; but, if Cooper wished, he would place him in charge of a preparatory school, and provide him with an usher.[38] The proposal was wholly mortifying to the reluctant scholar, and he turned it down; proposing, however, a Mr. Stack for the position "as the best classical teacher in America."

By this time—May, 1819—it was obvious that all dates for the opening of the University had been premature, and that the classical school as a nursery for the higher institution ought to be opened at once. Stack, therefore, was offered and accepted the post; and twenty students were enrolled.[39]

Meanwhile, work went ahead on the University proper. Jefferson hired two Italian sculptors from Leghorn through the good offices of the American consul there, and brought them under contract to America to do the marble work.[40] Much grief and controversy were to ensue from the pair.

In spite of mounting troubles, of recalcitrant workmen and reluctant professors, of failure of funds, Jefferson's indomitable will and enthusiasm overcame all difficulties, and the great project forged slowly but surely ahead.

CHAPTER 70

A Philosophy of Life

JEFFERSON'S ideas on the education of men were radical and advanced beyond his time; but they lagged considerably when he contemplated women. "A plan of female education," he confessed, "has never been a subject of systematic contemplation with me." He had hitherto considered it only insofar as his own daughters' education was concerned; and there, since they were intended for country life, he thought it wise to give them a solid basis in order that they might be in a position to educate their own daughters, or even their sons, "should their fathers be lost, or incapable, or inattentive."

He considered the greatest obstacle in the path of a good education "the inordinate passion prevalent for novels.... When this poison infects the mind," he wrote, "it destroys its tone and revolts it against wholesome reading. Reason and fact, plain and unadorned, are rejected.... The result is a bloated imagination, sickly judgment, and disgust towards all the real businesses of life." He qualified his harsh judgment of "this mass of trash" to admit there were certain novels that might form "interesting and useful vehicles of a sound morality." Such were certain works of Marmontel, Madame Genlis and the writings of Maria Edgeworth.

He applied the same strictures to poetry; though he exempted Pope, Dryden, Shakespeare, Molière, Racine and a few others from his blanket condemnation. He evidently did not consider the Greek and Roman authors as being "poets" in his special definition of the term.

Indispensable in the education of women was a knowledge of French, dancing, drawing and music. But he subscribed to the French rule that married women must forswear dancing. "This," he said, "is founded in solid physical reasons, gestation and nursing leaving little time to a married lady when this exercise can be either safe or innocent." [1]

If he thus largely omitted women from his educational scheme, it was perhaps because they were not voting citizens, and therefore it was not as necessary for them to be as informed as men. He invariably equated education and citizenship, and considered one the requisite preliminary for the other.

It grieved him that his fellow citizens were so illiterate in the science of political economy; and it was almost as a missionary to the gentiles that he zealously promoted Destutt Tracy's volume on Political Economy. The ignorance of its doctrines, he maintained, had "threatened irreparable disaster during the late war, and by the parasite institution of banks is now consuming the public industry. The flood, with which they [the banks] are deluging us, of nominal money, has placed us compleatly without any certain measures of value, and, by interpolating a false measure is deceiving and ruining multitudes of our citizens." [2]

What he particularly admired in Tracy's philosophy was his insistence "on the certainty of the operations of the human understanding. He rests them on our sensations, of which we are very certain, and on this basis erects demonstrations irresistibly cogent, I think, against Scepticism, a disease of the mind so uncomfortable that it is charity to exhibit its cure, if there exists one." [3] Certain scepticism—with whose tenets Jefferson had only the most superficial acquaintance—was completely foreign to his own practical, positive mind.

He had placed Tracy's volume on Logic in 1816 with Joseph Milligan, the printer, for translation and publication; but Milligan had not even completed the task of translation by the beginning of 1818. In disgust, Jefferson took it away from him and turned it over to Robert Walsh, a littérateur and printer, who had visited him at Monticello the year before and fallen wholly under the spell of his charm, hospitality and encyclopedic knowledge.[4] Walsh took the book and pushed the task of translation and publication through to completion. As with Tracy's other books which Jefferson had devotedly sought to bring to the attention of his fellow countrymen, this volume dropped out of sight in a sea of indifference.

For the same reasons that he became a disciple of Tracy, Jefferson recoiled from the iron doctrines of Ricardo and advised against any attempt to bring his gloomy theory of rent to the attention of Americans. Ricardo's reasoning is "muddy," he exclaimed, and would not stand the test of time.[5]

This might not be censorship; but it came perilously close to it. A much more glaring instance of Jefferson's willingness to keep doctrines he personally disapproved of from the attention of the public, and even to tamper with the text—when it was impossible to prevent publication—appeared in a letter he wrote advocating the reprinting in America of Baxter's *History of England*. Baxter was a Whig who had suffered prosecution in England for his opinions; and his book, said Jefferson, might serve American readers as a substitute for Hume's poisonous ideas.

Hume's book, Jefferson acknowledged, had it been free "from political bias," would have been "the most perfect example of fine history which has ever flowed from the pen of man"; but unfortunately its bias and distortions were such that it promoted "wrong and lasting impressions in the minds of youthful readers.... As it is quite impracticable," he continued, "to put down such a book as this, we can only sheathe its poison by some antidote." Baxter provided that antidote by himself reprinting Hume's text; but, said Jefferson complacently, wherever Hume erred, "*he then alters the text silently*," in such skillful fashion that the innocent reader is not even aware that Hume's text has been tampered with. Jefferson not only did not see anything morally wrong in this outrageous perversion of another man's ideas, but wholeheartedly approved of it! [6]

As for himself, Jefferson developed what he described as "a canine appetite for reading. And I indulge it," he told Adams, "because I see in it a relief against the *taedium senectutis;* a lamp to lighten my path through the dreary wilderness of time before me, whose bourne I see not." [7]

That "bourne," of whose specifications he admitted he had no knowledge, was beginning to loom larger and larger in his consciousness as the years moved him closer to the passage into it. He hated religious controversies as "episodical, verbal, or personal, cavils." And he hated Calvinism and all metaphysics. "Our saviour," he wrote indignantly, "did not come into the world to save metaphysicians only, his doctrines are levelled to the simplest understanding. . . ." [8]

Any discussion of Unity and Trinity he dismissed with contempt and worthy only of the consideration of "the *genus irritable vatum*"—the priesthood. "This is food for the fools," he exclaimed, "amusement to the wise, and quiet to the patriot, while the light of the age will prevent danger from the flame it kindles." [9]

He rarely ever discussed the immortality of the soul or even whether a soul as distinct from the body truly existed. But he *did* avow that nothing is known to us but matter, as perceived by the senses. Sensation and thought are unseen, and are present in the animalcule observed under the microscope. There is no reason, he declared, why they cannot *inhere* in matter itself by fiat of the Creator.

While therefore finding no proof or even necessity for an independent soul, he believed in a teleological purpose behind the universe, and even argued from that purpose that it was doubtful whether any species of plant or animal, once in existence, could ever cease to exist. If the latter were true, he maintained, then *all* species might some day disappear, "and the earth be left without life or intellect, for the habitation of which it is so peculiarly prepared."

He spoke of a "Creator," yet he did not mean that there had been a creation of the world in time. Rather, he believed in the Aristotelian idea of the co-eternity of the universe and God, and that God had set the universe in motion. He believed that no particle of existing matter had ever been destroyed, but had merely been subject to change and flux in a "never ending circle." He dismissed all ideas of evolution and growth in the physical universe—as opposed to mental evolution—ideas which Cuvier was beginning to disseminate. The earth, Jefferson was convinced, had been created "at once, in all the perfection in which it now exists." And logically, since no species ever became extinct, those species like the mammoth of which only the fossil bones have been found, ought still to breathe and have their being somewhere in the unexplored sections of the world.[10]

The letter in which he expounded these doctrines, addressed to Adrian Van der Kemp, a Dutch scientist residing in the United States, is perhaps the most complete statement of Jefferson's beliefs he ever permitted himself. None of them was original, as he himself was ready to admit. They represented a coat of many colors that included Aristotle (filtered through Thomas Aquinas), Locke, Helvetius, Tracy, Laplace and many others. It was a strange mixture; wholly mechanistic in ingredients, yet granting a place to a God as the original mover; optimistic as to man's mental evolution, yet denying the possibility of a physical evolution; speaking of a "Creator" and His will and of a teleological purpose in nature, yet eliminating both Creator and purpose from any practical applications in the universe. For all his preoccupation with these high matters, Jefferson never really thought them through.

Sometimes, indeed, his personal morality had more than a tinge of the Puritanism he invariably derided and, for all his disclaimers of interference in the personal habits and morality of others, he was willing to enforce his own conceptions by law—for their good, of course. He had on occasion favored a tax on whisky in order to discourage its drinking by the poor. By the same token, he rejoiced "as a Moralist" at the prospect of a reduction of the duties on wine. He had always considered that particular tax as "the most exceptionable article in Mr. Hamilton's original tariff." It was an error, he declared, to consider it as a tax merely on the rich. As a matter of fact, it prohibited the use of wines to the middle classes and condemned them to "the poison of whisky, which is desolating their houses." [11] He said nothing of the fact that, as a prodigious importer of wines, the tax imposed a heavy burden on himself.

When it came to the religious beliefs of others, however, Jefferson rose to some of his noblest utterances. He thought, indeed, that there was a "universal spirit of religious intolerance, inherent in every sect, disclaimed by all while feeble, and practiced by all when in power." The worst example of this was the persecution of the Jews by the other sects. "Our laws," he assured Mordecai M. Noah, who had sent him a copy of his discourse on the consecration of a synagogue in New York City, "have applied the only antidote to this vice, protecting our religions, as they do our civil rights by putting all on an equal footing. But more remains to be done. For altho' we are free by the law, we are not so in practice. Public opinion erects itself into an Inquisition, and exercises its office with as much fanaticism as fans the flames of an Auto da fé. The prejudice still scowling on your section of our religion, altho' the elder one, cannot be unfelt by yourselves. It is to be hoped that individual dispositions will at length, mould themselves to the model of the law, and consider the moral basis on which all our religions rest, as the rallying point which unites them in a common interest; while the peculiar dogmas branching from it are the exclusive concern of the respective sects embracing them, and no rightful subject of notice to any other." [12]

The death of Abigail Adams, that stern yet remarkable Puritan old lady, saddened him; and he hastened to send his condolences to his old friend thus deprived of his prop and comfort.[13]

Yet, if largely hospitable to *all* religious beliefs—provided they left his own religious convictions alone—Jefferson displayed no such tolerance in other matters. John Trumbull, his friend of Parisian days, had finally executed his long contemplated project of a heroic-sized painting of the signing of the Declaration of Independence, and its unveiling had stirred a storm of controversy over the features and depiction of the several signers. But Jefferson defended the handling warmly, sight unseen. He only hoped that Trumbull had given to James Wilson's countenance "its haggard lineaments. If you have not, touch it again. It ought to be preserved as the eikon of the non-concurrents. He refused to sign."[14]

He hated the tribe of doctors, particularly those trained in Philadelphia. "I have in absolute abhorrence," he wrote, "the fanciful and ephemeral theories under which dashing practitioners are so wantonly sporting with human life. Our country is overrun with young lads from the Philadelphia school, who with their mercury & lancet in hand are vying with the sword of Bonaparte which shall have shed most human blood."[15]

He hailed the news of Republican victories in Connecticut and in Boston, the last fortress of Federalism. But his exultation was tempered with certain misgivings for the future. Now that the Federalist party seemed wholly extinct, "what," he asked, "are to be our future parties? For parties must be wherever men are free, and wherever their minds & faces are unlike." He scanned the jumbled horizon of maverick Republicans for the answer. Duane, John Randolph, Henry Clay, the Clintons of New York—all held within their passions and tempers the seeds of disruption. Perhaps, he thought, the party split would come between those who thought Congress ought to be the stronger, and those who upheld the Executive.

By now he was himself disgusted with Congress as a group of lawyers talking all action to death. "The never-ending debates of Congress," he wrote Dearborn, "make me almost willing to try Bonaparte's dumb legislature. However it will last my time as it is, and perhaps yours."[16]

But the chief interest and absorbing passion of his life was the University. As the bill in the legislature designating Central College as that institution approached a vote he was literally "atiptoe" with excitement. The final passage, in spite of all the crosscurrents of local intrigues and religious opposition, gratified him; at the same time, the grudging financial support voted made him fear that the institution would prove merely a paper one.[17]

How to allocate the scanty funds posed a serious problem, but Jefferson and Cabell both agreed that it was better to devote the entire amount to the building operations and hold off the actual opening of the University until it could be done "with that degree of splendor necessary to give it a prominent character."[18]

This decision brought to a halt all attempts to obtain professors. It was fortunate, therefore, that both young Ticknor and Nathaniel Bowditch, the famous mathematician-astronomer, had rejected his earlier offers of posts.[19] And a new complication arose concerning the hesitant Cooper. Some of the Board of Visitors had heard he was addicted to drink.[20] But from distant New York Jefferson's old political friend, Samuel L. Mitchill, wrote to recommend for the chair of Hebrew and Oriental languages Dr. Jonas Horwitz from whom, he said, "some of our most distinguished clergymen in New York, have received lessons."[21]

All these plans now had to be left in abeyance, as work on the buildings continued. While it is true that Jefferson incorporated some of the ideas and suggestions he had received from Thornton and Latrobe, the plan of the University and most of its details were entirely his own. He spent his days and part of his nights at his drafting board. He worked out carefully detailed plans, elevations and specifications. He proposed an addition to his previous group of buildings in the form of an astronomical observatory, "with an Astronomer resident at it, employed solely in the business of Observation." This building he thought should be located on the nearby mountain of Montalto as commanding a fine horizon. He continued to work on the great Rotunda, and drafted a proposal for an Anatomical Theater to house the School of Medicine. All his drawings were made with professional competence and meticulous care.[22]

Meanwhile, renewed efforts were made to get the legislature to vote additional funds so that the University buildings, as they were finished, might be put to use. But a combination of indifference and savage opposition met every attempt. The proponents of William and Mary College, bypassed by this new institution, worked unceasingly to hamstring the rival. Jefferson did not worry about them; he was more alarmed over the activities of "the priests of the different religious sects, who dread the advance of science as witches do the approach of day-light; and scowl on the fatal harbinger announcing the subversion of the duperies on which they live. In this the Presbyterian clergy take the lead. The tocsin is sounded in all their pulpits, and the first alarm denounced is against the particular creed of Doctr. Cooper; and as impudently denounced as if they really knew what it is."[23]

Actually, and Jefferson was well aware of it, the clergy were using the hapless Cooper as a stick with which to beat Jefferson himself, whose views were somewhat similar to those of the Doctor.

If the clergy were vehemently opposed to Jefferson and his University, others paid their respects to him as the leading man of his age. "All the Literary Gentlemen of this part of the Country," wrote John Adams humorously, "have an Ambitious Curiosity to see the Philosopher and Statesman of Monticello—and they all apply to me for Introductions."[24]

The crowds continued to stream up the mountain to visit the sage and to be entertained. Nor were they all reverent pilgrims. The growing grandchildren attracted the younger set as well. What a time they have at Monticello! exclaimed one of the young visitors. "Famous kick-up dancing" in the south pavilion to the sound of harpsichord and violin until midnight!

But dancing proved not the only excitement. On April 9, 1819, the south pavilion caught fire and burnt to the ground in a furious wind. Fortunately, the wind shifted its direction away from the main buildings; though the north pavilion caught momentarily. Jefferson rushed out to aid in saving the north structure, but fell down among the loose boards and scraped his shin. When John Quincy Adams, who had read of the fire and the accident in the press, solicitously inquired, Jefferson dismissed both as of small consequence. He was more interested in the offer of the Italian sculptor, Cardelli, to come to Monticello to take a portrait bust of him.[25]

The burning of the pavilion may not have been serious, but Jefferson's financial involvements were. And this time it proved to be no fault of his own. In 1817, Jefferson had applied to the Richmond branch of the Bank of the United States, of which his old friend Wilson Cary Nicholas was a director, for a loan of $3,000. A new audit of Jefferson's old accounts as Minister to France had disclosed him to be in debt to the United States. The loan was granted; and, as usual, he was compelled the following year to apply for a renewal. But he could not obtain an endorser, and Nicholas generously offered to act as one.[26]

Less than a month after this gesture, Nicholas in turn applied to Jefferson to act as *his* endorser; and this on two notes for the total sum of $20,000. It was an embarrassing situation in which Jefferson found himself. Nicholas was a bosom friend and he had just signed for Jefferson; but $20,000 was an enormous sum. Nicholas assured him that his estate was worth far more than that, should he die before the notes were met; and Jefferson, with many misgivings, affixed his signatures, "reposing myself," he wrote Nicholas, "with entire confidence in your care." [27]

That confidence was not justified. The following year, when the notes fell due, Nicholas wrote Jefferson that the first of them would have to go to protest; but assured him he would not suffer thereby. This was an easy assurance. After much frantic negotiation—in which Nicholas seemingly made no move—the bank accepted Jefferson's offer to cover his own endorsement, first, by a blanket mortgage on Monticello and all his other property; second, by conveyance of the Bedford plantation to his grandson, Thomas Jefferson Randolph, as trustee for the bank's benefit.[28]

At the same time, Jefferson was incapacitated by the severest attack of rheumatism he had ever experienced; and this new calamity added to his sufferings. He appealed desperately to Nicholas to ward off disaster by efforts of his own. "A call on me to the amount of my endorsements for you," he wrote pathetically, "would indeed close my course by a catastrophe I had never contemplated." [29] But Nicholas's affairs were so involved that he could do nothing; and his own bank—though he was a director—knew that he was in a state of bankruptcy.

With all his earthly possessions mortgaged, and no hope of Nicholas ever meeting his debts, it is no wonder that Jefferson suffered an attack of indigestion and stoppage of bowels that caused his family for several days to fear for his life.[30]

He had always prided himself on his good digestion, which he attributed to his course of life. He ate vegetables chiefly, and very little meat. He drank sparingly, and only light wines, of which three to four glasses at dinner constituted his quota. His teeth were still untouched, his hearing good, and he used spectacles only at night, except for fine print. Occasionally he suffered from his old complaint of headaches; but he was remarkably free from colds; a fact which he attributed to his sixty-year practice of bathing his feet in cold water every morning. His wrist, however, fractured in France, was growing increasingly stiff, and made writing slow and painful.[31]

But he was getting old, and the worry over the Nicholas notes hastened the aging process. For the rest of his life he sought vainly to untangle himself from their toils, but never succeeded.

The troubles and successive deaths of old friends also saddened him and warned him that his own span of life was necessarily brief. In 1817, he had wondered audibly as to the present condition of his ancient coterie in Paris, whether they were living or dead. They were, he commented to Trumbull, "now scattered & estranged but not so in either my memory or affections." [32]

Now came a voice from the dead; from no less a person than Maria Cosway. Her packet of news was sad enough. Her husband had been stricken with paralysis in London, and she had hastened from her religious retreat in Italy to nurse him. Angelica Church was dead, and Madame de Corny, though still alive, was very ill. "Strange changes over & over again all over Europe," she concluded. "You only are proceeding on well." [33]

To which the former exponent of the Heart over the Head could only return resignedly: "Such is the state of our former coterie—dead, diseased, dispersed. . . . Mine is the next turn, and I shall meet it with good will." [34]

If he could thus philosophically look forward to his own dissolution, he did not permit the contemplation to interfere with his present active engagement in life or its manifold problems. His current difficulties with banks only served to exacerbate his eternal warfare with those institutions. He would, he avowed violently, abolish all paper money issued by them, and forfeit the charter of any bank that refused to submit, even if it were the Bank of the United States itself. He would interdict forever the power to issue paper in the future and, in the meantime, pass stay laws against executions based on it.[35] This last provision, had his advice been heeded, would have lightened the load of the Nicholas paper on himself.

He firmly believed in a written constitution, which should be treated with veneration and not merely as an ordinary law, to be broken at convenience.[36] Such was the Constitution of the United States. But it had taken his election in 1800 to fix its principles on the government. That revolution, he asserted, was "as real a revolution in the principles of our government as that of 1776 was in its form; not effected indeed by the sword, as that, but by the rational and peaceable instrument of reform, the suffrage of the people." Unfortunately, the Judiciary had not heeded the will of the people, and was illegally driving the nation into "consolidation." Jefferson's own construction of the Constitution was simple: "That each department is truly independent of the others, and has an equal right to decide for itself what is the meaning of the constitution in the cases submitted to its action; and especially, where it is to act ultimately and without appeal." [37]

He also laid down rigid rules of finance for the government to follow: "1. never to borrow without laying a tax sufficient to pay principal and interest within a fixed period, and I would fix that period at 10. years, & that tax should be solemnly pledged to the lenders. 2. never to borrow or tax without appropriating the money to its specific object." [38]

He defined *liberty* in its full extent as "unobstructed action according to our will: but rightful Liberty is unobstructed action according to our will, within the limits drawn around us by the equal rights of others." This more limited definition follows John Stuart Mill's famous characterization very closely.

From liberty he moved to a consideration of "a pure republic" which "is a state of society in which every member, of mature and sound mind, has an equal right of participation, personally, in the direction of the affairs of the society. Such a regimen," he qualified, "is obviously impractical beyond the limits of an encampment, or of a very small village." In all other cases where it is necessary to act by deputy, "then their government continues republican in proportion only as the functions they still exercise in person, are more or fewer," and as they have the right to appoint their deputies directly, for limited purposes and for short periods.[39]

Jefferson's own personal beliefs were always a matter of profound concern to him; and, though hiding them from the public view and consequent attack, he never omitted an opportunity to discuss them confidentially with his friends.

He was an Epicurean, he told Short. "I consider the genuine (not the imputed) doctrines of Epicurus as containing everything rational in moral philosophy which Greece and Rome have left us." The Stoics, aside from Epictetus, abounded in "hypocrisy and grimace." Cicero, though his style was beautiful and enchanting, was "diffuse, vapid, rhetorical." Plato, eloquent enough, was incomprehensibly mystical and had been deified because of "certain sects usurping the name of Christians," who reared on his foundations "fabrications as delirious, of their own invention," which they "fathered blasphemously" on Jesus.

Jesus, indeed, was the greatest of all reformers; and when what is really his doctrine is abstracted "from the rubbish in which it is buried... we have the outlines of a system of the most sublime morality which has ever fallen from the lips of man; outlines which it is lamentable he did not live to fill up."

To rescue this pure system of Jesus from the artificial systems of the sects, as exemplified in the doctrines of the immaculate conception, his deification, miraculous powers, resurrection and visible ascension, the Trinity, original sin, atonement, election and others, was "a most desirable object, and one to which Priestley has successfully devoted his labors and learning."

Jefferson had sometimes thought of translating Epictetus afresh, add to him the doctrines of Epicurus and an abstract of the Evangelists to make up a new system of morality. He had indeed, years before, hastily extracted the true sayings of Jesus from the Evangelists; but that was as far as he had been able to go in the project. "With one foot in the grave," he concluded with a sigh, "these are now idle projects for me." [40]

He considered Calvin and Hopkins as insane and the strait jacket as their only proper remedy. "Were I to be the founder of a new sect," he exclaimed, "I would call them Apiarians, and, after the example of the bee, advise them to extract the honey of every sect. My fundamental principle would be the reverse of Calvin's, that we are to be saved by our good works which are within our power, and not by our faith which is not within our power." [41]

In all these animadversions on government, philosophy, religion and the universe, Jefferson did not for a moment lose sight of his own project of the University. It was encountering stormy weather, and he bent every effort to bring it safely to port.

Though there was no money to open the University proper, at least he was able to start the preparatory school. He was enthusiastic about the instructor he had hired to take charge of it, and thought him probably the finest teacher in the United States. The attending pupils were boarded in Charlottesville with a Frenchman named Laporte, and were compelled to converse in French so as to learn the language rapidly and thoroughly. Jefferson himself laid down the menu for their daily nourishment. Breakfast consisted of bread and butter, coffee or milk; dinner of soup, meat and a great variety of vegetables; supper of bread and coffee or milk. The youngsters, he was careful to specify, must drink only water; "a young stomach needing no stimulating drinks, and the habit of using them being dangerous." [42]

He hailed the arrival of the two Italian sculptors, the Raggis. Finally, he was convinced, he had obtained artisans who knew how to cut Ionic and Corinthian columns properly. But tragedy impended. When the newcomers examined the native quarry from which the stone was mined, they pronounced it of poor quality and of no use for the classic capitals. Nor were they proficient in plain work, as against the ornamental. Jefferson was nonplused. "They have cost us a great deal of money," he complained, "& how to avoid its becoming a loss, & how to get our work done, is the difficulty." [43]

He tried setting the Italians at work on what they *could* do; but soon found they were getting nowhere. The pair finally made an astounding proposition to him; they would return to Italy, make the capitals there of proper marble, and have them shipped back to the United States. Jefferson countered with an offer to pay the passage money for Michele Raggi's wife and her brother, who was an "ornatist," to come to Virginia. This was on Raggi's assurance that his brother-in-law was sufficiently competent in all the fields in which he himself was lacking.[44]

Old as Jefferson was—and he was now approaching seventy-seven—he used to ride daily down the mountain and inspect the work on the University. With Edmund Bacon, his overseer, to accompany him, the two men surveyed the original forty-acre plot. The ex-President placed the pegs in the ground, while Bacon carried the line. He personally watched every bit of material as it was brought in, examined it for soundness and strength, and directed the workmen in their operations.[45]

He kept prodding the legislature and grumbled loudly over their "higgling" with the University. Private subscriptions also were coming in "slow & grudgingly," and often there was not enough money on hand to pay the wages of the workmen. Dr. Cooper, temporarily at Columbia, South Carolina, had finally agreed to take a salary of $1,500 a year to act as the institution's first professor; but even that had not been raised, and he kept up a steady stream of complaints from that vantage point.[46]

The chief cause for the heartbreaking delays lay in the increasing opposition of certain groups who, for different reasons, either did not want a University at all or did not wish one at Charlottesville and under Jefferson's control. In the first category were the vested interests of William and Mary; in the second, a combination of the counties further to the west and the Presbyterian clergy and laymen who saw in the new institution an extension of Jefferson's "atheistic" views.[47]

One of the sticks which the religious bodies used to beat both Jefferson and the University was the proposed appointment of Cooper to the chief post. An Evangelical magazine published a violent attack on Cooper's radical theological views and denounced his employment as a teacher of the young. Cooper offered to resign his still untenanted post rather than embarrass the University.[48]

But Jefferson refused the offer and bade him "be of good heart." The loudest-mouthed, he wrote back, were the least considerable in numbers and influence. The two chief sects—the Baptists and Methodists—were friendly, republican in politics and supported the government or refused to meddle. So were the Anglicans. Only the Presbyterian clergy were "bitterly federal and malcontent with their government. They are violent, ambitious of power, and intolerant in politics as in religion and want nothing but licence from the laws to kindle again the fires of their leader John Knox, and to give us a 2d blast from his trumpet. Having a little more monkish learning than the clergy of other sects, they are jealous of the general diffusion of science, and therefore hostile to our Seminary, lest it should qualify their antagonists of the other sects to meet them in equal combat. Not daring to attack the institution with the avowal of their real motives, they peck at you, at me, and every feather they can spy out." But, concluded Jefferson, "they have no weight, even with their own followers," who in the main "are good citizens & friendly." [49]

But Jefferson had written too hastily, it seems. For the Board of Visitors of the University was not as ready to dismiss the outcry as of no weight as he was. On April 3, 1820, the Board held a meeting, and what passed may easily be surmised from the action they took and Jefferson's unwilling retraction. It was decided, and so Cooper was informed, that there had been such delay and uncertainty as to the opening of the University that it was deemed advisable to make changes in his contract of employment.[50]

Cooper was hotly indignant. He had never published anything in this country on theological matters, he said. It was true that thirty-five years before, in England, he had written in denial of the Trinity and of the existence of a soul apart from the body. But the latter opinion, he exclaimed, was shared with him by the vast majority of medical men. In any event, Columbia (S.C.) College had just appointed him to the chairs of geology, law and chemistry at a salary double what Virginia offered him. Therefore he was willing to accept the Board's offer of $1,500 to terminate his contract; though he regretted the storm that had been raised on his account.[51]

This abrupt dismissal of the liberal and learned Dr. Cooper as a sop to religious prejudice was a staggering blow to Jefferson. Cooper, he wrote bitterly, "has more science in his single head than all the Colleges of New England, New Jersey, and I may add Virginia put together." [52] His pet project was obviously off to a very bad start.

It is no wonder then, that with this sharp recrudescence of bigotry, he was particularly careful when sending a copy of his old Syllabus on Jesus to William Short to express more than his usual anxieties over its confidential nature. In the accompanying letter he also threw a new and interesting sidelight on his own convictions.

The Syllabus, he declared, was not to be understood as identifying Jefferson in full with all the doctrines of Jesus. "I am a Materialist," he avowed; "he [Jesus] takes the side of Spiritualism; he preaches the efficacy of repentance towards forgiveness of sin; I require a counterpoise of good works to redeem it, etc., etc. It is the innocence of His character, the purity and sublimity of His moral precepts, the eloquence of His inculcations, the beauty of the apologues in which He conveys them, that I so much admire; sometimes, indeed, needing indulgence to eastern hyperbolism." [53]

He refused to concern himself with incomprehensibles. "When I meet with a proposition beyond finite comprehension," he told Adams, "I abandon it as I do a weight which human strength cannot lift, and I think ignorance, in these cases, is truly the softest pillow on which I can lay my head." [54]

CHAPTER 71

Seeds of Disunion

IN 1819, the great question of the century reared its head. Missouri, carved out of the Louisiana Territory, now claimed entrance to the Union as a state. That would have been comparatively simple, except for one thing. The proposed constitution for the new state permitted slavery within its borders.

Yet, when the bill was first offered in Congress for the admission of Missouri, no one suspected the storm that would arise. It came suddenly in the form of an amendment in the House prohibiting any further importation of slaves and providing for the emancipation of children born to slave parents once they reached the age of twenty-five. In this revised form, the bill passed the House, but failed in the Senate.

The fat was in the fire. Congress shortly thereafter adjourned, but the question of slavery or no slavery for Missouri—or, for that matter, for any of the states to be admitted in the future—became the burning issue of the hour. The great debate that ended in secession and bloody war was now commenced.

By the beginning of 1820, after Congress had reassembled, threats and counterthreats were already heating the air to incandescence. Alarmed at the monstrous genie that had been uncorked, a sufficient number of northern Republicans, though themselves opposed to slavery, joined with the embattled Southerners to work out a compromise arrangement. Missouri was to be admitted as a slave state and Maine, cutting itself off from its ancient parent, Massachusetts, as a free state. Thereby the number of free and slave states in the Union were exactly balanced at twelve each. At the same time, slavery was forever prohibited in that section of the Louisiana Territory which lay north of latitude 36° 30′.

Almost immediately the storm was allayed, though here and there could be heard ominous rumblings of discontent. But Jefferson was clearer-headed than most. He had seen with a sense of shock and alarm this sudden raising of the lid, and caught a glimpse of the tremendous passions that had escaped their old confinement. Here was something new in American life; a division along coincident moral and geographical lines that put into the shade any former division in the country.

He raised his voice in prophetic horror. "This momentous question," he warned, "like a fire bell in the night, awakened and filled me with terror. I considered it at once as the knell of the Union. It is hushed, indeed, for the moment. But this is a reprieve only, not a final sentence. A geographical line, coinciding with a marked principle, moral and political, once conceived and held up to the angry passions of men, will never be obliterated; and every new irritation will mark it deeper and deeper." [1]

He had never feared to this extent the old schism of Federalist and Republican, since that had cut across state lines; and all the states were united by their constituent groups in the national parties. This new schism was of a different order. He foresaw that the passions and severance would grow and grow, until they "would kindle such mutual and mortal hatred, as to render separation preferable to eternal discord. I have been," he wrote sorrowfully, "among the most sanguine in believing that our Union would be of long duration. I now doubt it much, and see the event at no great distance, and the direct consequence of this question; not by the line which had been so confidently counted on; the laws of nature control this; but by the Potomac, Ohio and Missouri, or more probably, the Mississippi upwards to our northern boundary. My only comfort and confidence is, that I shall not live to see this; and I envy not the present generation the glory of throwing away the fruits of their fathers' sacrifices of life and fortune, and of rendering desperate the experiment which was to decide ultimately whether man is capable of self-government? This treason against human hope, will signalize their epoch in future history, as the counterpart of the medal of their predecessors." [2]

With such prophetic foresight and moving exhortation did Jefferson seek to warn his fellow countrymen of the road on which they had embarked. Yet he did not remain wholly above the battle, even though he meant to allay passions. His sympathies in the struggle were all with the South, in spite of his dislike for the institution of slavery. Indeed, he was able to find some ingenious, if fallible, arguments to justify the admission of Missouri and other territories without any constitutional prohibition against slavery, while at the same time holding to his own adverse views on the institution.

"Of one thing I am certain," he wrote, "that as the passage of slaves from one State to another, would not make a slave of a single human being who would not be so without it, so their diffusion over a greater surface would make them individually happier, and proportionately facilitate the accomplishment of their emancipation, by dividing the burthen on a greater number of coadjutors." [3]

He placed most of the blame for the split on the Federalists; and the more he thought on the question, the more his indignation rose against the anti-slavery forces. For all his clearheadedness on the other phases of the question, he was singularly blind to the moral forces that were coming to the fore in the country. Later in the year he was writing that the problem had "just enough of the semblance of morality to throw dust into the eyes of the people, & to fanaticise them; while with the knowing ones it is simply a question of power. The Federalists, unable to rise again under the old division of whig and tory, have invented a geographical division which

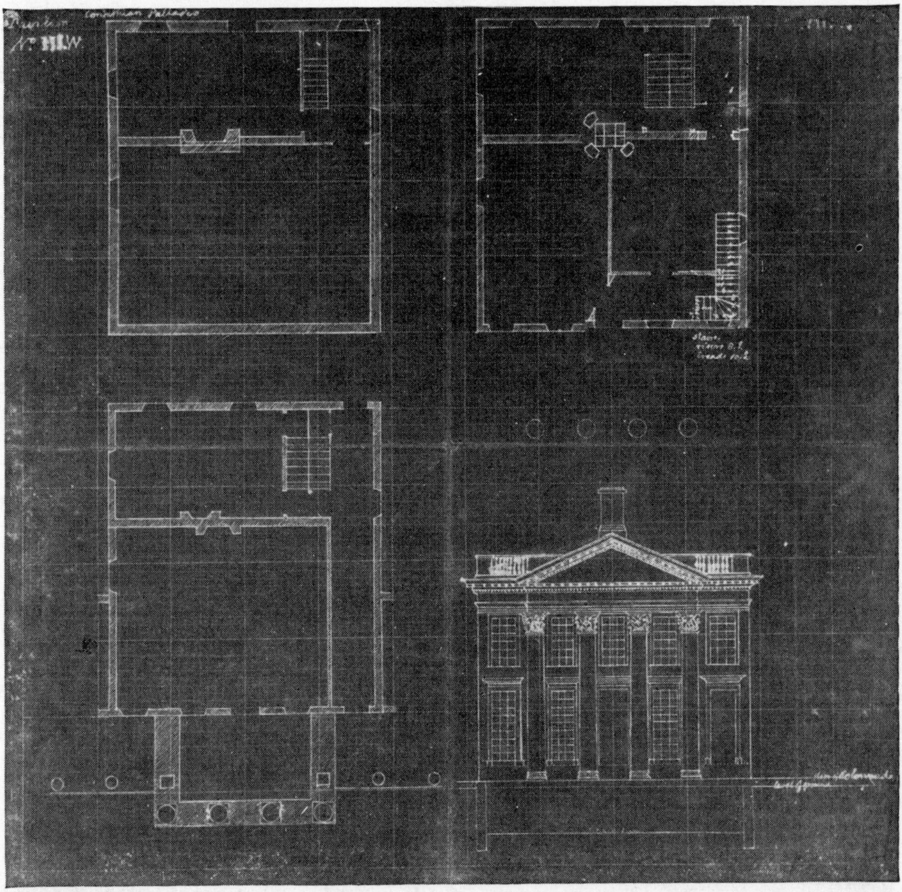

Courtesy the Jefferson Papers, University of Virginia Library

ARCHITECTURAL SKETCHES FOR UNIVERSITY OF VIRGINIA BUILDINGS BY JEFFERSON

could the dead feel any interest in Monuments or other remembrances of them, when, as Anacreon says Ολιγη δε κεισομεσθα
Κονις, οστεων λυθεντων

the following would be to my Manes the most gratifying.

On the grave

a plain die or cube of 3.f without any mouldings, surmounted by an Obelisk of 6.f. height, each of a single stone: on the faces of the Obelisk the following inscription, & not a word more

'Here was buried
Thomas Jefferson
Author of the Declaration of American Independance
of the Statute of Virginia for religious freedom
& Father of the University of Virginia.'

because by these, as testimonials that I have lived, I wish most to be remembered. ~~[illegible]~~ to be of the coarse stone of which my columns are made, that no one might be tempted hereafter to destroy it for the value of the materials.

my bust by Ciracchi, with the pedestal and truncated column on which it stands, might be given to the University if they would place it in the Dome room of the Rotunda.

on the Die of the Obelisk might be engraved
Born Apr. 2. 1743. O.S.
Died ——

Courtesy the Library of Congress

JEFFERSON'S DESIGN FOR HIS OWN TOMBSTONE

gives them 14. states against 10. and seduces their old opponents into a coalition with them. Real morality is on the other side." And he repeated his argument that further diffusion of the slaves would make for their happiness and future emancipation.

His son-in-law, Thomas Mann Randolph, had been elected Governor of Virginia, and proposed a plan for the eventual emancipation and deportation of all slaves in the state. Though Jefferson realized that Virginia was not ripe for such a sweeping solution, he approved of the proposition as helping to focus attention on the problem.[4] Certainly he did not believe that Congress or any other national body had the constitutional right to interfere with the "peculiar" institution within the confines of any state.

As he approached the end of his life, his affection for his native state grew in intensity, in spite of certain objectionable features he was sensible enough to see and understand. The earlier nationalism was slowly evaporating; though he was willing to admit that some of his new sentiments were "perhaps illiberal and many of them founded on prejudice." One of them was his "decided preference for the Virginia character and principles. All the science in the world would not to me as a parent compensate the loss of that open, manly, character, which Virginians possess and in which the most liberal and enlightened of the Eastern people are deplorably deficient. I have known many of their conspicuous men intimately, and I have never yet seen one who could march directly to his object. Some view at home or at the seat of Government entered all their projects & subjected them continually to the commission of acts which would tinge with shame the face of a Virginian." Therefore he strongly urged that his grandson, Francis Eppes, "complete his Education within the limits of Virginia." [5]

Yet it was impossible, for all Jefferson's local patriotism, to find a proper place at which to educate young Francis in his native state. The next best thing, then, was to send him to Columbia College, in the sister state of South Carolina, where Dr. Cooper was now the head. Accordingly, Francis was enrolled at Columbia, and Jefferson furnished him with advice on his studies, proposing especially for his attention Tracy's Commentaries on Montesquieu as "the best elementary book on government which has ever been published," and advising him to learn only those sciences which would be useful to him in his future pursuits, and not to waste his time on other subjects. With a radical viewpoint that anticipated the most extreme modern elective system, Jefferson asserted that "this will certainly be the fundamental law of our University, to leave every one free to attend whatever branches of instruction he wants, and to decline what he doesn't want." [6]

Also, Jefferson was compelled to admit that the state of New York, under the governorship of De Witt Clinton, was making "gigantic exertions" for the public education of its citizens. Stung by this discrepancy between the northern state and his own Virginia, he urged on his son-in-law, the new Governor, to lay before the legislature as soon as it met, the reports for the financing of the University. By such speedy action, Jefferson hoped to avoid any chance for "caballing, circulating false rumors, and other maneuvres by the enemies of the institution." [7]

Unfortunately, those enemies were not to be caught napping, and it was long before funds were forthcoming or the University could publicly open its doors. Jefferson called it "the Hobby of my old age," and avowed that it would be "based on the illimitable freedom of the human mind, to explore and to expose every subject susceptible of its contemplation." [8] But, as so often the case with Jefferson's noble phrases, these were inconsistent with other statements of his, notably the one quoted above in which he wished only "useful" learning to be taught to college students, or with his own previous cavalier dismissal of many branches of human contemplation as mystical and incomprehensible.

Yet, such are the curious convolutions of the human mind, Jefferson wished to introduce an intensive study of Anglo-Saxon into his University, and purchased every volume he could lay hands on for the furtherance of that object.[9] He had a passion for Anglo-Saxon himself, and therefore conceived it to be "useful"; rationalizing it as essential for the study of the old English law of liberty, which later degenerated into the "common law" through the infiltration of Norman feudal ideas.

Nicholas's unpaid notes cast a huge shadow over Jefferson's last years. But even without them, his finances were as always in a parlous state. Once again he was writing the old familiar apology for being unable to meet his debts, and blaming it as usual on low prices for his crops.[10]

But this time the ancient song did not soothe the creditor's savage breast and Jefferson was compelled to seek a loan from his son-in-law, John W. Eppes, who gave him $4,000, to be repaid within two years by a transfer of Negroes from his father-in-law's plantations. Eppes obviously realized that the cash would never be forthcoming. Jefferson had scruples about selling Negroes for any reason other than "delinquency or on their own request"; but Eppes made the transaction palatable. He would, he agreed, let them remain together as families, and turn them over with the ground to his own son, young Francis, when he came of age. To this Jefferson gladly assented, and set aside twenty men, women and children as payment.[11]

More and more, during the few years left, due notes and the discount of notes—never cash payments—fill the pages of his account books until, in March, 1823, he estimated his debts as amounting to $19,000, *exclusive* of bank notes and a sizable sum still due on the old Wayles estate.[12]

On January 26, 1821, having reached the age of maturity and looking back over his long and eventful life, Jefferson thought it time to write his

Autobiography. Yet it was not an autobiography in the ordinary sense, for it covered only the earlier years of his life, terminating with his services in France; and it restricted itself largely, with rare exceptions, to cold political ideas. Nor was it intended for the general public—he had long disavowed any attempt to write his own history. It was rather a private document for himself and his family. Therefore, in a hand still firm and legible, in spite of his stiffening wrist, he inscribed on the first sheet: "At the age of 77. I begin to make some memoranda and state some recollections of dates & facts concerning myself, for my own more ready reference & for the inform[atio]n of my family." [13]

He realized his time was getting short and, as he told a friend, "when I look back over the ranks of those with whom I have lived and loved, it is like looking over a field of battle. All fallen. Nor do I feel it as a blessing to be reserved for this afflicting spectacle." [14]

The one spectacle he still wished ardently to see seemed destined to elude his view—the opening of the University. But he exhorted Cabell to continue his efforts in the recalcitrant legislature. "What service can we ever render [Virginia]," he demanded eloquently, "equal to this? What object of our lives can we propose so important? What interest of our own which ought not to be postponed to this? Health, time, labor, on what in the single life which nature has given us, can these be better bestowed than on this immortal boon to our country?"

By his "country," Jefferson still meant Virginia, and not the United States. With the Missouri question still agitating the nation, it was essential, he wrote, to keep the youth of Virginia at home and not expose them in northern colleges to become, as he ironically put it, "deeply impressed with the sacred principles of our Holy Alliance of restrictionists," and with the "lessons of anti-Missourianism." [15]

He kept harping on this appeal to the fears and prejudices of the Virginia legislators. There were in northern colleges, he estimated, "five hundred of our sons, imbibing opinions and principles in discord with those of their own country. This canker is eating on the vitals of our existence, and if not arrested at once, will be beyond remedy." [16]

The remedy, of course, was to get the University under way at once, and to bring the imperiled Virginia youths home immediately.

He was getting more and more intemperate over the Missouri issue, even though it had seemingly been settled by the Compromise. "Our anxieties in this quarter are all concentrated in the question," he told John Adams, "what does the Holy Alliance in and out of Congress mean to do with us on the Missouri question?" The "Holy Alliance" was his sarcastic designation for the combination of Northern Republicans and Federalists on the issue of slavery. The real question is, he pursued further: "Are our slaves to be presented with freedom and a dagger? For if Congress has the power to regulate the conditions of the inhabitants of the States, within the States, it will be but another exercise of that power, to declare that all shall be free." This, to Jefferson, meant the equally abhorrent alternatives: an intersectional war modeled on the ancient Grecian struggles, or a servile war with black pitted against white.[17]

To which Adams countered that "Slavery in this Country I have seen hanging over it like a black cloud for half a Century." He was terrified by the phenomenon, but always said to Southerners: "I will vote for forcing no measure against your judgements. What we are to see God knows and I leave it to him, and his agents in posterity."

Then he turned to a less controversial question—at least with Jefferson. "I have long been decided in opinion that a free government and the Roman Catholick religion can never exist together in any nation or Country." [18]

To Jefferson, however, there was a much more serious threat to free government nearer at home. "The great object of my fear," he wrote with passion, "is the federal judiciary. That body, like gravity, ever acting, with noiseless foot, and unalarming advance, gaining ground step by step, and holding what it gains, is ingulphing insidiously the special governments into the jaws of that which feeds them." [19]

It was a striking simile, and one which conveyed—even to Jefferson himself—a certain helpless fascination in the presence of a monstrous force. He had fought the Judiciary ever since the days of the "midnight" appointments; and he had been beaten back every time—for the impeachment of Pickering could not be considered as a victory of principle. He had heard Marshall enunciate the hated doctrine that the courts were the final arbiters of the Constitution; he had been summoned peremptorily as President before the august bench; and he was now witnessing state laws made subservient to the sanctity of private contracts.

Impeachment had been tried—and found wanting. It was "a mere scarecrow," he declared contemptuously. The *only* way in which to halt the hitherto irresistible power was to make judges removable on "the simple concurrence of the two other coordinate branches"—by which he meant Congress and the Executive.[20]

In the face of the menace, he hailed every pamphlet, every book that purported to expose the fallacious nature of the judicial pretension; and he was willing for the first time to permit a letter of condemnation from himself—"cooked-up" for the occasion—to be published in the press as a puff for a book. The volume for which he broke his long-standing rule was *Construction Construed*, by the great Republican theoretician, John Taylor of Caroline. Jefferson did not always agree with the radical purity and unbending logic of his friend, but in this instance his praise was unreserved. The book, he wrote, "is the most logical retraction of our governments to the original and true principles of the constitution creating them, which has appeared since the adoption of that instrument." [21]

What particularly excited his anger and alarm against the Supreme Court at this moment was the bold new doctrine which Marshall enunciated in the famous case of Cohens v. Virginia—that the Court had appellate jurisdiction in a case between a sovereign State and a private party. Jefferson wrote immediately to the law printer for a copy of the proceedings, adding significantly: "A more important case I presume you have never published." [22]

His attacks on the tribunal grew ever more unrestrained. He called it "this parricide tribunal," and the Cohens decision "that insult to human reason." He groped around for remedies, sometimes shifting ideas in midstream. After decrying impeachment as a useless remedy, he was now willing to have Congress, if its protest by resolution were unheeded, to impeach the entire Court "and set the whole adrift." A little later, he proposed a different remedy: a Constitutional amendment that would limit judicial tenures to six years; the incumbents to be reappointable by the President only with the consent of *both* Houses.

"Independant as they feel themselves of the nation and all its authorities," he wrote bitterly, "they already openly avow the daring and impudent principle of consolidation & arrogate to themselves the authority of ultimately construing the constitution for all the other departments and for the nation itself. It is that body which is to sap the independance of the states, to generalize first, and then to monarchise the federal authority." [23]

Elsewhere he likened the Court to a Roman Caesar and the Pope in its assumption of infallibility. "But the battle of Bunker's hill," he cried wrathfully, "was not fought to set up a Pope." [24]

His complaints grew also in volume against another great cross he had to bear—the inordinate weight of his private correspondence. He kept an exact diary of letters received and answered. In 1820, he had received 1,267 letters, many of them, he complained to Adams, "requiring answers of elaborate research, and all to be answered with due attention and consideration.... Is this life? At best it is but the life of a mill-horse, who sees no end to his circle but in death." [25]

Yet, for all his stiff and painful wrist, he meticulously answered every one, even those which came from strangers. Occasionally he would refuse to enter into a controversy or to estimate the beauties of a poem; but it never occurred to him to adopt his friend Adams's summary course of not answering at all. Nor could he resist a good swinging religious discussion, even though he had reason to rue it later.

Perhaps the most surprising of his new correspondencies was with no less a person than Timothy Pickering, the prime evil spirit of the extreme Federalists, the man who had verged perilously close to treason, and who had fought Jefferson personally and politically for many years.

Pickering wrote first, calling attention to the general opinion that Jefferson was "one of the learned unbelievers in revelation," and wondering if he realized the influence his name had in such matters on youthful admirers. With tongue in cheek, he added that though they had differed politically in the past, there had been nothing personal in the matter.[26]

With equal tongue in cheek, Jefferson replied that he felt exactly the same way. As for his influence, "no one sees with greater pleasure than myself the progress of reason in its advances towards rational Christianity." [27] The day will come, he told Pickering now, when "the incomprehensible jargon of the Trinitarian arithmetic" will be dismissed by all sensible men; to which he later added to Adams, "the mystical generation of Jesus, by the Supreme Being as His Father, in the womb of a virgin...." [28]

He substituted for these mysticisms an almost mystical devotion of his own "for the luminous advance of sciences, of which we see the dawn." It might perhaps be regretted that his age had seen only the dawn instead of the glorious fulfillment, but he consoled himself with the thought that each age has its turn, and since *they* had advanced sharply over preceding ages, why envy additional advances to those who would come after? [29]

Books were essential if knowledge was to flow on unimpeded. And, for the present, that knowledge was secreted within the covers of learned volumes published abroad. He therefore lent the weight of his name and of his inchoate University to a movement started at Harvard for the removal of the tariff on foreign books. This, he declared in a petition to Congress, was "an unfair impediment to the American student," and did not serve its avowed purpose of encouraging literature at home. It was more like "burying the fountain to increase the flow of its waters." [30]

In a letter to his friend, Dr. Benjamin Waterhouse, Jefferson finally avowed himself a Unitarian; expressing the hope "that there is not a *young man* now living in the United States who will not die an Unitarian." For the first time he set forth his own religious creed as a complete system.

He believed, he said, "1. That there is one only God, and he all perfect. 2. That there is a future state of rewards and punishments. 3. That to love God with all thy heart and thy neighbor as thyself, is the sum of religion."

Against this creed he opposed the doctrines of Calvin: 1. That there were *three* Gods. 2. That good works and the love of neighbor are as nothing. 3. That faith is everything. 4. That reason in religion is unlawful. 5. That there is a pre-election of those who are to be saved and those who are to be damned.[31]

But when the enthusiastic doctor proposed that this statement be published to the world, Jefferson shrank back in great alarm. "Into what a nest of hornets would it thrust my head!" he cried.[32]

He hated all dogmas and claimed that they "have been the bane and ruin of the Christian church, its own fatal invention which, thro' so many ages, made of Christendom a slaughter house, and at this day divides it into castes of inextinguishable hatred to one another. Witness the present internecine rage of all other sects against the Unitarian. The religions of antiquity had no particular formulas of creed, those of the modern world none; except those of the religionists calling themselves Christians, and even among these, the Quakers have none. And hence alone the harmony the quiet, the brotherly affections, the exemplary and unschismatising society of the Friends. And I hope the Unitarians will follow their happy example." [33]

It was in part because of his Unitarian beliefs—suspected, even though not publicly avowed—that the University had such hard sledding. An incautious remark of Jefferson to the effect that the sects "may well be afraid of the progress of the Unitarians to the South" spread like a prairie fire, and the enraged synods and Bible societies rose in arms against the infidel.[34]

If it had been difficult for Cabell to get the legislature to supply funds before, now it was heart-breaking. "Would it be believed in future times," he wrote despairingly, "that such efforts are necessary to carry such a bill, for such an object!!" [35]

Nor was the *religious* opposition all they had to contend with. There were *political* influences at work as well. One of Jefferson's prime projects for the University was the great central Rotunda he envisaged as the dominating, yet co-ordinating structure for the whole. But the people of Richmond feared that the erection of such a magnificent building at Charlottesville would induce the legislature to quit them and move the capital to the University town. It became the subject of fierce philippics in the Assembly sessions by the local legislators. Harvie shouted that "he would never vote another Dollar to the University but on condition that it should not be applied to that building." Johnson, on the Board of Visitors itself, was similarly opposed.

But Jefferson was equally adamant. He left it to Cabell to neutralize Harvie; but, as he advised Madison, also on the Board, "we must manage our dissenting brother [Johnson] softly; he is of too much weight to be given up." [36]

He was disgusted with the legislature. "There is some flaw," he gloomily told Cooper, "not yet detected in our principle of representation which fails to bring forth the wisdom of our country into its councils. It is impossible to foretell to what this will lead; but certainly to a state of disgradation [*sic*], which I thank heaven I am not to live to witness." [37]

The funds were refused for the Rotunda; and Jefferson lashed out again at the dissidents as "truly the *Parliamentum indoctissimum* that was ever assembled in this state." His only comfort was that the recent elections had changed a majority of the members, and that the University had gained some valuable friends in the forthcoming session.[38]

In spite of the lack of funds, of troubles with workmen who failed often to comprehend the scope of Jefferson's plans, the buildings slowly and painfully moved from blueprint to substance. On the Doric pavilions

Jefferson employed the human faces that fringed the classic Baths of Diocletian. He admired these, but he liked perhaps even more the motif of the oxskulls, which belonged, however, to a different classic order. He therefore refused to mix the two in the "public" buildings, where he felt bound "to follow authority strictly." But he felt free to follow the dictates of his own fancy at home; and intended in the middle room he was completing at Poplar Forest to alternate the human faces and the "mitred ox-sculls." In a second room he proposed a five-inch frieze in the Ionic style of the temple of Fortuna Virilis.[39]

He was quite pleased with his endeavors, even though "the keystone of the arch, the Rotunda," was still lacking. The University was well worth a visit, he boasted, "as a specimen of classical architecture which would be remarked in Europe." The cost already totaled $200,000 and another $50,000 was required. It was here that the legislature had balked, and again he thought that the Presbyterian clergy were chiefly responsible.

"This is rather the most numerous of our present sects," he exploded to Short, "and the most ambitious, the most intolerant & tyrannical of all our sects. They wish to see no instruction of which they have not the exclusive direction. Their present aim is ascendancy only, their next exclusive possession and establishment. They dread the light which this University is to shed on the public mind, and its obstruction to their ambition. But there is a breeze advancing from the North, which will put them down. Unitarianism has not yet reached us; but our citizens are ready to recieve reason from any quarter. The Unity of a supreme being is so much more intelligible than the triune arithmetic of the counterfeit [*sic*] Christians that it will kindle here like a wild-fire." He expected all men under forty to harken; though "*female* fanaticism might hold out a while longer."[40]

Goaded by the unrelenting opposition of the sects, Jefferson was ready now to doff his former cloak of private neutrality in religious affairs, and don the mantle of missionary proselytization on behalf of the Unitarians.

As the newly elected legislature opened its sessions, the sky began to lighten somewhat. The finances of the University had been placed by previous legislatures in a complicated pattern of extended loans rather than outright subsidies; and the problem now arose whether it would be better to obtain a remission of the debts or new funds with which to build the Library and its Rotunda. By all means, the latter! cried Jefferson. Let us finish the buildings; the remission of the debt "will come of itself.... The great object of our aim from the beginning has been to make the establishment the most eminent in the United States, in order to draw to it the youth of every state, but especially of the South and West." To achieve that ideal, it was necessary to attract a notable faculty from Europe as well as from this country. "Had we built a barn for a College, and log huts for accommodations," he queried, "should we ever have had the assurance to propose to an European Professor of that character to come to it? Why give up this important idea, when so near its accomplishment that a single lift more effects it?" [41]

Thus he encouraged Cabell, whose heart was failing. Yet, admitted Jefferson later, if it were a question of having to yield either the University or the Primary Schools, he would give up the University. "It is safer," he said, "to have a whole people respectably enlightened, than a few in a high state of science and the many in ignorance. This last is the most dangerous state in which a nation can be." Look at Europe for the proof of this.[42]

Now it was Cabell's turn to encourage Jefferson; and when the test came, the latter reversed himself and was ready to let the Primary Schools lie in abeyance, if only the University could be completed and its debt remitted. *Then*, he said, we could "come forward heartily as the patrons of the Primaries on some plan which will allow us a fairer share of the common fund." [43]

In February, 1823, Cabell exultingly announced the end of the long, hard struggle. As a result of the spring elections, where aid to the University had been the chief issue, the electorate had unequivocally given its mandate; and the new legislature now passed the University Bill and granted a loan of $60,000 for the building of the controversial library. But, warned Cabell, "we must never come here again for money to erect buildings." [44]

As soon as the glorious news reached Jefferson, he wasted not a moment to authorize construction on the Rotunda full speed ahead.[45] The long-awaited end was in sight.

He was not so happy, however, when he heard that his grandson, Francis Eppes, aged twenty-one, was contemplating marriage. "The European period of full age at 25 years," he believed, remembering his own experience, "is certainly more conformable with the natural maturity of the body and mind of man than ours of 21. The interruption of studies, and filling our houses with children are the consequences of our habits of early marriage." Nevertheless, he warned the worried father, we must acquiesce. The girl was a worthy one, Francis had assured his grandfather that he would continue his studies, and Jefferson was ready to provide him with a house at Poplar Forest as well as a plantation. Unfortunately, he could not deed the property over to him, since it was mortgaged to a bank as part of his security on the fatal Nicholas indebtedness.[46]

For all his dogmatic assertions on the uses of education as a panacea for the world, Jefferson nevertheless was sensible enough to qualify them on occasion. Nor did he believe that a communistic society was the pattern for a country like the United States. In an important letter he made his position clear on these two vital issues:

That, on the principle of a communion of property, small societies may exist in habits of virtue, order industry and peace, and consequently in a state of as much happiness as heaven has been pleased to deal out to imperfect humanity, I can readily concieve, and indeed have seen its proofs in various small societies which have been constituted on that principle. But I do not feel authorised to conclude from these, that an extended society, like that of the US. or of an individual state, could be governed happily on the same principle. I look to the diffusion of light and education as the resource most to be relied on for ameliorating the condition, promoting the virtue and advancing the happiness of man. That every man shall be made virtuous, by any process whatever, is indeed no more to be expected, than that every tree be made to bear fruit, and every plant nourishment. The briar and bramble can never become the vine and olive; but their asperities may be softened by culture, and their properties improved to usefulness in the order and economy of the world. And I do hope, in the present spirit of extending to the great mass of mankind the blessings of instruction, I see a prospect of great advancement in the happiness of the human race; and that this may proceed to an indefinite, altho' not to an infinite degree.[47]

On November 12, 1822, Jefferson suffered an accident. Descending one of his terraces at Monticello, a decayed step gave way and he fell, breaking his left forearm and dislocating the bones of the wrist. He called in a surgeon who set the injured arm and ordered him to remain at home until Christmas. Though the bones eventually knit, he never recovered the full use of his left hand and fingers. At the age of seventy-nine, healing was difficult. Coupled with the pain and stiffness in his right hand from the ancient accident, writing became an even more tedious and torturing business than before.[48]

CHAPTER 72

Declining Years

WITH one arm almost useless and the other in a bad way, Jefferson had not yet completed the chapter of his accidents. Barely had he been permitted by his physician out of the house when he went riding and was thrown, escaping by a miracle with no more than severe bruises. Undaunted, he rode again. This time the horse slipped in fording a river and his master, entangled in the reins and crippled, was almost drowned. Next came a fever that confined him to bed for three weeks. And, to cap the climax, a flash flood swept away the mill dam he was building, and he had laboriously to start all over again.[1]

Yet, through all these disablements and misfortunes, his beloved University remained ever in his thoughts. He wished to capture the public imagination for it; and to do this, he felt compelled to obtain teachers whose names possessed the glamor of distance. For all his incessant comments on the superiority of America to Europe, he sought his men abroad rather than at home.[2] Oxford, Edinburgh, Cambridge—these were names to conjure with. Ticknor, in his grand tour, was to seek out their celebrities for shipment to Virginia; and later, a special emissary, young Francis W. Gilmer, was commissioned to do the same.

When Gilmer, in the following year, reported sorrowfully that the salaries demanded were far out of the reach of the still unopened institution, Jefferson wrote in great alarm that foreign teachers *must* be obtained, otherwise both the Legislature and the general public would think little of the University. He urged therefore "that if you cannot get men of the first order of science, it would be better you should bring the best you can get, altho' of a secondary grade. They would be preferable to secondaries of our own country, because the stature of these is known to be inferior to some in other seminaries; whereas those you would bring would be unknown, would be readily imagined such as we had expected, and might set us agoing advantageously, until we could mend our hold." [3]

In other words, practical considerations and the pressure of competition were forcing Jefferson into a position not too far removed from certain practices not unknown today. Fortunately, Gilmer was able finally to assemble five willing professors of better than secondary grade, pack them in triumph on board ship, and eventually land them in Virginia.

Jefferson's genius for compromise and moving backward a little in order to gain a more tenacious position later, was similarly in evidence when it came to meeting the fierce opposition of the sects. Dr. Cooper had been sacrificed; though this had not been Jefferson's doing. But another means of placating the "genus irritabile vatum" was his own idea.

He explained the strategy to Cooper. Priestcraft, he wrote, had attempted to blacken the University as "an anti-religious institution. We disarmed them of this calumny however in our last report by inviting the different sects to establish their respective divinity schools on the margin of the grounds of the University, so that their students might attend its schools & have the benefit of its library, to be entirely independent of it at the same time, and no ways incorporated with it. One sect, I think, may do it, but another, disdaining equality, ambitioning nothing less than a soaring ascendancy, will despise our invitation."[4] The latter, of course, was the Presbyterian.

In the same way he bowed to pressure to permit a professorship of theology. When he came to make out a catalogue of volumes to be purchased for the University library, he found himself at a loss for the chapter on books of divinity. He appealed, therefore, to Madison for help. He was sufficiently familiar, he said, with the good moral writers, Christian as well as Pagan; but the writers on religious metaphysics, like Duns Scotus and others, were terra incognita.[5]

He also sought to placate the high-spirited youth of Virginia when they ultimately entered his institution. They were not amenable to such strict supervision and discipline as obtained in a northern college like Harvard; and he wished to avoid their kicking over the traces. The best method, he considered, was to let them elect freely whatever courses they wished, and "by avoiding too much government, by requiring no useless observances."[6]

The affairs of the University, his several crippling accidents, "age and debility," and perhaps the knowledge that his debts could no longer be surmounted by his own unaided efforts, forced Jefferson to turn over the management of his estates and all business matters to his grandson, Thomas Jefferson Randolph, son of Thomas Mann and Martha Randolph.[7]

Indeed, the problem of meeting his endorsement of Nicholas's notes for $20,000 harried him night and day. He had staved off the day of judgment by heavy borrowings, by a loan from one son-in-law, John Wayles Eppes, and the pledge of Varina, the estate of his other son-in-law, Thomas Mann Randolph. In spite of these maneuvers, Jefferson feared he would have to start selling his own lands on a heavy scale.[8]

But Thomas Mann Randolph had himself become a problem both to his father-in-law and to his wife and children. The strange traits, the black moods, the jealous tempers of some years ago, were now beginning to cloud his mind and send him into incalculable rages. No longer Governor of Virginia, he had time to brood on what he conceived to be his wrongs, and began to fasten them unerringly on Jefferson and poor Martha. Whether he took to drink as well is unknown; as is also the exact nature of the fancied grievances that eventually drove him to a hermitlike existence and a hatred of his entire family.

Monroe, who had heard something of the state of affairs, offered his services as a mediator; but Jefferson was unwilling to discuss the matter by letter, preferring to wait instead for a chance for private conversation. "In the mean while no time is lost," he wrote Monroe. "For as long as the party continues his present habits there could be neither satisfaction nor safety in his society; and his reclamation from them, I believe to be absolutely desperate. This however does not lessen our sense of the kindness and friendship of your wish to relieve us from the most constant and poignant affliction of our lives." [9]

Yet, some months later, Jefferson was sending Randolph to New York to pledge his Varina estate for Jefferson's benefit.[10] Perhaps this incessant involvement in the tangled debts of his father-in-law, the fear that nothing would remain to himself in his old age, had something to do with the final catastrophe.

At various times, Jefferson received requests from ambitious writers for materials wherewith to write his biography. Jefferson invariably refused, and generalized his reasons. "I do not think," he told one such aspirant, "a biography should be written, or at least not published, during the life of the person the subject of it. It is impossible that the writer's delicacy should permit him to speak as freely of the faults or errors of a living, as of a dead character. There is still however a better reason. The letters of a person, especially of one whose business has been chiefly transacted by letters, form the only full and genuine journal of his life; and few can let them go out of their own hands while they live. A life written after these hoards become opened to investigation must supersede any previous one." [11] To no one did this apply so completely as to Jefferson.

Yet he urged and implored his Republican friend, Judge William Johnson, to continue writing his history of parties in the United States as a counterweight to that "five-volumed libel"—John Marshall's *Life of Washington*—as well as other historical ventures whereby the "tories" were diligently seeking to subvert history for their own purposes. Among such projects which Jefferson thought was in contemplation was the life of Hamilton by "a man who, to the bitterness of the priest, adds the rancor of the fiercest federalism. Mr. Adams' papers, too, and his biography, will descend of course to his son, whose pen, you know, is pointed, and his prejudices not in our favor."

As against these Jefferson offered his own "letters (all preserved) [which] will furnish the daily occurrences and views from my return from Europe in 1790, till I retired finally from office. These will command more conviction than anything I could have written after my retirement. . . . Selections from these, after my death, may come out successively as the maturity of circumstances may render their appearance seasonable." [12]

Johnson in return seized upon the reference to John Quincy Adams, and made it the subject of a diatribe against "both Father & Son," complaining that the son had been too liberally rewarded by the Republicans for his accession to their ranks. To which Jefferson answered not a word. Instead, he attacked at length the Supreme Court and the decision rendered by Marshall in Cohens v. Virginia.[13]

In so doing, he ran afoul of his own faithful friend, Madison. The latter, with striking vigor, insisted that the Constitution "intended the Authority vested in the Judicial Department as a final resort in relation to the States, for cases resulting to it in the exercise of its functions." He avowed that he had never yielded his original opinion on the Court's powers as he had long ago stated it in the 39th paper of the *Federalist*, and that he repudiated the "ingenious reasonings of Col: Taylor agst. this construction of the Constitution."

He admitted that the Court had abused its powers, but declared that such abuse of trust did not disprove their existence. "I should prefer," he concluded, "a resort to the Nation for an amendment of the Tribunal itself, to continual appeals from its controverted decisions to that Ultimate Arbiter."[14]

Such an affirmation of the Court's powers ran counter to all of Jefferson's thinking, and would have evoked a violent rejoinder had it been advanced by anyone else but Madison. Instead, he vented his feelings to Samuel H. Smith, demanding that "the true old republicans stand to the line, and . . . die on it if necessary."[15]

The final overthrow of Napoleon had unleashed a new force in Europe —the so-called Holy Alliance of the great Powers who, with the exception of England, avowed their intention to maintain the status quo and all existing monarchies, to enforce order and prevent any further revolutions, and to keep religion in its accepted forms intact. Even Alexander of Russia, whom Jefferson had apostrophized in the past as the one benevolent monarch and an ornament to the human race, joined the Alliance (he was one of its chief architects, in fact) and Jefferson suffered all the pangs of disillusionment.

Watching the rapid unfoldment, Jefferson saw the match being put to a train "which will blow up despotism from the face of the earth. The insurrection beginn[in]g in any one spot will spread like wild fire over the civilized world. The great contest between men & monarchs must now be decided. . . . And I trust it will end with the extermination of the Holy conspirators agt the human race and leave not a wreck [*sic*] of their existence behind."[16]

That spark was shortly to be applied—in remote South America. The last of a series of revolts from European domination was sweeping the continent, and the twin heroes, Bolivar and San Martin, were pushing Spain and Portugal into the sea. The monarchs of the Holy Alliance, and in particular, Louis of France, were perturbed at these new successes of the republican principle and seriously considered a combined invasion of the rebellious continent to crush the upstart republics once for all.

President Monroe, surveying the distant situation, was equally perturbed. He had rarely sought Jefferson's advice during his Presidency; now he did. "The moment is peculiarly critical," he wrote to Monticello, "as respects the present state of the world, & our relations with the acting parties in it, in Europe, & in this hemisphere, & it would have been very gratifying to me to have had an opportunity of free communication with you, on all the interesting subjects connected with it." Unable to see him personally, he therefore rapidly outlined the situation, past and present, and asked: "Can we, in any form, take a bolder attitude, in regard to it, in favor of liberty, than we then did? Can we afford greater aid to that cause, by assuming any such attitude, than we now do, by the force of our example? These are subjects, on which I should be glad to have your sentiments." [17] He sent a similar request to Madison.

For all his private boldness, when thus asked to take a semiofficial stand, Jefferson became most cautious. He feared the power of the Holy Alliance and did not wish to attract its angry lightnings in the direction of the United States. "I have ever deemed it fundamental for the United States," he replied, "never to take active part in the quarrels of Europe. Their political interests are entirely distinct from ours. Their mutual jealousies, their balance of power, their complicated alliances, their forms and principles of government, are all foreign to us. They are nations of eternal war." [18]

This was all very well while Europe was alone embroiled (France had invaded Spain to relieve her monarch from the liberal constitution forced on him by his own subjects). But it shortly appeared that, once this was accomplished, *both* nations would send an expeditionary force to South America to recapture the revolted colonies.

George Canning, the British Minister, who viewed with alarm any strengthening of the French-Spanish axis, bethought himself of a plan to prevent a reaccession of strength to it through the recapture of the American possessions. He called for Richard Rush, the American Minister to England, laid before him the secret proposals of the Holy Alliance with respect to South America, and offered to co-operate with the United States in a public support of the independence of that continent.

Rush promptly dispatched Canning's proposals to Monroe and John Quincy Adams, the Secretary of State. Immediately recognizing their supreme importance, Monroe turned again to Jefferson and Madison for advice. He asked specific questions: (1) Shall we entangle ourselves in European politics? (2) If there need be an exception—is this such a one? (3) Has England finally decided to take a stand on the side of liberty against despotism? [19]

Jefferson also recognized the importance of the question and the decision that must be made on it. That question, he wrote to Monroe, then vacationing at his home in Oakhill,

> is the most momentous which has ever been offered to my contemplation since that of Independence. That made us a nation, this sets our compass and points the course which we are to steer through the ocean of time opening on us. ... Our first and fundamental maxim should be, never to entangle ourselves in the broils of Europe. Our second, never to suffer Europe to intermeddle with cis-Atlantic affairs. America, North, and South, has a set of interests distinct from those of Europe, and peculiarly her own. She should therefore have a system of her own, separate and apart from that of Europe. While the last is laboring to become the domicil of despotism, our endeavor should surely be, to make our hemisphere that of freedom. One nation, most of all, could disturb us in this pursuit; she now offers to lead, aid, and accompany us in it. By acceding to her proposition, we detach her from the bands, bring her mighty weight into the scale of free government, and emancipate a continent at one stroke, which might otherwise linger long in doubt and difficulty. Great Britain is the nation which can do us the most harm of any one, or all on earth; and with her on our side we need not fear the whole world.

Thus arguing, Jefferson advised that we go along with Canning in making the proposed joint declaration; that Monroe give the requisite assurances insofar as it lay within his authority; and that, since war might follow with the Holy Alliance, the entire matter ought to be laid before Congress.[20]

Madison, at Montpellier, offered similar and even bolder advice. So that the three great Republican leaders, one the President and two of them ex-Presidents, concurred in this novel policy that was destined to have such portentous implications for the future of America.

But John Quincy Adams, the late convert to Republicanism, saw certain deeper meanings in the situation than the others. He distrusted Canning's motives, and foresaw that any joining of the two Powers might give a handle to fears of the Holy Alliance that we intended to intermeddle with the affairs of Europe. He therefore argued Monroe into issuing a statement on his own, asserting the principles contemplated, but, by refusing to tie the United States to England, make it a peculiarly American policy and thereby quiet any suspicion of our intervention in European affairs.

Monroe assented, and enunciated what has since become known as the "Monroe Doctrine" in his Annual Message to Congress on December 2, 1823. It was a bold step thus to stand alone against all Europe, and to dissociate this country from the protective cover of British power. In a sense, perhaps, Monroe did not fully realize the significance or the daring of his position; for he thought he was truly following Jefferson's advice. "I have concurr'd thoroughly," he wrote his ancient friend in Monticello, "with the sentiments express'd in your late letter, as I am persuaded you will find, by the message, as to the part we ought to act, toward the Allied Powers, in regard to So. America."[21]

But Jefferson knew better; for he had bottomed his assent to a declaration on the sole ground that England was to be included, and that she would thenceforth be our ally, instead of an enemy, as in the past.

Jefferson had adhered pretty strictly to his determination not to solicit public office for his friends and acquaintances from either Madison or Monroe; but, like all rules, this one had exceptions. Two instances arose in which he felt compelled to exercise his influence.

One concerned Colonel Bernard Peyton of Richmond, on whom he looked "almost with the eyes of a father." Peyton wanted either the Post Office or the Collector's post in Richmond, whichever first became vacant; and Jefferson pushed his application to Monroe in the most extravagant terms. "Grant me this," he begged, "and as I never have, so I never will again put your friendship to the trial as to myself."[22]

In August, 1824, the Post Office became available, and Jefferson joyfully wrote to the President soliciting the vacancy for Peyton. But Monroe had other plans, and coldly replied that at least two other applicants had been recommended to him by people, so he implied, with greater claims to consideration.[23]

The same equivocal situation arose in the case of William Duane, the old Republican editor of the *Aurora* who had wielded the bludgeon with such telling effect in the good cause, but who had since come to blows within the party itself. He implored Jefferson to help him with a hostile administration and Jefferson, before he knew the result of his entreaty for Peyton, complied.[24] Here, too, Monroe's response was a cold denial; not, he hastened to say, because of Duane's attacks on himself, but because any favor shown Duane would give offense to good Republicans in Pennsylvania.[25]

Jefferson was cut to the quick. The hurt was deep and irremediable. Monroe, who had once looked up to him and worshiped him almost as a god, whom he had trained in politics and raised to the heights, now turned him down on two small favors. The aged ex-President displayed his feelings with unwonted candor.

"I am indeed sorely and deeply wounded by the result of my late solicit[atio]n for you," he wrote bitterly to Peyton. "I had thought its success as certain as that the sun will rise tomorrow.... As respects the public, I supposed that 60. years of faithful service would weigh with them as much as a broken leg. And that six and forty years, not of friendship merely, but of affection and service warm from the heart, would have kindled as kind feelings as a transient acquaintance with my competitor. It was the first opportunity too I had ever given of obliging me. I have miscalculated, and shall better understand my place hereafter."[26]

It was a mortal blow, and one that Jefferson never got over; though he continued an outward friendship with Monroe. At the time that it came, he was afflicted with an "imposthume" or abcess under the jaw which locked it so tightly that he had to be fed liquid nourishment through a tube. The combination of man's ingratitude and physical suffering put him in a melancholy mood. "It is become impossible for me to ask anything further from the govmt," he told Thomas Leiper, who also requested his intervention. To Duane he repeated his determination never to ask another favor; and to everyone he begged that they burn his letters. As for Peyton, perhaps the next administration, once Monroe was out, might do something. In the event Jefferson died before the event occurred, he asked Richard Rush to consider Peyton's cause as a legacy to him.[27]

But to Monroe, Jefferson never disclosed his hurt, locking it up in an armor of courteous silence; and even, after Monroe's retirement from office shortly thereafter, continued to disclose a pleasant countenance to him. So much that the outer world noted with a kind of awe the spectacle of the three ex-Presidents—Jefferson, Madison and Monroe—walking together and seated together in a tavern in Charlottesville, where admiring crowds gathered to hear them talk.[28]

In the Presidential election of 1824 Monroe, bowing to the tradition established by Jefferson, retired from office. Several attempts were made by inquiring politicians and the merely curious to find out whom Jefferson favored for the Republican nomination; but to all such attempts he insisted on his absolute neutrality. He did, however, indicate that he thought John Quincy Adams and William H. Crawford would be the probable candidates, and indirectly hinted that he preferred Crawford.[29] In spite of the second Adams's conversion to Republicanism, Jefferson could not help remembering those earlier "monarchical" principles as exemplified in the attacks on Tom Paine.

All that he wished now in the way of politics was to see three amendments to the Constitution: (1) a limitation on the Presidential term; (2) direct election of the President by the people; (3) power to Congress to establish internal improvements, *provided* they were employed within each state in proportion to its contributions to the Federal Treasury. "If I can see these three great amendments prevail," he declared, "I shall consider it as a renewed extension of the term of our lease, shall live in more confidence, and die in more hope."[30]

More and more Jefferson, as was natural with one who was entering his eighty-second year, began to live in the memory of past stirring events and glories. But so, unfortunately, did others. Timothy Pickering, who recently had written to Jefferson to discuss Unitarianism and to disclaim personal enmity, now appeared in the public prints with a violent attack and "elaborate philippic" against John Adams, Thomas Jefferson, Elbridge Gerry and other ancient foes, based on deeds and sayings of thirty years before.

"I could not have believed," wrote Jefferson angrily, "that for so many years, and to such a period of advanced age, he could have nourished passions so vehement and viperous."

What roused Jefferson particularly was the attack on himself and the claim that Washington had reprimanded Jefferson for the Mazzei letter, and that he had humbled himself in turn. "I do affirm," he retorted vehemently, "that there never passed a word, written or verbal, directly or indirectly, between General Washington and myself on the subject of that letter. . . . The whole story is a fabrication, and I defy the framers of it, and all mankind, to produce a scrip of a pen between General Washington and myself on the subject." [31] Which was technically correct.

He refused, however, to join in the public interchange of angry communications on the subject of Pickering's shotgun assault, and left it to the Adamses to bear the brunt of the battle.

Between reminiscences of the past, his several ailments, and the University, Jefferson's life was a busy one. The Virginia legislature had remitted the debt of the University, but attached a rider to it—which Jefferson indignantly called a "Scotch gift"—making the loan subject to reinstatement. How was it possible, he exclaimed, under such uncertainties to obtain good professors? Only the "young scions & sciolists from the schools of the north" who were accustomed to "job-work" and "uncertainty of tenure" would come on those terms; and the University would become a second-rate institution.[32]

John Adams, however, disapproved of Jefferson's obsession with celebrities and European cachet. "I do believe," he wrote strongly, "there are sufficient scholars in America, to fill your professorships and tutorships with more active ingenuity and independent minds than you can bring from Europe. The Europeans are all deeply tainted with prejudices, both ecclesiastical and temporal, which they can never get rid of." [33]

Jefferson was watching with intense interest the proposal of the moribund William and Mary College to remove from what had become the backwater of Williamsburg to a more active site, such as Richmond. Only eleven students were then wandering solitary through its halls, and it was a question of closing altogether or changing location. "Give them no alarm," Jefferson advised Cabell; "let them petition for the removal; let them get the old structure completely on wheels, and not till then put in our claim to its reception." [34] In other words, incorporate the old College into the new.

He was waiting impatiently for the $50,000 which the Assembly had voted for the use of his University. If that came through, he expected to be able to open the doors to students and faculty on February 1, 1825, "splendidly and with effect. If we do not get it, we set out pitifully indeed, without a book, or a single article of apparatus of any kind. A juster debt was never claimed, and on its allowance hangs the fate of our University." [35]

Meanwhile, young Francis Gilmer was in England and Scotland seeking professors for the institution; and his reports were consistently gloomy. The well-known men were accustomed to salaries far beyond what the University could afford to pay, and Jefferson wrote in desperation to get young unknowns then. "I consider," he told Madison, "that his return without any professors will compleatly quash every hope of the inst[itutio]n." [36]

But later came more cheerful news. The youthful emissary had succeeded in rounding up a fairly good stable of professors; and he brought back with him in November, 1824, five men: George Long for Ancient Languages, George Blaetterman for the Modern tongues, Thomas H. Key for Mathematics, Charles Bonnycastle for Natural Philosophy, and Robley Dunglison for Anatomy and Chemistry.[37]

The report lifted Jefferson's spirits. But there still remained one opening which he was at a loss how to fill. That was the chair of Ethics. He explained his problem to Madison: "This subject has been so exclusively confined to the Clergy, that when forced to seek one not of that body it becomes difficult. But it is a branch of science of little difficulty to any ingenious man. Locke, Stewart, Brown, Tracy for the general science of mind furnish material abundant; and that of Ethics is still more trite. I should think any person, with a general educ[atio]n worthy of a place among his scientific brethren might soon qualify himself." [38] To Jefferson ethics was merely a matter of general knowledge, common sense and a decent disposition.

Now that the main body of professors were on the way to the United States, Jefferson wasted no time in setting the machinery of the University in motion. He asked the University Proctor, Arthur S. Brockenbrough, to insert an advertisement in the Virginia newspapers, notifying the public and prospective students that the great day for the opening of its doors was near at hand.[39]

Lafayette had finally come to his "second country" on a triumphal tour. Jefferson welcomed him with public pomp and ceremony to Charlottesville, and with private enthusiasm to Monticello. "But what recollections, dear friend," he wrote Lafayette as soon as he heard of his arrival, "will this call up to you and me! What a history have we to run over from the evening that yourself, Meusnier, Bernau, and other patriots settled, in my house in Paris, the outlines of the constitution you wished! And to trace it through all the disastrous chapters of Robespierre, Barras, Bonaparte, and the Bourbons!"

As for the University, it was still no Athens; "but everything has its beginning, its growth, and end; and who knows with what future delicious morsels of philosophy . . . the world may, some day, be gratified and instructed?" [40]

During his stay in Charlottesville, Lafayette went up to Monticello to eat and drink, sleep and talk of the "good old times" until the small hours of the morning; while officially Jefferson gave a luncheon in his honor in the still unfinished Rotunda of the University and spoke fitting words for the glorious occasion.[41]

Young Ticknor, now teaching at Harvard, revisited Monticello at the end of 1824, accompanied by his wife and the great Daniel Webster. The rising statesman left his own account of the visit, which related largely to his discussions with the elderly ex-President on political matters. Ticknor touched more on the intimate aspects. Both Webster and Ticknor were Federalists—or rather Whigs, as the new amalgam of old Federalists and dissident Republicans were soon to be called—and they had been surprised on first meeting with Madison to discover "a degree of good-sense in his conversation which we had not anticipated from his school of politics and course of life."

But for Jefferson, in spite of his politics, Ticknor had always had a sense of reverence. Returning to the scene of his earlier visit, he found nothing which "marks the residence of an Ex-King." Living with the retired sage were his daughter, Martha J. Randolph, and her four daughters and *their* families. He makes no mention of Thomas Mann Randolph; the split had already occurred.

Going down to the University grounds, Ticknor was struck with their spaciousness and the beautiful architecture of the buildings, so much superior to his own Harvard. He was sceptical of the success of the system that Jefferson proposed, but was willing to watch the experiment unfold.

"Mr. Jefferson," he wrote, "is entirely absorbed in it, and its success would make a *beau finale* indeed to his life. He is now eighty-two years old, very little altered from what he was ten years ago, very active, lively, and happy, riding from ten to fifteen miles every day, and talking without the least restraint, very pleasantly, upon all subjects. In politics, his interest seems nearly gone. He takes no newspaper but the Richmond Enquirer, and reads that reluctantly; but on all matters of literature, philosophy, and general interest, he is prompt and even eager. He reads much Greek and Saxon. I saw his Greek lexicon, printed in 1817; it is much worn with use, and contained many curious notes....

"Mr. Jefferson seems to enjoy life highly, and very rationally; but he said well of himself the other evening, 'When I can neither read nor ride, I shall desire very much to make my bow.' I think he bids fair to enjoy both, yet nine or ten years."[42] Unfortunately, Ticknor's prophecy was not to be fulfilled.

Even the Republicans differentiated between Jefferson and his two successors in the Presidency. As Francis Gilmer was to write: "We adore Mr. Jefferson, admire Mr. Madison, and esteem Mr. Monroe."[43]

CHAPTER 73

The End and the Beginning

AS the year of 1825 dawned, the University was still not opened; and a new headache assailed Jefferson. To his troubles over the chair of Ethics was added a long and exasperating search for someone to assume the much more important—to him—chair of Law.

He offered it first to young Gilmer, recently returned from his mission in England. Gilmer turned it down. "What are we to do?" Jefferson asked in despair of Madison. "I abhor the idea of a mere Gothic lawyer who has no idea beyond his Coke Littleton, who could not associate in conversation with his Colleagues, nor utter a single Academical idea to an enquiring stranger." [1]

He also hated the idea of giving the all-important post to a "Richmond" lawyer. They are "rank Federalists," he cried, "as formerly denominated, and now Consolidationists." But if they had to yield the position to one of them, at least the governing Board had "a duty to guard against danger by a previous prescription of the texts to be adopted." [2]

He was willing enough to leave the question of the proper textbooks in all other fields to the Professors, but *not* in Law. Here he felt that it was essential to indoctrinate the students in accordance with what he conceived to be proper principles. He explained his position on the censorship of texts to Cabell: "There is one branch in which we are the best judges, in which heresies may be taught, of so interesting a character to our own state and to the US. as to make it a duty in us to lay down the principles which shall be taught. It is that of Government. Mr. Gilmer being withdrawn, we know not who his Successor may be. He may be a Richm[on]d lawyer, or one of that school of quondam federalism, now Consolidation. It is our duty to guard against the dissemination of such principles among our youth, and the diffusion of that poison, by a previous prescription of the texts to be followed in their discourse."

Indeed, he was preparing a resolution for the next meeting of the Board of Visitors on the subject; but he proposed not to say a word about it in advance, except to Cabell and Madison. "I have always found," he said significantly, "that the less such things are spoken of beforehand, the less obstruction is contrived to be thrown in their way." [3]

The texts which he now proposed for the School of Law and Civil Polity included Locke's *Essay on Civil Government*, Sidney's *Discourses on Government*, the Declaration of Independence, the *Federalist*, the Virginia Resolutions of 1799, and Washington's Farewell Address. It is the duty of the Board, so read his resolution, "to pay special attention to the principles of government which shall be inculcated therein, and to provide that none shall be inculcated which are incompatible with those on which the Constitutions of this state, and of the US. were *genuinely based in the common opinion*." [4]

Jefferson did not italicise that last curious phrase; but it is illuminating. Jefferson seemingly meant by it that the *interpretation* of the Constitutions ought firmly to remain in the hands of those whose beliefs were like his own, and that Marshall's Supreme Court decisions should not be cited in the classroom to the opposite effect.

Madison cautiously concurred in Jefferson's conception of the way in which to teach "the true doctrines of liberty as exemplified in our Political System"; though he expressed some critical doubts as to the orthodox texts to be employed.[5]

The search for a proper Law Professor continued unabated. Jefferson peremptorily rejected a proposal to call in James Kent, the great New York judge and later author of the classic *Commentaries*. For Kent was a Federalist and, avowed Jefferson, "an angel from heaven who should inculcate such principles in our school of govmt should be rejected by me." [6]

The chair of Ethics was finally accepted by George Tucker, but the chair in Law continued a headache. It was offered in turn to sound Republicans like Judge Philip P. Barber, Henry St. George Tucker, Judge Dabney Carr, Judge William Dade and a host of others; but all refused unless it was not to be a full-time job.[7] On this, however, Jefferson remained adamant.

Finally, his pressure on Francis W. Gilmer became so unrelenting that the young man reluctantly accepted, and the search was ended.[8]

In the interim, there had been a national election, and John Quincy Adams received a plurality over his rivals, General Andrew Jackson, Henry Clay and William H. Crawford, to the last of whom Jefferson had privately inclined. Since no one had a majority, the election was thrown into the House where, through the efforts of Clay, John Quincy Adams was chosen. Jefferson sent formal congratulations to John Adams, the father of the new President, and much more sincere condolences to Crawford. What had happened in the Congressional balloting, he confided, had "very much damped" his confidence in the discretion of his friends, and disclosed their ignorance of character and inattention to the right qualifications. It all argued ill for the future, he concluded gloomily. Perhaps it was time for him to "exit" from the human stage.[9]

Of this dichotomy, fortunately, old John Adams knew nothing. He received the congratulations for his son at face value and with a feeling of solid comfort. "I look back with rapture," he exclaimed in reply, "to those golden days when Virginia and Massachusetts lived and acted together like a band of brothers and I hope it will not be long before they may say redeunt saturnia regna when I hope the world will hear no more of Hartford Convention or Virginia Armories." [10] He did not live long enough to witness the blighting of his hopes.

The election of the younger Adams as a "Consolidationist" and the rise of a new spirit of nationalism caused Jefferson some unhappy moments. He thought he saw a trend in the new coalition of Eastern and Western States toward a greater centralization and a breach in the rigid principle of the division of authority between the Federal Government and the States. He could only hope that the current majority would eventually see the error of its ways and return to "the old principle of a limited government." [11]

The occasion for these animadversions on the future was a request from an old Virginia neighbor who had emigrated to Kentucky and found himself involved in a hot political squabble over paper money and debtors' relief laws. The name of Jefferson had been used by the proponents to inculcate "unsound principles." Would Jefferson deny them?

Jefferson evaded taking any position in the controversy. "Quiet is my wish," he replied, "with the peace and good will of the world. With its contentions I have nothing to do." [12]

Thus dismissing the world—as he had been in the habit of doing for decades whenever it suited his purpose—Jefferson concentrated all his attention on the University.

For a while the fantastic chapter of hostilities and accidents that had dogged the University from the beginning seemed without end. William and Mary threatened to move to Richmond and become a powerful rival. The five intrepid professors who had embarked from England had not yet been heard from and were feared lost at sea. A steady rain set in and turned all roads leading into Charlottesville into impassable swamp.

The University had been scheduled to open on February 1, 1825; but the red-letter day came and went without a sign. Students who had intended enrolling despaired of the new institution and went elsewhere.

On March 7th, however, all the obstacles had been surmounted. The legislature refused William and Mary's petition. The missing faculty turned up safe and sound. A final donation from the legislature permitted the purchase of a library and laboratory equipment. And, even though the rains continued, determined students came straggling in by twos and threes. Since the stages could not get through the boggy roads, they hired horses to plod knee-deep in mud. Fifty to sixty of these hardy pioneers were present by the opening day.[13]

Fruition was at hand to half a century of dreams and unremitting labors. Yet all was still not well. The schools of Languages and of Mathematics had about thirty students each; but the school of Natural Philosophy was sparsely attended. Very few of the young men had a sufficient grounding in mathematics. And "they are half idle," complained Jefferson, "all for want of books." [14]

But somehow or other the University slowly pushed forward. Each day saw several more students come straggling in and by the end of June, some ninety were in attendance. Jefferson thought them "a very fine parcel of young men, but so defectively prepared, that we have been obliged for the present year, to relax in our laws of reception." Nevertheless he exulted that "our scale of educ[atio]n comprehends every branch of useful knowledge, and our Professors are of the first order of science, so that I hope it will prove a great blessing to my country." [15]

He realized to the full the parlous state of education in Virginia, and he refused to adopt the provincial outlook of some of his neighbors in sneering at what they called "imported science." He would ask it from "every soil," he avowed. Nor were the regular classical studies in a better state. The teachers in the Latin schools of Virginia, he insisted, were of such poor caliber that they would not have been able to qualify even as sophomores in the English schools of Eton and Westminster.[16]

For all his talk of electives and treating the students as mature young men who knew what they wanted and could choose freely for themselves, Jefferson proved a rigid disciplinarian as Rector of the University. The single vacation which he permitted the scholars during the entire year was the month and a half between December 15th and January 31st. When the students asked for an additional ten days beginning on July 4th, the petition was refused. He disapproved of too many vacations, wrote Jefferson; they break up the continuity of studies and represent an irreparable loss of time for young men.[17]

An application was made to teach dancing and the use of the small sword to the boys. He approved of the first, but not of the second. "Dancing," he commented, "is generally, and justly I think, considered among *innocent* accomplishments; while we cannot so consider the art of stabbing and pistolling our friends, or dexterity in the practice of an instrument exclusively used for killing our fellow-citizens *only* and never against the public enemy." [18]

But Jefferson failed to realize that young men—and particularly Virginia young men—can not be subjected to overstrict restraints without an explosion. On October 1st, a group of fourteen students got uproariously drunk, masked themselves and sallied riotously out upon the campus. Two Professors, George Long and Thomas H. Key, sought to intervene; but were met with insulting language and a hail of brickbats.

The next day the faculty met in solemn conclave and demanded the names of the rioters from the general student body. The students refused in a written statement that added insult to injury. Whereupon the two aggrieved Professors tendered their resignations. The Board of Visitors, hurriedly convened by Jefferson, refused to accept the resignations and descended upon the campus in stately array. At their presence, the guilty fourteen finally stepped forward. Three were expelled and the others suspended or reprimanded. The disorder, which must have reminded Jefferson of his own student days, was ended; the honor of the Professors was satisfied; and peace descended on the campus.[19]

A few days later Jefferson could report with satisfaction that everything was running smoothly; that "the Students are attending their schools more assiduously, and looking to their Professors with more respect." By February of the following year, there were 150 in attendance, and the University could be said to be flourishing.[20]

Unfortunately, Jefferson's health during this period was rapidly deteriorating. One of the students, Matthew Maury, was shocked at the alteration in his appearance and feared that he could not long survive. He suffered from diabetes, was unable now either to walk or ride over 200 yards, and his memory began to fail.[21] Dr. Dunglison, the imported professor who taught anatomy at the University, treated the ailing Rector for a while with good results, but the complaint kept recurring. Dunglison refused to accept payment for his services; but Jefferson insisted. "The fragment of life remaining to me," he wrote to the doctor, "is likely to be past in sickness and suffering. The young physicians in our neighborhood will probably be good ones in time. But time & experience as well as science are necessary to make a skilful physician, and Nature is preferable to an unskilful one." He wished to avail himself of Dunglison's skill and experience; but only if he would consent to be paid.[22]

"Eighty two years old," wrote Jefferson painfully and despondently to Samuel Smith, "my memory gone, my mind d[itt]o, for over five months confined to the house by a painful complaint, which, permitting me neither to walk nor to sit, obliges me to be constantly reclined, and to write in that posture, when I write at all." Smith had asked his advice as to certain legal matters. "I am dead as to that," he ended, "and my friends and the world must so consider me." [23]

Yet such was the resiliency of his nature that at the first reprieve in his condition, Jefferson emerged from gloom and foreboding to his more natural state of optimism. A month later, he was bragging over his excellent eyesight and his continued reading of the classics which, he averred, he unwillingly laid aside to take up a current book.[24]

Age merely fortified him in his materialistic philosophy and abhorrence of "all metaphysical reaching. . . . The business of life," he asserted, "is with matter. That gives us tangible results. Handling that, we arrive at the knolege of the axe, the plough, the steam-boat, and everything useful in life. But, from metaphysical speculations, I have never seen one useful result." [25]

Nor, in spite of his pathetic dismissal of himself from the affairs of the world in October, did his mind in December show any relaxation of its former keenness. The growing tide of public opinion in favor of federal action on internal improvements alarmed him, and he drafted a "Solemn Declaration and Protest of the Commonwealth of Virginia" which he sent to Madison for adoption by the legislature.

Virginia, the Declaration asserted, reaffirmed the historical division of powers between the Federal and State governments. It viewed with apprehension the recent usurpations of the former and its claim "to construct roads, open canals, & effect other internal improvements within the territories and jurisdictions exclusively belonging to the several states." Once more Virginia was to disavow "as most false and unfounded" the doctrine that the right to levy taxes and provide for the general welfare gave the general government unlimited powers.

Virginia, however, so Jefferson added, did not wish to "raise the banner of disaffection, or of separation from their sister-states." Yet the threat was plainly there, unless the Federal Government retracted.

Jefferson was willing enough to give to the central government a power over internal improvements, *provided* the power was granted by a Constitutional amendment, and *provided* it was "sufficiently guarded against abuses, compromises, and corrupt practices, not only of possible, but of probable occurrence." [26]

But the Resolution was never put before the Assembly. The current, which seemed to have been running so strongly just a week before, now suddenly shifted. Jefferson suppressed his solemn statement and advised that Virginia adopt a wait-and-see attitude.[27]

If the whole affair may seem to have been a tempest in a teapot, it must be remembered that even today certain of the states and influential private groups are contesting a proposed plan of federal aid to education on the same grounds—that it represents an encroachment on the sovereignty of the States. There was also a fear in the minds of Jefferson and others more extreme than he. Where would such an exercise of power stop? Internal improvements were well enough; but would not the next step be an inference in the "local" problem of slavery?

If trouble was thus ominously visible on the public horizon, disaster struck Jefferson more intimately at home. The long pending affair of his son-in-law, Thomas Mann Randolph, had finally come to a head. Randolph's personal finances had steadily been on the downgrade; by the middle of 1825 it was obvious that they were "beyond recovery." Jefferson, with his own finances in an almost equally desperate state, could do nothing to help. Randolph's mind, already unbalanced, now snapped almost completely. He blamed Jefferson for his supposed refusal to extend aid; he thought that everyone, including his own wife and children, were hostile and secretly in alliance against him. Brooding on his fancied wrongs, he secreted himself alone in a small home on the edge of the estate, and refused to see family or friends.

Jefferson was sick at heart. His sole remaining daughter was unhappy;

the children, now chiefly grown, were at loggerheads; and the whole warm refuge of family life he had laboriously built for himself during the previous years was now tumbling about his ears. He made a last desperate and moving appeal to Randolph. He explained why it was impossible for him to sink what little funds and unencumbered property he had in the bottomless morass of Randolph's debts. Others were in similar trouble at the time, he pointed out. It was due, "not by their own errors, but by that of our legislators, in subjecting the proportions between the money of the country, and its other property to the gambling operations of money brokers."

Let Randolph go into bankruptcy, he suggested, and he would then offer all he had to "the comfortable maintenance of yourself and the family, and to a future provision for them. I have no other use for property." Only return to the bosom of your family, he begged Randolph, and "resume the place in society which is still yours." [28]

Randolph replied in what was evidently a repetition of his dark accusations against Jefferson, his wife and everyone else. The letter, however, has vanished, and it is probable that Jefferson destroyed it as unfit for future eyes. It is known, however, that Randolph accused his father-in-law of indifference or worse to his plight. Jefferson explained that his reserve was not unfriendly, but merely a delicacy against intermeddling; and that increasing deafness often made it impossible for him to hear what was being said at the table. Nor had he been annoyed, as Randolph seemingly believed, at the latter's public employment of some of Jefferson's political sentiments during the trial of a case. "Let me beseech you, dear Sir," he concluded, "to return and become again a member of the family . . . rather than to continue in solitude, brooding over your misfortunes." [29]

But Randolph's mental condition was too far disordered for explanation or appeal. He continued to brood over his wrongs and his mind continued to darken. Jefferson tried again to get him to return at the beginning of 1826. Randolph returned no answer; merely scrawling at the bottom of the letter a note that betrays only too well the strength of his persecution complex.

"I never slept a night from Monticello while my wife was there. But I left it early & returned after dark. After my misfortune I wished to avoid the supercilious looks of Mr. Jefferson's various guests. I still had the house in which I had so long kept my books & papers. Thither I went at an early hour every day & constantly returned when I could cross the river or the rains were not too heavy to brave." [30]

Having failed in all his attempts to effect a reconciliation, Jefferson made certain in his will that his own estate was sufficiently protected against the machinations of his son-in-law and held intact for the benefit of his wife and their children. But he failed to reckon with the cunning and pertinacity of a diseased mind.

Two days after Jefferson's death, Nicholas P. Trist, one of his executors, hearing of some measures that Randolph contemplated, evidently sought to dissuade him from his course. Randolph was not to be dissuaded, though he *did* halt an intemperate letter he had intended to send to poor Martha in her bereavement. "As I do not consider myself a member of the family at all," he replied to Trist, "and cannot reside at Monticello again, I do not feel myself bound to consult with any member of it upon what I do, or what I write, or what I say." [31]

Young Thomas Jefferson Randolph, his son and Jefferson's favorite grandson, complained on July 28, 1826, that he was "in a perfect hell of trouble . . . my father having filed the most atrocious bill against me, charging every form and variety of fraud to set aside the sale of his property and making it an act of duty to my own character to allow him another term to bring forward his proofs." [32]

The senior Randolph failed to pursue his legal action, and almost two years later both his family and the executors were still trying to convince him to return to them. He yielded sufficiently to take up quarters in the north pavilion at Monticello, but made it a condition that he live wholly by himself, "in his room, at his own charge, making no part of the family, and receiving nothing from it in any way whatever."

When these remarkable conditions were met, he returned to the theme of his solitude, which he required for "mental quietude. . . . I must acknowledge," he ended, "that it is painfull to me in a family, because it constantly recalls past scenes which it is better for me to forget." [33]

On such a note did Jefferson's dreams of family solidarity end.

It was not enough that Jefferson had Randolph's financial and mental state to contend with; there were his own financial difficulties that could no longer be evaded. The bankruptcy and death of Wilson Cary Nicholas, which left him liable on his endorsements, coupled with the failure of his estates to meet his regular obligations, brought matters to a climax. Young Thomas Jefferson Randolph, his grandson, to whom he had confided the management of his affairs, finally acknowledged defeat in his efforts to cope with the situation.

As disaster stared him in the face, Jefferson clutched at a possible method of relief. Bankruptcy was impossible; his lands were already mortgaged to the hilt, and his daughter and his many grandchildren would thereby be left penniless. But why not put up the property at a lottery? Thereby, he thought, a sum could be realized sufficient to pay mortgages and debts and still leave a comfortable excess for the benefit of his family. The winners would get the lands, the slaves and the other appurtenances.

The consent of the legislature was necessary for the running of a lottery, but Jefferson saw no reason why it could not be obtained. The scheme would injure no one, while to him "it is almost a question of life and death." In January, 1826, therefore, he sent his grandson to Richmond to seek the necessary bill of authorization.[34]

Cabell pledged his help, and a meeting was called at which most of the Judges of the Court of Appeals attended to offer their services. A bill was drafted for immediate introduction into the legislature.[35]

Meanwhile Jefferson drew up a most curious disquisition on Lotteries, evidently for use in connection with the application. Their morality, he wrote, was unimpeachable, and they had received official approval on many former occasions. He recapitulated his own career, and the services he had rendered the nation and the state; alleging that his present hardships were due solely to the extended absences from his private affairs occasioned by his public activities.

The service which most entitled him to the gratitude of Virginia, he asserted, had been his action when Vice-President (in conjunction with Gallatin) in holding the Republicans in Congress in line against Federalist usurpations until the state legislatures of Virginia and Kentucky, "by their celebrated resolutions, saved the constitution at its last gasp. No person who was not a witness of the scenes of that gloomy period," he wrote, "can form any idea of the afflicting persecutions and personal indignities we had to brook. They saved our country however." All that he now asked in return was permission to employ a lottery which would not cost the state a single cent.[36]

Thus, in his dire extremity, was Jefferson compelled to abase himself and recall himself to the gratitude of his country, like any old soldier begging for bread and showing his wounds.

Should his application be denied, he told Cabell pathetically, "I must sell house and all here and carry my family to Bedford where I have not even a log hut to put my head into." If granted, "I can save the house of Monticello and a farm adjoining to end my days in and bury my bones." [37]

But the news that came from Richmond dashed his hopes. Opposition had been steadily growing to give permission for lotteries, and even Jefferson's political friends were indisposed to make an exception in his behalf. Cabell and some others thought instead to grant him an interest-free loan from the State in the sum of $80,000 to run for the remainder of his life, but that was abandoned as impracticable.[38]

Jefferson's mortification was extreme. He realized now, what too many have realized before and since, that nations and public bodies can speedily forget their heroes and that gratitude is not a marketable commodity. "It is a part of my mortification," he wrote his grandson, "to perceive that I had so far overvalued myself as to have counted on it with too much confidence. I see in the failure of this hope, a deadly blast of all my peace of mind, during my remaining days." [39]

Cabell and other staunch friends of Jefferson in the Assembly, however, refused to relax their efforts. The lower House finally and reluctantly, by a bare majority of four votes, granted leave to bring in the lottery bill on February 9th. Cabell was furious at the slim margin of the victory. "I blush for my country," he cried, "and am humiliated to think how we shall appear on the pages of history." But on the 20th, he was able to write exultantly that the Senate opposition had collapsed. The measure went through by thirteen votes to four; and became "a law of the land." [40]

With the legal hurdles surmounted, the next step was to put the lottery into operation. A board of three managers was appointed, and an advertisement appeared in the Richmond *Enquirer*, offering tickets in the "Jefferson Lottery" for sale.[41]

But the sale did not catch on. The returns were so disappointing that indignant friends sought to raise money by straight public subscription. Young Thomas Jefferson Randolph journeyed north to arouse interest; Governor John Tyler of Virginia, stung at the ingratitude of his fellow Virginians, presided at public meetings where, as he later ironically related, "we had eloquent speeches and the expenditure of a vast deal of breath, but that was all. The money did not come." [42]

The North was more generous than his own state. Pledges came in from New York, Philadelphia, Baltimore and elsewhere in varying sums. It may be, as his biographer, Randall, was to write, that Jefferson died in the happy belief that enough funds had been raised to save his estates from seizure by creditors. Actually, some of the pledged money never materialized, and what did was not sufficient to pay his enormous debts. These amounted to the staggering sum of $107,273.63.[43]

It was well that Jefferson did not foresee the mournful vicissitudes that overtook his beloved Monticello. Almost a century was to pass before the ruined and overgrown mountaintop, passing through alien hands, was finally restored to its pristine splendor by the indefatigable efforts of a group of associated Jeffersonian disciples.

The days of the Sage of Monticello were now numbered. As his eighty-third birthday approached, his health rapidly failed. Arthritis, rheumatism and chronic diarrhea sapped his vitality. On March 19, 1826, feeling the end not far off, he made his will. Hopeful that all, or most of his lands could still be saved, he devised the western part of Poplar Forest to Francis Eppes, the son of his deceased daughter, Maria. He commended his aged sister, the widowed Anna Scott, to Martha's care. To Madison he left his "gold-mounted walking stick of animal horn"; to the University of Virginia those of his books of which it had no duplicates; to his grandson, Thomas Jefferson Randolph, his literary and other papers. To three slaves he gave their freedom, and to two apprentices a similar emancipation on reaching twenty-one.

His particular fear was that his son-in-law, the embittered and half-insane Thomas Mann Randolph, might lay hands on the estate. With great care, therefore, he bequeathed the entire remainder of his possessions to his grandson and his friends, Nicholas P. Trist and Alexander Garrett, to hold in trust during Thomas Mann's lifetime, "for the sole and separate use and behoof of my dear daughter Martha Randolph, and her heirs," with the fee going to her on the death of her alienated husband. But Jefferson tenderly commended the broken man to her care and protection as long as he lived.[44]

As for himself, he wished only a simple grave in the little burial plot on the mountainside, with a plain monument overhead. "Could the dead feel any interest in Monuments or other remembrances," he wrote in his instructions, quoting a line from Anacreon in the original Greek, "the following would be to my Manes the most gratifying."

Drawing with a still steady hand a picture of what he wished, he described it also in words:

> On the grave, a plain die or cube of 3. f. without any mouldings, surmounted by an Obelisk of 6. f. height, each of a single stone: on the faces of the Obelisk the following inscription, & not a word more:
>
> *Here was buried*
> *Thomas Jefferson*
> *Author of the Declaration of American Independance*
> *of the Statute of Virginia for religious freedom & Father*
> *of the University of Virginia.*

He gave no reason for choosing these three particular events out of all the achievements of a long, fruitful and magnificent life; simply that, "because of these, as testimonials that I have lived, I wish most to be remembered. [The Monument] to be of the coarse stone of which my columns are made, that no one might be tempted hereafter to destroy it for the value of the materials. My bust by Ceracchi, with the pedestal and truncated column on which it stands, might be given to the University if they would place it in the Dome room of the Rotunda. On the Die of the Obelisk might be engraved:

Born Apr. 2, 1743 O. S.
Died ——[45]

The Declaration of Independence, the Statute for Religious Freedom, and the University of Virginia. These were the landmarks of his life in Jefferson's own mind; these were the things through which he wished to go down to posterity. Not his Governorship, nor his years as Secretary of State, nor his Presidency. Not even the purchase of Louisiana.

The set of his thought is clearly discernible. He chose unerringly those points in his career when he performed some service in the unending struggle for the liberation of the human mind. Freedom from political tyranny, freedom from religious tyranny, and finally, as the capstone and climax, freedom through education from *all* the tyrannies that have ever clouded and restrained the human spirit in its march down the ages toward an indefinitely approachable perfectibility.

Jefferson may have been unduly optimistic; but he was optimistic in the noblest of causes. Freedom! Liberty! The words may today have lost some of their original luster in the darkened aspect of the world, but to Jefferson they burned with a pure and holy flame. Of man's ultimate victory he had no doubts; and he died steadfast in the conviction that the future must inevitably be good.

His instructions were religiously followed, and the blank date was eventually filled in. But the precautions which Jefferson took against vandalism proved unavailing. The valueless stone was overthrown and broken; and today a careful copy rears its pointed head in the tiny graveyard—the shrine and goal of thousands of visitors from every point of the inhabited globe.

With his house thus set in order against eternity, with his body racked with impending dissolution, Jefferson nevertheless kept up his activities almost to the final day.

A political legislature refused by an overwhelming vote any further funds for the University. The day he heard the news, Jefferson mounted horse, rode down the mountain to the campus and ordered all work to cease except on the "circular room for the books, and the anatomical theater." [46]

Two months later, however, the work was still continuing, though at a very slow pace. By this time—it was May 20th—Jefferson was no longer able to make the long trip down into the valley, and he sent notes instead of "strong urgency." The great Dome was leaking, the wells had failed, and the faculty demanded gas light instead of oil lamps. "A stimulus must be applied, and very earnestly applied," he exhorted General Cocke, one of his fellow members on the Board of Visitors, "or consultations and orders are nugatory. Come then, dear Sir, to our aid as soon as possible." [47]

His mind was still alert, but his physical powers were fast failing. Yet he persisted, against all the expostulations of his family, in riding almost to the very end. He would be lifted upon the back of his favorite steed, Old Eagle, aged like his master, and would ride alone about the grounds.[48]

Almost to the end, too, requests still were made on him to exercise his supposed influence with the national government to obtain office for the applicants. He turned them down with bitter explanation: "I had worn out the knees of my pantaloons in the humiliating posture of an eternal suppliant at the feet of the govmt begging favors for others. I became tired of it, and thought I ought at length to pay some respect to my own character and to rise from the ground. Since that time I have sollicited for nobody nor answered any letters requesting me to resume that painful attitude." [49]

By June, he could barely hobble, though he continued to ride. On June 12th, he watched a "shew of horsemanship." On June 13th, he purchased a book. And, on June 21st, he wrote his last memorandum in the final account book: "Isaacs for cheese 4.84." [50] From that day on, he wrote no more.

Life was ebbing now. In far-off Braintree, another life was coming to a close—John Adams. It was a grim and tragic race for these two old warriors of an earlier and fabulous era. June waned and July brought its blazon of summer flowers and heat.

On the Fourth of July, 1826, while jubilant bells tolled the tidings of that earlier Fourth when the Declaration of Independence was announced to the world, John Adams quietly passed away. His last words were: "Thomas Jefferson still survives!" [51]

He was wrong. At ten minutes before ten in the morning, on that same Fourth of July, at Monticello, the author of the Declaration had already departed. He went peacefully, and in the presence only of Alexander Garrett and Colonel Carr. Throughout the nation, there were holiday rejoicings over the sign manual of the independence it had achieved; but the two men who had done so much to bring it about lay dead. As the news slowly percolated through towns, hamlets and countryside, the nation turned to mourning and grief, knowing that a great era had at last come to an end.

In Monticello, Garrett and Carr unskillfully laid the mortal remains of Jefferson out in a shroud, and performed the last sad offices. Martha, the sole remaining daughter, shed no tears, though it would have been better for her had she been able to find release. Family, friends and slaves moved in an atmosphere of hush and silence.

Down in the valley, at the University that was his visible monument, the students held a meeting in the Rotunda he had builded to testify to their great loss. Most of the young men had known him personally, and had partaken of his generous hospitality up the mountain. "I never saw young men so deeply affected by any circumstance in my life," wrote an observer.[52]

Late in the afternoon of the following day, to the accompaniment of scattered rain, the body was laid in its burial plot with a brief service by the Episcopalian clergyman of the parish. Aged eighty-three, after one of the most extraordinary lives in history, Thomas Jefferson had departed from the mortal stage and assumed his place among the immortals.

Notes, Chapters 39-73

CHAPTER 39

[1] Horatio Gates to Jefferson, Jan. 5, 1794; Gates Papers, N. Y. H. S.
[2] *Literary Diary of Ezra Stiles*, May 21, 1794, III, 524.
[3] Weather Bk., Jan. 22, Mar. 11, 17, Apr. 2, 1794; LC.
[4] Jefferson to Gates, Feb. 3, 1794; Gates Papers, N. Y. H. S.
[5] Jefferson to Edmund Randolph, Feb. 3, 1794; *Works*, Ford, VIII, 137-9.
[6] Land roll of slaves, Nov., 1794; Farm Bk., Mass. H. S. Randall, *Jefferson*, II, 237-8.
[7] Farm Bk., 1794; Mass. H. S.
[8] *Garden Book*, 208-9.
[9] Jefferson to John Taylor, May 1, 1794; *Works*, Ford, VIII, 145-6.
[10] "Plan for Garden"; Dreer Coll., Pa. H. S.
[11] Farm Bk., Mass. H. S.
[12] Jefferson to Madison, Feb. 15, 1794; Madison Papers, LC., v. 17, p. 20. This section is omitted from printed version in *Works*, Ford, VIII, 139.
[13] Acct. Bk., Nov. 18, 1794; N. Y. Pub. Lib.
[14] Jefferson to Adams, Apr. 25, 1794; *Works*, Ford, VIII, 144-5.
[15] "Diary for 1795"; Farm Bk., Mass. H. S. Jefferson to Edmund Randolph, Sept. 7, 1794; *Works*, Ford, VIII, 152-3.
[16] Jefferson to John Taylor, Dec. 29, 1794; *Writings*, Mont., XVIII, 197.
[17] "Report on Commerce" [Dec. 16, 1793]; *Works*, Ford, VIII, 98-117.
[18] Richard Peters to Jefferson, Mar. 13, 1794; Jefferson Project, Princeton Univ.
[19] Jefferson to Madison, Apr. 3, 1794; *Works*, Ford, VIII, 141-3.
[20] Jefferson to Monroe, Apr. 24, 1794; *ibid*, VIII, 143-4. Madison had written the details in a letter to Jefferson dated Apr. 14, 1794; Madison Papers, LC., v. 17, p. 51.
[21] Adams to Jefferson, May 11, 1794; Jefferson Papers, LC., v. 97, p. 16633.
[22] Jefferson to Tench Coxe, May 1, 1794; *Works*, Ford, VIII, 147-8.
[23] Jefferson to Madison, May 15, 1794; *ibid*, VIII, 150-2.
[24] Jefferson to Madison, Oct. 30, 1794; Madison Papers, LC., v. 17, p. 89.
[25] *Gazette of the U. S.*, Aug. 7, Sept. 6, 1794.
[26] Jefferson to Giles, Dec. 17, 1794; *Works*, Ford, VIII, 155.
[27] Jefferson to Madison, Dec. 28, 1794; *ibid*, VIII, 156-9.
[28] Washington to Henry Lee, Aug. 26, 1794; Washington, *Writings*, XXXIII, 479.
[29] Edmund Randolph to Jefferson, Aug. 26, 1794; Jefferson Papers, LC., v. 97, pp. 16675-6.
[30] Jefferson to Edmund Randolph, Sept. 7, 1794; *Works*, Ford, VIII, 152-3.
[31] Jefferson to Henry Remsen, Oct. 30, 1794; Franklin Papers, Yale Univ. (copy).
[32] Jefferson to Wythe, Oct. 24, 1794; Jefferson Papers, LC., v. 98, p. 16749.
[33] Farm Bk., 1795; Mass. H. S. Jefferson to Martha J. Randolph, Jan. 22, 1795; Jefferson Papers, Morgan Lib.
[34] Jefferson to James Brown, Apr. 18, 1795; *Works*, Ford, VIII, 166-7. To same, May 7, 1795; Jefferson MSS., Va. H. S.
[35] Jefferson to M. de Meusnieur, Apr. 29, 1795; *Works*, Ford, VIII, 173-6.
[36] Jefferson to Henry Knox, June 1, 1795; Jefferson Papers, LC., v. 98, pp. 16868-9. See also to Wythe, Apr. 18, 1795; *ibid*, v. 98, p. 16840.
[37] Jefferson to Maria Cosway, Sept. 8, 1795; to Mme. de Tessé, Sept. 6, 1795; both in Jefferson Papers, LC.
[38] Rochefoucauld-Liancourt, *Travels through the U. S.* (London, 1799), 69 ff.
[39] Jefferson to Madison, Feb. 23, 1795; Madison Papers, LC., v. 18, p. 28. Madison to Jefferson, Mar. 23, 1795; *ibid*, v. 18, p. 35.
[40] Washington to Jefferson, Mar. 15, 1795; Washington, *Writings*, XXXIV, 146-9.
[41] "Notes on Professor Ebeling's letter of July 30, 1795" (undated, but Ebeling's letter

is marked received, Oct. 15, 1795); Jefferson Papers, LC., v. 98, pp. 16893-5. Ebeling's request is in *ibid*, v. 98, pp. 16898-901.

[42] Adams to Abigail Adams, Feb. 8, 1796; Adams, *Letters to his Wife*, II, 195.

[43] Hammond to Grenville, Aug. 3, 1794; Hammond Corresp., N. Y. Pub. Lib.

[44] "Notes on Jay's Treaty"; Jefferson Papers, LC., v. 98, pp. 16750-9. For Jefferson's views on the Treaty, see his letters to Monroe, Sept. 6, 1795 (*Works*, Ford. VIII, 186-9) and to Mazzei, Sept. 8, 1795 (Jefferson Project, Princeton Univ.).

[45] Jefferson to Madison, Sept. 21, 1795; *Works*, Ford, VIII, 191-3. Jefferson thought that the pamphleteer "Curtius" was Hamilton in another disguise. Actually it was Noah Webster.

[46] Jefferson to Giles, Dec. 31, 1795; Jefferson Papers, Morgan Lib. Printed with some minor errors in *Works*, Ford, VIII, 201-4.

[47] *Ibid.*

[48] Jefferson to Edward Rutledge, Nov. 30, 1795; Rutledge Papers, Pa. H. S. See also to Mazzei, *supra;* to Tench Coxe, Sept. 10, 1795; *Works*, Ford, VIII, 189-90.

CHAPTER 40

[1] Farm Bk., Apr. 26, 1796; Mass. H. S.

[2] Jefferson to T. M. Randolph, Jan. 18, 1796; Jefferson Papers, LC., v. 99, p. 17028.

[3] Jefferson to Archibald Stuart, Jan. 3, 1796; *Works*, Ford, VIII, 212-14.

[4] Jefferson to Wythe, Jan. 16, 1796; *ibid*, VIII, 214-18.

[5] *Transactions of the Amer. Philos. Soc.*, v. 4, no. 30, pp. 246-60.

[6] Jefferson to Archibald Stuart, May 26, 1796; *Va. Mag.*, VIII, 122.

[7] Jefferson to Benjamin Hawkins, Mar. 22, 1796; Jefferson Papers, LC., v. 100, pp. 17093-4. To Volney, Apr. 10, 1796; *ibid*, v. 100, p. 17120. To T. M. Randolph, *ibid*, v. 100, p. 17121. To Martha J. Randolph, Feb. 14, 1796; Jefferson Papers, Morgan Lib.

[8] Jefferson to Hawkins, *supra*. For an extended study of Jefferson's plans see F. Kimball, *Jefferson—Architect*, *passim.*

[9] Jefferson to Giles, Mar. 19, 1796; Randall, *Jefferson*, II, 302. To T. M. Randolph, Nov. 28, 1796; Jefferson Papers, Mass. H. S. To Martha J. Randolph, Mar. 27, 1797; Jefferson Papers, Morgan Lib.

[10] Jefferson to Maria J. Eppes, Mar. 8, 1799; S. N. Randolph, *Domestic Life*, 257.

[11] Jefferson to Monroe, Mar. 21, 1796; *Works*, Ford, VIII, 229-30.

[12] Jefferson to Madison, Mar. 27, 1796; *ibid*, VIII, 230-2.

[13] Jefferson to Mazzei, Apr. 24, 1796; Jefferson Papers, LC., v. 100, pp. 17129-31. Printed in *Works*, Ford, VIII, 235-41, with changes in punctuation. See also *Wm. & Mary Quart.*, 2nd ser., XXII, 28-9.

[14] *Works*, Ford, VIII, 238-40 n.

[15] Jefferson to Washington, June 19, 1796; *ibid*, VIII, 245-9.

[16] Washington to Jefferson, July 6, 1796; Washington, *Writings*, XXXV, 118-22.

[17] Jefferson to Madison, Aug. 3, 1797; *Works*, Ford, VIII, 331-4.

[18] Madison to Jefferson, Aug. 5, 1797; Madison Papers, LC., v. 20, p. 58.

[19] Washington to John Langhorne, Sept. 25, 1797; John Nicholas to Washington, Oct. 15, Dec. 9, 1797, enclosing a copy of note from Peter Carr to John Scott; Washington, *Writings*, XXXVI, 52-3.

[20] Washington to John Nicholas, Mar. 8, 1798; *ibid*, XXXVI, 182-3.

[21] Jefferson to Monroe, June 12, 1796; *Works*, Ford, VIII, 243-5.

[22] Madison to Jefferson, May 22, 1796; Madison Papers, LC., v. 19, p. 68.

[23] Beckley to Madison, June 20, 1796; Madison Papers, N. Y. Pub. Lib.

[24] Jefferson to Jonathan Williams, July 3, 1796; *Works*, Ford, VIII, 249-51.

[25] Beckley to Monroe, Oct. 17, 1796; Monroe Papers, N. Y. Pub. Lib.

[26] Jefferson to T. M. Randolph, Nov. 28, 1796; Jefferson Papers, LC., v. 95, p. 16280.

[27] "Deed of Trust," Nov. 21, 1796; *ibid*, v. 101, pp. 17247, 17250.

[28] Madison to Jefferson, Dec. 5, 1796; Madison Papers, LC., v. 19, p. 104.

[29] Madison to Jefferson, Dec. 10, 1796; *ibid*, v. 19, p. 106.

[30] Madison to Jefferson, Dec. 25, 1796; *ibid*, v. 19, p. 112.

[31] Jefferson to Madison, Dec. 17, 1796; *Works*, Ford, VIII, 254-6.

[32] Jefferson to Edward Rutledge, Dec. 27, 1796; *ibid*, VIII, 256-9.

[33] *Philadelphia General Advertiser (Aurora)*, Dec. 2, 1796.

[34] *Ibid*, Dec. 12, 1796.

[35] *Ibid.* See *N. Y. Times*, July 19, 1948.

[36] Jefferson to T. M. Randolph, Jan. 9, 1797; Jefferson Papers, LC., v. 101, pp. 17286-7. "Summary of his public services" [Sept. 1800?]; *ibid*, v. 219, p. 39161. Since neither of these important documents has been published in full (Ford printed part of the "Summary" and omitted the postscript), it might be well to quote from the latter. The subject of the contested election had been revived in a campaign biography of Jefferson which appeared in Pleasant's newspaper of Sept. 2, 1800. "The writer," Jefferson commented, "speaks of one false return & the suppression of another preventing my being declared President. I know not on what this is founded. The return of 2. electors on the republican ticket of Pensvã was delayed artfully so that two from the Federal ticket, who were *in truth* not elected at all, gave their votes: one of these however voted for me, so that I lost but one vote by that maneuvre. This made an apparent difference of 2. viz. 68 & 71, when the real vote was 69. & 70. so that mr Adams was duly elected by a majority of a single voice."

[37] Madison to Jefferson, Jan. 8, 1797; Madison Papers, LC., v. 20, p. 4.

[38] Madison to Jefferson, Dec. 19, 1796; Madison, *Writings*, VI, 296-302.

[39] Jefferson to Adams, Dec. 28, 1796; *Works*, Ford, VIII, 259-61 (original in Emmet Coll., N. Y. Pub. Lib.).

[40] Jefferson to Madison, Jan. 1, 1797; *ibid*, VIII, 262-4.

[41] Madison to Jefferson, Jan. 15, 1797; Madison Papers, LC., v. 20, p. 9. Madison kept Jefferson's letter, and permitted Nicholas P. Trist to make a copy of it in 1827.

[42] Jefferson to Madison, Jan. 30, 1797; *Works*, Ford, VIII, 279-80.

[43] Adams to Dalton, Jan. 19, 1797; Emmet Coll., N. Y. Pub. Lib.

[44] Jefferson to Madison, Jan. 22, 1797; *Works*, Ford, VIII, 271-4.

[45] Jefferson to Madison, Jan. 16, 1797; *ibid*, VIII, 269. To Henry Tazewell, Jan. 16, 1797; *ibid*, VIII, 270-1. To Madison, Jan. 30, 1797; Madison Papers, LC., v. 20, p. 22.

CHAPTER 41

[1] "The Answer" and "The Warning"; Hamilton, *Works*, VI, 215-29, 229-59.

[2] Jefferson to Madison, Jan. 22, 1797; *Works*, Ford, VIII, 273.

[3] Jefferson to Madison, Jan. 8, 1797; *ibid*, VIII, 268-9.

[4] Jefferson to Archibald Stuart, Jan. 4, 1797; *ibid*, VIII, 265-6.

[5] Jefferson to Madison, Jan. 22, 1797; *supra.* To T. M. Randolph, Jan. 22, 1797; Jefferson Papers, LC., v. 101, p. 17292.

[6] Anas, *Works*, Ford, I, 334-6. For Adams's version of the incident, see his letter to Elbridge Gerry, Apr. 6, 1797; Adams, *Works*, VIII, 538-40.

[7] Hamilton to King, Feb. 15, 1797; C. R. King, *Rufus King*, II, 148.

[8] Hamilton to McHenry, Mar. 22, 1797; Hamilton, *Works*, X, 241-3.

[9] Acct. Bk., Mar. 3, 10, June 10, 1797; N. Y. Pub. Lib.

[10] Anas, 1797-1800; *Works*, Ford, I, *passim.*

[11] Jefferson to T. M. Randolph, Mar. 23, 1797; Jefferson Papers, LC., v. 101, p. 17328.

[12] Jefferson to John Brown, Apr. 5, 1797; *ibid*, v. 101, p. 17350.

[13] Jefferson to Volney, Jan. 8, 1797; *Writings*, Mont., IX, 363-4.

[14] Jefferson to Giroud, May 22, 1797; *ibid*, IX, 387-8.

[15] Rush to Jefferson, Feb. 4, 1797; Jefferson Papers, LC., v. 101, pp. 17309-10.

[16] Jefferson to Volney, Apr. 9, 1797; *ibid*, v. 101, pp. 17356-7.

[17] Jefferson to Peregrine Fitzhugh, Apr. 9, 1797; *Writings*, Mont., IX, 380.

[18] Jefferson to Volney, Apr. 9, 1797; *supra.*

[19] J. Q. Adams to Abigail Adams, July 29, 1797; J. Q. Adams, *Writings*, II, 194.

[20] Wm. Sullivan, *Familiar Letters on Public Characters*, 148.

[21] Jefferson to T. M. Randolph, May 19, 1797; Jefferson Papers, LC., v. 101, p. 17384.

[22] May 16, 1797; Richardson, *Messages of the Presidents*, I, 233-9.

[23] Jefferson to T. M. Randolph, May 19, 1797; *supra.* To same, May 26, 1797; Jefferson Papers, LC., v. 101, p. 17399.

[24] Jefferson to T. M. Randolph, June 1, 1797; *ibid*, v. 101, p. 17412.

[25] Wythe to Jefferson, Feb. 1, 1797; *ibid*, v. 101, p. 17307.

[26] Jefferson to Madison, May 18, 1797; *Works*, Ford, VIII, 288-91.

[27] Jefferson to Martha J. Randolph, May 18, 1797; Jefferson MSS., Morgan Lib.

[28] Jefferson to Thomas Pinckney, May 29, 1797; *Works*, Ford, VIII, 291-4.

[29] Jefferson to Peregrine Fitzhugh, June 4, 1797; *ibid*, VIII, 300.

[30] Jefferson to Elbridge Gerry, June 21, 1797; Franklin Papers, Yale Univ. Printed in *Works*, Ford, VIII, 313-15.

[31] Jefferson to Edward Rutledge, June 24, 1797; *Works*, Ford, VIII, 316-19.

[32] Jefferson to Madison, June 15, 1797; *ibid*, VIII, 306-8.

[33] Jefferson to Burr, June 17, 1797; *ibid*, VIII, 309-13.

[34] Jefferson to Martha J. Randolph, June 8, 1797; Jefferson MSS., Morgan Lib.

[35] Monroe to Jefferson [Oct., 1797]; Monroe, *Writings*, III, 86-7.

[36] Madison to Jefferson, Jan. 21, 1798; Madison Papers, LC., v. 20, p. 79.

[37] Acct. Bk., June 19, 1797; N. Y. Pub. Lib.

[38] Jefferson to John Taylor, Oct. 8, 1797; *Writings*, Mont., XVIII, 202-3.

[39] Acct. Bk., Dec. 14, 23, 1797; Jan. 8, Mar. 23, May 23, 29, June 25, 1798; Sept. 6, 1799; Oct. 22, 1800; N. Y. Pub. Lib. Callender to Jefferson, Sept. 28, 1797; Jefferson Papers, LC., v. 102, p. 17492.

[40] Callender to Jefferson, Mar. 21, 1798; Ford, *Jefferson and Callender*, 9.

[41] "Petition to Va. House of Delegates" [Aug., 1797]; *Works*, Ford, VIII, 322-31.

[42] Jefferson to John Taylor, Dec. 23, 1797; *ibid*, VIII, 348-9.

[43] Jefferson to Monroe, Dec. 27, 1797; *ibid*, VIII, 349-52.

[44] Jefferson to Martha J. Randolph, Dec. 27, 1797; Jefferson MSS., Morgan Lib.

CHAPTER 42

[1] Jefferson to T. M. Randolph, Jan. 11, 1798; Jefferson Papers, LC., v. 102, p. 17554.

[2] Jefferson to Madison, Feb. 15, 1798; *Works*, Ford, VIII, 368-70.

[3] Monroe to Jefferson, Feb. 19, 1798; Monroe, *Writings*, III, 103 (abbreviations written out).

[4] Jefferson to Peregrine Fitzhugh, Feb. 23, 1798; *Works*, Ford, VIII, 377. See also to Hugh Williamson, Feb. 11, 1798; *ibid*, VIII, 367-8: "I sincerely wish that the whole Union may accommodate their interests to each other, & play into their hands mutually as members of the same family, that the wealth & strength of any one part should be viewed as the wealth & strength of the whole."

[5] Quoted in Phila. *Aurora*, Feb. 2, 1798.

[6] Phila. *Aurora*, Aug. 3, 1798.

[7] *Ibid*, Mar. 12, Mar. 17, Aug. 3, 1798.

[8] Jefferson to Monroe, Mar. 8, 1798; *Works*, Ford, VIII, 381. To Madison, Mar. 15, 1798; *ibid*, VIII, 383-4.

[9] Jefferson to Madison, Mar. 21, 1798; *ibid*, VIII, 386-8. To T. M. Randolph, Mar. 22, 1798; *Wm. & Mary Quart.*, ser. 2, v. 6, pp. 335-6.

[10] Jefferson to Madison, Mar. 29, 1798; *Works*, Ford, VIII, 391-4.

[11] Jefferson to Edmund Pendleton, Apr. 2, 1798; *ibid*, VIII, 394-7.

[12] Jefferson to Madison, Apr. 5, 1798; *ibid*, VIII, 397-9.

[13] Jefferson to Madison, Apr. 6, 1798; *ibid*, 401-3. To John Wayles Eppes, Apr. 11, 1798; Jefferson MSS., U. of Va.

[14] Jefferson to Madison, Apr. 26, 1798; *Works*, Ford, VIII, 411-13.

[15] Madison to Jefferson, Apr. 29, 1798; Madison Papers, LC., v. 20, p. 108.

[16] Jefferson to Madison, May 10, 17, 1798; *Works*, Ford, VIII, 417-19, 420.

[17] Jefferson to St. George Tucker, May 9, 1798; photostat, Tucker-Coleman Coll., Colonial Williamsburg Archives. To J. W. Eppes, May 6, 1798; Jeff MSS., U. of Va. It is interesting to note that whereas Jefferson had formerly addressed Tucker as "Citizen" (Sept. 15, 1795), he now cautiously superscribed him as "Dear Sir."

[18] Jefferson to T. M. Randolph, May 3, 1798; Jefferson Papers, LC., v. 103, p. 17748.

[19] Jefferson to Madison, May 24, June 14, 1798; Rives Papers, LC.

[20] The best account of Dr. Logan's voyage is in his own *Memoirs*, edited by D. N. Logan. Jefferson's certificate was dated June 4, 1798; pp. 54-6.

[21] Quoted in Logan, *Memoirs*, 59-60 n.

[22] Logan to Deborah Logan, Sept. 9, 1798; *ibid*, 79-80.

[23] *Ibid*, 85, 86 n. Logan's wife, Deborah, insists that Jefferson used to visit her secretly

during her husband's absence abroad, to comfort her over the abuse heaped on him, and that he came by a circuitous route to throw off the Federalist spies who, he claimed, constantly dogged his footsteps, *ibid*, 75.

[24] Jefferson to Martha J. Randolph, May 31, 1798; Jefferson MSS., Morgan Lib.

[25] Jefferson to John Taylor, June 1, 1798; *Works*, Ford, VIII, 430-3.

[26] Jefferson Papers, LC., cited in Beveridge, *John Marshall*, II, 346-7.

[27] *Green Bag*, VIII, 482-3.

[28] Jefferson to Madison, June 7, 21, 1798; *Works*, Ford, VIII, 433-6, 439-43.

[29] Henry Tazewell to Jefferson, July 5, 1798; Jefferson Papers, LC., v. 104, pp. 17823-4.

[30] Jefferson to Samuel Smith, Aug. 22, 1798; *Works*, Ford, VIII, 443-7. The original is in private hands, of which a photostat has been made for the Jefferson Project, at Princeton. Another copy is in the Amer. Philos. Soc., while an imperfect letterpress is in the Jefferson Papers, LC., v. 104, pp. 17844-6.

[31] Draft MS. of Jefferson to Samuel Smith, *supra;* Jefferson Papers, LC., v. 104, p. 17917. The sentence quoted does not appear in any of the other copies.

[32] John Brown to Jefferson, Sept. 15, 1798; Jefferson Papers, LC., v. 104, pp. 17867-9.

[33] "The Enforcement of the Alien and Sedition Laws," by Frank M. Anderson, in *Amer. Hist. Assoc. Reports* (1912), pp. 115-26, is a careful study of the prosecutions under the Acts.

[34] Callender to Jefferson, Sept. 22, 1798; W. C. Ford, *Jefferson and Callender*, 10.

[35] Jefferson to George Mason, Oct. 11, 1798; *ibid*, 10-11 n. Callender to Jefferson, Nov. 19, 1798; *ibid*, 12-15.

CHAPTER 43

[1] It was not until Dec. 11, 1821, that Jefferson, rather reluctantly, acknowledged his authorship of the Kentucky Resolutions (to J. C. Breckinridge; *Works*, Ford, VIII, 459-60 n.). By this time, however, his memory was not altogether accurate, and he reconstructed certain episodes that later investigations have modified considerably. In 1887, two new accounts appeared, which cleared up some of the points at issue, but managed in the process to create new difficulties ("The Kentucky Resolutions in a New Light" by S. N. Randolph in *The Nation*, v. 44, pp. 382-4; and *The Kentucky Resolutions of 1798*, by E. D. Warfield). The latest and best account has been given by Adrienne Koch and Harry Ammon, "The Virginia and Kentucky Resolutions" in *Wm. & Mary Quart.*, 3rd ser., v. 5, pp. 145-75.

[2] Koch and Ammon, *supra*, feel that Madison *did* have knowledge of the Resolutions during the period of genesis and writing; but the evidence does not seem to support this belief. On Oct. 5, 1798, Jefferson asked W. C. Nicholas to consult with Madison on the Resolutions, without anything to indicate that Madison was already aware of their contents (Jefferson Papers, LC., v. 104, p. 17877) and it does not appear that Nicholas did so. The first *attested* meeting between Jefferson and Madison since the Spring of 1798 was only a few days before Oct. 26th (Jefferson to Madison, Oct. 26, 1798; *Works*, Ford, VIII, 456), at which, though it is certain the two men discussed the problem, Madison still had no copy of the Resolutions. Jefferson did not actually place them in Madison's hands until Nov. 17th (Jefferson to Madison, Nov. 17, 1798; *Works*, Ford, VIII, 456-7).

[3] The text of Jefferson's rough draft and fair copy of the Kentucky Resolutions are arranged in parallel columns in *Works*, Ford, VIII, 458-79.

[4] W. C. Nicholas to Jefferson, Oct. 4, 1798; Jefferson Papers, LC., v. 104, p. 17877.

[5] Jefferson to W. C. Nicholas, Oct. 5, 1798; *ibid*, v. 104, p. 17878. Jefferson had failed to make a copy at the time of writing; but wrote it down from memory immediately after the original was dispatched.

[6] W. C. Nicholas to John Breckinridge, Oct. 10, 1798; Breckinridge Papers, LC.

[7] "Draft Petition," Dec. 24, 1798; Jefferson Papers, LC., v. 232, pp. 42018-9.

[8] Jefferson to Madison, Oct. 26, 1798; *Works*, Ford, VIII, 456.

[9] "A Bill for the relief of sufferers" [1798]; Jefferson Papers, LC., v. 232, p. 42035.

[10] Jefferson to S. T. Mason, Oct. 11, 1798; *Works*, Ford, VIII, 449-51.

[11] *The Palladium*, Frankfort, Ky., Nov. 13, 1798.

[12] *Ky. Resolutions*, Nov. 10, 1798; *Works*, Ford, VIII, facsimile insert, 458-9.

[13] Quoted in E. D. Warfield, *The Kentucky Resolutions of 1798*, 94.

[14] Breckinridge to Henry Tazewell, Dec. 2, 1798; Breckinridge Papers, LC.

[15] Jefferson to Madison, Nov. 17, 1798; *Works,* Ford, VIII, 456-7. Original in Rives Papers, LC., where the year was mistakenly written as 1799.

[16] Such, at least, is indicated by two letters from Jefferson to Madison. On Oct. 26, 1798, Jefferson sent him his Jury bill and promised to send a copy "of the other paper" by his foreman, Richardson (see notes 7 and 8, *supra*). Evidently this document was too important to send by mail. But Richardson was detained at Monticello by press of work and did not go (to Madison, Nov. 17, 1798, *supra*).

[17] *Va. Report of 1799-1800*, 22-3.

[18] Jefferson to W. C. Nicholas, Nov. 29, 1798; *Works,* Ford, VIII, 483.

[19] Madison to Jefferson, Dec. 29, 1798; Madison Papers, LC.

[20] Jefferson to John Taylor, Nov. 26, 1798; *Works,* Ford, VIII, 479-83.

[21] Quoted in Warfield, *Ky. Resolutions of 1798,* 111-12.

[22] Burr to Jefferson, Feb. 3, 1799; Jefferson Papers, LC., v. 105, p. 17953.

CHAPTER 44

[1] Jefferson to T. M. Randolph, Dec. 4, 1798; Jefferson Papers, LC., v. 104, p. 17900.

[2] Jefferson to Martha J. Randolph, Dec. 27, 1798; Jefferson MSS., Morgan Lib.

[3] Phila. *Aurora*, Jan. 2, 1799.

[4] Jefferson to Madison, Jan. 3, 1799; *Works,* Ford, IX, 3-5.

[5] Jefferson to Madison, Jan. 16, 1799; *ibid*, IX, 6-9.

[6] Jefferson to Gerry, Jan. 26, 1799; *ibid*, IX, 15-26.

[7] Jefferson to Pendleton, Jan. 29, 1799; *ibid*, IX, 27-9. Original in Washburn Papers, Mass. H. S. He repeated his request, with a sense of urgency, in another letter, dated Feb. 14, 1799; *ibid*, IX, 45-50; the original also in Washburn Papers.

[8] Jefferson to Pendleton, Feb. 14, 1799; *supra.*

[9] Jefferson to Madison, Feb. 5, 1799; *Works,* Ford, IX, 34.

[10] Jefferson to Madison, Feb. 12, 1799; *ibid*, IX, 39-40.

[11] Jefferson to Monroe, Feb. 19, 1799; *ibid*, IX, 55-7. Phila. *Aurora*, Feb. 20, 1799.

[12] Jefferson to Madison, Feb. 26, 1799; *Works,* Ford, IX, 59-61.

[13] Jefferson to Thomas Lomax, Mar. 12, 1799; *ibid*, IX, 62-4.

[14] Jefferson to Edmund Pendleton, Apr. 22, 1799; *ibid*, IX, 64-6. Original in Washburn Papers, Mass. H. S.

[15] Jefferson to Tench Coxe, May 21, 1799; *Works,* Ford, IX, 68-70.

[16] Jefferson to Wm. Green Mumford, June 18, 1799; Teachers College Lib., Columbia Univ. Photostat in Jefferson Project, Princeton.

[17] Jefferson to Henry Remsen, rec. May 17, 1799; Franklin Papers, Yale Univ.

[18] Jefferson to Remsen, Oct. 14, 1799; Mar. 4, 1800; *ibid.*

[19] Jefferson to Tench Coxe, May 21, 1799; *supra.*

[20] W. C. Nicholas to Jefferson, Aug. 20, 1799; Nicholas P. Trist Papers, LC.

[21] Jefferson to Madison, Aug. 23, 1799; Rives Papers, LC. A much garbled version, with the most important sections omitted, transcribed from the nearly illegible press copy in the Jefferson Papers, LC., is in *Works,* Ford, IX, 77-8. The full text, with comment, has been published by Koch and Ammon, in *Wm. & Mary Quart., op. cit.*

[22] Madison to Nicholas P. Trist, Dec. 23, 1832; Madison Papers, LC., v. 87, p. 16.

[23] On a copy of the letter described in Note 21, which Madison later made for Nicholas P. Trist, and now in the U. of Va., he penned the comment: "The visit invited took the place of an answer to the letter." Jefferson had written to W. C. Nicholas to come; Aug. 26, 1799, *Works,* Ford, IX, 78-9.

[24] Jefferson to W. C. Nicholas, Sept. 5, 1799; *Works,* Ford, IX, 79-81.

[25] Breckinridge to Jefferson, Dec. 13, 1799; Jefferson Papers, LC., v. 105, pp. 18094-5.

[26] Warfield, *Kentucky Resolutions of 1798,* 123-6.

[27] See Chap. 43, note 13.

[28] "Draft Resolutions"; Breckinridge Papers, LC., v. 18, pp. 3011-16. Koch and Ammon, *op. cit.*, p. 169, do not believe Breckinridge drafted the second set.

[29] Monroe to Madison, Nov. 22, 1799; Monroe, *Writings*, III, 159-60. Jefferson to Madison, Nov. 22, 1799; *Works,* Ford, IX, 89-90.

[30] Jefferson to Madison, Nov. 26, 1799; Rives Papers, LC.

[31] Jefferson to John Taylor, Nov. 26, 1799; *Mass. H. S. Colls.*, Seventh Ser., I, 66-8. Along similar lines to Madison, Nov. 22, 1799; *Works*, Ford, IX, 89-90.

[32] "Report of 1800," Madison, *Writings* (Cong. ed.), IV, 540 ff.

[33] Jefferson to Monroe, Feb. 6, 1800; *Works*, Ford, IX, 113. To same, Mar. 26, 1800; Jefferson Papers, LC., v. 106, pp. 18230-1.

[34] Jefferson to Philip N. Nicholas, Apr. 7, 1800; *Works*, Ford, IX, 127-9.

CHAPTER 45

[1] Jefferson to Monroe, Jan. 12, 1800; *Works*, Ford, IX, 90-2.

[2] Jefferson to Priestley, Jan. 8, 27, 1800; *ibid*, IX, 95-9, 102-5.

[3] Priestley to Jefferson, May 8, 1800; Chinard, *Correspondence of Jefferson and Du Pont*, 11-12.

[4] Jefferson to Priestley, Aug. 11, 1800; Jefferson Papers, LC., v. 107, p. 18330.

[5] Dupont to Jefferson [Aug. 27, 1798]; Malone, *Correspond. between Jefferson and Du Pont*, 1-2.

[6] Jefferson to T. M. Randolph, Jan. 17, 1799; Jefferson Papers, LC., v. 104, p. 17925.

[7] Jefferson to Dupont [Jan. 17, 1800]; Malone, *op. cit.*, 3-4.

[8] Jefferson to Dupont, Apr. 12, 1800; Chinard, *op. cit.*, 11-12.

[9] Dupont to Jefferson, Apr. 21, June 15, 1800; Malone, *op. cit.*, 10-13, 16. Dupont, *National Education in the U. S.* (trans. by P. S. Du Pont, 1923).

[10] Jefferson to Wm. Dunbar, Jan. 16, 1800; Jefferson Papers, LC., v. 106, p. 18136.

[11] Jefferson to Benjamin Hawkins, Mar. 14, 1800; *Works*, Ford, IX, 123-6. He sent a similar inquiry to David Campbell of Tennessee for information as to the Cherokee dialect, Mar. 14, 1800; Jefferson Papers, LC., v. 106, p. 18216.

[12] Jefferson to Wythe, Feb. 28, 1800; *Works*, Ford, IX, 115-17.

[13] Jefferson to Wythe, Apr. 7, 1800; Jefferson Papers, LC., v. 106, p. 18239.

[14] Wythe to Jefferson, Dec. 7, 1800; *ibid*, v. 108, pp. 18459-60. Pendleton to Jefferson, June 17, 1800; *ibid*, v. 108, pp. 18470-5; replying to Jefferson's letter of Apr. 19, 1800; *ibid*, v. 107, p. 18261.

[15] Jefferson to Martha J. Randolph, Feb. 17, 1800; S. N. Randolph, *Domestic Life*, 262-3.

[16] Jefferson to Rev. Samuel Miller, Feb. 25, 1800; Sales Catalogue, Thos. F. Madigan, 1939.

[17] Jefferson to Dr. Wm. Bache, Feb. 2, 1800; Jefferson Papers, LC., v. 106, pp. 18167-8.

[18] Jefferson to John Breckinridge, Jan. 29, 1800; *Works*, Ford, IX, 105-7.

[19] Jefferson to T. M. Randolph, Feb. 2, 1800; *ibid*, IX, 110-13. To Samuel Adams, Feb. 26 [1800]; *ibid*, IX, 114-15.

[20] Jefferson to Martha J. Randolph, Jan. 21, 1800; Jefferson MSS., Morgan Lib.

[21] Jefferson to Madison, Mar. 4, 1800; *Works*, Ford, IX, 118-23.

[22] Jefferson to Monroe, Apr. 13, 1800; Monroe Papers, LC., v. 6, p. 956.

[23] Edward Livingston to Jefferson, Apr. 11, 1800; Jefferson Papers, Box 2, N. Y. Pub. Lib.

[24] Jefferson to T. M. Randolph, May 7, 1800; Jefferson Papers, LC., v. 107, p. 18277. For full details of the N. Y. election see Schachner, *Burr*, chap. XIII.

[25] Hamilton to Jay, May 7, 1800; Hamilton, *Works*, X, 371-4.

[26] Wm. Jay, *Life of John Jay*, I, 414.

[27] Hamilton to Sedgwick, May 10, 1800; Hamilton, *Works*, X, 375-6.

[28] Phila. *Aurora*, May 1, 1800.

[29] Jefferson to Monroe, Mar. 26, 1800; Monroe Papers, LC., v. 6, p. 953.

[30] Jefferson to Monroe, Apr. 13, 1800; *ibid*, v. 6, p. 956.

[31] Quoted in Phila. *Aurora*, Mar. 31, 1800.

[32] *Diary of Rev. Thomas Robbins* (I. N. Tarbox, ed.), I, 145.

[33] *The Voice of Warning*... [John M. Mason, D.D.], N. Y., 1800.

[34] *Serious Considerations on the Election of a President*... [Rev. Dr. Linn], N. Y., 1800.

[35] Quoted in the Hudson *Bee*, Sept. 7, 1802.

[36] Abraham Labagh to Jefferson, Nov. 9, 1800; Tucker-Coleman Coll., Colonial Williamsburg Arch.

[37] Jefferson to Monroe, May 26, 1800; *Works*, Ford, IX, 135-7.

[38] *Address to the People of the United States*... [John Beckley], Phila., 1800.

[39] Jefferson to Gen. Knox, Apr. 8, 1800; Knox Papers, Mass. H. S. To same effect to

Wm. Hamilton, Apr. 22, 1800; *Works*, Ford, IX, 129-31; in which he tells how former friends had crossed the street to avoid meeting him.

[40] *Autobiography of Benjamin Rush* (G. W. Corner, ed.), 151-2.

[41] Jefferson to Rush, Sept. 23, 1800; Jefferson MSS., Am. Philos. Soc. (italics added). Printed in *Works*, Ford, IX, 146-9, with some minor changes.

[42] Jefferson to T. M. Randolph, May 7, 1800; "Jefferson Papers," *Mass. Hist. Soc. Colls.*, Seventh Ser., I, 76-8.

[43] Jefferson to Short, Apr. 13, 1800; Short Papers, Wm. & Mary College.

[44] Acct. Bk., Aug. 23, 1800; N. Y. Pub. Lib.

[45] Jefferson to Madison, Aug. 29, 1800; Rives Papers, LC.

[46] Jefferson to Pierce Butler, Aug. 11, 1800; *Works*, Ford, IX, 137-8.

[47] Jefferson to Gideon Granger, Aug. 13, 1800; *ibid*, IX, 138-41.

[48] Callender to Jefferson, Aug. 14, 1800; Ford, *Jefferson and Callender*, 25.

[49] Acct. Bk., Oct. 23, 1800; N. Y. Pub. Lib.

[50] Jefferson to J. W. Eppes, Apr. 21, 1800; MS., N. Y. H. S.

[51] Monroe to Jefferson, Sept. 9, 1800; Monroe, *Writings*, III, 205.

[52] Monroe to Jefferson, Sept. 15, 1800; *ibid*, III, 208-9.

[53] Jefferson to Monroe, Sept. 20, 1800; *Works*, Ford, IX, 145-6.

[54] Jefferson to Monroe, Nov. 24, 1801; *ibid*, IX, 315-19.

[55] Jefferson to Samuel Smith, Oct. 17, 1800; privately owned; photostat in Princeton Project.

[56] Jefferson to Madison, Nov. 9, 1800; Rives Papers, LC. Similarly to Monroe, Nov. 8, 1800; *Works*, Ford, IX, 149-50.

CHAPTER 46

[1] *National Intelligencer*, Nov. 28, 1800.

[2] Margaret B. Smith, *First Forty Years of Washington Society*, 12.

[3] Gallatin to Mrs. Gallatin, Jan. 15, 1801; Adams, *Gallatin*, 252-5.

[4] *First Forty Years of Washington Society*, 5-6.

[5] Diary of John Randolph; Typed copy by Wm. Cabell Bruce, on deposit in Va. State Lib.

[6] Hamilton to James A. Bayard, Aug. 6, 1800; Hamilton, *Works* (Lodge, ed.), X, 387.

[7] George Cabot to Hamilton, Aug. 10, 1800; *ibid* (J. C. Hamilton, ed.), VI, 454.

[8] Mrs. Gallatin to Gallatin, May 7, 1800; *Adams*, Gallatin, 243: "Burr says he has no confidence in the Virginians; they once deceived him and they are not to be trusted."

[9] Burr to Jefferson, Dec. 23, 1800; Jefferson Papers, LC., v. 108, p. 18525.

[10] Dallas to Gov. McKean, Dec. 1, 1800; McKean Papers, Pa. H. S.

[11] Jefferson to Benjamin Rush, Dec. 14, 1800; MSS., Amer. Philos. Soc.

[12] Dwight Foster to Caleb Strong, Dec. 12, 1800; *Am. Hist. Rev.*, IV, 330-1, C. C. Pinckney, *Thomas Pinckney*, 156.

[13] Jefferson to T. M. Randolph, Dec. 12, 1800; *Mass. H. S. Colls., Seventh Ser.*, I, 80.

[14] Peter Freneau to Jefferson, Dec. 2, 1800; *Am. Hist. Rev.*, IV, 120.

[15] Jefferson to Madison, Dec. 19, 1800; *Works*, Ford, IX, 157-9.

[16] *Ibid.*

[17] Gouverneur Morris, *Diary* (A. C. Morris, ed.), II, 396-7. See Schachner, *Hamilton*, pp. 400-2, and *Burr*, pp. 192-6 for Hamilton's attempt to sway the Federalists against Burr and in favor of Jefferson.

[18] Jefferson to Burr, Dec. 15, 1800; *Works*, Ford, IX, 154-6.

[19] Burr to Jefferson, Dec. 23, 1800; Jefferson Papers, LC., v. 108, p. 18525.

[20] Hamilton to James A. Bayard, Dec. 27, 1800, Jan. 16, 1801; Hamilton, *Works* (J. C. Hamilton, ed.), VI, 499-500, 419-24. Troup to King, Dec. 31, 1800; King, *Correspondence*, III, 358-9.

[21] Hamilton to Oliver Wolcott, Dec. 17, 1800; Hamilton, *Works*, X, 393 ff.

[22] Burr to Samuel Smith, Dec. 16, 1800; Davis, *Burr*, II, 75.

[23] Ogden to Peter Irving, Nov. 24, 1802; N. Y. *Morning Chronicle*, Nov. 25, 1802.

[24] Samuel Smith to Burr, Jan. 11, 1800 [1801]; Samuel Smith Papers, LC. On July 9, 1804, when the matter came up again, Smith indignantly denied to John Smith that he had called Burr a "scoundrel" and declared that none of Burr's "*Correspondence, or Conversation with me would warrant the Charge made against him of having Intrigued with the Federal party*

for his Election"; *ibid.* Yet, on interrogatories in a libel suit by Burr against Cheetham, in Mar., 1805, while repeating that he knew of no such intrigues, he admitted he *did* have a conversation with Burr in Philadelphia "from which it appeared to the Deponent that the Plaintiff was determined to serve as President if the H— of Representatives should elect him"; *ibid.* At this time (1805) Smith, who had been in Jefferson's Cabinet, was confronted with a definite political situation.

[25] Joseph H. Nicholson to a Constituent, Jan. 15, 1801; MS., Pa. H. S.

[26] Monroe to Jefferson, Jan. 6, 1801; Monroe to Col. John Hoomes, Feb. 14, 1801; Monroe, *Writings,* 253-5, 258-60.

[27] Jefferson to Gov. McKean, Mar. 9, 1801; McKean Papers, Pa. H. S.

[28] Jefferson to Tench Coxe, Dec. 31, 1800; *Works,* Ford, IX, 162-3. To Craven Peyton, Jan. 15, 1801; Jefferson Papers, U. of Va. McKean to Jefferson, Jan. 10, 1801; Jefferson Papers, LC., v. 108, pp. 18606-7.

[29] Madison to Jefferson, Jan. 10, 1801; Madison, *Writings,* VI, 410-16.

[30] Gallatin's Plan, 1801; Gallatin, *Writings,* I, 18-23.

[31] H. H. Brackenridge to Jefferson, Jan. 19, 1801; Jefferson Papers, LC., v. 109, pp. 18645-9.

[32] Jefferson to R. R. Livingston, Dec. 14, 1800; *Works,* Ford, IX, 150-4.

[33] Jefferson to T. M. Randolph, Jan. 23, 1801; Jefferson Papers, LC., v. 109, p. 18668.

[34] Acct. Bk., Feb. 3, 1801; N. Y. Pub. Lib.

[35] Jefferson to Martha J. Randolph, Feb. 5, 1801; Jefferson Papers, LC., v. 109, p. 18705. To same, Jan. 16, 1801; Jefferson MSS., Morgan Lib.

[36] Adams to Elbridge Gerry, Feb. 7, 1801; Adams, *Works,* IX, 98. Jefferson was mistaken in his belief that Adams's influence was being used in his behalf; to T. M. Randolph, Jan. 23, 1801; *Writings,* Mont., XVIII, 233.

[37] Jefferson to T. M. Randolph, Jan. 29 [1801]; *Writings,* Mont., XVIII, 237. His earlier estimate, also to Randolph, Jan. 9, 1801, gave the Federalists only five sure States, and listed three—Maryland, Delaware and Vermont—as divided; Jefferson Papers, LC., v. 108, p. 18599.

[38] Robert C. Harper's *Circular Letter,* Feb. 24, 1801; *Bayard Papers* (Donnan, ed.), in *Annual Report of Amer. Hist. Assoc.,* II, 132-7.

[39] Gallatin to Mrs. Gallatin, Feb. 12, 1801; Adams, *Gallatin,* 260-1.

[40] Uriah Tracy to Mr. Gould, Feb. 16, 1801; MS., Pa. H. S.

[41] John Randolph to St. George Tucker, Feb. 11, 1801; W. C. Bruce, *Randolph,* I, 168. H. G. Otis to his wife, Feb. 11, 1801; Morrison, *Otis,* I, 207-8.

[42] Gallatin to James Nicholson, Feb. 14, 1801; Adams, *Gallatin,* 261-2.

[43] Gallatin to James Nicholson, Feb. 16, 1801; *ibid,* 262.

[44] Jefferson to Monroe, Feb. 15, 1801; *Works,* Ford, IX, 178-80.

[45] Anas, Feb. 12, 1801; *ibid,* I, 361-2.

[46] Bayard to Hamilton, Mar. 8, 1801; Hamilton, *Works* (J. C. H., ed.), VI, 522-4.

[47] "Interrogatories of James A. Bayard, *in re* Gillespie vs Smith," Apr. 3, 1806; Davis, *Burr,* II, 129-33. Even more direct evidence of Bayard's belief that Jefferson had agreed to the bargain is contained in a letter he wrote the day of the final vote to Allan McLane, the Federalist office-holder in whose behalf Smith later claimed Bayard had intervened. "Mr. Jefferson is our President. Our opposition was continued till it was demonstrated that Burr could not be brought in, and even if he could he meant to come in as a Democrat. In such case to evidence his sincerity he must have swept every officer in the U. States. I have direct information that Mr. Jefferson will not pursue that plan." The original of this letter was given in later years by McLane to T. M. Randolph for copying; and on the copy Jefferson wrote that it was authentic. The copy is in Jefferson Papers, LC., v. 109, p. 18739.

[48] "Interrogatories of Gen. Samuel Smith"; Apr. 15, 1806; Davis, *Burr,* II, 133-7.

[49] Gallatin to his wife, Feb. 17, 1801; Adams, *Gallatin,* 262.

CHAPTER 47

[1] Jefferson to John Dickinson, Mar. 6, 1801; *Works,* Ford, IX, 201-2.

[2] Marshall to Chas. C. Pinckney, Mar. 4, 1801; *Am. Hist. Rev.,* v. 53, no. 3, pp. 518-20. Beveridge, in his *Marshall,* III, 11, 18, completely distorted the sense by omitting the "not" before Marshall's classing of Jefferson with the "terrorists."

[3] Words by Rembrandt Peale and music by John I. Hawkins. "The People's Friend" was

sung at the German Reformed Church in Philadelphia on Mar. 4, 1801. The text was sent to Jefferson by Chas. W. Peale, Rembrandt's father, on Mar. 8, 1801; Jefferson Papers, LC., v. 110, pp. 18848, 18896-8.

[4] Jefferson to Madison, Oct. 26, 1800; *Works*, Ford, IX, 161-2.

[5] Actually, what Jefferson meant by the phrase, which he had coined, were those appointments made by Adams after Dec. 12th, when Jefferson conceived that the news of his own election had been confirmed; "Memorandum," May [10], 1803; Jefferson Papers, LC., v. 119, p. 20545.

[6] Jefferson to Madison, Dec. 19, 1800; *Works*, Ford, IX, 157-60.

[7] The details of the inauguration are taken largely from the *National Intelligencer*, Mar. 6, 1801; and Edward Thornton (of the British Legation) to Lord Grenville, Mar. 4, 1801; Adams' *Hist. of the U. S.*, I, 198. By this time the famous account of John Davis (*Travels*, 177) to the effect that Jefferson rode alone to the Capitol without a single guard or attendant and hitched his horse unaided to the palisades in front, has been so thoroughly exploded that it is unnecessary once again to examine it in detail.

[8] Monroe to Jefferson, Mar. 3, 1801; Monroe, *Writings*, III, 261-4.

[9] Jefferson to Horatio Gates, Mar. 8, 1801; Emmet Coll., N. Y. Pub. Lib. See also to Dickinson, Mar. 6, 1801, *supra*, in which Jefferson asserted: "I hope to see shortly a perfect consolidation, to effect which, nothing shall be spared on my part, short of the abandonment of the principles of our revolution."

[10] "Inaugural address," Mar. 4, 1801; J. D. Richardson, *Messages of the Presidents*, I, 321-4.

[11] M. B. Smith, *The First Forty Years*, 12.

[12] *Ibid*, 384-5. *National Intelligencer*, Mar. 20, 1801.

[13] Marshall to C. C. Pinckney, Mar. 4, 1801; *supra*.

[14] W. P. and J. P. Cutler, *Rev. Manasseh Cutler*, II, 43-5.

[15] George Cabot to Rufus King, Mar. 20, 1801; C. R. King, *Rufus King*, III, 407.

[16] Yrujo to Jefferson, Mar. 13, 1801; *Jefferson Correspondence*, Bixby Coll. Yrujo added some more intimate details: he had been commissioned by Jefferson to find him a good cook in Philadelphia, and had tried to lure away the cook of William Bingham, the famous gourmet, society arbiter and supposedly wealthy. The cook would have been glad to go, said Yrujo, but Bingham owed him $800 in wages, & he feared he would "loose every farthing if he was to leave him."

[17] Robert Troup to King, Aug. 8, 1801; C. R. King, *Rufus King*, III, 496.

[18] "Oration at New Haven," July 7, 1801; Pamphlet published 1801.

[19] Jefferson to Moses Robinson, Mar. 23, 1801; *Writings*, Mont., X, 236-7.

[20] Monroe to Jefferson, Mar. 18, 1801; Monroe, *Writings*, III, 268-74. (Abbreviations written out.)

[21] Jefferson to Monroe, Feb. [Mar.] 7, 1801; *Works*, Ford, IX, 202-5.

[22] Jefferson to Samuel Smith, Mar. 9, 1801; *ibid*, IX, 207-8.

[23] Jefferson to Madison, Mar. 12, 1801; *ibid*, IX, 208-10.

[24] Jefferson to Samuel Smith, Apr. 17, 1801; privately owned MS., photostat in U. of Va.

[25] Jefferson to Meriwether Lewis, Feb. 23, 1801; Jefferson Papers, LC., v. 109, p. 18776. Lewis accepted Mar. 10, 1801; *ibid*, v. 110, p. 18909.

[26] Jefferson to T. M. Randolph, Mar. 12, 1801; *ibid*, v. 110, p. 18923.

[27] Jefferson to J. W. Eppes, Mar. 27, 1801; privately owned MS., photostats in U. of Va. & in N. Y. Pub. Lib.

[28] Jefferson to Benjamin S. Barton, Feb. 14, 1801; *Works*, Ford, IX, 177-8.

[29] Adams to Jefferson, Mar. 24, 1801; Jefferson Papers, LC., v. 111, p. 19055.

[30] "Memorandum," May [10], 1803; *ibid*, v. 119, p. 20545.

[31] "Memoranda," 1801; *ibid*, v. 119, p. 20542, 20568. Anas, Mar. 8, 1801; *Works*, Ford, I, 363-4.

[32] "Memorandum," May [10], 1803; *supra*.

[33] Jefferson to —— [Mar., 1801]; Appointment Book, State Dept., Nat. Arch.

[34] Jefferson to Benjamin Rush, Mar. 24, 1801; *Works*, Ford, IX, 229-32.

CHAPTER 48

[1] Jefferson to W. C. Nicholas, June 11, 1801; *Works*, Ford, IX, 264-6.

[2] Jefferson to Levi Lincoln, Aug. 26, 1801; *ibid*, IX, 289-91.

[3] Lincoln to Jefferson, June 15, 1801; Jefferson Papers, LC., v. 113, pp. 19459-62.

[4] Jefferson to John Dickinson, July 23, 1801; to Thomas McKean, July 24, 1801; *Works*, Ford, IX, 280-2, 282-5.

[5] Jefferson to Merchants of New Haven, July 12, 1801; *ibid*, IX, 270-4.

[6] *Amer. Hist. Rev.*, III, 290.

[7] Jefferson to Maria J. Eppes, Jan. 4, 1801; *Works*, Ford, IX, 166.

[8] Monroe to [Madison], May 23, 1801; Monroe Papers, N. Y. Pub. Lib.

[9] Jefferson to George Clinton, May 17, 1801; *Works*, Ford, IX, 254-5.

[10] Burr to Gallatin, June 28, 1801; Adams, *Gallatin*, 283.

[11] Gallatin to Jefferson, Sept. 12, 1801; Gallatin, *Writings*, I, 47-8.

[12] Gallatin to Jefferson, Sept. 14, 1801; *ibid*, I, 51-3.

[13] Jefferson to Gallatin, Sept. 18, 1801; *ibid*, I, 54.

[14] Jefferson to Burr, Nov. 18, 1801; *Works*, Ford, IX, 313-14.

[15] Callender to Jefferson, Feb. 23, 1801; Jefferson Papers, LC., v. 109, pp. 18770-1.

[16] Callender to Madison, Apr. 27, 1801; W. C. Ford, *Jefferson and Callender*, 35.

[17] Anas, Mar. 9, 1801; *Works*, Ford, I, 365.

[18] Samuel Smith to Callender, Apr. 12, 1801; *Jefferson and Callender*, 33-4.

[19] Jefferson to Monroe, May 26, 1801; *Works*, Ford, IX, 259-60. Acct. Bk., May 28, 1801; N. Y. Pub. Lib.

[20] Jefferson to Monroe, May 29, 1801; *Works*, Ford, IX, 262-3.

[21] Monroe to Jefferson, June 1, 1801; *Jefferson and Callender*, 39.

[22] Jefferson to Monroe, July 15, July 17, 1802; *Works*, Ford, IX, 387-90, 390 n. Monroe to Jefferson, July 7, July 26, 1802; Misc. Letters, Dept. of State, Nat. Arch.

[23] Jefferson to R. R. Livingston, May 31, 1801; *Works*, Ford, IX, 257-8 n.

[24] Jefferson to Duane, May 23, 1801; *ibid*, 255-8. To Madison, July 19, 1801; Madison Papers, LC., v. 23, p. 21. Madison to A. J. Dallas, July 20, 1801; Jefferson Papers, LC., v. 114, p. 19661. Jefferson even drafted a message to the Senate, on the subject, but evidently decided against sending it; *Works*, Ford, IX, 257-9 n.

[25] Paine to Jefferson, Oct. 1, 1800; Paine, *Writings* (P. S. Foner, ed.), II, 1412.

[26] Jefferson to Paine, Mar. 18, 1801; *Works*, Ford, IX, 212-14.

[27] Paine to Jefferson, June 9, 1801; Paine, *Writings*, II, 1419.

[28] Jefferson to Pierpoint [Pierpont] Edwards, July 21, 1801; Dreer Coll., Pa. H. S.

[29] Jefferson to Priestley, Mar. 21, 1801; *Works*, Ford, IX, 216-19.

[30] Jefferson to St. George Tucker, June 3, 1801; Jefferson Papers, LC., v. 113, p. 19386. To T. M. Randolph, June 4, 1801; *ibid*, v. 113, p. 19390.

[31] The *Port Folio*, Oct. 2, 1802.

[32] Gallatin to Jefferson, Mar. 14, 1801; Jefferson Papers, LC., v. 110, pp. 18953-4.

[33] Jefferson to T. M. Randolph, May 14, 1801; *ibid*, v. 112, p. 19296.

[34] Jefferson to George Logan, Mar. 21, 1801; *Works*, Ford, IX, 219-20.

[35] Jefferson to T. M. Randolph, June 18, 1801; Jefferson Papers, LC., v. 113, p. 19483.

[36] Jefferson to Madison, Aug. 28, 1801; Madison Papers, LC., v. 23, p. 45.

[37] Gallatin to Jefferson, June 12, July 25, 1801; Gallatin, *Writings*, I, 27-8, 28-9.

[38] Jefferson to Gallatin, July 26, 1801; Gallatin Papers, N. Y. H. S.

[39] Gallatin to Jefferson, Aug. 10, 1801; Gallatin, *Writings*, I, 30-5.

[40] Jefferson to Gallatin, Aug. 14, 1801; Gallatin Papers, N. Y. H. S.

[41] John Taylor to W. C. Nicholas, Sept. 5, 1801; "Jefferson Papers," *Mass. H. S. Colls.*, 100-3.

CHAPTER 49

[1] Anas, *Works*, Ford, I, 365-6.

[2] Madison to Wm. Eaton, May 20, 1801; *Amer. State Papers: For. Rel.*, II, 347-8.

[3] Jefferson to W. C. Nicholas, June 11, 1801; *Works*, Ford, IX, 264-6.

[4] Madison to Chas. Pinckney, June 9, 1801; to R. R. Livingston, Sept. 28, 1801; *Amer. State Papers: For. Rel.*, II, 510.

[5] May 20-June 19, 1798; Adams, *Hist. of U. S.*, I, 356-7.

[6] Jefferson to W. C. C. Claiborne, July 13, 1801; *Works*, Ford, IX, 274-7.

[7] Jefferson to Gallatin, Sept. 18, 1801; Aug. 30, 1802; Gallatin Papers, N. Y. H. S.

[8] Rush to Jefferson, Mar. 12, 1803; Jefferson Papers, Mass. H. S.

[9] Jefferson to Gallatin, Sept. 18, 1801; *Works*, Ford, IX, 304-6.

[10] Jefferson to Gallatin, Sept. 5, 1801; Gallatin Papers, N. Y. H. S. To same effect to Robert Smith, Sept. 5, 1801; Jefferson Papers, LC., v. 116, p. 19983.
[11] Jefferson to Short, Oct. 3, 1801; *Works*, Ford, IX, 306-10.
[12] Jefferson to Robert Smith, Aug. 14, 1801; Jefferson Papers, LC., v. 115, p. 19837. To same effect to Gallatin, Aug. 14, 1801; Gallatin Papers, N. Y. H. S.
[13] Gallatin to Jefferson, Aug. 18, 1801; Jefferson Papers, LC., v. 115, pp. 19864-5.
[14] Jefferson to Gallatin, Aug. 28, 1801; Gallatin Papers, N. Y. H. S.
[15] "Memoranda on Neutral Rights," Sept. 9, 1801; Jefferson Papers, LC., v. 116, p. 19991.
[16] Jefferson to R. R. Livingston, Sept. 9, 1801; *Works*, Ford, IX, 295-302.
[17] Madison to Chas. Pinckney, June 9, 1801; *Amer. State Papers: For. Rel.*, II, 476.
[18] *Amer. State Papers: For. Rel.*, II, 440-58.
[19] Anas, Oct. 22, 1801; *Works*, Ford, I, 369.
[20] Jefferson to Martha J. Randolph, May 28, 1801; Jefferson Papers, Morgan Lib.
[21] Jefferson to Dr. Rush, Dec. 20, 1801; *Works*, Ford, IX, 346.
[22] Jefferson to T. M. Randolph, Nov. 16, 1801; Jefferson Papers, LC., v. 118, p. 20289.
[23] The correspondence is in Jefferson Papers, LC., v. 116, *passim*. See particularly, Jefferson to Waterhouse, Sept. 2, 1801; v. 116, p. 19963.
[24] Jefferson to John D. Burke, June 21, 1801; *Works*, Ford, IX, 267-8.
[25] Enoch Edwards to Jefferson, Aug. 31, 1801; Jefferson Papers, LC., v. 116, p. 19930a. Jefferson to Edwards, Oct. 11, 1801; *ibid*, v. 117, p. 20131.
[26] Acct. Bk., May-Oct. 31, 1801; N. Y. Pub. Lib. "Accts. of President's Household with John Barnes, Apr. 27-July 6, 1801"; Jefferson MSS., U. of Va.
[27] George Flower's Diary; Chicago Hist. Soc. Photostat in Princeton Project.
[28] "Circular to the Heads of the Depts.," Nov. 6, 1801; *Works*, Ford, IX, 310-12.
[29] Jefferson to Maria J. Eppes, Dec. 14, 1801; Jefferson Papers, LC., v. 118, p. 20418. To Steven T. Mason, Oct. 28, 1801; *ibid*, v. 117, p. 20191. To Peter Carr, Oct. 25, 1801; *ibid*, v. 117, p. 20178.
[30] Jefferson to Gideon Granger, Oct. 31, 1801; *ibid*, v. 117, p. 20210.
[31] Jefferson to Gov. Joseph Bloomfield, Dec. 5, 1801; Jefferson Papers, Box 1, N. Y. Pub. Lib.
[32] Gallatin to Jefferson [rec] Nov. 16, 1801; Gallatin, *Writings*, I, 69-73.
[33] Jefferson to Martha J. Randolph, Nov. 27, 1801; Jefferson Papers, Morgan Lib.
[34] Cheetham to Jefferson, Dec. 10, Dec. 29, 1801; Jefferson Papers, LC., v. 118, pp. 20394-400; v. 119, pp. 20511-12.
[35] Jefferson to Pres. of the Senate, Dec. 8, 1801; *Writings*, Mont., X, 300.
[36] Jefferson to Rush, Dec. 20, 1801; *Works*, Ford, IX, 343-6.
[37] *Gazette of the U. S.*, Dec. 11, 15, 1801.
[38] "Draft Message," Jefferson Papers, LC. Jefferson had already informed Edward Livingston of N. Y. on Nov. 1, 1801, that "I affirm that act [Sedition] to be no law because in opposition to the Constitution; and I shall treat it as a nullity wherever it comes in the way of my [power?]"; Jefferson Papers, LC., v. 117, p. 20222.
[39] *The Port Folio*, Mar. 28, 1801.
[40] Jefferson to Madison, Nov. 12, 1801; *Works*, Ford, IX, 321 n.
[41] Gallatin to Jefferson, Nov., 1801; Gallatin, *Writings*, I, 68.
[42] "Reports of U. S. Attys.," Misc. Letters, State Dept., Nat. Arch.
[43] "First Annual Message," Dec. 8, 1801; Richardson, *Messages of the Presidents*, I, 326-32.
[44] Jefferson to Mazzei, Dec. 30, 1801; Maruzzi Arch., Pisa. Printed in *Va. Mag.*, v. 51, p. 124.

CHAPTER 50

[1] Dupont to Jefferson, Dec. 17, 1801; *Jefferson and Dupont de Nemours* (D. Malone, ed.), 30-6.
[2] Jefferson to Dupont, Jan. 18, 1802; *Works*, Ford, IX, 342-4 n.
[3] Jefferson to John Dickinson, Dec. 19, 1801; *Writings*, Mont., X, 301-3.
[4] *Life, Journals & Correspond. of Manasseh Cutler*, II, 54-5. Jefferson to T. M. Randolph, Jan. 1, 1802; Jefferson Papers, LC., v. 119, p. 20599.
[5] "Dr. Mitchill's Letters from Washington"; *Harper's Mag.*, v. 58, pp. 743-4.
[6] *Ibid;* v. 58, p. 744.
[7] Jefferson to Levi Lincoln, Jan. 1, 1802; *Works*, Ford, IX, 346-7.

[8] Levi Lincoln to Jefferson, Jan. 1, 1802; Jefferson Papers, LC., v. 119, p. 20600. Jefferson to Baptist Congregation, Jan. 1, 1802; S. Padover, *Complete Jefferson*, 518-19.

[9] *Annals of Cong.*, 7th Cong., 1st Sess., pp. 23, 25-8.

[10] *Ibid*; pp. 33, 41.

[11] Bayard to Bassett, Jan. 25, 1802; *Papers of James Bayard*, 147. Jackson to Jefferson, Dec. 28, 1801; Jefferson Papers, LC., v. 119, p. 20503.

[12] Jefferson to J. W. Eppes, Jan. 22, 1802; MS., N. Y. H. S.

[13] Gouverneur Morris to R. Livingston, Aug. 21, 1802; Morris, *Diary and Letters*, II, 426.

[14] For a discussion of Burr's votes, see Schachner, *Burr*, 222-4.

[15] Jefferson to T. M. Randolph, Feb. 21, 1802; Jefferson Papers, LC., v. 121, p. 20836.

[16] Bayard to Hamilton, Apr. 12, 1802; Hamilton, *Works* (J. C. Hamilton, ed.), VI, 539. Hamilton to Gouverneur Morris, Mar. 4, 1802; Hamilton, *Works* (Lodge, ed.), X, 427-8.

[17] Monroe to Jefferson, Feb. 13, 1802; Monroe, *Writings*, III, 336-8.

[18] Jefferson to Monroe, June 2, 1802; *Works*, Ford, IX, 373-5. To Rufus King, July 13, 1802; *ibid*, IX, 383-7.

[19] Monroe to Jefferson, June 11, 1802; Monroe, *Writings*, III, 351-3.

[20] Jefferson to J. W. Eppes, Jan. 1, 1802; Jefferson MSS., U. of Va.

[21] Jefferson to Charles W. Peale, Jan. 16, 1802; Jefferson Papers, LC., v. 120, p. 20680.

[22] Jefferson to Page, Feb. 20, Apr. 2, May 7, 1802; *Works*, Ford, IX, 350-6, 352-3 n. See also Jefferson to Gallatin, Aug. 28, 1801; Gallatin Papers, N. Y. H. S., and Page to Jefferson, Mar. 27, 1802; Jefferson Papers, LC., v. 121, p. 20968.

[23] Jefferson to Maria J. Eppes, Mar. 3, 1802; Jefferson Papers, LC., v. 121, p. 20875.

[24] Jefferson to T. M. Randolph, Mar. 12, 28, 1802; *ibid*, v. 121, pp. 20904-5, 20971.

[25] Jefferson to James Dinsmore, Mar. 19, 1802; *ibid*, v. 121, p. 20932.

[26] Acct. Bk., Mar. 4, 1801-Mar. 4, 1802; N. Y. P. L. "State of the Apparent Monthly Balances-Advances on the Presidents a/c with J. Barnes," Mar. 31, 1801-May 3, 1803; Jefferson MSS., U. of Va. Acct. Bk., Jan. 23, 1809; Mass. H. S.

[27] Annals of Cong., 7th Cong., 1st Sess., pp. 989, 1015-16, 1073.

[28] *Ibid*, pp. 250, 1129.

[29] Jefferson to Gallatin, Apr. 1, 1802; *Works*, Ford, IX, 358-61.

[30] Jefferson to Monroe, Mar. 31, 1802; Monroe Papers, N. Y. Pub. Lib. The Convention was ratified in the Senate on May 3, 1802; *Annals of Cong.*, 7th Cong., 1st Sess., p. 303.

[31] Annals of Cong., 7th Cong., 1st Sess., pp. 259, 304, 1293.

[32] Gideon Granger to Jefferson, May 11, 14, 17, 23, 1802; Jefferson Papers, LC., v. 123, pp. 21230, 21239, 21243, 21264.

[33] Jefferson to Levi Lincoln, Mar. 24, 1802; *Works*, Ford, IX, 357-8.

[34] Jefferson to Volney, Apr. 20, 1802; Jefferson Papers, LC., v. 122, pp. 21086-8.

[35] Jefferson to Cheetham, Apr. 23, 1802; *ibid*, v. 122, p. 21104.

[36] Jefferson to Matthew Cary, May 4, 1802; *ibid*, v. 123, p. 21184.

[37] Jefferson to Rodney, Apr. 24, 1802; *Works*, Ford, IX, 368-9.

[38] Jefferson to Joel Barlow, May 3, 1802; *ibid*, IX, 370-2.

[39] Jefferson to Mme. Corny, Apr. 23, 1802; Jefferson Papers, LC., v. 122, pp. 21105-6. A few days later, Angelica Church called on Jefferson for help to her son, whose ship and cargo had been seized by the Portuguese; Apr. 27, 1802; *ibid*, v. 122, p. 21138.

[40] Wm. Duane to Jefferson, Oct. 18, 1802; *ibid*, v. 126, pp. 21850-1.

[41] Gallatin to Jefferson, Aug. 3, Sept. 21, 1802; *ibid*, v. 125, p. 21545; v. 126, pp. 21762-3.

[42] Jefferson to Gideon Granger, Aug. 29, 1802; *Works*, Ford, IX, 393-4.

[43] Jefferson to Madison, July 30, 1802; Misc. Letters, Dept. of State, Nat. Arch.

[44] Jefferson to Madison, Aug. 9, 1802; *ibid.*

[45] Gallatin to Jefferson, Aug. 16, 1802; Gallatin, *Writings*, I, 86-90.

[46] Jefferson to Madison, Aug. 23, 1802; Jefferson Papers, LC., v. 125, p. 21656. Jefferson to Robert Smith, Aug. 30, 1802; *ibid*, v. 126, p. 21688.

[47] Robert Smith to Jefferson, Sept. 14, 1802; *ibid*, v. 126, pp. 21742-4. Jefferson to Smith, Sept. 17, 20, 1802; *ibid*, v. 126, pp. 21750, 21756. To Gallatin, *ibid*, v. 126, p. 21757.

[48] Jefferson to Robert Smith, Oct. 16, 1802; *ibid*, v. 126, p. 21839.

[49] Anas, *Works*, Ford, I, 370-1.

[50] Jefferson to Latrobe, Nov. 2, 1802; Jefferson Papers, LC., v. 127, pp. 21927-8.

[51] Gallatin to Jefferson [rec.] Nov. 21, 1802; *ibid*, v. 127, pp. 21983-5.

[52] Latrobe to Jefferson, Dec. 4, 1802; *ibid*, v. 127, pp. 22026-7. Jefferson to Congress, Dec. 27, 1802; *ibid*, v. 128, p. 22105.

[53] Jefferson to Gallatin, Sept. 13, 1802; *Works*, Ford, IX, 394.
[54] Jefferson to Gallatin, Oct. 13, 1802; *ibid*, IX, 398-9.

CHAPTER 51

[1] Adams, *Hist. of U. S.*, I, 367. Henry Adams's great work, based on the archives of the European Powers, gives the fundamental background of the cession of Louisiana.
[2] Napoleon to Decrès, June 4, 1802; *ibid*, I, 399.
[3] Jefferson to Monroe, May 29, 1801; *Works*, Ford, IX, 263. Madison to Chas. Pinckney, June 9, 1801; to R. R. Livingston, Sept. 28, 1801; *Am. State Papers: For. Rel.*, II, 510.
[4] King to Madison, Nov. 20, 1801; R. R. Livingston to Madison, Dec. 31, 1801; *Am. State Papers: For. Rel.*, II, 511, 513.
[5] Dupont to Jefferson, Apr. 13, 1802; *Jefferson and Du Pont de Nemours* (Chinard, ed.), 43.
[6] Jefferson to Dupont, Apr. 21, 1802; *ibid*, 44.
[7] Dupont to Jefferson, Apr. 24, 1802; *ibid*, 44-6.
[8] Jefferson to R. R. Livingston, Apr. 18, 1802; *Works*, Ford, IX, 363-8.
[9] Jefferson to R. R. Livingston, May 5, 1802; *Jefferson and Du Pont* (Chinard), 54.
[10] Jefferson to Dupont, Apr. 25, 1802; *Jefferson and Dupont* (D. Malone, ed.), 46-9.
[11] Dupont to Jefferson, Apr. 30, 1802; *ibid*, 52-61.
[12] Dupont to Jefferson, May 12, 1802; *ibid*, 61-7.
[13] Livingston to King, Jan. 25, 1802; "Letters of R. R. Livingston," by E. A. Parsons, in *Amer. Antiquarian Soc. Proc.*, v. 52, pp. 376-7.
[14] Livingston to King, Mar. 27, 1802; *ibid*, v. 52, p. 379.
[15] King to Livingston, July 12, 1802; Rufus King Papers, N. Y. H. S.
[16] Livingston to Madison, Apr. 24, 1802; *Am. State Papers: For. Rel.*, II, 515-6. Chevalier d'Azara to Livingston, June 2, 1802; *ibid*, II, 519.
[17] Livingston to Madison, Sept. 1, 1802; *ibid*, II, 525.
[18] Dupont to Jefferson, Aug. 16, 1802; *Jefferson and Du Pont* (Chinard), 61-2. To same, Oct. 4, 1802; *Jefferson and Dupont* (Malone), 68-71.
[19] Daniel Clark to Madison, June 22, 1802; Monroe Papers, LC.
[20] Jefferson to Madison, Aug. 30, 1802; Jefferson Papers, LC., v. 126, p. 21692.
[21] King of Spain to Intendant of New Orleans, July 14, 1802; Seville Archives, quoted in Channing, *Hist. of U. S.*, IV, 326-7.
[22] Yrujo to Madison, Nov. 27, 1802; State Dept. MSS., Nat. Arch. Yrujo to Morales, Nov. 26, 1802; Gayarré, *Hist. of La.*, III, 576. Madison wrote to Chas. Pinckney, Nov. 27, 1802, to demand at Madrid an immediate countermand of Morales' orders; *Am. State Papers: For. Rel.*, II, 527.
[23] Jefferson to Livingston, Oct. 10, 1802; *Works*, Ford, IX, 396-8.
[24] Pichon to Talleyrand, Dec. 22, 1802; Adams, *Hist. of U. S.*, I, 429.
[25] Jefferson to Madison, Aug. 30, 1802; Madison Papers, LC., v. 24, p. 100. To same, Sept. 6, 1802; *ibid*, v. 24, p. 104.
[26] Jefferson to Gallatin, Aug. 3, 1802; Jefferson Papers, LC., v. 125, p. 21545.
[27] Gallatin to Jefferson [rec. Nov. 21, 1802]; *ibid*, v. 127, pp. 21983-5.
[28] Jefferson to Priestley, Nov. 29, 1802; *Works*, Ford, IX, 404-6.
[29] Jefferson to Short, to George V. Erving, July 16, 1802; Jefferson Papers, Mo. H. S.
[30] Wm. Duane to Jefferson, Nov. 27, 1802; Jefferson Papers, LC., v. 127, p. 22004.
[31] Dec. 11, 1802; *Harper's Mag.*, v. 58, p. 745.
[32] Jefferson to Paine, Jan. 13, 1803; *Works*, Ford, IX, 417-18.
[33] Paine to Jefferson, Jan. 12, 1803; Jefferson Papers, LC., v. 128, p. 22200. Paine had already suggested to Jefferson that the United States purchase Louisiana [rec. Dec. 25, 1802]; *ibid*, v. 128, pp. 22125-6.
[34] Wm. Plumer to Jeremiah Smith, Dec. 9, 1802; Plumer MSS., LC.
[35] Dec. 13, 1802; *Life, Journals & Corresp. of Manasseh Cutler*, II, 113.
[36] "Second Annual Message," Dec. 15, 1802; *Works*, Ford, IX, 406-15.
[37] Plumer's MS. Autobiography, LC. The autobiography was written in 1827.
[38] *Ibid.*
[39] *Ibid.*
[40] *Am. State Papers: For. Rel.*, II, 469, 471.

[41] *Annals of Cong.*, 7th Cong., 2nd Sess., 339, 342.
[42] *Ibid*, 255-6.
[43] *Ibid*, 311, 366.
[44] *Ibid*, 367, 370-1.
[45] Jefferson to Monroe, Jan. 10, 1803; *Works*, Ford, IX, 416-17.
[46] *Annals of Cong.*, 7th Cong., 2nd Sess., 371-4.
[47] Jefferson to Monroe, Jan. 13, 1803; *Works*, IX, 418-21.
[48] Jefferson to Priestley, Jan. 29, 1804; *ibid*, X, 69-72.
[49] Gallatin to Jefferson, Jan. 13, 1803; Gallatin, *Writings*, I, 111-14.
[50] Levi Lincoln to Jefferson, Jan. 10, 1803; Jefferson Papers, LC., v. 128, pp. 22189-90. Jefferson to Gallatin [Jan., 1803]; Gallatin, *Writings*, I, 114-15.

CHAPTER 52

[1] Jefferson to T. M. Randolph, Jan. 17, 1803; Jefferson Papers, LC., v. 129, p. 22219.
[2] Jefferson to Richard Derby, Mar. 6, 1803; *ibid.*
[3] Jefferson to Mme. de Tessé, Jan. 30, 1803; *ibid*, v. 129, pp. 22267-8.
[4] Jefferson to Maria Cosway, Jan. 31, 1803; *ibid*, v. 129, p. 22273.
[5] Jefferson to M. de Cepede, Feb. 24, 1803; *ibid*, v. 130, pp. 22397-8.
[6] Jefferson to Rush, Apr. 21, 1803; Jefferson Papers, Mass. H. S. Printed in *Works*, Ford, IX, 457-8 n.
[7] "Syllabus . . . of the Doctrines of Jesus"; *Works*, Ford, IX, 457-63. It had already been outlined in different form in a letter from Jefferson to Priestley, Apr. 9, 1803; *ibid*, 458-9 n.
[8] Jefferson to Martha J. Randolph, Apr. 25, 1803; Jefferson Papers, LC., v. 131, p. 22631. See also to Priestley, Apr. 24, 1803; *ibid*, v. 131, p. 22630; to "three or four particular friends"; Apr. 21, 1803; *ibid*, v. 131, p. 22616; to Levi Lincoln, Apr. 26, 1803; *Works*, Ford, IX, 459 n.
[9] Priestley to Jefferson, May 7, 1803; Jefferson Papers, LC., v. 131, p. 22679.
[10] Jefferson to Edward Dowse, Apr. 19, 1803; *ibid*, v. 131, p. 22605. Printed in *Writings*, Mont., X, 378.
[11] Jefferson to Christopher Ellery, May 9, 1803; Jefferson Papers, LC., v. 131, p. 22684. Printed in *Works*, Ford, IX, 466-8 under the erroneous date of May 19, 1803.
[12] Jefferson to Gov. Wm. H. Harrison, Feb. 27, 1803; *Writings*, Mont., X, 368-73. To same effect to Henry Dearborn, Sec. of War, Dec. 29, 1802; Jefferson Papers, LC., v. 128, pp. 22110-12.
[13] Jefferson to Gov. W. C. C. Claiborne, May 24, 1803; *Writings*, Mont., X, 390-6. He also wrote to James Jackson, with instructions for the use of agents among the Indians, Feb. 16, 1803; Jefferson Papers, LC., v. 129, pp. 22365-6. The recipient is erroneously listed in *Writings*, Mont., X, 357, as *Andrew* Jackson.
[14] Jefferson to André Michaux [Jan., 1793]; *Works*, Ford, VII, 208-12.
[15] "Message on Expedition to the Pacific," Jan. 18, 1793; *ibid*, IX, 421-34.
[16] Jefferson to Caspar Wistar, Feb. 28, 1803; *ibid*, IX, 422 n.
[17] Jefferson to Lewis Harvie, Feb. 29, 1803; Jefferson Papers, LC., v. 130, p. 22420. Harvie to Jefferson, Mar. 12, 1803; *ibid*, v. 130, p. 22478.
[18] Jefferson to Peyrouse, July 3, 1803; *Works*, Ford, IX, 429-30 n.
[19] Jefferson to Meriwether Lewis, June 20, 1803; *ibid*, IX, 423-9 n. Gallatin at this point was even ahead of Jefferson. He foresaw the necessity of taking possession of Upper Louisiana and the Missouri country in order to keep them from falling into the hands of Great Britain. He foresaw also that some day it would be essential to provide for the expansive overflow of the American people; to Jefferson, Apr. 13, 1803; Jefferson Papers, LC., v. 131, pp. 22582-3. The real purposes of the expedition were even masked from the American public, it being given out that only an exploration of the Mississippi was intended; Jefferson to Lewis, Apr. 27, 1803; *ibid*, v. 112, p. 19216.
[20] Jefferson to R. R. Livingston, Feb. 3, 1803; *Works*, Ford, IX, 441-3. See also Madison to same, Jan. 18, 1803; *Amer. State Papers: For. Rel.*, II, 529.
[21] Jefferson to Dupont, Feb. 1, 1803; *Works*, Ford, IX, 436-43.
[22] Madison to Jefferson, Mar. 14, 1803; Jefferson Papers, LC., v. 130, p. 22481.
[23] Livingston to Madison, Mar. 18, 1803; *Amer. State Papers: For. Rel.*, II, 548.
[24] Talleyrand to Livingston, Mar. 21, 1803; *ibid*, II, 550.

25 Livingston to Talleyrand, Mar. 11 [23], 1803; *ibid*, II, 550-1.

26 Livingston to Rufus King, Jan. 20, Feb. 3, 1803; "Letters of R. R. Livingston," in *Amer. Antiq. Soc. Proc.*, v. 52, pp. 386, 388.

27 Madison to Livingston and Monroe, Mar. 2, 1803; *Amer. State Papers: For. Rel.*, II, 540-4.

28 Jefferson to Sir John Sinclair, June 30, 1803; quoted in Adams, *Hist. of U. S.*, I, 445-6.

29 Anas, Apr. 8, 1803; *Works*, Ford, I, 372.

30 Anas, May 7, 1803; *ibid*, I, 372-3.

31 Jefferson to John Bacon, Apr. 30, 1803; *ibid*, IX, 463-4.

32 Barbé-Marbois, *Hist. of Louisiana*, 263.

33 *Ibid*, 274.

34 Livingston to Madison, Apr. 11, 1803; *Amer. State Papers: For. Rel.*, II, 552.

35 Livingston to Madison, Apr. 13, 1803; *ibid*, II, 552-4. Monroe to Madison, Apr. 15, 1803; Monroe, *Writings*, IV, 9-12.

36 Monroe to Madison, Apr. 15, 1803; *supra.*

37 T. Jung, *Lucien Bonaparte et ses Mémoires*, II, 121 ff.

38 Livingston to King, Apr. 27, 1803; *Letters of Livingston*, 399-401.

39 Monroe's Memorandum on La., Apr. 27-May 9, 1803; Monroe, *Writings*, IV, 12-19.

40 Livingston to King, May 7, 1803; *Letters of Livingston*, 402-3.

CHAPTER 53

1 Livingston and Monroe to Madison, May 13, 1803; *Amer. State Papers: For. Rel.*, II, 558-60.

2 Barbé-Marbois, *Hist. of La.*, 283, 286.

3 Adams, *Hist. of U. S.*, II, 43-4.

4 Livingston to Madison, May 20, 1803; *Amer. State Papers: For. Rel.*, II, 560-1.

5 Livingston and Monroe to Madison, June 7, 1803; *ibid*, II, 563-4.

6 Livingston to Jefferson, June 2, 1803; Jefferson Papers, LC., v. 132, pp. 22792-3.

7 D'Azara to Talleyrand, June 6, 1803, Adams, *Hist. of U. S.*, II, 58.

8 Talleyrand to Bournonville, June 22, 1803; *ibid*, II, 61-2.

9 Jefferson to Rush, Feb. 28, 1803; *Works*, Ford, IX, 452-4.

10 The correspondence between Jefferson and Craven Peyton on the Henderson quarrel is extensive and may be found in the Jefferson Papers, U. of Va., commencing on Oct. 27, 1802 and running well into 1804.

11 Jefferson to Maria J. Eppes, Jan. 18, 1803; Randall, *Jefferson*, III, 44-5.

12 T. M. Randolph to Jefferson, May 22, 1803; Jefferson Papers, LC., v. 131, p. 22736. Jefferson to Randolph, July 5, 1803; *ibid*, v. 133, p. 22946.

13 John Page to Jefferson, Apr. 25, 1803; *ibid*, v. 131, pp. 22632-3. Jefferson to T. M. Randolph, May 5, 1803; *ibid*, v. 131, pp. 22670-1.

14 Acct. Bk., Mar. 4, 1803; N. Y. Pub. Lib.

15 Acct. Bk., Mar. 20, 1804; Mass. H. S. See also Jefferson to Joseph Yznardy, May 10, 1803; Jefferson Papers, LC., v. 131, p. 22691.

16 Gov. McKean to Jefferson, Feb. 7, 1803; Jefferson Papers, LC., v. 129, pp. 22325-6.

17 Jefferson to McKean, Feb. 19, 1803; McKean Papers, Pa. H. S. Printed in *Works*, Ford, IX, 449-52.

18 Jefferson to Levi Lincoln, June 1, 1803 (with article enclosed); Jefferson Papers, LC., v. 132, p. 22780. Printed in *Works*, Ford, IX, 469-74; but without the postscript in which Jefferson asks Lincoln to prune it and adapt it to "the character and feelings of a Massachusetts writer." The article appeared in the Boston *Chronicle*, June 27, 1803.

19 Jefferson to Gallatin, Jan., 1803; *Works*, Ford, X, 3 n.

20 *Works*, Ford, X, 3-12.

21 Robert Smith to Jefferson (enclosing his own draft of an amendment), July 9, 1803; *ibid*, X, 3-5 n.

22 Anas, July 16, 1803; *ibid*, I, 373-5.

23 Jefferson to Gates, July 11, 1803; Emmet Coll., N. Y. Pub. Lib. Printed in *Works*, Ford, X, 12-14.

[24] Jefferson Papers, LC., v. 135, pp. 23267-71, v. 137, pp. 22690-1, 23694, 23695, 23696-704 *et passim.*

[25] Jefferson to John C. Breckinridge, Aug. 12, 1803; MS., Wm. L. Clements Lib. Published in *Works,* Ford, X, 5-7 n.

[26] Jefferson to Breckinridge, Aug. 10, 1803; *Works,* Ford, X, 7-8 n. To Madison, Sept. 7, 1803; Jefferson Papers, LC., v. 135, p. 23273. To Dearborn, Aug. 23, 1803; *ibid,* v. 134, p. 23195. To Madison, Aug. 18, 1803; Rives Papers, LC.

[27] W. C. Nicholas to Jefferson, Sept. 3, 1803; Jefferson Papers, LC.

[28] Jefferson to Nicholas, Sept. 7, 1803; *Works,* Ford, X, 10-11, n.

[29] Jefferson to Gallatin, Aug. 23, 1803; Gallatin Papers, N. Y. H. S. Gallatin to Jefferson, Aug. 31, 1803; Jefferson Papers, LC., v. 134, pp. 23238-43.

[30] Livingston to Monroe, Sept. 11, 1803; Monroe to Livingston, Oct. 9, 1803; *Amer. Art Assoc. Catalogue,* Apr. 15, 1937.

[31] Yrujo to Madison, Sept. 4, 27, 1803; *Amer. State Papers: For. Rel.*, II, 569.

[32] Madison to Yrujo, Oct. 4, 1803; Pichon to Madison, Oct. 14, 1803; *ibid,* II, 569-70, 571-2.

[33] Gallatin to Jefferson, Jan. 18, 1803; Gallatin, *Writings,* I, 117.

[34] Jefferson to Robert Smith, Oct. 10, 1803; Jefferson Papers, LC., v. 135, p. 23366.

[35] "Third Annual Message"; *Works,* Ford, X, 23-44.

[36] Jefferson to Rush, Oct. 14, 1803; *ibid,* X, 32.

[37] Wm. Plumer, MS. Autobiography; LC.

[38] *Ibid.* Plumer, *Memorandum of Proceedings in the U. S. Senate* (E. S. Brown, ed.), 13.

[39] *Annals of Cong.*, 8th Cong., 1st Sess., 18, 31.

[40] *Ibid,* 385-7.

[41] *Ibid,* 387-419.

[42] *Ibid,* 432-3, 458, 468-9.

[43] *Ibid,* 498-9, 510.

[44] Jefferson to John Randolph, Oct. 25, 1803; Jefferson Papers, LC., v. 136, p. 23449. Randolph to Jefferson, Oct. 25, 1803; *ibid,* v. 136. p. 23451.

[45] *Annals of Cong.*, 8th Cong., 1st Sess., 514, 545-6.

[46] Jefferson to Madison, Sept. 14, 1803; *Works,* Ford, X, 30-1.

[47] Anas, Oct. 4, 1803; *ibid,* I, 375.

[48] Jefferson to Gallatin, Oct. 29, 1803; *ibid,* X, 45-6. Gallatin reported that only 300 regulars could be spared from Fort Adams, but that the Western States would easily raise 5,000 volunteers; to Jefferson, Oct. 28, 1803; Jefferson Papers, LC., v. 136, pp. 23458-61.

[49] Jefferson to Dearborn, Oct. 29, 1803; Jefferson Papers, LC., v. 136, p. 23495.

[50] Jefferson to Page, Nov. 25, 1803; *ibid,* v. 136, p. 23570.

CHAPTER 54

[1] Livingston to Madison, Nov. 15, 1803; *Amer. State Papers: For Rel.*, II, 573-4.

[2] Madison to Livingston, Mar. 31, 1804; *ibid,* II, 575-8.

[3] Talleyrand to Chevalier de Santivanes, 5 Germinal, year 13; *ibid,* II, 659-60.

[4] Madison to Livingston, Mar. 31, 1804; *ibid,* II, 575.

[5] Jefferson to Gallatin, Nov. 9, 1803; *Works,* Ford, X, 46 n.

[6] *Annals of Cong.*, 8th Cong., 1st Sess., 223, 256.

[7] *Ibid,* 1055-6, 1193-4, 1199, 1229-30, 1293-1300.

[8] *Amer. State Papers: For. Rel.*, II, 583.

[9] Jefferson to David Williams, Nov. 14, 1803; *Writings,* Mont., X, 428-31.

[10] Jefferson to Jean Baptiste Say, Feb. 1, 1804; *ibid,* XI, 1-3.

[11] Jefferson to Andrew Ellicott, Dec. 23, 1803; Jefferson Papers, LC., v. 137, p. 23653.

[12] See B. H. Latrobe's *Journal* for his account of the lengthy proceedings.

[13] "Report on Public Buildings," Feb. 22, 1804; Jefferson Papers, LC., v. 138, p. 23947. See also Jefferson to B. H. Latrobe, Feb. 26, 1804; Jefferson Papers, LC., v. 138, p. 23968a. To Chas. W. Peale, Mar. 1, 1804; *ibid,* v. 138, p. 23988. To same, Aug. 19, 1804; *ibid,* v. 142, p. 24760.

[14] King to Madison, Apr. 10, 1802; Adams, *Hist. of U.S.*, II, 361.

[15] "Notes" [1809]; Jefferson Papers, LC., v. 111, p. 19124. See also "Rules of Etiquette" [Nov., 1803]; *Works,* Ford, X, 47-8.

[16] Merry to Hawkesbury, Dec. 6, 1803; Adams, *Hist. of U.S.*, II, 369-70.

[17] Yrujo to Cevallos, Feb. 7, 1804; *ibid*, II, 370-1.

[18] *Ibid*. Pichon to Talleyrand; *ibid*, II, 372. Madison gravely inquired of Rufus King in London what the ceremonial usage in such cases was abroad. "Our wish would be," he wrote, "to unfetter social intercourse as well as public business as much as possible from ceremonious clogs, by substituting the pell mell; but this may be rendered difficult by the pretentions & expectations opposed to it"; Dec. 18, 1803; *King's Life & Correspondence*, IV, 332-3.

[19] Jefferson to Martha J. Randolph, Jan. 23, 1804; Jefferson MSS., Morgan Lib.

[20] Jefferson to Short, Jan. 23, 1804; *Am. Hist. Rev.*, XXXIII, 832-5.

[21] Turreau to Talleyrand, Jan. 27, 1804; Adams, *Hist. of U.S.*, II, 274.

[22] John Walker to Henry Lee, Mar. 28, 1805; Jefferson Papers, LC., v. 155, pp. 27117-21.

[23] "Burwell Memoir," LC.

[24] Walker to Jefferson, Feb. 4, 1786; Jefferson Papers, Mo. H.S.

[25] Jefferson to Walker, Apr. 13, 1803; photostat in Va. Hist. Soc. of a copy of the letter. But the copy has a certification at the bottom by Bishop James Madison and by Chief Justice John Marshall, dated May 13, 1806, that they had seen the original and that this was a true copy.

[26] *The Port Folio*, Dec. 8, 1804.

[27] "Burwell's Memoir," LC.

[28] Walker to Henry Lee, Mar. 28, 1805; Jefferson Papers, LC., v. 148, pp. 25833-4.

[29] The letter to Lincoln, perhaps dated July 1, 1805, has vanished. So has a copy of it which Jefferson enclosed to Robert Smith, accompanied by an explanatory letter from which the textual quotation is taken, dated July 1, 1805; *Jefferson Correspondence, Bixby Coll.*, 114-15. The original is in the Huntington Lib.

[30] Henry Lee to Jefferson, Sept. 8, 1806; Jefferson Papers, LC., v. 161, pp. 28252-3.

[31] Monroe to Jefferson, Sept. 4, 1809; *ibid*, v. 188, p. 33464. Hugh Nelson to Jefferson, Sept. 4, 1809; *ibid*, v. 188, p. 33465.

[32] Acct. Bk., Mass. H.S.

[33] Jefferson to J. W. Eppes, Mar. 15, 1804; Randall, *Jefferson*, III, 98.

[34] Jefferson to W. C. Nicholas, May 3, 1804; Jefferson Papers, Mo. H.S.

[35] Abigail Adams to Jefferson, May 20, 1804; Jefferson MSS., Morgan Lib.

[36] Jefferson to J. W. Eppes, June 4, 1804; Randall, *Jefferson*, III, 99-100. The original is in the Huntington Lib.

[37] Jefferson to Abigail Adams, June 13, 1804; *Works*, Ford, X, 84-6.

[38] Abigail Adams to Jefferson, July 1, 1804; Jefferson Papers, LC., v. 141, pp. 24548-9.

[39] Jefferson to Abigail Adams, July 22, 1804; *Works*, Ford, X, 86-8 n.

[40] Abigail Adams to Jefferson, Aug. 18, 1804; Jefferson Papers, LC., v. 142, pp. 24758-9.

[41] Jefferson to Abigail Adams, Sept. 11, 1804; *Works*, Ford, X, 88-90 n.

[42] Abigail Adams to Jefferson, Oct. 25, 1804; Jefferson Papers, LC., v. 144, pp. 25042-3.

[43] Acct. Bk., Nov. 17, Dec. 8, 1803; N. Y. Pub. Lib.

CHAPTER 55

[1] Anas, Jan. 26, 1804; *Works*, Ford, I, 377-81.

[2] De Witt Clinton to Jefferson, Nov. 26, 1803; Jefferson Papers, LC., v. 136, p. 23574.

[3] Jefferson to De Witt Clinton, Dec. 2, 1803; *Works*, Ford, X, 54-5.

[4] Jefferson to Gideon Granger, Mar. 9, 1814; *ibid*, XI, 383-90.

[5] The details of the election in New York may be found in Schachner, *Burr*, Chap. 16. See also Henry Adams, *New England Federalism*, for the Federalist Conspiracy.

[6] Pickering to George Cabot, Jan. 29, 1804; Adams, *N. E. Federalism*, 338-42.

[7] Pickering to King, Mar. 4, 1804; Lodge, *George Cabot*, 447-9.

[8] Jefferson to Gideon Granger, Apr. 16, 1804; *Works*, Ford, X, 74-6.

[9] Jefferson to Elbridge Gerry, Mar. 3, 1804; *ibid*, X, 73-4.

[10] Tazewell to Jefferson, Mar. 8, 1804; Jefferson Papers, LC., v. 139, pp. 24000-1.

[11] Jefferson to Gallatin, July 12, 1803; *Works*, Ford, X, 15-16.

[12] Jefferson to Gallatin, Dec. 13, 1803; *ibid*, X, 56-8.

[13] *Annals of Cong.*, 7th Cong., 2nd Sess., 460, 544, 641-2, 268.

[14] *Cranch's (U.S.) Reports*, I, 153.

[15] *Annals of Cong.*, 8th Cong., 1st Sess., 790, 794-6.

[16] *Ibid*, 319-22, 328-45, 359-61.

[17] *Ibid*, 367-8.
[18] Plumer's Autobiography; MS., LC.
[19] *Annals of Cong.*, 8th Cong., 1st Sess., 145-6.
[20] Jefferson to Joseph H. Nicholson, May 13, 1803; *Writings*, Mont., X, 390.
[21] Nathaniel Macon to Nicholson, Aug. 6, 1803; Nicholson MSS., LC.
[22] *Annals of Cong.*, 8th Cong., 1st Sess., 806-25, 875-6, 1093, 1171-82, 1237-40.
[23] Plumer to Treadwell, Nov. 6, 1804; Plumer MSS., LC. Plumer, *Memorandum of Proceedings*, Nov. 26, 1804; pp. 203-4.
[24] *Annals of Cong.*, 8th Cong., 2nd Sess., 100-218, 664-9.
[25] Madison to Monroe, Jan. 5, 1804; *Amer. State Papers: For. Rel.*, II, 730-2.
[26] Jefferson to Monroe, Jan. 8, 1804; *Works*, Ford, X, 59-68.
[27] Anas, Feb. 18, 1804; *ibid*, I, 382.
[28] Jefferson to Gallatin, Feb. 22, 1804; Jefferson Papers, LC., v. 138, p. 23948. To same, June 9, 1804; Gallatin, *Writings*, I, 196.
[29] Jefferson to Robert Smith, Apr. 27, 1804; *Works*, Ford, X, 77-9.
[30] Jefferson to Madison, Apr. 27, 1804; Madison Papers, LC., v. 27, p. 35.
[31] Jefferson to Madison, Aug. 18, 1804; Jefferson Papers, LC., v. 142, p. 24752.
[32] Jefferson to Armstrong, May 26, 1804; *Works*, Ford, X, 79-81.

CHAPTER 56

[1] Indenture from Peyton to Jefferson, May 4, 1804; Jefferson to Peyton, Feb. 25, 1804; Peyton v. Henderson, Suit in Chancery, May 1804; Jefferson MSS., U. of Va.
[2] Reply to article in Washington *Federalist*, May 18, 1804; draft dated May 21, 1804; Jefferson Papers, LC., v. 140, pp. 24347-8.
[3] Lafayette to Jefferson, Sept. 1, 1803; Jefferson to Lafayette, Jan. 1804; Chinard, *Lafayette and Jefferson*, 223-4, 226-7. Jefferson to Say, Feb. 1, 1804; *Writings*, Mont., XI, 1-3.
[4] Burwell's Memoir; MS., LC. Jefferson to Caspar Wistar, June 7, 1804; Jefferson Papers, LC., v. 141, p. 24408.
[5] Jefferson to Stephen Cathalan, Mar. 22, 1804; Jefferson Papers, LC., v. 139, p. 24057.
[6] Jefferson to Priestley, Jan. 29, 1804; *Works*, Ford, X, 69-72.
[7] Jefferson to Henry Fry, June 17, 1804; Jefferson Papers, LC., v. 141, p. 24473.
[8] Jefferson to Bishop James Madison, June 29, 1804; *ibid*, v. 141, p. 24529.
[9] Jefferson to Ferdinand Fairfax, Sept. 13, 1804; *ibid*, v. 143, p. 24869.
[10] Jefferson to Claiborne, Aug. 30, 1804; *ibid*, v. 143, pp. 24805-6.
[11] Jefferson to Madison, Aug. 7, 15, 1804; *Works*, Ford, X, 93, 95.
[12] Jefferson to Madison, Sept. 25, 1804; Jefferson Papers, LC., v. 143, p. 24902.
[13] Monroe to Jefferson, Sept. 25, 1804; *ibid*, v. 143, pp. 24914-7. Madison to Jefferson, Aug. 28, 1804; *ibid*, v. 143, p. 24800.
[14] Charles Pinckney to Cevallos, July 5, 1804; *Amer. State Papers: For. Rel.*, II, 620.
[15] Cevallos to Pinckney, July 8, 1804; Pinckney to Cevallos, July 14, 1804; *ibid*, II, 620-1.
[16] Madison to Monroe, Nov. 9, 1804; Madison, *Works*, II, 208.
[17] Jefferson to Madison, Apr. 23, 1804; Jefferson Papers, Mass. H.S.
[18] Jefferson to Robert Smith, Sept. 6, 1804; Jefferson Papers, LC., v. 143, p. 24845.
[19] Annual Message, Nov. 8, 1804; *Works*, Ford, X, 105-17.
[20] Jefferson to Gallatin, Sept. 1, 1804; Gallatin, *Writings*, I, 207.
[21] Jefferson to John Randolph, Nov. 19, 1804; *Works*, Ford, X, 118-22.
[22] Plumer's MS Autobiography, LC.
[23] Jefferson to Wm. Heath, Dec. 13, 1804; Jefferson Papers, LC., v. 145, p. 25267.
[24] Jefferson to John Taylor, Jan. 6, 1805; *Works*, Ford, X, 124-6.
[25] Short to Jefferson, Nov. 5, 1804; Jefferson to Short, Nov. 10, 1804; Jefferson Papers, LC., v. 144, pp. 25089-90, 25126 (facsimile).
[26] Plumer's *Memorandum of Proc. in U. S. Senate*, 193, 212.
[27] J. Q. Adams, *Memoirs* (C. F. Adams, ed.), I, 317, 330.
[28] Jefferson to Littleton W. Tazewell, Jan. 5, 1804; Jefferson MSS., U. of Va.
[29] Jefferson to Tazewell, Mar. 13, 1825; Jefferson Papers, LC., v. 229, p. 40901.
[30] Jefferson to Joseph Nicholson, Jan. 29, 1805; *Writings*, Mont., XI, 59-62.
[31] Jefferson to W. C. Nicholas, Dec. 4, 1804; *Works*, Ford, X, 123-4.

[32] *Annals of Cong.*, 8th Cong., 2nd Sess., 1684.
[33] *Ibid*, 1694-8.

CHAPTER 57

[1] J. Q. Adams, *Memoirs*, I, 373.
[2] *Works*, Ford, X, 127-8 n.
[3] Henry Dearborn to Jefferson, Jan. 12, 1805; Jefferson Papers, LC., v. 146, p. 25461.
[4] Second Inaugural Address, Mar. 4, 1805; *Works*, Ford, X, 127-36.
[5] Jefferson to Benjamin Waterhouse, Mar. 9, 1805; Jefferson Papers, LC., v. 148, p. 25743.
[6] Jefferson to Craven Peyton, Feb. 4, 1805; Peyton to Jefferson, rec. June 25, 1805; Jefferson MSS., U. of Va.
[7] M. B. Smith, *Forty Years of Washington Soc.*, 391, 387-8.
[8] Acct. Bk., 1804-6, *passim;* Mass. H. S.
[9] License from Register of City of Washington to Jefferson, May 7, 1805; Jefferson Papers, Mo. H. S.
[10] Jefferson to Edward Preble, July 6, 1805; Jefferson Papers, LC., v. 151, p. 26328.
[11] Jefferson to Dr. George Logan, May 11, 1805; *Works*, Ford, X, 141-3.
[12] Jefferson to James Bowdoin, April 27, 1805; *ibid*, X, 140-1.
[13] *Annals of Cong.*, 8th Cong., 2nd Sess., 1674-6, 1684-6.
[14] Jefferson to Gov. Robert Williams of Miss. Terr., July 6, 1805; Jefferson Papers, LC., v. 151, p. 26329.
[15] Pinckney and Monroe to Cevallos, Feb. 5, 1805; *Amer. State Papers: For. Rel.*, II, 640.
[16] Armstrong to Monroe, Mar. 12, 18, 1805; *ibid*, II, 636.
[17] Pinckney and Monroe to Cevallos, May 18, 1805; Cevallos to Pinckney and Monroe, May 20, 1805; *ibid*, II, 667.
[18] Erving to Madison, Dec. 7, 1805; Adams, *Hist. of U. S.*, III, 38.
[19] Jefferson to Martha J. Randolph, Oct. 22, 1805; Jefferson MSS., Morgan Lib.
[20] Merry to Mulgrave, Sept. 30, 1805; Adams, *Hist. of U. S.*, III, 97.
[21] Jefferson to Madison, Aug. 17, 1805; Jefferson Papers, LC., v. 152, p. 26531.
[22] Madison to Jefferson, Sept. 1, 1805; *ibid*, v. 152, p. 26608. Jefferson had already proposed the idea to Madison, Aug. 4, 1805; *Works*, Ford, X, 168-9.
[23] Jefferson to Madison, Aug. 27, 1805; *Works*, Ford, X, 172-4.
[24] Memorials from Merchants; *Amer. State Papers: For. Rel.*, II, 737-41, 749-73.
[25] Report of George W. Erving, Sept. 1, 1804 to Sept. 26, 1805; *ibid*, II, 777-98.
[26] Monroe to Madison, Oct. 18, 1805; *ibid*, III, 106-8.
[27] Jefferson to Madison, Oct. 23, 1805; *Works*, Ford, X, 176-7 n. To same effect to Gallatin, Oct. 23, 1805; Gallatin, *Writings*, I, 257.
[28] Cabinet Decision [Nov. 14, 1805]; *Works*, Ford, X, 180-1.
[29] Fifth Annual Message, Dec. 3, 1805; *ibid*, X, 181-98.
[30] Plumer's Register, Dec. 5, 1805; MS., LC.
[31] "Confidential Message on Spain," Dec. 6, 1805; *Works*, Ford, X, 198-205.
[32] "Decius" Letters; *Richmond Enquirer*, Aug. 15, 1806.
[33] Draft Resolutions (2 sets); *Works*, Ford, X, 199-201 n.
[34] "Decius" Letters; *supra.*
[35] MS. Note; Jefferson Papers, LC., v. 233, p. 41748.
[36] Burwell's Memoir; MS., LC.
[37] Plumer's *Memorandum of Proc.*, Jan. 2, 1806; p. 366.
[38] "Militia Bill," *Works*, Ford, X, 213-17.
[39] Jefferson to Wm. Burwell, Jan. 15, 1806; Franklin Papers, Yale Univ.
[40] Notes on "a revisal of the law respecting citizens" [n.d.]; Jefferson Papers, LC., v. 155, p. 27102.
[41] Jefferson to Gallatin, June 26, 1806; *Works*, Ford, X, 273.

CHAPTER 58

[1] *Annals of Cong.*, 9th Cong., 1st Sess., 55-7, 88, 166.
[2] *Ibid*, 412-13.
[3] *Ibid*, 449-51.
[4] *Ibid*, 441-2, 458-60.

[5] *Ibid*, 566-7.
[6] Benjamin Tallmadge to Manasseh Cutler, Feb. 19, 1806; Cutler, *Life of Cutler*, II, 326.
[7] *Annals of Cong.*, 9th Cong., 1st Sess., 769, 778.
[8] Jefferson to Monroe, Mar. 16, 1806; Jefferson Papers, LC., v. 157, p. 27562.
[9] Wm. Duane to Jefferson, Mar. 12, 1806; *ibid*, v. 157, pp. 27548-9.
[10] George Logan to Jefferson, Mar. 12, 1806; *ibid*, v. 157, p. 27550. See also Thomas Leiper to Jefferson, Mar. 23, 1806; *ibid*, v. 157, pp. 27600-3.
[11] Jefferson to Nathaniel Macon, Mar. 22, 1806; *ibid*, v. 157, p. 27597. Printed in *Works*, Ford, X, 248-9 under the erroneous date of Mar. 26th.
[12] Jefferson to Wm. Duane, Mar. 22, 1806; *Works*, Ford, X, 240-3.
[13] *Annals of Cong.*, 9th Cong., 1st Sess., 823-4, 877-8.
[14] Jefferson to Monroe, Mar. 18, 1806; Jefferson Papers, LC., v. 157.
[15] W. C. Nicholas to Jefferson, Apr. 2, 1806; *ibid.*
[16] Plumer's MS. Autobiography; LC.
[17] Plumer's Register, Feb. 14, 1806; LC.
[18] Monroe to Madison, Jan. 28, Mar. 31, 1806; *Amer. State Papers: For. Rel.*, III, 111-12, 115.
[19] Monroe to Madison, Apr. 18, Apr. 20, 1806; *ibid*, III, 116, 117.
[20] Jefferson to Thomas Cooper, Feb. 18, 1806; Jefferson Papers, LC., v. 156, p. 27424.
[21] Jefferson to W. C. Nicholas, Mar. 24, Apr. 13, 1806; *Works*, Ford, X, 243-4, 244-5 n.
[22] Jefferson to Alexander of Russia, Apr. 19, 1806; *ibid*, X, 249-51.
[23] Madison to Monroe and Pinkney, May 17, 1806; *Amer. State Papers: For. Rel.*, III, 119-24.
[24] Jefferson to Monroe, May 4, 1806; *Works*, Ford, X, 259-64.
[25] Monroe and Pinkney to Madison, Sept. 11, Nov. 11, 1806; *Amer. State Papers: For. Rel.*, III, 133-5, 137.
[26] *Amer. State Papers: For. Rel.*, III, 151.
[27] Plumer's *Memorandum of Proceedings*, Mar. 16, 1806; p. 453.
[28] Turreau to Talleyrand, May 10, 1806; Adams, *Hist. of U. S.*, III, 205-6.
[29] Jefferson to J. Holmes Freeman, Feb. 7, Feb. 26, 1806; Jefferson Papers, U. of Va. *Garden Bk.*, 310.
[30] Jefferson to T. M. Randolph, June 23, 1806; Franklin Papers, Yale Univ.
[31] Jefferson to Madison, Feb. 5, 1806; Misc. Letters, State Dept., Nat. Arch.
[32] Gallatin to Jefferson, Mar. 11, 1806; Jefferson Papers, LC., v. 157, pp. 27545-6.
[33] Jefferson to Gallatin, Aug. 15, 1806; *Works*, Ford, X, 281-2. Anas, May 1, 1805; *ibid*, I, 398-9.
[34] Anas, Apr. 15, 1806; *ibid*, I, 391-5.
[35] Jefferson to Samuel Smith, May 4, 1806; *ibid*, X, 264-5.
[36] Merry to Lord Harrowby, Aug. 6, 1804; Mar. 29, 1805; Adams Transcripts, LC.
[37] Yrujo to Casa Calvo, May 23, 1805; "Hispanic-American Phases of the 'Burr Conspiracy,'" by I. J. Cox, in *Hisp. Amer. Hist. Rev.*, XII, 157.
[38] For full details of the "Burr Conspiracy" see Schachner, *Burr*, *Chaps.* 19-26.
[39] "Your Friend" to Jefferson, rec. Dec. 1, 1805; Jefferson Papers, LC., v. 154, p. 26942.
[40] Daveiss to Jefferson, Jan. 10, 1806; *ibid*, v. 155, pp. 27210-2.
[41] Gallatin to Jefferson, Feb. 12, 1806; *ibid*, v. 156, pp. 27401-2.
[42] Jefferson to Daveiss, Feb. 15, 1806; *Works*, Ford, X, 231-2.
[43] Daveiss to Jefferson, Feb. 10, 1806; Jefferson Papers, LC., v. 156, pp. 27393-4.
[44] Daveiss to Jefferson, Mar. 28, 1806; *ibid*, v. 157, pp. 27620-2.
[45] Plumer's MS. Autobiography, LC.
[46] *Ibid.*
[47] Jefferson to Robert Smith, May 19, 1806; Jefferson Papers, LC., v. 159, pp. 27819-20.

CHAPTER 59

[1] Jefferson to Barnabas Bidwell, July 5, 1806; Jefferson Papers, LC., v. 160, pp. 27995-6. (Omitted from published version in *Writings*, Mont., XI, 114.)
[2] Bidwell to Jefferson, July 28, 1806; *ibid*, v. 160, pp. 28111-12.
[3] Jefferson to Page, July 3, 1806; *ibid*, v. 159, p. 27987.
[4] Jefferson to Martha J. Randolph, July 6, 1806; Jefferson MSS., Morgan Lib.

[5] Jefferson to Martha J. Randolph, Oct. 20, 1806; *ibid.*

[6] "Propositions for consideration & consultation respecting Yrujo," July 9, 19, 1806; Jefferson Papers, LC., v. 160, p. 28018.

[7] Jefferson to W. A. Burwell, Sept. 17, 1806; *Works*, Ford, X, 286-91.

[8] Jefferson to George Morgan, Sept. 19, 1806; *ibid*, X, 291-3.

[9] Monroe to Jefferson, July 8, 1806; Monroe, *Writings*, IV, 477-8.

[10] Beckley to Monroe, July 13, 1806; Monroe Papers, N. Y. Pub. Lib.

[11] Gallatin to Jefferson, Oct. 13, 1806; Jefferson Papers, LC., v. 161, p. 28347. Jefferson to Gallatin, Oct. 12, 1806; *Works*, Ford, X, 294-5.

[12] See Jefferson Papers, LC., v. 161, *passim.*

[13] Jefferson to Monroe, Oct. 26, 1806; *Works*, Ford, X, 296-8.

[14] Burr to Wilkinson, July 29, 1806; Schachner, *Burr*, 322-3. The original cipher and the key were in the possession of Gabriel Wells of New York City.

[15] May 6, 1806; McCaleb, *Aaron Burr Conspiracy*, 121.

[16] Wilkinson to Jefferson, Oct. 20, 21 (2 letters), 1806; Letters in Relation to Burr Conspiracy, LC.

[17] Salcedo to Iturrigaray, Dec. 3, 1806; Bexar Arch., U. of Tex.

[18] Jefferson to Wilkinson, Dec. 19, 1806; Jefferson Papers, LC., v. 162, pp. 28422-7.

[19] Anas, Oct. 22, 1806; *Works*, Ford, I, 401-2.

[20] Anas, Oct. 24, 1806; *ibid*, I, 402-3.

[21] Anas, Oct. 25, 1806; *ibid*, I, 403.

[22] Jefferson to T. M. Randolph, Nov. 3, 1806; Jefferson Papers, Mass. H. S.

[23] Claiborne to Madison, Nov. 18, 25, 1806; *Claiborne's Official Letter Books* (D. Rowland, ed.), IV, 37, 37-8.

[24] Anas, Nov. 25, 1806; *Works*, Ford, I, 404-5. "Proclamation," Nov. 27, 1806; *ibid*, X, 301-2.

[25] "Sixth Annual Message," Dec. 2, 1806; *ibid*, X, 302-20.

[26] "Special Message," Dec. 3, 1806; *ibid*, X, 320-2.

[27] Jefferson to Chas. W. Peale, Dec. 21, 1806; Jefferson Papers, LC., v. 163, p. 28611.

[28] Jefferson to Caesar A. Rodney, Dec. 5, 1806; *Works*, Ford, X, 322-3.

[29] Jefferson to John Langdon, Dec. 22, 1806; Jefferson Papers, LC., v. 163, p. 28617.

[30] Jefferson to John Dawson, Dec. 19, 1806; *ibid*, v. 163, p. 28595.

[31] *Annals of Cong.*, 9th Cong., 2nd Sess., 114, 1249.

[32] *Ibid*, 626.

[33] *Ibid*, 357-8.

[34] Jefferson to Wilkinson, Jan. 3, 1807; *Works*, Ford, X, 332-5.

[35] "Special Message on Burr," Jan. 22, 1807; *ibid*, X, 346-56.

[36] Jefferson to Wilkinson, Feb. 3, 1807; *ibid*, X, 335-6 n.

[37] Madison to Monroe and Pinkney, Feb. 3, 1807; *Amer. State Papers: For. Rel.*, III, 153-6.

[38] Monroe and Pinkney to Madison, Jan. 3, 1807; *ibid*, III, 142-7.

[39] Monroe to John Taylor, Sept. 10, 1810; Monroe Papers, LC.

[40] Samuel Smith to W. C. Nicholas, Mar. 4, 1807; Nicholas MSS., LC.

[41] Samuel Smith to W. C. Nicholas, Mar. 4, 1807 (2nd letter); *ibid.*

[42] Jefferson to Madison, Feb. 1, 1807; Rives Papers, LC. See also to Gallatin, Feb. 1, 1807; Gallatin Papers, N. Y. H. S.

[43] "Notes" [1807]; Jefferson Papers, LC., v. 137, p. 23712.

[44] "Draft Observations" [Mar. 21, 1807]; *ibid*, v. 163, pp. 28702-3.

[45] Anas, Mar. 17, 1807; *Works*, Ford, I, 409.

[46] Jefferson to Monroe, Mar. 21, 1807; *ibid*, X, 374-7.

[47] Jefferson to T. M. Randolph, Feb. 18, 1807; Jefferson Papers, Mass. H. S.

[48] Jefferson to T. M. Randolph, Feb. 19, 1807; Jefferson Papers, LC., v. 165, p. 29024.

[49] Jefferson to Martha J. Randolph, Mar. 6, 23, 1807; Jefferson Papers, Mass. H. S. Same to same, Mar. 20, 1807; Jefferson MSS., Morgan Lib., in which Jefferson also alludes to his own illness and "periodical headaches for 7 straight days, from 9-10 AM to dark, that neither calomel nor bark helps."

[50] J. Q. Adams, *Diary*, I, 495.

[51] Jefferson to Madison, May 8, 1807; *Writings*, Mont., XI, 204.

[52] Gallatin to Jefferson, Apr. 16, 1807; Jefferson Papers, LC., v. 166, p. 29311.

[53] Madison to Jefferson, Apr. 17, 1807; *ibid*, v. 166, p. 29314.

[54] Jefferson to Madison, Apr. 21, 1807; *Works*, Ford, X, 389.

[55] Madison to Monroe and Pinkney, May 20, 1807; *Amer. State Papers: For. Rel.*, III, 166-73.

CHAPTER 60

[1] "*Chesapeake* Proclamation" [July 2, 1807]; *Works*, Ford, X, 434-47.
[2] Jefferson to Gov. Wm. H. Cabell of Va., June 29, 1807; *ibid*, X, 432-3.
[3] Jefferson to George Clinton, July 6, 1807; *ibid*, X, 448-9.
[4] Nicholson to Gallatin, July 14, 1807; Adams, *Gallatin*, 360-1.
[5] Gallatin to Nicholson, July 17, 1807; Gallatin, *Writings*, I, 338.
[6] Jefferson to Short, June 12, 1807; Jefferson-Short Papers, Wm. & Mary College.
[7] Anas, July 2, 1807; *Works*, Ford, I, 410.
[8] Anas, July 5, 1807; *ibid*, I, 411.
[9] Anas, July 26, 1807; *ibid*, I, 411.
[10] Jefferson to Dearborn, July 7, 1807; *ibid*, X, 449-50.
[11] William Tatham to Jefferson, July, 1807. The whole indigestible mass of reports are in Misc. Letters, Dept. of State, Nat. Arch.
[12] Jefferson to Wm. H. Cabell, July 16, 1807; *Works*, Ford, X, 280-1.
[13] Jefferson to T. M. Randolph, July 5, 1807; Jefferson Papers, LC., v. 168, p. 29649.
[14] Nicholson to Gallatin, July 14, 1807; *supra*. See also W. C. Nicholas to Jefferson, July 7, 1807; Jefferson Papers, LC., v. 168, pp. 29669-70.
[15] Nathaniel Macon to Gallatin, Aug. 2, 1807; Adams, *Gallatin*, 362-3.
[16] Jefferson to Cabell, July 24, 1807; *Writings*, Mont., XI, 294-6.
[17] Jefferson to Thomas Appleton, July 9, 1807; Jefferson Papers, LC., v. 168, p. 29688.
[18] Jefferson to T. M. Randolph, July 13, 1807; *ibid*, v. 168, p. 29718.
[19] Jefferson to James Bowdoin, July 10, 1807; *Works*, Ford, X, 453-5.
[20] Jefferson to Dearborn, July 17, 1807; Jefferson Papers, LC., v. 169, p. 29752.
[21] Robert Smith, Secretary of Navy, stood alone in the Cabinet against Jefferson in insisting on "an immediate call of Congress & a demand of the punishment of the offending British Officers." (To Jefferson, July 17, 1807; *ibid*, v. 169, pp. 29755-9.) His brother, Senator Samuel Smith, was equally indignant over what seemed Jefferson's shilly-shallying. He served notice on Gallatin that if the Administration was not adequately prepared for war, "the particular departments which have been remiss will not find defenders in Congress. The Democratic party will not defend through thick & thin." (July 26, 1807; *ibid*, v. 169, pp. 29821-3.)
[22] Jefferson to Wm. Duane, July 20, 1807; *Works*, Ford, X, 470-2.
[23] Jefferson to Madison, Aug. 16, 1807; *ibid*, X, 476-7.
[24] Jefferson to Robert Fulton, Aug. 16, 1807; *ibid*, X, 477-8.
[25] Jefferson to Fulton, July 21, 1813; Franklin Papers, Yale Univ.
[26] Jefferson to Thomas Paine, Sept. 6, 1807; *Works*, Ford, X, 492-3.
[27] Trumbull, *Autobiography*, 246-53. *N. Y. Evening Post*, Dec. 12, 1807.
[28] Madison to Monroe, July 6, 1807; *Amer. State Papers: For. Rel.*, III, 183-5.
[29] Jefferson to Monroe, May 29, 1807; *Writings*, Mont., XI, 211-12.
[30] Jefferson to Dupont, May 2, 1808; *Jefferson and Dupont* (Malone, ed.), 102-3.
[31] Monroe to Jefferson [June, 1807]; Monroe Papers, LC., v. 15, p. 2615.
[32] Erskine to Canning, July 21, 1807; Adams, *Hist. of U. S.*, IV, 37.
[33] Canning to Monroe, July 25, Aug. 3, 1807; *Amer. State Papers: For. Rel.*, III, 187, 188.
[34] Monroe to Madison, Oct. 10, 1807; *ibid*, III, 191-3.
[35] Canning to Monroe and Pinkney, Oct. 17 [15], 1807; *ibid*, III, 197.
[36] Jefferson to Cathalan, June 29, 1807; Jefferson Papers, LC., v. 168, p. 29606.
[37] Jefferson to Martha J. Randolph, Jan. 5, 1808; Jefferson MSS., Morgan Lib.
[38] "Memoranda" [May 13, 1807]; Franklin Papers, Yale Univ.
[39] Jefferson to Latrobe, Apr. 22, 1807; Jefferson Papers, LC.
[40] Latrobe to Jefferson, May 21, 1807; Latrobe, *Journal*, 137-41.
[41] Jefferson to Latrobe, Apr. 25, 1808; Padover, *Jefferson and the Capital*, 414-16.
[42] Jefferson to Martha J. Randolph, Oct. 12, 1807; Jefferson MSS., Morgan Lib.
[43] Jefferson to T. M. Randolph, Oct. 26, 1807; Jefferson Papers, LC., v. 172, p. 30353.

CHAPTER 61

[1] Jefferson to Joseph C. Cabell, Mar. 18, 1807; Jefferson Papers, LC., v. 166, p. 29184.
[2] Jefferson to R. R. Livingston, Mar. 24, 1807; *Writings*, Mont., XI, 170-2.
[3] Jefferson to Levi Lincoln, Mar. 25, 1807; Jefferson Papers, LC., v. 166, p. 29214.
[4] Jos. H. Nicholson to Jefferson, Feb. 18, 1807; *ibid*, v. 165, p. 29020.
[5] *Annals of Congress*, 9th Cong., 2nd Sess., 44, 403.
[6] Jefferson to Daniel Brent, Jan. 23, 1807; to Bollman, Jan. 25, 1807; "Substance of a communication... by Dr. Bollman to the President," Jan. 23, 1807; "Bollman's Report to Jefferson," Jan. 26, 1807; Jefferson Papers, LC., v. 164, pp. 28852, 28864, 28865-70, 28875-84.
[7] 4 *Cranch Reports, U. S.*, 125-6.
[8] Jefferson to Bowdoin, Apr. 2, 1807; *Writings*, Mont., XI, 185-6.
[9] Jefferson to Giles, Apr. 20, 1807; *ibid*, XI, 187-91.
[10] Giles to Jefferson, Apr. 6, 1807; Jefferson Papers, LC., v. 166, pp. 29264-5.
[11] Jefferson to Hay, May 20, 1807; *Works*, Ford, X, 394-401.
[12] Hay to Jefferson, May 25, 31, 1807; Jefferson Papers, LC., v. 167, pp. 29452-3, 29482-3.
[13] Hay to Jefferson, June 14, 1807; *ibid*, v. 168, pp. 29533-5.
[14] *Ibid*.
[15] Jefferson to Hay, May 26, 1807; *Works*, Ford, X, 394-5 n.
[16] Jefferson to Hay, June 2, 1807; *ibid*, X, 396-7 n.
[17] Hay to Jefferson, June 9, 1807; Jefferson Papers, LC.
[18] Jefferson to Hay, June 12, 1807; *Works*, Ford, X, 398-400 n.
[19] Jefferson to Hay, June 17, 1807; *ibid*, X, 400-2 n.
[20] Jefferson to Hay, June 19, 1807; *Writings*, Mont., XI, 233-6. To Caesar A. Rodney, June 19, 1807; Jefferson Papers, LC., v. 168, p. 29546.
[21] Jefferson to Wilkinson, June 21, 1807; *Works*, Ford, X, 336-7 n.
[22] John Smith to Jefferson, July 6, 1807; Jefferson Papers, LC., v. p. 29657.
[23] John Randolph to Joseph H. Nicholson, June 25, 28, 1807; Nicholson MSS., LC.
[24] Hay to Jefferson, Sept. 1, 1807; Jefferson Papers, LC., v. 170, p. 30067.
[25] Jefferson to Hay, Sept. 4, 1807; *ibid*, v. 170, p. 30084.
[26] Hay to Jefferson, Oct. 15, 1807; Jefferson Papers, LC.
[27] Jefferson to Wilkinson, Sept. 20, 1807; *Works*, Ford, X, 499-500.
[28] Jefferson to House of Representatives [Sept. 20, 1807?]; Jefferson Papers, LC., v. 163, p. 28701.
[29] Seventh Annual Message, Oct. 27, 1807; Richardson, *Messages of the Presidents*, I, 425-30.
[30] First and Second Drafts; *Works*, Ford, X, 506-7.
[31] Gallatin to Jefferson, Oct. 21, 1807; Gallatin, *Writings*, I, 358-61.
[32] Jefferson to Martha J. Randolph, Nov. 23, 1807; Jefferson MSS., Morgan Lib.
[33] Monroe to Madison, Oct. 10, 1807; *Amer. State Papers: For. Rel.*, III, 191.
[34] Jefferson to T. M. Randolph, Nov. 30, 1807; Jefferson Papers, LC., v. 172, p. 30506.
[35] Messages, Dec. 7, Dec. 18, 1807; *Works*, Ford, X, 528-9, 530-1.
[36] Gallatin to Jefferson, Dec. 18, 1801; Jefferson Papers, LC., v. 173, p. 30617.
[37] *Annals of Cong.*, 10th Cong., 1st Sess., 1216, 1221-2, 50-1, 2814-15. Jefferson to T. M. Randolph; Jefferson Papers, LC., v. 173, p. 30641.

CHAPTER 62

[1] J. Q. Adams, *Diary*, Dec. 18, 1807; I, 491. Erskine to Canning, Dec. 21, 1807; Adams, *Hist. of U.S.*, IV, 175-6.
[2] *Annals of Cong.*, 10th Cong., 1st Sess., 2815-7, 2834-5, 2839-42, 2870-4.
[3] Jefferson to Gideon Granger, Jan. 22, 1808; Jefferson Papers, LC., v. 174, p. 30814.
[4] *Conn. Courant*, Dec. 30, 1807.
[5] *N. E. Palladium*, Oct. 14, 1808.
[6] John Kelly to Wm. Taylor, Jan. 6, 1808; Wm. Taylor Papers, LC.
[7] Justice Joseph Story of the Supreme Court, an eminent Constitutional authority and at the same time a confirmed Federalist, later wrote in his autobiography: "I have ever considered the embargo a measure, which went to the utmost limit of constructive power under the Constitution. It stands upon the extreme verge of the Constitution, being in its

very form and terms an unlimited prohibition, or suspension of foreign commerce." (*Life and Letters*, I, 185-6.)

[8] Jefferson to N. J. Legislature, Dec. 10, 1807; Jefferson Papers, LC., v. 173, pp. 30582-3.

[9] Jefferson to T. M. Randolph, Jan. 26, 1808; *ibid*, v. 174, p. 30841.

[10] Monroe to Jefferson, Feb. 27, 1808; *ibid*, v. 175, pp. 31055-6.

[11] Jefferson to Monroe, Feb. 18, 1808; *Works*, Ford, XI, 9-11.

[12] Jefferson to Monroe, Mar. 10, 1808; *ibid*, XI, 11-14 n.

[13] Monroe to Jefferson, Mar. 22, 1808; Monroe, *Writings*, V, 27-35.

[14] Monroe to John Taylor, Sept. 10, 1810; *ibid*, V, 121-49.

[15] Jefferson to Chas. Thomson, Jan. 11, 1808; *Works*, Ford, XI, 6-7. To T. M. Randolph, Jan. 26, 1808; *supra*.

[16] Rev. Samuel Miller to Jefferson, Jan. 18, 1808; Jefferson Papers, LC., v. 174, pp. 30802-3. Jefferson to Miller, Jan. 23, 1808; *Works*, Ford, XI, 7-9.

[17] Rose to Madison, Jan. 26, 1808; *Amer. State Papers: For. Rel.*, III, 213-14.

[18] Madison to Rose, Mar. 5, 1808; *ibid*, III, 214-17.

[19] Rose to Madison, Mar. 17, 1808; *ibid*, III, 217-20.

[20] Pickering to T. Williams, Jan. 18, 1808; Pickering MSS., Mass. H. S. George Cabot, to whom he had earlier written along the same lines, wholly approved, Dec. 31, 1807; H. C. Lodge, *George Cabot*, 374-5.

[21] Pickering to Rose, Mar. 13, 1808; *New England Federalism* (H. Adams, ed.), 366.

[22] Pickering to Gov. Sullivan, Feb. 16, 1808; published as pamphlet, Boston, 1808.

[23] "Journal of Capt. Henry Massie" [June, 1808]; *Tyler's Mag.*, IV, 84.

[24] Henry's letters to H. W. Ryland (Craig's secretary) are quoted in Adams, *Hist. of U. S.*, IV, 243-7.

[25] J. Q. Adams, *To the Citizens of hte U. S.* (1828); *National Intelligencer*, Oct. 21, 1828. Jefferson to Wm. B. Giles, Dec. 25, 1825; *Works*, Ford, XII, 418-24, gives an account of the meeting with Adams, but confuses the dates, which led to Adams's later clarification. This in turn started a feud between Adams and those members of the Essex Junto who were still alive, and with the sons of those who were not. See also *Am. Hist. Rev.*, XVII, 70-103, 332-55.

[26] Rose to Canning, Jan. 27, 1808; Adams, *Hist. of U. S.*, IV, 188-9.

[27] *Ibid.*

[28] Jefferson to T. M. Randolph, Jan. 26, 1808; Jefferson Papers, LC., v. 174, p. 30841. To Monroe, Apr. 11, 1808; *Works*, Ford, XI, 14-19 n.

[29] Madison to Rose, Mar. 5, 1808; *Amer. State Papers: For. Rel.*, III, 214. Rose to Madison, Mar. 17, 1808; *ibid*, III, 217.

[30] Jefferson to Dupont, May 2, 1808; Jefferson Papers, LC., v. 177, p. 31379.

[31] Jefferson to Joseph Eggleston, Mar. 7, 1808; *ibid*, v. 175, p. 31085. To same effect to Levi Lincoln, Mar. 23, 1808; *Writings*, Mont., XII, 21.

[32] *Commonplace Bk.*, 391-2. The entry is undated, and it may possibly have been made during the War of 1812 when Jefferson, then in retirement, again advocated domestic manufactures. But it is more plausible to place it during the period of the Embargo, when he was ready to go to any extremes to ensure the success of his favorite measure.

[33] *Richmond Enquirer*, Feb. 26, 1808.

[34] *National Intelligencer*, June 27, 1808.

[35] Proclamation, Apr. 19, 1808; Richardson, *Messages of the President*, I, 450-1.

[36] Jefferson to Madison, May 17, 1808; Jefferson Papers, LC., v. 177, p. 31436.

[37] Jefferson to Gov. Daniel D. Tompkins, Aug. 15, 1808; *Writings*, Mont., XII, 131-3.

[38] Jefferson to Gallatin, May 20, 1808; *ibid*, XII, 59-60.

[39] Gallatin to Jefferson, May 28, 1808; Gallatin, *Writings*, I, 393.

[40] Gallatin to Jefferson, July 29, 1808; *ibid*, I, 396-9.

[41] Jefferson to Secretary of Navy, July 16, 1808; *Writings*, Mont., XII, 93. For some reason known only to themselves, the editors of this edition of Jefferson's *Writings* persist in making Jacob Crowninshield Jefferson's Secretary of Navy.

[42] Draft Circular, enclosed in Jefferson to Gallatin, May 16, 1808; Gallatin Papers, N. Y. H. S.

[43] Gallatin to Jefferson, July 15, 1808 (2 letters); Jefferson Papers, LC., v. 179, pp. 31691, 31692.

[44] Jefferson to Gov. James Sullivan, July 16, 1808; *ibid*, v. 179, p. 31696.

[45] Sullivan to Jefferson, July 21, 1808; *ibid*.

46 Jefferson to Dearborn, Aug. 9, 1808; Works, Ford, XI, 40-1.

47 Jefferson to Madison, Mar. 11, 1808; *ibid*, XI, 12-18. Madison to Pinkney, Apr. 30, 1808; *Amer. State Papers: For. Rel.*, III, 222.

48 Pinkney to Madison, Mar. 11, 1808; *Amer. State Papers: For. Rel.*, III, 228-30.

49 Jefferson to Elisha Tracy, Aug. 9, 1808; Franklin Papers, Yale Univ. One protest against the embargo was signed by 929 electors of Windham Co., Conn., Tucker-Coleman Coll., Williamsburg Arch. Others came from Newburyport, Boston and Providence, demanding—some of them—that Congress be convened in special session to lift the embargo; Misc. Letters, Dept. of State, Nat. Arch. For the type of threatening letter Jefferson was receiving, see one from Boston signed *John Lane Jones*, Aug. 8, 1808, commencing: "You infernal villain How much longer are you going to keep this damned Embargo on to starve us poor people..."; Jefferson MSS., Huntington Lib.

50 Robert Smith to Gallatin, Aug. 1, 1808; Adams, *Gallatin*, 373.

51 Gallatin to Jefferson, Sept. 16, 1808; Gallatin, *Writings*, I, 418.

52 Gallatin to Jefferson, Aug. 17, 1808; *ibid*, I, 405-7.

53 Jefferson to Thomas Leib, June 23, 1808; *Works*, Ford, XI, 33-5.

54 Jefferson to David B. Warden, July 16, 1808; Jefferson Papers, LC., v. 179, p. 31699.

55 *Lambert's Travels*, II, 64-5.

CHAPTER 63

1 Gallatin to Jefferson, Aug. 6, 1808; Jefferson Papers, LC., v. 179, pp. 31828-9.

2 Wm. Plumer to Jefferson, July 22, 1808; Plumer MSS., LC., v. 3, pp. 440-1.

3 W. C. Nicholas to Jefferson, Oct. 28, 1808; Jefferson Papers, LC.

4 Monroe to Jos. H. Nicholson, Sept. 24, 1808; Nicholson MSS., LC.

5 John G. Jackson to Jefferson, Oct. 9, 1808; Jefferson Papers, LC., v. 181, p. 32182.

6 Jefferson to Jackson, Oct. 13, 1808; *ibid*, v. 181, p. 32202.

7 Robt. Smith to Jefferson, Nov. 1, 1808; *ibid*, v. 182, p. 32325.

8 Jefferson to Gallatin, Aug. 11, 1808; *Works*, Ford, XI, 41-2.

9 Jefferson to Madison, Sept. 6, 1808; *ibid*, XI, 49.

10 Napoleon to Champagny, Feb. 2, 1808; *Adams, Hist. of U.S.*, IV, 293.

11 Armstrong to Madison, Feb. 15, 1808; *ibid*, IV, 295-6.

12 Jefferson to Dearborn, Aug. 12, 1808; *Works*, Ford, XI, 42-3.

13 Jefferson to Short, July 8, 1808; Jefferson Papers, LC., v. 178, p. 31643.

14 Jefferson to Short, Aug. 2, 1808; *ibid*, v. 179, p. 31807. To same, Aug. 29, 1808; *ibid*, v. 180, p. 31973. To Madison, July 29, 1808; Madison Papers, LC., v. 34, p. 113.

15 Jefferson to Emperor of Russia, Aug. 29, 1808; *Works*, Ford, XI, 47-8.

16 Jefferson to Short, Mar. 8, 1809; *ibid*, XI, 102-4. To Armstrong, Mar. 6, 1809; Jefferson Papers, Box 3, N. Y. Pub. Lib.

17 Jefferson to Page, Sept. 6, 1808; Jefferson MSS., U. of Va. The italics are in the original.

18 St. George Tucker to Jefferson, Oct. 5, 1808; Jefferson Papers, LC., v. 181, pp. 32174-5.

19 John Page to Jefferson, Sept. 13, 1808; *ibid*, v. 181, p. 32060.

20 Jefferson to Gallatin, Oct. 10, 1808; *ibid*, v. 181, p. 32183.

21 Gallatin to Jefferson, Oct. 12, 1808; *ibid*, v. 181, p. 32201.

22 St. George Tucker to Jefferson, Oct. 21, 1808; *ibid*, v. 182, pp. 32254-5.

23 Jefferson to St. George Tucker, Dec. 8, 1808; *ibid*, v. 183, p. 32512. To same, Dec. 25, 1808; *ibid*, v. 184, p. 32625.

24 Adams, *Gallatin*, 390.

25 Burwell to Jefferson, Nov. 21, 1808; Jefferson Papers, LC., v. 182, p. 32401. Jefferson to Burwell, Nov. 22, 1808; *Works*, Ford, XI, 75-8.

26 Gallatin to Jefferson, Nov. 15, 1808; Jefferson Papers, LC., v. 182, p. 32372.

27 Jefferson to Dr. George Logan, Dec. 27, 1808; *Writings*, Mont., XII, 219.

28 Gallatin's Draft; *Works*, Ford, XI, 59-62 n. Jefferson to Gallatin, Oct. 30, 1808; *ibid*, XI, 58-9 n.

29 "Eighth Annual Message," Nov. 8, 1808; *ibid*, XI, 56-72.

30 *Annals of Cong.*, 10th Cong., 2nd Sess., 16-17, 19-22, 26.

31 *Ibid*, 105-6.

[32] *Ibid*, 474, 482, 486, 1024-5.
[33] *Ibid*, 345, 436, 451-2.
[34] Jefferson to T. M. Randolph, Nov. 22, 1808, Dec. 13, 1808; Jefferson Papers, LC., v. 182, p. 32402; v. 183, p. 32550.
[35] Jefferson to Gallatin, Dec. 24, 1808; *ibid*, v. 184, p. 32621.
[36] John Taylor to Jefferson, Dec. 23, 1808; *ibid*, v. 184, pp. 32614-6.
[37] Jefferson to Abraham Bishop, Nov. 13, Dec. 8, 1808; *New Haven Col. Hist. Soc. Papers*, v. 1, pp. 143, 144. Bishop to Jefferson, Dec. 14, 1808; *ibid*, v. 1, p. 145.
[38] *N. E. Palladium*, Jan. 3, 1809.
[39] Adams, *Hist. of U. S.*, IV, 411-13.
[40] George Cabot to Pickering, Oct. 5, 1808; Lodge, *Cabot*, 308. H. G. Otis to Josiah Quincy, Dec. 15, 1808; Quincy, *Life of Quincy*, 164.
[41] Gov. Jonathan Trumbull to Dearborn, Feb. 4, 1809; Adams, *Hist. of U. S.*, IV, 417-18.
[42] Jefferson to T. M. Randolph, Jan. 2, 1809; Jefferson Papers, LC., v. 184, p. 32735. See also to C. L. Bankhead, Jan. 19, 1809; Jefferson MSS., Va. H. S.
[43] Jefferson to Monroe, Jan. 28, 1809; *Works*, Ford, XI, 93-6.
[44] Jefferson to T. M. Randolph, Feb. 7, 1809; *ibid*, XI, 96-7.
[45] Jefferson to Gen. Armstrong, Mar. 6, 1809; Jefferson Papers, Box 2, N. Y. Pub. Lib.
[46] Jefferson to Dupont, Mar. 2, 1809; Malone, *Jefferson and Dupont*, 121-3.
[47] *Annals of Cong.*, 10th Cong., 2nd Sess., 456-61.
[48] Jefferson to James Mease, Jan. 15, 1809; Jefferson Papers, LC., v. 185, p. 32807.
[49] Jefferson to T. M. Randolph, Jan. 17, 1809; Jefferson Papers, LC., v. 185, p. 32818a. To Craven Peyton, Jan. 9, 1809; Jefferson MSS., U. of Va.
[50] Jefferson to Abraham Venable, Jan. 23, 1809; *Works*, Ford, XI, 91-2. To Madison, May 29, 1809; *ibid*, XI, 92-4 n.
[51] Jefferson to James Ronaldson, Feb. 13, 1809; Jefferson Papers, LC., v. 186, p. 33015. To Caleb Kirk, Feb. 13, 1809; *ibid*, v. 186, p. 33016. Kirk to Jefferson, Feb. 17, 1809; *ibid*, v. 186, pp. 33047-50. James Mease to Jefferson, Feb. 27, 1809; *ibid*, v. 186, pp. 33137-8.
[52] M. B. Smith, *Forty Years*, 410.
[53] Weather Bk., Mar. 11, 1809; LC.

CHAPTER 64

[1] Jefferson to Madison, Mar. 17, 1809; *Writings*, Mont., XII, 266-8.
[2] Jefferson Papers, LC., v. 187, *passim*.
[3] MS. and Printed Broadside, Mar., 1809; Henley-Smith Papers, LC.
[4] Jefferson to Madison, May 22, 1809; Madison Papers, LC., v. 37, p. 92.
[5] Jefferson to T. M. Randolph, Jan. 31, 1809; *Writings*, Mont., XVIII, 262-4.
[6] H. W. Pierson, *Jefferson at Monticello*, 29, 45-52, 56, 70-4, 86, 93-9. This valuable little book consists chiefly of the dictated reminiscences of Edmund Bacon. Other illuminating sidelights on the daily life of Jefferson and his family may be found in the reminiscences of his Negro servant, Isaac Jefferson; Jefferson MSS., U. of Va. With considerable pride Isaac declared that "nary man in this town walked so straight as my master." Jefferson would wear "Vaginny cloth & a red waist coat . . . & small clothes: arter dat he used to wear red breeches too." But Isaac added a touch of realism. On being shown a published picture of Jefferson, the former slave shook his head. "Old master," he declared, "never dat handsome in dis world." He substantiated Bacon's account of Martha as a "mighty peacable woman: never holler for servant; make no fuss nor racket." But he disagreed on Thomas Mann, her husband. The latter he thought to be a fine master.
[7] Jefferson to John S. Barnes, Apr. 27, 1809; Jefferson Papers, LC., v. 187, p. 33275.
[8] Jefferson to Levi Lincoln, Mar. 11, 1809; *ibid*, v. 187, p. 33197.
[9] Jefferson to Madison, Mar. 17, 1809; *supra*.
[10] Jefferson to James Jay, Apr. 7, 1809; *Writings*, Mont., XII, 271.
[11] Jefferson to Madison, Apr. 27, 1809; Rives Papers, LC.
[12] Jefferson to Madison, Mar. 30, 1809; *ibid*.
[13] Jefferson to Madison, Apr. 18, 1809; *Works*, Ford, XI, 106-7.
[14] Jefferson to W. C. Nicholas, May 25, 1809; *ibid*, XI, 107-8.
[15] Jefferson to Freneau, May 22, 1809; Jefferson Papers, LC., v. 187, p. 33305.
[16] Jefferson to John Wyche, May 19, 1809; *Writings*, Mont., XII, 282.

[17] Jefferson to B. S. Barton, Sept. 21, 1809; *ibid*, XII, 312-14. To John S. Barnes, Aug. 3, 1809; Jefferson Papers, LC., v. 188, p. 33416.

[18] Jefferson to Madison, Oct. 9, 1809; Madison Papers, LC., v. 39, p. 30.

[19] Lafayette to Jefferson, June 12, 1809; Chinard, *Letters of Lafayette and Jefferson*, 287-8.

[20] Lafayette to Jefferson, Nov. 16, 1810; *ibid*, 318-21.

[21] Jefferson to Lafayette, Jan. 20, 1811; *ibid*, 321-3.

[22] Jefferson to James Fishback, Sept. 27, 1809; Jefferson Papers, Box 2, N. Y. Pub. Lib.

[23] Jefferson to Claiborne, Sept. 10, 1809; Jefferson Papers, LC., v. 188, p. 33470.

[24] Jefferson to Wm. Lambert, Sept. 10, 1809; *ibid*, v. 188, p. 33471. To Meriwether Lewis, Aug. 16, 1809; *ibid*, v. 188, p. 33429. To Madison, Aug. 17, 1809; Madison Papers, LC., v. 38, p. 78.

[25] Jefferson to Gallatin, Oct. 11, 1809; *Works*, Ford, XI, 124-6.

[26] Gallatin to Jefferson, Nov. 11, 1809; Jefferson Papers, LC., v. 189, pp. 33555-6.

[27] Jefferson to Rush, Sept. 22, 1809; *ibid*, v. 188, p. 33495. The manuscript is badly mutilated.

[28] Jefferson to Madison, Nov. 30, 1809; *ibid*, v. 189, p. 33576.

[29] Jefferson to Joel Barlow, Jan. 24, 1810; *Works*, Ford, XI, 131-2. See also to Walter Jones, Mar. 5, 1810; *ibid*, XI, 137-9.

[30] Jefferson to Wm. A. Burwell, Feb. 25, 1810; *Jefferson Correspondence: Bixby Coll.*, 192-4.

[31] Jefferson to Henry Dearborn, July 16, 1810; *Works*, Ford, XI, 142-5.

[32] Jefferson to John Langdon, Mar. 5, 1810; *Writings*, Mont., XII, 373 ff.

[33] Jefferson to Kosciusko, Feb. 26, 1810; *ibid*, XII, 369-70.

[34] Jefferson to Gov. John Tyler, May 26, 1810; *ibid*, XII, 391-4.

[35] Tyler to Jefferson, May 12, 1810; L. G. Tyler, *The Letters and Times of the Tylers*, I, 244-7.

[36] Jefferson to Tyler, May 26, 1810; *supra*.

[37] Jefferson to Madison, May 25, 1810; *Works*, Ford, XI, 139-41. See the letters from Gov. Claiborne to Jefferson giving some of the background of the "Batture" case; *Claiborne's Letter Bks.*, IV, *passim*. See also, W. B. Hatcher, *Edward Livingston*, for an extended consideration of the proceedings.

[38] Jefferson to Gallatin, Aug. 16, 1810; *Writings*, Mont., XII, 409-13. He also asked Wm. B. Giles to prevent the Senate from doing anything that might prove "injurious to a fair trial"; Nov. 12, 1810; *ibid*, XII, 175-6.

[39] Jefferson to Barnes, June 15, 1809; Jefferson Papers, LC., v. 187, p. 33346.

[40] Jefferson to Kosciusko, Feb. 26, 1810; *supra*.

[41] Jefferson to George Hay, June 18, 1810; Jefferson Papers, LC., v. 190, p. 33841.

[42] Hay to Jefferson, July 15, 1810; *ibid*, v. 190, pp. 33866-7.

[43] Jefferson to Hay, Aug. 1, 1810; *ibid*, v. 190, p. 33896.

[44] Livingston v. Jefferson, 15 *Fed. Cas.* 8411 (1811). The ethical basis for Tyler's sitting in a case involving the man who was not only a personal friend, but had been directly responsible for his appointment to the bench, is doubtful, to say the least. This must be set in opposition to the angry protestations by Jefferson and later commentators to the incident in the trial of Burr, when Justice Marshall attended a social function to which Burr had also been invited.

[45] Jefferson to Madison, Oct. 15, 1810; *Works*, Ford, XI, 150-4.

[46] Jefferson to Gallatin, Sept. 27, 1810; Jefferson Papers, LC., v. 191, p. 33981.

[47] The court records, the briefs, and the voluminous correspondence are in the Jefferson MSS., U. of Va.

CHAPTER 65

[1] Jefferson to Wm. Plumer, July 12, 1810; Tucker-Coleman Coll., Colonial Wmsburg Arch. Jefferson to Madison, June 27, 1810; Jefferson Papers, LC., v. 190, p. 33850.

[2] Jefferson to Madison, May 13, 1810; *Writings*, Mont., XII, 389.

[3] Jefferson to Wm. Thornton, Apr. 27, May 24, 1810; Jefferson Papers, LC., v. 190, pp. 33755, 33792.

[4] Farm Bk., Mass. H. S.

[5] Pierson, *Jefferson at Monticello*, 124-5. "Reminiscences of Isaac Jefferson," U. of Va.

[6] Jefferson to J. W. Eppes, Sept. 18, 1812, July 16, 1814; *Huntington Lib. Quarterly*, VI, 342-5, 348. Unfortunately, the building is no longer in existence; it burnt down in 1845.

[7] Jefferson to Judge Innes, Sept. 18, 1813; Jefferson Papers, Mass. H. S.
[8] John Randolph's Diary; Va. State Lib. (copy).
[9] Jefferson to P. Minor, Sept. 24, 1811; Jefferson Papers, Mass. H. S.
[10] Jefferson to Jeremiah A. Goodman, Feb. 3, 1814; original at Monticello, photostat in U. of Va.
[11] Jefferson to Jos. C. Cabell, June 27, 1810; Jefferson MSS., U. of Va.
[12] Jefferson to Wm. Duane, Aug. 12, Sept. 16, 1810; *Writings*, Mont., XII, 404-9, 413-17.
[13] Destutt Tracy, *A Commentary and Review of Montesquieu's Spirit of Laws* (Phila., 1811), 12-13, 19, 33, 43.
[14] Jefferson to Destutt Tracy, Jan. 26, 1811; *Works*, Ford, XI, 181-9.
[15] Jefferson to Duane, Mar. 28, 1811; *ibid*, XI, 189-95.
[16] Jefferson to Wm. Wirt, Mar. 30, 1811; Jefferson Papers, LC., v. 193, p. 34265. Wirt to Jefferson, Apr. 10, 1811; *ibid*, v. 193, p. 34281. Jefferson to Wirt, Apr. 15, 1811; *ibid*, v. 193, p. 34288.
[17] Jefferson to Duane, Apr. 30, 1811; *Works*, Ford, XI, 195-7 n.
[18] Duane to Jefferson, July 5, 1811; Jefferson Papers, LC., v. 193, p. 34364.
[19] Jefferson to Gov. Milledge, Jan. 5, 1811; *ibid*, v. 193, p. 34348.
[20] Jefferson to J. W. Eppes, Jan. 5, 1811; *Works*, Ford, XI, 160-1.
[21] Jefferson to J. W. Eppes, Mar. 24, 1811; Jefferson MSS., Huntington Lib.
[22] Jefferson to Madison, Apr. 7, 1811; Rives Papers, LC.
[23] Jefferson to Dupont, Apr. 15, 1811; *Works*, Ford, XI, 203-4.
[24] Jefferson to Wm. A. Burwell, Aug. 19, 1811; *Jefferson Correspondence: Bixby Coll.*, 198-9.
[25] Rush to Jefferson, Aug. 26, 1811; Jefferson Papers, LC., v. 193, pp. 34419-21.
[26] Jefferson to Charles Clay, Aug. 23, 1811; *Writings*, Mont., XIII, 80-1. To J. W. Eppes, Sept. 6, 1811; Jefferson Papers, LC., v. 194, p. 34441. To Wm. Lambert, Dec. 29, 1811; *ibid*, v. 194, p. 34537. Weather Bk., Sept. 17, 1811; LC. To H. Dearborn, Nov. 15, 1811; *Writings*, Mont., XIII, 110-12.
[27] "Notes on Rivanna River Canal," 1811; Jefferson Papers, LC., v. 194, pp. 34545-55.
[28] Jefferson to George Hay, Dec. 28, 1811; *ibid*, v. 194, p. 34535.
[29] Jefferson to J. W. Eppes, Sept. 6, 1811; *ibid*, v. 194, p. 34441.
[30] Rush to Jefferson, Jan. 2, 1811; *ibid*, v. 192, pp. 34150-2.
[31] Jefferson to Rush, Jan. 16, 1811; *Works*, Ford, XI, 165-73.
[32] Jefferson to Rush, Dec. 5, 1811; Jefferson Papers, LC., v. 194, pp. 34511-12. The letter is printed in the Ford and the Monticello editions, but both omit, for some unexplained reason, the name of the neighbors who brought the good news from Braintree to Monticello.
[33] Rush to Jefferson, Dec. 17, 1811; *ibid*, v. 194, pp. 34523-5.
[34] Adams to Rush, Dec. 25, 1811; Adams, *Works*, X, 10-12.

CHAPTER 66

[1] Adams to Jefferson, Jan. 1, 1812; Jefferson Papers, LC., v. 194, p. 34564.
[2] Jefferson to Adams, Jan. 21, 1812; *Works*, Ford, XI, 218-21.
[3] Jefferson to Rush, Jan. 21, 1812; *ibid*, XI, 218-19 n.
[4] Adams to Jefferson, Feb. 3, 1812; Jefferson Papers, LC., v. 195, pp. 34636-7.
[5] Rush to Jefferson, Feb. 3, 1812; *ibid*, v. 195, p. 34638.
[6] Jefferson to Rush, Mar. 6, 1813; *Writings*, Mont., XIII, 225-6.
[7] Adams to Jefferson, May 1, 1812; Jefferson Papers, LC., v. 196, p. 34808.
[8] Jefferson to James Pleasants, Feb. 9, 1812; Tucker-Coleman Coll., Colonial Williamsburg Arch.
[9] Jefferson to Madison, Apr. 17, 1812; *Works*, Ford, XI, 232-6.
[10] Jefferson to Madison, June 29, 1812; Jefferson Papers, LC., v. 196, p. 34889. (omitted from *Works*, Ford, XI, 262-4). The original is in Rives Papers, LC.
[11] Jefferson to Patrick Gibson, Apr. 12, 1812; *ibid*, v. 195, p. 34764.
[12] Jefferson to Wm. Duane, Apr. 20, 1812; *ibid*, v. 195, p. 34787.
[13] Jefferson to Judge John Tyler, June 17, 1812; *Writings*, Mont., XIII, 165-8.
[14] Adams to Jefferson, June 28, 1812; Adams, *Works*, X, 17-20.
[15] Jefferson to Rush, Mar. 6, 1813; *Writings*, Mont., XIII, 225-6. To Adams, May 27, 1813; *ibid*, XIII, 249.

[16] Jefferson to Kosciusko, June 28, 1812; *Works*, Ford, XI, 258-62.
[17] Jefferson to John Melish, Jan. 13, 1813; *ibid*, XI, 274-80.
[18] Jefferson to Wm. Duane, Aug. 4, 1812; *ibid*, XI, 264-7.
[19] Jefferson to Madison, Nov. 6, 1812; *ibid*, XI, 270-1.
[20] Jefferson to John Hollins, Sept. 16, 1812; Jefferson Papers, LC., v. 196, p. 34947.
[21] Jefferson to Madison, Aug. 12, 1812; Rives Papers, LC.
[22] Jefferson to Elbridge Gerry, June 11, 1812; Franklin Papers, Yale Univ.
[23] Jefferson to James Ronaldson, Oct. 11, 1812; Jefferson Papers, LC., v. 196, p. 34969.
[24] Jefferson to John Barnes, Oct. 8, 1812; *ibid*, v. 196, p. 34968. To Philip Barbour, Oct. 12, 1812, Jan. 4, 1813; *ibid*, v. 197, pp. 34971, 35054-8 (re Rivanna canal). To Archibald Thweatt, May 27, 1812; Jefferson MSS., U. of Va. (This referred to litigation with "the old drunkard [Samuel] Scott" over a fifty acre plot, and became infinitely complicated.) To Monroe, Nov. 3, 1812; Jefferson Papers, LC., v. 197, p. 34994.
[25] Jefferson to Short, Oct. 17, 1812; Jefferson-Short Papers, Wm. & Mary Coll.
[26] Jefferson to Richard M. Johnson, Jan. 29, 1813; Jefferson Papers, LC., v. 197, p. 35094.
[27] Jefferson to Thos. Cooper, July 10, 1812; *Writings*, Mont., XIII, 176.
[28] Jefferson to M. de Bécourt, Feb. 6, 1813; Jefferson Papers, LC., v. 197, p. 35105.
[29] Jefferson to Thos. Cooper, July 10, 1812; *supra*.
[30] Jefferson to Duane, Jan. 22, 1813; *Writings*, Mont., XIII, 213-15.
[31] Jefferson to Duane, Apr. 4, 1813; *ibid*, XIII, 231.
[32] Jefferson to Monroe, June 19, 1813; Monroe Papers, LC., v. 19, p. 3441.
[33] Jefferson to Monroe, May 30, 1813; *Writings*, Mont., XIII, 250-2. To Madison, June 18, 1813; *ibid*, XIII, 259-61. Monroe to Jefferson, June 16, 1813; Monroe, *Writings*, V, 268-71.
[34] Jefferson to Madison, June 21, 1813; *ibid*, XIII, 265-8.
[35] Jefferson to Archibald Robertson, Apr. 30, 1813; Jefferson MSS., U. of Va. To Brown & Robertson, Aug. 27, 1813; *ibid*. To Short, Apr. 25, 1813; Jefferson-Short Papers, Wm. & Mary Coll.
[36] G. Duvall to Madison, Sept. 5, 1812; Madison Papers, LC., v. 49, p. 32.
[37] Jefferson to Madison, Feb. 21, 1813; *Works*, Ford, XI, 281-4.
[38] Jefferson to Mrs. Trist, May 10, 1813; Jefferson Papers, Mo. H. S.
[39] The extant correspondence between the brothers is chiefly in the Jefferson MSS., U. of Va., and may be conveniently found in Mayo, *Jefferson and his unknown brother, Randolph*. Tales of Randolph's simple-mindedness are in Isaac Jefferson's Reminiscences, U. of Va., and in Edgar Wood, *Albemarle County in Virginia*, 237-8.
[40] Jefferson's Deposition, Sept. 15, 1815; Jefferson MSS., U. of Va.
[41] Jefferson to Richard Rush, May 31, 1813; *Works*, Ford, XI, 291-3.
[42] Jefferson to Margaret de Bonneville, Apr. 3, 1813; Jefferson Papers, LC., v. 198, p. 35183.
[43] Adams to Jefferson, June 25, 1813; *ibid*, v. 198, pp. 35288-9.
[44] Adams to Jefferson, June 14, 1813; *ibid*, v. 198, p. 35267. (Printed with minor variations in Adams, *Works*, X, 42-3.)
[45] Jefferson to Adams, June 27, 1813; *ibid*, v. 198, p. 35291. (Printed with variations in *Writings*, Mont., XIII, 279-84.)
[46] Adams to Jefferson, June 30, 1813; Adams, *Works*, X, 46-9.
[47] Adams to Jefferson, July 9, 1813; *ibid*, X, 49-52.
[48] Jefferson to Adams, Aug. 22, 1813; *Works*, Ford, XI, 323-34.
[49] Jefferson to Abigail Adams, Aug. 22, 1813; Jefferson Papers, LC., v. 199, p. 35403. Abigail Adams to Jefferson, Sept. 20, 1813; *ibid*, v. 199, p. 35459.
[50] Jefferson to Adams, Oct. 28, 1813; *Works*, Ford, XI, 341-50.
[51] Jefferson to John Waldo, Aug. 16, 1813; *Writings*, Mont., XIII, 338-47.
[52] Jefferson to Lafayette, Nov. 30, 1813; *Works*, Ford, XI, 356-60. To Humboldt, Dec. 6, 1813; *ibid*, XI, 350-5.

CHAPTER 67

[1] Joseph C. Cabell to Jefferson, Jan. 12, 1813; *Early History of the Univ. of Va.* (J. W. Randolph, ed.), 6.
[2] Cabell to Jefferson, Feb. 17, 1813; *ibid*, 7-8.
[3] Jefferson to Cabell, Nov. 7, 1813; *ibid*, 8-9.
[4] Jefferson to Wm. Cocke, Apr. 17, 1813; Jefferson Papers, LC., v. 198, p. 35203.
[5] Jefferson to James Martin, Sept. 20, 1813; *Works*, Ford, XI, 335-8.

[6] Jefferson to J. W. Eppes, June 24, Sept. 11, Nov. 6, 1813; *ibid*, XI, 297-306, 306-15 n., 315-32 n. A paragraph relating to the Bank of the United States and Jefferson's expectation that its charter would never be renewed was included in the final letter, but was then stricken out (see draft copy in Jefferson MSS., U. of Va.). See also Jefferson to J. C. Cabell, Jan. 17, 1814 (Jefferson MSS., U. of Va.) for additional arguments by him along the same lines. He had hoped, he wrote, that "good old Virginia" might start the cure for paper money "by passing a law that after a certain time, suppose of 6. months, no bank bill of less than 10.D. should be permitted; that after some other reasonable term there should be none less than 20.D. and so on, until these only should be left in circulation whose size would be above the common transactions of any but merchants."

[7] Jefferson to T. M. Randolph, Nov. 14, 1813; Jefferson Papers, LC., v. 200, pp. 35522-3.

[8] Jefferson to Logan, Oct. 3, 1813; *Works*, Ford, XI, 338-41.

[9] Jefferson to Horatio G. Spofford, Mar. 17, 1814; *Writings*, Mont., XIV, 118-20.

[10] Jefferson to Adams, Jan. 24, 1814; Jefferson Papers, LC., v. 200, p. 35638.

[11] *Ibid.*

[12] Jefferson to Archibald Robertson, June 21, 1814; Jefferson MSS., U. of Va. Obviously the year of 1755 was written in error for some other year; which one, however, it is difficult to say.

[13] Jefferson to Dr. Cooper, Jan. 16, 1814; *Writings*, Mont., XIV, 61.

[14] Jefferson to J. C. Cabell, Sept. 23, 1814; Jefferson MSS., U. of Va.

[15] Jefferson to Caspar Wistar, Aug. 17, 1813; Jefferson Papers, LC., v. 199, p. 35388. To Correa, Apr. 19, 1814; *ibid*, v. 201, p. 35738.

[16] Francis Calley Gray, *Thomas Jefferson in 1814*, 67.

[17] *Ibid*, 68. Ticknor, *Life, Letters and Journals*, I, 34-6.

[18] Ticknor, *op. cit.*, I, 36-7.

[19] *Ibid*, 37-8.

[20] Jefferson to B. F. Barton, Apr. 3, 1814; Jefferson Papers, LC., v. 201, p. 35722.

[21] Jefferson to Thomas Law, June 13, 1814; *Writings*, Mont., XIV, 138-44.

[22] Jefferson to Miles King, Sept. 26, 1814; *ibid*, XIV, 196-8.

[23] Jefferson to J. C. Cabell, Jan. 31, 1814; *Works*, Ford, XI, 382.

[24] Jefferson to Dr. Cooper, Jan. 16, 1814; *supra.*

[25] Jefferson to Dr. Cooper, Oct. 7, 1814; *Writings*, Mont., XIV, 199-202.

[26] Jefferson to Peter Carr, Sept. 7, 1814; Jefferson Papers, LC., v. 202, pp. 35947-50.

[27] Cabell to Jefferson, Feb. 14, Feb. 21, 1816; *Early Hist. of the Univ. of Va.*, 56, 57-60.

[28] Cabell to Jefferson, Feb. 26, 1816; *ibid*, 60-1.

[29] Jefferson to Francis Gilmer, Nov. 23, 1814; Jefferson MSS., U. of Va.

[30] Jefferson to Adams, July 5, 1814; *Works*, Ford, XI, 393-400.

[31] Adams to Jefferson, July 16, 1814; Adams, *Works*, X, 100-5.

[32] Jefferson to Adams, July 5, 1814; *supra.*

[33] Jefferson to Girardin, Dec. 21, 1814; Jefferson MSS., Am. Philos. Soc.

[34] Jefferson to Short, Aug. 20, 1814; *Writings*, Mont., XVIII, 283.

[35] Jefferson to Samuel H. Smith, Sept. 21, 1814; *Works*, Ford, XI, 427-30.

[36] Acct. Bk., Apr. 29, 1815; Mass. H. S.

CHAPTER 68

[1] Jefferson to Jeremiah A. Goodman, Dec. 10, 1814; Jefferson Papers, LC., v. 202, p. 36078.

[2] Jefferson to Madison, Oct. 15, 1814; *Works*, Ford, XI, 432-6. To Monroe, Jan. 1, 1815; *ibid*, XI, 442-6. To Wm. H. Crawford, Feb. 11, 1815; *ibid*, XI, 450-4.

[3] Jefferson to Lafayette, Feb. 14, 1815; *ibid*, XI, 454-64.

[4] Monroe to Jefferson, Feb. 15, 1815; Jefferson Papers, LC., v. 203, p. 36151.

[5] Jefferson to Madison, Mar. 23, 1815; *Works*, Ford, XI, 464-8.

[6] Jefferson to Dupont, Feb. 28, 1815; Malone, *Jefferson and Dupont*, 150-3.

[7] Jefferson to David B. Warden, Warden Papers, Md. H. S.

[8] Jefferson to Samuel H. Smith, May 8, 1815; Henley-Smith Papers, LC.

[9] Jefferson to Short, Mar. 25, 1815; Jefferson MSS., Huntington Lib.

[10] Jefferson to Short, May 15, 1815; *Writings*, Mont., XVIII, 287.

[11] Jefferson to Thomas Leiper, June 12, 1815; *Works*, Ford, XI, 475-80.

[12] Jefferson to Mazzei, Aug. 9, 1815; *ibid*, XI, 483.

[13] Jefferson to Caesar A. Rodney, Mar. 16, 1815; Jefferson Papers, LC., v. 203, pp. 36194-5.

[14] Jefferson to George W. Campbell, Oct. 15, 1815; *ibid*, v. 205, p. 36473. See also to Gallatin, Oct. 16, 1815; Gallatin, *Works*, V, 408.

[15] Jefferson to Monroe, July 15, 1815; Monroe Papers, LC., v. 23, p. 4081.

[16] Jefferson to Benjamin Waterhouse, Oct. 13, 1815; Jefferson Papers, LC., v. 205, p. 36464.

[17] Jefferson to George Watterston, May 7, 1815; *ibid*, v. 204, pp. 36275-6. To John Vaughan, Mar. 1, 1815; *ibid*, v. 203, p. 36169. To Ticknor, July 4, 1815; Jefferson Papers, Mass. H. S. To Adams, June 10, 1815; *Writings*, Mont., XIV, 299-302.

[18] Jefferson to Madison, Mar. 24, 1815; Madison Papers, LC., v. 58, p. 92.

[19] Jefferson to J. F. Oliviera Fernandez, Dec. 16, 1815; Jefferson Papers, LC., v. 205, p. 36543.

[20] Adams to Jefferson, Oct. 20, 1815; *ibid*, v. 205, p. 36481.

[21] Jefferson to Adams, Aug. 10, 1815; *Works*, Ford, XI, 484-8.

[22] Adams to Jefferson, Aug. 24, 1815; Adams, *Works*, X, 172.

[23] Adams to Jefferson, May 3, 1816; *ibid*, X, 213-16.

[24] Jefferson to Adams, Aug. 1, 1816; *ibid*, X, 222-3.

[25] Jefferson to Wm. Caruthers, Mar. 15, 1815; Jefferson Papers, LC., v. 203, p. 36192.

[26] Jefferson to Martha J. Randolph, Aug. 31, 1815; Jefferson MSS., Morgan Lib.

[27] Weather Bk., Sept. 18, 1815; LC. Peachy Gilmer to F. W. Gilmer, Oct. 3, 1815; Davis, *Gilmer*, 90.

[28] Jefferson to John Milledge, Sept. 22, 1815; Jefferson Papers, LC.

[29] Jefferson to A. Partridge, Jan. 2, 1816; *Writings*, Mont., XIV, 374-9. To Joseph Correa, Jan. 1, 1816; Jefferson Papers, LC., v. 205, pp. 36574-5. Dupont to Jefferson, Dec. 10, 1815; Malone, *Jefferson and Dupont*, 226. Jefferson to Charles Clay, Nov. 18, 1815; copy of privately owned letter in Jefferson MSS., U. of Va.

[30] Jefferson to Chas. Yancey, Jan. 6, 1816; *Works*, Ford, XI, 493-7.

[31] Jefferson to Benjamin Austin, Jan. 9, 1816; *ibid*, XI, 500-5.

[32] Jefferson to Jos. C. Cabell, Feb. 2, 1816; Jefferson Papers, LC., v. 199, p. 35493. The letter itself, without the addenda, is printed in *Writings*, Mont., XIV, 421.

[33] Jefferson to Wm. H. Crawford, June 20, 1816; *Works*, Ford, XI, 537-41.

[34] Jefferson to Samuel Kercheval, July 12, 1816; *Works*, Ford, XII, 3-15.

[35] Jefferson to Kercheval, Oct. 8, 1816; *ibid*, XII, 17 n.

[36] See, as another example, Jefferson to Dr. Logan, May 19, 1816; *ibid*, XI, 525-7.

[37] Jefferson to Chas. Thomson, Jan. 19, 1816; *ibid*, XI, 498-500.

[38] *Ibid*. He nevertheless placed himself unreservedly in the hands of a comparative stranger, F. A. Vander Kamp: "Ridicule," he declared to him, "is the only weapon which can be used against unintelligible propositions. Ideas must be distinct before reason can act upon them; and no man ever had a distinct idea of the trinity. It is a mere Abracadabra of the mountebanks calling themselves the priests of Jesus." (July 30, 1816; Jefferson Papers, LC., v. 207, p. 36985.)

[39] Jefferson to Mrs. S. H. Smith, Aug. 6, 1816; Henley-Smith Papers, LC. See also to Joseph Delaplaine, Nov. 23, 1816; Jefferson Papers, LC., v. 209, p. 37201.

[40] Jefferson to Short, May 5, 1816; Jefferson Papers, LC., v. 207, pp. 36844-5. See also to Delaplaine, Feb. 9, 1816; *ibid*, v. 206, p. 36678: "To become my own biographer is the last thing in the world I would undertake. No. If there has been any thing in my course worth the public attention, they are better judges of it than I can be myself, and to them it is my duty to leave it."

[41] Jefferson to Joseph Milligan, Apr. 6, 1816; *Writings*, Mont., XIV, 456-66. To Thomas Ritchie, Mar. 8, Apr. 6, 1816; Jefferson Papers, LC., v. 206, pp. 36736, 36784. To Dupont, Aug. 3, 1816; Malone, *Jefferson and Dupont*, 187-91.

[42] Jefferson to Cabell, asking him to translate the works of another French economist, Jean Baptiste Say, Feb. 28, 1816; Cabell, *Early Hist. of the Univ. of Va.*, 62.

[43] Jefferson to Adams, Oct. 14, 1816; *Writings*, Mont., XV, 73-8.

CHAPTER 69

[1] Jefferson to Monroe, Feb. 4, 1816; *Works*, Ford, XI, 514-18.

[2] Jefferson to Dupont, Apr. 24, 1816; *ibid*, XI, 519-25.

[3] Jefferson to Barbé-Marbois, June 14, 1817; *Writings*, Mont., XV, 130.

[4] Jefferson to Wm. Lee, Aug. 24, 1816; Jefferson Papers, LC., v. 208, p. 37032.

[5] Jefferson to Isaac H. Tiffany, Aug. 26, 1826; *Writings*, Mont., XV, 65-6.

[6] Jefferson to Monroe, Oct. 16, 1816; *Works*, Ford, XII, 39-41.

[7] Jefferson to Thomas Appleton, July 18, 1816, June 30, 1820; *ibid*, XII, 16-20, 26-7 n. To G. Carmigniani, July 18, 1816; *ibid*, XII, 20-2 n.

[8] Jefferson to Burwell, Feb. 6, 1817; Jefferson Papers, LC., v. 209, p. 37268. See also to Wm. Duane, Jan. 24, 1817; *ibid*, v. 209, p. 37248.

[9] Adams to Jefferson, Feb. 2, 1817; *ibid*, v. 209, pp. 37264-5.

[10] Jefferson to Adams, Jan. 11, 1817; *Works*, Ford, XII, 46-9.

[11] Adams to Jefferson, Feb. 2, 1817; *supra.*

[12] Jefferson to Chas. Thomson, Jan. 29, 1817; *Works*, Ford, XII, 51-3.

[13] Jefferson to Wm. Sampson, Jan. 26, 1817; *ibid*, XII, 49-51.

[14] Jefferson to Monroe, Apr. 8, 1817; Jefferson Papers, LC., v. 209, p. 37363. To Cathalan, June 6, 1817; *ibid*, v. 210, pp. 37451-2.

[15] Jefferson to Gallatin, June 16, 1817; *Works*, Ford, XII, 70-4.

[16] Jefferson to Cabell, Sept. 9, 1817; Cabell, *Early Hist. of the Univ. of Va.*, 79-80.

[17] "A Bill for establishing a system of public education" [Sept. 9, 1817]; Jefferson MSS., U. of Va. Printed with some variations in *Writings*, Mont., XVII, 418-41.

[18] Jefferson to Cabell, Sept. 10, 1817; Cabell, *Early Hist of the Univ. of Va.*, 80-1.

[19] Jefferson to Cabell, Oct. 24, 1817; Jefferson Papers, LC., v. 211, p. 37688.

[20] Jefferson to Monroe, Dec. 13, 1817; Jefferson MSS., U. of Va. To Cabell, Dec. 18, 1817; *ibid.*

[21] Cabell to Jefferson, Dec. 29, 1817; Cabell, *Early Hist. of the Univ. of Va.*, 89-94.

[22] Cabell to Jefferson, Feb. 13, 1818; *ibid*, 122-3.

[23] Jefferson to Cabell, Jan. 6, 1818; Tucker-Coleman Coll., Colonial Wmsburg Arch. To same, Feb. 16, 1818; Cabell, *op. cit.*, 124-5. To same, Feb. 26, 1818; *ibid*, 128-9.

[24] Cabell to Jefferson, Feb. 20, 22, 1818; Cabell, *op. cit.*, 125-6, 127.

[25] Jefferson to Francis Gilmer, Apr. 10, 1818; Jefferson MSS., U. of Va.

[26] "Report of the Commissioners," Aug. 1-4, 1818; *ibid.* With some variations it appeared in the later pamphlet, and is printed in Cabell, *op. cit.*, 432-47. For the incident of the map, etc., see Bruce, *Hist. of Univ. of Va.*, I, 218.

[27] Jefferson to Thos. Cooper, Aug. 7, Sept. 12, 1818; Jefferson Papers, LC., v. 213, pp. 38059, 38082. To Wm. Alston, Oct. 6, 1818; *ibid*, v. 213, p. 38093. To Martha J. Randolph, Aug. 14, 1818 (2 letters); Jefferson MSS., Morgan Lib.

[28] Jefferson to Hugh Chisolm, Aug. 31, 1817; Jefferson MSS., U. of Va.

[29] Jefferson to J. W. Eppes, May 1, 1817; Jefferson MSS., Huntington Lib.

[30] Memorandum Bk., with specifications, calculations, plans and pen and ink drawings; Jefferson MSS., U. of Va.

[31] Jefferson to J. W. Eppes, Aug. 6, 1817; Jefferson MSS., Huntington Lib.

[32] Jefferson to Latrobe, June 12, 1817; Jefferson Papers, LC., v. 210, p. 37469. See also to Wm. Thornton, May 9, 1817; Jefferson MSS., U. of Va.: "Will you set your imagination to work and sketch some designs for us?"

[33] Thornton to Jefferson, May 27, 1817; Jefferson Papers, LC., v. 210, pp. 37440-2. Latrobe to Jefferson, July 24, 1817; *ibid*, v. 210, p. 37535. In a letter dated Aug. 12, 1817, Latrobe thought Jefferson's east-and-west arrangement of the dormitories in his "academical village" unfortunate and insisted they be pivoted to the north and south. F. Kimball is convinced that the idea of a Rotunda was first proposed by Latrobe and had not previously occurred to Jefferson. The point is arguable, but Jefferson's drawings and descriptions of the dome in the Huntington Lib. MSS. might be dated as May-June, 1817—*before* he received Latrobe's letter. Furthermore, the idea of a dome had always fascinated him (*vide* Monticello and Washington) and, as he had declared on several previous occasions, a library was one of the essentials he predicated for his College.

[34] Jefferson to Madison, Nov. 15, 1817; Madison Papers, LC., v. 64, p. 113.

[35] Cooper to Jefferson, Sept. 17, Dec. 7, 1817; Jefferson MSS., U. of Va.

[36] Jefferson to J. W. Eppes, Feb. 6, 1818; Jefferson MSS., Huntington Lib.

[37] Cooper to Jefferson, Oct. 6, 1818; Jefferson MSS., U. of Va.

[38] Jefferson to Cooper, Apr. 2, 1819; *ibid.*

[39] Jefferson to W. C. Nicholas, May 4, 1819; *ibid.*

[40] Contract between Thomas Appleton and Messrs. Michele and Jacopo Raggi, Feb. 17, 1819; photostat, U. of Va. Jefferson to A. S. Brockenbrough, July 2, 1819; Jefferson MSS., U. of Va.

CHAPTER 70

[1] Jefferson to Nathaniel Burwell, Mar. 14, 1818; *Works*, Ford, XII, 90-3.

[2] Jefferson to Gallatin, Nov. 24, 1818; Chinard, *Jefferson and les Idéologues*, 182.

[3] Jefferson to Robert Walsh, Feb. 19, 1818; Jefferson Papers, LC., v. 212, p. 37871.

[4] Jefferson to Milligan, Jan. 3, 1818; *ibid*, v. 212, p. 37778. To Walsh, Jan. 9, 1818; Jefferson MSS., U. of Va. Walsh to Francis Gilmer, Nov. 4, 1817; Gilmer Papers, U. of Va.

[5] Jefferson to Milligan, Jan. 12, 1819; Jefferson Papers, LC., v. 214, p. 38228.

[6] Jefferson to Matthew Cary, Nov. 22, 1818; *ibid*, v. 214, pp. 38150-1 (italics in the text added).

[7] Jefferson to Adams, May 17, 1818; *Works*, Ford, XII, 94-6.

[8] Jefferson to Salma Hales, July 26, 1818; Jefferson Papers, LC., v. 213, p. 38048.

[9] Jefferson to Gallatin, Feb. 15, 1818; *ibid*, v. 212, p. 37862.

[10] Jefferson to Van der Kemp, Feb. 9, 1818; *ibid*, v. 212, pp. 37850-3.

[11] Jefferson to Baron de Neuville, Dec. 13, 1818; facsimile in Jefferson Papers, Box 1, N. Y. Pub. Lib. To Wm. H. Crawford, Nov. 10, 1818; *Works*, Ford, XII, 100-2.

[12] Jefferson to Mordecai M. Noah, May 28, 1818; Jefferson Papers, LC., v. 213, p. 37988.

[13] Jefferson to Adams, Nov. 13, 1818; *Works*, Ford, XII, 102-3.

[14] Jefferson to Trumbull, Nov. 18, 1818; Jefferson Papers, LC., v. 214, p. 38142.

[15] Jefferson to Dr. Andrew Kean, Nov. 11, 1818; *ibid*, v. 214, p. 38143.

[16] Jefferson to Henry Dearborn, May 17, 1818; *ibid*, v. 213, p. 37978.

[17] Jefferson to Adams, Jan. 19, 1819; *ibid*, v. 214, p. 38237. W. C. Rives to Jefferson, Jan. 20, 1819; v. 214, pp. 38238-9. Jefferson to W. C. Nicholas, Jan. 28, 1819; *ibid*, v. 214, p. 38250.

[18] Jefferson to Cabell, Feb. 19, 1819; *ibid*, v. 214, p. 38279.

[19] Jefferson to Ticknor, Oct. 25, 1818; *ibid*, v. 213, p. 38113. To Bowditch, Oct. 26, 1818; *ibid*, v. 213, p. 38116.

[20] Jefferson to Correa, Mar. 2, 1819; *ibid*, v. 215, p. 38304.

[21] S. L. Mitchill to Jefferson, May 10, 1819; *ibid*, v. 215, pp. 38385-6.

[22] The MS. plans and specifications are in the U. of Va. library.

[23] Jefferson to Correa, Apr. 11, 1820; Jefferson Papers, LC., v. 217, p. 38767.

[24] Adams to Jefferson, May 21, 1819; *ibid*, v. 215, p. 38408.

[25] H. B. Trist to N. P. Trist, May 13, 1819; Nicholas P. Trist Papers, LC., v. 1, pp. 55534-5. Acct. Bk., Apr. 9, 1819; Mass. H. S. J. Q. Adams to Jefferson, Apr. 24, 1819; Jefferson Papers, LC., v. 215, p. 38379. Jefferson to J. Q. Adams, May 10, 1819; *ibid*, v. 215, p. 38391.

[26] Jefferson to W. C. Nicholas, Mar. 26, 1818; Jefferson Papers, LC., v. 212, p. 37909. Nicholas to Jefferson, Mar. 30, 1818; v. 212, p. 37915.

[27] Nicholas to Jefferson, Apr. 19, 1818; *ibid*, v. 213, p. 37945. Jefferson to Nicholas, May 1, 1818; *ibid*, v. 213, p. 37962.

[28] Nicholas to Jefferson, Aug. 5, 1819; *ibid*, v. 216, p. 38530. Jefferson to Joseph Marx, Aug. 24, 1819; *Works*, Ford, XII, 134-5. Marx to Jefferson, Sept. 2, 1819; Jefferson Papers, LC., v. 216, p. 38560. Indenture between Jefferson and T. J. Randolph, Sept. 15, 1819; Jefferson Papers, Mass. H. S.

[29] Jefferson to Nicholas, Aug. 11, 1819; Jefferson Papers, LC., v. 216, p. 38535.

[30] H. B. Trist to N. P. Trist, Oct. 19, 1819; Nicholas P. Trist Papers, v. 1, p. 55554. Thomas Mann Randolph thought this was the first time Jefferson had ever endorsed for anyone; but he was mistaken. Jefferson had done so on several occasions. (To N. P. Trist, Aug. 15, 1819; *ibid*, v. 1, pp. 55546-7.)

[31] Jefferson to Dr. Vine Utley, Mar. 21, 1819; *Works*, Ford, XII, 116-18. To Cathalan, May 26, 1819; Jefferson Papers, LC., v. 215, pp. 38412-13.

[32] Jefferson to John Trumbull, Jan. 10, 1817; Franklin Papers, Yale Univ.

[33] Maria Cosway to Jefferson, Apr. 7, 1819; Jefferson Papers, Mass. H. S.

[34] Jefferson to Maria Cosway, Dec. 27, 1820; *ibid*.

[35] Jefferson to Wm. C. Rives, Nov. 28, 1819; *Works*, Ford, XII, 149-50. See also to Adams, Nov. 7, 1819; *ibid*, XII, 144-6.

[36] Jefferson to Lafayette, Mar. 8, 1819; Jefferson Papers, LC., v. 215, p. 38313.

[37] Jefferson to Spencer Roane, Sept. 6, 1819; *Works*, Ford, XII, 135-40.

[38] Jefferson to Lewis Williams, Feb. 18, 1820; Jefferson Papers, LC., v. 217, p. 38713.

[39] Jefferson to Isaac H. Tiffany, Apr. 4, 1819; *ibid*, v. 215, p. 38353.

[40] Jefferson to Short, Oct. 31, 1819; *ibid*, v. 216, p. 38596. (Printed in *Works*, Ford, XII, 140-4, with minor errors.)

[41] Jefferson to Thomas B. Parker, May 15, 1819; *ibid*, v. 215, p. 38400.

[42] Jefferson to John H. Cocke, July 17, 1819; Jefferson MSS., U. of Va. To P. Laporte, June 4, 1819; MS., Harvard Univ., photostat in U. of Va.

[43] Jefferson to Madison, July 7, 1819; Madison Papers, LC., v. 66, p. 77. To James Breckinridge, July 8, 11, 16, 1819; Jefferson MSS., U. of Va.

[44] Michele and Giacomo Raggi to Jefferson (in Italian), rec. Sept. 17, 1819; Jefferson MSS., U. of Va. Memo of conversation between Jefferson and Michele Raggi, Nov. 4, 1819; *ibid.*

[45] Pierson, *Jefferson at Monticello*, 19-22.

[46] Jefferson to Cabell, Jan. 22, 1820; *Works*, Ford, XII, 154-5. To Madison, Feb. 16, 1820; Madison Papers, LC., v. 67, p. 50.

[47] Short to Jefferson, Mar. 27, 1820; Jefferson Papers, Mass. H. S.

[48] Cooper to Jefferson, Mar. 1, 1820; Jefferson MSS., U. of Va.

[49] Jefferson to Cooper, Mar. 13, 1820; *ibid.*

[50] Minutes of the Board, Apr. 3, 1820; Jefferson to John H. Cocke, Apr. 9, 1820; *ibid.*

[51] Cooper to Jefferson, Apr. 24, May 3, 1820; *ibid.*

[52] Jefferson to J. W. Eppes, June 30, 1820; *ibid.*

[53] Jefferson to Short, Apr. 13, 1820; *Writings*, Mont., XV, 243-8. Jefferson, however, never capitalized the references to Jesus as they are printed in the text.

[54] Jefferson to Adams, Mar. 14, 1820; *ibid*, XV, 241.

CHAPTER 71

[1] Jefferson to John Holmes, Apr. 22, 1820; *Works*, Ford, XII, 158-60. See also Isaac Briggs to his wife, describing a visit to Jefferson, Nov. 21, 1820; photostat in U. of Va.

[2] Jefferson to Short, Apr. 13, 1820; *Writings*, Mont., XV, 243-8.

[3] Jefferson to John Holmes, *supra.*

[4] Jefferson to Warden, Dec. 20, 1820; Warden Papers, Md. H. S.

[5] Jefferson to J. W. Eppes, June 12, 1820; "Some Family Papers of Jefferson," *Scribner's Mag.*, XXXVI, 579-80.

[6] Jefferson to Francis Eppes, Oct. 6, 1820, June 27, 1821; Jefferson MSS., Huntington Lib. To same, Dec. 13, 1820; Jefferson Papers, LC., v. 218, pp. 39026-7.

[7] Jefferson to T. M. Randolph, Nov. 20, 1820; Jefferson Papers, Mass. H. S.

[8] Jefferson to Destutt Tracy, Dec. 26, 1820; *Works*, Ford, XII, 181-4.

[9] MS. List of Books, Jefferson to James Leitch, Oct. 21, 1820; McGregor Coll., U. of Va.

[10] Jefferson to John C. Wells, May 13, 1820; *Glimpses of the Past*, 124.

[11] Jefferson to J. W. Eppes, June 30, July 29, Aug. 19, 1820; Jefferson MSS., U. of Va.

[12] Acct. Bks., 1821-23; Mass. H. S.

[13] Autobiography, Jan. 6-July 29, 1821; Jefferson Papers, LC., v. 219, pp. 39061-80. This is the first part; later parts continue through the succeeding volumes of the Papers. The whole has been printed as a unit in *Works*, Ford, I, and elsewhere.

[14] Jefferson to James W. Wallace, July 10, 1821; Jefferson Papers, LC., v. 220, p. 39325.

[15] Jefferson to Cabell, Jan. 31, 1821; *Writings*, Mont., XV, 310-13.

[16] Jefferson to James Breckinridge, Feb. 15, 1821; *ibid*, XV, 314-18.

[17] Jefferson to Adams, Jan. 22, 1821; *Works*, Ford, XII, 198-200.

[18] Adams to Jefferson, Feb. 3, 1821; Jefferson Papers, LC., v. 219, p. 39198-9.

[19] Jefferson to Spencer Roane, Mar. 9, 1821; *Works*, Ford, XII, 201-2. See also to C. Hammond, Aug. 18, 1821; *Writings*, Mont., XV, 330.

[20] Jefferson to James T. Austin, Feb. 13, 1821; Jefferson Papers, LC., v. 219, p. 39201.

[21] Jefferson to Spencer Roane, June 27, 1821; *Works*, Ford, XII, 202-3.

[22] Jefferson to John E. Hall, Aug. 8, 1821; Jefferson Papers, LC., v. 220, p. 39360.

[23] Jefferson to J. W. Eppes, Oct. 23, 1821; *ibid*, v. 221, pp. 39433-4. To Nathaniel Macon, Aug. 19, 1821; *Works*, Ford, XII, 206-8.

[24] Jefferson to Benjamin Ruggles, May 3, 1822; Jefferson Papers, LC., v. 222, p. 39612.

[25] Jefferson to Adams, June 27, 1822; *Works*, Ford, XII, 240-1 n.

[26] Pickering to Jefferson, Feb. 12, 1821; Pickering and Upham, *Life of Timothy Pickering*, IV, 324-7.

27 Jefferson to Pickering, Feb. 27, 1821; *ibid*, IV, 327-8.
28 Jefferson to Adams, Apr. 11, 1823; *Writings*, Mont., XV, 430.
29 Jefferson to C. Crozet, Nov. 23, 1821; Jefferson Papers, Mass. H. S.
30 Draft Petition to Congress, Nov. 30, 1821; Jefferson MSS., U. of Va.
31 Jefferson to Waterhouse, June 26, 1822; *Works*, Ford, XII, 241-3.
32 Jefferson to Waterhouse, July 19, 1822; *ibid*, XII, 243-4 n.
33 Jefferson to Rev. Thomas Whittemore, June 5, 1822; MS., Tufts Coll. Library.
34 Cabell to Jefferson, Jan. 14, 1822; Cabell, *op. cit.*, 233-4.
35 Cabell to Jefferson, Feb. 11, 1822; *ibid*, 242-4.
36 Jefferson to Madison, Apr. 7, 1822; Jefferson Papers, LC., v. 222, p. 39588.
37 Jefferson to Cooper, Mar. 9, 1822; *ibid*, v. 221, p. 39568.
38 Jefferson to N. P. Trist, June 14, 1822; *Bixby Coll.—Jefferson Correspondence*, 272-3.
39 Jefferson to Wm. Coffee, July 10, 1822; Jefferson Papers. Mass. H. S. See also Jefferson to Tucker, Aug. 24, 1822; Tucker-Coleman Coll., Colonial Wmsburg. Arch.
40 Jefferson to Short, Oct. 19, 1822; Jefferson Papers, LC., v. 223, p. 39778.
41 Jefferson to Cabell, Dec. 28, 1822; Cabell, *op. cit.*, 260-2.
42 Jefferson to Cabell, Jan. 13, 1823; *ibid*, 266-8.
43 Jefferson to Cabell, Jan. 26, 1823; *ibid*, 270-1.
44 Cabell to Jefferson, Jan. 9, Feb. 3, 5, 1823; *ibid*, 265-6, 273, 274.
45 Jefferson to Cabell, Mar. 12, 1823; *ibid*, 278-9.
46 Jefferson to J. W. Eppes, July 28, 1822; Jefferson MSS., Huntington Lib.
47 Jefferson to Cornelius C. Blatchley, Oct. 21, 1822; Jefferson Misc. MSS., N. Y. H. S.
48 Jefferson to Madison, Nov. 22, 1822; Madison Papers, LC., v. 70, p. 85. Randall, *Jefferson*, III, 487.

CHAPTER 72

1 Jefferson to Edmund Bacon, Aug. 18, 1823; Jefferson Papers, Mass. H. S.
2 Jefferson to Madison, Mar. 14, 1823; Jefferson Papers, LC., v. 223, p. 39946.
3 Jefferson to F. W. Gilmer, Oct. 12, 1824; Gilmer MSS., U. of Va. See also to Madison, Oct. 6, 1824, Madison Papers, LC., v. 73, p. 90.
4 Jefferson to Cooper, Apr. 12, 1823; Jefferson Papers, LC., v. 224, p. 39995. Some modern commentators, reading merely the printed Report of the Visitors, have assumed from it that Jefferson was willing to make religious study an integral part of his University.
5 Jefferson to Madison, Aug. 8, 1824; Madison Papers, LC., v. 73, p. 51. Madison obliged with a list, Sept. 10, 1824; Madison, *Writings*, IX, 202-7.
6 Jefferson to Ticknor, July 16, 1823; *Writings*, Mont., XV, 454-7.
7 Jefferson to James Lindsay, June 14, 1823; Jefferson MSS., Va. H. S.
8 Jefferson to Remsen, Dec. 19, 1823; Franklin Papers, Yale Univ. To Thomas Leiper, May 31, 1823; *Works*, Ford, XII, 286-9.
9 Jefferson to Monroe, June 14, 1823; Monroe Papers, N. Y. Pub. Lib.
10 Jefferson to Remsen, Oct. 26, Dec. 19, 1823; Franklin Papers, Yale Univ.
11 Jefferson to Robert Walsh, Apr. 5, 1823; Jefferson MSS., U. of Va.
12 Jefferson to Judge Wm. Johnson, Mar. 4, 1823; *Works*, Ford, XII, 277-80. In spite of Jefferson's urgings and the offer of his papers, Johnson's history never appeared. Neither did the lives of Hamilton and Adams. All waited for another generation; Hamilton's by his son, John C. Hamilton; Adams's by his grandson, Charles Francis Adams, and Jefferson's by Tucker and Randall.
13 Wm. Johnson to Jefferson, Apr. 11, 1823; Jefferson Papers, LC., v. 224, pp. 39984-8. Jefferson to Johnson, June 12, 1823; *Works*, Ford, XII, 252-9 n.
14 Madison to Jefferson, June 27, 1823; Madison Papers, LC., v. 71, p. 74.
15 Jefferson to Samuel H. Smith, Aug. 2, 1823; *Works*, Ford, XII, 300-2.
16 Jefferson to Geo. W. Erving, Apr. 11, 1823; Jefferson Papers, LC., v. 224, p. 39981.
17 Monroe to Jefferson, June 2, 1823; *ibid*, v. 224, pp. 40059-60.
18 Jefferson to Monroe, June 11, 1823; *Works*, Ford, XII, 292.
19 Monroe to Jefferson, Oct. 17, 1823; Monroe, *Writings*, VI, 323-5.
20 Jefferson to Monroe, Oct. 24, 1823; *Works*, Ford, XII, 318-21.
21 Monroe to Jefferson, Dec. 4, 1823; Monroe, *Writings*, VI, 342.
22 Jefferson to Monroe, Feb. 20, 1824; *Works*, Ford. XII, 343-6.
23 Jefferson to Monroe, Aug. 25, 1824; Jefferson Papers, LC., v. 227, p. 40558. Monroe to Jefferson, Aug. 26, 1824; *ibid*, v. 227, pp. 40562-3.

[24] Jefferson to Duane, May 31, 1824; Franklin Papers, Yale Univ.

[25] Monroe to Jefferson, July 12, 1824; Jefferson Papers, LC., v. 226, p. 40505.

[26] Jefferson to Col. Peyton, Sept. 3, 1824; Jefferson Papers, Mass. H. S.

[27] Jefferson to Thomas Leiper, Oct. 27, 1824; *Works*, Ford, XII, 345 n. To Richard Rush, undated, *ibid*, XII, 344-5 n. To Duane, Oct. 24, 1824; Jefferson Papers, LC., v. 227, p. 40650.

[28] Pierson, *Jefferson at Monticello*, 123.

[29] Jefferson to Richard Rush, June 5, 1824; *Works*, Ford, XII, 355-6.

[30] Jefferson to Robert J. Garnett, Feb. 14, 1824; *ibid*, XII, 341-3.

[31] Jefferson to Martin Van Buren, June 29, 1824; *ibid*, XII, 357-72.

[32] Jefferson to Cabell, Jan. 23, 1824; photostat, U. of Va.

[33] Adams to Jefferson, Jan. 22, 1825; Adams, *Works*, X, 414-15.

[34] Jefferson to Cabell, May 16, 1824; *Writings*, Mont., XVI, 35-42. To Gilmer, June 5, 1824; Gilmer MSS., U. of Va.

[35] Jefferson to Sen. James Barbour, May 2, 1824; Barbour Papers, N. Y. Pub. Lib.

[36] Jefferson to Madison, Oct. 6, 1824; *op. cit.*

[37] Jefferson to Madison, Nov. 20, 1824; Madison Papers, LC., v. 73, p. 114.

[38] Jefferson to Madison, Nov. 30, 1824; Jefferson Papers, LC., v. 227, p. 40692.

[39] Jefferson to A. S. Brockenbrough, Jan. 9, 1825; Jefferson MSS., U. of Va.

[40] Jefferson to Lafayette, Oct. 9, 1824; *Works*, Ford, XII, 378-80.

[41] Draft Address of Welcome, Nov. 4, 1824; Jefferson Papers, LC., v. 227, p. 40660.

[42] Ticknor to Wm. H. Prescott, Dec. 16, 1824; Ticknor's *Journals*, I, 348-9. Webster's account of the visit appeared in his *Correspondence*, I, 364 ff., and has already been adverted to in connection with the political matters he discussed with Jefferson.

[43] MS. "Sketches of American Statesmen," quoted in Davis, *Gilmer*, 354.

CHAPTER 73

[1] Jefferson to Madison, Jan. 23, 1825; Rives Papers, LC.

[2] Jefferson to Madison, Feb. 1, 1825; *ibid.*

[3] Jefferson to Cabell, Feb. 3, 1825; Cabell, *op. cit.*, 339-41.

[4] Draft Resolution, Mar. 4-5, 1825; Jefferson MSS., U. of Va.

[5] Madison to Jefferson, Feb. 8, 1825; Rives Papers, LC. Jefferson to Madison, Feb. 12, 1825; *ibid.*

[6] Jefferson to Gilmer, Jan. 20, 1825; Jefferson Papers, LC., v. 228, p. 40817.

[7] The long and involved hunt for a professor of law may be studied in the Jefferson Papers, LC., in the U. of Va., and in Cabell, *op. cit.*

[8] Jefferson to Gilmer, Oct. 11, 1825; Jefferson MSS., U. of Va.

[9] Jefferson to John Adams, Feb. 15, 1825; Jefferson Papers, LC., v. 228, pp. 40853-4. To Crawford, Feb. 15, 1825; *ibid*, v. 228, p. 40854.

[10] Adams to Jefferson, Feb. 25, 1825; *ibid*, v. 228, p. 40871. The Latin is from Vergil's famous "prophetic" Eclogue, in which he hailed the return of the golden Saturnian age to earth.

[11] Jefferson to George Thompson, June 23, 1825; Amer. Art Assn.—Anderson Galleries Catalogue, Apr. 14, 1932.

[12] George Thompson to Jefferson, June 2, 1825; *Glimpses of the Past*, 126-30. Jefferson to Thompson, June 22, 1825; *ibid*, 130-2.

[13] Cabell to Jefferson, Feb. 7, 1825; Cabell, *op. cit.*, 341-2. Jefferson to John Patterson, Mar. 22, 1825; Jefferson Papers, LC., v. 229, p. 40911.

[14] Jefferson to Madison, Mar. 22, 1825; Madison Papers, LC., v. 74, p. 53.

[15] Jefferson to Littleton W. Tazewell, Mar. 13, 1825; Jefferson Papers, LC., v. 229, p. 40901. To George Thompson, June 22, 1825; *supra.*

[16] Jefferson to Dr. Robert Greenhow, Apr. 29, 1825; Jefferson Papers, LC., v. 229, p. 40980. To Thomas Campbell, Apr. 29, 1825; *ibid*, v. 229, p. 40981.

[17] Jefferson to Robley Dunglison, June 29, 1825; Jefferson MSS., U. of Va.

[18] Jefferson to Xaupy, Sept. 1, 1825; Jefferson Papers, LC., v. 230, p. 41141.

[19] Jefferson to Joseph Coolidge, Jr., Oct. 13 [1825]; *Writings*, Mont., XVIII, 342-6. Minutes of Board of Visitors, Oct. 4-7, 1825; *ibid*, XVIII, 360-499. Key and Long to Rector and Visitors, Oct. 4, 1825; Jefferson MSS., U. of Va.

[20] Jefferson to Madison, Oct. 18, 1825; Feb. 17, 1826; Madison Papers, LC., v. 75, pp. 57, 108.

[21] Matthew Maury to his mother, Aug. 6, 1825; *Intimate Virginiana*, 95.

[22] Jefferson to Dr. Dunglison, July 2, 8, Nov. 26, 1825; privately owned; copies in U. of Va.

[23] Jefferson to Samuel Smith, Oct. 22, 1825; Jefferson Papers, Mass. H. S.

[24] Jefferson to F. A. Van der Kemp, Nov. 30, 1825; Jefferson Papers, LC., v. 230, p. 41235.

[25] Jefferson to Sheldon Clark, Dec. 5, 1825; Jefferson Papers, LC., v. 230, p. 41244.

[26] Jefferson to Madison, Dec. 24, 1825; *Works*, Ford, XII, 416-18, 418-21 n. See also to Giles, Dec. 26, 1825; *ibid*, XII, 424-8.

[27] Jefferson to Madison, Jan. 2, 1826; *ibid*, XII, 431-2.

[28] Jefferson to T. M. Randolph, June 5, 1825; Jefferson Papers, LC., v. 229, p. 41034.

[29] Jefferson to T. M. Randolph, July 9, 1825; *ibid*, v. 229, pp. 41076-7.

[30] Jefferson to T. M. Randolph, Jan. 8, 1826; *Works*, Ford, XII, 432-3. Randolph's penciled notes, undated, *ibid*, XII, 433-4 n.

[31] T. M. Randolph to N. P. Trist, July 6, 1826; copy, Trist Papers, LC., v. 3, p. 55918.

[32] T. J. Randolph to Dabney S. Carr, July 18, 1826; Jefferson MSS., U. of Va.

[33] T. M. Randolph to Trist, Mar. 10, 11, 1828; Trist Papers, LC., v. 5, pp. 56143, 56146. Trist to T. M. Randolph, Mar. 10, 1828; *ibid*, v. 5, p. 56145.

[34] Jefferson to Cabell, Jan. 20, 1826; Randall, *Jefferson*, III, 527.

[35] Cabell to Jefferson, Jan. 30, 1826; Cabell, *op. cit.*, 360-1.

[36] "Thoughts on Lotteries," Feb., 1826; *Works*, Ford, XII, 435-50.

[37] Jefferson to Cabell, Feb. 7, 1826; *ibid*, XII, 450-3.

[38] Cabell to Jefferson, Feb. 3, 1826; Cabell, *op. cit.*, 362.

[39] Jefferson to T. J. Randolph, Feb. 8, 1826; Randall, *Jefferson*, III, 531.

[40] Cabell to Jefferson, Feb. 10, 20, 1826; Cabell, *op. cit.*, 370, 375-6. See also Jefferson to Wm. F. Gordon, Feb. 22, 1826; Jefferson Papers, Mass., H. S., in which Jefferson claimed that the majority for leave to bring in the bill was only *one*.

[41] Notice of Lottery; Richmond *Enquirer*, Apr. 28, 1826. Jefferson to Thomas Ritchie, Mar. 13, 1826; *Works*, Ford, XII, 465 n. Some of the original lottery tickets are in Jefferson Papers, LC., v. 231, p. 41413.

[42] John Tyler to H. A. Wise, Mar. 8, 1859; *Wm. & Mary Quart.*, ser. 2, v. 8, p. 275.

[43] Statement of Debts, July 4, 1826; Trist Papers, LC. (The Inventory of his Assets is in Will Bk. #8, Albemarle Co. Court House.) Randall, *Jefferson*, III, 536-9.

[44] Jefferson's Will, Mar. 19, 1826; *Writings*, Mont., XVII, 456-70.

[45] Instructions for Grave Monument; Jefferson Papers, LC., v. 231, p. 41473 a.

[46] Jefferson to Madison, Feb. 17, 1826; *Works*, Ford, XII, 455-9.

[47] Jefferson to John H. Cocke, May 20, 1826; Jefferson MSS., U. of Va.

[48] Randall, *Jefferson*, III, 538-9.

[49] Jefferson to Patrick Gibson, Feb. 22, 1826; Jefferson Papers, LC., v. 231, p. 41348.

[50] Acct. Bk., 1826; Mass. H. S.

[51] Adams, *Works*, I, 636.

[52] Alexander Garrett to his wife, July 4, 1826; Jefferson MSS., U. of Va. H. H. Worthington to Reuben B. Hicks, July 5, 1826; *ibid*.

General Bibliography

The number of volumes that have been written on and around Jefferson is truly staggering; the manuscripts, scattered in collections great and small throughout the country, run literally into the hundreds of thousands. The two decades that the author has devoted to the research, contemplation and writing of three related lives—Aaron Burr, Alexander Hamilton and Thomas Jefferson—have now been brought to a conclusion. It is his belief that through the clash of personalities and political ideas of these three key figures the formative years of the American nation may be studied to advantage.

The published writings of Thomas Jefferson have thus far been woefully inadequate. The best to date is the compilation by Paul Leicester Ford, chiefly political in character. The worst are the more numerous volumes known either as the Monticello or the Memorial edition. Errors of transcription, of dates, of attributions abound on almost every page. Fortunately, the monumental edition of *The Papers of Thomas Jefferson,* under the direction of Julian P. Boyd, as editor, and Lyman C. Butterfield and others as associates, is now well under way. The three volumes already published out of a total of fifty-two are models of clarity, accuracy and meticulous editing; the success of the entire venture seems well assured.

Most of the abbreviations in the Notes appended to this book should furnish no difficulty to the inquiring student. Some few which may are herewith listed:

Works, Ford: *The Federal Edition of the Works of Jefferson,* edited by P. L. Ford.

Writings, Mont.: *The Monticello or Memorial Edition of the Writings of Jefferson,* edited by Lipscomb and Bergh.

LC.: The Library of Congress.

The author has received almost uniformly cordial co-operation from busy librarians and custodians of the great manuscript collections. His grateful thanks are herewith rendered to each and every one of them. They helped make an almost impossible task possible.

Thanks are also extended to the institutions and individuals who have permitted investigation of their treasures and gave permission to print excerpts therefrom.

New York, June 1, 1951

NATHAN SCHACHNER

MANUSCRIPT COLLECTIONS

American Philosophical Society
 Jefferson MSS.
Boston Public Library
 Jefferson MSS.
Clements (Wm. L.) Library
 Misc. Jefferson MSS.
Colonial Williamsburg, Inc. Archives
 Tucker-Coleman Collection
Historical Society of Pennsylvania
 Barton, Benjamin S., Papers
 Dreer Collection
 Etting Papers
 Gilpin Papers
 Jefferson MSS. (misc.)
 Logan, Maria Dickinson, Collection
 McKean Papers
 Parker Papers
 Peters MSS.
 Rittenhouse Photostats
 Rutledge Papers
Huntington (Henry E.) Library
 Jefferson MSS.
 Jefferson, Peter, Accounts
 Jefferson, Thomas, Account Bk., 1775
Library of Congress
 Adams, Henry, Transcripts from British, French and Spanish Archives
 Breckinridge Papers
 Burr, Aaron, Misc. Folder
 Burwell, William A., Private Memoir
 East Florida Papers
 Gallatin, Albert, Treasury Book, 1802–11
 Hamilton, Alexander, MSS.
 Henley-Smith Papers
 Jefferson, Thomas
  Account Bks. for years 1767–70, 1773, 1779–82
  Bible
  Papers (bound in 236 vols.)
  Weather Bk., 1776–1820
  Rare Book Collection
  Commonplace Books
 Letters in Relation to Burr's Conspiracy
 Madison, James, Papers
 Mazzei, Philip, Papers
 Monroe, James, Papers
 Nicholas, Wilson Cary, Papers
 Nicholson, Joseph H., Papers
 Papers of the Continental Congress
 Paris, Affaires Etrangères, Correspondence Politique, États-Unis (Steven's and Doysie's transcripts)
 Pendleton Letters, Mays Collection

Plumer, William
MS. Autobiography
Letters
Memorandum of the Proceedings of the Senate of the United States
MS. Register
Rives, William C., Papers
Shippen Papers
Short, William, Papers
Smith, Samuel H., Papers
Thomson, Charles, Papers
Trist, Nicholas P., Papers

Maryland Historical Society
Warden, David B., Papers

Massachusetts Historical Society
Bowdoin, James, Papers
Jefferson Papers
Account Bks., 1771-72, 1774, 1776-78, 1783-90, 1804-26
Coolidge Collection
Farm Book
Garden Book
Weather Bks., 1784-94, 1802-16
Knox Papers
Lincoln, Levi, Papers
Pickering Papers
Smith, W. S., Papers
Washburn Papers

Missouri Historical Society
Bixby Collection
Clark Papers

Morgan Library
Jefferson MSS.

National Archives
Department of State
American Letters
Appointment Book
Communications
Domestic Letters
Instructions to Ministers
Miscellaneous Records
Report Books

New York Historical Society
Gallatin Papers
Gates Papers
Jefferson MSS. (misc.)
King, Rufus, Papers
Steuben Papers

New York Public Library
Emmet Collection
Jefferson MSS.
Jefferson, Account Bk., 1791-1803
Madison MSS.
Mazzei Papers
Monroe MSS.
Myers Collection

University of Virginia
- Carr Papers
- Cary Papers
- Edgehill-Randolph Papers
- Jefferson MSS., Photostats and Microfilms
- Lee Collection
- McGregor Papers
- Maury Deposit

University of Wisconsin
- Draper MSS.

Virginia Archives
- Albemarle Court House
- Cumberland Court House

Virginia Historical Society
- Jefferson MSS.
- Lee Papers

Virginia State Library
- Journals of the Burgesses
- Journals of the House of Delegates
- Letters of the Governors
- Randolph, John, Diary and Papers (typed copies by Wm. Cabell Bruce)

William and Mary College
- Jefferson-Short Papers
- William Short–Peyton Short Papers

Yale University
- Franklin Papers

NEWSPAPERS

Albany Register
Columbian Centinel
Dunlap's Pennsylvania Packet and Advertiser
Gazette of the United States
Maryland Gazette
National Gazette
National Intelligencer
New England Chronicle
New England Palladium
New York American Citizen and Advertiser
New York Bee
New York Commercial Advertiser
New York Evening Post
Pennsylvania Gazette
Philadelphia Aurora (and General Advertiser)
Porcupine's Gazette
Port Folio, The
Richmond Enquirer
Virginia Gazette
Washington Federalist

PRINTED DOCUMENTS AND BOOKS

Abernethy, Thomas P., *Western Lands and the American Revolution*, 1937
Adams, Mrs. (Abigail), *Letters of* (Chas. F. Adams, *ed.*), 2 v., 1841
Adams, Henry, *History of the United States of America during the Administrations of Thomas Jefferson and James Madison*, 8 v. in 4, 1930
——— *The Life of Albert Gallatin*, 1879
——— *Documents relating to New-England Federalism* (*ed.*), 1905
Adams, Herbert, *Thomas Jefferson and the University of Virginia*, 1888
Adams, James Truslow, *The Living Jefferson*, 1936
Adams, John, *Letters of, Addressed to his Wife* (Chas. F. Adams, *ed.*), 2 v., 1841
——— *Works* (Chas. F. Adams, *ed.*), 10 v., 1850–56
Adams, John Quincy, *The Writings of* (W. C. Ford, *ed.*), 7 v., 1913–17
Adams, Randolph G., *Three Americanists*, 1939
Agricultural History, "Jefferson as an Agriculturist," by August C. Miller, Jr., v. 16 (1942)
Albemarle County Historical Society, Papers of the, "Thomas Walker of Albemarle," by Natalie J. Disbrow, v. 1 (1940–41)
——— "A Dissertation on Education in the Form of a Letter from James Maury to Robert Jackson, July 17, 1762" (Helen C. Bullock, *ed.*), v. 2 (1941–42)
Ambler, Charles H., *Sectionalism in Virginia from 1776 to 1861*, 1910
——— *Thomas Ritchie*, 1913
American Antiquarian Society Proceedings, "The Letters of Robert R. Livingston," by Edward A. Parsons, v. 52 (1942)
American Historical Association Reports, "The Enforcement of the Alien and Sedition Laws," by Frank M. Anderson, 1912
American Journal of Archaeology, "Thomas Jefferson, Archaeologist," by Karl Lehmann-Hartleben, ser. 2, v. 47 (1943)
American Philosophical Society, Proceedings of the, "Jefferson and the American Philosophical Society," by Gilbert Chinard; "Jefferson and the Arts," by Fiske Kimball; "Thomas Jefferson and the Classics," by Louis B. Wright; v. 87 (July, 1943)
American State Papers: Foreign Relations, v. 1–3, 1833
Ames, Fisher, *Works of* (Seth Ames, *ed.*), 2 v., 1854
Anderson, Dice R., *William Branch Giles*, 1914
Annals of Congress: The Debates and Proceedings in the Congress of the United States (Gales and Seaton, *eds.*), 1834–56
Austin, James, T., *Life of Elbridge Gerry*, 2 v., 1828

Bakeless, John, *Lewis & Clark*, 1947
Barbé-Marbois, Francois, *Histoire de la Louisiane*, 1829
Beard, Charles A., *Economic Origins of Jeffersonian Democracy*, 1915
Becker, Carl, *The Declaration of Independence*, 1942
Beckley, John, *Address to the People of the United States . . .*, 1800
Bell, Sadie, *The Church, the State, and Education in Virginia*, 1930
Bemis, Samuel Flagg, *Jay's Treaty*, 1924
Berman, Eleanor D., *Thomas Jefferson among the Arts*, 1947
Betts, Edwin M., *ed.*, *Thomas Jefferson's Garden Book*, 1944
Beveridge, Albert J., *The Life of John Marshall*, 4 v., 1916–19
Biddle, Alexander, *Old Family Letters*, 1892
Biddle, Charles, *Autobiography of*, 1883
Bishop, Abraham, *An Oration on the Extent and Power of Political Delusion*, 1800
Bland, Richard, *An Enquiry into the Rights of the British Colonies . . .*, 1769

Boorstin, Daniel J., *The Lost World of Thomas Jefferson*, 1948
Bowers, Claude G., *Jefferson and Hamilton*, 1925
——— *Jefferson in Power*, 1936
——— *The Young Jefferson*, 1945
Boyd, Julian P., *The Declaration of Independence*, 1943
Brant, Irving, *James Madison, The Virginia Revolutionist*, 1941
——— *James Madison, The Nationalist*, 1948
Brock, Robert A., *The Vestry Book of Henrico Parish*, 1874
Brock, Robert K., *Archibald Cary of Ampthill*, 1937
Brown, Everett S., *ed.*, *William Plumer's Memorandum of Proceedings in the United States Senate, 1803–1807*; 1923
Brown, Glenn, *History of the United States Capital*, 2 v., 1902
Bruce, Philip A., *History of the University of Virginia*, 5 v., 1920–22
Bruce, William C., *John Randolph of Roanoke*, 2 v., 1922
Buffalo Historical Society Publications, "A Bundle of Thomas Jefferson's Letters," VII (1904)
Bullock, Helen D., *My Head and My Heart*, 1945
Burk, John (with Skelton Jones and Louis Hue Girardin), *The History of Virginia*, 4 v., 1804–16
Burnett, Edmund C., *Letters of Members of the Continental Congress*, 8 v., 1921–36
——— *The Continental Congress*, 1941

Cabell, Nathaniel F., *Early History of the University of Virginia, as contained in the Letters of Thomas Jefferson and Joseph C. Cabell*, 1856
Caldwell, Lynton K., *The Administrative Theories of Hamilton and Jefferson*, 1944
Campbell, Charles, *ed.*, *The Bland Papers*, 2 v. in 1, 1840
Carpenter, T., *reporter*, The Trial of Col. Aaron Burr, 3 v., 1807
Channing, Edward, "Kentucky Resolutions of 1798," in *American Historical Review*, XX (1915)
——— *The Jeffersonian System*, 1906
Chastellux, Francois Jean, Marquis de, *Voyages dans L'Amérique*, 2 v., 1786
Cheetham, James, *A View of the Political Conduct of Aaron Burr*, 1802
Chinard, Gilbert, *Honest John Adams*, 1933
——— *Houdon in America*, 1930
——— *Les Amitiés américaines de Madame d'Houdetot*, 1924
——— *The Commonplace Book of Thomas Jefferson*, 1926
——— *The Correspondence of Jefferson and Du Pont de Nemours*, 1931
——— *The Letters of Lafayette and Jefferson*, 1929
——— *The Literary Bible of Thomas Jefferson*, 1928
——— *Thomas Jefferson: Apostle of Americanism*, 1929
——— *Trois Amitiés Françaises de Jefferson*, 1927
——— *Volney et L'Amérique*, 1923
Claiborne, W. C. C., Official Letter Books of (Dunbar Rowland, *ed.*), 6 v., 1917
Clark, Col. George Rogers, *Sketch of his Campaign in the Illinois*, 1869
Clinton, De Witt (Grotius), *A Vindication of Thomas Jefferson*, 1800
Collections of the Connecticut Historical Society, v. 2, 1870, "Correspondence of Silas Deane, 1774–76"
Collections of the Illinois State Historical Library, Virginia Series, v. 3 (1912), v. 4 (1926), "George Rogers Clark Papers"
Continental Congress, Journals of the (W. C. Ford, G. Hunt and J. C. Fitzpatrick, *eds.*), 34 v., 1904–37
Conway, Moncure Daniel, *Omitted Chapters of History . . . Edmund Randolph*, 1889
——— *The Life of Thomas Paine*, 1909
Corwin, Edwin S., *John Marshall and the Constitution*, 1919

Coxe, Tench, *Strictures on the Letter imputed to Mr. Jefferson, addressed to Mr. Mazzei*, 1800
Cresson, W. P., *James Monroe*, 1946
Culbreth, David M. R., *The University of Virginia*, 1908
Curtis, William E., *The True Thomas Jefferson*, 1901
Cutler, Wm. P. and Julia P., *Life, Journals and Correspondence of Rev. Manasseh Cutler*, 2 v., 1888

Daughters of the American Revolution Magazine, LV, "The Manuscript from which Jefferson Wrote the Declaration of Independence," by John C. Fitzpatrick
Daveiss, J. H., *A View of the President's Conduct Concerning the Conspiracy of 1806*, 1807
Davis, John, *Travels of Four Years and a Half in the United States of America*, 1803
Davis, Matthew L., *Memoirs of Aaron Burr*, 2 v., 1852
Davis, Richard Beale, *Francis Walker Gilmer, Life and Learning in Jefferson's Virginia*, 1939
Dickore, Marie, *Two Letters from Thomas Jefferson to his Relatives the Turpins*, 1941
Donaldson, Thomas, *The House in which Thomas Jefferson wrote the Declaration of Independence*, 1898
Dumbauld, Edward, *Thomas Jefferson, American Tourist*, 1946
Dupont de Nemours, Pierre S., *National Education in the United States of America* (B. G. Dupont, *trans.*), 1923

Eckenrode, H. J., *Separation of Church and State in Virginia*, 1910
——— *The Revolution in Virginia*, 1916
Eelking, Max von, *Memoirs and Letters and Journals of Major General Riedesel*, 2 v., 1868
Essays in Honor of William E. Dodd (Avery Craven, *ed.*), "Contemporary Opinion in Virginia of Thomas Jefferson," by Maude H. Woodfin

Farrand, Max, *ed.*, *The Records of the Federal Convention of 1787*, 4 v., 1937
Fauquier Historical Society Bulletin, No. 4 (1924), pp. 343–50
Flippin, Percy S., *The Royal Government in Virginia*, 1919
Force, Peter, *ed.*, *American Archives; Fourth and Fifth Series*, 1848
Ford, Worthington C., "Letters of William Duane," in *Massachusetts Historical Society Proceedings*, 2nd series, v. 20 (1906)
——— *The United States and Spain in 1790*, 1890
——— *Thomas Jefferson and James Thomson Callender*, 1897
Forman, Samuel E., *The Life and Writings of Thomas Jefferson*, 1905
——— *The Political Activities of Philip Freneau*, 1902
Franklin, Benjamin, *The Writings of* (Albert H. Smyth, *ed.*), 10 v., 1906–7
Frary, I. T., *Thomas Jefferson, Architect and Builder*, 1931

Gallatin, Albert, *The Writings of* (Henry Adams, *ed.*), 3 v., 1879
Garlick, Richard C., *Philip Mazzei, Friend of Jefferson*, 1933
Genet, George Clinton, *Washington, Jefferson and "Citizen" Genet*, 1899
Gibbs, George, *Memoirs of the Administrations of Washington and John Adams*, 2 v., 1846
Goodwin, Rutherford, *A Brief and True Report concerning Williamsburg in Virginia*, 1940
Granger, Gideon (Algernon Sydney), *A Vindication of the Measures of the Present Administration*, 1803
Gray, Francis Calley, *Thomas Jefferson in 1814*, 1924

Graydon, Alexander, *Memoirs of a Life*, 1811
Grigsby, Hugh B., *The Virginia Convention of 1776*, 1855
Griswold, Rufus W., *The Republican Court*, 1859

Hall, Lieut. Francis, *Travels in Canada and the United States* ..., 1819
Hamilton, Alexander, *The Works of* (H. C. Lodge, *ed.*), 12 v., 1903
——— *The Works of* (J. C. Hamilton, *ed.*), 7 v., 1851
Hamilton, John C., *History of the Republic of the United States* ..., 7 v., 1857–64
Harley, Lewis R., *The Life of Charles Thomson*, 1900
Hart, S. A., *ed.*, *Zebulon Pike's Arkansas Journey*, 1832
Hastings, George E., *The Life and Works of Francis Hopkinson*, 1926
Hatcher, William B., *Edward Livingston*, 1940
Hazelton, John H., *The Declaration of Independence*, 1906
Hazen, Charles D., *Contemporary American Opinion of the French Revolution*, 1897
Hening, William W., *The Statutes at Large; being a Collection of all the Laws of Virginia*, 13 v., 1823
Henry, William Wirt, *Patrick Henry*, 3 v., 1891
Hilldrup, Robert L., *The Life and Times of Edmund Pendleton*, 1939
Hirst, Francis W., *Life and Letters of Thomas Jefferson*, 1926
Hogarth, William, *The Analysis of Beauty*, 1753
Honeywell, Roy J., *The Educational Work of Thomas Jefferson*, 1931
Hoslett, Schuyler Dean, "Jefferson and England, The Embargo as a Measure of Coercion," in *Americana*, v. 34 (1940)
Humphreys, Frank L., *Life and Times of David Humphreys*, 2 v., 1917

Jacob, John J., *A biographical sketch ... of the late Capt. Michael Cresap*, 1826
Jacobs, James Ripley, *Tarnished Warrior, Major-General James Wilkinson*, 1938
Jay, John, *The Correspondence and Public Papers of* (Henry P. Johnston, *ed.*), 4 v., 1890–93
Jay, William, *The Life of John Jay*, 2 v., 1833
Jefferson, Thomas, *Calendar of the Correspondence of*, 3 v., U. S. Bureau of Rolls and Library, Bulletins nos., 6, 8, 10
——— *Correspondence, printed from the originals in the Collections of William K. Bixby* (W. C. Ford, *ed.*), 1916
——— *Germantown Letters* (C. F. Jenkins, *ed.*), 1906
——— *Library—Catalogue* (President), 1829
——— *The Papers of* (Julian P. Boyd and Lyman C. Butterfield, *eds.*), 52 v. in preparation, 1950–
——— *The Works of* (P. L. Ford, *ed.*), 10 v., 1892–99
——— *The Works of* (*Federal Edition*, P. L. Ford, *ed.*), 12 v., 1904
——— *The Writings of* (*Monticello Edition*, Lipscomb and Bergh, *eds.*), 20 v., 1905
——— *The Writings of* (H. A. Washington, *ed.*), 9 v., 1853–54
Jones, Howard M., *America and French Culture*, 1927
Jones, Joseph, *of Virginia*, Letters of (W. C. Ford, *ed.*), 1889
Johnson, Allen, *Jefferson and His Colleagues*, 1921

Kames, Lord Henry H., *Elements of Criticism*, 1774
Kennedy, John P., *Journals of the House of Burgesses of Virginia, 1761–65*, 1907
Kent, William, *Memoirs and Letters of James Kent*, 1898
Kentucky State Historical Society Register, "Letters of John Brown" and "Letters of Samuel Brown," v. 35 (1937)
Kimball, Fiske, *The Life Portraits of Jefferson and their Replicas*, 1944
——— *Thomas Jefferson and the First Monument of the Classical Revival in America*, 1915

——— *Thomas Jefferson, Architect*, 1916
——— "Thomas Jefferson as an Architect: Monticello and Shadwell," in *The Architectural Quarterly of Harvard University*, v. 2 (1914)
Kimball, Marie, *Jefferson, The Road to Glory*, 1943
——— *Jefferson, War and Peace*, 1947
——— *Jefferson: The Scene of Europe*, 1950
——— *The Furnishings of Monticello*, 1940
——— *Thomas Jefferson's Cook Book*, 1938
King, Charles R., *The Life and Correspondence of Rufus King*, 6 v., 1894–1900
Kite, Elizabeth S., *L'Enfant and Washington, 1791–1792*, 1929
Koch, Adrienne, *Jefferson and Madison*, 1950
——— *The Philosophy of Thomas Jefferson*, 1943
——— (and Harry Ammon), "The Virginia and Kentucky Resolutions...," in *The William and Mary Quarterly, 3rd series*, v. 5 (1948)

Lafayette, General, *Memoirs, Correspondence and Manuscripts of*, 3 v., 1837
Lambeth, Wm. A. and W. H. Manning, *Thomas Jefferson as an Architect and a Designer of Landscapes*, 1913
Latrobe, Benjamin H., *The Journal of Latrobe...*, 1905
Lee, Henry, *Memoirs of the War in the Southern Department of the United States*, 1870
——— *Observations on the Writings of Thomas Jefferson*, 1832
Lehmann, Karl, *Thomas Jefferson, American Humanist*, 1947
Lewis and Clarke, *History of the Expedition of...*, 2 v., 1817
Lingley, Charles R., *The Transition in Virginia from Colony to Commonwealth*, 1910
Linn, Rev. Dr., *Serious Considerations on the Election of a President...*, 1800
Lloyd, Thomas, *reporter, Trials for Misdemeanor of W. S. Smith and S. G. Ogden*, 1807
Lodge, Henry C., *Life and Letters of George Cabot*, 1877
Logan, Deborah N., *Memoir of Dr. George Logan of Stenton*, 1899
Long, Orie W., *Thomas Jefferson and George Ticknor*, 1933
Lee, The Letters of Richard Henry (J. C. Ballagh, *ed.*), 2 v., 1912

Maclay, William, *The Journal of*, 1927
Mcleod, Julia H., "Jefferson and the Navy," in *Huntington Library Quarterly*, v. 8 (1945)
Macmillan, Margaret B., *The War Governors in the American Revolution*, 1943
Madison, James, *The Writings of* (Gaillard Hunt, *ed.*), 9 v., 1900–10
Malone, Dumas, *Jefferson, the Virginian*, 1948
——— *Correspondence between Thomas Jefferson and Pierre Samuel du Pont de Nemours (ed.)*, 1930
Marshall, John, *The Life of George Washington*, 5 v., 1807
Mason, Rev. John M., *The Voice of Warning, to Christians, on the ensuing Election of a President of the United States*, 1800
Massachusetts Historical Society Collections, 7th Series, v. 1 (1900), "The Jefferson Papers"
Massachusetts Historical Society Proceedings, v. 51 (1917–18), "Journal of William Loughton Smith"
Maury, Ann, *Memoirs of a Huguenot Family*, 1853
Maury, Anne Fontaine, *Intimate Virginiana*, 1941
Mayo, Bernard, *ed., Thomas Jefferson and his unknown brother, Randolph*, 1942
Mazzei, Philip, Memoirs of the Life and Peregrinations of the Florentine (H. R. Marraro, *trans.*), 1942

McCaleb, Walter F., *The Aaron Burr Conspiracy*, 1903
McIlwaine, H. R., *ed.*, *Journals of the Council of the State of Virginia*, 2 v., 1931
——— *Legislative Journals of the Council of Colonial Virginia*, 3 v., 1919
——— *Official Letters of the Governors of the State of Virginia*, vol. 2, *The Letters of Thomas Jefferson*, 1928
Mississippi Valley Historical Review, The, XXX, No. 2 (Sept., 1943); XXXIV (1948), "Jefferson and Virginia's Pioneers," by Anthony M. Lewis
Missouri Historical Society, Glimpses of the Past, Correspondence of Thomas Jefferson, 1788–1826, III (1936)
Monroe, James, *The Writings of* (S. M. Hamilton, *ed.*), 7 v., 1898–1903
More Books—The Bulletin of the Boston Public Library, Apr., 1943
Morison, Samuel E., *The Life and Letters of Harrison Gray Otis*, 2 v., 1913
Morris, Gouverneur, *A Diary of the French Revolution* (B. C. Davenport, *ed.*), 2 v., 1939
Morse, John T., Jr., *Thomas Jefferson*, 1883
Morton, Louis, *Robert Carter of Nomini Hall*, 1941
Mott, Frank L., *Jefferson and the Press*, 1943
Muzzey, David S., *Thomas Jefferson*, 1918

New Haven Colony Historical Society Papers, v. I (1865), pp. 143–5
New York Historical Society Collections, Publication Fund Series, "The Deane Papers," 5 v. (1886–90)
——— "The Papers of Charles Thomson," v. XI (1878)
Nock, Albert J., *Jefferson*, 1926

Osborne, J. A., *Williamsburg in Colonial Times*, 1935

Padover, Saul K., *Thomas Jefferson*, 1942
Padover, Saul K., *ed.*, *Thomas Jefferson and the National Capital*, 1946
Paine, Thomas, *The Complete Writings of* (P. S. Foner, *ed.*), 2 v., 1945
Palmer, John M., *General Von Steuben*, 1937
Parton, James, *Life of Thomas Jefferson*, 1874
Patton, John S., *Jefferson, Cabell and the University of Virginia*, 1906
Patton, John S. and Sallie J. Doswell, *Monticello and its Master*, 1925
Peyster, Frederic de, *A Biographical Sketch of Robert R. Livingston*, 1876
Philips, Edith, *Louis Hue Girardin and Nicholas Gouin Dufief and their relations to Thomas Jefferson*, 1926
Pickering, Octavius and Charles W. Upham, *The Life of Timothy Pickering*, 4 v., 1867–73
Pierson, Hamilton W., *Jefferson at Monticello*, 1862
Pinkney, William, *The Life of William Pinkney*, 1853
Plumer, William, Jr., *Life of William Plumer*, 1857
Political Science Quarterly, v. 55 (1940), "The Economic Philosophy of Thomas Jefferson," by Joseph Dorfman
Price, Richard, *Observations on the Nature of Civil Liberty*, 1776
Purcell, Richard J., *Connecticut in Transition*, 1918

Quincy, Edmund, *Life of Josiah Quincy*, 1868

Randall, Henry S., *The Life of Thomas Jefferson*, 3 v., 1858
Randolph, Sarah N., *The Domestic Life of Thomas Jefferson*, 1871
Randolph, Thomas J., *ed.*, *Memoir, Correspondence and Miscellanies, from the Papers of Thomas Jefferson*, 4 v., 1829

Riedesel, Mrs. General, *Letters and Journals relating to the War of the American Revolution*, 1867
Rives, William C., *History of the life and times of James Madison*, 3 v., 1868-73
Robertson, David, *Reports of the Trials of Colonel Aaron Burr*, 2 v., 1808
Rochefoucauld-Liancourt, Duc de la, *Travels through the United States of North America . . .*, 1799
Rowland, Kate Mason, *The Life of George Mason*, 2 v., 1892
Rush, Benjamin, *The Autobiography of* (G. W. Corner, *ed.*), 1948

Schachner, Nathan, *Aaron Burr, a Biography*, 1937
——— *Alexander Hamilton*, 1946
Schoepf, Johann D. (A. J. Morrison, *trans.*), *Travels in the Confederation, 1783-1784*, 2 v., 1911
Schouler, James, *Thomas Jefferson*, 1919
Scribner's Magazine, v. 36 (1904), "Some Family Letters of Thomas Jefferson"
——— v. 83 (1928), "Jouett Outrides Tarleton," by Virginius Dabney
Sears, Louis M., *Jefferson and the Embargo*, 1927
Shepperson, Archibald B., *John Paradise and Lucy Ludwell*, 1942
Simcoe, Lt. Col. John G., *A History of the Operations of . . . the Queen's Rangers*, 1844
Slaughter, P., *Memoir of Col. Joshua Fry*, 1880
Smith, Margaret Bayard, *The First Forty Years of Washington Society*, 1906
Smyth, J. F. D., *A Tour in the United States of America*, 2 v., 1784
Southern Bivouac, The, n. s. II (1886-7), "Jefferson-Short Correspondence"
Stanard, W. G., *Extracts from the Records of Henrico County, Va., 1677-1771*
Stephenson, N. W. and W. H. Dunn, *George Washington*, 2 v., 1940
Stiles, Ezra, *The Literary Diary of* (Franklin B. Dexter, *ed.*), 3 v., 1901
Stillé, Charles J., *The Life and Times of John Dickinson*, 1891
Story, William W., *ed.*, *Life and Letters of Joseph Story*, 2 v., 1851
Sullivan, William, *Familiar Letters on Public Characters and Public Events*, 1834
Swem, Earl G., *Virginia Historical Index*, 2 v., 1934-36

Tarleton, Lt. Col. (Bonastre), *A History of the Campaigns of 1780 and 1781 in the Southern Provinces of North America*, 1787
Taylor, John (Curtius), *A defence of the measures of the administration of Thomas Jefferson*, 1805
Thomas, Charles Mason, *American Neutrality in 1793*, 1931
Thwaites, R. G., *ed.*, *Official Journals of Lewis and Clark Expedition*, 7 v., 1904
Ticknor, George, *Life, Letters, and Journals of*, 2 v., 1909
Tompkins, Hamilton B., *Bibliotheca Jeffersoniana . . .*, 1887
Tracy, Destutt de, *A Commentary and Review of Montesquieu's Spirit of Laws*, 1811
——— *A Treatise on Political Economy*, 1817
Trumbull, John, *Autobiography, Reminiscences and Letters of*, 1841
Tucker, George, *The Life of Thomas Jefferson*, 2 v., 1837
Tyler, Lyon G., *The Letters and Times of the Tylers*, 3 v., 1884-96
——— *Williamsburg, the Old Colonial Capital*, 1907
Tyler's Quarterly Historical and Genealogical Magazine, passim

United States, Catalogue of the Library of the, 1815
United States Department of Agriculture, Agricultural History Series, No. 7, "Jefferson and Agriculture," by Everett E. Edwards, 1943

Van Doren, Carl, *Benjamin Franklin*, 1938

Van Ness, William Peter (Aristides), *An Examination of the Various Charges exhibited against Aaron Burr*, 1803

Virginia Assembly, Proceedings of the, on the Answers of Sundry States to their Resolutions, passed in December, 1798, 1800

Virginia Historical Register, v. 3 (1850), "Memoir of John Page"

Virginia Historical Society Collections, n. s., v. 6 (1887), "George Gilmer Papers"

Virginia, Journals of the House of Delegates of, 1776–90, 1827–28

Virginia Magazine of History and Biography, The, passim

Virginia State Papers, Calendar of, v. 1 (W. P. Palmer, *ed.*), 1875

Warfield, Ethelbert, D., *The Kentucky Resolutions of 1798*, 1887

Washington, George, *The Writings of* (John C. Fitzpatrick, *ed.*), 39 v., 1931–44

Wayland, John W., *ed.*, *The Fairfax Line: Thomas Lewis's Journal of 1746*, 1925

Wells, William V., *The Life and Public Services of Samuel Adams*, 3 v., 1865

Wertenbaker, Thomas J., *Patrician and Plebeian in Virginia*, 1910

Wharton, Anne H., *Social Life in the Early Republic*, 1902

Wharton, Francis, *ed.*, *The Revolutionary Diplomatic Correspondence of the United States*, 6 v., 1889

White, Leonard D., *The Federalists*, 1948

Wilkinson, General James, *Memoirs of My Own Times*, 3 v., 1816

William and Mary College Quarterly Historical Magazine, series 1, 2 and 3, passim

Williamson, George C., *Richard Cosway, R. A.*, 1905

Wilstach, Paul, *Jefferson and Monticello*, 1925

Wiltsie, Charles M., *The Jeffersonian Tradition in American Democracy*, 1935

Wirt, William, *The Life of Patrick Henry*, 1831

Wise, W. H., Jr. and J. W. Cronin, *Presidential Bibliographical Series No. 3*, 1935

Woods, Edgar, *Albermarle County in Virginia*, 1901

Woolery, William K., *The Relation of Thomas Jefferson to American Foreign Policy, 1783–1793*, 1927

Wortman, Tunis, *A Solemn Address to Christians & Patriots, upon the Approaching Election . . .*, 1800

Index

A

B

D

E

F

G

H

M

N

O

P

R

S

T

U

V

(1)